KT-420-025

Egypt

Matthew D Firestone

Michael Benanav, Thomas Hall, Anthony Sattin

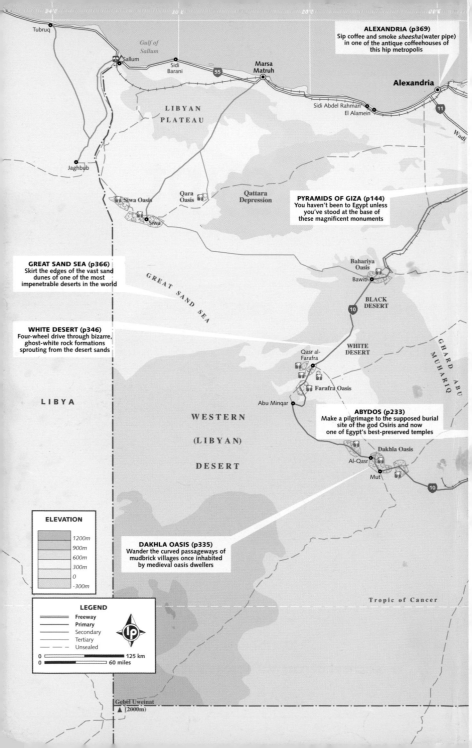

Tubruq

Gulf of Sallum

Sallum

Sidi Barani

55

Marsa Matruh

ALEXANDRIA (p369)
Sip coffee and smoke *sheesha* (water pipe) in one of the antique coffeehouses of this hip metropolis

Alexandria

Sidi Abdel Rahman
El Alamein

11

Wadi

LIBYAN PLATEAU

Jaghbub

Siwa Oasis

Siwa

Qara Oasis

Qattara Depression

PYRAMIDS OF GIZA (p144)
You haven't been to Egypt unless you've stood at the base of these magnificent monuments

Bahariya Oasis

Bawiti

GREAT SAND SEA (p366)
Skirt the edges of the vast sand dunes of one of the most impenetrable deserts in the world

G R E A T   S A N D   S E A

BLACK DESERT

10

WHITE DESERT (p346)
Four-wheel drive through bizarre, ghost-white rock formations sprouting from the desert sands

Qasr al-Farafra

WHITE DESERT

G H A R D   A B U   M U H A R I Q

LIBYA

Farafra Oasis

Abu Minqar

ABYDOS (p233)
Make a pilgrimage to the supposed burial site of the god Osiris and now one of Egypt's best-preserved temples

W E S T E R N

(L I B Y A N)

D E S E R T

Dakhla Oasis

Al-Qasr

Mut

10

ELEVATION

	1200m
	900m
	600m
	300m
	0
	-300m

DAKHLA OASIS (p335)
Wander the curved passageways of mudbrick villages once inhabited by medieval oasis dwellers

Tropic of Cancer

LEGEND
Freeway
Primary
Secondary
Tertiary
Unsealed

LP

0 ————— 125 km
0 ————— 60 miles

Gebel Uweinat
▲ (2000m)

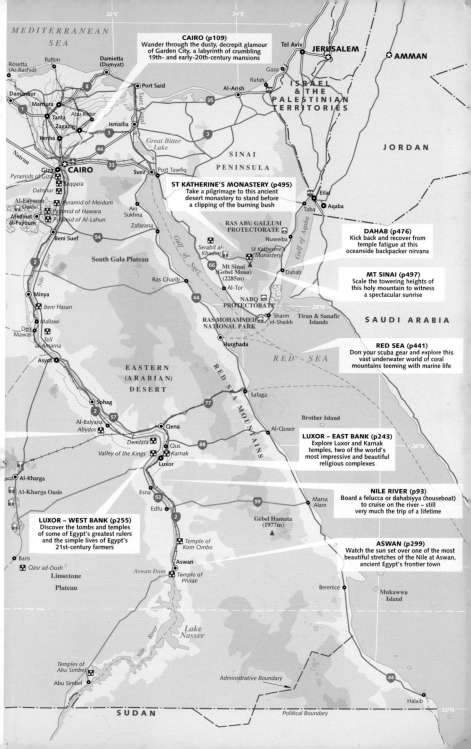

CAIRO (p109)
Wander through the dusty, decrepit glamour of Garden City, a labyrinth of crumbling 19th- and early-20th-century mansions

ST KATHERINE'S MONASTERY (p495)
Take a pilgrimage to this ancient desert monastery to stand before a clipping of the burning bush

DAHAB (p476)
Kick back and recover from temple fatigue at this oceanside backpacker nirvana

MT SINAI (p497)
Scale the towering heights of this holy mountain to witness a spectacular sunrise

RED SEA (p441)
Don your scuba gear and explore this vast underwater world of coral mountains teeming with marine life

LUXOR – EAST BANK (p243)
Explore Luxor and Karnak temples, two of the world's most impressive and beautiful religious complexes

NILE RIVER (p93)
Board a felucca or dahabiyya (houseboat) to cruise on the river – still very much the trip of a lifetime

LUXOR – WEST BANK (p255)
Discover the tombs and temples of some of Egypt's greatest rulers and the simple lives of Egypt's 21st-century farmers

ASWAN (p299)
Watch the sun set over one of the most beautiful stretches of the Nile at Aswan, ancient Egypt's frontier town

MEDITERRANEAN SEA

Rosetta (Ar-Rashid)
Baltim
Damietta (Dumyat)
Damanhur
Mansura
Tanta
Zagazig
Abu Kebir
Itenha
Ismailia
Port Said
Al-Arish
Rafah
Gaza
Tel Aviv
JERUSALEM
AMMAN
ISRAEL & THE PALESTINIAN TERRITORIES
JORDAN

Giza
CAIRO
Suez
Port Tawfiq
Great Bitter Lake
SINAI PENINSULA
Pyramids of Giza
Saqqara
Dahshur
Al-Fayoum Oasis
Pyramid of Meidum
Pyramid of Hawara
Medinat al-Fayoum
Pyramid of Al-Lahun
Ain Sukhna
Zafarana
Serabit al-Khadim
Mt Sinai (Gebel Musa) (2285m)
St Katherine's Monastery
Eilat
Taba
Aqaba
RAS ABU GALLUM PROTECTORATE
Nuweiba
Beni Suef
Ras Gharib
Al-Tor
Dahab
NABQ PROTECTORATE
Minya
Beni Hasan
Mallawi
Deir al-Mawas
Tell al-Amarna
RAS MOHAMMED NATIONAL PARK
Sharm el-Sheikh
Tiran & Sanafir Islands
SAUDI ARABIA
Hurghada

Asyut
EASTERN (ARABIAN) DESERT
RED SEA MOUNTAINS
RED SEA
Sohag
Al-Balyana
Abydos
Qena
Dendara
Valley of the Kings
Qus
Karnak
Luxor
Al-Kharga
Al-Kharga Oasis
Esna
Edfu
Temple of Kom Ombo
Baris
Qasr ad-Dush
Limestone Plateau
Aswan Dam
Aswan
Temple of Philae
Berenice
Mukawwa Island
Brother Island
Safaga
Al-Quseir
Marsa Alam
Gebel Hamata (1977m)

Lake Nasser
Temples of Abu Simbel
Abu Simbel
Administrative Boundary
Halaib
Political Boundary
SUDAN

South Gala Plateau
Gulf of Suez
Gulf of Aqaba
Nile River
Natrun

On the Road

MATTHEW D FIRESTONE Coordinating Author

Sometimes a picture really does speak a thousand words, which is convenient given that sunrise at the top of Mt Sinai (p497) awed me with its brilliance, and left me utterly speechless. Fortunately, my Bedouin guide recognised my trance-like state and snapped this photo just as the morning light washed away the stars and ignited the sky.

ANTHONY SATTIN Too often the tombs and temples in Luxor and Aswan are so packed you can do no more than dodge the crowds, which adds to the joy of finding yourself somewhere a little more remote. Most of the ancient sites between Abydos and Cairo are empty these days but the difficulties of reaching them can dampen the thrill. Now without the need to travel in a police convoy on the Luxor–Aswan route, reaching somewhere like Gebel Silsila (p296) is a lot easier and well worth the effort.

THOMAS HALL Third dive of the afternoon, crystal-clear and bath-warm water, hanging out 30 feet below the surface watching turtles, sharks and a veritable smorgasbord of incredibly colourful little Nemos dart by, soon to ascend back to the boat for ice-cold gin-and-tonics and a simple, filling dinner served by the cook – yawn, just another average day diving in the Red Sea (p441).

MICHAEL BENANAV I love experiencing the intense personality changes that the Western Desert (p326) undergoes every day. Its brutal midday heat provides the perfect excuse to nap somewhere shady; its sunsets are vibrant and alluring; at night it's quiet and kind and, with a dazzling starscape overhead, so easy to be psyched to be alive.

For full author biographies see p551

Egypt Highlights

Egypt is a behemoth of a destination that quickly brings out the explorer in all of us. The vast grandeur and beauty of this ancient land is evident in the lofty heights of Mt Sinai, the silent depths of the Red Sea, the ancient tombs of Luxor and the open expanses of the Siwa Oasis. In a land where time is measured by dynasties, and distance by the setting sun, it is best to travel slowly, and lose yourself in the infinite expanse of sand and sea.

ARIADNE VAN ZANDBERGEN

1 LUXOR'S WEST BANK

Wake before dawn on Luxor's West Bank and see the abode of death – the tombs of kings, queens and nobles – come to life. Deir al-Bahri (Temple of Hatshepsut, pictured above; p267) and all the other tombs are open from 6am, at which time most of the crowds are still slumbering in their hotels.

Anthony Sattin, Lonely Planet Author

SARA-JANE CLELAND

2 SIWA OASIS

It's impossible not to relax in Siwa (p355), the Dahab of the desert. With cold springs and palm groves to keep you cool in the day, and the best cafe/restaurant scene in the Western Desert to entertain you at night, it's easy to spend enough time in Siwa to make the long drive there worthwhile.

Michael Benanav, Lonely Planet Author

ARIADNE VAN ZANDBERGEN

3 STEP PYRAMID

Everyone knows about *the* Pyramids, but did you know about the *other* pyramids? While the majority of tourists are fending off camel drivers and souvenir touts at the Pyramids of Giza, savvy travellers are exploring the earlier monuments at both Saqqara and Dahshur. Of particular interest is the Step Pyramid of Zoser (pictured above; p198), which is regarded by archaeologists as the oldest pyramid in the world. Also not to be missed is the Red Pyramid (p205), believed to be the first true pyramid, and the inspiration for the Great Pyramid at Giza.

Matthew D Firestone, Lonely Planet Author

RED SEA

Egypt is more than sun, sand, pyramids and the Nile – the Red Sea (p441) is regarded as one of the premier scuba-diving destinations in the world. Whether you've logged hundreds of dives or you're looking to get certified, don't miss Egypt's remarkable underwater world. One highlight in particular is the *Thistlegorm* (p451), a huge underwater wreck discovered by Jacques Cousteau. After descending to 30m and penetrating the cargo hold, you'll find yourself among a living museum of World War II memorabilia including motorcycles, jeeps, tanks and armoury.

Matthew D Firestone, Lonely Planet Author

MARK WEBSTER

MT SINAI

Even if you're not normally an early riser, do not miss the sunrise from the top of Mt Sinai (p497). Truth be told, you're going to have to climb through the night if you want to be at the summit in time for the first rays of sunshine. But there are few mountains in the world that can top Sinai in terms of significance, especially since the peak is sacred to Jews, Christians and Muslims alike.

Matthew D Firestone, Lonely Planet Author

FRANS LEMMENS

ANDERS BLOMQVIS

6 RAMESSEUM

Visit some of the less popular ancient temples. Many of the sites between Cairo and Luxor see few visitors because of the difficulty of travel in this area. But even in Luxor some sites are missed out completely by tour groups – not because they are not worth visiting, but because there is too much to see in a day or two. So mix the must-see sights, places such as the Valley of the Kings and Karnak Temple, with some others. The funerary Temple of Seti I (p258) doesn't get the crowds, but even somewhere as important as the Ramesseum (p270), the memorial temple of Ramses II, has been empty on my last couple of visits.

Anthony Sattin, Lonely Planet Author

ASWAN SUNSET

Watch the sun set over Aswan (p299): there is something about the way the river is squeezed between rocks here, the proximity of the desert, the lonely burial places of the Aga Khan and of forgotten princes up on the rise on the west bank, that makes sunset here more poignant than anywhere else along the Egyptian Nile.

Anthony Sattin, Lonely Planet Author

7

JOHN ELK III

SHEESHA

Smoke a *sheesha*. The bubbling water pipe is as essential to life in Egypt as the Nile itself. Keep it real with macho molasses-flavoured tobacco at a traditional *ahwa* (coffeehouse; p170) or go upscale with a fresh-fruit-cocktail treatment at one of Cairo's numerous chic lounges.

**Zora O'Neill,
Lonely Planet Author**

8

ARIADNE VAN ZANDBERGEN

CHRISTINE OSBORNE

9

COPTIC SITES

Seek out one of the many Coptic sites along the Nile, some at least 1600 years old and still used as churches, convents and monasteries. They tend to be overwhelmed on feast days, when thousands of faithful come to pray, but at other times they can be sleepy places full of beauty and fascination, perhaps nowhere more so than Deir al-Muharraq (p227), north of Asyut.

**Anthony Sattin,
Lonely Planet Author**

DAHAB

If you're looking for a slice of Thailand in the Middle East, there is no better place to kick back and slow things down a bit than Dahab (p476). Although it has expanded beyond its humble origins as a beach-side hippy colony, Dahab is still ruled by independent travellers. Whether you're looking to dive the Red Sea, trek through the interior or spend most of your days smoking *sheesha* by the sea, chances are you're going to get stuck here for longer than you planned.

**Matthew D Firestone,
Lonely Planet Author**

10

RELAX IN A MOSQUE

The quiet, shady arcades of a medieval mosque, such as Al-Azhar Mosque (pictured above; p129), are the perfect place to take a break from modern Cairo – kick your shoes off and stay a while. The Mosque of Amr ibn al-As (p128) has plenty of room, while the Mosque of Al-Maridani (p136) is filled with trees.

Zora O'Neill, Lonely Planet Author

11

PYRAMIDS OF GIZA

Although they're Egypt's most iconic images, nothing can prepare you for the sense of awe and wonderment you'll feel when you first lay eyes on the Pyramids of Giza (p144) and the Sphinx (p151). Towering over both the urban sprawl of Giza and the desert plains beyond, these ancient monuments are at the top of every traveller's itinerary, and they never fail to amaze. Bring lots of water, an empty memory card, and a lot of patience! Although you'll have to fend off lots of touts to enjoy this ancient funerary complex in peace, no trip to Egypt is complete without a visit to Giza.

Matthew D Firestone, Lonely Planet Author

12

DONALD C. & PRISCILLA ALEXANDER EASTMAN

SOUQS

Commercial insanity reigns in Egypt's souqs, where bargaining is part of everyday life. Haggle for dusty antiques, new bicycles, secondhand shirts, vintage sunglasses…or perhaps you'd like to buy a donkey?

Zora O'Neill, Lonely Planet Author

13

FRANS LEMMENS

14

JOHN ELK III

PETRA

Hewn from rose-coloured rock, legendary Petra (p492), in Jordan, is one of the most impressive archaeological sites in the region and only a hop and a skip away from Sinai. From the iconic Treasury, location of the Holy Grail in *Indiana Jones*, to the mountaintop Monastery, Petra shouldn't be missed.

Matthew D Firestone, Lonely Planet Author

CHRIS MELLC

15 ABU SIMBEL

Spend the night in Abu Simbel (p323) and visit the Great Temple of Ramses II (p324). Explore the growing town and its attractions, not least local musician Fikry Kachif's simple hotel Eskaleh (see p325), dedicated to all aspects of Nubian culture.

Rafael Wlodarski, Lonely Planet Author

Contents

Regional Map Contents

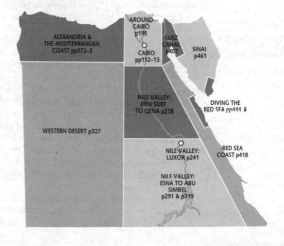

Destination Egypt

A land of magnificent World Heritage Sites and a thousand tourist clichés, Egypt was enticing visitors millennia before Mr Thomas Cook sailed his first steamers up the Nile. It was in Egypt that the Holy Family sheltered, Alexander conquered and Mark Antony flirted. Napoleon stopped long enough to pilfer a few obelisks, the Ottomans paused to prop up the great and barbarous pasha Mohammed Ali, and the British stayed around to get the train system running and furnish every spare nook of the British Museum. And all this was long, long after Menes united the two states of Upper and Lower Egypt, and set the stage for one of the greatest civilisations the world has ever known.

Lingering over coffee in one of Alexandria's cosmopolitan cafes or sipping a calming glass of *shai* (tea) after a frenzied shopping episode in Cairo's Khan al-Khalili are activities as popular today as they were back when 19th-century tourists started to arrive en masse. Magnificent monuments are everywhere – the pointed perfection of the Pyramids, soaring minarets of Cairo's skyline and majestic tombs and temples of Luxor are just a few of the wonders that generations of visitors have admired during their city sojourns, jaunts up and down the Nile and expeditions through spectacularly stark desert landscapes.

Beyond the graceful symmetry and calculated order of the country's ancient pyramid and temple complexes, Egypt is bursting at the seams. More than half a century on from the great Nasser-led revolution, Egypt is in a pretty bad state. Unemployment is rife, the economy is of the basket-case variety and terrorist attacks are starting to occur with worrying regularity. Once home to the all-powerful pharaohs, the country has largely been reduced to a dependent state of the USA, having received more than US$30 billion dollars in military aid and economic assistance over the past three decades.

The list of woes continues: torture and ill-treatment of prisoners in detention by police, described by Amnesty International as 'systematic'; the issue of child labour, particularly within the lucrative national cotton industry (UNICEF reports over one million children are believed to work in this industry alone); regularly reported cases of 'administrative detention' of individuals without trial, which has brought criticism from both local media and international human rights organisations; continuing restrictions on women under personal-status laws, which, for example, deny the freedom to travel without permission; rampant inflation, leading to food shortages within the poorest communities; and constant environmental threats, with polluted waterways, overpopulation, unregulated emissions and soil salinity being of serious concern.

Against the backdrop of America's 'War on Terror', Egypt has weathered a storm of internal strife, and struggled to define its identity as a moderate Islamic country. On one hand, Egypt was a member of former US President George W Bush's ill-fated 'Coalition of the Willing', and the sultry belly dancing of underground pop sensation Dina helped spark a debate on the nation's traditional views of sexuality. On the other hand, Egyptian opinion polls have shown outrage over Bush's support of Israel, and the emergence of televangelist Amr Khaled is credited with encouraging young girls to start wearing the headscarf.

While it remains to be seen whether or not the Barack Hussein Obama presidency will redefine America's image in the region, the promise of change is alive and well. Several months after taking the oath of office, President

FAST FACTS

Population: 83 million

Population growth rate: 1.6%

Inflation: 18.3%

GDP: US$443 billion

Main exports: Petroleum, petroleum products, cotton

Average annual income: US$4200

Average male life expectancy: 69 years

Average female life expectancy: 74 years

Male literacy rate: 83%

Female literacy rate: 59%

Estimated number of taxis in the Cairo area: 50,000

Obama made good on his word to deliver a speech in a major Islamic capital. The venue for this historic address was none other than Cairo University, and Egyptians from all walks of life tuned in to hear the words of a Western emissary, whose middle name means 'good' or 'handsome' in the Arabic language. Pledging a new beginning between America and Muslims around the world, Obama sought to forge a relationship based on mutual interest and respect.

Unfortunately, it's politics as usual on the home front, with more than a quarter of a century having passed since Hosni Mubarak and his wife Suzanne first set up house in the presidential palace. While he has drawn a small measure of political legitimacy from a series of highly contested elections alongside the continued implementation of martial law (first declared in 1981 following the assassination of former President Sadat), the fact remains that Mubarak is one of Africa's longest-serving 'Big Men'. Born in 1928, Mubarak is now well into his golden years, though his health is something of a closely guarded state secret.

Mubarak's imminent demise raises some serious questions about the future political and economic stability of Egypt. While it's widely believed that Mubarak's younger son, Gamal, is being groomed for the role of president, the Mubarak family continues to deny such allegations. Regardless of who takes control of the country, the next president (or pseudo-monarch) will have to address some very real issues, including Islamic fundamentalism, domestic terrorism, the Israeli-Palestinian conflict and the changing economic scene, which are all to some degree interconnected.

Indeed, the last couple of years have been marked by further terror attacks in Cairo, riots over the price of wheat and border instability with the Gaza Strip. To his credit, Mubarak has carefully walked a thin line in his attempts to maintain order at home while brokering peace between Israel and the Palestinian Territories, though critics are quick to describe his actions as being little more than chasing rats off a sinking ship. One bright note for visitors has been the lifting of decade-old restrictions that forced travellers into tourist convoys in the Nile Valley, which will ultimately foster more independent travel throughout the country.

Of course, one of the many reasons why Egypt remains such a fascinating tourist destination is that it is very much a country in flux. Egypt may be famous the world over for the Pyramids of Giza and the Valley of the Kings, but these ancient monuments are just part of the equation. Whether in the suffocating density of Cairo's city streets or the harsh elements of the open desert, the Egyptians are an incredibly resilient people who find humour and optimism in the most unlikely of circumstances. While your travels in Egypt won't always be easygoing and hassle-free, they'll certainly be eye-opening, to say the least.

Getting Started

Egypt is the most traveller-friendly country in North Africa and the Middle East. Most of the tourist spots are well connected by cheap buses, and many are also linked by trains and planes. Accommodation is plentiful, particularly in the budget and top-end categories, and decent eateries are thick on the ground in nearly every corner of the country. Unlike in some other parts of the region, enjoying a beer, meeting the locals and accessing the internet are all things that can be taken for granted. Predeparture planning will usually guarantee your accommodation of choice but on the whole it's not necessary – unless you're on a tight timetable, it's usually more enjoyable to leave your itinerary in the lap of the gods. After all, there are a lot of them to call on...

WHEN TO GO

The best time to visit Egypt depends on where you want to go. Generally speaking, winter (December to February) is the tourist high season and summer (June to August) is the low season in all parts of the country except on the coasts, and to a lesser degree in Cairo. Hotel prices reflect this.

In terms of weather, June to August is unbearable almost anywhere south of Cairo, especially around Luxor and Aswan, where daytime temperatures soar up to 40°C. Summer in Cairo is almost as hot and the combination of heat, dust, pollution, noise and crush makes walking the city streets a real test of endurance. On the other hand, a scorching sun might be exactly what's wanted for a week or two of slow roasting on the beaches of southern Sinai, the Alexandrian coast or the Red Sea – just be prepared to fight for hotel rooms with locals on their summer holidays and Gulf Arabs escaping the even greater heat in their home countries.

See Climate Charts (p508) for more information.

When visiting somewhere such as Luxor, winter is easily the most comfortable time. Cairo isn't quite as pleasant, with often overcast skies and chilly evenings, while up on the Mediterranean coast Alexandria is subject to frequent downpours resulting in flooded, muddy streets. Even Sinai's beaches are a little too chilly for sunbathing in January. The happiest compromise for an all-Egypt trip is to visit in spring (March to May) or autumn (September to November).

Most of Egypt's religious and state holidays (for dates see p513) last only one or two days at most and should not seriously disrupt any travel plans. Buses, however, may be fully booked around the two *eids* (feasts) and on Sham an-Nessim. Ramadan, the Muslim month of fasting, can be seriously disruptive to your best-laid travel plans. During daylight hours many cafes and restaurants are closed, while bars cease business completely for the duration. Offices also operate at reduced and very erratic hours.

COSTS & MONEY

By international standards Egypt is still fairly cheap, though admission fees, guided tours and private transportation can really hike up the costs.

If you're a hard-core budget traveller, it's possible to get by on about US$20 a day or maybe less, though you will have to stick to the cheapest hotels, eat the staple snacks of *fuul* and *ta'amiyya*, use the cheapest local transport and limit your sightseeing. At the other end of the scale, Egypt has plenty of accommodation charging upwards of US$200 a night, and some of the better restaurants will set you back US$20 per person or more.

DON'T LEAVE HOME WITHOUT...

There is very little that you might need and won't be able to find in Egypt. That said, you may not have the same degree of choice as at home.

- Sunglasses, sunscreen and a hat
- A torch (flashlight)
- Earplugs if you're a light sleeper (bus rides are rarely quiet, Cairo is a very noisy city and throughout the country dawn is accompanied by the amplified voice of the muezzin calling the faithful to prayer)
- A sweater or light jacket for winter evenings in desert areas
- Contact-lens solution, roll-on mosquito repellent, tampons and contraceptives (all sometimes difficult to find and expensive)
- Checking the travel advisories for a current security update (p511)

Taking a middle route, if you stay in a modest hotel with a fan and private bathroom, eat in low-key restaurants frequented by locals (allowing for occasional meals at more upmarket eateries), and aim to see a couple of sites each day, you'll be looking at between US$30 and US$50 a day.

It is inexpensive to get around the country: the 10-hour train ride between Cairo and Luxor can cost less than US$10 in 2nd class, and even domestic flights on EgyptAir can cost less than US$100. However, the cost of private taxis and chartered minibuses between tourist destinations can quickly add up, though these are often the safest and most comfortable way to travel.

The major expense is going to be the entry fees to tourist sites. Foreigners are seen as dollars on legs, so places where they flock tend to be pricey. A complete visit to the Giza Pyramids costs more than US$50 in admission charges, while seeing the mummies at the Egyptian Museum costs about US$25. However, if you have a valid International Student Identity Card (ISIC), you can rack up some good discounts. Of course, no card will make you exempt from the demands for baksheesh, which can seriously drain your wallet if you're not careful.

A service charge of between 10% and 15% is applied in most upmarket restaurants and hotels, to which value-added tax (VAT) and municipal taxes are also added. In other words, the price that you are quoted at a hotel or read on a menu could be almost 25% higher when it comes to paying the bill.

HOW MUCH?

Meal in a cheap restaurant E£15 to E£25

Meal in a good restaurant E£65 to E£125

Glass of tea E£2 to E£3

Short taxi hop E£5 to E£10

Average museum admission E£30

TRAVELLING RESPONSIBLY

When backpackers first started blazing the hippie trail across the old Silk Road during the 1960s and 1970s, sustainability was an implicit concept that few people needed to give much thought. Travel at the time was nearly always slow, overland and utterly dependant on local economies.

Things change, however, and sometimes in dramatic ways. Today, travel is one of the world's fastest-growing industries, and is one of the largest single contributors to the Egyptian economy. But this growth has also placed enormous stress on both the environment and traditional communities, and threatens to destroy the very destinations that tourists are seeking out.

One of the simplest things you can do before embarking on a trip to Egypt is to learn about pressing conservation and environmental issues – for more information, see the Environment chapter, p88. While travelling around the country, don't be afraid to ask questions – usually the best source of information about an area is from those actually living there.

TIPS FOR TRAVELLING RESPONSIBLY

Take only photographs, leave only footprints – the following is a list of Lonely Planet author-tested tips for minimising the impact of your stay and limiting your ecological footprint.

Learn the language Although English is widely spoken as a second language in Egypt, it's well worth making an effort to learn a bit of Arabic. Knowing the basic greetings will win the respect of locals, and a firm command of the numbers will give you some bargaining power.

Sail the Nile The only choice for Cleopatra is still the best way to go for 21st-century travellers. Until recently feluccas were the only sail-powered option but there are now a growing number of dahabiyyas (houseboats), most of them operating between Esna and Aswan.

Rent a bike The opening of the bridge across the Nile in Luxor has seen a huge rise in the number of coaches and taxis on the West Bank, with all the usual issues of pollution. But bikes are easy to rent on both sides of the river and slow travelling gives you a different perspective on the country.

Don't bribe guards Do give them a present if you want – they are paid so little that any amount will be welcome – but don't bribe them to let you bend or break rules that are meant to protect local sites.

Don't touch the ruins The deterioration of temples, pyramids and monuments due to rampant overtourism has reached critical levels. Unless drastic measures are taken, a large percentage of reliefs and paintings may be gone in another generation.

Dress conservatively Rural areas in the deserts are home to very conservative communities that do not see many travellers. Be cautious with revealing dress, showing affection in public and any behaviour that may offend sensibilities.

Use a pump For many travellers, drinking bottled water is a necessity. However, you can go easy on the plastic by bringing your own pump and filtering the tap water.

Community preservation is one area where travellers can make the biggest individual difference. While in Egypt, talk to the locals about their customs and practices. Indeed, the best window into a local culture might be sitting next to you on the bus or sharing a bench with you in a cafe. And you never know where a conversation will take you.

Finally, one of the most immediate benefits of tourism is the financial boost. A great way of stimulating local economies in a sustainable manner is to frequent businesses that are dedicated to these aims. For a list of eco-friendly businesses in Egypt, see the GreenDex, p571.

TRAVEL LITERATURE

In an Antique Land by Amitav Ghosh is a wonderfully observant account of the author's lengthy stay in a Delta village. It's entertaining, educational and one of the few travel books that is not patronising towards its subject.

The Pharaoh's Shadow by Anthony Sattin is travel literature with a twist. Sattin searches for 'survivals' of Pharaonic traditions and practices in the Egypt of today, encountering magicians, snake catchers, mystics and sceptics along the way. Also by Anthony Sattin, *Florence Nightingale's Letters from Egypt* tells of the five-month trip that the famous 'Lady with the Lamp' took through Egypt in the winter of 1849–50. The book is packed with 19th-century images.

The Blue Nile and *The White Nile* by Alan Moorhead form a two-volume tour de force describing the search for sources of the Nile.

Flaubert in Egypt: A Sensibility on Tour, translated and edited by Francis Steegmuller, includes choice excerpts from Flaubert's diary as he made his way up the Nile. Detailed descriptions of Upper Egyptian dancing girls and prostitutes spice up his accounts of ancient sites.

A Thousand Miles Up the Nile by Amelia Edwards is a travel classic describing a 19th-century journey from Cairo to Abu Simbel and back on a dahabiyya.

Letters from Egypt by Lucie Duff Gordon is the journal of a solo woman traveller who lived in Luxor for seven years from 1862 to 1869.

Travels with a Tangerine: A Journey in the Footnotes of Ibn Battutah by Tim Mackintosh-Smith sees the modern-day author following the route taken by the medieval adventurer; three great chapters are set in Egypt.

Cairo: The City Victorious by Max Rodenbeck offers a broad history of Cairo and a commentary on modern social life – it's great for helping foreigners adjust their attitudes to the city.

PREDEPARTURE FILM VIEWING

In recent years taxes levied on foreign film companies have kept the cameras away (that's Tunisia standing in for Egypt in *The English Patient* and *Raiders of the Lost Ark,* Arizona in *Stargate,* and computer-generated imagery in the remake of *The Mummy*). But even if they haven't been shot on location, there are plenty of films that evoke the country and its colourful history splendidly. All make great predeparture viewing.

The Ten Commandments (1956) with Charlton Heston, Yul Brynner and Anne Baxter is an enduring classic about the Exodus of the Israelites out of Egypt.

Cleopatra (1963) starring Elizabeth Taylor and Richard Burton almost bankrupted 20th Century Fox, though the film remains the best onscreen adaptation of the famous love affair between Mark Antony and Cleopatra.

The Spy Who Loved Me (1977) starring Roger Moore as James Bond follows the exploits of the original international man of mystery as he travels

TOP PICKS

JOURNEYS

Given the array of transport options – from donkey to luxury dahabiyya – Egypt is one place where the journey itself can be the adventure. These are just a few worth experiencing while you're here.

- Taxi (p182) or bus ride (p180) through the chaos of Cairo
- Camel or horse ride from Giza to Saqqara (p145)
- Cycling around the West Bank in Luxor (p288)

- Felucca down the Nile between Luxor and Aswan (p99)
- Donkey cart around Siwa Oasis (p366)
- Jeep expedition through the Great Sand Sea (p328)

SLEEPS

Whatever your budget and style, there's accommodation in Egypt to suit you.

- Beach camp – Penguin Village, Dahab (p480)
- Boutique hotel – Talisman Hotel, Cairo (p161)
- Budget hotels – Hotel Luna, Cairo (p160) and Nefertiti Hotel, Luxor (p278)

- Ecolodges – Basata, Mahash (p491) and Adrére Amellal, Siwa (p362)
- Hotel with a view – Desert Lodge, Dakhla (p342)
- Luxury hotel – Al-Moudira, Luxor (p282)

to Egypt and meets the lovely Agent Triple X in front of the Pyramids of Giza.

Based on an Agatha Christie novel, *Death on the Nile* (1978) featuring Peter Ustinov and Jane Birkin follows the murder investigation of Belgian detective Hercule Poirot as he travels along the Nile.

Al-Mohager (The Emigrant; 1994) by Egyptian director Youssef Chahine is a beautiful avant-garde Arabic film that relates the journey through life of a man who has been rejected by his family.

Although it doesn't actually show Egypt, *The English Patient* (1996) with Ralph Fiennes and Kristin Scott Thomas depicts a love story set against the North Africa campaign of WWII.

The Yacoubian Building (2006), an onscreen adaptation of the best-selling Egyptian novel by Alaa al-Aswany, is a scathing commentary on the modern decay of Egypt's political system.

Transformers 2: Revenge of the Fallen (2009) isn't exactly critically acclaimed cinema but Shia Labeouf and Megan Fox do look pretty dashing as they're racing alongside giant robots in Luxor and Giza.

INTERNET RESOURCES

Al-Ahram Weekly (http://weekly.ahram.org.eg) Electronic version of the weekly English-language newspaper. Almost the whole paper is online and the archives are fully searchable and free to access.

Egypt: The Complete Guide (www.egypt.travel) The official site of the Egyptian Tourist Authority is updated fairly regularly with magazine-type features, news and a huge range of resources and links.

Lonely Planet (www.lonelyplanet.com) Includes summaries on travelling to Egypt, the Thorn Tree forum, travel news and links to the most useful travel resources on the web.

Red Sea Guide & Search Engine (www.red-sea.com) This site does exactly what the name suggests: provides heaps of travel tips and water-sports information and links.

State Information Service (www.sis.gov.eg) A large amount of information on tourism, geography and culture, plus a great many useful links.

Theban Mapping Project (www.thebanmappingproject.com) Professor Kent Weeks' website dedicated to all things to do with the Valley of the Kings. One of the best Egyptology websites out there.

Itineraries
CLASSIC ROUTES

EGYPT BENEATH THE SURFACE

More than One Month / Cairo to Sinai plus Siwa & Petra

In a month or more you could cover most of Egypt's main sights and still have time to explore the Western Desert and even southern Jordan.

While in **Cairo** (p109), include a visit to **Coptic Cairo** (p125), the oldest part of modern-day Cairo and the Christian heartland of the city.

Before heading south to Aswan, take an early train north to Alexandria and a bus for **Siwa Oasis** (p355), one of Egypt's most idyllic spots. After hanging out in this tranquil haven, backtrack along the Mediterranean coast to **Alexandria** (p369) and spend a couple of days in its wonderful cafes and museums.

Take the sleeper train (or plane) to **Aswan** (p299), then back to **Luxor** (p239) and eventually **Dahab** (p476). Here, you should slow down and enjoy the laid-back Bedouin vibe of Sinai, pausing only to arrange the obligatory **dive trip** (p447) and/or **desert safari** (p479). Finally, say goodbye (temporarily) to Egypt on a brief excursion to Jordan and the ancient Nabataean city of **Petra** (p492), one of the 'New Seven Wonders of the World'.

If you have more than a month, you could comfortably cover over 2000km and visit Egypt's far-flung desert oases in addition to Jordan's ancient city of Petra.

WHISTLE-STOP NILE TOUR   One to Two Weeks / Cairo to Abu Simbel

On a punishing schedule, one to two weeks is just enough time to traverse the length of the Nile Valley and see some of Egypt's most famous sights.

Two days in **Cairo** (p109) will allow you to see the astounding **Pyramids of Giza** (p144), seek out the treasures in the **Egyptian Museum** (p183) and shop till you drop in **Khan al-Khalili** (p130). Catch the overnight train (or a quick flight) to **Luxor** (p239), arriving early in the morning – the perfect time to head over to the **West Bank** (p255) to see the monuments of the ancient necropolis of Thebes. In two days you can visit most major sights, including the **Valley of the Kings** (p258), the **Valley of the Queens** (p273) and **Deir al-Bahri** (Temple of Hatshepsut; p267). Spend the afternoons and evenings cooling off on the **East Bank** (p243), but be sure to save time for the spectacular **temples of Karnak** (p243) and **Luxor** (p250).

You can either jump on a morning train to **Aswan** (p299), or spend a few days sailing down the Nile on a budget-friendly **felucca** (p101) or a luxurious five-star **cruiser** (p105). From Aswan, you absolutely must visit **Abu Simbel** (p323), the grandest of all Pharaonic monuments, which is perched on the edge of Lake Nasser. With a day or two to spare, you can explore Aswan's other highlights including the **Nubia Museum** (p302) and the **Unfinished Obelisk** (p303) before hightailing it back to Cairo.

The 1000km Whistle-Stop Nile Tour will race you along the lifeline of Egypt – the Nile River – teasing you with a brief taste of what this country can offer.

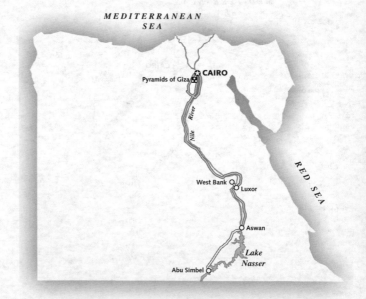

TRAVELLING AT A STEADY PACE

**Two Weeks to One Month /
Cairo to Sinai**

Two weeks to a month is an ideal amount of time to get the most out of the Nile Valley while including the Sinai Peninsula on your journey.

Starting in **Cairo** (p109), be sure to add the **Step Pyramid of Zoser** (p198) at Saqqara and the **Bent** (p205) and **Red Pyramids** (p205) at Dahshur to your itinerary, as well as the twisting alleyways and splendid mosques of the medieval quarters of **Islamic Cairo** (p162). Take your time and spend a moment or two relaxing in one of the area's fabulous *ahwa*s (coffeehouses), where you can alternate between sips of strong Turkish-style coffee and puffs of apple-scented *sheesha* (water pipe).

Next, take a train or fly straight down to **Aswan** (p299), from where you can take trips to the island **Temple of Isis** (p315) at Philae and the **West Bank** (p305), home to ancient monasteries and tombs that cling to the edges of the desert. Then, move into relaxation mode with a slow felucca or cruiser, sailing up to **Kom Ombo** (p296), site of a fine Ptolemaic-era temple dedicated to Sobek, and **Edfu** (p293), site of a fine Ptolemaic-era temple dedicated to Horus.

From here you can move on to **Luxor** (p239) before catching a bus across the Eastern Desert to the resort town of **Hurghada** (p423), where you can catch a ferry to **Sharm el-Sheikh** (p466) and on to the backpacker paradise of **Dahab** (p476). Around here you can delight in the underwater world before visiting the Greek Orthodox **St Katherine's Monastery** (p495) and climbing to the top of **Mt Sinai** (p497), revered by Muslims, Christians and Jews alike.

Whether you have two weeks or 40 days and 40 nights, you can experience at a steady pace this 1500km jaunt through the Nile Valley and Sinai.

ROADS LESS TRAVELLED

EXPLORING THE WESTERN DESERT Two Weeks / Luxor to Siwa

Taking inspiration from films such as *Lawrence of Arabia* and *The English Patient*, would-be desert rovers should opt for two weeks of getting sand-happy in the amazing **Western Desert** (p326).

Begin your journey by taking a bus from **Luxor** (p239) to **Al-Kharga Oasis** (p329), the southernmost oasis in the Western Desert loop. Spend a day here exploring the **Al-Kharga Museum of Antiquities** (p330) as well as the profusion of Graeco-Roman temples, tombs and other interesting ruins scattered around the oasis.

Shun the cities for two weeks in favour of getting swept up in deserts, though be sure to take time to chill out and cool down in the stunning oases.

From Al-Kharga, make your way northwest to **Dakhla Oasis** (p335) for the experience of seeing the fascinating hivelike, mud-walled settlements of **Balat** (p340) and **Al-Qasr** (p341). Next, head north to either **Farafra Oasis** (p343) or **Bahariya Oasis** (p347), both of which are great places to organise trips out into the stunning **White Desert** (p346).

Real desert addicts can then strike west across several hundred kilometres of open desert to **Siwa Oasis** (p355), one of the most surreal spots in the entire country. Perched on the edge of the **Great Sand Sea** (p366), Siwa is renowned for its dates and olives, and serves as a convenient base for exploring some of the most stunning yet accessible sandscapes in Egypt.

EXPLORING THE SINAI PENINSULA

Two Weeks / Sharm el-Sheikh to Taba

If you really want to get a taste of all the Sinai has to offer, spend about two weeks exploring its incredible desert landscapes and serene underwater world.

Starting in **Sharm el-Sheikh** (p466), the gateway to Sinai, hop on a bus to **Dahab** (p476), a laid-back town dubbed the 'Ko Samui of the Middle East'. From here, you can easily arrange all of your camel and jeep safaris to such natural wonders as the **Coloured Canyon** (p479) and the **Ras Abu Gallum Protectorate** (p483).

If you're looking to get wet, a diving trip to **Ras Mohammed National Park** (p464), home to some of the world's most spectacular reefs, is a must. Serious divers can arrange trips to more remote reefs or to the world-famous **Thistlegorm** (p451), a wrecked British supply ship that was sunk during WWII with a full cargo of military goods.

After waiting 24 hours for your body to release all that nitrogen, lace up your hiking boots and head to the **St Katherine Protectorate** (p495). Head first to **St Katherine's Monastery** (p495), which is a must for the complete biblical experience – it has the burning bush, a famous Byzantine church and a stunning icon collection. Afterwards, arrange a trek through the protectorate with a Bedouin guide, but save some energy for a night-time ascent of **Mt Sinai** (p497) in order to catch the spectacular sunrise.

After your mountain-climbing excursions, choose any of Sinai's far-flung beaches to relax and recover – a good place to start is at any of the camps along the coast from **Nuweiba** to **Taba** (p490).

In about two weeks, you could explore the underwater and desert landscapes of the Sinai Peninsula, the crossroads of Africa.

TAILORED TRIPS

THE ANCIENT EGYPT TRAIL

If you're interested in the Pharaonic era, it greatly adds to the travel experience to tour Egypt in a chronological fashion.

Start in **Cairo** (p109), making Saqqara the first port of call to view the **Step Pyramid of Zoser** (p198), the prototype of all pyramids to come. Next, travel to

Dahshur to view the **Bent Pyramid** (p205) and **Red Pyramid** (p205) before returning to Giza to see the final article in the **Great Pyramid of Khufu** (p149). Visit the **Egyptian Museum** (p183), focusing on the Old Kingdom galleries.

Your next stop should be **Luxor** (p239), moving into the era of the Middle and New Kingdoms. The temple complex of **Karnak** (p243) offers a history lesson set in stone. Cross to the West Bank, and explore the **Valley of the Kings** (p258) and the **Valley of the Queens** (p273), viewing the tombs in chronological order to witness the development of tomb painting. Before leaving the West Bank, visit **Medinat Habu** (p273) for the most complete expression of the Pharaonic golden age.

Travel north by train or taxi to Al-Balyana for **Abydos** (p233), the ancient burial ground of Osiris and home to the sublime **Temple of Seti I** (p234). Finally, return to Cairo and revisit the Egyptian Museum, this time to see the Middle and New Kingdom galleries.

EGYPT FROM BELOW

Egypt isn't just about pyramids and deserts, and it only takes a quick plunge in the Red Sea to find yourself in another world.

If you're a certified diver, set aside as much time as possible to **dive** (p441) Egypt's incredible number and variety of sites. One of the best ways to do this is to explore the Red Sea on a **live-aboard** (p456), which allows you access to some of the country's most far-flung and pristine locales. The challenging dive spots in the **south** (p452) and **far south** (p453) have restricted access and see no more than a smattering of divers each year. If you don't have your licence, you can always spend a few busy days in **Dahab** (p476) studying up for your PADI certification (see p456). Don't leave before diving the infamous

Bells & Blue Hole (p447), a gaping underwater sinkhole that simulates the feeling of skydiving. Also check out the **Canyon** (p447), a long, narrow trench filled with corals and schools of exotic fish.

Regardless of where you base yourself, organise a trip to **Ras Mohammed National Park** (p449), the crown jewel of Egypt's underwater offerings. With so many spots, it can be difficult to choose a site, though you can't go wrong with **Shark Observatory** (p449). And don't miss the hulking mass that is the **Thistlegorm** (p451), regarded by some as the top wreck dive in the world.

IMPRINTS OF ANCIENT CULTURE

With a rich and diverse heritage stretching back several millennia, Egypt is a treasure trove of ancient cultural sites that beckon to be explored.

It goes without saying that the **Pyramids of Giza** (p144) and the temples and tombs at **Luxor** (p250) are the best evidence of Pharaonic Egypt. However, don't let these sights overshadow all of the other cultures that have touched Egypt over the millennia.

Although its legendary library is no more, it's worth visiting **Alexandria** (p369), on the Mediterranean, if only to stand on the hallowed grounds of this fabled Graeco-Roman city. The Romans left their mark throughout the country, though perhaps nowhere as striking as in the oases of the **Western Desert** (p326), which prospered in Roman times as part of an expansive caravan network.

It should come as no surprise that various religions have their roots in the deserts of Egypt. The first sight that should immediately come to mind is **Mt Sinai** (p497), the holy mountain where it is said Moses received the Ten Commandments. Egypt also houses the holiest Coptic Christian sights, namely the **Red Sea Monasteries** (p418) of St Anthony and St Paul. These monasteries are the oldest in Egypt and the entire Christian world, and continue to function today as centres of worship.

Finally, don't forget the contributions of the Nubians, whose cultural influences are still felt today throughout the country. There is no better place to get a sense of their unique heritage than at the **Nubia Museum** (p302) in Aswan.

History

The history of Egypt is as rich as the land, as varied as the landscape, as lively as the character of its people. And it is as long as the Nile, longer than most in the world. While much of Europe was still wrapped in animal skins and wielding clubs, Egyptians enjoyed a sophisticated life, dedicated to maintaining order in the universe and to making the most of their one great commodity, the Nile.

THE NILE
The Nation's Gift

The Greek historian Herodotus observed that Egypt was the gift of the Nile and although it might now be a cliché, it also happens to be true. Ancient Egyptians called it simply *iteru*, the river. Without the Nile, Egypt as we know it would not exist.

The exact history is obscure, but many thousands of years ago the climate of North Africa changed dramatically. Patterns of rainfall also changed and Egypt, formerly a rich savannah, became increasingly dry. The social consequences were dramatic. People in this part of Africa lived as nomads, hunting, gathering and moving across the region with the seasons. But when their pastures turned to desert, there was only one place for them to go: the Nile.

Rainfall in east and central Africa ensured that the Nile in Egypt rose each summer; this happened some time towards the end of June in Aswan. The waters would reach their height around the Cairo area in September. In most years, this surge of water flooded the valley and left the countryside hidden. As the rains eased, the river level started to drop and water drained off the land, leaving behind a layer of rich silt washed down from the hills of Africa.

Egyptians learned that if they planted seed on this fertile land, they could grow a good crop. As more people settled along the valley, it became more important to make the best use of the annual floodwater, or there would not be enough food for the following year. A social order evolved to organise the workforce to make the most of this 'gift', an order that had farmers at the bottom, bureaucrats and governors in the middle and, at the top of this pyramid, the pharaoh.

Egyptian legend credited all this social development to the good king Osiris, who, so the story went, taught Egyptians how to farm, how to make the best use of the Nile and how to live a good, civil life. The myth harks back to an idealised past, but also ties in with what we know of the emergence of kingship: one of the earliest attributions of kingship, the predynastic Scorpion Macehead, found in Hierakonpolis around 3000 BC, shows an irrigation

Egyptians called the vast areas of barren desert *deshret* (red land) and the narrow banks of the Nile *kemet* (black land).

The Penguin Guide to Ancient Egypt by William J Murnane is one of the best overall books on the lifestyle and monuments of the Pharaonic Period, with illustrations and descriptions of the major temples and tombs.

TIMELINE

c 250,000 BC	c 3100 BC	2650–2323 BC
Earliest human traces in Egypt. The valley is surrounded by savannah, providing ample food for groups of hunter-gatherers until climate change turns lush countryside to desert and forces settlement along the fertile Nile.	Legend credits a pharaoh named Narmer with uniting the people between the Mediterranean and the First Cataract at Aswan. Memphis emerges as the first capital of a united Upper Egypt and Lower Egypt.	This period of great pyramid building at Giza and Saqqara suggests that for at least part of each year, presumably when the Nile flooded, a substantial workforce was available for civic projects.

ritual. This suggests that even right back in early times, making use of the river's gift was a key part of the role of the leader.

Source Stories

The rise of the Nile was a matter of continual wonder for ancient Egyptians, as it was right up to the 19th century, when European explorers settled the question of the source. There is no evidence that ancient Egyptians knew where this lifeline came from. In the absence of facts, they made up stories.

One of the least convincing of all Egyptian myths concerning the rise of the Nile places the river's source in Aswan, beneath the First Cataract. From here, they believed, the river flowed north to the Mediterranean and south into Africa.

The river's life-giving force was revered as a god, Happy. He was an unusual deity in that, contrary to the slim outline of most gods, Happy was most often portrayed as a pot-bellied man with hanging breasts and a headdress of papyrus. Happy was celebrated at a feast each year when the Nile rose. In later images, he was often shown tying papyrus and lotus plants together, a reminder that the Nile bound people together.

But the most enduring and endearing of all Egyptian myths concerning the river is devoted to the figure of Isis, the mourning wife. Wherever the river originated, the annual rising of the Nile was explained as being tears shed by the mother goddess at the loss of the good king Osiris.

The Complete Pyramids: Solving the Ancient Mysteries by Mark Lehner and Richard H Wilkinson is a readable reference to the famous threesome of Giza and the other 70-plus triangular-sided funerary monuments besides.

Matters of Fact

Wherever it came from, the Nile was the beginning and end for most Egyptians. They were born beside it and had their first postnatal bath in its waters. It sustained them throughout their lives, made possible the vegetables in the fields, the chickens, cows, ducks and fish on their plates, and filled their drinking vessels when they were thirsty. When it was very hot or at the end of a day's work, it was the Nile that provided relief, a place to bathe. Later, when they died, if they had the funds, their body would be taken along the river to the cult centre at Abydos. And it was water from the Nile that the embalmers used when they prepared the body for burial. But burial was a moment of total separation from this life source for, if you were lucky, you were buried away from the damp, where the dry sands and rocks of the desert would preserve your remains throughout eternity.

Not everything about the river was generous – it also brought dangers in many forms: the crocodile, the sudden flood that washed away helpless children and brought the house down on your head, the diseases that thrived in water, and the creatures (among them the mosquito) that carried them. The river also brought the taxman, for it was on the level of flood that the level of tax was set. The formula was simple. Bureaucrats watched the rise of the river on Elephantine Island, where a gauge had been cut along the side

Ramses: The Son of Light by Christian Jacq is the first of a five-volume popular hagiography of the famous pharaoh. The prose is simplistic, but Jacq is an Egyptologist so the basics are accurate.

2125–1650 BC	1650–1550 BC	1550–1186 BC
Thebes emerges as capital of Upper Egypt and as the pre-eminent seat of religious power. When the Theban ruler Montuhotep II defeats his northern rival and establishes the Middle Kingdom, Thebes becomes its capital.	The Hyksos – western Asian tribes who settled in northern Egypt – establish control over the Egyptian Nile Valley, ushering in the Second Intermediate Period, a time of great technological and social innovation.	Ahmose, prince of Thebes, defeats the Hyksos c 1532 BC and begins a period of expansion into Nubia and Palestine. Over the next two centuries, Tuthmosis III and his New Kingdom successors expand the empire.

of the rock. Each year's flood was recorded at its height. If the water rose to the level of 14 cubits, there would be enough food to go around. If it rose to 16, there would be an abundance – and abundance meant good taxation. And if there were, say, only eight cubits, then it was time to prepare for the worst because famine would come and many would follow Osiris to the land of spirits beyond the valley.

The Dictionary of Ancient Egypt by Ian Shaw and Paul Nicholson gives an authoritative overview of ancient Egypt.

The river also dictated the rhythm of life and everything started with the beginning of the inundation: New Year fell as the waters rose. This was a time of celebration and also, for some, of relaxation. As the land was covered with water and a boat was needed to travel from one village to the next, farmers found time to catch up on long-neglected chores, fixing tools and working on their houses. This was also the period of the corvée, the labour system by which it is thought many civic projects were built, among them the pyramids, the canal cut through from the Nile to the Red Sea and, in the 19th century, the Suez Canal.

Old Habits

Even when the old gods were long dead, and roads and railways ran alongside the river, the Nile exerted its magic and its power. In the 18th and 19th centuries it was the way in which foreigners uncovered the mysteries of the past, sailing upriver when the winds blew from the north, and finding themselves face to face with unimaginable splendour. Even then, Egyptians clung to their habits and their dependence on the river. In the 1830s, the British Orientalist Edward Lane recorded that 17 June was still called the Night of the Drop. 'It is believed,' he wrote, 'that a miraculous drop then falls into the Nile; and causes it to rise.' Lane also recorded the custom of creating a figure of a girl, the 'Bride of the Nile', out of mud, which was then washed away as the river rose, an echo of an ancient ceremony in which effigies – and perhaps also young women – were sacrificed to the rising river.

J Baines and J Malek's Atlas of Ancient Egypt, B Manley's The Penguin Historical Atlas of Ancient Egypt and BJ Kemp's Anatomy of a Civilisation are all great Egypt resources.

Some 100 years later, in 1934, the Egyptologist Margaret Murray spent a mid-September night in a Coptic village, celebrating the night of the high Nile, giving thanks 'to the Ruler of the river, no longer Osiris, but Christ; and as of old they pray for a blessing upon their children and their homes.'

This kind of spiritual bond with the river was broken when dams and barrages stopped the annual flood. But Egyptians, whether they live along the river or in one of the new satellite cities in the desert, remain as dependent on the Nile as ever. Now, instead of praying to the 'Ruler of the river', they put their faith in engineers, who, like kings of old, help them make the most of the water; and in politicians, who are currently renegotiating water-sharing agreements with Nile-basin neighbours. Wherever they pin their hopes, they know that, as ever, their happiness, their very existence, depends on water flowing past Aswan on its way to the Mediterranean.

1352–1336 BC	1294–1279 BC	1279–1213 BC
Akhenaten establishes a new monotheism and a short-lived capital at Akhetaten. But by the death of his heir, Tutankhamun, in 1327 BC, Thebes is again the capital and power is restored to the priests of Amun.	Seti I restores some of the empire and also initiates a period of neoconservatism: his temple at Abydos copies styles of the Old Kingdom. He then constructs the finest tomb in the Valley of the Kings.	Seti's son, Ramses II, constructs more buildings than any other pharaoh. He makes Avaris, the old Hyksos capital and his home town, the centre of Egyptian trade, but adds to the glory of Thebes.

CHRISTIAN EGYPT

Coptic tradition states that Christianity arrived in Egypt in AD 45 in the form of St Mark. According to this tradition, St Mark, originally from Cyrene in modern-day Libya, was in Alexandria when his sandal broke. He took it to a cobbler, Ananias, who hurt his hand while working on the sandal and shouted 'O One God', at which St Mark recognised his first convert to the new religion. While there is no way to prove the story, there is no denying the basic truth that Christianity arrived early in Egypt, direct from Palestine.

The country had long been open to foreign religious influences and nowhere more so than Alexandria. At the height of their power, ancient Egyptians had exported their religions – Amun of Thebes was known and feared throughout the Mediterranean. And even in times of weakness, the cult of the goddess Isis spread throughout the Roman Empire. But Egyptians were also open to foreign religious ideas. The Persians did little to impose their gods on the country when they sacked Thebes in the 6th century BC and made Egypt part of their empire. Two centuries later, Alexander the Great viewed things differently, at least in the north of the country: while he built shrines to Amun at Karnak and was happy to be welcomed as pharaoh by the priests at Memphis, he also encouraged Greeks and Jews to bring their gods to his new city. Alexandria under the Macedonian's successors, the Ptolemies, became a centre for multiculturalism, where people of many different beliefs and religions lived and worshipped side by side.

It wasn't always a happy coexistence. The city's history is scarred by fights between devotees of different religions, as St Mark discovered to his cost: he was executed for speaking out against the worship of the city's pagan god Serapis. And at times, decrees came from Rome that litigated against Christians, the worst coming from Emperor Diocletian. The persecution was so extreme and cost so many lives (some Coptic historians have estimated 144,000) that the Coptic Church calendar, the Era of Martyrs, begins with the year of Diocletian's accession, AD 284. But change was not far away.

In AD 293, Diocletian found himself sharing power with Constantine. In 312, just as Constantine went into battle against his opponents, he had a vision of a cross blazing in the sky, on which was written, *In This Conquer*. When he emerged victorious, becoming ruler of the empire, Constantine converted to Christianity and, in 324, made Christianity the imperial religion.

By then, Egypt's Christians had absorbed much from both the form and the content of the ancient pagan religion. It is impossible to make direct parallels, but the rise of the cult of Mary appears to have been influenced by the popularity of Isis: both were said to have conceived through divine intervention. According to the late Coptic musicologist Dr Ragheb Moftah, the way in which the Coptic liturgy was performed seems to have evolved from ancient rites and in it, even today, we can hear an echo of ancient Egypt's rituals. Even the physical structure of Coptic churches echoes the layout of

Coptic Egypt by Christian Cannuyer tells the story from the earliest preachings by Mark the Evangelist in 1st-century-AD Alexandria to 21st-century Christianity in Egypt.

The best source for accurate plans of the Theban tombs can be found in Reeves and Wilkinson's 1996 book *The Complete Valley of the Kings*, supplemented by Siliotti's *Guide to the Valley of the Kings*.

1184–1153 BC	945–715 BC	663 BC
Ramses III provides a stable moment in an unstable century, controlling the Libyans, defeating the 'Sea People', a mix of Mediterranean tribes, and suppressing internal dissent. After his death, power slips from the throne.	Libyan settlers become increasingly powerful in the Delta, eventually taking power as the 22nd and 23rd dynasties, but the Egyptian Nile is divided among a series of princes.	After a series of diplomatic and military confrontations, Ashurbanipal, King of the Assyrians, attacks Egypt, sacks Thebes and loots the Temple of Amun. Devastated Egypt is ruled by Libyan princes from Sais in the Delta.

CHRONOLOGY OF THE PHARAOHS

This is not a complete listing but it does include the most significant rulers mentioned throughout this book. See also p47 for a Pharaonic who's who.

EARLY DYNASTIC PERIOD
1st Dynasty	**3100–2890 BC**
including:	
Narmer (Menes)	c 3100 BC
2nd Dynasty	**2890–2686 BC**

OLD KINGDOM
3rd Dynasty	**2686–2613 BC**
including:	
Zoser	2667–2648 BC
Sekhemket	2648–2640 BC
4th Dynasty	**2613–2494 BC**
including:	
Sneferu	2613–2589 BC
Khufu (Cheops)	2589–2566 BC
Djedefra	2566–2558 BC
Khafre (Chephren)	2558–2532 BC
Menkaure (Mycerinus)	2532–2503 BC
Shepseskaf	2503–2498 BC
5th Dynasty	**2494–2345 BC**
including:	
Userkaf	2494–2487 BC
Sahure	2487–2475 BC
Neferirkare	2475–2455 BC
Shepseskare	2455–2448 BC
Raneferef	2448–2445 BC
Nyuserra	2445–2421 BC
Unas	2375–2345 BC
6th Dynasty	**2345–2181 BC**
including:	
Teti	2345–2323 BC
Pepi I	2321–2287 BC
Pepi II	2278–2184 BC
7th–8th Dynasties	**2181–2125 BC**

FIRST INTERMEDIATE PERIOD
9th–10th Dynasties	**2160–2025 BC**

MIDDLE KINGDOM
11th Dynasty	**2055–1985 BC**
including:	
Montuhotep II	2055–2004 BC
Montuhotep III	2004–1992 BC

610–595 BC	525 BC	518 BC
Late Period pharaoh Necho encourages foreign trade by strengthening ties (and his navy) in the Mediterranean, cutting a canal to the Red Sea and sending an expedition to sail around Africa.	The Persian king Cambyses makes Egypt part of his empire and rules as pharaoh, launching an attack against Nubia and then on Siwa, in which his army disappears into the desert.	Cambyses' successor, Darius I, visits Egypt, completes the canal to the Red Sea and introduces the camel, which transforms the possibilities of desert travel and the experience of modern visitors to Egypt.

12th Dynasty	**1985–1795 BC**
including:	
Amenemhat I	1985–1955 BC
Sesostris I	1965–1920 BC
Amenemhat II	1922–1878 BC
Sesostris II	1880–1874 BC
Sesostris III	1874–1855 BC
Amenemhat III	1855–1808 BC
Amenemhat IV	1808–1799 BC
13th–14th Dynasties	**1795–1650 BC**
SECOND INTERMEDIATE PERIOD	
15th–17th Dynasties	**1650–1550 BC**
NEW KINGDOM	
18th Dynasty	**1550–1290 BC**
including:	
Ahmose	1550–1525 BC
Amenhotep I	1525–1504 BC
Tuthmosis I	1504–1492 BC
Tuthmosis II	1492–1479 BC
Tuthmosis III	1479–1425 BC
Hatshepsut	1473–1458 BC
Amenhotep II	1427–1400 BC
Tuthmosis IV	1400–1390 BC
Amenhotep III	1390–1352 BC
Akhenaten	1352–1336 BC
Tutankhamun	1336–1327 BC
Horemheb	1323–1295 BC
19th Dynasty	**1295–1186 BC**
including:	
Ramses I	1295–1294 BC
Seti I	1294–1279 BC
Ramses II	1279–1213 BC
Seti II	1200–1194 BC
20th Dynasty	**1186–1069 BC**
including:	
Ramses III	1184–1153 BC
THIRD INTERMEDIATE PERIOD	
21st Dynasty	**1069–945 BC**
including:	
Psusennes I	1039–991 BC

331 BC	**323 BC**	**c 310–250 BC**
Alexander invades Egypt and visits the capital, Memphis, and the oracle at Siwa. He then lays out a city, Alexandria, that will become the pivot of a new Hellenic culture in the Mediterranean.	On Alexander's death in Babylon, his general Ptolemy is given control of Egypt. Alexander's body is buried in Alexandria, Ptolemy's new capital. Ptolemy builds the Museion and Library and perhaps also the Pharos.	Under Ptolemaic patronage and with access to a library of 700,000 written works, scholars in Alexandria calculated the earth's circumference, discovered it circles the sun and wrote the definitive edition of Homer's work.

earlier pagan temples in the use of three different sacred spaces, the innermost one containing the altar reserved for priests. This is hidden from the rest of the congregation by the iconostasis, with its images of saints, just as ancient priests were hidden behind walls decorated with gods and pharaohs.

The early need to hold hidden prayer, the desire to follow Jesus' example of retreat from the world, the increasing difficulty of reconciling spiritual values with the demands and temptations of urban life, and perhaps also the memory of pagan hermits, led some Christians to leave the Nile Valley and seek spiritual purity in the desert. The man credited with being the first is St Paul, born in Alexandria in AD 228, who is said to have fled to the Eastern Desert to escape persecution and died there in AD 343. Although there are 5th-century accounts of the man, there is still some controversy as to whether St Paul existed. There is no such problem with the man he is said to have inspired.

St Anthony was the son of wealthy landowners, but found himself orphaned at an early age. As an adult, he sold his inheritance, gave the proceeds to the poor and retreated to the desert near St Paul. Other Christians soon followed, inspired by his example and perhaps also to escape persecution. The hermit moved further up into the hills, hiding alone in a cave, while leaving his followers to a life of collective retreat – a first monastery – in the valley below. Although there may have been earlier religious communities in the desert, especially one in Palestine, Copts credit St Anthony with creating a new way of life that sought salvation through retreat. It was left to St Pachomius, born around AD 285, to order the life of these hermits into what we would now recognise as monasteries, which has proved to be one of the most important movements in Christianity.

Egypt's Christians played a decisive role in the evolution of the young religion. In a series of meetings with Christians from across the empire, Copts argued over the nature of divinity, the duties of a Christian, the correct way to pray and many other aspects of religious life. In one matter in particular, Copts found themselves isolated. Many Christians argued that, as Jesus was born, there must have been a time when he was not divine and part of God. The Coptic clergy, particularly one Athanasius, argued that this idea of a dual nature was a throwback to polytheism. The crunch came in 325 at a council in Nicea, organised by the emperor, at which the Alexandrians triumphed: the Nicene Creed stated unequivocally that Father and Son are one. With this success, Alexandria confirmed its status as the centre of Mediterranean culture.

In 391, Emperor Theodosius issued an edict that banned people from visiting pagan temples, but also even looking at pagan statues. While the edict was ignored in some places, it was taken seriously in Alexandria, where the Temple of Serapis still stood in the city centre. The golden statue of the god remained in his sanctuary, adored by the faithful, until the Christian patriarch of Alexandria stirred a crowd and led them in an attack on the

The site of Luxor Temple has been a place of worship for the last 3500 years and remains one today: the Mosque of Abu al-Haggag is situated high above the great court.

246–221 BC	170–116 BC	30 BC
Ptolemy III Euergetes I begins a building program that includes the Serapeum in Alexandria and the Temple of Horus at Edfu. His successor continues his work, adding a new tomb to Alexander in Alexandria.	Ptolemy VIII Euergetes II's reign is characterised by violence and brutality, but also by the opening of the Edfu Temple and by building at Philae and Kom Ombo.	After Antony and Cleopatra are defeated at Actium, the queen commits suicide, bringing an end to the Ptolemies and the start of Roman rule, with Egypt initially the personal property of the Octarian (the future emperor Augustus Caesar).

temple: the god was toppled from his plinth – proving false the prophets who foresaw doom should he be damaged – and then dragged through the streets and burned. The crowd is also believed to have set fire to the temple library, which had contained one of the largest collections of scrolls in the world since the Alexandrian 'mother library' had been burned during an attack by Julius Caesar. The patriarch then built a church over the ruins.

Constantine had moved his capital to the city of Byzantium, renamed Constantinople (now Istanbul), in 330 and from that moment power seeped from Alexandria. More than a century later, in 451, the Egyptians were officially sidelined at the Council of Chalcedon. Refusing to accept that Jesus had one person but two natures, which again seemed a revival of polytheism, the Egyptians split with the rest of Christianity, their patriarch was excommunicated and soon after Alexandria was sacked.

Yet in spite of the religious split, Egypt was still part of the Byzantine Empire, ruled by a foreign governor, and its fortunes were tied to the empire. This caused ever-greater tension, which peaked in the reign of Emperor Justinian (528–565). Alexandrians stoned the emperor's governor, who retaliated by sending his army to punish the people. In 629, a messenger travelled to the emperor in Byzantium from Arabia. He had been sent by a man named Mohammed to reveal a new religion, Islam. The messenger was murdered on the way. Ten years later, Arab armies invaded Egypt.

Under their brilliant leader Amr ibn al-As, the Arabs swept through a badly defended and ill-prepared Egypt, defeated the Byzantine army near Babylon (see p126) and found the gates of Alexandria opened to them without a fight.

Amr didn't force Egyptians to convert to the new religion, but did levy a tax on nonbelievers and showed preference to those who did convert. Slowly, inevitably, the population turned, although how fast is open to dispute. Eventually, however, some monasteries emptied and Coptic writing and language, the last version of the language of the pharaohs, stopped being spoken in public. Christian communities remained strongest in the new capital, Cairo, and in the valley south as far as the ancient capital, Thebes (Luxor). Increasingly Christians also fell back on the monasteries. In places such as Wadi Natrun and studded along the Nile Valley, monastic communities hid behind their high walls, preserving the old language, the old traditions and, in their libraries, some of the old wisdom.

By the middle of the 19th century, even the monasteries were under threat and European travellers sailing up the Nile were shocked to discover monks swimming naked up to their boats to beg for food and money. The decline continued until the 20th century. By then, only around 10% of Egyptians were Christians and the great monasteries were at their lowest ebb. Ironically Christianity has responded to threats by enjoying something of a revival. Modernising influences in the early 20th century sparked a cultural renewal

Ancient Egypt: The Great Discoveries by Nicholas Reeves is a chronology of 200 years of marvellous finds, from the Rosetta Stone (1799) to the Valley of the Golden Mummies (1999).

AD 45

According to Coptic tradition, St Mark arrived in Alexandria this year and converted the first Egyptian, an Alexandria cobbler, to Christianity. The new religion was certainly established in Egypt by the end of the century.

c 271

St Anthony begins his retreat from the world, leaving home near Beni Suef and living in a cave in the Eastern Desert. He soon attracts others, whom he organises into a loose community and Christianity's first monks.

391

Fifty years after the Byzantine emperor Constantine spoke against the religion of the pharaohs, his successor Theodosius makes paganism a treasonable offence and Alexandria's Temple of Serapis burns, along with its library of scrolls.

that breathed new life into, among other things, the long-defunct tradition of icon painting. Islamist violence aimed at Copts in the 1980s and 1990s had the effect of significantly increasing the number of monks. At St Anthony's Monastery numbers rose from 24 in 1960 to 69 in 1986, in St Bishoi from 12 to 115. But the majority of Christians in Egypt still live in towns and cities along the Nile, still coping with continual threat from Muslim extremists, still cut off from the rest of the world's Christians and still, as ever, proud of their claim to be the true heirs of ancient Egypt.

THE MAMLUKS

Many of the tales recounted each night by Sherezade in *The Thousand and One Nights* are set in Mamluk-era Egypt, particularly in Cairo, referred to as 'Mother of the World'.

Every Egyptian army had its contingent of foreign soldiers, sometimes mercenaries, often slaves. When Psammetichus II sent an expedition into Nubia in 593 BC, a large contingent of Greek mercenaries went with them and left graffiti on the walls of Abu Simbel to tell us about it. In fact, no ruler of Egypt seems ever to have embarked on a large-scale campaign without foreign fighters. And often even the rulers were foreign – Macedonians such as Ptolemy I (323–283 BC), Romans such as Octavian (30 BC–AD 14) and even Kurds such as Salah ad-Din (1171–93), the Saladin of Crusader fame.

Saladin had created a dynasty, the Ayyubids, and reinstated Sunni Islam after the Shia rule of the Fatimids (969–1171). One of the last rulers of his dynasty, a man named Sultan as-Salih, brought the innovation of a permanent Turkic slave-soldier class. Most sultans relied on friends and relatives to provide a measure of security. As-Salih was so despised by all that he thought it wise to provide his own protection and did so by purchasing a large number of slaves from the land between the Urals and the Caspian. These men were freed on arrival in Egypt – their name, Mamluks, means 'owned' or 'slave' – and formed into a warrior class, which came to rule Egypt.

The sixth Fatimid caliph, El Hakim, was notorious for his unusual behaviour: convinced that a woman's place was in the home, he banned the manufacture of women's shoes.

Mamluks owed their allegiance not to a blood line but to their original owner, the emir. New purchases maintained the groups. There was no system of hereditary lineage; instead it was rule by the strongest. Rare was the sultan who died of old age. Natural-born soldiers, Mamluks fought a series of successful campaigns that gave Egypt control of all of Palestine and Syria, the Hejaz and much of North Africa, the largest Islamic empire of the late Middle Ages. Because they were forbidden to bequeath their wealth, Mamluks built on a grand scale, endowing Cairo with the most exquisite mosques, schools and tombs. During their 267-year reign (1250–1517), the city was the intellectual and cultural centre of the Islamic world.

The contradictions in the Mamluk constitution are typified in the figure of Sultan Qaitbey, who was bought as a slave-boy by one sultan and witnessed the brief reigns of nine more before clawing his way to power. As sultan he rapaciously taxed all his subjects and dealt out vicious punishments with his own hands, once tearing out the eyes and tongue of a court chemist who had failed to transform lead into gold. Yet Qaitbey marked his ruthless sultanship

451	640	832
At the Council of Chalcedon, Egyptian Christians refuse to accept the Imperial view that Jesus Christ had two natures, human and divine. The Coptic Church has been separated from the rest of Christianity ever since.	An Arab army under Amr ibn al-As sweeps through Egypt and establishes a base at Babylon (now part of Cairo). The following year, Amr captures the Byzantine capital, Alexandria.	The caliph Al-Mamun, son of Haroun ar-Rashid, arrives to suppress a Coptic uprising, but also forces a way into the Pyramid of Cheops in the hope of finding treasure. None is recorded as being found.

with some of Cairo's most beautiful monuments, notably his mosque, which stands in the Northern Cemetery (p140).

The funding for the Mamluks' great buildings came from trade. A canal existed that connected the Red Sea with the Nile at Cairo, and thus the Mediterranean, forming a vital link in the busy commercial route between Europe and India and east Asia. In the 14th and 15th centuries, the Mamluks worked with the Venetians to control east–west trade and both grew fabulously rich from it.

The end of these fabled days came about for two reasons at the beginning of the 16th century: Vasco da Gama's discovery of the sea route around the Cape of Good Hope freed European merchants from the heavy taxes charged by Cairo; and the Ottoman Turks emerged as a mighty new force, looking to unify the Muslim world. In 1516 the Mamluks, under the command of their penultimate sultan Al-Ghouri, were obliged to meet the Turkish threat. The battle, which took place at Aleppo in Syria, resulted in complete defeat for the Mamluks. In January of the following year the Turkish sultan Selim I entered Cairo and although the Mamluks remained in power in Egypt, they never again enjoyed their former prominence or autonomy.

FOREIGN INVADERS

The story of ancient Egypt is the story of Egypt's relationships with its neighbours, for its wealth attracted some and its strategic location on the Mediterranean and Red Seas, and on the trade routes between Africa and Asia, attracted others. When it was strong, it controlled the gold of Nubia and the trade route across the Levant – not for nothing was the image of Ramses II crushing the Hittites at Kadesh splashed across so many temple walls. When it was weak, it caught the attention of the power of the moment. In 663 BC, the Assyrian leader Ashurbanipal sacked Thebes. A century later the Persians were in control of the Nile. In 331 BC, Alexander the Great moved against the Egyptians and incorporated them into his Hellenic empire. In 30 BC, Octavian, the future emperor Augustus Caesar, annexed the country as his own property. Arab armies stormed through in the 7th century AD just as Ottoman ones did in the 16th century. However, by the end of the 18th century, the arrival of Europeans heralded the start of a very different age.

Napoleon & Description de l'Egypte

When Napoleon and his musket-armed forces blew apart the scimitar-wielding Mamluk cavalry at the Battle of the Pyramids in 1798, which he claimed he was doing with the approval of the Ottoman sultan, he dragged Egypt into the age of geopolitics. Napoleon professed a desire to revive Egypt's glory, free it from the yoke of tyranny and educate its masses, but there was also the significant matter of striking a blow at Britain. Napoleon found a way to strike at British interests by capturing Egypt and in the process taking control of the quickest route between Europe and Britain's fast-growing empire in the East.

Zayni Barakat by Gamal al-Ghitani is full of intrigue, backstabbing and general Machiavellian goings-on in the twilight of Mamluk-era Cairo.

Favoured punishments employed by the Mamluks included *al-tawsit*, in which the victim was cut in half at the belly, and *al-khazuq* (impaling).

At the Battle of the Pyramids, Napoleon's forces took just 45 minutes to rout the Mamluk army, killing 1000 for the loss of just 29 of their own men.

868	969	1171
Turkish general Ahmed ibn Tulun arrives as a governor for the Abbasid caliph in Baghdad, but ends up establishing his own Tulunid dynasty.	The Shiite general Jawhar lays the foundations for a new palace-city, Al-Qahira (Cairo), where a new university-mosque, Al-Azhar, is founded in 971. Two years later the Fatimid caliph, Al-Muizz, settles here from Tunis.	Saladin, the caliph's Kurdish vizier, seizes power, restores Sunni rule and establishes the Ayyubid dynasty. In 1176 he begins work on a citadel in Cairo, home to the city's rulers for the next seven centuries.

Napoleon's forces weren't always successful. In 1798, a British fleet under Admiral Nelson had been criss-crossing the Mediterranean trying to find the French force and, on 1 August, they found them at anchor in Aboukir Bay, off the coast of Alexandria. Only three French warships survived the ensuing Battle of the Nile. Encouraged by the British, the Ottoman sultan sent an army that was trounced by the French, which put paid to any pretence that the French were in Egypt with the complicity of Constantinople. Despite these setbacks, the French still maintained rule.

During Napoleon's time in the newly conquered Egypt, he established a French-style government, revamped the tax system, brought in Africa's first printing press, implemented public-works projects and introduced new crops and a new system of weights and measures. He also brought 167 scholars and artists, whom he commissioned to make a complete study of Egypt's monuments, crafts, arts, flora and fauna, and of its society and people. The resulting work was published as the 24-volume *Description de l'Egypte*, which did much to stimulate the study of Egyptian antiquities.

However, relations between the occupied and occupier deteriorated rapidly and there were regular uprisings against the French in Cairo. When the British landed an army, also at Aboukir, in 1801, the French agreed to an armistice and departed.

The Albanian Mercenary

The French and then British departure left Egypt politically unstable, a situation that was soon exploited by a lieutenant in an Albanian contingent of the Ottoman army, named Mohammed Ali. Within five years of the French evacuation, he had fought and conspired his way to become pasha (governor) of Egypt. Although he was nominally the vassal of Constantinople, like so many governors before him, he soon realised that the country could be his own.

The sultan in Constantinople was too weak to resist this challenge to his power. And once he had defeated a British force of 5000 men, the only threat to Mohammed Ali could come from the Mamluk beys (leaders). Any danger here was swiftly and viciously dealt with. On 1 March 1811, Mohammed Ali invited some 470 Mamluk beys to the Citadel to feast his son's imminent departure for Mecca. When the feasting was over the Mamluks mounted their lavishly decorated horses and were led in procession down the narrow, high-sided defile below what is now the Police Museum. As they approached the Bab al-Azab, the great gates were swung closed and gunfire rained down from above. After the fusillades, Mohammed Ali's soldiers waded in with swords and axes to finish the job. Legend relates that only one Mamluk escaped alive, leaping over the wall on his horse.

Mohammed Ali's reign is pivotal in the history of Egypt. Having watched the old Mamluk army flounder against modern European weapons and tactics, he recognised the need to modernise his new army, as well as his new country.

The Great Pyramid of Khufu (built in 2570 BC) remained the tallest artificial structure in the world until the building of the Eiffel Tower in 1889.

1250	1468	1517
Mamluk slave warriors, most of Turkish or Kurdish origin, seize control of Egypt. Although their rule was often harsh and anarchic, they graced the capital with some of its most impressive and beautiful monuments.	The Mamluk sultan Qaitbey begins a 27-year reign that brings stability and wealth to the country. Qaitbey is a prodigious builder, constructing a notable tomb complex in Cairo and a fort on the site of the Pharos in Alexandria.	Turkish sultan Selim I takes Cairo, executes the last Mamluk sultan and makes Egypt a Turkish province. For almost 300 years, it will be ruled, however weakly, from Istanbul.

Under his uncompromising rule, Egypt abandoned its medieval-style feudalism and looked to Europe for innovation. In his long reign (he died in 1848), Mohammed Ali modernised the army, built a navy, built roads, cut a new canal linking Alexandria with the Nile, introduced public education, improved irrigation, built a barrage across the Nile and began planting Egypt's fields with the valuable cash crop, cotton. His heirs continued the work, implementing reforms and social projects, foremost of which were the building of Africa's first railway, opening factories and starting a telegraph and postal system. Egypt's fledgling cotton industry boomed as production in the USA was disrupted by civil war, and revenues were directed into ever-grander schemes. Grandest of all was the Suez Canal, which opened in 1869 to great fanfare and an audience that included European royalty, including Empress Eugenie of France. In the same year that Khedive (Viceroy) Ismail announced that Egypt was now part of Europe, not Africa, Thomas Cook led the first organised package tour to see the wonders of ancient Egypt. It was the start of an industry that was to become one of Egypt's core businesses – mass tourism.

Khedive Ismail had taken on more debt than even Egypt's booming economy could handle and European politicians and banks were quick to exploit his growing weakness. Six years after opening the canal, Ismail was forced to sell his controlling share to the British government and soon after that, bankruptcy and British pressure forced him to abdicate. This sort of foreign involvement in Egyptian affairs created great resentment, especially among a group of officers in the Egyptian army, who moved against the new khedive. In 1882, under the pretext of restoring order, the British fleet bombarded Alexandria, and British soldiers defeated a nationalist Egyptian army.

The Veiled Protectorate

The British had no desire to make Egypt a colony: their main reason for involvement was to ensure the safety of the Suez Canal. So they allowed the heirs of Mohammed Ali to remain on the throne, while real power was concentrated in the hands of the British agent, Sir Evelyn Baring. By appointing British 'advisors' to Egyptian ministries and himself advising the khedive, Baring operated what became known as the veiled protectorate, colonisation by another name.

British desire to ensure the safety of their passage to India coloured Egyptian policy for the next few decades. For instance, it became increasingly obvious that controlling Egypt meant controlling the Nile and therefore an Egyptian force was sent to protect that interest in Sudan. When they came up against the Islamist uprising of the Mahdi, and following the death of General Charles Gordon in Khartoum in 1885, British troops became involved on the middle Nile.

The protectorate did much to achieve its ends. The canal was secure, Egypt's finances were bolstered, the bureaucracy and infrastructure improved,

The opera *Aida* was originally commissioned for the opening ceremony of the Suez Canal, but Verdi was late delivering and it was first performed on Christmas Eve, 1871, two years after the opening.

Famed as an American icon, the monument now known as the Statue of Liberty was originally intended to stand at the mouth of the Suez Canal.

1798	**1805**	**1856**
Napoleon invades, bringing a group of scholars, who produce the first full description of Egypt's antiquities. The British force the French to leave but their legacy, a fascination with ancient Egypt, lives on.	An Albanian mercenary, Mohammed Ali, exploits the power vacuum left by the French to seize power and establish a new 'Egyptian' dynasty; he begins a modernisation program that transforms the country.	Africa's first railway, between Tanta and Cairo, is built by British engineer Robert Stephenson. The line extended to Suez in 1858 and was popular with Europeans heading to India and the Far East until the opening of the Suez Canal.

and there were some social advances, but it remained that Egypt and its resources were being used to further British foreign policy. This situation became even more frustrating for Egyptians with the outbreak of WWI. When Turkey, still officially sovereign of Egypt, sided with Germany and against Britain, the British felt the need to make Egypt an official protectorate.

The Egyptians' desire for self-determination was strengthened by the Allies' use of the country as a barracks during a war that most Egyptians regarded as having nothing to do with them. Popular national sentiments were articulated by riots in 1919 and, more eloquently, by the likes of Saad Zaghloul, the most brilliant of an emerging breed of young Egyptian politicians, who said of the British, 'I have no quarrel with them personally but I want to see an independent Egypt'. The British allowed the formation of a nationalist political party, called the Wafd (Delegation), and granted Egypt its sovereignty, but this was seen as an empty gesture. King Fuad enjoyed little popularity among his people and the British still kept a tight rein on the administration.

The British and their Allies came to Egypt in greater numbers following the outbreak of WWII. The war wasn't all bad news for the Egyptians – certainly not for shopkeepers and businessmen who saw thousands of Allied soldiers pouring into the towns and cities with money to burn on 48-hour leave from the desert. But there was a vocal element who saw the Germans as potential liberators. Students held rallies in support of Rommel, and a small cabal of Egyptian officers, including future presidents Nasser and Sadat, plotted to aid the German general's advance on their city.

Rommel pushed the Allied forces back almost to Alexandria, which had the British hurriedly burning documents in such quantities that the skies over Cairo turned dark with the ash, but the Germans did not break through. Instead, the British maintained a military and political presence in Egypt until a day of flames almost seven years after the war.

INDEPENDENT EGYPT
Emerging from the Ashes

On 26 January 1952, a day that came to be known as Black Saturday, Cairo was set on fire. After years of demonstrations, strikes and riots against foreign rule, an Anglo-Egyptian showdown over a police station in the Suez Canal zone provided the spark that ignited the capital. Shops and businesses owned or frequented by foreigners were torched by mobs and many landmarks of 70 years of British rule were reduced to charred ruins within a day.

While the smoke cleared, the sense of agitation remained, not just against the British but also against the monarchy that most Egyptians regarded as too easily influenced by the British. King Farouk assumed the monarchy would survive the turmoil because it could count on the support of the Egyptian army. But a faction within the officer corps, known as the Free Officers, had long been planning a coup. On 20 July 1952, the leader of the Free Officers, Colonel

As a young Egyptian officer during WWII, Anwar Sadat was imprisoned by the British for conspiring with German spies.

One of the most notable casualties of Black Saturday was Shepheard's, Cairo's most famous hotel, and host to European royalty and Hollywood stars. A new Shepheard's was built beside the Nile in 1957.

1869	1882	1902
Khedive Ismail, Mohammed Ali's grandson, opens the Suez Canal. The British, who had preferred a railway, soon take control of the waterway as the quickest route to their empire in the East.	British troops invade to suppress nationalist elements in the army. Although they officially restore power to the khedive, Britain effectively rules Egypt in what becomes the 'veiled protectorate'.	Inauguration of the Aswan Dam, the world's largest at that time, and the Asyut Barrage, which help control the Nile flood. The Egyptian Museum is also opened on what is now Cairo's Midan Tahrir.

Gamal Abdel Nasser, heard that a new minister of war knew of the group and had planned their arrest. Two nights later, army units loyal to the Free Officers moved on key posts in the capital and by the following morning the monarchy had fallen. King Farouk, descendant of the Albanian Mohammed Ali, departed from Alexandria harbour on the royal yacht on 26 July 1952, leaving Egypt to be ruled by Egyptians for the first time since the pharaohs.

Colonel Nasser became president in elections held in 1956. With the aim of returning some of Egypt's wealth to its much-exploited peasantry, but also in an echo of the events of Russia in 1917, the country's landowners were dispossessed and many of their assets nationalised. Nasser also moved against the country's huge foreign community and, although he did not force them to emigrate, his new measures persuaded many to sell up and ship out.

In the year of his inauguration, Nasser successfully faced down Britain and France in a confrontation over the Suez Canal, which was mostly owned by British and French investors. On 26 July, the fourth anniversary of King Farouk's departure, Nasser announced that he had nationalised the Suez Canal to finance the building of a great dam that would control the flooding of the Nile and boost Egyptian agriculture. A combined British, French and Israeli invasion force, intended to take possession of the canal, resulted in diplomatic embarrassment and undignified retreat after the UN and US applied pressure. Nasser emerged from the conflict a hero of the developing world, a sort of Robin Hood and Ramses rolled into one, and the man who had finally and publicly shaken off the colonial yoke.

Cairo: The City Victorious by Max Rodenbeck is the most authoritative and entertaining read on the convoluted and picturesque 1000-year history of the Egyptian capital.

Neighbours & Friends

Nasser's show of strength in 1956 led to many years of drum-beating and antagonism between Egypt and its Arab friends on one side, and their unwelcome neighbour Israel on the other. On June 1967 Israel launched a surprise attack and destroyed Egypt's air force before it even got into the air. With it went the confidence and credibility of Nasser and his nation.

Relations with Israel had been hostile ever since its founding in 1948. Egypt had sent soldiers to fight alongside Palestinians against the newly proclaimed Jewish state and ended up on the losing side. Although privately Nasser acknowledged that the Arabs would probably lose another war against Israel, for public consumption he gave rabble-rousing speeches about liberating Palestine. But he was a skilled orator and by early 1967 the mood engendered throughout the Arab world by these speeches was beginning to catch up with him. Soon other Arab leaders started to accuse him of cowardice and of hiding behind the UN troops stationed in Sinai since the Suez Crisis. Nasser responded by ordering the peacekeepers out and blockading the Strait of Tiran, effectively closing the southern Israeli port of Eilat. He gave Israel reassurances that he wasn't going to attack but meanwhile massed his forces east of Suez. Israel struck first.

1914	1922	1922
When Turkey sides with Germany in the war, Britain moves to make Egypt an official British protectorate. A new ruler, Hussein Kamel, takes the title of Sultan of Egypt.	Britain ends the protectorate and grants Egypt independence, but reserves the right to defend Egypt, its interests in Sudan and, most importantly, the Suez Canal, where Britain continues to maintain a large military presence.	Howard Carter discovers the tomb of Tutankhamun. The first great Egyptological discovery in the age of mass media, the tomb contains more than 3000 objects, which take 10 years to record and remove.

When the shooting stopped six days later, Israel controlled all of the Sinai Peninsula and had closed the Suez Canal (which didn't reopen for another eight years). A humiliated Nasser offered to resign, but in a spontaneous outpouring of support, the Egyptian people wouldn't accept this move and he remained in office. However, it was to be for only another three years; abruptly in November 1970, the president died of a heart attack.

Anwar Sadat, another of the Free Officers and Egypt's next president, instigated a reversal of foreign policy. Nasser had looked to the Soviet Union for inspiration, but Sadat looked to the US, swapping socialist principles for capitalist opportunism. Having kept a low profile for a decade and a half, the wealthy resurfaced and were joined by a large, new, moneyed middle class who grew rich on the back of Sadat's much-touted *al-infitah* (open-door policy). Sadat also believed that to revitalise Egypt's economy he would have to deal with Israel. But first he needed bargaining power, a basis for negotiations.

On 6 October 1973, the Jewish holiday of Yom Kippur, Egypt launched a surprise attack across the Suez Canal. Its army beat back Israel's superior forces and crossed their supposedly impregnable line of fortifications. Although these initial gains were later reversed, Egypt's national pride was restored and Sadat's negotiating strategy had succeeded.

In November 1977, a time when Arab leaders still refused to talk publicly to Israel, Sadat travelled to Jerusalem to negotiate a peace treaty with Israel. The following year, he and the Israeli premier signed the Camp David Agreement, in which Israel agreed to withdraw from Sinai in return for Egyptian recognition of Israel's right to exist. There was shock in the Arab world, where Sadat's rejection of Nasser's pan-Arabist principles was seen as a betrayal. As a result, Egypt lost much prestige among the Arabs, who moved the HQ of the Arab League out of Cairo, and Sadat lost his life. On 6 October 1981, at a parade commemorating the 1973 war, one of his soldiers, a member of an Islamist group, broke from the marching ranks and sprayed the presidential stand with gunfire. Sadat was killed instantly.

Mubarak & the Rise of the Islamist Movement

Sadat was succeeded by another of the Free Officers, Hosni Mubarak, a former airforce general and vice president. Less flamboyant than Sadat and less charismatic than Nasser, Mubarak has been called unimaginative and indecisive, but has managed to carry out a balancing act on several fronts, abroad and at home. To the irritation of more hard-line states such as Syria and Libya, Mubarak rehabilitated Egypt in the eyes of the Arab world without abandoning the treaty with Israel. At the same time, he managed to keep the lid on the Islamist extremists at home. In the early 1990s the lid blew off.

Theories abound regarding the rise of fundamentalist Islamist groups in Egypt. Some believe this rise is more to do with harsh socio-economic condi-

---

Both Egypt and Israel were able to claim victory in the October 1973 war. The Egyptians boast of having broken the Israeli hold on Sinai while the Israelis were fighting their way towards Cairo when the UN imposed a ceasefire. This sense of victory helped make the Camp David peace talks possible.

No God but God: Egypt and the Triumph of Islam by Geneive Abdo is one of the best books on the Egyptian Islamist movement. It examines the movement as a response to a general increase in Muslim piety and the ineptitude of governance in the post-Nasser era.

1952	1967	1970
Anti-British sentiment leads to many foreign buildings in Cairo being burned. By the summer, Nasser and his fellow Free Officers have overthrown King Farouk and established the Republic of Egypt.	Egypt, Syria and Jordan are defeated by Israel in what becomes known as the Six Day War. Egypt loses control of the Sinai Peninsula and Nasser resigns, only to be returned to power by popular demand.	Fifty-two-year-old Gamal Abdel Nasser, Egyptian president since 1956, dies of a heart attack and is replaced by his fellow revolutionary, Anwar Sadat.

tions, despite the use of religion by Islamist groups. More than 30 years after the revolution, government promises had failed to keep up with the population explosion and a generation of youths was living in squalid, overcrowded housing, without jobs and many feeling little or no hope for the future. With a political system that allowed little chance to voice legitimate opposition, many felt the only hope lay with Islamist parties such as the Muslim Brotherhood and their calls for change. Denied recognition by the state as a legal political entity, in the 1980s and 1990s the Islamists turned to force. There were frequent attempts on the life of the president and his ministers, and clashes with the security forces. The matter escalated from a domestic issue to a matter of international concern when Islamists began to target one of the state's most vulnerable and valuable sources of income: tourists.

Several groups of foreign tourists were shot at, bombed or otherwise assaulted throughout the 1990s, including the 1997 fire-bomb attack on a tour bus outside the Egyptian Museum in Cairo, followed a few weeks later by the killing of holidaymakers at the Temple of Hatshepsut in Luxor by members of the Gama'a al-Islamiyya (Islamic Group), a Muslim Brotherhood splinter group.

The brutality of the massacre and its success at deterring foreign visitors destroyed grassroots support for militants, and the Muslim Brotherhood declared a ceasefire the following year. Things were relatively quiet until October 2004, when bombs at Taba, on the border with Israel, and the nearby Ras Shaytan camp, killed 34 and signalled the start of an unsettled 12 months.

In 2005 President Mubarak bowed to growing international pressure to bring the country's political system in line with Western-style democracy, and proposed a constitutional amendment (subsequently approved by parliament and ratified at a national referendum) that aimed to introduce direct and competitive presidential elections. While some pundits saw this as a step in the right direction, others suspected it was a sham, particularly as popular opposition groups such as the Muslim Brotherhood were still banned and other independent candidates were required to have the backing of at least 65 members of the lower house of parliament. As the lower house was dominated by the National Democratic Party (NDP), the possibility of real change was slight. When the Kifaya! (Enough!) coalition of opposition groups protested at these restrictions, security forces cracked down. Ayman Nour, the leader of the popular Ghad (Tomorrow) party, was jailed on forgery charges. Local human rights organisations questioned the validity of the charges and expressed concern for Nour's safety, while the US released a statement declaring it was 'deeply troubled' by the conviction.

At this stage the banned Muslim Brotherhood began holding its own rallies and there were two isolated terrorist incidents in Cairo aimed at foreign tourists, both carried out by members of the same pro-Islamist family. Soon afterwards, three bombs at the popular beach resort of Sharm el-Sheikh claimed

A History of Egypt by PJ Vatiokis is the best one-volume history available, although it's a decidedly modern history with a focus on the 19th and 20th centuries.

The trilogy of *The Mummy* (1999), *The Mummy Returns* (2001) and *The Scorpion King* (2002) was written by Stephen Sommers. The films feature fabulous art direction and far-fetched plots set in ancient and early-20th-century Egypt.

1971

The Aswan High Dam is completed. Eleven years in the making, it extends Lake Nasser to some 510km, forces the relocation of 50,000 Nubians and many monuments, and extends Egypt's farmland by 30%.

1973

In October, Egyptian forces attack and cross the Israeli defences along the Suez Canal. Although the Egyptians are repulsed and Israel threatens Cairo, the war is seen as an Egyptian success.

1981

President Sadat is assassinated, an event precipitated by his having signed the Camp David peace accord with Israel in 1978. He is replaced by Vice President Hosni Mubarak.

the lives of 88 people, most of them Egyptian. Various groups claimed responsibility, tourism took an immediate hit and Egyptians braced themselves for the possibility of further terrorist incursions and domestic unrest.

In 2005 Mubarak won the country's first multicandidate presidential election with 89% of the vote, after a turnout of just 23% of the 32 million registered voters. There were many reports from observers, such as the Egyptian Organization for Human Rights (EOHR), of disorganisation, intimidation and abusive security forces at the polls, and opposition parties and candidates (including Ayman Nour) alleged the vote was unfair and the result invalid. Still, other observers noted the process was a great improvement on previous elections.

In subsequent parliamentary elections in November 2005, the Muslim Brotherhood independents won 88 seats in the 444-seat national parliament (six times the number they had previously held), making the Brotherhood a major player on the national political scene despite its officially illegal status.

The past and present are described and ruminated over by the archaeologists leading the ongoing harbour explorations in *Alexandria Rediscovered* by Jean-Yves Empreur.

Egypt Today

Despite election backlash, domestic terrorism and the threat of an Islamist uprising, the biggest challenge facing President Mubarak is simply the hands of time. One of the few surviving Free Officers who overthrew the monarchy in 1952, Mubarak is nearing his mid-eighties, and concern about his health is mounting. But, media censorship in Egypt has not made it easy for critics to press the issue.

When the national paper *Al-Dastur* ran rumours of the president's ill health in September 2007, the editor was arrested for damaging the public interest, and some US$350 million was withdrawn from the Egyptian stock market by nervous foreign investors. The constitution states that power passes to the vice president, but Mubarak has always refused to appoint one. Many rumours surround the president's son, Gamal Mubarak, but the succession is far from clear.

Whoever takes the helm of the sinking ship, there is no denying that Egypt is in serious economic crisis, and has been for many years. The national economy has had to cope with a massive growth in population, rise in unemployment, and decline in the value of the Egyptian currency. Lower taxes, reduced energy subsidies and increased privatisation have facilitated a higher GDP and a booming stock market, but the living standards for the average Egyptian have not kept pace. In response, the masses have taken to the streets over stagnant wages and rising commodity prices, a threatening combination that has been further aggravated by the global economic slowdown.

Many commentators recognised that Gamal Mubarak's 2007 wedding in Sharm el-Sheikh removed one of the last obstacles to him becoming the next president. While most Egyptians marry young, Mubarak was still unmarried in his early 40s.

Pharaonic Egypt Dr Joann Fletcher

Despite its rather clichéd image, there is so much more to ancient Egypt than temples, tombs and Tutankhamun. As the world's first nation-state, predating the civilisations of Greece and Rome by several millennia, Egypt was responsible for some of the most important achievements in human history – it was where writing was invented, the first stone monuments erected and an entire culture set in place, which remained largely unchanged for thousands of years.

All this was made possible by the Nile River, which brought life to this virtually rainless land. In contrast to the vast barren 'red land' of desert that the Egyptians called *deshret*, the narrow river banks were known as *kemet* (black land), named after the rich silt deposited by the river's annual floods. The abundant harvests grown in this rich earth were then gathered as taxes by a highly organised bureaucracy working on behalf of the king (pharaoh). They redirected this wealth to run the administration and to fund ambitious building projects designed to enhance royal status. Although such structures have come to symbolise ancient Egypt, the survival of so many pyramids, temples and tombs have created a misleading impression of the Egyptians as a morbid bunch obsessed with religion and death, when they simply loved life so much that they went to enormous lengths to ensure it continued for eternity.

The depth of this conviction suffused almost every aspect of the ancient Egyptians' lives and gave their culture its incredible coherence and conservatism. They believed they had their gods to take care of them, and each pharaoh was regarded as the gods' representative on earth, ruling by divine approval. Absolute monarchy was integral to Egyptian culture and the country's history was shaped around the lengths of each pharaoh's reign. Thirty royal dynasties ruled over a 3000-year period, now divided into the Old, Middle and New Kingdoms separated by intermittent periods of unrest (Intermediate periods) when the country split into north (Lower Egypt) and south (Upper Egypt).

When this split finally became permanent at the end of the New Kingdom (around 1069 BC), foreign powers were gradually able to take control of the government. Yet even then Egyptian culture was so deeply rooted that the successive invaders could not escape its influence, and Libyans, Nubians and Persians all came to adopt traditional Egyptian ways. The Greeks were so impressed with the ancient culture that they regarded Egypt as the 'cradle of civilisation', and even the occupying Romans adopted the country's ancient gods and traditions. It was only at the end of the 4th century AD, when the Roman Empire adopted Christianity, that ancient Egypt finally died; their gods were taken from them, their temples were closed down and all knowledge of the 'pagan' hieroglyphs that transmitted their culture was lost for some 1400 years.

Dr Joann Fletcher of the University of York is an Egyptologist, writer, and a consultant to museums and the media. For more biographical information, see p552.

Although the Narmer Palette is in many ways Egypt's earliest historical document, it is also a giant piece of cosmetic equipment, designed as a surface on which to prepare eye make-up.

PHARAONIC WHO'S WHO

Egypt's Pharaonic history is based on the regnal years of each king, or pharaoh, a word derived from *per-aa*, meaning palace. Among the many hundreds of pharaohs who ruled Egypt over a 3000-year period, the following are some of the names found most frequently around the ancient sites.

Narmer c 3100 BC First king of a united Egypt after he conquered the north (Lower) Egypt, Narmer from south (Upper) Egypt is portrayed as victorious on the famous Narmer Palette in the Egyptian Museum. He is perhaps to be identified with the semimythical King Menes, founder of Egypt's ancient capital city Memphis. See also Room 43 – Atrium, p184; and Memphis, p194.

Zoser (Djoser) c 2667–2648 BC As second king of the 3rd dynasty, Zoser was buried in Egypt's first pyramid, the world's oldest monumental stone building, designed by the architect Imhotep. Zoser's statue in the foyer of the Egyptian Museum shows a long-haired king with a slight moustache, dressed in a tight-fitting robe and striped *nemes* (headcloth). See also Room 48 – Early Dynastic Period, p185, and p198.

The subterranean chambers beneath Zoser's pyramid were decorated with bright turquoise-blue tiles, some of which can be seen in the upper rooms of the Egyptian Museum.

Sneferu c 2613–2589 BC The first king of the 4th dynasty, and held in the highest esteem by later generations, Sneferu was Egypt's greatest pyramid builder. He was responsible for four such structures, and his final resting place, the Red (Northern) Pyramid at Dahshur, was Egypt's first true pyramid and a model for the more famous pyramids at Giza. See also Pyramid of Meidum, p208.

Khufu (Cheops) c 2589–2566 BC As Sneferu's son and successor, Khufu was second king of the 4th dynasty. Best known for Egypt's largest pyramid, the Great Pyramid at Giza, his only surviving likeness is Egypt's smallest royal sculpture, a 7.5cm-high figurine in the Egyptian Museum. The gold furniture of his mother Hetepheres is also in the museum. See also p149 and Room 37, p185.

Khafre (Khephren, Chephren) c 2558–2532 BC Khafre was a younger son of Khufu who succeeded his half-brother to become fourth king of the 4th dynasty. He built the second of Giza's famous pyramids and although he is best known as the model for the face of the Great Sphinx, his diorite statue in the Egyptian Museum is equally stunning. See also p149 and Room 42, p185.

Menkaure (Mycerinus) c 2532–2503 BC As the son of Khafre and fifth king of the 4th dynasty, Menkaure built the smallest of Giza's three huge pyramids. He is also well represented by a series of superb sculptures in the Egyptian Museum, which show him with the goddess Hathor and deities representing various administrative divisions (nomes) of Egypt. See also p151, and Rooms 47 & 46 – Old Kingdom, p185.

Sneferu was a great inspiration to later pharaohs. Excavations at Dahshur have revealed that incense was still being offered to Sneferu's memory 2000 years after his death.

Pepi II c 2278–2184 BC As fifth king of the 6th dynasty, Pepi II was a child at his accession; his delight with a dancing pygmy was recorded in the Aswan tomb of his official Harkhuf. As one of the world's longest-reigning monarchs (96 years), Pepi contributed to the decline of the Pyramid Age. See also p203 and p307.

Montuhotep II c 2055–2004 BC As overlord of Thebes, Montuhotep II reunited Egypt and his reign began the Middle Kingdom. He was the first king to build a funerary temple at Deir al-Bahri, in which he was buried with five of his wives and a daughter, with further wives and courtiers buried in the surrounding area. See also p186 and p267.

Sesostris III (Senwosret, Senusret) c 1874–1855 BC The fifth king of the 12th dynasty, Sesostris III reorganised the administration by taking power from the provincial governors (nomarchs). He strengthened Egypt's frontiers and occupied Nubia with a chain of fortresses, and is recognisable by the stern, 'careworn' faces of his statues. His female relatives were buried with spectacular jewellery. See also Black Pyramid, p205.

Amenhotep I c 1525–1504 BC As second king of the 18th dynasty, Amenhotep I ruled for a time with his mother Ahmose-Nofretari. They founded the village of Deir el-Medina for the workers who built the tombs in the Valley of the Kings, and Amenhotep I may have been the first king to be buried there. See also Room 56 – Royal Mummy Room, p188, and the open-air museum, p249.

Regarded as the most magnificent of the pharaohs, Amenhotep III seems to have appreciated literature, judging by the discovery of small glazed bookplates bearing his name.

Hatshepsut c 1473–1458 BC As the most famous of Egypt's female pharaohs, Hatshepsut took power at the death of her brother-husband Tuthmosis II and initially ruled jointly with her nephew-stepson Tuthmosis III. After taking complete control, she undertook ambitious building schemes, including obelisks at Karnak Temple and her own spectacular funerary temple at Deir al-Bahri. See also Room 12 – Hathor Shrine, p187; and p267.

Tuthmosis III c 1479–1425 BC As sixth king of the 18th dynasty, Tuthmosis III (the Napoleon of ancient Egypt) expanded Egypt's empire with a series of foreign campaigns into Syria. He built extensively at Karnak, added a chapel at Deir al-Bahri and his tomb was the first in the Valley of the Kings to be decorated. See also Room 12 – Hathor Shrine, p187; Inner Temple, p247; and p264.

Amenhotep III c 1390–1352 BC As ninth king of the 18th dynasty, Amenhotep III's reign marks the zenith of Egypt's culture and power. He is the creator of Luxor Temple and the largest ever funerary temple marked by the Colossi of Memnon, and his many innovations, including Aten worship, are usually credited to his son and successor Amenhotep IV (later 'Akhenaten'). See also Luxor Museum, p252, and Colossi of Memnon, p256.

Akhenaten (Amenhotep IV) c 1352–1336 BC Changing his name from Amenhotep to distance himself from the state god Amun, Akhenaten relocated the royal capital to Amarna with his wife Nefertiti . While many still regard him as a monotheist and benign revolutionary, the evidence suggests he was a dictator whose reforms were political rather than religious. See also p187, p225 and p254.

Nefertiti c 1338–1336 BC (?) Famous for her painted bust in Berlin, Nefertiti ruled with her husband Akhenaten, and while the identity of his successor remains controversial, this may have been Nefertiti herself, using the throne name 'Smenkhkare'. Equally controversial is the suggested identification of her mummy in tomb KV 35 in the Valley of the Kings. See also Room 3 – Amarna Room, p187; Tell al-Amarna, p225; and Luxor Museum, p252.

Tutankhamun c 1336–1327 BC As the 11th king of the 18th dynasty, Tutankhamun's fame is based on the great quantities of treasure discovered in his tomb in 1922. Most likely the son of Akhenaten by minor wife Kiya, Tutankhamun reopened the traditional temples and restored Egypt's fortunes after the disastrous reign of his father. See also Luxor Museum, p252, and p262.

Horemheb c 1323–1295 BC As a military general, Horemheb restored Egypt's empire under Tutankhamun and after the brief reign of Ay eventually became king himself, marrying Nefertiti's sister Mutnodjmet. His tomb at Saqqara was abandoned in favour of a royal burial in a superbly decorated tomb in the Valley of the Kings. See also p263.

Seti I c 1294–1279 BC The second king of the 19th dynasty, Seti I continued to consolidate Egypt's empire with foreign campaigns. Best known for building Karnak's Hypostyle Hall, a superb temple at Abydos and a huge tomb in the Valley of the Kings, his mummy in the Egyptian Museum is one of the best preserved examples. See also Room 56 – Royal Mummy Room, p188; p234; Great Hypostyle Hall, p246; and p265.

Ramses II c 1279–1213 BC As son and successor of Seti I, Ramses II fought the Hittites at the Battle of Kadesh and built temples including Abu Simbel and the Ramesseum, once adorned with the statue that inspired poet PB Shelley's 'Ozymandias'. The vast tomb of his children was rediscovered in the Valley of the Kings in 1995. See also p187; Room 56 – Royal Mummy Room, p188; Memphis, p194; p235; p261; boxed text, p261; p322; and p324.

Ramses III c 1184–1153 BC As second king of the 20th dynasty, Ramses III was the last of the warrior kings, repelling several attempted invasions portrayed in scenes at his funerary temple Medinat Habu. Buried in a finely decorated tomb in the Valley of the Kings, his mummy was the inspiration for Boris Karloff's *The Mummy*. See also p273.

Taharka 690–664 BC As fourth king of the 25th dynasty, Taharka was one of Egypt's Nubian pharaohs and his daughter Amenirdis II high priestess at Karnak, where Taharka undertook building work. A fine sculpted head of the king is in Aswan's Nubian Museum, and he was buried in a pyramid at Nuri in southern Nubia. See also p246.

Alexander the Great 331–323 BC During his conquest of the Persian Empire, the Macedonian king Alexander invaded Egypt in 331 BC. Crowned pharaoh at Memphis, he founded Alexandria, visited Amun's temple at Siwa Oasis to confirm his divinity and after his untimely death in Babylon in 323 BC his mummy was eventually buried in Alexandria. See also p188; Barque Shrine of Amun, p252; p355; and p369.

Ptolemy I 323–283 BC As Alexander's general and rumoured half-brother, Ptolemy seized Egypt at Alexander's death and established the Ptolemaic line of pharaohs. Ruling in traditional style for 300 years, they made Alexandria the greatest capital of the ancient world and built many of the temples standing today, including Edfu, Philae and Dendera. See also p369.

Cleopatra VII 51–30 BC As the 19th ruler of the Ptolemaic dynasty, Cleopatra VII ruled with her brothers Ptolemy XIII then Ptolemy XIV before taking power herself. A brilliant politician who restored Egypt's former glories, she married Julius Caesar then Mark Antony, whose defeat at Actium in 31 BC led to the couple's suicide. See also p370 and Graeco-Roman Museum, p376.

EVERYDAY LIFE

With ancient Egypt's history focused on its royals, the part played by the rest of the ancient population is frequently ignored. The great emphasis on written history also excludes the 99% of the ancient population who were unable to write, and it can often seem as if the only people who lived in ancient Egypt were pharaohs, priests and scribes.

Nefertiti had a taste for beer. She is shown drinking in several tomb scenes at Amarna and even had her own brewery at the site, which produced a quick-fermenting brew.

Many of the treasures found in the tomb of Tutankhamun bear the names of his predecessors Akhenaten and the mysterious 'Smenkhkare', and were apparently buried with Tutankhamun simply to get rid of all trace of this unpopular family.

Although synonymous with ancient Egypt, Cleopatra VII was actually Greek by descent, one of the Ptolemaic dynasty of pharaohs who originated from Macedonia where Cleopatra was a popular royal name.

The silent majority are often dismissed as little more than illiterate peasants, although these were the very people who built the monuments and produced the wealth on which the culture was based.

Fortunately Egypt's climate, at least, is democratic, and has preserved the remains of people throughout society, from the mummies of the wealthy in their grand tombs to the remains of the poorest individuals buried in hollows in the sand. The worldly goods buried with them for use in the afterlife can give valuable details about everyday life and how it was lived, be it in the bustling, cosmopolitan capital Memphis or in the small rural settlements scattered along the banks of the Nile.

Eugen Strouhal's *Life in Ancient Egypt* (Cambridge University Press, 1992) is one of the most informative and best illustrated books dealing with domestic life. Drawing on the author's medical expertise, the chapter on health and medicine is particularly good.

Domestic Life

In Egypt's dry climate, houses were traditionally built of mudbrick, whether they were the back-to-back homes of workers or the sprawling palaces of the royals. The main differences were the number of rooms and the quality of fixtures and fittings. The villas of the wealthy often incorporated walled gardens with stone drainage systems for small pools, and some even had en-suite bathroom facilities – look out for the limestone toilet seat found at Amarna and now hanging in the Egyptian Museum in Cairo.

Just like the mudbrick houses in rural Egypt today, ancient homes were warm in winter and cool in summer. Small, high-set windows reduced the sun's heat but allowed breezes to blow through, and stairs gave access to the flat roof where the family could relax or sleep.

Often whitewashed on the outside to deflect the heat, interiors were usually painted in bright colours, the walls and floors of wealthier homes further enhanced with gilding and inlaid tiles. Although the furniture of most homes would have been quite sparse – little more than a mudbrick bench, a couple of stools and a few sleeping mats – the wealthy could afford beautiful furniture, including inlaid chairs and footstools, storage chests, beds with linen sheets and feather-stuffed cushions. Most homes also had small shrines for household deities and busts of family ancestors, and a small raised area seems to have been reserved for women in childbirth.

Chickens, described as miraculous birds that 'give birth every day', were first imported from Syria around 1450 BC.

The home was very much a female domain. The most common title for women of all social classes was *nebet per* (lady of the house), emphasising their control over most aspects of domestic life. Although there is little evidence of marriage ceremonies, monogamy was standard practice for the majority, with divorce and remarriage relatively common and initiated by either sex. With the same legal rights as men, women were responsible for running the home and although there were male launderers, cleaners and cooks, it was mainly women who cared for the children, cleaned the house, made clothing and prepared food in small open-air kitchens adjoining the home.

The staple food was bread, produced in many varieties, including the dense calorie-laden loaves mass-produced for those working on government building schemes. Onions, leeks, garlic and pulses were eaten in great quantities along with dates, figs, pomegranates and grapes. Grapes were also used, along with honey, as sweeteners. Spices, herbs, nuts and seeds were also added to food, along with oil extracted from native plants and imported almonds and olives. Although cows provided milk for drinking and making butter and cheese, meat was only eaten regularly by the wealthy and by priests allowed to eat temple offerings once the gods had been satisfied. This was mostly beef, although sheep, goats and pigs were also eaten, as were game and wild fowl. Fish was generally dried and salted and, because of its importance in workers' diets, a fish-processing plant existed at the pyramid builders' settlement at Giza.

Wine jars were sometimes inscribed with the intended purpose of their contents, from 'offering wine' or 'wine for taxes' to 'wine for merry-making'.

Although the wealthy enjoyed wine (with the best produced in the vineyards of the Delta and western oases, or imported from Syria), the standard beverage was a rather soupy barley beer, which was drunk throughout society by everyone, including children. The ancient Egyptians' secret to a contented life is summed up by the words of one of their poems: 'it is good to drink beer with happy hearts, when one is clothed in clean robes'.

Public Life/At Work

The majority of ancient Egyptians were farmers, whose lives were based around the annual cycle of the Nile. This formed the basis of their calendar with its three seasons – *akhet* (inundation), *peret* (spring planting) and *shemu* (summer harvest). As the flood waters covering the valley floor receded by October, farmers planted their crops in the silt left behind, using irrigation canals to distribute the flood waters where needed and to water their crops until harvest time in April.

Agriculture was so fundamental to life in both this world and the next that it was one of the main themes in tomb scenes. The standard repertoire of ploughing, sowing and reaping is often interspersed with officials checking field boundaries or calculating the grain to be paid as tax in this pre-coinage economy. The officials are often accompanied by scribes busily recording all transactions, with hieroglyphs now known to have been first developed c 3250 BC as a means of recording produce.

A huge civil service of scribes worked on the pharaoh's behalf to record taxes and organise workers and, in a society where less than 1% were literate, scribes were regarded as wise and were much admired. Taught to read and write in the schools attached to temples where written texts were stored and studied, the great majority of scribes were male. However, some women are also shown with documents and literacy would have been necessary to undertake roles they are known to have held, including overseer, steward, teacher, doctor, high priestess, vizier and even pharaoh on at least six occasions.

Closely related to the scribe's profession were the artists and sculptors who produced the stunning artefacts synonymous with ancient Egypt. From colossal statues to delicate jewellery, all were fashioned using simple tools and natural materials.

Building stone was hewn by teams of labourers supplemented by prisoners, with granite obtained from Aswan, sandstone from Gebel Silsila, alabaster from Hatnub near Amarna and limestone from Tura near modern Cairo. Gold came from mines in the Eastern Desert and Nubia, and both copper and turquoise were mined in the Sinai. With such precious commodities being transported large distances, trade routes and border areas were patrolled by guards, police (known as *medjay*) and the army, when not out on campaign.

Men also plied their trade as potters, carpenters, builders, metalworkers, jewellers, weavers, fishermen and butchers, with many of these professions handed down from father to son. (This is especially well portrayed in the tomb scenes of Rekhmire, see p270.) There were also itinerant workers such as barbers, dancers and midwives, and those employed for their skills as magicians. Men worked alongside women as servants in wealthy homes, performing standard household duties, and thousands of people were employed in the temples, which formed the heart of every settlement – a combination of town hall, college, library and medical centre. As well as a hierarchy of priests and priestesses, temples employed their own scribes, butchers, gardeners, florists, perfume makers, musicians and dancers, many of whom worked on a part-time basis.

BBC History website www.bbc.co.uk/history /ancient/egyptians has a number of articles covering Egyptian daily life, including a look at what was available for women outside the home.

A contract from AD 206 states that Isadora the castanet dancer and two other women hired to perform at a six-day festival received 36 drachmae a day, well above the average wage.

The first recorded workers' strike in history occurred in 1152 BC when royal tomb builders refused to go back to work because their supplies of moisturising oil had not been delivered.

OILS, PERFUMES & COSMETICS

Most Egyptians seem to have bathed regularly and used moisturising oils to protect their skin from the drying effects of the sun. These oils were sometimes perfumed with flowers, herbs and spices, and Egyptian perfumes were famous throughout the ancient world for their strength and quality. Perfume ingredients are listed in ancient texts, along with recipes for face creams and beauty preparations, and cosmetics were also used to enhance the appearance. Responsible for the familiar elongated eye shape, eye-paint also had a practical use, acting like sunglasses by reducing the glare of bright sunlight and explaining why builders are shown having their eyes made up during work. Both green malachite and black galena (kohl) were used in crushed form, mixed with water or oil and stored ready for use in small pots. Red ochre prepared in a similar fashion was used by women to shade their lips and cheeks. Some Egyptians were also trained to apply cosmetics and perform manicures and pedicures.

Although most people kept their cosmetic equipment in small baskets or boxes, the wealthy had beautifully decorated chests with multiple compartments, pull-out drawers and polished metal mirrors with which they could inspect their carefully designed appearance.

Clothing, Hairstyles & Jewellery

Personal appearance was clearly important to the Egyptians, with wigs, jewellery, cosmetics and perfumes worn by men and women alike. Garments were generally linen, made from the flax plant before the introduction of cotton in Ptolemaic times. Status was reflected in the fineness and quantity of the linen, but as it was expensive, surviving clothes show frequent patching and darning. Laundry marks are also found; male launderers were employed by the wealthy, and even a few ancient laundry lists have survived, listing the types of garments they had to wash in the course of their work.

The most common garment was the loincloth, worn like underpants beneath other clothes. Men also wore a linen kilt, sometimes pleated, and both men and women wore the bag-tunic made from a rectangle of linen folded in half and sewn up each side. The most common female garments were dresses, most wrapped sari-like around the body, although there were also V-neck designs cut to shape, and detachable sleeves for easy cleaning.

> Hair colour had great significance for the Egyptians and, in a largely dark-haired population, redheads were regarded as dangerous and described as 'followers of Seth', the god of chaos.

Linen leggings have also been found, as well as socks with a gap between the toes for wearing with sandals made of vegetable fibre or leather. Royal footwear also featured gold sequins, embroidery and beading, with enemies painted on the soles to be crushed underfoot.

Plain headscarves were worn to protect the head from the sun or during messy work; the striped *nemes* (headcloth) was only worn by the pharaoh, who also had numerous crowns and diadems for ceremonial occasions.

Jewellery was worn by men and women throughout society for both aesthetic and magical purposes. It was made of various materials, from gold to glazed pottery, and included collars, necklaces, hair ornaments, bracelets, anklets, belts, earrings and finger rings.

> By Roman times Isis had become the most important of all Egypt's gods and by the 1st century AD her worship had even spread as far as London.

Wigs and hair extensions were also popular and date back to c 3400 BC, as does the use of the hair dye henna *(Lawsonia inermis)*. Many people shaved or cropped their hair for cleanliness and to prevent head lice (which have even been found in the hair of pharaohs). The clergy had to shave their heads for ritual purity and children's heads were partially shaved to leave only a side lock of hair as a symbol of their youth.

GODS & GODDESSES

Initially representing aspects of the natural world, Egypt's gods and goddesses grew more complex through time. As they began to blend together and adopt each other's characteristics, they started to become difficult to identify, although their distinctive headgear and clothing can provide clues as to who they are. The following brief descriptions should help travellers spot at least a few of the many hundreds who appear on monuments and in museums.

Amun The local god of Thebes (Luxor) who absorbed the war god Montu and fertility god Min and combined with the sun god to create Amun-Ra, King of the Gods. He is generally portrayed as a man with a double-plumed crown and sometimes the horns of his sacred ram.

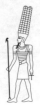

Amun

Anubis God of mummification, patron of embalmers and guardian of cemeteries, Anubis is generally depicted as a black jackal or a jackal-headed man.

Apophis The huge snake embodying darkness and chaos was the enemy of the sun god Ra and tried to destroy him every night and prevent him reaching the dawn.

Anubis

Aten The solar disc whose rays end in outstretched hands, first appearing in texts c 1900 BC and becoming chief deity during the Amarna Period c 1360–1335 BC.

Atum Creator god of Heliopolis who rose from the primeval waters and ejaculated (or sneezed depending on the myth) to create gods and humans. Generally depicted as a man wearing the double crown, Atum represented the setting sun.

Bastet Cat goddess whose cult centre was Bubastis; ferocious when defending her father Ra the sun god, she was often shown as a friendly deity, personified by the domestic cat.

Aten

Bes Grotesque yet benign dwarf god fond of music and dancing; he kept evil from the home and protected women in childbirth by waving his knives and sticking out his tongue.

Geb God of the earth generally depicted as a green man lying beneath his sister-wife Nut the sky goddess, supported by their father Shu, god of air.

Hapy God of the Nile flood and the plump embodiment of fertility shown as an androgynous figure with a headdress of aquatic plants.

Bes

Hathor Goddess of love and pleasure represented as a cow or a woman with a crown of horns and sun's disc in her guise as the sun god's daughter. Patron of music and dancing whose cult centre was Dendara, she was known as 'she of the beautiful hair' and 'lady of drunkenness'.

Horus Falcon god of the sky and son of Isis and Osiris, he avenged his father to rule on earth and was personified by the ruling king. He can appear as a falcon or a man with a falcon's head, and his eye *(wedjat)* was a powerful amulet.

Isis Goddess of magic and protector of her brother-husband Osiris and their son Horus, she and her sister Nephthys also protected the dead. As symbolic mother of the king she appears as a woman with a throne-shaped crown, or sometimes has Hathor's cow horns.

Hapy

Khepri God of the rising sun represented by the scarab beetle, whose habit of rolling balls of dirt was likened to the sun's journey across the sky.

Khnum Ram-headed god who created life on a potter's wheel; he also controlled the waters of the Nile flood from his cave at Elephantine and his cult centre was Esna.

Khons Young god of the moon and son of Amun and Mut. He is generally depicted in human form wearing a crescent moon crown and the 'sidelock of youth' hairstyle.

Maat Goddess of cosmic order, truth and justice, depicted as a woman wearing an ostrich feather on her head, or sometimes by the feather alone.

Mut Amun's consort and one of the symbolic mothers of the king; her name means both 'mother' and 'vulture' and she is generally shown as woman with a vulture headdress.

Nekhbet Vulture goddess of Upper Egypt worshipped at el-Kab; she often appears with her sister-goddess Wadjet the cobra, protecting the pharaoh.

Hathor

Nut Sky goddess usually portrayed as a woman whose star-spangled body arches across tomb and temple ceilings. She swallows the sun each evening to give birth to it each morning.

Osiris God of regeneration portrayed in human form whose main cult centre was at Abydos. As the first mummy created, he was magically revived by Isis to produce their son Horus, who took over the earthly kingship while Osiris became ruler of the underworld and symbol of eternal life.

Ptah Creator god of Memphis who thought the world into being. He is patron of craftsmen, wears a skullcap and usually clutches a tall sceptre (resembling a 1950s microphone).

Ra Supreme sun god generally shown as a man with a falcon's head topped by a sun disc, although he can take many forms (eg Aten, Khepri) and other gods merge with him to enhance their powers (eg Amun-Ra, Ra-Atum). Ra travelled through the skies in a boat, sinking down into the underworld each night before re-emerging at dawn to bring light.

Horus

Sekhmet Lioness goddess of Memphis whose name means 'the powerful one'. As a daughter of sun god Ra she was capable of great destruction and was the bringer of pestilence; her priests functioned as doctors.

Seth God of chaos personified by a mythological, composite animal. After murdering his brother Osiris he was defeated by Horus, and his great physical strength was harnessed to defend Ra in the underworld.

Sobek Crocodile god representing Pharaonic might, he was worshipped at Kom Ombo and the Fayuum.

Taweret Hippopotamus goddess who often appears upright to scare evil from the home and protect women in childbirth.

Thoth God of wisdom and writing, and patron of scribes. He is portrayed as an ibis or baboon and his cult centre was Hermopolis.

TEMPLES

Isis

Although many gods had their own cult centres, they were also worshipped at temples throughout Egypt. Built on sites considered sacred, existing temples were added to by successive pharaohs to demonstrate their piety. This is best seen at the enormous complex of Karnak (p243), the culmination of 2000 years of reconstruction.

Surrounded by huge enclosure walls of mudbrick, the stone temples within were regarded as houses of the gods where daily rituals were performed on behalf of the pharaoh. As the intermediary between gods and humans, the pharaoh was high priest of every temple, although in practice these powers were delegated to each temple's high priest.

Khepri

As well as the temples housing the gods (cult temples), there were also funerary (mortuary) temples where each pharaoh was worshipped after death. Eventually sited away from their tombs for security reasons, the best examples are on Luxor's West Bank, where pharaohs buried in the Valley of the Kings had huge funerary temples built closer to the river. These include Ramses III's temple at Medinat Habu (p273), Amenhotep III's once-vast temple marked by the Colossi of Memnon (p256) and the best known example built by Hatshepsut into the cliffs of Deir al-Bahri (p267).

TOMBS & MUMMIFICATION
Tombs

Nut

Initially, tombs were created to differentiate the burials of the elite from the majority, whose bodies continued to be placed directly into the desert sand. By around 3100 BC the mound of sand heaped over a grave was replaced by a more permanent structure of mudbrick, whose characteristic bench-shape is known as a mastaba, after the Arabic word for bench.

As stone replaced mudbrick, the addition of further levels to increase height created the pyramid, the first built at Saqqara for King Zoser (see Zoser's Funerary Complex, p198). Its stepped sides soon evolved into the familiar smooth-sided structure, with the Pyramids of Giza (p144) the most famous examples.

Osiris

Pyramids are generally surrounded by the mastaba tombs of officials wanting burial close to their pharaoh in order to share in an afterlife, which was still the prerogative of royalty; see Cemeteries (p152), Tomb of Akhethotep & Ptahhotep (p202), Mastaba of Ti (p202) and Tombs of Mereruka & Ankhmahor (p203). It was only when the power of the monarchy broke down at the end of the Old Kingdom that the afterlife became increasingly accessible to those outside the royal family, and as officials became more independent they began to opt for burial in their home towns. With little room for grand superstructures along many of the narrow stretches beside the Nile, an alternative type of tomb developed, cut tunnel-fashion into the cliffs that border the river. Most were built on the west bank, the traditional place of burial where the sun was seen to sink down into the underworld each evening.

These simple rock-cut tombs consisting of a single chamber gradually developed into more elaborate structures complete with an open court-yard, offering a chapel and entrance facade carved out of the rock, with a shaft leading down into a burial chamber; see Tomb of Kheti (p223), Tomb of Baqet (p223), Tomb of Khnumhotep (p223) and Tombs of the Nobles (p306).

Ra

The most impressive rock-cut tombs were those built for the kings of the New Kingdom (1550–1069 BC), who relocated the royal burial ground south to the religious capital Thebes (modern Luxor) to a remote desert valley on the west bank, now known as the Valley of the Kings (see p258). There is evidence suggesting the first tomb (KV 39) here may have been built by Amenhotep I. The tomb of his successor Tuthmosis I was built by royal architect Ineni, whose biographical inscription states that he supervised its construction alone, 'with no one seeing, no one hearing'. In a radical departure from tradition, the offering chapels that were once part of the tomb's layout were now replaced by funerary (mortuary) temples built some distance away to preserve the tomb's secret location.

Sekhmet

The tombs themselves were designed with a long corridor descending to a network of chambers decorated with scenes to help the deceased reach the next world. Many of these were extracts from the Book of the Dead, the modern term for works including The Book of Amduat (literally, 'that which is in the underworld'), The Book of Gates and The Litany of Ra. These describe the sun god's nightly journey through the darkness of the underworld, the realm of Osiris, with each hour of the night regarded as a separate region guarded by demigods. In order for Ra and the dead souls who accompanied him to pass through on their way to rebirth at dawn, it was essential that they knew the demigods' names in order to get past them. Since knowledge was power in the Egyptian afterlife, the funerary texts give 'Knowledge of the power of those in the underworld, knowl-edge of the hidden forces, knowing each hour and each god, knowing the gates where the great god must pass and knowing how the powerful can be destroyed'.

Sobek

Mummification

Although mummification was used by many ancient cultures across the world, the Egyptians were the ultimate practitioners of this highly complex procedure, which they refined over 4000 years.

Their preservation of the dead can be traced back to the very earliest times, when bodies were simply buried in the desert away from the limited areas of cultivation. In direct contact with the sand, the hot, dry conditions allowed body fluids to drain away while preserving the skin, hair and nails intact. Accidentally uncovering such bodies must have had a profound effect upon those able to recognise people who had died years before.

Taweret

As society developed, those who would once have been buried in a hole in the ground demanded tombs befitting their status. But as the bodies were no longer in direct contact with the sand, they rapidly decomposed. An alternative means of preservation was therefore required. After a long process of experimentation, and a good deal of trial and error, the Egyptians seem to have finally cracked it around 2600 BC when they started to remove the internal organs, where putrefaction begins.

As the process became increasingly elaborate, all the organs were removed except the kidneys, which were hard to reach, and the heart, considered to

Thoth

The textiles used to wrap mummies are often described as 'bandages', although all kinds of recycled linen was used for the purpose, from old shirts to boat sails.

be the source of intelligence. The brain was generally removed by inserting a metal probe up the nose and whisking until it had liquefied sufficiently to be drained down the nose. All the rest – lungs, liver, stomach and intestines – were removed through an opening cut in the left flank. Then the body and its separate organs were covered with natron salt (a combination of sodium carbonate and sodium bicarbonate) and left to dry out for 40 days, after which they were washed, purified and anointed with a range of oils, spices and resins. All were then wrapped in layers of linen, with the appropriate amulets set in place over the various parts of the body as priests recited the necessary incantations.

With each of the internal organs placed inside its own burial container (one of four Canopic jars), the wrapped body with its funerary mask was placed inside its coffin. It was then ready for the funeral procession to the tomb, where the vital Opening of the Mouth ceremony reanimated the soul and restored its senses (see p59). Offerings could then be given and the deceased wished 'a thousand of every good and pure thing for your soul and all kinds of offerings'.

Research is starting to reveal that the Egyptians were experimenting with mummification as early as 4300 BC, almost 1000 years earlier than previously believed.

The Egyptians also used their mummification skills to preserve animals, both much-loved pets and creatures presented in huge numbers as votive offerings to the gods with which they were associated. Everything from huge bulls to tiny shrews were mummified, with cats, hawks and ibis preserved in their millions by Graeco-Roman times.

ART IN LIFE & DEATH

Ancient Egyptian art is instantly recognisable and its distinctive style remained largely unchanged for more than three millennia. With its basic characteristics already in place at the beginning of the Pharaonic Period c 3100 BC, the motif of the king smiting his enemies on the Narmer Palette (see Room 43 – Atrium, p184) was still used in Roman times.

Despite being described in modern terms as 'works of art', the reasons for the production of art in ancient Egypt are still very much misunderstood. Whereas most cultures create art for purely decorative purposes, Egyptian art was primarily functional. This idea is best understood when gazing

HEALTH

With average life expectancy around 35 years, the ancient Egyptians took health care seriously, and used a blend of medicine and magic to treat problems caused mainly by the environment. Wind-blown sand damaged eyes, teeth and lungs; snakes and scorpions were a common danger; parasitic worms lurked in infected water; and flies spread diseases. Medicines prescribed for such problems were largely plant- or mineral-based, and included honey (now known to be an effective antibacterial) and 'bread in mouldy condition' – as described in the ancient medical texts – which provided a source of penicillin.

By 2650 BC there were dentists and doctors, with specialists in surgery, gynaecology, osteopathy and even veterinary practice trained in the temple medical schools. The pyramid builders' town at Giza had medical facilities capable of treating fractures and performing successful surgical amputations.

Magic was also used to combat illness or injury, and spells were recited and amulets worn to promote recovery. Most popular was the *wedjat*-eye of Horus, representing health and completeness, while amulets of the household deities Bes and Taweret were worn during the difficult time of childbirth. Mixtures of honey, sour milk and crocodile dung were recommended as contraceptives, and pregnancy tests involving barley were used to foretell the sex of the unborn child. Magic was also used extensively during childhood, with the great mother goddess Isis and her son Horus often referred to in spells to cure a variety of childhood ailments.

at the most famous and perhaps most beautiful of all Egyptian images, Tutankhamun's death mask (see Room 3, p190), which was quite literally made to be buried in a hole in the ground.

The majority of artefacts were produced for religious and funerary purposes and, despite their breathtaking beauty, would have been hidden away from public gaze, either within a temple's dark interior or, like Tut's mask, buried in a tomb with the dead. This only makes the objects – and those who made them – even more remarkable. Artists regarded the things they made as pieces of equipment to do a job rather than works of art to be displayed and admired, and only very occasionally in 3000 years did an artist actually sign their work.

This concept also explains the appearance of carved and painted wall scenes, whose deceptively simple appearance and lack of perspective reinforces their functional purpose. The Egyptians believed it was essential that the things they portrayed had every relevant feature shown as clearly as possible. Then when they were magically reanimated through the correct rituals they would be able to function as effectively as possible, protecting and sustaining the unseen spirits of both the gods and the dead.

Figures needed a clear outline, with a profile of nose and mouth to let them breathe, and the eye shown whole as if seen from the front, to allow the figure to see. This explains why eyes were often painted on the sides of coffins to allow the dead to see out and why hieroglyphs such as snakes or enemy figures were sometimes shown in two halves to prevent them causing damage when re-activated.

The vast quantities of food and drink offered in temples and tombs were duplicated on surrounding walls to ensure a constant supply for eternity. The offerings are shown piled up in layers, sometimes appearing to float in that air if the artist took this practice too far. In the same way, objects otherwise hidden from view if portrayed realistically appear to balance on top of the boxes that actually contained them.

While working within such restrictive conventions, the ancient artists still managed to capture a feeling of vitality. Inspired by the natural world around them, they selected images to reflect the concept of life and rebirth, as embodied by the scarab beetles and tilapia fish thought capable of self-generation. Since images were also believed to be able to transmit the life force they contained, fluttering birds, gambolling cattle and the speeding quarry of huntsmen were all favourite motifs. The life-giving properties of plants are also much in evidence, with wheat, grapes, onions and figs stacked side by side with the flowers the Egyptians loved so much. Particularly common are the lotus (water lily) and papyrus, the heraldic symbols of Upper and Lower Egypt often shown entwined to symbolise a kingdom united.

Colour was also used as a means of reinforcing an object's function, with bright primary shades achieved with natural pigments selected for their specific qualities. Egypt was represented politically by the White Crown of Upper Egypt and the Red Crown of Lower Egypt, fitted together in the dual crown to represent the two lands brought together. The country could also be represented in environmental terms by the colours red and black, the red desert wastes of *deshret* contrasting with the fertile black land of *kemet*. For the Egyptians, black was the colour of life, which also explains the choice of black in representations of Osiris, god of fertility and resurrection in contrast to the redness associated with his brother Seth, god of chaos. Colour does not indicate ethnic origins, however, since Osiris is also shown with green skin, the colour of vegetation and new life. Some of his fellow gods are blue to echo the ethereal blue of the sky, and the golden yellow of the sun is regularly employed

Temple rituals included the burning or smashing of wax or clay figurines of anyone who threatened divine order, from enemies of the state to enemies of the sun god.

One of the most common souvenirs of a trip to Egypt in the 19th century was a mummy, either whole or in bits – heads and hands were particularly popular as they fitted easily into luggage.

Although cats were considered sacred, X-ray examinations have revealed that some at least were killed to order by strangulation prior to their mummification for use as votive offerings.

for its protective qualities. Even human figures were initially represented with different coloured skin tones, the red-brown of men contrasting with the paler, yellowed tones of women, and although this has been interpreted as indicating that men spent most of the time working outdoors whereas women led a more sheltered existence, changes in artistic convention meant everyone was eventually shown with the same red-brown skin tone.

The choice of material was also an important way of enhancing an object's purpose. Sculptors worked in a variety of different mediums, with stone often chosen for its colour – white limestone and alabaster (calcite), golden sandstone, green schist (slate), brown quartzite and both black and red granite. Smaller items could be made of red or yellow jasper; orange carnelian or blue lapis lazuli; metals such as copper, gold or silver; or less costly materials such as wood or highly glazed blue faïence pottery.

All these materials were used to produce a wide range of statuary for temples and tombs, from 20m-high stone colossi to gold figurines a few centimetres tall. Regardless of their dimensions, each figure was thought capable of containing the spirit of the individual they represented – useful insurance should anything happen to the mummy. Amulets and jewellery were another means of ensuring the security of the dead. While their beauty would enhance the appearance of the living, each piece was also carefully designed as a protective talisman or a means of communicating status. Even when creating such small-scale masterpieces, the same principles employed in larger-scale works of art applied, and little of the work that the ancient craftsmen produced was either accidental or frivolous.

There was also a standard repertoire of funerary scenes, from the colourful images that adorn the walls of tombs to the highly detailed vignettes illuminating funerary texts. Every single image, whether carved on stone or painted on papyrus, was designed to serve and protect the deceased on their journey into the afterlife.

Initially the afterlife was restricted to royalty and the texts meant to guide the pharaohs towards eternity were inscribed on the walls of their burial chambers. Since the rulers of the Old Kingdom were buried in pyramids, the accompanying funerary writings are known as the Pyramid Texts – see Pyramid & Causeway of Unas (p200), Pyramid of Teti (p202) and Other Pyramids (p203).

In the hope of sharing in the royal afterlife, Old Kingdom officials built their tombs close to the pyramids until the pharaohs lost power at the end of the Old Kingdom. No longer reliant on the pharaoh's favour, the officials began to use the royal funerary texts for themselves. Inscribed on their coffins, they are known as Coffin Texts – a Middle Kingdom version of the earlier Pyramid Texts, adapted for nonroyal use.

This 'democratisation' of the afterlife evolved even further when the Coffin Texts were literally brought out in paperback, inscribed on papyrus and made available to the masses during the New Kingdom. Referred to by the modern term the *Book of the Dead,* the Egyptians knew this as the *Book of Coming Forth by Day,* with sections entitled 'Spell for not dying a second time', 'Spell not to rot and not to do work in the land of the dead' and 'Spell for not having your magic taken away'. The texts also give various visions of paradise, from joining the sun god Ra in his journey across the sky, joining Osiris in the underworld or rising up to become one of the Imperishable Stars, the variety of final destinations reflecting the ancient Egyptians' multifaceted belief system. These spells and instructions acted as a kind of guidebook to the afterlife, with some of the texts accompanied by maps, and images of some of the gods and demons that would be encountered en route together with the correct way to address them.

The ancient Egyptians were very good at faking certain materials, with wooden pots painted to resemble costly stone and painted linen used for priestly vestments instead of real panther skin.

Since it was thought that images of living things could reanimate in the afterlife, the nose and mouth of unpopular figures were often defaced to prevent them inhaling the breath of life needed to live again in the next world.

The same scenes were also portrayed on tomb walls; the New Kingdom royal tombs in the Valley of the Kings (p256) are decorated with highly formal scenes showing the pharaoh in the company of the gods and all the forces of darkness defeated. Since the pharaoh was always pharaoh, even in death, there was no room for the informality and scenes of daily life that can be found in the tombs of lesser mortals (see Tombs of the Nobles, p256).

This explains the big difference between the formal scenes in royal tombs and the much more relaxed, almost eclectic nature of nonroyal tomb scenes, which feature everything from eating and drinking to dancing and hairdressing. Yet even here these apparently random scenes of daily life carry the same message found throughout Egyptian art – the eternal continuity of life and the triumph of order over chaos. As the pharaoh is shown smiting the enemy and restoring peace to the land, his subjects contribute to this continual battle of opposites in which order must always triumph for life to continue.

In one of the most common nonroyal tomb scenes, the tomb owner hunts on the river (see Tombs of Menna & Nakht, p269). Although generally interpreted on a simplistic level as the deceased enjoying a day out boating with his family, the scene is far more complex than it first appears. The tomb owner, shown in a central position in the prime of life, strikes a formal pose as he restores order amid the chaos of nature all around him. In his task he is supported by the female members of his family, from his small daughter to the wife standing serenely beside him. Dressed far too impractically for a hunting trip on the river, his wife wears an outfit more in keeping with a priestess of Hathor, goddess of love and sensual pleasure. Yet Hathor is also the protector of the dead and capable of great violence as defender of her father, the sun god Ra, in his eternal struggle against the chaotic forces of darkness.

Some versions of this riverside hunting scene also feature a cat. Often described as a kind of 'retriever' (whoever heard of a retriever cat?), the cat is one of the creatures who was believed to defend the sun god on his nightly journey through the underworld. Similarly, the river's teeming fish were regarded as pilots for the sun god's boat and were themselves potent symbols of rebirth. Even the abundant lotus flowers are significant since the lotus, whose petals open each morning, is the flower that symbolised rebirth. Once the coded meaning of ancient Egyptian art is understood, such previously silent images almost scream out the idea of 'life'.

Another common tomb scene is the banquet at which guests enjoy generous quantities of food and drink – see Tombs of Menna & Nakht (p269) and Tombs of Sennofer & Rekhmire (p270). Although no doubt reflecting some of the pleasures the deceased had enjoyed in life, the food portrayed was also meant to sustain their souls, as would the accompanying scenes of bountiful harvests which would ensure supplies never ran out. Even the music and dance performed at these banquets indicate much more than a party in full swing – the lively proceedings were another way of reviving the deceased by awakening their senses.

The culmination of this idea can be found in the all-important Opening of the Mouth ceremony, performed by the deceased's heir, either the next king or the eldest son. The ceremony was designed to reanimate the soul (ka), which could then go on to enjoy eternal life once all its senses had been restored. Noise and movement were believed to reactivate hearing and sight, while the sense of smell was restored with incense and flowers. The essential offerings of food and drink then sustained the soul that resided within the mummy as it was finally laid to rest inside the tomb.

For a straightforward approach to ancient Egypt's artistic legacy, Cyril Aldred's *Egyptian Art* (Thames & Hudson, 1985) remains a standard work, while a useful guide to the way hieroglyphs were used in art is provided by Richard Wilkinson's *Reading Egyptian Art: A Hieroglyphic Guide to Ancient Egyptian Painting and Sculpture* (Thames & Hudson, 1994).

The eyes of cats in tomb scenes were occasionally painted with gold leaf, giving them a realistic reflective quality and linking them to the sun god's protective powers. This is also the theme of the 2009 novel *The Glittering Eye* by LJ Adlington (Hodder).

HIEROGLYPHS

Hieroglyphs, meaning 'sacred carvings' in Greek, are the pictorial script used by the ancient Egyptians. The script was developed as a means of recording produce and recent discoveries at Abydos dating to around 3250 BC make this the earliest form of writing yet found, even predating that of Mesopotamia.

The impact of hieroglyphs on Egyptian culture cannot be overestimated, as they provided the means by which the state took shape. They were used by a civil service of scribes working on the king's behalf to collect taxes and organise vast workforces. With literacy in Egypt at the time running at less than 1%, scribes were considered wise and part of society's elite.

Within a few centuries, day-to-day transactions were undertaken in a shorthand version of hieroglyphs known as hieratic, whereas hieroglyphs remained the perfect medium for monumental inscriptions. They were in constant use for more than 3500 years until the last example was carved at Philae temple on 24 August AD 394. Covering every available tomb and temple surface, hieroglyphs were regarded as 'the words of the Thoth', the ibis-headed god of writing and patron deity of scribes, who, like the scribes, is often shown holding a reed pen and ink palette.

The small figures of humans, animals, birds and symbols that populate the script were believed to infuse each scene with divine power. In fact certain signs were considered so potent they were shown in two halves to prevent them causing havoc should they magically reanimate. Yet the ancient Egyptians also liked a joke, and their language was often onomatopoeic – for example, the word for cat was *miw* after the noise it makes, and the word for wine was *irp,* after the noise made by those who drank it.

Evolving from a handful of basic signs, more than 6000 hieroglyphs have been identified, although less than 1000 were in general use. Although they may at first appear deceptively simple, the signs themselves operate on several different levels and can best be understood if divided into three categories – logograms (ideograms), determinatives and phonograms. While logograms represent the thing they depict (eg the sun sign meaning 'sun'), and determinatives are simply placed at the ends of words to reinforce their meaning (eg the sun sign in the verb 'to shine'), phonograms are less straightforward and are the signs that represent either one, two or three consonants. The 26 signs usually described in simple terms as 'the hieroglyphic alphabet' are the single consonant signs (eg the owl pronounced 'm', the zig-zag water sign 'n'). Another 100 or so signs are biconsonantal (eg the bowl sign read as 'nb'), and a further 50 are triconsonantal signs (eg 'nfr' meaning good, perfect or beautiful).

Unfortunately there are no actual vowels as such, and the absence of any punctuation can also prove tricky, especially since the signs can be arranged either vertically to be read down or horizontally to be read left to right or right to left, depending which way the symbols face.

Although they can seem incredibly complex, the majority of hieroglyphic inscriptions are simply endless repetitions of the names and titles of the pharaohs and gods, surrounded by protective symbols. Names were of tremendous importance to the Egyptians and as vital to an individual's existence as their soul (ka), and it was sincerely believed that 'to speak the name of the dead is to make them live'.

The loss of one's name meant permanent obliteration from history, and those unfortunate enough to incur official censure included commoners and pharaohs alike. At times it even happened to the gods themselves, a fate which befell the state god Amun during the reign of the 'heretic' pharaoh Akhenaten, who in turn suffered the same fate together with his god Aten when Amun was later restored.

PHARAONIC CARTOUCHES

Ramses II
(Usermaatre Setepenre)

Amenhotep III (Nebmaatre)

Tuthmosis III
(Menkheperre)

Hatshepsut (Maatkare)

In order to prevent this kind of obliteration, names were sometimes carved so deeply into the rock it is possible to place an outstretched hand right inside each hieroglyph, as is the case of Ramses III's name and titles at his funerary temple of Medinat Habu.

Royal names were also followed by epithets such as 'life, prosperity, health', comparable to the way in which the name of the Prophet Mohammed is always followed by the phrase 'peace be upon him'. For further protection, royal names were written inside a rectangular fortress wall known as a *serekh*, which later developed into the more familiar oval-shaped cartouche (the French word for cartridge).

Although each pharaoh had five names, cartouches were used to enclose the two most important ones: the 'prenomen' or 'King of Upper and Lower Egypt' name assumed at the coronation and written with a bee and a sedge plant; and the 'nomen' or 'Son of Ra' name, which was given at birth and written with a goose and a sun sign.

As an example, Amenhotep III is known by his nomen or Son of Ra name 'Amun-hotep' (meaning Amun is content), although his prenomen or King of Upper and Lower Egypt name was Neb-maat-Re (meaning Ra, lord of truth). His grandson had the most famous of all Egyptian names, Tut-ankh-amun, which literally translates as 'the living image of Amun', yet he had originally been named Tut-ankh-aten, meaning 'the living image of the Aten' – a change in name that reflects the shifting politics of the time.

Gods were also incorporated into the names of ordinary people and as well as Amunhotep there was Rahotep (the sun god Ra is content) and Ptahhotep (the creator god Ptah is content). By changing 'hotep' (meaning 'content') to 'mose' (meaning 'born of'), the names Amenmose, Ramose and Ptahmose meant that these men were 'born of' these gods.

In similar fashion, goddesses featured in women's names. Hathor, goddess of love, beauty and pleasure, was a particular favourite, with names such as Sithathor (daughter of Hathor). Standard male names could also be feminised by the simple addition of 't', so Nefer (good, beautiful or perfect) becomes Nefert, which could be further embellished with the addition of a verb, as in the case of the famous name Nefertiti (goodness/beauty/perfection has come).

Others were known by their place of origin, such as Panehesy (the Nubian), or could be named after flora and fauna – Miwt (cat), Debet (hippopotamus) and Seshen (lotus), which is still in use today as the name Susan.

> Struggling with their hieroglyphs, student scribes were advised to 'Love writing and shun dancing, make friends with the scroll and palette, for they bring more joy than wine!'

> Fond of word play, the Egyptians often incorporated hieroglyphs into their designs to spell out names or phrases – the basket, beetle and sun disc featured in some of Tutankhamun's jewellery, for example, spells out his throne name 'neb-kheperu-re'.

PHARAONIC GLOSSARY

akh – usually translated as 'transfigured spirit', produced when the ka (soul) and ba (spirit) united after the deceased was judged worthy enough to enter the afterlife

Ammut – composite monster of the underworld who was part crocodile, part lion, part hippo and ate the hearts of the unworthy dead; her name means 'The Devourer'

ba – usually translated as 'spirit', which appeared after death as a human-headed bird, able to fly to and from the tomb and into the afterlife

Book of the Dead – modern term for the collection of ancient funerary texts designed to guide the dead through the afterlife, developed at the beginning of the New Kingdom and partly based on the earlier Pyramid Texts and Coffin Texts

Canopic jars – containers usually made of limestone or calcite to store the preserved entrails (stomach, liver, lungs and intestines) of mummified individuals

cartouche – the protective oval shape (the name derived from the French word for cartridge), which surrounded the names of kings and queens and occasionally gods

cenotaph – a memorial structure set up in memory of a deceased king or queen, separate from their tomb or funerary temple

Coffin Texts – funerary texts developed from the earlier Pyramid Texts, which were then written on coffins during the Middle Kingdom

coregency – a period of joint rule by two pharaohs, usually father and son

cult temple – the standard religious building(s) designed to house the spirits of the gods and accessible only to the priesthood, usually located on the Nile's east bank

deshret – 'red land', referring to barren desert

djed pillar – the symbolic backbone of Osiris, bestowing strength and stability and often worn as an amulet

false door – the means by which the soul of the deceased could enter and leave the world of the living to accept funerary offerings brought to their tomb

funerary (mortuary) temple – the religious structures where the souls of dead pharaohs were commemorated and sustained with offerings, usually built on the Nile's west bank

Heb-Sed festival – the jubilee ceremony of royal renewal and rejuvenation, which pharaohs usually celebrated after 30 years' rule

Heb-Sed race – part of the Heb-Sed festival when pharaohs undertook physical feats such as running to demonstrate their prowess and fitness to rule

hieratic – ancient shorthand version of hieroglyphs used for day-to-day transactions by scribes

hieroglyphs – Greek for 'sacred carvings', referring to ancient Egypt's formal picture writing used mainly for tomb and temple walls

hypostyle hall – imposing section of temple characterised by densely packed monumental columns

ka – usually translated as 'soul', this was a person's 'double', which was created with them at birth and which lived on after death, sustained by offerings left by the living

kemet – 'black land', referring to the fertile areas along the Nile's banks

king lists – chronological lists of each king's names kept as a means of recording history

lotus (water lily) – the heraldic plant of Upper (southern) Egypt

mammisi – the Birth House attached to certain Late Period and Graeco-Roman temples and associated with the goddesses Isis and Hathor

mastaba – Arabic word for bench, used to describe the mudbrick tomb structures built over subterranean burial chambers and from which pyramids developed

name – an essential part of each individual given at birth, and spoken after their death to allow them to live again in the afterlife

naos – sanctuary containing the god's statue, generally located in the centre of ancient temples

natron – mixture of sodium carbonate and sodium bicarbonate used to dry out the body during mummification and used by the living to clean linen, teeth and skin

nemes – the yellow-and-blue striped headcloth worn by pharaohs, the most famous example found on Tutankhamun's golden death mask

nomarch – local governor of each of Egypt's 42 nomes

nome – Greek term for Egypt's 42 provinces – 22 in Upper Egypt and later 20 added in Lower Egypt

obelisk – monolithic stone pillar tapering to a pyramidal top that was often gilded to reflect sunlight around temples and usually set in pairs

Opening of the Mouth ceremony – the culmination of the funeral, performed on the mummy of the deceased by their heir or funerary priest using spells and implements to restore their senses

Opet festival – annual celebration held at Luxor Temple to restore the powers of the pharaoh at a secret meeting with the god Amun

papyrus – the heraldic plant of Lower (northern) Egypt whose reedlike stem was sliced and layered to create paperlike sheets for writing

pharaoh – term for an Egyptian king derived from the ancient Egyptian word for palace, *per-aa*

pylon – monumental gateway with sloping sides forming the entrance to temples

Pyramid Texts – funerary texts inscribed on the walls of late Old Kingdom pyramids and restricted to royalty

sacred animals – living creatures thought to represent certain gods – eg the crocodile (identified with Sobek), the cat (identified with Bastet) – and often mummified at death

sarcophagus – derived from the Greek for 'flesh eating' and referring to the large stone coffins used to house the mummy and its wooden coffin(s)

scarab – the sacred dung beetle believed to propel the sun's disc through the sky in the same way the beetle pushes a ball of dung across the floor

Serapeum – vast network of underground catacombs at Saqqara in which the Apis bulls were buried, later associated with the Ptolemaic god Serapis

serdab – from the Arabic word for cellar, a small room in a mastaba tomb containing a statue of the deceased to which offerings were presented

shabti (or ushabti) – small servant figurines placed in burials designed to undertake any manual work in the afterlife on behalf of the deceased

shadow – an essential part of each individual, the shadow was believed to offer protection, based on the importance of shade in an extremely hot climate

sidelock of youth – characteristic hairstyle of children and certain priests in which the head is shaved and a single lock of hair allowed to grow

solar barque – the boat in which the sun god Ra sailed through the heavens, with actual examples buried close to certain pyramids for use by the spirits of the pharaohs

Uraeus – an image of the cobra goddess Wadjet worn at the brow of royalty to symbolically protect them by spitting fire into the eyes of their enemies

Weighing of the Heart (The Judgement of Osiris) – the heart of the deceased was weighed against the feather of Maat with Osiris as judge; if light and free of sin they were allowed to spend eternity as an *akh,* but if their heart was heavy with sin it was eaten by Ammut and they were damned forever

The Culture

THE NATIONAL PSYCHE

If there's one characteristic that links the majority of Egyptians, from the university professor in Alexandria to the shoeshine boy in Luxor, it's an immense pride in simply being Egyptian.

It's hard sometimes for outsiders to see where that pride could come from, given the pervasive poverty, low literacy levels, high unemployment, housing shortages, infrastructure shortfalls and myriad other pitfalls that face the country. But aiding every Egyptian in the daily struggle is every other Egyptian, and indeed there is a real sense that everybody's in it together. Large extended families and close-knit neighbourhoods act as social support groups, strangers fall easily into conversation with each other, and whatever goes wrong somebody always knows someone somewhere who can help fix it.

Religion also cushions life's blows. Islam permeates Egyptian life. It's manifested not in a strictly authoritarian manner as in Saudi Arabia – Egyptians love enjoying themselves too much for that – but it's there at an almost subconscious level. Ask after someone's health and the answer is *Alhamdulallah* (Fine. Praise to God). Arrange to meet tomorrow and it's *inshallah* (God willing). Then, if your appointee fails to turn up, God obviously didn't mean it to be.

And when all else fails there's humour, and Egyptians are renowned for it. Jokes and wisecracks are the parlance of life. Comedy is the staple of the local cinema industry and backbone of TV scheduling. The stock character is the little guy who through wit and a sharp tongue always manages to prick pomposity and triumph over the odds. Laughter lubricates the wheels of social exchange and one of the most enjoyable aspects of travel in Egypt is how much can be negotiated with a smile.

LIFESTYLE

There's no simple definition of Egyptian society. On the one hand there's traditional conservatism, reinforced by poverty, in which the diet is one of *fuul, ta'amiyya* and vegetables; women wear the long, black, all-concealing *abeyya* and men wear the gownlike *galabiyya;* cousins marry cousins; going to Alexandria constitutes the trip of a lifetime; and all is 'God's will'. On the other hand, there are sections of society whose members order out from McDonald's; whose daughters wear slinky black numbers and flirt outrageously; who think nothing of regular trips to the USA; and who never set foot in a mosque until the day they're laid out in one.

The bulk of the Egyptian populace falls somewhere between these two extremes. The typical urban family lives in an overcrowded suburb in a six-floor breeze-block apartment building with cracking walls and dodgy plumbing. If they're lucky they may own a small car (Fiat or Lada), which will be 10 or more years old. Otherwise the husband will take the metro to work or, more likely, fight for a handhold on one of the city's sardine-can buses. He may well be a university graduate (about 40,000 people graduate each year), although a degree is no longer any guarantee of a job. He may also be one of the million-plus paper-pushing civil servants, earning a pittance to while away each day in an undemanding job. This at least allows him to slip away from work early each afternoon to borrow his cousin's taxi for a few hours to bring in some much-needed supplementary income.

Statistics, background information and the lowdown on what's going on in Egypt is available to the public at the CIA World Factbook (www.cia.gov).

Fifty per cent of Egyptians live or work within 150km of Cairo.

His wife remains at home cooking, looking after the three or more children, and swapping visits with his mother, her mother and various other family members.

Meanwhile life in rural Egypt, where just over half the country's population lives, is undergoing a transformation. The population density on the agricultural land of the Nile Valley, on which most cities and villages are built, is one of the highest in the world. What little land remains is divided into small plots (averaging just 0.6 hectares), which don't even support a medium-sized family. As much as 50% of the rural population no longer makes its living off the land. For those who do, the small size of their plots prevents the mechanisation needed to increase yields. As a result, they increasingly rely on animal husbandry or are forced to look for other ways of surviving. So the farmer you see working his field is probably spending his afternoons working as a labourer or selling cigarettes from a homemade kiosk in an effort to make ends meet.

The countryside remains the repository of traditional culture and values. Large families are still the norm, particularly in Upper Egypt, and extended families still live together. High rates of female illiteracy are standard. Whether all this will change with the steady diet of urban Cairene values and Western soap operas currently beamed into village cafes and farmhouses each night remains to be seen.

Shahhat: An Egyptian by Richard Critchfield has become an anthropology classic, even though much of its content was debunked as a copy of a 1930s ethnographic study. So long as you keep this in mind it's still a good read, especially if you're spending time on Luxor's West Bank.

ECONOMY

Over the last few decades, the Egyptian government has struggled to reform the centralised economy it inherited from Nasser. In recent years, personal and corporate tax rates have been reduced, energy subsidies have been cut and several enterprises have been privatised. Despite these achievements, living standards for the average Egyptian are still abysmally low.

In response to the stagnating quality of life, the government has continued to subsidise basic commodities, which has created a spiralling budget deficit. As a result, the economy has been slowly collapsing, which has deterred vital foreign investment. Recently, Egyptians took to the streets to protest over

---

BACKHAND ECONOMY – THE ART OF BAKSHEESH

Tipping in Egypt is called baksheesh, but it's more than just a reward for services rendered. Salaries and wages in Egypt are much lower than in Western countries, so baksheesh is an essential means of supplementing income. It's far from a custom exclusively reserved for foreigners. Egyptians have to constantly dole out the baksheesh too – to park their cars, receive their mail, ensure they get fresh produce at the grocers and to be shown to their seat at the cinema.

For travellers who are not used to tipping, demands for baksheesh for doing anything from opening doors to pointing out the obvious in museums can be quite irritating. But it is the accepted way in Egypt. Just use your discretion, always remembering that more things warrant baksheesh here than anywhere in the West.

In hotels and restaurants, a 12% service charge is included at the bottom of the bill. However, since the money goes into the till, it's necessary to leave an additional tip for the waiter, usually 10% to 20%. Services such as opening a door, delivering room service or carrying your bags warrant at least E£1. A guard who shows you something off the beaten track at an ancient site or an attendant at a mosque who looks after your shoes should receive a couple of pounds. Baksheesh is not necessary when asking for directions.

We suggest carrying lots of small change with you (trust us – you'll need it!) and also to keep it separate from bigger bills as flashing your cash will lead to demands for greater baksheesh.

low wages and the rising cost of living, problems that have not been helped by the global economic crisis.

Of course, there is hope that Egypt can recoup these financial losses, in particular through growth in the energy sector, since the country is sitting on enormous natural gas reserves that foreign countries such as the US are eagerly eyeing.

POPULATION

Although the latest census results show that Egypt's population growth rate is falling, the number of citizens continues to increase by around one million every nine months. The Nile Valley is in danger of becoming one giant sprawling city, and Greater Cairo alone is home to nearly 20 million people. Parts of the city continue to house the world's highest density of people per kilometre. The strain placed on the city's decaying infrastructure is more than it can cope with.

The State Information Service (www.sis.gov.eg) has a huge amount of information on tourism, geography and culture.

SPORT

Egypt is football obsessed. The country hosts the Egyptian Premier League, which is regarded as one of the top 20 most competitive leagues in the world. The two most popular clubs are Ahly and Zamalek, both of which are located in Cairo, and inspire fervent loyalty in their fans. The Egyptian national team hasn't qualified for the FIFA World Cup since 1990 (and its 2009 loss to Algeria in a qualifier match sparked passionate protests and riots in Egypt and abroad). But it has won the African Nations Cup six times, including in 2008.

MULTICULTURALISM

Most Egyptians will proudly tell you that they are descendants of the ancient Egyptians, and while there is a strand of truth in this, any Pharaonic blood still flowing in modern veins has been seriously diluted. The country has weathered invasions of Libyans, Persians, Greeks, Romans and, most significantly, the 4000 Arab horsemen who invaded in AD 640. Following the Arab conquest, there was significant Arab migration and intermarriage with the indigenous population. The Mamluks, rulers of Egypt between the 13th and 16th centuries, were of Turkish and Circassian origins, and then there were the Ottoman Turks, rulers and occupiers from 1517 until the latter years of the 18th century.

The official site of the Egyptian Tourist Authority (www.egypt.travel) has magazine-type features, news and a huge range of resources and links.

Beside the Egyptians, there are a handful of separate indigenous groups with ancient roots. The ancestors of Egypt's Bedouins are believed to have migrated from the Arabian Peninsula, before settling the Western and Eastern Deserts and Sinai. The number of Bedouin in Egypt these days is estimated around 500,000, but their nomadic way of life is under threat as the interests of the rest of the country increasingly intrude on their once-isolated domains (see p486).

In the Western Desert, particularly in and around Siwa Oasis, are a small number of Berbers who have retained much of their own identity. They are quite easily distinguished from other Egyptians by the dress of the women, who usually don the *meliyya* (head-to-toe garment with slits for the eyes). Although many speak Arabic, they have preserved their own native tongues.

In the south are the tall, dark-skinned Nubians. They originate from Nubia, the region between Aswan in southern Egypt and Khartoum in Sudan, an area that almost completely disappeared in the 1970s when the High Dam was created and the subsequent build-up of water behind it drowned their traditional lands.

MEDIA

As in the West the media is big business in Egypt. The biggest daily newspapers are all pro-government or 'nationalist', including *Al-Akhbar*, the biggest seller with a circulation of around one million; *Al-Ahram*, the oldest daily in the Arab world (founded in 1877); and *Al-Gomhurriya*, set up by the military regime following the 1952 coup. Battling against them is an array of independents, including the weekly opposition publications *Al-Arabi* and the Islamist *Al-Ahrar*, as well as the business-slanted *Al-Alam al-Yom*. Although there are red lines not to be crossed (no criticism of the military, no presidential sleaze, nothing detrimental to 'national unity'), editors are given a degree of licence to publish what they will – which they do, often irrespective of whether a story happens to be true or not.

Illiteracy of around 50% means TV is the medium with the most penetration. In addition to the state channels (whose most popular output is Arabic films and home-grown soap operas), Egypt has its own satellite channels (ArabSat, NileSat 101, NileSat 202) including a couple of private operations (Al-Mehwar and Dream), both set up by well-known, politically connected businessmen. Quality of programming has markedly improved in recent years, forced to evolve by competition from other Arab and foreign channels such as CNN, Al-Jazeera and even transmissions from the old enemy to the north, Israel, whose channels many Egyptians furtively tune to for the better-quality US-made soaps and comedies.

Check out www.arabist .net for interesting news and articles relating to Egypt and the rest of the Arab world.

RELIGION

About 90% of Egypt's population is Muslim. Islam prevails in Egyptian life at a low-key, almost unconscious level. Few pray the specified five times a day, but almost all men heed the amplified call of the muezzin (mosque official) each Friday noon, when the crowds from the mosques block streets and footpaths. The vast majority of the 10% of Egypt that isn't Muslim is Coptic Christian. The two communities enjoy a more-or-less easy coexistence, although flare-ups in Minya and Alexandria in 2005 seemed to herald the introduction of tensions in this historically peaceful relationship. The 2009 pig cull in response to the threat of H1N1 (swine flu) was also seen by some as an attempt by the government to fan sectarian flames.

Islam

Islam is the predominant religion of Egypt. It shares its roots with Judaism and Christianity. Adam, Abraham (Ibrahim), Noah, Moses and Jesus are all accepted as Muslim prophets, although Jesus is recognised as a prophet and not the son of God. Muslim teachings correspond closely to the Torah (the foundation book of Judaism) and the Christian Gospels. The essence of Islam is the Quran and the Prophet Mohammed, who was the last and truest prophet to deliver messages from God (Allah) to the people.

Islam was founded in the early 7th century by Mohammed, who was born around AD 570 in Mecca. Mohammed is said to have received his first divine message at about the age of 40. The revelations continued for the rest of his life and were transcribed to become the holy Quran. To this day not one dot of the Quran has been changed, making it, Muslims believe, the direct word of Allah.

Mohammed started preaching in 613, three years after the first revelation, but could only attract a few dozen followers. Having attacked the ways of Meccan life, especially the worship of a wealth of idols, he made many enemies. In 622 he and his followers retreated to Medina, an oasis town some 360km from Mecca. This Hejira, or migration, marks the start of the Muslim calendar.

Mohammed died in 632 but the new religion continued its rapid spread, reaching all of Arabia by 634 and Egypt in 642.

Islam means 'submission' and this principle is visible in the daily life of Muslims. The faith is expressed by observance of the five 'pillars of Islam':

- Publicly declare that 'there is no god but God, and Mohammed is His Prophet'.
- Pray five times a day: at sunrise, noon, mid-afternoon, sunset and night.
- Give *zakat* (alms) for the propagation of Islam and to help the needy.
- Fast during daylight hours during the month of Ramadan.
- Complete the hajj (the pilgrimage to Mecca).

The first pillar is accomplished through prayer, which is the second pillar and an essential part of the daily life of a believer. Five times a day the muezzins bellow out the call to prayer through speakers on top of the minarets. It is perfectly permissible to pray at home or elsewhere; only the noon prayer on Friday need be conducted in the mosque. It is preferred that women pray at home.

The fourth pillar, Ramadan, is the ninth month of the Muslim calendar, when all believers fast during the day. Pious Muslims do not allow anything to pass their lips in daylight hours. Although many Muslims do not follow the injunctions to the letter, most conform to some extent. However, the impact of the fasting is often lessened by a shift in waking hours: many only get up in the afternoon when there are just a few hours of fasting left to observe. They then feast through the night until sunrise. The combination of abstinence and lack of sleep means that tempers are often short during Ramadan.

'The evening meal during Ramadan, called *iftar*, is always a celebration'

Although there are no public holidays until Eid al-Fitr, it is difficult to get anything done during Ramadan because of erratic hours. Almost everything closes in the afternoon or has shorter daytime hours; this does not apply to businesses that cater mostly to foreign tourists but some restaurants and hotels may be closed for the entire month. Although non-Muslims are not expected to fast, it is considered impolite to eat or drink in public during fasting hours. The evening meal during Ramadan, called *iftar* (breaking the fast), is always a celebration. In some parts of town, tables are laid out in the street as charitable acts by the wealthy to provide food for the less fortunate. Evenings are imbued with a party atmosphere and there's plenty of street entertainment, often through until sunrise. (For information about Islamic holidays and festivals, see p514.)

One of the most influential Islamic authorities in Egypt is the Sheikh of Al-Azhar, a position currently held by Mohammed Sayyed Tantawi. It is the role of the supreme sheikh to define the official Islamic line on any particular matter from organ donations to heavy-metal music.

Coptic Christianity

Egyptian Christians are known as Copts. The term is the Western form of the Arabic *qibt,* derived from the Greek *aegyptios* (Egyptian).

Before the arrival of Islam, Christianity was the predominant religion in Egypt. St Mark, companion of the apostles Paul and Peter, began preaching Christianity in Egypt around AD 45 and although it did not become the official religion of the country until the 4th century, Egypt was one of the first countries to embrace the new faith.

Egyptian Christians split from the Orthodox Church of the Eastern (or Byzantine) Empire, of which Egypt was then a part, after the main body of the church described Christ as both human and divine. Dioscurus, the patriarch of Alexandria, refused to accept this description, and embraced the theory that Christ is totally absorbed by his divinity and that it is blasphemous to consider him human.

The Coptic Church is ruled by a patriarch (presently Pope Shenouda III), other members of the religious hierarchy and an ecclesiastical council of laypeople. It has a long history of monasticism and can justly claim that the first Christian monks, St Anthony and St Pachomius, were Copts.

The Coptic language, which has its origins in Egyptian hieroglyphs and Ancient Greek, is still used in religious ceremonies, sometimes in conjunction with Arabic for the benefit of the congregation. Today the Coptic language is based on the Greek alphabet with an additional seven characters taken from hieroglyphs.

The Copts have long provided something of an educated elite in Egypt, filling many important government and bureaucratic posts. Furthermore, they've always been an economically powerful minority, and the majority of Copts are wealthy and influential.

With that said, there are also a lot of Copts at the very bottom of the heap: the *zabbalin*, the garbage-pickers of Cairo, who collect and sort through most of the city's rubbish, have always been Copts.

Other Creeds

Other Christian denominations are represented in Egypt, each by a few thousand adherents. In total, there are about one million members of other Christian groups. Among Catholics, apart from Roman Catholics of the Latin rite, the whole gamut of the fragmented Middle Eastern rites is represented, including the Armenian, Syrian, Chaldean, Maronite and Melkite rites. The Anglican communion comes under the Episcopal Church in Jerusalem. The Armenian Apostolic Church has around 10,000 members, and the Greek Orthodox Church is based in Alexandria.

Egypt was once home to a significant number of Jews. Historical sources record that there were 7000 Jews living in Cairo as far back as 1168. In Mamluk times there was a Jewish quarter, Haret al-Yahud, in the vicinity of the Mosque of Al-Azhar.

The first 40 years of the 20th century constituted something of a golden age for Egyptian Jews as their numbers reached an all-time peak of 80,000, and they came to play a bigger role in society and the affairs of state.

However, the reversal began with the creation of Israel in 1948. Not long afterwards, the exodus received further impetus with the nationalisation that followed Gamal Abdel Nasser's seizure of power. Today, it's estimated there are no more than 200 Jews left in Egypt.

WOMEN IN EGYPT

Some of the biggest misunderstandings between Egyptians and Westerners occur over the issue of women. Half-truths and stereotypes exist on both sides: many Westerners assume all Egyptian women are veiled, repressed victims, while a large number of Egyptians just see Western women as sex-obsessed and immoral.

For many Egyptians of both genders, the role of a woman is specifically defined: she is the mother and the matron of the household. The man is the provider. However, as with any society, generalisations can be misleading and the reality is far more nuanced. There are thousands of

Though women received the vote in 1956, restrictive personal-status laws prohibited a woman leaving her husband's house without his permission or a court order up until 1979.

UNDERSTANDING THE LACK OF VIOLENT CRIME IN EGYPT *Hassan Ansah*

Social scientists commonly argue that crime and poverty are bedfellows that are intractably interwoven. However, despite the overwhelming and at times grinding poverty experienced by the majority of Egyptians, the country's violent crime rate is lower than the United States and Britain. Of course, this brings about the question of why Egypt has a relative lack of violent crime, particularly rape and murder. This is especially puzzling in Cairo, where millions of people contend daily with dense living conditions, a high unemployment rate and urban malaise. To answer this lingering question, it is important to realise that crime, like any other social dynamic, is the reflection of a country's cultural norms.

While many developed nations in the West have a tendency to view Islamic societies such as Egypt with a wary eye, there is a lot to be learnt from a country that puts faith in a higher power. In Egypt, the majority of the people seem united in their enduring focus on the afterlife (a local holy man once joked that everyone in Egypt lives partly in their coffin!), a conservative tradition that permeates virtually every aspect of life. This conservatism has established and maintained a system of moral values and principles that has in part tapered the violent crime rate in Egypt. Crime in Egypt is rarely random and almost never targeted towards foreigners.

Although the Egyptian government sets out to create a manageable and law-abiding society, it is the family and the community that establishes and maintains the safe environment found throughout the country. Within Egypt, nothing functions outside of the realm of religion, which is often regarded as the fabric that holds the entire country together. The family ethos, maintained and fostered by Islamic law, facilitates channels of cooperation, arbitration, conflict resolution and economic assistance within the greater community. Furthermore, these same interactions are also used as enforcement mechanisms for common moral values, which certainly serve as a deterrent for crime within the community. Not surprisingly, breaking these informal moral ethical codes often comes with a heavy price – certain individuals may not be able to find a job, a spouse, a home, or even negotiate the bureaucracy of state institutions.

Unlike the West where conflicts often take place behind closed doors in the shadows of official court rooms, in Egypt renegotiations and fights often occur in public with a theatrical hint to them in order to injure, shore up, or improve one's public reputation. For example, a man will pick a quiet evening to shout from the street to a friend reprimanding him for not repaying a personal loan, thus sharing with the entire community that the man is dishonourable and irresponsible. Or, in the instance of spousal abuse, a woman will go to the roof of her building, shouting to the entire neighbourhood that her husband has beaten her.

As a result, this community-enforced moral code creates an extremely discouraging environment for a would-be criminal. In fact, it is arguably these deeply interconnected and informal social networks that temper the towering poverty experienced by most Egyptians. As one Cairene puts it, perhaps it is the 'deeply embedded nosiness' of Egyptians that helps to maintain the peace.

Hassan Ansah is a freelance writer and journalist who has taught at the Western International University in Phoenix, Arizona, and at the American University of Cairo (AUC).

Hakmet abu Zeid became the first woman in the Egyptian cabinet in 1962, assuming the post of social affairs minister.

middle- and upper-middle-class professional women in Egypt who, like their counterparts in the West, juggle work and family responsibilities. Among the working classes, where adherence to tradition is strongest, the ideal may be for women to concentrate on home and family, but economic reality means that millions of women are forced to work (but are still responsible for all the domestic chores).

The issue of sex is where the differences between Western and Egyptian women are most apparent. Premarital sex (or, indeed, any sex outside marriage) is taboo in Egypt. But, as with anything forbidden, it still happens. Nevertheless, it is the exception rather than the rule – and that goes for men as well as women.

For women the issue is potentially far more serious. With the possible exception of the upper classes, women are expected to be virgins when they marry and a family's reputation can rest upon this point. In such a context the restrictions placed on a girl – no matter how onerous they may seem to a Westerner – are to protect her and her reputation from the potentially disastrous attentions of men.

ARTS

To the Arab world, Egypt (or more specifically Cairo) is a powerhouse of film, TV, music and theatre. While little of this culture has had any impact on the West, a great many Egyptian actors and singers are superstars and revered cultural icons to Arabic-speakers around the world.

Literature

Awarded the Nobel prize for Literature in 1988, Naguib Mahfouz can claim to have single-handedly shaped the nature of Arabic literature in the 20th century. Born in 1911 in Cairo's Islamic quarter, Mahfouz began writing when he was 17. His first efforts were influenced by the European greats, but over the course of his career he developed a voice that was uniquely Arab, and drew its inspiration from the talk in the coffeehouses and the dialect of Cairo's streets. In 1994 he was the victim of a knife attack that left him partially paralysed. The attack was a response to a book that Mahfouz had written, which was a thinly disguised allegory of the life of the great religious leaders including Mohammed. In 2006, Mahfouz died after falling and sustaining a head injury.

On the strength of what's available in English, it's easy to view Egyptian literature as beginning and ending with Mahfouz but he's only the best known of a canon of respected writers. Others include Taha Hussein, a blind author and intellectual who spent much of his life in trouble with whichever establishment happened to be in power; the Alexandrian Tewfiq Hakim; and Yousef Idris, a writer of powerful short stories. Unfortunately, none of these authors has gained the international attention they deserve and they're only published in English by the American University in Cairo Press, a small Cairo-based academic publishing house that publishes an impressive line-up of Egyptian novelists as well as a large (and excellent) nonfiction list.

Egypt's women writers are enjoying more international success than the men. Nawal al-Saadawi's fictional work *Woman at Point Zero* has been published, at last count, in 28 languages. An outspoken critic on behalf of women, she is marginalised at home – her nonfiction book *The Hidden Face of Eve*, which criticises the role of women in the Arab world, is banned in Egypt. For many years following its publication, Saadawi was forced to stay out of the country after reportedly receiving death threats from Islamist groups. Those interested in learning more about her fascinating and inspirational life should read her autobiography *Walking Through Fire*, which was published in 2002.

Salwa Bakr is another writer who tackles taboo subjects such as sexual prejudice and social inequality. Her work includes the novels *The Golden Chariot* and *The Man from Bashmour*.

All of this is a world away from Egypt's current best-known cultural export, Ahdaf Soueif. Though Egyptian, born and brought up in Cairo, she's something of an anomaly in that she writes in English as well as Arabic. She lives and is published in London, where she's part of the UK literary scene. So far, most of her work has yet to appear in Arabic. Her wonderful 1999 novel *The Map of Love* was short-listed for the UK's most prestigious literary prize, the Booker. Her other novels are *Aisha*, *Sandpiper* and *In the Eye of the Sun*.

On their return from a women's suffrage conference in Rome in 1923, pioneer Arab feminists Huda Sharawi and Saiza Nabarawi threw away their *abeyya*s at Ramses Station in Cairo. Many in the crowd of women who had come to welcome them home followed suit.

Apricots on the Nile: A Memoir by Collette Rossant brings to life a young girl's childhood in 1930s and '40s Cairo.

In *Khul-Khaal: Five Egyptian Women Tell Their Stories*, edited by Nayra Atiya, five women from different backgrounds speak out. It's an often harrowing but revealing portrait of women's lives in Egypt.

The most controversial novel to hit the Egyptian literary scene in recent years is Sonallah Ibrahim's *Zaat,* a scathing piece of satire on contemporary Egyptian life. Ibrahim became a cause célèbre in 2003 when he declined to accept the country's most prestigious literary prize, the Arab Novel Conference Award, which was being presented by the Egyptian Ministry of Culture and the Egyptian Supreme Council for Culture. Ibrahim labelled the award 'worthless'.

For those who are new to Egyptian writers, the following is a short list of must-read books, all of which are (or have been) available in English-language translations.

EGYPTIAN CLASSICS

Beer at the Snooker Club by Waguih Ghali is a fantastic novel of youthful angst set against a backdrop of revolutionary Egypt and literary London. It's the Egyptian *Catcher in the Rye.*

The Cairo Trilogy by Naguib Mahfouz is usually considered Mahfouz' masterpiece; this generational saga of family life is rich in colour and detail, and has earned comparisons with Dickens and Zola.

Yousef Idris is best known for his short stories, but the novel *City of Love and Ashes* is set in January 1952 as Cairo struggles free of British occupation.

The Harafish by Naguib Mahfouz would be our desert-island choice if we were allowed only one work by Mahfouz. This is written in an episodic, almost folkloric style that owes much to the tradition of *The Thousand and One Nights.*

Albert Cossery, who passed away in 2008, made Paris his home for 60 years; his novels are widely available in French, less so in English, not at all in Arabic. His novel *Proud Beggars* is worth a read.

Zayni Barakat by Gamal al-Ghitani is a drama set in Cairo during the waning years of the Mamluk era. It was made into an extremely successful local TV drama in the early 1990s.

EGYPTIAN CONTEMPORARY NOVELS

The 2002 blockbuster *The Yacoubian Building* by Alaa al-Aswany is a bleak and utterly compelling snapshot of contemporary Cairo and Egypt seen through the stories of the occupants of a Downtown building. The world's biggest-selling novel in Arabic, it is reminiscent (though not at all derivative) of the novels of Rohinton Mistry. If you read only one contemporary Egyptian novel before or during your visit, make it this one.

Author Alaa al-Aswany *(The Yacoubian Building)* is a professional dentist whose first office was located in the real-life Yacoubian Building, which is on Sharia Suleiman Basha in Downtown Cairo.

It should be said that this book is groundbreaking more for its plot and characters than the actual language. The story itself is really just an elaborate soap opera, though it's remarkable in that it depicts Egypt in a particular time and place, and introduces archetypes that hadn't previously been captured in Arabic literature. Al-Aswany's more recent *Friendly Fire,* a novella and collection of short stories, is another of his works with a focus on contemporary life in Egypt.

Other recommended books include the following:

The Golden Chariot by Salwa Bakr is a short novel in which inmates in a women's prison exchange life stories. It's surprisingly upbeat, funny and even bawdy.

No One Sleeps in Alexandria by Ibrahim Abdel Meguid is an antidote to the mythical Alexandria of Lawrence Durrell. It portrays the city in the same period as the *Quartet* but as viewed by two poor Egyptians.

The Tent by Miral al-Tahawy is a bleak but beautiful tale of the slow descent into madness of a crippled Bedouin girl.

Love in Exile by Bahaa Taher is a meditation on the themes of exile, disillusionment, failed dreams and the redemptive power of love. Taher was born in Egypt in 1935, but lived for many years in Switzerland, and is one of the most outspoken figures within the local literary scene. The novel may be too mannered for some readers' tastes.

Taxi by Khalid al-Khamissi is one of the most popular books to hit the Egyptian shelves in years, and is rumoured to have outsold the *The Yacoubian Building*. The book details the author's conversations with cab drivers, which results in an amusing discourse on the trials and tribulations of daily Egyptian life.

EGYPT IN WESTERN NOVELS

The Alexandria Quartet by Lawrence Durrell is essential reading perhaps, but to visit Alexandria looking for the city of the *Quartet* is a bit like heading to London hoping to run into Mary Poppins.

Baby Love by Louisa Young is a smart, hip novel that shimmies between Shepherd's Bush in London and the West Bank of Luxor, as a former belly dancer, now single mother, skirts romance and a violent past.

City of Gold by Len Deighton is a thriller set in wartime Cairo, elevated by solid research. The period detail is fantastic and brings the city to life.

Death on the Nile by Agatha Christie draws on Christie's experiences of a winter in Upper Egypt. An absolute must if you're booked on a cruise.

Although the well-known film of the same name bears little resemblance to the novel, Michael Ondaatje's *The English Patient* – a story of love and destiny in WWII – remains a beautifully written, poetic novel.

The Mark of the Pasha by Michael Pearce is the latest in an ever-expanding series of lightweight historical mystery novels featuring the 'Mamur Zapt', Cairo's chief of police. A bit like Tintin but without the pictures.

Egypt during the war serves as the setting for the trials and traumas of a despicable bunch of expats in *The Levant Trilogy* by Olivia Manning. It has some fabulous descriptions of life in Cairo during WWII, and was filmed by the BBC as *Fortunes of War* starring Kenneth Branagh and Emma Thompson.

Moon Tiger by Penelope Lively is an award-winning romance, technically accomplished, very moving in parts, with events that occurred in Cairo during WWII at its heart.

The Photographer's Wife by Robert Sole is one of three historical romances by this French journalist set in late-19th-century Egypt. They're slow-going but it's worth persevering for the fine period detail and emotive stories.

Crocodile on the Sandbank is the first of a bestselling series of crime fiction novels by American Egyptologist, Elizabeth Peters. Lightweight but highly entertaining, it and its successors recount the various adventures of Amelia Peabody Emerson, a feisty archaeologist and amateur sleuth excavating in Egypt at the start of the 20th century.

For everything you've ever wanted to know about the art of smoking *sheesha* (water pipe), check out the guide at www.smoking-hookah .com.

Cinema
EGYPTIAN CINEMA

In the halcyon years of the 1940s and 1950s, Cairo's film studios turned out more than 100 movies annually, filling cinemas throughout the Arab world. These days, only about 20 films are made each year. The chief reason for the decline, according to the producers, is excessive government taxation and restrictive censorship. Asked what sort of things they censor, one film industry figure replied, 'Sex, politics, religion – that's all'. However, at least one Cairo film critic has suggested that another reason for the demise of local film is that so much of what is made is trash. The ingredients of the typical Egyptian film are shallow plot lines, farcical slapstick humour, over-the-top acting and perhaps a little belly dancing.

One Egyptian director who consistently stood apart from the mainstream detritus was Yousef Chahine. Born in 1926, he directed over 35 films and was accorded messiah-like status by critics in Egypt. He has been called Egypt's Fellini and was honoured at Cannes in 1997 with a lifetime achievement award. Chahine's films are also some of the very few Egyptian productions that are subtitled in English or French. Chahine passed away at his home in Cairo in 2008.

His later and more well-known works are 1999's *Al-Akhar* (The Other), 1997's *Al-Masir* (Destiny) and 1994's *Al-Muhagir* (The Emigrant), effectively banned in Egypt because of Islamist claims that it portrays scenes from the life of the Prophet. Others to look out for are *Al-Widaa Bonaparte* (Adieu Bonaparte), a historical drama about the French occupation, and *Iskandariyya Ley?* (Alexandria Why?), an autobiographical meditation on the city of Chahine's birth. Chahine also contributed to *11'09"01 September 11,* a short film of 11 minutes, nine seconds, and one frame about the World Trade Center bombing.

The father-and-son team of screenwriter Wahis Hamed and director Marwan Hamed adapted Alaa al-Aswany's bestselling *The Yacoubian Building* into a feature film. The budget of over US$3 million was the largest ever seen in Egypt.

EGYPT IN WESTERN CINEMA

With the exception of Michael Bay's *Transformers 2: Revenge of the Fallen* (2009), Egypt hasn't been seen much at the cinema in recent years. True, a large part of the Oscar-sweeping *The English Patient* (1996) was set in the Western Desert and Cairo, but this was silver-screen trickery, achieved with scenic doubles – the Egyptian locations were filmed in Tunisia, and the building interiors were filmed in Venice. The same goes for *The Mummy* (1999), *The Mummy Returns* (2001) and *The Scorpion King* (2002), all of which used Morocco and computer graphics to stand in for Egypt. (The original 1932 version, however, with Boris Karloff, does feature footage shot at Cairo's Egyptian Museum.)

It's not that Egypt is unphotogenic – quite the opposite. Its deserts, temples and colourful bazaars appear beguilingly seductive on a wide screen. So much so that the country experienced a surge in tourism in the wake of *The English Patient,* despite the best attempts of the Tunisian tourist authority to set the record straight. But extortionate taxes levied on foreign film companies keep the cameras away. It wasn't always so, and the 1970s and 1980s in particular resulted in a number of films on location in Egypt, most of which you should still be able to find.

Five Graves to Cairo (1943) is a wartime espionage thriller directed by Billy Wilder *(Some Like It Hot)* featuring a British corporal holed up in a Nazi-controlled hotel in the Western Desert.

In the classic wartime thriller *Ice Cold in Alex* (1958), a British ambulance officer and crew flee Rommel's forces across the Western Desert and dream of an ice-cold beer in a little bar in Alexandria.

In *The Spy Who Loved Me* (1977) the Pyramids, Islamic Cairo and Karnak provide glamorous backdrops for the campy, smirking antics of Roger Moore as James Bond.

Agatha Christie's whodunit, *Death on the Nile* (1978), has Poirot investigating the murder of an heiress on board a Nile cruiser. It's gorgeous scenery but the real mystery is how the boat manages to sail from Aswan down to Karnak in Luxor and back up to Abu Simbel all in the same day.

The Awakening (1980) is a horror film about an ancient Egyptian queen possessing modern souls, loosely based on Bram Stoker's *The Jewel of the Seven Stars.*

Sphinx (1980), adapted from a bestselling novel by Robin Cook *(Coma),* is a tale about antiquities smuggling shot entirely in Cairo and Luxor, but from which no one emerges with any credit, except the location scout.

The Aussie film *Gallipoli* (1981) is about the fateful WWI battle and includes an extended middle section devoted to the young soldiers' training in Egypt in the shadow of the Pyramids.

Ruby Cairo (1992), one of the last Hollywood productions to brave the bureaucracy, is the limp tale of a wife who tracks down her missing-presumed-dead husband to a hideaway in Egypt. The real star of the film is Cairo, where no cliché is left unturned, including camels, pyramids and feluccas.

Transformers 2: Revenge of the Fallen (2009) put the director's chair back in Egypt, though at times it's difficult to distinguish Giza and Luxor from the saturated overlay of computer graphics.

Music
CLASSICAL

Classical Arabic music peaked in the 1940s and '50s. These were the golden days of a rushing tide of nationalism and then, later, of Nasser's rule when Cairo was the virile heart of the Arab-speaking world. Its singers were icons, and through radio their impassioned words captured and inflamed the spirits of listeners from Algiers to Baghdad.

Chief icon of all was Umm Kolthum, the most famous Arab singer of the 20th century. Her protracted love songs and *qasa'id* (long poems) were the very expression of the Arab world's collective identity. Egypt's love affair with Umm Kolthum was such that on the afternoon of the first Thursday of each month, streets would become deserted as the whole country sat beside a radio to listen to her regular live-broadcast performances. She had her male counterparts in Abdel Halim Hafez and Farid al-Attrache, but they never attracted anything like the devotion accorded to 'As-Sitt' (the Lady). She retired after a concert in 1972, and when she died in 1975, her death caused havoc, with millions of grieving Egyptians pouring onto the streets of Cairo.

Amr Diab's *Nour El Ain* (Mind's Eye) is the highest selling album ever released by an Arabic artist.

The Umm Kolthum Museum (p125) opened in Cairo in 2002.

POPULAR

As Egypt experienced a population boom and the mean age decreased, a gap in popular culture developed, which the memory of the greats couldn't

---

RECOMMENDED LISTENING

Together, the following tapes/CDs give a pretty good taste of what Egyptian music is all about. Some of these are available internationally on CD or MP3.

Aho by Hakim 'Hey People' – an anthemic shout rooted in a traditional *shaabi* (from the word for popular) sound.

Layli Nahari by Amr Diab This catchy album from the Egyptian heart-throb skyrocketed to the top of the charts across the Arab world. Highly sing-along-able.

Khosara by Abdel Halim Hafez The riff from this song sounds remarkably like that in the track 'Big Pimpin' by US rapper Jay Z.

Inta Omri by Umm Kolthum One hour long and an absolute classic. Also try *Fakharuni* and *Al-Atlal*.

Lo Laki by Ali Hameida Pivotal The 1988 track that set the formula for much of the Egyptian pop to follow.

Al-Darb fil Iraq by Shaaban Abdel Rahim *Shaabi*est of *shaabi* singers, Rahim is hugely popular for singing the words that few others in the spotlight would dare say.

Nagham al-Hawa by Warda Algerian by birth but an honorary Cairene by residency. This double CD includes one of her best songs, 'Batwanes Beek'.

Taam el-Beyout by Mohammed Mounir Latest album by the thinking-person's pop star, a Nubian who fuses traditional Arabic music with jazz. His lyrics are admired above all others.

Zakma by Ahmed Adawiyya Social comment (the title means 'crowded') from the 1970s when Adawiyya's irreverent sound was at the peak of its popularity.

fill. Enter Ahmed Adawiyya, who did for Arabic music what punk did to popular music in the West. Throwing out traditional melodies and melodramas, his backstreet, streetwise and, to some, politically subversive songs captured the spirit of the times and dominated popular culture throughout the 1970s.

Adawiyya set the blueprint for a new kind of music known as *al-jeel* (the generation), characterised by a clattering, hand-clapping rhythm overlaid with synthesised twirling and a catchy, repetitive vocal. Highly formulaic, poorly recorded and mass-produced on cheap cassettes, this form of Egyptian pop was always tacky and highly disposable. That's changing fast as in recent years, the Cairo sound is getting ever more chic and slickly produced as the big-name artists look towards the international market. Head of the pack is Amr Diab, the foremost purveyor of Western-style pop, who is often described as the Arab world's Ricky Martin.

The Egyptian Center for Culture & Art (www .egyptmusic.org) aims to safeguard, foster and spread oral and traditional arts.

Adawiyya's legacy also spawned something called *shaabi* (from the word for popular), which is considered the real music of the working class. Indeed, it's much cruder than *al-jeel*, and its lyrics are often satirical or politically provocative. The acceptable face of *shaabi* is TV-friendly Hakim, whose albums regularly sell around the million mark.

The majority of current big sellers in Cairo cassette and CD shops hail from Lebanon, Syria, Tunisia and even Iraq. The consolation is that Egypt still provides the best backing musicians, songwriters and production facilities in the Arab world, not to mention the biggest audiences.

Architecture

Early in the 21st century, architecture in Egypt is in a sad state. In fact, according to one published survey, the highest rate of depression in 2000 in Egypt was among architects.

Among the very few named artists known from ancient Egypt, Men worked as a sculptor for Amenhotep III while his son Bek worked for Amenhotep's son and successor Akhenaten, claiming he was 'the apprentice whom his majesty himself taught'.

Besides Cairo's Opera House (p173) and Alexandria's Bibliotheca Alexandrina (p380) – both foreign designs – the country possesses few buildings of architectural worth that postdate the 1950s. The only exceptions are works by the influential Hassan Fathy, author of the seminal work *Architecture for the Poor* and designer of utopian projects such as New Gurna (p274) on Luxor's West Bank and the Fathy-influenced practice of Rami el-Dahan and Soheir Farid, responsible for the pavilion at the new Al-Azhar Park in Cairo (see p141).

This depressing reality wasn't always so. Cairo and Alexandria possess a splendid legacy of late-19th- and early-20th-century apartment blocks, villas and public buildings. Even more splendid is the capital's fantastic legacy of medieval architecture. Starting with the Mosque of Amr ibn al-As (p128) in AD 642, the earliest existing Islamic structure in Cairo, it's possible to trace the development of Muslim architecture through more than 1000 years. Sadly, these grand monuments are often overshadowed by chock-a-block brick and concrete high-rises. Unfortunately, a demographic shift from rural to urban and a lack of space mean that this architectural trend is not likely to be reversed anytime soon.

The Metropolitan Museum of Art (www .metmuseum.org) has an excellent web resource on the art of ancient Egypt.

Painting

While Egypt has produced one or two outstanding painters, contemporary art has been very much much in the doldrums. The problem stems from the Egyptian art-school system, where a student's success largely depends on their ability to emulate the artistic styles favoured or practised by their professors. Not surprisingly, some of the most interesting work comes from artists with no formal training at all. Such artists are often shunned by the state-run galleries but there are several private exhibition spaces that are happy to show nonconformist work. Anyone seriously interested in contemporary art should visit the Mashrabia or Townhouse galleries (p155) in Cairo.

For more information, see Liliane Karnouk's *Modern Egyptian Art 1910–2003*, or pick up Fatma Ismail's *29 Artists in the Museum of Egyptian Modern Art*.

Dance

BELLY DANCING

Tomb paintings in Egypt prove that the tradition of formalised dancing goes back as far as the pharaohs. During medieval times, dancing became institutionalised in the form of the *ghawazee*, a cast of dancers who travelled with storytellers and poets and performed publicly or for hire, rather like the troubadours of medieval Europe. Performances were often segregated, with women dancers either performing for other women or appearing before men veiled.

The arrival of 19th-century European travellers irrevocably changed this tradition. Religious authorities, outraged that Muslim women were performing for 'infidel' men, pressured the government to impose heavy taxes on the dancers. When high prices failed to stop Western thrill-seekers, the dancers were banished from Cairo. Cut off from their clientele, many turned to prostitution to survive.

For intrepid male travellers, this only increased the lure and they went out of their way to fulfil their erotic fantasies. Visitors such as French author Gustave Flaubert, who travelled through Egypt in 1849 and wrote *Flaubert in Egypt*, supplied lurid accounts of their experiences, titillating his

One of Egypt's most famous belly dancers, Soheir el-Babli, renounced show business and adopted the Islamic veil in 1993, setting off a wave of religiously motivated resignations among the country's belly-dance artists.

SISTERS ARE DANCIN' IT FOR THEMSELVES   *Louisa Young*

'Why did you make the heroine of your novels a belly dancer?' is a question I get asked with some regularity. 'Because she gets to hang out in low dives and swanky hotels, wear fabulous outfits and consider the historical background to a woman's power over her own body, from Salome to contemporary prostitution, via Flaubert and sexual tourism in the developing world', is my reply.

It's easy to forget, when you're being dragged up onto a tiny nightclub stage by a strapping Ukrainian lass in a sequinned bikini, that belly dancing is older than the hills, deeply private and an icon of postfeminism. Men and foreigners tend to see it as a sexual show but for many Arab women – and an increasing number of Western women – it is a personal activity incorporating identity, history and community alongside fun, exercise and girl-bonding.

The Babylonian goddess Ishtar, when she went down to the underworld to get her dead husband Tammuz back, danced with her seven veils at each of the seven entrances. Ancient Egyptian wall paintings, the Bible, Greek legend and *The Thousand and One Nights* are full of women dancing by and for themselves and each other. Salome's dance for Herod – the seven veils again – was so powerful because she was bringing into public what normally only happened in the women's quarters.

Arab domestic dancing nowadays tends to involve tea, cakes, female friends and relations, little girls and old ladies, a scarf around the hips and a lot of laughter and gossip. Western versions, particularly in the US and Germany, are the bastard children of aerobics classes, women's groups, New Age Goddess awareness, and the perennial female weakness for fancy underwear and showing off in it. Belly dancing is extremely good exercise – for the back, the figure, stamina, sex life. It's also good for the soul – it's an art, and requires the distilled concentration, self-respect and 'heart' necessary to art.

Louisa Young is an author whose work includes the novels Baby Love, Desiring Cairo *and* Tree of Pearls.

European readers and helping to cement the less-than-respectable reputation of Egyptian dance:

> They both wore the same costume – baggy trousers and embroidered jacket, their eyes painted with kohl. The jacket goes down to the abdomen, whereas the trousers, held by an enormous cashmere belt folded over several times, begin approximately at the pubis, so that the stomach, the small of the back and the beginning of the buttocks are naked, seen through a bit of black gauze held in place by the upper and lower garments. The gauze ripples on the hips like a transparent wave with every movement they make.

Belly dancing began to gain credibility and popularity in Egypt with the advent of cinema, when dancers were lifted out of nightclubs and put on the screen before mass audiences. The cinema imbued belly dancing with glamour and made household names of a handful of dancers. It also borrowed liberally from Hollywood, adopting Tinseltown's fanciful costumes of hip-hugging bikini bottoms, sequined bras and swaths of diaphanous veils.

'dancers were lifted out of nightclubs and put on the screen before mass audiences'

Also imported from the Western movie industry was the modern phenomenon of the belly dancer as a superstar capable of commanding Hollywood-style fees for an appearance. Dancers such as Samia Gamal and Tahia Carioca, who became the stars of B&W films of the 1930s and '40s, can still be seen today as the old films are endlessly rerun on Egyptian TV. Such is the present-day earning power of the top dancers that in 1997 a series of court cases was able to haul in E£900 million in back taxes from 12 of the country's top artists.

Despite its long history, belly dancing is still not considered completely respectable, and is slowly dying out according to many aficionados. In the early 1990s, Islamist conservatives patrolled weddings in poor areas of Cairo and forcibly prevented women from dancing or singing, cutting off a vital source of income for lower-echelon performers. In an attempt to placate the religious right, the government joined in and declared that bare midriffs, cleavage and thighs were out. At the same time, a number of high-profile entertainers donned the veil and retired, denouncing their former profession as sinful. Since then, bellies have once more been bared but the industry has not recovered.

Food & Drink

The reputation of Egyptian cuisine takes a constant battering, largely because it's compared with regional heavyweights such as those of Lebanon, Turkey and Iran. Truth be told, Egypt does not have a well-established culinary heritage, and lacks the diversity and regionalisation of dishes found elsewhere in the Middle East. But this ill-reputation is unfortunate simply because the food here is good, honest peasant fare that packs an occasional – and sensational – knockout punch.

Whether you're a hard-core carnivore or a devoted vegetarian, you'll never fail to find cheap and hearty fare in Egypt. True to their Middle Eastern roots, Egyptian meals typically centre on lightly spiced lamb or chicken, though there's enough coastline to reel in the fruits of the sea. Of course, even meat lovers will wait in line for hot and crispy falafel, the ubiquitous Middle Eastern vegetarian staple. Regardless of your culinary preference, you can always count on stacks of freshly baked pita and heaping bowls of rice to accompany any meal.

There is always room for dessert in Egypt. This is one culinary arena where the country really shines, especially when you accompany your plate of delectable treats with a cup of dark, thick and knock-your-socks-off-strong coffee. And, just when your stomach is about to explode, signal your waiter to bring you an apple-scented *sheesha* (water pipe) – a few long, drawn-out puffs can not only settle the stomach but also relax the mind and calm the nerves.

> *The New Book of Middle Eastern Food* by Egyptian-born Claudia Roden brought the cuisines of the region to the attention of Western cooks when it was first released in 1968. It's still an essential reference, now updated and expanded, as fascinating for its cultural insights as for its great recipes.

STAPLES & SPECIALITIES
Mezze

Largely vegetable based and always bursting with colour and flavour, mezze (a selection of hot and cold starters) aren't strictly Egyptian (many hail from the Levant), but they have been customised here in a more limited and economical form. They're the perfect start to any meal, and it's usually perfectly acceptable for diners to order an entire meal from the mezze list and forego the mains.

Bread

'*Aish* (bread) is the most important staple of the national diet. Usually made with a combination of plain and wholemeal flour with sufficient leavening to form a pocket and soft crust, it's cooked over an open flame. Locals use it in lieu of cutlery to scoop up dips, and rip it into pieces to

---

TRAVEL YOUR TASTEBUDS

- *Fatta* – dish involving rice and bread soaked in a garlicky-vinegary sauce with lamb or chicken, which is then oven cooked in a *tagen* (clay pot). It's very heavy; after eating retire to a chaise longue.

- *Mahshi kurumb* – these rice- and meat-stuffed cabbage leaves are decadently delightful when correctly cooked with plenty of dill and lots of sinful *samna* (clarified butter).

- *Molokhiyya* – a soup made from mallow. Properly prepared with rabbit broth and plenty of garlic, it's quite delicious.

- *Hamam mahshi* – pigeons (smaller than European) usually stuffed with *fireek* (green wheat) and rice. This dish is served at all traditional restaurants and can be fiddly to eat; beware the plentiful little bones.

wrap around morsels of meat. *Shammy,* a version made with plain flour only, is the usual wrapping for *ta'amiyya* (see p83).

Salads

For a basic overview of Egyptian food in addition to recipes for the country's most popular dishes, check out www .foodbycountry.com.

Simplicity is the key to Egyptian salads, which have crunchy fresh ingredients (including herbs) often tossed in oil and vinegar, and are eaten with relish as a mezze or as an accompaniment to a meat or fish main. Two salads are found on menus throughout the country: oriental salad, a colourful mix of chopped tomatoes, cucumber, onion and pepper; and the Middle East's signature salad, *tabbouleh* (bulgur wheat, parsley and tomato, with a sprinkling of sesame seeds, lemon and garlic). Less common but equally delicious is a salad made of boiled beetroot with a tangy oil and vinegar dressing.

Vegetables & Soups

In Egypt, there's none of the Western practice of preparing vegetables that are out of season – here tomatoes are eaten when they're almost bursting out of their skins with sweet juices, corn is picked when it's golden and plentiful, and cucumbers are munched when they're soft and sweet.

There are a number of vegetables that are particular to Middle Eastern cuisine, including *molokhiyya,* a green leafy vegetable known in the West as mallow. Here it's made into a slimy and surprisingly sexy soup with a glutinous texture and earthy flavour. Usually served as an accompaniment to roast chicken, it inspires an almost religious devotion among locals.

Vegetable soups are extremely popular, as are soups made with pulses. *Shurba ads* (lentil soup) is made with red or yellow lentils and is always served with wedges of lemon on the side. *Fuul nabbed* (broad bean soup) is almost as popular.

Meats

Dozens of recipes for tasty Egyptian dishes can be found at www .egyptianfood.org.

Kofta and kebab are two of the most popular dishes in Egypt. *Kofta,* spiced minced lamb or beef peppered with spices and shaped into balls, is skewered and grilled. It is the signature element of the Egyptian favourite *daoud basha,* meatballs cooked with pine nuts and tomato sauce in a *tagen.* Kebab is skewered and flame-grilled chunks of meat, normally lamb (the chicken equivalent is called *shish tawouq*). The meat usually comes on a bed of *badounis* (parsley), and may be served in upmarket restaurants with grilled tomatoes and onions; otherwise you eat it with bread, salad and tahini.

Firekh (chicken) roasted on a spit is a commonly spotted dish, and in restaurants is typically ordered by the half. *Hamam* (pigeon) is also extremely popular, and is best served as *tagen* with onions, tomatoes and rice or cracked wheat.

Seafood

When in Alexandria, along the Red Sea and in Sinai, you'll undoubtedly join the locals in falling hook, line and sinker for the marvellous array of fresh seafood on offer. Local favourites are *kalamaari* (squid); *balti,* fish that are about 15cm long, flattish and grey with a light belly; and the larger, tastier *bouri* (mullet). You'll also commonly find sea bass, bluefish, sole, *subeit* or *gambari* (shrimp) on restaurant menus. The most popular ways to cook fish are to bake them with salt, grill them over coals or fry them in olive oil.

Desserts & Sweets

If you have a sweet tooth, be prepared to put it to good use on your travels in Egypt. The prince of local puds is undoubtedly *muhalabiyya*, a concoction like blancmange, made using ground rice, milk, sugar and rose or orange water and topped with chopped pistachios and almonds. Almost as popular are *ruz bi laban* (rice pudding) and *omm ali* (layers of pastry filled with nuts and raisins, soaked in cream and milk, and baked in the oven). Seasonal fresh fruit is just as commonly served and provides a refreshing finale to any meal.

Best of all are the pastries, including *kunafa*, a vermicelli-like pastry over a vanilla base soaked in syrup that is often associated with feasts and is always eaten at Ramadan. The most famous of all pastries is baklava, made from delicate filo drenched in honey or syrup. Variations on baklava are flavoured with fresh nuts or stuffed with wickedly rich clotted cream *(eishta)*.

The popular Egyptian dessert of *omm ali* is said to have been introduced into the country by Miss O'Malley, an Irish mistress of Khedive Ismail.

DRINKS
Tea & Coffee

Drinking *shai* (tea) is the signature pastime of the country, and it is seen as strange and decidedly antisocial not to swig the tannin-laden beverage at regular intervals throughout the day. *Shai* will either come in the form of a teabag plonked in a cup or glass of hot water (Lipton is the usual brand) or a strong brew of the local leaves (the brew of choice is El Arosa).

It is always served sweet; to moderate this, order it *sukar shwaiyya* – with 'a little sugar'. If you don't want any sugar, ask for *min ghayr sukar*. Far more refreshing, when it's in season, is *shai* served with mint leaves: ask for *shai na'na'*. Be warned that you'll risk severe embarrassment if you ask for milk anywhere but in tourist hotels and restaurants. In these places, ask for *b'laban*.

Turkish and Arabic coffee (*ahwa*; the word is also used for coffeehouse) aren't widely consumed in the region; instant coffee (always called *neskaf*) is far more common. If you do find the real stuff, it's likely to be a thick and powerful Turkish-style brew that's served in small cups and drunk in a couple of short sips. As with tea, you have to specify how much sugar you want: *ahwa mazboot* comes with a moderate amount of sugar but is still fairly sweet; if you don't want any sugar ask for *ahwa saada*.

The website www .foodtimeline.org offers an impressive overview of the history of food from Mesopotamia through the Middle Ages.

Beer & Wine

For beer in Egypt just say 'Stella'. It's been brewed and bottled in Cairo now for more than 100 years. A yeasty and highly drinkable lager, it has a taste that varies enormously by batch. Since 1998, the standard Stella has been supplemented by sister brews including Stella Meister (a light lager) and Stella Premium (for the beer snob in us all). Most locals just stick to the unfussy basic brew – it's the cheapest (around E£10 in restaurants) and, as long as it's cold, it's not bad. Since the late 1990s there's been a worthy 'competitor' on the market called Saqqara, though this is actually owned by the same brewery as Stella.

There's a growing viticulture industry around Alexandria but the product is so far pretty unimpressive; Grand de Marquise is by far the best of a lacklustre bunch, producing an antipodean-style red and a chablis-style white. Obelisk is a newcomer to the scene and has a quaffable cabernet sauvignon, a Pinot blanc and a dodgy rosé. The country's oldest winery, Gianaclis, produces three decidedly headache-inducing tipples: a dry red known as Omar Khayyam, a rosé called Rubis D'Egypte and a gasoline-like dry white called Cru des Ptolémées.

BEFORE THERE WAS STARBUCKS

The coffeehouse, known as *ahwa* (the Arabic word means both coffee and the place in which it's drunk), is one of the great Egyptian social institutions. Typically just a collection of cheap tin-plate-topped tables and wooden chairs in a basic room open to the street, the *ahwa* is a relaxed and unfussy place where the average Joe (or Ahmed) will hang out for part of each day, whiling away the hours reading the papers, meeting friends or sipping tea. The hubbub of conversation is usually accompanied by the incessant clacking or slamming of *domina* (dominoes) and *towla* (backgammon) pieces, and the burbling of smokers drawing heavily on their *sheesha*s.

The *sheesha* is a tradition, an indulgence and a slightly naughty habit all wrapped into one gloriously fragrant and relaxing package. A feature of coffeehouses from Alexandria to Aswan, it's a pastime that's as addictive as it is magical. Traditionally *ahwa*-going has been something of an all-male preserve, and older men at that, but in recent years *sheesha* smoking has become extremely fashionable. It's now common to see young, mixed-sex groups of Egyptians in *ahwa*s, especially in Cairo and Alexandria. In fact, *sheesha* is sweeping the world – from New York to London and Tokyo to Sydney, *sheesha* bars can be found all over these days.

When you order a water pipe you'll need to specify the type of tobacco and molasses mix you would like. Most people opt for tobacco soaked in apple juice *(tufah)* but it's also possible to order strawberry, melon, cherry or mixed-fruit flavours. Some purists order their tobacco unadulterated, but in doing this they miss out on the wonderfully sweet and fragrant aroma that makes the experience so memorable. Once you've specified your flavour, a decorated bulbous glass pipe filled with water will be brought to your table, hot coals will be placed in it to get it started and you will be given a disposable plastic mouthpiece to slip over the pipe's stem. Just draw back and you're off. The only secret to a good smoke is to take a puff every now and again to keep the coals hot; when they start to lose their heat the waiter (or dedicated water-pipe minder) will replace them. Bliss!

Of course, it's worth mentioning that even though the smoke from *sheesha* is filtered through water and tastes nothing like the tobacco from cigarettes, it's still smoke nevertheless. Studies vary, but since you're pulling large volumes of smoke into your lungs with each puff, it has been estimated that a one-hour *sheesha* session delivers as much tar as smoking an entire pack of cigarettes. Consider yourself warned. The good news is that *sheesha* isn't nearly as addictive as cigarettes, so it's unlikely that you'll be stealing away in the morning hours to puff one before breakfast. Certainly the intoxicating scents of roasted coffee and apple tobacco are a seductive blend, and about as authentically Egyptian as you can get.

These wines average between E£100 and E£150 per bottle in restaurants throughout the country. Imported wines are both hard to find and prohibitively expensive.

Water

Don't even *think* of drinking from the tap in Egypt – the dreaded 'Nile Piles' is enough to ruin any traveller's day. Cheap bottled water is readily available in even the smallest towns.

With that said, there is some debate regarding the drinkability of water in Cairo. Although we'll leave it to you to see whether or not your body can cope, according to one Cairo expat: 'You can drink the water in Cairo, I swear. It just tastes less than delicious.'

Did you know that the delicious drink *karkadai*, made from boiling hibiscus leaves, is famous for 'strengthening the blood' (lowering blood pressure)?

Other Drinks

Over the hot summer months many *ahwa*-goers forgo their regular teas and coffees for cooler drinks such as the crimson-hued, iced *karkadai*, a wonderfully refreshing drink boiled up from hibiscus leaves; *limoon* (lemon juice); or *zabaady* (yoghurt beaten with cold water and salt). In winter many prefer *sahlab*, a warm drink made with semolina powder, milk and chopped nuts; or *yansoon*, a medicinal-tasting aniseed drink.

Juice stands are recognisable by the hanging bags of netted fruit (and carrots) that adorn their facades and are an absolute godsend on a hot summer's day. Standard juices *(asiir)* include *moz* (banana), *guafa* (guava), *limoon* (lemon), *manga* (mango), *bortuaan* (orange), *rumman* (pomegranate), *farawla* (strawberry) and *asab* (sugar cane). A glass costs between 50pt and E£2 depending on the fruit used.

CELEBRATIONS

Egyptians love nothing more than a celebration and food plays an important role when it comes to giving thanks for a birth, celebrating an engagement or marriage, bringing in a harvest or marking a significant religious holiday.

The most important religious feasts occur during Ramadan, the Muslim holy month. *Iftar,* the evening meal prepared to break the fast, is a special feast calling for substantial soups, chicken and meat dishes, and other delicacies. It's often enjoyed communally in the street or in large, specially erected tents.

Family celebrations are always accompanied by a flurry of baking. *Ataïf* (pancakes dipped in syrup) are eaten on the day of a betrothal and biscuits known as *kahk bi loz* (almond bracelets) are favourites at wedding parties. The birth of a son is marked by serving an aromatic rice pudding with aniseed called *meghlie. Moulids* (saints' festivals; see p512) also involve copious eating of sweet pastries.

WHERE & WHEN TO EAT & DRINK

In Egypt, one rule stands firm: the best food is always served in private homes. If you are fortunate enough to be invited to share a home-cooked meal, make sure you take up the offer. But be warned that you will most likely be stuffed to the point of bursting – the minute you look close to cleaning your plate, you will be showered with more food, which no amount of protesting can stop.

The only place we'd recommend branching out and trying other regional cuisines is Cairo, as well as in tourist cities such as Luxor, Sharm el-Sheikh and Dahab. Otherwise, look for where the locals are eating. In Alexandria, for instance, you should follow their lead and dine out in the local seafood restaurants – they're some of the best in the region.

When you do eat out, you'll find that locals usually dine at a later hour than is the norm in the West; it's usual to see diners arrive at a restaurant at 10pm or even later in the big cities, particularly in summer. They also dine in large family groups, order up big, smoke like chimneys and linger over their meals.

The main meal of the day is usually lunch – see p507 for restaurants' and cafes' business hours. Tipping is expected in almost every eatery and restaurant and 10% is the norm.

Quick Eats

Once you've sampled the joys of Egyptian street food you'll never again be able to face dining out on the bland international snack food served up by the global chains.

The national stars of the snack-food line-up are *fuul* and *ta'amiyya,* and they are both things of joy when served and eaten fresh. *Fuul,* an unassuming peasant dish of slow-cooked fava beans cooked with garlic and garnished with parsley, olive oil, lemon, salt, black pepper and cumin, is the national dish. It's absolutely delicious stuffed into *shammy* and eaten as a sandwich. *Ta'amiyya* (better known outside Cairo as felafel) is mashed broad beans and spices rolled into balls and deep fried.

The Complete Middle East Cookbook by Tess Mallos is full of easy-to-follow recipes and devotes an entire chapter to the cuisine of Egypt.

Egyptian Cooking: A Practical Guide by Samia Abdennour is published by Hippocrene and is readily available in Egypt.

TOP PICKS

■ **Qadoura** (p387) in Alexandria. The best seafood in the country, especially when the sea has been bountiful.

■ **Sabaya** (p166) in Cairo. Lebanese food as impressive as anything you'll find in Beirut.

■ **Oasis Café** (p282) in Luxor. Sophisticated decor and a colonial ambience complement the eclectic menu at this tourist favourite.

■ **Al-Fanar** (p474) in Sharm el-Sheikh. Serving arguably the best pizza in Egypt, this place has stunning ocean views and a chic Bedouin-inspired ambience to match.

■ **Funny Mummy** (p482) in Dahab. A popular seaside tourist spot serving Western and Asian favourites beneath a palm-tree canopy.

Almost as popular as *fuul* and *ta'amiyya* is *shwarma*, the local equivalent of the Greek *gyros* sandwich or the Turkish *döner kebap*; strips are sliced from a vertical spit of compressed lamb or chicken, sizzled on a hot plate with chopped tomatoes and garnish, and then stuffed into a *shammy*.

You should also look out for shops sporting large metal tureens in the window: these specialise in the vegetarian delight *kushari*, a delicate mix of noodles, rice, black lentils and dried onions, served with an accompanying tomato sauce that's sometimes fiery with chilli. Although the entire concoction is somewhat reminiscent of your mum's leftovers thrown together in a dish, it's extremely cheap and filling and authentically Egyptian to boot. Don't forget to splash a healthy amount of the provided garlicky vinegar on your *kushari*.

The local variation of the pizza is *fiteer*, which has a thin, flaky pastry base. Try it topped with salty haloumi cheese, or even with a mixture of sugar-dusted fruit.

Picturesque as some of them are, avoid the street carts trundled around by vendors. These guys sell anything from sandwiches to milk puddings but the food has often been out in the sun all day long, not to mention exposed to fumes, dust and all manner of insect life.

VEGETARIANS & VEGANS

Though it's quite usual for the people of the Middle East to eat vegetarian meals, the concept of vegetarianism is quite foreign. Say you're a vegan and Egyptians will either look mystified or assume that you're confessing to some sort of socially aberrant behaviour.

Fortunately, it's not difficult to order vegetable-based dishes. You'll find that you can eat loads of mezze and salads, *fuul, kushari, ta'amiyya,* the occasional omelette or oven-baked vegetable *tagen*s with okra and eggplant. When in doubt, you can always order a stack of pita bread and a bowl of hummus, which can easily be a meal itself. If your diet enables you to eat fish, note that fresh seafood is nearly always available in tourist towns and along the coasts.

The main cause of inadvertent meat eating is meat stock, which is often used to make otherwise vegetarian *tagen*s and soups. Your hosts or waiter may not even consider such stock to be meat, so they will reassure you that the dish is vegetarian. Be vigilant. See also the Language chapter (p541) for some useful phrases.

EATING WITH KIDS

It's usual for Egyptians to eat out as a family group and you'll often see children and teenagers dining with their parents and friends in restaurants

---

DOS & DON'TS

- Remember to always remove your shoes before sitting down on a rug or carpet to eat or drink tea.

- Avoid putting your left hand into a communal dish if you're eating Bedouin style – your left hand is used for, well, wiping yourself in the absence of toilet paper.

- Be sure to leave the dining area and go outside or to the toilet before blowing your nose in a restaurant.

- Make sure you refrain from eating, drinking or smoking in public during the daytime in the holy month of Ramadan (international hotels are an exception to this rule).

- Always sit at the dinner table next to a person of the same sex unless your host(ess) suggests otherwise.

---

until the early hours. Waiters are uniformly accepting of children and they will usually go out of their way to make them feel welcome (offerings of fried potato chips being a tried-and-true method). Best of all, the cuisine of the region is very child-friendly, being simple yet varied.

Letting the youngest members of the party choose from the mezze dishes is a good idea, kebabs (particularly *shish tawouq*) are perennial favourites and roast chicken is usually a safe bet, especially when put into fresh bread to make a sandwich. And of course the snack foods tend to go down a treat, particularly *fiteer*, *kushari* and *ta'amiyya*. Fresh juice and soft drinks are almost always available to quench Junior's thirst, too.

Some places have high chairs, but they're in the minority. Kids menus are usually only seen at Western-style hotel restaurants.

For more information on travelling with children, see p507.

For younger readers, www.historyforkids.org has a great overview of food in ancient Egypt.

HABITS & CUSTOMS

Egyptians eat a standard three meals a day. When it comes to breakfast, Kellogg's has yet to make inroads – for much of the populace the morning meal consists of bread and cheese, maybe olives or a fried egg at home, or a *fuul* sandwich on the run. Lunch is the day's main meal, taken from 2pm onwards, but more likely around 3pm or 4pm when dad's home from work and the kids are back from school. Whatever's served, the women of the house (usually the mother) will probably have spent most of her day in the kitchen preparing it, it'll be hot and there'll probably be plenty to go around. Whatever's left over is usually served up again later in the evening as supper.

EAT YOUR WORDS

Below is a selection of dishes you are likely to come across in Egypt. Note that because of the imprecise nature of transliterating Arabic into English, spellings will vary; for example, what we give as *kibbeh* may appear variously as 'kibba', 'kibby' or even 'gibeh' on a menu. See also the Language chapter (p541) for a list of basic food items, useful phrases, and pronunciation guidelines.

Food Glossary

MEZZE

baba ghanoug	ba·ba gha·*noog*	a lumpy paste of mashed eggplant mixed with tomato and onion and sometimes, in season, pomegranate; done well, it has a delicious smoky taste
besara	be·*sā*·ra	purée of broad beans served as a dip

hummus	*Hum·*mus	cooked chickpeas ground into a paste and mixed with tahini, garlic and lemon; this is available in every restaurant and at its best it should be thick and creamy
kibbeh	*kib·*be	minced lamb, bulgur wheat and pine seeds shaped into a patty and deep-fried
kibbeh nayeh	*kib·*be *nay·*e	ground lamb and cracked wheat served raw like steak tartare
kibda	*kib·*da	liver, often chicken liver *(kibda firekh)*, usually sautéed in lemon or garlic; done correctly it should have an almost pâté-like consistency
labneh	*lab·*ne	a cheesy yoghurt paste, which is often heavily flavoured with garlic or sometimes, even better, with mint
loubieh	*lu·*bi·e	French bean salad with tomato, onion and garlic
mahshi	*maH·*shi	minced meat, rice, onion, parsley and herbs stuffed into vine leaves (in summer), cabbage (in winter), peppers, courgettes or white and black eggplants; the mixture is baked and is delicious when just cooked and hot, but less so when cold
mokh	mokh	brains served crumbed and deep-fried or whole, garnished with salad
muttabel	mut·*ta·*bel	similar to *baba ghanoug* but the blended eggplant is mixed with tahini, yoghurt and olive oil to achieve a creamier consistency
sambousak	san·*boo·*sak	pastry filled with salty white cheese or spicy minced meat with pine kernels
shanklish	shank·*leesh*	a salad of small pieces of crumbled, tangy, eye-wateringly strong cheese mixed with chopped onion and tomato
tabbouleh	tab·*boo·*le	a salad of bulgur wheat, parsley and tomato, with a sprinkling of sesame seeds, lemon and garlic
tahina/tahini	ta·*Hee·*na/ta·*Hee·*nee	paste made of sesame seeds and served as dip
wara einab	wa·ra' ai-nab	stuffed vine leaves, served both hot and cold

MAIN COURSES

fasoolyeh	fa·*sool·*ye	a green-bean stew
hamam	*Ham·*aam	pigeon, usually baked or grilled and served stuffed with rice and spices; it's also served as a stew *(tagen)*, cooked in a deep clay pot
kebab	ke·*baab*	skewered chunks of meat (usually lamb) cooked over a flame grill
kofta	*kof·*ta	minced meat and spices grilled on a skewer
shish tawouq	shish ta·*wooq*	kebab with pieces of marinated, spiced chicken instead of lamb

DESSERTS

asabeeh	a·*sa·*beeh	rolled filo pastry filled with pistachio, pine and cashew nuts and honey; otherwise known as 'lady's fingers'
baklava	ba·*kla·*wa	generic term for any layered, flaky pastry with nuts, drenched in honey
barazak	ba·ra·zak	flat, circular cookies sprinkled with sesame seeds; very crisp and light
isfinjiyya	is·fin·*zhiy·*ya	coconut slice
kunafa	ku·*naa·*fa	vermicelli-like strands of cooked batter over a creamy sweet cheese base baked in syrup

muhalabiyya	mu·hal·a·*biy*·ya	blancmange-like concoction made with ground rice, milk, sugar and rose or orange water and topped with chopped pistachios and almonds
mushabbak	mu·*shab*·bak	lace-shaped pastry drenched in syrup
zalabiyya	za·la·*beey*·ya	pastries dipped in rose water

Environment

THE LAND

The Nile Valley is home to most Egyptians, with some 90% of the population confined to the narrow carpet of fertile land bordering the great river. To the south the river is hemmed in by mountains and the agricultural plain is narrow, but as the river flows north the land becomes flatter and the valley widens to between 20km and 30km.

Egypt has four of the world's five officially identified types of sand dunes, including the *seif* (sword) dunes, so named because they resemble the blades of curved Arab swords.

To the east of the valley is the Eastern Desert (this is also known as the Arabian Desert), a barren plateau bounded on its eastern edge by a high ridge of mountains that rises to more than 2000m and extends for about 800km. To the west is the Western Desert (also known as the Libyan Desert), which officially comprises two-thirds of the land surface of Egypt. If you ignore the political boundaries on the map, it stretches right across the top of North Africa under its better-known and highly evocative name, the Sahara.

Cairo also demarcates Egyptian geography as it lies roughly at the point where the Nile splits into several tributaries and the valley becomes a 200km-wide delta. Burdened with the task of providing for the entire country, this Delta region ranks among the world's most intensely cultivated lands.

To the east, across the Suez Canal, is the triangular wedge of Sinai. A geological extension of the Eastern Desert, terrain here slopes from the high mountain ridges, which include Mt Sinai and Gebel Katarina (the highest mountain in Egypt at 2642m) in the south, to desert coastal plains and lagoons in the north.

WILDLIFE

Egypt is about 94% desert – such a figure conjures up images of vast, barren wastelands where nothing can live. However, there are plenty of desert regions where fragile ecosystems have adapted over millennia to extremely hostile conditions. For more information on desert flora, see the boxed text, p462.

RESPONSIBLE TRAVEL

Tourism is vital to the Egyptian economy and the country would be a mess without it. At the same time, millions of visitors a year can't help but add to the ecological and environmental overload. As long as outsiders have been stumbling upon or searching for the wonders of ancient Egypt, they have also been crawling all over them, chipping bits off or leaving their own contributions engraved in the stones. Needless to say, this is not sustainable.

Mass tourism threatens to destroy the very monuments that visitors come to see. At sites such as the Valley of the Kings, thousands of visitors a day mill about in cramped tombs designed for one occupant. The deterioration of the painted wall reliefs alarms archaeologists, whose calls for limits on the numbers of visitors have largely fallen on deaf ears.

Even the Pyramids, which have so far survived 4500 years, are suffering. Cracks have begun to appear in inner chambers and, in cases like these, authorities have been forced to limit visitors and to close the great structures periodically to give them some rest and recuperation. It is likely only a matter of time before similar measures are enforced elsewhere.

In the meantime it's up to the traveller to be aware of these serious concerns. Don't be tempted to baksheesh guards so you can use your flash in tombs. Don't clamber over toppled pillars and statues. Don't touch painted reliefs. It's all just common sense.

Animals

Egypt is home to about 100 species of mammals, though you'd be lucky to see anything other than camels, donkeys, horses and buffalo. Although Egypt's deserts were once sanctuaries for an amazing variety of larger mammals, such as the leopard, cheetah, oryx, aardwolf, striped hyena and caracal, all of these have been brought to the brink of extinction through hunting. Creatures such as the sand cat, the fennec fox and the Nubian ibex are rarely sighted, and Egyptian cheetahs and leopards have most likely already been wiped out.

There are three types of gazelle in Egypt: the Arabian, dorcas and white. Unfortunately, Arabian gazelles are thought to be extinct, and there are only individual sightings of dorcas and white gazelles, despite that herds were common features of the desert landscape only 35 years ago.

The zorilla, a kind of weasel, lives in the Gebel Elba region. In Sinai you may see the rock hyrax, a small creature about the size of a large rabbit, which lives in large groups and is extremely sociable.

Less loveable are the 34 species of snake in Egypt. The best known is the cobra, which featured prominently on the headdress of the ancient pharaohs. Another well-known species is the horned viper, a thickset snake that has horns over its eyes. There are also plenty of scorpions, although they're largely nocturnal and rarely seen. Be careful if you're lifting up stones as they like to burrow into cool spots.

Natural Selections: A Year of Egypt's Wildlife, written and illustrated by Richard Hoath and published locally by the American University in Cairo Press, is a passionate account of the birds, mammals, insects and marine creatures that make Egypt their home.

BIRDS

About 430 bird species have been sighted in Egypt, of which about one-third actually breed in Egypt, while most of the others are passage migrants or winter visitors. Each year an estimated one to two million large birds migrate via certain routes from Europe to Africa through Egypt. Most large birds, including flamingos, storks, cranes, herons and all large birds of prey, are protected under Egyptian law.

The most ubiquitous birds are the house sparrow and the hooded crow, while the most distinctive is the hoopoe. This cinnamon-toned bird has a head shaped like a hammer and extends its crest in a dramatic fashion when it's excited. Hoopoes are often seen hunting for insects in gardens in central Cairo, though they're more common in the countryside.

For information on birdwatching in Egypt, see p506.

The Egyptian tortoise, native to the Mediterranean coastal desert, is one of the world's smallest tortoises; most males are less than 9cm long.

MARINE LIFE

See Watching Wildlife (p443) in the Diving the Red Sea chapter for details on Egypt's marine life.

Plants

The lotus that symbolises ancient Egypt can be found, albeit rarely, in the Delta area, but the papyrus reed, depicted in ancient art as vast swamps where the pharaohs hunted hippos, has disappeared from its natural habitats. Except for one clump found in 1968 in Wadi Natrun, papyrus is now found only in botanical gardens.

More than 100 varieties of grass thrive in areas where there is water, and the date palm can be seen in virtually every cultivable area. Along with tamarisk and acacia, the imported jacaranda and poinciana (red and orange flowers) have come to mark Egyptian summers with their vivid colours.

Birding Egypt (www .birdingegypt.com) serves the Egyptian birding community by listing top birding sites, rarities and travel tips.

NATIONAL PARKS

Egypt currently has 23 'protected areas', although just what the status of 'protected area' means varies wildly. Take for instance the Nile Islands Protected

ALTERNATIVE ENERGY: EGYPT'S WAVE OF THE FUTURE *Hassan Ansah*

People have often complained that Egypt is surrounded by some of the world's most lucrative oil producers, yet the country itself isn't endowed with such profitable resources. Yes, Egypt is loaded with historical monuments unmatched by any other country in the world but some local entrepreneurs would love a little more access to the earth's black gold. Fortunately, the future just may give Egypt a level playing field in terms of energy resources, namely in the form of alternative energy.

One of Egypt's most acclaimed achievements is the High Dam in Aswan, which gave the country the opportunity to generate a large portion of its electricity cleanly and freely. For a country that still relies heavily on thermal power plants, which are notorious for emitting noxious fumes directly into the atmosphere, increased reliance on hydropower was definitely a step in the right direction. Hydropower projects are under way in towns like Qanater and Nag Hammadi, which will hopefully set a precedent for further investment in this industry.

Another form of alternative energy that has huge potential in Egypt is wind power, more precisely large-scale wind farms. One of the largest wind farms in all of Africa and the Middle East is located in the town of Zafarana, approximately halfway between Cairo and Hurghada. Here, along the windswept Red Sea coast, the average wind speed is 9m/s, which allows a production capability of over 150MW. Due to the success of this project, numerous other plans for construction of wind farms in towns along the coast are under way.

There is also a growing business sector in Egypt for diverse forms of solar power usage, particularly in remote areas that are unable to access the unified power grid. A good example of this is the use of photovoltaics, which are high-powered reflectors that can produce voltage when exposed to sunlight. Photovoltaics are extremely advantageous in that they can be easily utilised for anything from illuminating roads to strengthening scattered mobile phone signals. Considering that Egypt basks in sunshine virtually year-round, there is an incredible amount of potential in this field.

Of course, despite the progress that has been made so far in the renewable energy industry within Egypt, significant problems and obstacles for its development remain. For instance, there are still heavy government regulations within the energy industry that protect existing large companies and hinder entrepreneurial innovation. Although government officials and businesses argue that nothing can compete with the cheapness and safe returns of electricity or natural gas, it's impossible to deny the impending global energy crisis, rising pollution levels and the threat of global warming.

Fortunately, government regulations may just be a temporary obstacle, especially considering Egypt's mushrooming population and increased energy needs. As more and more countries start to take drastic steps to reach sustainability in a time of depleting resources, there's reason to be optimistic that Egypt will follow suit. Furthermore, as an influential player in both Africa and the Middle East, Egypt is in a unique position to be able to induce a change in attitude beyond its borders.

Hassan Ansah is a freelance writer and journalist who has taught at the Western International University in Phoenix, Arizona, and at the American University in Cairo (AUC).

You can download a Wadi Rayyan Protected Area atlas, which contains 15 chapters of photos and maps, at http://www.eiecop.org/ambiente2/projects_2/wadiel rayan_atlas.htm.

Area, which runs all the way from Cairo to Aswan: nobody is clear which islands are included and most are inhabited and cultivated without restriction. Other sites are closed to the public while some, such as Ras Mohammed National Park (p464) in the Red Sea, are popular tourist destinations that have received international plaudits for their eco smarts.

The problem, as always, is a lack of funding. The Egyptian Environmental Affairs Agency (EEAA) has neither the high-level support nor the resources needed to provide effective management of the protectorates. Some help has arrived through foreign donorship and assistance: the Italians at Wadi Rayyan; the EU at St Katherine; and the US Agency for International Development (USAID) at the Red Sea coast and islands.

UNDER A BLACK CLOUD

Cairo is close to claiming the dubious title of the world's most polluted city. Airborne smoke, soot, dust, and liquid droplets from fuel combustion constantly well exceed World Health Organisation (WHO) standards, leading to skyrocketing instances of emphysema, asthma and cancer among the city's population. A startling feature article by Ursula Lindsey published in *Cairo* magazine asserted that as many as 20,000 Cairenes die each year of pollution-related disease and that close to half a million contract pollution-related respiratory diseases every year.

The government blames the city's pollution on its dry, sandy climate, which leads, it says, to a thick dust rarely cleared by rain. It hasn't commented on other contributing factors such as the increase in 'dirty' industry and Cairo's ever-burgeoning population, a result of people moving to the city from rural areas in search of work.

Cars are, of course, a major offender. Some estimates place over two million cars in the greater Cairo area, and it's clear that this number is increasing every year. Very few run on unleaded petrol; most are poorly maintained diesel-run Fiats and Peugeots that spew out dangerous fumes.

Though factories are officially required to undertake environmental impact assessments and the government lays out a system of incentives and penalties designed to encourage industrial polluters to clean up their acts, few have done so and little is being done to prosecute offenders. Laws designed to have emission levels of vehicles tested don't appear to be regularly enforced. Organisations such as USAID are trying to turn the situation around, funding initiatives such as the Cairo Air Improvement project, costing several hundreds of millions of US dollars.

The seriousness of the situation is particularly apparent each October and November, when the infamous 'black cloud' appears over the city. A dense layer of smog that is variously blamed on thermal inversion, rice straw burning in the Delta, automobile exhaust, burning rubbish and industrial pollution, it is a vivid reminder of an increasingly serious environmental problem.

Egypt has a number of notable national parks:

Lake Qarun Protected Area (p209) Scenic oasis lake important for wintering water birds.

Nabq Protectorate (p476) Southern Sinai coastal strip with the most northerly mangrove swamp in the world.

Ras Mohammed National Park (p464) Spectacular reefs with sheer cliffs of coral; a haven for migrating white storks in autumn.

Siwa Reserve (p355) Three separate areas of natural springs, palm groves, salt lakes and endangered dorcas gazelles.

St Katherine Protectorate (p495) Mountains rich in plant and animal life including Nubian ibex and rock hyrax.

Wadi Rayyan Protected Area (p210) Uninhabited Saharan oasis with endangered wildlife.

White Desert (p346) White chalk monoliths, fossils and rock formations.

Zerenike Protectorate (p502) A lagoon on Lake Bardawil that harbours migrating water birds.

ENVIRONMENTAL ISSUES

Ill-planned touristic development remains one of the biggest threats to Egypt's environment, particularly along the Red Sea coast and in Sinai. Following decades of frenzied development along the Red Sea coast, damaged coral reefs now run along most of its length. In Sinai, the coastline near Sharm el-Sheikh is already the site of a building boom and half-finished and unattractive resorts are clamouring for every speck of seafront. Whether the businesspeople investing here will make good on their promises to protect the reefs around the area remains to be seen.

The opening of the Nile bridge in Luxor (previously there was only a ferry) and the destruction of large parts of the West Bank has finally happened. After more than 50 years of trying to move people off the hillside, this has happened under the present governor. Large residential areas in Luxor are also being demolished to clear areas around historical

At www.hepca.com you can learn about the efforts of HEPCA (Hurghada Environmental Protection and Conservation Association) to conserve the Red Sea's reefs through public awareness campaigns, direct community action and lobbying efforts.

sites, despite protests from some locals and organisations (see also boxed text, p272).

Fortunately, there have been some positive developments. A National Parks office (see boxed text, p425) has opened in Hurghada and it is hoping to rein in some of the more grandiose development plans in the Marsa Alam area. And new 'green' guidelines for running hotels are being trialled under a joint US-Egyptian Red Sea Sustainable Tourism Initiative (RSSTI). Recommendations focus on energy use, water conservation, and handling and disposal of waste, including simple measures such as installing foot-pedal taps at sinks, which make it harder to leave water running.

Finally, Egypt now has a growing number of high-profile ecolodges – including the fabulous Basata in Sinai (p491) and Adrére Amellal at Siwa (p362) – which may be the harbingers of a new, environmentally responsible trend in Egyptian tourism.

Cruising
the Nile

Feluccas voyage down the River of Life

A cruise on the Nile River has always ranked among the world's most exciting and most romantic travel experiences. The combination of the world's longest river and its extraordinary monuments; the stunningly fertile valley and the barren beauty of the surrounding desert; the light; the heat; and the joy of slow travel in a superfast world: it all adds up to one of the highlights of any trip to Egypt.

The Nile Basin covers 3.35 million sq km – an incredible 10% of the African continent – and is shared by 10 countries, but Egypt is the main beneficiary of this mighty river. Rain seldom falls on this part of the Nile Valley, so without the river, the country would simply not exist. Ancient Egyptians recognised this fact when they likened their land to a lotus – the delta was the flower, the oasis of Al-Fayoum the bud, and the river and its valley the stem that supported them all.

But rather than the practical use of the waterway, the Nile's beauty strikes travellers most: the soft light of its mornings, the lushness of the plants and trees that grow along its banks, the thrill of flights of birds that shuttle up- or down-river on their migrations, the patience of fishermen, rowing out in the morning to cast their nets, the greatness of it all.

Spending a few days on and close to the Nile, one gains an understanding of the fundamentals of ancient Egyptian religion. Wake up at dawn to witness the sun come up in all its majesty on the east bank, hear the countryside wake up and see the fishermen already at work. During the day gaze upon the all-important Nile that makes everything possible, with the light getting warmer and softer all afternoon, until the glowing sun sets over the west bank and everything is put to rest until the following day.

HISTORY OF NILE TRAVEL

Until decent roads and a railway were laid in the late 19th century, the Nile was Egypt's main highway and the simplest and quickest way to move cargo, send messages or visit other areas of the country. Away from the river, the desert terrain was difficult to negotiate, slow and dangerous. Such was the ease of boat travel on the Nile that, despite incredible feats of engineering, the ancient Egyptians only began to use the wheel about 1000 years after they built the Pyramids. River travel was so central to the Egyptian psyche that it seemed perfectly obvious that the sun god Ra travelled through the sky in a boat and that the dead would sail to the afterlife.

NILE FACTS

As the world's longest river, the Nile cuts through an incredible 6680km of Africa as it winds its way north towards the Mediterranean Sea. It has two main sources: Lake Victoria in Uganda, out of which flows the White Nile; and Lake Tana in the Ethiopian highlands, from which the Blue Nile emerges. The two rivers meet at Khartoum in Sudan. Some 320km further north, they are joined by a single tributary, the Atbara. From here, the river flows northwards to its end without any other source and almost no rain adding to its waters.

Ancient Barques

The earliest boats are likely to have been simple skiffs made of papyrus bundles. These would probably have been used for hunting and travelling short distances throughout the Pharaonic period. Ancient Egyptians also developed more elaborate wooden boats powered by multiple sets of oars, a long narrow sail and a steering

Vibrant dahabiyya sails

ANTHONY SATTIN

THE BEST ON THE NILE

Close to the Nile in luxury Enjoying a private cruise on a refurbished dahabiyya (p103).

Economy cruise Taking a felucca trip from Aswan to Edfu (p101).

Nubian treat Sailing to Abu Simbel on the elegant *Kasr Ibrim* (p108).

Nostalgia trip Reliving Agatha Christie's Egypt on the Nile's last steamer, the *Sudan* (p106).

Five-star plutocracy Style and luxury on Oberoi's award-winning *Philae* (p107).

Family fun Combining luxury cruising and sightseeing with kid-friendly cooking on the *Sun Boat III* (p107).

oar that later evolved into a rudder. The most elaborate surviving example of an ancient boat appears to have been part of Pharaoh Khufu's funerary goods and can be seen at the Solar Barque Museum (p149) at the Pyramids of Giza. Numerous models of simpler boats were found in tombs and are now on display at Cairo's Egyptian Museum (p183).

Glorious Dahabiyyas

By the Middle Ages, when Cairo had become Egypt's capital and one of the world's wealthiest trading centres, one Italian traveller estimated that there were as many as 36,000 ships on the Nile. Some were simple, lateen (triangular) sailed cargo boats, given the Italian name felucca; others were elaborate vessels for the rich, the Rolls Royces of their era. These were dahabiyyas, described by medieval historians as lavishly decorated, two-masted wooden boats with private cabins and bathrooms.

For wealthy Europeans travelling along the Nile in the first half of the 19th century, the dahabiyya was the preferred mode of transport. A trip from Cairo to Abu Simbel on one of these elegant vessels took the better part of two months, and a large part of the preparations for any trip on the Nile was the renting and kitting out of one's home away from home.

top five
TRAVEL ACCOUNTS ON THE NILE

The sensual experience
Flaubert in Egypt by Gustave Flaubert –
Francis Steegmuller's brilliant translation of
Flaubert's letters and notes describes how
the exotic sights and sensual pleasures on his
long journey along the Nile changed his life
forever.

The spiritual discovery
*Letters from Egypt, A Journey on the Nile
1849–1850* by Florence Nightingale, edited by
Anthony Sattin – Florence's wonderful letters
home describe her delight in the monuments
and reveal her spiritual journey, which paved
the way for her imminent fame.

Classical Egyptology
A Thousand Miles Up the Nile by Amelia B
Edwards – Edwards was so absorbed by the
remains of ancient Egyptian civilisation she
came across on her journey that she founded
the London-based Egypt Exploration Fund,
which still finances archaeological missions
today.

Ancient encounter
The Histories by Herodotus – Egyptian customs,
curious manners, tall tales and a few facts from
a curious Greek historian in the 5th century BC.

The long journey
Old Serpent Nile: A Journey to the Source by
Stanley Stewart – a view from the ground as
Stewart travels from the Nile Delta to its source
in the Mountains of the Moon, in Uganda,
during the late 1980s.

Mass Tourism

In the 1850s, Nile travel was changed forever with the arrival of regular steamers on the river. Thomas Cook, a printer from Britain, took advantage of this innovation in 1869 when he brought his first group of tourists to Egypt. Package tourism was born and steamers gradually edged out dahabiyyas, making travel on the Nile relatively cheap and accessible for ever-growing numbers of visitors.

Today a trip on the famous river is part of almost every package itinerary to Egypt. From the humble steamer, cruisers have now grown into huge floating hotels, some with nightclubs and dip pools. Visitors can fly directly to Upper Egypt from Europe, spend five days on the Nile and be back home again within a week. The cruise ships have become so huge and plentiful that the dahabiyya has made a comeback. Old dahabiyyas were restored and many new

A peaceful early morning on the river in Aswan
IZZET KERIBAR

ones are being built, offering longer tailor-made trips that allow passengers to swim in the Nile, stop at smaller fascinating sites and see the larger ones in more intimacy.

ITINERARIES & SITES

Large cruisers stick to rigid itineraries on the busy Luxor–Aswan stretch of the Nile. On these trips, generally lasting from three to six nights, days are spent visiting monuments, and relaxing by the pool or on deck. By night there is a variety of entertainment: cocktails, dancing and fancy-dress parties – usually called a *galabiyya* (man's robe) party, as passengers are encouraged to 'dress like an Egyptian' – are all part of the fun. Actual sailing time is minimal on most of these trips – often as little as four hours each day, depending on the itinerary.

Feluccas and dahabiyyas determine their own schedules and do not need special mooring spots, so can stop at small islands or antiquities sites often skipped by the big cruisers. But even these boats usually have their preferred mooring places, which they will use for each trip. Using sail power instead of large engines, a far greater proportion of time is spent in motion. Night-time entertainment is more likely to be stargazing, listening to the sounds of the river, and occasionally music from the crew or villagers.

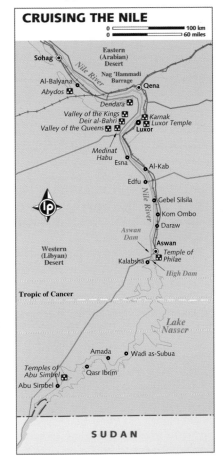

The stretch of the Nile between Luxor and Aswan has the greatest concentration of well-preserved monuments in the country, which is why it also has the greatest number of boats and tourists (sailing in both directions). The government currently forbids any boat to sail north of Abydos, a hangover from the Islamist insurgency of the 1990s (see boxed text, p220). Feluccas and dahabiyyas rarely sail between Luxor and Esna because police permits are difficult to get and because the big boats usually have priority using the busy Esna lock. Dahabiyya operators will bus passengers down to Esna from Luxor. Felucca trips generally start in Aswan and end south of Esna; captains can arrange onward transport to Luxor, but this will cost extra.

The following are the most common stops on cruise itineraries.

Luxor

Given the crowded mooring scene, often with eight or 10 boats tied up together (so

Sunset casts a warm light on the hypostyle hall in Kom Ombo (p296)

JOHN E

the view from your cabin can be someone else's cabin), and the wide choice of hotels, it is best to keep on-board time in Luxor to a minimum.

The capital of Egypt's glorious New Kingdom pharaohs, home to Tutankhamun, Ramses II and many other famous names, Luxor is blessed with many remarkable monuments. Most cruises only cover the bare minimum and, if you are interested in seeing the sights, it pays to spend an extra day or two here away from the boat. Highlights include the **Temples of Karnak** (p243), **Luxor Temple** (p250), the **Luxor Museum** (p252), the **Valley of the Kings** (p258), the **Tombs of the Nobles** (p268), **Deir al-Bahri** (p267) and **Medinat Habu** (p273).

The Luxor governor has plans to build a dock south of Luxor bridge, where cruise ships will be obliged to moor, away from the Corniche. Passengers would be brought by bus to Luxor. Work had not started on this at the time of writing.

The columns of the Temple of Khnum (p291)

IZZET KER

NORTH OF LUXOR

The area north of Luxor was excluded from cruise itineraries for years because of Islamist violence, but the archaeological sites at **Dendara** (p236) and **Abydos** (p233) are beginning to appear on tour schedules again. Usually this means taking a seven- or eight-day cruise, instead of the usual four- or five-day trip. Not all boats offer this option so sites are uncrowded and there are fewer cruisers at mooring docks. It is also possible to take a day cruise to Dendara (see p276). Feluccas and dahabiyyas rarely sail north of Luxor.

Between Luxor & Aswan

This most famous stretch of the river is studded with stunning architecture and varied scenes of great natural beauty. All cruisers stop to visit the Ptolemaic temples of **Esna** (p291), **Edfu** (p293) and **Kom Ombo** (p296). On the shorter cruises, all three sites are visited in a single day. While none of the sites is so large that this is unrealistic, exploring three great temples is a lot to jam into one day and the rushed visit means that you will be moored longer at Luxor or Aswan.

Dahabiyyas and feluccas take longer to cover the distance between the three temples, usually seeing only one a day. Most dahabiyyas (and some feluccas) also stop at the rarely visited and highly recommended sites of **Al-Kab** (p292) and **Gebel Silsila** (p296). Cruisers do not have moorings here, so visitors may be limited to your fellow passengers, giving a taste of how it might have been for 19th-century travellers.

Aswan

The Nile is squeezed between rocks and a series of islands at Aswan, which makes it particularly picturesque, especially with the desert crowding in on both sides of the river. If you embark here you will probably spend only one night in town, but some cruisers stay moored for two nights. Most itineraries include a visit to **Philae** (p315), site of the Temple of Isis, the **High Dam** (p316) and the Northern Quarries, site of the **Unfinished Obelisk** (p303). Occasionally cruisers offer a felucca ride around **Elephantine Island** (p303) as an excursion; if not, it is worth organising your own. Some also offer an optional half-day tour (generally by plane) to **Abu Simbel** (p323). At the time of writing, a dock was being built north of Aswan to moor all the cruise ships out of town, so they no longer block the view from the Corniche. Passengers will be brought by bus to Aswan.

Intricate bas-relief in the Tomb Chapels of the Divine Adorers at Medinat Habu (p273)

MARK DAFFEY

A traditional felucca glides into Aswan

WAYNE WAL

Lake Nasser

The lake was created when the High Dam was built near Aswan, and covers much of Egyptian Nubia, once home to hundreds of tombs, temples and churches (see p318 for details of Nubian history and culture). Some monuments were moved from their original sites prior to the building of the dam and are grouped together at four locations: **Kalabsha** (p321), **Wadi as-Subua** (p322; accessible only by boat), **Amada** (p322; accessible only by boat) and, of course, **Abu Simbel** (p324).

Because there are currently only six cruisers sailing on Lake Nasser, moorings are never crowded and monuments – with the exception of the Temple of Ramses II at Abu Simbel – are not overrun. Itineraries are generally three nights/four days from Aswan to Abu Simbel, or four nights/five days from Abu Simbel to Aswan.

SAILING A FELUCCA

For many travellers, the only way to travel on the Nile is slowly, on board a traditional felucca (Egyptian sailing boat). Except for swimming, this is as close as you can get to the river, zigzagging from one bank to the other, watching the seemingly timeless activity on the land – fishermen throwing their nets, water buffaloes staring at passers-by, women doing dishes, *fellaheen* (farmers) working their fields, and children swimming and stargazing at night. The small size of the boat limits the number of passengers and means a far more intimate experience of the river and the monuments alongside it; the low prices mean that these trips are open to all budgets.

A Slow Journey

Most felucca trips begin at Aswan; the strong northward current means that boats are not marooned if the wind dies. Trips go to Kom Ombo (two days/one night), Edfu (three days/two nights – the most popular option) or Esna (four days/three nights). Feluccas no longer sail past the Esna lock to Luxor. Many of the felucca captains are Nubian and will take you for tea in their village along the way. (Women should dress modestly, including covering arms and legs.)

Feluccas are not allowed to sail after 8pm, so most stop at sunset and set up camp for the night on the boat or on an island. Night-time entertainment ranges from stargazing and the crew singing to partying, depending on you and your fellow passengers.

Although it can be difficult to keep small children amused on a sailing boat all day, felucca trips make great family holidays, especially with older kids. Egyptians love children, and the captain and crew will enjoy

---

PLANNING YOUR FELUCCA TRIP

Toilet facilities Let it be clear that there are no toilet facilities on the boat, so you will need to go to the toilet overboard or find somewhere private on shore.

Ensure that your boat is riverworthy Check that the captain has what appears to be a decent, riverworthy boat, and the essential gear: blankets (it gets cold at night), cooking implements and a sunshade. If a different boat or captain is foisted on you at the last minute, be firm in refusing.

Establish whether the price includes food To be sure you're getting what you paid for, go with whoever does the shopping.

Agree on the number of passengers beforehand Ask to meet fellow passengers, because you are going to be sharing a small space.

Decide on the drop-off point before you set sail Many felucca captains stop 30km south of Edfu in Hammam, Faris or Ar-Ramady and arrange for 'special' shared taxis – which take you to the temple of Edfu and then straight to a hotel of the captain's choice in Luxor for E£25 to E£30 per person (it should be E£15).

Don't hand over your passport Captains can use a photocopy to arrange the permit.

Take plenty of bottled water

Bring comfort essentials It can get bitterly cold at night, and the supply of blankets on board won't be enough, so bring a sleeping bag. Insect repellent is a good idea. A hat and sunscreen are essential.

Take your rubbish with you Wherever you stop, be sure to clean up after yourself.

having them aboard. Just keep in mind that you will have to bring your own life jackets and other safety equipment.

Find the Captain

Officially there are 3400 feluccas in Aswan, so arranging a felucca trip is quite daunting, particularly when faced with the legions of touts on Aswan's Corniche. The small hotels can be just as aggressive in trying to rope you in. While it is easier to let the hotels do the organising, remember that they get a percentage of the price, which makes it more costly, or either comes out of the captain's fee or your food allowance.

If you want to be sure of what you're getting it's best to arrange things yourself. Many of the better captains on the river can be found having a *sheesha* (water pipe) or a drink in Nileside restaurants such as the Aswan Moon (p312), Emy, near the Panorama restaurant (p312), or on Elephantine Island (p303). Meet a few captains before choosing one you get on with well. Women alone or in a group should try to team up with a few men if possible, as some women travellers have reported sailing with felucca captains who had groping hands, and there have been some rare reports of assault.

Officially, feluccas can carry a minimum of six passengers and a maximum of eight. Expect to pay around E£50 per person to Kom Ombo, E£90 to Edfu and E£120 to Esna. On top of this you need to add E£5 to E£10 per person for the captain to arrange the police registration. Food will cost around E£70 per person for two nights, E£90 for three and E£100 for four nights. You can get boats for less, but take care; if it's much cheaper you'll either have a resentful captain and crew, or you'll be eating little more than bread and *fuul* (fava bean paste) for three days. Do not hand out the whole agreed amount until you get to your destination because there have been several reports of trips being stopped prematurely for a so-called breakdown.

If you want help, see Hakeem Hussein at Aswan's tourist office (p302). He can recom-

A MOST TEMPESTUOUS LAKE

'The Nile, when he makes a reach, looks like a great sea, he is so wide, and when the wind freshens, you see a fleet of little cangias coming out, like water-lilies, upon the river (you don't know from where), or like fairy boats, a fleet of *efreets* coming up the Nile, doubling a cape, cutting in among each other. There are islands and headlands and creeks, just like a sea, and sometimes, when the wind blows against the current, he is no longer the solemn Nile, but a most tempestuous lake, with white horses, and turbulent little waves. But he is always beautiful.'

From Florence Nightingale's Letters from Egypt: A Journey on the Nile 1849–1850

Enjoy floating along the Nile's calming waters

JANE SWEE

The dahabiyya crew jumps into action

ANTHONY SATTIN

mend some reputable operators (or at least advise you against some who are shady). The tourist police and the tourist office should be the first port of call if you have any problems.

DAHABIYYAS, THE GOLDEN BOATS

'The choice between a dahabiyya and a steamer is like the choice between travelling with post-horses and travelling by rail. One is expensive, leisurely, delightful; the other is cheap, swift, and comparatively comfortless.' When the 19th-century traveller Amelia Edwards wrote these lines in *A Thousand Miles Up the Nile*, package steamer tours were already crowding dahabiyyas off the Nile, and for most of the 20th century, dahabiyyas were not seen on the river. But a few smart companies recognised that some people wanted to sail in pre-steamer style – and were prepared to pay for it. Many others have followed and, although dahabiyyas are still relatively rare, there is a good choice of boats and operators. We have listed five companies. All have boats that are beautifully appointed, with an antique feel, tasteful decor and double lateen sails. They also have water filters, their own generators and hook-ups to get electricity at certain moorings. Some are privately chartered for honeymooners, extended families or groups of friends. With such small numbers of passengers, this is the most luxurious way to see the monuments without crowds. As most dahabiyyas have flexible itineraries and personalised service, it is also the best way to feel truly independent while travelling in comfort. For the time being, police regulations forbid most boats from sailing between Luxor and Esna. Prices include all meals and usually also transfers to and from airports/train stations. Some include entrance to monuments and

A dahabiyya deck – perfect for relaxing and taking in the scenery

ANTHONY SA

guide fees, but you should check when booking your trip. Trips are best arranged before you depart for Egypt.

Meroe (☎ 010 657 8322; www.nourelnil.com; 5-night trip per person from €1000; ⬚ ⬚) A replica of a 19th-century dahabiyya indistinguishable from the original, the beautifully finished *Meroe* is the coolest dahabiyya currently on the Nile and is rare for being owner-operated. It has room for 20 passengers in 10 comfortable, stylish white cabins with private bathroom, and large windows overlooking the Nile. Because it is newly built, plumbing and water filtration are good, and there is plenty of storage for clothes and suitcases. During the day, when not visiting an ancient site or a local market, there is plenty of space on deck to read in your own corner, to watch the scenery or to dive off and swim in the strong current of the Nile. The chef buys from farmers and markets on the way, so the food is simple but totally fresh and delicious: plenty of fresh vegetables, farm-bred chicken, duck and fish. This tailor-made trip, with moorings at small islands and outside villages, is a unique way to see the Nile, reminiscent of another age. If there is no wind, the dahabiyya is towed by a motor boat. The same owners have three other boats, *El Nil* (10 cabins), *Malouka* and *Assouan* (both eight cabins). All boats only run from Esna to Aswan (five nights).

Lazuli (☎ 010 364 7011; www.lazulinil.com; per person per week from €1850; ⬚) There are now three *Lazulis* on the Nile, one with five cabins and two with six. The long, elegant boats have two lateen sails, a spacious deck with deck chairs, cushions and a long table at which most meals are served. The cabins are comfortable with compact but modern private bathrooms. The same company also offers trips in four larger *sandales* (sailing boats smaller than dahabiyyas): *Al Karim, Al Shaba, Al Sindbad* and *Al Qurna,* with four to nine cabins, some with private bathroom and all with fan. They cost from €1410 per person for a week. All cruises take six days and five nights from Esna to Aswan.

Belle Époque Dahabiyyas (☎ 02-516 9649; www.dahabiya.com; prices upon request; ⚡) The Belle Époque Company, which also runs several boats on Lake Nasser, has six air-conditioned dahabiyyas, and some more under construction: *El Bey* (The Lord), *El Hanem* (The Lady), *Zahra* (Flower), *Nesma* (Breeze), *Amber* and *Musk,* each with six individually decorated cabins in a colonial style. Some of the boats are chartered by Bales and upmarket American companies; others can be booked by individuals. The atmosphere is more formal than on the other dahabiyyas, and there is a motor on board for windless days.

La Flâneuse du Nil (☎ in France 00 331 42 86 16 00; www.la-flaneuse-du-nil.com, in French; 3-night trip per person from €640, 4 nights from €790; ⚡) One of the newcomers, La Flâneuse has been quickly picked up by several up-market British tour operators and with good reason. The company currently only has one boat, but it is well fitted and well run. Like original dahabiyyas, it relies on sails (or tugs) to move, but does have air-con in the seven cabins. Tours are shorter than some, taking four nights from Esna to Aswan and three nights from Aswan back to Esna.

Princess Donia (☎ 010 686 1688; www.princessdonia.com; 5-night trip per person from €650; ⚡) British-owned and Egyptian-run, the Princess Donia leaves Esna for Aswan on Friday. There is a large suite at the stern and four cabins, all with flat-screen TV. En-suite bathrooms have power showers and hair driers. The boat lacks some of the intimacy of other dahabiyyas, with the staff in uniform, but cabin prices are competitive.

CRUISERS

There are more than 270 cruisers plying the waters between Aswan and Luxor – so many that there is a moratorium on the launching of new boats. Like Egyptian hotels they range from slightly shabby to sumptuous, but almost all have some sort of pool, a large rooftop area for sunbathing and watching the scenery, a restaurant, a bar, air-con, TV, minibars and en-suite bathrooms. Few people are aware that the government has imposed that each cruiser now has at least two armed soldiers on board, who guard the boat at the back and in the front.

In general, travelling on one of these floating hotels means entering the package-holiday world: a cruise remains the easiest way to see the Nile in comfort on a midrange budget and can be ideal for families with older children who want to splash in a pool between archaeological visits, or for people who want to combine sightseeing with relaxation. The downside

A fine dahabiyya salon   ANTHONY SATTIN   Striking double-lateen dahabiyya sails   ANTHONY SATTIN

CRUISE TIPS

When to travel All cruisers (except those on Lake Nasser) must pass through a lock at Esna. This is closed for two weeks each December and June when water levels in the Nile are lowered for the cleaning of irrigation canals. The exact dates can change each year, so check with your tour operator or cruise company to avoid having to transfer from Luxor by road.

Where to start Most cruises starting from Luxor are a day longer than those starting from Aswan, partly because they are going against the Nile's strong current. If you want to spend longer in Luxor or are concerned about cost, start from Aswan and head north.

Know your boat Ask the name of your boat before you book. If your hotel or travel agency cannot tell you, look elsewhere.

Cabin choice Try to avoid the lowest deck. Most boats listed here have decent views from all cabins, but the banks of the Nile are high – and get higher as the river level drops – and you want to see as much as possible. Ask for a deck plan when booking.

Sailing time Many Nile cruise passengers are surprised by how little time is spent cruising – the boats' large engines cover distances relatively quickly and cruise times are often only four hours per day.

Mooring misery The vast majority of cruisers end up mooring next to each other (one of the exceptions being the *Sudan*, below), so you may have to cross four or five boats to get to your own, or you may find that your large cabin window looks directly onto another ship.

Healthy cruising In general, the more expensive the boat, the better the standard of hygiene and all cruise boats listed here filter their water, but many passengers still get stomach upsets. (See p535 for more tips.)

is that monuments are almost always seen with large groups and the itineraries are generally inflexible. Boats are almost always moored together, and the sheer volume of traffic means that generators and air-con units overwhelm the peace of the river. The consensus from our research is that scrimping on cruises means substandard hygiene, no pool, cubby-hole cabins and lots of hidden extras, which makes a felucca trip a far better option.

The only way around this is to book an all-inclusive package to Egypt. Not only are the prices usually lower than those listed here but, in the case of cut-price cruises, the agency guarantees the reliability of the boat. The best deals are from Europe. Avoid booking through small hotels in Egypt; they often send customers on substandard boats and, because the hotels are not licensed as travel agencies, you have no recourse if there are problems.

With so many (largely indistinguishable) boats to choose from, we have only listed the most noteworthy, with high-season prices, which include all meals, entrance to monuments and guides. Prices vary considerably according to the time of year, the state of tourism, and how you book.

Between Luxor & Aswan

M/S Sudan (☎ France 00 33 1 7300 8188; www.steam-ship-sudan.com; 3-night cruise s/d from €750/990, 4-night cruise from €945/1265; ✕) The *Sudan* was built as part of Thomas Cook's steamer fleet in 1885 and was once owned by King Fouad. It was also used as a set in the film *Death on the Nile*. It has been refurbished and offers 23 cabins, all with private bathroom, air-con and access to the deck. It's unusual in that it has no pool, but it's also unique because it has so much history and character, something sorely missing on most cruisers. Its configuration means it cannot moor to other cruisers, so night-time views are good. Note that the management does not accept children under seven.

M/S Sun Boat III (www.abercrombiekent.co.uk; per person per night from US$575; ) Abercrombie & Kent's most intimate cruiser is the beautiful *Sun Boat III,* with 14 cabins and four suites decorated in a contemporary Egyptian style, straight out of a style magazine. The 11-night itinerary includes visits to Dendara and Abydos. Dinner on board is à la carte or a set menu with two European choices and one Egyptian. There is also the option of in-room dining. The boat is impeccably run and operates a no-mobile-phone policy in public areas. Facilities include a pool and exercise machines. The company also operates the 40-cabin, deluxe M/S *Sun Boat IV* and the 32-cabin *Nile Adventurer,* back in service after a complete refit. All A&K boats have excellent Egyptologists as guides and a private mooring dock in Luxor, Aswan and Kom Ombo.

M/S Philae (www.oberoihotels.com; per person per night from €150;) Designed to resemble a Mississippi paddle boat, the award-winning *Philae* runs four- and six-night cruises. Its interior is filled with wood panelling and antiques, and all rooms have a balcony. The old-world feel is backed up by state-of-the-art water filtration, a library and all the comforts of a good five-star hotel. Prices more than double in high season.

M/S Nile Goddess (www.sonesta.com/nilecruises; s/d/tr per night from US$240/300/405;) One of the top boats in the Sonesta's five cruisers (and joined by a new dahabiyya), the *Nile Goddess* is a large, plush, five-star vessel featuring lots of marble and gilt. Sonesta's sister ship, the M/S *Sun Goddess* is slightly cheaper, the M/S *Moon Goddess* and *Star Goddess* are even plusher and more expensive.

M/S Beau Soleil (www.msbeausoleil.com; per person per night from US$95;) The five-star *Beau Soleil* is more reasonably priced than many others and recommended for its good service and facilities. The smallest cabins are 15 sq metres (large for such a boat) and many of the cabins have their own balcony from where you can watch the scenery go by.

M/S Florence (☎ 02-450 2327; http://florencestmaria.com; per person per night from US$90;) Not a beautiful boat compared to some others listed here, the *Florence* is included because it's one of the more reasonably priced options and comes recommended from a number of sources.

M/S Darakum Not a boat you can book direct, but one that is offered by a number of international agencies. New, spacious and top end, if not super-luxurious, the *Darakum* has 44

An outing on the Nile is an unforgettable Egypt experience

JULIET COOMBE

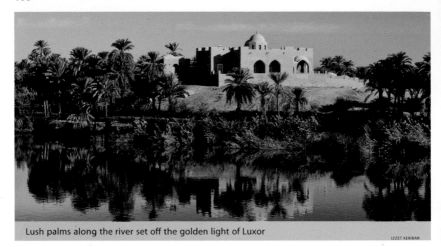

Lush palms along the river set off the golden light of Luxor

IZZET KERIBAR

cabins and eight suites, plus a swimming pool. The decor is more 1970s than New Kingdom and you have to be quick to get a sunbed, but prices come right down out of high season.

Lake Nasser

Of the handful of boats currently cruising on Lake Nasser, a few stand out above the rest.

Kasr Ibrim & Eugénie (☎ 02-516 9653/4/5; www.kasribrim.com.eg; d per person per night on 3- to 4-day trip from US$190; ⊠) Both run by Belle Époque Travel, these boats were the brainchild of Mustafa al-Guindi, a Cairene of Nubian origin who is almost single-handedly responsible for getting Lake Nasser opened to tourists. The boats are stunningly designed: *Eugénie* is modelled on an early-20th-century hunting lodge; *Kasr Ibrim* is all 1930s Art Deco elegance. Each has a pool, a hammam (bathhouse) and fantastic French cuisine. In addition, passengers are pampered with treats such as evening cocktails and classical music in front of the temples at Abu Simbel.

Prince Abbas (☎ 097 314 660, 012 220 6747; ⊠ ⊠) The *Prince Abbas* is a five-star deluxe ship with a library, a gym, a sun deck with a plunge pool and a jacuzzi. The spacious staterooms have TV, a music system, a minibar, picture windows and a private bathroom.

Ta Seti (☎ 097-231 0907; www.african-angler.net; 3-night trip per person in safari boat from €300, in houseboat from €455) Tim Baily worked in safaris south of the Sahara before setting up African Angler, the first company to run Lake Nasser safaris. He has a staff of skilled guides, expert in the flora, fauna and fish life of the lake and owns several styles of small boat. The two-cabin houseboats have toilet and shower, the two-bunk safari boat is more basic, while the mothership carries the kitchen and supplies. There are departures from Aswan each Tuesday.

Nubiana (☎ 012 104 0255; www.lakenasseradventure.com; 4-night trip per person from UK£750; ⊠) A newcomer to the lake, the *Nubiana* is a small motorboat with three cabins and one suite. Cabins are small but bright and there are two shared bathrooms, an upper lounge and a sun deck. An English-speaking guide accompanies the trip and transfers back to Aswan are included. A speedboat can also be arranged for fishing trips or waterskiing. The same company also organises five-day boat trekking trips from Aswan to Abu Simbel from UK£410 per person and six-day fishing safaris from £660 per angler.

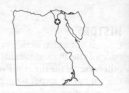

Cairo

Let's address the drawbacks first. The crowds on a Cairo footpath make Manhattan look like a ghost town. You will be hounded by papyrus sellers at every turn. Your life will flash before your eyes each time you venture across a street. And your snot will run black from the smog.

But it's a small price to pay to visit the city Cairenes call *Umm ad-Dunya* – the Mother of the World. This city has an energy, palpable even at three in the morning, like no other. It's the product of its 20 million inhabitants waging a battle against the desert and winning (mostly), of 20 million people simultaneously crushing the city's infrastructure under their collective weight and lifting the city's spirit up with their uncommon graciousness and humour.

One taxi ride can span millennia, from the resplendent mosques and mausoleums built at the pinnacle of the Islamic empire, to the 19th-century palaces and grand avenues (which earned the city the nickname 'Paris on the Nile'), to the brutal concrete blocks of the Nasser years – then all the way back to the days of the pharaohs, as the Pyramids of Giza hulk on the western edge of the city. The architectural jumble is smoothed over by an even coating of beige sand, and the sand is a social equaliser as well: everyone, no matter how rich, gets dusty when the spring khamsin blows in.

So blow your nose, crack a joke and learn to look through the dirt to see the city's true colours. If you love Cairo, it will love you back.

HIGHLIGHTS

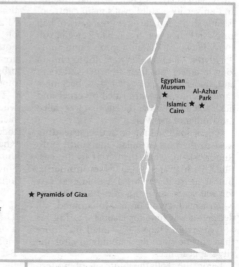

- Tip your head back and gape at the **Pyramids of Giza** (p144) and cross an item off your life to-do list

- Give your regards to Tutankhamun and his cohorts in the mazelike **Egyptian Museum** (p183)

- Visit the great medieval mosques of **Islamic Cairo** (p128) – or just get lost in the narrow alleys (p157)

- Relax to the click of backgammon and the bubble of the *sheesha* (water pipe) at an Egyptian coffeehouse, known as an **ahwa** (p170)

- Escape the city noise in the greenery of **Al-Azhar Park** (p141) with its splendid sunset view

Egyptian Museum ★
Al-Azhar Park ★
Islamic ★ ★ Cairo
★ Pyramids of Giza

- TELEPHONE CODE: 02 | - POPULATION: MORE THAN 20 MILLION

CAIRO

HISTORY

Cairo is not a Pharaonic city, though the presence of the Pyramids leads many to believe otherwise. At the time the Pyramids were built, the capital of ancient Egypt was Memphis, 20km southeast of the Giza Plateau.

The core foundations of the city of Cairo were laid in AD 969 by the Fatimid dynasty, but the city's history goes further back than that. There was an important ancient religious centre at On (modern-day Heliopolis). The Romans built a fortress at the port of On, which they called Babylon, while Amr ibn al-As, the general who conquered Egypt for Islam in AD 642, established the city of Fustat nearby. Fustat's huge wealth was drawn from Egypt's very rich soil and the taxes imposed on the heavy Nile traffic. Descriptions left by 10th-century travellers tell of public gardens, street lighting and buildings up to 14 storeys high. Yet in the 10th century, when the Fatimids marched in from modern-day Tunisia, they spurned Fustat and instead set about building a new city.

Construction began on the new capital, probably on purpose, when the planet Mars (Al-Qahir, 'the Victorious') was in the ascendant; thus arose Al-Madina al-Qahira, 'the city victorious', the pronunciation of which Europeans corrupted to Cairo.

Many imposing buildings from the Fatimid era remain today: the great Al-Azhar Mosque and university is still Egypt's main centre of Islamic study, and the three great gates of Bab an-Nasr, Bab al-Futuh and Bab Zuweila still straddle two of Islamic Cairo's main thoroughfares. The Fatimids were not to remain long in power, but their city survived them and, under subsequent dynasties, became a capital of great wealth, ruled by cruel and fickle sultans. This was the city that was called the Mother of the World.

Cairo finally burst its walls, spreading west to the port of Bulaq and south onto Rhoda Island, while the desert to the east filled with grand funerary monuments. But at heart it remained a medieval city for 900 years, until the mid-19th century, when Ismail, grandson of Mohammed Ali, decided it was time for change. During his 16-year reign (1863–79), Ismail did more than anyone since the Fatimids to alter the city's appearance.

Before the 1860s the future site of modern central Cairo was a swampy plain subject to the annual flooding of the Nile. When the French-educated Ismail came to power, he was determined to remake his capital into a city of European standing. This could only be done by starting afresh. For 10 years the former marsh became one vast building site as Ismail invited architects from Belgium, France and Italy to design and build a new European-style Cairo beside the old Islamic city.

Since the revolution of 1952 the population of Cairo has grown spectacularly – although at the expense of Ismail's vision. Building maintenance fell by the wayside as apartments were overcrowded. In the 1960s and 1970s, urban planners concreted over the sparsely populated west bank of the Nile for desperately needed new suburbs. In more recent decades, growth has crept beyond Muqattam Hills on the east and the Pyramids on the west. Luxe gated communities, sprawling housing blocks and full satellite cities, complete with malls and megastores, spring up from the desert every year: 6th of October City, New Cairo and others are the new Egyptian dream. Whether the desert and the economy can sustain them remains to be seen.

ORIENTATION

Finding your way around Cairo's sprawl is not as difficult as it may at first seem. Midan Tahrir is the centre. The noisy, busy Downtown area, where most cheap eating and sleeping options are, lies northeast of Tahrir, centred on Midan Talaat Harb. Midan Ramses, location of the city's main train station, marks the northernmost extent of Downtown. Beyond are teeming middle- and working-class suburbs such as Shubra, perhaps the true soul of modern-day Cairo.

Downtown's eastern edge is Midan Ataba, where Islamic Cairo takes over. This is the medieval heart of the city, still beating strong today. At its centre is the great bazaar of Khan al-Khalili and Al-Azhar Mosque and university. Further east are the Northern and Southern Cemeteries, vast necropolises now inhabited by both the living and the dead.

South of Midan Tahrir, the tree-lined streets of Garden City are prime embassy territory. Then you're out of central Cairo and into a succession of ramshackle neighbourhoods loosely termed Old Cairo, the site of Roman Babylon and Arab Fustat. Buried in here is the small, walled enclave of Coptic Cairo, a feature on many tourist agendas. Well beyond

CAIRO IN...

Two Days

Start day one with the magnificent exhibits at the **Egyptian Museum** (p183). When you've reached Pharaonic overload, leave the museum and wander around the Downtown area, stopping to grab a cheap and delicious lunch at any of the local spots. In the afternoon, make your way to historic **Khan al-Khalili** (p130), and practise your haggling skills with the cheerful stall owners. While there, don't forget to have the obligatory mint tea and a *sheesha* at **Fishawi's** (p170), Cairo's oldest running cafe. When the sun sets, head to Zamalek, where you can dine like a pasha at any of the neighbourhood's well-heeled establishments.

On day two make an early start and hire a taxi for the day to take you to **Dahshur** (p204), **Memphis** (p194) and **Saqqara** (p198). Bring a picnic to eat at the foot of the **Step Pyramid** (p198), or alternatively have lunch along **Pyramids Road** (p168). In the afternoon visit the only remaining Ancient Wonder of the World, the **Pyramids of Giza** (p144). After this, it's on to the **Citadel View** (p166) in Al-Azhar Park for a lavish dinner overlooking the medieval city.

Four Days

For days one and two, follow the Two Days itinerary.

Start day three by taking a taxi to the **Mosque of Ibn Tulun** (p139) and the **Gayer-Anderson Museum** (p140) in Islamic Cairo. Indulge in a bit of shopping at **Khan Misr Touloun** (p176) before catching a taxi to Midan al-Hussein to visit historic **Al-Azhar Mosque** (p129) and the **Al-Ghouri Complex** (p135). Have a late lunch in the Khan al-Khalili, then rest up before strolling through **Garden City at twilight** (p157). At sundown, take an hour's **felucca ride** (p156), then head back to Garden City for dinner, which should put you within easy stumbling distance of Cairo's late-night **drinking** (p170) and **dancing** (p172) establishments in Gezira and Zamalek.

On your last day take the river bus to **Coptic Cairo** (p125) in the morning, then catch the metro back to Midan Tahrir. Walk over the Qasr el-Nil Bridge to Gezira and check out the **Museum of Modern Egyptian Art** (p142) and the **Mahmoud Mukhtar Museum** (p142) before strolling along the bank of the Nile to the neighbourhood of Zamalek for a late lunch, and perhaps some shopping. After a rest at your hotel, bid farewell to the city by having a late dinner and watching the best belly dancers in the world shake their stuff on the **Nile Maxim boat** (p173) or at the wonderfully sleazy **Palmyra** (p173).

that is the green residential suburb of Ma'adi, an expat enclave.

West of all these districts is the Nile, obstructed by two sizable islands. The more central of these, connected directly to Downtown by three bridges, is Gezira, home to the Cairo Tower and the Cairo Opera House. The northern half of Gezira is an affluent district called Zamalek, historically favoured by the city's European residents and home to many embassies. The southern island is Rhoda, although its northern part goes by the name of Manial.

The west bank of the Nile is newer (lots more concrete) and more residential than areas along the east bank, but it's also the wealthier, trendier part of the city. The primary districts from north to south are Mohandiseen, Agouza, Doqqi and Giza, which stretches 10km out to the foot of the Pyramids.

Maps

The American University in Cairo (AUC) Press publishes *Cairo Maps: The Practical Guide* (E£30), a book-sized but lightweight collection of 40 street maps, with index.

INFORMATION
Bookshops

American University in Cairo (AUC) Bookshop
Downtown (Map pp120-1; ☎ 2797 5370; Sharia Mohammed Mahmoud; ☻ 9am-6pm Sat-Thu); Zamalek (Map pp146-7; ☎ 2739 7045; 16 Sharia Mohammed Thakeb; ☻ 10am-6pm Sat-Thu, 1-6pm Fri) The best English-language bookshop in Egypt, with stacks of material on the politics, sociology and history of Cairo, Egypt and the Middle East. Plenty of guidebooks and some fiction.

Anglo-Egyptian Bookshop (Map pp120-1; ☎ 2391 4337; 165 Sharia Mohammed Farid, Downtown; ☻ 9am-1.30pm & 4.30-8pm Mon-Sat) Good selection of books on Egypt and the Middle East.

CAIRO

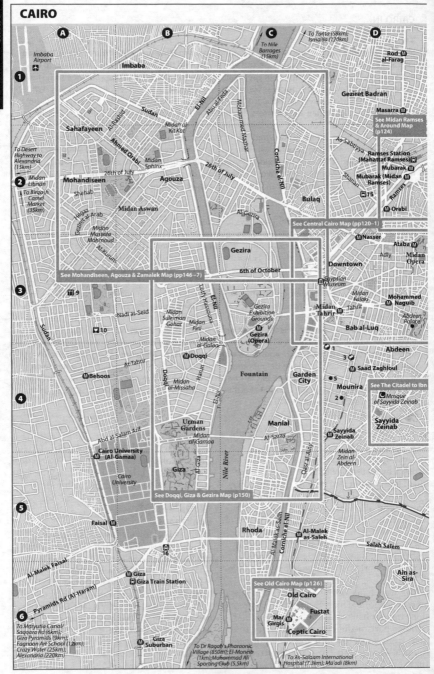

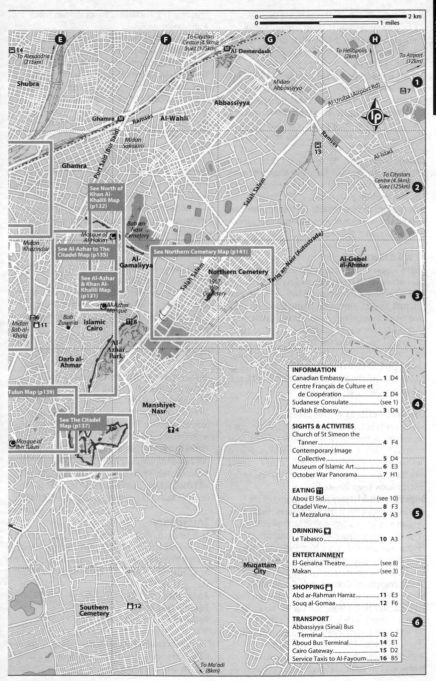

INFORMATION
Canadian Embassy..............................**1** D4
Centre Français de Culture et
de Coopération.................................**2** D4
Sudanese Consulate.....................(see 1)
Turkish Embassy..................................**3** D4

SIGHTS & ACTIVITIES
Church of St Simeon the
Tanner..**4** F4
Contemporary Image
Collective..**5** D4
Museum of Islamic Art.....................**6** E3
October War Panorama......................**7** H1

EATING
Abou El Sid......................................(see 10)
Citadel View...**8** F3
La Mezzaluna.......................................**9** A3

DRINKING
Le Tabasco...**10** A3

ENTERTAINMENT
El-Genaina Theatre.......................(see 8)
Makan..(see 3)

SHOPPING
Abd ar-Rahman Harraz...................**11** E3
Souq al-Gomaa..................................**12** F6

TRANSPORT
Abbassiyya (Sinai) Bus
Terminal...**13** G2
Aboud Bus Terminal.......................**14** E1
Cairo Gateway..................................**15** D2
Service Taxis to Al-Fayoum...........**16** B5

Diwan (Map pp146-7; ☎ 2736 2578; 159 Sharia 26th of July, Zamalek; ☺ 9am-11.30pm) Fabulous: English, French and German titles, from novels to travel guides to coffee-table books. It also has a kids' section, large music wing and a small cafe.

Lehnert & Landrock (Map pp120-1; ☎ 2392 7606; 44 Sharia Sherif, Downtown; ☺ 10am-7pm Mon-Sat) A good place for maps, books about Cairo and Egypt (some secondhand), vintage postcards and reprints of old photographs. There are branches opposite the Egyptian Museum (Map pp120-1) and outside the Sphinx-side entrance to the Pyramids (Map p152).

Shorouk (Map pp120-1; ☎ 2393 0643; 1 Midan Talaat Harb, Downtown; ☺ 10am-10pm) Find Arabic and English bestsellers, plus a lot of magazines at this two-storey shop.

Zamalek Bookshop (Map pp146-7; ☎ 2736 9197; 19 Sharia Shagaret ad-Durr, Zamalek; ☺ 9am-8pm Mon-Sat) Small but packed with magazines, English-language crime fiction and airport-style novels.

NEWS-STANDS

Cairo's best news-stands face each other on the corner of Sharias 26th of July and Hassan Sabry in Zamalek (Map pp146-7). You can get just about anything from these stands. Downtown, good news-stands are situated on Sharia Mohammed Mahmoud opposite AUC (Map pp120-1) and on Midan Tahrir (Map pp120-1). The bookshops at the Nile Hotel (Map pp120-1), the Cairo Marriott (Map pp146-7) and the Semiramis InterContinental (Map pp120-1) are also decent.

Cultural Centres & Libraries

Many centres will ask for ID (preferably your passport) before they will allow you in. For event schedules, check *Al-Ahram Weekly* and the monthly *Egypt Today*, but don't expect much activity during the summer, when many institutions keep limited hours.

British Council & Library (www.britishcouncil.org .eg) Agouza (Map pp146-7; ☎ 3300 1666; 192 Sharia el-Nil; ☺ 8am-8pm Sun-Thu, 9am-4.30pm Sat); Heliopolis (Map p155; ☎ 19789; 4 Sharia el-Minia, off Sharia Nazih Khalifa; ☺ 9am-8pm Sun-Wed, 9am-4.30pm Thu) Organises performances, exhibitions and talks and has a useful library; its Agouza office has a strong collection of modern British art.

Centre Français de Culture et de Coopération (www.ambafrance-eg.org/cfcc) Heliopolis (off Map p155; ☎ 2419 3857; 5 Sharia Shafik al-Dib, Ard al-Golf; ☺ 10am-10pm Sun-Thu); Mounira (Map pp112-13; ☎ 2794 7679; 1 Sharia Madrassat al-Huquq al-Fransiyya; ☺ 11am-7pm Sun-Tue, Thu & Fri, 11am-8pm Wed) Regularly puts on films, lectures and exhibitions, opens its libraries to the public and screens French-language

news from TV5. The Mounira branch also runs French- and Arabic-language courses.

Egyptian Centre for International Cultural Cooperation (Map pp146-7; ☎ 2736 5410; 11 Sharia Shagaret ad-Durr, Zamalek; ☺ 10am-3pm & 4-9pm Sat-Thu) Organises concerts of Egyptian composers, as well as good classical and colloquial Arabic classes.

El Sawy Culture Wheel (El Sakia; Map pp146-7; ☎ 2736 8881; www.culturewheel.com; Sharia 26th of July, Zamalek; ☺ 9am-9pm) Excellent lively space that hosts concerts, art exhibitions, theatre, films and even yoga classes and children's puppet shows. Tickets for shows are on sale at Cilantro coffee shops around town.

Goethe Institut (www.goethe.de) Doqqi (Map p150; ☎ 3748 4501; 5 Sharia Hussein Wassef); Downtown (Map pp120-1; ☎ 2575 9877; 5 Sharia al-Bustan; ☺ library 1-7pm Sun-Wed) Seminars and lectures in German on Egyptology and other topics, plus visiting music groups, art exhibitions and film screenings. The library has more than 15,000 (mainly German) titles. The Doqqi location focuses on language classes.

Great Cairo Library (Map pp146-7; ☎ 2736 2271; 15 Sharia Mohammed Mazhar, Zamalek; ☺ 9am-4pm Sat-Thu) The city's best public library, stocked with a collection of art, science and other reference books, mainly in English. It also has English-language magazines for browsing. Show your passport to enter.

Instituto Cervantes (Map p150; ☎ 3337 1962; www .elcairo.cervantes.es; 20 Sharia Boulos Hanna, Doqqi; ☺ 9am-4pm Sun-Thu) Spanish language and cultural institute, screening films and organising lectures.

Istituto Italiano di Cultura (Map pp146-7; ☎ 2735 8791; www.iiccairo.esteri.it; 3 Sharia Sheikh al-Marsafy, Zamalek; ☺ library 10am-4pm Sun, Tue & Thu) A busy program of films and lectures (sometimes in English) and art exhibitions, plus a library.

Netherlands-Flemish Institute (Map pp146-7; ☎ 2738 2520; www.nvic.leidenuniv.nl; 1 Sharia Mahmoud Azmy, Zamalek; ☺ 9am-2pm Sun-Thu) This centre hosts art exhibitions and is well regarded for its weekly lectures, delivered on a wide variety of topics and usually in English.

Emergency

In the case of an accident or injury, call the As-Salam International Hospital (opposite). For details on lost credit cards, see p516. For anything more serious, contact your embassy (see p511).

Ambulance (☎ 123)
Fire service (☎ 180)
Police (☎ 122)

The **main tourist police office** (Map pp120-1; ☎ 2390 6028, emergency 126) is on the 1st floor of a building in the alley just left of the main tourist office in Downtown. This should be your first port of call for minor emergencies, including theft; there are other offices by the Pyramids, across from Mena House (Map p152) and in Khan al-Khalili (Map p131).

Internet Access

Internet access is fairly cheap in Cairo, averaging around E£5 per hour. While there are cybercafes scattered throughout town, they're not exactly plentiful. These are the most conveniently located:

4U Internet Café (Map pp120-1; ☎ 2575 9304; 1st fl, 6 Midan Talaat Harb, Downtown; ☺ 24hr) Under the Lialy Hostel.

Five St@rs Net (Map pp120-1; ☎ 2574 7881; 1st fl, 6 Midan Talaat Harb, Downtown; ☺ 24hr) Opposite 4U Internet; dodgier computers.

Hany Internet Café (Map pp120-1; ☎ 2395 1985; 16 Sharia Abdel Khalek Sarwat, Downtown; ☺ 10am-8pm) Bargain rates and open windows, so relatively smoke-free.

InterClub (Map pp120-1; ☎ 2579 1860; 12 Sharia Talaat Harb, Downtown; ☺ 8am-2am) Nice flat-screens, with printing, faxing and scanning services; in alley next to Estoril restaurant.

Memories Net (Map pp120-1; ☎ 018 169 6471; 12 Sharia Mahmoud Bassiouni, Downtown; ☺ 10am-2am) Cool cave ambience located down an alley.

Sigma Net (Map pp146-7; ☎ 2738 0516; Sharia Gezirat al-Wusta, Zamalek; ☺ 24hr) Opposite Golden Tulip Flamenco Hotel. Fast connections and good air-con.

Zamalek Center (Map pp146-7; ☎ 2736 4004; 25 Sharia Ismail Mohammed, Zamalek; ☺ 24hr) A bit smoky, but has the best rates in the area; offers other business services too.

Internet Resources

Cairo, Egypt (www.cairotourist.com) Virtual tours of Pharaonic, Coptic, Islamic and modern Cairo; hotel and restaurant listings are not kept up to date, however.

cairolive.com (www.cairolive.com) Online news aggregator and magazine with views on Cairo's cultural events, political developments and general news. Useful kids' section.

Egy.com (www.egy.com) A great website by Egyptian social historian and journalist Samir Raafat, with articles on architecture, events and people in 19th- and 20th-century Cairo, with an interesting section on the city's Jewish community.

Guardian's Egypt (www.guardians.net) Great site covering the Giza, Dahshur and Saqqara pyramid sites. Has photos, articles about recent discoveries, and bulletins from Dr Zahi Hawass, the secretary-general of the Supreme Council of Antiquities.

Yallabina (www.yallabina.com) Devoted to the Big Mango's nightlife, with restaurant and bar reviews, plus listings for concerts, events and films.

Media

The monthly magazine *Egypt Today* (E£15; also online at www.egypttoday.com) covers major social and economic issues and also includes basic listings. The *Daily Star Egypt* comes as an insert in the *International Herald-Tribune* (E£10); a spin-off of the quality Beirut paper, it's the most informative news in English. The flimsy daily *Egyptian Gazette* (50pt) and the more substantial *Al-Ahram Weekly* (E£1) are the other English-language rags. For a hipper perspective, pick up a free copy of the *Croc*, a monthly listings flyer found at many restaurants and galleries; it includes restaurant reviews and other informative articles.

Medical Services

HOSPITALS

Many of Cairo's hospitals suffer from antiquated equipment and a cavalier attitude to hygiene, but there are several exceptions. Your embassy should be able to recommend doctors and hospitals. Other options: .

Anglo-American Hospital (Map p150; ☎ 2735 6162/5; Sharia Hadayek al-Zuhreyya, Gezira) West of the Cairo Tower.

As-Salam International Hospital Ma'adi (off Map pp112-13; ☎ 2524 0250, emergency 2524 0077; Corniche el-Nil); Mohandiseen (Map pp146-7; ☎ 3303 0502; 3 Sharia Syria) The Ma'adi branch has a better reputation.

PHARMACIES

In Egyptian pharmacies almost any medicine can be obtained without prescription. Some pharmacies are major drop-in centres, while others can be contacted by phone. The pharmacies operate 24 hours, have English-speaking staff and will deliver to your hotel.

Al-Ezaby (Map pp146-7; ☎ 19600)

Ali & Ali Downtown (☎ 2365 3880); Mohandiseen (☎ 3302 1421)

Delmar (Map pp120 1; ☎ 2575 1052; Downtown) At the corner of Sharia 26th of July and Sharia Mohammed Farid.

New Victoria Pharmacy (☎ 2735 1628; Zamalek)

Seif Pharmacy (☎ 19199)

Money

For general information about money, foreign exchange bureaus and transferring funds, see p515. For banking hours, see p507. The Banque Misr branches located at the Nile

Hotel and Mena House Oberoi hotels are open 24 hours. Hotel branches of the big banks are happy to change your cash, but rates are slightly better at independent exchange bureaus, of which there are several along Sharia Adly in Downtown and on Sharia 26th of July in Zamalek. These tend to be open from 10am to 8pm Saturday to Thursday.

American Express (Amex; www.americanexpress .com.eg; ⊕ 9am-5pm Sat-Thu) Downtown (Map pp120-1; ☎ 2574 7991; 15 Sharia Qasr el-Nil); Downtown (Map pp120-1; ☎ 2578 5001; Nile Hotel); Heliopolis (off Map p155; ☎ 2418 2144; 33 Sharia Nabil al-Wakkad, Ard al-Golf) All offices will hold mail for cardholders and give cash advances on gold and platinum cards.

Citibank (www.citibankegypt.com) Garden City (Map p150; ☎ 2795 1873; 4 Sharia Ahmad Pasha); Zamalek (Map pp146-7; ☎ 2736 5622; 4A Sharia al-Gezira)

Thomas Cook (☎ emergency 010 140 1367; www .thomascookegypt.com; ⊕ 8am-4.30pm Sat-Thu) Airport (☎ 2265 4447); Downtown (Map pp120-1; ☎ 2574 3776; 17 Sharia Mahmoud Bassiouni); Heliopolis (Map p155; ☎ 2416 4000; 7 Sharia Baghdad, Korba); Mohandiseen (Map pp146-7; ☎ 3344 0008; 10 Sharia 26th of July); Zamalek (Map pp146-7; ☎ 2735 9223; 3 Sharia Abu al-Feda)

ATMS

ATMs are located on all major streets, in shopping malls and in the foyers of five-star hotels. The only place they're hard to find is in Islamic Cairo – the most convenient machine here is below El Hussein (Map p131) in Khan al-Khalili. The ones in hotels are the most reliable.

Post

Marked with green-and-yellow signs, post offices are numerous, though not all have signs in English explaining which window is meant for what business.

Express Mail Service (EMS; Map pp120-1; ☎ 2390 5874; fax 2390 4250; ⊕ 24hr) Opposite the poste restante office. Most post offices also have an EMS counter.

Main post office (Map pp120-1; Midan Ataba; ⊕ 8am-10pm Sat-Thu)

Post traffic centre (Map p124; Midan Ramses; ⊕ 8.30am-3pm Sat-Thu) Come here to send packages abroad. Bring your passport. Leave your package unsealed, to be inspected; someone will then wrap the parcel for you for a small charge, or you can supply your own tape. The process is bureaucratic, but not utterly maddening.

Poste restante (Map pp120-1; ⊕ 8am-2.30pm Sat-Thu) On the side street to the right of the main post office, with the entrance on the cross street one block down. Mail is usually held for three weeks. It's divided into three

sections: letters (window 10), packages (window 1) and registered mail (upstairs). Take your passport.

Zamalek post office (Map pp146-7; Sharia Brazil; ⊕ 8am 3pm Sat Thu)

Telephone & Fax

Cardphones Menatel cardphones are all over the city, although the practice of placing them on street corners (or streets, for that matter) can make it hard to hear.

Faxes These can be sent to/from the Telephone centrales on Midan Tahrir, Sharia Adly and Sharia Alfy. You can also send and receive them from the EMS main office in Ataba (see left) and from a couple of internet cafes (see p115).

Telephone centrales Downtown (Map pp120-1; fax 2578 0979; 13 Midan Tahrir; ⊕ 24hr); Downtown (Map pp120-1; fax 2393 3903; 8 Sharia Adly; ⊕ 24hr); Downtown (Map pp120-1; fax 2589 7635; Sharia Alfy; ⊕ 24hr); Downtown (Map pp120-1; Sharia Ramses; ⊕ 24hr); Zamalek (Map pp146-7; Sharia 26th of July) The branch on Sharia Alfy is next to the Windsor Hotel. The Sharia Ramses branch is opposite Sharia Tawfiqiyya.

Tourist Information

Cairo International Airport tourist office Terminal I (☎ 2265 3642; ⊕ 24hr); Terminal II (☎ 2265 2269; ⊕ 24hr)

Main tourist office (Map pp120-1; ☎ 2391 3454; 5 Sharia Adly; ⊕ 8.30am-7pm)

Pyramids tourist office (Map p152; ☎ 3383 8823; Pyramids Rd; ⊕ 8.30am-5pm) Opposite Mena House Oberoi.

Ramses Station tourist office (Map p179; ☎ 2579 0767; ⊕ 9am-7pm) Next to the Abela Sleeping Train office.

Travel Agencies

The streets around Midan Tahrir teem with travel agencies, but don't expect amazing deals. Instead, watch out for dodgy operators (see p510). Amex and Thomas Cook (see p115) offer reliable service. Other recommendations:

Backpacker Concierge (☎ 016 350 7118; www .backpackerconcierge.com) An excellent boutique start-up that offers customised travel packages with a strong emphasis on culturally and environmentally responsible service. Although they don't have an official office, they are incredibly tech savvy, and can communicate with you via phone, email, Facebook and even Twitter. Their most popular packages are desert safaris and Nile cruises, but there are myriad possibilities here for individually catered holidays.

Egypt Panorama Tours (☎ 2359 0200; www.eptours .com; 4 Rd 79, Ma'adi; ⊕ 9am-5pm) Opposite Ma'adi metro station, this is one of the best and most reputable agencies in town, though it's a long way from Downtown. Fortunately it will book tickets, tours and hotel rooms over the phone and courier the documents to you, if necessary, for a reasonable fee. Efficient staff speak excellent English. It's good for cheap airfares, four- and five-star hotel deals and tours within Egypt and around the Mediterranean.

Misr Travel (Map pp120-1; ☎ 2393 0259; www.misr travel.net; 7 Sharia Talaat Harb, Downtown) The official Egyptian government travel agency, which also has offices in most of the luxury hotels.

Travco (Map pp146-7; ☎ 2736 2042; www.travcotravel .com; 13 Sharia Mahmoud Azmy, Zamalek) The highly regarded Zamalek branch of an Egyptwide travel group.

DANGERS & ANNOYANCES

You can walk almost wherever you like in Cairo, at any time of day or night, as long as you are properly dressed and a little street-wise. That said, single women should still be careful when walking alone at night.

Terrorism

In February 2009, Cairo was the scene of three separate acts of terrorism that were specifically aimed at tourists. Although none of the attacks were deemed sophisticated by Egyptian security officials, a 17-year-old French girl was brutally killed when a bomb exploded in Khan al-Khalili market. The second incident involved the stabbing of an American teacher in the face, while the third was a failed firebombing of a passing train on the Cairo metro. The motivation behind these attacks was not clear, though they did coincide with Egyptians protesting the closure of the border with the Gaza strip.

On 7 April 2005, Khan al-Khalili was the scene of a suicide bombing that killed two French tourists and one American tourist, in addition to injuring 11 Egyptians and seven other foreign nationals. Three weeks later, another man suspected of involvement in the attack was being trailed by police when he leapt off the 6th of October Bridge onto Gezira Island. The landing detonated the nail bomb that he was carrying, resulting in his death along with injuries to seven others. A few hours later, two women opened fire on a tourist coach near the Citadel, injuring three, before one of the shooters turned the gun on herself.

The Mujahedeen of Egypt and the Abdullah Azzam Brigades claimed responsibility for these attacks, citing the government's clampdown on dissidents in the wake of the Sinai Peninsula bombings of October 2004 (see p460 for more information). Shortly after, government antiterrorism squads detained more than 200 individuals for questioning, which eventually lead to the prosecution of nine plotters on 20 August, 2007.

Overall security is currently good in the area but it's advisable to be aware of the history, and to check travel advisories before your trip.

Theft

Theft is not a big problem, but it pays to be safe. We regularly receive letters from readers who have had items stolen from locked hotel rooms and even from safes, so think about keeping money and valuables on you or locked in a suitcase. Pickpockets are rare, but do sometimes operate in crowded spots such as Khan al-Khalili, the Birqash camel market, the metro and buses. If anything does get stolen go straight to the tourist police (p114).

Scams & Hassles

Scams in Cairo are so numerous that there's no way to list them all. There are roughly four types: hotel scams (see p159), overcharging on tours to elsewhere in Egypt, shopping cons and funny business involving tickets to monuments.

The worst scams afflicting Cairo are associated with tours. Rather than making arrangements in Cairo, you are almost always better off booking tours in the place you'll be taking them. Reputable agencies (see opposite) are completely outnumbered by dodgy operators. Despite the steady pressure you'll receive, we can't emphasise enough that it's *not* a good idea to book flights, felucca cruises and the like through Cairo hotels – you will inevitably pay more to cover their commission on the transaction. Also be wary of travel agencies in the Downtown area. Many rent space to unscrupulous types who will charge well over the odds for arrangements they make. If you return to complain, the agency will say that you booked through a freelance agent unassociated with the company. And finally: never, ever book a tour through a tout you meet on the street or in a souvenir shop.

Shopping scams are nearly as prevalent, but less nefarious. For the most part, they are conversation-starters to lure you into stores. Most of these routines would be dully obvious, if not for the special conviction with which the

CAIRO

more talented con artists deliver them. Around the Egyptian Museum, for instance, a charming chap approaches foreigners to ask if they're looking for the museum entrance or the bus to the Pyramids. If the answer is yes, he asserts that it's prayer time/lunchtime/any-inventive-reason time and that the museum is temporarily closed and the bus isn't running. Then he suggests that while they're waiting, they may be interested in going to the nearby 'Government Bazaar', which happens to be having its annual sale that day. Needless to say, there's a sale every day, it's not much of a sale, the bazaar isn't government run and he'll collect a commission on anything you purchase…

When you're in Downtown or Islamic Cairo, locals may start walking next to you, offering help or chatting. These are usually touts who want to direct you into shops where they'll earn a commission. They can be persistent, but telling them you just want to walk and know where you're going, with a joke thrown in to keep everything amicable, will save you a lot of hassle.

Other shopping scams include the old 'two for five pounds' hard sell (when you go to pay, the stallholder will say that he meant five *British* pounds), the dried-banana-leaf-instead-of-papyrus con and the safflower-not-saffron spice trade.

When visiting monuments in Islamic Cairo, it pays to know that, with two exceptions, all mosques are free to enter, as they are places of worship. But some caretakers will claim an admission price – if you're not sure it's legit, ask if there is a ticket ('fee taz-*kar*-a?') and politely refuse payment if there is none. In officially ticketed monuments, some guards will attempt to resell a previous visitor's ticket (cadged by another guard inside, assuring the visitor it's 'normal' to hand it over). If it is not torn out of the book in front of you, it's reused. As it doesn't affect what you pay, it's up to you whether you object, but doing so might send a larger signal that most tourists prefer business on the up-and-up.

Most common is a stream of people asking for baksheesh (alms, tip); this is legitimate and expected, but be firm and don't pay more than you want to (E£5 per monument is reasonable, plus another E£2 or E£3 if you climb a minaret).

Finally, be aware that fake International Student Identity Cards (ISIC) are sold by scam artists in Downtown. For more information on ISIC cards see p510.

SIGHTS

Cairo's sights are spread all over the city, so it makes sense to do things in one area before moving on to the next – but don't try to cram too much into one day, or you'll soon be overwhelmed. The awe-inspiring but cluttered Egyptian Museum requires at least half a day, but could easily merit a second visit. Khan al-Khalili and most of the medieval monuments are in Islamic Cairo, and you'll need a full day or several shorter visits to appreciate them. Definitely allow a few hours of aimless wandering in this area (even if it comes at the expense of 'proper' sightseeing), as the back lanes give the truest sense of the city. The Pyramids and tombs of Giza, Saqqara and Dahshur require a whole extra day. Coptic Cairo can be toured in a morning – made especially easy by Metro access – and you'll

---

HOW TO BLEND IN

Even if your skin colouring allows it, it's next to impossible to 'pass' as a native Cairene. But you can look more like a resident expat, thus deflecting attention onto the more obvious tourists walking behind you – and giving you more opportunity to enjoy the good things about Cairo. Here's how:

■ Carry your stuff in a plastic shopping bag or a generic tote. Nothing screams 'tourist' like a multipocketed, extra-zippered, heavy-duty-nylon backpack with visible water bottle.

■ Wear impractical shoes. This is a city. Fashion counts.

■ Cover up your legs – this goes for men and women. Islamic rules aside, Egyptians simply have a higher level of modesty, and it's clear you haven't been here long if you don't feel embarrassed to show your knees in public.

■ Carry a copy of *Al-Ahram Weekly* – or the Arabic *Al-Ahram*, if you want to go deep undercover.

■ Learn and use the local nonverbal cues (see boxed text, p164).

likely soak up Downtown's atmosphere just by going to and from your hotel, or by hanging out there in the evenings.

Central Cairo

Though the Egyptian Museum is found here, the part of town between Midan Ramses and Midan Tahrir, which locals call Wust al-Balad, is better known for its practical offerings: budget hotels, eateries and a dazzling stream of window displays (don't use that shoe store/lingerie shop/prosthetic-limbs dealer as a landmark; trust us – there's another one just a block away). Occasionally try to look away from the traffic and fluorescent-lit shops and up at the elegant Empire-style office and apartment buildings that drip faded glamour (or is that an air-conditioner leaking?). It's a wonderful part of town to explore – just be prepared for total sensory overload after a few hours.

MIDAN TAHRIR & AROUND

With half-a-dozen major arteries converging, Midan Tahrir (Liberation Sq) is the fulcrum of modern-day Cairo, and as a result the site of some serious traffic and pedestrian jams. But the square is one of the few central spaces that isn't hemmed in by buildings and overpasses, making it an excellent spot to have a look around and orient yourself.

One of the most distinctive location aids is the Nile Hotel (p161), the blue-and-white slab that stands between Midan Tahrir and the Nile. When it was built in 1959 it was the first modern hotel in Cairo, replacing a former British Army barracks. Due north is the neo-classical bulk of the Egyptian Museum (p183), painted a lurid shade of pink, while south is the **Arab League Building** (Map pp120–1), the occasional gathering place of leaders from around the Middle East.

If continuing around Midan Tahrir anti-clockwise, you'll see the ornate white palace of the **Ministry of Foreign Affairs**. Adjacent **Omar Makram Mosque** (Map pp120–1) is the place where anybody who's anybody has a funeral. The rest of the south side is occupied by the monstrous **Mogamma** (Map pp120–1), home to 18,000 civil servants – this is where you come for visa extensions (see p520).

If the Soviet-funded Mogamma symbol-ises Egypt's quasi-socialist past, then the next building around, across four-lane Qasr al-Ainy, represents the current energy of pri-vate enterprise: the **American University in Cairo** (AUC; Map pp120–1), the college of choice for the sons and daughters of Egypt's stratos-pherically wealthy. In 2008, a new campus opened in the eastern suburb of New Cairo, though that won't stop average Egyptians from imagining the Western-inspired de-bauchery that goes on behind the tall fences. This campus has an attractive courtyard and a good bookshop (p111). You must hand over your passport to enter at the gate on Sharia Mohammed Mahmoud, opposite the enter-prisingly sited McDonald's.

The buildings then break for Sharia Tahrir, which leads 300m east to a busy square (Midan Falaki) with the indoor veg-and-meat **Souq Bab al-Luq** to one side. Continuing east brings you to Midan al-Gomhuriyya, a scraggly grass square skirted by speeding traffic. The great building to the east, dominating the square, is Abdeen Palace, former residence of the rulers of Egypt.

Abdeen Palace

Begun in 1863 and employing Europe's most lavish architects and designers, **Abdeen Palace** (Qasr Abdeen; Map pp120–1; ☎ 2391 0042; Midan al-Gomhuriyya; adult/student E£10/5; ☷ 9am-2.45pm Sat-Thu) was a centrepiece of Khedive Ismail's plan for a modern Cairo, inspired by Paris' recent makeover; the khedive even called in master-mind French planner Baron Haussmann as a consultant. He wanted the palace finished for the 1869 opening of the Suez Canal, to impress visiting dignitaries, but its 500 rooms weren't completed until 1874. It was the royal residence until the monarchy was abolished in 1952, then became the presidential pal-ace. President Mubarak prefers his digs in Heliopolis, but uses Abdeen for official oc-casions. One section, though not the ritzy royal chambers, is open to the public (enter on Sharia Mustafa Abdel Raziq); its halls are filled with a vast array of weaponry, ranging from ceremonial daggers to howitzers.

DOWNTOWN

In the commercial heart of Cairo, glitzy shops and thousands of small businesses are wedged into the ground floors of glorious (if dust-caked) buildings that represent every archi-tectural fantasy of the 19th and early 20th centuries. The two main streets, Sharia Talaat Harb and Sharia Qasr el-Nil, intersect at the traffic circle of Midan Talaat Harb, where cars

CENTRAL CAIRO

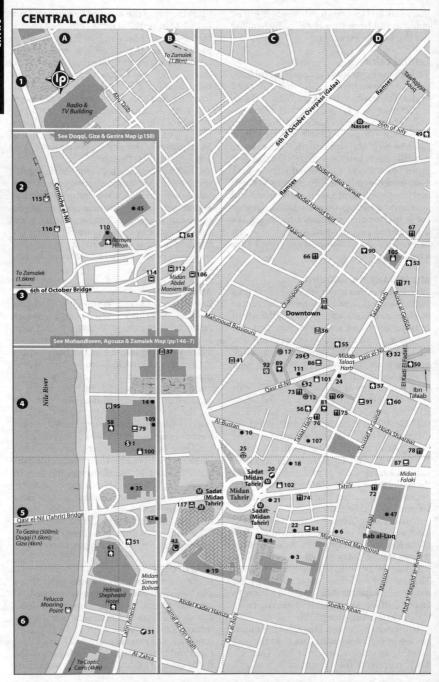

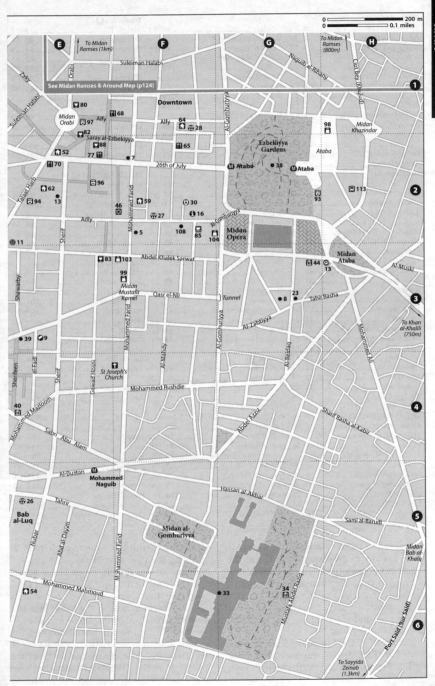

CAIRO

whiz around a statue of tarboosh-sporting Mr Harb, founder of the National Bank. On the square is Groppi's (p169), in its heyday one of the most celebrated patisseries this side of the Mediterranean and *the* venue for ritzy society functions and concert dances. Gold mosaics around the doorway are, alas, the only remaining glitter.

Just south of the square on Sharia Talaat Harb, Café Riche (p165) was once a hang-out for Egyptian writers and intellectuals. Nasser allegedly met with his collaborators here while planning the 1952 Revolution.

North of the square, shops along Sharia Qasr el-Nil sell a drag queen's dream of footwear. The street itself boasts some particularly fine architecture, notably the **Italian Insurance building** (Map pp120–1), on the corner of Qasr el-Nil and Sharia Sherifeen, and the Cosmopolitan Hotel (p161), a short block off Qasr el-Nil. The area around the hotel and the neighbouring **Cairo Stock Exchange** has been pedestrianised, so you can savour both the turn-of-the-century architecture and some relative quiet.

Over on Sharia Talaat Harb, **Cinema Metro** (Map pp120–1) is a 1930s movie palace: when it first opened, with *Gone with the Wind*, it boasted a Ford showroom and a diner. One block east of the cinema, along Sharia Adly, **Shar Hashamaim Synagogue** (Map pp120–1) is one of the few remaining testaments to Cairo's once-thriving Jewish community. While the stark art nouveau architecture is intimidating enough, the heavy police presence makes for a rather tense scene. The interior is open daily to the public. You will need to present a passport and pass through a rigorous security check.

Further east on Adly is the faded Groppi Garden (p169) – actually the first Cairo outpost of Italian chocolatier Giacomo Groppi, and site of the city's first outdoor cinema. During WWII it was known as a place where Egyptians and Europeans mixed easily – particularly Allied troops and the local ladies.

A block north of Adly is Sharia 26th of July, named for the date Egypt's last king, Farouk, abdicated. As far as Cairenes are concerned, the street's major attraction is El-Abd Bakery (p164), packed every morning to midnight with locals jostling for cakes, sweets and delicious pastries (there's also a branch on Sharia Talaat Harb).

Another block north, pedestrianised Sharia Saray al-Ezbekiyya and Sharia Alfy are Downtown's nightlife centre, with kebab joints, seedy bars, dubious belly-dancing joints, countless opportunities for sidewalk *sheesha* smoking and a 24-hour eating place in Akher Sa'a (p165).

East along Sharia 26th of July leads to **Ezbekiyya Gardens** (Map pp120–1), which look nicer than they ever have – but are open only to those who pay (E£2). The famous Shepheard's Hotel was once located opposite – it was the preferred accommodation of the British colonial classes for a century, until it was destroyed by Black Saturday rioters in 1952 (see p42). Next to the gardens Midan Opera marks the site of the old opera house, which burnt down in 1971 – rebuilt as a towering car park. Beyond the car park, to the east, is Midan Ataba.

MIDAN ATABA
Here, 'modern European' Cairo runs up against the old medieval Cairo of Saladin (Salah ad-Din), the Mamluks and the Ottomans. A mass of buses and hawkers, the area seems like one traffic-clogged bazaar – though the goods now are vinyl shoes and acetate ball gowns, not fine silks and gold as in centuries past. Off the southwest side, past the flyover, the domed **main post office** (Map pp120–1) has a pretty courtyard. A window immediately on your right is where you buy tickets to the neighbouring **Postal Museum** (Map pp120–1; ☎ 2391 0011; 2nd fl, Midan Ataba; admission E£2; ☉ 8am-3pm), a beautifully maintained collection of stamps, uniforms and even tiny scale models of great post offices throughout Egypt.

On the north side of the square, behind the modernist white Cairo Puppet Theatre (p157), are the stalls of the Ezbekiyya Book Market (p174).

Further east beyond that is Midan Khazindar and running north from there is Sharia Clot Bey (aka Sharia Khulud), named after a French physician who introduced Western ideas about public health to Mohammed Ali's Egypt. That didn't stop the street from becoming the diseased heart of Cairo's red-light district, known as 'the Berka' ('the blessing', with ladles of irony), an area of brothels, peepshows and cabarets. These days it's a shabby but charming street with arcades over the pavements sheltering sepia-toned coffeehouses and eating places. It eventually comes out onto Midan Ramses.

MIDAN RAMSES & AROUND
The northern gateway into central Cairo, Midan Ramses (Map p124) is a byword for bedlam. The city's main north–south access collides with overpasses and numerous arterial roads to swamp the square with an unchoreographed slew of minibuses, buses, taxis and cars. Commuters swarming from the train station add to the melee.

The eponymous Ramses, a multistorey Pharaonic colossus of red granite, stood sentinel amid the traffic to greet new visitors to the city until 2006, when he was removed to protect him from further pollution damage – a process that required major machinery and road closures. He will stand at the entrance of the Grand Egyptian Museum (GEM) in Giza, slated to open (perhaps) in 2012. For more information, see p154.

Ramses Station (Mahattat Ramses; Map p124) is an attractive marriage of Islamic style and industrial-age engineering. At its

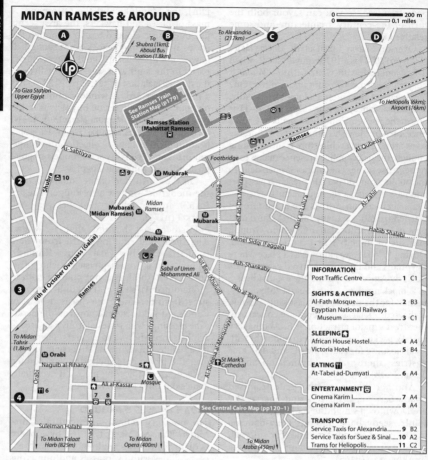

MIDAN RAMSES & AROUND

INFORMATION
Post Traffic Centre........................... **1** C1

SIGHTS & ACTIVITIES
Al-Fath Mosque............................... **2** B3
Egyptian National Railways
  Museum....................................... **3** C1

SLEEPING
African House Hostel........................ **4** A4
Victoria Hotel.................................. **5** B4

EATING
At-Tabei ad-Dumyati........................ **6** A4

ENTERTAINMENT
Cinema Karim I................................. **7** A4
Cinema Karim II............................... **8** A4

TRANSPORT
Service Taxis for Alexandria............ **9** B2
Service Taxis for Suez & Sinai.......**10** A2
Trams for Heliopolis........................**11** C2

eastern end it houses the **Egyptian National Railways Museum** (Map p124; ☎ 2576 3793; Midan Ramses; admission E£10, Fri & public holidays E£20; ❂ 9am-2pm Tue-Sun) with a beautiful but somewhat dilapidated collection of old locomotives, including one built for Empress Eugénie on the occasion of the opening of the Suez Canal.

On the south side of the square is Cairo's pre-eminent orientation aid, **Al-Fath Mosque** (Map p124). Completed in the early 1990s, the mosque's minaret is visible from just about anywhere in central and Islamic Cairo.

GARDEN CITY & RHODA

Garden City (Map p150) was developed in the early 1900s along the lines of an English garden suburb. Its curving, tree-lined streets were designed for tranquillity, while its proximity to the British embassy was no doubt intended to convey security. Many of the enclave's elegant villas have fallen prey to quick-buck developers, but enough grand architecture and lush trees survive to make a wander through the streets worthwhile – at sunset, the air of faded romance is palpable (see p157).

Or you can walk directly (if a bit less scenically) south along the noisy Corniche el-Nil. It takes only 20 minutes to walk from Midan Tahrir to the small Manial Bridge. Crossing this, you arrive at the **Manial Palace Museum** (Mathaf al-Manial; Map p150; ☎ 2368 7495; Sharia al-Saray, Manial; adult/student E£25/12; ❂ 9am-4pm, during Ramadan 9am-3pm). One of Cairo's most eccentric tourist sites, the palace was built by the uncle of King

Farouk, Prince Mohammed Ali, in the early 20th century. Apparently he couldn't decide which architectural style he preferred, so he went for the lot: Ottoman, Moorish, Persian and European rococo. The palace contains, among other things, Farouk's horde of hunting trophies and the prince's collection of medieval manuscripts, clothing and other items. The gardens are planted with rare tropical plants collected by the prince on his travels. If you don't want to walk to the museum, a taxi from Midan Tahrir should cost E£4. Note that the museum was closed at the time of research, though it's scheduled to reopen during the life of this book.

A 15-minute walk south along the eastern side of the island, past lush plant nurseries, takes you to its southern tip, home to Monastirli Palace, the Umm Kolthum Museum and a Nilometer (see below). From there, it's an easy walk on to Old Cairo.

Monastirli Palace & Umm Kolthum Museum

Set in a peaceful Nileside garden, **Monastirli Palace** (Map p126) was built in 1851 for an Ottoman pasha whose family hailed from Monastir, in northern Greece. The *salamlik* (greeting area) that he built for public functions is now an elegant venue for concerts, while the other part is now the **Umm Kolthum Museum** (Map p126; ☎ 2363 1467; Sharia al-Malek as-Salih, Rhoda; adult/student E£6/3; ☼ 10am-5pm). Dedicated to the most famous Arab diva, the small museum is more like a shrine, given the reverence with which the singer's signature rhinestone-trimmed glasses and glittery gowns are hung under spotlights in display cases. There's a multimedia room where you can listen to her music, and a short film shows key moments of her life, from the beginning when she performed disguised as a Bedouin boy, to her magnetic performances that brought Cairo to a standstill, to her funeral, when millions of mourners flooded the streets.

Nilometer

Built in AD 861, the **Nilometer** (Map p126; Sharia al-Malek as-Salih, Rhoda; admission E£10; ☼ 10am-5pm) was designed to measure the rise and fall of the river, and thus predict the fortunes of the annual harvest. If the water rose to 16 cubits (a cubit is about the length of a forearm) the harvest was likely to be good, inspiring one of the greatest celebrations of the medieval era; any

higher, though, and the flooding could be disastrous, and lower levels presaged hunger. The Turkish-style pencil-point dome is a Farouk-era reconstruction of an earlier one wrecked by Napoleon's troops. The measuring device, a graduated column, sits below the level of the Nile at the bottom of a flight of precipitous steps, which the guard will cheerfully let you descend for a little baksheesh.

Old Cairo

Broadly speaking, Old Cairo (Misr al-Qadima, with a glottal-stop 'Q'; Map p126) incorporates the area south of Garden City down to the quarter known to foreigners as Coptic Cairo. Most visitors head straight to the latter. From there, you can also visit the Mosque of Amr ibn al-As.

In this traditional part of Cairo appropriate dress is essential. Visitors of either sex wearing shorts or showing their shoulders will not be allowed into churches or mosques. The liveliest time to visit is on a Sunday, when Cairene Copts come for services; but if you want a quiet wander, avoid Sunday and Friday as well. The churches do not charge admission, but most have donation boxes.

The easiest way of getting here is by metro: trains run every few minutes, and Mar Girgis station is right outside the Coptic Cairo compound. It's much better than a crowded bus (though the trip back to Tahrir isn't as bad because you can board the bus at the terminal, beside the Mosque of Amr ibn al-As, and be sure of a seat). A slow but pleasant option is to take the orange-and-green river bus *(autobees nahri)* from the Maspero dock (Map pp120–1) to its last stop at Misr al-Qadima in Old Cairo. From there it's a 10-minute walk east to the main cluster of churches. The service runs at 8am, 2pm and 9pm and costs E£1.

COPTIC CAIRO

Coptic Cairo (Map p126) is the heartland of Egypt's indigenous Christian community, a haven of tranquillity and peace that reveals layers of history. Archaeologists have found traces of a small Nileside settlement on this site from as early as the 6th century BC. In the 2nd century AD the Romans established a fortress here, called 'Babylon in Egypt'. The name Babylon is most likely a Roman corruption of 'Per-hapi-en-on' (Estate of the Nile God at On), a Pharaonic name for ancient Heliopolis.

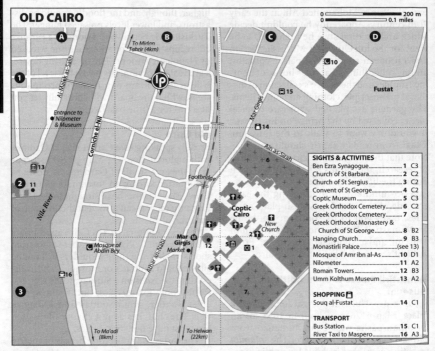

OLD CAIRO

SIGHTS & ACTIVITIES	
Ben Ezra Synagogue.................... 1	C3
Church of St Barbara.................. 2	C2
Church of St Sergius................... 3	C2
Convent of St George................. 4	C2
Coptic Museum.......................... 5	C3
Greek Orthodox Cemetery......... 6	C2
Greek Orthodox Cemetery......... 7	C3
Greek Orthodox Monastery &	
Church of St George............... 8	B2
Hanging Church.......................... 9	B3
Monastirli Palace....................(see 13)	
Mosque of Amr ibn al-As......... 10	D1
Nilometer................................ 11	A2
Roman Towers.......................... 12	B3
Umm Kolthum Museum............ 13	A2

SHOPPING	
Souq al-Fustat........................ 14	C1

TRANSPORT	
Bus Station............................. 15	C1
River Taxi to Maspero............. 16	A3

Babylon has always been a stronghold of Christianity. At one time there were more than 20 churches clustered within less than 1 sq km, though just a handful survive today. They are linked by narrow cobbled alleyways running between high stone walls: the place feels similar to parts of Jerusalem's Old City. That might not be mere coincidence, because when Jews were exiled from their holy city in AD 70, some found refuge in Egypt; the country's oldest synagogue is here in Coptic Cairo. There are three entrances to the Coptic compound: a sunken staircase beside the footbridge over the metro gives access to most churches and the synagogue; the main gate in the centre is for the Coptic Museum; and another doorway further south leads to the Hanging Church.

Roman Towers

The main entrance to the Coptic compound lies between the remains of the two round **towers** (Map p126) of Babylon's western gate. Built in AD 98 by Emperor Trajan, these were part of riverfront fortifications: at the time, the Nile would have lapped right up against them. Excavations around the southern tower have revealed part of the ancient quay, several metres below street level. The Greek Orthodox Monastery and Church of St George sit on top of the northern tower.

Coptic Museum

This **museum** (Map p126; ☎ 2363 9742; www.coptic museum.gov.eg; Sharia Mar Girgis; adult/student E£50/25; ⊙ 9am-4pm), founded in 1908, houses Coptic art from Graeco-Roman times to the Islamic era in a collection drawn from all over Egypt. Reopened after thorough renovation in 2006, it is a beautiful place, as much for the elaborate woodcarving in all the galleries as for the treasures they contain. These include a sculpture that shows obvious continuity from the Ptolemaic period, rich textiles and whole walls of monastery frescoes. There's a pleasant garden out front; a small cafe was not yet open at the time of research.

Hanging Church

Just south of the museum on Sharia Mar Girgis (the main road parallel with the metro), a stone facade inscribed with Coptic and Arabic marks the entrance to the **Hanging Church** (Al-Kineesa al-Mu'allaqa; Map p126; Sharia Mar Girgis; ☺ Coptic Mass 8-11am Fri, 9-11am Sun). Still in use for Mass and by parishioners who come to pray over a collection of saints' relics and an icon of Mary, this 9th-century (some say 7th-century) structure is called the Hanging or Suspended Church as it is built on top of the Water Gate of Roman Babylon. Steep stairs lead to a 19th-century facade topped by twin bell towers. In a small inner courtyard, vendors sell taped liturgies and videos of the Coptic pope, Shenouda III.

With its three barrel-vaulted, wooden-roofed aisles, the interior of the church feels like an upturned ark. Ivory-inlaid screens hiding the altar have intricate geometric designs that are distinguishable from Islamic designs only by the tiny crosses worked into the pattern. In front of them, a fine pulpit used only on Palm Sunday stands on 13 slender pillars that represent Christ and his disciples; one of the pillars, darker than the rest, is said to symbolise Judas. In the baptistry, off to the right, a panel has been cut out of the floor to reveal the Water Gate below.

Greek Orthodox Monastery & Church of St George

Back on the street, the first doorway north of the museum gate leads to the **Greek Orthodox Monastery** and **Church of St George** (Map p126). St George (Mar Girgis) is one of the region's most popular Christian saints. A Palestinian conscript in the Roman army, he was executed in AD 303 for resisting Emperor Diocletian's decree forbidding the practice of Christianity. There has been a church dedicated to him in Coptic Cairo since the 10th century; this one dates from 1909. The interior has been gutted by fires, but the stained-glass windows and blue-green tile ceiling remain bright and colourful. The neighbouring monastery is closed to visitors. The Coptic *moulid* (saints' festival) of Mar Girgis is held here on 23 April.

Convent of St George

Down a sunken staircase by the footbridge, along the alleyway, the first doorway on your left leads into the courtyard of the **Convent of St George** (Map p126). The convent is closed to visitors, but you can step down into the main hall and the chapel. Inside the latter is a beautiful wooden door, almost 8m high, behind which a small room is still occasionally

used for the chain-wrapping ritual that symbolises the persecution of St George during the Roman occupation. Occasionally, visitors wishing to be blessed are wrapped in chains by the resident nuns, who intone the requisite prayers. Usually, though, the nuns will merely offer to show you a chain that they claim was used to bind early martyrs.

Churches of St Sergius & St Barbara

To get to the **Church of St Sergius** (Abu Serga; Map p126; ☺ 8am-4pm), walk down the lane that the Convent of St George is on, following it around to the right. Duck under the low arch and walk a few steps more to the entrance, below street level. This is the oldest church inside the walls, with 3rd- and 4th-century pillars. It is said to be built over a cave where Joseph, Mary and the infant Jesus sheltered after fleeing to Egypt to escape persecution from King Herod of Judea, who had embarked upon a 'massacre of the first born'. The cave in question (now a crypt) is reached by descending steps to the left of the altar. Every year, on 1 June, a special mass is held here to commemorate the event.

Further along the alley, a passage leads to the left, where another church dedicated to St George is being restored; the passage ends at a shiny new church – a surprise in the middle of all the ancient stones (as are its superlative restrooms). Returning to the main walkway, the **Church of St Barbara** (Map p126) is at the corner; she was beaten to death by her father for trying to convert him to Christianity. Her relics supposedly rest in a small chapel left of the nave.

Beyond the church an iron gate leads to the large, peaceful (if a bit litter-strewn) **Greek Orthodox cemetery** (Map p126). Women on their own should be careful – we've heard reports of flashers lurking among the gravestones.

Ben Ezra Synagogue

To the right of the cemetery entrance, the 9th-century **Ben Ezra Synagogue** (Map p126; admission free, donations welcome) occupies the shell of a 4th-century Christian church. In the 12th century the synagogue was restored by Abraham Ben Ezra, rabbi of Jerusalem – hence its name. Tradition marks this as the spot where the prophet Jeremiah gathered the Jews in the 6th century after Nebuchadnezzar destroyed the Jerusalem temple. The adjacent spring is supposed to mark the place where the pharaoh's daughter found Moses in the reeds, and where Mary drew water to wash Jesus. In 1890, a cache of more than 250,000 papers, known as the Geniza documents, was uncovered in the synagogue; from them, researchers have been able to piece together details of the life of the North African Jewish community from the 11th to 13th centuries.

MOSQUE OF AMR IBN AL-AS

Sharia Mar Girgis leads north past Souq al-Fustat (p176), a covered market with quality crafts shops and a pricey cafe, to the **Mosque of Amr ibn al-As** (Map p126; Sharia Sidi Hassan al-Anwar, Old Cairo), the first mosque built in Egypt, constructed in AD 642 by the general who conquered Egypt for Islam. On the site where Ibn al-As pitched his tent, the original structure was only palm trunks thatched with leaves. It expanded to its current size in AD 827, and has been continuously reworked since then – recently, a wood roof was installed to mimic the original style more closely. The oldest section is to the right of the sanctuary; the rest of the mosque is a forest of some 200 different columns, the majority taken from ancient sites. There's little else to see, but the vast space is a pleasant place to rest.

Islamic Cairo

If you can, walk from Downtown Cairo east to this district, the core of the medieval city. In just 1.5km, centuries fall away – as you near Midan al-Hussein, traditional *galabiyyas* (men's full-length robes) begin to outnumber modern suits, buildings and crowds press closer on all sides, and the din comes less from car traffic and more from the cries of street vendors and the creak of cart wheels. Here

the aromas of mint and cumin mix with the stink of livestock, petrol and sewage – the real smell of the city. The effect can be disorientating and the casual visitor can lose not just a sense of direction but also a sense of time. Of all Cairo's districts, this is undoubtedly the most fascinating.

Although the atmosphere is different from Downtown, and certainly there is a profusion of minarets on the skyline, the term 'Islamic Cairo' is a bit of misnomer, as this area is not significantly more religious than other parts of the city. But it is Islamic in the sense that for many centuries, it was one of the power centres of the Islamic empire, a nexus of commerce and political intrigue. And the monuments that remain are some of the most resplendent examples of architecture inspired by the glory of Islam.

The Ministry of Culture is in the middle of an ambitious, costly and slow restoration program. Some conservation architects are concerned that monuments are being superficially rebuilt, with lashings of cement and no vision as to how the spaces will be used and maintained. Likewise, the new emphasis on tourist-friendliness and tidiness could transform the district from an architecturally significant and intact precinct with a vibrant human presence to a sanitised heritage theme park. Certainly the complaints have merit, but it's also true that some parts of Islamic Cairo are receiving much-needed help in the process. Vast Al-Azhar Park, once an enormous rubbish heap, is hard to argue with as an improvement.

The best way to explore is to spend a couple of days wandering through the narrow streets and twisting alleyways – ideally once

---

ISLAMIC CAIRO HIGHLIGHTS

■ Soak up the atmosphere in Al-Azhar Mosque (opposite), the centre of Sunni Islamic education for more than a millennium.

■ Take in the view from the south end of Bein al-Qasreen (p134) – with a few camels, you could be in a 19th-century etching.

■ Compare the Mosque of Ibn Tulun (p139) to its image on your E£5 note, and pop into the adjacent Gayer-Anderson Museum (p140), a private home furnished with quirky art and collectibles.

■ Sip tea at the Platonic ideal of the *ahwa* (coffeehouse), Fishawi's Coffeehouse (p170) – a great place to rest before or after trawling Khan al-Khalili (p130) for deals.

■ Climb the minarets at Bab Zuweila (p136) to survey the view over the whole medieval district.

on a weekday to feel the throng of commerce at its height, and again on a quieter Friday morning or Sunday, when most shops are shut (see p157 for a suggested walk) and you can pause to admire a delicately carved minaret without being run down by an overburdened donkey cart.

VISITING ISLAMIC CAIRO

With more than 800 listed monuments and few signposts or other concessions to the visitor, Islamic Cairo can be a daunting place. We've divided it into six segments with maps, each taking about half a day to cover – plus Al-Azhar Park, which borders the district and makes a good place to rest after touring. The magnificent Museum of Islamic Art (p136) deserves another half-day when it opens again *(inshallah)*.

Al-Azhar & Khan al-Khalili (right) The geographical and symbolic centre of medieval Cairo.

North of Khan al-Khalili (p130) A monument-studded walk to the old city gates and back.

Al-Azhar to the Citadel (p134) Through the Darb al-Ahmar district to Mohammed Ali's seat of power.

The Citadel (p137) Home to Egypt's rulers for 700 years.

The Citadel to Ibn Tulun (p138) Two magnificent mosques and a couple of smaller gems.

Northern Cemetery (p140) Cairo's famous City of the Dead.

Al-Azhar Park (p141) Great views from this green space.

Appropriate dress in this traditional part of Cairo is not just polite but necessary if you want to enter mosques, where legs and shoulders must be covered. Shoes must be removed before entering prayer halls, so bring footwear that can be easily slipped off but that is robust enough to survive potholes and odd puddles. Caretakers at mosques and museums expect tips, so bring plenty of small change – E£5 should be sufficient at each place, but throw in a little extra if someone takes you up a minaret. Some enterprising people have taken to claiming entry fees at mosques, but except for Sultan Hassan and Ar-Rifai, this is not sanctioned – see p117 for how to handle this and other scams.

Caretakers are usually around from 9am until early evening, but may follow their own whims. Mosques are usually closed to visitors during prayer times.

For more thorough preparation, look for *Islamic Monuments in Cairo: The Practical Guide* by Caroline Williams (E£75), or *Historic Cairo: A Walk Through the Islamic City,* by British architect Jim Antoniou (E£75). Those serious about their architecture may like to get a copy of Nicholas Warner's *The Monuments of Historic Cairo: A Map and Descriptive Catalogue* (E£300), which covers 500 buildings, complete with historical data and renovation details. All are published by AUC Press.

GETTING TO ISLAMIC CAIRO

Islamic Cairo covers a large area. The centre of the action, and the easiest place to reach, is Al-Azhar and Khan al-Khalili. The best approach is on foot from Downtown, so you can see the transition from the modern city; head for Midan Ataba then bear east under the elevated motorway along Sharia al-Azhar, or throw yourself into the crowds on Sharia al-Muski. Or hail a taxi and ask for 'Al-Hussein' – the name of the *midan* (square) and the mosque at the mouth of the bazaar (pay E£6 from Downtown). Most places in the following pages can be reached from there, although for the Citadel and Mosque of Ibn Tulun it may be easier to take a taxi (E£10 from Downtown) to the Citadel entrance.

AL-AZHAR & KHAN AL-KHALILI

The best place to get acquainted with Islamic Cairo is the area around Al-Azhar Mosque and the great bazaar, Khan al-Khalili, which panders shamelessly to Western preconceptions of the Orient.

Al-Azhar Mosque

Founded in AD 970 as the centrepiece of the newly created Fatimid city, **Al-Azhar Mosque** (Gami' al-Azhar; Map p131; Sharia al-Azhar; ⏰ 24hr) is one of Cairo's earliest mosques and its sheikh is the highest theological authority for Egyptian Muslims. A madrassa was established in AD 988, growing into a university that is the world's second-oldest educational institution (after the University of al-Kairaouine in Fez, Morocco). At one time the university was one of the world's pre-eminent centres of learning, drawing scholars from Europe and across the Arab world, and it is still the most prestigious place to study Sunni theology.

The mosque is a harmonious blend of architectural styles, the result of numerous enlargements over a thousand years. The central courtyard is the earliest part, while, from south to north, the three minarets date from

CAIRO

the 14th, 15th and 16th centuries; the latter, with its double finial, was added by Sultan al-Ghouri, whose mosque and mausoleum stand nearby. The tomb chamber, located through a doorway on the left just inside the entrance, has a beautiful mihrab (a niche indicating the direction of Mecca) and should not be missed.

Midan al-Hussein

The square between the two highly venerated mosques of Al-Azhar and Sayyidna al-Hussein was one of the focal points of Mamluk Cairo and remains an important space at feast times, particularly on Ramadan evenings and during the *moulids* (see boxed text, p512) of Hussein and the Prophet Mohammed, when people throng the brightly lit *midan,* where music and Sufi chanting blares until the early morning. The square is a popular meeting place at other times too, and the *ahwas* with outdoor seating at the entrance to the khan are often packed with equal parts locals and tourists.

One of the most sacred Islamic sites in Egypt, the **Mosque of Sayyidna al-Hussein** (Map p131) is the reputed burial place of the head of Hussein, the grandson of the Prophet whose death in Karbala, Iraq, cemented the rift between the Sunni and Shia branches of Islam. Never mind that the Umayyad Mosque in Damascus claims the same Shiite relic, and that both mosques were established by Sunnis – the site is still so holy that non-Muslims are not allowed inside. Most of the building dates from about 1870, except for the beautiful 14th-century stucco panels on the minaret. The modern-looking metal sculptures in front are elegant Teflon canopies that expand to cover worshipers during Friday prayer times.

Khan al-Khalili

Jaded travellers often dismiss Khan al-Khalili (Map p131) as a tourist trap, and there's no ignoring the flotillas of tour buses parked on the square, and all the touts and tat that come with them. But it's worth remembering that Cairenes have plied their trades here since the khan was built in the 14th century, and parts of the market, such as the gold district, are still the first choice for thousands of locals to do business.

Open from early morning to sundown (except Friday morning and Sunday), the agglomeration of shops – many arranged around small courtyards, in the original me-

dieval 'minimal' layout – stock everything from soap powder to semiprecious stones, not to mention stuffed-toy camels and alabaster pyramids. The khan used to be divided into fairly rigid districts, but that has been lost since the tourist trade became paramount; the only distinct areas are now the gold sellers, the coppersmiths and the spice dealers (see Map p131). Apart from the clumsy 'Hey mister, look for free' touts, the merchants of Khan al-Khalili are some of the greatest smooth-talkers you will ever meet. Almost anything can be bought here and if one merchant doesn't have what you're looking for, he'll happily find somebody who does.

There are few specific things to see in the khan but **Fishawi's Coffeehouse** (Map p131; ⊙ 24hr except during Ramadan), in an alley one block west of Midan al-Hussein, is an absolute must. Hung with huge mirrors and packed day and night, it claims to have been open continuously since the year 1773, except during Ramadan, when everyone is fasting. Entertainment comes in the form of roaming salesmen hawking wallets, carved canes, pistol-shaped cigarette lighters and packet after packet after packet of tissues. For a full review of the coffeehouse, see p170.

The other landmark, in the southwest area of the khan, is **Midaq Alley** (Zuqaq al-Midaq; Map p131). Its name the title of one of Naguib Mahfouz' best-known works, the tiny stepped alley may not be populated with the same colourful characters as the novel, but the way of life here is little changed from the author's 1940s depiction. Such is the alley's fame that the street sign is kept in the coffeehouse at the foot of the steps and is produced only on payment of baksheesh.

Sharia al-Muski

Congested and fabulous, the market street known as Sharia al-Muski (Map p131) begins in the khan (where it's formally called Sharia Gawhar al-Qaid) and runs parallel to Sharia al-Azhar to Midan Ataba. It's the 'real life' counterpoint to Khan al-Khalili's touristy maze, lined with carts selling cheap shoes, plastic toys, bucket-sized bras and some truly shocking lingerie.

NORTH OF KHAN AL-KHALILI

From Midan al-Hussein walk up the road that leads along the western side of the Mosque of Sayyidna al-Hussein. Stick to it as

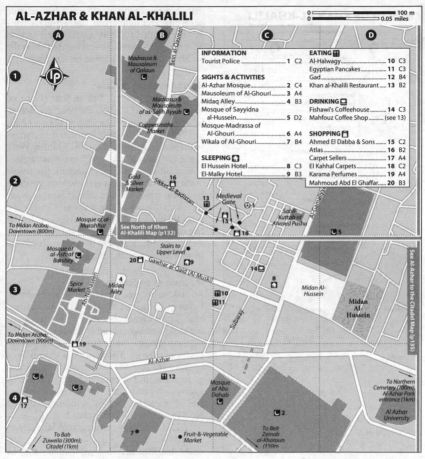

AL-AZHAR & KHAN AL-KHALILI

0 100 m
0 0.05 miles

INFORMATION		
Tourist Police	1	C2

SIGHTS & ACTIVITIES		
Al-Azhar Mosque	2	C4
Mausoleum of Al-Ghouri	3	A4
Midaq Alley	4	B3
Mosque of Sayyidna al-Hussein	5	D2
Mosque-Madrassa of Al-Ghouri	6	A4
Wikala of Al-Ghouri	7	B4

SLEEPING		
El Hussein Hotel	8	C3
El-Malky Hotel	9	B3

EATING		
Al-Halwagy	10	C3
Egyptian Pancakes	11	C3
Gad	12	B4
Khan al-Khalili Restaurant	13	B2

DRINKING		
Fishawi's Coffeehouse	14	C3
Mahfouz Coffee Shop	(see 13)	

SHOPPING		
Ahmed El Dabba & Sons	15	C2
Atlas	16	B2
Carpet Sellers	17	A4
El Kahhal Carpets	18	C2
Karama Perfumes	19	A4
Mahmoud Abd El Ghaffar	20	B3

it doglegs left into the district known as the Gamaliyya. This avenue, **Sharia al-Gamaliyya** (Map p132), was an essential thoroughfare in medieval Cairo; today it looks more like a back alley, with many of the Mamluk-era buildings obscured by restorers' webs of wooden scaffolding.

The 1408 **Mosque of Gamal ad-Din** (Map p132) is a monument that has received somewhat overzealous restoration attention. It's raised above a row of shops, the rent from which was intended for the mosque's upkeep. Adjacent (go left down the lane) is the fully restored yet empty – **Wikala al-Bazara** (Map p132; Sharia al-Tombakshiyya; adult/student E£20/10; ☺ 8am-6pm summer, 9am-5pm winter), one of about 20 remaining *wikala*s (merchants' inns) in the medieval

city, down from about 360 in the 17th century, when this one was built. The Gamaliyya was the medieval warehouse district, with many of these *wikala*s, all built to the same plan: storerooms and stables surrounding a courtyard, with guestrooms for traders on the upper floors; heavy front gates protected the merchandise at night.

Further north on Sharia al-Gamaliyya, on the opposite side of the street, the Mamluk **Khanqah & Mausoleum of Sultan Beybars al-Gashankir** (Map p132) is distinguished by its stubby minaret, topped with a small ribbed dome. Built in 1310, this is one of the city's first *khanqah*s (Sufi monasteries). Thanks to a multipart 'baffled' entrance, it is serene inside. Beybars al-Gashankir is entombed in a room

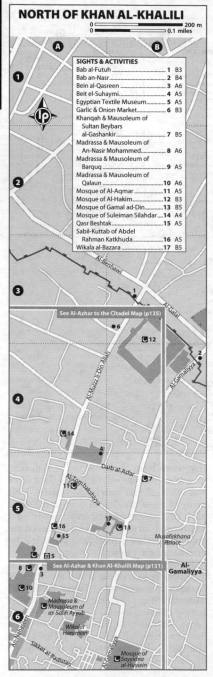

NORTH OF KHAN AL-KHALILI

SIGHTS & ACTIVITIES		
Bab al-Futuh	1	B3
Bab an-Nasr	2	B4
Bein al-Qasreen	3	A6
Beit el-Suhaymi	4	A5
Egyptian Textile Museum	5	A5
Garlic & Onion Market	6	B3
Khanqah & Mausoleum of Sultan Beybars al-Gashankir	7	B5
Madrassa & Mausoleum of An-Nasir Mohammed	8	A6
Madrassa & Mausoleum of Barquq	9	A5
Madrassa & Mausoleum of Qalaun	10	A6
Mosque of Al-Aqmar	11	A5
Mosque of Al-Hakim	12	B3
Mosque of Gamal ad-Din	13	B5
Mosque of Suleiman Silahdar	14	A4
Qasr Beshtak	15	A5
Sabil-Kuttab of Abdel Rahman Katkhuda	16	A5
Wikala al-Bazara	17	B5

that shimmers with black-and-white marble panelling and light from stained-glass windows. He ruled for only a year, then wound up strangled – his name was excised from the building facade by order of his successor.

Northern Walls & Gates

The square-towered **Bab an-Nasr** (Gate of Victory; Map p132) and the rounded **Bab al-Futuh** (Gate of Conquests; Map p132) were built in 1087 as the two main northern entrances to the walled Fatimid city of Al-Qahira. Walk along the outside and you'll see what an imposing bit of military architecture the whole thing is. When current renovations are done (any year now), visitors should be able to get access to the top of the walls and inside the gates themselves, and see inscriptions left by Napoleon's troops as well as carved animals and Pharaonic figures on the stones scavenged from the ruins of ancient Memphis.

Mosque of Al-Hakim

Al-Hakim became the sixth Fatimid ruler of Egypt at the age of 11. His tutor nicknamed him 'Little Lizard' because of his frightening looks and behaviour. Hakim later had the man murdered, along with scores of others in his 24-year reign. Those nearest to him lived in constant fear for their lives: a victorious general rushing unannounced into the royal apartments was confronted by a bloodied Hakim standing over a disembowelled page boy. The general was beheaded.

Hakim reputedly often patroled the streets in disguise, riding a donkey. Most notoriously, he punished dishonest merchants by having them dealt with by a well-endowed black servant. His death was as bizarre as his life. On one of his solitary nocturnal jaunts up onto the Muqattam Hills, Hakim simply disappeared; his body was never found. To one of his followers, a man called Al-Darizy, this was proof of Hakim's divine nature. From this seed Al-Darizy founded the sect of the Druze that continues to this day.

Completed in 1013, the vast Mosque of Al-Hakim (Map p132) is one of Cairo's older mosques but it was rarely used for worship. Instead it functioned as a Crusaders' prison, a stable, a warehouse, a boys' school and, most appropriately, considering its notorious founder, a madhouse. An Ismaili Shiite group restored the mosque in the 1980s, but with its open-plan square and spare decora-

CAIRO

MUSEUMS: THE BEST OF THE REST

The mammoth Egyptian Museum gets all the fanfare, but the city also holds a number of lesser-known gems – ones that require half an hour or two, rather than a lifetime. And you'll always have the places to yourself.

Agricultural Museum (p144) So frozen in time, this whole museum should be in a museum.

Mahmoud Mukhtar Museum (p143) Elegant sculpture, elegant building – and there's even a tomb in the basement!

Mr & Mrs Mahmoud Khalil Museum (p144) Never thought you'd see a Picasso in Cairo, did you?

Museum of Islamic Ceramics (p142) Simply beautiful, with attractive, uncrowded displays and a gorgeous house as the setting.

tion, it's not particularly interesting. The real masterpieces are the two stone minarets, the earliest surviving in the city (thanks in part to a post-earthquake restoration in 1304 by Beybars al-Gashankir).

Sharia al-Muizz li-Din Allah

Sharia al-Muizz (its shortened name; Map p132), which takes its name from the Fatimid caliph who conquered Cairo in AD 969, is the former grand thoroughfare of medieval Cairo, once chock-a-block with storytellers, entertainers and food stalls. These days the street is getting totally redone, from new pavement on up to the tips of the minarets of the monuments along its length. During morning vehicle-free hours, visitors may comfortably gawk at the sites without fear of being flattened by traffic. The drawback, though, is that this is now more squarely a tourist destination and touts have found their way up from the khan. First-timers will likely be impressed at the streetscape; return visitors may be taken aback at the extent of the changes.

Heading south from the gates, a **garlic-and-onion market** (Map p132) gives way to a variety of small places selling *sheesha*s, braziers and pear-shaped cooking pots for *fuul* (fava beans). Soon the stock expands to crescent-moon minaret tops, coffee ewers and other copper products, hence its more popular name, Sharia an-Nahaseen (Street of the Coppersmiths). On the right, about 200m south, is the **Mosque of Suleiman Silahdar** (Map

p132), built comparatively late, in 1839, during the reign of Mohammed Ali. It's distinguished by its thin, Turkish-inspired minaret and the graceful, curvaceous lines along its facade, with a rounded *sabil-kuttab* (water fountain and school) on the corner.

Darb al-Asfar & Beit el-Suhaymi

Just south of Suleiman's *sabil*, the narrow lane Darb al-Asfar (Map p132) runs east. Its new paving stones and elaborate *mashrabiyya* (wooden lattice screens) are a sample of the renovation goals for the whole area. Walking down here conjures the Middle Ages – if the Middle Ages were clean. The first few buildings you pass are part of **Beit el-Suhaymi** (Map p132; Darb al-Asfar; admission E£25; ⏰ 9am-5pm), a family mansion and caravanserai (merchants' inn) built in the 17th and 18th centuries. From the street, it's nothing; after jogging through a narrow hall, you arrive at a peaceful courtyard surrounded by a warren of reception halls, storerooms and baths. It has been thoroughly restored, though barely furnished (fire extinguishers, a precaution required by the extensive new woodwork, are the most prominent item on display). As a result it feels a bit ghostly – especially considering some 30 families were evicted to make way for the renovation.

The changes on Darb al-Asfar have been heavily debated. One definite benefit has been that the street has been reclaimed for residents. As on Sharia al-Muizz, many of the ground-floor spaces used to be small workshops and factories – noisy and sometimes unsafe for kids. Now those who still live here, at least, can enjoy the privacy of the lane as it was originally built.

Back on Sharia al-Muizz, just 50m south of the junction with Darb al-Asfar, is the petite **Mosque of Al-Aqmar** (Map p132). Built in 1125 by one of the last Fatimid caliphs, it is the oldest stone-facaded mosque in Egypt. Several features appear here that became part of the mosque builders' essential vocabulary, including *muqarnas* (stalactite-like decorative stone) vaulting and the ribbing in the hooded arch.

Sabil-Kuttab of Abdel Rahman Katkhuda

Further south along the street, where the road splits, the Sabil-Kuttab of Abdel Rahman Katkhuda (Map p132) is one of the iconic structures of Islamic Cairo, depicted in scores of paintings and lithographs. Building this

CAIRO

fountain-school combo was an atonement for sins, as it provided two things commended by the Prophet: water for the thirsty and enlightenment for the ignorant. This one was built in 1744 by an emir notorious for his debauchery. There's nice ceramic work inside, so it's worth trying to find the caretaker with the key. He often sits in **Qasr Beshtak** (Palace of Amir Beshtak; Map p132), down the little alley to the east, then through the archway at the bottom. The palace is a rare example of 14th-century domestic architecture, originally five floors high, now largely ruined but with splendid rooftop views.

Bein al-Qasreen

The part of Sharia al-Muizz immediately south of the *sabil-kuttab* is known as Bein al-Qasreen (Between the Two Palaces; Map p132), a reminder of the great palace complexes that flanked the street during the Fatimid era. The palaces fell into ruin and were replaced by the works of subsequent rulers. Today three great abutting Mamluk complexes line the west of the street, providing one of Cairo's most impressive assemblies of minarets, domes and striped stone facades.

First comes the **Madrassa & Mausoleum of Barquq** (Map p132). Barquq seized power in 1382, when Egypt was reeling from plague and famine; his Sufi school was completed four years later. Enter through the bold black-and-white marble portal into a vaulted passageway. To the right, the inner court has a colourful ceiling supported by four porphyry Pharaonic columns. Barquq's daughter is buried in the splendid domed tomb chamber; the sultan himself preferred to rest in the Northern Cemetery (see p141), surrounded by Sufi sheikhs.

Barquq's neighbour to the south is the **Madrassa & Mausoleum of An-Nasir Mohammed** (Map p132), built in 1304 by a Mamluk sultan both despotic and exceedingly accomplished. The Gothic doorway was plundered from a church in Acre (now Akko, Israel) when An-Nasir and his army ended Crusader domination there in 1290 – note how the word 'Allah' has been inscribed at the point of the arch. The lacy pattern on the carved stucco minaret, a North African style, reveals more foreign influence. Buried in the mausoleum (on the right as you enter but usually locked) is An-Nasir's mother and favourite son; An-Nasir Mohammed is

interred next door in the mausoleum of his father, Qalaun.

Built in just 13 months, the 1279 **Madrassa & Mausoleum of Qalaun** (Map p132) is both the earliest and the most splendid of the three buildings. Although it was closed for restoration at the time of research, it is scheduled to open during the shelf life of this book. The mausoleum, on the right, is a particularly intricate assemblage of inlaid stone and stucco, patterned with stars and floral motifs and lit by stained-glass windows. The complex also includes a *maristan* (hospital), which Qalaun ordered built after he visited one in Damascus, where he was cured of colic. The Arab traveller and historian Ibn Battuta, who visited Cairo in 1325, was impressed that Qalaun's hospital contained 'an innumerable quantity of appliances and medicaments'. He also described how the mausoleum was flanked by Quran reciters day and night chanting requiems for the dead within.

Bein al-Qasreen to the City Centre

Soon a last cluster of copper workshops gives way to gold jewellers, signifying re-entry into the precincts of Khan al-Khalili. At the junction with Sharia al-Muski, beside two mosques, a left turn leads back to Midan al-Hussein, while heading right will eventually take you to Midan Ataba (1.2km); straight ahead is Sharia al-Azhar, the easiest place to find a taxi.

AL-AZHAR TO THE CITADEL

South of Sharia al-Azhar, Sharia al-Muizz li-Din Allah continues as a market street 400m down to the twin-minareted gate of Bab Zuweila (p136). From there two routes lead to the Mosque-Madrassa of Sultan Hassan (p138): east along Sharia Ahmed Mahir Pasha, or south through Sharia al-Khayamiyya. Either way, it's a long (at least 40 minutes), dusty, interesting walk to the main entrance of the Citadel.

Ottoman Houses

Leaving Al-Azhar Mosque, turn left and then left again into an alley between the southern wall of the mosque and a row of shops housed in the vaults of a 15th-century merchants' building. At the top of this road lies **Beit Zeinab al-Khatoun** (House of Zeinab Khatoun; Map p135; ☎ 2735 7001; Sharia Mohammed Abduh; admission E£10; ⏱ 9am-

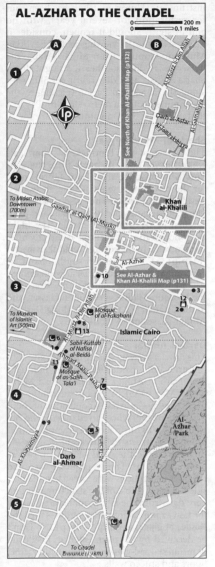

AL-AZHAR TO THE CITADEL

houses the Arabic Oud House; you may hear rehearsals. Between the two houses is Al-Khatoun (p176), one of the city's better shops for stylish handicrafts and homewares.

Al-Ghouri Complex

On the south side of Sharia al-Azhar, opposite the khan, the grand **Mosque-Madrassa of Al-Ghouri** (Map p131), with its red-chequered minaret, and the elegant **Mausoleum of Al-Ghouri** (Map p131) together form an exquisite monument to the end of the Mamluk era. Qansuh al-Ghouri, the penultimate Mamluk sultan, ruled for 16 years. At the age of 78, he rode to Syria at the head of his army to battle the Ottoman Turks. The head of the defeated Al-Ghouri was sent to Constantinople; his body was never recovered. His mausoleum (dating from 1505) contains the body of Tumanbey, his short-lived successor, hanged by the Turks at Bab Zuweila. The mausoleum, which has been under restoration for a number of years, may reopen as a cultural centre. Across the street at the mosque, don't be put off by the scaffolding: the interior, small but with soaring ceilings, is beautifully decorated; it's also possible to climb the minaret (for baksheesh; ignore claims of 'tickets'). Also part of the complex, the **Wikala of Al-Ghouri** (Map p131; ☎ 2511 0472; adult/student E£15/10; ⏱ 9am-8pm Sat-Thu), 100m east, is another of the doomed sultan's legacies. Similar to the Wikala al-Bazara (see p131) but more sympathetically restored, the upper rooms are artists' ateliers while the former stables are craft shops. The courtyard serves as a theatre for Sufi dance performances (see p173).

Carpet & Clothes Market

The street between the mosque and the mausoleum, as well as the alleys just west and south

6pm), a small but interesting Ottoman-era house with a rooftop affording superb views of the surrounding minaret-studded skyline. Across a peaceful little plaza, **Beit al-Harrawi** (Map p135; ☎ 2510 4174; admission E£10; ⏱ 9am-6pm) is another fine 18th-century mansion, but too sparse inside to warrant the admission charge. It is sometimes used as a concert venue and

of the mosque-madrassa, were historically the city's silk market, and the small passageways are still filled with **carpet sellers** (Map p131). Heading south into the district called Al-Ghouriyya, Sharia al-Muizz becomes a busy market for household goods and cheap clothing. On the right, less than 50m south of the mosque, Cairo's last **tarboosh (fez) maker** (Map p135) shapes the red felt hats on heavy brass presses. Once worn by every *effendi* (gentleman), the tarboosh is now mainly bought by hotels and tourist restaurants. They sell for between E£15 and E£60. Further down on the left is the delicate Ottoman-style **Sabil of Muhammed Ali Pasha** (Map p135). The 1820 fountain was the first in Cairo to have gilded window grilles and calligraphic panels in Ottoman Turkish. Although it has been meticulously restored, it was closed to the public at last pass; check if it's open, as there is also access to a cistern below. Across the street, the red-and-white-striped **Mosque of Al-Mu'ayyad** (Map p135), built on the site where its patron Mamluk sultan had earlier been imprisoned, displays a particularly grand entrance portal, dripping with stalactite vaulting. The interior is equally lavish.

Bab Zuweila

Built at the same time as the northern gates (10th century), beautiful **Bab Zuweila** (Map p135; adult/student E£20/10; ☉ 8.30am-5pm) is the only remaining southern gate of medieval Al-Qahira. Visitors may climb the ramparts, where some intriguing exhibits about the gate's history are in place. The two minarets atop the gate, also open to visitors, offer one of the best available views of the area. In Mamluk times, the space in front of the gate was the site of executions, a popular form of street theatre, with some victims being sawn in half or crucified. The spirit of a healing saint was (and still is) said to reside behind one towering wooden door, which supplicants have studded with nails and teeth as offerings over the centuries.

From here, you can detour to the Museum of Islamic Art or continue to the Citadel by two possible routes.

Museum of Islamic Art

West of Bab Zuweila 500m, the **Museum of Islamic Art** (Map pp112-13; ☎ 2390 1520; Sharia Bur Said) holds one of the world's finest collections of Islamic applied art: a trove of manuscripts, woodwork, textiles and astronomy

instruments. Unfortunately it has been shut for restoration for several years, with no end in sight. Should it reopen, consider it nearly as essential viewing as the Egyptian Museum. Coming from Midan Ataba, the museum is 700m southeast, straight down Sharia al-Qala'a. Midan Tahrir is 1.5km west along Sharia Sami al-Barudi (passing by the Mohammed Naguib metro station). Pay E£4 for taxi to or from Downtown.

Sharia al-Khayamiyya

The 'Street of the Tentmakers', Sharia al-Khayamiyya, takes its name from the artisans who produce the bright fabrics used for the ceremonial tents at funerals, wakes, weddings and feasts. They also make appliqué wall hangings and bedspreads, and print original patterns for tablecloths. The highest concentration of artisans is directly after Bab Zuweila, in the covered **tentmakers market** (Map p135). About 800m south, Sharia al-Khayamiyya intersects Sharia Mohammed Ali; a left turn here will take you directly to the Mosque-Madrassa of Sultan Hassan and to the Citadel, but the detour along Darb al-Ahmar passes more monuments.

Darb al-Ahmar

This district grew up during the 14th and 15th centuries and is named for its main thoroughfare, Darb al-Ahmar (Sharia Ahmad Mahir Pasha; Map p135), or 'Red Road'. In the district's heyday Cairo had a population of about 250,000, most of whom lived outside the city walls in this tightly packed residential area of twisting streets and dark cul-de-sacs. As the area inside the walls of Al-Qahira was built-up, patrons of new mosques, palaces and religious institutions were forced to build outside the gates. Most of the structures around here date from the late Mamluk era. One of the best examples from this period is the 1481 **Mosque of Qijmas al-Ishaqi** (Map p135). Don't be deceived by the plain exterior: inside are beautiful stained-glass windows, inlaid marble floors and stucco walls.

About 150m further on the right, the 1339 **Mosque of Al-Maridani** (Map p135) incorporates architectural elements from several periods: eight granite columns were taken from a Pharaonic monument; the arches contain Roman, Christian and Islamic designs; and the Ottomans added a fountain and wooden housing. Trees in the courtyard, attractive *mashrabiyya* and a lack of visitors make this a peaceful place to stop.

The **Blue Mosque** (Mosque of Aqsunqur; Map p135), built in 1347, gets its popular name from the combination of blue-grey marble on the exterior and the flowery Ottoman tiling, not applied until 1652, inside. The minaret affords an excellent view of the Citadel, while over to the east, just behind the mosque, you can see the remains of Saladin's city walls, being excavated as part of the Al-Azhar Park project.

THE CITADEL

Sprawling over a limestone spur on the eastern edge of the city, the **Citadel** (Al-Qala'a; Map p137; ☎ 2512 1735; Sharia Salah Salem; adult/student E£50/25; ☺ 8am-5pm Oct-May, 8am-6pm Jun-Sep, mosques closed during Fri prayers) was home to Egypt's rulers for 700 years. Their legacy is a collection of three very different mosques, several palaces (housing some underwhelming museums; admission fee included) and a couple of terraces with views over the city. This is one of the most popular tourist attractions in Cairo, so be prepared for heavy crowds and

heavier security, including metal detectors and bag searches.

Saladin began building the Citadel in 1176 to fortify the city against the Crusaders, who were then rampaging through Palestine. Following their overthrow of Saladin's Ayyubid dynasty, the Mamluks enlarged the complex, adding sumptuous palaces and harems. Under the Ottomans (1517–1798) the fortress expanded westwards and a new main gate, the Bab al-Azab, was added, while the Mamluk palaces deteriorated. Even so, when Napoleon's French expedition took control in 1798, the emperor's savants regarded these buildings as some of the finest Islamic monuments in Cairo. This didn't stop Mohammed Ali – who rose to power when the French left – from demolishing them. The only Mamluk structure left standing was a single mosque, used as a stable. Mohammed Ali completely remodelled the rest of the Citadel and crowned it with the Turkish-style mosque that currently dominates Cairo's eastern skyline.

After Mohammed Ali's grandson Ismail moved his residence to the Abdeen Palace (p119), the Citadel became a military garrison.

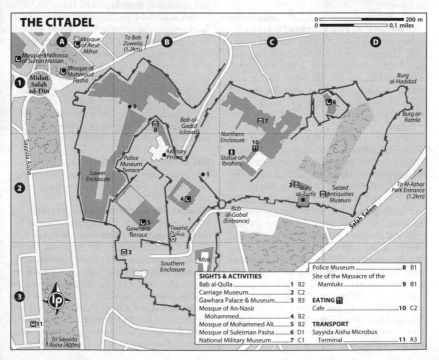

THE CITADEL

0 . . . 200 m
0 . . . 0.1 miles

The British army was barracked here during WWII, and Egyptian soldiers still have a small foothold, although most of the Citadel has been given over to tourists.

Mosque of Mohammed Ali

The fortress is dominated by the Mosque of Mohammed Ali (Map p137). Modelled along classic Turkish lines, with domes upon domes upon domes, it took 18 years to build (1830–48), and its interior is all twinkling chandeliers and luridly striped stone. Perhaps the most evocative description of it is in Olivia Manning's *The Levant Trilogy*: 'Above them Mohammed Ali's alabaster mosque, uniquely white in this sand-coloured city, sat with minarets pricked, like a fat, white, watchful cat'. Other writers have called it unimaginative and graceless and compared it to a toad. Beyond criticism, the mosque's patron lies in the marble tomb on the right as you enter. Note the glitzy clock in the central courtyard, a gift from King Louis-Philippe of France in thanks for the Pharaonic obelisk that adorns the Place de la Concorde in Paris. It was damaged on delivery and has yet to be repaired.

Dwarfed by Mohammed Ali's mosque, the 1318 **Mosque of An-Nasir Mohammed** (Map p137) is the Citadel's sole surviving Mamluk structure. The interior is a little sparse because the Ottoman sultan Selim I had it stripped of its marble, but the old wood ceiling and *muqarnas* show up nicely, and the twisted finials of the minarets are interesting for their covering of glazed tiles, something rarely seen in Egypt.

Facing the entrance of the Mosque of An-Nasir Mohammed, a mock-Gothic gateway leads to a grand terrace, with superb views all the way to the Pyramids at Giza. Immediately below, in the Citadel's Lower Enclosure (closed to the public), the steep-sided roadway leading to Bab al-Azab was the site of the infamous massacre of the Mamluks (see p38). The flyblown **Police Museum** (Map p137), located at the northern end of the terrace, includes displays on famous political assassinations, complete in some cases with the murder weapon.

South of Mohammed Ali's mosque is another terrace with good views. Beyond, the dull **Gawhara Palace & Museum** (Map p137) is a lame attempt to evoke 19th-century court life, and it's often closed anyway.

Northern Enclosure

Entrance to the Northern Enclosure is via the 16th-century Bab al-Qulla (entrance fee is included in the Citadel entrance fee). Past an overpriced cafe lies Mohammed Ali's one-time Harem Palace, now the lavish **National Military Museum** (Map p137) and perhaps the best-tended exhibition in the country. Endless plush-carpeted halls are lined with dioramas depicting great moments in warfare, from Pharaonic times to the 20th-century conflicts with Israel – kitschy fun to start, then eventually a bit depressing.

East of the cafe a narrow road leads to an area with a few smaller museums, along the humble lines of the **Carriage Museum** (Map p137). Devotees of Islamic architecture might appreciate the 1528 **Mosque of Suleiman Pasha** (Map p137), a far more tasteful example of the Ottoman-style domed mosque.

Getting to/from the Citadel

To walk from Midan Ataba to the Citadel's entrance gate, it's almost 4km through the furniture and musical-instruments districts. From Midan Ataba go straight down Sharia al-Qala'a and its continuation, Sharia Mohammed Ali, to Midan Salah ad-Din, then walk to Sharia Salah Salem via Sharia Sayyida Aisha. A taxi will cost E£12. Minibus 150 (E£1.10) runs from Midan Ataba. This and other services drop you only at Midan Salah ad-Din, still a 15-minute walk from the entrance; taking a taxi (E£3) from here is easier on the legs, but only marginally quicker due to the complicated traffic-flow on the highway. A microbus to Sayyida Aisha from Salah ad-Din gets you closest – to the intersection with Salah Salem.

THE CITADEL TO IBN TULUN

The route takes in two of Islamic Cairo's largest mosques, plus a few tiny surprises.

Mosque-Madrassa of Sultan Hassan

Massive yet elegant, the great structure of the **Mosque-Madrassa of Sultan Hassan** (Map p139; Midan Salah ad-Din; admission E£25; ☽ 8am-5pm Oct-May, 8am-6pm Jun-Sep) is regarded as the finest piece of early-Mamluk architecture in Cairo. It was built between 1356 and 1363 by the troubled Sultan Hassan, a grandson of Sultan Qalaun; he took the throne at the age of 13, was deposed and reinstated no less than three times, then assassinated shortly before the mosque was completed. Tragedy also shadowed the construction when

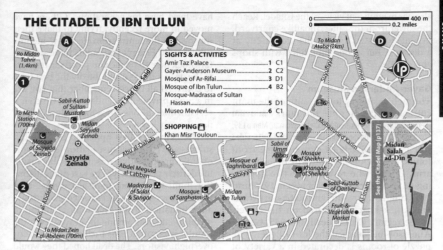

THE CITADEL TO IBN TULUN

SIGHTS & ACTIVITIES
Amir Taz Palace 1 C1
Gayer-Anderson Museum 2 C2
Mosque of Ar-Rifai 3 D1
Mosque of Ibn Tulun 4 B2
Mosque-Madrassa of Sultan
Hassan 5 D1
Museo Mevlevi 6 C1

SHOPPING
Khan Misr Touloun 7 C2

---

one of the minarets collapsed, killing some 300 onlookers. Beyond the striking, recessed entrance, a dark passage leads into a square courtyard whose soaring walls are punctured by four *iwans* (vaulted halls), one dedicated to teaching each of the four main schools of Sunni Islam. At the rear of the eastern *iwan,* an especially beautiful mihrab is flanked by stolen Crusader columns. To the right, a bronze door leads to the sultan's mausoleum.

Opposite the grand mosque, the **Mosque of Ar-Rifai** (Map p139; admission E£20) is constructed on a similarly grand scale, begun in 1869 and not finished until 1912. Members of modern Egypt's royal family, including Khedive Ismail and King Farouk, are buried inside, as is the last shah of Iran. Their tombs lie to the left of the entrance.

Museo Mevlevi & Amir Taz Palace

Walking west along busy Sharia as-Salbiyya eventually leads to the Mosque of Ibn Tulun. A short detour north on Sharia Suyufiyya brings you to two little-visited but rewarding buildings. The **Amir Taz Palace** (Map p139; ☎ 2514 2581; 17 Sharia Suyufiyya; admission free; ⏰ 8am-4pm) is the restored home of one of Sultan al-Nasir Muhammad's closest advisers, who later controlled the throne through Sultan Hassan. Now used as a cultural centre, the home is not as extensive as Beit el-Suhaymi, but admission is free, and there are a couple of small exhibits, a beautiful wood ceiling in the loggia and clean bathrooms.

A little further down the street, behind a green door with an Italian Institute sign,

the **Museo Mevlevi** (Map p139; Sharia Suyufiyya; admission free; ⏰ 8am-4pm) centres on a meticulously restored Ottoman-era theatre for whirling dervishes. Hidden behind stone facades, the beautiful wood structure feels like a little jewel box. Downstairs, see the remains of the madrassa that forms the building's foundation; the thorough notes are a rare model of thoughtful excavation.

Mosque of Ibn Tulun

Another 250m west on Sharia as-Salbiyya, the **Mosque of Ibn Tulun** (Map p139; ⏰ 8am-6pm) is easily identified by its high walls topped with neat crenulations that resemble a string of paper dolls. Built between AD 876 and 879 by Ibn Tulun, who was sent to rule the outpost of Al-Fustat in the 9th century by the Abbasid caliph of Baghdad, it is the city's oldest intact, functioning Islamic monument. It's also one of its most beautiful, despite a rather ham-fisted restoration using cement on the mud-brick-and-timber structure. Ibn Tulun drew inspiration from his homeland, particularly the ancient Mosque of Samarra (Iraq), on which the spiral minaret is modelled. He also added some innovations of his own: according to architectural historians, this is the first structure to use the pointed arch, a good 200 years before the European Gothic arch. The mosque covers 2.5 hectares, large enough for the whole community of Al-Fustat to assemble for Friday prayers.

The mosque's geometric simplicity is best appreciated from the top of the minaret, which also has magnificent views of the Citadel. Reach the tower from the outer, moatlike courtyard, originally created to keep the secular city at a distance, but at one time filled with shops and stalls.

Gayer-Anderson Museum

Through a gateway to the south of the main entrance of the mosque, this quirky **museum** (Beit al-Kritliyya, the House of the Cretan Woman; Map p139; ☎ 2364 7822; Sharia ibn Tulun; adult/student E£30/15, video E£20; ⏰ 9am-5pm) gets its current name from John Gayer-Anderson, the British major and army doctor who restored the two adjoining 16th-century houses between 1935 and 1942, filling them with antiquities, artworks and knick-knacks acquired on his travels in the region. On his death in 1945, Gayer-Anderson bequeathed the lot to Egypt. The puzzle of rooms is decorated in a variety of styles: the Persian Room has exquisite tiling, the Damascus Room has lacquer and gold, and the Queen Anne Room displays ornate furniture and a silver tea set. The enchanting *mashrabiyya* gallery looks down onto a magnificent *qa'a* (reception hall) which has a marble fountain, decorated ceiling beams and carpet-covered alcoves. The rooftop terrace has been lovingly restored, with more complex *mashrabiyya*. You may find the interior familiar – the museum was used as a location in the James Bond film *The Spy Who Loved Me*. Across the street, Khan Misr Touloun (see p176) is a good handicrafts emporium.

From here, it's rewarding to keep walking another 750m west to the popular quarter of Sayyida Zeinab, where there's a metro station.

NORTHERN CEMETERY

The Northern Cemetery (Al-Qarafa; Map p141) is the more interesting half of a vast necropolis known popularly as the City of the Dead. The titillating name refers to the fact that the cemeteries are not only resting places for Cairo's dead, but for the living too. However, visitors expecting morbid squalor will be surprised to discover that the area is more 'town' than 'shanty', complete with power lines, a post office and multistorey buildings.

Some estimates put the number of living Cairenes here at 50,000; others, at 10 times this number. As Max Rodenbeck notes in *Cairo: The City Victorious*, some of the tomb dwellers, especially the paid guardians and their families,

have lived here for generations. Others have moved in more recently, trying to make their way back to the centre from bleak low-income suburbs. On Fridays and public holidays visitors flock here to picnic and pay their respects to the dead – this is undoubtedly the best time to come. At all times, remember that you are in a more private, residential space, which is a very low-income one; dress modestly and don't flaunt costly jewellery or gadgets.

The cemetery first appealed to Mamluk sultans and emirs because it afforded the sort of building space that was unavailable inside the densely packed city. The vast mausoleums they built were more than just tombs; they were also meant as places for entertaining – a continuation of the Pharaonic tradition of people picnicking among the graves. Even the humblest family tombs included a room for overnight visitors. The dead hoped they would be remembered; the city's homeless thanked them for free accommodation. This coexistence of the living and the dead was happening as far back as the 14th century; in some tombhouses, cenotaphs serve as tables and washing is strung between headstones.

The easiest way to the Northern Cemetery is heading east from Midan al-Hussein along Sharia al-Azhar. As you breast the top of the hill, bear right, walk below the overpass and go straight along the road between the tombs. Follow this road to the left, then right. You'll pass by the crumbling, domed **Tomb of Emir Tashtimur** (Map p141) on your left. About 150m further on, a narrow lane goes left, passing under a stone archway. This is the gate to the former compound of Qaitbey, whose splendid mosque is immediately ahead.

Mosque of Qaitbey

Sultan Qaitbey, a prolific builder, was the last Mamluk leader with any real power in Egypt. He ruled for 28 years and, though he was as ruthless as any Mamluk sultan, he was also something of an aesthete. His mosque (Map p141), completed in 1474 and featured on the E£1 note, is widely agreed to mark the pinnacle of Islamic building in Cairo. Behind the boldly striped facade, the interior has four *iwans* around a central court lit by large, lattice-screened windows. Panelled in cool marble, it's one of the most pleasant places in Cairo to sit and relax. The adjacent tomb chamber contains the cenotaphs of Qaitbey and his two sisters. The true glory, however, is

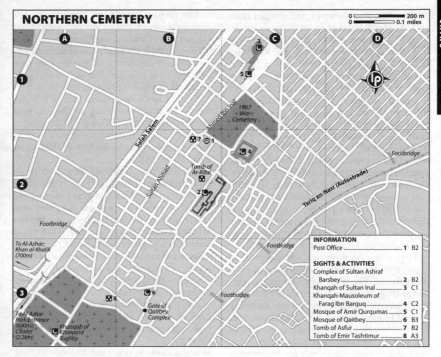

above, where the exterior of the dome is carved with interlaced star and floral designs; its intricacy and delicacy were never surpassed in Cairo or anywhere else in the Islamic world – climb the minaret for the best view.

Other Monuments

From Qaitbey cross the square and continue north. After about 350m the street widens and on the right a stone wall encloses a large area of rubble-strewn ground that was formerly the **Complex of Sultan Ashraf Barsbey** (Map p141). Though not as sophisticated as the one topping the Mosque of Qaitbey, the dome here is carved with a beautiful star pattern. Inside is some fine marble flooring and a beautiful minbar (pulpit) inlaid with ivory. The guard will let you in for baksheesh (ask the ever-present children if he's not around).

Two hundred metres further north is the **Khanqah-Mausoleum of Farag Ibn Barquq** (Map p141), built by a son of Sultan Barquq, whose great madrassa and mausoleum stand on Bein al-Qasreen (p134). Completed in 1411 the *khanqah* is a fortresslike building with high, sheer facades and twin minarets and domes.

In the courtyard, monastic cells lead off the arcades. Two tomb chambers – one for women, one for men – are each topped with domes; their ceilings are painted in mesmerising red-and-black geometric patterns.

Northern Cemetery to al-Hussein

Two large adjacent complexes northwest – the 1507 **Mosque of Amir Qurqumas** (Map p141) and the 1456 **Khanqah of Sultan Inal** (Map p141) – are beautiful, thanks to restoration work, but they are not always open.

Rather than just retracing your steps from Ibn Barquq, walk straight ahead from the entrance, passing the post office on your left, until you come to the small, elongated **Tomb of Asfur** (Map p141); turn left immediately after. A straight walk 850m down Sharia Sultan Ahmed will bring you back to the road leading to the underpass – or you can continue another kilometre down Sharia Salah Salem to Al-Azhar Park's main entrance.

AL-AZHAR PARK

Islamic Cairo's eastern horizon changed substantially when **Al-Azhar Park** (Map pp112-13;

CAIRO

☎ 2510 7378; www.alazharpark.com; admission E£10; ☺ 9am-midnight) opened in 2005. With funds from the Aga Khan Trust for Culture, what had been a mountain of centuries' worth of collected garbage was transformed into a beautifully landscaped swath of green, the city's first (and only) park of significant size. It's hard to convey just how dramatically different the park is from any other public space in Cairo: a profusion of gardens, emerald grass, even a lake (part of a larger public water-supply system) cover the grounds, while ambient Arabic music drifts softly from speakers and fountains bubble in front of sleek modern Islamic architecture. In addition to a couple of small cafes and an open-air theatre (p173), there's an excellent restaurant here (Citadel View; see p166) capitalising on the park's awesome views across the medieval city and beyond – a sunset visit is essential.

Depending on your outlook, the park is a gorgeous respite or a weirdly isolated elite playground. The atmosphere may change, but as long as the only entrance is on Sharia Salah Salem, which requires a taxi to reach (pay E£12 from Tahrir), it's an expensive trek for most people. The entrances on the downhill side, in the Darb al-Ahmar district, were shut at last visit, apparently for renovation work being carried out on the Ayyubid gates and walls.

Zamalek & Gezira

Uninhabited until the mid-19th century, Gezira (Arabic for 'island') was a narrow strip of alluvial land rising up out of the Nile. After he built modern-day Downtown, Khedive Ismail dedicated his energy to a great palace on the island, with the rest of the land as a royal garden. During the development boom of the early 20th century, the palace grounds were sold off, while the palace was made into a hotel (now the core of the Cairo Marriott).

The northern third of the island is the stylish residential district of Zamalek; the rest, still called Gezira, is largely occupied by sports clubs and parks.

ZAMALEK

A leafy neighbourhood of old embassy mansions and 1920s apartment blocks, Zamalek (Map pp146–7) has few tourist sites, but it's a pleasant place to wander around and an even better place to eat, drink and shop.

The main street, Sharia 26th of July, cuts across the island, and its junction with Sharia Hassan Sabry (heading south) and Sharia Brazil (to the north) is the focal point of the area. Just a couple of doors east of Hassan Sabry on Sharia 26th of July, Simonds (see p169) is one of the city's oldest European-style cafes.

Further east along Sharia 26th of July, towards the bridge to Bulaq, are the excellent bookshop Diwan (p114) and – in the ground floor of a lavish apartment complex built by Swiss hotelier Charles Baehler in 1927 – cafe Cilantro (p169).

Immediately south of Sharia 26th of July, and overlooking the Nile, is the Cairo Marriott (p163). This converted palace has a lush, shady garden where you can enjoy your coffee or beer. Behind the hotel, the **Museum of Islamic Ceramics** (Map pp146–7; ☎ 2737 3298; 1 Sharia Sheikh al-Marsafy, Zamalek; adult/student E£25/15; ☺ 10am-1.30pm & 5.30-9pm Sat-Thu) is a beautiful small museum. It's housed in a gorgeous 1924 villa, where the intricately carved walls (and vintage bathroom) are as fascinating as the colourful plates, tiles and even 11th-century hand grenades on display. The garden and back of the building are given over to the **Gezira Art Centre** (Map pp146–7), with several galleries hosting rotating contemporary exhibitions.

GEZIRA

Gezira (Map p150) is best approached across Qasr el-Nil Bridge from Midan Tahrir, a popular strolling spot for couples at sunset. This brings you to **Midan Saad Zaghloul**, presided over by the statue of tarbooshed Mr Zaghloul himself, a 1930s nationalist leader. North of the *midan* on the banks of the Nile two lush **formal gardens** (Map p150; admission E£10) have outdoor cafes where local families and young couples partake of tea and *sheesha*. Below the gardens, the **pedestrian corniche** (admission E£2) is lively in the evenings.

Off the west side of the *midan*, the well-groomed **Gezira Exhibition Grounds** (Map p150) are dominated by the Cairo Opera House (Map p150). Built in 1988 with money from Japan, the building is a modern take on traditional Islamic design. See p173 for details.

Across from the Cairo Opera House, the **Museum of Modern Egyptian Art** (Map p150; ☎ 2736 6667; admission E£10; ☺ 10am-2pm & 5.30-10pm Tue-Sun) houses a vast – perhaps too vast – collection of 20th- and 21st-century Egyptian art. Even after a 2005 renovation, it still can be difficult to ap-

THE MIRACLE ON THE MOUNTAIN

Looking around some parts of Cairo, you'd think garbage is never collected – but it certainly is, by tens of thousands of people known as *zabbaleen*. The *zabbaleen* are Coptic Christians, and their district at the base of the Muqattam Hills not only contains all the city's refuse, sorted into recyclable bits, but also one of the most surprising churches in the country.

In fact, the **Church of St Simeon the Tanner** (Kineesat Samaan al-Kharraz; Map pp112-13; ☎ 2512 3666; Manshiyet Nasr), on a ridge above 'Garbage City', is just a part of a whole complex carved into the cliffs. It seats 5000 (that the buses carrying worshippers fit through the lanes below is a miracle in itself) and is ringed with biblical scenes carved into the rock. Look over the ridge and you can see the whole sprawling city; look down, and you see real, live pigs rooting around the *zabbaleen* backyards, recycling the edible trash.

But this church is not old (nor are any of the others here, though some are tucked in spooky hermits' caves). Completed in 1994, St Simeon is a belated honour for a 10th-century ascetic who prayed to make Muqattam move at the behest of Fatimid caliph Al-Muizz li-Din Allah (per Matthew 17:20: 'If ye have faith as a grain of mustard seed, ye shall say unto this mountain, Remove hence to yonder place; and it shall remove…'). Today the church is a major site of Coptic pilgrimage.

To make your own trek to this modern marvel, tell your taxi driver 'Manshiyet Nasr' or 'Madeenat az-Zabbaleen'; after turning off the highway toward Muqattam, make the first left, going slightly uphill. Once you're in the *zabbaleen* district (which is surprisingly tidy, considering), anyone you pass will wave you in the right direction – they all know where you're headed. Pay E£60 for a round-trip taxi from Downtown, with an hour's waiting time. If you'd like to go with a guide, consider **Ibrahim Morgan** (☎ 012 347 6343; morgan_eg@yahoo.com), recommended by Lonely Planet readers.

preciate the work given the cramped rooms, collected dust and lack of signage. The museum's prize items are all on the ground floor: Mahmoud Mukhtar's deco-elegant bronze statue *Bride of the Nile* is here, along with Mahmoud Said's *Al Madina* (The City, 1937). Though Said has a slew of kitschy imitators, he was one of the first artists to depict folk life in vivid colour, and his commitment inspired Naguib Mahfouz to pursue his own career in writing. Throughout the museum, it is interesting to observe how Western trends such as pop art have manifested themselves in Egypt – almost always with a much sharper social or political message. Upstairs is a small cafe and a gift shop selling a few postcards and posters.

Elsewhere in the exhibition grounds, the **Hanager Arts Centre** (Map p150; ☎ 2735 6861; admission free; ۞ 10am-10pm Tue-Sun) and the **Palace of Arts** (Map p150; ☎ 2737 0603, 736 7627; admission free; ۞ 10am-1.30pm & 5.30-10pm Sat-Thu) host rotating exhibits and performances.

Leave the complex from the rear entrance near the Galaa Bridge and you'll see a modest gate across the road, which leads to the **Mahmoud Mukhtar Museum** (Map p150; ☎ 2735 2519; admission E£5; ۞ 10am-1.30pm & 5-10pm Tue-Sun). Mukhtar (1891–1934) was the sculptor laureate

of independent Egypt, responsible for Saad Zaghloul on the nearby *midan* and the *Egypt Reawakening* monument outside the Giza Zoo. His collected work ranges from tiny caricatures (look for *Ibn al-Balad*, a spunky city kid) to life-size portraits. Mukhtar's tomb sits in the basement. Egyptian architect Ramses Wissa Wassef (1911–74) designed the elegant building – originally open, to capture natural light, but this was changed presumably to keep the cleaning budget down.

North of the Cairo Opera House and Ahly Stadium, the **Cairo Tower** (Burg Misr; Map p150; ☎ 2735 7187; Sharia el-Borg; adult/child under 6 E£60/free, video E£20; ۞ 8am-midnight) is the city's most famous landmark after the Pyramids. Resembling a 185m-high wickerwork tube, the tower was built in 1961 as a thumb to the nose at the Americans, who had given Nasser the money used for its construction to buy US arms. The 360-degree views from the top are clearest in the late morning, after the haze burns off, or late afternoon. An occasionally revolving restaurant on top serves food (E£100 lunch or dinner, including entrance), or you can get a soft drink at the cafeteria (E£80, including entrance). You might encounter quite a queue at dusk.

Mohandiseen, Agouza & Doqqi

A map of Cairo in Baedecker's 1929 guide to Egypt shows nothing on the Nile's west bank other than a hospital and the road to the Pyramids. The hospital is still there, set back from the corniche in Agouza, but it's now hemmed in on all sides by midrise buildings that shot up during the 1960s and 1970s when Mohandiseen, Agouza and Doqqi were created to house Egypt's emerging professional classes. The three districts remain middle-class bastions, home to families who made good during the years of Sadat's open-door policy – though some sections of Mohandiseen are Cairo's ritziest. Unless you happen to find concrete and traffic stimulating, the main attractions here are some good restaurants (p168), bars and upscale shopping on Sharia Suleiman Abaza and Sharia Libnan.

What little history there is floats on the river in the form of the **houseboats** moored off Sharia el-Nil just north of Zamalek Bridge in Agouza (Map pp146–7). Known as dahabiyyas, these floating two-storey structures once lined the Nile all the way from Giza to Imbaba. During the 1930s some boats were casinos, music halls and bordellos. Many of the surviving residences still have a bohemian air, as chronicled in Naguib Mahfouz' novel *Adrift on the Nile*.

AGRICULTURAL MUSEUM

It may sound dull, but the **Agricultural Museum** (Map p150; ☎ 3761 6785; off Sharia Wizarat al-Ziraa, Doqqi; adult/student E£20/10; ☑ 9am-2pm Tue-Sun) is far from it. Spread over several buildings, the displays tell you all you've ever wanted to know about agriculture in Egypt, from Pharaonic times onwards, and so much more: dioramas depict traditional weddings, glass cases are packed with wax cucurbits, and in one mothball-scented wing, a specimen of every bird in Egypt has been stuffed and pinned to a board. Dusty and a bit spooky, it's a true hall of wonders. It's about 1km from the Doqqi metro station.

MR & MRS MAHMOUD KHALIL MUSEUM

A noted politician during the 1940s, Mohammed Mahmoud Khalil amassed one of the Middle East's finest collections of 19th- and 20th-century European work. The wonderful **Mr & Mrs Mahmoud Khalil Museum** (Map p150; ☎ 3338 9720; 1 Sharia Kafour, Doqqi; admission with ID card or passport only, adult/student E£25/12; ☑ 10am-5pm Tue-Sun, 10am-3pm holidays) includes sculptures by Rodin and paintings by the likes of Delacroix, Gauguin, Toulouse-Lautrec, Manet, Monet and Pissarro. There are also some Rubens, Sisleys and a Picasso. The paintings are housed in Khalil's former villa, later taken over by President Sadat. It's just a few minutes' walk south of the Cairo Sheraton.

Pyramids of Giza

Amid all the hype about the New Wonders of the World, the Pyramids of Giza just sat there – as they have for 4000 years, both outliving the other six ancient wonders and living up to all the hype that has been lavished on them over the millennia. Their extraordinary shape, impeccable geometry and sheer bulk invite the obvious question: 'How were we built, and why?'

Centuries of research have given us parts of the answer to this double-barrelled question. We know they were massive tombs constructed on the orders of the pharaohs by teams of workers tens-of-thousands strong. This is supported by the discovery of a pyramid-builders' settlement, complete with areas for large-scale food production and medical facilities. Ongoing excavations on the Giza Plateau are providing more evidence that the workers were not the slaves of Hollywood tradition, but a highly organised workforce of Egyptian farmers. During the annual flood season, when the Nile covered their fields, the same farmers could have been redeployed by the highly structured bureaucracy to work on the pharaoh's tomb. The Pyramids can almost be seen as an ancient job-creation scheme, with the flood waters also making it easier to transport building stone to the site.

But despite the evidence, some still won't accept that the ancient Egyptians were capable of such astonishing achievements. Pyramidologists – for the study of the structures has become a 'science' in its own right – point to the carving and placement of the stones, precise to the millimetre, and argue the numerological significance of the structures' dimensions as evidence that the Pyramids were variously constructed by angels, the devil or visitors from another planet. It's easy to laugh at such seemingly out-there ideas, but visit the Giza Plateau and you'll see why so many people believe such awesome structures could only have unearthly origins.

THE PYRAMIDS AS A FUNERARY COMPLEX
It was neither an obsession with death, nor a fear of it, that led the ancient Egyptians to build such incredible mausoleums as the pyramids. Rather it was their belief in eternal life and their desire to be at one with the cosmos. The pharaoh was the son of the gods, but it was also his role to conduct the gods' powers to his people. Set between the earth and the sky, connecting the worlds mortal and divine, he was therefore honoured in life and worshipped in death. The pyramid was a fitting tomb for such an individual. A funerary temple attached to each pyramid allowed the pharaoh to be worshipped after his demise, with daily rounds of offerings to sustain his soul. A long covered causeway connected the funerary temple to a 'valley temple' built on the quayside, where the flood waters would reach each year (a superb model of the Abu Sir pyramids illustrates all this on the 1st floor of the Egyptian Museum). The complex also provided a constant visible reminder of the eternal power of the gods, as well as the absolute power of the pharaoh for whom it was built.

PRACTICALITIES
It can be a bit of a shock to visit the **Giza Plateau** (Map p152; adult/student E£50/25; ☎ 8am-4pm winter, 8am-6pm summer) and realise that the sandy mound that's home to the Pyramids is actually plonked in the middle of the congested city suburb of Giza. There are two entrances: one via a continuation of Pyramids Rd (Sharia al-Haram) at the foot of the Great Pyramid of Khufu, and another below the Sphinx, in the village of Nazlet as-Samaan. Most independent visitors enter from Pyramids Rd, as this is where the bus and minibus from Downtown stop. Follow the road up from the roundabout towards the Pyramids and firmly ignore anyone who tries to distract you (see right). Continue along the tarmacked road, up to the temporary ticket office (an unofficial-looking hut) to your right.

There are extra entry charges for the Solar Barque Museum and the interiors of the Pyramids (two of the three are open to visitors, rotating every few years). Before visiting, you could check http://drhawass.com, antiquities director Dr Zahi Hawass' website, which usually posts news about tomb and Pyramid openings.

Note that climbing the Pyramids, a must for European visitors in the 19th and 20th centuries, is dangerous and is now strictly forbidden.

Bathrooms are at the cafe at the base of the Sphinx, as well as in a very dodgy trailer on the plateau itself, adjacent to the ticket office for the Great Pyramid (pay the 'attendant' E£1 max).

THE HASSLE
With battalions of buses, armies of touts and legions of visitors from every part of the globe – all to a soundtrack of gargling camels and cries of 'Buy postcards?' – the tourist scene at the Pyramids is intense. But it helps to remember that it's not a modern phenomenon. The Pyramids have been attracting tourists since they were built, and a local was probably there offering them a ride on a donkey.

Also, it used to be worse. Now an aggressive campaign – involving a very tall concrete wall, razor wire and sentries on camelback – has cut down the number of touts, camel drivers and other hustlers on the plateau itself. The bad news is that, because the people of Nazlet as-Samaan still rely on renting horses and camels for a living, the line of skirmish has just moved further away from the Pyramids. While your taxi or minibus is stopped in traffic on Pyramids Rd, young men might try to jump in with you to explain that the road ahead is closed – and the best way to proceed, conveniently, is on horseback. They might also tell you the 'walk-in entrance' is near their stables, or suggest that they can get you into the Pyramids area without a ticket. Note that genuine tickets have a hologram seal, and ignore everyone until you get one in your hands. Once on the plateau, you just have to negotiate with guys for camel rides and avoid the rogue antiquities cop who will try to usher you into the 'ruin' of the old police station.

CAMELS & HORSES
The blocks just behind the Sphinx-side entrance are filled with milling horses and

CAIRO

MOHANDISEEN, AGOUZA & ZAMALEK

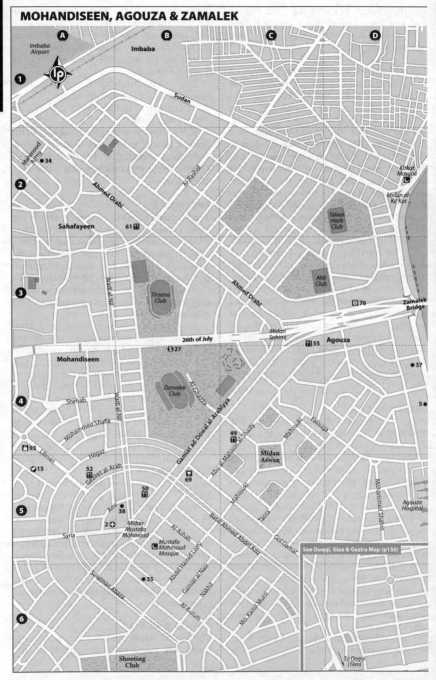

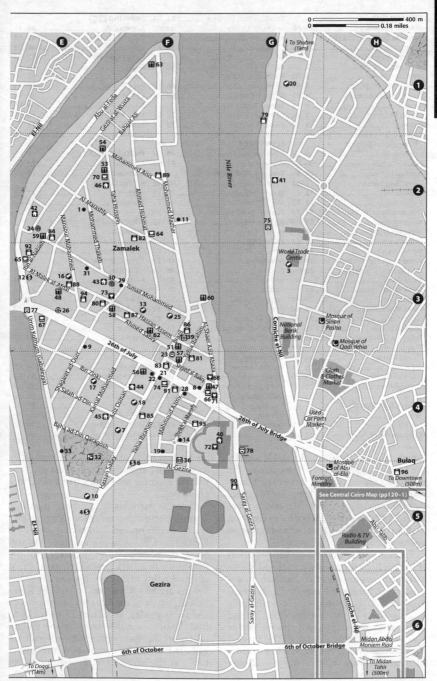

CAIRO

camels. There's also a smaller stable area by the Mena House entrance. Considering the extraordinary amount of hassle the horse-owners give tourists, it's tempting to ignore them completely; however, the distance between the three pyramids is a lot to cover on foot, so the service is a real one, should you be interested.

Tourism authorities have set 'official' prices (E£35 per hour for camels, horses and horse-carts), but, as one officer said with an apologetic shrug, 'you're still expected to bargain'. Women should be a little wary of overfriendly camel-owners trying to clamber up behind them, and everyone should choose to ride only healthy-looking animals. If you are ever held hostage on a camel – asked to pay more than agreed before you're let down – call over

the nearest tourist police, or go to the office by the Mena House and complain (E£20 or E£25 is a fair fee for a quick trot around and photo op).

If you're particularly interested in riding, hiring a horse from one of the village stables is a far better option than taking one at the Pyramids. Once you're mounted, you will be off on your own in the desert with the Pyramids as a background. General expat opinion holds that the best stables near the Sphinx are **NB** (☎ 3382 0435), owned by Naser Breesh, who's praised for his healthy steeds and good guides; his place can be tricky to find: head down the street by the Sphinx poster off the main square where horses are gathered, or ask for directions to the Sphinx Club, as the stables are just behind it. **MG**

(☎ 3385 3832) and **AA** (☎ 3385 0531), near the coach park, are both decent as well. Expect to pay around E£35 per hour (hand over the money after the ride, and tip your guide an additional E£5 or E£10), and keep your Pyramids site ticket or you'll be charged again to enter. Moonlight rides around the Pyramids are a favourite outing but under new regulations you can't ride very close to the site after 6pm.

GREAT PYRAMID OF KHUFU (CHEOPS)

The oldest pyramid in Giza and the largest in Egypt, the **Great Pyramid of Khufu** (Map p152; adult/student E£100/50) stood 146m high when it was completed around 2570 BC. After 46 windy centuries, its height has been reduced by 9m. About 2.3 million limestone blocks, reckoned to weigh about 2.5 tonnes each, were used in the construction.

Tickets, sold from a kiosk in front and slightly to the east (city side) of the pyramid, are limited to 300 per day: 150 on sale starting at 7.30am and 150 at 1pm. During the winter you'll probably need to queue early, especially on Wednesday and Thursday, when tour groups from the Red Sea visit Cairo for the day. Note that only Egyptian pounds are accepted, and cameras are not allowed into the pyramid – you must surrender them to the guards at the entrance, who will ask for baksheesh before returning them (E£1 is fine).

There isn't much to see inside the pyramid, but the experience of climbing through the ancient structure is unforgettable – though impossible if you suffer the tiniest degree of claustrophobia. The elderly and unfit should not attempt the climb, as it is very steep.

Past the entrance, on the north face, a passage descends to an unfinished tomb (usually closed) about 100m along and 30m deep in the bedrock. Before you reach this, about 20m after the entrance, another passage, 1.3m high and 1m wide, ascends for about 40m to reach the Great Gallery, an impressive area 47m long and 8.5m high. At the start of the gallery, a small horizontal passage leads into the so-called Queen's Chamber.

As you continue through the Great Gallery, notice how precisely the blocks in the ceiling fit together. In the 10m-long King's Chamber at the end, the walls are built of red granite blocks. The ceiling itself consists of nine huge slabs of granite, which weigh more than 400 tonnes. Above these slabs, four more slabs are separated by gaps, which are designed to distribute the enormous weight away from the chamber. Good airflow from the modern ventilation system (built into two ancient air shafts) will help you breathe easier as you contemplate the tremendous weight suspended above you.

Outside, on the eastern side of the pyramid, three small structures some 20m high resemble pyramid-shaped piles of rubble. These are the Queens' Pyramids, the tombs of Khufu's wives and sisters. You can enter some of them, but they're quite steamy inside.

SOLAR BARQUE MUSEUM

South of the Great Pyramid is the fascinating **Solar Barque Museum** (Map p152; adult/student E£50/25; ☉ 9am-4pm Oct-May, 9am-5pm Jun-Sep). Five pits near the Great Pyramid of Khufu contained the pharaoh's solar barques (boats), which may have been used to convey the mummy of the dead pharaoh across the Nile to the valley temple, from where it was brought up the causeway and into the tomb chamber. The barques were then buried around the pyramid to provide transport for the pharaoh in the next world.

One of these ancient cedar-wood vessels, possibly the oldest boat in existence, was unearthed in 1954. It was carefully restored from 1200 pieces of wood and encased in a glass museum to protect it from damage from the elements. Visitors to the museum must help this process by donning protective footwear to keep sand out.

There are plans to move the boat to the nearby Grand Egyptian Museum, whenever it opens – for more information, see the boxed text on p154.

PYRAMID OF KHAFRE (CHEPHREN)

Southwest of the Great Pyramid, the **Pyramid of Khafre** (Map p152; adult/student E£30/15) seems larger than that of his father, Khufu. At just 136m high, it's not, but it stands on higher ground and its peak is still capped with a limestone casing. Originally all three pyramids were totally encased with polished white stone, which would have made them gleam in the sun. Over the centuries, this casing has been stripped for use in palaces and mosques, exposing the softer inner-core stones to the elements.

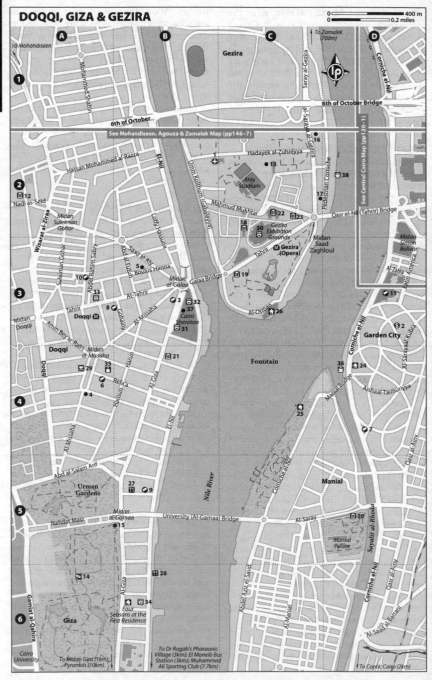

DOQQI, GIZA & GEZIRA

To Mohandiseen

Gezira

6th of October Bridge

6th of October

See Mohandiseen, Agouza & Zamalek Map (pp146–7)

Hadayek al-Zuhreyya

Ahly Stadium

Nadi as-Seid

Mahmud Mukhtar

Gezira Exhibition Grounds

Qasr el-Nil (Tahrir) Bridge

Midan Saad Zaghloul

Midan Simon Bolivar

Midan Suleiman Gohar

Gezira (Opera)

Garden City

Midan al-Galaa

Galaa Bridge

Al-Orman

Doqqi

Midan Doqqi

Cairo Sheraton

Midan al-Missaha

Fountain

Manial Bridge

Urman Gardens

Nile River

University (Al-Gamaa) Bridge

Al-Saray

Manial

Midan al-Gamaa

Four Seasons at the First Residence

Manial Palace

Giza

Cairo University

To Midan Giza (1km); Pyramids (10km)

To Dr Ragab's Pharaonic Village (3km); El Moneib Bus Station (3km); Muhammad Ali Sporting Club (7.7km)

To Coptic Cairo (2km)

To Zamalek (700m)

0   400 m
0   0.2 miles

The chambers and passageways of this particular pyramid are less elaborate than those in the Great Pyramid, but are almost as claustrophobic. The entrance descends into a passage and then across to the burial chamber, which still contains Khafre's large granite sarcophagus. Tickets are sold at the kiosk in front of the pyramid.

Back outside, to the east of the pyramid, are the substantial remains of **Khafre's funerary temple** (Map p152) and the flagged paving of the causeway that provided access from the Nile to the tomb.

PYRAMID OF MENKAURE (MYCERINUS)

At 62m (originally 66.5m), this pyramid (Map p152) is the smallest of the trio. A gash in the north face is the result of an attempt by Saladin's son Malek Abdel Aziz to dismantle the pyramid in AD 1186. He gave up after eight months, having achieved little. Outside the pyramid you'll see the excavated remains of **Menkaure's funerary temple** and, further east, the ruins of his **valley temple**. Visitors are no longer allowed inside the pyramid, and it's a long slog out here – you're excused if you skip it.

THE SPHINX

Legends and superstitions abound about the Sphinx (Map p152), and the mystery surrounding its long-forgotten purpose is almost as intriguing as its appearance. On seeing it for the first time, many visitors agree with English playwright Alan Bennett, who noted in his diary that seeing the Sphinx is like meet-

ing a TV personality in the flesh: he's smaller than one had imagined.

Known in Arabic as Abu al-Hol (Father of Terror), the feline man was dubbed the Sphinx by the ancient Greeks because it resembled the mythical winged monster with a woman's head and lion's body who set riddles and killed anyone unable to answer them. (It even has a little tail.)

The Sphinx was carved from the bedrock at the bottom of the causeway to the Pyramid of Khafre; geological survey has shown that it was most likely carved during this pharaoh's reign, so it probably portrays his features, framed by the *nemes* (striped headcloth worn by royalty).

As is clear from the accounts of early Arab travellers, the nose was hammered off sometime between the 11th and 15th centuries, although some still like to blame Napoleon for the deed. Part of the fallen beard was carted off by 19th-century adventurers and is now on display in the British Museum in London. These days the Sphinx has potentially greater problems: the monument is suffering the stone equivalent of cancer and is being eaten away from the inside; pollution and rising groundwater are the most likely causes. A succession of restoration attempts unfortunately sped up the decay rather than halting it. The Sphinx' shiny white paws are the result of the most recent effort.

Just below the Sphinx an expensive **cafe** (tea & soda from E£15, fresh juice from E£20) boasts an outdoor terrace and truly amazing view. It's technically outside the site but, as long as you

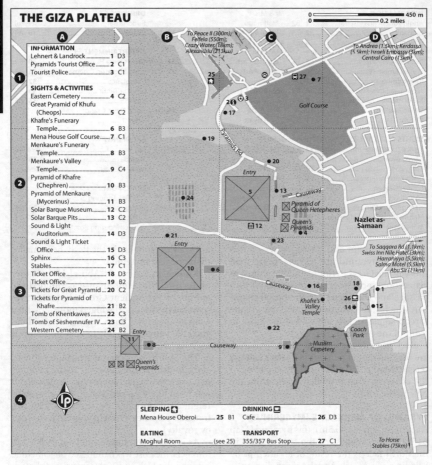

THE GIZA PLATEAU

INFORMATION	
Lehnert & Landrock	**1** D3
Pyramids Tourist Office	**2** C1
Tourist Police	**3** C1

SIGHTS & ACTIVITIES	
Eastern Cemetery	**4** C2
Great Pyramid of Khufu (Cheops)	**5** C2
Khafre's Funerary Temple	**6** B3
Mena House Golf Course	**7** C1
Menkaure's Funerary Temple	**8** B3
Menkaure's Valley Temple	**9** C4
Pyramid of Khafre (Chephren)	**10** B3
Pyramid of Menkaure (Mycerinus)	**11** B3
Solar Barque Museum	**12** C2
Solar Barque Pits	**13** C2
Sound & Light Auditorium	**14** D3
Sound & Light Ticket Office	**15** D3
Sphinx	**16** C3
Stables	**17** C1
Ticket Office	**18** D3
Ticket Office	**19** B2
Tickets for Great Pyramid	**20** C2
Tickets for Pyramid of Khafre	**21** B2
Tomb of Khentkawes	**22** C3
Tomb of Seshemnufer IV	**23** C3
Western Cemetery	**24** B2

SLEEPING		DRINKING	
Mena House Oberoi	**25** B1	Cafe	**26** D3

EATING		TRANSPORT	
Moghul Room	(see 25)	355/357 Bus Stop	**27** C1

have your ticket, the guards will let you leave and come back in again.

TOMB OF KHENTKAWES

This rarely visited imposing structure (Map p152), opposite the Great Pyramid and south of Khafre's causeway, is the tomb of Menkaure's powerful daughter. The tomb is a rectangular building cut into a small hill. A corridor at the back of the chapel room leads down to the burial chambers; the descent can be hazardous.

CEMETERIES

Private cemeteries consisting of several rows of tombs are organised around the Pyramids in a grid pattern. Most tombs are closed to the public, but those of Qar, Idu and Queen Meresankh III, in the **eastern cemetery** (Map p152), are accessible, although it can sometimes be difficult to find the guard who has the keys.

The Tomb of Iasen, in the **western cemetery** (Map p152), contains interesting inscriptions and wall paintings that offer a glimpse of daily life during the Old Kingdom. The **tomb of Seshemnufer IV** (Map p152), just south of the Great Pyramid, also has a burial chamber you can climb down into.

SOUND & LIGHT SHOW

The Sphinx narrates the somewhat cheesy **sound and light show** (☎ 3385 2880; www.soundand light.com.eg; admission E£75), but it's neat to see the Pyramids so dramatically lit. Though there's officially no student discount, you may be able to negotiate one. Schedules were as follows at the time of writing, but check the website for the latest. Note that this is the winter schedule; in summer shows start two hours later.

Day	6.30pm	7.30pm	8.30pm	9.30pm
Mon	English	French	Spanish	
Tue	English	Italian	French	
Wed	English	French	German	Spanish
Thu	Japanese	English	French	Arabic
Fri	English	French	Italian	
Sat	English	Spanish	Italian	
Sun	German	French	Russian	English

GETTING THERE & AWAY

Bus 355/357 runs from Heliopolis to the Pyramids via central Cairo every 20 minutes. It picks up from the road (not the island) under the overpass at Midan Abdel Moniem Riad. There's no sign so you'll have to ask a local where to stand. Be alert, as you'll probably have to flag the bus down. It also passes through Tahrir, and can usually be flagged down from the bus shelter near the northwestern metro stairs; see Map pp120–1 for the exact position. The bus is a white one, with 'CTA' on its side. A ticket costs E£2 and the trip takes about 45 minutes.

Microbuses also go from Midan Abdel Moniem Riad, near the Ramses Hilton; just ask for 'Haram' and somebody will point you to the right line of vehicles. The fare is E£1.50 and you'll be dropped off about 250m short of the Mena House Oberoi hotel (also where buses 355 and 357 terminate).

By far the most straightforward way to go is in a yellow metered taxi from the rank on Midan Tahrir. It's usually about E£20, the same price you'd be lucky to bargain a black-and-white-cab driver down to – plus you get air-con. Avoiding the city-centre traffic by taking the metro to the Giza stop (E£1) doesn't work so well; from there, a taxi to the Pyramids *should* cost only E£8, but many drivers have caught on to this cost-saving tactic and quickly quote outrageous prices.

Returning to Cairo, taxis leaving from either entrance will try for at least E£40, so you'll need to bargain hard – or else walk down Pyramids Rd until you encounter a less voracious driver, or just take the bus.

Around the Pyramids

Tours to the Pyramids often include the two communities on the Maryutia Canal, which runs north-south about 1.5km east of the plateau. One is worth your time, perhaps even an independent trip. The other, not so much.

HARRANIYYA

Along the Maryutia Canal south of Pyramids Rd, Harraniyya (off Map p152) is one of several villages that have now blurred into one long stretch of half-developed green farmland. The main (er, only) attraction is **Wissa Wassef Art Centre** (☎ 3381 5746; www.wissa-wassef-arts.com; Saqqara Rd; ☟ 10am-5pm). The mudbrick complex is the work of architect Ramses Wissa Wassef; it won an Aga Khan prize for its refined traditional style. The artisans who work here in open studios (closed Friday) are known for their distinctive tapestries depicting rural scenes. Crude imitations are standard in souvenir shops; the ones for sale and on display in the museum here are in a completely different class, like paintings in wool. There's pottery and batik fabric, done to equally good effect. The place has the feeling of a sanctuary – quiet and refreshingly green.

To get here, take a microbus (E£1) or taxi (E£10) from Pyramids Rd in the direction of Saqqara and get off when you see the blue 'Harraniyya' sign, after about 3.5km, or 10 minutes. The centre is by the canal on the west side of the road.

KERDASSA

As the source of many of the scarves, *galabiyya*s and weavings sold in the bazaars of Cairo, Kerdassa is often touted as an insider shopping destination, to buy 'direct from the source'. But the dismal setting of semirural poverty adjacent to a new strip mall, plus the price of a taxi ride (E£15 from the Pyramids), cancels out the minor savings. You could also flag down a microbus (E£1) heading north on the canal from Pyramids Rd – the village is about 5.5km, roughly 15 minutes, along.

Heliopolis

It's only a suburb of Cairo, but were it to stand alone as a town in its own right, Heliopolis (Misr al-Gedida, or 'New Cairo'; Map p155) would be considered one of the gems of North Africa. A Belgian industrialist conceived the district in the early 20th century as a 'garden city', home to the colonial officials who ruled Egypt. With whitewashed Moorish-style buildings with dark wood balconies, grand arcades and terraces, it's the European vision

CAIRO

THE GRAND EGYPTIAN MUSEUM

In 2002, amidst much pomp and circumstance, Egyptian President Mubarak laid the ceremonial foundation for the **Grand Egyptian Museum** (GEM; www.gem.gov.eg), the cornerstone of an ambitious project aimed at redefining the Giza Plateau. Located just two kilometres from the Great Pyramids, the GEM is intended to serve as a state-of-the-art showcase for the country's finest antiquities. In addition to relieving the Egyptian Museum (see p183) of its overcrowded displays, the GEM will also provide proper climate control, something that the Egyptian Museum is at present sorely lacking.

Things got off to a good start following the largest architectural competition in history, which resulted in 1557 entries from 82 countries. The winning bid was from the Heneghan Peng firm in Ireland, which envisioned a translucent stone wall running along the entire length of the museum's main facade, and lining up in perfect precision with the Great Pyramids of Khufu and Menkaure. In 2006, the Statue of Ramses II was moved from Ramses Square in downtown Cairo to the anticipated entrance of the GEM. In 2008, preliminary excavation began, which prompted the press announcement that the GEM would open to the public in no more than 36 months.

But at the time of research the project was suffering from severe construction delays, fuelled in part by the global recession, which has hit Egypt particularly hard. While museum officials have pushed the opening date back to 2012, it is very likely that the doors of the GEM will remain closed much longer than originally anticipated. There are also growing concerns, frequently echoed in Egyptian media, that the price tag on the GEM is rapidly ballooning above the initial estimate of US$550 million.

Construction delays and bureaucratic hurdles aside, the GEM will eventually boast provisional space for more than 100,000 artefacts, and it's believed that around five million domestic and foreign tourists will visit annually. Perhaps even more important is the simple fact that Egypt's ancient treasures will be housed in a world-class structure that will ensure their continued preservation for future generations.

of the 'Orient' in stone. Since the 1950s, overcrowding has filled in the spaces between the villas with apartment buildings festooned with satellite dishes, but the area still has a relaxed, almost Mediterranean air. With all its trees and outdoor cafes, it's a pleasant place for an evening's wander – and many Egyptians think so too, as Heliopolis has become 'downtown' for people living in dull satellite cities further east. Weekend nights can be very lively.

The main street is Sharia al-Ahram, on which stands the **Uruba Palace** (Map p155), once a grand hotel graced by the likes of King Albert I of Belgium and now Mubarak's offices – a short commute, as he lives just up the street. From the palace, at the first intersection with the splendid Sharia Ibrahim Laqqany (detour left for some fantastic architecture), is the open-air cafeteria **Amphitrion** (Map p155), as old as Heliopolis itself and a popular watering hole for Allied soldiers during the world wars. At the end of the street, the **Basilica** (Map p155) is a miniature version of Istanbul's famous Aya Sofya, dubbed the 'jelly mould' by local expats. Baron Empain, the man who founded Heliopolis, is buried here.

South, on Sharia al-Uruba (Airport Rd), you can't miss the extraordinary **Baron's Palace** (Qasr al-Baron; Map p155), a Hindu-style temple modelled on the temples of Angkor Wat in Cambodia, with Buddhas, geishas, elephants and serpents adorning the exterior. The fantastical look of the place contributed to a citywide panic in 1997 about 'Satanists' allegedly holding rituals here – it turned out they were a bunch of upper-class teenage heavy-metal fans. A decade later, the ruin is still very much off-limits.

OCTOBER WAR PANORAMA

Built with help from North Korean artists, the **October War Panorama** (Map pp112-13; ☎ 2402 2317; Sharia al-Uruba; admission E£20; ☯ shows 9.30am, 11am, 12.20pm, 6pm & 7.30pm Wed-Mon) is a memorial to the 1973 'victory' over Israel. A large 3D mural and diorama depicts the Egyptian forces breaching of the Bar Lev Line on the Suez Canal, while a stirring commentary (in Arabic only) recounts the heroic victories. Interestingly it skips over the successful Israeli counterattacks. Both sides accepted a UN-brokered ceasefire, and Sinai was returned by negotiation six years later. The exhibition is

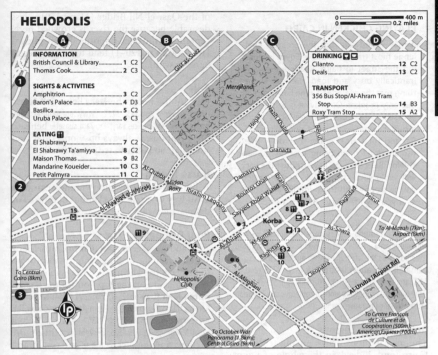

HELIOPOLIS

0 — 400 m
0 — 0.2 miles

INFORMATION
British Council & Library...................**1** C2
Thomas Cook...**2** C3

SIGHTS & ACTIVITIES
Amphitrion..**3** C2
Baron's Palace......................................**4** D3
Basilica...**5** C3
Uruba Palace...**6** C3

EATING 🍴
El Shabrawy..**7** C2
El Shabrawy Ta'amiyya.....................**8** C2
Maison Thomas....................................**9** B2
Mandarine Koueider..........................**10** C3
Petit Palmyra.......................................**11** C2

DRINKING 🍷 🍺
Cilantro...**12** C2
Deals...**13** C2

TRANSPORT
356 Bus Stop/Al-Ahram Tram
Stop..**14** B3
Roxy Tram Stop..................................**15** A2

about 2.5km southwest of the Baron's Palace, on the same road; walk, take one of the buses along Sharia al-Uruba or get a taxi.

GETTING THERE & AWAY
Cairo's trams (25pt, 30 to 40 minutes) run to Heliopolis from just north of Midan Ramses (see Map p124). They're a little rattletrap, but often faster than the bus. Get off where the line branches, just before Midan Roxy. Or take airport bus 356 (E£2) from Midan Abdel Moniem Riad (see Map pp120–1). The ride takes between 30 and 45 minutes. Get off outside the Heliopolis Club (the first stop after reaching the street with tram tracks). Trams and buses usually run every 20 minutes.

ACTIVITIES
For more details of activities around town, check *Al-Ahram Weekly* or the monthlies *Egypt Today* and the *Croc*.

Art Galleries
With a fresh generation of artists and new media, Cairo's art scene is more active and diverse than it ever has been. In addition to

galleries, the city's cultural centres (p114) often mount interesting exhibitions too.

Cairo Atelier (Map pp120-1; ☎ 2574 6730; 2 Sharia Karim al-Dawla, Downtown; ☉ 10am-1pm & 5-10pm Sat-Thu) Off Sharia Mahmoud Bassiouni, as much a clubhouse as an exhibition space, frequented by Cairo's art-world old guard.

Contemporary Image Collective (Map pp112-13; ☎ 2794 1686; 20 Sharia Safeya Zaghloul, Mounira; ☉ 11am-6pm Sun-Thu) Excellent exhibits documenting Egyptian life and occasionally shows videos on its rooftop.

Karim Francis Art Gallery Downtown (Map pp120-1; ☎ 2391 6357; 1 Sharia Sherifeen; ☉ 2-9pm Sat-Thu); Zamalek (Map pp146-7; ☎ 2736 2183; www.karimfrancis .com; 3rd fl, Baehler's Mansions, 157 Sharia 26th of July; ☉ 4-11pm Tue-Sun) Francis is one of Cairo's more influential curators.

Mashrabia Gallery of Contemporary Art (Map pp120-1; ☎ 2578 4494; 8 Sharia Champollion, Downtown; ☉ 11am-8pm Sat-Thu) One of the first independent galleries, Mashrabia is bit cramped but represents the bigger names in painting and sculpture.

Townhouse Gallery of Contemporary Art (Map pp120-1; ☎ 2576 8086; www.thetownhousegallery.com; 10 Sharia Nabrawy, Downtown; ☉ 10am-2pm & 6-9pm Sat-Wed, 6-9pm Fri) Set amid car-repair shops, Townhouse

---

PLAYING CHICKEN IN CAIRO

It may sound silly, but the greatest challenge most travellers face in Egypt is crossing the street in Cairo. Roads are always frantically busy and road rules are something that the average Cairene has heard of, but only in jokes. Our advice is to position yourself so that one or more locals forms a buffer between you and oncoming traffic, and then cross when they do – they usually don't mind being used as human shields. Basically, you have to trust the cars will avoid you – never, ever hesitate once you've stepped off the sidewalk, and cross as if you own the road. But do it fast!

---

is Cairo's most cutting-edge space, with emphasis on video and multimedia installations. It also has a large workshop situated across the street, for classes and confabs.
Zamalek Art Gallery (Map pp146-7; ☎ 2735 1240; 11 Sharia Brazil, Zamalek; ☺ 10.30am-9pm Sat-Thu) A light-filled space showing work of contemporary Egyptian artists, usually figurative.

Belly-Dancing Lessons

The most famous belly-dancing teacher in Cairo (and, indeed, in the whole of Egypt) is **Mme Raqia Hassan** (☎ 3748 2338; raqiahassan@hotmail.com). Many of the country's best dancers have learned their craft from Mme Hassan. She runs a small studio in her Doqqi apartment, where either she or one of her protégés will give you (or a group, if you can get one together) lessons. Some of the city's gyms and health clubs will organise group courses – try **Samia Allouba Dance & Fitness Centre** (Map pp146-7; ☎ 3302 0572; 6 Sharia Amr) in Mohandiseen. Costs for lessons vary depending on the size of your group and the length of time.

Felucca Rides

One of the most pleasant things to do on a warm day is to go out on a felucca, Egypt's ancient broad-sail boat, with a supply of beer and a small picnic just as sunset approaches. The best spot for hiring is the Dok Dok landing stage (Map p150) on the corniche in Garden City, across from the Four Seasons. Subject to haggling, a boat and captain should cost about E£30 per hour irrespective of the number of people on board; your captain will appreciate additional baksheesh (possibly in liquid form). The mooring point in Gezira just north

of the Qasr el-Nil Bridge (Map p150) is less desirable because the river is crowded here; captains at the dock opposite the Shepheard Hotel (Map pp120-1) tend to be tougher to bargain with.

Golf

Run by the hotel, the **Mena House Golf Course** (Map p152; ☎ 3383 3222; www.oberoihotels.com; Pyramids Rd, Giza; prices vary; ☺ 7am-sunset), beneath the Pyramids, is always busy on Friday and Saturday, so better to tee off midweek.

Horse Riding

A horse ride out by the Pyramids can be a great way to escape the clamour of Cairo. For details, see p145.

Pool & Snooker

Pool and snooker are popular in Cairo. Many venues are in the wealthier suburbs away from the city centre. The most central snooker and pool halls are on the top floor of the **Ramses Hilton Mall** (Map pp120-1; ☎ 2577 7444; east of the Ramses Hilton, Downtown; ☺ 2pm-4am). In Zamalek **Aristocrat** (Map pp146-7; ☎ 2736 6344; 2nd fl, 15 Sharia Ismail Mohammed; per hr E£25; ☺ 24hr) is a little more mellow, and doubles as a bar and restaurant.

Swimming

Finding a place to cool off in the city can be difficult. Cairenes who can afford it swim in sporting clubs, which do not admit nonmembers. Some hotels do allow day use for nonguests, at a price. Best options:
Cairo Marriott (Map pp146-7; ☎ 2728 3000; 16 Sharia Saray al-Gezira, Zamalek; day use E£125) The Marriott has a good pool in a garden setting. The fee includes use of gym and sauna.
Muhammad Ali Sporting Club (off Map pp112-13; ☎ 010 568 6000; Corniche el-Nil, Sharia Saied Giza, Moneib; day use Fri & Sat adult/child £50/25, Sun-Thu E£25/15) Major social scene – a mix of expats and Egyptians – at this cool Nileside pool with beanbag chairs, beers and bikinis. It's located way south on the west bank, about even with Ma'adi – a taxi will cost E£20 from the centre.
Nile Hotel (Map pp120-1; ☎ 2578 0444; 1113 Corniche el-Nil, Downtown; day use E£125) The Hilton's pool is large, relatively deep and surrounded by shady trees.

CAIRO FOR CHILDREN

Cairo can be exhausting for kids, but there is much they will enjoy. If you have a few days in the city it may be worth buying *Cairo, the Family Guide*, by Lesley Lababidi and Lisa

Sabbahy (AUC Press, E£70), revised in 2006. Most children will enjoy pretending to be a pirate on a Nile felucca (opposite), gawking at the treasures of Tutankhamun in the Egyptian Museum (p183), investigating the Pyramids at Giza (p144) and Dahshur (p204), as well as the maze of Khan al-Khalili (p130). A number of child-oriented activities and theme parks are also worth considering.

The long-running **Cairo Puppet Theatre** (Masrah al-Ara'is; Map pp120-1; ☎ 2591 0954; admission E£5; ⏰ 6.30-8.15pm Thu, 10.30am-1pm Fri & Sun) is opposite Ezbekiyya Gardens in Downtown. The shows are in Arabic, but are colourful and

---

DIY WALKING CAIRO

Contrary to first impressions of careening buses and crammed sidewalks, Cairo is an excellent city for walking. Really.

It's especially good for aimless, mapless wandering: districts are relatively compact, the terrain is level and the scenery changes quickly enough to keep things interesting. Streets are safe, and you will never accidentally wander into a 'bad' neighbourhood. We heartily encourage stowing the guidebook and letting yourself get at least a little lost in Cairo's winding back lanes.

Feel free to walk in the street (most people do), be considerate when taking photos, and keep your ears open for local cues such as hissing (see boxed text, p164). And, at least once, accept a stranger's invitation to tea or soda. These are some of the best places to stroll, over the course of a day.

Islamic Cairo in the Morning

Start early – before 7.30am – with tea at Fishawi's (p170) and watch the khan slowly wake up. If you do want to work in a little sightseeing, take a quick stroll up Bein al-Qasreen (p134) to admire the buildings without the crush of traffic and commerce. But the better, more aimless amble is to the south: take the small alley behind Sharia al-Azhar, heading in the direction of Al-Azhar Park, then head south, roughly following the old walls built by Saladin that are being excavated as part of the park development. The tiny workshops produce shoes, parquet flooring, mother-of-pearl inlay boxes and more. But it's also a residential district, where families on upper floors run baskets down to the *ba'al* (grocer) for supplies, and knife-sharpeners and junk traders (the men who shout 'Beeeeeee-kya!') roll through the lanes. Keeping your general bearings with the park to your left, you can wander all the way down to the Citadel. Near the end, you'll wind up on the southern stretch of Darb al-Ahmar (p136). To loop back to Sharia al-Azhar, go via Sharia al-Khayamiyya (p136).

Garden City at Twilight

The interlocking circles that form the streets of Garden City are maddening if you want to get anywhere, but they're perfect for strolling just for the sake of admiring the crumbling mansions in this colonial-era district. The best time to visit is the hour before sundown, when the dust coating the architectural curlicues turns a warm, glamorous gold and the starlings shrill in the fruit trees.

You can start at the north end (get the brutalist concrete Canadian embassy behind you right away!) and wind south. Keep an eye out for wrought-iron dragons on cobwebbed gates, a rare Turkish-style wood-front home and the last real garden in Garden City, behind the Four Seasons hotel.

You'll wind up, conveniently, near the Dok Dok felucca landing stage (opposite).

Downtown after Midnight

This is less walking than cafe-hopping, when the air is cool and the streets are thronged. Wander around Midan Orabi, where you can perch on any random planter and someone will come and sell you tea. From here Sharia Alfy and the smaller streets on either side are your playground for snacking, *sheesha*-smoking and maybe even some lavish tipping of belly dancers (see p173). No matter how late you're out, you can wind up the night at the 24-hour Odeon Palace Hotel bar (p171).

animated enough to entertain non-Arabic speakers of all ages.

Fun Planet (Map pp146-7; Arkadia Mall, Corniche el-Nil, Bulaq; first 3 games E£10, each subsequent game E£3-5; ☻ 3-11pm Sat-Thu & 1-11pm Fri) is an indoor amusement centre offering loads of rides and games and will appeal to teenagers. Citystars Centre (see p176) also has a big indoor fun park.

The **National Circus** (Map pp146-7; ☎ 3347 0612; Sharia el-Nil, Agouza, near the Zamalek Bridge; admission E£30-50; ☻ box office 11am-10pm, performances 10pm-midnight) is a traditional circus with clowns, acrobats, lions and tigers and lots of glitter. It's usually here during the cooler months; it tours the country at other times of the year. Not far away, children can feed the hippos, see countless kinds of camels and meet local kids at the **Cairo Zoo** (Guineenat al-Haywanet; Map p150; ☎ 3570 8895; Midan al-Gamaa, Giza; admission 50pt; ☻ 9am-4pm).

The aqua park **Crazy Water** (off Map pp112-13; ☎ 3781 4564; admission children 3-10 yr E£25, children 10 yr & older E£35-45; ☻ 10am-10pm) has half-a-dozen water slides, a wave pool, a kiddies' pool, and a playground area with sand, slides and tunnels. To get to the park from the Pyramids, drive 15km on the Cairo–Alexandria road from its intersection with Pyramids Rd, then turn left towards 6th of October City.

The theme park **Dr Ragab's Pharaonic Village** (off Map pp112-13; ☎ 3571 8675; www.pharaonicvillage .com; 3 Sharia al-Bahr al-Azam, Corniche, Moneib; per person from US$15; ☻ 9am-6pm Sep-Jun, 9am-9pm Jul & Aug) is cheesy but offers a child-friendly glimpse of what life in ancient Egypt would have been like, with a boat trip past actors in Pharaonic costumes, a playground and an art centre where kids can make mini reed boats. Take a taxi (E£20 from Downtown), or walk the 800m from the Sakiat Mekki metro stop. Note that the price of admission varies according to your planned itinerary.

Fagnoon Art School (☎ 3815 1014; Saqqara Rd, Sabil Umm Hashim; per day E£25; ☻ 10am-7pm) is a wonderful art centre in the fields between Giza and Saqqara. Children can slosh paint around, model clay, work with wrought iron or print and paint on textiles, all in the shadow of the Saqqara step pyramid. You can bring your own food and drink, although *fiteer* (pancake/ pizza), coffee and water are usually on sale. To get here, take a microbus from the Pyramids Rd 12.5km in the direction of Saqqara and asked to be dropped off at Sabil Umm Hashim.

The pleasant **Gabalaya Park & Aquarium** (Fish Garden; Map pp146-7; Sharia Umm Kolthum, Zamalek; admis-sion E£1; ☻ 10am-5pm) has landscaped gardens with aquariums set in rocks (though not many actual fish). It's a great central spot to escape the crowds.

Overlooking Islamic Cairo, Al-Azhar Park (p141) is home to one of the few children's playgrounds in the central city.

When only bribery will help, try Mandarine Koueider (see p168) for delectable, distracting ice cream. Or cut straight to toys at **Mom & Me** (Map pp146-7; ☎ 2736 5751; 20A Sharia Mansour Mohammed, Zamalek) or **Toys R Us** (Map pp146-7; ☎ 2578 0820; Ground fl, Arkadia Mall, Bulaq).

TOURS

Numerous companies and individuals offer tours of sights within and around Cairo. We recommend Salah Muhammad's **Noga Tours** (☎ 012 313 8446; www.first24hours.com), as he employs excellent English-speaking guides, Egyptologists and drivers. Mohamed Anwar's specialised **museum tours** (☎ 012 340 7724) also have a good reputation. To hire a taxi for the day and dispense with a guide, try the friendly **Fathy el-Menesy** (☎ 2486 4251), who owns a well-maintained Peugeot and speaks English, as does **Abu Mu'azz** (☎ 010 563 2078). Alternatively, ask at your hotel about taxi hire. Fathy el-Menesy charges between E£200 and E£250 for a full day, and Noga Tours charges around US$25 (plus entry fees) per person for a day-long trip to the Giza Pyramids, Memphis and Saqqara. Its half-day tour of Dahshur costs around US$20 per person.

FESTIVALS & EVENTS

For general information on festivals and public holidays see p512.

Arabic Music Festival At the Cairo Opera House in November.

Belly dance festival (www.nilegroup.net) At the Mena House Oberoi hotel in June. Check the website for details.

Cairo International Film Festival (www.cairofilmfest .org) At the Cairo Opera House in November/December.

Moulid an-Nabi Birthday of Prophet Mohammed, 12 Rabi al-Awwal (26 February 2010, 15 February 2011, 4 February 2012). A citywide party with sweets, and kids in new clothes; in the week beforehand, Midan al-Hussein is the venue for the most intense Sufi *zikrs* (sessions of dancing and chanting carried out to achieve oneness with God). For more information on Moulids, see boxed text, p512.

Ramadan Ninth month of the Islamic calendar (11 August 2010, 1 August 2011, 20 July 2012). By day everything slows down: shops and offices open late and close early, and just before sunset the streets empty as everyone goes home to break the fast. But the nights, particularly in Islamic Cairo, buzz until dawn.

Sham an-Nassim First Monday after Coptic Easter. Literally meaning 'sniffing the breeze' (ie to welcome spring), it's a ritual that came from Pharaonic tradition via the Copts, and is celebrated by all Cairenes, who picnic at the zoo, in parks, by the Pyramids and on riverbanks and even traffic islands.

SLEEPING

Cairo has a few gem hotels, and something for every budget, but it certainly pays to shop around before the start of your trip, and make reservations in advance whenever possible. This is definitely not a city where you want to be hauling your luggage and dodging wild traffic for any longer than is absolutely necessary.

Budget crash pads are chock-a-block but in the midrange the choices are not as numerous. Paying slightly more may get you amenities such as satellite TV, but it doesn't guarantee quality and comfort – a few budget (under E£120) options outclass some midrange places that coast on package-tour bookings. Breakfast is usually included in the rate in both price categories, and prices are somewhat negotiable, especially in the summer, when tourists are fewer. In Cairo, as well as elsewhere in Egypt, consider the rates quoted here a guideline.

On the upper end, impressive luxury hotels line the banks of the Nile and, if your wallet has adequate padding, this is definitely one city where you may want to enjoy these establishments. Also, feel free to treat these hotels as locals do: as places of respite from the city din, with clean bathrooms and other comforts. You can soak up lobby air-con for hours, and many of the pools are open to nonguests for a fee (see p156). Rates vary according to season and other factors including miscellaneous service charges.

Downtown

If you're on a budget, or just want to be in the thick of things and near great cheap eateries, you're best off in Downtown. Most of the city's hostels and midrange hotels are located on or around Sharia Talaat Harb in old, usually decrepit, apartment blocks. (Grimy stairs and shaky elevators aren't necessarily a reflection of the hotels above.) Many have balconies and windows overlooking noisy main

---

CAIRO HOTEL SCAMS

In short, all scams are attempts to distract you from your lodging of choice. Hotels do not open and close with any great frequency in Cairo, and if it's listed in this book it is very unlikely to have gone out of business by the time you arrive.

At the airport, you may be approached by a man or woman with an official-looking badge. These people are not government tourism reps, they are hotel touts, and they can be shameless. For instance, they'll ask if you've booked a hotel. If you have, they'll offer to call the hotel to confirm that a room is waiting for you. Of course, they don't call the hotel – they call a friend who says that there is no booking and that his establishment is full. Concerned, the tout will offer to find you an alternative…

Some taxi drivers will stall by telling you that they don't know where your hotel is. In that case tell them to let you out at Midan Talaat Harb – from here it's a short walk to most budget hotels. Other lines include telling you the hotel you're heading for is closed/very expensive/horrible/a brothel and suggesting a 'better' place, for which they earn a commission, which will then be added to your bill.

The most complex scam is when a stranger (often on the airport bus) asks you your name and where you're staying. After a chat, the person says goodbye and isn't seen again. What they next do is call a friend, who goes and stands outside the hotel you've booked. When you arrive, he or she will ask 'Are you…?', using the name you volunteered back at the airport. When you answer in the affirmative, you'll be told that the hotel has been flooded/closed by the police/totally booked out and that the owners have organised a room for you elsewhere.

Finally, when checking in, never pay for more than a night in advance. No decent hotel will ever ask for more substantial cash. We've had letters from readers asked to stump up for two nights on arrival and then when they've decided to check out after one night (because of grotty toilets, no hot water, whatever), they've been unable to get a refund.

streets; request a rear room if you're a light sleeper. Plumbing sometimes dates from the Pharaonic era; better hotels will have individual hot-water heaters in each bathroom. On the flipside, there are also a few noteworthy top-end sleeps that are a world away from the never-ending Cairo mayhem.

BUDGET

African House Hostel (Map p124; ☎ 2591 1744; www .africanhousehostel.com; 3rd fl, 15 Sharia Emad ad-Din; s/d US$22/29, s/d/tr with shared bathroom US$12/18/24; ☐) The African House offers an affordable way to stay in one of the city's most gorgeous mid-19th-century buildings (First Lady Suzanne Mubarak has her offices here). You want a room on the upper floor, where the balconies are. Paint is peeling in spots, and the toilets occasionally run, but the staff are very nice and the kitchen is enormous.

Lotus Hotel (Map pp120-1; ☎ 2575 0966; www.lotus hotel.com; 12 Sharia Talaat Harb; s/d US$22/29, with shared bathroom US$16/23; ✖ ☐) The sister hotel to the slightly more upmarket Windsor Hotel, the Lotus is a 1950s concrete monolith with some surprising art deco flourishes strewn about. Rooms are a bit on the dingy side, and have certainly seen brighter decades. But the communal spaces are time warps full of character and can quickly transport you back to a less complicated era.

Sara Inn Hostel (Map pp120-1; ☎ 23922940; www.sarainn hostel.com; 21 Sharia Youssef al-Guindi; dm E£40, s/d from E£110/140, with shared bathroom E£70/100; ✖ ☐) This is another decent option offering both dorms and private rooms for shoestringing travellers. The Sara Inn is a small but personable place where you can easily get to know the staff. Plenty of well-strewn rugs and tapestries give a relaxed and cosy feel.

Wake UP! Cairo Hostel (Map pp120-1; ☎ 2636 3325; www.wakeupcairohostel.com; Marouf Tower, 33A Sharia Ramses, Downtown; dm E£45, d E£140, d/tr with shared bathroom E£110/150; ✖ ☐) A new Downtown hostel with very enthusiastic management (the capital letters in the name should be your first clue), Wake UP! is just 200m from the Egyptian Museum. Dorm rooms are a steal if you're not fussy about privacy, though slightly pricier rooms are still cheap and fairly cheerful. The staff are a treat, and while they are quick to sell you a tour, they're just as quick to provide solid and helpful advice free of charge.

Lialy Hostel (Map pp120-1; ☎ 2575 2802; 3rd fl, 8 Midan Talaat Harb; s/d E£60/80) Lialy's position on Midan Talaat Harb puts it right in the thick of the action, and it's tough to beat the price. Ten simple rooms share three bathrooms; everything is clean but the hot water sometimes runs out (rough in the winter), and the rooms are fan-cooled (rough in the summer). There's a small collection of books to read, a large breakfast room with satellite TV and free use of the kitchen.

our pick **Pension Roma** (Map pp120-1; ☎ 2391 1088; www.pensionroma.com.eg; 4th fl, 169 Sharia Mohammed Farid; s/d with shared bathroom E£60/96, d/tr with shower E£123/162) Run by a French-Egyptian woman with impeccable standards, the Roma brings dignity, even elegance, to the budget-travel scene. Towering ceilings, dark-wood floors and filmy white curtains create a feeling of timeless calm. Evening meals are an option. Book ahead, as the place is very popular with repeat guests, many of whom could afford to stay at more expensive hotels but prefer the old-Cairo atmosphere here.

Meramees Hostel (Map pp120-1; ☎ 2396 2518; http:// merameeshotel.net; 32 Sabri Abou Alam; s/d with shared bathroom E£75/110; ✖ ☐) This well-positioned hostel is easy-going, and the casual *majlis* (meeting room) makes a good place to hang out after a hot day's sightseeing. The rooms themselves have high ceilings, wooden floorboards, large windows and French doors leading onto balconies. Communal bathrooms and a kitchen are kept clean, and the management definitely seems to have travellers' interests in mind.

Hotel Luna (Map pp120-1; ☎ 2396 1020; www.hotel lunacairo.com; 5th fl, 27 Sharia Talaat Harb; r E£110-150, with shared bathroom E£100; ✖ ☐) The owner of this modern, backpacker-friendly place is one of the most fastidious in the city, and his sparkling rooms offer many small comforts, such as bedside lamps and bathmats. In the newer 'Oasis' wing, even the paint and furniture are colour-coordinated in soothing pastels – a rare sight indeed in Egypt. Excellent shared kitchen too.

MIDRANGE

Carlton Hotel (Map pp120-1; ☎ 2575 5022; www.carlton hotelcairo.com; 21 Sharia 26th of July; s/d half board from US$28/42; ✖ ☐) The rooms at this old-fashioned place near Cinema Rivoli are reasonably priced (and the staff often seem ready to make a deal), but vary in size and degree of dilapidation. The ones that have been renovated have shiny white paint, clean wooden floors, satellite TV and private bathrooms.

There's a restaurant (two free meals are included in the price of your stay), a coffeehouse and a welcoming rooftop cafeteria where you can enjoy a cold beer.

our pick **Hotel Osiris** (Map pp120-1; ☎ 2794 5728; http://hotelosiris.free.fr; 12th fl, 49 Sharia Nubar; s/d from €25/30; ☒ ☐) On the top floor of a commercial building, the Osiris' rooms enjoy views across the city. The French-Egyptian couple who run the place keep the tile floors and white walls spotless, and the pretty hand-sewn appliqué bedspreads tidily arranged on the supercomfy mattresses. Breakfast, served on a side terrace or the roof, involves fresh juice and crepes and omelettes. Its location in Bab al-Luq is quiet at night.

Cosmopolitan Hotel (Map pp120-1; ☎ 2392 384; fax 393 3531; 1 Sharia ibn Taalab; s/d US$44/55; ☒) Gloomy Spanish Inquisition–look furniture, mysteriously spotted carpeting and reports of surly service would normally get this place dropped from the list. But its prime location, on a tranquil pedestrian street in Downtown, is tough to beat, as is its gorgeous art nouveau facade and entry staircase. If you could choose anywhere in Cairo, this might not be it – but if it's already booked as part of a package, you could do worse.

Windsor Hotel (Map pp120-1; ☎ 2591 5277; www.windsor cairo.com; 19 Sharia Alfy; s/d with shower & hand basin US$37/48, s/d full bathroom US$46/59, deluxe with bath & shower US$62/74; ☒ ☐) Practically speaking, the rooms at the Windsor are dim, with low ceilings and noisy air-conditioners. But with the beautifully maintained elevator, worn marble stairs and a hotel restaurant, where the dinner bell chimes every evening at 7.30pm, the place is hard for nostalgia buffs to resist. The entrance (to both the hotel and the bar) is on the back side, in the narrow street just south of Sharia Alfy.

Grand Hotel (Map pp120-1; ☎ 2575 7700; grandhotel@link .net; 17 Sharia 26th of July; s/d from US$48/66; ☒ ☐) This busy seven-storey palace managed to survive conversion to a midrange place without completely losing its old-fashioned luxury character. The hundred or so rooms still have good parquet floors, and there a few remaining art deco flourishes about, though the shiny white-tile bathrooms are a wonderful modern addition. Entry is around the back in a tiny plaza.

Victoria Hotel (Map p124; ☎ 2589 2290; www.victoria .com.eg; 66 Sharia al-Gomhuriyya; s/d from US$56/70; ☒ ☐) Not far from Ramses Station, the Victoria is a grand old palace with the happy addition of utterly silent air-con, as well as comfy beds and satellite TV. Off long halls lined with clouded mirrors, the rooms have antique furniture and nice high ceilings – but no balconies, unfortunately. The place is not in central Downtown, but that keeps prices lower – and you're very close to the Ataba and Orabi metro stops.

Talisman Hotel (Map pp120-1; ☎ 2393 9431; www .talisman-hotel.com; 5th fl, 39 Sharia Talaat Harb; s/d from US$85/95; ☒ ☐) Thanks to double-pane windows, Downtown traffic is a distant memory once you're inside this luxurious cocoon, one of the only real boutique hotels in the city. The 24 rooms are an impeccable mix of Egyptian handicrafts, rococo furniture and jewel-tone colours. Turn into the alley opposite the A L'Americaine Coffee Shop; enter the first building entrance on the right and use the lift on the left side of the foyer.

TOP END

Nile Hotel (Map pp120-1; ☎ 2578 0444; www.thenilehotels .com; 1113 Corniche el-Nil; r from US$170; ☒ ☐ ☒) Formerly known as the Nile Hilton, this midcentury-built modern monolith has been around long enough that its sleek concrete look is coming back into style. Fortunately, the recent renovation that accompanied its corporate rebranding has made the Nile Hotel more attractive than ever. The unbeatable location, off Midan Tahrir and adjacent to the Egyptian Museum, completes the package.

Conrad Cairo (Map pp146-7; ☎ 2580 8000; http://cairo .conradmeetings.com; 1191 Corniche el-Nil; r from US$195; ☒ ☐ ☒) While the Nile Hilton is no more, the Conrad Cairo is still running strong, and continues to uphold the luxury moniker of Conrad Hilton. Primarily aimed at business travellers and visiting dignitaries, the Conrad is packed with meeting rooms, event spaces and a full entertainment centre and casino. Even if you're not travelling on the company dime, it's a good choice for modernity and luxury seekers alike who are looking for a well-heeled spot along the Corniche.

Garden City

Just south of Midan Tahrir, this area is in some ways just as convenient as Downtown (still an easy walk away), but it's a lot quieter and much less congested. Budget options are limited, though some of Cairo's finest luxury spots enjoy enviable locations along the banks of the Nile.

BUDGET

Garden City House (Map pp120-1; ☎ 2542 0600; www .gardencityhouse.com; 23 Sharia Kamal ad-Din Salah; s/d/tr E£125/166/212, s/d with shared bathroom from E£77/116; 🔀) This pension is untouched by time – not great in some ways (rooms could use a fresh coat of paint), but a boon in others, such as the gentlemanly staff (nice for solo women). Shared bathrooms can be small and stifling; private bathrooms are much more spacious. The handy location is steps from Tahrir, but you can walk out and not be immediately accosted by touts.

TOP END

Semiramis InterContinental (Map pp120-1; ☎ 2795 7171; www.ichotelsgroup.com/intercontinental; Corniche el-Nil; r from US$135; 🔀 🔀 🖳 🖳) The elegant foyer at the Semiramis InterContinental is a popular Cairo meeting place, and its 1st-floor restaurants are among the best in the city. Compared with other Garden City top-end offerings, however, the InterCon is a bit faded and past its prime, though its five-star quarters are reasonably priced if you book in advance online.

Grand Hyatt Cairo (Map p150; ☎ 2365 1234; http:// cairo.grand.hyatt.com; off Corniche el-Nil, Rhoda; s/d from US$200/225; 🔀 🖳) The new favourite of high-falutin tourists from the Gulf, the Hyatt is nothing but glitz and glamour. It has by far the best Nileside terrace in town, as well as a gargantuan rooftop pool. Rooms are minimalist chic, with brushed-gold trim and large marble bathrooms even in the standard layout. In 2008, the hotel's Saudi owner made international headlines by banning the sale of alcohol on the premises, and subsequently pouring an estimated US$1 million worth of booze into the Nile. The Egyptian tourism board countered by threatening to remove their rating (three-star hotels and above must serve alcohol), and the ban was partially retracted. At the time of research, compromise was the order of the day – you could enjoy alcohol either in the privacy of your own room, or at the sky bar.

our pick **Four Seasons at Nile Plaza** (Map p150; ☎ 2791 7000; www.fourseasons.com/caironp; 1089 Corniche el-Nil; r from US$360; 🔀 🖳 🖳) Of the two Four Seasons properties in Cairo (the other is the First Residence in Giza), this one may be marginally less posh, but it has a much handier location – you can walk to the Egyptian Museum in about 15 minutes. Rooms are nothing short of impeccable, with lavish bathrooms fit for royalty, and enormous picture windows that open out to the river. The Omar Nagdi canvas behind reception is just one piece of a big collection of modern Egyptian art that graces the property.

Islamic Cairo

We can't rationally recommend bunking here without pointing out the strong negatives of crazy crowds, touts like locusts and more than the usual number of mosques with amplified calls to prayer. But, if you want to plunge in at Cairo's deep end, this is certainly the place to shock your senses.

El-Malky Hotel (Map p131; ☎ 2589 1093; 4 Midan al-Hussein; s/d from E£60/70; 🔀) This is definitely the nicer of the two habitable options in the neighbourhood, though rooms are extremely varied. The nicer spots have balconies overlooking the surrounding madness, while the cheaper rooms are concrete prisons with no windows to the outside world. The rooftop views here are stunning, and the onsite coffee shop is a good place to linger over a *sheesha*.

El Hussein Hotel (Map p131; ☎ 2591 8089; Midan al-Hussein; s/d E£105/130; 🔀) Off either side of an open-ended hallway (where street noise reverberates), the basic rooms are dreary even by optimistic standards. But if you park yourself in a front-facing one with a balcony, the people-watching below is so mesmerising you may not want to sleep anyway. There's a top-floor restaurant, but don't expect alcohol in these parts. Entrance is in the back alley, one block off the square.

Zamalek

For a good night's sleep, the relatively quiet enclave of Zamalek is the best in the city. This is also where many of Cairo's best restaurants, shops, bars and coffee shops are located, and most of the city's sights are a short taxi ride away. As this is the embassy district, don't come here expecting too much in the budget range.

BUDGET

Mayfair Hotel (Map pp146-7; ☎ 2735 7315; www.mayfair cairo.com; 2nd fl, 9 Sharia Aziz Osman; s/d from E£140/160, with shared bathroom E£100/120; 🔀 🖳) Housed in an art deco building on a quiet street, the Mayfair has benefited greatly from a recent renovation, and is now one of the best deals in Zamalek.

The large terrace is a great place to relax and soak up the Cairo sunshine, though the single rooms are on the smallish side. Still, the young staff are very welcoming, and generous balconies and attractive wooden floors are a plus in the larger double rooms.

MIDRANGE

Pension Zamalek (Map pp146–7; ☎ 2735 9318; pension zamalek@msn.com; 6 Sharia Salah ad-Din; s/d E£125/175; ✸) With a warm welcome from mum and the kids watching TV in the living room, you'll feel as if you've moved in with a family if you stay at this clean and quiet pension a few blocks off the main drag. It has 14 kitschily furnished, slightly dim rooms (four with aircon) and shared bathrooms. Discounts are available for long stays.

President Hotel (Map pp146–7; ☎ 2735 0718; www.presidenthotelcairo.com; 22 Sharia Taha Hussein; s/d from US$55/65; ✸ 💻) Judging by the lobby, this is a thoroughly modern three-star place with glittering mirrors and plush carpeting. But rooms don't live up to the promise – the newish bathrooms make the rest look a little shabby. But there is a good top-floor bar and a very tasty patisserie in the lobby, which supplies the breakfasts – for the right guest, this makes up for a lot.

Hotel Longchamps (Map pp146–7; ☎ 2735 2311; www.hotellongchamps.com; 5th fl, 21 Sharia Ismail Mohammed; s US$54–62, d US$78–89; ✸) The old-European-style Longchamps has a residential feel. Rooms are spacious and well maintained, and guests gather to chat on the greenery-covered, peaceful rear balcony around sunset, or lounge in the restaurant (where alcohol – and a full breakfast buffet – is served). If you want your own balcony and a small bathtub, pay extra for an 'executive' room. Book well ahead.

Golden Tulip Flamenco Hotel (Map pp146–7; ☎ 2735 0815; www.flamencohotels.com; 2 Sharia Gezirat al-Wusta; s US$76–86, d US$86–96; ✸ 💻) This popular business-class place is comfortable and well equipped, and serves as a more fiscally reasonable alternative to Zamalek's five-star heavyweights. Standard rooms are a bit cramped if you're travelling as a pair, though it's only an extra $US10 to upgrade to the more spacious 'superior' class, which nets you a balcony overlooking the houseboats on the Nile.

TOP END

Cairo Marriott Hotel (Map pp146–7; ☎ 2728 3000; www.marriott.com/caieg; 16 Sharia Saray al-Gezira; r from US$175; ✸ 💻 ✎) This 19th-century pleasure palace is arguably the most atmospheric hotel in Cairo, at least in the lobby and other public areas. Unfortunately, all of the rooms are in two modern towers, though ongoing renovations have added key touches including plasma-screen TVs and extra-plush beds. A popular retreat for guests and nonguests alike, the Marriott offers a positively regal garden restaurant, a resort-quality pool and a sophisticated casino that attracts its fair share of high-rollers.

Sofitel El Gezirah (Map p150; ☎ 2737 3737; www.sofitel.com; Sharia al-Orman; r from US$225; ✸ ✸ 💻 ✎) This misplaced cylindrical tower is an unfortunate eye sore that dominates the very southern tip of Gezira Island. While it was something of the runt of the upmarket hotel litter for many years, the Sofitel has at long last been completely overhauled, and its interior is now an impressive mix of French and local styles. There are superb panoramas to be had from its plush rooms, though even non-guests can stop by and enjoy the views while having a drink at the floating bar on the Nile.

Giza & Harraniyya

Because the Nile's west bank is inconvenient for sightseeing, the only reason to stay here is for absolute luxury – or if you're determined to pitch a tent.

Salma Motel (off Map p152; ☎ 3381 5062, 010 270 4442; Saqqara Rd, Harraniyya; camping per person E£25, cabins E£90) The only camping option in Cairo is miles from the centre, adjacent to the Wissa Wassef Art Centre (p153). As it's close to a canal, mosquitoes can be a problem, whether you're in a camping spot or one of the double cabins. Breakfast is not included in the rate, nor offered. To get here, take a microbus or taxi from Pyramids Rd in the direction of Saqqara and get off when you see the blue 'Harraniyya' sign.

Swiss Inn Nile Hotel (off Map p152; ☎ 3776 6501; www.swissinn.net; 110 El Bahr El Aazam; s/d from €30/45; ✸ 💻 ✎) A decent midrange option about halfway between Downtown and the Giza Plateau, the Swiss Inn is a brand new and fairly comfortable spot for anyone needing an affordable yet modern base in this part of town. Although lacking in personality, the cookie-cutter rooms are offset by the wonderful rooftop *sheesha* bar, where you can smoke your pipe while gazing out at the Great Pyramids.

CAIRO

SILENT COMMUNICATION IN CAIRO

Cairenes have a whole array of nonverbal ways of getting a point across – and if you know some of them, you'll be much less likely to get offended, run over or neglected in a restaurant.

First, 'no' is often communicated with a simple upward nod or a brusque *tsk* sound – which can seem a bit rude if you're not expecting it. But if you use it casually to touts on the street, they're more likely to leave you alone.

Another signal that's often misinterpreted by foreigners is a loud hissing sound. No, that guy isn't commenting on your hot bod (well, OK, sometimes he might be) – he's trying to get your attention so you don't get trampled by his donkey cart coming down the narrow lane. Translate a hiss as 'Heads up – comin' through'.

But the most essential gesture to learn is the one for asking for the bill at a restaurant. Make eye contact with your waiter, hold out your hand palm up, then make a quick chopping motion across it with the side of your other hand, as if to say 'Cut me off'. Works like a charm.

---

our pick **Mena House Oberoi** (Map p152; ☎ 3377 3222; www.menahouseoberoi.com; Pyramids Rd; r garden wing from €150, r palace wing from €195; ✖ ▢ ▨) Built in 1869 as Khedive Ismail's hunting lodge, the stately Mena House offers two time warps in one: the public areas sport dazzling Islamic decoration and perpetually smell of jasmine, but the grandest palace-wing rooms are *Arabian Nights*, with whimsical tapestry bedspreads and opulent mirrors. You really have to go for a Pyramids view in the palace wing as rooms in the new garden wing are dully modern. The swimming pool is suitably capacious.

EATING

With some of the best restaurants in the country, Cairo is the place to sample not only refined versions of Egyptian classics, but also all the pizza, pasta and even Thai food you've been craving. Whether you spend E£5 or E£250 on dinner, there is a taste to suit every budget, making this a difficult city to go hungry in.

At one end of the spectrum are the scores of street carts, *kushari* counters, and fruit-and-veg markets where the majority of Cairenes feed themselves. You'll see Pizza Hut, KFC and McDonald's, but these glossy places are out of the reach of many locals; for visitors, they're a source of clean bathrooms, at least. But don't write off everything that looks like fast food: Egyptian minichains often serve some of the most delicious and cheap meals you'll have. Look for them along the main avenues in Downtown and along Sharia 26th of July in Zamalek.

Assuming you're dressed to impress – Cairo's upmarket dining scene is as trendy and sophisticated as any – most swank dining options are at the luxury hotels, and the chefs are usually imported straight from the relevant country, along with all the ingredients. At these and some slightly more modest midrange places, expect to pay an additional 22% or so for tax and service (a few extra pounds' cash tip is always appreciated to help bolster low wages). At lunchtime feel free to stop by unannounced, though dinner reservations are generally recommended.

Many restaurants tend to double as bars and nightclubs, with guests proceeding from multicourse meals into boozing and grooving. If a place like this has notably scrumptious food, we list it here, but if the scene's more the thing, it's under Drinking (p169).

Too tired to leave the hotel? You can get just about anything delivered, and even order online through **Otlob.com** (www.otlob.com), with service from more than 60 of the city's most popular restaurants.

Downtown

Forget fine dining. This is predominantly cheap-and-cheerful territory, plus a few nostalgic favourites.

BUDGET

El-Abd Bakery (Map pp120-1; 35 Sharia Talaat Harb; pastries E£1-6; ⏰ 8am-midnight) For pastries head for Cairo's most famous bakery, easily identified by the crowds of people outside tearing into their sweets and savoury pies. There's another branch on the corner of Sharia 26th of July and Sharia Sherif.

our pick **At-Tabei ad-Dumyati** (Map p124; ☎ 2575 4211; 31 Sharia Orabi; dishes E£2-10; ⏰ 7am-1am) About

200m north of Midan Orabi, this place offers some of the cheapest local meals in Cairo. Start by picking four salads from a large array, then order *shwarma* or *ta'amiyya*, along with some lentil soup or *fuul*. There are also branches in the food court of the Talaat Harb Complex (Map pp120–1) and in Mohandiseen (Map pp146–7).

Akher Sa'a (Map pp120-1; ☎ 2575 1668; 8 Sharia Alfy; dishes E£2-10; ⏰ 24hr) A frantically busy *fuul* and *ta'amiyya* takeaway joint with a no-frills cafeteria next door, Akher Sa'a has a limited menu but its food is fresh and good. The sign's in Arabic only; there's a Christian bookstore next door. A branch at 14 Sharia Abdel Khalek Sarwat has a fast-food-style set-up downstairs (note the genius giant-*ta'amiyya* 'burger') but glacial table service upstairs.

Gad (Map pp120-1; ☎ 2576 3583; 13 Sharia 26th of July; dishes E£2-12; ⏰ 9am-2am) This fast-food eatery is usually packed to the rafters with a constant stream of young Cairenes sampling its fresh and well-priced food. The *fiteer* with Greek cheese is scrumptious and the quarter chicken with rice and salad is both tasty and good value. You can sit upstairs or take away from the front counters. It has branches throughout the city, including opposite Khan al-Khalili (Map p131).

Abu Tarek (Map pp120-1; 40 Sharia Champollion; dishes E£3-10; ⏰ 8am-midnight) 'We have no other branches!' proclaims this veritable temple of *kushari* – no, the place has just expanded, decade by decade, into the upper storeys of its building, even as it has held onto the un-official Best Kushari title. The line moves fast; it's worth eating in to get the proper dose of garlicky vinegar, which isn't packed with takeout orders.

Fatatri at-Tahrir (Map pp120-1; 166 Sharia Tahrir; dishes E£9-15; ⏰ 7am-1am) This tiny place just off Midan Tahrir has been serving sweet and savoury *fiteer* to Downtown residents, AUC students and legions of backpackers for decades. It's reliable and delicious, though it can get very crowded in the afternoon.

MIDRANGE
Abu al-Hassan al-Haty (Map pp120-1; 3 Sharia Halim; mains E£15-25) With its foggy mirrors, dusty chandeliers and waiters who look older than the building itself, this is a beautiful relic of Downtown – it's often used as a set for period TV shows. The food (all grilled items) is a bit secondary, but perfectly palatable.

Felfela Restaurant (Map pp120-1; ☎ 2392 2833; 15 Sharia Hoda Shaarawi; dishes E£15-40; ⏰ 8am-midnight) Attracting tourists, coach parties and locals since 1963, Felfela is an institution that can deliver a reliable, if not wildly delicious, meal and good service. A bizarre jungle theme rules the decor, but the food is straight-down-the-line Egyptian and consistently decent, especially the mezze and grilled chicken.

Café Riche (Map pp120-1; ☎ 2392 9793; 17 Sharia Talaat Harb; dishes E£15-40; ⏰ 9am-1am) This narrow restaurant was the favoured drinking spot of Cairo's intelligentsia. It's a bit less lively now, but nonetheless a reliable and nostalgic spot to enjoy a meal (even a European-style breakfast) and a glass of wine, surrounded by framed portraits of Cairo luminaries on the wood-panelled walls.

our pick **Emara Hati al-Gish** (Map pp120-1; ☎ 2796 2964; 32 Sharia Falaki; mains E£20-30; ⏰ 11am-11pm) Carnivores will salivate instantly upon entering this place, where the air is heavy with the smell of charcoal-cooked meat. The *kastileeta* (lamb chops) are particularly splendid, and the *mouza* (shins) good for gnawing. There's another branch in Mohandiseen, at 164 Sharia 26th of July, off Midan Sphinx (Map pp146–7).

Sangria (Map pp146-7; ☎ 2579 6511; Casino ash-Shaggara, Corniche el-Nil, Bulaq; meals E£25-60; ⏰ 1pm-3am) Adjacent to the club Absolute, Sangria has great Nile views from its 1st-floor terrace (where the stylish scene is) and a large garden area, which often has a more casual crowd, including children. Hip music adds to the ambience – the place is as much a bar as a restaurant.

Le Bistro (Map pp120-1; ☎ 2392 7694; 8 Sharia Hoda Shaarawi; mains E£30-45; ⏰ noon-11pm) Tucked away below street level, Le Bistro tries to evoke summery France with a blue-and-white colour scheme and Gallic crooners on the stereo. The food may not quite match its European ideal, but Francophone Cairenes love it, and steak *frites* can make a nice change from kebab.

Estoril (Map pp120-1; ☎ 2574 3102; off Sharia Talaat Harb; mezze E£7-35; mains E£35-65) Walking into Estoril (from an alley next to the Amex office) can be a little awkward: stroll through clouds of cigarette smoke, past booths crammed with Cairo's arts-and-letters set, then get the attention of a waiter, which is no mean feat. Once seated, though, you'll feel like one of the club, scooping up simple mezze and ordering beer after beer. It's not uncommon to see women alone here, and the bar in the back is a good place to perch for a shorter stay.

CAIRO

Garden City

This is the place to come if you're looking for a formal feast. The luxury hotels lining the banks of the Nile here have some truly excellent restaurants.

TOP END

El Sakya (Map p150; ☎ 2365 1234; Grand Hyatt Cairo, off Corniche el-Nil; dishes E£45-100; ☽ noon-1am) Dotted with big white umbrellas and jutting over the water, the terrace restaurant at the Grand Hyatt is a great place to take in a view of the Nile – and perhaps some local movie stars, as this is a popular place to schmooze. The menu draws from all the hotel's restaurants, so you can take your pick of Indian, Italian, American and more. Note that following a partial ban by the hotel's Saudi owner, alcohol is not available on the terrace.

Bird Cage (Map pp120-1; ☎ 2795 7171; Semiramis InterContinental, Corniche el-Nil; mains E£45-105; ☽ noon-1am) Spicy means *spicy* at Cairo's best Thai restaurant, a soothing, wood-panelled space that's a favourite with wealthy Cairenes. Standards such as fish cakes and grilled beef salad are delicious and beautifully presented, as are more nouvelle offerings like *pla pow* (sea bass wrapped in banana leaves).

Sabaya (Map pp120-1; ☎ 2795 7171; Semiramis InterContinental, Corniche el-Nil; mezze E£15-30, mains E£50-110; ☽ 7.30pm-1am) Lebanese cuisine is Egypt's most common 'ethnic' food, but it's rarely done as well as it is here, where the diverse and delicate mezze come with fresh-baked pillows of pita, and mains such as *fatta* are served in individual cast-iron pots. The setting is very sleek, but considering portion sizes and sharing is the norm, the prices are not as high as you would expect.

Bella (Map p150; ☎ 2791 7000; Four Seasons at Nile Plaza, Corniche el-Nil; mains E£60-125; ☽ 12.30am-midnight) The top-billed restaurant at the Four Seasons is an elegant Italian-inspired affair highlighted by an open kitchen, two wood-burning stoves and lashings of contemporary art at every turn. Evening dinners are accompanied by a hedonistic antipasti buffet; it's wise to save room for the rich risottos and handmade semolina pastas.

Revolving Restaurant (Map p150; ☎ 2365 1234; Grand Hyatt Hotel, off Corniche el-Nil; dishes E£65-130; ☽ 7pm-1am) Located on the 41st floor of the Grand Hyatt, the Revolving Restaurant boasts some impressive stats: at 30m in diameter, the room rotates 360 degrees in 75 minutes, and takes in views of the Pyramids, the Nile and most of Cairo. While the revolving experience is enough of a reason to visit, the French haute cuisine prepared here in the show kitchen is nothing less than exquisite.

Islamic Cairo

There are plenty of fast-food joints around Midan al-Hussein but the restaurants in this part of town are limited – you really have to like grilled meat, and not be too squeamish about hygiene.

BUDGET

Al-Halwagy (Map p131; Midan al-Hussein; dishes E£5-30; ☽ 24hr) Not directly on the square, but just behind a row of buildings, this good *ta'amiyya*, *fuul* and salad place has been around for nearly a century. You can eat at pavement tables or hide away upstairs.

Egyptian Pancakes (Map p131; Midan al-Hussein; dishes E£10-15; ☽ 24hr) Adjacent to Al-Halwagy (above), this popular place serves up made-to-order *fiteer* topped with your choice of cheese, egg, tomato, olives and ground meat. For dessert, choose your toppings from raisins, coconut and icing sugar.

MIDRANGE

Khan el-Khalili Restaurant & Mahfouz Coffee Shop (Map p131; ☎ 2590 3788; 5 Sikket al-Badistan; snacks E£10-20, mains E£15-50; ☽ 10am-2am) The luxurious Moorish-style interiors of this restaurant and adjoining cafe are a popular haven from the khan's bustle and hassle. The place may be geared entirely to tourists but the food is reasonably good, the air-con is strong and the toilets are clean. Look for the metal detector in the lane, immediately west of the medieval gate.

Citadel View (Map pp112-13; ☎ 2510 9151; Al-Azhar Park; entrées E£10-20, mains E£20-75; ☽ noon-1am) Eating at this gorgeous restaurant – on a vast multilevel terrace, with Cairo's elite seated around you and the whole city sprawled below – feels almost like visiting a luxury resort. Fortunately the prices are not so stratospheric, and the food, all traditional Egyptian grill items, is quite good.

Zamalek

Zamalek has some of Cairo's best and most stylish restaurants. Cheap dining is not one of the island's fortes but there are a few possibilities, including the Baraka *shwarma* stand (Map pp146–7) on Sharia Brazil.

BUDGET

Didos Al Dente (Map pp146-7; ☎ 2735 9117; 26 Sharia Bahgat Ali; pasta E£10-25) A noisy, crowded pasta joint with a small outdoor space, Didos rings with the clatter of dishes and often has crowds waiting out front for a table. It's popular with students from the nearby AUC dorm and it comes pretty close to living up to its claim of making the best noodles in town. No alcohol.

MIDRANGE

Maison Thomas (Map pp146-7; ☎ 2735 7057; 157 Sharia 26th of July; sandwiches E£12-40, pizzas E£25-40; ☻ 24hr) A little slice of Europe, with loads of brass and mirrors, and waiters in long white aprons serving crusty baguette sandwiches. But this institution is best known for its pizza, with generous toppings. There's a branch in Heliopolis (Map p155).

La Mezzaluna (Map pp146-7; ☎ 2735 2655; Sharia Aziz Osman; mains E£18-40; ☻ 7am-11pm) Head down a tiny alley to find this funky bi-level space that's frequented by Cairo bohemians. The menu is roughly Italian, from conventional combos such as tomato and basil to the 'Illy pasta' (beef bacon, cream, radicchio and coffee). Salads are enormous. No alcohol is served, but the little patio out front is a quiet place to take coffee. There's also an outpost in Mohandiseen (Map pp112–13).

Crave (Map pp146-7; ☎ 2736 3870; 22A Sharia Taha Hussein; mains E£18-50; ☻ noon-1am) This little black-and-white eatery looks extremely chic but it has a welcoming (rather than snooty) staff and a reasonably priced menu of pizzas, pasta and the like. Score one of the comfy corner couch set-ups, and you could find yourself lounging here for quite some time.

ourpick **Abou El Sid** (Map pp146-7; ☎ 2735 9640; 157 Sharia 26th of July; mezze E£12-25, mains E£25-70; ☻ noon-2am) Cairo's first hipster Egyptian restaurant, Abou El Sid is as popular with tourists as it is with upper-class natives looking for a taste of their roots – Omar Sharif has been known to savour the chicken with *molokhiyya* (stewed leaf soup), but you can also enjoy a sugar-cane-and-tequila cocktail at the big bar, or a postprandial *sheesha*. It's all served amid hanging lamps, kitschy gilt 'Louis Farouk' furniture and fat pillows. The entrance is on the west side of the Baehler's Mansions com-

plex; look for the tall wooden doors. There's another branch in Mohandiseen, on Midan Amman (Map pp112–13; ☎ 3749 7326). Reservations are a must.

L'Aubergine (Map pp146-7; ☎ 2738 0080; 5 Sharia Sayyed al-Bakry; entrées E£14-25, mains E£30-70; ☻ noon-2am) This white-walled, candlelit bistro devotes half its menu to vegetarian dishes, such as blue-cheese ravioli and aubergine moussaka. You can't go wrong with most of the cheesier, creamier items, and the calming soundtrack accompanying dinner is a soothing contrast to the average Cairo street noise.

Sabai Sabai (Map pp146-7; ☎ 2735 1846; 21 Sharia al-Shaer Aziz Abaza; entrées E£8-35, mains E£35-70) Even if you're not craving Thai food, you might want to visit this mellow little restaurant for its quiet outdoor terrace. Salads and appetisers have all the requisite lemon grass and herbs, and the curries have just the right balance between searing heat and rich flavour. Taxi drivers may know the street by its old name, Sharia Maahad al-Swissry; the entrance is to the right of the hotel.

Sequoia (Map pp146-7; ☎ 2576 8086; 3 Sharia Abu al-Feda; mezze E£15, mains E£35-80, minimum Sat-Wed E£50, Thu-Fri E£75; ☻ 1pm-1am) At the very northern tip of Zamalek, this sprawling Nileside lounge is a major scene, with art exhibits by Townhouse Gallery, low cushions for nursing a *sheesha* and everything from Egyptian-style mezze to sushi on the menu, washed down with a healthy bar list. Bring an extra layer – evenings directly on the water can be surprisingly cool.

TOP END

ourpick **La Bodega** (Map pp146-7; ☎ 2735 6761; 1st fl, Baehler's Mansions, 157 Sharia 26th of July, Zamalek; mains E£70-135; ☻ noon-2am) Make a reservation well in advance – or show up early and take your chances at the door – if you want to score a much coveted table at this trendsetting culinary kingpin. A combination bar, restaurant and lounge, La Bodega sprawls across several rooms, incorporating both handsome colonial dining halls and edgier modern interiors. The menu is equally eclectic, drawing heavily from European and regional traditions, and served up with a dollop of Latin flare.

SELF-CATERING

Zamalek's best grocery is **Alfa Market** (Map pp146-7; ☎ 2737 0801; 4 Sharia al-Malek al-Afdal), with both local foods and imported items, while **Sekem** (Map pp146-7; ☎ 2738 2724; Sharia Ahmed Sabry) sells organic products and tofu. There's a 24-hour **Metro Supermarket** (Map pp146-7) on Sharia Ismail Mohammed, and several shops on Sharia 26th of July sell good-quality produce. Pork products such as prosciutto are available from the deli counter at Maison Thomas (p167).

For a sweet treat, **Mandarine Koueider** (Map pp146-7; ☎ 2735 5010; 17 Sharia Shagaret ad-Durr; per scoop E£3.25; ☯ 9am-11pm) is the place to get your fix of delectable ice cream. Definitely shell out extra for the *zabadi bi-tut* (yoghurt with blackberry). There's another branch in Heliopolis (Map p155).

Mohandiseen & Doqqi

These grey concrete suburbs look bland and flavourless, but it's possible to find some excellent restaurants among the plethora of fast-food outlets.

BUDGET

Al-Omda (Map pp146-7; ☎ 3346 2701; 6 Sharia al-Ghazza, Mohandiseen; dishes E£8-30; ☯ noon-2am) A mini-empire taking up the better part of a block, Al-Omda offers numerous ways to put grilled meats into your system. At the takeout joint on the corner, get a *shish tawouq* sandwich with spicy pickles. Or else you can sit down in the old-style 'Oriental' restaurant around the corner to your left, or head upstairs to the neon-lit cafe and get a *sheesha* with the trendy crowd.

MIDRANGE

Samakmak (Map pp146-7; ☎ 3302 7308; 24 Sharia Ahmed Orabi, Mohandiseen; dishes E£30-75; ☯ 10am-4am) Shielded from a noisy street by a phalanx of shrubbery, a few tables with blue-checked cloths set a cheery note in a garden at the Cairo branch of the respected Alexandrian fish restaurant. There's no menu – just pick from mullet, crabs, squid and more (priced per kilo) in the iced-up display, then specify how you want it prepared. It arrives at the table accompanied by salads and rice. No alcohol.

Cedars (Map pp146-7; ☎ 3345 0088; 42 Sharia Geziret al-Arab, Mohandiseen; mezze E£10-25, mains E£45-75; ☯ noon-1am) This chic Lebanese restaurant is a favourite with Mohandiseen's lunching ladies, then with a younger crowd later in the evening. Rattan chairs dot the spacious terrace, where there's *sheesha* along with the

better-than-average food: peppery *muhammara* (red-pepper salad), fresh and salty *ayran* (yoghurt drink) and big sandwiches stuffed with French fries. You can also get full meals from the grill.

Giza & Pyramids Road

There are a number of good eateries in this part of Cairo, any of which will serve you well if you happen to be heading to/from the Pyramids or simply passing through the neighbourhood.

El-Mashrabiah (Map p150; ☎ 3748 2801; 4 Sharia Ahmed Nessim, Giza; mains E£10-35; ☯ noon-1am) Excellent Egyptian food is served with formality at this intimate eatery. Located a few steps below street level, the dining room is further darkened by ornate carved panelling, deep leather banquettes and waiters dressed in sombre suits. Meat lovers will find themselves in seventh heaven: the kofta and *tagens* (stew cooked in a deep clay pot) are good, as is the rabbit with *molokhiyya* and the duck with starchy taro root. But vegetarians don't get much to work with. No alcohol is served.

Andrea (off Map p152; ☎ 3383 1133; 59 Tir'at al-Maryutia, Saqqara; entrées E£5-15, mains E£20-25; ☯ 10am-1am) Take a trip to the country at this restaurant 1.5km north of Pyramids Rd on the west side of Maryutia Canal. At the entrance women pat out bread dough and tend the spit-roasted chicken the place is justly famous for. There's little else on the menu aside from this and salads, but everything is slow-roasted, which gives you ample time to enjoy a few Stellas. Weather permitting, seating is in a large garden with playground equipment and a swimming pool that is great for the kiddies. But with greenery come mosquitoes, so lay on the repellent beforehand. A taxi from central Cairo should cost about E£25, or E£10 from the Pyramids/Mena House area. Make sure your driver doesn't take you to the unrelated Andrea Gardenia, south of Pyramids Rd.

Fish Market (Map p150; ☎ 3570 9693; Americana Boat, 26 Sharia el-Nil, Giza; dishes E£25-60; ☯ noon-2am) After selecting some of the finest and freshest seafood in town from the large display counter, most guests tuck into delicious mezze while their fish is simply but expertly cooked. With its wonderful Nile views, laid-back feel and efficient service, this permanently docked boat-turned-restaurant is a hidden gem.

Moghul Room (Map p152; ☎ 3377 3222; Mena House Oberoi, Pyramids Rd; mains E£85-165; ☯ 7-11.45pm daily &

12.30-2.45pm Fri) Cairo's best Indian restaurant specialises in mild North Indian–style curries and kebabs, with an emphasis on tandoori dishes. Though it's a long taxi ride from Downtown, the opulent decor, good food and live sitar music make it worthwhile. There's a wide range of vegetarian options (from E£35 to E£45) and an extensive wine list.

Heliopolis

In addition to the Amphitrion (p153) and branches of major chains, the following places are a good break if you happen to be in the neighbourhood.

El Shabrawy (Map p155; ☎ 2258 6954; Sharia Ibrahimy; dishes E£4-15; ☻ 8am-2am) Locals love this place for its *makaroneh* – big bowls of noodles with a rich meat sauce – but the place also serves dishes such as egg-fried cauliflower and *aggah* (a cross between an omelette and a giant *ta'amiyya*), most of which are vegetarian. It's signed in Arabic only – look for the red awning. The Shabrawy *ta'amiyya* stand (Map p155) on the opposite side of the street is also popular.

Petit Palmyra (Map p155; ☎ 2417 1720; 27 Sharia al-Ahram; mezze E£10-20, mains E£15-40; ☻ 11am-2am) Old-school Heliopolis, with stiffly starched serviettes, puffy chairs, sepia-toned photos on the wall and someone tickling the ivories while you eat. Egyptian-Levantine staples such as stuffed pigeon are great; a few European dishes such as penne puttanesca are decent.

DRINKING

Cairo isn't a 'dry' city, but locals tend to run on caffeine by day, available at both traditional *ahwa*s and European-style cafes. Drinking beer or spirits typically doesn't start till the evening hours, and then it's limited to hotel bars and some cheaper dives. Liquor is expensive and wine is barely drinkable, but beer is widely available and cheap. Note that drinking on the street is absolutely taboo, and wandering around drunk is in poor taste as well. During Ramadan alcohol is served only to foreigners.

Cafes & Patisseries

At the start of the millennium, espresso crash-landed in Cairo, and the city hasn't been the same since. Every reasonably well-to-do neighbourhood supports several coffee bars offering every kind of caffeinated drink, as well as snacks, sweets and free wi-fi. If it weren't for the gaggles of headscarf-wearing teenage girls who crowd the banquettes after school, it would be hard to locate yourself in Egypt. And yes, there are even a couple of Starbucks outlets, though Cairenes thus far seem to be sticking primarily to their home-grown haunts.

DOWNTOWN

Groppi's (Map pp120-1; Midan Talaat Harb; coffee & pastries from E£5; ☻ 7am-midnight) Distinctly *not* part of the new coffee wave, Groppi's high point was more than 50 years ago when it was one of the most celebrated patisseries this side of the Mediterranean, as well as the preferred venue of ritzy society functions and concert dances. Today, the offerings are sadly poor and overpriced, and the tearoom reeks of cheap tobacco. The only hint of glitter remaining is in the beautiful mosaics around the doorway, but it nevertheless continues to appeal to hardcore nostalgia buffs.

Groppi Garden (Map pp120-1; Sharia Adly; coffee & pastries from E£5; ☻ 7am-midnight) Same bland coffee and uninteresting pastries as the other Groppi, but the garden terrace here is a relatively peaceful place for a cup of tea and a *sheesha*. The cafe was a favoured relaxation spot for Allied troops in WWII, and was immortalised in Olivia Manning's *The Levant Trilogy* as '…a garden of indulgences where the Levantine ladies came to eye the staff officers who treated it as a home away from home.'

Cilantro (Map pp120-1; 31 Sharia Mohammed Mahmoud; coffees & teas E£5-20, sandwiches E£10-35; ☻ 9am-2am) This popular, sparkling-clean cafe – part of a locally owned chain – does excellent Italian-style coffee and coffee drinks alongside exotic teas and fruit blends. Downstairs, order to go and grab a packaged sandwich, cake or salad from the open fridge; for table service head upstairs (smoky but with a couple of outside balcony seats). While some readers justifiably complain about the high prices and fairly indifferent service, Cilantro is beloved by locals as a bastion of peace and calm. There are other branches just about everywhere you turn: Zamalek (Map pp146–7), Heliopolis (Map p155) and Doqqi (Map p150), to name a few. All offer free wi-fi, strong air-con and a stash of magazines and newspapers.

ZAMALEK

Simonds (Map pp146-7; 112 Sharia 26th of July; coffees & pastries from E£7; ☻ 7am-10pm) The recent overhaul

CAIRO

of this century-old French-style cafe has divided locals: some say that all the faded charm has been thoroughly sterilised, while others welcome the fresh coat of paint and bold new look. Whatever your opinion, at least the coffee is still good.

Coffee Roastery (Map pp146-7; 140 Sharia 26th of July; cappuccino E£7; 24hr) Its fast-food menu, blaring music videos and young staff make this an extremely popular meeting place for groups of young locals. The coffee, served in 30 different ways, is surprisingly good. Don't bother with the food.

Euro Deli (Map pp146-7; 22 Sharia Taha Hussein; cappuccino E£9, sandwiches E£12-22; 24hr) Bright, busy and slick cafe with free wi-fi and good wraps, pastas and fries. For breakfast, there are chewy Montreal-style bagels – try the local variation, topped with *labneh* (yoghurtlike white cheese served with olive oil) and cucumber.

Arabica Café (Map pp146-7; 2735 7982; 20 Sharia al-Marashly, Zamalek; cappuccino E£7, breakfast E£12-24; 9am-11pm) Funky and lived-in, this upstairs cafe is frequented by teens and older students, who gather to study and doodle on the paper-topped tables. And unlike at slicker competitors, you can actually get some Egyptian food here along with your latte – breakfast options include *fuul* and *shakshouka* (spicy scrambled eggs), and you can order sweet or savoury *fiteer* anytime.

Ahwas

Cairo's *ahwa*s are essential places to unwind, chat and breathe deeply over a *sheesha*. Dusty floors, rickety tables and the clatter of dominoes and *towla* (backgammon) define the most traditional places, but newer, shinier places – where women smoke as well – have expanded the concept, not to mention the array of *sheesha* flavours, which now include everything from mango to guava and mint to rose.

Even though coffee *(ahwa)* gave its name to the cafe, *shai* (tea) is far more common than the inky-black Turkish-style brew, usually drunk in the morning if at all. Or you can order lemonade, hot herbal infusions or, in the winter, rich, milky *sahlab* (see p82).

There's an *ahwa* for every possible subculture. We list the most famous ones here but half the joy of the *ahwa* is discovering 'yours'. Look in back alleys all over Downtown (sports fans gather south of Sharia Adly; intellectuals, at Midan Falaki); there's a nice traditional joint down

the lane behind Al-Azhar Mosque; and some mall food courts can be surprisingly fun. Most *ahwa*s are open from 8am to 2am; a few serve beer, but generally it's a nonalcoholic scene.

DOWNTOWN

Horreyya (Map pp120-1; Midan Falaki, Bab al-Luq; tea & sheesha E£8, beer E£10, 8am-2am) The Horreyya (there's no real sign outside – look for a pale-pink facade and plywood over some of the windows) is one of the city's classic *ahwa*s. Here you stare dreamily through the *sheesha* smoke up at the high ceilings, down at the sawdust-strewn floor and out across a great cross-section of customers. Bonus: there are regular, ongoing chess matches here that attract some truly gifted players. Another bonus: beer is also available, but it's only allowed to be quaffed in designated areas, far away from the boards.

Zahret al-Bustan (Map pp120-1; Sharia Talaat Harb, Downtown; tea & sheesha E£9, 8am-2am) Formerly the haunt of intellectuals, journalists and writers, this coffeehouse has more recently become a favourite with backpackers and students from the nearby AUC.

Abu Aly Bar (Map pp120-1; Nile Hotel, 1113 Corniche el-Nil, Downtown; minimum charge E£35, entrées E£12-15; 10am-1.30am) For an upscale *sheesha* experience, head to the open-air terrace at this modern *ahwa*, featuring live music, delectable snacks and superbly brewed coffee.

ISLAMIC CAIRO

Fishawi's Coffeehouse (El Fishawy; Map p131; off Midan al-Hussein, Islamic Cairo; tea & sheesha around E£10; 24hr, during Ramadan 5pm-3am) Probably the oldest *ahwa* in the city, and certainly the most celebrated, Fishawi's is a great place to watch the world go by, particularly in the wee hours of the morning. Despite being swamped by foreign tourists and equally wide-eyed out-of-town Egyptians, it is a regular *ahwa*, serving up *shai* and *sheesha* to stallholders and shoppers alike. Unfortunately, prices seem to vary without rhyme or reason, so ask your waiter before ordering anything.

Bars
LOCAL BARS

For those who want to see Cairo's underbelly, try the few Downtown bars that serve beer and local spirits. They can seem unwelcoming: none are suitable for women on their own, and the toilets are pretty foul. It also doesn't help that there are no clear 'bar' signs; 'cafeteria' is the common euphemism, and the entrances are screened off so passers-by can't see in. A Stella will set you back on average between E£8 and E£12, though it's not uncommon for foreigners to be overcharged extravagant amounts.

Cairo (Map pp120-1; 3 Sharia Saray al-Ezbekiyya, Downtown; 24hr) Walk through the restaurant to the 1st-floor bar. The beer is not always icy but the atmosphere is fun, if slightly sleazy.

Cafeteria Stella (Map pp120-1; cnr Sharia Hoda Shaarawi & Sharia Talaat Harb, Downtown; until midnight) Marked with a tiny red neon sign, this spit'n'sawdust-style place gets good reviews from Downtown expats, who find it a more cheerful and welcoming place than similar bars nearby.

Cafeteria Port Tawfiq (Map pp120-1; Midan Orabi, Downtown) Dark and reasonably inviting, which is very typical of Cairo's Downtown scene.

Cap d'Or (Map pp120-1; Sharia Abdel Khalek Sarwat, Downtown) Quite run-down and lit with fluorescent bulbs – but you're not going for the decor. The staff and regulars are used to seeing foreigners.

WESTERN-STYLE BARS

As in any other busy city, bars open and close and go in and out of favour. The most reliable are those in hotels but the flavour-of-the-week places can generate the most high-rolling fun. By far the best place to go boozing is Zamalek, where several bars are within staggering distance of one another. Many places also have full menus, so you can snack as you go. The fancier places can have door policies as strict as the nightclubs, so dress well and go in mixed groups. Drink prices range from around E£10 to E£15 for a Stella to as high as E£25 to E£30 for a well-mixed cocktail at some of the more elite spots.

Downtown

Odeon Palace Hotel (Map pp120-1; 6 Sharia Abdel Hamid Said, Downtown; 24hr) Its green carpet singed from *sheesha* coals, this rooftop bar is favoured by Cairo's heavy-drinking theatre and cinema clique, and is a great place to watch the sun go down (or come up).

Le Grillon (Map pp120-1; 8 Sharia Qasr el-Nil, Downtown) Nominally a restaurant, this bizarre faux patio is all about beer, *sheesha* and gossip about politics and the arts scene. The illusion of outdoors is created with wicker furniture, fake vines and lots of ceiling fans. The entrance is in the back of a courtyard between two buildings.

Windsor Bar (Map pp120-1; 19 Sharia Alfy, Downtown; 6pm-1am) Alas, most of the Windsor's regular clientele has passed on, leaving a few hotel guests, a cordial, polyglot bartender and a faint soundtrack of swing jazz and Umm Kolthum. Colonial history has settled in an almost palpable film on the taxidermist's antelope heads, the barrel-shape chairs and the dainty wall sconces. Solo women will feel comfortable here.

Zamalek, Gezira & Mohandiseen

Buddha Bar (Map p150; Sharia al-Orman, Zamalek; 5pm-2am) A swish new addition to the Sofitel, Cairo's instalment of the world-famous Buddha Bar is where you can party with the beautiful people while sipping lychee martinis and listening to chill-out beats.

Deals (Map pp146-7; 2 Sharia Sayyed al-Bakry, Zamalek; 4pm-2am) A small cellar bar that never looks open actually gets too packed for comfort late in the evening and at weekends. It's pleasant enough at quieter times. There are other branches in Mohandiseen (Map pp146-7) and Heliopolis (Map p155).

Marriott Garden Café (Map pp146-7; Cairo Marriott, 16 Sharia Saray al-Gezira, Zamalek; 6.30am-10pm) The Marriott's garden terrace is one of the most comfortable spots in town to relax over a drink. Big cane chairs, fresh air and good-quality wine and beer make it deservedly popular. You can eat here, too. The only downside is that it's pricey.

La Bodega (Map pp146-7; 2735 6761; 1st fl, Baehler's Mansions, 157 Sharia 26th of July, Zamalek; noon-2am) This vast, amber-lit lounge doubles as a restaurant, but it's the long brass-top bar and original cocktails that garner most of the attention. The place draws most of Cairo's celebrity scenesters, who look gorgeous against the belle époque backdrop. One wing is sectioned off and dubbed 'Barten', where the crowd is younger and the music louder. Reservations are recommended.

L'Aubergine (Map pp146-7; 1st fl, 5 Sharia Sayyed al-Bakry, Zamalek; noon-2am) Wear your tightest black T-shirt and your sharpest eyewear to this minimalist bar that's just a little hipper than other fab nightspots, catering to jazz cats, expats and moodier AUC students.

Le Tabasco (Map pp112-13; 3336 5583; 8 Midan Amman, Mohandiseen; minimum charge E£50; 1pm-2am)

Perennially chic, Le Tabasco is a basement grotto with good electronica and moody lighting – most of the well-dressed, slightly older patrons are here to air-kiss and nibble on assorted international snacks. Reservations are a good idea.

Pub 28 (Map pp146-7; 28 Shagarat el-Dorr, Zamalek; ☺ 5pm-2am) The ex-pats in Zamalek are always coming and going, though this wooden, Brit-inspired drinking den has been serving up cold pints and whiskey on the rocks for quite some time, and certainly isn't in danger of packing up anytime soon.

ENTERTAINMENT

Western-style clubs, cinemas that screen English-language films and five-star cabarets with floorshows abound in Cairo. Live music is somewhat more limited, but whether you're in for rock, local folk or jazz, it can be a welcoming scene because it's relatively small. Theatre is mainly in Arabic.

Nightclubs

There aren't enough clubbers in Cairo to pack more than one place at a time, so what's hot varies according to the night of the week. Occasionally a club will host a special one-off party for which a ticket is required; they're free or very cheap, but the challenge is getting one. Keep an ear to the ground and ask likely Egyptians you meet. Many places start as restaurants and only shift into club mode after midnight, at which point the door policy gets stricter. Big packs of men (and sometimes even single men) are always a no-no – go in as mixed a group if you can, and ideally make reservations.

Absolute (Map pp146-7; ☎ 2579 6512; Corniche el-Nil, Bulaq; ☺ 1pm-3am) One of Cairo's most elite clubs but also one of its best, Absolute absolutely requires reservations. With a big dance floor and solid DJs, it draws a flashy crowd for which bottle service is the norm.

Club 35 (Map p150; ☎ 3573 8500; Four Seasons at the First Residence, 35 Sharia al-Giza, Giza; ☺ 7pm-3am) If you go before midnight, the place doesn't look all that promising, as it's still in soft-jazz Asian-fusion-bistro mode. But later, the light show gets livelier, as does the music, and it rivals Latex for weekend crowds.

Latex (Map pp120-1; ☎ 2578 0444; Nile Hotel, 1113 Corniche el-Nil, Downtown; ☺ 10pm-4am) The grande dame of Cairo's club scene, the Nile Hotel's basement party zone has changed hands several times over the years, but it still manages to keep up with the times. The music is always some variation on house, with the occasional Arabic pop hit thrown in, and the crowd is largely 20-somethings.

Cinemas

For what's showing, check the listings in *Al-Ahram Weekly* or online at www.yallabina .com; cinemas usually have four or five sessions a day, some starting at 10am or as late as 12.30am. Tickets typically cost around E£25 and can be cheaper at daytime sessions (when more women attend shows at the lower-rent places). Also check schedules at the many cultural centres (p114). The following regularly screen English-language films:

Cairo Sheraton Cinema (Map p150; ☎ 3760 6081; Cairo Sheraton, Midan al-Galaa, Doqqi) The closest Cairo has to an art-house cinema.

Cinema Karim I & II (Map p124; ☎ 2592 4830; 15 Sharia Emad ad-Din, Downtown) Cheap tickets and action flicks make it popular with young males (not a place for unaccompanied women). The entrance to Karim II is around the corner from Karim I.

Cinema Metro (Map pp120-1; ☎ 2393 7061; 35 Sharia Talaat Harb, Downtown) Once Cairo's finest, now one of its scruffiest.

Cinema Tahrir (Map p150; ☎ 3335 4726; 122 Sharia Tahrir, Doqqi) Comfortable, modern cinema where single females shouldn't receive hassle.

Citystars Centre (off Map pp112-13; ☎ 2480 2013; Sharia Omar ibn Khattab, Nasr City) A 13-screen megaplex at the mall.

Good News Grand Hyatt (Map p150; ☎ 2532 2800; Grand Hyatt Annex, off Corniche el-Nil, Rhoda) This cinema has three screens and occasionally subtitles Arabic films in English.

Theatre & Live Music

For theatre and classical and folk music schedules, check the 'ET Calendar' in *Egypt Today* or the *Egyptian Gazette*; for bands, pick up a copy of the *Croc* monthly. Also keep an eye out for the SOS Music Festival (www.sosmusic festival.com), a periodic free show of local bands that draws a devoted crowd.

After Eight (Map pp120-1; ☎ 2574 0855; www.after 8cairo.com; 6 Sharia Qasr el-Nil, Downtown; ☺ 8pm-2am) A funky, poorly ventilated venue that gets packed for everything from jazz trios to a Frank Sinatra impersonator to the wildly popular DJ Dina, who mixes James Brown, '70s Egyptian pop and the latest cab-driver favourites; the clientele is equally eclectic. Reserve online (the website's style in no way reflects the club's).

Cairo Opera House (Map p150; ☎ 2739 8144; Gezira Exhibition Grounds, Gezira) The opera complex has five halls. Performances by the Cairo Opera and the Cairo Symphony Orchestra tend to be held in its Main Hall while recitals, theatre and dance from Egypt and the rest of the world in its Small Hall, Gomhouria Theatre, Arab Music Institute and an open-air theatre. Jacket and tie are required by males for Main Hall performances (travellers have been known to borrow them from staff). Programs are available at the information window (right of the main entrance).

Cairo Jazz Club (Map pp146-7; ☎ 3345 9939; www.cairojazzclub.com; 197 Sharia 26th of July, Agouza; ⏰ 5pm-3am) The city's liveliest stage, with modern Egyptian folk, electronica, fusion and more seven nights a week, usually starting around 10pm. You must book a table ahead (online is easiest), and no one under 25 is admitted.

El Genaina Theatre (Map pp112-13; ☎ 2362 6748; www.mawred.org; Al-Azhar Park, Sharia Salah Salem, Islamic Cairo) The park's 300-seat open-air theatre hosts touring Western artists, stars from the Middle East and locals; shows are often free (though you must pay the park entrance fee).

Makan (Map pp112-13; ☎ 2792 0878; www.egyptmusic.org; 1 Sharia Saad Zaghloul, Mounira) The Egyptian Centre for Culture & Art runs this intimate space dedicated to traditional music. Don't miss the Mazaher ensemble, performing the traditional women's *zar*, a sort of musical trance and healing ritual (usually Wednesday, 9pm; E£20).

Also check the schedule at El Sawy Culture Wheel (p114), where two concert halls host the city's bigger rock and jazz bands. The Citadel (p137) often has free major concerts in the summer as well.

Dance
BELLY DANCING
If you see only one belly dancer in your life, it had better be in Cairo, the art form's true home. The best dancers perform at Cairo's five-star hotels, usually to an adoring crowd of wealthy Gulf Arabs. Shows typically begin around midnight, although the star might not take to the stage until 2am or later. Admission is steep; expect to pay upwards of E£250 to E£350, which includes food but not drinks. Cairo's divas are often getting in tiffs with their host hotels or their managers, so their venues may change from what's given below.

At the other end of the scale, you can watch a less nuanced expression of the art form for just a few pounds at several clubs along Sharia Alfy in Downtown. They're seedy, the mikes are set on the highest reverb, and most of the dancers have the appearance and grace of amateur wrestlers. But it can be fun, especially if you can maintain enough of a buzz to join in the dancing onstage (a perk if you shower the dancer and the band with enough E£5 notes), but not so fun if you fall for the myriad overcharging tactics, such as fees for unordered snacks and even napkins (expect to pay about E£15 to £20 for a Stella, after about E£5 to £10 cover charge). Like at the hotels, nothing happens till after midnight.

Haroun al-Rashid (Map pp120-1; ☎ 3795 7171; Semiramis InterContinental, Corniche el-Nil, Garden City; ⏰ 11pm-4am Tue-Thu & Sun) This old-fashioned-looking five-star club – all red curtains and white marquee lights – is where the famous Dina undulates (though often not on Wednesday nights – call to check).

Casablanca (Map p150; ☎ 3336 9700; Midan al-Galaa, Doqqi) Located in the Cairo Sheraton, where Soraya is the star.

Palmyra (Map pp120-1; off Sharia 26th of July, Downtown; admission E£6) The furthest on the 'other end of the scale' is Palmyra, a cavernous, dilapidated 1950s dancehall in an alley off Sharia 26th of July. It has a full Arab musical contingent, belly dancers who get better the more money is thrown at them, and an occasional singer or acrobat. In addition to the entrance fee, there's a minimum charge of E£30, which basically covers a beer and a *sheesha*.

Scheherazade (Map pp120-1; 1 Sharia Alfy, Downtown; admission E£5) Worth visiting for the gorgeous interior alone, all Orientalist fantasia complete with red velvet drapes – this doesn't inspire a classier air in the patrons, however.

Nile Maxim (Map pp146-7; ☎ 2728 3000; opposite Cairo Marriott Hotel, Sharia Saray al-Gezira, Zamalek; minimum charge E£170; ⏰ sailings at 7.30pm & 10.45pm) The best of the Nile cruise boats, run by the Marriott, is a relatively economical way to see a big-name star such as Randa or Asmahan, along with an à la carte menu. Go for the later sailing, as the show is less rushed.

SUFI DANCING
Al-Tannoura Egyptian Heritage Dance Troupe (☎ 2512 1735; admission free; ⏰ 7pm winter, 8pm Mon, Wed &

Sat summer) Egypt's only Sufi dance troupe – far more raucous and colourful than white-clad Turkish dervishes – puts on a mesmerising performance at the Wikala of Al-Ghouri (p135). It's a great opportunity to see one of the medieval spaces in use; arrive about an hour ahead to secure a seat.

SHOPPING

Faced with the mountains of chintzy souvenirs and the over-eager hustlers trying to sell them to you over endless glasses of tea, it's tempting to keep your wallet firmly shut in Cairo. But then you'd be missing out on some of Egypt's most beautiful treasures. The trick is knowing where to look. Though they're touristy and stocked with goods from China, the tiny shops of Khan al-Khalili (p130) do yield a few specific treasures, such as gorgeous silks. Downtown along Sharia Qasr el-Nil is more for checking out street fashion in the mass-market shops. Zamalek is the best place to actually buy – its shady streets have some gem boutiques for housewares and clothing, and not all of them are as expensive as you'd expect – look especially on Sharia al-Marashly and Sharia Mansour Mohammed. For upscale imported goods (and all the people-watching that affords), Mohandiseen is the place to go, especially along Sharia Suleiman Abaza and Sharia Abd al-Hamid Lotfy.

Antiques & Interiors

Shop owners have begun commissioning stylish home items from traditional artisans, with some beautiful results. As for antiques, some are stratospherically priced – but neat Egypt-specific items such as old advertising signs are often a good deal. Sikket al-Badistan, the central east–west route through Khan al-Khalili, is home to several notable antiques shops.

Loft (Map pp146-7; ☎ 2736 6931; www.loftegypt.com; 12 Sharia Sayyed al-Bakry, Zamalek; ۞ 10am-10pm Mon-Sat) In a rambling apartment, this eclectic store stocks local regional curiosities from small brass candlesticks to antique divans. Here's where to pick up large painted tabletop trays like those in chic restaurants around town.

Ahmed El Dabba & Sons (Map p131; ☎ 2590 7823; 5 Sikket al-Badistan, Islamic Cairo) The most respected antiques dealer in Khan al-Khalili is a warren of Louis XV furniture and glass cases filled with gleaming jewellery and snuff boxes. This

is where the treasures stashed in 19th-century Downtown apartments all end up.

Makan (Map pp146-7; ☎ 2738 2632; www.makanegypt .com; 4 Sharia Ismail Mohammed, Zamalek; ۞ 10am-11pm) This cool housewares shop features clever applications of traditional crafts – check out the lights made from tambourines. Some items are minimalist; others, like the painted wood picture frames, have a folk-art aesthetic. Upholstery fabric is sold by the yard.

Noubi Nabil (Map pp146-7; ☎ 2735 3233; 106-126 Sharia 26th of July, Zamalek; ۞ 10am-2pm & 4-10pm) Elephant sculptures guard the entrance to this corner shop, a trove of antique silk rugs, cut-glass bowls, old silver and fine china. The overflow is in a smaller place just across 26th of July.

Books & CDs

For new books, see p111.

L'Orientale (Map pp120-1; ☎ 2576 2440; www .orientalecairo.com; Shop 757, Basement, Nile Hotel Shopping Mall, Corniche el-Nil, Downtown; ۞ 10am-8pm Mon-Sat, 10am-5pm Sun) This is a great outlet for rare books on Egypt and the Middle East, as well as lithographs, maps and engravings. Another branch (L'Orientaliste) is on Sharia Qasr el-Nil.

Ezbekiyya Book Market (Map pp120-1; Ezbekiyya Gardens, Downtown) The 50 or so stalls here have the occasional treasures, but browsing the messy piles can be a chore.

The latest hit played in taxi cabs might be available only on cassette; look for sidewalk kiosks selling these. **Sawt al-Qahira** (Map pp120-1; ☎ 2392 1916; Midan Opera, Downtown; ۞ 10am-11pm), in an arcade set back from Sharia al-Gomhurriya, stocks the classic crooners on CD.

The best music section outside the malls is at Diwan (p114).

Carpets & Rugs

Unlike Morocco, Turkey or Iran, Egypt has no rich tradition of carpet weaving. The standard products are brown striped camel-hair Bedouin rugs, and flat-weave kilims with geometric patterns – all stocked by numerous shops in the tight squeeze of alleys behind the Mosque of Al-Ghouri, across the road from Khan al-Khalili, or some of the places mentioned in the Handicrafts & Souvenirs section (opposite).

El Kahhal Carpets (Map p131; ☎ 2590 9128; Sikket al-Badistan, Islamic Cairo; ۞ 10am-8pm Mon-Sat) Located in the khan, this super-elegant shop has the finest imported stock in the city, with both antiques and new made-to-order designs.

The rugs and wall hangings at Wissa Wassef Art Centre (p153) are in a class by themselves.

Clothing & Jewellery

Egyptian-cotton clothing can be a good buy. For real local fashion (mostly polyester), cruise the main avenues Downtown; the arcade between Sharia Abdel Khalek Sarwat and Sharia Adly just west of Midan Opera is crammed with hijabs in every pattern imaginable. If shopping for jewellery, note that gold and silver is sold by weight (check the daily rate in the *Egyptian Gazette*), plus a little extra for labour; antique silver can be quite expensive (and unfortunately is easily faked). The centre of Khan al-Khalili is still the main district for gold and silver, and where you should go for a custom cartouche with your name in hieroglyphics. The stores listed here offer something a bit different.

Mix & Match (Map pp146-7; ☎ 2736 4640; 11 Sharia Brazil, Zamalek; ⏲ 10am-8pm) Well made and locally designed, these separates for women in wool, silk and cotton are reasonably priced and often feature subtle Middle Eastern details. A branch two blocks south, at 11 Sharia Hassan Sabry, stocks larger sizes.

Mobaco (Map pp146-7; ☎ 2738 2790; 8 Sharia Ahmed Sabry, Zamalek) Not as interesting as Mix & Match in design, but inexpensive and with a great range of colours. There's always a flattering long cotton or linen skirt available, and men can choose from a rainbow of polo shirts sporting a camel logo. There are stores throughout the city, including at the Nile Hotel and the Semiramis (both Map pp120–1).

Atlas (Map p131; ☎ 2591 8833; abdelazizsalah@hotmail.com; Sikket al-Badistan, Islamic Cairo) In business since 1948, the Atlas family specialises in silk. Sold by the yard, it's both beautiful and sturdy, and holds its dye better than anything you might find for less. Kaftans and slippers are also available, and you can order custom clothing with any of the fabrics.

Sami Amin (Map pp146-7; ☎ 2738 1837; www.samiamin.com; 15A Sharia Mansour Mohammed, Zamalek) Cool chunky brass-and-enamel jewellery as well as leather bags, belts and shoes, many imprinted with tribal patterns. And all at bargain prices – bags and sandals start at just E£35.

Friction (Map pp146-7; ☎ 2736 9204; 18B Sharia al-Marashly, Zamalek; ⏲ 11am-8.30pm Sat-Thu) Friction's shop-window mannequins scandalise with underwear-as-outerwear; inside, it's club music and cool clothes from Turkish and Scandinavian designers – still nothing you could wear on the street here, but welcome at better night spots.

Nagada (Map p150; ☎ 3748 6663; www.nagada.net; 13 Sharia Refa'a, Doqqi; ⏲ 10am-6.30pm) Handwoven, colour-saturated silks, cottons and linens are the mainstay of this luxe shop in a grand villa – buy by the yard, or in boxy, drapey women's and men's apparel. There's also very pretty handmade pottery from Al-Fayoum.

Beymen (Map p150; ☎ 2791 7000; Four Seasons at Nile Plaza, 1089 Corniche el-Nil, Garden City; ⏲ 10am-11pm) This Turkish department store is the last word in luxury shopping in Cairo, stocking Prada et al alongside its chic house brand. There's a disproportionately huge selection of scarves and perfume, and great people-watching in the cafe.

Dina Maghawry (Map pp146-7; ☎ 012 322 3896; www.dinamaghawry.com; 1st fl, 16 Sharia Sayyed al-Bakry, Zamalek; ⏲ 11am-9.30pm Sat-Thu, 3-9.30pm Fri) This boutique showcases the local designer's delicate cascading necklaces trimmed with semi-precious stones and other elegant but modern pieces. Not cheap, but gorgeous work.

Handicrafts & Souvenirs

These fixed-price shops often stock familiar Egyptian crafts for not much more than you'd pay in Khan al-Khalili, and often with better quality. Expect *muski* glass (fragile and gem-coloured), inlaid wood and papyrus. For *sheesha* fittings, visit the copper district just north of the Madrassa & Mausoleum of Barquq, or Sharia Ahmad Mahir Pasha east of Bab Zuweila.

Egypt Crafts Fair/Fair Trade Egypt (Map pp146-7; ☎ 2736 5123; www.fairtradeegypt.org; 1st fl, 27 Sharia Yehia Ibrahim, Zamalek; ⏲ 9am-8pm Sat-Thu, 10am-6pm Fri) Crafts sold here are produced in income-generating projects throughout the country. Items for sale include Bedouin rugs, hand-woven cotton, pottery from Al-Fayoum and beaded jewellery from Aswan. The cotton bedcovers and shawls are particularly lovely, and prices are excellent.

Nomad (Map pp146-7; ☎ 2736 1917; 1st fl, 14 Sharia Saray al-Gezira, Zamalek; ⏲ 10am-7pm) This gem of a place specialises in jewellery and traditional Bedouin crafts and costumes, particularly from Siwa. Items include appliquéd tablecloths and cushion covers, dresses made in the oases, woven baskets, silk slippers and chunky silver jewellery. To find it, go past the Egyptian

Water Works office to the 1st floor and ring the bell. There are smaller branches in the Cairo Marriott (Map pp146–7), Grand Hyatt (Map p150) and Nile Hotel (Map pp120–1).

Oum El Dounia (Map pp120-1; ☎ 2393 8273; 1st fl, 3 Sharia Talaat Harb, Downtown; ۞ 10am-7pm) At a great central location, Oum El Dounia sells an attractive range of locally made glassware, Bedouin jewellery, cotton clothes, bags, embroidered shawls and light fittings. It also stocks a small range of maps, postcards and English- and French-language books about Cairo and Egypt, as well as CDs.

Al-Khatoun (Map p135; ☎ 2514 7164; www.alkhatoun .net; 3 Sharia Mohammed Abduh, Islamic Cairo; ۞ 11am-9pm) This gorgeous store stocks an ever-changing array of very chic light-fittings, alabaster pots, tablecloths, jewellery, clothes and shawls, all designed and made in Egypt.

Khan Misr Touloun (Map p139; ☎ 2365 2227; Midan ibn Tulun; ۞ 10am-5pm Mon-Sat) This shop opposite the Mosque of Ibn Tulun is stacked with a desirable jumble of crafts from all over Egypt, including wooden chests, jewellery, pottery, puppets, scarves and even hip T-shirts emblazoned with popular Egyptian product logos.

Said Delta Papyrus Centre (Map p135; ☎ 2512 0747; 3rd fl, 21 Sharia al-Muizz li-Din Allah, Islamic Cairo; ۞ 10am-9pm) A spin-off of Dr Ragab (the father of quality papyrus painting), Said has a vast selection, from ancient Egyptian scenes to cool Cairo skylines. He'll do a cartouche with your name in about half an hour. Prices are negotiable and quite reasonable, provided you arrive without a tout. (The shop is up two flights and down a dim hallway.)

Wady Craft Shop (Map pp146-7; ☎ 2738 0826; 5 Sharia Michel Lutfallah, Zamalek; ۞ 9am-5pm) This charity store next to the Marriott hotel sells cotton bags, aprons, tablecloths, inlay coasters and silk-screened tea towels – all work done by organisations of refugees, prisoners and others in need of aid.

Mahmoud Abd El Ghaffar (Al Wikalah; Map p131; ☎ 2589 7443; 73 Sharia Gawhar al-Qaid, Islamic Cairo) One of the best dealers in belly-dancing outfits in the city; the really nice stuff is upstairs. Look for the entrance down a little lane just off the main street.

Appliqué work is one case where it can be more rewarding to head to the source: the tent-makers bazaar, Sharia al-Khayamiyya (p136), where scores of shops sell intricately embroidered bedspreads, pillow covers and wall hangings, as well as canvas-weight striped fabric and thinner stamped cotton (around E£7 to E£10 per metre).

Household Linens

Egyptian cotton is a badge of quality in sheets and towels, though little of it is turned into fine products locally. An exception is the gorgeous hand-embroidered sheets and robes by Malaika at **Mounaya** (Map pp146-7; ☎ 2736 4827; 16 Sharia Mohammed Anis, Zamalek; ۞ 11am-8pm Mon-Thu & Sat, noon-8pm Fri). You can also find decent linens for less than you'd pay at home at the frumpy **Galerie Hathout** (Map pp120-1; ☎ 2393 6782; 114 Sharia Mohammed Farid, Downtown; ۞ 11am-7pm Mon-Sat).

Malls, Souqs & Markets

Street markets in Cairo are both social and functional – a great place for bargains and interacting with locals in a lively public space. Cairenes are also crazy for malls, and a new one opens every couple of years, inevitably drawing the crowds and shops away from the older places.

Souq al-Gomaa (Friday Market; Map pp112-13; Islamic Cairo; ۞ 6am-noon Fri) In the Southern Cemetery south of the Citadel, this sprawling weekly market is all the craziness of a medieval bazaar in a modern setting: under a highway flyover, expect new bicycles, live donkeys, toilets and broken telephones. Savvy pickers can find some great antiques and vintage duds. Go before 10am, when the crush of people can get overwhelming. You'll need a taxi to get there (about E£12 from Downtown); tell the driver 'Khalifa', the name of the neighbourhood.

Souq al-Fustat (Map p126; Sharia Mar Girgis, Old Cairo; ۞ 8am-4pm) A new market built for tourists, this is nonetheless a nice collection of shops, with vendors of antique carpets, modern ceramics, richly embroidered *galabiyyas* and wooden toys along with a branch of Sami Amin (p175). Sales pressure is pleasantly low.

Wikalat al-Balah (Souq Bulaq, Bulaq Market; Map pp146-7; north of Sharia 26th of July, Bulaq) The main draw is secondhand clothing, mostly well organised, clean and with marked prices (especially on Sharia al-Wabur al-Fransawi). Further in, you'll find good textiles, car parts and military surplus.

Citystars Centre (off Map pp112-13; ☎ 2480 0500; Sharia Omar ibn Khattab, Nasr City; ۞ 11am-1am) Cairo's most lavish mall is the current landing spot for every new international chain, from Starbucks to Wagamama. There's a kids' theme park and a big cinema. It's about 12km east of Downtown – a E£12 taxi ride.

Arkadia Mall (Map pp146-7; Corniche el-Nil, Bulaq; 10am-11pm) The biggest mall in central Cairo, with bars and a top-floor arcade. Here you'll find all the usual international brands, plus a good food court.

Perfume

Cairenes adore scent, and this is one of the few cities where you'll find perfumers occupying kiosks in the subway – perfectly good (and nonpushy) places to shop, though you can find somewhat better quality at a few specialists, such as **Karama Perfumes** (Map p131; ☎ 2590 2386; 112 Sharia al-Azhar, Islamic Cairo), which is very popular with locals for scent copies as well as its own blends and basic essences; look for the open-sided corner shop at the corner of Sharia al-Muizz. At less reputable places, 'essences' are diluted with vegetable oil – be sceptical if a salesman rubs the scent furiously into your skin while applying a sample.

Spices

Spices are a good buy, particularly *kuzbara* (coriander), *kamoon* (cumin), *shatta* (chilli), *filfil iswid* (black pepper) and *karkadeh* (hibiscus). Buy whole spices, never ground, for freshness, and skip the 'saffron' – it's really safflower and tastes of little more than dust. The shops that sell these items also deal in henna, soaps and herbal treatments.

Abd ar-Rahman Harraz (Map pp112-13; ☎ 2512 6349; 1 Midan Bab al-Khalq, Islamic Cairo) The sheikh of herbalist and medicinal plants, this is an interesting place. Look for the neglected taxidermy in the window on the corner.

Attara Ahl al-Beit (Map pp146-7; ☎ 2735 4955; Sharia Hassan Assem, Zamalek) This small but excellent shop is just west of Sharia Shagaret ad-Durr.

The streets around Midan Falaki also contain several large perfume shops, as does the southwest corner of Khan al-Khalili.

Tailoring

Given cheap labour and skilled tailors, Cairo is a good place to get a bespoke suit. Bring magazine clips of suit designs, as local tailors aren't always up on trends. You may also need to bring your own fabric (at least 3m for a jacket and a pair of pants, plus another

metre for extra pants). The best quality is at Salem (below); cheaper shops on Midan Opera sell Egyptian-made textiles. Allow three days to a week, plus another day for final adjustments.

Orange Square (Map pp146-7; ☎ 2735 2887; 4A Sharia Ibn al-Nabieh, Zamalek; noon-8pm) With books to select designs from and a decent stock of fabric, this trendy operation is the easiest place to get a suit made. But not the cheapest: prices start at E£1800.

Samir El Sakka (Map pp120-1; ☎ 2392 6196; 31 Sharia Abdel Khalek Sarwat, Downtown; 10am-1.30pm & 5.30-8.30pm Mon-Fri) This old-school tailor trained in Rome; he stocks a small selection of fabrics. Prices start around E£1000.

Salem (Map pp146-7; ☎ 3345 2232; 30 Sharia Libnan, Mohandiseen; 11an-6pm) The finest suit fabrics from England and Italy are available here.

GETTING THERE & AWAY
Air

For international airfare details see p524; for domestic flights see p528. For information on airline offices in Cairo see p524.

CAIRO INTERNATIONAL AIRPORT

For information on the airport see p180. For flight information call ☎ 0900 77777 from a landline in Egypt or ☎ 27777 from a mobile phone.

EGYPTAIR OFFICES

EgyptAir Airport (☎ 2265 7256); Doqqi (Map p150; ☎ 2748 9122; Cairo Sheraton, Midan el-Galaa); Downtown (Map pp120-1; ☎ 2393 0381; cnr Sharia Talaat Harb & Sharia al-Bustan); Downtown (Map pp120-1; ☎ 2392 7680; 6 Sharia Adly); Downtown (Map pp120-1; ☎ 2577 2410; Nile Hotel, 1113 Corniche el-Nil)

Bus

Cairo's main bus station is **Cairo Gateway** (Mina al-Qahira, Turgoman Garage; Map pp112-13; Sharia al-Gisr, Bulaq), 1km northwest of the intersection of Sharia Galaa and Sharia 26th of July. It's a five-minute walk from the Orabi metro stop – or pay E£5 or so for a taxi from Tahrir or Talaat Harb. The flashy new station maintains separate windows for each bus company, so you might have to do some comparison-shopping. It is advisable to book most tickets in advance, particularly for popular routes such as Sinai, Alexandria and Marsa Matruh in summer. Companies don't offer student discounts.

There are four other bus stations, less frequently used now that Cairo Gateway has been revamped to handle more traffic:

Aboud (Map pp112-13; Sharia El-Tir'a El-Boulakia, Shubra) is the starting point for buses to the Delta. Shuttle taxis run between here and Midan Ramses (2km to the south), or alternatively you can walk east from the Rod al-Farag metro stop, about 800m.

El-Moneib is the small station where buses from Al-Fayoum terminate. It is located on the Giza corniche after Sharia al-Bahr al-Azam and just south of Dr Ragab's Pharaonic Village. A taxi will cost E£15 from Downtown, or you can walk from Sakiat Mekki metro station, about 800m.

Al-Mazah is in Heliopolis near the airport (a taxi will cost E£30, or you can take the Merghani line of the Heliopolis tram and walk a couple of blocks north). Some international services depart from here, and some other services stop here en route out of Cairo.

Abbassiyya (Sinai Station; Map pp112-13; Sharia Ramses, Abbassiyya) is where all of the services from Sinai used to arrive, and there's a very slim chance you might still get dropped here – it's about E£15 in a taxi to the centre.

AROUND EGYPT
Alexandria & the Mediterranean Coast
From Cairo Gateway, **West & Mid Delta Bus Co** (☎ 2432 0049) travels to Alexandria (E£25 to E£35, three hours) hourly at 45 minutes past the hour starting at 4.45am and running till 8.45pm; after that, departures go at 15 minutes past, 9.15pm to 1.15am.

Al-Fayoum
Buses and service taxis for Al-Fayoum (E£6 to E£8, two hours) leave from El-Moneib station in Giza, as well as from Aboud, every half-hour 6am to 7pm.

Sinai
All Sinai buses leave from Cairo Gateway.

East Delta Travel Co (☎ 2574 2814) has services running to Sharm el-Sheikh (E£65 to E£75, five to six hours) at 6.30am, 10am, 3pm, 7pm, 11pm, 11.30pm, midnight, 1am and 1.45am. Dahab (E£60 to E£70, nine hours) service goes at 7.15am, 1pm, 5pm and 12.15am.

There are three daily buses to Nuweiba (E£70 to E£80, seven to eight hours) and Taba (E£70 to E£80, six to seven hours), leaving at 6.30am, 9.30am and 10.15pm. A daily service

to St Katherine's Monastery leaves at 10.30am (E£60, six to seven hours).

Superjet (☎ 2290 9017) has services to Sharm el-Sheikh at 7.30am, 3.15pm, 10.45pm (E£65 to E£75, five to six hours).

Suez Canal
All Suez buses depart from Cairo Gateway. East Delta Travel Co travels to Ismailia (E£20, three hours) and Suez (E£15 to E£20, two hours) every 30 minutes between 6am and 8pm. Buses to Port Said (E£25, three hours) leave every 30 minutes between 6am and 9.30am and then every hour until 9.30pm.

Luxor
Upper Egypt Bus Co (☎ 2576 0261) buses depart from Cairo Gateway. There's daily service to Luxor (E£100, 10 to 11 hours) at 5pm and 9pm, though you're much better off getting the train.

Red Sea
Superjet departs from Cairo Gateway for Hurghada (E£70, six hours) at 7.30am, 2.30pm and 11.45pm.

Upper Egypt Bus Co runs to Hurghada (E£60 to E£70, six hours) departing at 8am, 9.30am, noon, 1.30pm, 3pm, 5pm, 6.30pm, 8pm, 9pm, 10pm, 11pm, 11.30pm, 12.30am and 1am.

There are Upper Egypt services running to Al-Quseir (E£80 to E£85, ten to eleven hours) at 1.30pm, 6.30pm, 8pm, 10pm and 11pm.

Western Oases
All Western Oases buses leave from Cairo Gateway. Note that to get to Siwa you must take a bus to Alexandria, and then another onwards. For journeys to the oases take food and water as sometimes these buses don't stop anywhere useful for breaks.

Upper Egypt Bus Co services go to Dakhla (E£55, eight to 10 hours) via Al-Kharga Oasis (E£40, seven to eight hours) at 7am, 8am and 6pm; and to Bahariyya (E£30, four to five hours) at 6pm.

INTERNATIONAL
For information about buses to Libya, Israel and Jordan see p525.

Service Taxi
Most service taxis depart from lots around Ramses Station and Midan Ulali (see Map

p124). Exceptions are Delta and Suez services, which leave from just north of Midan Ulali, and Alexandria services, which leave from south of Ramses Station (Map p124). For specific details, see specific destinations chapters.

Train

Ramses Station (Mahattat Ramses; Map p124; ☎ 2575 3555; Midan Ramses) is Cairo's main train station. It has a **left luggage office** (Map p179; per piece per day E£2.50; �9 24hr), a **post office** (Map p179; �9 8am-8pm), ATMs, a pharmacy and a **tourist information office** (Map p179; �9 9am-7pm).

For general details about the types of trains and tickets available, including student discounts, see p534. Also try www.egyptrail .gov.eg, which may be running fully by the time you read this.

ALEXANDRIA

There are more than 15 trains daily between Cairo and Alexandria, from 6am to 11pm. The best trains running between Cairo and Alexandria are the Special and Spanish trains (1st/2nd class E£50/35, 2½ hours), which make few stops. The French train (1st/2nd class E£35/22; 3½ to four hours) makes multiple stops. First class *(ula)* is well worth the additional cost as you get roomier assigned seats and a much cleaner bathroom.

LUXOR & ASWAN

The excellent overnight wagons-lit service to Upper Egypt departs from Giza Station (Map pp112–13), right next to the Giza metro stop; you can purchase tickets at the office in a trailer to the right of the station entrance, but the larger **Abela Egypt Sleeping Train Ticket Office** (Map p179; ☎ 2574 9474; www.sleepingtrains.com; �9 8.30am-9pm) keeps longer hours and can take credit cards. Tickets for same-day travel must be purchased before 6pm, although in the high season (from about October to April) you should book several days in advance. The offices take payment in cash (euros or dollars only) or, for a small surcharge, credit card (Visa only).

The sleeping car services depart Giza at 8.25pm and 8.45pm daily. The former stops at fewer towns along the way, arriving in Luxor at 5am and in Aswan at 8.05am. The latter train gets in about 40 minutes behind. There is also a third sleeping car, departing at 9.10pm from Ramses and arriving at 6.30am in Luxor and 9.45am in Aswan; the agents try to steer people away from this train because it's slower, but it might be ideal if you want to sleep later. To either Luxor or Aswan, tickets cost US$60 per person one-way in a double cabin, US$80 in a single cabin and US$45 for kids ages four to 10. There are no student discounts. If you wish to get off at Luxor and continue to Aswan a few days later this must be specified when booking. The price includes an aeroplane-style dinner and breakfast.

Aside from the sleeping train, foreigners can travel to Luxor and Aswan only on train 980, departing Ramses daily at 7.30am; train 996, at 10pm; and train 1902, at 12.30am. To Luxor, 1st/2nd class fares are E£79/41; to Aswan, E£94/47. The trip to Luxor takes 10 hours; to Aswan, around 12.

Student discounts of 30% are available in both classes. You must buy your tickets at least a couple of days in advance.

SUEZ CANAL

Delays on this route are commonplace; going by bus is much more efficient. If you're determined to travel by train, see p416 for more information.

GETTING AROUND

Overcrowded buses and minibuses are the most common form of transport for the majority of Cairenes; anyone with means takes taxis. By Western standards, taxis are very cheap, although the fare can mount up if you

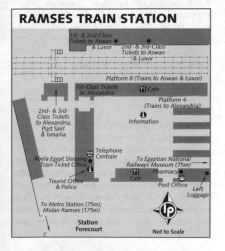

RAMSES TRAIN STATION

1st- & 2nd-Class Tickets to Aswan & Luxor

2nd- & 3rd-Class Tickets to Aswan & Luxor

Platform 8 (Trains to Aswan & Luxor)

1st-Class Tickets to Alexandria

Cafe

Platform 4 (Trains to Alexandria)

2nd- & 3rd-Class Tickets to Alexandria, Port Said & Ismailia

Information

Telephone Centrale

Abela Egypt Sleeping Train Ticket Office

To Egyptian National Railways Museum (75m)

Tourist Office & Police

Cafe

Pharmacy

Post Office

Left Luggage

To Metro Station (75m); Midan Ramses (175m)

Station Forecourt

Not to Scale

CAIRO

travel any distance – to the Pyramids, say – in which case the bus or the excellent metro can be better.

To/From the Airport

Cairo International Airport (www.cairo-airport.com) Terminal 1 (☎ 2265 5000); Terminal 2 (☎ 2265 2222) is on the northeastern fringes of Heliopolis, 20km northeast of the city centre. Terminal 1 services EgyptAir's international and domestic flights and Terminal 2 services all international carriers except Saudi Arabian Airlines. Terminal 3 (immediately adjacent to Terminal 2) was not yet fully operational at the time of writing. You'll find ATMs and exchange booths in all arrivals halls.

BUS

Don't believe anyone who tells you that there is no bus to the city centre – there are two, plus a minibus.

Air-con bus 356 (E£2, plus E£1 per large luggage item, one hour) runs at 20-minute intervals from 7am to midnight between Midan Abdel Moniem Riad (behind the Egyptian Museum) in central Cairo and Terminal 1 at the airport. Less comfortable options are minibus 27 (6am to midnight) and the 24-hour bus 400 (both 50pt).

If you arrive at Terminal 1, you'll see the bus parking area to the side of the arrivals hall, beyond the Air Mall. During the construction of Terminal 3, buses are bypassing Terminal 2, so the situation is trickier: catch a shuttle bus to the car park (clearly marked, running constantly), then cross the road and walk left to the bus shelter. Flag down any bus from here; it will carry on to Terminal 1, where you can change if necessary. By the time you read this, though, Terminal 3 may very well be complete, and presumably the buses will stop in the parking area between Terminals 2 and 3.

TAXI

The going rate for a taxi from the airport to central Cairo is E£45 to E£70; unfortunately the metered yellow cabs (p182) are seldom seen at this end of the trip. (Heading to the airport from the centre, you can get one of these, or bargain a black-and-white down to E£35 or E£40, taking into account that drivers must pay E£5 to enter the airport grounds.) It's better to get away from the arrivals hall and all the touts before talking to anyone, as walking away can sometimes bring the price down. Triple-check the agreed fare, as there is an irritating tendency for drivers to nod at what you say and claim a higher fare later.

If you don't want to bargain and would prefer a clean and comfortable ride, head for the limousine counter, where you can organise a car at a fixed price of E£65 to E£80. There's a lot to be said for this option, particularly after a long international flight.

In the traffic-free early hours of the morning (when so many flights seem to arrive), the journey to central Cairo takes 20 minutes. At busier times of the day it can take an hour, with the worst traffic on Sharia Uruba.

Bus & Minibus

Cairo is thoroughly served by a network of lumbering sardine-cans-on-wheels and smaller, shuttle-size minibuses (on which, theoretically, there's no standing allowed), but visitors will find only a few uses for them: they're good for a slow but cheap trip to the Pyramids or from the airport, but elsewhere you can travel more efficiently and comfortably by metro and/or taxi. Signs are in Arabic only, so you'll have to know your numerals. There is no known map of any of the city's bus routes.

Nonetheless, the view from a window seat on *any* bus is invariably fascinating. For general take-me-anywhere sightseeing, start at the central Midan Abdel Moniem Riad, behind the Egyptian Museum, where services leave for just about everywhere in the city; another major hub is Midan Ataba (see Map pp120–1). Just pick a neighbourhood and ask bystanders where to stand. Tickets cost between 50pt and E£2 depending on distance and whether there's air-con (mint-green buses often have it).

Car

Driving in Cairo can't in any way be recommended – not only is it harrowing, but you're only contributing to the already hideously clogged streets. Lane markings are ignored and brakes are scorned; traffic lights are discretionary unless enforced by a policeman. At night some drivers use their headlights exclusively for flashing oncoming vehicles. But Cairo drivers do have road rules: they look out for each other and are tolerant of the type of driving that elsewhere might provoke road rage. Things only go awry when an inexperienced driver – like an international visitor, perhaps – is thrown into the mix.

For more information about cars and driving in Egypt see p531.

HIRE

The only reason we expect you might rent a car is to drive directly out of the city. The major options:

Avis (www.avisegypt.com) Airport (☎ 2265 4249); Downtown (Map pp120-1; ☎ 2579 2400; Nile Hotel, 1113 Corniche el-Nil)

Budget (☎ 2265 2395; www.budget.com; Terminal 1, Cairo Airport)

Europcar (www.europcar.com/car-EGYPT.html; Terminal 1, Cairo Airport)

Hertz (www.hertzegypt.com) Airport (☎ 2265 2430); Downtown (Map pp120-1; ☎ 2575 8914; Ramses Hilton, Corniche el-Nil)

The rates of these big guns match international charges and finding a cheap deal with local dealers is virtually impossible. You are much better off organising via the web before you arrive.

Metro

The metro is blissfully efficient and the stations are cleaner than many of Cairo's other public places. It's also inexpensive and, outside rush hours (7am to 9am and 3pm

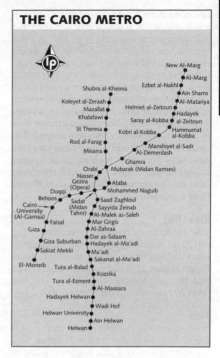

THE CAIRO METRO

to 6pm), not too crowded. Two lines are in operation, with a fabled third line perpetually 'under construction'. The 35-station main line stretches for 43km from the southern suburb of Helwan up to Al-Marg; the second line connects Shubra with Giza, stopping at the Cairo Opera House en route. See the Cairo Metro map, p181.

Metro stations are easily identified by signs with a big red 'M' in a blue star. Tickets cost E£1 to any stop; keep your ticket handy to feed into the turnstile on the way out. Trains run every five minutes or so from around 6am until 11.30pm.

The first (and often second) carriage on each train is reserved for women. If you want to ride in this carriage, make sure you're standing where the front of the train will stop, as it won't hang around long in the station.

Microbus

Increasingly Cairenes use private microbuses (*meekro*) – small vans with 10 or so seats – rather than public buses and minibuses. No destinations are marked, which

---

USEFUL METRO STATIONS

Ataba The closest stop to Khan al-Khalili.
Gezira (Opera) Underneath the Cairo Opera House, closest to Zamalek.
Giza Connected to the Giza train station, for departures to Upper Egypt.
Mar Girgis In the middle of Coptic Cairo.
Mohammed Naguib Close to the Abdeen Palace and the Museum of Islamic Art.
Mubarak Beneath Midan Ramses and Ramses Railway Station.
Nasser Sharia 26th of July and Sharia Ramses; closest to Downtown nightlife.
Sadat Beneath Midan Tahrir, close to the Egyptian Museum.

CAIRO

can make them hard to use at first. To catch a *meekro*, position yourself beside the road that leads where you want to go and, as a bus approaches, yell out your destination. At the same time, a kid is usually leaning off the running board yelling the *meekro*'s end terminal. If it's going where you want to go and there are seats free, it'll stop. Some microbus terminals are near Midan Ataba and in Sayyida Aisha (Map p137), the closest transit hub to the Citadel. Fares vary according to distance, from 50pt to E£2, paid after you take your seat. This often requires passing your money to passengers ahead and receiving your change the same way (which is always done scrupulously).

River Bus

The Downtown river-bus terminal (Map pp120–1) is at Maspero, on the Corniche in front of the big round TV building. Boats depart at 8am, 2pm and 9pm for Manial, Giza and Misr al-Qadima (Old Cairo). The trip takes 50 minutes and the fare is E£1.

Taxi

Aside from the midafternoon rush, taxis are readily available and will come to a screeching halt with the slightest wave of your hand. Standard black-and-white taxis are unmetered, and navigating the system requires the confidence that you are paying adequately. Given how cheap the fares are, a cabbie can with a few words plant the seed of doubt that you've paid too little, so it's important not to get drawn into a dialogue over the fare. Following are some sample fares from Downtown:

Destination	Fare (E£)
Cairo Gateway	5-10
The Citadel	12-15
Heliopolis	10-17
Khan al-Khalili	6-10
Midan Ramses	4-8
The Pyramids	25-40
Zamalek	6-10

Hiring a taxi for a longer period runs between E£15 and E£25 per hour, depending on your bargaining skills. For information on black-and-white taxi etiquette see p533.

But there has been a life-changing shift with the arrival of **yellow taxis** (☎ 19730, 16516), which can be called ahead, have air-con and always use meters. There aren't enough of them to hail in the street, but you can always get one from the rank on the south side of Midan Tahrir. With a minimum charge of E£3.50, they're pricier than black-and-whites for short distances, but for a trip to the Pyramids, for instance, they can actually work out more cheaply (drivers still appreciate a 10% or so tip, though).

Tram

Known to Cairenes, confusingly, as 'metros', rattly old-fashioned trams run from central Cairo to Heliopolis (25pt, 30 to 45 minutes). The terminal is just north of Midan Ramses (see Map p124); the line goes to Midan Roxy on the southern edge of Heliopolis (see Map p155), at which point it divides into three – Nouzha (through central Heliopolis on Sharia al-Ahram; sign written in red), Al-Mirghani (heads further east; sign in yellow) and Abdel Aziz Fahmy (west side; sign in blue).

Egyptian Museum

The Egyptian Museum is one of the world's most important museums of ancient history and one of its great spectacles. Here, the treasures of Tutankhamun lie alongside the grave goods, mummies, jewellery, eating bowls and toys of Egyptians whose names are lost to history. To walk around the museum is to embark on an adventure through time.

The museum has its origins in the work of French archaeologist Auguste Mariette. The Egyptian ruler Mohammed Ali had banned the export of antiquities in 1835. In 1858, his successor Said Pasha allowed Mariette to create the Egyptian Antiquities Service, and to base its activities around a new museum in Bulaq, which was moved to the current purpose-built museum in 1902.

The number of exhibits long ago outgrew the available space and the place is virtually bursting at the seams. Many stories are told about the museum's basement store, some of whose sculptures have now sunk into the soft flooring and are currently being excavated. A Grand Egyptian Museum has been planned, close to the Pyramids in Giza, but progress has been very slow and it is unlikely to open before 2012. When it does, many of the museum's highlights will be relocated to a state-of-the-art facility with the blessing that is climate control, something sorely lacking in the current building. For more information on the Grand Egyptian Museum, see p154.

Until 1996, museum security involved locking the door at night. When an enterprising thief stowed away overnight and helped himself to treasures, the museum authorities installed alarms and detectors, at the same time improving the lighting on many exhibits. Some improvements have since been made to display cases but much of the collection remains in early-20th-century cases with poor or nonexistent labels. This, together with the enormity of the collection and the fact that it is arranged chronologically, means that one of the most rewarding ways of visiting is simply to walk around and see what catches your eye. There's no missing the highlights – they usually have crowds around them – but be sure to stop and see some of the lesser items, all of which will help bring the world of the pharaohs back to life.

The design for the planned Grand Museum of Egypt features a spectacular alabaster facade that will be illuminated at night.

PRACTICALITIES

Don't hope to see everything in the **Egyptian Museum** (Map p185; ☎ 579 6748; www .egyptianmuseum.gov.eg; Midan Tahrir, Downtown; adult/student E£60/30; ☷ 9am-6.45pm) in one go. It simply cannot be done. Instead, plan on making at least two visits, maybe tackling one floor at a time, or decide on the things you absolutely must see and head straight for them. In peak season (much of winter and all public holidays), there's no best time to visit as the museum heaves with visitors throughout the day; lunchtime and late afternoons can be a little quieter.

There are several queues to brave before entering, which in peak season can start to form an hour before opening time. At busy periods, the fivefold admission procedure is as painfully slow as it sounds:

- queue near the gate to pass through a metal detector and have your bags X-rayed
- queue at the booth to your right to buy a ticket
- queue at the cloakroom on the left to leave bags, cameras and videos
- queue at the automatic ticket barriers to enter the building
- queue inside for a second metal detector and have your bags searched again.

Note that the **Royal Mummy Room** (adult/student E£100/50, tickets from museum upper fl, beside Room 50; 🕑 9am-6.20pm) closes before the rest of the museum.

Official guides can usually be found near the gate or after the cloakroom and will take you around for upwards of E£60 per hour. You can also rent audio guides inside (E£30) in English, Arabic and French, although with at least three different numbering systems in use, it isn't always easy to match the item to the commentary.

HIGHLIGHTS OF THE EGYPTIAN MUSEUM

The following are our favourite, must-see exhibits, for which you need at least half a day but preferably a little more.

Tutankhamun Galleries (1st fl; p189)
Old Kingdom Rooms (Ground fl, Rooms 42, 37 & 32; opposite)
Amarna Room (Ground fl, Room 3; p187)
Royal Tombs of Tanis (1st fl, Room 2; p191)
Royal Mummy Room (1st fl, Room 56; p188)
Graeco-Roman Mummies (1st fl, Room 14; p191)
Yuya & Thuyu Rooms (1st fl, Room 43; p191)
Ancient Egyptian Jewellery (1st fl, Room 4; p191)
Animal Mummies (1st fl, Rooms 53 & 54; p192)
Pharaonic Technology (1st fl, Room 34; p191)

MUSEUM TOUR: GROUND FLOOR

Before entering the museum, wander through the garden; to your left lies the **tomb of Mariette** (1821–81), with a statue of the man, arms folded, shaded under a spreading tree. Mariette's tomb is overlooked by an **arc of busts** of two dozen Egyptological luminaries including Champollion, who cracked the code of hieroglyphs; Maspero, Mariette's successor as director of the Egyptian Antiquities Service; and Lepsius, the pre-eminent 19th-century German Egyptologist.

The Egyptian government established the Service des Antiques de l'Egypte in 1835 to halt the plundering of archaeological sites and to arrange the exhibition of all the artefacts it owned. Its most enduring legacy is this museum.

The ground floor of the museum is laid out roughly chronologically in a clockwise fashion starting at the entrance hall. For room numbers see Map p185.

ROOM 43 – ATRIUM

The central atrium is filled with a miscellany of large and small Egyptological finds. In the area before the steps lie some of the collection's oldest items. In the central cabinet No 8, the double-sided **Narmer Palette** is of great significance. Dating from around 3100 BC it depicts Pharaoh Narmer (also known as Menes) wearing the crown of Upper Egypt on one side of the palette, and the crown of Lower Egypt on the other, suggesting the first union of Upper and Lower Egypt under one ruler. Egyptologists take this as the birth of ancient Egyptian civilisation and his reign as the first of the 1st dynasty. This, then, is the starting point of more than 3000 years of Pharaonic history in which more than 170 rulers presiding over 30 dynasties and during which time almost everything in this building was fashioned. Seen like this, the Narmer Palette, found at the Temple of Horus in Kom al-Ahmar near Edfu, is the foundation stone of the Egyptian Museum.

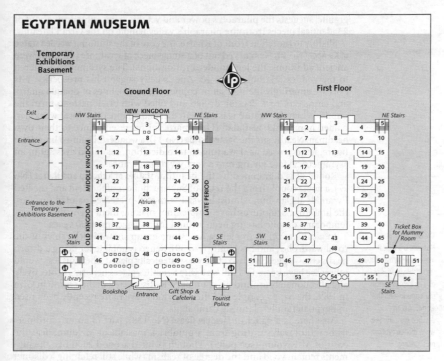

ROOM 48 – EARLY DYNASTIC PERIOD

In glass cabinet No 16 is the **limestone statue of Zoser (Djoser)**, the 3rd-dynasty pharaoh, whose chief architect Imhotep designed the revolutionary Step Pyramid at Saqqara. The statue, discovered in 1924 in its serdab (cellar) in the northeastern corner of the pyramid, is the oldest statue of its kind in the museum. The seated, near-life-size figure has lost its original inlaid eyes but is still impressive in a tight robe and striped headcloth over a huge wig.

ROOMS 47 & 46 – OLD KINGDOM

Look for the three exquisite **black schist triads** that depict the pharaoh Menkaure (Mycerinus), builder of the smallest of the three Pyramids of Giza, flanked either side by a female figure. The hardness of the stone makes the sculptor's skill all the greater and has helped ensure the triads' survival through the ages. The figure to the pharaoh's right is the goddess Hathor, while each of the figures on his left represents a nome (administrative division) of Egypt, the name of which is given by the symbol above their head. These triads (plus one other that is not held by this museum) were discovered at the pharaoh's valley temple, just east of his pyramid at Giza.

ROOMS 42, 37 & 32 – MASTERPIECES OF THE OLD KINGDOM

In the centre of Room 42 is one of the museum's masterpieces, a smooth, black, dioritic, larger-than-life-size **statue of Khafre (Chephren)**. The builder of the second pyramid at Giza sits on a lion throne, and is protected by the wings of the falcon god Horus. The choice of stone, which is harder than marble or

The Illustrated Guide to the Egyptian Museum in Cairo is written by Dr Zahi Hawass, the secretary-general of Egypt's Supreme Council of Antiquities, and published by the excellent American University in Cairo Press. Available all over the city, it costs E£150 and features colour photographs and useful itineraries.

granite, suggests the pharaoh's power and yet this is the only survivor out of 23 identical pieces from the pharaoh's valley temple on the Giza Plateau.

Slightly to the left in front of Khafre, the core of the stunning **wooden statue of Ka-Aper** (No 40) was carved out of a single piece of sycamore (the arms were ancient additions, the legs modern restorations). The sycamore was sacred to the goddess Hathor, while Ka-Aper's belly suggest his prosperity. His eyes are amazingly lifelike, set in copper lids with whites of opaque quartz and corneas of rock crystal, drilled and filled with black paste to form the pupils. When this statue was excavated at Saqqara in 1860, local workmen named him Sheikh al-Balad (Headman), for his resemblance to their own headman. Nearby sits the **Seated Scribe** (No 44), a wonderful painted limestone figure, hand poised as if waiting to take dictation, his inlaid eyes set in an asymmetrical face giving him a very vivid appearance.

Room 32 is dominated by the beautiful **statues of Rahotep and Nofret** (No 27), a noble couple from the reign of Sneferu, builder of the Bent and the Red Pyramids at Dahshur. Almost life-size with well-preserved painted surfaces, the limestone sculptures have simple lines making them seem almost contemporary, despite having been around for a staggering 4600 years.

In a cabinet off to the left, a limestone group shows **Seneb**, 'chief of the royal wardrobe', and his family (No 39). Seneb is notable for being a dwarf: he sits cross-legged, his two children strategically placed where his legs would otherwise have been. His full-size wife Senetites places her arms protectively and affectionately around his shoulders. Rediscovered in their tomb in Giza in 1926, the happy couple and their two kids have more recently been used in Egyptian family-planning campaigns.

Also here is a panel of **Meidum Geese** (No 138), part of an extraordinarily beautiful wall painting from a mudbrick mastaba at Meidum, near the oasis of Al-Fayoum (see p205). Though painted around 2600 BC, the pigments remain vivid and the degree of realism (while still retaining a distinct Pharaonic style) is astonishing – ornithologists have had no trouble identifying the species.

Room 37, entered via Room 32, contains furniture from the Giza Plateau **tomb of Queen Hetepheres**, wife of Sneferu and mother of Khufu (Cheops), including a carrying chair, bed, bed canopy and a jewellery box. Her mummy has not been found but her shrivelled internal organs remain inside her Canopic chest. A glass cabinet holds a miniature ivory statue of her son Khufu, found at Abydos. Ironically, at under 8cm, this tiny figure is the only surviving representation of the builder of Egypt's Great Pyramid.

ROOM 26 – MONTUHOTEP II

The seated statue in the corridor on your right, after leaving Room 32, represents Theban-born **Montuhotep II** (No 136), first ruler of the Middle Kingdom period. He is shown with black skin (representing fertility and rebirth) and the red crown of Lower Egypt. This statue was discovered by Howard Carter under the forecourt of the pharaoh's temple at Deir al-Bahri in Thebes in 1900, when the ground gave way under his horse – a surprisingly recurrent means of discovery in the annals of Egyptology.

ROOMS 21 & 16 – SPHINXES

These **grey-granite sphinxes** are very different from the great enigmatic Sphinx at Giza – they look more like the Cowardly Lion from *The Wizard of Oz*, with a fleshy human face surrounded by a great shaggy mane and big ears. Sculpted for Pharaoh Amenemhat III (1855–1808 BC) during the 12th dynasty, they were moved to Avaris by the Hyksos and then to the Delta city of Tanis by Ramses II (see p215). Also here is an extra-

The Global Egyptian Museum is a virtual museum with over 1000 searchable images of objects kept in various museums around the world, plus an excellent detailed glossary. See www.globalegyptian museum.org.

ordinary wood figure of the *ka* (spirit double) of the 13th-dynasty ruler Hor Auibre.

ROOM 12 – HATHOR SHRINE

The centrepiece of this room is a remarkably well-preserved vaulted **sandstone chapel**, found near the Theban temple of Deir al-Bahri. Its walls are painted with reliefs of Tuthmosis III, his wife Meritre and two princesses, making offerings to Hathor, who suckles the pharaoh. The life-size cow statue suckles Tuthmosis III's son and successor Amenhotep II, who also stands beneath her chin.

Hatshepsut, who was coregent for part of Tuthmosis III's reign, eventually had herself crowned as pharaoh. Her life-size **pink granite statue** stands to the left of the chapel. Although she wears a pharaoh's headdress and a false beard, the statue has definite feminine characteristics. The large reddish-painted limestone head in the corridor outside this room is also of Hatshepsut, originally from one of the huge Osiris-type statues that adorned the pillared facade of her great temple at Deir al-Bahri. Also here are wall decorations from the temple showing the famed expedition to Punt, perhaps Somalia or Eritrea.

ROOM 3 – AMARNA ROOM

Akhenaten (1352–1336 BC), the 'heretic pharaoh', did more than build a new capital at Tell al-Amarna, close the temples of the traditional state god Amun and promote the sun god Aten in his place. He also ushered in a period of great artistic freedom, as a glance around this room will show. Compare these great torsos with their strangely bulbous bellies, hips and thighs, their elongated faces and thick lips, with the sleek, hard-edged Middle Kingdom sculpture of previous rooms.

Perhaps most striking of all is the **unfinished head of Nefertiti** (No 161), wife of Akhenaten. Worked in brown quartzite, it's an incredibly delicate and sensitive portrait and shows the queen to have been extremely beautiful – unlike some of the relief figures of her elsewhere in the room, in which she appears with exactly the same strange features as her husband. The masterpiece of this period, the finished bust of Nefertiti, can be seen in the Neues Museum in Berlin.

ROOM 10 – RAMSES II

At the foot of the northeast stairs is a fabulous large, **grey-granite representation of Ramses II**, builder of the Ramesseum and Abu Simbel. But here in this statue he is tenderly depicted as a child with his finger in his mouth nestled against the breast of a great falcon, in this case the Canaanite god Horus.

ROOM 34 – GRAECO-ROMAN ROOM

It is best to visit these last rooms after seeing the upper floor, because this is the end of the ancient Egyptian story. By the 4th century BC, Egypt had been invaded by many nations, mostly recently by the Macedonian Alexander the Great. Egypt's famously resistant culture had become porous, as will be obvious from the **stelae** on the back wall, and on the large **sandstone panel** on the right-hand wall inscribed in three languages: official Egyptian hieroglyphics; the more popularly used demotic; and Greek, the language of the new rulers. This trilingual stone is similar in nature to the more famous Rosetta Stone (see p395), now housed in London's British Museum. A cast of the stone stands near the museum entrance (Room 48). Also, notice the **bust** situated immediately to the left as you enter this room: a typically Greek face with curly beard and locks, but wearing a Pharaonic-style headdress.

www.ancientegypt.co.uk is a fabulous website hosted by the British Museum that has loads of interactive online games and information about ancient Egypt for children. It is guaranteed to keep aspiring Egyptologists occupied for hours.

ROOMS 50 & 51 – ALEXANDER THE GREAT

On the official museum plan this area is labelled 'Alexander the Great' but currently there's nothing here that relates directly to the Macedonian conqueror who became pharaoh. However, there is a beautiful small marble **statuette of the Greek goddess Aphrodite**, carved at the end of the 1st century BC and found in Alexandria. Egyptians identified her with Isis.

MUSEUM TOUR: FIRST FLOOR

Exhibits here are grouped thematically and can be viewed in any order, but assuming that you've come up the southeast stairs, we'll enter the Tutankhamun Galleries at Room 45. This way, you'll experience the pieces in roughly the same order that they were laid out in the tomb (a poster on the wall outside Room 45 illustrates the tomb and treasures as they were found). But if you are fascinated by mummies, see some of the most amazing ones on display in the Royal Mummy Room, best visited before entering the Tutankhamun Galleries.

ROOM 56 – ROYAL MUMMY ROOM

The **Royal Mummy Room** (adult/student E£100/50, ticket office beside stairs off room 50; ✆ 9am-6.20pm) houses the remains of some of Egypt's most illustrious pharaohs and queens from the 17th to 21st dynasties, 1650 to 945 BC. They lie in individual glass showcases (kept at a constant 22°C) in a suitably sombre, tomblike environment. Talking above a hushed whisper is forbidden (somewhat counterproductively, a guard will bellow 'silence' if you do) and tour guides are not allowed to enter, although some do.

Displaying dead royalty has proved highly controversial in the past. Late President Anwar Sadat took the Royal Mummies off display in 1979 for political reasons, but the subsequent reappearance of 11 of the better-looking mummies in 1994 has done wonders for tourism figures and a second mummy room has now been added. The extra admission charge is steep but well worth it if you have any interest in mummies or in ancient Egypt's great rulers. Parents should be aware that the mummies can be a frightening sight for young children.

Take time to study the faces of some of the first room's celebrated inmates, beginning with the brave Theban king **Seqenenre II** who died violently, possibly during struggles to reunite the country at the end of the Second Intermediate Period (1650–1550 BC). His wounds are still visible beneath his curly hair and his twisted arms reflect the violence of his death. The perfectly wrapped mummies of **Amenhotep I** and **Queen Merit Amun** show how all royal mummies would once have looked, bedecked with garlands. Hatshepsut's brother-husband **Tuthmosis II** lies close by, as does **Tuthmosis IV** with his beautifully styled hair – he was the first pharaoh to have his ears pierced. Here too is **Seti I**, often described as the best-preserved royal mummy. His son **Ramses II**, in the middle of the room, might argue with that, his haughty profile revealing the family's characteristic curved nose, his hair dyed in old age with yellow henna. Ramses II's 13th son and successor **Merenptah** has a distinctly white appearance caused by the mummification process.

The new mummy room (same ticket) is located across the building, off room 46. The corridor display relates some of the most famous mummy discoveries, including the 1881 Deir al-Bahri cache of royal mummies. Many of the mummies in this section date from the 20th and 21st dynasties, the end of the New Kingdom and the start of the Third Intermediate

The Treasures of the Egyptian Museum, edited by Francesco Tiradritti, is an excellent reference published by the American University in Cairo Press. Available in most of Cairo's English-language bookshops and at the museum bookshop, it features 416 pages of stunning colour photographs and costs E£300.

> **MYTH BUSTING**
>
> In January 2005 the National Geographic Society arranged for 1700 CT scans of the mummy of Tutankhamun to be taken at his tomb in Luxor's Valley of the Kings. The scans were then given to three teams of researchers (from Paris, New York and Egypt), who used them to model busts showing what the boy pharaoh might have looked like on the day of his death 3300 years ago. Unveiling the startlingly similar-looking busts to a packed international press conference, Dr Zahi Hawass, secretary-general of Egypt's Supreme Council of Antiquities, stated that the scans had shown that Tut was healthy and well fed at the time of his death and that there was no evidence of foul play, contradicting the oft-repeated theory that he had been murdered at the behest of Ay, the commoner who ruled Egypt as regent while Tut was growing up. The scans showed that one of Tut's legs had been fractured shortly before his death, leading to conjecture that this had led to infection or a fat embolism that eventually killed him.

Period (c 1186–945 BC). In the mummy room, the small raised spots visible on the face of **Ramses V** may have been caused by smallpox. His predecessors **Ramses III and IV** lie nearby. Since her cheeks had burst apart due to overpacking during the mummification process, the appearance of **Queen Henettawy** (c 1025 BC) owes as much to modern restorers as to ancient embalmers, who decorated her linen shroud with an image of Osiris. The mummy of **Queen Nesikhonsu** still conveys the queen's vivid features. **Queen Maatkare** lies nearby with her pet baboon. Also here are the mummies of several youths, including **Prince Djedptahiufankh**.

TUTANKHAMUN GALLERIES

The treasure of the young New Kingdom pharaoh, Tutankhamun, are among the world's most famous antiquities. The tomb and treasures of this pharaoh, who ruled for only nine years during the 14th century BC (1336–1327 BC), were discovered in 1922 by English archaeologist Howard Carter. Its well-hidden location in the Valley of the Kings, below the much grander but ransacked tomb of Ramses VI, had long prevented its discovery (see p262). Many archaeologists now believe that up to 80% of these extraordinary treasures were made for Tutankhamun's predecessors, Akhenaten and Smenkhkare – some still carry the names of the original owners. Perhaps with Tutankhamun's death everything connected with the Amarna Period was simply chucked in with him to be buried away and forgotten.

About 1700 items are spread throughout a series of rooms on the museum's 1st floor, and although the gold shines brightest, sometimes the less grand objects give more insight into the pharaoh's life. The following are some of the highlights.

Room 45

Flanking the doorway as you enter are two life-size **statues of Tutankhamun**, found in the tomb antechamber. A large black-and-white photograph shows them in situ. The statues are made of wood coated in bitumen, their black skin suggesting an identification with Osiris and the rich, black river silt, symbolising fertility and rebirth.

Room 40

Note **Tutankhamun's wig box** of dark wood, with strips of blue and orange inlay, the wooden mushroom-shaped support inside once holding the pharaoh's short curly wig.

Moisturising oils were very popular; even troops were anointed with perfumes as a mark of honour. One Spartan king stormed out of a banquet when his fellow Egyptian guests had overdone the perfume. He thought them decadent and effeminate.

Rooms 35 & 30

The **pharaoh's lion throne** (No 179) is one of the museum's highlights. Covered with sheet gold and inlaid with lapis, cornelian and other semiprecious stones, the wooden throne is supported by lion legs. The colourful tableau on the chair back depicts Ankhesenamun applying perfume to husband Tutankhamun, under the rays of the sun (Aten), the worship of which was a hangover from the Amarna period. Evidence of remodelling of the figures suggests that this was the throne of his father and predecessor, Akhenaten. The robes are modelled in beaten silver, their hair of glass paste.

Many **golden statues** were placed in the tomb to help the pharaoh on his journey in the afterlife, including a series of 28 gilt-wood protective deities and 413 *shabti*, attendants who would serve the pharaoh in the afterlife. Only a few of them are displayed here.

Room 20

Despite the magnificence of his burial artefacts, Tutankhamun only ruled Egypt for nine years and made little impression in the annals of its history.

This room contains exquisite **alabaster jars** and **vessels** carved into the shape of boats and animals.

Rooms 10 & 9

The northern end of this gallery is filled with the pharaoh's three elaborate **funerary couches**, one supported by the cow-goddess Mehetweret, one by two figures of the goddess Ammit, 'the devourer' who ate the hearts of the damned, and the third by the lioness god Mehet. The huge **bouquet** of persea and olive leaves in Room 10, near the top of the stairs, was originally propped up beside the two black and gold guardian statues in Room 45.

The alabaster chest contains four **Canopic jars**, the stoppers of which are in the form of Tutankhamun's head. Inside these jars, four miniature gold coffins (now in Room 3) held the pharaoh's internal organs. The chest was placed inside the golden Canopic shrine with the four gilded goddesses: Isis, Neith, Nephthys and Selket, all portrayed with protective outstretched arms.

Most people walk right past Tutankhamun's amazing **wardrobe**. The pharaoh was buried with a range of sumptuous tunics covered in gold discs and beading, ritual robes of 'fake fur', a large supply of neatly folded underwear and even socks to be worn with flip-flop-type sandals, 47 pairs of which were buried with him. From these and other objects, the Tutankhamun Textile Project has worked out that the pharaoh's vital statistics were chest 79cm (31in), waist 74cm (29in) and hips 109cm (43in).

Rooms 8 & 7

These galleries just barely accommodate four massive **gilded wooden shrines**. These fitted one inside the other, like a set of Russian dolls, encasing at their centre the sarcophagi of the boy pharaoh.

Room 3

This is the room everybody wants to see as it contains the pharaoh's golden sarcophagus and jewels; at peak times, prepare to queue. Tutankhamun's astonishing **death mask** has become an Egyptian icon. Made of solid gold and weighing 11kg, the mask covered the head of the mummy, where it lay inside a series of three sarcophagi. The mask is an idealised portrait of the young pharaoh; the eyes are fashioned from obsidian and quartz, while the outlines of the eyes and the eyebrows are delineated with lapis lazuli.

No less wondrous are the two **golden sarcophagi**. These are the inner two sarcophagi – the outermost coffin, along with the pharaoh's mummy, remains in his tomb in the Valley of the Kings. The smallest coffin is, like the mask, cast in solid gold and inlaid in the same fashion. It weighs 110kg. The slightly larger coffin is made of gilded wood.

ROOM 4 – ANCIENT EGYPTIAN JEWELLERY

Even after Tutankhamun's treasures, this stunning collection of royal jewellery takes the breath away. The collection covers the period from early dynasties to the Romans and includes belts, inlaid beadwork, necklaces, semiprecious stones and bracelets. Among the most beautiful is a **diadem of Queen Sit-Hathor-Yunet**, a golden headband with a rearing cobra inset with semiprecious stones. Also of note is Pharaoh Ahmose's gold dagger and Seti II's considerable gold earrings.

ROOM 2 – ROYAL TOMBS OF TANIS

This glittering collection of gold- and silver-encrusted objects came from six intact 21st- and 22nd-dynasty tombs unearthed at the Delta site of Tanis (p215) by the French in 1939. The tombs' discovery rivalled Carter's finding of Tutankhamun's tomb but news of the find was overshadowed by the outbreak of WWII. The gold **death mask of Psusennes I** (1039–991 BC) is shown alongside his silver inner coffin and another silver coffin with the head of a falcon belonging to the pharaoh Shoshenq II (c 890 BC).

ROOM 14 – GRAECO-ROMAN MUMMIES

This room contains a small sample of the stunning portraits found on Graeco-Roman mummies, popularly known as the **Fayoum Portraits** (see boxed text, p208). These faces were painted onto wooden panels, often during the subject's life, and placed over the mummies' embalmed faces. These portraits express the personalities of their subjects more successfully than the stylised elegance of most other ancient Egyptian art, and are recognised as the link between ancient art and the Western portrait tradition.

ROOM 34 – PHARAONIC TECHNOLOGY

Interesting for gadget buffs, this room contains a great number of everyday objects that helped support ancient Egypt's great leap out of prehistory. Some are still in use in Egypt today. **Pharaonic boomerangs** were apparently used for hunting birds.

ROOM 43 – YUYA & THUYU ROOMS

Before Tutankhamun's tomb was uncovered, the tomb of Yuya and Thuyu (the parents of Queen Tiy, and Tutankhamun's great-grandparents) had yielded the most spectacular find in Egyptian archaeology. Discovered virtually intact in the Valley of the Kings in 1905, the tomb contained a vast number of treasures, including five ornate sarcophagi and the remarkably well-preserved mummies of the two commoners who became royal in-laws. Among many other items on display are such essentials for the hereafter as beds and sandals, as well as the fabulous gilded **death mask of Thuyu**.

ROOM 48 – PYRAMID MODEL

This excellent large-scale model of one of the Abu Sir pyramids perfectly illustrates the typical pyramid complex with its valley temple, high-walled causeway, mortuary temple and mini-satellite pyramid – well worth studying before a trip to Giza. Case No 82 contains the much-copied blue faience **hippopotamus** from the Middle Kingdom, a symbol of the Nile's fertility.

Cosmetics played an important role in the daily life of both women and men; the tomb builders of Deir al-Medina are shown having their eye paint applied during working hours as protection against glare and various eye diseases.

ROOM 53 – ANIMAL MUMMIES

Animal cults grew in strength throughout ancient Egypt, as the battered and dust-covered mummified cats, dogs, crocodiles, birds, rams and jackals in Room 53 suggest.

ROOM 37 – MODEL ARMIES

The Animal Mummy Project is dedicated to the Egyptian Museum's animal mummies, including raising funds to help pay for a climate-controlled room and special cases to conserve the poor beasts. Check out www .animalmummies.com for more.

Discovered in the Asyut tomb of governor Mesheti and dating from about 2000 BC (11th dynasty), these are two sets of 40 **wooden warriors** marching in phalanxes. The darker soldiers (No 72) are Nubian archers from the south of the kingdom, each wearing brightly coloured kilts of varying design, while the lighter-skinned soldiers (No 73) are Egyptian pikemen.

ROOMS 32 & 27 – MIDDLE KINGDOM MODELS

These sensational lifelike models were mostly found in the tomb of Meketre, an 11th-dynasty chancellor in Thebes, and, like some of the best of Egyptian tomb paintings, they provide a fascinating portrait of daily life in Egypt almost 4000 years ago. They include fishing boats, a slaughterhouse, a carpentry workshop, a loom and a model of Meketre's house (with fig trees in the garden). Most spectacular is the 1.5m-wide scene of Meketre sitting with his sons, four scribes and various others, counting cattle.

Around Cairo

Held hostage by Cairo's endless charms (or perhaps desperate to flee in search of more relaxed locales), too few travellers explore the capital's surrounding countryside. However, those who manage to escape from the urban sprawl discover a serene landscape of luscious green fields and palm groves that end abruptly at the edges of the vast desert. And importantly, the outskirts of Cairo are home to some of the oldest and most impressive ancient sites in Egypt.

On the southern edge of the city limits lies the city of Memphis, which was once the mighty capital of the Old Kingdom. Unfortunately, little remains of this famed city of power and wealth, though the surrounding desert pays eloquent visual testimony to the early pharaohs' dreams of eternal life. Here, on the edge of expansive sand seas, are the impressive necropolises of Saqqara, Abu Sir and Dahshur. Despite being overshadowed by their more famous neighbours at Giza, the Step Pyramid at Saqqara and the Red and Bent Pyramids at Dahshur are among the most stunning monuments of ancient Egypt.

The southern outskirts of Cairo are also home to the lush oasis of Al-Fayoum, which harbours ancient monuments, abundant wildlife and a spectacular desert rich in fossils. Northwest of the city, memorable day trips include the Birqash camel market, where Sudanese traders dispose of the last of their camels; and the monasteries of Wadi Natrun, which lure urban Copts to follow in the pilgrimage footsteps of their ancestors. And of course, if you're looking to take a break from sightseeing and unwind with the locals, there's nothing quite like a raucous trip on the Nile Barrages with a boatload of Cairenes kicking up their heels.

HIGHLIGHTS

- Explore the half-buried ruins of **Saqqara** (p198), home to the famous Step Pyramid of Zoser

- Penetrate the heart of the Red Pyramid, part of the ancient pyramid complex at **Dahshur** p204)

- Immerse yourself in the sights, sounds and (most importantly) smells of the **Birqash camel market** (p211)

- Meet the astonishing monks of the desert monasteries of **Wadi Natrun** (p212)

- Search for the fossilised forebears of whales amid the desert sands of **Wadi al-Hittan** (p210)

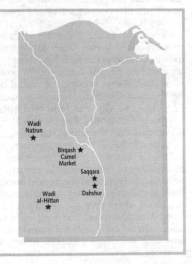

Wadi Natrun ★

Birqash ★ Camel Market

Saqqara ★

Wadi al-Hittan ★

Dahshur ★

MEMPHIS & THE EARLY PYRAMIDS

Although most tourists associate Egypt with the Pyramids of Giza, there were, at the time of writing, known to be 118 ancient pyramids scattered around the country, with more being discovered every few years or so. The majority of these monuments are spread out along the desert between the Gaza Plateau and the oasis of Al-Fayoum, and include the must-see Step Pyramid of Zoser at Saqqara and the Red and Bent Pyramids of Dahshur. These three pyramids, which predate the complex at Giza, represent the formative steps of architecture that reached fruition in the Great Pyramid of Khufu (Cheops).

MEMPHIS

☎ 02

Around 3100 BC, the legendary pharaoh Narmer (Menes) unified the two lands of Upper and Lower Egypt, and founded Memphis, symbolically on the spot where the Nile Delta met the valley. For most of the Pharaonic period, Memphis was the capital of Egypt, though the seat of power was later moved to Thebes (now Luxor) during the era of the New Kingdom.

Originally known as *Ineb-hedj*, meaning 'White walls', the contemporary name of Memphis derives from *Men-nefer*, meaning 'Established and beautiful'. Indeed, the city was filled with palaces, gardens and temples, making it one of the greatest cities of the ancient world. In the 5th century BC, long after its period of power, Greek historian and traveller Herodotus still described Memphis as 'a prosperous city and cosmopolitan centre'. Even after Thebes became the capital during the New Kingdom, Memphis remained Egypt's second city, and prospered until it was finally abandoned during the first Muslim invasions in the 7th century AD.

Although the city was once an area replete with royal pyramids, private tombs and the necropolises of sacred animals, centuries of builders quarrying for stone, annual floods of the Nile and greed-stricken antiquity hunters succeeded where even the mighty Persians failed: Memphis has almost completely vanished. The foundations of the ancient city have long since been ploughed under, and even the enormous temple of the creator god, Ptah, is little more than a few sparse ruins frequently waterlogged due to the high water table. Today, there are few clues as to Memphis' former grandeur and importance and, sadly, it's difficult to imagine that any sort of settlement once stood here.

Nonetheless, a visit to Memphis is worthwhile just to stand on the hallowed grounds of one of the world's greatest cities. Furthermore, Memphis is home to a noteworthy open-air **museum** (Mit Rahina; adult/student E£30/15, parking E£5; ☽ 8am-4pm Oct-Apr, to 5pm May-Sep, to 3pm during Ramadan), which is built around a magnificent fallen colossal limestone statue of Ramses II. Highlights of the museum include an alabaster sphinx of the New Kingdom, two statues of Ramses II that originally adorned Nubian temples, and the huge travertine beds on which the sacred Apis bulls were mummified before being placed in the Serapeum at Saqqara.

Getting There & Away

The tiny village of Memphis is 24km south of Cairo and 3km from Saqqara. While it is worth visiting as part of a tour of Saqqara and Dahshur, only those seriously into Egyptology would want to trek down here by public transport – getting to Memphis is a pain in the neck and a lengthy process.

For those determined to do it themselves, the cheapest way is to take a crowded 3rd-class train from Cairo's Ramses Station to Al-Badrashein village, then walk for about half an hour, catch a Saqqara microbus and ask to be dropped off at Memphis. Unless you have plenty of time, enjoy discomfort or have overspent, we strongly recommend taking a tour or hiring a taxi for a day instead.

For more information on visiting Memphis and the pyramids at Saqqara and Dahshur by private vehicle, see boxed text, p196.

PYRAMIDS OF ABU SIR

Lying between Giza and Saqqara and surrounded by sand dunes, the **pyramids of Abu Sir** (off Saqqara Rd) form the necropolis of the 5th dynasty (2494–2345 BC). Unfortunately, most of the remains have not withstood the ravages of time as well as their bigger, older brethren at Giza, and today the pyramids are slumped and lack geometric precision.

After being closed for many years, Abu Sir was officially opened to the public at the beginning of 1999, with the construction of a gatehouse. But in reality visitors don't always

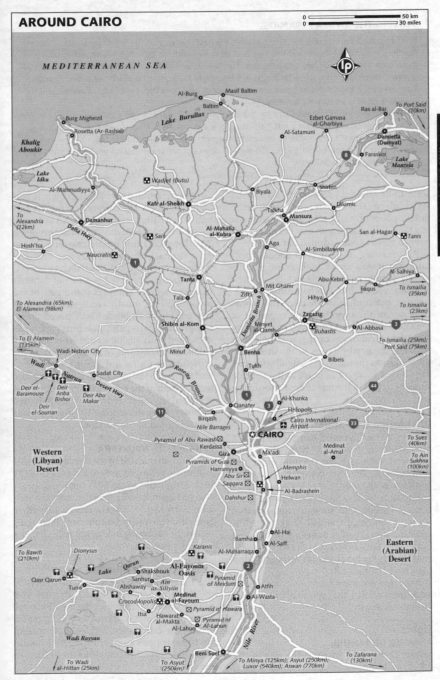

AROUND CAIRO

0 — 50 km
0 — 30 miles

MEDITERRANEAN SEA

Al-Burg
Masif Baltim
Baltim
Lake Burullus
To Port Said (10km)
Ras al-Bar
Burg Migheizil
Rosetta (Ar-Rashid)
Ezbet Gamasa al-Gharbiya
Al-Satamuni
Damietta (Dumyat)
Khalig Aboukir
8
Faraskor
Lake Manzela
Lake Idku
Al-Mahmudiyya
Wadjet (Buto)
Biyala
Shirbin
Dikirnis
Hosh'Isa
Kafr al-Sheikh
Talkha
Mansura
To Alexandria (12km)
Damanhur
Delta Hwy
Sais
Al-Mahalla al-Kubra
Aga
San al-Hagar
Tanis
Naucratis
1
Aga
Al-Simbillawein
To Alexandria (65km); El Alamein (98km)
Tanta
Mit Ghamr
Abu Kebir
Al-Salhiya
Tala
Zifta
Hihya
Faqus
To Ismailia (35km)
To El Alamein (135km)
Shibin al-Kom
Minyet al-Qamh
Zagazig
Bubastis
Al-Abbasa
3
To Ismailia (23km)
Wadi Natrun City
Minuf
Benha
Tukh
Bilbeis
To Ismailia (25km); Port Said (75km)
Wadi Natrun
Sadat City
Desert Hwy
Deir el-Baramouse
Deir Anba Bishoi
Deir Abu Makar
44
Deir el-Sourian
11
Birqash
Nile Barrages
Qanater
3
Al-khanka
Heliopolis
33
Cairo International Airport
To Suez (40km)
Western (Libyan) Desert
Pyramid of Abu Rawash
Giza
CAIRO
Medinat al-Amal
To Ain Sukhna (100km)
Kerdassa
Ma'adi
Pyramids of Giza
Harraniyya
Memphis
Abu Sir
Helwan
Saqqara
Al-Badrashein
Dahshur
Bamha
Al-Hai
Eastern (Arabian) Desert
To Bawiti (210km)
Dionysus
Karanis
Al-Maharraqa
Al-Saff
Al-Fayoum Oasis
2
Lake Qarun
Shakshouk
Sanhur
Pyramid of Meidum
Atfih
Qasr Qarun
Tunis
Abshaway
Ain as-Siliyin
Medinat al-Fayoum
Al-Wasta
Crocodilopolis
Itsa
Pyramid of Hawara
Hawarat al-Makta
Pyramid of Al-Lahun
Al-Lahun
Wadi Rayyan
Beni Suef
Nile River
To Wadi al-Hittan (25km)
To Asyut (250km)
To Minya (125km); Asyut (250km); Luxor (540km); Aswan (770km)
To Zafarana (130km)

VISITING THE 'OTHER PYRAMIDS'

Even if you're a fiercely independent traveller, the best way to visit the 'other pyramids' – namely the Step Pyramid of Zoser and the Red and Bent Pyramids at Dahshur – is to either take part in an organised tour or hire a taxi for the day. The main reason for giving in to the comfort of a private vehicle is that these pyramids are extremely frustrating to reach via public transport. Furthermore, a tour shouldn't cost too much money, and you can easily add Memphis and the pyramids of Abu Sir to your itinerary.

If you're looking to escape Cairo for the day, organised tours can be easily arranged through your accommodation, and it's not hard to find a cab driver willing to offer their services for the day (though it's preferable to make arrangements via your accommodation). A private car should cost between E£150 and E£250 for the day (around seven hours) excluding entry fees and the obligatory baksheesh.

---

seem to be allowed access (with no specific reason given) and there is no set ticket price, despite police officially treating the pyramids as a tourist site. Faced with this, baksheesh will have to serve as your admission fee.

Appreciating Abu Sir is all about expectations – if you arrive with grand visions on the same size and scale as Giza or even Saqqara, you're going to be severely disappointed. But come if you're interested in visiting one of the prominent necropolises of the Old Kingdom, and you'll be surprised by the relative calmness of the archaeological sight and the nearby dunes. With virtually no other tourists (or touts) to contend with, you can enjoy a moment of peace at the humble ruins, and revel in the serene desolation of the surrounding desert.

Orientation & Information

There are four pyramid complexes at Abu Sir – Sahure, Nyuserra, Neferirkare and Raneferef. Although the Pyramid of Sahure is in ruins, its funerary complex is the most complete of the four.

Entrance to Abu Sir is through the gatehouse off Saqqara Rd, though remember that it's not guaranteed you will be permitted to enter the site. If you're travelling by horse or camel from Giza to Saqqara, you will pass reasonably close to the pyramids without having to deal with the guards.

Note that there are no facilities at Abu Sir aside from a toilet that you may or may not be allowed to use.

Sights
PYRAMID OF SAHURE
Sahure (2487–2475 BC) was the first of the 5th-dynasty pharaohs to be buried at Abu

Sir. His pyramid, originally 50m high, is now badly damaged. The entrance corridor is only half a metre high, and slopes down to a small room. From there, you can walk through a 75m-long corridor before crawling 2m on your stomach through Pharaonic dust and spider webs to reach the burial chamber.

The better-preserved remains of Sahure's funerary temple complex stand east of the pyramid. This must have been an impressive temple, with black-basalt-paved floors, red-granite date-palm columns and walls decorated with 10,000 sq metres of superbly detailed reliefs (some of these are now in the museums of Cairo and Berlin). It was connected by a 235m-long causeway to the valley temple, built at the edge of the cultivation and bordered by water. From the pyramid, on a clear day, you can see some 10 other pyramids stretching out to the horizon.

PYRAMID OF NYUSERRA
The most dilapidated of the finished pyramids at Abu Sir belonged to Nyuserra (2445–2421 BC). Originally some 50m high, this pyramid has been heavily quarried over the millennia. In fact, Nyuserra reused his father Neferirkare's valley temple, and then redirected the causeway to lead not to his father's pyramid, but to his own.

PYRAMID OF NEFERIRKARE
The Pyramid of Neferirkare (2475–2455 BC), the third pharaoh of the 5th dynasty and Sahure's father, resembles the Step Pyramid at Saqqara. However, the present-day complex is only the core as the original outer casing has been stripped away, reducing the pyramid from its original planned height of 72m to today's 45m.

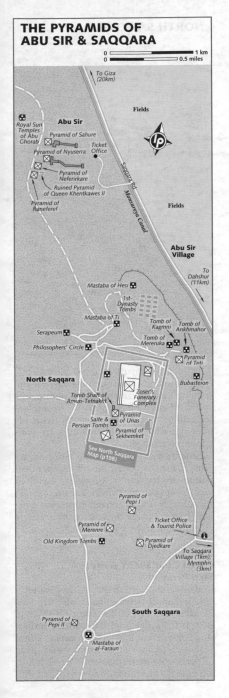

THE PYRAMIDS OF ABU SIR & SAQQARA

AROUND CAIRO

In the early 20th century in Neferirkare's funerary temple, archaeologists found the so-called Abu Sir Papyri, a highly important archive of Old Kingdom documents written in hieratic script, a shorthand form of hieroglyphs. They relate to the cult of the pharaohs buried at the site, recording important details of ritual ceremonies, temple equipment, priests' work rotas and the temple accounts.

South of Neferirkare's pyramid lies the badly ruined **Pyramid of Queen Khentkawes II**, wife of Neferirkare and mother of both Raneferef and Nyuserra. In her nearby funerary temple, Czech archaeologists discovered another set of papyrus archive documents. In addition, two virtually destroyed pyramids to the south of the queen's pyramid may have belonged to the queens of Nyuserra.

PYRAMID OF RANEFEREF

On a diagonal, just west of Neferirkare's pyramid, are the remains of the unfinished Pyramid of Raneferef (also known as Neferefre), who is believed to have reigned for four years before Nyuserra. However, work was so little advanced at the time of his death that the tomb was only completed as a mastaba (a mudbrick structure in the shape of a bench above tombs, which was the basis for later pyramids).

In the adjoining mudbrick cult building, Czech archaeologists found fragments of statuary, including a superb limestone figurine of Raneferef protected by Horus (now in the Egyptian Museum) along with papyrus fragments relating to the Abu Sir temple archives.

ROYAL SUN TEMPLES OF ABU GHORAB

Just northwest of the Abu Sir pyramids lies the site of Abu Ghorab, which is home to two royal sun temples dedicated to the worship of Ra, the sun god of Heliopolis. The Abu Sir Papyri describe six such temples but only two, built for Pharaohs Userkaf (2494–2487 BC) and Nyuserra, have ever been discovered.

Both of these temples follow the traditional plan of a valley temple, and contain a causeway and a large stone enclosure. This enclosure contains a large limestone obelisk standing some 37m tall on a 20m-high base. In front of the obelisk, the enormous alabaster altar can still be seen. Made in the form of a solar disc flanked by four 'hotep' signs (the hieroglyphic sign for 'offerings' and 'satisfied'), the altar itself reads 'The sun god Ra is satisfied'.

Getting There & Away

Abu Sir is some distance off the main Saqqara road and there's no way to reach it by public transport. The best way to visit is as part of an organised tour or by private taxi. The other option is to ride a horse or camel from Giza to Saqqara, which will grant you a decent glimpse of Abu Sir while en route.

SAQQARA

Covering a 7km stretch of the Western Desert, Saqqara, the huge cemetery of ancient Memphis, was an active burial ground for more than 3500 years, and is Egypt's largest archaeological site. The necropolis is situated high above the Nile Valley's cultivation area, and is the final resting place for deceased pharaohs and their families, administrators, generals and sacred animals. Old Kingdom pharaohs were buried within Saqqara's 11 major pyramids, while their subjects were buried in the hundreds of smaller tombs found in the great necropolis. Not surprisingly, the name Saqqara is most likely derived from Sokar, the Memphite god of the dead.

Most of Saqqara, except for the Step Pyramid, was buried in sand until the mid-19th century, when the great French Egyptologist Auguste Mariette uncovered the Serapeum. Since then, it has been a gradual process of rediscovery: the Step Pyramid's massive funerary complex was not discovered until 1924 and it is still being restored. French architect Jean-Philippe Lauer, who began work here in 1926, was involved in its restoration for an incredible 75 years until his death in 2001. In more recent years, a string of new discoveries has captured international media, including a whole slew of mummies and even a new pyramid. For more information, see the boxed text, p204.

Orientation & Information

The main monuments are in an area around the Step Pyramid known as **North Saqqara** (adult/student E£50/25, parking E£2; ☉ 8am-4pm Oct-Apr, to 5pm May-Sep, to 3pm during Ramadan). About 1km south of the Step Pyramid is a group of monuments known as South Saqqara, with no official entry fee or opening hours as these are rarely visited.

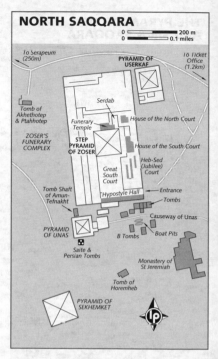

NORTH SAQQARA

0 ——————— 200 m
0 ——————— 0.1 miles

To Serapeum (250m)
PYRAMID OF USERKAF
To Ticket Office (1.2km)
Serdab
Tomb of Akhethotep & Ptahhotep
House of the North Court
Funerary Temple
ZOSER'S FUNERARY COMPLEX
STEP PYRAMID OF ZOSER
House of the South Court
Heb-Sed (Jubilee) Court
Great South Court
Tomb Shaft of Amun-Tefnakht
Hypostyle Hall
Entrance
Tombs
Causeway of Unas
PYRAMID OF UNAS
B Tombs
Boat Pits
Saïte & Persian Tombs
Monastery of St Jeremiah
Tomb of Horemheb
PYRAMID OF SEKHEMKET

At North Saqqara, facilities include toilets, drink stands and souvenir stalls, but you shouldn't expect anything but monuments and sand at South Saqqara. Before exploring either complex, check at the ticket office to see which monuments are open – this constantly changes.

Saqqara is one of the most popular attractions in the Cairo area, though independent visitors are few and far between. Organised tour groups can overwhelm the site, though they quickly rush in and out during the morning hours, leaving the ruins comparatively quiet during midday and early afternoon.

Sights
ZOSER'S FUNERARY COMPLEX
Step Pyramid

In the year 2650 BC, Imhotep, the pharaoh's chief architect (later deified) built the Step Pyramid (Map p198) for Zoser (2667–2648 BC). It is Egypt's (and the world's) earliest stone monument, and its significance cannot be overstated. Previously, temples were made of perishable materials, while royal tombs were usually underground rooms topped with

SAQQARA HALF-DAY ITINERARY

Enter through the hypostyle hall and gaze on the **Step Pyramid**, the world's oldest pyramid. Run the rejuvenation race in Zoser's **Heb-Sed Court**, wonder at the ancient graffiti in the **Houses of the North and South** and stare into Zoser's stone eyes in the eerie **Serdab** (cellar). Walk anticlockwise around the Step Pyramid, visit the mastaba tomb of 5th-dynasty father and son **Akhethotep** and **Ptahhotep**, with its beautiful painted reliefs of animals, battle scenes and the two men receiving offerings, then head south towards the causeway of Unas.

Moving away from the Step Pyramid, descend 25m into the **Pyramid of Teti** to see the famous Pyramid Texts inside, and then pop into the nearby tombs of **Mereruka** and **Ankhmahor**. To complete your visit, move on to the most wonderful tomb of all, the **Mastaba of Ti**, with its fascinating tomb reliefs of daily life in the Old Kingdom, which show people trading, building ships, milking cows and rescuing their livestock from crocodiles. Of course, if you want to extend your stay and get off the beaten path, the rarely visited monuments at **South Saqqara** are just 1km away across the sands.

mudbrick mastabas. However, Imhotep developed the mastaba into a pyramid *and* built it in hewn stone. From this flowed Egypt's later architectural achievements.

The pyramid was transformed from mastaba into pyramid through six separate stages of construction and alteration. With each stage, the builders gained confidence in their use of the new medium and mastered the techniques required to move, place and secure the huge blocks. This first pyramid rose in six steps to a height of 60m, and was encased in fine white limestone.

The Step Pyramid is surrounded by a vast funerary complex, enclosed by a 1645m-long panelled limestone wall, and covers 15 hectares. Part of the enclosure wall survives today at a height of about 5m, and a section near the entrance was restored to its original 10m height. Fourteen false doors, formerly of wood but now carved from stone and painted to resemble real wood, hinges and sockets, allowed the pharaoh's ka (attendant spirit) to come and go at will.

The complex is entered at the southeastern corner via a vestibule and along a colonnaded corridor into the broad hypostyle hall. The 40 pillars in the corridor are the original 'bundle columns', ribbed to resemble a bundle of palm or papyrus stems. The walls have been restored, but the protective ceiling is modern concrete. The roof of the hypostyle hall is supported by four impressive columns and there's a large, false, half-open ka door.

Great South Court

The hypostyle hall leads into the Great South Court (Map p198), a huge open area flanking the south side of the pyramid, with a section of wall featuring a frieze of cobras. The cobra (uraeus) represented the goddess Wadjet, a fire-spitting agent of destruction and protector of the pharaoh. It was a symbol of Egyptian royalty, and a rearing cobra always appeared on the brow of a pharaoh's headdress or crown.

Near the base of the pyramid is an altar, and in the centre of the court are two stone B-shaped boundary markers, which delineated the ritual race the pharaoh had to run, a literal demonstration of his fitness to rule. The race was part of the Jubilee Festival (Heb-Sed), which usually occurred after 30 years' reign, and involved the pharaoh's symbolic rejuvenation and the recognition of his supremacy by officials from all over Egypt. The construction of the Heb-Sed featured within Zoser's funerary complex was therefore intended to perpetuate his revitalisation for eternity.

The buildings on the eastern side of the pyramid are also connected with the royal jubilee, and include the **Heb-Sed (Jubilee) Court** (Map p198). Buildings on the east side of the court represent the shrines of Lower Egypt, and those on the west represent Upper Egypt. All were designed to house the spirits of Egypt's gods when they gathered to witness the rebirth of the pharaoh during his jubilee rituals.

North of the Heb-Sed Court are the **House of the South Court** (Map p198) and **House of the North Court** (Map p198), representing the two main shrines of Upper and Lower Egypt, and symbolising the unity of the country. The heraldic plants of the two regions were chosen to decorate the column capitals: papyrus in the north and lotus in the south.

READING THE PHARAONIC SCENES Dr Joann Fletcher

When visiting temples and tombs, the endless scenes of pharaohs – standing sideways, presenting a never-ending line of gods with the same old offerings – can start to get a bit much. Look closer, however, and these scenes can reveal a few surprises.

As the little figures on the wall strike their eternal poses, a keen eye can find anything from pharaohs ploughing fields to small girls pulling at each other's hair. A whole range of activities that we consider modern can be found among the most ancient scenes, including hairdressing, perfumery, manicures and even massage – the treasury overseer Ptahhotep (p202) certainly enjoyed his comforts, and is seen inhaling deeply from a jar of perfume, while his feet are massaged and fingers manicured. There are similar scenes elsewhere at Saqqara, with a group of men in the Tomb of Ankhmahor (p203) enjoying both manicures and pedicures.

With the title 'overseer of royal hairdressers and wigmakers' commonly held by the highest officials in the land, hairdressing scenes can also be found in the most unexpected places. Not only does Ptahhotep have his wig fitted by his manservants, similar hairdressing scenes can even be found on coffins, as on the limestone sarcophagus of 11th-dynasty Queen Kawit (in Cairo's Egyptian Museum, p183), which shows her wig being deftly styled.

Among its wealth of scenes, the Theban Tomb of Rekhmire (p270) shows a banquet at which the female harpist sings, 'Put perfume on the hair of the goddess Maat'. And in the Deir al-Medina tomb of the workman Peshedu (p272), his family tree contains relatives whose hair denotes their seniority, the eldest shown with the whitest hair as opposed to with wrinkles.

As in many representations of ancient Egyptians, black eye make-up is worn by both male and female, adult and child. As well as its aesthetic value, it was also used as a means of reducing the glare of the sun – think ancient sunglasses. Even manual workers wore it: the Deir al-Medina Tomb of Ipy (p272) once contained a scene in which men building the royal tombs were having eye paint applied while they worked. Difficult to imagine on a building site today!

The House of the South also features one of the earliest examples of tourist graffiti. In the 47th year of Ramses II's reign, nearly 1500 years after Zoser's death, Hadnakhte, a treasury scribe, recorded his admiration for Zoser while 'on a pleasure trip west of Memphis' in about 1232 BC. His hieratic script, written in black ink, is preserved behind perspex just inside the building's entrance.

Serdab

A stone structure right in front of the pyramid, the serdab (a small room containing a statue of the deceased to which offerings were presented; Map p198) contains a slightly tilted wooden box with two holes drilled into its north face. Look through these and you'll have the eerie experience of coming face to face with Zoser himself. Inside is a near-life-size, lifelike painted statue of the long-dead pharaoh, gazing stonily out towards the stars. However, it's worth noting that this statue is only a copy – the original is in Cairo's Egyptian Museum.

The original entrance to the Step Pyramid is directly behind the serdab, and leads down to a maze of subterranean tunnels and chambers

quarried for almost 6km through the rock. The pharaoh's burial chamber is vaulted in granite, and others are decorated with reliefs of the jubilee race and feature some exquisite blue faïence tile decoration. Although the interior of the pyramid is unsafe and closed to the public, part of the blue-tiled decoration can be seen in the Egyptian Museum.

PYRAMID OF USERKAF

Northeast of the funerary complex is the Pyramid of Userkaf (Map p198), the first pharaoh of the 5th dynasty, which is closed to the public for safety reasons. Although the removal of its limestone casing has left little more than a mound of rubble, it once rose to a height of 49m. Furthermore, its funerary temple was once decorated with the most exquisite naturalistic relief carvings, judging from one of the few remaining fragments (now in the Egyptian Museum) showing birds by the river.

PYRAMID & CAUSEWAY OF UNAS

What appears to be another big mound of rubble, this time to the southwest of Zoser's funerary complex, is actually the Pyramid of Unas (Map p198), the last pharaoh of the 5th dynasty (r 2375–2345 BC). Built only 300 years after the inspired creation of the Step Pyramid, this unassuming pile of loose blocks and debris once stood 43m high.

From the outside, the Pyramid of Unas is not much to look at, though the interior marked the beginning of a significant development in funerary practices. For the first time, the royal burial chamber was decorated, its ceiling adorned with stars and its white alabaster-lined walls inscribed with beautiful blue hieroglyphs.

The aforementioned hieroglyphs are the funerary inscriptions that are now known as the Pyramid Texts, comprising 283 separate 'spells' chosen by Unas to protect his soul. The inscriptions include rituals, prayers and hymns, as well as lists of items, such as a list of food and clothing Unas would require in the afterlife. Unfortunately, deterioration of the interior led to the pyramid's permanent closure in 1998.

The 750m-long causeway running from the east side of Unas' pyramid to his valley temple (now marked by little more than a couple of stone columns at the side of the road leading up to the site) was originally roofed and decorated with a great range of painted relief scenes, including a startling image of people starving (now preserved in the Louvre in Paris).

The two 45m-long boat pits of Unas lie immediately south of the causeway, while on either side of the causeway are numerous tombs – more than 200 have been excavated. Of the several better-preserved examples usually open to visitors are the tombs of one of Unas' queens, Nebet, and that of Princess Idut, who was possibly his daughter. There are also several brightly painted tombs of prominent 5th- and 6th-dynasty officials. These include the Tomb of Mehu, the royal vizier (minister), and the Tomb of Nefer, the supervisor of singers.

B Tombs

Several beautiful tombs (Map p198) have been cleared in the area east of the Pyramid of Unas. Although not quite as famous as the tombs north of the Step Pyramid, this set includes a number of interesting Pharaonic attendants. These include the joint Tomb of Niankhkhnum and Khnumhotep, overseers

of the royal manicurists to Pharaoh Nyuserra; the Tomb of Neferherenptah, the overseer of the royal hairdressers; and the Tomb of Irukaptah, overseer of the royal butchers.

Saite & Persian Tombs

Around the sides of the Pyramid of Unas are several large shaft tombs (Map p198) of the Saite (664–525 BC) and Persian (525–404 BC) eras. These are some of the deepest tombs in Egypt, although as with just about everywhere else in the country, the precaution against grave robbers failed. However, the sheer size of the tombs and the great stone sarcophagi within, combined with their sophisticated decoration, demonstrate that the technical achievements of the later part of Egyptian history were equal to those of earlier times.

To the north of the pyramid is the enormous tomb shaft of the Saite general Amun-Tefnakht. On the south side of the pyramid is a group of three Persian tombs – the entrance is covered by a small wooden hut to which a guard in the area has the key. If you don't have your own torch, he'll lead you down a 25m-deep winding staircase to the vaulted tombs of three officials: the admiral Djenhebu to the west, chief royal physician Psamtik in the centre and Psamtik's son, Pediese, to the east.

MONASTERY OF ST JEREMIAH

Uphill from the causeway of Unas, southeast of the boat pits, are the half-buried remains of this Coptic monastery (Map p198), which dates from the 5th century AD. Unfortunately, little is left of the structure, which was ransacked by invading Arabs in 950. More recently, the wall paintings and carvings were removed to the Coptic Museum in Cairo (p126).

PYRAMID OF SEKHEMKET

Closed to the public because of its dangerous condition, the unfinished pyramid (Map p198) of Zoser's successor Sekhemket (2648–2640 BC) is a short distance west of the ruined monastery. The project was abandoned for unknown reasons when the great limestone enclosure wall was only 3m high, despite the fact that the architects had already constructed the underground chambers in the rock beneath the pyramid as well as the deep shaft of the south tomb. An unused travertine sarcophagus was found in the sealed burial chamber, and a quantity of gold, jewellery and a child's body were discovered in the south tomb. Recent surveys have also revealed another mysterious large complex to the west of Sekhemket's enclosure, but this remains unexcavated.

TOMB OF AKHETHOTEP & PTAHHOTEP

Akhethotep and his son Ptahhotep were senior royal officials during the reigns of Djedkare (2414–2375 BC) and Unas at the end of the 5th dynasty. Akhethotep served as vizier, judge, supervisor of pyramid cities and supervisor of priests, though his titles were eventually inherited by Ptahhotep, along with his tomb (Map p198). The joint mastaba has two burial chambers, two chapels and a pillared hall.

The painted reliefs in Ptahhotep's section are particularly beautiful, and portray a wide range of animals, from lions and hedgehogs to the domesticated cattle and fowl that were brought as offerings to the deceased. Ptahhotep himself is portrayed resplendent in a panther-skin robe inhaling perfume from a jar. Ever the fan of pampering himself, he is having his wig fitted, his feet massaged and his fingers manicured (some Egyptologists prefer to interpret this detail as Ptahhotep inspecting an important document, which would be in keeping with his official status).

PHILOSOPHERS' CIRCLE

Nearby is this sad-looking group of Greek statues (Map p197), which are arranged in a semicircle and sheltered by a spectacularly ugly concrete shelter. This is the remnant of a collection of philosophers and poets set up as a wayside shrine by Ptolemy I (323–283 BC) as part of his patronage of learning. From left to right are Plato, Heraclitus, Thales, Protagoras, Homer, Hesiod, Demetrius of Phalerum and Pindar.

SERAPEUM

The Serapeum (Map p197), which is dedicated to the sacred Apis bull, is one of the highlights of visiting Saqqara. The Apis bulls were by far the most important of the cult animals entombed at Saqqara. The Apis, it was believed, was an incarnation of Ptah, the god of Memphis, and was the calf of a cow struck by lightning from heaven. Once divinely impregnated, the cow could never again give birth, and her calf was kept in the Temple of Ptah at Memphis and worshipped as a god.

The Apis was always portrayed as black, with a distinctive white diamond on its forehead, the image of a vulture on its back and a scarab-shaped mark on its tongue. When it died, the bull was mummified on one of the large travertine embalming tables discovered at Memphis, then carried in a stately procession to the subterranean galleries of the Serapeum at Saqqara, and placed in a huge stone sarcophagus.

The first Apis burial took place in the reign of Amenhotep III (1390–1352 BC), and the practice continued until 30 BC. The enormous granite and limestone coffins could weigh up to 80 tonnes each. Until the mid-19th century, the existence of the sacred Apis tombs was known only from classical references. But, having found a half-buried sphinx at Saqqara, and using the description given by the Greek historian Strabo in 24 BC, in 1851 Auguste Mariette uncovered the avenue leading to the Serapeum. However, only one Apis sarcophagus was found intact.

MASTABA OF TI

Northeast of the Philosophers' Circle is the Mastaba of Ti (Map p197), which was discovered by Mariette in 1865. It is perhaps the grandest and most detailed private tomb at Saqqara, and one of our main sources of knowledge about life in Old Kingdom Egypt. Its owner, Ti, was overseer of the Abu Sir pyramids and sun temples (among other things) during the 5th dynasty. In fact, the superb quality of his tomb is in keeping with his nickname, Ti the Rich.

A life-size statue of the deceased stands in the tomb's offering hall (as with the Zoser statue, the original is in the Egyptian Museum). Ti's wife, Neferhetpes, was priestess and 'royal acquaintance'. Together with their two sons, Demedj (overseer of the duck pond) and Ti (inspector of royal manicurists), the couple appear throughout the tomb alongside detailed scenes of daily life. As men and women are seen working on the land, preparing food, fishing, building boats, dancing, trading and avoiding crocodiles, their images are accompanied by chattering hieroglyphic dialogue, all no doubt familiar to Ti during his career as a royal overseer: 'Hurry up, the herdsman's coming', 'Don't make so much noise!', 'Pay up – it's cheap!'.

PYRAMID OF TETI

The avenue of sphinxes excavated by Mariette in the 1850s has again been hidden by desert sands, but it once extended to the much earlier Pyramid of Teti (Map p197). Teti (2345–2323 BC) was the first pharaoh of the 6th dynasty, and his pyramid was built in step form and cased in limestone. Unfortunately, the pyramid was robbed for its treasure and its stone, and today only a modest mound remains. The interior fared better, and is similar in appearance to that of the Pyramid of Unas (p200). Within the intact burial chamber, Teti's basalt sarcophagus is well preserved, and represents the first example of a sarcophagus with inscriptions.

TOMBS OF MERERUKA & ANKHMAHOR

Near the Pyramid of Teti is the tomb (Map p197) of his highest official, Mereruka, vizier and overseer of priests. It's the largest Old Kingdom courtier's tomb, with 32 chambers covering an area of 1000 sq metres. The 17 chambers on the eastern side belong to Mereruka, and include a magnificent six-columned offering hall with a life-size statue of Mereruka appearing to walk right out of the wall to receive the offerings.

Other rooms are reserved for Mereruka's wife, Princess Seshseshat (Teti's daughter), and their eldest son, Meriteti (whose name means 'Beloved of Teti'). Much of the tomb's decoration is similar to that of the Mastaba of Ti, with an even greater number of animals portrayed – look out for the wide-mouthed, sharp-tusked hippos as you enter – along with a charming scene of domestic bliss as husband and wife are seated joyfully on a bed as Seshseshat plays them music on her harp.

Further east, the tomb (Map p197) of the 6th-dynasty vizier and palace overseer, Ankhmahor, contains more interesting scenes of daily life. Most unusual here are images of surgical procedures, earning the tomb its alternative title, the Doctor's Tomb. As two boys are circumcised the hieroglyphic caption says, 'Hold him firmly so he does not fall'!

TOMB OF HOREMHEB

Originally designated as the final resting place of General Horemheb, this tomb (Map p198) became irrelevant in 1323 BC when its intended occupant seized power from Pharaoh Ay. Soon afterwards, Pharaoh Horemheb commissioned the building of a new tomb in the Valley of the Kings. Although the tomb at Saqqara was never put to use, it did yield a number of exquisite reliefs that are currently displayed around the world.

MASTABA OF AL-FARAUN

Known as the Pharaoh's Bench, this unusual funerary complex (Map p197) belongs to the last 4th-dynasty pharaoh, the short-lived Shepseskaf (2503–2498 BC). Shepseskaf was the son of Menkaure, builder of Giza's third great pyramid, though he failed to emulate the glory of his father. Occupying an enclosure once covering 700 sq metres, Shepseskaf's rectangular tomb was built of limestone blocks, and originally covered by a further layer of fine, white limestone and a lower layer of red granite. Inside the tomb, a 21m-long corridor slopes down to storage rooms and a vaulted burial chamber.

PYRAMID OF PEPI II

This pyramid (Map p197) once interred the remains of Pepi II (2278–2184 BC), whose 94-year reign at the end of the 6th dynasty might have been the longest in Egyptian history. Despite his longevity, Pepi II's 52m-high pyramid was of the same modest proportions as those of his predecessor, Pepi I. Although the exterior is little more than a mound of rubble, the interior is decorated with more passages from the Pyramid Texts.

OTHER PYRAMIDS

South Saqqara is also home to the pyramids of **Djedkare**, **Merenre** and **Pepi I** (Map p197). Known as the 'Pyramid of the Sentinel', the 25m-high Djedkare pyramid contains the remains of the last ruler of the 5th dynasty, and can be penetrated from the north side. The pyramids of Merenre and Pepi I are little more than slowly collapsing piles of rock, though the latter is significant as 'Memphis' appears in one of its names.

Getting There & Away

Saqqara is about 25km south of Cairo and is best visited in a taxi, combined with a visit to Memphis and Dahshur – see the boxed text, p196, for more details.

Alternatively, competent riders can hire a horse or camel for the day in Giza, and make the three-hour ride to Saqqara – see p145 for more details.

If you're coming from Cairo or Giza, and are determined to do it on your own, you have several options, including the time-consuming and hassle-rich combination of train, bus and foot via Al-Badrashein. One of the cheapest transport options is to take a bus or minibus to

---

ARCHAEOLOGY IN ACTION

If you thought major Egyptological discoveries were a thing of the past, think again. Saqqara, perhaps more than any other site in Egypt, has been snapping up headlines in recent years following a slew of astonishing findings.

In 2005, Egyptian archaeologists unearthed a 2300-year-old mummy buried in sand at the bottom of a 6m shaft. The perfectly preserved mummy was wearing a golden mask, and was encased in a wooden sarcophagus covered in brightly coloured images of gods and goddesses. Describing the find, Dr Zahi Hawass, secretary-general of Egypt's Supreme Council of Antiquities, said: 'We have revealed what may be the most beautiful mummy ever found in Egypt.'

In 2006, the graves of three royal dentists were discovered after the arrest of tomb raiders led archaeologists to the site. Just two months later, the mummified remains of a doctor were found alongside surgical tools dating back more than 4000 years.

In 2007, archaeologists unveiled the tombs of a Pharaonic butler and a scribe that had been buried for more than 3000 years. The scribe's mudbrick tomb contained several wooden statues and a door with intricate hieroglyphics, while the butler's limestone grave contained two painted coffins. Of particular interest were the blue and orange painted murals that adorned the butler's tomb, and depicted scenes of people performing rituals and monkeys eating fruit.

In 2008, Saqqara made global headlines following the discovery of a new pyramid. Although little remains aside from the 3m-tall, square-shaped foundation, it's estimated that the pyramid once reached a height of approximately 15m, and may be more than 4300 years old.

A year after the discovery, archaeologists entered for the first time and discovered the mummy of Queen Sesheshet. The mother of Teti, first pharaoh of the 6th dynasty, Sesheshet ruled Egypt for just over a decade and was one of just a handful of female pharaohs. While the burial chamber had been raided in antiquity, the mummy survived along with its coverings of linen, pottery and gold sheet.

The discoveries continue. At the time of writing 20 intact mummies were found in niches along the walls of a burial chamber dating back at least 2600 years.

Although archaeologists have been excavating Saqqara for more than a century, it's estimated that only one-third of the total site has been uncovered. According to Dr Hawass, who believes that some 70% of Egypt's ancient monuments remain buried, 'the sands of Saqqara reveal lots of secrets.'

Saqqara Rd and get off at the microbus stop. From there, you will transfer vehicles and get off at the turn-off to the Saqqara site (Haram Saqqara; don't ask for Saqqara village as you'll end up in the wrong place). You'll then have to walk 1.5km to the ticket office.

Getting Around

It's easy to walk around North Saqqara, though it can be a hot and sweaty slog through the sand to South Saqqara. It's also possible to hire a camel, horse or donkey from near the Serapeum to take you on a circuit of the sites for between E£25 and E£50. You'll need to pay more the further into the desert away from North Saqqara you go.

DAHSHUR

About 10km south of Saqqara in a quiet bit of desert is **Dahshur** (adult/student E£25/15; 🕑 8am-4pm Oct-Apr, to 5pm May-Sep, to 3pm during Ramadan),

an impressive 3.5km-long field of 4th- and 12th-dynasty pyramids. Although there were originally 11 pyramids at Dahshur, only the two Old Kingdom ones, the incredibly striking Bent and Red Pyramids, remain intact, as well as three Middle Kingdom pyramid complexes.

Pharaoh Sneferu (2613–2589 BC), father of Khufu and founder of the 4th dynasty, built Egypt's first true pyramid here, the Red Pyramid, as well as an earlier version, the Bent Pyramid. These two pyramids are the same height, and together are also the third-largest pyramids in Egypt after the two largest at Giza. Before founding the necropolis at Dahshur, Sneferu also began the Pyramid of Meidum (p208).

Although the entire plain was previously an off-limits military zone, part of the complex was opened to tourism in 1996. Today, many cluey travellers are adding Dahshur to their itinerary for three reasons: the pyramids here are just as impressive as their counterparts at Giza, the site is much more peaceful (no camel touts in sight) and the entry fee is significantly cheaper.

Orientation & Information
Admission is paid at a small gatehouse on the edge of the complex. The Bent Pyramid, and its surrounds, is still a militarised zone, meaning that it can only be admired at a distance. Fortunately, the wonderful Red Pyramid is open to visitors, and penetrating its somewhat dank interior is a true Indiana Jones-esque experience.

Note that there are no facilities at Dahshur aside from a toilet that you may or may not be allowed to use.

Sights
BENT PYRAMID
Experimenting with ways to create a true, smooth-sided pyramid, Sneferu's architects began with the same steep angle and inward-leaning courses of stone they used to create step pyramids. When this began to show signs of stress and instability around halfway up its eventual 105m height, they had little choice but to reduce the angle from 54° to 43° and begin to lay the stones in horizontal layers. This explains why the structure has the unusual shape that gives it its name. Most of its outer casing is still intact, and inside (closed to visitors) are two burial chambers, the highest of which retains its original ancient scaffolding of great cedar beams to counteract internal instability. There is also a small subsidiary pyramid to the south as well as the remains of a small funerary temple to the east. About halfway towards the cultivation to the east are the ruins of Sneferu's valley temple, which yielded some interesting reliefs.

RED PYRAMID
The world's oldest true pyramid is the North Pyramid, which is better known as the Red Pyramid. It derives its name either from the red tones of its weathered limestone, after the better-quality white limestone casing was removed, or perhaps from the red graffiti and construction marks scribbled on its masonry in ancient times. Having learnt from their experiences building the Bent Pyramid, the same architects carried on where they had left off, building the Red Pyramid at

the same 43° angle as the Bent Pyramid's more gently inclining upper section. The entrance – via 125 extremely steep stone steps and a 63m-long passage – takes you down to two antechambers with stunning 12m-high corbelled ceilings and a 15m-high corbelled burial chamber in which fragmentary human remains, possibly of Sneferu himself, were found.

BLACK PYRAMID
Of the three Middle Kingdom pyramid complexes built by Amenemhat II (1922–1878 BC), Sesostris III (1874–1855 BC) and his son Amenemhat III (1855–1808 BC), only the oddly shaped Black Pyramid of Amenemhat III is worth a look.

The towerlike structure appears to have completely collapsed due to the pilfering of its limestone outer casing in medieval times, but the mudbrick remains contain a maze of corridors and rooms designed to deceive tomb robbers. Thieves did manage to penetrate the burial chambers but left behind a number of precious funerary artefacts that were discovered in 1993.

Getting There & Away
The only way to visit Dahshur is by taxi or organised tour, which can easily be combined with a visit to Memphis, Abu Sir and Saqqara – see the boxed text, p196, for more details.

AL-FAYOUM OASIS

This large semi-oasis, about 70km wide and 60km long, is an extremely fertile basin watered by the Nile via hundreds of capillary canals and is home to more than two million people. The region also harbours a number of important archaeological sites, particularly Qasr Qarun and the Pyramid of Meidum, as well as scenic Lake Qarun and Wadi Rayyan. Unfortunately, tight security restrictions have essentially crushed tourism in the region, and independent travel in Al-Fayoum can be frustratingly slow and at times prohibited.

MEDINAT AL-FAYOUM
☎ 084 / pop 515,000
The largest town on the Al-Fayoum Oasis was a favourite holiday spot for 13th-dynasty

---

SECURITY IN AL-FAYOUM

This relatively quiet corner of Egypt has some of the most heavy-handed security restrictions in the whole of the country, a result of the clampdown that occurred after the massacre of tourists in Cairo and Luxor in 1997. Many of the Islamist terrorists involved in the Luxor massacre came from Al-Fayoum, and Islamist groups such as the Muslim Brotherhood and Gama'a al-Islamiyya have a strong local following. This poses a real problem for foreigners, who will often find they are not allowed to leave their hotel rooms without a dedicated tourist-police escort or use local transport. If you intend to explore the Al-Fayoum area, be advised that you will have to deal with more hassles than usual, though it's worth suffering a little extra abuse for the chance to explore this little-visited oasis.

---

pharaohs, who built a series of pleasure palaces in the area. Centuries later, the Greeks, who believed the crocodiles in Lake Qarun were sacred, called the area Crocodilopolis, and built a temple in honour of Sobek, the crocodile-headed god. During Ptolemaic and Roman times, pilgrims came from across the ancient world to feed the sacred beasts.

These days Medinat al-Fayoum (Town of the Fayoum) is a less-than-appealing mix of crumbling concrete, horn-happy drivers, choking fumes, swirling dust and crowded streets. Needless to say, there is little reason to spend any more time here than is absolutely necessary, though it's a convenient enough base for visiting the major sights in the region.

Orientation & Information

The Bahr Yusuf canal acts as the city's main artery, and most commercial activities take place along it. Banks in the town include Bank of Alexandria and Banque du Caire.

Located at the Governorate Building, the **Fayoum Tourism Authority** (☎ 634 2313; Sharia Saad Zaghloul) can organise guides to take travellers around the oasis's sites. From Al-Fayoum, you'll be looking at a cost of around E£300 to E£400 for a guide and taxi for the day, which should allow you to visit the Pyramid of Meidum, Lake Qarun and Wadi Rayyan.

For more information on the oasis, obtain a copy of *The Fayoum: History and Guide* by R Neil Hewison (AUC Press).

The bus and taxi stations are a short hike from the city centre.

Sights

As far as sights go, there's the **Obelisk of Senusert**, which you'll pass coming in from Cairo at the centre of a roundabout to the northeast of town. Although it looks lost among the cars

and buses, it's supposedly the only obelisk in Egypt with a rounded top, and it also features a cleft in which a golden statue of Ra was placed, reflecting the sun's rays in the four directions of the wind.

Fayoum is also famous for its **waterwheels**, which in total number more than 200, and have become a prominent symbol of the town. Since Pharaonic times, these devices have kept the town well irrigated despite its irregular topography of rolling hills and steep depressions. Although some of the rickety waterwheels look as if they were built thousands of years ago, the vast majority are modern constructions.

The **Governorate Building** (Sharia Saad Zaghloul; ☉ closed irregularly) houses a modest display on the history and fauna of the oasis.

Sleeping & Eating

If you're not excited about the prospect of bedding down in Fayoum, there are other options to consider along the shores of Lake Qarun (p209).

Palace Hotel (☎ 635 1222; Bahr Yusuf; s/d from E£65/80; ✖) Although it maintains a certain air of respectability, this ageing relic has seen better dynasties. The rooms themselves are clean if slightly musty, and you'll get a decent night's sleep if you're not too fussy. The Palace is 200m west of the park; to find it, look up from street level – it's the pink building with a sign on the 2nd floor, and is entered via a tiled open-air arcade behind a watch kiosk.

Honeyday Hotel (☎ 634 0105; 105 Sharia Gamal Abdel Nasser; s/d from E£85/105; ✖) Although it lacks the central location of the Palace, the Honeyday is near the bus station, which is certainly convenient if you're hauling heavy bags. It's a fairly nondescript high-rise with little charm, but the rooms themselves are a bit nicer than the bland exterior lets on. There is

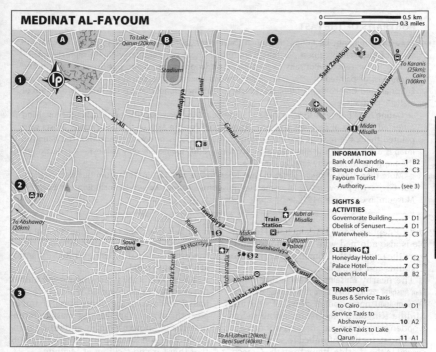

MEDINAT AL-FAYOUM

0   0.5 km
0   0.3 miles

INFORMATION	
Bank of Alexandria 1	B2
Banque du Caire 2	C3
Fayoum Tourist	
Authority ....(see 3)	

SIGHTS &	
ACTIVITIES	
Governorate Building.........3	D1
Obelisk of Senusert...........4	D1
Waterwheels 5	C3

SLEEPING	
Honeyday Hotel 6	C2
Palace Hotel 7	C3
Queen Hotel 8	B2

TRANSPORT	
Buses & Service Taxis	
to Cairo 9	D1
Service Taxis to	
Abshaway 10	A2
Service Taxis to Lake	
Qarun 11	A1

AROUND CAIRO

also a small restaurant here serving cheap and hearty Egyptian fare, which fills the stomach without making too much of a show.

Queen Hotel (☎ 634 6819; Sharia Minshaat Lutfallah; s/d from E£175/215; ❄) The Queen is undoubtedly the most comfortable option in town, which is one reason it can be difficult to get a room here. Relatively clean and spacious rooms have private bathrooms, minifridges and satellite TV, and serve as a nice base if you want to spend a day or two exploring the oasis. Even if you're not staying here, you could try the on-site restaurant, which serves comparatively decent food. Though don't expect a cold beer in these parts.

There are several very basic cafes and assorted eateries on the canal-side road just west of the park. The region is famous for its lush fields of vegetables and sugar cane, as well as its groves of citrus fruits, nuts and olives, so definitely pick up some fresh produce at any of the shops and markets around town.

Getting There & Away
Buses to Cairo (E£6 to E£8, two to three hours) leave every half-hour from 7am until 7pm from the train station on the west side of Gamal Abdel Nasser Rd (the Cairo road). These buses take you to the Ahmed Helmy bus station behind Cairo's Ramses train station, stopping en route at Al-Monieb station on Midan Giza.

Getting Around
Green-and-white minibuses (25pt) cover all areas of Medinat al-Fayoum between the western and eastern bus stations.

KARANIS
At the edge of the oasis depression, 25km north of Medinat al-Fayoum on the road to Cairo, lie the ruins of ancient Karanis. Founded by Ptolemy II's mercenaries in the 3rd century BC, the town was once a mudbrick settlement with a population in the thousands.

Today, little of the ancient city remains intact aside from a few walls, though Karanis is home to two well-preserved **Graeco-Roman temples** (adult/student E£32/16; ❄ 9am-4pm) in the southern part of town. The larger and more interesting temple was built in the 1st century BC, and is dedicated to two local crocodile

---

PORTRAITS OF THE PAST

Al-Fayoum may not be famous for much these days, but it was here that caches of what are some of the world's earliest portraits were found. These extraordinarily lifelike representations, known as the 'Fayoum Portraits', were painted on wooden panels and put over the faces of the mummies, or painted directly onto linen shrouds covering the corpses. This fusion of ancient Egyptian and Graeco-Roman funerary practices laid the foundation for the Western tradition of realistic portraiture.

Dating from between 30 BC and AD 395, the paintings were executed in a technique involving a heated mixture of pigment and wax. Remarkable for the skill of the anonymous artists who painted them, the realistic and eerily modern-looking faces bridge the centuries. The haunting images are made all the more poignant by their youth (some are only babies) – a reflection of the high infant-mortality rates at the time.

More than 1000 of these portraits have been found, not just in Al-Fayoum but also throughout Egypt. They now reside in numerous museums around the world, including the Egyptian Museum in Cairo (see p191).

---

gods, Pnepheros and Petesouchos. The temple is also adorned with inscriptions dating from the reigns of the Roman emperors Nero, Claudius and Vespasian.

The nearby **Museum of Kom Aushim** (Mathaf Kom Aushim; ☎ 650 1825; Cairo rd; adult/student E£16/8; ☺ 9am-4pm) has good displays of Old and Middle Kingdom objects, including sacred wooden boats, Canopic jars, and wooden and ceramic statuettes entombed to serve the deceased in the afterlife. Items from the Graeco-Roman period, which give context to Karanis, are exhibited on the 1st floor.

To get here, catch one of the Cairo-bound buses from Medinat al-Fayoum (E£5 to E£7).

PYRAMID OF MEIDUM

About 30km to the northeast of Medinat al-Fayoum is the ruin of the first true pyramid attempted by the ancient Egyptians, namely the **Pyramid of Meidum** (adult/student E£32/16; ☺ 8am-4pm). It began as an eight-stepped structure, with the steps later filled in and an outer casing added, forming the first true pyramid shell. However, there were serious design flaws and, sometime after completion (possibly as late as the last few centuries BC), the pyramid's own weight caused the sides to collapse. Today, only the core of the 'Collapsed' Pyramid of Meidum stands, though it is still an impressive sight to behold.

Pharaoh Huni (2637–2613 BC) was responsible for commissioning the pyramid, although it was his son Sneferu who was responsible for the actual building. Interestingly,

it is likely that Sneferu's architects learnt from their mistakes since they then went on to build the more successful Bent and Red Pyramids at Dahshur (p204).

The guard at the nearby house will unlock the entrance of the pyramid, from where steps lead 75m down to the empty burial chamber. Near the pyramid are the large mastaba tombs of some of Sneferu's family and officials, including his son Rahotep and wife Nofret. Note that there are no facilities at Meidum.

To reach the pyramid, take any service taxi or bus running between Cairo and Beni Suef, and ask to be dropped off at the Meidum turn-off (E£13 to E£15). From here you will still have about 6km to go but it can be difficult to get a lift.

A much better option is to hire a taxi from Medinat al-Fayoum, and visit Meidum in conjunction with the surrounding pyramids. Prices are highly negotiable but you should aim for between E£100 and E£200 for the complete circuit excluding entry fees and baksheesh.

PYRAMID OF HAWARA

About 8km to the southeast of Medinat al-Fayoum, off the Beni Suef road, stands the dilapidated mudbrick **Pyramid of Hawara** (adult/student E£32/16; ☺ 8am-4pm). This is the second pyramid of Amenemhat III, his other being the towerlike Black Pyramid at Dahshur (p204). Much like Pharaoh Sneferu 800 years before him, it's believed that Amenemhat III built Hawara at a gentler angle after his first pyramid at Dahshur showed signs of instability.

Although the Pyramid of Hawara was originally covered with white limestone casing, sadly only the mudbrick core remains today, and even the once-famous temple has been quarried. Herodotus described the temple (300m by 250m) as a 3000-room labyrinth that surpassed even the Pyramids of Giza. Strabo claimed it had as many rooms as there were provinces, so that all the pharaoh's subjects could be represented by their local officials in the presentation of offerings.

The Greeks and Romans also used the area as a cemetery: the dead were mummified in an Egyptian way, but the mummies' wrappings incorporated a portrait-style face (see boxed text, opposite). Widespread excavations left little more than pieces of mummy cloth and human bones sticking up through the mounds of rubble.

The Pyramid of Hawara is notable among archaeologists for its interior, which revealed several technical developments: corridors were blocked using a series of huge stone portcullises; the burial chamber is carved from a single piece of quartzite; and the chamber was sealed by an ingenious device using sand to lower the roof block into place.

Be advised that it hasn't been possible to enter the pyramid since 1882. Note also that there are no facilities at Hawara.

Buses between Medinat al-Fayoum and Beni Suef pass through Hawarat al-Makta. From there, it is just a short walk to the pyramid. Alternatively, you can visit in a private taxi as part of a grand circuit taking in other pyramids (see Pyramid of Meidum, opposite).

PYRAMID OF AL-LAHUN

About 10km southeast of Hawara, on the Nile side of the narrow fertile passage that connects Al-Fayoum to the Nile, are the ruins of the **Pyramid of Al-Lahun** (adult/student E£32/16; 8am-4pm), built by Pharaoh Sesostris II (1880–1874 BC). The pyramid was once covered in precious limestone, but ancient tomb robbers stripped it of all its rock and treasures, except for the amazing solid-gold uraeus that is now displayed in the jewellery room (Room 4) of the Egyptian Museum in Cairo. Note that there are no facilities at Al-Lahun.

To reach the pyramid, take any service taxi or bus running between Cairo and Beni Suef, and ask to be dropped off at the village of Al-Lahun. From here, you will have to walk for another 2km. You can also visit via private taxi.

LAKE QARUN
☎ 084

Prior to the 12th-dynasty reigns of Sesostris III and his son Amenemhat III, the Al-Fayoum region was entirely covered by Lake Qarun. In an early effort at land reclamation, however, both pharaohs dug a series of canals linking Qarun to the Nile, and drained much of the lake. Over the past few centuries, the lake has regained some of its former grandeur due to the diversion of the Nile to create more agricultural land. However, since Lake Qarun presently sits at 45m below sea level, it has suffered from increasing salinity. Remarkably, the wildlife has adapted, and today the self-proclaimed 'world's most ancient lake' supports a unique ecosystem. There's a good chance you'll spot countless varieties of birds here including a large colony of flamingos.

Sights

Although few foreign tourists visit the lake, Qarun is a popular weekend spot for vacationing Cairenes looking to cool down. Even if you're not up for a swim, the sight of an expansive lake on the edge of the desert is quite striking, and makes a nice diversion from a morning spent pyramid-hopping.

At the western end of Lake Qarun, near the village of Qasr Qarun, are the ruins of ancient Dionysus, once the starting point for caravans to the Western Desert oasis of Bahariya. Although little remains of this historic settlement, a **Ptolemaic temple** (adult/student E£32/16; 8am-4pm), built in 4 BC and dedicated to Sobek, the crocodile-headed god of Al-Fayoum, is still standing. If you're feeling adventurous, you can go down to the underground chambers (beware of snakes), and up to the roof for a view of the desert, the sparse remains of Ptolemaic and Roman settlements, and the oasis.

Sleeping

New Panorama Village (☎ 683 0746; s/d from E£250/275;) While lacking the character of its principle lakeside competitor (the Helnan Auberge Fayoum), the New Panorama Village is still an attractive spot for a night or two. True to its moniker, the premises are designed along the lines of an Egyptian village, albeit one with balcony-lined chalets that front the incongruous waters of this mirage-worthy desert lake. The restaurant specialises in fresh fish from the lake waters, and fresh fowl from the lake shores.

our pick **Helnan Auberge Fayoum** (☎ 698 1200; www.helnan.com; r from US$75; 🛇 🔊) This opulent colonial-style hotel, constructed in the late 1930s, was where world leaders met after WWII to decide on the borders of the Middle East. Later, it served as King Farouk's private hunting lodge, though these days it primarily caters to wealthy Cairene families looking for some fresh air. Although it recently changed ownership, and underwent extensive renovations to modernise the premises, the Helnan Auberge Fayoum remains a quiet refuge from the bump and grind of Cairo that is steeped in a rich and visible history.

Getting There & Away

To reach Lake Qarun, take any service taxi or pick-up from Medinat al-Fayoum (Map p207) to Shakshouk (E£1), the major settlement on the lake. From here, you will see English signs pointing the way to the massive Helnan Auberge Fayoum, which is easily recognisable from a distance.

To reach Qasr Qarun, take any service taxi or pick-up from Medinat al-Fayoum (Map p207) to Abshaway (E£1), just south of the lake. Here you will need to change to any service taxi or pick-up heading to the village (E£1), located just past Tunis. The Ptolemaic temple is off to the left of the road shortly before the settlement begins.

While Lake Qarun is accessible by public transport, it's recommended that you visit the area by private vehicle. Having the freedom provided by your own wheels will allow you to cruise around the lake, in addition to visiting the spectacular Wadi Rayyan Protected Area and Wadi al-Hittan.

WADI RAYYAN & WADI AL-HITTAN

In the 1960s Egyptian authorities created three lakes in the Wadi Rayyan depression, southwest of Lake Qarun, to hold excess water from agricultural drainage. This was intended to be the first step in an ambitious land-reclamation project, though not everything went to plan when the water started to become increasingly brackish. On the bright side, Wadi Rayyan is particularly conducive to large colonies of birds, and today the entire depression is administered as a quasi national park.

The **Wadi Rayyan Protected Area** (admission per person US$3 plus E£5 per vehicle, camping per person E£10) is primarily a major nesting ground for both endemic and migrating birds, though it's also something of a weekend picnic spot for escaping Cairenes, especially near 'the Waterfalls', where one lake drains into the other. Here, you'll also find a visitors centre and a couple of small cafes serving cold drinks and light meals.

Be advised that you technically need permission in advance from the tourist police in Medinat al-Fayoum to visit here, though in a pinch a little baksheesh can help smooth things over at any of the roadside checkpoints. Also, don't be surprised if you're given a police escort to the park entrance, who will also likely expect baksheesh in return for their service.

Some 55km further south into the desert is Wadi al-Hittan (Valley of the Whales), where the skeletons of primitive whales have been lying for about 40 million years. These fossilised remains are of *Archaeoceti*, a now extinct suborder of modern whales that has helped to shed light on the evolution of land-based to sea-going mammals. Although still part of the Wadi Rayyan Protected Area, the Valley of the Whales now receives additional support from various agencies after being declared a Unesco World Heritage Site in 2005.

The Valley of the Whales is also home to a small network of walking tracks leading out to more than a dozen skeletons, in addition to a wilderness campsite complete with basic toilets and fire pits. There are also plans to expand tourist infrastructure at the site, which should help generate the revenue needed to continue ongoing excavations.

Getting There & Away

In the past, getting out here was something of an expedition that required a convoy of 4WD vehicles. But Wadi al-Hittan has greatly benefited from the construction of a new 2WD-accessible road that connects the site to Wadi Rayyan.

The Wadi Rayyan Protected Area is not accessible by public transport; you'll either need your own vehicle, or hire a taxi in Medinat al-Fayoum. Prices vary, but you can plan on E£150 to E£250 if you're just visiting Wadi Rayyan, and upwards of E£300 to E£400 if you want to extend your trip to Wadi al-Hittan.

For drivers heading to Wadi Rayyan, follow the road to the end of Lake Qarun, and take the wide asphalt road to the left just after you see the mudbrick domes of the village of Tunis on a ridge to your left. This road heads south and leads straight to the visitors centre where you must pay your entrance fee.

If going on to Wadi al-Hittan, continue past the visitors centre for roughly 10km – go slow along this stretch as you're looking for the signed turn-off. Once you've found the road, continue straight through the dune fields for approximately 60km until arriving at the entrance to the Valley of the Whales, where you pay your fees.

THE ROAD TO ALEXANDRIA

The Cairo–Alexandria Desert Hwy (known usually as the Desert Hwy) roughly separates the green fields of the Delta and the harsh sands of the Western Desert. Previously desolate, large swathes of the area's prairie-type expanses have been greened to create farms, and several new satellite towns have been established in order to ease the population pressure on Cairo. However, it's the desert life of the past that draws most tourists to this stretch, namely the famous Birqash camel market and the historic Coptic monasteries of Wadi Natrun.

BIRQASH CAMEL MARKET

Egypt's largest **camel market** (souq al-gamaal; admission E£20; ☻ 6am-noon daily) is held at Birqash, a small village 35km northwest of Cairo. Until 1995 the market was held in Cairo's western suburb of Imbaba, but when land became too precious for camels, one of Cairo's age-old institutions was relocated to the edge of the Western Desert. Like all Egypt's animal markets, the Birqash camel market is not for animal lovers, nor for the faint of heart. But if you've got a strong stomach (and better yet a weak sense of smell), a visit to Birqash can make an unforgettable day trip.

Hundreds of camels are sold here every day, most having been brought up the Forty Days Rd from western Sudan to just north of Abu Simbel by camel herders, and from there to the market in Daraw (see p299). Unsold camels are then hobbled and crammed into trucks for the 24-hour drive to Birqash. By the time they arrive, many are emaciated, fit only for the knacker's yard. Traders stand no nonsense and camels that get out of line are beaten relentlessly.

In addition to those from Sudan, there are camels from various parts of Egypt (including Sinai, the west and the south) and sometimes from as far away as Somalia. They are traded for cash or other livestock, such as goats, sheep and horses, and sold for farm work or slaughter.

While at the market, watch out for pick-pockets. Women should dress conservatively – the market is very much a man's scene, with the only female presence other than the occasional traveller being the local tea lady. When you arrive, pick a strategic spot and settle in to watch the negotiations. The best area is around the middle of the lot; there are not as many camels at the entrance, and at the very back, and it's noticeably scruffier there.

If you're interested in buying a camel (either for transportation or for meat – what you do with it is up to you), smaller ones cost several thousand Egyptian pounds, while bigger beasts sometimes go for as much as E£5000 to E£10,000. Negotiations tend to take place early in the day, with the peak of action being between 7am and 10am, especially on Fridays. By early afternoon the market is quite subdued as everyone returns home either on camelback or empty-handed.

Getting There & Away

Using public transport, the cheapest way to get to Birqash involves getting yourself to the site of the old camel market at Imbaba, from where microbuses filled with traders and potential buyers shuttle back and forth to Birqash.

To get to the old camel market, take a minibus from Midan Abdel Moniem Riad (see Map pp120–1) to Imbaba, from where you can catch a connecting microbus. Easier still, take a taxi from central Cairo all the way to the old site (about E£10); Imbaba airport (matar Imbaba) is the closest landmark. Once at Imbaba, ask a local to show you where to get the microbus (E£1) to Birqash. From Imbaba, the road winds through fields dotted with date palms, dusty villages, orange orchards and patches of encroaching urban sprawl before climbing the desert escarpment to the market. Microbuses from Birqash back to Imbaba leave when full: depending on the time of the day, you could wait up to two hours or so.

The easiest way to get to and from the market is to hire a private taxi for the morning. The market is an easy half-day trip (one to 1½ hours) from Cairo, and one hour in the hot and dusty market is usually enough for most people. The return trip will cost somewhere between E£75 and E£125, depending on your bargaining skills.

WADI NATRUN

Wadi Natrun, about 100km northwest of Cairo, was of great importance to ancient Egyptians, for this was where they found natron, a substance that was crucial to the mummification process. Natron comes from large deposits of sodium carbonate that are left when the valley's salt lakes dry up every summer. Today, natron is used on a larger scale by the chemical industry.

Wadi Natrun is primarily known for its historic Coptic Christian monasteries. Besides their solitude and serenity, the monasteries are worth visiting for the Coptic art they contain, particularly at Deir el-Sourian.

History

A visit to the monasteries of Wadi Natrun reveals clues to the survival of the Coptic Church, for the desert has long been the protector of the faith. It was there that thousands of Christians retreated to escape Roman persecution in the 4th century. They lived in caves, or built monasteries, and developed the monastic tradition that was later adopted by European Christians.

The focal point of the monasteries was the church, around which were built a well, storerooms, a dining hall, kitchen, bakery and the monks' cells. These isolated, unprotected communities were fortified after destructive raids in 817 by Arab tribes on their way to conquer North Africa. Of the 60 monasteries once scattered over the valley, only four remain.

The religious life they helped protect is now thriving. The Coptic pope is still chosen from among the Wadi Natrun monks, and monasticism is experiencing a revival, with young professional Copts once again donning robes and embroidered hoods to live within these ancient walls in the desert. Even today, some monks still retreat into caves in the surrounding countryside for weeks and months at a time.

Information

Each monastery has different opening times, with some closed completely during the three annual fasting periods (Lents) at Easter,

Christmas and in August. Before going, it is worth checking with their Cairo residences that visits are possible.

As a general rule, you can visit all of the monasteries without prior notice, the only exception being Deir Abu Makar. Males wishing to stay overnight (women are not allowed to do so) need written permission from the monasteries' Cairo residences:

Deir Abu Makar (☎ 02-577 0614)
Deir Anba Bishoi (☎ 02-591 4448)
Deir el-Baramouse (☎ 02-592 2775)
Deir el-Sourian (☎ 02-592 9658)

Sights

DEIR ANBA BISHOI

St Bishoi founded two monasteries in Wadi Natrun: this one (which bears his name) and neighbouring Deir el-Sourian. **Deir Anba Bishoi** (☼ daily incl during Lents) is built around a church that contains the saint's body, said to be perfectly preserved in its sealed, tubelike container. Each year on 17 July, the tube is carried in procession around the church. According to the monks, the bearers clearly feel the weight of a whole body. The church also contains the cell where St Bishoi tied his hair to the ceiling to stop himself sleeping during prayers.

There's a lovely internal garden with an impressive vegetable patch, an enormous new cathedral and an interesting fortified keep that you enter via a drawbridge. This contains a well, kitchens, two churches and storerooms that can hold provisions for a year. On the roof, trap doors open to small cells that acted as makeshift tombs for those who died during frequent sieges. The rooftop is a splendid place to watch the desert sunset.

DEIR EL-SOURIAN

About 500m northwest of Deir Anba Bishoi, **Deir el-Sourian** (☼ 3-6pm Mon-Fri, 9am-6pm Sat & Sun during Lents) is named after wandering Syrian monks who bought the monastery from the Copts in the 8th century, and is the most picturesquely situated of the monasteries. Since the 16th century it has been solely occupied by Coptic monks. Its Church of the Virgin was built around a 4th-century cave that had been occupied by St Bishoi, and is worth visiting for its superb series of 11th-century wall paintings.

DEIR ABU MAKAR

Nearly 20km southeast of Deir Anba Bishoi, **Deir Abu Makar** (☼ daily but only by prior arrangement, closed during Lents) was founded around the cell where St Makarios spent his last 20 or so years. Structurally, it suffered more than other monasteries at the hands of raiding Bedouin, but it is famous as most of the Coptic popes over the centuries have been selected from among its monks. It is the last resting place of many of those popes and also contains the remains of the 49 Martyrs, a group of monks killed by Bedouin in 444. Deir Abu Makar is understandably the most secluded of the monasteries, so permission to visit must be requested in advance.

DEIR EL-BARAMOUSE

Until recently, when a good road was built to Deir Anba Bishoi to the southeast, **Deir el-Baramouse** (Fri-Sun, closed during Lents) was the most isolated of the Wadi Natrun monasteries. These days more than 100 monks live here, and there are now six modern churches and a restored medieval fortress (not open to the public) within its compound. There are also remnants of 13th-century wall frescoes in its oldest church, the Church of the Virgin Mary.

Sleeping

If you have both a Y-chromosome and the necessary written consent, then you're welcome to spend the night in any of the monasteries listed above. Since all four places are major destinations for Coptic Christians on religious pilgrimages, a night's stay is generally a sombre affair defined by regular prayer sessions. Even if you're not devout, it is good manners to attend these religious services, and to leave a generous donation with the monks at the time of your departure.

If you weren't able to obtain written permission, or you have two X-chromosomes, you can easily access the monasteries on a day trip from Cairo (see below).

Getting There & Away

You can catch a West Delta Co bus to the less-than-inviting town functioning as a gateway to the monasteries that goes by the grandiloquent name of Wadi Natrun City. These buses leave from Cairo's Turgoman Garage (p177) every 30 minutes between 6am and 10pm and cost E£5 to E£10. From the bus lot at Wadi Natrun City, you'll have to negotiate with a taxi driver to take you around the monasteries; expect to pay around E£20 per hour. On Fridays and Sundays, when the monasteries

are crowded with pious Copts, you can easily pick up a lift. The last bus back to Cairo leaves at 6pm.

A taxi from Cairo should cost about E£150 to E£200 there and back, including a couple of hours driving around the monasteries.

If you have your own vehicle and you're coming from Cairo, take Saqqara Rd and turn onto the Cairo–Alexandria Desert Hwy. After about 95km (just after the rest house and petrol station), turn left into the wadi, drive another 4km or so to Wadi Natrun City and continue on, following the signs pointing to the monasteries.

THE NILE DELTA

North of Cairo, the Nile River divides into two branches that enter the Mediterranean at the old ports of Damietta and Rosetta, forming one of the most fertile and, unsurprisingly, most cultivated regions in the world. Laced with countless waterways, the lush, fan-shaped Nile Delta is (and has always been) the agricultural heartland of Egypt. If you have the time, it's worth the effort (and it is an effort) to get off the beaten path and explore the unique environment and culture of the Delta region.

NILE BARRAGES

It's great fun taking a ride on one of the ramshackle river buses that ply the Nile between Cairo and Qanater (Arabic for 'Barrages'), 16km to the north of the city where the Nile splits in two. The trip, which takes 90 minutes each way, is best done on Fridays or public holidays, when large groups of young people and smaller family parties pack the boats and the tawdry but highly atmospheric funfair and public gardens at Qanater. On the boats, Arabic pop blares and the younger passengers sing along, clap their hands, dance and decorously flirt. It's an immensely enjoyable half-day jaunt – particularly when the sun is out and the sky is clear.

The barrages were begun in the early 19th century. The series of basins and locks, on both main branches of the Nile and the two side canals, guaranteed a year-round flow of water into the Delta region and led to a great increase in cotton production.

The Damietta Barrage consists of 71 sluices stretching 521m across the river; the Rosetta

---

EXPLORING THE DELTA

The Delta region played just as important a part as Upper Egypt in the early history of the country, but few archaeological remains record this. While the desert and dryness of the south helped preserve its Pharaonic sites, the amazing fertility of the Delta region had the opposite effect. Over the centuries, as the ancient cities, temples and palaces of the Delta fell into ruin; they were literally ploughed into oblivion by the fellaheen (peasant farmers).

The attraction of this area is the chance to encounter communities rarely visited by foreigners, where you can gain insight into the Egyptian farmer's way of life. The region is also impossibly green and scenic, which can be therapeutic if you've spent too much time surrounded by swirling sand and barren rock. If you do intend spending any time in this region, we strongly recommend reading Amitav Ghosh's excellent *In an Antique Land,* an account of the author's lengthy stay in a Delta village.

Service taxis and buses crisscross the region but if you want to really explore the countryside, you'll have to hire a car. Officially, you're not supposed to leave the main roads for security reasons but there have been no recent reports of any real security concerns (check the current situation). The most you risk is some questioning from the police, who will likely expect baksheesh for their troubles. Another great way to explore the Delta is to take a ride on a river bus (see the Nile Barrages, p213), which is essentially the Egyptian version of the 'booze cruise' (sans booze of course!).

In summary, don't let the effort involved dissuade you from exploring this region. Indeed, this is one part of Egypt where you should put the book down, leave the well-trodden tourist trail behind and strike out in search of your own unique travel experience.

Barrage is 438m long with 61 sluices. The area between the two at Qanater is 1km wide and filled with straggly gardens, riverside cafes and souvenir stands. The Cairene equivalent of America's Coney Island or Britain's Blackpool, it's particularly popular with young males, whose pastime of choice is to ride motor scooters and bikes at breakneck speed up and down the promenade, dodging indignant pedestrians and scaring the saddles off the poor horses pulling *calèches* (horse-drawn carriages) full of families along the Corniche.

The best way to reach the barrages is to take a privately run river bus (E£6 return) from the river taxi station in front of the Radio and TV Building (Maspero station), just north of the Ramses Hilton in central Cairo.

ZAGAZIG & BUBASTIS

Just outside the city of Zagazig – that's pronounced za-a-zi, not zag-a-zig – are the ruins of Bubastis, one of Egypt's most ancient cities. The great deity of the ancient city of Bubastis was the elegant cat goddess Bastet. Festivals held in her honour are said to have attracted more than 700,000 revellers who sang, danced, feasted, consumed great quantities of wine and offered sacrifices to the goddess.

Although there's not much to see in Zagazig itself, serious Egyptology buffs will enjoy a visit to the ruined **Temple of Bubastis** (adult/student E£15/10; ☼ 8am-4pm). The temple was begun by the great pyramid builders Khufu and Khafre during the 4th dynasty, and pharaohs of subsequent dynasties made their additions over about 17 centuries. Although this architectural gem once rose above the city, today the temple is now just a pile of rubble. However, the cat cemetery 200m down the road, which consists of a series of underground galleries where many bronze statues of cats were found, is morbidly fun to explore.

Zagazig and Bubastis are only 80km northeast of Cairo, and serve as an easy day trip from the capital. If you get stuck, you could try one of the budget hotels clustered around the train station, though they're of questionable cleanliness and security, and the lack of English signage is a deterrent.

A far better option is the **Marina** (☎ 055-231 3934; 58 Gamal Abdel Nasser; s/d from E£250/275;) a somewhat upmarket affair near the Al-Fatr Mosque that caters to local business travellers. Fairly standard rooms are comfortable despite being unmemorable, though the views from the nearby bridge are very attractive, particularly when the mosque is lit up at night.

Trains running between Cairo and Port Said call in Zagazig, though it's far easier and cheaper to access the town by bus or service taxi. There are frequent departures in both directions between Zagazig's train station and Cairo's Aboud terminal (p178; E£4 to E£6, one to two hours). From the train station in Zagazig, the temple is about 1km southeast along Sharia Farouq. Taxis (E£1) can whisk you away to the site in under a minute.

TANIS

Just outside the village of San al-Hagar, 70km northeast of Zagazig, are the partly excavated ruins of the ancient city of Tanis. Although its modern name is derived from Greek, this ancient city was Djanet to the Egyptians and Zoan to the Hebrews.

For several centuries Tanis was one of the largest cities in the Delta, and became a site of great importance after the end of the New Kingdom, especially during the Late Period (747–332 BC). Cinema buffs are also quick to point out that Tanis is where Indiana Jones discovered the 'Lost Ark'.

Much like Bubastis, the ruins of Tanis are really only of interest to those with a strong interest in Egyptology, though it is a relatively quick and somewhat painless day trip from Cairo.

Owing to its poor state of preservation, Tanis receives few foreign visitors. However, this means that you won't have to pay an entry charge and you'll probably have the site to yourself. You can always wander around the ruins as you like, which can be a lonely and somewhat eerie experience.

Although many of the blocks and statues found here date from the Old and Middle Kingdoms, they had been brought from other sites for reuse by later kings. The earliest buildings at Tanis actually date from the reign of Psusennes I (1039–991 BC), who surrounded the Temple of Amun with a great enclosure wall. His successors added a temple to Mut, Khons and the Asiatic goddess Astarte, together with a sacred lake, and temple building continued until Ptolemaic times.

Tanis is most famous for its **royal tombs**, created by the kings of the 21st dynasty after the Valley of the Kings was abandoned at the end of the New Kingdom (c 1069 BC). In 1939 the French discovered six royal tombs here, including that of Psusennes I and several of his successors. Although the tombs themselves might seem relatively unimpressive today, they once contained some of the most spectacular treasure ever found in Egypt – gold

and silver coffins, mummy masks and jewellery, which can now be seen in the Egyptian Museum (p191).

To reach Tanis, take a service taxi or bus from Cairo (E£5 to E£10, one to two hours) to the town of Faqus, which is about 35km south of Tanis. Alternatively, the train heading for Al-Salhiya takes about 1½ hours to get there; these leave Cairo's Ramses station (p179) approximately every two to three hours. Ticket costs for an adult/student are E£20/15 (2nd class only).

From Faqus, take a service taxi or bus (E£1) to the village of San al-Hagar, or alternatively hire a taxi (E£20) to take you to the site.

TANTA AREA

The largest city in the Delta, Tanta is a major centre for Sufism, and is home to a large mosque dedicated to Sayyed Ahmed al-Badawi, a Moroccan Sufi who fought the Crusaders in the 13th century. The *moulid* (saints' festival) held in honour of Sayyed Ahmed al-Badawi follows the October cotton harvest and is one of the biggest in Egypt, drawing crowds of more than one million people.

While the city itself is of little interest to foreign travellers, this area of the western Delta was once home to the ancient cities of Sais, Naucratis and Wadjet. Although these cities have been wiped off the map, anyone with a historical interest in the Delta region might be interested in knowing where they once stood.

Northwest of Tanta, on the east bank of the Rosetta branch of the Nile, once stood the legendary city of **Sais** (Sa al-Hagar), Egypt's 26th-dynasty capital. Sacred to Neith, goddess of war and hunting and protector of embalmed bodies, Sais dates back to the start of Egyptian history, and was replete with palaces, temples and royal tombs. However, the city was destroyed in 525 BC by the Persian emperor Cambyses, who reportedly exhumed the mummies of previous rulers from the ground and had them publicly whipped and burned.

West of Tanta, more than halfway along the road to Damanhur, once stood the city of **Naucratis**, which was given to the Greeks to settle during the 7th century BC.

Northeast of Damanhur and northwest of Tanta was the Egyptian cult centre of **Wadjet** (known as Buto to the Greeks), which honoured the cobra goddess of Lower Egypt. Cobras were once worshipped here by devout followers.

Most visitors to the Tanta area generally pass through en route to either Cairo or Alexandria, though Tanta itself is a large city with a good range of accommodation. Hotels cluster around the train station, though the best of the lot is the **New Arafa Hotel** (☎ 040-340 5040; Midan al-Mahatt; s/d from E£160/175; ☒). Arriving passengers are greeted with modern rooms that are well insulated from the bustling city streets, and there is a decent bar and restaurant on the premises.

From Cairo's Turgoman Garage (p177), you can also take buses to the Gomla bus station in Tanta (E£7 to E£12, one to two hours); these leave every hour between 7am and 7pm. From there, you can hop in a taxi to Tanta's centrally located train station (E£1), about 2km south, or hire a driver for an hour or two (E£20 to E£40) to drive you around the area.

Nile Valley: Beni Suef to Qena

He who rides the sea of the Nile must have sails woven of patience.

Egyptian Proverb

In a hurry to reach the treasures of Luxor and the pleasures of the south, it is easy to dismiss this first segment of Upper Egypt. But the less-visited parts of Egypt almost always repay the effort of a visit and the valley from Cairo to Luxor is no exception.

Much of the green and brown land south of Cairo is still worked by hand, often using tools known to the ancients, although even in remote rural areas of the Nile Valley, farmers must learn to grapple with the issues of modernity, particularly problems with pumps and water shortages. The region's sprawling provincial towns were the scene of considerable violence during the Islamist unrest of the 1990s and, although they may no longer deserve their reputation for trouble, they are considerably less developed than Cairo and Luxor.

But however much a backwater this part of the valley is now, it still carries vivid reminders of the important role it played in Egypt's destiny – from the lavishly painted tombs of early provincial rulers to the remains of the doomed city Akhetaten and the monasteries of the early Christian period. Close to Qena is Dendara, one of the most complete surviving temple complexes. But most mysterious of all is Abydos, the supposed resting place of the god Osiris' head, and a sacred Egyptian burial ground.

Because of the violence of the 1990s, security remains tight in places and individual travel is often difficult, but now rarely impossible.

NILE VALLEY: BENI SUEF TO QENA

HIGHLIGHTS

- Admire lithe dancing girls and muscular wrestlers in the finely painted **tombs of Baqet** and **Kheti** (p223 in Beni Hasan
- Visit the early Coptic monastery of **Deir al-Muharraq** (p227), to see why the Copts claim to be heirs to the ancient Egyptians
- Gaze upon some of ancient Egypt's finest temple reliefs at the **Temple of Seti I** (p234) in Abydos
- Marvel at one of the best-preserved temple complexes in Egypt in Dendara's magnificent **Temple of Hathor** (p236)
- Hang out in the elegant colonial centre of **Minya** (p220)

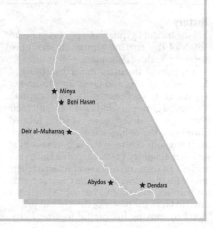

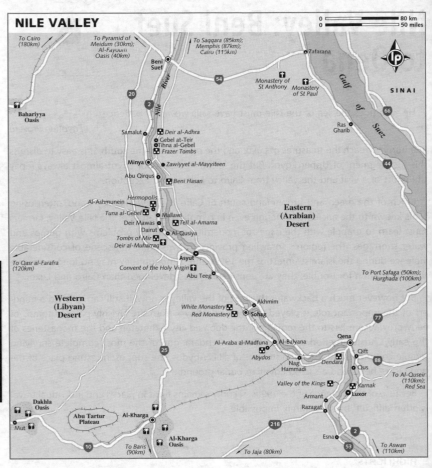

History

For the ancient Egyptians, Upper Egypt began south of the ancient capital of Memphis, beyond present-day Saqqara.

The ancients divided the area that stretched between Beni Suef and Qena into 15 nomes (provinces), each with its own capital. Provincial governors and notables built their tombs on the desert edge. Abydos, located close to modern Sohag, was once the predominant religious centre in the region as well as one of the country's most sacred sites: Egypt's earliest 1st dynasty rulers were interred there and it flourished well into the Christian era.

The New Kingdom Pharaoh Akhenaten tried to break the power of the Theban priesthood by moving his capital to a new city, Akhetaten (near modern Mallawi), one of the few places along the Nile not already associated with a deity.

Christianity arrived early in Upper Egypt. Sectarian splits in Alexandria and the popularity of the monastic tradition established by St Anthony in the Eastern Desert encouraged priests to settle in the provinces. The many churches and monasteries that continue to function in the area are a testament to the strength of the Christian tradition: this area has the largest Coptic communities outside Cairo.

Dependant on agriculture, much of the area remained a backwater throughout the Christian and Islamic periods, although Qena and Asyut flourished as trading hubs: Qena was the jumping-off point for the Red Sea port of Safaga, while Asyut linked the Nile with the Western Desert and the Darb al-Arba'een caravan route.

Today much of the region remains poor. Agriculture is still the mainstay of the economy, but cannot absorb the population growth. The lack of any real industrial base south of Cairo has caused severe economic hardship, particularly for young people who drift in increasing numbers into the towns and cities in search of work. Resentment at their lack of hope was compounded by the loss of remittances from Iraq: many people from this region had found work there in the 1980s, but lost it with the outbreak of the first Gulf War. Religious militants exploited the violence that exploded in the 1990s and directed it towards the government, in a bid to create an Islamic state. The security forces responded by dishing out some heavy-handed tactics. The violence eventually petered out but the causes of the unrest – poverty and thwarted hopes – remain.

Getting There & Away

Trains are recommended for getting in and out of this part of the country. There are frequent services heading north to Cairo and south to Luxor and Aswan. Officially foreigners are only allowed on selected services. In practice, if you cannot buy a ticket in the station, you may be able to buy one on the train. Private vehicles and taxis are the only viable alternative, but they can be slower, thanks to heavy-handed police measures; for more information, see below, and the boxed text, p220.

Getting Around

Wherever possible, try to stick to trains in this part of Egypt. A good network of buses, service taxis and pick-up taxis links towns and villages, but the police may put them off limits to foreigners. If you have to travel by vehicle, armed police may accompany you. If they do, you should try to allow extra time for delays at the checkpoints, where the escort will need to change vehicles (see boxed text, p220).

BENI SUEF

☎ 082 / pop 193,048

Beni Suef is a provincial capital, 120km south of Cairo. From antiquity until at least the 16th century it was famous for its linen, and in the 19th century was still sufficiently important

to have an American consulate, but there is now little to capture the traveller's interest. It is close to the Pyramid of Meidum (p208) and the oasis area of Al-Fayoum (p205), but both places can be just as easily visited from Cairo. There's a small **museum** (adult/student E£20/10; ☒ 8am-4pm), next to the governorate building. The lower floor displays local antiquities and the upper floor contains Coptic and Islamic objects from the area. One of the curators, Soad fayez Mahrouz, may be on hand to explain the displays.

There is a **post office** (Sharia Safiyya Zaghloul; ☒ 8.30am-2.30pm Sat-Thu) and a **Bank of Alexandria** (Sharia Sa'ad Zaghloul, just off Midan al-Gomhuriyya; ☒ 9am-2pm Sun-Thu).

Sleeping & Eating

Semiramis Hotel (☎ 232 2092; fax 231 6017; Sharia Safiyya Zaghloul; s/d/tr E£51.50/75.50/83.50; ☒) The best place to stay in town, as it has been for at least 80 years, is this two-star hotel just north of the train station. Rooms have private bathroom and TV. Its restaurant serves a filling kebab or chicken meal for around E£35.

There are cheap *kushari, fuul* (fava bean paste) and *ta'amiyya* stands around the train station.

Getting There & Away

There are frequent train connections north to Cairo and Giza, and south to Minya.

Should you be allowed to board a bus, the bus station is along the main road, Sharia Bur Said, south of the town centre. Buses run from about 6am to 6pm to Cairo, Minya and Al-Fayoum.

From Beni Suef, a road runs east across the desert to Zafarana on the Red Sea. There is a daily bus to Zafarana (E£25, three to four hours). The bus will stop at the turn-off to the Monastery of St Anthony (p418), about 130km east of Beni Suef. From there it is a further 12km to the monastery.

GEBEL AT-TEIR & FRAZER TOMBS

The clifflike Gebel at-Teir (Bird Mountain) rises on the east bank of the Nile, some 93km south of Beni Suef and 20km north of Minya. **Deir al-Adhra** (Monastery of the Virgin) is perched 130m above the river. The mountain takes its name from a legend that all Egyptian birds paused here on the monastery's annual feast day. The monastery was formerly known as the Convent of the Pulley, a reminder of the

NILE VALLEY TROUBLES

Northern Upper Egypt was the centre of an Islamist insurgency that saw more than a thousand deaths, mostly of policemen and militants in the early and mid-1990s. Tourists were often caught up in this violence, victims of Gama'a al-Islamiyya, the 'Islamic Group', who tried to topple the government by attacking one of its main foreign-currency sources, tourism. Unsurprisingly, tourism ground to a halt and Nile cruise boats stopped running between Cairo and Luxor after several incidents of militants shooting at people on their open upper decks. The few foreigners who did venture here were accompanied by heavily armed police escorts.

No foreigners have been attacked in the area since the late 1990s. The group's more moderate leaders declared the use of violence to be a mistake and Western embassies in Egypt have lifted their travel advisories, but security continues to be heavy-handed and cruises between Cairo and Luxor are still banned. Recently the Interior Ministry eased restrictions on foreigners travelling in the region. But ultimate responsibility rests with local officials, many of whom prefer to err on the side of caution. So while you may be able to board a bus or take a taxi in Minya, you may be refused permission to leave your hotel in Qena. And to make things more confusing, the situation can change day by day: what was law at the time of writing may not be law when you go travelling. With the public agitating over issues such as the price of bread and factory closures, it's likely that efforts to protect visitors will continue to be erratic and heavy-handed.

This situation will affect your journey. A group of heavily armed policemen may make your journey safer (although some believe they make you more of a target), but they will also restrict your movements and alter the experience of your visit. They may also add to the expense of your trip because, if you are escorted, you are likely to be forced to travel by private taxis, not shared taxis or microbuses. The most likely inconvenience will be delay: the stretch between Asyut and Minya is still littered with checkpoints and crossing them can be very slow.

But security is relaxing and our experience of travelling between Luxor and Cairo was mixed. In some places we were stopped by police as we stepped off a train and not even allowed to walk out of our hotel without an escort. In others we were surprised to find little insistence and there were times when we were left alone completely. Our advice is to go only if you are prepared for setbacks, extra expense and delays: this is not a place to be worrying about getting to Cairo in time for your flight home. A sense of humour will also help.

time when rope was the only way of reaching the cliff top.

Coptic tradition claims that the Holy Family rested here for three days on their journey through Egypt. A cave-chapel built on the site in the 4th century AD is ascribed to Helena, mother of Byzantine Emperor Constantine. A 19th-century building encloses the cave, whose icon of the virgin is said to have miraculous powers. The monastery, unvisited for most of the year, is mobbed during the week-long Feast of the Assumption, 40 days after Coptic Easter.

The village is closest to Minya and a service taxi or microbus from Minya to Samalut (if the police allow it) costs E£5 to E£10. From Samalut, pick-ups run to the Nile boat landing (E£1), where you can take the car ferry or, if it is running, the felucca (both E£2). Pick-ups run from the east-bank landing to Deir al-Adhra, but there are usually not many

passengers, so prepare to pay extra to avoid a long wait. A private taxi from Minya should cost E£30 to E£55 for the return trip but may be as much as E£100, depending on your haggling ability and the driver's mood.

Five kilometres south of Tihna al-Gebel, the **Frazer Tombs** date back to the 5th and 6th dynasties. These Old Kingdom tombs are cut into the east-bank cliffs, overlooking the valley. Only two tombs are open and both, very simple, contain eroded images and hieroglyphs but no colourful scenes and are likely to appeal only if you have a passion for rarely visited sites.

MINYA
☎ 086 / pop 236,043
Minya, the 'Bride of Upper Egypt' (Arous as-Sa'id), sits on the boundary between Upper and Lower Egypt. A provincial capital 245km south of Cairo, it was the capital of

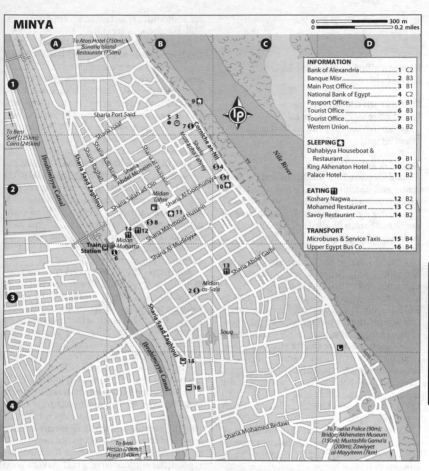

the Upper Egyptian cotton trade, but its factories now process sugar and produce soap and perfume.

When Minya was caught up in the Islamist insurgency of the 1990s, the government sent tanks and armoured personnel carriers. Some police posts from that period still dot the town centre, but the violence has abated and security stepped down, which is good news for visitors because Minya has one of the most pleasant town centres in Upper Egypt. With broad tree-lined streets, a wide corniche and some great, if shabby, early-20th-century buildings, central Minya has retained the feel of a more graceful era. At the time of our visit, this was one of the most relaxed places to visit between Cairo and Luxor.

Information

EMERGENCY
Ambulance (☎ 123)
Tourist police (☎ 236 4527; Amarat el-Gama'a)

MEDICAL SERVICES
Mustashfa Gama'a (University Hospital; ☎ 236 6743, 234 2505; Midan Suzanne Mubarak/ Corniche an-Nil)

MONEY
Bank of Alexandria (Sharia al-Gomhuriyya; ⏰ 9am-2pm Sun-Thu) Changes foreign currency.
Banque Misr (Midan as-Sa'a; ⏰ 8.30am-2pm Sun-Thu) Has an ATM.
National Bank of Egypt (Sharia al-Gomhuriyya; ⏰ 9am-2pm Sun-Thu) Has an ATM.

Western Union (☎ 236 4905; Sharia al-Gomhuriyya; ⏱ 9am-7pm Sat-Thu)

POST
Main post office (⏱ 8.30am-2pm Sat-Thu) Off Corniche an-Nil.

TOURIST INFORMATION
Tourist office Corniche an-Nil (☎ 236 0150; ⏱ 9am-3.30pm Sat-Thu); train station (☎ 234 2044) Supposedly 24 hour but rarely staffed.

Sights & Activities
Beyond the pleasure of walking around the town centre and watching the Nile flow against the background of the Eastern Hills, Minya doesn't have many sights. The new **Akhenaten Museum** on the east bank is heading towards completion and is due to open soon. If the Egyptian authorities can swing it, it will be home, for some months at least, to the iconic bust of Queen Nefertiti (now in Berlin) as well as other treasures from nearby Tell al-Amarna.

Hantours (horse-drawn carriages; E£25 to E£35 per hour) can be rented for a leisurely ride around the town centre or along the corniche. There is a **souq** (market) at the southern end of the town centre and the streets that run from it to Midan Tahrir are among the liveliest. *Lunches* (motor boats; E£50 per hour) and feluccas (E£30 per hour) can be rented at the landing opposite the tourist office for trips along the river and to Banana Island, which is good for a picnic.

On the east bank about 7km southeast of town, a large Muslim and Christian cemetery, called **Zawiyyet al-Mayyiteen** (Place of the Dead), consists of several hundred mudbrick mausoleums. Stretching for 4km from the road to the hills and said to be one of the largest cemeteries in the world, it is an interesting sight.

Sleeping & Eating
Minya has a decent selection of hotels, but these days many are not accepting foreigners or are suffering from the lack of custom. Eating options are few. Apart from the basic places listed here, your best bet is to eat in the hotels.

Palace Hotel (☎ 324 021; Midan Tahrir; s/d E£25/40) Central location, high ceilings, hand-painted Pharaonic murals, old tourism posters and time-warp atmosphere should make this Minya's best budget hotel. But rooms are noisy, bathrooms communal and the owners are sometimes reluctant to accept foreigners. Still, the decor is great.

Dahabiyya Houseboat & Restaurant (☎ 236 3596/5596; Corniche an-Nil; s/d E£35/70) This old Nile sailing boat has been moored along the Corniche near the tourist office for many years, but recently refurbished, it is Minya's most unusual address, with a restaurant on the upper deck and accommodation below. The small cabins are all equipped with fan and TV, but tend to be noisy as the restaurant (dishes E£8 to E£15) is open until the last person leaves.

King Akhenaton Hotel (☎ 236 5917/8; www.king akhenaton.com; Corniche an-Nil; s/d with Nile view E£120/150; ✷) One of two hotels in town that are booming, the 48-room Akhenaton is comfortable and central, although there have been complaints about the service here. Rooms have satellite TV and fridge and some have Nile views. Breakfast is buffet style. Staff may be able to arrange transport.

Aton Hotel (☎ 234 2993/4; fax 234 1517; Corniche an-Nil; s/d US$60/70; ✷ ▣) Still referred to locally as the Etap (its former incarnation) and still Minya's top hotel, the friendly, comfortable Aton is about 1km north of the town centre, on the west bank of the Nile and across the road from the more expensive and less interesting Mercure Nefertiti. Many of the well-equipped bungalow rooms have great Nile views. There are two good restaurants, a bar and pool.

Banana Island Restaurant (☎ 234 2993/4; Corniche an-Nil; dishes E£30-45) The main restaurant of the Aton Hotel is year-round dependable for friendly service and good Egyptian cuisine, from lentil soup and grills to hot bread-and-milk pudding. Alcohol is served. If the weather is good, the outdoor terrace grill makes a good alternative, though not everyone will enjoy the widescreen TV.

Savoy Restaurant (Midan al-Mahatta; dishes E£5-20), a busy corner restaurant, serves good rotisserie chicken and kebabs in the fan-cooled restaurant or you can take away. Just down the street, **Koshary Nagwa** (Sharia al-Gomhuriyya; dishes E£5-15) serves good, basic *kushari*. The popular **Mohamed Restaurant** (Sharia al-Hussaini; dishes E£5-15) serves basic grills and salads on a street packed with food options, from juice stands to a bakery and patisserie.

Getting There & Away
BUS
The **Upper Egypt Bus Co** (☎ 236 3721; Sharia Saad Zaghloul) has hourly services to Cairo (E£12,

four hours) from 6am. Foreigners are currently banned from the Asyut service. Buses leave for Hurghada at 10.30am and 10.30pm (E£50, six hours).

SERVICE TAXI
At the time of writing, the police and drivers were discouraging foreigners from using service taxis because of possible delays at checkpoints. One to Cairo is the most likely (E£15). A private service will cost around E£350. If you can get there, a seat to Asyut costs E£10.

TRAIN
The **tourist office** (☎ 236 2722) in the station may be able to help with information. Trains to Cairo (three to four hours) have only 1st- and 2nd-class carriages and leave at 5.55am, 6.30am, 8.50am, 4.30pm (which goes on to Alexandria) and 6.50pm. Tickets in 1st-class cost E£35 to E£45, in 2nd-class E£29 to E£34.

Trains heading south leave fairly frequently, with the fastest trains departing from Minya between around 11pm and 1am. Foreigners are officially only allowed to take the two Wagons Lit trains that come from Cairo, but you might be allowed to buy a ticket on the other trains. Seven 1st-/2nd-class trains go all the way to Luxor (E£67/37) and Aswan (E£78/44), stopping at Asyut (E£16/8), Sohag (E£21/13) and Qena (E£31/19).

BENI HASAN
The necropolis of **Beni Hasan** (adult/student E£30/20; ⏰ 8am-5pm) occupies a range of east-bank limestone cliffs some 20km south of Minya. It is a superb and important location and has the added attraction of a new rest house, which is usually open for drinks. Most tombs date from the 11th and 12th dynasties (2125–1795 BC), the 39 upper tombs belonging to nomarchs (local governors). Many remain unfinished and only four are currently open to visitors, but they are worth the trouble of visiting for the glimpse they provide of daily life and political tensions of the period.

A guard will accompany you from the ticket office, so baksheesh is expected (at least E£10). Try to see the tombs chronologically, as follows.

Tomb of Baqet (No 15)
Baqet was an 11th-dynasty governor of the Oryx nome (district). His rectangular tomb chapel has seven tomb shafts and some well-preserved wall paintings. They include Baqet and his wife on the left wall watching weavers and acrobats – mostly women in diaphanous dresses in flexible poses. Further along, animals, presumably possessions of Baqet, are being counted. A hunting scene in the desert shows mythical creatures among the gazelles. The back wall shows a sequence of wrestling moves that are still used today. The right (south) wall is decorated with scenes from the nomarch's daily life, with potters, metalworkers and a flax harvest, among others.

Tomb of Kheti (No 17)
Kheti, Baqet's son, inherited the governorship of the Oryx nome from his father. His tomb chapel, with two of its original six papyrus columns intact, has many vivid painted scenes that show hunting, linen production, board games, metalwork, wrestling, acrobatics and dancing, most of them watched over by the nomarch. Notice the yogalike positions on the right-hand wall, between images of winemaking and herding.

Tomb of Amenemhat (No 2)
Amenemhat was a 12th-dynasty governor of Oryx. His tomb is the largest and possibly the best at Beni Hasan and, like that of Khnumhotep, its impressive facade and interior decoration mark a clear departure from the more modest earlier ones. Entered through a columned doorway and with its six columns intact, it contains beautifully executed scenes of farming, hunting, manufacturing and offerings to the deceased, who can also be seen with his dogs. As well as the fine paintings, the tomb has a long, faded text in which Amenemhat addresses the visitors to his chapel: 'You who love life and hate death, say: Thousands of bread and beer, thousands of cattle and wild fowl for the ka of the hereditary prince…the Great Chief of the Oryx Nome…'.

Tomb of Khnumhotep (No 3)
Khnumhotep was governor during the early 12th dynasty, and his detailed 'autobiography' is inscribed on the base of walls that contain the most detailed painted scenes. The tomb is famous for its rich, finely rendered scenes of plant, animal and bird life. On the left wall farmers are shown tending their crops while a scribe is shown recording the harvest. Also on

the left wall is a representation of a delegation bringing offerings from Asia – their clothes, faces and beards are all distinct.

If the police allow it, follow a cliffside track that leads southeast for about 2.5km, then some 500m into a wadi to the rock-cut temple of **Speos Artemidos** (Grotto of Artemis). Known locally as Istabl Antar (the Stable of Antar, an Arab warrior-poet and folk hero), it deserves neither its Greek nor Arab names for it dates back to the 18th dynasty. Started by Hatshepsut (1473–1458 BC) and completed by Tuthmosis III (1479–1425 BC), it was dedicated to the lion-goddess Pakht. There is a small hall with roughly hewn Hathor-headed columns and an unfinished sanctuary. On the walls are scenes of Hatshepsut making offerings and, on its upper facade, an inscription describing how she restored order after the Hyksos, even though she reigned long after the event. Expect to be accompanied by a police escort and a guard (who will want baksheesh).

Getting There & Away

A taxi from Minya will cost anything from E£50 to E£100, depending on your bargaining skills and how long you stay at the site. Currently private taxis are not escorted by police. It may also be possible to take a microbus from Minya to Abu Qirqus and a pick-up from there to the ferry landing. Return boat tickets are on a sliding scale from E£5 per person if there are eight or more passengers, to E£15 if you're by yourself.

BENI HASAN TO TELL AL-AMARNA

Forty-eight kilometres south of Minya on the west bank, **Mallawi** is infamous in Egypt as the home town of President Sadat's assassin (see p44), Khalid al-Islambouli. A centre of armed rebellion throughout the early 1990s, the town is now calmer, but there's little to linger over, even in the two-storey **museum** (adult/student E£25/15; ☉ 9am-3pm Sat-Tue & Thu, to noon Fri), which displays tomb paintings, glassware, sculpture including a limestone statue of a Ptolemaic priest, baboon and pencil-thin ibis mummies, and other artefacts from nearby Hermopolis and Tuna al-Gebel, in no particular chronological order.

Eight kilometres north of Mallawi, near the town of Al-Ashmunein, **Hermopolis** is the site of the ancient city of Khemenu. Capital of the 15th Upper Egyptian nome, its name (Eight Town) refers to four pairs of snake and frog gods that, according to one Egyptian creation myth, existed here before the first earth appeared out of the waters of chaos. This was also an important cult centre of Thoth, god of wisdom and writing, whom the Greeks identified with their god Hermes, hence the city's Greek name, 'Hermopolis'.

Little remains of the wealthy ancient city, the most striking ruins being two colossal 14th-century-BC quartzite statues of Thoth as a baboon. These supported part of Thoth's temple, which was rebuilt throughout antiquity. A Middle Kingdom temple gateway and a pylon of Ramses II, using stone plundered from nearby Tell al-Amarna, also survive. The most interesting ruins are from the Coptic basilica, which reused columns and even the baboon statues, though first removing their giant phalluses. The 'open-air museum' is officially free, but if you arrive with a police escort you will be expected to pay baksheesh.

Several kilometres south of Hermopolis and then 5km along a road into the desert, **Tuna al-Gebel** (adult/student E£15/10; ☉ 8am-5pm) was the necropolis of Hermopolis. Given the lack of tourists in the area, check with the Minya tourist office (p222) that the site is open.

At one time Tuna al-Gebel belonged to Akhetaten, the short-lived capital of Pharaoh Akhenaten (see opposite), and along the road you pass one of 14 stelae marking the boundary of the royal city. The large stone stele carries Akhenaten's vow never to expand his city beyond this western limit of the city's farmlands and associated villages, nor to be buried anywhere else. To the left, two damaged statues of the pharaoh and his wife Nefertiti hold offering tables; the sides are inscribed with figures of three of their daughters.

South of the stele, which is located about 5km past the village of Tuna al-Gebel, are the **catacombs** and tombs of the residents and sacred animals of Hermopolis. The dark catacomb galleries once held millions of mummified ibis, the 'living image of Thoth', and thousands of mummified baboons, sacrificed and embalmed by the Ptolemaic and Roman faithful. The subterranean cemetery extends for at least 3km, perhaps even all the way to Hermopolis. You need a torch to explore the galleries.

The nearby **Tomb of Petosiris** was built by a high priest of Thoth from the early Ptolomaic period. His temple-like tomb, like his sarcophagus in the Egyptian Museum in Cairo, shows early Greek influence. The wonderful coloured reliefs of farming and the deceased being given offerings also show Greek influence, with the figures wearing Greek dress.

The guard may open several other tombs (for a tip), the most interesting being the **Tomb of Isadora**, a wealthy woman who drowned in the Nile during the rule of Antoninus Pius (AD 138–161). The tomb has few decorations, but does contain the unfortunate woman's **mummy**, its teeth, hair and fingernails clearly visible.

Getting There & Away
The easiest and at times the only way to get around these sites is by taxi from Minya, perhaps continuing on to Asyut if the security situation allows. Expect to pay E£100 to E£200, depending on the time you want to spend and your bargaining skills.

The slow 2nd- and 3rd-class trains to or from Minya and Asyut stop in Mallawi and you may be allowed on. The bus service from Minya is currently stopped. If the security situation allows, for Hermopolis you could take a local microbus or service taxi from Mallawi to Al-Ashmunein; the turn-off to the site is 1km from the main road. From the junction you can either walk the short distance to Hermopolis or coax your driver to go a bit further. Tuna al-Gebel is 7km west of Hermopolis and, depending on the security situation and the time of day, you should be able to flag down a pick-up truck to get there.

TELL AL-AMARNA
In the fifth year of his reign, Pharaoh Akhenaten (1352–1336 BC) and his queen Nefertiti abandoned the gods and priests of Karnak and established a new religion based on the worship of Aten, god of the sun disc.

They also built a new city, Akhetaten, Horizon of the Aten, on the east bank of the Nile, in the area now known as Tell al-Amarna, a beautiful yet solitary crescent-shaped plain, which extends about 10km from north to south. Bounded by the river and backed by a bay of high cliffs, this was the capital of Egypt for some 30 years.

Akhetaten was abandoned for all time after Akhenaten's death. His successor, a son by a minor wife, changed his name from

Tutankhaten to Tutankhamun (1336–1327 BC), moved the capital back to Thebes, reestablished the cult of Amun at Thebes, restored power to the Theban priesthood and brought an end to what is known as the Amarna Period. Akhetaten fell into ruin, its palaces and temples quarried during the reign of Ramses II for buildings in Hermopolis and other cities.

Archaeologists value the site because, unlike most places in Egypt, it was occupied for just one reign. Many visitors are attracted by the romance of Akhenaten's doomed project but the ruins, scattered across the desert plain, are hard to understand, the tombs nowhere near as interesting or well preserved as others along the Nile (although the remains of the north palace and the Great Temple of Aten can still be identified), and the visit can be disappointing.

Tell al-Amarna Necropolis
Two groups of cliff tombs, about 8km apart, make up the **Tell al-Amarna necropolis** (adult/student E£25/15; ⊙ 8am-4pm Oct-May, to 5pm Jun-Sep), which features some coloured, though defaced, wall paintings of life during the Aten revolution. Remains of temples and private or administrative buildings are scattered across a wide area: this was, after all, an imperial city.

There used to be a bus for touring the site but it was not running at the time of our visit. As the site is so large, the only viable way of visiting is to come by private taxi or with your own car.

In all, there are 25 tombs cut into the base of the cliffs, numbered from one to six in the north, and seven to 25 in the south. Not all are open to the public and only five (No 3 to 6 and the royal tomb) currently have light. Even if you have transport, the guards may be unwilling to open the unlighted tombs and the lighted tombs contain some of the best reliefs. You will be expected to tip the guards (at least E£10 per person). Many visitors find the southern tombs a disappointment after the hassle of getting there. Be sure to bring water as there is currently no possibility of buying any at the site.

NORTHERN TOMBS
Tomb of Huya (No 1)
Huya was the steward of Akhenaten's mother, Queen Tiye, and relief scenes to the right and left of the entrance to his tomb show Tiye

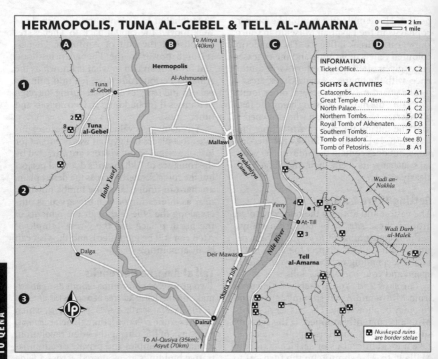

HERMOPOLIS, TUNA AL-GEBEL & TELL AL-AMARNA

0 ——— 2 km
0 ——— 1 mile

INFORMATION
Ticket Office..........................1 C2

SIGHTS & ACTIVITIES
Catacombs..............................2 A1
Great Temple of Aten...........3 C2
North Palace..........................4 C2
Northern Tombs.....................5 D2
Royal Tomb of Akhenaten......6 D3
Southern Tombs.....................7 C3
Tomb of Isadora................(see 8)
Tomb of Petosiris..................8 A1

Numkeyed ruins are border stelae

dining with her son and his family. On the right wall of this columned outer chamber, Akhenaten is shown taking his mother to a small temple he has built for her and, on the left wall, sitting in a carrying chair with Nefertiti.

Tomb of Meryre II (No 2)

Meryre II was superintendent of Nefertiti's household, and to the left of the entrance, you will find a scene that shows Nefertiti pouring wine for Akhenaten.

Tomb of Ahmose (No 3)

Ahmose's title was 'Fan-bearer on the King's Right Hand'. Much of his tomb decoration was unfinished: the left-hand wall of the long corridor leading to the burial chamber shows the artists' different stages. The upper register shows the royal couple on their way to the Great Temple of Aten, followed by armed guards. The lower register shows them seated in the palace listening to an orchestra.

Tomb of Meryre I (No 4)

High priest of the Aten, Meryre is shown, on the left wall of the columned chamber, being

carried by his friends to receive rewards from the royal couple. On the right-hand wall, the royal couple are shown making offerings to the Aten disc; note here the rare depiction of a rainbow.

Tomb of Pentu (No 5)

Pentu, the royal physician, was buried in a simple tomb. The left-hand wall of the corridor is decorated with images of the royal family at the Great Temple of Aten and of Pentu being appointed their physician.

Tomb of Panehsy (No 6)

The tomb of Panehsy, chief servant of the Aten in Akhetaten, retains the decorated facade most others have lost. Inside, scenes of the royal family, including Nefertiti driving her chariot and, on the right wall of the entrance passage, Nefertiti's sister Mutnodjmet, later married to Pharaoh Horemheb (1323–1295 BC), with dwarf servants. Panehsy appears as a fat old man on the left wall of the passage between the two main chambers. Two of the first chamber's four columns were removed by the Copts, who added a nave to the inner wall and created a chapel – the remains of painted angel wings can be seen on the walls.

SOUTHERN TOMBS
Tomb of Mahu (No 9)
This is one of the best preserved southern tombs. The paintings show interesting details of Mahu's duties as Akhenaten's chief of police, including taking prisoners to the vizier (minister), checking supplies and visiting the temple.

Tomb of Ay (No 25)
This is the finest tomb at Tell al-Amarna. Ay's titles were simply 'God's Father' and 'Fan-bearer on the King's Right Hand' and he was vizier to three pharaohs before becoming one himself (he succeeded Tutankhamun and reigned 1327–1323 BC). His wife Tiyi was Nefertiti's wet nurse. The images here reflect the couple's importance, with scenes including Ay and Tiyi worshipping the sun and Ay receiving rewards from the royal family, including red-leather riding gloves. Ay wasn't buried here, but in the west valley beside the Valley of the Kings (p266) at Thebes.

ROYAL TOMB OF AKHENATEN
Akhenaten's own **tomb** (additional ticket adult/student E£20/10) is in a ravine about 12km up the Royal Valley (Wadi Darb al-Malek), the valley that divides the north and south sections of the cliffs and where the sun was seen to rise each dawn. A well-laid road leads up the bleak valley. The guard will need to start up the tomb's generator. Very little remains inside the tomb. The right-hand side chamber has damaged reliefs of Akhenaten and his family worshipping Aten. A raised rectangular outline in the burial chamber once held the sarcophagus, which is now in the Egyptian Museum in Cairo (after being returned from Germany). Akhenaten himself was probably not buried here, although members of his family certainly were. Some believe he was buried in KV 55 in Luxor's Valley of the Kings, where his sarcophagus was discovered. The whereabouts of his mummy remains a mystery.

Getting There & Away
Even if the security situation allows it, getting to Tell al-Amarna by public transport remains a challenge and, until the site bus starts running, is pointless: the site is so large that it is impossible to visit on foot. So for now you need to take a taxi from either Asyut, Minya or Mallawi and cross on the irregular car ferry (E£15 per car). Expect to pay as much as E£150 to E£250 depending on where you start and how long you want to stay. Be sure to specify which tombs you want to visit or your driver may refuse to go to far-flung sites.

AL-QUSIYA
pop 69,388
Located about 8km southwest of the small rural town of Al-Qusiya, 35km south of Mallawi, is the Coptic complex of Deir al-Muharraq. About 7km further northwest, on an escarpment at the edge of the desert, lie the Tombs of Mir. There are no hotels in Al-Qusiya and police are unlikely to let you stay at the large guest house just outside the pseudo-medieval crenellated walls of Deir al-Muharraq. Happily, both sites can be visited in an easy day trip from Minya or Asyut, the latter being just an hour away by car.

Sights
DEIR AL-MUHARRAQ
Deir al-Muharraq, the **Burnt Monastery**, is a place of pilgrimage, refuge and vows where the strength of Coptic traditions can be experienced. The 120 resident monks believe that Mary and Jesus inhabited a cave on this site for six months and 10 days after fleeing from Herod. This was their longest stay at any of the numerous places where they are said to have rested in Egypt. Coptic tradition claims the **Church of al-Azraq** (Church of the Anointed) sits over the cave and is the world's oldest Christian church, consecrated around AD 60. More certain is the presence of monastic life here since the 4th century. The current building dates from the 12th to 13th centuries. Unusually, the church contains two iconostases. The one to the left of the altar came from an Ethiopian Church of Sts Peter and Paul, which used to sit on the roof. Other objects from the Ethiopians are displayed in the hall outside the church.

The **keep** beside the church is an independent 7th-century tower, rebuilt in the 12th and 20th centuries. Reached by drawbridge, its four floors can serve as a minimonastery, complete with its own small **Church of St Michael**, a refectory, accommodation and even burial space behind the altar.

Monks believe the monastery's religious significance is given in the Book of Isaiah.

In that day there will be an altar to the Lord in the midst of the land of Egypt, and a pillar to the Lord at its border. It will be a sign and a witness to the Lord of Host in the land of Egypt; when they cry to the Lord because of oppressors he will send them a saviour, and will defend and deliver them. And the Lord will make himself known to the Egyptians; and the Egyptians will know the Lord in that day and worship with sacrifice and burnt offering, and they will make vows to the Lord and perform them.

Isaiah 19:19-21

The monastery has done much to preserve Coptic tradition: monks here spoke the Coptic language until the 19th century (at that time there were 190 of them) and while other monasteries celebrate some of the Coptic liturgy in Arabic (for their Arabic-speaking congregation), here they stick to Coptic.

Also in the compound, the **Church of St George** (Mar Girgis) was built in 1880 with permission from the Ottoman sultan, who was still the official sovereign of Egypt. It is decorated with paintings of the 12 apostles and other religious scenes, its iconostasis is made from marble and many of the icons are in Byzantine style. Tradition has it that the icon showing the Virgin and Child was painted by St Luke.

Remember to remove shoes before entering either church and respect the silence and sanctity of the place. For a week every year (usually 21–28 June), thousands of pilgrims attend the monastery's annual feast, a time when visitors may not be admitted.

You will usually be escorted around the monastery and, while there is no fee, donations are appreciated. Visits sometimes finish with a brief visit to the new church built in 1940 or the nearby gift shop or, sometimes, with a cool drink in the monastery's reception room.

TOMBS OF MIR

The necropolis of the governors of Cusae, the **Tombs of Mir** (adult/student E£25/15; 🕙 9am-5pm Sat-Wed), as they are commonly known (sometimes also Meir), were dug into the barren escarpment during the Old and Middle Kingdoms. Nine tombs are decorated and open to the public; six others were unfinished and remain unexcavated.

Tomb No 1 and the adjoining tomb No 2 are inscribed with 720 Pharaonic deities, but as the tombs were used as cells by early Coptic hermits, many faces and names of the gods were destroyed. In tomb No 4 you can still see the original grid drawn on the wall to assist the artist in designing the layout of the wall decorations. Tomb No 3 features a cow giving birth.

Getting There & Away

At the time of writing, the bus from Minya to Asyut had been stopped. If it runs, or if you are allowed to come from Asyut, you will be dropped at Al-Qusiya, about 50 minutes' drive from Asyut. From Al-Qusiya you may be able to get a local microbus (E£3) to the monastery.

Few vehicles from Al-Qusiya go out to the Tombs of Mir, so you'll have to hire a taxi to take you there. Expect to pay E£35 to E£45, depending on your bargaining skills and how long you spend at the site. A taxi from Asyut to Mir will cost E£50 to E£70. Ideally, you could combine this with a visit to the monastery.

ASYUT

☎ 088 / pop 389,307

Asyut, 375km south of Cairo, was settled during Pharaonic times on a broad fertile plain bordering the west bank of the Nile and has preserved an echo of antiquity in its name. As Swaty, it was the ancient capital of the 13th nome of Upper Egypt. Surrounded by rich agricultural land and sitting at the end of one of Africa's great caravan routes, from sub-Saharan Africa and Sudan to Asyut via Al-Kharga Oasis (see the boxed text, p331), it has always been important commercially, if not politically. For centuries one of the main commodities traded here was slaves: caravans stopped here for quarantine before being traded, a period in which slavers used to prepare some of their male slaves for the harem.

Much of modern Asyut is an agglomeration of high-rises that resemble an eastern European new town rather than an ancient Egyptian entrepôt. In the late 1980s this was one of the earliest centres of Islamist fomentation. In the summer and autumn of 2000, it was also the scene of an apparition in which the Virgin Mary appeared to Copts and

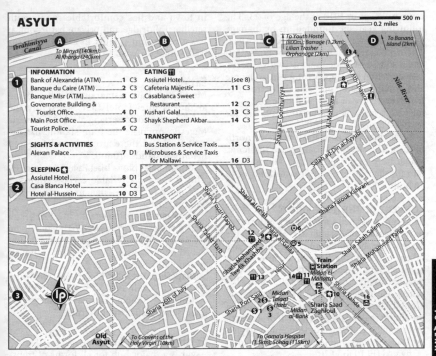

ASYUT

INFORMATION	
Bank of Alexandria (ATM)	**1** C3
Banque du Caire (ATM)	**2** C3
Banque Misr (ATM)	**3** C3
Governorate Building &	
Tourist Office	**4** D1
Main Post Office	**5** C3
Tourist Police	**6** C2
SIGHTS & ACTIVITIES	
Alexan Palace	**7** D1
SLEEPING	
Assiutel Hotel	**8** D1
Casa Blanca Hotel	**9** C2
Hotel al-Hussein	**10** D3

EATING	
Assiutel Hotel	(see 8)
Cafeteria Majestic	**11** C3
Casablanca Sweet	
Restaurant	**12** C2
Kushari Galal	**13** C3
Shayk Shepherd Akbar	**14** C3
TRANSPORT	
Bus Station & Service Taxis	**15** C3
Microbuses & Service Taxis	
for Mallawi	**16** D3

Muslims, in the words of one witness, 'with flashes of heavenly lights and spiritual doves'. Although the town has been quiet for several years, the police continue to maintain a visible presence around hotels.

Information
EMERGENCY
Ambulance (☎ 123)
Police (☎ 122)
Tourist police (☎ 232 3328; Sharia Farouk Kidwani)

MEDICAL SERVICES
Gama'a Hospital (☎ 233 4500; University of Asyut)

MONEY
Bank of Alexandria (Sharia Port Said; ⊗ 9am-2pm & 6-8pm Sun-Thu) Has an ATM.
Banque du Caire (Midan Talaat Harb; ⊗ 9am-2pm Sun-Thu) Has an ATM.
Banque Misr (Midan Talaat Harb; ⊗ 9am-2pm Sun-Thu) Has an ATM.

POST
Main post office (Sharia Nahda; ⊗ 8.30am-2.30pm Sat-Thu)

TOURIST INFORMATION
Tourist office (☎ 231 0010; 1st fl, Governorate Bldg, Sharia ath-Thawra; ⊗ 8.30am-3pm Sun-Thu) The very welcoming staff at the tourist office can provide maps of the city and help arrange onward travel.

Sights
For a city of such history, Asyut has surprisingly little to show for itself, partly because most of the city still remains unexcavated and the ancient tombs in the hills on the edge of the irrigation are currently unvisited.

Until the Nile-side **Alexan Palace**, one of the city's finest 19th-century buildings, has been renovated and opened, the most accessible monument to Asyut's period of wealth is the **Asyut Barrage**. Built over the Nile between 1898 and 1902 to regulate the flow of water into the Ibrahimiyya Canal and assure irrigation of the valley as far north as Beni Suef, it also serves as a bridge across the Nile. As the barrage still has strategic importance, photography is forbidden, so you should keep your camera out of sight.

On the east bank, 200m beyond the barrage, is the **Lillian Trasher Orphanage** (http://ltokids .tripod.com). American-born Lillian Trasher came to Egypt in 1910 at the age of 23. The following year she founded an orphanage in Asyut and stayed until her death in 1961. The orphanage is a Christian organisation and a source of pride in a city with a heavy concentration of Copts. Visitors are welcome and donations are appreciated. Microbuses from the centre of town will take you close for E£2; a taxi will cost up to E£10. Ask for 'Malga Trasher'.

Banana Island (Gezirat al-Moz), to the north of town, is a shady, pleasant place to picnic. You'll have to bargain with a felucca captain for the ride: expect to pay around E£40 an hour.

CONVENT OF THE HOLY VIRGIN

At Dirunka, located some 11km southwest of Asyut, this **convent** was built near another of the caves where the Holy Family are said to have taken refuge during their flight into Egypt. Some 50 nuns and monks live at the convent, built into a cliff situated about 120m above the valley. One of the monks will happily show you around. During the Moulid (saints' festival) of the Virgin (held in the second half of August), up to a million pilgrims come to pray, carrying portraits of Mary and Jesus. You will need to go by taxi (E£10 to E£20).

Sleeping

As a large provincial centre, Asyut has a selection of hotels but many are overpriced and noisy.

Youth Hostel (☎ 232 4846; Lux Houses, 503 Sharia al-Walidiyya; dm with/without student card E£3.25/5.25) The youth hostel, with its entrance off a side street, is Asyut's best budget option, with friendly staff. Avoid coming here during Egyptian college breaks, when it gets very crowded.

Hotel al-Hussein (☎ /fax 234 2532; Midan el-Mahatta; s/d E£60/80) The Hussein is comfortable and conveniently overlooks the bus station, but noise means you won't want to stay longer than one night.

Casa Blanca Hotel (☎ 233 7662; fax 233 1600; Sharia Mohammed Tawfiq Khashba; s/d E£132/176; 🕸) Sharing an air of neglect and underuse with the similarly rated Akhenaten Hotel across the road, rooms are gloomy but clean, with private bathroom and TV. Friendly staff. The disco is currently not running.

Assiutel Hotel (☎ 231 2121; fax 231 2122; 146 Sharia al-Nil; s/d US$47/66; 🕸) Overlooking the Nile, this three-star hotel is the best place

in town and has comfortable rooms with satellite TV, fridge and private bathroom. It has a restaurant (mains E£15 to E£30), as well as one of Asyut's only bars.

Eating

Most hotels have restaurants, the best being at the Assiutel Hotel (left), currently the only place in town serving alcohol. Cafeteria Majestic, opposite the train station, has decent food and there are the usual *fuul* and *ta'amiyya* stands around.

Kushari Galal (Sharia Talaat Harb; dishes from E£5) This is the most reliable carbohydrate intake place in town – delicious, convenient and open late.

Casablanca Sweet Restaurant (☎ 234 2727; Sharia Mohammed Tawfiq Khashba; dishes E£7-12) Come here for savoury *fiteer* (Egyptian pancakes), pizzas (though nothing to do with the Italian variety) and sweet crepes.

Shayk Shepherd Akbar (Sharia Saad Zaghloul; dishes E£8-20) A few minutes' walk from the train station, this popular cafe-restaurant serves good salads, chicken and grills.

Getting There & Away

Asyut is a major hub for all forms of transport, but the police may still prefer you to take the train or a private taxi. There is no service taxi to Luxor, but there is to Minya (E£10). A private taxi to Luxor should cost around E£150 each way. Should the security situation change, the **bus station** (☎ 233 0460) near the train station has services to Cairo, Luxor and west to the New Valley. The exception is the 9am service to Hurghada (E£35).

Note that it was not possible to get to Mallawi from here at the time of writing, but this situation is likely to change.

TRAIN

The train station has an English-speaking **information desk** (☎ 233 5623). There are several daytime trains to Cairo (1st/2nd class E£45/26, four to five hours) and Minya (E£19/10, one hour), and about 10 daily south to Luxor (E£53/30, five to six hours) and Aswan (E£59/38, eight to nine hours). All stop in Sohag (E£26/14, one to two hours) and Qena (E£37/25, three to four hours). You may find yourself being restricted to certain 'tourist trains'.

SOHAG

☎ 093 / pop 190,132

The city of Sohag, 115km south of Asyut, is one of the major Coptic Christian areas of Upper Egypt. Although there are few sights in the city, the nearby White and Red Monasteries, and the town of Akhmim across the river, are all of interest. Police presence here is stronger than in Asyut and Minya and travellers are still being discouraged from staying. You may be stopped from getting off the train, be escorted wherever you go or may be banned from leaving your hotel after dark. Given the possible restrictions, Sohag still looks best as a day trip from Luxor.

The helpful **tourist office** (☎ 460 4913; Governorate Bldg; ⏱ 8.30am-3pm Sun-Thu), in the building beside the new museum on the east bank, can help arrange visits to the monasteries. Sohag tourist police can be contacted on ☎ 460 4800. There are ATMs and cash or travellers cheques may be changed at the **Bank of Alexandria** (Sharia al-Gomhuriyya; ⏱ 9am-2pm & 6-8pm Sun-Thu) or the **Banque du Caire** (Sharia al-Gomhuriyya; ⏱ 9am-2pm Sun-Thu). There is also a **post office** (Sharia al-Gomhuriyya; ⏱ 8.30am-2.30pm Sat-Thu).

Sights

At the time of writing the new **Sohag Museum** was still not open but it will eventually display local antiquities, including those from ongoing excavations of the temple of Ramses II in Akhmim. Until then, apart from the weekly Monday morning livestock market, there is little in town to delay visitors.

Currently the best reason to stop at Sohag is to visit two early Coptic monasteries, which trumpet the victory of Christianity over Egypt's pagan gods. The **White Monastery** (Deir al-Abyad; ⏱ 7am-dusk), on rocky ground above the old Nile flood level, 12km northwest of Sohag, was founded by St Shenouda around AD 400 and dedicated to his mentor, St Bigol. White limestone from Pharaonic temples was reused, and ancient gods and hieroglyphs still look out from some of the blocks. It once supported a huge community of monks and boasted the largest library in Egypt, but today the manuscripts are scattered around the world and the monastery is home to 23 monks. The fortress walls still stand though they failed to protect the interior, most of which is in ruins. Nevertheless,

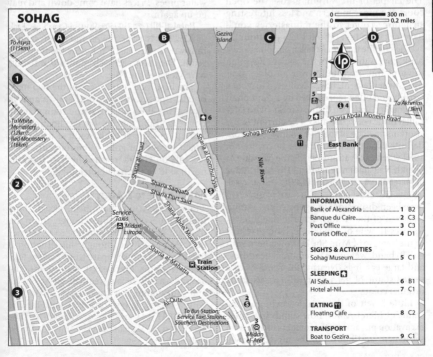

SOHAG

INFORMATION
Bank of Alexandria	**1** B2
Banque du Caire	**2** C3
Post Office	**3** C3
Tourist Office	**4** D1

SIGHTS & ACTIVITIES
Sohag Museum	**5** C1

SLEEPING 🛏
Al Safa	**6** B1
Hotel al-Nil	**7** C1

EATING 🍴
Floating Cafe	**8** C2

TRANSPORT
Boat to Gezira	**9** C1

it is easy to make out the plan of the church inside the enclosure walls. Made of brick and measuring 75m by 35m, it follows a basilica plan, with a nave, two side aisles and a triple apse. The nave and apses are intact, the domes decorated with the Dormition of the Virgin and Christ Pantocrator. Nineteen columns, taken from an earlier structure, separate the side chapels from the nave. Visitors wanting to assist in services may arrive from 4am.

The **Red Monastery** (Deir al-Ahmar; 7am-midnight), 4km southeast of Deir al-Abyad, is hidden at the rear of a village. Founded by Besa, a disciple of Shenouda who, according to legend, was a thief who converted to Christianity, it was dedicated to St Bishoi. The older of the monastery's two chapels, St Bishoi and St Bigol's, dates from the 4th century AD and contains some rare frescoes. At the time of writing these were being restored by a team sponsored by the American Research Center in Egypt and USAID. While some of the chapel is hidden by scaffolding, frescoes visible in the right-hand nave suggest the superior quality of this early work. The chapel of the Virgin, across the open court, is a more modern and less interesting structure. To get to the monasteries you'll have to take a taxi (about E£25 per hour).

The satellite town of **Akhmim**, on Sohag's east bank, covers the ruins of the ancient Egyptian town of Ipu, itself built over an older predynastic settlement. It was dedicated to Min, a fertility god often represented by a giant phallus, equated with Pan by the Greeks (who later called the town Panopolis). The current name contains an echo of the god's name, but more definite links to antiquity were uncovered in 1982 when excavations beside the Mosque of Sheikh Naqshadi revealed an 11m-high **statue of Meret Amun** (adult/student E£20/10; 8am-6pm). This is the tallest statue of an ancient queen to have been discovered in Egypt. Meret Amun (Beloved of the Amun) was the daughter of Ramses II, wife of Amenhotep and priestess of the Temple of Min. She is shown here with flail in hand, wearing a ceremonial headdress and large earrings. Nearby, the remains of a seated statue of her father still retains some original colour.

Little is left of the temple itself, and the statue of Meret Amun now stands in a huge excavation pit, among the remains of a Roman settlement and houses of the modern town.

Another excavation pit has been dug across the road.

Akhmim was famed in antiquity for its textiles – one of its current weavers calls it 'Manchester before history'. The tradition continues today and opposite the statue of Meret Amun, across from the post office, a green door leads to a small **weaving factory** (knock if it is shut). Here you can see weavers at work and buy hand-woven silk and cotton textiles straight from the bolt (silk E£65 to E£75 per metre, cotton E£30) or packets of ready-made tablecloths and serviettes.

A taxi to Akhmim should cost around E£25 per hour. The microbus costs E£2 and takes 15 minutes.

Sleeping & Eating

Sohag doesn't have the charm of Minya or the facilities of Luxor, but it does have a couple of good hotels.

Al Safa (230 7701/2; fax 230 7704; Sharia al-Gomhuriyya, West Bank; s/d/tr E£165/193/220;) A relatively new West Bank block. Rooms are comfortable and the riverside terrace is popular in the evening for snacks, soft drinks and water pipes. Prices have come down and may go up again.

Hotel al-Nil (230 7509; Sharia al-Gamah, East Bank; s/d E£250/325;) The newest and smartest hotel in town, on the east bank near the new museum. The rooms are well equipped and most have views of the Nile.

The best food options are in the two main hotels. Budget *kushari, fuul* and *ta'amiyya* places line the roads near the train station. For something fancier, try the floating cafe tied up on the east bank, south of the bridge, which is good for grills. More romantic, there is a cafe on Gezira, reached by boat from the north side of the new Hotel al-Nil.

Getting There & Away

Travel restrictions have been eased along this stretch of the Nile, though there are frequent checkpoints along the road. Service taxis don't run yet (though this situation is likely to change) so, apart from private taxi, train remains the easiest way of moving around and there is a frequent service north and south along the Cairo–Luxor main line, with a dozen daily trains to Asyut (1st/2nd class E£31/14) and Luxor (E£21/13). The service to Al-Balyana is very slow (3rd class only E£5.50).

AL-BALYANA

☎ 093 / pop 46,997

Al-Balyana is the jumping-off point for the village of **Al-Araba al-Madfuna**, 10km away, site of the necropolis of Abydos and the magnificent Temple of Seti I, one of the most beautiful monuments in Egypt. Security here has been heavy-handed in the past, but has recently relaxed and, although you may be stopped at the checkpoint, you should be able to move around as you like.

Should you need to change money, try the tiny Banque Misr kiosk at the entrance to Abydos Temple, which may open when tourists arrive, but cannot be relied upon.

As you're unlikely to be able to stay in Al-Balyana, you will be limited to travelling here by private taxi or on a day trip, most easily from Luxor.

Abydos

As the main cult centre of Osiris, god of the dead, **Abydos** (ancient name Ibdju; adult/student E£30/15; ⏰ 7am-6pm) was *the* place to be buried in ancient Egypt. It was used as a necropolis

from predynastic to Christian times (c 4000 BC–AD 600), more than 4500 years of constant use. The area now known as Umm al-Qa'ab (Mother of Pots) contains the mastaba tombs of the first pharaohs of Egypt, including that of the third pharaoh of the 1st dynasty, Djer (c 3000 BC). By the Middle Kingdom his tomb had become identified as the tomb of Osiris himself.

Abydos maintained its importance because of the cult of Osiris, god of the dead (see boxed text, p235). Although there were shrines to Osiris throughout Egypt, each one the supposed resting place of another part of his body, the temple at Abydos was the most important, being the home of his head. It was a place that most Egyptians would try to visit in their lifetime – or have themselves buried here. Failing that, they would be buried with small boats to enable their souls to make the journey after death.

One of the temple's more recent residents was Dorothy Eady. An Englishwoman better known as 'Omm Sety', she believed she was a reincarnated temple priestess and lover of Seti I. For 35 years she lived at Abydos and provided

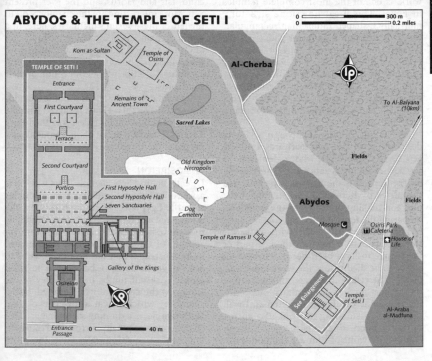

ABYDOS & THE TEMPLE OF SETI I

KING LISTS *Dr Joann Fletcher*

Ancient Egyptians constructed their history around their pharaohs. Instead of using a continuous year-by-year sequence, events were recorded as happening in a specific year of a specific pharaoh: at each pharaoh's accession they started at year 1 until the pharaoh died, then began again with year 1 of the next pharaoh.

So it was vital to have reliable records listing each reign. While a number of so-called king lists can be seen in Cairo's Egyptian Museum, the Louvre in Paris and the British Museum, the only one remaining in its original location was created by Seti I in his Abydos Temple. With an emphasis on the royal ancestors, Seti names 75 of his predecessors beginning with the semi-mythical Menes (usually regarded as Narmer), yet in typical Egyptian fashion he rewrites history by excluding those considered 'unsuitable', from the foreign Hyksos pharaohs of the Second Intermediate Period and the female pharaoh Hatshepsut to the Amarna pharaohs: Amenhotep III is immediately followed by Horemheb, and thus Akhenaten, Smenkhkare, Tutankhamun and Ay are simply erased from the record.

archaeologists with information about the working of the temple, in which she was given permission to perform the old rites. She died in 1981 and was buried in the desert.

TEMPLE OF SETI I

The first structure you'll see at Abydos is the striking Cenotaph or Great Temple of Seti I, which, after a certain amount of restoration work, is one of the most complete temples in Egypt. This great limestone structure, unusually L-shaped rather than rectangular, was dedicated to the six major gods – Osiris, Isis and Horus, Amun-Ra, Ra-Horakhty and Ptah – and also to Seti I (1294–1279 BC) himself. In the aftermath of the Amarna Period, it is a clear statement of a return to the old ways. As you roam through Seti's dark halls and sanctuaries an air of mystery surrounds you.

The temple is entered through a largely destroyed **pylon** and two **courtyards**, built by Seti I's son Ramses II, who is depicted on the portico killing Asiatics and worshipping Osiris. Beyond is the **first hypostyle hall**, also completed by Ramses II. Reliefs depict the pharaoh making offerings to the gods and preparing the temple building.

The **second hypostyle hall**, with 24 sandstone papyrus columns, was the last part of the temple to have been decorated by Seti, although he died before the work was completed. The reliefs that were finished are of the highest quality. Particularly outstanding is a scene on the rear right-hand wall showing Seti standing in front of a shrine to Osiris, upon which sits the god himself. Standing in front of him are the goddesses

Maat, Renpet, Isis, Nephthys and Amentet. Below is a frieze of Hapi, the Nile god.

At the rear of this second hypostyle hall are **sanctuaries** for each of the seven gods (right to left: Horus, Isis, Osiris, Amun-Ra, Ra-Horakhty, Ptah and Seti), which once held their cult statues. The Osiris sanctuary, third from the right, leads to a series of inner chambers dedicated to the god, his wife and child, Isis and Horus, and the ever-present Seti. More interesting are the chambers off to the left of these seven sanctuaries: here, in a group of chambers dedicated to the mysteries of Osiris, the god is shown mummified with the goddess Isis hovering above him as a bird, a graphic depiction of the conception of their son Horus.

Immediately to the left of this, the corridor known as **Gallery of the Kings** is carved with the figures of Seti I with his eldest son, the future Ramses II, and a long list of the pharaohs who preceded them (see boxed text, above).

THE OSIREION

Directly behind Seti's temple, the Osireion is a weird, wonderful building that continues to baffle Egyptologists, though it is usually interpreted as a cenotaph to Osiris. Originally thought to be an Old Kingdom structure, on account of the great blocks of granite used in its construction, it has now been dated to Seti's reign, its design is believed to be based on the rock-cut tombs in the Valley of the Kings. At the centre of its columned 'burial chamber', which lies at a lower level than Seti's temple, is a dummy sarcophagus. This chamber was originally surrounded by water, but thanks to a rising water table, the entire

---

THE CULT OF OSIRIS

The most familiar of all ancient Egypt's myths is the story of Isis and Osiris, preserved in the writings of the Greek historian Plutarch (c AD 46–126) following a visit to Egypt. According to Plutarch, Osiris and his sister-wife Isis ruled on earth, bringing peace and prosperity to their kingdom. Seething with jealousy at their success, their brother Seth invited Osiris to a banquet and tricked him into climbing inside a chest. Once Osiris was inside, Seth sealed the coffin and threw it into the Nile, drowning his brother. Following the murder, the distraught Isis retrieved her brother-husband's body, only to have it seized back by Seth who dismembered it, scattering the pieces far and wide. But Isis refused to give up and, taking the form of a kite, searched for the separate body parts, burying each piece where she found it, which explains why there are so many places that claim to be Osiris' tomb.

Another version of the story has Isis collecting the parts of Osiris and reassembling them to create the first mummy, helped by Anubis, god of embalming. Then, using her immense magic, she restored Osiris to life for long enough to conceive their son Horus. Raised to avenge his father, Horus defeated Seth. While Horus ruled on earth, represented by each pharaoh, his resurrected father ruled as Lord of the Afterlife. A much-loved god, Osiris came to represent the hope for salvation after death, a concept as important to life-loving ancient Egyptians as it was to early Christians.

---

structure is now flooded, making inspection of the funerary and ritual texts carved on its walls hazardous.

TEMPLE OF RAMSES II

Just northwest of Seti I's temple is the smaller and less well preserved structure built by his son Ramses II (1279–1213 BC). Although following the rectangular plan of a traditional temple, it has sanctuaries for each god Ramses considered important, including Osiris, Amun-Ra, Thoth, Min, the deified Seti I and, of course, Ramses himself. Although the roof is missing, the reliefs again retain a significant amount of their colour, clearly seen on figures of priests, offering bearers and the pharaoh anointing the gods' statues. You may not be allowed to visit this site.

Sleeping & Eating

You may now be allowed to stay in Al-Balyana, but given the nervousness of the local police, the situation may change. There are a couple of hotels and some cafes and food stands around the town.

House of Life (☎ 012 733 0071; www.ancientegyptian healing.com; opposite Temple of Seti I; B&B/full board per person €15/25) The only hotel functioning at the time of our visit, this simple Dutch-, Egyptian- and US-run house overlooking the temple has six rooms, sharing three bathrooms. There's a big terrace, and guests can access the internet and washing machine. The partners claim to have been trained in ancient Egyptian heal-

ing and run sessions in the house and out of Egypt. Essential oils and other products are on sale. Desert trips can be arranged.

Osiris Park Cafeteria (Temple of Seti I; ☺ 7am-10pm) Right in front of the temple, this is the only reliable option within sight of the temple. The food is overpriced and consists mostly of snacks, although chicken meals (E£35) are sometimes available and the welcome is friendly and the drinks cold. There is also a surprisingly good range of books and brochures about the temple.

Getting There & Away

The most common way of getting to Al-Balyana is by tour bus. A private taxi from Luxor should cost around E£300 return, depending on how long you want at the temple. Now that the convoy has been lifted on this stretch of the road, you can travel at any time during daylight. A train leaves Luxor at 6am and 8.25am (1st/2nd class E£18/13, three hours). A private taxi to the temple will cost about E£50. There is a train back to Luxor at 5pm (3rd class only E£8).

QENA

☎ 096 / pop 201,191

Ninety-one kilometres east of Al-Balyana, 62km north of Luxor, Qena sits at the intersection of the main Nile road and the road running across the desert to the Red Sea towns of Port Safaga and Hurghada. A scruffy market town and provincial capital, it was off-limits

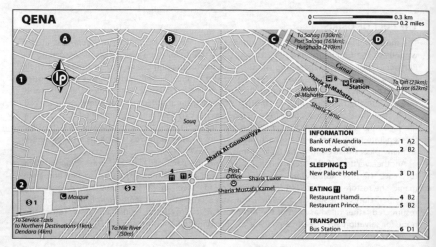

QENA

INFORMATION
Bank of Alexandria...............1 A2
Banque du Caire....................2 B2

SLEEPING
New Palace Hotel..................3 D1

EATING
Restaurant Hamdi.................4 B2
Restaurant Prince.................5 B2

TRANSPORT
Bus Station...........................6 D1

for a long time. Security has now been lifted, but there is still little reason to stop, unless it is to get to the spectacular temple complex at Dendara, located just outside the town. This is still best done as a day trip from Luxor. Train or private taxi are the best ways of travelling independently. If you need money, visit the **Bank of Alexandria** (off Sharia Luxor; 8.30am-2pm & 6-8pm Sun-Thu) or **Banque du Caire** (Sharia Luxor; 9am-2.30pm Sun-Thu).

Dendara

Although built at the very end of the Pharaonic period, the **Temple of Hathor** (adult/student E£25/15; 7am-6pm) at her cult site of Dendara is one of the iconic Egyptian buildings, mostly because it remains virtually intact, with a great stone roof and columns, dark chambers, underground crypts and twisting stairways all carved with hieroglyphs.

Dendara was an important administrative and religious centre as early as the 6th dynasty (c 2320 BC). The goddess Hathor had been worshipped here since the Old Kingdom. But this great temple was only begun in the 30th dynasty, with much of the building undertaken by the Ptolemies and completed during the Roman period.

Few deities have such varied characteristics. Hathor was the goddess of love and sensual pleasures, patron of music and dancing: the Greeks appropriately associated her with their goddess Aphrodite. Like most Egyptian gods, Hathor was known by a range of titles, including 'the golden one', 'she of the beautiful hair' and 'lady of drunkenness', representing the joyful intoxication involved in her worship. As the 'Lady of the West' she was also protector of the dead. She is usually represented as a woman, a cow or a woman with a headdress of cow's horns and sun disc, as she was the daughter of the sun-god Ra. She was also a maternal figure and as wife of Horus was often portrayed as the divine mother of the reigning pharaoh. In a famous statue from Deir al-Bahri in Luxor she even appears in the form of a cow suckling Amenhotep II (1427–1400 BC). Confusingly, she shared many of these attributes with the goddess Isis, who was also described as the mother of the king. In the end Isis essentially overshadowed Hathor as an ubermother when the legend of Isis and Osiris expanded to include the birth of Horus.

TOURING THE TEMPLE

All visitors must pass through the new visitors centre, with ticket office and bazaar. While it is still mostly unoccupied, before long this will involve running the gauntlet of hassling traders in order to get to the temple. One advantage is a clean, working toilet. At the time of our visit it was not possible to buy food or drinks at the site.

Beyond the towering gateway and mud walls, the temple was built on a slight rise. The entrance leads into the **outer hypostyle hall**, built by Roman emperor Tiberius, the first six of its 24 great stone columns adorned

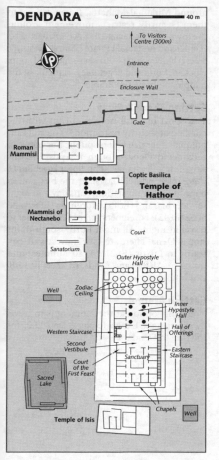

DENDARA

0 —— 40 m

To Visitors Centre (300m)

Entrance

Enclosure Wall

Gate

Roman Mammisi

Coptic Basilica

Temple of Hathor

Mammisi of Nectanebo

Court

Sanatorium

Outer Hypostyle Hall

Well

Zodiac Ceiling

Inner Hypostyle Hall

Western Staircase

Hall of Offerings

Second Vestibule

Eastern Staircase

Court of the First Feast

Sanctuary

Sacred Lake

Chapels

Well

Temple of Isis

turnover of pharaohs, the stonemasons seem to have been reluctant to carve the names of those who might not be in the job for long. Things reached an all-time low in 80 BC when Ptolemy XI murdered his more popular wife and stepmother Berenice III after only 19 days of co-rule. The outraged citizens of Alexandria dragged the pharaoh from his palace and killed him in revenge.

Beyond the second hypostyle hall, you will find the **Hall of Offerings** leads to the **sanctuary**, the most holy part of the temple, home to the goddess' statue. A further Hathor statue was stored in the crypt beneath her temple, and brought out each year for the New Year Festival, which in ancient times fell in July and coincided with the rising of the Nile. It was carried into the Hall of Offerings, where it rested with statues of other gods before being taken to the roof. The western staircase is decorated with scenes from this procession. In the open-air kiosk on the southwestern corner of the roof, the gods awaited the first reviving rays of the sun-god Ra on New Year's Day. The statues were later taken down the eastern staircase, which is also decorated with this scene.

The theme of revival continues in two suites of rooms on the roof, decorated with scenes of the revival of Osiris by his sister-wife, Isis. In the centre of the ceiling of the northeastern suite is a plaster cast of the famous 'Dendara Zodiac', the original now in the Louvre, Paris. Views of the surrounding countryside from the roof are magnificent. The graffiti on the edge of the temple was left by Napoleon's commander Desaix, and other French soldiers, in 1799.

The **exterior walls** feature lion-headed gargoyles to cope with the very occasional rainfall and are decorated with scenes of pharaohs paying homage to the gods. The most famous of these is on the rear (south) wall, where Cleopatra stands with Caesarion, her son by Julius Caesar.

Facing this back wall is a small **temple of Isis** built by Cleopatra's great rival Octavian, the Emperor Augustus. Walking back towards the front of the Hathor temple on the west side, the palm-filled Sacred Lake supplied the temple's water. Beyond this, to the north, lie the mudbrick foundations of the **sanatorium**, where the ill came to seek a cure from the goddess.

Finally there are the two **mammisi** (birth houses), the first built by the 30th-dynasty Egyptian pharaoh, Nectanebo I (380–362 BC),

on all four sides with Hathor's head, defaced by Christians but still an impressive sight. The walls are carved with scenes of Tiberius and his Roman successors presenting offerings to the Egyptian gods: the message here, as throughout the temple, is the continuity of tradition, even under foreign rulers. The ceiling at the far left and right side of the hall, currently being cleaned, is decorated with zodiacs.

The inner temple was built by the Ptolemies, the smaller **inner hypostyle hall** again has Hathor columns and walls carved with scenes of royal ceremonials, including the founding of the temple. But notice the 'blank' cartouches that reveal much about the political instability of late Ptolemaic times – with such a rapid

and decorated by the Ptolemies, the one nearest the temple wall built by the Romans and decorated by Emperor Trajan (AD 98–117). Such buildings celebrated divine birth, both of the young gods and of the pharaoh himself as son of the gods. Between the *mammisi* lie the remains of a 5th-century AD **Coptic basilica**.

Dendara is 4km southwest of Qena on the west side of the Nile. Most visitors arrive from Luxor. A return taxi from Luxor will cost you about E£200. There is also a day cruise to Dendara from Luxor (see p276). If you arrive in Qena by train, you will need to take a taxi to the temple (E£25 to E£35 to the temple and back with some waiting time).

Sleeping & Eating

The police will not allow you to stay the night, but even if you could the choices are limited and Qena is close enough to Luxor for commuting.

New Palace Hotel (☎ 010 303 5514; off Midan al-Mahatta; s/d E£80/100; ⌗) Behind the Mobil petrol station, this hotel is a poor option when you could be staying in Luxor but prices include breakfast.

Food choices are similarly limited, with several *fuul*, *kushari* and *ta'amiyya* places

around Midan al-Mahatta. If you can get to them (security restricts movement around the town), try **Restaurant Hamdi** (Sharia Luxor; dishes E£10-22) and **Restaurant Prince** (Sharia al-Gomhurlyya; dishes E£10-20), which both serve meals of soup, chicken, kofta and vegetables. A picnic at the temple might be preferable.

Getting There & Away

Transport has still not caught up with the relaxing of security restrictions. You still cannot take a service taxi or public bus between Luxor and Qena, though it's possible this situation will change. The **Upper Egypt Bus Co** (☎ 532 5068; Midan al-Mahatta), at the bus station opposite the train station, runs day and night services to Cairo (E£45), Hurghada (E£50) and Suez (E£45). Foreigners might find it easier to travel at night. All main north–south trains stop at Qena. There are 1st-/2nd-class air-con trains to Luxor (E£21/14, 40 minutes) and trains to Al-Balyana (2nd/3rd class E£15/8, two hours).

Getting Around

Your only option at the moment is to travel by private taxi. Expect to pay at least E£25 for the ride to Dendara.

Nile Valley: Luxor

> Royal Thebes, Egyptian treasure-house of countless wealth, Who boasts her hundred gates, through each of which, With horse and car, two hundred warriors march.
>
> *Homer, The Iliad, Book IX*

The city's governor would like you to know that Luxor is the world's greatest open-air museum, but that comes nowhere near describing this extraordinary place. There is simply nothing in the world that comes close to the grandeur of ancient Thebes.

Although the city has grown rapidly, the setting is still breathtakingly beautiful, the Nile flowing between the modern town and the west-bank necropolis, backed by the enigmatic Theban escarpment. Scattered across the landscape is an embarrassment of riches, from the temples of Karnak and Luxor on its East Bank to the temples of Deir al-Bahri and Medinat Habu, the Colossi of Memnon and the Valley of the Kings on the West Bank.

Thebes' wealth and power was already legendary in antiquity and by the end of the 18th century it had begun to lure curious travellers from Europe. Since then, fuelled by tales of great treasure and pharaohs' curses, ever greater numbers have made the pilgrimage to the site.

Visiting the main sights, today's traveller risks being surrounded by coachloads of tourists as they are herded through tombs and temples at a furious pace. But with a little planning and flexibility, it is possible to avoid the worst of the crowds and get the most from the magic of the Theban landscape and its unparalleled archaeological heritage.

HIGHLIGHTS

■ Imagine yourself in an exotic garden with gigantic papyrus-shaped stone columns in the **great hypostyle hall** (p246) at Karnak

■ Glimpse the good life of an ancient Egyptian aristocrat, so good he wanted it represented on his tomb walls, in the **Tombs of the Nobles** (p268) hoping it would continue after his death

■ Marvel at the wonderful architecture of the **Luxor Temple** (p250) and return later at night for a detailed view of the beautifully lit carvings on the walls

■ Wander through the best-preserved Theban temple, **Medinat Habu** (p273), in the soft, late-afternoon light

■ Sense the spirituality in an uncrowded ancient temple, at the beautifully restored and rarely visited **Temple of Seti I** (p258)

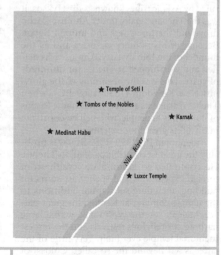

★ Temple of Seti I
★ Tombs of the Nobles
★ Karnak
★ Medinat Habu
Nile River
★ Luxor Temple

■ TELEPHONE CODE: 095

■ POPULATION: 451,350

HISTORY

Palaeolithic tools found in the Theban hills indicate that there have been human settlements in the area for at least half a million years, but Thebes (ancient Waset) only became important in the Middle Kingdom period (2055–1650 BC). During the chaos of the First Intermediate Period (2160–2025 BC), the small village of Thebes eventually grew strong enough to overpower the northern capital Heracleopolis. The 11th-dynasty Theban prince Montuhotep II (2055–2004 BC) reunited the country, moved his capital to Thebes and increased Karnak's importance as a cult centre to the local god Amun with a temple dedicated to him. Montuhotep's funerary temple at Deir al-Bahri served as an inspiration for Queen Hatshepsut's temple 500 years later. The 12th-dynasty pharaohs (1985–1795 BC) moved their administrative capital back north to Al-Lisht, situated about 30km south of Memphis, but much of their immense wealth from expanded foreign trade and agriculture, and tribute from military expeditions made into Nubia and Asia, went to the priesthood of Amun and Thebes, which remained the religious capital. This 200-year period was one of the richest times throughout Egyptian history, which witnessed a great flourishing of architecture and the arts, and major advances in science.

After the Second Intermediate Period (1650–1550 BC), when much of Egypt was ruled by Asiatic tribes known as the Hyksos, it was the Thebans again, under Ahmose I, who drove out the foreigners and unified Egypt. Because of his military victories and as the founder of the 18th dynasty, Ahmose was deified and worshipped at Thebes for hundreds of years. This was the beginning of the glorious New Kingdom (1550–1069 BC), when Thebes reached its apogee. It was home to tens of thousands of people, who helped construct many of its great monuments.

Amenhotep III (1390–1352 BC) was probably the greatest contributor of all to Thebes. He continued to accumulate wealth from foreign expeditions and spent vast sums on building, including substantial additions to the temple complex at Karnak, his great palace, Malqata, on the West Bank, with a large harbour for religious festivals and the largest memorial temple ever built. Very little of the latter is left beyond the so-called Colossi of Memnon, the largest monolithic statue ever carved. His son Amenhotep IV (1352–1336 BC), who later renamed himself Akhenaten, moved the capital from Thebes to his new city of Akhetaten (Tell al-Amarna), worshipped one god only (Aten the solar god), and brought about dramatic changes in art and architecture. The temples in Thebes were closed until his death, but the powerful priesthood was soon after reinstated under Akhenaten's successor, Tutankhamun (1336–1327 BC), who built very little but became the best-known pharaoh ever when his tomb was discovered full of treasure in 1922. Ramses II (1279–1213 BC) may have exaggerated his military victories, but he too was a great builder and added the magnificent hypostyle hall to Karnak, other halls to Luxor Temple, and built the Ramesseum and two magnificent tombs in the Valley of the Kings for himself and his many sons.

The decline of Pharaonic rule was mirrored by Thebes' gradual slide into insignificance: when the Persians sacked Thebes, it was clear the end was nigh. Mudbrick settlements clung to the once mighty Theban temples, and people hid within the stone walls against marauding desert tribes. Early Christians built churches in the temples, carved crosses on the walls and scratched out reliefs of the pagan gods. The area fell into obscurity in the 7th century AD after the Arab invasion, and the only reminder of its glorious past was the name bestowed on it by its Arab rulers: Al-Uqsur (The Fortifications), giving modern Luxor its name. By the time European travellers arrived here in the 18th century, Luxor was little more than a large Upper Egyptian village, known more for its 12th-century saint, Abu al-Haggag, buried above the mound of Luxor Temple, than for its half-buried ruins.

The growth of Egyptomania changed that. Napoleon arrived in 1798 wanting to revive Egypt's greatness and, with the publication of the *Description de l'Egypte,* did manage to revive interest in Egypt. European exhibitions of mummies, jewellery and other spectacular funerary artefacts from Theban tombs (often found by plundering adventurers rather than enquiring scholars) made Luxor an increasingly popular destination for travellers. By 1869, when Thomas Cook brought his first group of tourists to Egypt, Luxor was one of the highlights. Mass tourism had arrived and Luxor regained its place on the world map.

Most recently, Dr Zahi Hawass, the secretary-general of the Supreme Council of

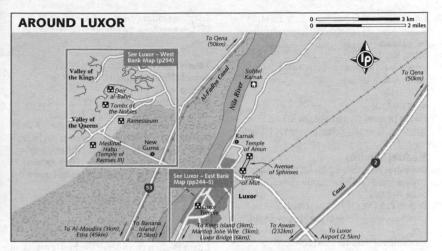

AROUND LUXOR

Antiquities, has stated that this tourism is the greatest threat to the Egyptian monuments, and that if nothing is done they will be destroyed in less than 100 years. Many plans and projects to protect and manage the sites are under way, and Luxor is now a city in flux: on both banks, huge swaths of houses and in places entire villages are being demolished to clear the areas around the historical sites. Most dramatically, most of the villages that clung to the side of the Theban hills have been bulldozed (see also boxed text, p272). On a positive note, visitors centres are being built at the main sights and replicas of some of the most beautiful but fragile tombs are planned.

ORIENTATION

Luxor today is divided into three separate areas for visitors: the city of Luxor itself, the temple complex at Karnak, a couple of kilometres to the northeast, and the monuments and necropolis of ancient Thebes on the west bank of the Nile.

In Luxor city (Map pp244–5) there are five main thoroughfares: Sharia as-Souq, Sharia al-Mahatta, Sharia Maabad al-Karnak, Corniche an-Nil, and Sharia Televizyon, a bustling area around which many of the budget hotels are clustered.

On the West Bank (Map p254) the village of Al-Gezira, close to the ferry landing, is becoming a hub of shops, midrange hotels and restaurants. Most monuments are further west, with tombs and temples strung out at the edge of the desert.

INFORMATION
Bookshops

Luxor has two excellent English-language bookshops. Opposite Aboudi and the New Winter Palace, on the Corniche, is a kiosk selling a good selection of foreign press.

AA Gaddis Bookshop (Map pp244-5; ☎ 238 7042; Corniche an-Nil; ⊗ 9am-10pm Mon-Sat, 10.30am-10pm Sun, closed Jun & Jul) Next door to the Old Winter Palace Hotel; extensive selection of books on Egypt, postcards and souvenirs.

Aboudi Bookshop (Map pp244-5; ☎ 237 3390; next door to AA Gaddis, Tourist Bazaar, Corniche an-Nil; ⊗ 8am-10pm) Has an excellent selection of guidebooks, maps, postcards and fiction.

Emergency

Ambulance (☎ 123)

Police (Map pp244-5; ☎ 237 1500, 237 3845; cnr Sharia Maabad al-Karnak & Sharia al-Matafy)

Tourist police (Map pp244-5; ☎ 237 6620; Midan al-Mahatta) On the left coming out of the train station.

Internet Access

You can find internet access everywhere in Luxor, including in many hotels. Prices range from E£5 to E£10 per hour.

EAST BANK

Aboudi Bookshop (Map pp244-5; ☎ 237 3390; Corniche an-Nil; ⊗ 9am-10pm)

Gamil Centre (Map pp244-5; lower level, Corniche an-Nil; ⊗ 24hr) In front of the Old Winter Palace Hotel.

Heroes Internet (Map pp244-5; Sharia Televizyon; ⊗ 24hr)

Lotus Internet Café (Map pp244-5; ☎ 238 0419; Sharia as-Souq; ⊙ 9am-midnight) Located next door to the restaurant.
Salem Net (Map pp244-5; ☎ 236 4652; ⊙ 24hr) Good connection and air-conditioned room next to the train station, opposite the Anglo Hotel.

WEST BANK
Europa Internet (Map pp244-5; ☎ 012 866 5558; main street, Al-Gezira; ⊙ 8am-2am) Very fast connection.

Medical Services
Dr Boutros (Map p254; ☎ 231 0851; Kom Lolah) Excellent English- and French-speaking doctor, who works on the West Bank.
Dr Ihab Rizk (☎ 012 216 0846) English-speaking cardiologist, who will come to your hotel, on the East Bank.
International Hospital (Map pp244-5; ☎ 228 0192/4; Sharia Televizyon) The best place in town.

Money
Most major Egyptian banks have branches in Luxor. Unless otherwise noted, usual opening hours are 8.30am to 2pm and 5pm to 6pm Sunday to Thursday. ATMs can be found all over town, including at most banks and five-star hotels.
American Express (Map pp244-5; ☎ 237 8333; Corniche an-Nil; ⊙ 9am-4.30pm) Beside the entrance to the Old Winter Palace Hotel.
Bank of Alexandria (Map pp244-5; Corniche an-Nil) Near Hotel Mercure.
Banque du Caire (Map pp244-5; Corniche an-Nil)
Banque Misr (Map pp244-5; Sharia Dr Labib Habashi) Around the corner from Hotel Mercure. There is another branch on Sharia Televizyon.
Broxelles Exchange (Map pp244-5; ☎ 237 1300; Sharia al-Mahatta; ⊙ 8am-10pm)
National Bank of Egypt (Map pp244-5; Corniche an-Nil)
Thomas Cook (Map pp244-5; ☎ 237 2196; Corniche an-Nil; ⊙ 8am-8pm) Below entrance to Old Winter Palace Hotel.

Post
Main post office (Map pp244-5; Sharia al-Mahatta; ⊙ 8.30am-2.30pm Sat-Thu)

Telephone
There are cardphones scattered throughout the town. Cards are available from kiosks and shops. There are several mobile phone shops on Sharia al-Mahatta and Sharia Televizyon that sell tourist SIM cards.

Telephone office (Map pp244-5; Corniche an-Nil; ⊙ 8am-8pm) Below the entrance to Old Winter Palace Hotel.

Tourist Information
Airport office (off Map pp244-5; ☎ 237 2306; ⊙ 8am-8pm)
Corniche office (Map pp244-5; ☎ 928 0004; Corniche an-Nil, opposite Luxor Museum; ⊙ 8am-8pm)
Main tourist office (Map pp244-5; ☎ /fax 237 3294; Midan al-Mahatta; ⊙ 8am-8pm) New and very helpful tourist information, particularly Mourad Gamil, opposite the train station. Also has an internet cafe, hotel bookings, tours and tickets for the sound and light show in Karnak.
Train station office (Map pp244-5; ☎ 237 0259; ⊙ 8am-8pm)

DANGERS & ANNOYANCES
Luxor is often considered the hassle capital of Egypt, and although the governor is cleaning up the town in every possible way, the scams and hassle remain, so much so that several package tour hotels tell their clients it is too dangerous to leave their hotel. The most common scams are asking for extra baksheesh at the monuments, overcharging for a *calèche* (horse-drawn carriage) or felucca, charging European prices for taxi rides, and touts in the souq or station targeting new arrivals. A frequent scam is that taxi or *calèche* drivers tell tourists there is a local souq that is less touristy than the souq behind the Luxor Temple. They then drive around town and pull up at the same old souq. The tourist office or the tourist police will need a written report from you if anything happens, and will try to take action.

In recent years Luxor has also become a known destination for female sex tourism, popular with some often-older Western women looking for sex with young Egyptians. Because of this, individual women travellers looking for nothing more risqué than an ancient temple or a desert sunset can find themselves seriously hassled. There have also been many cases of women being lured or tricked into marriage, or into giving away their savings to these gigolos, only to find themselves confined to a room under the watchful eye of their new mother-in-law while their young husband goes out looking for more fun. Another alarming new trend is for taxi or *calèche* drivers to offer prostitutes to foreign clients.

SIGHTS – EAST BANK

Luxor's East Bank is still a busy provincial city, despite the presence of an ever-increasing number of tourists. The governor has made huge efforts to clean up the town centre but not everyone is happy. Many locals feel that their interests have been placed second in the drive to boost tourism, and have raised concerns over the relocation and compensation efforts.

Sharia al-Mahatta has a slight Parisian air, the souq is clean and protected from the sun, while buildings are being cleared from around the temples of Luxor and Karnak. The project to clear the 3km-long alley of the sphinxes between the two temples has been the most controversial. The parameters have not been made clear and rumours swirl around the city, the wildest being a suggestion that everything between the river and the railway line – most of pre-1960s Luxor – will be pulled down. A number of historic, although not ancient, buildings have been razed, among them the 19th-century colonial palaces on the Corniche and the French House next to Karnak Temple.

The city centre, where hotels, bars and restaurants are concentrated, is easily walkable when the heat is not intense. At its heart is Luxor Temple, an elegant architectural masterpiece, its courtyards and sanctuaries dedicated to the Theban triad, Amun, Mut and Khonsu. Rather than start here, it makes sense to visit the awe-inspiring temple complex of Karnak early in the morning. Here, for more than 1500 years, pharaohs vied for the gods' attention by outdoing each other's architectural feats. Luxor Temple can be visited later and is even open at night.

Complementing the monuments are two excellent museums. Luxor Museum, currently the best-designed museum in the country, has a fascinating collection of artefacts discovered in this antiquities-rich area. The nearby Mummification Museum displays animal and human mummies and explains in detail how ancient Egyptians perfected the embalming process.

Temples of Karnak

More than a temple, **Karnak** (Map p241; Sharia Maabad al-Karnak; adult/student E£65/40; ⏰ 6am-5pm Oct-Apr, to 6pm May-Sep) is an extraordinary complex of sanctuaries, kiosks, pylons and obelisks dedicated to the Theban gods and the greater glory of pharaohs. Everything is on a gigantic scale: the site covers over 2 sq km, large enough to contain about 10 cathedrals, while its main structure, the Temple of Amun, is the largest religious building ever built. This was where the god lived on earth, surrounded by the houses of his wife Mut, and their son Khonsu, two other huge temple complexes on this site. Built, added to, dismantled, restored, enlarged and decorated over nearly 1500 years, Karnak was the most important place of worship in Egypt during the New Kingdom. It was called Ipet-Sut, meaning 'The Most Esteemed of Places'; Karnak is its Arabic name meaning 'fortified settlement'. New Kingdom records show that the priests of the Temple of Amun had 81,000 people working in or for the temple, owned 421,000 head of cattle, 65 cities, 83 ships and 276,400 hectares of agricultural land, giving an idea of its economic, as well as spiritual, significance.

With so many additions, the site can be very confusing; trying to understand this immense monument has vexed travellers for centuries. As Amelia Edwards, the 19th-century writer and artist who journeyed up the Nile, succinctly put it:

> It is a place that has been much written about and often painted; but of which no writing and no art can convey more than a dwarfed and pallid impression … The scale is too vast; the effect too tremendous; the sense of one's own dumbness, and littleness, and incapacity, too complete and crushing.

The most important place of worship was the massive **Amun Temple Enclosure** (Precinct of Amun; Map pp248–9), dominated by the great Temple of Amun-Ra, which contains the famous hypostyle hall, a spectacular forest of giant papyrus-shaped columns. On its southern side is the Mut Temple Enclosure, once linked to the main temple by an avenue of ram-headed sphinxes. To the north is the Montu Temple Enclosure, which honoured the local Theban war god. The 3km-long paved avenue of human-headed sphinxes that once linked the great Temple of Amun at Karnak with Luxor Temple is now again being cleared.

The earliest structures at Karnak go back to the Middle Kingdom period: the White Chapel of Sesostris (Senruset) I (1965–1920 BC),

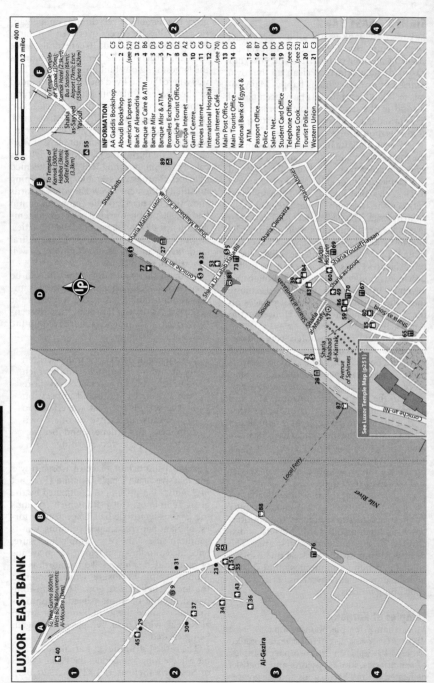

LUXOR – EAST BANK

INFORMATION

AA Gaddis Bookshop	1 C5
Aboudi Bookshop	2 C5
American Express	(see 52)
Bank of Alexandria	3 D2
Banque du Caire & ATM	4 B6
Banque Misr	5 D3
Banque Misr & ATM	6 C6
Broxelles Exchange	7 D5
Corniche Tourist Office	8 D2
Europa Internet	9 A2
Gamil Centre	10 C5
Heroes Internet	11 C6
International Hospital	12 C7
Lotus Internet Café	(see 70)
Main Post Office	13 D5
Main Tourist Office	14 D5
National Bank of Egypt & ATM	15 B5
Passport Office	16 B7
Police	17 D4
Salem Net	18 D5
Student Card Office	19 D6
Telephone Office	(see 52)
Thomas Cook	(see 52)
Tourist Police	20 E5
Western Union	21 C3

Nile River

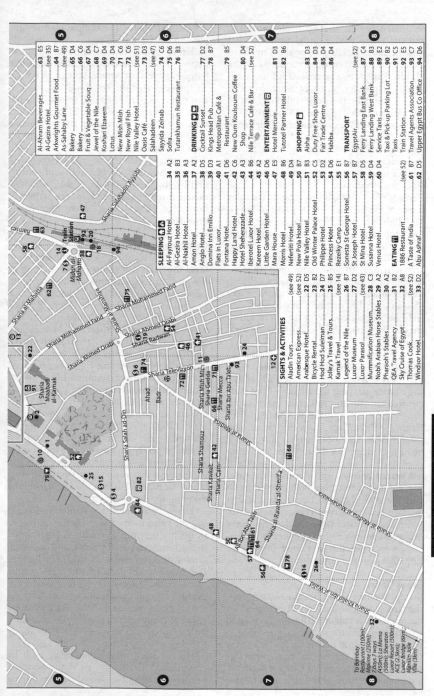

SIGHTS & ACTIVITIES

Aladin Tours	(see 49)
American Express	(see 52)
Arabesque Hotel	22 D5
Bicycle Rental	23 B2
Hod Hod Suleiman	24 D7
Jolley's Travel & Tours	25 B5
Karnak Travel	(see 14)
Legend of the Nile	26 B7
Luxor Museum	27 D2
Luxor Parasol	(see 43)
Mummification Museum	28 C3
Nobi's Arabian Horse Stables	29 A2
Pharaoh's Stables	30 A2
QEA Travel Agency	31 B2
Sky Cruise of Egypt	32 A8
Thomas Cook	(see 52)
Windsor Hotel	33 D2

SLEEPING

Al-Fayrouz Hotel	34 A2
Al-Gezira Hotel	35 B3
Al-Nakhil Hotel	36 A3
Amon Hotel	37 A2
Anglo Hotel	38 D5
Domina Inn Emilio	39 D3
Flats in Luxor	40 A1
Fontana Hotel	41 D6
Happy Land Hotel	42 C6
Hotel Sheherazade	43 A3
Iberotel Luxor Hotel	44 B6
Kareem Hotel	45 A2
Little Garden Hotel	46 D6
Mara House	47 E5
Morris Hotel	48 B6
Nefertiti Hotel	49 D4
New Pola Hotel	50 B7
Nile Valley Hotel	51 B3
Old Winter Palace Hotel	52 C5
Philippe Hotel	53 D2
Princess Hotel	54 D6
Rezeley Camp	55 E1
Sonesta St George Hotel	56 B7
St Joseph Hotel	57 D2
St Mina Hotel	58 D5
Susanna Hotel	59 D4
Venus Hotel	60 D4

EATING

1886 Restaurant	(see 52)
A Taste of India	61 B7
Abu Ashraf	62 D5
Al-Ahram Beverages	63 E5
Al-Gezira Hotel	(see 35)
Arkwrights Gourmet Food	64 B7
As-Sahaby Lane	(see 49)
Bakery	65 D4
Bakery	66 C6
Fruit & Vegetable Souq	67 D4
Jewel of the Nile	68 C7
Koshari Elzaeem	69 D4
Lotus	70 D4
New Mish Mish	71 C6
New Royal Fish	72 C6
Nile Valley Hotel	(see 51)
Oasis Café	73 D3
Salahadeen	(see 47)
Sayyida Zeinab	74 C6
Sofra	75 D6
Tutankhamun Restaurant	76 B3

DRINKING

Cocktail Sunset	77 D2
Kings Head Pub	78 B7
Metropolitan Café & Restaurant	79 B5
New Oum Koulsoum Coffee Shop	80 D4
Nile Terrace Café & Bar	(see 52)

ENTERTAINMENT

Hotel Mercure	81 D3
Tutotel Partner Hotel	82 B6

SHOPPING

Aisha	83 D3
Duty Free Shop Luxor	84 D3
Fair Trade Centre	85 D4
Habiba	86 D4

TRANSPORT

EgyptAir	(see 52)
Ferry Landing East Bank	87 C4
Ferry Landing West Bank	88 B3
Service Taxis	89 E2
Taxi & Pick-up Parking Lot	90 B2
Taxis	91 C5
Train Station	92 E5
Travel Agents Association	93 C7
Upper Egypt Bus Co Office	94 D6

NILE VALLEY: LUXOR

reconstructed in the open-air museum, and the 12th-dynasty foundations of what was the most sacred part of the Temple of Amun, the sacred barque sanctuary and the Middle Kingdom Court (behind the sixth pylon). However, most of what you can see was built by the powerful pharaohs of the 18th to 20th dynasties (1570–1090 BC), who spent fortunes on making their mark in this most sacred of places. Later pharaohs extended and rebuilt the complex, as did the Ptolemies and early Christians. Basically the further into the complex you venture, the older the structures.

Wandering through this gigantic complex is one of the highlights of any visit to Egypt. The light is most beautiful in the early morning, and the temple is quieter then, as later in the morning the tour groups and loads of day-trippers from Hurghada arrive. It pays to visit more than once, to be able to make sense of the overwhelming jumble of ancient remains. As almost every pharaoh left his or her mark here, it can feel like a crash course in the evolution of ancient Egyptian artistic and architectural styles.

AMUN TEMPLE ENCLOSURE – MAIN AXIS

The **Quay of Amun** was the dock where the large boats carrying the statues of the gods moored during the festivals. From tomb paintings such as those in the Tomb of Nakht (see p269) we know that there were palaces to the north of the quay surrounded by lush gardens. On the east side is a ramp sloping down to the processional **avenue of ram-headed sphinxes**, which leads to the massive unfinished **first pylon**, built by Nectanebo I of the 30th dynasty. On the inside is a massive mudbrick construction ramp, onto which the blocks of stone for the pylon were dragged up with rollers and ropes. When Napoleon's expedition visited there were still blocks on the ramp.

Great Court

Behind the first pylon lies the Great Court, the largest area of the Karnak complex. To the left is the **Temple of Seti II** with three small chapels that held the sacred barques of Mut, Amun and Khonsu during the lead-up to the Opet Festival. In the southeastern corner (far right) is the well-preserved **Temple of Ramses III**, a miniature version of the pharaoh's temple at Medinat Habu. The temple plan is simple and classic: pylon, open court, vestibule with four Osirid columns and four columns, hypostyle hall with eight columns and three barque chapels for Amun, Mut and Khonsu. At the centre of the court are two rows of five columns. Only one still stands 21m tall with a papyrus-shaped capital, and a small alabaster altar at the middle: all that remains of the **Kiosk of Taharka**, the 25th-dynasty Nubian pharaoh.

The **second pylon** was begun by Horemheb, the last 18th-dynasty pharaoh, and continued by Ramses I and Ramses II, who also raised three colossal red-granite **statues** of himself on either side of the entrance; one is now destroyed.

Great Hypostyle Hall

Beyond the second pylon is the awesome **Great Hypostyle Hall** (Map pp248–9), one of the greatest religious monuments ever built. Covering 5500 sq metres – enough space to contain both Rome's St Peter's Basilica and London's St Paul's Cathedral – the hall is an unforgettable forest of 134 towering papyrus-shaped stone pillars. It symbolised a papyrus swamp, of which there were so many along the Nile. Ancient Egyptians believed that these plants surrounded the primeval mound on which life was first created. Each summer when the Nile began to flood, this hall and its columns were under several feet of water. Originally, it would have been brightly painted – some colours remain – and roofed, making it pretty dark away from the lit main axis. The size and grandeur of the pillars and the endless decorations are overwhelming: take your time, sit for a while and stare at the dizzying spectacle.

The hall was planned by Ramses I and built by Seti I and Ramses II. Note the difference in quality between the delicate raised relief in the northern part, by Seti I, and the much cruder sunken relief work, added by Ramses II in the southern part of the hall. The cryptic scenes on the inner walls were intended for the priesthood and the royalty who understood the religious context, but the outer walls are easier to comprehend, showing the pharaoh's military prowess and strength, and his ability to bring order to chaos.

On the back of the **third pylon**, built by Amenhotep III, to the right the pharaoh is shown sailing the sacred barque during the Opet Festival (see boxed text, p250). Tuthmosis I (1504–1492 BC) created a narrow court between the third and fourth pylons, where four obelisks stood, two each for Tuthmosis I and Tuthmosis III (1479–1425 BC). Only the bases remain except for one, 22m high, raised for Tuthmosis I.

Inner Temple

Beyond the **fourth pylon** is the Hypostyle Hall of Tuthmosis III built by Tuthmosis I in precious wood, and altered by Tuthmosis III with 14 columns and a stone roof. In this court stands one of the two magnificent 30m-high obelisks erected by Queen Hatshepsut (1473–1458 BC) to the glory of her 'father' Amun. The other is broken but the upper shaft lies near the sacred lake (right). The **Obelisk of Hatshepsut** is the tallest in Egypt, its tip originally covered in electrum (a commonly used alloy of gold and silver). After Hatshepsut's death, her stepson Tuthmosis III eradicated all signs of her reign (see boxed text, p269) and had them walled into a sandstone structure.

The ruined **fifth pylon**, constructed by Tuthmosis I, leads to another colonnade now badly ruined, followed by the small **sixth pylon**, raised by Tuthmosis III, who also built the pair of red-granite columns in the vestibule beyond, carved with the lotus and the papyrus, the symbols of Upper and Lower Egypt. Nearby are two huge statues of Amun and the goddess Amunet, carved in the reign of Tutankhamun.

The original **sacred barque sanctuary** of Tuthmosis III, the very core of the temple where the god Amun resided, was replaced by a granite one, that was built and decorated with well-preserved painted reliefs by Alexander the Great's successor and half-brother: the fragile, dim-witted Philip Arrhidaeus (323–317 BC).

East of the shrine of Philip Arrhidaeus, is the oldest known part of the temple, the **Middle Kingdom Court**, where Sesostris I built a shrine, of which the foundation walls have been found. On the northern wall of the court is the **Wall of Records**, a running tally of the organised tribute the pharaoh exacted in honour of Amun from his subjugated lands.

Great Festival Hall of Tuthmosis III

At the back of the Middle Kingdom Court is the Festival Hall of Tuthmosis III, the Akh-Menou, Brilliant of Monuments. It is an unusual structure with uniquely carved stone columns imitating tent poles, perhaps a reference to the pharaoh's life under canvas on his frequent military expeditions abroad. The columned vestibule that lies beyond, generally referred to as the **Botanical Gardens**, has wonderful, detailed relief scenes of the flora and fauna that the pharaoh had encountered during his campaigns in Syria and Palestine, and had brought back to Egypt.

For the many people not allowed inside the temple's sacred enclosure, Tuthmosis III built a small **chapel** onto the back of the temple wall behind his festival hall, at either side of which can be seen the enormous bases for two of Hatshepsut's obelisks that once stood here. Beyond this, further to the southeast, Ramses II built a similar chapel, the **Temple of the Hearing Ear**, again with a base for a single obelisk standing 32.2m tall and which Ramses usurped from Tuthmosis III. Removed from Karnak on the orders of the Emperor Constantine (AD 306–337) and bound for Constantinople, the obelisk was redirected to Rome to stand in the Circus Maximus. It was re-erected in 1588 on the orders of Pope Sixtus V where it now stands, in front of the church of St John (Giovanni) Lateran.

Against the northern enclosure wall of the Amun Temple Enclosure is the well-preserved cult **Temple of Ptah**, started by Tuthmosis III and finished by the Ptolemies and the Romans. Access to the inner chambers is through a series of five doorways, which lead to two of the temple's original statues. The headless figure of Ptah, the creator god of Memphis, is in the middle chapel behind a locked door – the custodian will often unlock it for some baksheesh. To his left is the eerily beautiful black granite statue of his goddess-wife Sekhmet (the spreader of terror), bare-breasted and lioness-headed.

AMUN TEMPLE ENCLOSURE – SOUTHERN AXIS

The secondary axis of the Amun Temple Enclosure, running south from the third and fourth pylons, is a walled processional way from the seventh to the 10th pylon, leading to the Mut Temple Enclosure. The courtyard between the Hypostyle Hall and the **seventh pylon**, built by Tuthmosis III, is known as the **cachette court**, as thousands of stone and bronze statues were discovered here in 1903. The priests had the old statues and temple furniture they no longer needed buried around

AMUN TEMPLE ENCLOSURE

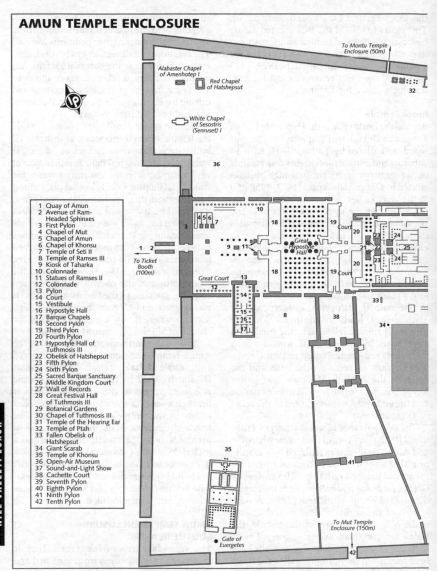

To Montu Temple Enclosure (50m)

Alabaster Chapel of Amenhotep I

Red Chapel of Hatshepsut

White Chapel of Sesostris (Senruset) I

To Ticket Booth (100m)

To Mut Temple Enclosure (150m)

Gate of Euergetes

1 Quay of Amun
2 Avenue of Ram-Headed Sphinxes
3 First Pylon
4 Chapel of Mut
5 Chapel of Amun
6 Chapel of Khonsu
7 Temple of Seti II
8 Temple of Ramses III
9 Kiosk of Taharka
10 Colonnade
11 Statues of Ramses II
12 Colonnade
13 Pylon
14 Court
15 Vestibule
16 Hypostyle Hall
17 Barque Chapels
18 Second Pylon
19 Third Pylon
20 Fourth Pylon
21 Hypostyle Hall of Tuthmosis III
22 Obelisk of Hatshepsut
23 Fifth Pylon
24 Sixth Pylon
25 Sacred Barque Sanctuary
26 Middle Kingdom Court
27 Wall of Records
28 Great Festival Hall of Tuthmosis III
29 Botanical Gardens
30 Chapel of Tuthmosis III
31 Temple of the Hearing Ear
32 Temple of Ptah
33 Fallen Obelisk of Hatshepsut
34 Giant Scarab
35 Temple of Khonsu
36 Open-Air Museum
37 Sound-and-Light Show
38 Cachette Court
39 Seventh Pylon
40 Eighth Pylon
41 Ninth Pylon
42 Tenth Pylon

300 BC. Most statues were sent to the Egyptian Museum in Cairo, but some remain, standing in front of the seventh pylon, including four of Tuthmosis III on the left.

The well-preserved **eighth pylon**, built by Queen Hatshepsut, is the oldest part of the north–south axis of the temple, and one of the earliest pylons in Karnak. Carved on it is a text

she falsely attributed to Tuthmosis I, justifying her taking the throne of Egypt.

The **ninth** and **10th pylons** were built by Horemheb, who used some of the stones of a demolished temple that had been built to the east by Akhenaten (before he decamped to Tell al-Amarna), some of which can be seen on display in the wonderful Luxor Museum (p252).

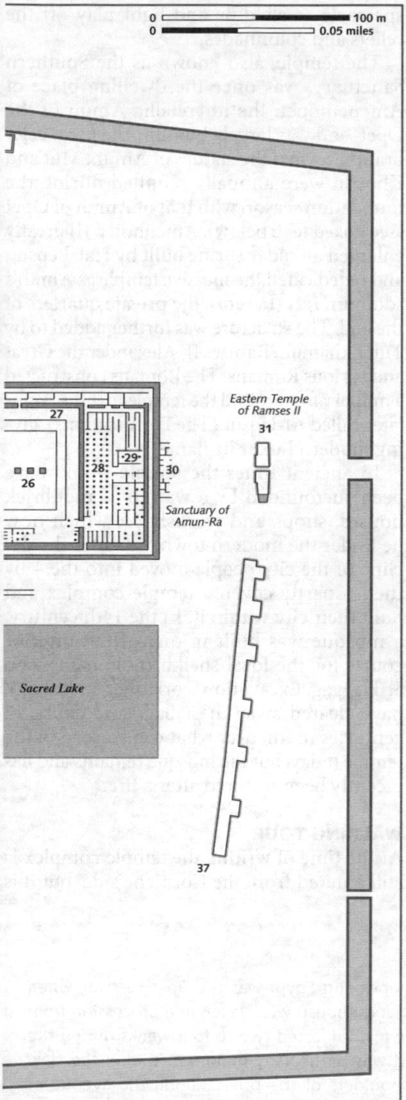
0 100 m
0 0.05 miles
Eastern Temple of Ramses II
27
31
29
28
30
26
Sanctuary of Amun-Ra
Sacred Lake
37

East of the seventh and eighth pylons is the **sacred lake** (Map pp248–9), where, according to Herodotus, the priests of Amun bathed twice daily and nightly for ritual purity. On the northwestern side of the lake is part of the **Fallen Obelisk of Hatshepsut** showing her coronation, and a **Giant Scarab** in stone dedicated by Amenhotep III to Khepri, a form of the sun god.

In the southwestern corner of the enclosure is the **Temple of Khonsu**, god of the moon, and son of Amun and Mut. It can be reached from a door in the southern wall of the Hypostyle Hall of the Temple of Amun, via a path through various blocks of stone. The temple, mostly the work of Ramses III and enlarged by later Ramesside rulers, lies north of Euergetes' Gate and the avenue of sphinxes leading to Luxor Temple. The temple pylon leads via a peristyle court to a hypostyle hall with eight columns carved with figures of Ramses XI and the High Priest Herihor, who effectively ruled Upper Egypt at the time. The next chamber housed the sacred barque of Khonsu.

MUT TEMPLE ENCLOSURE

From the 10th pylon an avenue of sphinxes leads to the partly excavated southern enclosure – the Precinct of Mut. The badly ruined Temple of Mut was built by Amenhotep III and consists of a sanctuary, a hypostyle hall and two courts. Amenhotep also set up more than 700 black granite statues of the lioness goddess Sekhmet, Mut's northern counterpart, which are believed to form a calendar, with two statues for every day of the year, receiving offerings each morning and evening.

MONTU TEMPLE ENCLOSURE

A gate, usually locked, on the wall near the Temple of Ptah (in the Amun Temple Enclosure) leads to the Montu Temple Enclosure. Montu, the falcon-headed warrior god, was one of the original deities of Thebes. The main temple was built by Amenhotep III and modified by others. The complex is very dilapidated.

OPEN-AIR MUSEUM

Off to the left (north) of the first court of the Amun Temple Enclosure is Karnak's **open-air museum** (Map pp248-9; tickets at main ticket office, adult/student E£25/15; 🕓 6am-5.30pm summer, 6am-4.30pm winter). This museum is missed by most visitors but is definitely worth a look. The well-preserved chapels include the **White Chapel of Sesostris I**, one of the oldest and most beautiful monuments in Karnak, which has wonderful Middle Kingdom reliefs; the **Red Chapel of Hatshepsut**, its red quartzite blocks reassembled in 2000; and the **Alabaster Chapel of Amenhotep I**. The museum also contains a collection of statuary found throughout the temple complex.

NILE VALLEY: LUXOR

SOUND & LIGHT SHOW

Karnak's highly kitsch **sound and light show** (Map pp248-9; ☎ 238 6000, 238 2777; www.soundandlight.com.eg; adult/student E£100/60, video camera E£35; ☉ 6.30pm, 7.45pm & 9pm winter, 8pm, 9.15pm & 10.30pm summer) is a 1½-hour Hollywood-style extravaganza that recounts the history of Thebes and the lives of the many pharaohs who built here in honour of Amun. It's worth a visit particularly for the walk through the beautifully lit temple at night.

This was the schedule at the time of writing but check either at the temple or at the office for the sound and light show at the main tourist office, before heading there.

Day	Show 1	Show 2	Show 3
Monday	English	French	Spanish
Tuesday	Japanese	English	German (private)
Wednesday	German	English	French
Thursday	English	French	Arabic
Friday	English	French	
Saturday	French	English	German
Sunday	German	English	Italian

Luxor Temple

Largely built by the New Kingdom pharaohs Amenhotep III (1390–1352 BC) and Ramses II (1279–1213 BC), this **temple** (Map p251; Corniche an-Nil; adult/student E£50/30; ☉ 6am-9pm Oct-Apr, to 10pm May-Sep) is a strikingly graceful monument in the heart of the modern town. Visit early when the temple opens, before the crowds arrive or later at sunset when the stones glow. Whenever you go, be sure to return at night when the temple is lit up, creating an eerie

spectacle as shadow and light play off the reliefs and colonnades.

The temple, also known as the Southern Sanctuary, was once the dwelling place of Amenemopet, the ithyphallic Amun of the Opet, and was largely built for the Opet celebrations, when the statues of Amun, Mut and Khonsu were annually reunited during the inundation season with that of Amun of Opet (see boxed text, below). Amenhotep III greatly enlarged an older shrine built by Hatshepsut, and rededicated the massive temple as Amun's southern *ipet* (harem), the private quarters of the god. The structure was further added to by Tutankhamun, Ramses II, Alexander the Great and various Romans. The Romans constructed a military fort around the temple that the Arabs later called Al-Uqsur (The Fortifications), giving modern Luxor its name.

In ancient times the temple would have been surrounded by a warren of mudbrick houses, shops and workshops, which now lie under the modern town, but after the decline of the city people moved into the – by then – partly covered temple complex and built their city within it. In the 14th century, a mosque was built in one of the interior courts for the local sheikh (holy man) Abu al-Haggag. Excavation works, begun in 1885, have cleared away the village and debris of centuries to uncover what can be seen of the temple today, but the mosque remains and has recently been restored after a fire.

WALKING TOUR

At the time of writing the temple complex is still entered from the Corniche side, but it is

---

THE BEAUTIFUL FESTIVAL OF THE OPET

The most important annual religious festival in Thebes and Egypt was the Opet Festival, when the barque shrines of the Theban triad Amun, Mut and Khonsu were taken in a procession from Karnak Temple to their home at Luxor Temple. The festival lasted two to four weeks during the summer, the second month of the Nile flood, and was particularly important during the New Kingdom. The cult images were carried on the shoulders of the priests along the avenue of sphinxes, stopping for ceremonies and to rest at six barque shrines on the way, or taken by boat up the Nile, as seen on the reliefs in Amenhotep III's Colonnade in Luxor Temple and the outer wall of the Temple of Ramses III in the Great Court in Karnak. The statue of Amun was reunited with his ithyphallic form Amenemopet, symbolising fertility and rejuvenation. The ceremony reaffirmed the pharaoh's authority and his close ties with the 'King of Gods' Amun. The pharaoh, after all, was the living embodiment of the god Horus on earth. These days, during the *moulid* (saint's festival) of Abu al-Haggag (see boxed text, p252), one of the highlights of this three-day festival is a felucca pulled in procession through town and circling the temple, a modern survival of the ancient Opet Festival.

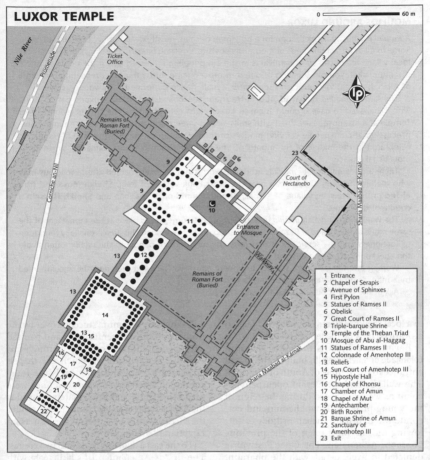

LUXOR TEMPLE

0 —————————— 60 m

1 Entrance
2 Chapel of Serapis
3 Avenue of Sphinxes
4 First Pylon
5 Statues of Ramses II
6 Obelisk
7 Great Court of Ramses II
8 Triple-barque Shrine
9 Temple of the Theban Triad
10 Mosque of Abu al-Haggag
11 Statues of Ramses II
12 Colonnade of Amenhotep III
13 Reliefs
14 Sun Court of Amenhotep III
15 Hypostyle Hall
16 Chapel of Khonsu
17 Chamber of Amun
18 Chapel of Mut
19 Antechamber
20 Birth Room
21 Barque Shrine of Amun
22 Sanctuary of
    Amenhotep III
23 Exit

said that this will change, and the entrance will be moved to the square in front of the mosque of Abu al-Haggag. The temple is less complex to understand than Karnak, but here again we walk back in time, and away from the tour groups the deeper we go into it. In front of the temple is the beginning of the **avenue of sphinxes** that ran all the way to the temples at Karnak 3km to the north, which is now being entirely excavated.

The massive 24m-high **first pylon** was raised by Ramses II and decorated with reliefs of his military exploits, including the Battle of Kadesh. The pylon was originally fronted by six colossal **statues of Ramses II**, four seated and two standing, but only two of the seated figures and one standing remain, and a pair

pink granite **obelisks**, of which one remains and the other stands in the Place de la Concorde in Paris. Beyond lies the **Great Court of Ramses II**, surrounded by a double row of columns with lotus-bud capitals, the walls of which are decorated with scenes of the pharaoh making offerings to the gods. On the south (rear) wall is a procession of 17 sons of Ramses II with their names and titles, and in front of them a beautiful relief, the first pylon of the temple with statues, obelisks and flags, reliefs of his military successes. In the northwestern corner of the court is the earlier **triple-barque shrine** built by Hatshepsut and usurped by her stepson Tuthmosis III for Amun, Mut and Khonsu. Over the southeastern side hangs the 14th-century **Mosque of Abu al-Haggag**, dedicated

MOULIDS AROUND LUXOR

A *moulid* is a birthday celebration for a holy man or saint, mostly dead but occasionally still alive. Some *moulids* attract hundreds of thousands of visitors getting *barakas* (blessings), others are very local village affairs. An air of carnival is in the air, people are dressed up for the occasion, there is a big market, you can see Sufis of different orders going into a trance by repeating the name of Allah, hear real folk music and see *tahtib*, a male dance performed with wooden staves.

The largest *moulid* is that of **Abu al-Haggag** (see boxed text, p250), Luxor's patron saint, who is believed to have brought Islam to Luxor eight centuries ago. The streets around Luxor Temple and his mosque are lined with stalls selling sweets and toys, and there is an impressive procession of craftspeople carrying models of their trade up to the mosque. Abu al-Haggag is celebrated in the middle of the month of Sha'aban, the month before Ramadan, when most *moulids* take place.

There are several smaller *moulids* around Luxor: **Abu'l Gumsan**, named after a religious man who died in 1984, on 27 Sha'aban near the West Bank village of Taref; **Sheikh Musa** and **Abu al-Jud** in the sprawling village of Karnak; **Sheikh Hamid** on 1 Sha'aban and **Sheikh Hussein** a couple of days later.

The week-long Christian *moulid* of **Mar Girgis** (St George) takes place at the monastery of the same name at the village of Razagat, culminating on 11 November. This area is officially forbidden to foreigners, but the service taxis that ferry the hundreds of people to the *moulid* often avoid the checkpoint by taking a desert track.

Women attending *moulids* should dress very conservatively and preferably be accompanied by a man, as groping and harassment do occur.

Ask at the tourist office (p242) for exact dates.

to a local sheikh, entered from Sharia Maabad al-Karnak, outside the temple precinct.

Beyond the court is the older splendid **Colonnade of Amenhotep III**, built as the grand entrance to the Temple of Amun of the Opet. The walls behind the elegant open papyrus columns were decorated during the reign of the young pharaoh Tutankhamun and celebrate the return to Theban orthodoxy following the wayward reign of the previous pharaoh, Akhenaten. The Opet Festival is depicted in lively detail, with the pharaoh, nobility and common people joining the triumphal procession. Look out for the drummers and acrobats doing back bends.

South of the Colonnade is the **Sun Court of Amenhotep III**, once enclosed on three sides by double rows of towering papyrus-bundle columns, the best preserved of which, with their architraves extant, are those on the eastern and western sides. In 1989 workmen found here a cache of 26 statues, buried by priests in Roman times, now moved to the Luxor Museum (see right).

Beyond lies the **Hypostyle Hall**, the first room of the original Opet temple, with four rows of eight columns each, leading to the temple's main rooms. The central **chamber** on the axis south of the Hypostyle Hall was the

cult sanctuary of Amun, stuccoed over by the Romans in the 3rd century AD and painted with scenes of Roman officials. Through this chamber, either side of which are **chapels** dedicated to Mut and Khonsu, is the four-columned **Antechamber**, where offerings were made to Amun, and immediately behind it the **Barque Shrine of Amun**, rebuilt by Alexander the Great, with reliefs portraying him as an Egyptian pharaoh.

To the east a doorway leads into two rooms. The first is Amenhotep III's **birth room** with scenes of his divine birth. You can see the moment of his conception, when the fingers of the god touch those of the queen and 'his dew filled her body', according to the accompanying hieroglyphic caption. The **sanctuary of Amenhotep III** is the last chamber; it still has the remains of the stone base on which Amun's statue stood, and although it was once the most sacred part of the temple, the busy street that now runs directly behind it makes it less atmospheric.

Luxor Museum

This wonderful **museum** (Map pp244–5; ☎ 238 0269; Corniche an-Nil; adult/student E£80/40; ◷ 9am-1pm & 4-9pm Oct-Apr, 9am-1pm & 5-10pm May-Sep) has a beautifully displayed collection, from the end of the

Old Kingdom right through to the Mamluk period, mostly gathered from the Theban temples and necropolis.

The ground-floor gallery has several masterpieces including a well-preserved limestone **relief of Tuthmosis III** (No 140), an exquisitely carved **statue of Tuthmosis III** in greywacke from the Temple of Karnak (No 2), an alabaster **figure of Amenhotep III** protected by the great crocodile god Sobek (No 155) and, one of the few examples of Old Kingdom art found at Thebes, a **relief of Unas-ankh** (No 183), found in his tomb on the West Bank.

A new wing was opened in 2004, dedicated to the glory of Thebes during the New Kingdom period. The highlight, and the main reason for the new construction, is the two **royal mummies**, Ahmose I (founder of the 18th dynasty) and the mummy some believe to be Ramses I (founder of the 19th dynasty and father of Seti I), beauti-

fully displayed without their wrappings in dark rooms. Other well-labelled displays illustrate the military might of Thebes during the New Kingdom, the age of Egypt's empire-building, including chariots and weapons. On the upper floor the military theme is diluted with scenes from daily life showing the technology used in the New Kingdom. **Multimedia displays** show workers harvesting papyrus and processing it into sheets to be used for writing. Young boys are shown learning to read and write hieroglyphs beside a display of a scribe's implements and an architect's tools.

Back in the old building, moving up via the ramp to the 1st floor, you come face to face with a seated **granite figure** of the legendary scribe Amenhotep (No 4), son of Hapu, the great official eventually deified in Ptolemaic times and who, as overseer of all the pharaoh's works under Amenhotep III (1390–1352 BC),

---

MAKING MUMMIES   *Dr Joann Fletcher*

Although the practice of preserving dead bodies can be found in cultures across the world, the Egyptians were the ultimate practitioners of this highly complex procedure that they refined over a period of almost 4000 years. Their preservation of the dead can be traced back to the very earliest times, when bodies were simply buried in the desert away from the limited areas of cultivation. In direct contact with the sand that covered them, the hot, dry conditions allowed the body fluids to drain away while preserving the skin, hair and nails intact. Accidentally uncovering such bodies must have had a profound effect upon those who were able to recognise people who had died sometimes years before.

A long process of experimentation to preserve the bodies without burying them in the sand began. It wasn't until around 2600 BC that internal organs, which is where putrefaction actually begins, began to be removed. As the process became increasingly elaborate, all the organs were removed except the kidneys, which were hard to reach, and the heart. The heart was considered the source of intelligence rather than the brain, which was generally removed by inserting a metal probe up the nose and whisking to reduce it to a liquid that could be easily drained away. All the rest – lungs, liver, stomach, intestines – were removed through an opening cut in the left flank. Then the body and its separate organs were covered with piles of natron salt and left to dry out for 40 days, after which they were washed, purified and anointed with a range of oils, spices and resins. All were then wrapped in layers of linen, with the appropriate amulets set in place over the various parts of the body as priests recited the incantations needed to activate the protective functions of the amulets.

With each internal organ placed inside its own Canopic jar, the wrapped body complete with its funerary mask was placed inside its coffin. It was then ready for the funeral procession to the tomb, where the vital Opening of the Mouth ceremony reanimated the soul and restored its senses; offerings were given, while wishing the dead 'a thousand of every good and pure thing for your soul and all kinds of offerings on which the gods live'.

The ancient Egyptians also used mummification to preserve animals, both as a means of preserving the bodies of much-loved pets and the far more widespread practice of mummifying animals to present as votive offerings to the gods with which they were associated. The Egyptians mummified everything from huge bulls to tiny shrews, with cats, hawks and ibis mummified in their millions by Graeco-Roman times; recent research reveals that such creatures were killed for that purpose.

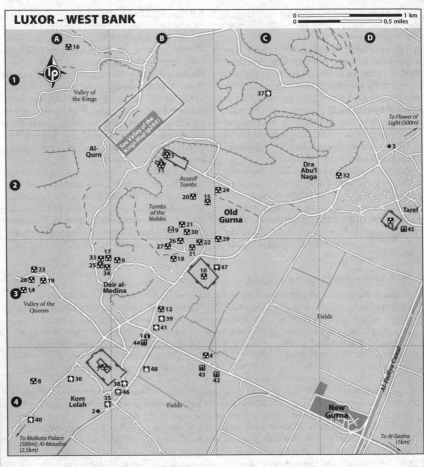

LUXOR – WEST BANK

was responsible for many of Thebes' greatest buildings. One of the most interesting exhibits is the **Wall of Akhenaten**, a series of small sandstone blocks named *talatat* or 'threes' by workmen – probably because their height and length was about three hand lengths – that came from Amenhotep IV's contribution at Karnak before he changed his name to Akhenaten and left Thebes for Tell al-Amarna. His building was demolished and about 40,000 blocks used to fill in Karnak's ninth pylon were found in the late 1960s and partially reassembled here. The scenes showing Akhenaten, his wife Nefertiti and temple life are a rare example of decoration from a Temple of Aten. Further highlights are treasures from Tutankhamun's tomb, including

shabti (servant) figures, model boats, sandals, arrows and a series of gilded bronze rosettes from his funeral pall.

A ramp back down to the ground floor leaves you close to the exit and beside a black-and-gold wooden head of the cow deity Mehit-Weret, an aspect of the goddess Hathor, which was also found in Tutankhamun's tomb.

On the left just before the exit is a small hall containing 16 of 22 statues that were uncovered in Luxor Temple in 1989. All are magnificent examples of ancient Egyptian sculpture but pride of place at the end of the hall is given to an almost pristine 2.45m-tall quartzite statue of a muscular Amenhotep III, wearing a pleated kilt.

Mummification Museum

Housed in the former visitors centre on Luxor's Corniche, the small **Mummification Museum** (Map pp244-5; ☎ 238 1501; Corniche an-Nil; adult/student E£50/25; ⏱ 9am-1pm & 4-9pm Oct-Apr, 9am-1pm & 5-10pm May-Sep) has well-presented exhibits explaining the art of mummification. On display are the well-preserved mummy of a 21st-dynasty high priest of Amun, Maserharti, and a host of mummified animals. Vitrines show the tools and materials used in the mummification process – check out the small spoon and metal spatula used for scraping the brain out of the skull. Several artefacts that were crucial to the mummy's journey to the afterlife have also been included, as well as some picturesque painted coffins. Presiding over the entrance is a beautiful little statue of the jackal god, Anubis, the god of embalming who helped Isis turn her brother-husband Osiris into the first mummy.

SIGHTS – WEST BANK

The West Bank is a world away from the noise and bustle of Luxor town on the east bank. Taking a taxi across the bridge, 6km south of the centre, or crossing on the old ferry, you are immediately in the lush countryside, with bright green sugarcane fields along irrigation canals and clusters of colourful houses, all against the background of the desert and the Theban hills. Coming towards the end of the cultivated land you start to notice huge sandstone blocks lying in the middle of fields, gaping black holes in the rocks and giant sandstone forms on the edge of the cultivation below. Magnificent memorial temples were built on the flood plains here, where the illusion of the pharaoh's immortality could be perpetuated by the devotions of his priests and subjects, while his body and worldly wealth, and the bodies of his wives and children, were laid in splendidly decorated hidden tombs excavated in the hills.

From the New Kingdom onwards, the necropolis also supported a large living population of artisans, labourers, temple priests and guards, who devoted their lives to the construction and maintenance of this city of the dead, and who protected the tombs full of treasure from eager robbers. The artisans perfected the techniques of tomb building, decoration and concealment, and passed the secrets down through their families. They all built their tombs here.

Until a generation ago, villagers used tombs to shelter from the extremes of the desert climate and, until recently, many lived in houses built over the Tombs of the Nobles. These beautifully painted houses were a picturesque sight to anyone visiting the West Bank. However, over the past 100 years or so the Supreme Council of Antiquities has been trying to relocate the inhabitants of Al-Gurna. A new village was built for them by Hassan Fathy at New Gurna (see p274), but the local people refused to move.

In spring 2007 the governor began a move to demolish their houses, the bulldozers moved

NILE VALLEY: LUXOR

BEST OF THE WEST

Our pick of the top West Bank sights that are currently open:

BEST TOMBS

Valley of the Kings

- Tuthmosis III (p264)
- Amenhotep II (p263)
- Horemheb (p263)

Valley of the Queens

- Amunherkhepshef (p273)

Tombs of the Nobles

- Nakht (p269)
- Sennofer (p270)
- Ramose (p270)

Deir al-Medina

- Sennedjem (p272)

BEST MEMORIAL TEMPLES

- Deir al-Bahri (Hatshepsut; p267)
- Medinat Habu (Ramses III; p273)
- Ramesseum (Ramses II; p270)
- Seti I (p258)

onto the hillside and families were moved to a huge new village of small breeze-block houses 8km north of the Valley of the Kings, as part of the city governor's master plan to make Luxor the largest open-air museum in the world. While some families say they are happy with the new facilities, many others say they miss their cooler, large mudbrick houses, the community spirit they enjoyed and, above all, being close to their work (public transport is only slowly becoming available). Others, including some archaeologists, have expressed concern that increased visitor numbers may actually threaten the monuments, and have questioned the Council of Antiquities ability to properly monitor such a large open-air museum.

What to Bring

Above all, bring plenty of water (though it is available at many of the sights) and a sun hat. Small change for baksheesh is much needed too, as guardians rely on tips to augment their pathetic salaries – a few Egyptian pounds

should be enough for them to either leave you in peace, or to open a door or reflect light on a particularly beautiful painting. A torch (flashlight) can come in handy.

Tickets

It is planned that every site will have its own visitors centre and ticket office, but at the time of writing the **Antiquities Inspectorate ticket office** (Map p254; main road, 3km inland from ferry landing; ☺ 6am-5pm), near Medinat Habu, still provided all tickets except for the Temple at Deir al-Bahri, the Assasif tombs (available at Deir al-Bahri ticket office), the Valley of the Kings and the Valley of the Queens. Check there first to see which tickets are available, and which tombs are open. All sites are officially open from 6am to 5pm. Photography is not permitted in any tombs and guards may confiscate film or memory cards.

Tickets at the ticket office are valid only for the day of purchase and no refunds are given. Prices (adult/student):

Dra Abu'l Naga (Roy & Shuroy) E£15/10
Deir al-Medina Temple & Tombs (except Peshedu) E£30/15
Medinat Habu (Temple of Ramses III) E£30/15
Ramesseum E£35/20
Temple of Merenptah E£15/10
Temple of Seti I E£30/15
Tomb of Ay (Western Valley) E£25/15
Tomb of Peshedu (Deir al-Medina) E£15/10
Tombs of the Nobles E£15/10 to E£30/10 per group of tombs

Colossi of Memnon

The two faceless **Colossi of Memnon** (Map p254) that rise majestically about 18m from the plain are the first monuments tourists see when they visit the West Bank. The enthroned figures have kept a lonely vigil over the changing landscape, and few visitors have any idea that these giants were only a tiny element of what was once the largest temple built in Egypt, Amenhotep III's memorial temple, believed to have covered an area larger than Karnak.

The pharaoh's memorial temple has now all but disappeared. It was built largely of mudbrick on the flood plain of the Nile, where it was flooded every year. The walls simply dissolved after it was abandoned and no longer maintained, and later pharaohs used

TACKLING THE WEST BANK

Little shade can be found at the archaeological remains on the West Bank and the midday heat is intense from April to October. Early morning visits are therefore ideal, but that is unfortunately also when most tour groups visit the Temple of Deir al-Bahri or the Valley of the Kings. In winter you can visit the two sites without the crowds during the afternoon, but they become very hot. This is our advice for getting the most out of your time on the West Bank:

■ The Valley of the Kings and Hatshepsut's temple may be the highlights of any visit to the West Bank, but they are also the most overrun by tour groups. Visit those sights early morning or late afternoon, and spend more time visiting some of the other splendid monuments, which see less visitors, like the Tombs of the Nobles, the Ramesseum, the Temple of Seti I or Medinat Habu.

■ Don't try to see it all in a day. Many small hotels have opened on the West Bank, offering good-value, comfortable accommodation, free from the hassles of the East Bank.

■ Keep tomb-viewing time to a minimum: visiting deep-cut tombs is exhausting and the air in some is far from fresh. Twenty minutes is ample time for most, bearing in mind that the humidity created by the breath of so many visitors creates a fungus that destroys the ancient pigments.

■ Take breaks: sipping a cold drink within view of a temple can be as sublime an experience as seeing your first tomb.

With all this in mind, here are some itineraries for those with limited time. The one- and two-day plans need a brisk pace and assume you have some sort of a vehicle.

■ One day: go via the Colossi of Memnon on the way to the Valley of the Kings. See some tombs, then spend an hour at Deir al-Bahri. Have lunch near the Tombs of the Nobles, after which you can visit a few tombs in that area for an hour. Late afternoon spend an hour at Medinat Habu.

■ Two days: the above at a slower pace, seeing more tombs, taking longer breaks and adding the Ramesseum.

■ Three days: spread out the previous offerings, walking along the mountain path from the Valley of the Kings to Deir al-Bahri; adding the Temple of Merenptah and its fascinating museum and the Temple of Seti I; horse riding through the fields from Al-Gezira to the desert at sunset.

■ Four days or more: take things at a leisurely pace; add the tombs at Deir al-Medina and Assasif, and some other Tombs of the Nobles; revisit the Valley of the Kings. Definitely take a sunset horse or camel ride. Drink tea and chat with villagers.

the stones for their monuments. Some tiny parts of the temple remain and more is being uncovered by excavation; the colossi are the only large-scale elements to have survived.

The magnificent colossi, each cut from a single block of stone and weighing 1000 tonnes, were already a great tourist attraction during Graeco-Roman times, when the statues were attributed to Memnon, the legendary African king who was slain by Achilles during the Trojan War. The Greeks and Romans considered it good luck to hear the whistling sound emitted by the northern statue at sunrise, which they believed to be the cry of Memnon greeting his mother Eos, the goddess of dawn. She in turn would weep tears of dew for his untimely death. All this was probably due to a crack in the colossus' upper body, which appeared after the 27 BC earthquake. As the heat of the morning sun baked the dew-soaked stone, sand particles would break off and resonate inside the cracks in the structure. After Septimus Severus (193–211 AD) repaired the statue in the 3rd century AD, Memnon's plaintive greeting was heard no more.

The temple was filled with thousands of statues (including the huge dyad of Amenhotep III and his wife Tiy that now dominates the central court of the Egyptian Museum in

Cairo), most of which were later dragged off by other pharaohs. A stele, also now in the Egyptian Museum, describes the temple as being built from 'white sandstone, with gold throughout, a floor covered with silver, and doors covered with electrum'. Other statues and fragments of wall reliefs can be seen at the nearby Temple of Merenptah.

The colossi are just off the road, before you reach the Antiquities Inspectorate ticket office, and are usually being snapped and filmed by an army of tourists. A new archaeological project is salvaging what remains of the temple.

Temple of Merenptah

Almost directly behind Amenhotep's temple lie the remains of the **Temple of Merenptah** (Map p254; adult/student E£15/10), who succeeded his father Ramses II in 1213 BC and ruled for 10 years. In the 19th century, the 'Israel Stele', now in the Egyptian Museum in Cairo, was found here, which is the only known Egyptian text to mention 'Israel' (which Merenptah claimed to have defeated).

The Swiss Institute in Egypt has done considerable work here, uncovering the temple's original plan and a large number of statues and reliefs. At the small **museum** near the entrance, the history of the temple is illustrated with text, plans and finds from excavations, a great help to understand the little that remains of the building. In a covered storage area east of the sacred lake are the statues found on the site, including 12 jackal-headed sphinxes, some of which retain their original colours. Merenptah pilfered these, and many other statues and large stone blocks, from Amenhotep III's temple nearby, often scratching out the latter's cartouche and replacing it with his own. Two display rooms in the centre of the temple house the reliefs of Merenptah with various gods that once stood atop the temple pylons (ask the caretaker to unlock them).

Temple of Seti I

At the northern end of the Theban necropolis lies the **Temple of Seti I** (Map p254). Seti I, who also built the superbly decorated temple at Abydos (see p233) and Karnak's magnificent hypostyle hall, died before this memorial temple was finished, so it was completed by his son Ramses II. The temple sees few visitors, despite its picturesque location near a palm grove and recent restoration after being severely damaged by floods in 1994.

The entrance is through a small door in the northeast corner of the reconstructed fortresslike enclosure wall. The first and second pylons and the court are in ruins, but recent excavations have revealed the foundations of the pharaoh's palace, just south of the court. The earliest found example of a palace within a memorial temple, its plan is similar to the better-preserved palace at the memorial temple of Ramses III at Medinat Habu. The walls of the columned portico at the west facade of the temple, and those of the hypostyle court beyond it, contain some superbly executed reliefs. Off the hypostyle are six shrines and to the south is a small chapel dedicated to Seti's father, Ramses I, who died before he could build his own mortuary temple.

Carter's House

Surrounded by a garden on what is otherwise a barren hill, where the road from Deir al-Bahri to the Valley of the Kings meets the road from Seti I's temple, stands the domed **house** (Map p254; admission free; ☉ 6am-5pm) where Howard Carter lived during his search for Tutankhamun's tomb (see p262). The house has been decorated with pictures and tools of the excavation. A cafe is expected to open shortly, making this a peaceful place to stop for a refreshment.

Valley of the Kings

Once called the Great Necropolis of Millions of Years of Pharaoh, or the Place of Truth, the **Valley of the Kings** (Wadi Biban al-Muluk; Map p260; www .thebanmappingproject.com; adult/student for 3 tombs excl Ramses VI, Ay & Tutankhamun E£80/40, Tomb of Ay available from the Antiquities Inspectorate office near Medinat Habu E£25/15, Tomb of Ramses VI E£50/25, Tomb of Tutankhamun E£100/60) has 63 magnificent royal tombs from the New Kingdom period (1550–1069 BC), all very different from each other. The West Bank had been the site of royal burials from the First Intermediate Period (2160–2025 BC) onwards. At least three 11th-dynasty rulers built their tombs near the modern village of Taref, northeast of the Valley of the Kings. The 18th-dynasty pharaohs, however, chose the isolated valley dominated by the pyramid-shaped mountain peak of Al-Qurn (The Horn). The secluded site enclosed by steep cliffs was easy to guard and, when seen from the Theban plain, appears to be the site of

TOMB BUILDING   *Dr Joann Fletcher*

Tombs were initially created to differentiate the burials of the elite from the people whose bodies were placed directly into the desert. By about 3100 BC the mound of sand heaped over these elite graves was replaced by a more permanent structure of mudbrick, whose characteristic bench shape is known as a 'mastaba' after the Arabic word for bench.

As stone replaced mudbrick, the addition of further levels to increase height gave birth to the pyramid, whose first incarnation at Saqqara is also the world's oldest monumental structure. Its stepped sides soon evolved into the more familiar smooth-sided structure, of which the Pyramids of Giza are the most famous examples.

It was only when the power of the monarchy broke down at the end of the Old Kingdom that the afterlife became increasingly accessible to those outside the royal family, and as officials became increasingly independent they began to opt for burial in their home towns. Yet the narrow stretches of fertile land that make up much of the Nile Valley generally left little room for grand superstructures, so an alternative type of tomb developed, cut tunnel-fashion into the cliffs that border the valley and which also proved more resilient against robbery. Most were built on the west side of the river, the traditional place of burial where the sun was seen to sink down into the underworld each evening.

These simple rock-cut tombs consisting of a single chamber gradually developed into more elaborate structures complete with an open courtyard, offering chapel and entrance facade carved out of the rock with a shaft leading down into an undecorated burial chamber. The most impressive rock-cut tombs were those built for the pharaohs of the New Kingdom (1550–1069 BC), who relocated the royal burial ground south to the remote valley now known as the Valley of the Kings. New evidence suggests that the first tomb in the valley may have been built for Amenhotep I (1525–1504 BC; KV 39). The tomb intended for his successor, Tuthmosis I (KV 20), demonstrated a radical departure from tradition: the offering chapel that was once part of the tomb's layout was built as a separate structure some distance away in an attempt to preserve the tomb's secret location. The tombs themselves were designed to resemble the underworld, with a long, inclined rock-hewn corridor descending into either an antechamber or a series of sometimes pillared halls, and ending in the burial chamber.

The tomb builders lived in their own village of Deir al-Medina and worked in relays. The duration of the ancient week was 10 days (eight days on, two days off) and the men tended to spend the nights of their working week at a small camp located on the pass leading from Deir al-Medina to the eastern part of the Valley of the Kings. Then they spent their two days off at home with their families.

Once the tomb walls were created, decoration could then be added; this dealt almost exclusively with the afterlife and the pharaoh's existence in it. The tombs were decorated with texts from the Book of the Dead and with colourful scenes to help guide the pharaoh on his or her journey through the afterlife. The Book of the Dead is the collective modern name for a range of works that deal with the sun god's nightly journey through the darkness of the underworld, the realm of Osiris and home of the dead. The Egyptians believed that the underworld was traversed each night by Ra, and it was the aim of the dead to secure passage on his sacred barque to travel with him for eternity.

the setting sun, associated with the afterlife by ancient Egyptians.

The tombs have suffered great damage from treasure hunters, floods and, in recent years, from mass tourism: carbon dioxide, friction and humidity produced by the average of 2.8g of sweat left by each visitor have affected the reliefs and the pigments of the wall paintings. The Department of Antiquities has installed dehumidifiers and glass screens in the worst-affected tombs, and introduced a rotation system for opening some tombs to the public while restoring others. Each tomb has a number that represents the order in which it was discovered. KV (short for Kings Valley) 1 belongs to Ramses VII; it has been open since Greek and Roman times, and was mentioned in the *Description de l'Egypte*, dating from the late 18th century. KV 62 – Tutankhamun's famous tomb, which was discovered by Howard

Carter in 1922 – was until recently the last one to be discovered, but in 2006 KV 63 was discovered, with a few empty sarcophagus. Lighting in the tombs was being installed at the time of writing so visitors will be able to visit at night, thus avoiding the heat of the day. Three replica tombs are planned in the near future: the tomb of Tutankhamun, Seti I and Nefertari (in the Valley of the Queens; see p273).

The large car park leads to an air-conditioned **visitors centre** (off Map p260; ☾ 6am-4pm winter, 6am-5pm summer), part of the site-management plan of the Theban Mapping Project, with a model of the Valley, a movie about Carter's discovery of the Tomb of Tutankhamun and computers offering information to individual travellers.

The road into the Valley of the Kings is a gradual, dry, hot climb, so be prepared if you are riding a bicycle. A rest house is being built near the visitors centre, and mineral water, soft drinks, ice creams and snacks are available from the stalls at the tourist bazaar near the entrance. A *tuf-tuf* (a little electrical train) ferries visitors between the visitors centre and the tombs (it can be hot during summer). The ride costs E£10. It's worth having a torch to illuminate badly lit areas.

Most of the tombs described here are usually open to visitors and are listed in the order that they are found when entering the site. If you want to avoid the inevitable crowds that tour buses bring to the tombs, head for those outside the entrance area.

Extra tickets for the tombs of Tutankhamun (adult/student E£100/50) and Ramses VI (adult/student E£50/25) are on sale at the second ticket office where the *tuf-tuf* arrives. The tomb of Ay (KV 23) also has its own ticket (E£25/15), from the ticket office near Medinat Habu.

TOMB OF RAMSES VII (KV 1)
Up a small wadi near the main entrance is the small, unfinished **tomb of Ramses VII** (1136–1129 BC; Map p260). Only 44.3m long – short for a royal tomb because of Ramses' sudden death – it consists of a corridor, a burial chamber and an unfinished third chamber. His architects hastily widened what was to have been the tomb's second corridor, making it a burial chamber, and the pharaoh was laid to rest in a pit covered with a sarcophagus lid. Niches for Canopic jars are carved into the pit's sides, a

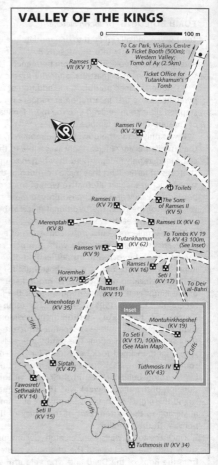

VALLEY OF THE KINGS

0 ——————— 100 m

feature unique to this tomb. Walls on the corridor leading to the chamber are decorated with fairly well preserved excerpts from the Book of Caverns and the Opening of the Mouth ritual, while the burial chamber is decorated with passages from the Book of the Earth.

TOMB OF RAMSES IV (KV 2)
The **tomb of Ramses IV** (Map p260) was already known in Ptolemaic times, evident from the graffiti on the walls dating back to 278 BC. Ramses IV (1153–1147 BC) died before the tomb was completed. The paintings in the burial chamber have deteriorated, but there is a wonderful image of the goddess Nut, stretched across the blue ceiling, and it is the only tomb to contain the text of the Book

of Nut, with a description of the daily path taken by the sun every day. The red granite sarcophagus, though empty, is one of the largest in the valley. The discovery of an ancient plan of the tomb on papyrus (now in the Turin Museum) shows the sarcophagus was originally enclosed by four large shrines similar to those in Tutankhamun's tomb (p262). The mummy of Ramses IV was later reburied in the Tomb of Amenhotep II (KV 35), and is now in the Egyptian Museum in Cairo.

TOMB OF RAMSES IX (KV 6)

Opposite Ramses II (right) is the most visited tomb in the valley, the **Tomb of Ramses IX** (1126–1108 BC; Map p260), with a wide entrance, a long sloping corridor, a large antechamber decorated with the animals, serpents and demons from the Book of the Dead, and then a pillared hall and short hallway before the burial chamber. On either side of the gate on the rear wall are two figures of Iunmutef priests, both dressed in priestly panther-skin robes and sporting a ceremonial side lock. The walls of the burial chamber feature the Book of Amduat, the Book of Caverns and the Book of the Earth; the Book of the Heavens is represented on the ceiling. Although unfinished it was the last tomb in the valley to have so much of its decoration completed, and the paintings are relatively well preserved. A number of wooden statues of the pharaoh and the gods were salvaged and taken to the British Museum in the 19th century, although the pharaoh's mummy had already been re-

moved in antiquity and reburied as part of the Deir al-Bahri cache.

TOMB OF RAMSES II (KV 7)

As befits the burial place of one of Egypt's longest-reigning pharaohs (67 years, from 1279 to 1213 BC), KV 7 (Map p260) is one of the biggest tombs in the valley. However, flash floods destroyed much of what must have been spectacular decoration, and left the rooms full of debris, so it is unlikely to open anytime soon. Based on the decorative scheme in his father Seti I's superb tomb, the walls of Ramses II's tomb would once have been just as brightly coloured, featuring scenes from the Litany of Ra, Book of Gates, the Book of the Dead and other sacred texts. In one of the side chambers off the burial chamber is a statue of Osiris similar to one found by Dr Kent Weeks in KV 5 (see boxed text, below), giving him yet more evidence for his theory that KV5 belongs to the many sons of Ramses.

Excavations have shown that Ramses II, following his father Seti I, had his sarcophagus made from alabaster, although his mummy was eventually buried in a wooden coffin in the Deir al-Bahri tomb cache; it's now in the Egyptian Museum in Cairo.

TOMB OF MERENPTAH (KV 8)

Ramses II lived for so long that 12 of his sons died before he did, so it was finally his 13th son Merenptah (1213–1203 BC) who succeeded him in his 60s. The second-largest tomb in the valley, **Merenptah's tomb** (Map p260)

THE GREATEST FIND SINCE TUTANKHAMUN

In May 1995, American archaeologist Dr Kent Weeks discovered the largest tomb in Egypt, believed to be the burial place of the many sons of Ramses II. It was immediately hailed as the greatest find since that of Tutankhamun, or as one London newspaper put it: 'The Mummy of all Tombs'.

In 1987 Weeks located the entrance to tomb KV 5, which Howard Carter had uncovered but dismissed as destroyed. Weeks' team cleared the entrance chambers, finding pottery, fragments of sarcophagi and wall decorations, which led him to believe it was the Tomb of the Sons of Ramses II.

Then in 1995 Weeks unearthed a doorway leading to an incredible 121 chambers and corridors, making the tomb many times larger and more complex than any other found in Egypt. Clearing the debris from this unique and enormous tomb is a painstaking and dangerous task. Not only does every bucketful have to be sifted for fragments of pottery, bones and reliefs, but major engineering work has to be done to shore up the tomb's structure. Progress is slow but Weeks speculates that it has as many as 150 chambers, and each year brings discovery of more chambers or new corridors. Progress of the excavation can be followed on the excellent website www.thebanmappingproject.com, or in Weeks' fascinating account in his book *The Lost Tomb*.

has been open since antiquity and has its share of Greek and Coptic graffiti. Floods have damaged the lower part of the walls of the long tunnel-like tomb, but the upper parts have well-preserved reliefs. As you enter the first long corridor, on the left is a striking relief of Merenptah with the god Ra-Horakhty followed by the Litany of Ra. Further down, the corridors are decorated with the Book of the Dead, the Book of Gates and the Book of Amduat. Beyond a shaft is a false burial chamber with two pillars decorated with the Book of Gates. Although much of the decoration in the burial chamber has faded, it remains an impressive room, with a sunken floor and brick niches on the front and rear walls.

The pharaoh was originally buried inside four stone sarcophagi, three of granite (the lid of the second still in situ, with an effigy of Merenptah on top) and the fourth, innermost, sarcophagus of alabaster. In a rare mistake by ancient Egyptian engineers, the outer sarcophagus did not fit through the tomb entrance and its gates had to be hacked away. Merenptah's mummy was removed in antiquity and was found in Amenhotep II's tomb (KV 35); it's now displayed in the Egyptian Museum.

TOMB OF TUTANKHAMUN (KV 62)

The story of the celebrated discovery of the famous tomb and all the fabulous treasures it contained far outshines its actual appearance, and it is one of the least impressive tombs in the valley. **Tutankhamun's tomb** (Map p260) is small and bears all the signs of a rather hasty completion and inglorious burial. The son of Akhenaten by a minor wife, he ruled briefly (1336–1327 BC) and died young, with no great battles or buildings to his credit, so there was little time to build a tomb.

The Egyptologist Howard Carter slaved away for six seasons in the valley, excavating thousands of tonnes of sand and rubble from possible sites, believing that he would find the tomb of Tutankhamun intact with all its treasures. Even his benefactor Lord Carnarvon lost hope, and with his funding about to be cut off Carter made one last attempt at the only unexplored area that was left, which was covered by workers' huts just under the already excavated Tomb of Ramses VI.

The first step was found on 4 November 1922, and on 5 November the rest of the steps and a sealed doorway came to light.

Carter wired Lord Carnarvon to join him in Egypt immediately for the opening of what he believed was the completely intact Tomb of Tutankhamun.

The tomb's priceless cache of treasures, although it had been partially robbed twice in antiquity, vindicated Carter's dream beyond even his wildest imaginings. Four chambers were found crammed with jewellery, furniture, statues, chariots, musical instruments, weapons, boxes, jars and food – even the later discovery that many had been stuffed haphazardly into the wrong boxes by necropolis officials 'tidying up' after the ancient robberies does not detract from their dazzling wealth. Some archaeologists believe that Tutankhamun was perhaps buried with all the regalia of the unpopular Amarna royal line, as some of it is inscribed with the names of his father Akhenaten and the mysterious Smenkhkare (1388–1336 BC), who some Egyptologists believe was Nefertiti ruling as pharaoh.

Most of the treasure is in the Cairo Museum, a few pieces are in Luxor Museum, and only Tutankhamun's mummy in its gilded wooden coffin is in situ. The burial chamber walls are decorated by chubby figures of the pharaoh before the gods, painted against a yellow-gold background. The wall at the foot end of the sarcophagus shows scenes of the pharaoh's funeral; the 12 squatting apes from the Book of Amduat, representing the 12 hours of the night, are featured on the opposite wall.

TOMB OF RAMSES VI (KV 9)

The intactness of Tutankhamun's tomb is largely thanks to the existence of the **tomb of Ramses VI** (Map p260). The tomb was actually begun for the ephemeral Ramses V (1147–1143 BC) and continued by Ramses VI (1143–1136 BC), with both pharaohs apparently buried here; the names and titles of Ramses V still appear in the first half of the tomb. Following the tomb's ransacking a mere 20 years after burial, the mummies of both Ramses V and Ramses VI were moved to Amenhotep II's tomb where they were found in 1898 and taken to Cairo.

Although the tomb's plastering was not finished, its fine decoration is well preserved, with an emphasis on astronomical scenes and texts. Extracts from the Book of Gates and the Book of Caverns cover the entrance corridor. These continue into the midsection of the tomb and well room, with the addition of the Book of the Heavens. Nearer the burial chamber the walls are decorated with extracts from the Book of Amduat. The burial chamber is beautifully decorated, with a superb double image of Nut framing the Book of the day and Book of the Night on the ceiling. This nocturnal landscape in black and gold shows the sky goddess swallowing the sun each evening to give birth to it each morning in an endless cycle of new life designed to revive the souls of the dead pharaohs. The walls of the chamber are filled with fine images of Ramses VI with various deities, as well as scenes from the Book of the Earth, with scenes that show the sun god's progress through the night, the gods who help him and the forces of darkness trying to stop him reaching the dawn; look out for the decapitated, kneeling figures of the sun god's enemies around the base of the chamber walls and the black-coloured executioners who turn the decapitated bodies upside down to render them as helpless as possible. On the beautifully decorated right wall of the burial chamber also try to pick out the ithyphallic figure (the one with a noticeable erection); the lines and symbols surrounding him represent a water clock. Plenty of Greek graffiti, from around AD 150, can be seen on the upper portions of the chamber.

TOMB OF RAMSES III (KV 11)

Ramses III (1184–1153 BC), the last of Egypt's warrior pharaohs, built one of the longest tombs in the Valley of the Kings. His **tomb** (Map p260), started but abandoned by Sethnakht (1186–1184 BC), is 125m long, much of it still beautifully decorated with colourful painted sunken reliefs featuring the traditional ritual texts (Litany of Ra, Book of Gates etc) and Ramses before the gods. Unusually here are the secular scenes, in the small side rooms of the entrance corridor, showing foreign tribute such as highly detailed pottery imported from the Aegean, the royal armoury, boats and, in the last of these side chambers, the blind harpists that gave the tomb one of its alternative names: 'Tomb of the Harpers'.

In the chamber beyond is an aborted tunnel where ancient builders ran into the neighbouring tomb. They shifted the axis of the tomb to the west and built a corridor leading to a pillared hall, with walls decorated with scenes from the Book of Gates. There is also ancient graffiti on the rear right pillar describing the reburial of the pharaoh during the 21st dynasty (1069–945 BC). The remainder of the tomb is only partially excavated and structurally weak.

Ramses III's sarcophagus is in the Louvre in Paris, its detailed lid is in the Fitzwilliam Museum in Cambridge and his mummy – found in the Deir al-Bahri cache – was the model for Boris Karloff's character in the 1930s film *The Mummy*. The mummy is now in Cairo's Egyptian Museum.

TOMB OF HOREMHEB (KV 57)

This **tomb** (Map p260) was discovered filled with ransacked pieces of the royal funerary equipment, including a number of wooden figurines that were taken to the Egyptian Museum in Cairo. Horemheb (1323–1295 BC), a general and military strongman under Tutankhamun, brought stability after the turmoil of Akhenaten's reign. He had already built a lavish tomb in Saqqara, but abandoned it for this tomb. The various stages of decoration in the burial chamber give a fascinating glimpse into the process of tomb decoration.

From the entrance, a steep flight of steps and an equally steep passage leads to a well shaft decorated with superb figures of Horemheb before the gods. Notice Hathor's blue-and-black striped wig and the lotus crown of the young god Nefertum, all executed against a grey-blue background. This leads to an undecorated pillared hall, and an antechamber. The six-pillared burial chamber decorated with part of the Book of Gates remains partially unfinished, showing how the decoration was applied by following a grid system in red ink over which the figures were drawn in black prior to their carving and painting. The pharaoh's empty red granite sarcophagus carved with protective figures of goddesses with outstretched wings remains in the tomb; his mummy is missing.

TOMB OF AMENHOTEP II (KV 35)

One of the deepest structures in the valley, this **tomb** (Map p260) has more than 90 steps down to a modern gangway, built over a deep pit designed to protect the inner, lower chambers from both thieves (which it failed to do) and the water from flash floods.

NILE VALLEY: LUXOR

Stars cover the entire ceiling in the huge burial chamber and the walls feature, as if on a giant painted scroll, text from the Book of Amduat. While most figures are of the same sticklike proportions as in the tomb of Amenhotep's father and predecessor Tuthmosis III, this is the first royal tomb in the valley to also show figures of more rounded proportions, as on the pillars in the burial chamber showing the pharaoh before Osiris, Hathor and Anubis. The burial chamber is also unique for its double level; the top level was filled with pillars, the bottom contained the sarcophagus.

Although thieves breached the tomb in antiquity, Amenhotep's (1427–1400 BC) mummy was restored by the priests, put back in his sarcophagus with a garland of flowers around his neck, and buried with 13 other royal mummies in the two side rooms, including Tuthmosis IV (1400–1390 BC), Amenhotep III, Merenptah, Ramses IV, V and VI and Seti II (1200–1194 BC), most of which are now at the Egyptian Museum.

TOMB OF TUTHMOSIS III (KV 34)

Hidden in the hills between high limestone cliffs and reached only via a steep staircase that crosses an even steeper ravine, this **tomb** (Map p260) demonstrates the lengths to which the ancient pharaohs went to thwart the cunning of the ancient thieves.

Tuthmosis III (1479–1425 BC), an innovator in many fields whose military exploits and stature has earned him the description 'the Napoleon of ancient Egypt', was one of the first to build his tomb in the Valley of the Kings. As secrecy was his utmost concern, he chose the most inaccessible spot and designed his burial place with a series of passages at haphazard angles and fake doors to mislead or catch potential robbers.

The shaft, now traversed by a narrow gangway, leads to an antechamber supported by two pillars, the walls of which are adorned with a list of more than 700 gods and demigods. As the earliest tomb in the valley to be painted, the walls appear to be simply giant versions of funerary papyri, with scenes populated by stick men. The burial chamber has curved walls and is oval in shape; it contains the pharaoh's quartzite sarcophagus that is carved in the shape of a cartouche.

Tuthmosis III's mummy, which shows he was a short man of around 1.5m, was one of

those found in the Deir al-Bahri cache and is now in the Egyptian Museum in Cairo.

TOMB OF SIPTAH (KV 47)

Discovered in 1905, the **tomb of Siptah** (1194–1188 BC; Map p260) was never completed but the upper corridors are nonetheless covered in fine paintings. The tomb's entrance is decorated with the sun disc, and figures of Maat, the goddess of truth, kneel on each side of the doorway. The corridor beyond features colourful scenes from the Litany of Ra with an elaborately dressed Siptah before various gods, including Ra-Horakhty (an aspect of the sun god Ra combined with Horakhty, a form of Horus the sky god). There are further scenes from the Book of Amduat, and figures of Anubis, after which the tomb remains undecorated. The tomb was reused in the Third Intermediate Period. But Siptah's mummy was moved for safety to the well-hidden tomb of Amenhotep II by 10th-century priests. There he lay with many other royal mummies, Seti II, Amenhotep III and Ramses IV, V and VI among them.

TOMB OF TAWOSRET/SETHNAKHT (KV 14)

Tawosret was the wife of Seti II and after his successor Siptah died she took power herself (1188–1186 BC). Egyptologists think she began the **tomb** (Map p260) for herself and Seti II but their burials were removed by her successor, the equally short-lived Sethnakht (1186–1184 BC), who completed the tomb by adding a second burial chamber for himself. The change of ownership can be seen in the tomb's decoration; the upper corridors show the queen, accompanied by her stepson Siptah, in the presence of the gods. Siptah's cartouche was later replaced by Seti II's. But in the lower corridors and burial chambers images of Tawosret have been plastered over by images or cartouches of Sethnakht.

The tomb has been open since antiquity and although the decoration has worn off in some parts, the colour and state of the burial chambers remains good, with astronomical ceiling decorations and images of Tawosret and Sethnakht with the gods. The final scene from the Book of Caverns adorning Tawosret's burial chamber is particularly impressive, showing the sun god as a ram-headed figure stretching out his wings to emerge from the darkness of the underworld. The two anonymous mummies found in the

Amenhotep II cache may belong to Tawosret and Sethnakht.

TOMB OF SETI II (KV 15)

Adjacent to Tawosret's/Sethnakht's tomb is a smaller **tomb** (Map p260) where it seems Sethnakht buried Seti II (1200–1194 BC) after turfing him out of KV 14. Open since ancient times judging by the many examples of classical graffiti, the tomb's entrance area has some finely carved relief scenes, although the rest was quickly finished off in paint alone. The walls have extracts from the Litany of Ra, the Book of Gates and the Book of Amduat and, unusually, on the walls of the well room, images of the type of funerary objects used in pharaohs' tombs, such as golden statuettes of the pharaoh within a shrine (just like the actual examples found in Tutankhamun's tomb, which are now in the Egyptian Museum in Cairo). The sky goddess Nut stretches out across the ceiling of the burial chamber. Seti II's mummy was found in the Amenhotep II tomb cache.

TOMB OF RAMSES I (KV 16)

Ramses I (1295–1294 BC) only ruled for a year so his **tomb** (Map p260) is a very simple affair. Originally called Paramessu, he was a military officer and vizier under Horemheb, and was later chosen as Horemheb's successor. His tomb has the shortest entrance corridor leading to a single, almost square, burial chamber, containing the pharaoh's open pink granite sarcophagus. Only the chamber is superbly decorated, very similar to Horemheb's tomb (KV 57), with extracts from the Book of Gates, as well as scenes of the pharaoh in the presence of the gods, eg the pharaoh kneeling between the jackal-headed 'Soul of Nekhen' and the falcon-headed 'Soul of Pe', symbolising Upper and Lower Egypt.

TOMB OF SETI I (KV 17)

As befits such an important pharaoh, Seti I (1294–1279 BC), son and heir of Ramses I, has one of the longest (137m) and most beautiful **tombs** (Map p260) in the valley. Its discovery by Giovanni Belzoni in 1817 generated almost the same interest as the discovery of Tutankhamun's tomb a century later. As the first royal tomb to be decorated throughout, its raised, painted relief scenes are similar to those found in the pharaoh's beautifully decorated temple at Abydos (p233) and the quality

of the work is superb. Two of its painted reliefs showing Seti with Hathor are now in the Louvre in Paris and Florence's Archaeological Museum, while Seti's alabaster sarcophagus was bought by Sir John Soane, and it can still be seen in the basement of his London house-turned-museum. Seti's mummy was found in the Deir al-Bahri mummy cache, and is now in the Egyptian Museum.

The first part of the pharaoh's burial chamber is decorated with texts from the Litany of Ra, and the Book of Amduat, with the Book of Gates featured in the first pillared hall. The walls of the burial chamber are adorned with the Book of Gates, the Book of Amduat and the Book of the Divine Cow, while the ceiling depicts vivid astronomical scenes featuring the various constellations.

The tomb is indefinitely closed for restoration (ongoing since 1991), but soon there should be a replica of this tomb including the missing parts that are now held in foreign museums (www.factum-arte.com/eng /con servacion/seti/seti_en.asp).

TOMB OF MONTUHIRKOPSHEF (KV 19)

The **tomb** (Map p260) of Ramses IX's son (c 1000 BC), whose name translates as 'The Arm of Montu is Strong', is located high up in the valley's eastern wall and seems to have been constructed for an earlier prince. It is small and unfinished but has fine paintings and few visitors. Its entrance corridor is adorned with life-size reliefs of various gods, including Osiris, Ptah, Thoth and Khonsu, receiving offerings from the young prince, who is shown in all his finery, wearing exquisitely pleated fine linen robes and a blue-and-gold 'sidelock of youth' attached to his black wig – not to mention his gorgeous make-up (as worn by both men and women in ancient Egypt).

TOMB OF TUTHMOSIS IV (KV 43)

The **tomb** (Map p260) of Tuthmosis IV (1400–1390 BC) is one of the largest and deepest tombs constructed during the 18th dynasty. It is also the first in which paint was applied over a yellow background, beginning a tradition that was continued in many tombs. Discovered in 1903 by Howard Carter (who less than 20 years later would find the tomb of Tuthmosis IV's great-grandson Tutankhamun), it is accessed by two long flights of steps leading down and around to the burial chamber where there's an enormous sarcophagus covered in

THE RETURN OF THE MUMMY

In 1881 the Egypt's antiquities authority made the greatest mummy find in history: the mummies of 40 pharaohs, queens and nobles, just south of Deir al-Bahri in tomb No 320. It seems that 21st-dynasty priests had them moved as a protection against tomb robbers to this communal grave, after 934 BC. The mummies included those of Amenhotep I, Tuthmosis I, II and III, Seti I and Ramses II and III, many of which are now on display at the Egyptian Museum in Cairo. Their removal from the tomb and procession down to the Nile, from where they were taken by barge to Cairo, was accompanied by the eerie sound of black-clad village women ululating to give a royal send-off to the remains. The episode makes for one of the most stunning scenes in Shadi Abdel Salam's 1969 epic *Al-Mummia* (The Mummy), one of the most beautiful films made in Egypt.

However, the cache had already been found a decade earlier by the Abdel Rassoul family from Gurna, who were making a tidy sum by selling contents from it. Mummies, coffins, sumptuous jewellery and other artefacts made their way to Europe and North America. One of the mummies ended up in a small museum in Niagara Falls, Canada, until the late 1990s, when the crossed arms and excellent state of the body were recognised by an Egyptologist as signs of possible royalty. When the museum closed in 1999, the mummy was acquired by the Michael Carlos Museum in Atlanta. CT scans, X-rays, radiocarbon dating and computer imaging attempted to identify the mummy, and although they could only suggest that it was from later than the Ramesside period, an uncanny resemblance to the mummified faces of Seti I and Ramses II was seized upon by some Egyptologists as proof that this was the missing mummy of Ramses I.

As a gesture of goodwill, the museum returned the mummy to Egypt in 2003, where it was welcomed home, at the Egyptian Museum, with songs and ceremonies. Later the mummy was taken to Luxor where, as befitting a pharaoh in the afterlife, it made the final stage of its journey under sail.

hieroglyphs. The walls of the well shaft and antechamber are decorated with painted scenes of Tuthmosis before the gods, and the figures of the goddess Hathor are particularly fetching in a range of beautiful dresses decorated with beaded designs.

On the left (south) wall of the antechamber there is a patch of ancient Egyptian graffiti dating back to 1315 BC, written by government official Maya and his assistant Djehutymose and referring to their inspection and restoration of Tuthmosis IV's burial on the orders of Horemheb following the first wave of robbery in the eighth year of Horemheb's reign, some 67 years after Tuthmosis IV died.

After the tomb was ransacked a second time it was decided it would be safer to rebury Tuthmosis' mummy in the tomb of his father Amenhotep II (KV 35). Tuthmosis' mummy, with pierced ears, is now displayed in the Egyptian Museum in Cairo.

TOMB OF AY (KV 23)

Although he succeeded Tutankhamun, Ay's brief reign from 1327 to 1323 BC tends to be associated with the earlier Amarna period and Akhenaten (some Egyptologists have suggested he could have been the father of Akhenaten's wife Nefertiti). Ay abandoned a grandiose tomb in Amarna (see p227) and took over another in the West Valley here. The West Valley played an important part in the Amarna story, as it was chosen as a new burial ground by Amenhotep III for his own enormous tomb (KV 22, partway up the valley), and his son and successor Akhenaten also began a tomb here, before he relocated the capital at Amarna, where he was eventually buried. It seems Tutankhamun too planned to be buried in the West Valley, until his early death saw his successor Ay 'switch' tombs. Tutankhamun was buried in a tomb (KV 62) in the traditional section of the Valley of the Kings, while Ay himself took over the tomb Tutankhamun had begun at the head of the West Valley. The **tomb** (Map p254) is accessed by a dirt road leading off from the car park at the Valley of the Kings that winds for almost 2km up a desolate valley past sheer rock cliffs. Recapturing the atmosphere (and silence) once found in the neighbouring Valley of the Kings makes it worth the visit.

Although only the burial chamber is decorated, it is noted for its scenes of Ay hippopotamus hunting and fishing in the marshes (scenes usually found in the tombs of nobles not royalty) and for a wall featuring 12 baboons, representing the 12 hours of the night, after which the West Valley or Wadi al-Gurud (Valley of the Monkeys) is named. This is so similar to the decoration in Tutankhamun's tomb that archaeologists suspect the same artists worked on both tombs. Although Ay's mummy has never been identified, his smashed-up sarcophagus has been restored for tourists.

Walk to Deir al-Bahri

The steep walk out of the Valley of the Kings and over the surrounding mountains down to Hatshepsut's mortuary temple at Deir al-Bahri guarantees great views over the ancient sites, fertile green fields, the Nile and across to the town of Luxor. The path starts beside KV 17, the tomb of Seti I, where the path is marked. The first few hundred metres are very steep, but then the path levels out. Ascending the path, souvenir hawkers and would-be guides will offer their services, but the route is pretty obvious. Walk along the ridge, taking a left where the path forks. After passing the police post on the left, you can see Deir al-Bahri down the sheer cliff to your right. Stick to the path that follows the ridge, ignoring the steep trail that plunges down the cliff face. Once you've almost completed a full circle you will find yourself at the ticket office to the temple.

The walk takes about 50 minutes, allowing time to enjoy the views and the amazing lunarlike landscape. Ideally the walk should be done in winter. In summer start very early as it gets incredibly hot up there. At all times take a hat, sun cream, lots of water and some decent walking shoes. If you tire on the ascent there are sometimes donkeys available to carry you to the top.

Deir al-Bahri

The eyes first focus on the dramatic rugged limestone cliffs that rise nearly 300m above the desert plain, a monument made by nature, only to realize that at the foot of all this immense beauty lies a man-made monument even more extraordinary, the dazzling **Temple of Hatshepsut** (Map p267; adult/student E£30/15; ◷ 6am-5pm). The almost modern-looking temple blends in beautifully with the cliffs from which it is partly cut, a marriage made in heaven.

Continuous excavation and restoration since 1891 have revealed one of ancient Egypt's finest monuments, but it must have been even more stunning in the days of Hatshepsut (1473–1458 BC), when it was ap-

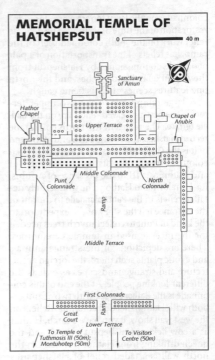

proached by a grand sphinx-lined causeway instead of today's noisy tourist bazaar, and when the court was a garden planted with a variety of exotic trees and perfumed plants – the ancient Egyptians called it *Djeser-djeseru* (Most Holy of Holies). If the design seems unusual, note that it did in fact feature all the things a memorial temple usually had, including the rising central axis and a three-part plan, but had to be adapted to the chosen site almost exactly on the same line with the Temple of Amun at Karnak, and near an older shrine to the goddess Hathor.

The temple was vandalised over the centuries: Tuthmosis III removed his stepmother's name whenever he could (see boxed text, p269), Akhenaten removed all references to Amun, and the early Christians turned it into a monastery, Deir al-Bahri (Monastery of the North), and defaced the pagan reliefs.

Deir al-Bahri has been designated as one of the hottest places on earth, so an early morning visit is advisable, also because the reliefs are best seen in the low sunlight. The complex is entered via the **great court**, where original ancient tree roots are still visible. The colonnades on the **lower terrace** were closed for restoration at the time of writing. The delicate relief work on the south colonnade, left of the ramp, has reliefs of the transportation of a pair of obelisks commissioned by Hatshepsut from the Aswan quarries to Thebes, and the north one features scenes of birds being caught.

A large ramp leads to the two upper terraces. The best-preserved reliefs are on the **middle terrace**. The reliefs in the north colonnade record Hatshepsut's divine birth and at the end of it is the **Chapel of Anubis**, with well-preserved colourful reliefs of a disfigured Hatshepsut and Tuthmosis III in the presence of Anubis, Ra-Horakhty and Hathor. The wonderfully detailed reliefs in the **Punt Colonnade** to the left of the entrance tell the story of the expedition to the Land of Punt to collect myrrh trees needed for the incense used in temple ceremonies. There are depictions of the strange animals and exotic plants seen there, the foreign architecture and strange landscapes as well as the different-looking people. At the end of this colonnade is the **Hathor Chapel**, with two chambers both with Hathor-headed columns. Reliefs on the west wall show, if you have a torch, Hathor as a cow licking Hatshepsut's hand, and the queen drinking from Hathor's udder. On the north wall is a faded relief of Hatshepsut's soldiers in naval dress in the goddess' honour. Beyond the pillared halls is a three-roomed chapel cut into the rock, now closed to the public, with reliefs of the queen in front of the deities, and with a small figure behind the door of Senenmut, the temple's architect and some believe Hatshepsut's lover.

The **upper terrace**, restored by a Polish-Egyptian team over the last 25 years, had 24 colossal Osiris statues, some of which are left. The central pink granite doorway leads into the Sanctuary of Amun, which is hewn out of the cliff.

On the south side of Hatshepsut's temple lie the remains of the **Temple of Montuhotep**, built for the founder of the 11th dynasty and one of the oldest temples so far discovered in Thebes, and the **Temple of Tuthmosis III**, Hatshepsut's successor. Both are in ruins.

Assasif Tombs

This group of tombs, located near Deir al-Bahri, belongs to 18th-dynasty nobles, and 25th- and 26th-dynasty nobles under the Nubian pharaohs. The area is under excavation by archaeologists, but of the many tombs

here only some are open to the public, including the **Tombs of Kheruef** and of **Mntophaat** (Map p254; adult/student E£30/15; ☉ 6am-4.30pm Oct-Apr, to 5pm May-Sep) and of **Pabasa** (Map p254; adult/student E£25/15; ☉ 6am-5pm); tickets are available at the ticket office of the Deir al-Bahri Temple. The tomb of Kheruef is the largest 18th-dynasty noble's tomb here in Thebes, and it has some of the finest examples of New Kingdom relief, but unfortunately the tomb is in poor condition. The tomb of Pabasa, a 26th-dynasty priest, has wonderful scenes of agriculture, hunting and fishing.

Dra Abu'l Naga

Hidden in the desert cliffs north of Deir al-Bahri lies yet another necropolis, **Dra Abu'l Naga** (Map p254), with 114 tombs of rulers and officials, most dating from the 17th dynasty to the late period (about 1550–500 BC). The area has been extensively plundered but two tombs escaped with their paintings mostly intact.

The **Tomb of Roy** (No 234; Map p254), a royal scribe and steward of Horemheb, is small with scenes of funerary offerings and agriculture, and a beautifully painted ceiling. A few metres away, the T-shaped **Tomb of Shuroy** (No 13; Map p254) contains some finely executed, but in places heavily damaged, paintings of Shuroy and his wife making offerings to the gods and a funeral procession led by a child mourner.

Tombs of the Nobles

The **tombs** (Map p254; ☉ 6am-5pm) in this area are some of the best, but least visited, attractions on the West Bank. Nestled in the foothills opposite the Ramesseum, there are more than 400 tombs belonging to nobles from the 6th dynasty to the Graeco-Roman period. Where the pharaohs decorated their tombs with cryptic passages from the Book of the Dead to guide them through the afterlife, the nobles, intent on letting the good life continue after their death, decorated their tombs with wonderfully detailed scenes of their daily lives.

Only 15 or so tombs are open to the public – they are divided into five groups and each requires a separate ticket from the Antiquities Inspectorate ticket office near Medinat Habu.

TOMBS OF KHONSU, USERHET & BENIA (NOS 31, 51 & 343)

Khonsu was First Prophet in the memorial temple of Tuthmosis III (1479–1425 BC).

FEMALE PHARAOHS

Pharaoh was an exclusively male title and in early Egyptian history there was no word for a Queen regent, but records show there actually were a few female pharaohs. From early dynastic times it seemed common practice that on the death of the pharaoh, if his heir was too young to rule or there was no heir, his wife, often also his stepsister or sister, would be appointed regent. It's not clear if this role was limited to a regency, or if they were created pharaoh, but what is sure is that they were often buried with all the honours reserved for a pharaoh.

The first queen to have ruled independently is thought to have been Merneith, who was the wife of the 1st-dynasty Pharaoh Djer (c 3000 BC), and mother of Den who ruled after her. Her name was found on a clay seal impression with all the names of the early kings, and she was buried with full royal honours at Abydos. Almost every dynasty had a woman who ruled for a short while under the title of 'King's Mother'. The 12th-dynasty Sobeknofru, daughter of Amenemhat III and wife and half-sister of Amenhotep IV, is thought to have ruled Egypt from 1799 to 1795 BC, and her titles included Female Horus, King of Upper and Lower Egypt, and Daughter of Ra.

Hatshepsut is the most famous of Egypt's female pharaohs. When her husband and half-brother Tuthmosis II died in 1479 BC, Hatshepsut became regent with her stepson Tuthmosis III. Later with the support of the Amun priesthood, she declared herself pharaoh, and her rule (1473–1458 BC) marked a period of peace and internal growth for Egypt. Sometimes she is shown in the regalia of the male pharaoh, including the false beard, sometimes she is clearly female. When Tuthmosis III finally took control in 1458 BC, he ordered all reference to her be wiped from Egyptian history, so her mummy has never been found, and her name and images were almost all erased.

Nefertiti, wife of the rebel pharaoh Akhenaten, was clearly involved in her husband's policies and is often depicted wearing kingly regalia. Some believe that she was in fact the mysterious Smenkhkare, known to have ruled for a few years after Akhenaten's death in 1336 BC. After Seti II died, his wife Tawosret, became co-regent with her stepson Siptah, and later proclaimed herself pharaoh (1188 to 1186 BC). She was buried in the Valley of the Kings (see p264).

About 1000 years later Cleopatra came to the throne at the age of 17, in 51 BC. It's thought that she first ruled jointly with her father Ptolemy XII and, after his death, with her younger brother Ptolemy XIII. To keep Egypt independent, she allied herself with the Roman Julius Caesar, whom she married and whose son she bore. After Caesar's death, she famously married another powerful Roman, Marc Antony, and fell with him to the might of Augustus Caesar.

Inside the first chamber of **Khonsu's tomb** (Map p254) are scenes of the Montu festival at Armant, about 20km south of Luxor, the festival of the god of war over which he presided. The sacred barque with the shrine of Montu is towed by two smaller boats. The gods Osiris and Anubis are also honoured, and in many scenes Khonsu is seen making offerings to them. The ceiling is adorned with images of ducks flying around and nests with eggs.

The **Tomb of Benia**, just behind that of Khonsu, is even more colourful. Benia was a boarder in the Royal Nursery and chief treasurer also during the reign of Tuthmosis III. There are many scenes of offering tables piled high with food and drinks overlooked by Benia, and sometimes by his parents. In a niche cut out at the end of the tomb is a statue

of Benia flanked by his parents, all three with destroyed faces.

TOMBS OF MENNA & NAKHT (NOS 52 & 69)
The beautiful and highly colourful wall paintings in the **Tomb of Menna** and the **Tomb of Nakht** (Map p254) emphasise rural life in 18th-dynasty Egypt. Menna was an estate inspector and Nakht was an astronomer of Amun. Their finely detailed tombs show scenes of farming, hunting, fishing and feasting. The Tomb of Nakht has a small museum area in its first chamber. Although this tomb is so small that only a handful of visitors are able to squeeze in at a time, the walls have some of the best-known examples of Egyptian tomb paintings. The paintings include some familiar scenes such as that of the three musicians, which shows up on a million souvenir

T-shirts, posters, postcards – and of course papyrus paintings.

TOMBS OF RAMOSE, USERHET & KHAEMHET (NOS 55, 56 & 57)

The **Tomb of Ramose** (Map p254), a governor of Thebes under Amenhotep III and Akhenaten, is fascinating because it is one of the few monuments dating from that time, a period of transition between two different forms of religious worship. The exquisite paintings and low reliefs show scenes in two different styles from the reigns of both pharaohs, depicting Ramose's funeral and his relationship with Akhenaten. The tomb was never actually finished, perhaps because Ramose died prematurely.

Next door is the **Tomb of Userhet** (Map p254), one of Amenhotep II's royal scribes, with fine wall paintings depicting daily life. Userhet is shown presenting gifts to Amenhotep II; there's a barber cutting hair on another wall; other scenes include men making wine and people hunting gazelles from a chariot.

The **Tomb of Khaemhet** (Map p254), Amenhotep III's royal inspector of the granaries and court scribe, has scenes on the walls showing Khaemhet making offerings, the pharaoh depicted as a sphinx, the funeral ritual of Osiris and images of daily country life as well as official business.

TOMBS OF SENNOFER & REKHMIRE (NOS 96 & 100)

The most interesting parts of the **Tomb of Sennofer** (Map p254), overseer of the Garden of Amun under Amenhotep II, are deep underground in the main chamber. The ceiling there is covered with clear paintings of grapes and vines, while most of the vivid scenes on the surrounding walls and columns depict Sennofer and the different women in his life, including his wife and daughters and his wet nurse. The guard usually has a kerosene lamp, but bring a torch just in case.

The **Tomb of Rekhmire**, governor under Tuthmosis III and Amenhotep II, is one of the best preserved in the area. In the first chamber, to the extreme left, are scenes of Rekhmire receiving gifts from foreign lands. The panther and giraffe are gifts from Nubia; the elephant, horses and chariot from Syria; and the expensive vases from Crete and the Aegean Islands. Beyond this is the unusual chapel. The west wall shows Rekhmire in-

specting the production of metals, bricks, jewellery, leather, furniture and statuary, while the east wall shows banquet scenes, complete with lyrics (the female harpist sings 'Put perfume on the hair of the goddess Maat').

TOMBS OF NEFERRONPET, DHUTMOSI & NEFERSEKHERU (NOS 178, 295 & 296)

Discovered in 1915, the highlight of the brightly painted **Tomb of Neferronpet** (also known as Kenro; Map p254), the scribe of the treasury under Ramses II, is the scene showing Kenro overseeing the weighing of gold at the treasury. Next door, the **Tomb of Nefersekheru**, an officer of the treasury during the same period, is similar in style and content to his neighbours. The ceiling is decorated with a huge variety of elaborate geometric patterns. From this long tomb, a small passage leads into the **Tomb of Dhutmosi**, which is in poor condition.

The Ramesseum

Ramses II called his massive **memorial temple** (Map p271; ☺ 6am-5pm) 'the Temple of Millions of Years of User-Maat-Ra'; classical visitors called it the Tomb of Ozymandias; and Jean-François Champollion, who deciphered hieroglyphics, called it the Ramesseum. Like other memorial temples it was part of Ramses II's funerary complex. His tomb was built deep in the hills, but his memorial temple was on the edge of the cultivation on a canal that connected with the Nile and with other memorial temples.

Unlike the well-preserved structures that Ramses II built at Karnak and Abu Simbel, his memorial temple has not survived the times very well. It is mostly in ruins, despite extensive restoration – a fact that would no doubt disappoint Ramses II. The Ramesseum is famous for the scattered remains of fallen statues that inspired the English poet Shelley's poem 'Ozymandias', using the undeniable fact of Ramses' mortality to ridicule his aspirations to immortality.

I met a traveller from an antique land
Who said: Two vast and trunkless legs of stone
Stand in the desert...Near them, on the sand,
Half sunk, a shattered visage lies, whose frown,
And wrinkled lip, and sneer of cold command,

THE RAMESSEUM

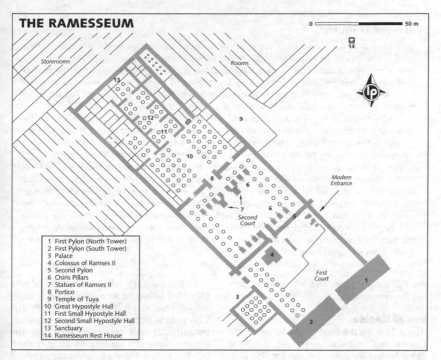

0 —————— 50 m

Storerooms

Rooms

Modern Entrance

Second Court

First Court

1 First Pylon (North Tower)
2 First Pylon (South Tower)
3 Palace
4 Colossus of Ramses II
5 Second Pylon
6 Osiris Pillars
7 Statues of Ramses II
8 Portico
9 Temple of Tuya
10 Great Hypostyle Hall
11 First Small Hypostyle Hall
12 Second Small Hypostyle Hall
13 Sanctuary
14 Ramesseum Rest House

Tell that its sculptor well those pas
sions read
Which yet survive, stamped on these
life-less things,
The hand that mocked them, and the
heart that fed:
And on the pedestal these words –
appear:
'My name is Ozymandias, king of
kings:
Look on my works, ye Mighty, and
despair!'
Nothing beside remains. Round the
decay
Of that colossal wreck, boundless and
bare
The lone and level sands stretch far
away.

Although it is more elaborate than other
temples, the fairly orthodox layout of the
Ramesseum, consisting of two courts, hypostyle hall, sanctuary, accompanying chambers and storerooms, is uncommon in that
the usual rectangular floor plan was altered
to incorporate an older, smaller temple –

that of Ramses II's mother, Tuya – off to
one side.

The entrance is through a doorway in the
northeast corner of the enclosure wall, which
leads into the second court, where one should
turn left to the **first pylon**. The **first** and **second
pylons** measure more than 60m across and
feature reliefs of Ramses' military exploits,
particularly his battles against the Hittites.
Through the first pylon are the ruins of the
huge **first court**, including the double colonnade that fronted the royal **palace**.

Near the western stairs is part of the **Colossus
of Ramses II**, the Ozymandias of Shelley's poem,
lying somewhat forlornly on the ground,
where it once stood 17.5m tall. The head of
another granite **statue of Ramses II**, one of a
pair, lies in the **second court**. Twenty-nine of
the original 48 columns of the **great hypostyle
hall** are still standing. In the smaller hall behind it, the roof, which features astronomical
hieroglyphs, is still in place.

There is a rest house-restaurant next to
the temple that is called, not surprisingly,
Ramesseum Rest House. It is a great place to
relax and have a cool drink or something to

OLD GURNA (QURNA)

Until early 2007 the entrances to some of the Tombs of the Nobles were hidden among the mudbrick houses of the village of Sheikh Abd al-Gurna. The houses, many with painted facades, were a picturesque sight against the backdrop of the Theban Hills and were often the sites of happy encounters between villager and visitor. As part of a government project to establish Luxor as the largest open-air museum in the world, the houses were demolished and almost all residents relocated to a new village north of the Valley of the Kings.

The UK-based Friends of Qurna Discovery, with the agreement of the Supreme Council for Antiquities, has fought to preserve and restore two properties – all that are left from Old Gurna – for **Qurna Discovery** (Map p254; www.qurna.org; Gurna; ☯ 8am-4.30pm, closed Fri). These will be devoted to explaining the history of life on the hillside in the last millennia. The *zawiya* (a family meeting, ceremonial and religious building) houses the permanent collection of the early-19th-century British artist Robert Hay's drawings of Gurna. These finely detailed works depict the ancient mudbrick structures and a way of life that are now lost, plus the famous tomb houses. The adjoining Daramalli house will be used to exhibit household objects and agricultural implements to show how Gurnawi families lived and worked. Historic photos will show the village and its residents as recorded from the 1850s to the 1950s. Entry to Qurna Discovery is free, but donations are much needed to complete the exhibits and to provide for the guards. More details from www.qurna.org.

eat. You can leave your bike here while exploring the surroundings.

Deir al-Medina

About 1km off the road to the Valley of the Queens and up a short, steep paved road is **Deir al-Medina** (Monastery of the Town; Map p254; adult/student E£30/15, extra ticket for Tomb of Peshedu adult/student E£15/10; ☯ 6am-5pm), named after a temple that was occupied by early Christian monks. Near the temple is the ruined settlement, the Workmen's Village. Many of the workers and artists who created the royal tombs lived and were buried here. Some of the small tombs have exquisite reliefs, making it worth a visit.

TEMPLE

The small Ptolemaic-era temple of Deir al-Medina is set just north of the Workmen's Village, along a rocky track. Measuring only 10m x 15m, it was built between 221 and 116 BC, the last of a series of earlier temples built on the same site. It was dedicated to Hathor, the goddess of pleasure and love, and to Maat, the goddess of truth and personification of cosmic order.

WORKMEN'S VILLAGE

Archaeologists have uncovered more than 70 houses in this village and many tombs, the most beautiful of which are now open to the public.

The beautifully adorned **Tomb of Inherka** (No 359) belonged to a 19th-dynasty servant who worked in the Place of Truth, the Valley of the Kings. The one-room tomb has magnificent wall paintings, including the famous scene of a cat (representing the sun god Ra) killing a snake (representing the evil serpent Apophis) under a sacred tree, on the left wall. There are also beautiful domestic scenes of Inherka with his wife and children. Right next to it is the **Tomb of Sennedjem** (No 1), a stunningly decorated 19th-dynasty tomb that contains two small chambers and some equally exquisite paintings. Sennedjem was an artist who lived during the reigns of Seti I and Ramses II and it seems he ensured his own tomb was as finely decorated as those of his masters. Due to the popularity and small size of both these tombs, only 10 people at a time are allowed inside; it's likely you'll find yourself in a queue.

While you wait, take a look at the 19th-dynasty **Tomb of Peshedu** (No 3) just up the slope from the other two tombs. Peshedu was another servant in the Place of Truth and can be seen in the burial chamber praying under a palm tree beside a lake. Close by is the **Tomb of Ipy** (No 217), a sculptor during the reign of Ramses II. Here scenes of everyday life eclipse the usual emphasis on ritual, with scenes of farming and hunting, and a depiction of Ipy's house in its flower- and fruit-filled garden.

Valley of the Queens

There are at least 75 tombs in the **Valley of the Queens** (Biban al-Harim; Map p254; adult/student E£35/20). They belonged to queens of the 19th and 20th dynasties and other members of the royal families, including princesses and the Ramesside princes. Only two were open at the time of writing, and the Tomb of Nefertari is closed for the foreseeable future but a replica will be built soon.

TOMB OF NEFERTARI (NO 66)

Hailed as the finest tomb in the Theban necropolis – and in all of Egypt for that matter – the **Tomb of Nefertari** (Map p254) was completely restored and reopened, but closed again until further notice.

Nefertari was one of the five wives of Ramses II, the New Kingdom pharaoh known for his colossal monuments, but the tomb he built for his favourite queen is a shrine to her beauty and, without doubt, an exquisite labour of love. Every centimetre of the walls in the tomb's three chambers and connecting corridors is adorned with colourful scenes of Nefertari in the company of the gods and with associated text from the Book of the Dead nearby. Invariably, the 'Most Beautiful of Them', as Nefertari was known, is depicted wearing a divinely transparent white gown and a golden headdress featuring two long feathers extending from the back of a vulture. The ceiling of the tomb is festooned with golden stars.

Like most of the tombs in the Valley of the Kings, this one had been plundered by the time it was discovered by archaeologists. Only a few fragments of the queen's pink granite sarcophagus remained, and of her mummified body, only traces of her knees were left.

TOMB OF AMUNHERKHEPSHEF (NO 55)

The valley's showpiece now is the **Tomb of Amunherkhepshef** (Map p254), with beautiful, well-preserved reliefs. Amunherkhepshef, the son of Ramses III, was still in his teens when he died. On the walls of the tomb's vestibule, Ramses holds his son's hand to introduce him to the gods that will help him on his journey to the afterlife. Amunherkhepshef can be seen wearing a kilt and sandals, with the sidelock of hair typical of young boys.

The mummified five-month-old foetus on display in a glass case in the tomb is the subject of many an inventive story, among them the suggestion that the foetus was aborted by Amunherkhepshef's mother when she heard of his death. It was actually found by Italian excavators in a valley to the south of the Valley of the Queens.

TOMB OF KHAEMWASET (NO 44)

Another of Ramses III's sons, Khaemwaset died young, although Egyptologists have little information about his age or cause of death. His **tomb** (Map p254) is filled with well-preserved, brightly coloured reliefs. Like that of his brother Amunherkhepshef, Khaemwaset's tomb follows a linear plan, and is decorated with scenes of the pharaoh introducing this deceased son to the various gods, and scenes from the Book of the Dead. The vestibule has an astronomical ceiling, showing Ramses III in full ceremonial dress, followed by his son wearing a tunic and the sidelock of hair signifying his youth.

TOMB OF TITI (NO 52)

Egyptologists are not sure which Ramesside pharaoh Titi was married to, however, in her **tomb** (Map p254) she is referred to as the royal wife, royal mother and royal daughter. Some archaeologists believe she was the wife of Ramses III, and her tomb is in many ways similar to those of Khaemwaset and Amunherkhepshef, who were perhaps her sons. The tomb consists of a corridor leading to a square chapel, off which is the burial chamber and two other small rooms. The paintings are faded but you can still make out a winged Maat kneeling on the left-hand side of the corridor, and the queen before Toth, Ptah and the four sons of Horus opposite. Inside the burial chamber are a series of animal guardians: a jackal and lion, two monkeys and a monkey with a bow.

Medinat Habu

Ramses III's magnificent memorial temple of **Medinat Habu** (Map p274; tickets from the Antiquities Inspectorate Office nearby; ☉ 6am-5pm) is perhaps one of the most underrated sites on the West Bank. With the Theban mountains as a backdrop and the sleepy village of Kom Lolah in front, it is a wonderful place to spend a few hours late afternoon.

The site was one of the first places in Thebes to be closely associated with the local god Amun. Although the complex is most famous for the funerary temple built by

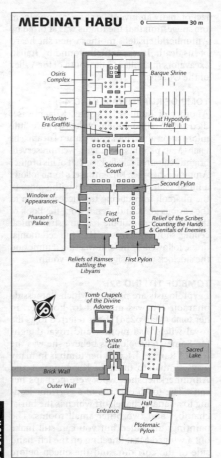

MEDINAT HABU 0 ⊏▭▭ 30 m

- Osiris Complex
- Barque Shrine
- Victorian-Era Graffiti
- Great Hypostyle Hall
- Second Court
- Second Pylon
- Window of Appearances
- Pharaoh's Palace
- First Court
- Relief of the Scribes Counting the Hands & Genitals of Enemies
- Reliefs of Ramses Battling the Libyans
- First Pylon
- Tomb Chapels of the Divine Adorers
- Syrian Gate
- Sacred Lake
- Brick Wall
- Outer Wall
- Entrance
- Hall
- Ptolemaic Pylon

Ramses III, Hatshepsut and Tuthmosis III also constructed buildings here. They were later added to and altered by a succession of rulers through to the Ptolemies. At Medinat Habu's height there were temples, storage rooms, workshops, administrative buildings and accommodation for priests and officials. It was the centre of the economic life of Thebes for centuries and was still inhabited as late as the 9th century AD, when a plague was thought to have decimated the town. You can still see the mudbrick remains of the medieval town that gave the site its name (medina means 'town' or 'city') on top of the enclosure walls.

The original **Temple of Amun**, which was built by Hatshepsut and Tuthmosis III, was later completely overshadowed by the enormous

Funerary Temple of Ramses III, the dominant feature of Medinat Habu.

Ramses III was inspired in the construction of his shrine by the Ramesseum of his illustrious forebear, Ramses II. His own temple and the smaller one dedicated to Amun are both enclosed within the massive outer walls of the complex.

Also just inside, to the left of the gate, are the **Tomb Chapels of the Divine Adorers**, which were built for the principal priestesses of Amun. Outside the eastern gate, one of only two entrances, was a landing quay for a canal that once connected Medinat Habu with the Nile.

You enter the site through the unique **Syrian Gate**, a large two-storey building modelled after an Asiatic fortress. If you follow the wall to the left you will find a staircase leading to the upper floors. There is not much to see in the rooms but you'll get some great views out across the village in front of the temple and over the fields to the south.

The well-preserved **first pylon** marks the front of the temple proper. Ramses III is portrayed in its reliefs as the victor in several wars. Most famous are the fine **reliefs** of his victory over the Libyans (who you can recognise by their long robes, sidelocks and beards). There is also a gruesome scene of scribes tallying the number of enemies killed by counting severed hands and genitals.

To the left of the **first court** are the remains of the **Pharaoh's Palace**; the three rooms at the rear were for the royal harem. There is a window between the first court and the Pharaoh's Palace known as the **Window of Appearances**, which allowed the pharaoh to show himself to his subjects.

The reliefs of the **second pylon** feature Ramses III presenting prisoners of war to Amun and his vulture-goddess wife, Mut. Colonnades and reliefs surround the **second court**, depicting various religious ceremonies.

If you have time to wander about the extensive ruins around the funerary temple you will see the remains of an **early Christian basilica** as well as a small **sacred lake**.

New Gurna

Hassan Fathy's mudbrick village of **New Gurna** (Map p254; www.fathyheritage.com) lies just past the railway track on the main road from the ferry to the Antiquities Inspectorate ticket office. It was built to rehouse the inhabitants of Old

Gurna, who lived on and around the Tombs of the Nobles (see boxed text, p272).

The buildings were stunning, with Hassan Fathy's signature domes and vaults, thick mud-brick walls and natural ventilation, but Fathy would probably cry if he went back today – much of the village is in tatters, although the beautiful mudbrick mosque and theatre survive. Unesco has recognised the need to safeguard the village and is considering its next step.

Getting There & Around

Most tourists cross to the West Bank by bus or taxi via the bridge, about 7km south of town. But the river remains the quickest way to go. The *baladi* (municipal) ferry costs E£1 for foreigners and leaves from a dock in front of Luxor Temple. Small motor launches (locally called *lunches*) also leave from wherever they can find customers and will take you across for E£10 to E£20 for a small group.

On the West Bank, the taxi lot is near the ferry landing. Voices call out the destinations of *kabouts* (pick-up trucks). If you listen out for Qurna you'll be on the right road to the ticket office (50pt). Pick-ups run back and forth between the villages, so you can always flag one down on your way to one of the sites, although you will have to walk from the main road to the entrance, which, in the case of the Valley of the Kings or Queens is quite far. If you want to have an entire pick-up for yourself, it'll cost around E£10. The driver is likely to stick to his normal route.

To hire a private taxi for the day, expect to pay between E£150 and E£250 per day, depending on the season, the state of tourism and your bargaining skills. Past the taxi lot are bicycles for rent for E£15 per day.

Donkeys and camels with guides can also be rented at the landing, but it's safer to rent them from a recognised stable (see right).

For an idea of the distances involved, from the local ferry landing it is 3km straight ahead to the ticket office, past the Colossi of Memnon; 4km to the Valley of the Queens; and 8km to the Valley of the Kings.

ACTIVITIES
Ballooning

Hot-air ballooning to see the sun rise over the ancient monuments on the West Bank and the Theban mountains is a great way to start the day. Unfortunately, in April 2009 a hot-air balloon crashed after hitting a cellphone tower and several tourists were injured. At the time of writing only a limited number of hot-air balloons were allowed to fly, so you will need to book early. **Hod Hod Suleiman** (Map pp244–5; ☎ 237 0116; Sharia Omar Ali, off Sharia Televizyon), **Sky Cruise of Egypt** (☎ 237 6515; Sharia Khalid ibn al-Walid) and **Sindbad Balloons** (☎ 010 330 7708; www .sindbadballoons.com) all offer early morning flights at varying prices, often depending on how many people are taken on board. Expect to pay from €80 to €150 per person, although it should be possible to bargain, particularly out of season.

Donkey, Horse & Camel Rides

Riding a horse, a donkey or a camel through the fields and seeing the sunset behind the Theban hills is a wonderful thing to do. The boys at the local ferry dock on the West Bank offer donkey and camel rides for about E£30 to E£40 for an hour, but beware. There are many reports of women getting hassled, and of overcharging at the end. The West Bank hotels also offer camel trips, which include visits to nearby villages for a cup of tea, and donkey treks around the West Bank. These trips, which start at around 7am (sometimes 5am) and finish near lunchtime, cost a minimum of about E£50 per person.

A BETTER LIFE FOR HORSES & DONKEYS

ACE (Animal Care in Egypt; off Map pp244–5; ☎ 928 0727; in the UK 0044-1732 700 710; www.ace-egypt.org.uk; at the start of Sharia al-Habil, near traffic police; donations welcome; ☒ 8am–noon & 1-5pm) was opened in 2000 by a British-run charity to give free treatment for the working animals of Egyptians, particularly donkeys and horses, and it is today a great veterinary hospital and animal welfare centre seeing up to 200 animals a day. For those distressed by the state of the horses in Luxor streets, you may like to see what is done here. The centre also runs an education program receiving 80 local children a day, aiming to impart a love and care for animals. This is a great place to visit, and foreign children can spend the day at the centre to help care for the animals. Volunteers and donations are very welcome.

Excellent horses can be found at **Nobi's Arabian Horse Stables** (Map pp244–5; ☎ 231 0024, 010 504 8558; www.luxorstables.com; approx per hr E£30; ☼ 7am-sunset), which also provides riding hats, English saddles and insurance. Nobi also has 25 camels and as many donkeys at the same price, and organises longer horse riding and camping trips into the desert or a week from Luxor to Kom Ombo along the West Bank. Call ahead to book, and he can arrange a hassle-free transfer to make sure you arrive at the right place, as often taxi drivers will try and take you to a friend's stable instead. Around the corner is **Pharaoh's Stables** (Map pp244–5; ☎ 231 0015; ☼ 7am-sunset) with horses, donkeys and camels (all E£30 to E£35 per hour).

Felucca Rides

As elsewhere in Egypt, the nicest place to be late afternoon is on the Nile. Take a felucca from either bank, and sail for a few hours, catching the soft afternoon light and the sunset, cooling in the afternoon breeze and calming down after sightseeing. Felucca prices range from E£30 to E£50 per boat per hour, depending on your bargaining skills.

A popular felucca trip is upriver to Banana Island, a tiny isle dotted with palms about 5km from Luxor. The trip takes two to three hours. Plan it in such a way that you're on your way back in time to watch a brilliant Nile sunset from the boat. Some travellers have complained that the felucca captain has added money for 'admission' to the island; make sure you are clear about what is included in the price you agree on.

Seaplane

Legend of the Nile (☎ 012 385 8389, 010 192 4232; Sharia al-Marwa) organises trips by seaplane to Luxor, Aswan, Abydos and Dendara. It was grounded at the time of writing, but was hoping to start tours again soon (see p275).

Swimming

After a hot morning of tombs and temples, a dip in a pool can seem like heaven. Most of the bigger hotels and some of the budget places have swimming pools. The **Iberotel** (Map pp244–5; Sharia Khaled Ibn Walid) has a great pool on a pontoon on the Nile that can be used for E£50, as does the nearby Isis hotel for E£30. The St Joseph, Karnak, Windsor, Domina Inn Emilio and Arabesque hotels have small rooftop pools that you can use

for E£20. Rezeiky Camp's slightly larger pool is E£15.

TOURS

Because of the bargaining and hassle involved, some people may find independent travel challenging at times, and a day tour in an air-conditioned tour bus, taking in the main sights, might be just the thing. These tours offer a good introduction to the city.

Most small budget hotels aggressively promote their own tours. Some of these are better than others and there have been complaints from a number of travellers that they ended up seeing little more than papyrus shops and alabaster factories from a sweaty car with no air-con. If you do decide to take one of these tours, expect to pay about E£75 to E£100 per person.

Several of the more reliable travel agents are all next to each other, next door to the Old Winter Palace Hotel. All offer the same kind of tours, so you can easily compare the prices.

Aladin Tours (Map pp244–5; ☎ 237 2386, 010 601 6132; http://nefertitihotel.com/tours; Nefertiti Hotel, Sharia as-Sahbi) This very helpful travel agency, run by the young, energetic Aladin, organises sightseeing tours in Luxor and around as well as in the Western Desert, plus boat trips and ferry tickets to Sinai.

American Express (Map pp244–5; ☎ 237 8333; www .americanexpress.com/egypt; Corniche an-Nil, next to Old Winter Palace Hotel; ☼ 8am-8pm) Offers a large menu of tours in and around Luxor. Prices range from E£250 to E£400 per person for a half-day.

Jolley's Travel & Tours (Map pp244–5; ☎ 237 2262; www.jolleys.com; ☼ 9am-10pm) This reputable company, next to the Old Winter Palace Hotel, also runs day trips to the main sites.

Karnak Travel (Map pp244–5; ☎ 010 303 0048) Government-run travel agency that offers a range of classic good-value tours in and around Luxor, with English-speaking guides, at fixed prices. It's at the tourist office opposite the train station.

Luxor Parasol (Map pp244–5; ☎ 010 397 1570; Hotel Sheherazade ☎ 016 487 1506; www.luxorparasol.com) British expat Christine Soliman offers a service escorting individual female travellers on sightseeing and shopping trips around Luxor.

QEA Travel Agency (Map pp244–5; ☎ 231 1667; Al-Gezira) A different approach from this British-run agency that runs tailor-made tours in and around Luxor, as well as further afield to the Red Sea or the Western Desert. A percentage of its profits go towards charitable projects in Egypt.

Thomas Cook (Map pp244–5; ☎ 237 2402; www .thomascookegypt.com; ☼ 8am-8pm) Next to the Old

Winter Palace, offers an array of tours. Prices range from E£250 to E£400 per person for a half-day.

The Iberotel Luxor Hotel (see p281) organises day cruises from 7am to 7pm on the *Lotus Boat* to Dendara from US$60, including lunch, tea, guide and admission fees. The **Nefertiti Hotel** (Map pp244-5; ☎ 010 601 6132; www.nefertitihotel .com/tours; Sharia Sahbi) also organises day cruises to Dendara. **Min Travel** (☎ in Cairo 02-2632 5987; www.min-travel.com) organises felucca day trips to Dendara from US$32 per person.

FESTIVALS & EVENTS

The town's biggest traditional festival is the **Moulid of Abu al-Haggag**. One of Egypt's largest *moulid*s (saints' festivals), it is held in honour of Luxor's patron sheikh, Yousef Abu al-Haggag, a 12th-century Iraqi who settled in Luxor. The *moulid* takes place around the Mosque of Abu al-Haggag, the town's oldest mosque, which is built on top of the northeastern corner of Luxor Temple. It's a raucous five-day carnival that takes place in the third week before Ramadan. See boxed text, p252, for details of other *moulid*s.

In February each year a **marathon** (☎ 02-2260 6930, 012 214 8839; www.egyptianmarathon.com) is held on the West Bank. It begins at Deir al-Bahri and loops around the main antiquities sites before ending back where it began.

SLEEPING

Luxor has a wide range of hotels for all budgets. Most package-tour hotels are on the East Bank, and so are the shops, restaurants and the hectic town life. The West Bank is developing at a fast rate and is certainly no longer as rural as it once was. But it is still a tranquil place, where the pace of life is much slower and where evenings are more often than not blissfully quiet. The situation in Luxor at the time of writing was moving fast. The area between Luxor and Karnak Temples on the east bank was being cleared, while on the west bank huge areas of the Gezira waterfront and around the monuments were being demolished, with hotels and restaurants disappearing in the process. Some of the places we have recommended here will have disappeared by the time you get there, so it is worth checking before you go. Prices for many hotels drop considerably in summer; prepare to bargain.

At all costs avoid the hotel touts who may pounce on you as you get off the train or bus –

they will get a 25% to 40% commission for bringing you into the hotel, but that will be added to your bill. Many hotels in the budget and midrange bracket offer free or cheap transfers from the airport or train station, so to avoid touts and bargaining with taxi drivers call ahead and arrange to be picked up.

Budget

Luxor has a good selection of budget places. Many boast both roof gardens and washing machines. The budget hotels on the West Bank are particularly good value, much quieter and often offering a more authentic meeting with locals.

EAST BANK

Princess Hotel (Map pp244-5; ☎ 012 431 3699; www .princesshotelluxor.com; Sharia Ahmed Orabi, off Sharia Televizyon; s/d/tr with shared bathroom E£20/30/45, with shower in the room E£30/40/60; 🌀 🖳) This relative newcomer on the budget hotel scene has been recommended by many readers. The 17-room hotel has clean rooms, a washing machine for guest use, wi-fi, a rooftop terrace and a kitchen, but check the rooms first as sizes vary. The French-Egyptian owners are always around and are very helpful.

Fontana Hotel (Map pp244-5; ☎ 228 0663, 010 733 3238; www.fontanaluxorhotel.com; Sharia Radwan, off Sharia Televizyon; s/d/tr E£35/45/60, with shared bathroom E£25/30/45; 🌀) An old stalwart of the budget hotel scene, this 25-room hotel has clean rooms, a washing machine for guest use, a rooftop terrace and a kitchen. All bathrooms are large and really clean, and toilet paper and towels are provided. The owner Magdi Soliman is always ready to help, and readers have written in to tell us how friendly and helpful his staff were.

Venus Hotel (Map pp244-5; ☎ 237 2625, 012 171 3599; Sharia Yousef Hassan; s/d with fan E£30/45, with aircon E£50/70; 🖳) The 25 rooms at the Venus are quite noisy and shabby, but there is a fun atmosphere in the hotel, which is still popular with budget tours. All rooms have clean private bathrooms, and most have air-con. There is a great rooftop terrace and a lively bar (Stella beer E£12).

St Mina Hotel (Map pp244-5; ☎ 237 5409; fax 237 6568; off Sharia Ramses; s/d E£40/70, with shared bathroom E£30/55; 🌀) A friendly, family-run hotel, the St Mina doesn't have the aura of hustle that plagues so many of Luxor's budget hotels. Its 20 rooms are clean, with air-con or fans.

Anglo Hotel (Map pp244-5; ☎ 238 1679; fax 238 1679; Midan al-Mahatta; s/d/tr E£50/60/90; ⌨) Right next to the train station, so a bit noisy at times, but the spacious rooms are excellent value, clean and well maintained, with air-con, satellite TV, private bathroom and telephone. The bar in the basement is popular with locals.

Happy Land Hotel (Map pp244-5; ☎ 227 1828; www.luxorhappyland.com; Sharia Qamr; s/d/tr with fridge & air-con E£70/80/110, s/d with shared bathroom E£30/45; ⌨ ▢) The Happy Land, another backpackers' favourite, offers clean rooms and spotless bathrooms, as well as very friendly service, a copious breakfast with fruit and cornflakes and a rooftop terrace. Competition among Luxor's budget hotels is fierce, and the Happy Land comes out well almost every time, it doesn't need to send touts to the station! Bikes can be rented for E£10 per day, and wi-fi and laundry facilities are free. Mr Ibrahim tries his utmost to make everyone appreciate his town. It sells ISIC cards.

our pick **Nefertiti Hotel** (Map pp244-5; ☎ 237 2386; www.nefertitihotel.com; Sharia as-Sahabi, btwn Sharia Maabad al-Karnak & Sharia as-Souq; s/d/tr US$9/13/16; ⌨ ▢) Aladin as-Sahabi runs his family's hotel and the attached Aladin Tours travel agency (see p276) with great care, offering recently renovated, midrange facilities at budget prices. No wonder this hotel is popular with our readers: the rooms are simple but cosy, the small private bathrooms are spotless, the breakfast is good and served on the roof terrace, and the staff is super friendly. The new domed rooms on the rooftop terrace are decorated in local style. You can sunbathe on the rooftop and enjoy the jacuzzi or have a drink with views of the West Bank and Luxor Temple. The top-floor lounge has satellite TV, wi-fi, a pool table and a small gym. On Saturday and Wednesday nights there is a folkloric show with dinner (E£75), with dervish dancing and snake charming, at the rooftop restaurant.

Rezeiky Camp (Map pp244-5; ☎ 238 1334; www.rezeikycamp.com.eg; Sharia Maabad al-Karnak; campsite per person E£25, vehicle E£20, s/d with fan E£55/110, with air-con E£65/120; ⌨ ▢ ⌨) Rezeiky Camp is the only place to pitch a tent in town, but it is pleasant enough, with a pool on your doorstep. There is a large garden with a restaurant and bar, and internet access. The motel-style rooms are not nice enough to make up for the inconvenient location, but the place is popular with overland groups, so call ahead to make sure there is space.

WEST BANK

Habu Hotel (Map p254; ☎ 231 1611, 012 358 0242; Kom Lolah; s/d E£40/60) If you like character in a hotel, the Habu is for you. It's a mudbrick warren of small, vaulted rooms and has stunning views over the entrance to Medinat Habu temple complex and the mountains beyond. Go for one of the three domed 1st-floor terrace rooms, which are practically in the forecourt of Medinat Habu and have a large terrace with palm-reed furniture. The downstairs restaurant has dusty ceiling fans and great old tourist posters. The downside? The less welcome saggy beds, mosquitoes, somnolent staff and waterlogged bathrooms.

Al-Gezira Hotel (Map pp244-5; ☎ 231 0034; www.el-gezira.com; Gezira al-Bayrat; s/d/tr E£80/120/150; ⌨) Different in style, as it is in a modern building overlooking the lush and fertile agricultural land in the village of Gezira al-Bayrat, this hotel is very much a home away from home. It is actually home to quite a few archaeologists during the winter season, and the charming owners really make everyone feel welcome, so much so that the hotel is often full. The 11 cosy and homey rooms are pristine, all with private bathrooms, overlooking the lake or a branch of the Nile. Management and staff are friendly and efficient, and the upstairs rooftop restaurant, where breakfast is served, has great Nile views as well as cold beer (E£12) and good traditional Egyptian food.

Marsam Hotel (Map p254; ☎ 237 2403, 231 1603; www.luxor-westbank.com/marsam_e_az.htm; Gurna; s/d E£75/150, with shared bathroom E£50/100) Built for American archaeologists in the 1920s, the Marsam, formerly the Sheikh Ali Hotel, is the oldest on the West Bank. The hotel is charming with 30 simple rooms set around a lovely courtyard, with ceiling fans and traditional palm-reed beds. A delicious breakfast with home-baked bread is served in the garden. Atmospheric and quiet, and close to almost all the West Bank sights, it is still popular with archaeologists, so you need to book ahead, particularly during the dig season (roughly October to March).

Kareem Hotel (Map pp244-5; ☎ 231 3530, 010 184 2083; www.elhakim-lodges.net; Al-Gezira; s/d/tr E£100/140/160, 3-room flat per week E£1000; ⌨) Newly opened hotel with 12 simple but very clean rooms in a quiet residential area. The owner is young and helpful and keeps the place spotless. The hotel has little character otherwise but offers good value, and has a little garden and a splendid rooftop terrace with a restaurant where the owner's sister cooks dishes and where cool beers are served.

Midrange

Luxor has an ever-growing selection of midrange hotels on both banks, often catering to families. If you are looking for a hotel with character, then check out the small mudbrick, traditional-style hotels on the West Bank. The East Bank hotels are often slick, modern places, popular with budget and adventure tour groups. There are some excellent bargains in this category, with good facilities at attractive rates. Out of season some incredibly cheap packages can be found, including flights from the UK.

EAST BANK

Little Garden Hotel (Map pp244-5; ☎ 227 9090, 012 103 8441; www.littlegardenhotel.com; Sharia Radwan, off Sharia Televizyon; s/d/tr/ste €14/18/24/23; ✖ ▣) This small hotel in a neat villa is well managed, with friendly staff, 24-hour room service, good cotton mattresses, air-con, satellite TV and sparklingly clean private bathrooms. There is also a small garden courtyard and a rooftop restaurant serving Asian foods and *sheesha* (water pipe) but no alcohol. Free transfers from the train station.

New Pola Hotel (Map pp244-5; ☎ 236 5081; www.newpolahotel.com; Sharia Khalid ibn al-Walid; s/d US$20/30; ✖ ▣ ✖) Great views and a small rooftop pool make the New Pola an excellent bargain. The decor is kitsch but the 81 air-con rooms are spotless and come with minibars, satellite TV and private bathrooms; half also have Nile views. The staff is very friendly and many clients are return customers.

Mara House (Map pp244-5; ☎ 236 5081; www.egyptwithmara.com; Sharia Salahadin Ayyubi, off Sharia Salakhana; per person €30; ✖ ▣) Irish Mara wanted to open a home for travellers and seems to have succeeded with spacious rooms, all including a sitting area and clean bathroom. The house, in a real Egyptian neighbourhood right behind the train station, can be hard to find but call for instructions or a free transfer. Mara also runs Salahadeen (p282), a popular Egyptian restaurant where the food is served as it is in Egyptian homes.

Philippe Hotel (Map pp244-5; ☎ 237 2284, 012 922 0336; www.philippeluxorhotel.com; Sharia Dr Labib Habashi; s US$20-22, d US$29-36; ✖ ✖) Near the Corniche, the Philippe is immensely popular with budget tours, offering comfortable and clean rooms with satellite TV, private bathrooms and air-con. The style is rather impersonal, but it is good value, and there is a roof terrace with a small pool. Front rooms are the best: most have small balconies and receive plenty of light.

St Joseph Hotel (Map pp244-5; ☎ 238 1707; sjhiey2002@hotmail.com; Sharia Khaled ibn al-Walid; s/d US$25/30; ✖ ✖) This popular and well-run three-star hotel has been a favourite with small groups for years thanks to its comfortable rooms with satellite TV, air-con and private bathrooms. There is also a (heated) rooftop pool and basement bar. Ask for a Nile view.

Susanna Hotel (Map pp244-5; ☎ 236 9915; www.susannahotelluxor.com; 52 Sharia Maabad al-Karnak; city view s/d/tr US$30/35/50, Nile view US$40/45/60; ✖ ✖) Set between the Luxor Temple and the souq, this new modern hotel has 45 spacious rooms with comfortable beds, air-con, satellite TV and great views. There is a good rooftop terrace restaurant with views over Luxor Temple and the Nile, perfect for a sunset drink as alcohol is available.

Domina Inn Emilio (Map pp244-5; ☎ 237 6666; www.emiliotravel.com; Sharia Yousef Hassan; s/d/tr €30/40/50; ✖ ▣ ✖) A good midrange hotel, the Emilio has 101 spacious rooms, all fully equipped with minifridge, satellite TV, private bathroom, air-con and 24-hour room service. Other extras include an AstroTurfed roof terrace with plenty of shade and a large pool, a sauna and a business centre.

Morris Hotel (Map pp244-5; ☎ 235 9833; www.hotelmorrisluxor.com; Sharia al-Hurriya, off Sharia ibn al-Walid; s/d/tr US$50/80/105; ✖ ▣ ✖) A four-star hotel recommended by some readers for its spacious rooms with classical decor with fridge, satellite TV and safe. The views over the Nile and West Bank from the terrace, where breakfast is served upon request, are delightful. The hotel has several international restaurants, a swimming pool and a piano bar.

Sheraton Luxor Resort (off Map pp244-5; ☎ 237 4544; www.starwoodhotels.com/sheraton; Sharia Khaled ibn al-Walid; s/d from US$75/90; ✖ ✖ ✖) This secluded three-storey building is set amid lush gardens at the far southern end of Sharia Khaled ibn al-Walid – close enough to walk to some restaurants but far enough away to avoid any street noise. Rooms are well appointed and those overlooking the Nile have great views, although the run-down garden bungalows should be avoided. The hotel has a shopping arcade and Italian restaurant, La Mama (see p283).

WEST BANK

Al-Fayrouz Hotel (Map pp244-5; ☎ 231 2709, 012 277 0565; www.elfayrouz.com; Al-Gezira; s E£90-110, d E£130-160, tr E£170-190, q E£190; 🆒 🖳) This tranquil hotel with 17 brightly painted rooms, overlooking fields, is a great base for exploring the monuments of the West Bank. Under Egyptian-German management, the simple, nicely decorated rooms are spotless and have private bathrooms; some also come with air-conditioning and a balcony with a view. The more expensive rooms are larger with a sitting area, and have more atmosphere. Meals can be had on the comfortable roof terrace or in the popular garden restaurant.

Amenophis Hotel (Map p254; ☎ 231 1228, 012 212 3719; www.luxor-westbank.com/amenophis_e.htm; Kom Lolah; s/d E£100/180, flat E£300, meals per person E£60; 🆒) This quiet hotel, in a large building near the Medinat Habu temple complex, is a good midrange choice, with spotless, comfortable rooms, all with air-con, satellite TV and private bathrooms, as well as flats with two double rooms, a kitchen and living area. The rooftop restaurant has stunning views over the temple, the mountains beyond and the fields.

Hotel Sheherazade (Map pp244-5; ☎ 231 1228, 012 212 3719; www.hotelsheherazade.com; Al-Gezira; s/d/tr E£150/220/230, flat E£300, 3-course meals per person E£40; 🆒) Mohammed Sanusy dreamt of building this place for several years, and he takes great pride in his hotel. The 17 comfortable and spacious rooms are decorated with local colour and furnishings and all have en suite bathrooms. The Moorish-style building is surrounded by a garden. The large restaurant is at the end of the garden and overlooks the canal. A pool is planned.

Nour al-Gurna (Map p254; ☎ 231 1430, 010 129 5812; www.nourelgournahotel.com; Gurna; s E£150, d E£200-250, ste E£300) Set in a palm grove, Nour al-Gurna has large mudbrick rooms, with fans, mosquito nets, small stereos, locally made furniture and tiled bathrooms. Romantic and original, with friendly management, this is a lovely centrally located hotel convenient for visiting West Bank sites.

Nour al-Balad (Map p254; ☎ 242 6111; Ezbet Bisily; s/d/ste E£200/250/300; 🆒) The sister hotel to Nour al-Gurna is even quieter and has more spacious rooms. To get there, follow the track behind Medinat Habu for 500m.

Amon Hotel (Map p244-5; ☎ 231 0912; fax 231 1353; Al-Gezira; s/d/tr E£150/200/250; 🆒) Charming family-run hotel in a modern building with spotless rooms, a lush exotic garden where it's pleasant to have breakfast or a drink, extremely helpful staff and delicious home-cooked meals. In the new wing the rooms are large with private bathrooms, ceiling fans, air-con and balconies overlooking the courtyard. In the old wing, some of the small rooms have private bathrooms, and all are air-con. On the top floor are three triple rooms with an adjoining terrace and stunning views over the Theban Hills and the East Bank. This hotel is also popular with archaeologists so book ahead. The sister hotel past Medinat Habu is even quieter, and the rooms more spacious.

Nile Valley Hotel (Map pp244-5; ☎ 231 1477, 012 796 4473; www.nilevalley.nl; Al-Gezira; s/d/tr E£178/238/306, with shared bathroom E£127/187/230, 2-room flat E£476; 🆒 🖳) Pleasant Dutch-Egyptian-run hotel in a modern block right near the ferry landing. The comfortable rooms almost all have ultraclean private bathrooms, satellite TV and air-con. Some rooms have Nile views but those overlooking the rear garden are quieter and slightly bigger. Upstairs is a good rooftop bar-restaurant with fantastic views of the Nile and Luxor Temple, and there is a pool and children's pool in the garden. This hotel is particularly family friendly, and has families staying here for a week or more.

Flower of Light (off Map p254; ☎ 231 4043, 010 232 4475; www.floweroflight.com; Al-Gurna; d E£200-205; 🆒 🖳 🖳) Small new ecolodge with mudbrick bungalows set in a shady and tranquil garden with a lovely swimming pool and a Bedouin-style tent where drinks are served. It's run by the Irish Glynn family, who run workshops and retreats about sacred ancient Egyptian wisdom and the Mystery School Teachings. The rooms are simply furnished with local furniture and textiles, and most have en suite bathrooms. Even if you are not doing a workshop this is a great place to stay as the Glynns enthusiastically share their knowledge to provide a different perspective on Egypt.

Al-Nakhil Hotel (Map pp244-5; ☎ 231 3922, 012 382 1007; www.el-nakhil.com; Al-Gezira; s/d/tr €25/35/40; 🆒 🖳) Nestled in a palm grove, the Nakhil or 'Palm Tree' is at the edge of Al-Gezira. The resort-style hotel has spotless, well-finished domed rooms, all with private bathrooms and air-con, and is very family-friendly, with family rooms and cots available for babies. It also has three rooms that can cater for disabled guests.

Desert Paradise Lodge (Map p254; ☎ 231 3036; www.desertparadiselodge.com; Qabawi, 1.5km from the crossroads to Valley of Kings; s/d €40/70; ☒ ☑) Far away from the crowds, off the road going to the Valley of the Kings and on the edge of the desert, this is a place for those who want to do the West Bank slowly and calmly. This beautiful small lodge has just nine spacious domed rooms, lots of communal space and charm, a garden and terraces overlooking the Theban hills. Note that 10% of the profit goes to animal welfare centre ACE (see boxed text, p275).

our pick Beit Sabée (Map p254; ☎ 010 632 4926, 010 570 5341; info@beitsabee.com; Kom Lolah; d €40-70, with air-con €50-80; ☒) More like a house than a hotel, Beit Sabée has appeared in design magazines for its cool use of Nubian colours and local furnishings with a twist. Near the farms around Medinat Habu, it offers quiet accommodation and a closer contact to the real Egypt. Set in a traditional-style two-storey mudbrick house, the eight bedrooms with en suite bathrooms are effortlessly stylish, and breakfast is served in the courtyard or on the roof. A good place to spend a few days.

our pick Malkata Palace (off Map p254; ☎ 012 773 4312, 010 116 8531; www.hughsowdenegypt.com; Malqata, 1.5km south of Medinat Habu; r per person E£300, meals E£100; ☒) Built right on the edge of the desert, on the site of the palace of Amenhotep III, this wonderful domed mudbrick house in traditional Egyptian style offers a unique stay on the West Bank. One of the four Egyptian retreats of British painter Hugh Sowden (all are for rent), either single rooms or the entire house with four bedrooms can be rented. You will need to book well ahead, and can't turn up on the spot. The house is decorated in local style and feels immediately like a home, with a great roof terrace overlooking the Theban hills. Delicious home-cooked meals are available also to nonresidents. It is a good walk from the sights, but local transport can be organised.

Top End

EAST BANK

Luxor has many four- and five-star hotels, all, with one notable exception, run by international hotel chains. Most are much cheaper when booked on the internet.

Iberotel Luxor Hotel (Map pp244-5; ☎ 238 0925; www.iberotel-eg.com; Sharia Khaled ibn al Walid; s/d with Nile view US$90/110, with city view US$80/105; ☒ ☒ ☑) Formerly the Novotel (and still called that locally), this squat high-rise at the southern tip of the Corniche has an indoor atrium, great Nile views and a floating swimming pool. Rooms are comfortable, if smallish and without much character, but its location on the Nile just a short distance from Luxor Temple is unbeatable.

Sofitel Karnak (Map p241; ☎ 237 8020; www.sofitel.com; Sharia az-Zinia Gebly; r US$110-250; ☒ ☒ ☑) Quiet and secluded, the enormous Sofitel Karnak has 351 Nubian-style bungalow rooms set in lush Nile-side gardens, 3km north of the Temples of Karnak. The hotel also boasts a very pleasant (heated) pool, tennis and squash courts and a fitness centre, sauna and jacuzzi, and it is near an 18-hole golf course. Shuttle buses go to Luxor town.

Old Winter Palace Hotel (Map pp244-5; ☎ 237 1197; www.sofitel.com; Corniche an-Nil; old wing r €180-350, ste €420-890, new wing pavilion r €108-120, ste €325; ☒ ☒ ☑) The Old Winter Palace was built to attract the aristocracy of Europe and is one of Egypt's most famous historic hotels. A wonderfully atmospheric Victorian pile, it has high ceilings, lots of gorgeous textiles, fabulous views over the Nile, an enormous garden with exotic trees and shrubs, a huge swimming pool, table-tennis tables and a tennis court. The rooms vary in size and decor, but are very comfortable, and the food is excellent as is the service. The New Winter Palace has been demolished and there are plans to upgrade the Old Winter Palace into a deluxe suite-only hotel.

Maritim Jolie Ville (off Map pp244-5; ☎ 227 4855; www.jolieville-hotels.com/luxor_welcome.php; Kings Island; s US$120-180, d US$130-210, ste US$450; ☒ ☒ ☑) Set amid lush gardens on Crocodile Island, 4km south of town, this is a great family hotel with a minizoo and playground in addition to the large heated swimming pool, tennis courts and feluccas. There are 320 well-furnished and comfortable, if architecturally unremarkable, bungalow-style rooms, and a hotel motorboat and bus shuttle guests to and from the centre of town. The hotel boasts several excellent restaurants.

Sonesta St George Hotel (Map pp244-5; ☎ 238 2575; www.sonesta.com/egypt_luxor; Sharia Khaled ibn al- Walid; s/d with Nile view US$250/270, with city view US$135/170;

⊠ ⊠ ⊠) This 224-room marble-filled hotel has a kitsch value that should not be overlooked, with lots of marble, faux Pharaonic columns and a flame-like fence around the roof, but it is a good lively place to stay. The hotel is well managed, has friendly staff, recently refurbished and comfortable rooms with great views, a heated swimming pool, a business centre and a good selection of restaurants. Rates are much cheaper when booked via the internet.

WEST BANK

ourpick Al-Moudira (Map pp244-5; ☎ 012 325 1307; www.moudira.com; Daba'iyya; r €220, ste €270; ⊠ ⊠ ⊠ ⊠) Al-Moudira is a true luxury hotel, with an individuality that is missing from so many other hotels in Luxor. A Moorish fantasy of soaring vaults, pointed arches and enormous domes, surrounded by lush green and birdsong, the hotel has 54 rooms grouped together around small courtyards. Each room is different in shape, size (all are very large though) and colour, each with its own hand-painted trompe l'oeil theme and with antiques found throughout Egypt. Cushioned benches and comfortable antique chairs invite pashalike lounging and the enormous vaulted bathrooms have the feel of a private hammam (bathhouse). The public spaces are even more spectacular with traditional *mashrabiyya* (wooden lattice) work combined with work by contemporary 'orientalist' artists. Set on the edge of the cultivated land and the desert, the hotel is truly spectacular, especially now that the staff are better trained. It's a long way from anywhere, but transport is fairly cheap.

Flat Rental

Families or those planning a prolonged stay in Luxor might consider a self-catering option. Flat rental is mushrooming in Luxor, on both banks, particularly as it is cheap and many foreigners are getting involved in the business. The downside of self-catering is sex tourism, as there is very little control as to whom people can take to their room, whereas in hotels foreigners are not allowed to take guests back to their room.

Several companies can arrange flat rentals, including **Flats in Luxor** (Map pp244-5; ☎ 010 356 4540; www.flatsinluxor.com; per week from £150; ⊠ ⊠ ⊠), run by a British-Egyptian couple

who started renting out their own flats but now also manage others. The websites www .luxor-westbank.com and www.luxor4flats .com also have a wide selection of flats and houses available.

EATING

Most people come to Luxor for monuments and not for its fine cuisine – a good thing as most restaurants, particularly in the hotels, are pretty mediocre. However, the food is gradually getting better, with a few restaurants upping the standards by doing what Egyptians do best: cook honest traditional Egyptian food. Outside the hotels few places serve alcohol or accept credit-card payment; exceptions are noted in the reviews. Unless otherwise noted, restaurants tend to open from about 9am until midnight.

Restaurants
EAST BANK

Oasis Café (Map pp244-5; ☎ 012 336 7121; Sharia Dr Labib Habashi; mains E£15-60; ⊙ 10am-10pm; ⊠) Set in a renovated 1930s building right in the centre of town, the Oasis is a good place to recover from the bustle of Luxor town, from the heat or from sightseeing. The dining rooms are cool with fans, high ceilings and old tiled floors, painted in soft colours with local artwork on the walls, and furnished with traditional-style furniture. With jazz softly playing, smoking and nonsmoking rooms, the *New Yorker* to read and friendly staff, this is the perfect place for lunch, to linger over a good morning latte or to spend the afternoon reading. The place is very Western, but in a nice way like your favourite cafe back home. The food is good too, with an extensive brunch menu and a regular menu of international dishes, including pastas (E£20 to E£30), grilled meats (E£47 to E£60), filling sandwiches (E£25), daily specials on the blackboard and a wide selection of pastries.

Salahadeen (off Map pp244-5; ☎ 236 5081; www .salahadeen.com; Mara Hotel, Sharia Salahadin Ayyubi, off Sharia Salakhana; dishes E£18-60; ⊙ 6pm-midnight; ⊠) Salahadeen offers a set menu of Egyptian dishes, served as if it were an Egyptian home – knives and forks are offered but guests are encouraged to eat in the Egyptian way by dipping bread in the various dishes. There are two choices, the 'platter' (E£85), which includes three courses with 14 dishes of fresh home-cooked food to share, or the 'Feast' (E£125) with five courses including 25 different dishes.

Most dishes consist of vegetables, and the vegetarian options are not cooked in a meat broth as in so many other places. The bar opens for pre-dinner drinks at 6pm, and alcohol is available in the restaurant, too.

New Mish Mish; ☎ 228 1756, 010 810 5862; Sharia Televizyon; mains E£20-25; ☺ 8am-midnight; ✂) The long-standing budget-traveller haunt, Mish Mish, has been upgraded with a swish contemporary and air-conditioned fast-food-style interior, serving good sandwiches (E£5 to E£12), salads (E£3 to E£10) and grilled meats (E£20 to E£25) including shwarma, mixed grill and stuffed pigeon, and good grilled and fried fish dishes (E£22 to E£30). There's no alcohol, but there is a selection of fresh fruit juices (E£4).

New Royal Fish (Map pp244-5; ☎ 010 183 9115; Sharia al-Nugum, off Sharia Televizyon; mains E£20-45; ☺ 10am-midnight) This straightforward restaurant in an alley off Sharia Televizyon is reputedly the best fish restaurant in town, with only locals and not another tourist in sight. The fresh fish is grilled or fried and served with rice and salads, but no alcohol. Great for a change!

ourpick Sofra (Map pp244-5; ☎ 235 9752; www.sofra .com.eg; 90 Sharia Mohammed Farid, off Sharia al-Manshiya; mains E£20-55; ☺ 11am-midnight) Sofra remains our favourite restaurant in Luxor. Located in a 1930s house, away from all the tourist tat, it is as Egyptian as can be, in menu and decor, and even in price. The ground floor has three private dining rooms and a salon, giving the feeling of being in someone's home. There is also a wonderful rooftop terrace, which is also a cafe, where you can come for a drink. The house is filled with antique oriental furniture, chandeliers and traditional decorations, all simple but cosy and very tasteful. The menu is large, featuring all the traditional Egyptian dishes, such as stuffed pigeon and excellent duck, as well as a large selection of salads, dips (E£4) and mezze. Alcohol is not available, but there are delicious fresh juices on offer, and *sheesha* afterwards. It's a real treat, with very friendly staff, and has been recommended by many readers.

Maxime (off Map pp244-5; ☎ 238 6315, 010 607 0538; btwn Isis & Sheraton, Sharia Khaled ibn al-Walid; mains E£22-50; ☺ 11.30am-midnight) This French-Egyptian run restaurant consistently serves good French bistro classics, with steaks that melt in your mouth. Vegetarian options are plentiful, and the place is popular with families with plenty of options for the little ones. The restaurant

is on the 1st and 2nd floors, and the only drawback is that the decor is as bland as the building. No alcohol.

Jewel of the Nile (Map pp244-5; ☎ 016 252 2394; Sharia al-Rawda al-Sherifa, 300m off Sharia Khaled ibn al-Walid; mains E£25-35, set menu E£50-60; ☺ 10am-midnight winter, 1pm-midnight summer; ✂ ▢) Laura and Mahmud offer traditional Egyptian food using organic vegetables from their own farm, as well as well-prepared British food for homesick Brits including steaks, cottage pie, apple crumble and an all-day English breakfast (E£25). On Sundays a traditional lunch is served all day with roast beef and Yorkshire pudding (E£50), and on Saturdays and Wednesdays at 5.30pm there is a popular quiz night in aid of local charities. The menu features a good selection of vegetarian dishes. You can dine in the small outside sitting area or the air-conditioned interior dining room. Alcohol available.

La Mama (off Map pp244-5; ☎ 237 4544; Sheraton Luxor Resort, Sharia Khaled ibn al-Walid; dishes E£25-80; ☺ 10.30am-11pm) The Italian restaurant on the terrace overlooking a little pond with wading birds, at the entrance to the Sheraton, is a good bet, particularly if you've got kids in tow. This is an Italian restaurant in 1970s style with red-and-white napkins, live Neapolitan music and a good selection of pizzas, pastas and mains, all served in clean five-star surroundings.

As-Sahaby Lane (Map pp244-5; ☎ 236 5509; www .nefertitihotel.com/sahabi.htm; Sharia as-Sahaby, off Sharia as-Souq; mains E£35-60; ☺ 9am-11.30pm) Great easy-going alfresco restaurant in the lane running between the souq and the street to Karnak Temple. Fresh and well-prepared Egyptian dishes like *tagens* (stews cooked in earthenware pots) are served as well as good pizzas and salads. The young staff is very friendly, always ready to help or up for a chat. This terrace is a great place to watch the world go by, or relax from shopping in the souq.

A Taste of India (Map pp244-5; ☎ 019 373 2727; Sharia St Joseph, off Sharia Khaled ibn al-Walid; dishes E£35-50; ☺ 10.30am-11pm; ✂) A small British-run Indian restaurant in neutral colours with plain wooden tables and chairs. On the menu are European versions of Indian dishes such as korma, masala sag (spinach) and jalfrezi (marinated meat curry with tomato, pepper and onion) dishes, as well as original Indian specials such as madras and vindaloo curries. For those not too fond of spice, a few international, read British, dishes such as steak and chips are available. The place is popular with expat Brits and vegetarians who come for spicy vegetable dishes.

Lotus (Map pp244-5; ☎ 238 0419, 012 788 7160; www.lotus-restaurantluxor.nl; Sharia as-Souq; mains E£35-65, kids menu E£17-22; ☒ 9am-midnight; ☒ ☐) This air-conditioned restaurant in the heart of Luxor serves mainly international cuisine. The chef is Dutch, but Egyptian specials also feature on the menu.

1886 Restaurant (Map pp244-5; ☎ 238 0422; Old Winter Palace Hotel, Corniche an-Nil; starters E£35-122, mains E£60-190; ☒ dinner only; ☒) The 1886 is the gourmet restaurant in town, serving inventive Mediterranean-French food and a few Egyptian dishes with a twist, in a grand old-style dining room with very formal waiters. Guests are expected to dress up for the occasion – men wear a tie and/or jacket (some are available for borrowing) – and the food is superb and light. Delicacies include risotto of crayfish, truffle and chanterelles, sea scallops in artichoke broth and potato and celery ravioli. A grand evening out!

WEST BANK

Restaurant Mohammed (Map p254; ☎ 012 385 0227; Kom Lolah; set menu E£20-40) With an outdoor terrace and laid-back atmosphere, Mohammed's is the perfect place to recharge batteries in the middle of a day exploring temples and tombs, or to linger in the evening. This is a family affair, the restaurant being attached to the owner's mudbrick house; the charming Mohammed Abdel Lahi serves with his son Azab, while his wife cooks. The menu is small but includes meat grills, delicious chicken and duck as well as stuffed pigeon, served with fries and excellent simple salads. Stella beer is available (E£10) and Egyptian wine. They can organise a picnic in the desert or on a felucca upon demand. Call ahead.

Al-Gezira Hotel (Map pp244-5; ☎ 231 0034; Al-Gezira; set menu E£30) This comfortable rooftop restaurant serves a set menu with Egyptian specialities, such as the infamous *molokhiyya* (stewed leaf soup; see p80) and *mahshi kurumb* (stuffed cabbage leaves) that must be ordered in advance. There are great views over the Nile and the bright lights of Luxor beyond. Beer and wine are available. Cool beers are on offer (E£12) as well as Egyptian wine (E£85).

Memnon (Map p254; ☎ 012 327 8747; opposite Colossi of Memnon; dishes E£19-40; ☒ 8am-11pm, later in summer) Excellent, laid-back restaurant with simple

but very well-prepared Egyptian fare, and if you want a change from that, there are some equally good Indian and Chinese dishes on the menu. Afterwards hang out and stare eternity in the face looking at the Colossi, while smoking a *sheesha*. Leave some space for the homemade mango sorbet, it's worth it.

Tutankhamun Restaurant (Map pp244-5; ☎ 231 0918, 016 461 6598; Al-Gezira; mains E£30-50; ☒ 11am-10pm) This top-floor restaurant was the first one here on the riverside just south of the local ferry dock and it's still going strong. Hagg Mahmoud was a former cook at one of the French archaeological missions, and he and his sons are still cooking excellent *tagens*, duck à l'orange, chicken with rosemary and other good dishes. The food is served on the great rooftop terrace with views of the Nile. Very good vegetarian dishes.

Nile Valley Hotel (Map pp244-5; ☎ 231 1477; Al-Gezira; meals E£35-50; ☒ 8am-11pm) A popular rooftop restaurant with a bird's-eye view of the action along the West Bank's waterfront, the Nile Valley has a wide-ranging menu of Egyptian and international specialities, but is also a good place to relax with a cold drink and a *sheeshu*.

Aux Trois Chacals (Map p254; ☎ 010 192 3130; opposite Colossi of Memnon; mains E£42-64; ☒ 11am-8pm) Almost invisible from the main road that leads to the Colossi is this small French family-run restaurant serving home cooking in the garden or on the beautiful rooftop terrace. This is a cosy place to pass a few hours or to have lunch with sandwiches (E£16), salads (E£15) or a good grill, not to mention the tasty couscous. No alcohol but it's probably the only place on the West Bank where you can get a Lavazza espresso. Dinner should be booked in advance.

Al-Moudira (off Map p254; ☎ 012 325 1307; Daba'iyya; mains E£75-95; ☒ 8am-midnight) In keeping with its flamboyant decor, Al-Moudira has the most sophisticated and the most expensive food on the West Bank, with great salads and grills at lunchtime and a more elaborate menu for dinner with a delicious Mediterranean-Lebanese cuisine. This is a great place for a romantic dinner in the courtyard, or by the fire in winter. Call ahead for reservations.

Quick Eats

EAST BANK

Sayyida Zeinab (Map pp244-5; Sharia Televizyon; dishes E£3-8; ☒ 10am-10pm) This tiny but spotless place is one of Luxor's best *kushari* joints. Takeaway only.

Abu Ashraf (Map pp244-5; ☎ 237 5936; Sharia al-Mahatta; dishes E£4-15; ☒ 8am-11pm) This large, popular restaurant and takeaway is just down from the train station. It serves roasted chicken (E£16), pizzas (E£20), good *kushari* (E£4 to E£10) and kebabs (E£20).

Koshari Elzaeem (Map pp244-5; Midan Hussan; ☒ 24hr) Popular *kushari* restaurant that also serves an Egyptian version of spaghetti (E£8 to E£15). There are a few tables but they fill up fast.

Self-Catering
Luxor has a number of good bakeries. Try the ones on Sharia Ahmed Orabi, at the beginning of Sharia Maabad al-Karnak and on Sharia Gedda (all Map pp244–5). On the West Bank try the food and fruit shops on the main street in Al-Gezira, or head for the wonderful weekly market **Souq at-Talaat** (Map p254; ☒ Tue mornings), in Taref opposite the Temple of Seti I.

Fruit & Vegetable Souq (Map pp244-5; Sharia as-Souq) This is the best place for fruit and veg, although the good stuff sells out early in the morning. On either side of the main street are little shops selling produce and groceries throughout the day.

Arkwrights Gourmet Food (Map pp244-5; ☎ 228 2335; www.arkwrights-luxor.com; Sharia al-Mahdy, off Sharia Khaled ibn al-Walid, near St Joseph Hotel; ☒ 6am-midnight) Amazing food store with fresh fruits and vegetables, freshly made breads and a large selection of Egyptian and imported food products. The quality of the produce is high, and this is the place to stock up for a more sophisticated picnic, as they recently started doing packed lunches, freshly made sandwiches and salads to take away.

Al-Ahram Beverages (Map pp244-5; ☎ 237 2445; Sharia Ramses) Al-Ahram Beverages is the Luxor outlet for the country's monopoly beer and wine producer.

DRINKING
East Bank
Metropolitan Café & Restaurant (Map pp244-5; lower level, Corniche an-Nil) A pleasant, popular outdoor cafe, right on the Nile, in front of the Old Winter Palace Hotel. Beers (Stella E£15) and a wide selection of cocktails are available, served on a terrace with rattan furniture and mist machines. The perfect place to enjoy a sundowner, but apart from some snacks with the drinks, the food is pretty mediocre.

New Oum Koulsoum Coffee Shop (Map pp244-5; Sharia as-Souq; ☒ 24hr) Pleasant *ahwa* (coffeehouse) right at the heart of the souq, on a large terrace with welcome mist machines, where you can recover from shopping and haggling in the souq and watch the crowds without any hassle. On the menu are fresh juices (E£10 to E£15), hot and cold drinks and a good *sheesha* (E£10) as well as 'professional Nespresso' coffee (E£15).

Kings Head Pub (Map pp244-5; ☎ 228 0489; Sharia Khaled ibn al-Walid; ☒) A relaxed and perennially popular place to have a drink and shoot pool, the Kings Head tries to capture the atmosphere of an English pub without being twee. The laid-back atmosphere also means that women can come here without being harassed.

Nile Terrace Café & Bar (Map pp244-5; ☎ 238 0422; Corniche an-Nil; ☒ 9am-7pm) The terrace in front of the Old Winter Palace Hotel is the most elegant place in Luxor to watch the sun slowly set over the Theban hills. Starched collars and gin and tonics are the rule here, but there is also ice-cold beer (E£35); or you can order afternoon tea if you prefer.

Cocktail Sunset (Map pp244-5; ☎ 238 0524; Corniche an-Nil, opposite Luxor Museum; ☒) On a pontoon, which rumour has it once belonged to King Farouk's father, on the Nile, this place is hugely popular for its congenial atmosphere, cocktails and ice-cold beers. There is a nice fashion store on the 1st floor.

West Bank
There are no real bars on the West Bank; drinking is done at restaurants or not at all.

Maratonga Cafeteria (Map p254; ☎ 231 0233; Kom Lolah; ☒ 6am-11pm) This friendly outdoor cafe-restaurant, in front of Medinat Habu, is the best place to sip a cold drink under a big tree after wandering through Ramses III's magnificent temple, or have a delicious *tagen* (E£35) or salad for lunch. The view is superlative and the atmosphere is relaxing.

Ramesseum Rest House (Map p254; beside the Ramesseum, Gurna) A friendly, laid-back place to relax after temple-viewing. In addition to the usual mineral water and soft drinks, Stella is sometimes available.

ENTERTAINMENT
East Bank
With tourism booming in Luxor, the town is busy at night. The Temple of Luxor is open

until 10pm and worth seeing at night; the souq is open late as well and more lively at night than in the day. In summer lots of locals stroll along the Corniche. Rumour has it that the sights will soon stay open longer so tourists can avoid the heat of the day for visits.

However, this is not exactly the place for clubbing, even if you're into dancing to outmoded disco music. There are some bars with a decent atmosphere, and most of the larger hotels put on a folkloric show several times each week, depending on the season and number of tour groups around. The best discos are at **Tutotel Partner Hotel** (Map pp244-5; ☎ 237 7990), one of the more popular options, while at **Hotel Mercure** (Map pp244-5; ☎ 238 0944; nonguest minimum E£50) the extra charge covers you for watching the belly-dancing show at 11.30pm too.

West Bank

If you want to avoid the bright lights of the town, the West Bank is the place to be. Nobi's Arabian Horse Stables (p276) and QEA (p276) arrange evening desert barbecues for groups of 10 or more and sometimes put on a horse-dancing show.

SHOPPING

The whole range of Egyptian souvenirs is available in Luxor town, but for alabaster it is best to head for the West Bank. The alabaster is mined about 80km northwest of the Valley of the Kings, and although the alabaster factories near the Ramesseum and Deir al-Bahri sell cheap handmade cups, vases and lights in the shape of Nefertiti's head, it is possible to find higher-quality bowls and vases, often unpolished, which are great buys. Take care when buying, as sometimes what passes for stone is actually wax with stone chips. Avoid going with a tour guide as his commission will invariably be added to your bill.

The *tagen* (clay pots) that are used in local cooking make a more unusual buy. Very practical, they can be used to cook on top of the stove or in the oven and they look good on the table too. Prices start at E£8 for a very small pot and go up to about E£40. They're on sale on the street just beside the police station in Luxor East Bank.

Habiba (Map pp244-5; ☎ 010 124 2026; www.habiba gallery.com; Sharia Sidi Mahmoud, off Sharia as-Souq; ☉ 10am-10pm) Run by an Australian woman who loves to

travel in Egypt and who wants to promote the best of Egyptian crafts, this tiny shop goes from strength to strength. It sells an ever-expanding selection of Bedouin embroidery, jewellery, leather work, wonderful Siwan scarves, cotton embroidered scarves from Sohag, the best Egyptian cotton towels (usually only for export), mirrors and brass lights – and all at fair-trade fixed prices. A world away from what is available in the nearby souq.

A new **branch** (off Map pp244-5; ☎ 010 306 2229; ☉ 10am-10pm) has opened near Karnak near Al-Fayed Perfume Store in the Sharia Hilton, that is also recommended.

Fair Trade Centre Luxor Outlet (Map pp244-5; ☎ 236 0870, 010 034 7900; www.egyptfairtrade.org; Sharia Maabad al-Karnak; ☉ 9am-10.30pm) A nonprofit shop that markets handicrafts from NGO projects throughout Egypt. It has a good selection of well-priced hand-carved wood and pottery from the nearby villages of Hejaza and Garagos, aromatic oils from Quz, beadwork from Sinai and hand-blown glass, Akhmim table linen, beading from the west bank in Luxor, recycled glass and recycled paper from Cairo.

Aisha (Map pp244-5; ☎ 016 184 6784; www.aisha -crafts.com; Sharia Yousef Hassan, opposite Domina Inn Emilio; ☉ 10am-4.30pm & 5.30-10pm) Beautiful shop that sells better quality and often fair-trade crafts from all over Egypt, including brass and copper lights, Bedouin jewellery, kilims, pottery and interesting scarves.

Caravanserai (Map p254; ☎ 012 327 8771; www .caravanserailuxor.com; Kom Lolah; ☉ 8am-10pm) This delightful shop, the only one of its kind on the West Bank, is kept by the friendly Hamdi and his family in a beautifully painted mudbrick house near Medinat Habu. He began travelling around Egypt and realised that making things was one of the few things poor people could do to earn money, so he decided to set up shop to encourage and help them, the women in particular. Hamdi buys almost everything people make, telling them what sells well, suggesting ways of improving their goods; above all he loves the people's creativity. The shop has the beautiful pottery from the Western Oases, Siwan embroideries, amazing appliqué bags and lots of other crafts that can be found almost nowhere else in Egypt.

Duty Free Shop Luxor (Map pp244-5; ☎ 237 6331; Sharia Yousef Hassan, off Sharia Maabad al-Karnak; ☉ 10am-2pm & 7-11pm) Within 48 hours of arriving in Egypt, you can enjoy duty-free shopping for cigarettes and alcohol at the downtown duty

---

NO MORE POLICE CONVOY AROUND LUXOR

Until early 2009 getting out of Luxor by road involved travelling in an armed police convoy. But now most convoys have been lifted. With the exception of the roads from Aswan–Abu Simbel, and Asyut–Cairo, it is now once again possible to travel by private taxi or car to Dendara and Abydos. You can also make the trip from Luxor to Aswan and stop for as long as you like at the temples along the way. But there are still security checks and if you do take a private car south to Aswan, or to Qena or Abydos, bear in mind that, in the morning, the driver will need to take your passport to the **Travel Agents Association** (Map pp244-5; cnr Sharia Televizyon & Sharia Ibn Abu Taleb) for a *tasrih* or permission, which is easy to get and free.

---

free, which has a good selection of the main brands. Bring your passport along.

GETTING THERE & AWAY
Air
EgyptAir (Map pp244-5; ☎ 238 0581; Corniche an-Nil; ☻ 8am-8pm) operates several daily flights between Cairo, Luxor and Aswan. A one-way ticket to Cairo costs E£200 to E£600. Tickets to Aswan cost E£160 to E£390 one-way. There are four flights per week to Sharm el-Sheikh (E£350 to E£625 one-way). Flights to Abu Simbel only operate in high season, but involve such long waits in Aswan that you're better off arranging a trip from there.

Bus
The **bus station** (off Map pp244-5; ☎ 237 2118, 232 3218) is out of town on the road to the airport, about 1km from the airport, but tickets for the **Upper Egypt Bus Co** (Map pp244-5; ☎ 232 3218, 237 2118; Midan al-Mahatta) buses can be bought at its office in town, south of the train station. A taxi from the town to the bus station will cost around E£25 to E£35, but it's a good idea to check because some buses leave from the office near the train station.

Buses heading to Cairo leave at 6.30pm from the office near the train station and 7pm from the bus station (E£100, 10 to 11 hours), but booking ahead is essential as the bus fills up quickly. Six daily buses head to Hurghada (E£30 to E£35, five hours) from 6.30am to 8pm. All stop in Qena (E£5, one to two hours) and Safaga (E£25 to E£30, 3½ to four hours) and go on to Suez (E£60 to E£70, 10 hours). For Al-Quseir and Marsa Alam, change at Safaga. A bus to Sharm el-Sheikh (E£120, 12 hours) and Dahab (E£130, 14 to 16 hours) leaves at 5pm. It is often full so try to reserve in advance. There are frequent buses to Qena (E£5 to E£7) between 6.30am and 8pm, but you pay for the taxi to get to the bus station

so it's cheaper to take the service taxi there. There is a daily bus to Port Said at 8pm (E£75, 12 hours) via Ismailia (E£70).

To go to the Western Desert oases take a train to Asyut, from where there are several buses a day to Kharga (E£15) and Dakhla (E£25). At the time of writing there were no buses between Luxor and Aswan.

Superjet (☎ 236 7732) runs buses from Luxor bus station at 8pm to Cairo (E£130) via Hurghada (E£45).

Cruise Ship or Dahabiyya
For information on the many cruise boats and increasing number of dahabiyyas (houseboats) that ply the Nile between Luxor and Aswan see p105 and p103.

Felucca
You can't take a felucca from Luxor to Aswan; most feluccas leave from Esna because of the Esna Lock. But unless you have a strong wind, it can take days to go more than a few kilometres in this direction. For more information, see p101.

Service Taxi
The station for service taxis and minibuses (Map pp244–5) on the east bank is on the north side of Sharia Maabad al-Karnak, near Rezeiky Camp, 2km from the centre of Luxor. Foreigners can again take service taxis from Luxor to Aswan (E£15) via Esna (E£3), Edfu (E£7), Kom Ombo (E£11), Hurghada (E£17) and Qena (E£3.50). There is no service to Asyut. The drivers are always ready to privatise the car to make special trips up the Nile to Aswan, stopping at the sights on the way; expect to pay about E£450 to E£500. To Asyut or to Hurghada, the going rate is about E£450. It is possible to take a private service taxi to Kharga via the direct road, avoiding Asyut, at E£700 for the car (maximum seven people).

Train

Luxor Station (Map pp244–5; ☎ 237 2018; www.egyptrail .gov.eg; Midan al-Mahatta) has left-luggage facilities, plenty of cardphones and a post office.

The **Abela Egypt Sleeping Train** (☎ 237 2015, in Cairo 02-2574 9474; www.sleepingtrains.com) goes daily to Cairo at 9.40pm and 12.50am (single/ double including dinner and breakfast US$80/120, child four to 19 years US$45, nine hours). No student discounts; tickets must be paid for in US dollars or euros.

The only other train to Cairo permitted for foreigners is the air-conditioned 85 leaving at 8.15pm and arriving in Cairo at 7.15am (E£165). Foreigners are allowed to take the 981 (adult 1st/2nd class E£79/41, student 1st/2nd class E£45/30, 10 hours), at 8.25pm, stopping at Qena (1st/2nd class E£21/15) and Balyana (E£19/14, three hours), but not further than Asyut E£53/30. Balyana is the stop for those who wish to visit Abydos, Qena for Dendara and Asyut if you want to travel to the Western Oases.

There are several trains to Aswan (adult 1st/2nd class E£41/25, student 1st/2nd class E£32/20, three hours) a day: the 996 at 7.30am, the 1902 at 9.30am and the 980 at 5.45pm.

GETTING AROUND
To/From the Airport

Luxor airport is 7km east of town. A sign at the airport announces the official tariffs to get a taxi to different parts of Luxor, between E£25 to E£50, but none of the taxi drivers will accept these prices: the asking price is often about E£70 to E£100 or more, and in low season when there is not enough work a fight between drivers may erupt. In short, it is a major hassle, so if you want peace of mind ask the hotel to arrange your transfer. There is no bus between the airport and the town.

Bicycle

The compact town lends itself to cycling, and distances on the generally flat West Bank are just far enough to provide some exercise but not exhaust (except when the weather is too hot). Cycling at night is inadvisable given the local habit of leaving headlights off.

Many hotels rent out bikes. Expect to pay from E£12 to E£15 per day and choose carefully – there's nothing worse than getting stuck with a broken chain halfway to the Valley of the Kings. A good place to rent is from restaurant **7 days 7 ways** (off Map pp244–5; ☎ 012 020 1876; www.bikerentalluxor.com; Sharia Sheraton; ☻ 8am-11pm), which also organises cycling tours around Luxor.

You can take bikes across to the West Bank on the *baladi* ferry (see p275). If you're based on the West Bank, there are several bike rentals near the ferry landing, or try renting from your hotel.

Felucca

There is a multitude of feluccas to take you on short trips around Luxor, leaving from various points all along the river. How much you pay depends on your bargaining skills, but you're looking at about E£20 to E£40 for an hour of sailing.

Hantour

Also called a *calèche*, horse and carriages cost about E£20 to E£50 per hour depending on your haggling skills (this is where you really need them). Expect to pay about E£20 to get to Karnak.

Pick-up Taxis

Kabout (pick-up trucks) and microbuses are often the quickest and easiest way to get about in Luxor. They ply fixed routes and will stop whenever flagged down. To get to the Temples of Karnak, take a microbus from Luxor station or from behind Luxor Temple for 50pt. Other routes run inside the town. For information about West Bank pick-ups, see p275.

Taxi

There are plenty of taxis in Luxor, but passengers still have to bargain hard for trips. A short trip around town is likely to cost at least E£10. Taxis can also be hired for day trips around the West Bank; expect to pay E£150 to E£250, depending on the length of the excursion and your bargaining skills.

Nile Valley: Esna to Abu Simbel

Where northern Upper Egypt is dominated by fast-growing cities and political problems, the country south of Luxor is both harder and calmer. The Nile is increasingly hemmed in by the desert, its banks lined with well-preserved Graeco-Roman temples at Esna, Edfu and Kom Ombo, its lush fields punctuated by palm-backed villages – it's the ideal place to glide through on a Nile sailing boat. Al-Kab provides the perfect contrast to the grandeur of the temples, for this once-great city has almost completely disappeared. Beyond Edfu the ribbon of cultivation on the Nile's east bank gives way to the Eastern Desert, while at Gebel Silsila, 145km south of Luxor, the river passes through a gorge, once thought to mark a cataract.

Aswan may be the regional capital and administrative centre, but this ancient ivory-trading post has a laid-back atmosphere that sets it apart from other tourist centres in Egypt. With the Nubia Museum, ancient remains, a vibrant souq, beautiful gardens and a unique Nubian-influenced local culture, it is a fascinating and relaxing place to spend time.

South of Aswan, the land is dominated by the High Dam and its offspring, Lake Nasser, the world's largest artificial lake. Remarkable monuments that would have been lost to the lake's waters now stand grouped on its shores and can be visited by boat. Most southerly and spectacular of all is the Great Temple of Ramses II at Abu Simbel, one of ancient Egypt's most awesome structures and a highlight of any visit to Egypt.

HIGHLIGHTS

- Marvel at the most completely preserved Egyptian temple and get lost in its inner chambers, all perfectly carved with sacred formulae, at the **Temple of Horus** (p294) at Edfu
- See where the pharaohs found their building blocks and get a sense of the connection between Egyptian religion and the Nile at the quarries and shrines of **Gebel Silsila** (p296)
- Wander around the rarely visited but fascinating ruins of the ancient settlement of **Abu** (p303) on Elephantine Island
- Sense Pharaoh Ramses II's vanity in the grandest temple he ever built, the awe-inspiring **Great Temple** (p324) at Abu Simbel
- Enjoy the peace of **Lake Nasser** (p321) and the rescued temples, and get an idea of the Nubian history and culture that were submerged by it at the **Nubia Museum** (p302) in Aswan

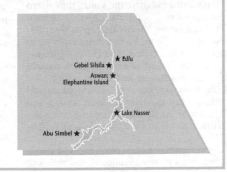

History

The Nile Valley south of Luxor was the homeland of the vulture and crocodile gods, a place of harsh nature and grand landscapes. Its cult places, centres such as Al-Kab and Kom al-Ahmar, date back to the earliest periods of Egyptian history – it was here that the Narmer Palette, the object around which the origins of the 1st dynasty have been constructed, was found; here that one of the earliest-known Egyptian temples, made of wood not stone, was found; and here that recently found Lascaux-type rock carvings (see boxed text, p297) have opened a window onto Egypt's remotest past.

Yet most of what one can see between Luxor and Aswan dates from the last period of ancient Egyptian history, when the country was ruled by the descendants of Alexander the Great's Macedonian general, Ptolemy I (323–283 BC). They ruled for some 300 years, respecting the country's ancient traditions and religion and setting an example to the Romans who succeeded them.

Although they were based in Alexandria and looked out to the Mediterranean, the Ptolemies pushed their way south into Nubia, the land that straddled what is now the border between Egypt and Sudan. They ensured peaceful rule in Upper Egypt by erecting temples in honour of the local gods, building in grand Pharaonic style to appease the priesthood and earn the trust of the people. The riverside temples at Esna, Edfu, Kom Ombo and Philae are as notable for their strategic locations, on ancient trade routes or key commercial centres, as for their artistic or architectural merit.

Aswan's history was always going to be different. However much the rulers in the north, whether Theban or Macedonian, may have wanted to ignore the south, they dared not neglect their southern border. Settlement on Elephantine Island, located in the middle of the Nile at Aswan, dates back to at least 3000 BC. Named Abu (Ivory) after the trade that flourished here, it was a natural fortress positioned just north of the First Nile Cataract, one of six sets of rapids that blocked the river between Aswan and Khartoum. At the beginning of Egypt's dynastic history, in the Old Kingdom (2686–2125 BC), Abu became capital of the first Upper Egyptian nome (province) and developed into a thriving economic and religious centre, its strategic importance underlined by the title accorded to its rulers, Keepers of the Gate of the South. By the end of ancient history, with Egypt part of a larger Roman Empire, the southern frontier town was seen as a place of exile for anyone from the north who stepped out of line.

Climate

Heading south from Luxor, the fertile, green Nile Valley narrows considerably and becomes more and more enclosed by the desert, which in some places edges dramatically close to the riverbanks. The climate also changes and becomes increasingly desertlike, with mostly warm, dry days in winter (December to February) – with an average temperature of about 26°C during the day – but often surprisingly cold nights. Summer (June to August) days are dry but often very hot, with temperatures hovering between 38°C and 45°C, making it difficult to visit sights outdoors. At the height of summer, temperatures hardly seem to drop during the night.

Getting There & Away

At the time of writing there are no buses between Aswan and Luxor. The train station will only sell tickets for a limited number of trains between Luxor and Aswan to foreigners, but they will also tell you to board any train you want and buy a ticket on board for E£6 extra. Service taxis and minibuses ply the road from Luxor to Aswan, or ferry passengers between cities along that stretch. With the convoy system no longer in place foreigners are now again able to travel in a service taxi, or to privatise a taxi for the day, and do the drive between Luxor and Aswan, stopping at the sights on the way. The best way is of course the slow way, sailing a felucca (traditional canvas-sailed boat) or a dahabiyya (houseboat), taking in the sights and the most glorious stretch of river.

There still *is* a convoy system in place between Aswan and Abu Simbel, and foreigners are only allowed to travel by bus, taxi or minibus in an armed convoy that leaves twice a day. The other option is to fly, or to take a cruise on Lake Nasser.

Getting Around

Foreigners are no longer restricted from travelling between towns in the far south of Egypt, except for Aswan to Abu Simbel. Service taxis and minibuses run between the towns, but the service-taxi station is often outside the town, and/or a few kilometres away from the sights. The easiest way is to either privatise a taxi for a day and visit sights en route, or to privatise a taxi once you are in the town and want to go to the sight. Security tightens inevitably if there has been any kind of incident in the town, even if it's not necessarily related to tourists or terrorism.

SOUTHERN UPPER EGYPT

ESNA

☎ 095 / pop 66,656

Most visitors come to Esna, 54km south of Luxor on the west bank of the Nile, for the Temple of Khnum, but the busy little farming town itself is quite charming. Beyond the small bazaar selling mainly tourist souvenirs are several examples of 19th-century provincial architecture with elaborate *mashrabiyyas* (wooden lattice screens). North of the temple is a beautiful but run-down Ottoman caravanserai, the Wekalat al-Gedawi, once the commercial centre of Esna. Merchants from Sudan, Somalia and central Africa stayed on the 2nd floor here, and a market was held regularly in the courtyard, with Berber baskets, Arab glue, ostrich feathers and elephant tusks all for sale. Opposite the temple is the Emari minaret from the Fatimid period, one of the oldest in Egypt, which escaped the mosque's demolition in 1960. An old oil mill, in the covered souq south of the temple, presses lettuce seed into oil, a powerful aphrodisiac since ancient times. Esna was until the early 20th century an important stop on the camel-caravan route between Sudan and Cairo, and between the Western Desert oases and the Nile Valley. It is now also known for the two Esna locks on the Nile, where cruise boats have to queue up to pass. The town makes for a pleasant morning excursion from Luxor, or a stop en route from Luxor to Aswan.

The post office and a branch of the Bank of Alexandria are on the street leading from the canal to the Nile. The **tourist police office** (☎ 240 0686) is in the tourist souq near the temple.

SOUTHERN UPPER EGYPT

0 _____ 20 km
0 _____ 10 miles

To Luxor (54km)
Esna
Wadi Hellal
53
Al-Kab (Nekheb)
Kom al-Ahmar (Hierakonpolis)
To Marsa Alam (220km)
Edfu
Temple of Horus
99
EASTERN ARABIAN DESERT
2
WESTERN (LIBYAN) DESERT
Speos of Horemheb
Kajuj
Gebel Silsila
Nile River
Temple of Kom Ombo
Kom Ombo
Daraw
Ballana
Eastern Desert
See Lower Nubia & Lake Nasser Map (p319)
Aswan Dam (First Cataract)
Aswan
Kalabsha, Beit al-Wali & Kertassi
Philae
To Abu Simbel (265km); Wadi Halfa, Sudan (360km)
High Dam
Lake Nasser

There is a busy **souq** (Map p292) on Monday, beside the canal, and an exchange kiosk near the dock.

Temple of Khnum

The Ptolemaic-Roman **Temple of Khnum** (adult/student E£20/15; ⏱ 6am-5pm Oct-May, to 6pm Jun-Sep) is situated about 200m from the boat landing, at the end of the tourist souq. The temple today sits in a 9m-deep pit, which represents 15 centuries of desert sand and debris, accumulated since it was abandoned during the Roman period. Most of the temple, which was similar in size to the temples of Edfu (see p293) and Dendara (see p236), is still covered. All that was excavated in the 1840s, all you can see now, is the Roman hypostyle hall.

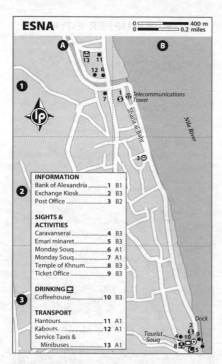

their speech different in every region but the lord of the wheel is their father too'.

On the walls Roman emperors dressed as pharaohs make offerings to the local gods of Esna. The northern wall has colourful scenes of the ruler catching fish in a papyrus thicket with the god Khnum, and next to this the emperor presents the temple to Khnum.

The back wall, to the northeast, the only remaining part of the original Ptolemaic temple, features reliefs of two Ptolemaic pharaohs, Ptolemy VI Philometor and Ptolemy VIII Euergetes (170–116 BC). A number of Roman emperors, including Septimus Severus, Caracalla and Geta, added their names near the hall's rear gateway.

Eating & Drinking

Few people linger in Esna, as most stop here on the road between Luxor and Aswan. There is nowhere to stay but there are a few *ahwa*s (coffeehouses) with a terrace, serving drinks, *sheesha* (water pipe) and some basic food, such as sandwiches with felafel, opposite the temple.

Getting There & Away

Trains are a pain because the train station is on the opposite (east) bank of the Nile, away from the town centre, but *kabouts* (pick-up trucks) go back and forth between the two. At the time of writing there are no buses to Luxor or Aswan. The busy *kabout* station is beside the canal, and a block further north is the service-taxi and minibus station. A seat in a service taxi or minibus to Luxor is E£3, to Edfu E£3.50 and to Aswan E£10. Arrivals are generally dropped off on the main thoroughfare into town along which *hantour* (horse-drawn carriage) drivers congregate in the hope of picking up a fare. They ask E£10 each way for the five- to 10-minute ride to the temple.

AL-KAB & KOM AL-AHMAR

Between Esna and Edfu are the ruins of two settlements, both dating back more than 3000 years, with traces of even earlier habitation.

The little-visited site of **Al-Kab** (adult/student E£30/20), ancient Nekheb, is one of the most important sites of ancient Egypt. It was the home of Nekhbet, the vulture goddess of Upper Egypt, one of two goddesses who protected the pharaoh right back to the Old Kingdom. There isn't much to see, but the remains of the 12m-thick mudbrick walls that

Khnum was the ram-headed creator god who fashioned humankind on his potter's wheel using Nile clay. Construction of the temple dedicated to him was started, on the site of an earlier temple, by Ptolemy VI Philometor (180–145 BC). The Romans added the hypostyle hall that can be visited today, with well-preserved carvings from as late as the 3rd century AD. A quay connecting the temple to the Nile was built by Marcus Aurelius (AD 161–180).

The central doorway leads into the dark, atmospheric vestibule, where the roof is supported by 18 columns with wonderfully varied floral capitals in the form of palm leaves, lotus buds and papyrus fans; some also have bunches of grapes, a distinctive Roman touch. The roof is decorated with astronomical scenes, while the pillars are covered with hieroglyphic accounts of temple rituals. Inside the front corners, beside the smaller doorways, are two hymns to Khnum. The first is a morning hymn to awaken Khnum in his shrine, and the second is a wonderful 'hymn of creation' that acknowledges him as creator of all, even foreigners: 'all are formed on his potter's wheel,

surrounded the town are impressive and date back to the Late Period (747–332 BC). The oldest of the sandstone temples within the walls dedicated to the god Thoth was built by Ramses II (1279–1213 BC) and the adjoining Temple of Nekhbet was built during the Late Period, both reusing blocks from much earlier temples from the Early Dynastic Period (from c 3100 BC) and the Middle Kingdom (2055–1650 BC).

To the northwest of the walls is an Old Kingdom cemetery. Across the road, past the ticket office and cut into the hill at the edge of the valley, are tombs of New Kingdom (1550–1069 BC) local governors. The most important is the **Tomb of Ahmose** (No 2), the 'Captain-General of Sailors', who fought under Ahmose I (1550–1525 BC). Ahmose, son of Ebana, left a detailed account of his bravery in the battle against the Hyksos. Further east were several temples dedicated to Nubian gods. A Ptolemaic temple has a staircase going up to two columned vestibules before a chapel carved into the rock. South of there is a small chapel, locally known as Al-Hammam (The Bathhouse), built by Setau, Viceroy of Nubia under Ramses II. At the centre of the wadi is a large vulture-shaped crag covered in inscriptions from predynastic times to the Old Kingdom. Some 3.5km further east into the desert is the small chapel of Nekhbet, built by Amenhotep III (1390–1352 BC) as a way station for the vulture goddess's cult statue when she passed through 'The Valley'. Her protective influence was no doubt appreciated, as this was one of the supply routes to the goldmines that gave Egypt much of its wealth.

Across the river lies **Kom al-Ahmar**, ancient Nekhen or Hierakonpolis, home of the falcon god Nekheny, an early form of Horus. This site can only be visited with special permission from the antiquities office at the entrance of the Temple of Horus at Edfu (p294); the director, Mr Zanan (☎ 010 374 6358), will grant permission at a cost of E£5600.

Although little remains of what was one of Egypt's most important cities in predynastic times, recent excavations have revealed a large settlement (with Egypt's earliest brewery!), a predynastic cemetery dating from around 3400 BC with elephant and cattle burials, together with the site of Egypt's earliest-known temple, a large timber-framed structure fronted by 12m-high imported wood pillars. A century ago, within this sacred enclosure, ar-

chaeologists discovered a range of ritual artefacts, among them two items of huge historical significance, the Narmer Palette and a superb gold falcon head of the god Horus, both now in Cairo's Egyptian Museum (see p183).

Close by is Egypt's oldest standing brick building, an enigmatic mudbrick enclosure known as 'the Fort', built by Khasekhemy (c 2686 BC). The impressive rock-cut tombs on the west bank were built by New Kingdom dignitaries.

Getting There & Away

Al-Kab and Kom al-Ahmar are 26km south of Esna. The best way of seeing these sites is to take a private taxi from Esna or Edfu, or on the way from Luxor to Aswan or vice versa. Dahabiyyas and some feluccas from Aswan to Esna (see p99 for more information) stop here too, but not the bigger cruise boats.

EDFU
☎ 097 / pop 69,000
Built on a rise above the broad river valley, the Temple of Horus at Edfu, having escaped destruction from Nile floods, is the most completely preserved Egyptian temple. One of the last ancient attempts at building on a grand scale, the temple dominates this west-bank town, 53km south of Esna. The temple's well-preserved reliefs have provided archaeologists with much valuable information about the temple rituals and the power of the priesthood. Walking through the large, gloomy chambers, visitors are sometimes overwhelmed by a sense of awe at the mysteries of ancient Egypt.

Modern Edfu, a centre for sugar and pottery, is a friendly, buzzing provincial centre. Although it is an agricultural town tourism is the biggest money earner and almost everyone seems to have an interest in the tourist bazaar, which all visitors must brave in order to reach the temple. As in other Egyptian towns, the main street is lined with mobile-phone shops, and the main square, the town's nerve centre, has a few simple but popular cafe-restaurants. A large Telephone centrale sits on the southern side of the square and the post office is behind it, just south of here, along the first street off to the left. On the main street, Sharia al-Maglis, is the Banque du Caire, with an ATM.

On the waterfront where the cruise boats dock are some pleasant cafe-restaurants, as well as more bazaars, the Bank of Alexandria,

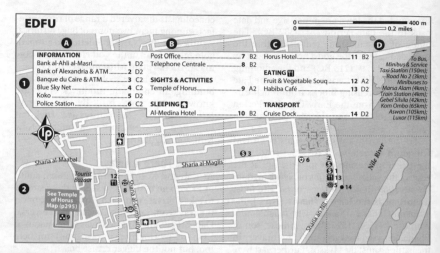

the Bank al-Ahli al-Masri and internet cafes **Koko** (☎ 010 440 1196; Sharia an-Nil; per hr E£10) and **Blue Sky Net** (Sharia an-Nil; per hr E£10).

The bus, minibus and service taxi station can be found at the entrance to town, next to the bridge over the Nile.

Temple of Horus

Edfu was a settlement and cemetery site from around 3000 BC onward, as it was the cult centre of the falcon god Horus of Behdet (the ancient name for Edfu), but the **Temple of Horus** (adult/student E£50/25; ☉ 7am-9pm Oct-May, to 10pm Jun-Sep) you see today is Ptolemaic. Started by Ptolemy III (246–221 BC) on 23 August 237 BC, on the site of an earlier and smaller New Kingdom structure, the sandstone temple was completed some 180 years later by Ptolemy XII Neos Dionysos, Cleopatra VII's father. In conception and design it follows the general plan, scale, or- namentation and traditions of Pharaonic archi- tecture, right down to the Egyptian attire worn by Greek pharaohs depicted in the temple's reliefs. Although it is much newer than cult temples at Luxor or Abydos, its excellent state of preservation helps to fill in many historical gaps; it is, in effect, a 2000-year-old example of an architectural style that was already archaic during Ptolemaic times.

Two hundred years ago the temple was buried by sand, rubble and part of the vil- lage of Edfu, which had spread over the roof. Excavation was begun by Auguste Mariette in the mid-19th century. Today the temple is entered via a long row of shops selling tourist tat, and a new visitors centre with the ticket office, clean toilets, a cafeteria and a room for showing a 15-minute film on the history of the temple in English.

Beyond the Roman *mammisi* (birth house), with some colourful carvings, the massive 36m-high **pylon** (gateway) is guarded by two huge but splendid granite statues of Horus as a falcon. The walls are decorated with colossal reliefs of Ptolemy XII Neos Dionysos, holding his enemies by their hair before Horus and about to smash their skulls; this is the classic propaganda pose of the almighty pharaoh.

Beyond this pylon, the **court of offerings** is surrounded on three sides by 32 columns, each with different floral capitals. The walls are decorated with reliefs, including the 'Feast of the Beautiful Meeting' just inside the en- trance, the meeting being that of Horus of Edfu and Hathor of Dendara, who visited each other's temples each year and, after two weeks of great fertility celebrations, were magically united.

A second set of Horus falcon statues in black granite once flanked the entrance to the temple's first or **outer hypostyle hall**, but today only one remains. Inside the entrance of the outer hypostyle hall, to the left and right, are two small chambers: the one on the right was the temple **library** where the ritual texts were stored; the chamber on the left was the **hall of consecrations**, a vestry where freshly laundered robes and ritual vases were kept. The hall itself has 12 columns, and the walls are decorated with reliefs of the temple's founding.

NILE VALLEY: ESNA TO ABU SIMBEL

The **inner hypostyle hall** also has 12 columns, and in the top left part of the hall is perhaps this temple's most interesting room: the temple **laboratory**. Here, all the necessary perfumes and incense recipes were carefully brewed up and stored, their ingredients listed on the walls.

On either side of the hall, doorways lead into the narrow **passage of victory**, which runs between the temple and its massive protective enclosure walls. This narrow ambulatory is decorated with scenes that are of tremendous value to Egyptologists in trying to understand the nature of the ancient temple rituals. Reliefs here show the dramatic reenactment of the battle between Horus and Seth at the annual Festival of Victory. Throughout the conflict, Seth is shown in the form of a hippopotamus, his tiny size rendering him less threatening. At the culmination of the drama, priests are shown cutting up a hippo-shaped cake and eating it to destroy Seth completely.

Back in the inner hypostyle hall, exit through the large central doorway to enter the **offering chamber**, or first antechamber, which has an altar where daily offerings of fruit, flowers, wine, milk and other foods were left. On the west side, 242 steps lead up to the rooftop and a fantastic view of the Nile and the surrounding fields. You may have to pay the guard a bit of baksheesh if you want to go up here.

The second antechamber gives access to the **sanctuary of Horus**, which still contains the polished-granite shrine that once housed the gold cult statue of Horus. Created during the reign of Nectanebo II (360–343 BC), this statue was reused by the Ptolemies in their newer temple. All around Horus' sanctuary are smaller shrines of other gods, including Hathor, Ra and Osiris, and, at the very back, a modern reproduction of the wooden barque in which Horus' statue would be taken out of the temple in procession during festive occasions.

On the eastern enclosure wall look for the remains of the Nilometer, which measured the level of the river and helped predict the coming harvest. For more on Nilometers and their importance in ancient Egypt, see boxed text, p317.

Sleeping & Eating

Al-Medina Hotel (☎ 471 1326; off Sharia al-Gumhuriya; s/d/tr with fan E£40/50/80) Threadbare, basic and with an erratic hot-water system, the hotel is run by staff who are considerably more willing than efficient.

Horus Hotel (☎ 471 5284/86; Sharia al-Gumhuriya; s/d/tr E£82/151/215) This hotel, opposite Omar Effendi department store, is the best option in town, but still pretty basic. It's on the upper floors of the building, with clean, bright rooms, with fans or with air-con, and clean, shared bathrooms. The staff are friendly and helpful, and the restaurant (set menu E£40) is one up on other eateries in town.

There is a kebab place on the main square, and several cafeterias on the waterfront, Sharia an-Nil, including internet cafe **Koko** (☎ 010 440 1196). At all of these places you should ask how much dishes cost before you order. There is a daily food and vegetable souq just off the main square.

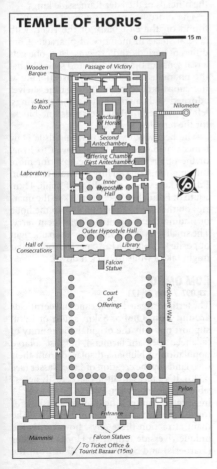

TEMPLE OF HORUS

0 ————— 15 m

Wooden Barque

Passage of Victory

Stairs to Roof

Nilometer

Sanctuary of Horus

Second Antechamber

Offering Chamber (First Antechamber)

Laboratory

Inner Hypostyle Hall

Outer Hypostyle Hall

Library

Hall of Consecrations

Falcon Statue

Court of Offerings

Enclosure Wall

Pylon

Entrance

Mammisi

Falcon Statues

To Ticket Office & Tourist Bazaar (15m)

Next door to Koko you will find the pleasant Habiba Café for tea and snacks and there are a few cafes, mostly men only, around the main square.

Getting There & Away

Edfu train station is on the east bank of the Nile, about 4km from town. There are frequent trains heading to Luxor and Aswan throughout the day, although most are 2nd and 3rd class only. To get to the town, you must first take a *kabout* from the train station to the bridge, then another into town. Each costs 50pt. Alternatively, hire an entire *kabout* to take you to the main square for about E£10 to E£15.

There are no more buses along the Aswan–Luxor road, so the only other option is to buy a seat in a service taxi or minibus: to Luxor (E£6.50, two hours), to Kom Ombo (E£3.50, 45 minutes), Aswan (E£5.50, 1½ hours) and Marsa Alam (E£25, three to four hours). A private minibus to Kom Ombo will cost E£60 per car, to Luxor and Aswan E£100 and to Marsa Alam on the Red Sea E£200.

Hantours take passengers from the waterfront to the temple or vice versa for E£10 to E£15, but you may have to bargain.

GEBEL SILSILA

At Gebel Silsila, about 42km south of Edfu, the Nile narrows considerably to pass between steep sandstone cliffs that are cluttered with ancient rock stelae and graffiti. Known in Pharaonic times as Khenu (Place of Rowing), it was an important centre for the cult of the Nile: every year at the beginning of the inundation season sacrifices were made here to ensure the fertility of the land. The Nile at its height flowing through the narrow gorge must have been a particularly impressive sight, which no doubt explains why the location was chosen as a cult centre. The gorge also marks the change from limestone to sandstone in the bedrock of Egypt. The sandstone quarries here were worked by thousands of men and, judging by the names of pharaohs inscribed in the caves, it seems they were worked from the 18th dynasty or earlier through to the Roman period. The quarries were for centuries the main source in Egypt of sandstone for temple building.

The most attractive monuments are on the west bank, where the rocks are carved with inscriptions and tiny shrines from all periods, as well as adorned with larger chapels. The southern side of the site is marked by a massive pillar of rock, known as the 'Capstan', so called because locals believe there was once a chain – silsila in Arabic, from which the place takes its name – that ran from the east to the west bank. Nearby are the three shrines built by Merenptah, Ramses II and Seti I during the New Kingdom. Further north, the main quarry has clear masons' marks and a group of elaborate private memorial chapels. Several stelae, including a large **Stelae of Shoshenq I**, mark the northern limit of the quarry and lead to the **Speos of Horemheb** (adult/student E£30/20; [clock] 7am-8pm), a rock-hewn chapel started by Horemheb (1323–1295 BC) and finished by the officials of the later Ramesside kings.

The more impressive quarries are to be found on the east bank of the river, with several stelae in memory of pharaohs from different periods and *ex votos*. Here one gets a real sense of the grandeur and scale of what the pharaohs undertook, by just looking at the cubist landscape of the gigantic shelves adorned with quarry marks and drawings, left by the removal of the sandstone blocks for the temples.

The best way to get to Gebel Silsila is by felucca or dahabiyya from Aswan to Esna, or the other way around. See p99 for more information. You can hire a private taxi from Edfu to take you to the village of Kajuj, 41km south of Edfu, then take the track to the quarries on the east bank of the Nile, in the hope of finding the antiquities department ferry. The small ferry leaves from the east bank right opposite the temple (E£10 per person), but it might take a while to track it down.

KOM OMBO

[phone] 097 / pop 71,121

The fertile, irrigated sugar cane and cornfields around Kom Ombo, 65km south of Edfu, support not only the original community of fellaheen (peasant farmers), but also a large population of Nubians displaced from their own lands by the creation of Lake Nasser (see p320). It's a pleasant little place, easily accessible en route between Aswan and Luxor. A huge cattle market is held on the outskirts of town, near the railway line, on Thursday. The main attraction these days, however, is the unique riverside temple to Horus the Elder (Haroeris) and Sobek, about 4km from the

LASCAUX ON THE NILE

In 2004 Belgian archaeologists discovered the oldest drawings in Egypt at a site 15km north of Kom Ombo. Palaeolithic animal illustrations, similar to those found in the Lascaux caves in France, have been discovered on huge Nubian sandstone rocks near the village of Qurta. Most of these fine paintings are of bovids in different positions. There are also gazelles, birds, hippos and fish in a naturalistic style, and a few stylised human figures with pronounced buttocks but no other particular features.

These discoveries represent some of the largest and finest examples of rock art ever found in Egypt. Many of the paintings were first carved in the rock surface, almost like a bas-relief, and then painted. It is thought they were produced by the Ballanan-Silsilian culture, dated to about 16,000 to 15,000 years ago, which corresponds climatologically with the end of a hyperarid period, before the return of the rains and the 'Wild Nile' stage of about 14,000 to 13,000 years ago. The artists appear to have been hunters and fishermen.

As the art is very fragile, the site is still closed to the public.

town's centre, which stands gloriously on a promontory overlooking the Nile.

In ancient times Kom Ombo was known as Pa-Sebek (Land of Sobek), after the crocodile god of the region. It became important during the Ptolemaic period, when its name was changed to Ombos and it became the capital of the first Upper Egyptian nome during the reign of Ptolemy VI Philometor. Kom Ombo was an important military base and a trading centre between Egypt and Nubia. Gold was traded here, but more importantly it was a market for African elephants brought from Ethiopia, which the Ptolemies needed to fight the Indian elephants of their long-term rivals the Seleucids, who ruled the largest chunk of Alexander's former empire to the east of Egypt.

Temple of Kom Ombo

Standing on a promontory at a bend in the Nile, where in ancient times sacred crocodiles basked in the sun on the riverbank, is the **Temple of Kom Ombo** (adult/student E£30/20; ⏲ 7am-8pm Oct-May, to 9pm Jun-Sep). Unique in Egypt, it has a dual dedication to the local crocodile god Sobek and Haroeris, from *har-wer*, meaning Horus the Elder. This is reflected in the temple's plan: perfectly symmetrical along the main axis of the temple, there are twin entrances, two shared hypostyle halls with carvings of the two gods on either side, and twin sanctuaries. It is assumed that there were also two priesthoods. The left (western) side of the temple was dedicated to Haroeris, the right (eastern) half to Sobek.

Reused blocks suggest an earlier temple from the Middle Kingdom period, and there

are remains of 18th-dynasty structures, but the main temple dates from Ptolemaic times, built by Ptolemy VI Philometor, though most of its decoration was completed by Cleopatra VII's father, Ptolemy XII Neos Dionysos. The temple's spectacular riverside setting has resulted in the erosion of part of its partly Roman forecourt and outer sections, but much of the complex has survived and is very similar in layout to the other Ptolemaic temples of Edfu and Dendara, albeit smaller.

The temple is entered through the Ptolemaic gateway on the southeast corner. Nearby, to the right of the temple wall, is a small **shrine to Hathor**, now used as storage for the **mummified crocodiles** and their clay coffins that were dug up from a nearby sacred-animal cemetery; four from the collection are on display. On the opposite side of the compound, to the left (southwest) corner of the temple are the remains of a small **mammisi**, decorated with reliefs, including one that depicts Ptolemy VIII Euergetes in a boat in a reed thicket before the god Min. Beyond this to the north you will find the deep well that supplied the temple with water, and close by is a small pool in which crocodiles, Sobek's sacred animal, were raised.

Passing into the temple's **forecourt**, where the reliefs are divided between the two gods, there is a double altar in the centre of the court for both gods. Beyond are the shared **inner and outer hypostyle halls**, each with 10 columns. Inside the **outer hypostyle hall**, to the left, is a finely executed relief showing Ptolemy XII Neos Dionysos being presented to Haroeris by Isis and the lion-headed goddess Raettawy, with Thoth looking on. The walls to the right

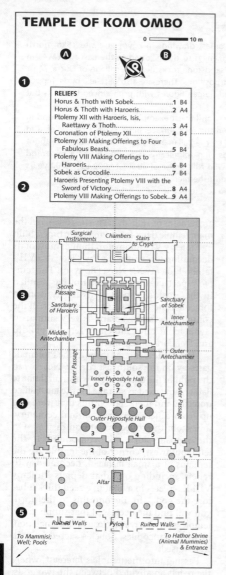

TEMPLE OF KOM OMBO

0 ————— 10 m

RELIEFS

Horus & Thoth with Sobek	1 B4
Horus & Thoth with Haroeris	2 A4
Ptolemy XII with Haroeris, Isis, Raettawy & Thoth	3 A4
Coronation of Ptolemy XII	4 B4
Ptolemy XII Making Offerings to Four Fabulous Beasts	5 B4
Ptolemy VIII Making Offerings to Haroeris	6 B4
Sobek as Crocodile	7 B4
Haroeris Presenting Ptolemy VIII with the Sword of Victory	8 A4
Ptolemy VIII Making Offerings to Sobek	9 A4

Surgical Instruments

Chambers

Stairs to Crypt

Secret Passage

Sanctuary of Haroeris

Sanctuary of Sobek

Inner Antechamber

Middle Antechamber

Outer Antechamber

Inner Passage

Outer Passage

Inner Hypostyle Hall

Outer Hypostyle Hall

Forecourt

Altar

Ruined Walls

Pylon

Ruined Walls

To Mammisi; Well; Pools

To Hathor Shrine (Animal Mummies) & Entrance

with a curved weapon, representing the sword of victory. Behind Ptolemy is his sister-wife and co-ruler Cleopatra II.

From here, three **antechambers**, each with double entrances, lead to the **sanctuaries of Sobek and Haroeris**. The now-ruined chambers on either side would have been used to store priests' vestments and liturgical papyri. The sanctuaries themselves are no longer completely intact, allowing you to see the **secret passage** between them that enabled the priests to give the gods a 'voice' to answer the petitions of pilgrims.

The **outer passage**, which runs around the temple walls, is unusual. Here, on the left-hand (northern) corner of the temple's back wall, is a puzzling scene, which is often described as a collection of '**surgical instruments**'. It seems more probable that these were implements used during the temple's daily rituals.

Sleeping & Eating

Foreigners are theoretically allowed to stay the night in Kom Ombo now, but there still isn't anywhere worth staying.

Al-Noba Restaurant (main rd; set menus E£25) A little way south of the service-taxi station, Al-Noba is the only sit-down eatery in this part of town and the only items on the menu are soup followed by a quarter chicken served with rice and vegetables.

Otherwise, the choice is between *ta'amiyya* and kebab stands. Snacks and drinks can be bought at the series of cafeterias and tourist bazaars, called Rural Home, in the shade of the trees between the temple and the Nile. Cafeteria Venus on the north side of the temple has cold beers in a pleasant garden setting, but foreigners are not always allowed to leave the temple compound to reach it.

Getting There & Away

The best way to visit the temple is to come on a tour or with a private taxi. A private taxi from Luxor taking in both Edfu and Kom Ombo and returning in the evening can cost from about E£400 to E£500; moving on to Aswan instead of returning will cost between E£450 and E£500. A private taxi from Aswan will cost from E£150 to E£200. Alternatively, buy a seat in a service taxi or minibus at E£12 to Luxor or E£6 to Aswan. At the time of writing, there are no buses between Aswan and Luxor.

show the crowning of Ptolemy XII by Nekhbet (the vulture goddess worshipped at the Upper Egyptian town of Al-Kab) and Wadjet (the snake goddess based at Buto in Lower Egypt), with the dual crown of Upper and Lower Egypt, symbolising the unification of Egypt.

Reliefs in the **inner hypostyle hall** show Haroeris presenting Ptolemy VIII Euergetes

THE FORTY DAYS ROAD

Large caravans of camels are brought through the desert from Sudan's Darfur and Kordofan provinces to Daraw, along the Forty Days Rd (Darb al-Arba'een), allegedly named for the number of days it took to walk.

At first, after the Persians introduced camels into the region (around the 6th century BC), the animals carried slaves, ostrich feathers, precious stones, animal skins and other goods from Africa, much appreciated by the pharaohs and their officials, or, later, distributed to the great empires in Greece, Persia and Rome.

Trading caravans were replaced by the faster railway at the end of the 19th century, but the camels still come, except now they are the cargo. Once in Daraw, they spend two days in quarantine, where they are inoculated against a number of diseases. After they have been sold by the Sudanese owners, most go on to the camel market in Birqash, about 35km northwest of Cairo (see p211), and from there they are sold again. Some are sold to Egyptian farmers, others are exported to other Middle Eastern countries, but many are slaughtered to provide meat for poorer Egyptians.

Trains are another option, but the train station is some way from the temple.

To get to the temple from the town centre, take a *kabout* to the boat landing on the Nile about 800m north of the temple (25pt to 50pt), then walk the remainder of the way. *Kabouts* to the boat landing leave from the service taxi station. A private taxi between the town and temple should cost about E£10 to E£15 return.

DARAW

Daraw, 8km south of Kom Ombo, appears to be like any other village in this part of Egypt, except for its remarkable **camel market** *(souq al-gimaal)*. Most of the camels are brought up in caravans from Sudan to just north of Abu Simbel (see boxed text, above), from where they're trucked to Daraw. The rest walk to the market in smaller groups, entering Egypt at Wadi al-Alagi and making their way through the Eastern Desert.

Camels are sold here each day of the week, but the main market days are Tuesday and Thursday, when sometimes as many as 2000 camels are brought down from Abu Simbel.

Definitely worth seeing is the Nubian museum called **Hosh al-Kenzi** (Kenzian House; ☎ 273 0970, opposite Dar Rasoul Mosque, Sharia al-Kunuz; admission E£15; ☻ 8am-noon). Built in 1912 by the father of the current resident, Haj Mohammed Eid Mohammed Hassanein, the house is constructed in traditional Nubian style and decorated with Nubian artefacts mostly made from palm trees. Next door is a workshop where the beaded curtains made from date pips, pieces of palm frond or various seeds

are still made for Nubian houses. Curtains like this are the main decoration but there is a wonderful sense of space and simplicity in these houses.

Getting There & Away

Trains between Aswan and Luxor usually stop at Daraw. By service taxi you are likely to be dropped at the station for minibuses and service taxis, which is 9km north of the town. Service taxis and minibuses running between Aswan and Kom Ombo stop in Daraw (if passengers want to get off). The E£6 fare is the same as for the whole stretch. The camel market is on a large lot, 2km from the Luxor–Aswan highway. Turn off at the main road into the town and ask for 'souq al-gimaal'.

ASWAN

☎ 097 / pop 226,013

On the northern end of the First Cataract and marking the country's ancient southern frontier, Aswan has always been of great strategic importance. In ancient times it was a garrison town for the military campaigns against Nubia, its quarries provided the valuable granite used for so many sculptures and obelisks, and it was a prosperous marketplace at the crossroads of the ancient caravan routes. The first document mentioning Aswan, rather than the older island settlement of Abu, date to the New Kingdom and use the ancient Egyptian word *swenet*, meaning 'trade', a name that later became the Arabic As-Suan, meaning markets.

Today, slower than most places in Egypt, laid-back and pleasant, it is the perfect place to linger for a few days, rest and recover from the rigours of travelling along the Nile. The river is wide, languorous and stunningly beautiful here, flowing gently down from Lake Nasser, around dramatic black-granite boulders and palm-studded islands. Colourful, sleepy Nubian villages run down to the water and stand out against the backdrop of the desert on the west bank. Aswan comes as a relief after Luxor, seemingly off the radar in an Egypt that wants to move on with mass tourism.

With so long a history, there is plenty to see in Aswan, but somehow the sightseeing seems less urgent and certainly less overwhelming than elsewhere in Egypt, allowing more time

to take in the magic of the Nile at sunset, to stroll in the exotic souq, one of the best outside Cairo, or to appreciate the gentleness of the Nubians. Most tour groups head straight for the Temple of Isis at Philae, taking in the Unfinished Obelisk and the dams on the way, but the rarely visited ruins of ancient Abu and the small Aswan Museum on Elephantine Island are fascinating, as are the exquisite botanical gardens and the Nubia Museum.

But Aswan is more than just a tourist town; a governorate capital, it has a large population of educated bureaucrats and a good university. Some days, when all the cruise boats seem to unload their tour groups at the same time, it is no longer as relaxed as it was a few years ago. But much of the time the heat, the sweet

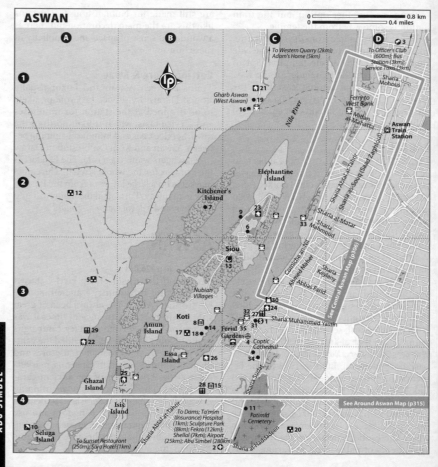

See Central Aswan Map (p306)

See Around Aswan Map (p315)

smells of spices and the slow pace take hold of the visitor. Few things are more calming than to glide on a felucca between the islands and the rocks at sunset or birdwatching in the early morning hours, or, failing that, to sit on the banks and watch the Nile go by.

The best time to visit Aswan is in winter, when the days are warm and dry. In summer the temperature hovers between 38°C and 45°C; it's too hot by day to do anything but sit by a fan and swat flies, or flop into a swimming pool.

ORIENTATION

Most of the city of interest to visitors is along the Nile or parallel to it. The train station is at the northern end of town, only 100m from the river and the Corniche an-Nil.

The street running north–south in front of the train station is Sharia as-Souq (also occasionally signposted as Sharia Saad Zaghloul). This is Aswan's market street, where the souq overflows with colourful, tempting and aromatic wares. Running parallel to it is Sharia Abtal at-Tahrir, where you'll find the youth hostel and a few budget and mid-range hotels. Most of Aswan's government buildings, banks, travel agencies, restaurants and top-end hotels are on Corniche an-Nil. From the Corniche, ferries and feluccas sail to the rock tombs on the west bank or to Elephantine Island.

INFORMATION

Bookshops

Stalls in the tourist bazaar at the exit of the Unfinished Obelisk (see p303) have some good books on Egypt and Nubia. If you're after international newspapers and maga-

zines, try the news-stand near the Philae Hotel on the Corniche.

Emergency

Ambulance (☎ 123)
Police (Map p306; ☎ 230 2043; Corniche an-Nil) Near Thomas Cook.
Tourist police (Map p306; ☎ 230 3436, 231 4393; Corniche an-Nil) Contact the tourist office (p302) first to help with translation.

Internet Access

Internet prices range from E£10 to E£15 per hour.
Aswan Internet Café (Map p306; ☎ 231 4472; Rowing Club, Corniche an-Nil; ☽ 9am-midnight Sun-Fri)
Aswanet Internet Café (Map p306; ☎ 231 7332; next to Keylany Hotel, 25 Sharia Keylany; ☽ 9am-11pm)
Nuba Nile Internet (p306; Sharia Abtal at-Tahrir; ☽ 24hr)

Medical Services

Mubarak Military Hospital (Map p300; ☎ 231 7985/4739; Sharia Sadat) The top hospital in town.
Ta'mim (Insurance) Hospital (off Map p300; ☎ 231 5112/6510; Sharia Sadat) Most recent hospital, with a good reputation.

Money

Unless otherwise noted, banking hours are 8.30am to 2pm and 5pm to 8pm Sunday to Thursday. There are ATMs all along the Corniche and around Sharia as-Souq, as well as at the train station.
American Express (Map p300; ☎ 230 6983; Corniche an-Nil; ☽ 9am-5pm Sun-Thu, to 2pm Fri & Sat)
Bank of Alexandria (Map p306; Corniche an-Nil)
Banque du Caire (Map p306; Corniche an-Nil) Branch and ATM.

NILE VALLEY: ESNA TO ABU SIMBEL

Banque Misr (Map p306; Corniche an-Nil; ⏰ 8am-3pm & 5-8pm) ATM and foreign-exchange booth next to main building.
Thomas Cook (Map p306; ☎ 230 4011; www.thomas cook.com.eg; Corniche an-Nil; ⏰ 8am-2pm & 5-9pm)

Post

Branch post office (Map p306; Sharia Abtal at-Tahrir; ⏰ 8am-2pm Sat-Thu) Opposite the Victoria Hotel.
Main post office (Map p306; Corniche an-Nil; ⏰ 8am-8pm Sat-Thu, 1-5pm Fri)

Telephone

There are cardphones along the Corniche and at the train station.
Telephone centrale (Map p300; Corniche an-Nil; ⏰ 24hr)

Tourist Information

Tourist office (Map p306; ☎ 231 2811, 010 576 7594; Midan al-Mahatta; ⏰ 8am-3pm & 7-9pm Sat-Thu, 9am-3pm & 6-8pm Fri) This tourist office has little material, and still no computer, but the manager, Hakeem Hussein, is knowledgeable and very helpful. He can deal with most questions, from organising a trip and advising on time-tables to giving an idea of prices for taxis and feluccas.

SIGHTS

Aswan's sights are spread out, mostly to the south and west of the town. The souq cuts right through the centre of town, parallel to the Nile. The Nubia Museum is within walking distance, just, but all other sights require transport. The sites on the islands and on the west bank involve a short boat trip.

Town & East Bank

Starting from the southern end, **Sharia as-Souq** appears very much like the tourist bazaars all over Egypt, with persistent traders (although perhaps less persistent than elsewhere in the country) trying to lure passers-by into their shops to buy T-shirts, perfume, spices, beaded *galabiyyas* (men's full-length robes) and roughly carved copies of Pharaonic statues. But a closer look reveals more exotic elements, with traders selling Nubian talismans for good luck, colourful Nubian baskets and skullcaps, Sudanese swords, African masques, and enormous stuffed crocodiles and desert creatures. This is also very much a living market, where Nubians from Elephantine Island and around Aswan shop for food and live produce, including fruit, vegetables, chickens and pigeons. Aswan is famous for the quality of its *fuul sudan* (peanuts), henna powder (sold in

different qualities) and dried hibiscus flowers, used to make the much-loved local drink *karkadai*. The pace is slow, particularly in the late afternoon, the air has a slight whiff of sandalwood and, as in ancient times, you may feel that Aswan is the gateway to Africa.

Walking along the Corniche and watching the sunset over the islands and the desert on the other side of the Nile is a favourite pastime in Aswan. The view from riverside cafe terraces may be blocked by cruise boats, but plans are under way to relocate them all to a dock that is under construction on the northern end of town; for now the best place to watch the sunset is from the Old Cataract (see p311) terrace once it's rebuilt, or from the Sunset Restaurant (see p312).

NUBIA MUSEUM

The **Nubia Museum** (Map p300; ☎ 231 9111; Sharia Abtal at-Tahrir; adult/student E£50/25; ⏰ 9am-1pm & 5-9pm) is a showcase of the history, art and culture of Nubia and is a real treat. Established in 1997, in cooperation with Unesco, the museum is a reminder of the history and culture of the Nubians, much of which was lost when Lake Nasser flooded their land after the building of the dams (see p319). Exhibits are beautifully displayed in huge halls, where clearly written explanations take you from 4500 BC through to the present day. As it is not on the tour-group circuit, the museum is little visited.

At the entrance to the main exhibition hall is a model of the Nile Valley and the main temple sites. The exhibits start with prehistoric artefacts and objects from the Kingdom of Kush and Meroe. Coptic and Islamic art displays lead to a description of the massive Unesco project to move Nubia's most important historic monuments away from the rising waters of Lake Nasser, following the building of the Aswan High Dam. Among museum highlights are 6000-year-old painted pottery bowls and an impressive quartzite statue of a 25th-dynasty priest of Amun in Thebes with distinct Kushite (Upper Nubian) features. The stunning horse armour found in tombs from the Ballana period (5th to 7th century BC) shows the sophistication of artisanship during this brief ascendancy. A fascinating display traces the development of irrigation along the Nile River, from the earliest attempts to control the flow of the river, right up to the building of the old Aswan Dam. A model of a Nubian house, complete with old furniture and mannequins wearing traditional silver jewellery, attempts to portray the folk culture of modern Nubia.

All this is housed in a well-designed modern building, loosely based on traditional Nubian architecture. In the museum garden there is a reconstructed Nubian house (which you can't enter, unfortunately) and a small 'cave' with prehistoric petroglyphs, which show giraffes and other wild animals once indigenous to the region. The site also incorporates an 11th-century Fatimid tomb, as well as a number of other tombs of sheikhs.

The museum entrance is about a five-minute walk from the EgyptAir office on Corniche an-Nil.

FATIMID CEMETERY

Behind the Nubia Museum is this vast **cemetery** (Map p300), a collection of low mudbrick buildings with domed roofs. Although most tombs are modern, some of the mausolea clustered towards the back of the cemetery go back to the Tulunid period (9th century). The old tombs are in bad shape and when the original marble inscriptions fell off after a freak late-19th-century rainstorm, they were taken to Cairo without anyone recording which tomb they had come from. As a result, the dates and names of tomb owners have been lost. The tombs are covered with domes built on a drum with corners sticking out like horns, a feature unique to southern Egypt. Some domes near the outer edges of the cemetery are decorated with flags and are in much better condition than the other ones. These belong to local saints; you may see Aswanis circumambulating a tomb, praying for the saint's intercession.

The municipality of Aswan has fenced off the Fatimid Cemetery. Enter from the main gate, a 10-minute walk from the Corniche along the road to the airport, and walk right through the cemetery to join the road to the Unfinished Obelisk; just aim for the four-storey building facing the back of the cemetery. The site's caretaker will often accompany you and show you the best-preserved tombs, for which he should be given a baksheesh of a few pounds.

UNFINISHED OBELISK

Aswan was the source of Egypt's finest granite, the hard stone ancient Egyptians used to make statues and embellish temples and pyramids.

In the **Northern Quarries** (Map p315; adult/student E£30/20; ⏰ 7am-4pm Oct-May, 8am-6pm Jun-Sep),

about 1.5km from town opposite the Fatimid Cemetery, is a huge discarded **obelisk**. Three sides of the shaft, which is nearly 42m long, were completed except for the inscriptions. At 1168 tonnes, the completed obelisk would have been the single heaviest piece of stone the Egyptians ever fashioned. However, a flaw appeared in the rock at a late stage in the process. So it lies where the disappointed stonemasons abandoned it, still partly attached to the parent rock, with no indication of what it was intended for.

Upon entering the quarry, follow the steps that lead down from the surrounding ramp into the pit of the obelisk, where there are ancient pictographs of dolphins and ostriches or flamingos, thought to have been painted by workers at the quarry.

No service taxis run past the site, but you can get one to the junction on Sharia al-Haddadeen and then walk (about 10 minutes). Private taxis will charge about E£12. You can also walk through Fatimid Cemetery to get to it.

SCULPTURE PARK

The atmospheric **Sculpture Park** (Map p315) on the lake between the High and old dam, houses the sculptures made by artists from around the world during the International Sculpture Symposium, held each spring at the Basma Hotel.

Sculpture aficionados can get here, taking the road to Shellal, and instead of turning right towards the ferry to Philae, taking the road up the hill. Continue until you reach the top; on the left is the quarry, on the right the sculptures. No service taxis come to the Sculpture Park, so you will have to organise a private taxi. You should expect to pay about E£25.

The River

ELEPHANTINE ISLAND

Aswan's earliest settlement lies opposite the town centre, just north of the First Cataract. **Elephantine Island** (Map p300) is the ancient **Abu** (meaning both elephant and ivory in ancient Egyptian), both names a reminder of the important role the island once played in the ivory trade. At the beginning of the 1st dynasty (about 3000 BC) a fortress was built on the island to establish Egypt's southern frontier. Abu soon became an important customs point and trading centre. It remained strategically significant throughout the Pharaonic

NILE VALLEY: ESNA TO ABU SIMBEL

period as a departure point for the military and commercial expeditions into Nubia and the south. During the 6th dynasty (2345–2181 BC) Abu gained its strength as a political and economics centre and, despite occasional ups and downs, the island retained its importance until the Graeco-Roman period.

As well as being a thriving settlement, Elephantine Island was the main cult centre of the ram-headed god Khnum (at first the god of the inundation, and from the 18th dynasty worshipped as the creator of humankind on his potter's wheel), Satet (Khnum's wife, and guardian of the southern frontier) and their daughter Anket. Each year the rushing of the waters of the flood were first heard here on Elephantine Island. Over time religious complexes took over more and more of the island, so residential areas moved either further north on the island or to the east bank. The temple town of Abu received its *coup de grâce* in the 4th century AD, when Christianity was established as the imperial Roman religion. From then on, worship of the ancient gods was gradually abandoned and defensive fortifications were moved to the east bank, today's city of Aswan.

The extensive ruins of Abu take up the southern end of the island. The northern tip is dominated by the deluxe and architecturally insensitive Mövenpick Resort Aswan.

Nubian Villages

Sandwiched between the ruins of Abu and the Mövenpick resort are two colourful Nubian villages, **Siou** and **Koti**. Their shady alleys and gardens make for a tranquil stroll – a north–south path crosses the middle of the island and links the two villages. At **Animalia** (Map p300; ☎ 231 4152, 010 545 6420; www.animalia-eg.com; main st, Siou; admission E£5, incl guided tour E£10; ⏰ 8am–7pm) Mohamed Sobhi, a Nubian guide, and his family have dedicated part of their large house to the traditions, flora and fauna and the history of Nubia. This small but charming museum has a collection of stuffed animals found in Nubia, samples of sedimentary rocks, great pictures of Nubia before it was flooded by Lake Nasser (see p321), a small shop selling Nubian crafts at fixed prices and a lovely roof terrace where drinks are served overlooking the gardens. Mohamed Sobhi is passionate and knowledgeable about Nubian culture and the natural world, and he also takes early-morning birdwatching trips (see p308).

Close to the wall separating the Mövenpick resort from Siou village, facing Kitchener's Island, is **Baaba Dool** (Map p300; ☎ Mustapha 010 497 2608; Siou; admission free), a gorgeous painted Nubian house, where the owner serves tea, sells Nubian handicrafts and can arrange live music and dancing or henna 'tattoos' (see boxed text, p308) done by local women. The roof terrace is the perfect place to watch the sunset on the west bank, with a multitude of birds flying around the island opposite.

Western women should be respectful of local tradition and wear modest clothes. More and more visitors prefer to enjoy the traditional set-up of the villages, and rent flats or houses here for a few days (see p312).

Aswan Museum & the Ruins of Abu

The ruins of the original town of Abu and the fascinating **Aswan Museum** (Map p300; adult/student E£25/15; ⏰ 8am–5pm Oct-Apr, 8.30am–6pm May-Sep) lie at the southern end of Elephantine Island. The older part of the museum is housed in the villa of Sir William Willcocks, architect of the old Aswan Dam. Built in 1898, the villa became a museum in 1912. The newer extension was added in 1998.

The main part of the museum houses a dusty collection of antiquities discovered in Aswan and Nubia, but most of the Nubian artefacts rescued from the temples flooded by Lake Nasser were moved to the Nubia Museum. The modern annexe, however, has a delightful collection of objects, from weapons, pottery and utensils to statues, encased mummies and sarcophagi from predynastic to late Roman times, found in the excavations on Elephantine Island. The well-displayed objects, with excellent labels in English and Arabic, are organised in separate glass cases, each explaining a particular facet of life on the island in ancient times: death, trade, religion, weaving, hunting, farming, cooking and so on. At the right of the main entrance, in a room by itself, lies the sarcophagus and mummy of a sacred ram, the animal associated with Khnum.

A path through the garden behind the museum leads to the evocative **ruins of ancient Abu**. Swiss and German teams, excavating here since the early 20th century, have made the site into an outdoor museum. Numbered plaques and reconstructed buildings mark the island's long history from around 3000 BC to the 14th century AD. The largest structure in the site is the partially reconstructed **Temple of Khnum** (plaque Nos 6, 12 and 13). Built in honour of the God of Inundation during the Old Kingdom, it was added to and used for more than 1500 years before being extensively rebuilt in Ptolemaic times. Other highlights include a small 4th-dynasty **step pyramid**, thought to have been built by Sneferu (2613–2589 BC; father of Khufu of Great Pyramid fame); a tiny **Ptolemaic chapel** (No 15), reconstructed from the Temple of Kalabsha (which is now just south of the High Dam); a reconstructed 18th-dynasty **temple** (No 2), built by Hatshepsut (1473–1458 BC) and dedicated to the goddess Satet; a **cemetery for sacred rams** (No 11), thought to have been the living embodiment of the god Khnum; and the ruins of an **Aramaic Jewish colony** dating from the 5th century BC.

Heavenly portents and priestly prophecies aside, in ancient times only the Nilometer could give a real indication of the likelihood of a bountiful harvest. When the Nilometer here in the southern frontier town recorded a high water level of the river, it meant a good harvest, which in turn meant more taxes. The **Nilometer of the Temple of Khnum** (No 7) is below the southern balustrade of the Khnum temple. Built in the 26th dynasty, its stone stairs lead down to a small basin for measuring the Nile's maximum level. Another stairway, with a scale etched into its wall, leads to the water from the basin's northern end. Descending to the river's edge from beneath a sycamore tree near the museum is the **Nilometer of the Satet Temple** (No 10). Built in late Ptolemaic or early Roman times and restored in the 19th century, its staircase is roofed over and niches in the walls would have had oil lamps to provide light. If you look hard as you descend to the river, you can see the names of Roman prefects carved into the left-hand wall.

An excellent guide, *Elephantine: The Ancient Town,* produced by the German archaeological mission on Elephantine, explains the long history of Abu and describes in detail the monuments according to their numbered plaques. It is available in English and German at the museum or, when it is open, at the German excavation house, adjacent to the site.

Getting There & Away
For information on ferries to Elephantine Island, see p308.

ASWAN BOTANICAL GARDENS
To the west of Elephantine Island is **Aswan Botanical Gardens** (Map p300; admission E£15; 8am-5pm Oct-Apr, to 6pm May-Sep), still often referred to by its old name, Kitchener's Island. The island was given to Lord Horatio Kitchener in the 1890s when he was commander of the Egyptian army. Indulging his passion for beautiful palms and plants, Kitchener turned the entire island into a stunning botanical garden, importing plants from the Far East, India and parts of Africa. Covering 6.8 hectares, it is filled with birds as well as hundreds of species of flora. The garden may have lost some of its former glory, but its majestic palm trees are still a stunning sight, particularly just before sunset when the light is softer and the scent of sandalwood floats on the breeze. Avoid coming here on Friday, when the place is invaded by picnicking extended families with stereos.

The island is most easily seen as part of a felucca tour. Alternatively, take the northernmost ferry to Elephantine Island and walk across the village to the other side of the island, where a few little feluccas wait on the island's western edge, to take visitors across. Expect to pay at least E£10 for a one-way trip.

The West Bank
As with the Botanical Gardens, it is easiest to visit the west bank as part of a felucca tour. The longer way is to take a ferry from Elephantine Island across to the landing for the Monastery of St Simeon. To get to the Tombs of the Nobles, or the Nubian village, take the public ferry that leaves from a landing opposite the train station, on the east bank. See p308 for more details.

AGA KHAN MAUSOLEUM
High up on the west bank stands the elegant **Tomb of Mohammed Shah Aga Khan** (Aga Khan Mausoleum, Map p300; closed to the public), the 48th imam (leader) of the Ismaili sect, who died in 1957, and of his wife the Begum, who died in 2000. Aswan was their favourite wintering place, and the family's white villa is in the garden beneath the tomb.

MONASTERY OF ST SIMEON
The fortresslike 7th-century **Monastery of St Simeon** (Map p300; Deir Amba Samaan; adult/student E£20/10; 8am-4pm Oct-May, 7am-5pm Jun-Sep) was first dedicated to the 4th-century local saint, Anba Hadra, who renounced the world on his

wedding day. It was rebuilt in the 10th century and dedicated to St Simeon. From here the monks travelled into Nubia, in the hope of converting the Nubians to Christianity, until Saladin (Salah ad-Din) destroyed the monastery in 1173.

Surrounded by desert sands, the monastery was built on two levels – the lower level of stone and the upper level of mudbrick – surrounded by 10m-high walls. The basilica has traces of frescos, and nearby is the chamber where St Simeon prayed with his beard tied to the ceiling in case he fell asleep. The cells, with their mastaba beds, once provided accommodation for about 300 resident monks and some 100 pilgrims. The last room on the right still has graffiti from Muslim pilgrims who stayed here en route to Mecca.

To get to the monastery from the boat landing, scramble up the desert track on foot (about 25 minutes) or hire a camel to take you up (negotiate with the camel drivers but expect to pay about E£30 per hour; agree in advance how much time you want to spend). Alternatively, you can take the ferry to the Tombs of the Nobles and ride a camel or donkey from there (see p308), but remember to bring water.

TOMBS OF THE NOBLES

The high cliffs opposite Aswan, just north of Kitchener's Island, are honeycombed with the tombs of the governors, the Keepers of the Gate of the South, and other dignitaries of ancient Elephantine Island. Known as the **Tombs of the Nobles** (Map p300; adult/student E£20/10; ☽ 8am-4pm Oct-May, to 5pm Jun-Sep), six are open to the public. The tombs date from the Old and Middle Kingdoms and most follow a simple plan, with an entrance hall, a pillared room and a corridor leading to the burial chamber. A set of stairs cutting diagonally across the hill takes you up to the tombs from the ferry landing.

Tombs of Mekhu & Sabni (Nos 25 & 26)

The adjoining tombs of father and son Mekhu (Tomb No 25) and Sabni (Tomb No 26), both governors, date from the long reign of 6th-dynasty Pharaoh Pepi II (2278–2184 BC). The reliefs in Sabni's tomb record how he led his army into Nubia, to punish the tribe responsible for killing his father during a previous military campaign, and to recover his father's body. Upon his return, Pepi II sent him his own royal embalmers and profes-

CENTRAL ASWAN

sional mourners, to show the importance accorded to the keepers of the southern frontier. Several reliefs in Sabni's tomb retain their original colours, and there are some lovely hunting and fishing scenes depicting him with his daughters in the pillared hall.

Tomb of Sarenput II (No 31)

Sarenput was the local governor and overseer of the priesthood of Satet and Khnum under 12th-dynasty Pharaoh Amenemhat II (1922–1878 BC). One of the most beautiful and best-preserved tombs, its colours are still vivid. A six-pillared entrance chamber leads into a corridor with six niches holding statues of Sarenput. The burial chamber has four columns and a niche with wall paintings showing Sarenput with his wife (on the right) and his mother (on the left), as well as hunting and fishing scenes.

Tomb of Harkhuf (No 34)

The tomb of Harkhuf, governor of the south during the reign of Pharaoh Pepi II, is hardly decorated, except for remarkable hieroglyphic texts about his three trading expeditions into central Africa, right of the entrance. Included here is Pepi II, then only a boy of eight, advising Harkhuf to take extra care of the 'dancing pygmy' he had obtained on his travels, as the pharaoh was very keen to see him in Memphis. My majesty desires to see this pygmy more than the gifts of Sinai or of Punt,' Harkhuf writes. Look carefully to see the tiny hieroglyph figure of the pygmy several times in the text.

Tomb of Hekaib (Pepinakht; No 35)

Hekaib, also known as Pepinakht, was overseer of foreign soldiers during the reign of Pharaoh

Pepi II. He was sent to quell rebellions in both Nubia and Palestine, and was even deified after his death, as is revealed by the small shrine of Hekaib built on Elephantine Island during the Middle Kingdom (c 1900 BC). There are fine reliefs showing fighting bulls and hunting scenes.

Tomb of Sarenput I (No 36)

The court of the tomb of Sarenput I, grandfather of Sarenput II and governor during the 12th-dynasty reign of Pharaoh Sesostris I (1965–1920 BC), has the remains of six pillars, decorated with reliefs. On either side of the entrance Sarenput is shown being followed by his dogs and sandal-bearer, his flower-bearing harem, his wife and his three sons.

KUBBET AL-HAWA

On the hilltop above the Tombs of the Nobles lies this small **tomb** (Map p300), constructed for a local sheikh. The steep climb up is rewarded with stunning views of the Nile and the surrounding area.

NUBIAN VILLAGE

The Nubian village of **Gharb Aswan** (West Aswan, Map p300) is so far a tranquil affair just north of the Tombs of the Nobles, but things might change soon. A tarmac road that peters out in the sand, at the Tomb of the Nobles, announces Aswan's expansion plans on the west bank. For now it's a pleasant place to be, particularly at night, after the souqs near the ferry landing have closed and most of the tourists have gone back to their hotel on the east bank. Beit al-Kerem (see p310) is a wonderful place to stay for a few nights.

NILE VALLEY: ESNA TO ABU SIMBEL

HENNA TATTOOS

Henna is the natural dye derived from the leaves of the *Lawsonia inermis* shrub, grown in southern Egypt and Nubia for millennia – traces of it have even been found on the nails of mummified pharaohs.

Like their ancestors, Nubian women use henna powder for their hair and also to decorate hands and feet prior to getting married. The intricate red-brown designs adorn the skin for a fortnight or so before fading away.

Women visitors will be offered henna 'tattoos' on their hands (or feet or stomachs, from E£30 per tattoo) at some of the Nubian villages on Elephantine Island or on the west bank of Aswan or in the souq – it looks great and you get to spend time with Nubian women. Always check who will apply the tattoos; this is women's work, but would-be Lotharios see this as a great opportunity to get close to a bit of foreign flesh.

Foreigners tend to prefer black to the traditional red henna tattoos, but beware, as this is in fact natural henna darkened with the very toxic hair dye PPD, which is banned in Europe. Avoid black henna completely, and visit www.hennapage.com to see the damage the dye can cause, from a light allergic reaction to chemical burns and sometimes even death.

WESTERN QUARRY

Isolated in the desert to the west of the Tomb of the Nobles is the ancient **Western Quarry** (Gebel Simaan), where stone for many ancient monuments – possibly including the Colossi of Memnon (see p256) – was quarried. The large **unfinished obelisk**, made for Pharaoh Seti I (1294–1279 BC), was decorated on three sides of its apex before it was abandoned. Nearby, the ancient quarry face and marks are clearly visible, along with the tracks on which the huge blocks were dragged down to the Nile.

Guides to the quarry can be found at the ferry landing, opposite the Tombs of the Nobles. Expect to pay at least E£60 to E£90, after bargaining, for the camel ride, half an hour each way. Take plenty of water, and keep an eye out for snakes.

ACTIVITIES
Birdwatching

Birdwatchers have long flocked to Aswan to watch birds in the winter period, but to be on the Nile very early in the morning, gliding along the edge of the islands, watching birds and hearing how they fit into ancient Egyptian history or into Nubian traditions, has a much wider appeal. **Mohamed Arabi** (☎ 012 324 0132; www.touregypt.net/featurestories/aswanbirding.htm; per person from US$30) is known as the 'Birdman of Aswan' and no bird escapes his eye. He has been taking twitchers and documentary makers for many years, but is also happy to take amateurs out into his small speedboat that glides into the channels between the islands, pointing out the vegetation; sunbirds; hoo-poes; purple, squacco, striated and night herons; pied kingfishers; little and cattle egrets; redshanks; and many other birds. You can call him direct, or book the trip via American Express (p301).

Mohamed Sobhi (see p304) does a similar trip in a normal motorboat for US$25 per person.

Feluccas & Ferries

The Nile looks fabulous and magical at Aswan, and few things are more relaxing than hiring a felucca before sunset and sailing between the islands, the desert and the huge black boulders, listening to the flapping of the sail and to Nubian boys singing from their tiny dugouts. On days when cruise boats dock together in town, hundreds of feluccas circle the islands, a good time to take a felucca a bit further out towards Seheyl Island (p314). The trustworthy **Gelal** (☎ 012 415 4902), who hangs out near Panorama Restaurant and the ferry landing, offers hassle-free tours on his family's feluccas at a fixed price (E£30 per boat for an hour, E£35 for a motor boat). Gelal is from Seheyl Island and can also arrange a visit to the island and lunch (E£30) in his house, as well as a swim on a safe beach (see opposite). According to the tourist office, a three- or four-hour tour costs at least E£90 to E£120. A two- to three-hour trip down to Seheyl Island costs about E£90.

Two public ferries (E£1) run to Elephantine Island; the one departing across from EgyptAir (Map p300) goes to the Aswan Museum, while the one across from Thomas Cook (Map p306) goes to Siou. A third public ferry (E£1) goes from the ferry landing across from the train station to West Aswan and the Tombs of the Nobles.

For details on taking an overnight felucca trip down the Nile, see boxed text, p101.

Swimming

Aswan is a hot place, and often the only way to cool down, apart from hiding in your air-conditioned room, is to swim. Joining the local kids splashing about in the Nile is not a good idea (see Schistosomiasis, p538). Schistosomiasis can only be caught in stagnant water; boatmen know where the current is strong enough (but not too strong) for it to be safe, among them a **beach for swimming** (Map p300) on the west bank opposite Seluga Island. To get there rent a motor boat (per person about E£50 and E£25 extra for lunch if you want to spend the day). Some hotels have swimming pools open to the public, generally from 9am to sunset. The cheapest by far is the Cleopatra Hotel (p310), which costs E£15, but the pool is small and overlooked by other buildings. The Mövenpick Resort (p311) and Isis Aswan (p311) charge nonguests E£100 to use their pools.

TOURS

Small hotels and travel agencies arrange day tours of the area's major sights. Half-day guided tours usually include the Temple of Isis at Philae, the Unfinished Obelisk and the High Dam, and start at E£300 (per person with three to five people) with Amex or Thomas Cook, including admission to all sites. Some budget hotels offer cheaper tours but are not licensed to guide groups. Travel agencies will also arrange felucca trips to Elephantine and Kitchener's Islands for about E£75 to E£100 per person, based on a group of three to five people, but it is cheaper to deal directly with the boatmen.

All travel agencies and most hotels in Aswan offer trips to Abu Simbel, but watch out for huge price differences, and check that the bus is comfortable and has air-con. Thomas Cook charges about E£1000 per person, including a seat in an air-con minibus, admission fees and guide, and E£1400 by air, including transfers, fees and guide. By contrast, budget hotels offer tours for about E£200 to E£300 in a smaller bus, though often not including the entrance fee or guide.

For more information about getting to Abu Simbel, see p325.

SLEEPING

Most visitors to Aswan stay on their cruise boats, so there has been little investment in hotels recently, but things are changing. The Old and New Cataract Hotels have been gutted, and are under complete restoration, to be turned into superdeluxe suite-only hotels. The other change is that quite a few houses on Elephantine Island and on the west bank are for rent, making for a very pleasant alternative to staying in a hotel on the east bank.

Prices vary greatly depending on the season; the rates mentioned here are high season, which extends from October through to April, but peaks in December and January. In the low season, and even until early November, you'll have no trouble finding a room at lower prices.

Hotel touts at the train station try to convince tired travellers that the hotel they have booked is now closed so that they can take them to another hotel and collect their commission. Ignoring them is the thing to do, as their commission will be added to your bill.

Budget

Baaba Dool (Map p300; ☎ 010 49/ 2608; Siou, Elephantine Island; r €10) A great place to unwind for a few days. A few rooms in this beautiful mudbrick house are painted in Nubian style, and have superb views over the Nile and the botanical gardens. Rooms are very basic but clean (bring a sleeping bag) and there are shared hot showers. Mustapha can arrange meals. Book ahead.

Abu Shleeb Hotel (Map p306; ☎ 230 3051; off Sharia Abbas Farid; s/d/tr E£45/55/65; ⚹) These small, clean rooms are in a modern, characterless building, but offer good value: all have private bathroom and hot water. Corner rooms have balconies, and there is a dusty restaurant on the ground floor with very sleepy staff.

Adam's Home (off Map p300; ☎ 010 640 4302; www .adamsnubyana.com; Sheikh Mohammed, Gharb Aswan; r E£50) A different experience awaits you at this beautiful Nubian House in the village of Sheikh Mohammed on the west bank, 7km north of Aswan, and about 2.5km south of the bridge. Overlanders have long known of this place, which provides camping facilities as well as little mudbrick rooms – bring your sleeping bag. This is a long way if you want to go sightseeing in Aswan, but it is the perfect place to immerse yourself in Nubian culture and tranquillity for a few days. Owner Yahya, a famous actor and theatre director, loves to share his passion for all things Nubian. Take a pickup truck from the Tomb of the Nobles to get there or a taxi from Aswan for about E£50.

Nuba Nile Hotel (Map p306; ☎ 231 3267; www.nuba nile.com; Sharia Abtal at-Tahrir; s/d E£60/75; 🔲 💻 💺) If the Keylany (below) is full, this friendly family-run hotel is the next best budget option, with clean, comfortable rooms, conveniently located just north of the square in front of the train station and beside a popular *ahwa* and internet cafe. Check the room before you agree, as they vary considerably: some are tiny, others have no windows, but all have private bathrooms, and most have air-con.

Memnon Hotel (Map p306; ☎ 230 0483, 010 193 5639; www.memnonhotel-aswan.com; Corniche an-Nil; s/d E£70/90; 🔲 💺) The Memnon has been around for a few years and it shows, but the clean, good-sized rooms have great Nile views. The rooftop has a small, not-very-attractive pool and no shade. The shabby hotel entrance is easily missed, on a dusty street off the Corniche, south of the Aswan Moon Restaurant (p312).

Hathor Hotel (Map p306; ☎ 231 4580; fax 303 462; www.hathorhotel.com; Corniche an-Nil; s/d E£80/100; 🔲 💻 💺) The 36 spotless rooms vary in size and some are gloomy, but all have a private bathroom and most have air-con (which is controlled at reception), all in all offering good value for money. The great rooftop terrace has a small swimming pool with a few poolside chairs and spectacular Nile views.

Orchida St George (Map p306; ☎ 231 5997; www .orchida-sg-hotel.com; 9 Sharia Muhammed Khalid; s/d/tr E£90/150/195; 🔲 💻) Friendly three-star hotel with clean rooms, all equipped with comfortable beds, spotless bathrooms, fridge, air-con and satellite TV. Room sizes differ considerably, so check before you commit.

Philae Hotel (Map p306; ☎ 231 2090; fax 232 4089; Corniche an-Nil; s/d Nile view E£100/150, rear view E£90/120; 🔲) Rooms at this well-established hotel have mostly all been renovated, with freshly painted walls, tiled floors and proper bathrooms; however, the Nile-view rooms on the lower floors are very noisy.

Keylany Hotel (Map p306; ☎ 231 7332; www.keylany hotel.com; 25 Sharia Keylany; s/d/tr US$16.50/24/32; 🔲 💻) Aswan's best budget hotel has simple but comfortable rooms furnished with pine fur-

niture, and spotless bathrooms with proper showers and hot water. The management and staff are friendly and endlessly helpful. The roof terrace has no Nile views but there is a burlap sunshade and furniture made from palm fronds, and it is a great place to hang out. Good internet place downstairs.

Midrange

Aswan has only a small selection of midrange hotels. There's not much to distinguish those at the bottom end of the scale from the better budget places, so if money's tight, look carefully before making a choice.

our pick Beit al-Kerem (Map p300; ☎ 019 239 9443, 012 384 2218; www.betelkerem.com; Gharb Aswan, west bank; s/d incl dinner on 1st night €35/45; 🔲) This modern hotel overlooking the desert and the Tomb of the Nobles is a great find, offering eight quiet and comfortable rooms with very clean shared bathrooms. The hotel boasts a wonderful rooftop terrace overlooking the Nile and Nubian village, and has a good restaurant (meals €8 to €11). The staff are very friendly and proud to be Nubian. Call ahead and Shaaban will come and fetch you or explain how to get there.

Ramses Hotel (Map p306; ☎ 230 4000; ramses hotel_aswan@yahoo.com; Sharia Abtal at-Tahrir; s/d/tr E£150/200/250; 🔲) A pleasant, conveniently located high-rise hotel, with little character but comfortable rooms with shower, toilet, TV and minifridge, and some have Nile views. Service is slow, but this place is good value for the price. The Nubian Underground disco (see p313) should be open in the basement by spring 2010.

Nile Hotel (Map p300; ☎ 231 4222; www.nilehotel -aswan.com; Corniche an-Nil; s/d/tr US$40/55/73, on Tue & Thu US$45/60/81; 🔲 💻) A very welcome new hotel in this price range, offering 40 well-appointed rooms with spotless private bathrooms, satellite TV and minibar, all with a window or balcony overlooking the Nile. The staff speak English and are very friendly and helpful. There is a restaurant, a small library with foreign novels and books about Egypt, and a business centre. Recommended.

Cleopatra Hotel (Map p306; ☎ 231 4003; fax 231 4002; Sharia as-Souq; s/d US$50/70; 🔲 💻 💺) Very central and well kept, the Cleopatra has 109 spacious, clean, albeit rather dark, rooms. It is popular with groups on cut-price package tours, because of its convenient location and the reasonably sized (but overlooked) rooftop pool.

A GREAT FEKRA (IDEA)

Fekra (Map p315; www.fekraculture.com; Gebal Shisha, Shallal; 3 nights half board per person US$235, 1 week half board US$480) is located on 40,000 sq metres of land on the lake between the old and the High Dam, and overlooks Philae Island. The Fekra Cultural Centre – *fekra* means thought or idea in Arabic – is a fascinating project of artists from around the world, to support Nubian and Upper Egyptian artists, and to promote an international cultural exchange through organising artistic events and workshops. It is a magical place for its energy and wonderful location: a Nubian-style mudbrick house right on the lake, perfectly peaceful and a great place for swimming. It has accommodation for 12 people and a few extra Bedouin tents, with shared bathrooms. The people coming for workshops take priority, but on other dates you can either book the house or a room in it. The rates include accommodation, breakfast, dinner, a private boat trip with breakfast and transport from and to train station or airport. Check the website for concerts, workshops or other happenings. In spring 2010 Fekra is also opening Underground (see p313), a platform for local artists and musicians, in downtown Aswan.

Sara Hotel (off Map p300; ☎ 232 7234; www.sarahotel-aswan.com; s/d US$50/80; ❉ ☑) Built on a clifftop overlooking the Nile about 2km beyond the Nubia Museum, the Sara is isolated but has fantastic views over the First Cataract and the Western Desert. It's worth putting up with the kitsch pastel decor for the spotlessly clean rooms, with satellite TV, friendly staff and a good-sized pool overlooking the Nile. Corner rooms have huge balconies. The cafeteria is hugely popular with Aswanis. A shuttle bus runs into town hourly. If you want to stay in Aswan for a few days of peace and quiet, the Sara is a good choice.

Marhaba Palace Hotel (Map p306; ☎ 233 0102; www.marhaba-aswan.com; Corniche an-Nil; s/d US$60/80; ❉) The Marhaba has small but cosy, tastefully decorated rooms, with comfortable beds, sumptuous bathrooms (for this price range) and satellite TV. Bright and welcoming, it overlooks a park on the Corniche and has two restaurants, friendly staff and a roof terrace with excellent Nile views.

Isis Aswan (Map p306; ☎ 231 5100; www.pyramisaegypt.com; Corniche an-Nil; s/d US$100/120; ❉ ☑) Built right on the riverbank, the Isis Aswan has a prime location in the centre of town. The 100 chalet-style rooms in the garden are clean and comfortable, popular with budget tour groups. The hotel has a reasonably good Italian restaurant, a great Nileside bar-terrace and a great figure-eight-shaped pool.

Top End

Pyramisa Isis Island Resort & Spa (Map p300; ☎ 231 7400; www.pyramisaegypt.com; r garden/Nile view €110/149; ❉ 🖳 ☑) An imposing four-star resort hotel on its own island (there are regular free shut-tle boats to town), with big, well-appointed rooms overlooking the Nile or the garden. Popular with tour groups, it has two huge swimming pools and several restaurants, usually with long queues at the enormous buffets. Very friendly staff.

Mövenpick Resort Aswan (Map p300; ☎ 230 3455; www.moevenpick-aswan.com; Elephantine Island; s/d from US$160/190; ❉ ☑) Hidden in a large garden, and characterised by an ugly tower – for many years now rumoured to be demolished 'soon' – the Mövenpick dominates the northern end of Elephantine Island. The hotel recently had a total makeover and has simple but very comfortable rooms, decorated in Nubian style and colours. It is set in lush, tranquil gardens and has a great swimming pool. Guests are transported to and from the town centre by a free ferry. Better rates when booked via website.

our pick **Sofitel Old Cataract Hotel & Spa** (Map p300; ☎ 231 6000; www.sofitel.com; Sharia Abtal at-Tahrir; r from US$250; ❉ ☑) The grande dame of hotels on the Nile, the Old Cataract brings you back to the days of Agatha Christie, who is said to have written part of her novel *Death on the Nile* here (the hotel featured in the movie). The splendid building, surrounded by well-tended exotic gardens on a rock above the river, commands fantastic views of the Nile and several islands, the ruins of Abu and the desert behind. At the time of writing both the Old and the more modern building of the New Cataract (saved from total demolition by President Mubarak because he wanted to preserve the place where he spent his honeymoon!) have been totally gutted. The hotels are due to reopen in summer 2010 as one deluxe-suite-only hotel with very spacious rooms of contemporary luxury

NILE VALLEY: ESNA TO ABU SIMBEL

in a Moorish-oriental decor, closer to the hotel's original style. The inevitable lavish spa is also being prepared.

Rentals

A number of flats are for rent on the west bank of Aswan, or on Elephantine Island, offering a good-value option for a longer stay, or even just for a night. Walk around on Elephantine Island and you will be offered houses for rent. If you want to book ahead, check **Beit al-Kerem** (www .betelkerem.com) for Nubian houses, or Mohamed Sobhi at **Animalia** (see p304). **Mohamed Arabi** (see p308) has four amazing **houses** (Map p300; ☎ 012 324 0132; per night from €100) for rent in his 10-acre garden and orchard on the west bank, all tastefully decorated in Nubian style, but with cool marble floors, clean bathrooms and a sitting room. These houses are very peaceful, and at night dinner with garden produce is served on a terrace on the Nile.

EATING

Aswan is a sleepy place and most tourists eat on board the cruise boats, but there are a few laid-back restaurants. Outside the hotels, few serve alcohol and few accept credit cards.

Restaurants

Panorama (off Map p306; ☎ 231 6169; Corniche an-Nil; dishes E£8-20) With its pleasant Nileside terrace, this is a great place to chill and sip a herbal tea or fresh juice. It also serves simple Egyptian stews cooked in clay pots, with salad, mezze and rice or chips, or an all-day breakfast.

Aswan Moon Restaurant (Map p306; ☎ 231 6108; Corniche an-Nil; meals E£12-30) The once-popular hang-out no longer serves alcohol, but it remains a pleasant place for dinner. The menu ranges from basic Egyptian and international dishes, including mezze (E£8), pizzas (E£25 to E£30) and grills (E£35).

Biti Pizza (Map p306; Midan al-Mahatta; dishes E£15-22; ☉ 10am-midnight; ☒) Biti is a popular air-conditioned restaurant that serves good Western-style pizzas, but more recommended are the delicious sweet and savoury *fiteer* (flaky Egyptian pizza), including the excellent tuna *fiteer* (E£20) or the fruit-and-nut dessert version (E£18).

Golden Pharaoh (Map p300; ☎ 231 0361, 010 229 2910; Corniche an-Nil; mains E£16-45; ☉ 9am-late; ☒) The newest arrival is this rather sophisticated eatery with an air-con dining room and a large terrace overlooking the Nile and the city. The menu includes Nubian and international dishes, and the place is already popular with Aswanis.

Chef Khalil (Map p306; ☎ 231 0142; Sharia as-Souq; meals E£25-60) Popular fish restaurant, just along from the train station, serving very fresh fish from Lake Nasser and the Red Sea, charged by weight, grilled, baked or fried to your choice and served with salad and rice or French fries. It's a small place, but worth the wait if it's full.

Al-Makka (Map p306; ☎ 230 3232; Sharia Abtal at-Tahrir, opposite Ramses Hotel; mains E£35-50; ☉ noon-2am) Popular with meat-eating local families, this place is famous for its excellent fresh kebabs and *kofta* (mincemeat and spices grilled on a skewer), as well as pigeon and chicken, all served with bread, salad and tahini. There is a sister store, Al-Madina (Map p306; ☎ 230 5696), with a similar menu, on Sharia as-Souq.

Salah ad-Din (Map p306; ☎ 231 0361, 010 229 2910; Corniche an-Nil; mains E£40; ☉ noon-late; ☒) This is the best of the Nileside restaurants, with several terraces and a freezing air-conditioned dining room. The menu has Egyptian, Nubian and international dishes, a notch better than most restaurants in Aswan. The service is efficient and the beers are cool (E£12). There is also a terrace to smoke a *sheesha*.

Nubian Beach (Map p300; west bank, past the Aga Khan Mausoleum; set menus per person E£45) Wonderful Nubian cafe-restaurant set in a quiet garden on the west bank of the Nile, against the backdrop of a towering sand dune. During the heat of the day or on cold winter nights, there is a beautifully painted room indoors. The food is simple but good, and alcohol is served – sometimes with live Nubian music.

Sunset (off Map p300; ☎ 233 0601, 012 166 1480; Sharia Abtal at-Tahrir, in Nasr City; set menus E£45-60; ☉ 9am-3am) This great cafe terrace and restaurant is the place to be at sunset, with spectacular views over the First Cataract. Sit on the huge shady terrace for a mint tea, or enjoy the small selection of excellent grills or pizzas (E£38). Or take a taxi after dark. Very popular with locals at night.

Quick Eats

Along Sharia as-Souq there are plenty of small restaurants and cafes, good for taking in the lively atmosphere of the souq.

Haramein Foul & Ta'amiyya (Map p306; Sharia Abtal at-Tahrir; dishes E£3-8) A tiny takeaway place hidden among the low-rise apartment blocks, this is where Aswanis go when they want good *fuul* (fava bean paste) and *ta'amiyya*.

Koshary Aly Baba Restaurant (Map p306; Sharia Abtal at-Tahrir; dishes E£4-20) A clean and popular takeaway place with good *kushari*, as well as *shwarma* and *kofta*.

El-Tahrer Pizza (Map p306; Midan al-Mahatta; dishes E£14-25) A popular cafe that serves pizza and *fiteer* at rock-bottom prices. Tea and *sheesha* (E£5) are also served.

Self-Catering

The souq is the best place to buy your own food. On Sharia as-Souq, as well as some of the small alleyways, small grocery shops stock canned goods, cheese and UHT milk. Fruit and vegetables are abundant when in season and are best bought in the morning, at their freshest.

Egypt Free Shop (Map p300; ☎ 231 4939; Corniche an-Nil; ⏱ 8am-2pm & 6-10pm) The only place to buy liquor, local beer and wine, but you need to show a passport; tax free only within 48 hours of arriving in Egypt.

ENTERTAINMENT

Palace of Culture (Map p306; ☎ 231 3390; Corniche an-Nil) Between October and February/ March, Aswan's folkloric dance troupe very sporadically performs Nubian *tahtib* (dance performed with wooden staves) and songs depicting village life. Call to check about performances.

Nubian shows are also performed for tourists at the **Mövenpick Resort Aswan** (Map p306; ☎ 230 3455; www.moevenpick-aswan.com; Elephantine Island) and at some of the smaller hotels like Beit al-Kerem (see p310). If you're lucky, you may be invited to a Nubian wedding on a weekend night. Foreign guests are deemed auspicious additions to the ceremony, but don't be surprised if you're asked to pay some money, between E£30 to E£50, to help defray the huge costs of the band and the food.

The only disco in town is at Pyramisa Isis Island Resort & Spa (see p311), but spring 2010 should see the opening of **Underground** (Map p306; ☎ 230 4000; basement, Ramses Hotel; ⏱ 8am-2pm & 6-10pm), a revival of a 1970s disco. The cool retro decor has been kept, and the venue will provide a much-needed space where local musicians can perform and young Nubians can hang out. Being a Fekra project (see boxed text, p311), it should be a place to watch.

Otherwise, strolling along the Corniche, watching the moon rise as you sit at a rooftop terrace or having a cool drink at one of the Nileside restaurants is about all that most travellers get up to in Aswan at night.

SHOPPING

Aswan's famous souq is a good place to pick up souvenirs and crafts. Handmade Nubian skullcaps (about E£10), colourful scarves (E£20 to E£50), and traditional baskets and trays (E£120 to E£90) in varying sizes are popular. The spices and indigo powder prominently displayed are also good buys, and most of the spice shops sell the dried hibiscus used to make the refreshing drink *karkadai*. However, beware of the safflower that is sold as saffron. Aswan is also famous for the quality of its henna powder and its delicious roasted peanuts. The higher grade of the latter go for E£20 per kilogram.

Hanafi Bazaar (Map p300; ☎ 231 4083; Corniche an-Nil; ⏱ 8am-10pm) With its mock Pharaonic facade, this is the oldest, no doubt also the most dusty, and best bazaar in town, with genuine Nubian swords, baskets, amulets, silk kaftans and beads from all over Africa, run by the totally laid-back Hanafi brothers.

GETTING THERE & AWAY
Air

Daily flights are available with **EgyptAir** (Map p300; ☎ 231 5000; Corniche an-Nil; ⏱ 8am-8pm) from Cairo to Aswan (one way E£223 to E£879, 1¼ hours). The one-way trip to Luxor is between E£156 and E£383 and takes 30 minutes. There are three to four flights a day to Abu Simbel, leaving between 6.15am and 9.15am, an hour later in summer. The round-trip ticket costs between E£192 and E£452, including bus transfers between the airport and the temple site.

Boat

For details about the five-star cruise boats and fishing safaris operating on Lake Nasser, see p108. For details on boat transport to Sudan, see p527.

Bus

The bus station is 3.5km north of the train station, but the tourist office advises against travelling by bus as it is too much of a hassle. At the time of writing, there are no buses to Luxor and travelling by bus to Abu Simbel is

---

POLICE CONVOYS

Driving north to Luxor no longer needs to be done in convoy, but at the time of writing there is still a twice-daily (4.30am and 11am) convoy to go Abu Simbel, compulsory for foreigners travelling there. Armed convoys congregate at the beginning of Sharia Sadat (Map p300), near the Coptic Cathedral. Be there at least 15 minutes in advance. It takes 3½ hours to Abu Simbel.

---

restricted to four foreigners per bus. Upper Egypt Bus Co has two daily buses to Abu Simbel (E£25, four hours, departing 8am and 5pm). A direct bus to Cairo (E£100, 14 hours) leaves at 6am and 3pm daily.

Service Taxi
Service taxis and minibuses leave from the bus station, 3.5km north of the train station. A taxi there will cost E£15, or 50pt in a communal taxi. A seat in a service taxi or minibus to Luxor costs E£18, to Kom Ombo E£5.50 and to Edfu E£11.

Train
From **Aswan Train Station** (Map p306; ☎ 231 4754) a number of daily trains run north to Cairo, but officially foreigners can only buy tickets in the station for one 1st-class train only (E£165, 14 hours, 6.45pm). However, no one will stop you boarding other trains if you buy the ticket on the train and pay E£6 extra. All trains heading north stop at Daraw (1st/2nd class E£20/13, 45 minutes), Kom Ombo (E£22/15, one hour), Edfu (E£25/17, two hours), Esna (E£35/20, 2½ hours) and Luxor (E£40/24, three hours). Student discounts are available on all of these trains.

   Abela Egypt Sleeping Train (☎ 230 2124; www .sleepingtrains.com) has two daily services to Cairo at 5pm and 7pm (single/double cabin per person including dinner and breakfast US$60/120, children aged four to nine years US$45, 14 hours). Note that there is no student discount and tickets must be paid for in US dollars.

GETTING AROUND
To/From the Airport
The airport is located 25km southwest of town. A taxi to/from the airport costs about E£35 to E£45.

Bicycle
Aswan is not a great town for cycling. However, there are a few places at the train-station end of Sharia as-Souq where you can hire bicycles for about E£12 to E£15 a day. Beit al-Kerem (see p310) runs cycling trips in the countryside.

Taxi
A taxi tour that includes Philae, the High Dam and the Unfinished Obelisk near Fatimid Cemetery costs around E£100 to E£150 for five to six people. Taxis can also take you on day trips to Daraw and/or Kom Ombo for about E£200. A taxi anywhere within the town costs E£5 to E£10.

   Service taxis (50pt) run along the major roads in Aswan.

AROUND ASWAN

ASWAN DAM
At the end of the 19th century Egypt's fast-growing population made it imperative to cultivate more agricultural land, which would only be possible by regulating the flow of the Nile. The British engineer Sir William Willcocks started construction of the old Aswan Dam in 1898 above the First Cataract. When completed in 1902, it was the largest dam in the world, measuring 2441m across, 50m tall and 30m wide, and was made almost entirely of Aswan granite.

   It was raised twice to meet the demand not only to increase the area of cultivable land but also to provide hydroelectric power. With the opening of the High Dam, it now only generates hydroelectricity for a nearby factory producing fertilisers, and otherwise serves as a tourist attraction on the way to the High Dam, 6km upstream. The road to the airport and all trips to Abu Simbel by road include a drive across the Aswan Dam.

SEHEYL ISLAND
The large island situated just north of the old Aswan Dam, **Seheyl** (adult/child E£25/15; 7am-4pm Oct-Apr, to 5pm May-Sep) was sacred to the goddess Anukis. Prior to the dam's construction, the Nile would rush noisily through the granite boulders that emerged from the riverbed just south of here, forming the First Cataract, called Shellal by

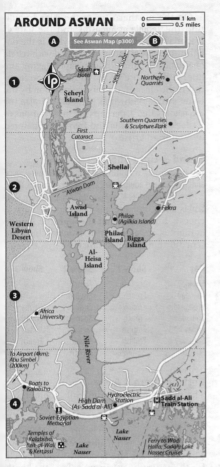

AROUND ASWAN

the Egyptians. Herodotus reported that an Egyptian official had told him that this was the source of the Nile, which flowed north and south from there. Now the waters flow slowly and Seheyl makes an ideal destination for a slightly longer felucca trip. On the island's southern tip is a cliff with more than **200 inscriptions**, most dating to the 18th and 19th dynasties, of princes, generals and other officials who passed by on their journey to Nubia. The most famous is the so-called 'famine stele' from the 3rd dynasty that recounts a terrible seven-year famine during the reign of Zoser (2667–2648 BC), which the pharaoh tried to end by making offerings to the Temple of Khnum on Elephantine Island.

Next to the inscriptions is a friendly Nubian village with brightly coloured houses. Several houses now welcome visitors, selling tea and good Nubian lunches as well as local crafts. It's a pleasant place to stroll around.

PHILAE (AGILKIA ISLAND)

The romantic aura and the grandeur of the **Temple of Isis** (adult/child E£50/25; 7am-4pm Oct-May, to 5pm Jun-Sep) on the island of Philae (fee-*leh*) lured pilgrims for thousands of years, and during the 19th century the ruins became one of Egypt's most legendary tourist attractions. After the building of the old Aswan Dam, Philae was swamped for six months of every year by the high waters, allowing travellers to take rowing boats and glide among the partially submerged columns to peer down through the translucent green at the wondrous sanctuaries of the mighty gods below.

After the completion of the High Dam, the temple would have entirely disappeared had Unesco not intervened. Between 1972 and 1980, the massive temple complex was disassembled stone by stone and reconstructed 20m higher on nearby Agilkia Island. Agilkia was then landscaped to resemble the sacred isle of Isis.

Although the cult of Isis at Philae goes back at least to the 7th century BC, the earliest remains on the island date from the reign of the last native king of Egypt, Nectanebo I (380–362 BC). The most important ruins were begun by Ptolemy II Philadelphus (285–246 BC) and added to for the next 500 years until the reign of Diocletian (AD 284–305). By Roman times Isis had become the greatest of all the Egyptian gods, worshipped right across the Roman Empire even as far as Britain. Indeed, as late as AD 550, well after Rome and its empire embraced Christianity, Isis was still being worshipped at Philae. Early Christians eventually transformed the main temple's hypostyle hall into a chapel and defaced the pagan reliefs, their inscriptions later vandalised by early Muslims.

Touring the Temple

The boat across to the temple leaves you at the base of the **Kiosk of Nectanebo**, the oldest part of the Philae complex. Heading north, you walk down the **outer temple court**, which has colonnades running along both sides; the western one is the most complete, with windows that originally overlooked the island of

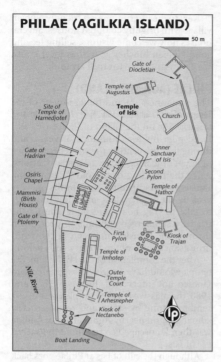

PHILAE (AGILKIA ISLAND)

0 — 50 m

Gate of Diocletian

Temple of Augustus

Site of Temple of Harnedjotef

Temple of Isis

Church

Gate of Hadrian

Inner Sanctuary of Isis

Osiris Chapel

Second Pylon

Mammisi (Birth House)

Temple of Hathor

Gate of Ptolemy

First Pylon

Kiosk of Trajan

Temple of Imhotep

Nile River

Outer Temple Court

Temple of Arhesnepher

Kiosk of Nectanebo

Boat Landing

On the northern tip of the island you'll find the **Temple of Augustus** and the **Gate of Diocletian**; east of the second pylon is the delightful **Temple of Hathor**, decorated with reliefs of musicians (including an ape playing the lute) and Bes, the god of childbirth. South of this is the elegant, unfinished pavilion by the water's edge, known as the **Kiosk of Trajan** (or 'Pharaoh's Bed'), perhaps the most famous of Philae's monuments and frequently painted by Victorian artists.

Sound & Light Show

Each evening a **sound and light show** (www.sound andlight.com.eg; adult/child E£70/50; ☺ shows 6.30pm, 7.30pm & 8.30pm Oct-May, 8pm, 9.15pm & 10.30pm May-Sep) is shown at Philae. The commentary is cheesy, but wandering through the temple at night is quite delightful. Double-check the schedule at the tourist office.

Day	Show 1	Show 2	Show 3
Monday	English	French	
Tuesday	French	English	
Wednesday	French	English	German
Thursday	French	Spanish	English
Friday	English	French	Italian
Saturday	English	Arabic	French
Sunday	German	French	English

Getting There & Away

The boat landing for the Philae complex is at Shellal, south of the old Aswan Dam. The only easy way to get there is by taxi or organised trip (which can be arranged by most travel agencies and major hotels in Aswan). The return taxi fare is about E£60. Tickets for the return boat trip are sold at the booth on the landing (E£10 per person, small extra baksheesh for the boatman, particularly if you want to stay a little longer).

HIGH DAM

Egypt's modern example of construction on a monumental scale, the controversial **Aswan High Dam** (As-Sadd al-Ali) contains 18 times the amount of material used in the Great Pyramid of Khufu and created Lake Nasser, the world's largest artificial lake.

From the 1940s it was clear that the old Aswan Dam, which only regulated the flow of water, was not big enough to counter the unpredictable annual flooding of the Nile. In 1952, when Gamal Abdel Nasser came to power, plans were drawn up for a new dam,

Bigga. At the end is the entrance of the Temple of Isis, marked by the 18m-high towers of the **first pylon** with reliefs of Ptolemy XII Neos Dionysos smiting enemies.

In the central court of the **Temple of Isis**, the *mammisi* is dedicated to Horus, son of Isis and Osiris. Successive pharaohs reinstated their legitimacy as the mortal descendants of Horus by taking part in rituals celebrating the Isis legend (see boxed text, p235) and the birth of her son Horus in the marshes.

The **second pylon** leads to a hypostyle hall, with superb column capitals, and beyond lie three vestibules, leading into the **Inner Sanctuary of Isis**. Two granite shrines stood here, one containing a gold statue of Isis and another containing the barque in which the statue travelled, but those were long ago moved to Florence and Paris, and only the stone pedestal for the barque remains, inscribed with the names of Ptolemy III and his wife, Berenice. A staircase, on the western side, leads up to the **Osiris Chapel** (closed at the time of writing), decorated with scenes of the gods bewailing the dead Osiris, as well as clear images of the Isis legend and the creation of Horus.

HIGH DAM FACTS

- Length: 3600m
- Width at base: 980m
- Height at highest point: 111m
- Number of workers involved in construction: 35,000
- Number of workers who died during construction: 451

6km south of the old one, but from the start there were political and engineering difficulties. In 1956, after the World Bank refused the promised loan for the project, Nasser ordered the nationalisation of the Suez Canal, which sparked the Suez Crisis in which France, the UK and Israel invaded the canal region. But Nasser got his way and also won additional funding and expertise from the Soviet Union.

Work started in 1960 and was finally completed in 1971.

The dam has brought great benefits to Egypt's farmers, increasing cultivable land by at least 30%. At the same time, the country's power supply has doubled. But there are downsides. The dam has stopped the flow of silt essential to the fertility of the land, and the much higher use of artificial fertilisers has led to increasing salinity of the agricultural areas. The groundwater tables have risen, too, and are damaging many monuments close to the Nile. The now perennially full irrigation canals have led to endemic infection with the bilharzia parasite, until recently a huge public health problem.

Most people visit the High Dam, 13km south of Aswan, as part of an organised trip to sights south of Aswan. There is a small pavilion with displays detailing the dimensions and the construction of the dam, and

FEAST, FAMINE OR WAR

Egypt's fate has always been closely intertwined with the amount of water in the Nile, and although the river flows through many countries, it is Egypt that has gained the most from its beneficence. Ancient Egyptians called their country Kemet (Black Land), after the fertile silt that the Nile's receding waters left in their wake. This annual dumping of a thick layer of dark, wet topsoil allowed ancient Egypt's agricultural system to develop and thrive, leading in turn to an accumulation of wealth and the flourishing of a sophisticated society and culture. When the floods failed and hunger turned to famine, the entire system broke down: consecutive years of inadequate flooding often coincided with the collapse of central authority or invasion by a foreign power.

Because of this dependence on the Nile, the Egyptians developed a highly organised irrigation system to help them deal with its unpredictability. Nilometers, a series of steps against which the rising water would be gauged, were used to measure the level of the flood, which was crucial for predicting soil fertility and crop yields. The Nilometer at Elephantine (see p305), on Egypt's southern frontier, was one of the first to show evidence of rising water in early June. Authorities also used the level of the flood to predict the size of the harvest and therefore to fix the level of taxes farmers should pay.

From the earliest times canals helped extend the reach of the flood plain, and devices were developed to help move water. These began as simple pots. Later, the *shadouf*, a long pole with a 'bucket' at one end and counterbalancing weight at the other, and the *saqia*, an animal-powered water wheel, helped farmers to move greater amounts of water and extend the area of cultivable land.

Since the building of the High Dam, Egypt has been freed from the uncertainties of the Nile's annual flood, but the supply of water is still not entirely within its control. At present Egypt's use of Nile water is governed by a 1959 treaty with Sudan that essentially divides the flow of the river between the two countries. The eight other countries around the Nile basin claim – not without reason – that this is unfair and are clamouring for a more equitable division of this precious resource. An international initiative to help resolve the issue has been under way since 1999 but Egypt, the largest and most powerful – and also the most Nile dependent – of the riparian states has so far blocked any changes to the 1959 treaty and has even threatened war if any country violates its terms.

on the western side is a monument honouring Soviet-Egyptian friendship and cooperation. Video cameras and zoom lenses cannot be used, although nobody seems to police this.

Getting There & Away

The quickest way to get to the High Dam is to take a taxi from Aswan (about E£25). Usually it is combined with a trip to the Temple of Kalabsha, which is about 3km from the western end of the dam and is visible from the dam on the western side of Lake Nasser.

LOWER NUBIA & LAKE NASSER

For thousands of years, the First Cataract marked the border between Egypt and Nubia, the land that stretched from Aswan to Khartoum. The Nile Valley on the Egyptian side was fertile and continuously cultivated, while the banks further south in Nubia were more rugged, with rocky desert cliffs and sand separating small pockets of agricultural land.

The building of the Aswan and High Dams irrevocably changed all that, and much of Nubia disappeared under the waters of Lake Nasser. The landscape now is dominated by the contrast of smooth desert and the calm green-brown water of the lake. Apart from the beauty and the peace of the lake itself, the main attraction of this region is the temples that were so painstakingly moved above the floodwaters in the 1960s. See the boxed text, p323, for more about this mammoth cultural rescue mission. The area between the First and the Second Cataract is generally known as Lower Nubia (ancient Egyptian Wawat), and further south between the Second and Sixth Cataracts is Upper Nubia (Kush).

To ancient Egyptians, Nubia was Ta-Sety, the Land of Bowmen, after the weapon for which the Nubians were famous. It was a crucial route for the trade with sub-Saharan Africa, and the source of much-needed raw materials, such as copper, ivory, ebony and gold. The modern name is thought to come from the ancient Egyptian word *nbw*, meaning 'gold'. Egypt was always interested in Nubia and its riches, and the two peoples'

history was always connected: when Egypt was strong it dominated Nubia and aggressively exploited its natural resources; when Egypt was weak, the Nubians enjoyed periods of growth and development.

Evidence of 10,000-year-old settlements has been found in northern Nubia. At Nabta Playa, located some 100km west of Abu Simbel, archaeologists have recently discovered the remains of houses, sculpted monoliths and the world's oldest calendar, made of small standing stones, dating from around 6000 BC. Until 3500 BC Nubia and Egypt both developed in roughly the same way, domesticating animals, growing crops and gradually adopting permanent settlements. Both people were ethnically linked, but the darker-skinned Nubians had more African features and spoke a Nilo-Saharan language, while the ancient Egyptian language is Afro-Asiatic.

With the unification of the land north of Aswan around 3100 BC, Egypt started to impose its authority on Nubia. From the beginning of the Old Kingdom, for nearly 5000 years, expeditions were sent to extract the region's considerable mineral wealth. During the First Intermediate Period (2160–2025 BC), central authority in Egypt collapsed, while Nubia became stronger, and Nubian soldiers played an important role in Egypt's civil war. The reunification of Egypt, at the start of the Middle Kingdom, saw Lower Nubia again annexed and a chain of fortresses built at strategic points along the Nile to safeguard trade.

During the New Kingdom, instead of fortresses, the Egyptians built temples in Nubia, dividing the whole of the region into five nomes, ruled on the pharaoh's behalf by his viceroy, who took the title King's Son of Kush. Taking advantage of Egypt's political disunity during the Third Intermediate Period (1069–945 BC), the tables were turned and Nubians extended their authority far to the north, ruling Egypt for a century as the 25th Kushite dynasty (747–656 BC). The 25th dynasty ended with the Assyrian invasion of Egypt, after which Nubian action was guided by its own best interests, sometimes siding with foreign invaders, sometimes with their Egyptian neighbours.

Christianity gradually spread to Nubia after the 5th century AD and lasted long after Islam had spread along the Egyptian Nile. In AD 652 Egypt's new Muslim authorities made a peace treaty with the Christian king of Nubia. That treaty lasted more or less until the 13th cen-

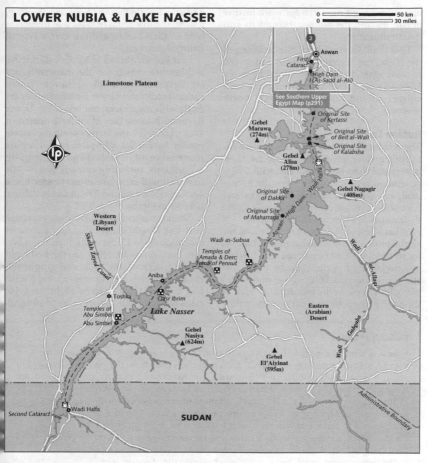

LOWER NUBIA & LAKE NASSER

0 — 50 km
0 — 30 miles

Limestone Plateau

Aswan

First Cataract

High Dam (As-Sadd al-Ali)

See Southern Upper Egypt Map (p291)

Original Site of Kertassi

Gebel Marawa (274m)

Original Site of Beit al-Wali

Original Site of Kalabsha

Gebel Alisa (278m)

Gebel Nagagir (408m)

Original Site of Dakka

Original Site of Maharraqa

Western (Libyan) Desert

Wadi as-Subua

Temples of Amada & Derr; Tomb of Pennut

Aniba

Qasr Ibrim

Toshka

Temples of Abu Simbel

Abu Simbel

Lake Nasser

Eastern (Arabian) Desert

Gebel Nasiya (624m)

Gebel El'Aiyinat (595m)

Wadi al-Allaqi

Wadi Gabgaba

Sheikh Zayed Canal

Aswan High Dam; Wadi Halfa

Second Cataract

Wadi Halfa

SUDAN

Administrative Boundary

---

tury, when Egyptians moved south again: the last Christian king of Nubia was replaced by a Muslim in 1305 and most of the population converted to Islam. In the 19th century Nubia was again important to Egyptian ambitions as the route for its supply of slaves. The rise of the Mahdist state in Sudan at the end of the 19th century led to Nubia being divided for the last time: with the defeat of the Mahdi and his successor, and the establishment of the Anglo-Egyptian government in Sudan in 1899, a border between Egypt and Sudan was established 40km north of Wadi Halfa.

Modern Nubia

Following the completion of the old Aswan Dam in 1902, and again after its height was raised in 1912 and 1934, the water level of the Nile in Lower Nubia gradually rose from 87m to 121m, partially submerging many of the monuments in the area and, by the 1930s, totally flooding a large number of Nubian villages. With their homes flooded, some Nubians moved north where, with government help, they bought land and built villages based on their traditional architecture. Most of the Nubian villages close to Aswan, such as Elephantine, West Aswan and Seheyl, are made up of people who moved at this time. Those who decided to stay in their home-land built houses on higher land, assuming they would be safe, but they saw their date plantations, central to their economy, destroyed. This meant that many Nubian men were forced to search for work further north, leaving the women behind to run the communities.

Less than 30 years later, the building of the High Dam forced those who had stayed to move again. In the 1960s, 50,000 Egyptian Nubians were relocated to government-built villages around Kom Ombo, 50km north of Aswan.

Nubian Culture

The Nubians have paid the highest price for Egypt's greater good. They have lost their homes and their homeland, and with a new generation growing up far from the homeland, as Egyptians, or even Europeans and Americans, they are now also gradually losing their distinctive identity and traditions.

What is left of Nubian culture then seems all the more vibrant. Nubian music, famous for its unique sound (see boxed text, below), was popularised in the West by musicians such as Hamza ad-Din, whose oud (lute) melodies are ethereally beautiful. As well as the oud, two basic instruments give the music

its distinctive rhythm and harmony: the *douff*, a wide, shallow drum or tabla that musicians hold in their hands; and the *kisir*, a type of stringed instrument.

Less known abroad is Nubia's distinctive architecture, which was the main influence on Egyptian mudbrick architect Hassan Fathy. Traditional Lower Nubian houses are made with mudbricks, but unlike the Upper Egyptian houses, they often have domed or vaulted ceilings, and further south the houses usually have a flat split-palm roof. They are plastered or whitewashed and covered with decorations, including ceramic plates. The basic forms of these houses can be seen in the Nubian villages around Aswan and in Ballana, near Kom Ombo.

Nubians also have their own marriage customs. Traditionally wedding festivities lasted for up to 15 days, although nowadays they are a three-day affair. On the first night of the festivities, the bride and groom celebrate separately with their respective friends and families. On the second night, the bride takes her party to the groom's home and both

---

NUBIAN MUSIC

It's one of those strange quirks, but it's almost easier to hear and buy Nubian music in the West than it is in Egypt, apart from in Aswan. Nubian music, very different to the more popular Egyptian music, is rarely heard on national TV and radio, and hard to find in music stores in Cairo. But Nubian artists sell CDs by the rackload in Europe and play to sell-out audiences.

The biggest name is Ali Hassan Kuban. A former tillerman from a small village near Aswan, Kuban grew up playing at weddings and parties and made the leap to a global audience after being invited to perform at a Berlin festival in 1989. Until his death in 2001, he toured all over Europe, as well as in Japan, Canada and the USA. He released several CDs on the German record label **Piranha** (www.piranha.de), including *From Nubia to Cairo* and *Walk Like a Nubian*.

The Nubian sound, unlike Arabic music with its jarring use of quarter tones, is easily accessible, particularly to a Western audience familiar with African music. It is rhythmic, warm and exotic, mixing simple melodies and soulful vocals. This can be heard at its best on a series of CDs by a loose grouping of musicians and vocalists recording under the name Salamat. Look out especially for *Mambo al-Soudani* (again on the Piranha label).

A slightly different facet of Nubian music is represented by Hamza ad-Din, a Nubian composer born in Wadi Halfa in 1929 and widely respected in the West for his semiclassical compositions written for the oud (lute). Inspired by his Sufi beliefs, Ad-Din's work is extremely haunting, especially *Escalay* (The Waterwheel), which you can find in a recording by the composer himself, or there's an excellent version of it by the Kronos Quartet on their CD *Pieces of Africa*.

Other names to look out for are the now-retired Sayyed Gayer, who sings poems and love songs accompanied only by the *douff* (drum), and Ahmed Monieb and Mohammed Hamam.

The best places to pick up CDs of Nubian music are from the music stores in the Aswan souq, where the sales assistants are happy to let you listen to different musicians. To hear authentic live Nubian music, try to get yourself invited to a Nubian wedding in Aswan. You can also head to Eskaleh in Abu Simbel (p325), where the renowned Nubian musician Fikry Kachef plays with his friends.

groups dance to traditional music until the wee hours. Then the bride returns home and her hands and feet are painted with beautiful designs in henna. The groom will also have his hands and feet covered in henna but without any design. On the third day, the groom and his party walk slowly to the bride's house in a *zaffer* (procession), singing and dancing the whole way. Traditionally the groom will stay at the bride's house for three days before seeing his family. The couple will then set up home.

Getting There & Away

Although all the sights except Qasr Ibrim have roads leading to them, the only sites foreigners are currently allowed to drive to are Kalabsha, Beit al-Wali and Kertassi. The road to Abu Simbel is open, but foreigners are only allowed to travel in buses or microbuses in a police convoy. Abu Simbel can be reached by plane from Aswan, Luxor or Cairo. For more details on travelling to Abu Simbel, see p325.

For the moment, the rest of the sights can only be reached by boat, which is in any case the best way to see Lake Nasser's dramatic monuments. **African Angler** organises safaris on the lake, fishing safaris and safaris around the shore of the lake. See p108 for details.

LAKE NASSER

Looking out over Lake Nasser's vast expanse of deep green-blue water, it's hard to believe that it is human-made. As the world's largest artificial lake, its statistics are staggering: with an area of 5250 sq km, it is 510km long and between 5km and 35km wide. On average it contains some 135 billion cu metres of water, of which an estimated six billion are lost each year to evaporation. Its maximum capacity is 157 billion cu metres of water, which was reached in 1996 after heavy rains in Ethiopia, forcing the opening of a special spillway at Toshka, about 30km north of Abu Simbel, the first time it had been opened since the dam was built. The Egyptian government has since embarked on a controversial project to build a new canal and irrigate thousands of acres in what is now the Nubian Desert between Toshka and the New Valley, a project President Mubarak has likened to the Suez Canal and Aswan High Dam in its scale.

Numbers aside, the contrast between this enormous body of water and the remote desert stretching away on all sides makes Lake Nasser a place of austere beauty. Because the level of the lake fluctuates it has been difficult to build settlements around its edges. Instead the lake has become a place for migrating birds to rest on their long journeys north and south. Gazelles, foxes and several types of snake (including the deadly horned viper) live on its shores. Many species of fish live in its waters, including the enormous Nile perch. Crocodiles – some reportedly up to 5m long – and monitor lizards also live in the lake's shallows. The main human presence here, apart from the fast-growing population of Abu Simbel town and the few tourists who visit, is limited to the 5000 or so fishermen who spend up to six months at a time in small rowing boats, together catching about 50,000 tonnes of small fish each year.

KALABSHA, BEIT AL-WALI & KERTASSI

As a result of a massive Unesco effort, the temples of **Kalabsha**, **Beit al-Wali** and **Kertassi** (adult/student E£30/15; 8am-5pm) were transplanted from a now-submerged site about 50km south of Aswan. The new site is on the west bank of Lake Nasser just south of the High Dam.

The **Temple of Kalabsha**, started in the late Ptolemaic period and completed during the reign of Emperor Augustus (30 BC–AD 14), was dedicated to the Nubian solar god Merwel, known to the Greeks as Mandulis. Later it was used as a church.

In the 1960s and '70s the West German government financed the transfer and reconstruction of the 13,000 blocks of the temple. In thanks, it was presented with the temple's west pylon, now in the Berlin Museum. During the rescue operation, evidence was found of older structures dating from the times of Amenhotep II (1427–1400 BC) and Ptolemy IX.

An impressive stone causeway leads from the lake to the first pylon of the temple, beyond which are the colonnaded court and the eight-columned hypostyle hall. Inscriptions on the walls show various emperors or pharaohs in the presence of gods and goddesses. Just beyond the hall is the sanctuary, consisting of three chambers, with stairs leading from one up to the roof, where there are superb views of Lake Nasser and the High Dam, across the capitals of the hall and court. An inner passage, between the temple and the encircling wall, leads to a well-preserved Nilometer.

The **Temple of Beit al-Wali** was rebuilt with assistance from the US government and was placed just northwest of the Temple of Kalabsha. The temple, mostly built by Ramses II, was cut into the rock and fronted by a brick pylon. On the walls of the forecourt, several fine reliefs detail the pharaoh's victory over the Nubians (on the south wall) and wars against the Libyans and Syrians (on the north wall). Ramses is gripping the hair of his enemies prior to smashing their brains while women plead for mercy. The finest scenes are those of Ramses on his throne, receiving the tribute paid by the defeated Nubians, including leopard skins, gold rings, elephant tusks, feathers and exotic animals.

Just north of the Temple of Kalabsha are the scant but picturesque remains of the **Temple of Kertassi**, with two Hathor columns, a massive architrave and four fine papyrus columns.

When the water level is low you can sometimes walk across to the site, otherwise you can find a motor boat on the western side of the High Dam (around E£30 for the return trip and an hour to visit).

WADI AS-SUBUA

The **temples of Wadi as-Subua** (adult/student E£35/20) were moved to this site, about 4km west of the original, now-submerged Wadi as-Subua, between 1961 and 1965.

Wadi as-Subua means 'Valley of Lions' in Arabic and refers to the avenue of sphinxes that leads to the **Temple of Ramses II**. Yet another monument built during the reign of the energetic pharaoh, the interior of the temple was hewn from the rock and fronted by a stone pylon and colossal statues. Behind the pylon is a court featuring 10 more statues of the pharaoh, beyond which lies a 12-pillared hall and the sanctuary. The central niche was once carved with relief scenes of Ramses making offerings to Amun-Ra and Ra-Horakhty. In Christian times this part was converted into a church, the pagan reliefs plastered over and painted with saints, so that now, with part of the plaster fallen away, Ramses II appears to be adoring St Peter!

About 1km to the north are the remains of the **Temple of Dakka**, begun by the Upper Nubian Pharaoh Arkamani (218–200 BC) using materials from much earlier structures and adapted by the Ptolemies and the Roman emperor Augustus. Originally situated 40km north of here, it is dedicated to the god of wisdom, Thoth, and is notable for its 12m-high

pylon, which you can climb for great views of the lake and the surrounding temples.

The **Temple of Maharraqa**, the smallest of the three at this site, originally stood 50km north at the ancient site of Ofendina. Dedicated to Isis and Serapis, the Alexandrian god, its decorations were never finished and all that remains is a small hypostyle hall, where in the northeast corner an usual spiral staircase of masonry leads up to the roof.

AMADA

Situated around 180km south of the High Dam there are two temples and a tomb at **Amada** (adult/student E£35/20).

The **Temple of Amada**, moved about 2.6km from its original location, is the oldest surviving monument on Lake Nasser. It was built jointly by 18th-dynasty pharaohs Tuthmosis III (1479–1425 BC) and his son Amenhotep II, with a hypostyle hall added by his successor, Tuthmosis IV (1400–1390 BC). Dedicated, like many temples in Nubia, to the gods Amun-Ra and Ra-Horakhty, it has some of the finest and best-preserved reliefs of any Nubian monument and contains two important historical inscriptions. The first, on a stele at the left (north) side of the entrance, describes the unsuccessful Libyan invasion of Egypt (1209 BC) during Pharaoh Merenptah's reign, and a second stele on the back wall of the sanctuary, describing Amenhotep II's military campaign (1424 BC) in Palestine, both no doubt designed to impress upon the Nubians that political opposition to the powerful Egyptians was useless.

The rock-cut **Temple of Derr**, built by Ramses II, stood on a curve of the Nile. The pylon and court have disappeared, but there are some well-preserved reliefs in the ruined pillared hall, illustrating the Nubian campaign of Ramses II, with the usual killing of his enemies, accompanied by his famous pet lion. Following cleaning, many of the scenes are once again brightly coloured.

Five minutes' walk away is the small rock-cut **Tomb of Pennut**, viceroy of Nubia under Ramses VI (1143–1136 BC), which was originally situated at Aniba, 40km southwest of Amada. This well-preserved Nubian tomb consists of a small offering chapel and a niche at the rear, with reliefs depicting events and personalities from Pennut's life, including him being presented with a gift by Ramses VI.

SAVING NUBIA'S MONUMENTS

As the plans for the High Dam were drawn up, worldwide attention focused on the many valuable and irreplaceable ancient monuments doomed by the waters of Lake Nasser. Between 1960 and 1980 the Unesco-sponsored Nubian Rescue Campaign gathered expertise and financing from more than 50 countries, and sent Egyptian and foreign archaeological teams to Nubia. Necropolises were excavated, all portable artefacts and relics were removed to museums and, while some temples disappeared beneath the lake, 14 were salvaged.

Ten of them, including the temple complexes of Philae, Kalabsha and Abu Simbel, were dismantled stone by stone and painstakingly rebuilt on higher ground. Four others were donated to the countries that contributed to the rescue effort, including the splendid Temple of Dendur, now reconstructed in the Metropolitan Museum of Art in New York.

Perhaps the greatest achievement of all was the preservation of the temples at Abu Simbel. Ancient magnificence and skill met with equally impressive modern technology as, at a cost of about US$40 million, Egyptian, Italian, Swedish, German and French archaeological teams cut the temples up into more than 2000 huge blocks, weighing from 10 to 40 tonnes each, and reconstructed them inside an artificially built mountain, 210m away from the water and 65m higher than the original site. The temples were carefully oriented to face the original direction, and the landscape of their original environment was re-created on and around the concrete, dome-shaped mountain.

The project took just over four years. The temples of Abu Simbel were officially reopened in 1968 while the sacred site they had occupied for more than 3000 years disappeared beneath Lake Nasser. A plaque to the right of the temple entrance eloquently describes this achievement: 'Through this restoration of the past, we have indeed helped to build the future of mankind.'

QASR IBRIM

The only Nubian monument visible on its original site, **Qasr Ibrim** once sat on top of a 70m-high cliff, about 60km north of Abu Simbel, but now has water lapping at its edges.

There is evidence that Ibrim was a garrison town from 1000 BC onward, and that around 680 BC the 25th-dynasty Pharaoh Taharka (690–664 BC), who was a Nubian by birth, built a mudbrick temple dedicated to Isis. During Roman times the town was one of the last bastions of paganism, its six temples converting to Christianity two centuries later than the rest of Egypt. It then became one of the main Christian centres in Lower Nubia and held out against the Muslims until the 16th century, when a group of Bosnian mercenaries, part of the Ottoman army, occupied the site. The mercenaries stayed on and eventually married into the local Nubian community, using part of the cathedral as a mosque.

Among the structural remains, the most impressive is an 8th-century sandstone cathedral built over Taharka's temple. The site is closed to visitors because of ongoing archaeological work.

ABU SIMBEL

☎ 097

The village of Abu Simbel lies 280km south of Aswan and only 40km north of the Sudanese border. The small settlement is laid-back and quiet. So far few tourists linger more than the few hours needed to visit the colossal temples for which it is famous, but things might be about to change. Those interested in the peace and tranquillity of the lake, in seeing the temples without the crowds, in wandering around a small nontouristy Egyptian town without a police escort, or in listening to Nubian music might choose to hang around for a few days.

Information

Abu Simbel Hospital (☎ 349 9237; main rd)

Ahly Bank (main rd; ⏱ 8.30am 2pm & 6-8pm Sun-Thu) Has an ATM.

Banque du Caire (main rd; ⏱ 8.30am-2pm & 6-8pm Sun-Thu) Has an ATM.

Banque Misr (main rd; ⏱ 8.30am-2pm & 6-8pm Sun-Thu) Has an ATM.

Main post office (⏱ 8.30am-2.30pm Sat-Mon) On the road to the temples.

Telephone centrale (⏱ 24hr) Off the main road.

Tourist police (☎ 340 0277) On the road to the temples.

Sights & Activities

Overlooking Lake Nasser, the two **temples of Abu Simbel** (adult/student E£90/45; 6am-5pm Oct-Apr, to 6pm May-Sep) are reached by road or, if you are on a cruise boat, from one of the jetties leading directly into the fenced temple compound.

GREAT TEMPLE OF RAMSES II

Carved out of the mountain on the west bank of the Nile between 1274 and 1244 BC, Ramses II's imposing temple was as much dedicated to the deified pharaoh himself as to Ra-Horakhty, Amun and Ptah. The four pharaoh's colossal statues fronting the temple are like gigantic sentinels watching over the incoming traffic from the south, undoubtedly designed as a warning of the strength of the pharaoh.

Over the centuries both the Nile and the desert sands imperceptibly shifted, and this temple was lost to the world until 1813, when it was rediscovered by chance by the Swiss explorer Jean-Louis Burckhardt. Only one of the heads was completely showing above the sand, the next head was broken off and, of the remaining two, only the crowns could be seen. Enough sand was cleared away in 1817 by Giovanni Belzoni for the temple to be entered.

From the temple's forecourt, a short flight of steps leads up to the terrace in front of the massive rock-cut facade, which is about 30m high and 35m wide. Guarding the entrance, three of the four famous colossal Ramses II statues sit majestically, staring out across the water into eternity – the inner left statue collapsed in antiquity and its upper body still lies on the ground. The statues, more than 20m high, are accompanied by smaller statues of the pharaoh's mother, Queen Tuya, his wife Nefertari and some of his favourite children.

Above the entrance, between the central throned colossi, is the figure of the falcon-headed sun god Ra-Horakhty. Unfortunately, the sun god has been subjected to the trials of time and he now lacks part of his leg and foot.

The roof of the large hall is decorated with vultures, which are protective figures symbolising the goddess Nekhbet, and is supported by eight columns, each fronted by an Osiride statue of Ramses II. Reliefs on the walls depict the pharaoh's prowess in battle, trampling over his enemies and slaughtering them in front of the gods. On the north wall

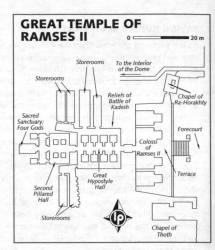

GREAT TEMPLE OF RAMSES II

is a depiction of the famous Battle of Kadesh (c 1274 BC), in what is now Syria, where Ramses inspired his demoralised army by his own courage, so that they won the war against the Hittites. The scene is dominated by a famous relief of Ramses in his chariot, shooting arrows at his fleeing enemies. Also visible is the Egyptian camp, walled off by its soldiers' round-topped shields, and the fortified Hittite town, surrounded by the Orontes River.

The next hall, the four-columned vestibule where Ramses and Nefertari are shown in front of the gods and the solar barques, leads to the sacred sanctuary, where Ramses and the triad of gods of the Great Temple sit on their thrones.

The temple is aligned in such a way that on 22 February and 22 October every year, the first rays of the rising sun reach across the Nile, penetrate the temple and move along the hypostyle hall, through the vestibule and into the sanctuary, where they illuminate the somewhat mutilated figures of Ra-Horakhty, Ramses II and Amun. Ptah, to the left, is never illuminated. (Until the temples were moved, this phenomenon happened one day earlier.)

TEMPLE OF HATHOR

Next to the Great Temple is the much smaller **Temple of Hathor**, with a rock-cut facade fronted by six 10m-high standing statues of Ramses and Nefertari, with some of their many children by their side. Nefertari here wears the costume of the goddess Hathor, and is, unusually, portrayed as the same height as her husband (instead of coming only up to his knees as most consorts were depicted).

Inside, the six pillars of the hypostyle hall are crowned with capitals in the bovine shape of Hathor. On the walls the queen appears in front of the gods very much equal to Ramses II, and she is seen honouring her husband. The vestibule and adjoining chambers, which have colourful scenes of the goddess and her sacred barque, lead to the sanctuary, with a weathered statue of Hathor as a cow emerging from the rock.

SOUND & LIGHT SHOW

A **sound and light show** (www.soundandlight.com.eg; adult/child E£80/45; ☺ shows 7pm, 8pm & 9pm winter, 8pm, 9pm & 10pm May-Sep) is performed nightly. Headphones are provided, allowing visitors to listen to the commentary in various languages. While the text is flowery and forgettable, the laser show projected onto the temples is stunning and well worth the detour.

Sleeping & Eating

Few people stay the night in Abu Simbel, but a few hotels allow those looking for ultimate peace and quiet to enjoy their stay.

Abu Simbel Village (☎ 340 0092; s/d E£90/120; 🗙) Abu Simbel's cheapest option, the faded Abu Simbel Village has basic vaulted rooms centred on a concrete courtyard.

our pick Eskaleh (Beit an-Nubi; ☎ 340 1288, 012 368 0521; d €50-70; 🗙 🖳) Part Nubian cultural centre with a library dedicated to Nubian history and culture, part small ecolodge in a traditional Nubian mudbrick house, Eskaleh is definitely the place to stay in town and something of a destination in its own right, if a bit pricey. The friendly owner, Fikry Kachif, a Nubian musician who lived in Abu Simbel before the dam was built, worked for years as a guide, but got tired of travelling and decided to set up shop beside the lake. Comfortable rooms are simply furnished with local furniture, and have fans, air-con and good private bathrooms. Nubian women prepare delicious home-cooked meals

(three-course lunch or dinner E£60) with organic produce from Fikry's garden and fish from the lake. At night the quiet is absolute, a rare thing on the tourist trail along the Nile. Sometimes Fikry plays with his friends, or he hosts performances of Nubian music and dance.

Seti Abu Simbel (☎ 400 720; www.setifirst.com; s/d US$145/200; 🗙 🖳 🖳) Abu Simbel's only five-star hotel has faded chalet-style rooms overlooking Lake Nasser – all pleasant enough but the service is slow and the food very mediocre, so it's not worth the prices being charged. The hotel is best booked through the Cairo-based travel agency Seti First (☎ 02-2736 9820). The restaurant here offers buffet breakfast (E£70), lunch (E£110) and dinner (E£150).

Toya (☎ 012 357 7539; Tariq al-Mabad; breakfasts E£8, mains E£15) New place in town serving breakfast for early arrivals, or simple local cuisine in a lovely garden or madly painted rooms inside. A good place to stop for a drink or to smoke a *sheesha*.

Along Abu Simbel's main road is a line-up of cheap cafes, with the Nubian Oasis and Wadi el-Nil among the most popular.

Getting There & Away

Foreigners travelling from Aswan to Abu Simbel by road must travel in police convoy. The police have deemed taxis off limits to foreigners, so luxury coach or minibus are your only options. Most people opt for a tour and get the admission and guide included.

You can avoid the convoy by taking a bus. Buses from Abu Simbel to Aswan leave at 6am, 9.30am, 1pm and 4pm from the Wadi el-Nil Restaurant on the main road. There is no advance booking, and tickets (E£21) are purchased on board. Note that the official limit is four foreign passengers per bus, although they will generally turn a blind eye to one or two extra.

EgyptAir has flights to Abu Simbel from Aswan; see p313 for flight details.

Western Desert

It's more ancient than the Pyramids, more sublime than any temple. Nearly as vast as your imagination, Egypt's Western Desert stretches from the Nile and the Mediterranean to the Sudanese and Libyan borders, rolling far into Africa oblivious to any lines drawn on the map. The Great Sand Sea starts here, a formidable khaki ocean undulating with some of the largest sand dunes on earth.

This desolate region is punctuated with five major oases boasting freshwater sources and supporting islands of verdant greenery. The valley floors lie speckled with crumbling Roman forts, once towering protectively over ancient caravan routes as they wound their way across North Africa. Flourishing palm plantations engulf medieval towns, and it's here out west that you will find the eerie rock formations of the White Desert, a dreamscape of eroded, snow-white pinnacles. Nearby, you can explore the charred mountains of the Black Desert, and bathe in innumerable crystal-clear springs as they gush from the valley floor. Away from the popular desert circuit road lies happily isolated Siwa, a tranquil paradise of springs and ancient ruins thickly carpeted with date palms.

Not many travellers peel themselves away from the popular Nile Valley routes to make the dusty trip out west. It's a shame. Paved roads now connect the oases, and while travel in this region takes time, the Western Desert offers some of the most jaw-dropping scenery and photogenic journeys in all Egypt.

HIGHLIGHTS

- Sleep under the blazing desert stars amid the unreal chalk-rock formations of the **White Desert** (p346)

- Soak in the tranquil, old-world ambience and unique culture of breathtaking **Siwa Oasis** (p355)

- Dip into one of the numerous cool and hot **natural springs** (see boxed text, p340) that lie peppered around the oases

- Wonder at the crumbling ruins of the medieval mudbrick fortified towns that protected oasis dwellers from marauding desert tribes in **Al-Qasr** (p341)

- Scramble over the ruins of Roman forts and the oldest Christian cemetery in the world around **Al-Kharga Oasis** (p330)

- Take the ultimate desert adventure, a multiday safari into the forebidding **Great Sand Sea** (p366) and beyond

★ Siwa Oasis

★ Great Sand Sea

★ White Desert

★ Al-Qasr

Al-Kharga Oasis ★

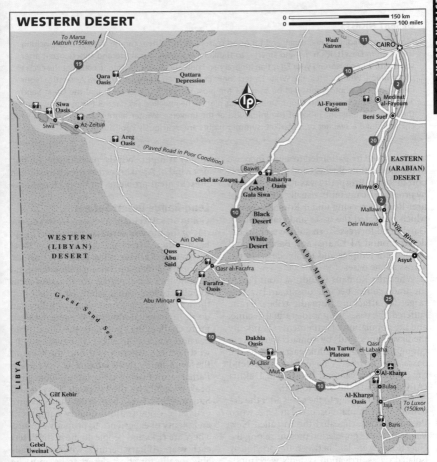

History

As with the Sahara and other deserts that stretch across northern Africa, the Western Desert was once a savannah that supported all manner of wildlife. Giraffes, lions and elephants roamed here in Palaeolithic times, when the landscape is thought to have looked much like the African Sahel. All that you see in the desert – the huge tracts of sand, the vast gravel plains, the fossil beds and limestone rocks – were once the happy hunting grounds that supported nomadic tribes. Gradual climate change led to desertification and turned this vast area into the arid expanse seen today. Only depressions in the desert floor have enough water to support wildlife, agriculture and human settlement.

The ancient Egyptians understood the nature of the desert, which they saw as being synonymous with death and exile. Seth, the god of chaos who killed his brother Osiris, was said to rule here. Despite their fears, it is believed the ancient Egyptians did maintain links with the oases throughout the Pharaonic era, although so far, with the exception of Dakhla Oasis, there is scant evidence of this before the Third Intermediate Period. But with the accession of a Libyan dynasty (22nd dynasty, 945–715 BC), focus moved to the west and the oases, with caravan routes to the Nile Valley. Many monuments in Al-Kharga and Baharia date from this period.

The oases enjoyed a period of great prosperity during Roman times, when new wells

---

DESERT NIGHTS

Most desert wildlife is nocturnal, and for good reason: daytime heat can be deadly. When visiting the Western Desert, it's fun – and smart – to think the way the animals do and experience it after sundown. When planning your Egyptian itinerary and how the desert fits into it, consider the cycles of the moon. When it's full, the White Desert looks like it's been transplanted from Antarctica (your long-exposure photographs will be some of the most surreal you ever take) and the Great Sand Sea swells with shadow and light. On moonless nights, the jewelled sky dazzles the eyes and awes the mind with instant proof of the infinitude of the universe. Winter nights can be surprisingly chilly, so take a sweater or a blanket; summer nights are deliciously cool but not cold.

---

and improved irrigation led to a vast increase in the production of wheat and grapes for export to Rome. Prosperity was also encouraged by provincial army units, usually consisting of non-Romans serving under Roman officers, which protected the oases and trade routes. Garrisoned fortresses can still be seen in the desert around Al-Kharga and Bahariya, and Roman-era temples and tombs lie scattered across all the oases.

When the Romans withdrew from Egypt, the trade routes became unsafe and were a target for attacking nomadic tribes. Trade suffered, the oases went into gradual decline, and the population of settlements shrank. By medieval times, raids by nomads were severe enough to bring Mamluk garrisons to the oases. The fortified villages built to defend the population can still be seen in Dakhla (Al-Qasr, Balat) and Siwa (Shali).

The biggest change to the oases after the departure of the Romans occurred in 1958, when President Nasser created the so-called New Valley to relieve population pressure along the Nile. Roads were laid between the previously isolated oases, irrigation systems were modernised and an administration was established. The New Valley Governorate is the largest in Egypt and one of the least densely populated: although conditions were right for people to migrate to the New Valley, there has never been enough work to attract significant numbers.

Climate

The ideal time to visit the Western Desert is in autumn (October/November) or early spring (March through mid-April). During summer (June through August), temperatures can soar as high as 52°C and although there is little humidity, the heat can be withering. Winter (December to February) is very pleasant, with average daytime highs of 20°C to 25°C, although it can get very cold (down to 0°C at

times) at night. Winds, particularly the hot, dry wind of April known as the khamsin, can present great problems for desert travellers.

Long-Range Desert Safaris

Going on safari in the Western Desert can be one of the most rewarding experiences Egypt has to offer. It can also be one of the most frustrating. Each oasis has good local guides, but many of them operate on a shoestring and have neither the expertise nor the equipment to pull off a long-range safari. This won't stop them from trying to persuade you they can do it. Included among the Western Desert's more challenging routes are the Great Sand Sea and remote Gilf Kebir (in Egypt's southwest corner), where you'll find the Cave of the Swimmers – made famous by *The English Patient* – and Gebel Uweinat, a 2000m-high peak trisected by the Egyptian, Libyan and Sudanese borders. These expeditions require extensive organisation, quality equipment and plenty of experience to properly execute. There are risks and people do die in the desert each year. Military permits, which are available locally for short desert treks, must be procured in Cairo for longer trips.

The following safari operators have solid international reputations, are among the more reliable in Egypt, and will treat the desert with the respect it deserves. Multiday expeditions run only between October and April.

Al-Badawiya (☎ 02-575 8076; www.badawiya.com) The three Ali brothers are Bedouin from Farafra, who have built up a significant business operating out of their Al-Badawiya Hotel and an office in downtown Cairo. With considerable experience in the Western Desert, they can mount tailored camel or jeep safaris from three to 28 days in length. They have tents, cooking equipment and bedding.

Dabuka Expeditions (☎ 6085 987 9896; www .dabuka.de) Dabuka is a German-based company that specialises in North African desert travel, not only through Egypt but also through Libya, Sudan, Tunisia and Jordan. In

Egypt it arranges multiday safaris into the Great Sand Sea, Gebel Uweinat and Gilf Kebir, as well as organising camel expeditions and running off-road driving courses.

Hisham Nessim (☎ 012 780 7999; www.raid4x4egypt .com) Rally driver and owner of the Aquasun hotels in Farafra and Sinai, Hisham Nessim has been driving in the desert for many years. With satellite phones, GPS and six 4WDs specially rigged for long-range desert travel, he is prepared to go to all corners of Egypt. He offers five programs (including self-drive) of seven to 14 days, or will tailor-make tours.

Khalifa Expedition (☎ 012 321 5445; www.khalifa exp.com) Khaled and Rose-Maria Khalifa have been running camel and jeep tours throughout the Western Desert from their base in Bahariya Oasis for well over a decade. Rose-Maria is a qualified speech therapist and foot masseuse, which perhaps explains why they also offer meditation tours for people more interested in communing with nature than looking at antiquities.

Pan Arab Tours (☎ 02-418 4409/419; www.pan arabtours.com) With more than 30 years' experience, Pan Arab Tours has developed expertise in taking visitors into Egypt's deserts. Used by archaeologists as well as tourists, the company has a number of specially equipped vehicles and offers six itineraries throughout the country, from two to eight days.

Zarzora Expedition (☎ 02-761 8105; www.zarzora .com) Captained by the very experienced Ahmed Al-Mestekawi, a retired colonel who used to conduct military desert patrols, Zarzora does expeditions to Siwa, Gilf Kebir and the Great Sand Sea. Ahmed has in-depth knowledge of the area and moonlights as a lecturer on the desert's environment and history.

AL-KHARGA OASIS

☎ 092 / pop 92,000

As the closest of the oases to the Nile Valley, Al-Kharga used to have the unenviable role as a place of banishment for mischievous Nile Valley citizens. Its remote location, punishing summer heat and destructive winds meant that the oasis was synonymous with misery and exile. It may seem strange, then, that its chief town, Al-Kharga, was chosen as the capital of the New Valley Governorate in the 1950s. Life in the oasis has improved somewhat since then, and with a smattering of fascinating ancient sites it's a worthwhile stopover.

Lying in a 220km-long and 40km-wide depression, Al-Kharga Oasis was at the crossroads of vital desert trade routes, including the famous Darb al-Arba'een (Forty Days Rd;

see boxed text, p331). Al-Kharga's influential location brought it great prosperity, and the arrival of the Romans improved things as wells were dug, crops cultivated and fortresses built to protect caravan routes from being attacked by desert nomads. Even as late as the 1890s, British forces were using lookout towers here to safeguard the 'back door' into Egypt. Today, attempts at modernising Wadi el-Gedid (the New Valley) with environmentally questionable land-reclamation efforts and intensive agriculture pose a bigger threat to the area than pillaging clans ever did.

AL-KHARGA

The busy city of Al-Kharga is the largest town in the Western Desert and also the posterchild of the government's efforts to modernise the oases. Unfortunately, visitors are unlikely to see the town's drab housing blocks and wide, bare boulevards as much of an improvement.

Still, the town makes a good base to explore some of the unique, gently crumbling sights found around this oasis valley floor. The museum showcases some intriguing ancient treasures, and a walk through the scruffy streets of the old souq (market) guarantees friendly conversations with locals (usually men).

Although there is no record of trouble in the oasis, expect a couple of policemen to station themselves at your hotel. Some travellers have even reported being trailed around town by police bodyguards. Most are perfectly courteous, and you can usually shake them by signing a paper refusing their protection.

Orientation

Al-Kharga is fairly spread out, with the bus station in the south-central part of town, the minibus stand in the southeast near the souq, and most of the hotels a fair hike away from both. If you're coming from Dakhla or Asyut, you may want to ask the driver to let you off early, near the hotel of your choice.

Information
EMERGENCY
Ambulance (☎ 123)
Tourist police (Map p332; ☎ 792 1367; Sharia Gamal Abdel Nasser)

INTERNET ACCESS
El-Radwan Hotel (Map p332; off Sharia Gamal Abdel Nasser; per hr E£2; ☺ 24hr)

Internet cafe (Map p332; 2nd fl, northwest cnr Midan Mudares; per hr E£1.5; ☉ 7.30am-11.30pm)

MEDICAL SERVICES
General hospital (Map p332; ☎ 792 0777; Sharia Basateen)

MONEY
Banque du Caire (Map p332; off Sharia Gamal Abdel Nasser) Very slow service, but there is an ATM.
National Bank of Egypt (p332; Sharia Gamal Abdel Nasser) Across from the museum; has an ATM out front.

POST & TELEPHONE
Private telephone shops are sprinkled all over Al-Kharga.
Main post office (Map p332; Sharia Abdel Moniem Riad; ☉ 8am-2.30pm Sat-Thu)
Telephone centrale (Map p332; Sharia Abdel Moniem Riad; ☉ 24hr)

TOURIST INFORMATION
New Valley Tourist Office (Map p332; ☎ 792 1206; Midan Nasser; ☉ 9am-2pm Sat-Thu) Find Mohsen Abd Al Moneam, a mother lode of knowledge about Kharga and Dakhla Oases. He arranges private transport to sights around Al-Kharga and to Luxor. If he's not in, phone his mobile: ☎ 010 180 6127.

Sights
AL-KHARGA MUSEUM OF ANTIQUITIES
Designed to resemble the architecture of nearby Bagawat, this two-storey **museum** (Map p332; Sharia Gamal Abdel Nasser; adult/student E£30/15; ☉ 8am-5pm) is housed in a cavernous, well-lit building made from local bricks. Inside is a small but interesting selection of archaeological finds from around Al-Kharga and Dakhla Oases. There's a particularly good selection of prehistoric objects, flints, ostrich eggs and tools tracing the prehistory of the oases in both English and Arabic. There's also a smattering of objects from Pharaonic, Greek and Roman antiquities. One fascinating find is a collection of wooden Roman panels (early versions of sticky notes) detailing farmers' accounts, marriages and contracts of the time. Also look for the exquisite false-door stele of 6th-dynasty governor Khent-ka (c 2700 BC), with the earliest known reference to Dakhla Oasis.

The upper floor contains objects from the Coptic, Islamic and Ottoman eras, with some fascinating jewellery, books, coins and textiles.

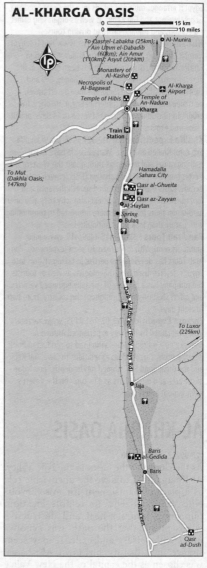

AL-KHARGA OASIS

0 — 15 km
0 — 10 miles

To Qasr el-Labakha (25km); Ain Umm el-Dabadib (60km); Ain Amur (110km); Asyut (205km)
Al-Munira
Monastery of Al-Kashef
Necropolis of Al-Bagawat
Temple of Hibis
Al-Kharga Airport
Temple of An-Nadura
Al-Kharga
Train Station
To Mut (Dakhla Oasis; 147km)
Hamadalla Sahara City
Qasr al-Ghueita
Qasr az-Zayyan
Al-Haytan
Spring
Bulaq
Darb al-Arba'een (Forty Days Rd)
To Luxor (225km)
Jaja
Baris al-Gedida
Baris
Darb al-Arba'een
Qasr ad-Dush

TEMPLE OF HIBIS
The town of Hebet ('the Plough', now corrupted into Hibis) was the capital of the oasis in antiquity, but all that remains today is the well-preserved limestone **Temple of Hibis** (Map p330; adult/student E£30/15; ☉ 8am-5pm Oct-Apr, to 6pm May-Sep). Once sitting on the edge of a sacred lake, the temple was dedicated to Amun of

THE WAY OF DUSTY DEATH

Al-Kharga Oasis sits atop what was once the only major African north–south trade route through Egypt's Western Desert: the notorious Darb al-Arba'een, or **Forty Days Rd**. A 1721km track linking Fasher in Sudan's Darfur province with Asyut in the Nile Valley, this was one of Africa's great caravan trails, bringing the riches of Sudan – gold, ivory, skins, ostrich feathers and especially slaves – north to the Nile Valley and beyond to the Mediterranean. It's thought to date back to the Old Kingdom, and the richness of the merchandise transported along this bleak track was such that protecting it was a priority. The Romans invested heavily here, building a series of fortresses – such as Qasr ad-Dush (p335), the Monastery of Al-Kashef (p332) and Qasr al-Ghueita (p334) – to tax the caravans and try to foil the frequent raids by desert tribesmen and, on occasion, Nubians.

Despite the dangers, Darb al-Arba'een flourished until well into the Islamic era, by which time it was Egypt's main source of slaves. Untold numbers of tragic human cargo died of starvation and thirst on the journey north. According to 19th-century European travellers, slavers travelled in the intense summer heat, preferring to expose their merchandise to dehydration on what British geographer GW Murray (author of the 1967 *Dare Me to the Desert*) called 'the way of dusty death', rather than risk the possibility of bronchitis and pneumonia from the cold desert winter.

Despite repeated attempts by the British to suppress the trade, slaves were brought north until Darfur became part of Sudan at the beginning of the 20th century. The Darb al-Arba'een withered and today its route has been all but lost.

Hibis (the local version of the god, who was sometimes given solar powers, becoming Amun-Ra), who appears with his usual companions, Mut and Khons. Construction of the temple began during the 25th dynasty, though the decorations and a **colonnade** were added over the next 300 years.

An **avenue of sphinxes** leads to a series of gateways, the colonnade of Nectanebo and then to a **court**, a **hypostyle hall** and an **inner sanctuary**. One of the reliefs in the hypostyle hall shows the god Seth battling with the evil serpent Apophis – an archetype of the St George and the dragon motif. Among the graffiti left by 19th-century European travellers is a lengthy inscription from 1818 by Frederic Cailliaud, who claimed to have been the first European to see the temple.

The temple has been closed for renovation, but is due to reopen some time in late 2009, *inshallah*. It's 2km north of town just to the left of the main road; pick-ups (50pt) heading to Al-Munira pass this way.

TEMPLE OF AN-NADURA

Located on a hill off the main road at the north end of town, the **Temple of An-Nadura** (Map p330; admission free) has strategic views of the area and once doubled as a fortified lookout. It was built during the reign of Roman emperor Antoninus Pius (AD 138–161) to protect the oasis, and inside you will find the remains of a sandstone temple with hieroglyphic inscrip-

tions. It later housed a Coptic church and was used as a fortress by the Ottomans.

The site is badly ruined, but the superb vistas are ideal for sunset adulation. The ruins lie perched on a rise off to the right of the main road before the Temple of Hibis.

NECROPOLIS OF AL-BAGAWAT

It may not look like much from afar, but this **necropolis** (Map p330; adult/student E£30/15; ☉ 8am-5pm Oct Apr, to 6pm May-Sep) is one of the earliest surviving and best-preserved Christian cemeteries in the world. About 1km north of the Temple of Hibis, it's built on the site of an earlier Egyptian necropolis, with most of the 263 mudbrick tombs appearing to date from the 4th to the 6th centuries AD. While many of the domed Coptic tombs are fairly plain, a few have vivid murals of biblical scenes inside and some have ornate facades. The **Chapel of Peace** has figures of the Apostles on the squinches of the domes, just visible through Greek graffiti. The **Chapel of the Exodus**, one of the oldest tombs, has the best-preserved paintings, including the Old Testament story of Moses leading the children of Israel out of Egypt, which is visible through some 9th-century graffiti. Another large family tomb (No 25) has a mural of Abraham sacrificing Isaac, and the smaller **Chapel of the Grapes** (Anaeed al-Ainab) is named after the images of grapevines that cover the walls. A guardian will be anxious to guide you to some of the

WESTERN DESERT

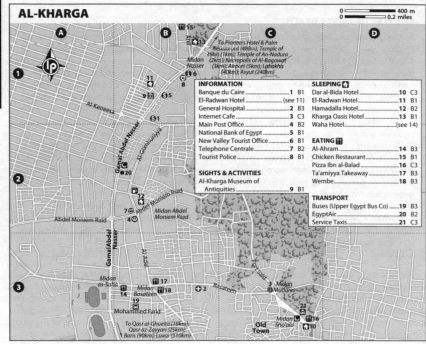

AL-KHARGA

0 — 400 m
0 — 0.2 miles

To Pioneers Hotel & Palm
Restaurant (400m), Temple of
Hibis (1km); Temple of An-Nadura
(2km); Necropolis of Al-Bagawat
(3km); Airport (5km); Labakha
(40km); Asyut (240km)

Midan
Nasser

Al-Keneesa

Gamal Abdel Nasser

Al-Gomhuriyya

Abdel Moniem Riad

Midan Abdel
Moniem Riad

Gamal Abdel Nasser

Abdel Moniem Raid

Al-Adel

Port-Said

Midan
as-Saha

Midan
Basateen

Midan
Mudares

Basateen

Mohammed Farid

To Qasr al-Ghueita (18km),
Qasr az-Zayyan (25km),
Baris (90km); Luxor (310km)

Old
Town

Midan
Sho'ala

INFORMATION

Banque du Caire...................1	B1
El-Radwan Hotel..............(see 11)	
General Hospital...................2	B3
Internet Cafe.......................3	C3
Main Post Office...................4	B2
National Bank of Egypt.........5	B1
New Valley Tourist Office......6	B1
Telephone Centrale...............7	B2
Tourist Police......................8	B1

SIGHTS & ACTIVITIES

Al-Kharga Museum of	
Antiquities........................9	B1

SLEEPING

Dar al-Bida Hotel................10	C3
El-Radwan Hotel.................11	B1
Hamadalla Hotel.................12	B2
Kharga Oasis Hotel..............13	B1
Waha Hotel.....................(see 14)	

EATING

Al-Ahram..........................14	B3
Chicken Restaurant.............15	B1
Pizza Ibn al-Balad...............16	C3
Ta'amiyya Takeaway............17	B3
Wembe............................18	B3

TRANSPORT

Buses (Upper Egypt Bus Co).....19	B3
EgyptAir...........................20	B2
Service Taxis.....................21	C3

more colourful tombs; he should be tipped (around E£5).

MONASTERY OF AL-KASHEF
Dominating the cliffs to the north of Al-Bagawat is the ruined Monastery of Al-Kashef (Deir al-Kashef; Map p330), named after Mustafa al-Kashef, a tax collector, and strategically placed to overlook what was one of the most important crossroads of the Western Desert – the point where the Darb al-Ghabari from Dakhla crossed the Darb al-Arba'een. The magnificent mudbrick remains date back to the early Christian era, although the site was occupied as early as the Middle Kingdom. Once five storeys high, much of it has collapsed, but you can see the tops of the arched corridors that criss-crossed the building. To get here, walk or drive on the left-hand track from the Necropolis of Al-Bagawat for about 1km.

Tours
Al-Kharga has few private outfits offering desert trips, but Mohsen, from the tourist office (see p330), is also an experienced guide highly recommended by travellers. If you

really dig archaeology, contact guide Sameh Abdel Rihem (☎ 010 296 2192), an expert on Kharga's antiquities who has a palpable love for sights both popular and esoteric around the oasis. For information on longer desert safaris, see p328.

Sleeping
HOTELS
You'd better recalibrate your hotel expectations for Al-Kharga before you arrive as, with a couple of exceptions, the choices are a little sad. On the upside, many places are nearly empty year-round, so getting a room is never a problem!

Waha Hotel (Map p332; ☎ 792 0393; Sharia an-Nabawi; s/d with shared bathroom E£18/25, with air-con E£30/40) This gritty, tenement-like hotel makes a great place to stay if you've lost your wallet, or want to use one of the shared toilets to re-enact the bathroom scene from the movie *Trainspotting*.

Hamadalla Hotel (Map p332; ☎ 792 0638; fax 792 5017; off Sharia Abdel Moniem Riad; s/d E£40/55, with air-con E£65/85) Popular with tour groups, Hamadalla has rooms that are clean, despite some torn carpeting and cracked plaster. It's only a minute's walk from some good felafel and streetside cafes. It sometimes sells Stella beer.

El-Radwan Hotel (Map p332; ☎ 792 1716, 012 747 2087; off Sharia Gamal Abdel Nasser; s/d E£45/65; ✷ ☐) Easily the best deal in town, El-Radwan gets everything important right (if you can overlook scuffed walls and a lack of decor). It's well located for the Museum of Antiquities and the tourist office, the staff is super-friendly and the clean rooms come with refrigerators and satellite TV. The 24-hour internet cafe off the lobby is a big bonus.

Dar al-Bida Hotel (Map p332; ☎ 792 9494, 010 308 2254; Midan Sho'ala; s/d/tr E£60/80/100, with shared bathroom E£55/75/95; ✷) Just to the left off Midan Sho'ala, Dar al-Bida is convenient if you're arriving late or leaving early by minibus. Rooms are cramped, shabby and overpriced, but the family that runs it is quite sweet.

Pioneers Hotel (off Map p332; ☎ 792 9751-3; www .solymar.com; Sharia Gamal Abdel Nasser; s/d half board from €66/84; ✷ ☐ ✷) An apt name: these guys pioneered the concept of luxury resorts in the Western Desert. While the salmon-pink, low-rise construction is reminiscent of a hollowed-out sponge cake, the hotel does offer a level of comfort that was until recently unimaginable in the oases: a swimming pool, a fitness area, an outdoor cafe, billiards and a children's playground all connected by ridiculously lush grass. It is the only place in Al-Kharga where you can count on getting alcohol.

Hamadalla Sahara City (Map p330; ☎ /62 0240; Kharga-Dush rd; s/d E£130/160; ✷) Hamadalla Sahara City shimmers like a gussied-up, garish pink-and-yellow mirage in the open desert, 15km south of Al-Kharga. Set around an urban-like hotel complex, it has domed bungalows clustered in small groups, each sporting neat, agreeable rooms with private bathrooms. It's a pain to get to without your own wheels, but the views of the desert rising over nearby Qasr al-Ghueita are damned impressive.

Kharga Oasis Hotel (Map p332; ☎ 792 4940; Midan Nasser; s/d E£175/260; ✷) Another modern homage to concrete, the 1960s Kharga Oasis is a favourite stopping-off point for desert adventurers. It sports generous and comfortable rooms and courteous staff and has a chic palm-filled garden and terrace. There are some new, traditionally styled mud-brick bungalows in the palm groves out back, which are nicer than the rooms in the main building.

CAMPING

Kharga Oasis Hotel (Map p332; ☎ 792 4940; Midan Nasser; sites per person E£45) The palm grove out the back of this hotel is your best bet in town for sleeping under your own canvas, at quite a cost. You can use the hotel's toilet and shower facilities, but be warned that the garden breeds aberrantly large swarms of mosquitoes at night.

Eating

If your palate needs a break from the staple Egyptian trinity of chicken, *fuul* (fava bean paste) and *ta'amiyya*, you'd be best to head for one of the better hotels. Otherwise, there's a smattering of basic eateries around Midan Sho'ala, Sharia al-Adel and near Midan Basateen. There's a cheap chicken restaurant at the northern end of town. Most restaurants are open for lunch and dinner.

Al-Ahram (Map p332; Waha Hotel, Sharia an-Nabawi; meals E£8-20) A small, friendly place serving roast chicken and *kofta* (minced meat and spices grilled on a skewer) accompanied by modest salads and vegetable dishes.

Pizza Ibn al-Balad (Map p332; Midan Sho'ala; pizzas E£10-30) Strike us down if this place doesn't serve some of the best darned *fit-eer* (Egyptian pizza/pancake) in the oases. Deservedly, it's one of the most popular places to eat. Choose from cheese, veggie and tuna or beef toppings.

Wembe (Map p332; Midan Basateen; meals E£10-30) This busy local eatery gets the thumbs up from people who are qualified to give such ratings, and serves the usual Egyptian comestibles: grilled meats, salads, rice and vegetables.

Palm Restaurant (off Map p332; ☎ 792 9751-3; fax 792 7983; Pioneers Hotel, Sharia Gamal Abdel Nasser; buffet dinners €10) If there is a group staying here, dinner tends to be a buffet; otherwise the restaurant offers an à la carte selection of continental dishes. None of the cooking here is particularly inspiring, but it's not bad for Al-Kharga.

Getting There & Away
AIR

The airport is 5km north of town. While **EgyptAir** (Map p332; ☎ 790 1334; Sharia Gamal Abdel Nasser) has been talking for years of restarting flights to Al-Kharga, the Petroleum Service Company has beaten it to it. The latter (usually) has Sunday flights on a 15-seat plane, leaving Cairo at 8am and returning from Al-Kharga at 4pm (E£500 one way, 1½ hours). Contact the tourist office (p330) for schedules and bookings.

BUS

Upper Egypt Bus Co (Map p332; ☎ 792 4587; Sharia Mohammed Farid) operates buses to Cairo (E£60, eight to 10 hours) daily at 6am, 9pm, 10pm, 11pm and midnight.

There are several buses bound for Asyut (E£16, three to four hours) leaving daily at 6am, 7am, 9am, 11am, 12pm, 2pm, 10pm and 12.30am.

Local buses to Baris (E£6, one hour) leave at 7am and 2.30pm daily. Buses to Dakhla (E£16, three hours) leave daily at 5am, 11am, 2pm, 11pm, 1am and 3.30am.

There's no bus service to Luxor. If heading that way, you can either catch a bus to Asyut and change there, or hire a private taxi (see below).

SERVICE TAXI

Most vehicles based at the **service taxi station** (Map p332; Midan Sho'ala) are microbuses but there are also a few Peugeot station wagons. Destinations include Asyut (E£12, three to four hours) and Dakhla (E£11, three hours).

TAXI

Thanks to the new road, special taxis can get you to Luxor (via Jaja) in three hours, but will set you back E£350 to E£400. Cairo (six to seven hours) costs E£700 for the car (maximum seven people), but expect a long, hot, cramped ride.

TRAIN

The Friday train between Al-Kharga and Luxor is no longer running, with no plans to resume service anytime soon. Seems bandits repeatedly stole sections of the track, also robbing travellers of the masochistically rewarding experience of crossing the desert by rail.

Getting Around

Microbuses (50pt) run along the main streets of Al-Kharga, especially Sharia Gamal Abdel Nasser. Taxis between any two points in town cost E£2.

AROUND AL-KHARGA

While the best-known sights near Al-Kharga lie along the good asphalt road that stretches south to Baris (Map p330), there are a few intriguing, harder-to-reach destinations north of town, too.

Qasr al-Ghueita & Qasr az-Zayyan

It is easy to see why the Romans chose the site, some 18km south of Al-Kharga, for **Qasr al-Ghueita** (Map p330; adult/student E£30/15; ⊗ 8am-5pm Oct-Apr, to 6pm May-Sep). The imposing Roman mudbrick fortress has survived millennia and still dominates the road to Baris. Its name means 'Fortress of the Small Garden', which seems a misnomer for a place surrounded by desert. But in antiquity, Qasr al-Ghueita was the centre of a fertile agricultural community renowned for its grapes. Soon, Ghueita may overlook an even more surprising patch of greenery: the golf resort that's planning to open nearby sometime in 2010.

The garrison's massive outer walls enclose a 25th-dynasty sandstone temple, dedicated to the Theban triad Amun, Mut and Khons. In later centuries, the fortress served as the perimeter for a village, with some houses surviving along the outer wall. Within the hypostyle hall, a series of reliefs show Hapy, the potbellied Nile god, holding symbols of the nomes (provinces) of Upper Egypt. An asphalt road leads 2km to the temple from the main road.

About 7km further south are the remains of **Qasr az-Zayyan** (Map p330; adult/student E£30/15; ⊗ 8am-5pm Oct-Apr, to 6pm May-Sep), another fortress enclosing a temple, though less impressive than Qasr al-Ghueita. Unlike many of the sights in this oasis, the fort is still situated beside a small but thriving village.

If you don't have a vehicle you can get to the temples by taking a bus heading for Baris (see left) or a covered pick-up going to Bulaq (E£1). There is an asphalt road linking the two temples, but 7km is a long hike if you're on foot – be sure to take plenty of water.

Baris

Baris, 90km south of Al-Kharga, was once one of the most important trading centres along the Darb al-Arba'een, but there is little left to remind you of that. Other than a few kiosks selling *fuul* and *ta'amiyya*, there is little of note apart from the mudbrick houses of **Baris al-Gedida**, about 2km north of the original town. Hassan Fathy, Egypt's most influential modern architect, designed the houses using traditional methods and materials and intended Baris al-Gedida to be a model for other new settlements. Work stopped at the outbreak of the Six Day War of 1967 and only two houses and some public spaces have ever been completed.

About 13km to the southeast of Baris is **Qasr ad-Dush** (Map p330; adult/student E£30/15; ☺ 8am-5pm Oct-Apr, to 6pm May-Sep), an imposing Roman temple-fortress completed around AD 177 on the site of the ancient town of Kysis. Dush was a border town strategically placed at the intersection of five desert tracks and one of the southern gateways to Egypt. It may also have been used to guard the Darb al-Dush, an east–west track to the Esna and Edfu temples in the Nile Valley. As a result it was solidly built and heavily garrisoned, with four or five more storeys lying underground. A 1st-century sandstone temple abutting the fortress was dedicated to Isis and Serapis. The gold decorations that once covered parts of the temple and earned it renown have long gone, but there is still some decoration on the inner stone walls.

Currently, Baris is not an ideal place to stay the night and you're better off staying at or near Al-Kharga, though a new hotel near Qasr ad-Dush, called Tabona Camp, may be open by the time you visit (check with the tourist office in Al-Kharga, p330).

GETTING THERE & AWAY
There are buses between Al-Kharga and Baris (E£6), leaving from Al-Kharga at 7am and 2.30pm daily, and from Baris at 6am and noon. The frequent microbuses and pick-up trucks are a more convenient option between Al-Kharga and Baris, and cost about E£3. To cover the 15km between Qasr ad-Dush and Baris, negotiate a special ride with a covered pick-up, usually available for E£30 to E£40, depending on waiting time. Hiring a private car for a day to see all the sights between Al-Kharga and Dush costs about E£17; this is best arranged through the tourist office (p330).

Qasr el-Labakha
Set amid a desertscape of duney desolation, **Qasr el-Labakha** (Map p327) is a micro-oasis some 40km north of Al-Kharga. Scattered among sandy swells and rocky shelfs are the remains of a towering four-storey Roman fortress, two temples, and a vast necropolis where over 500 mummies have been unearthed (you can still see human remains in

the tombs). A small camp, which is a perfect outpost for exploring the area, is run by the gentle-natured Sayed Taleb, who cleaned out the site's ancient aqueducts and uses them to water his garden. Day and overnight trips to Labakha can be arranged by the tourist office in Al-Kharga (see p330), with prices starting at around E£300 per vehicle.

About 20km west of Labakha lie the ruins at **Ain Umm el-Dabadib**, which has one of the most complex underground aqueduct systems built in this area by the Romans; keep going another 50km and you'll reach **Ain Amur** up on the Abu Tartur Plateau, the highest spring in the Western Desert (but don't plan on swimming). Trips to these sites qualify as serious desert excursions that require 4WD and experienced drivers, who can be contacted through Al-Kharga's tourist office (p330). Expect to pay about E£950 per vehicle to Ain Amur and back.

DAKHLA OASIS
☎ 092 / pop 95,000
With more than a dozen fertile hamlets sprinkled along the Western Desert circuit road, Dakhla lives up to most visitors' romantic expectations of oasis life. Lush palm groves and orchards support traditional villages, where imposing, ancient mudbrick forts still stand guard over the townships and allude to their less tranquil past.

The region has been inhabited since prehistoric times, with fossilised bones hinting at human habitation dating back 150,000 years. In Neolithic times, Dakhla was the site of a vast lake and rock paintings show that elephants, zebras and ostriches wandered its shores. As the area dried up, inhabitants migrated east to become the earliest settlers of the Nile Valley. In Pharaonic times, Dakhla retained several settlements and was a fertile land producing wine, fruit and grains. The Romans, and later Christians, left their mark by building over older settlements, and today's remaining medieval-era fortified towns attest to the more violent times of Bedouin and Arab raids.

MUT
At the centre of the oasis lies the town of Mut, settled since Pharaonic times (Mut was the god Amun's consort). Although now a

WESTERN DESERT

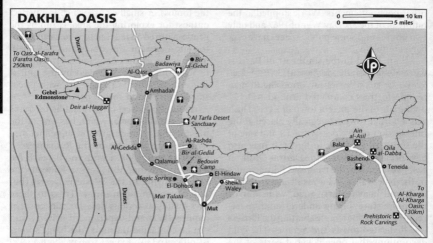

DAKHLA OASIS

modern Egyptian town, it has the most facilities in the area and makes the most convenient base for travellers. Mut's wide boulevards and the proximity of the palm groves all help to give it some charm, while the remains of the ruined old town show how it must have once looked.

Information
EMERGENCY
Ambulance (☎ 123)
Tourist police (off Map p338; ☎ 782 1687; Sharia 10th of Ramadan)

INTERNET ACCESS
Internet connections in Mut have been known to approach courier-pigeon speed. Some hotels now have internet terminals, though prices are much higher (E£10 per hour) than at the internet cafes.
Abo Ali Internet (Map p338; Sharia as-Sawra al-Khadra; per hr E£5; ☉ 6pm–midnight)
Mido Net (Map p338; Sharia Basateen; per hr E£2; ☉ 8am–3am)

MEDICAL SERVICES
General hospital (Map p338; ☎ 782 1555; off Sharia 10th of Ramadan)

MONEY
Banque Misr (Map p338; Sharia al-Wadi; ☉ 8.30am–2pm Sun–Thu) Has an ATM, exchanges cash and does cash advances on Visa and MasterCard, but does not change travellers cheques.

POST & TELEPHONE
Main post office (Map p338; Midan al-Gamaa; ☉ 8am–2pm Sat–Thu)
Telephone centrale (Map p338; Sharia as-Salam; ☉ 24hr)

TOURIST INFORMATION
Tourist office (Map p338; ☎ 782 1685 6; Sharia as-Sawra al-Khadra; ☉ 8am–3pm & some evenings) Friendly tourist-office director Omar Ahmad is a mine of knowledge about the oases. For urgent issues he can be contacted on his mobile: ☎ 012 179 6467.

Sights & Activities
ETHNOGRAPHIC MUSEUM
Dakhla's wonderful **museum** (Map p338; Sharia as-Salam; admission E£5; ☉ 8am–2pm Sat–Thu), attached to Dar al-Wafdeen Government Hotel, is only opened on request: ask at the tourist office or at the **Cultural Palace** (Map p338; ☎ 782 1311; Sharia al-Wadi), where the museum's manager, Ibrahim Kamel, can be found. The museum is laid out as a traditional home, with different areas for men, women and visitors. Displays of clothing, baskets, jewellery and other domestic items give an insight into oasis life.

OLD TOWN OF MUT
For much of old Mut's existence, the villagers lived with the threat of raiding Bedouin. Most houses here have no outside windows, thus protecting against intruders and keeping out the heat and wind of the desert. Often ignored by passing travellers, the

labyrinth of mudbrick houses and lanes that wind up the slopes of the hill is definitely worth exploring, even if you may sometimes stumble into less-than-appealing surrounds. From the top of the hill, at the **old citadel** (the original town centre; Map p338), there are great views of the new town and the desert beyond.

Tours

Dakhla has a few keen would-be desert guides (although they are not as aggressive as in Bahariya). Most hotels and restaurants will also offer to take you on a trek around the area. A typical day trip includes visits to Al-Gedida (p342) and Qalamun (p342), a drive through the dunes, visits to a spring and a tour of Al-Qasr for up to E£150 per person. Alternatively, aspiring taxi drivers can drive you to outlying sights for around E£200 for a full day.

An overnight trip around the same area, with Bedouin music, will cost about E£600 per person including food. The owners of the Bedouin Camp (right) are camel experts and can arrange long and short trips into the desert around Dakhla. You're looking at about E£100 for a day trip of any length, and E£300 to spend the night in the dunes. If you want to go further afield, check with the tourist office (opposite) to confirm whether the person taking you has the necessary permits – Dakhla is one of the closest oases to Gilf Kebir, but permits to go there are only issued from Cairo. For more information about desert safaris, see p328.

Sleeping

HOTELS

Mut has a decent selection of hotels, although most crowd the budget end of the spectrum. Recently, there's been a refreshing trend for hotels designed with Bedouin-influenced flair, using natural materials, mudbricks and palm logs.

Gardens Hotel (Map p338; ☎ 782 1577; Sharia al-Genayen; s/d with shared bathroom E£12/16, s/d/tr with shower E£15/25/24) Low prices and a good location help keep the rooms occupied at this ramshackle but popular budget hotel. The shared bathrooms can be pretty dire and single women may feel uncomfortable with the stares from resident Egyptian men. Breakfast is extra (E£5 to E£15) and the hotel rents bicycles for E£10 per hour.

Anwar Hotel (Map p338; ☎ 782 0070; Sharia Basateen; s/d/tr with fan E£30/50/70, with air-con E£40/60/80; 🖳) The friendly and sociable Mr Anwar runs this family establishment with gusto and offers relatively clean rooms above the popular restaurant of the same name (see p338). Noise from the nearby mosque can be an issue, and the younger Anwars are a bit overeager to sell their tours.

El-Forsan Hotel (Map p338; ☎ 782 1343; elforsanhotel.piczo.com; Sharia al-Wadi; s/d incl breakfast E£45/76, with air-con E£55/90; 🖳) While the main building is a typical concrete confabulation, the newer, domed mudbrick bungalows out back are a much more stylish option. There's a covered rotunda restaurant (meals E£15 to E£20) out back, along with a garden cafe boasting top views, where English-language movies or football matches are projected onto a screen every night. The staff has a good sense of humour and breakfast is included.

El-Negoom Hotel (Map p338; ☎ 782 0014; fax 782 3084; north of Sharia as-Sawra al-Khadra; s/d E£60/70, with air-con E£80/100; 🖳) On a quiet street behind the tourist office and near a selection of restaurants, this friendly hotel has a span of trim little abodes with bathrooms, some even with air-con and TV. This is one of the most dependable options in town.

Mebarez Hotel (Map p338; ☎ /fax 782 1524; Sharia as-Sawra al-Khadra; s/d E£80/130, with air-con E£90/140; 🖳) Safari groups and others doing an oases tour like to stay here, where the rooms offer a reasonable level of comfort and cleanliness. The top-floor rooms have great vistas over the oasis – ask for one facing away from the road.

Bedouin Camp & El-Dohous Village (Map p336; ☎ 785 0480; www.dakhlabedouins.com; s/d E£100/120) Al-Hag Abdel Hameed comes from a family of Bedouins who settled in the area a generation ago. El-Dohous Village has grown into a Disneyland of structures made from gently curving mudbrick and natural materials. There's a huge variety of rooms, from bell-shaped cave rooms to regular two-storey abodes, all carefully decorated with crafted pillows and local crafts. The hilltop restaurant (meals E£25) has outstanding views and there are plenty of cushioned chill-out areas strewn about the place. The nearby spring looks tempting but may stain clothes.

Bedouin Oasis Village (off Map p338; ☎ 782 0070, 012 669 4893; s/d E£70/150, full board E£100/200) This hilltop hotel at the north end of Mut has the most character of any place in town, with a deluge of domes, arches and vaults. There are quirky

WESTERN DESERT

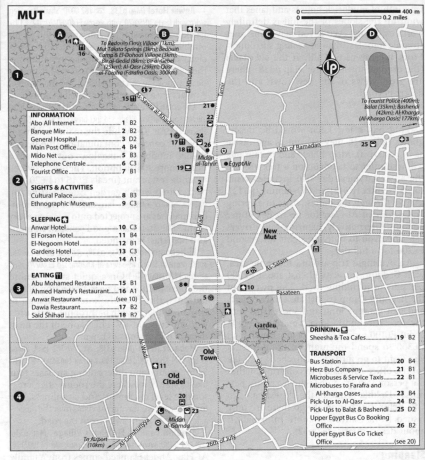

MUT

INFORMATION
Abo Ali Internet	**1**	B2
Banque Misr	**2**	B2
General Hospital	**3**	D2
Main Post Office	**4**	B4
Mido Net	**5**	B3
Telephone Centrale	**6**	C3
Tourist Office	**7**	B1

SIGHTS & ACTIVITIES
Cultural Palace	**8**	B3
Ethnographic Museum	**9**	C3

SLEEPING
Anwar Hotel	**10**	C3
El Forsan Hotel	**11**	B4
El-Negoom Hotel	**12**	B1
Gardens Hotel	**13**	C3
Mebarez Hotel	**14**	A1

EATING
Abu Mohamed Restaurant	**15**	B1
Ahmed Hamdy's Restaurant	**16**	A1
Anwar Restaurant	(see 10)	
Dawia Restaurant	**17**	B2
Said Shihad	**18**	B2

DRINKING
Sheesha & Tea Cafes	**19**	B2

TRANSPORT
Bus Station	**20**	B4
Herz Bus Company	**21**	B1
Microbuses & Service Taxis	**22**	B1
Microbuses to Farafra and Al-Kharga Oases	**23**	B4
Pick-Ups to Al-Qasr	**24**	B2
Pick-Ups to Balat & Bashendi	**25**	D2
Upper Egypt Bus Co Booking Office	**26**	B2
Upper Egypt Bus Co Ticket Office	(see 20)	

touches, too, like the whimsical carvings and sculptures around the courtyard. Temporarily closed for renovations at the time of writing, it will be worth checking out once it reopens.

CAMPING

You should be able to camp near the dunes west of Mut or in Al-Qasr, on a starlit plateau just north of town, but check first with the tourist office in Mut (see p336).

Eating & Drinking

There is no fancy dining in Mut, but there is some decent, fresh food (mostly of the chicken/kebab/rice variety) to be had. For an atmospheric tea or *sheesha* (water pipe), pop into one of the rowdy and popular outdoor

sheesha and tea cafes near Midan al-Tahrir. Most eateries are open from morning until night, though *ta'amiyya* takeaways usually close by noon.

Anwar Restaurant (Map p338; ☎ 782 0070; Sharia Basateen; meals E£2-25) A cafe-restaurant that's popular with locals, below the hotel of the same name. Anwar serves up *ta'amiyya* and *fuul*, in addition to the more substantial chicken-and-rice combo.

Abu Mohamed Restaurant (Map p338; ☎ 782 1431; Sharia as-Sawra al-Khadra; meals E£5-25; ☐) Abu Mohamed, brother of Ahmed Hamdy (see opposite), touts, cooks and serves in this simple roadside restaurant. His set meal includes good vegetables with kebab or pigeon (order ahead) and ends with homemade *bas-*

bousa (a sticky dessert). Cold beer, internet and bike hire (E£10 per hour) are available.

Dawia Restaurant (Map p338; Sharia as-Sawra al-Khadra; meals E£8-30) The wall-to-wall, sparkling-white tiles signal one of the cleanest places to eat in town. As well as the usual Egyptian victuals, Dawia throws caution to the wind: it fries up burgers and even experiments with several pasta dishes.

Said Shihad (Map p338; Sharia as-Sawra al-Khadra; meals E£10-20) Owner Said is on to a good thing here: grilling up a meat-centric feast nightly to a dedicated following of hungry locals. The lamb shish kebab is the thing to go for – perfectly succulent and served with potatoes in a tomato sauce, rice and tahini.

Ahmed Hamdy's Restaurant (Map p338; ☎ 782 0767; Sharia as-Sawra al-Khadra; meals E£10-30) On the main road into town is Ahmed Hamdy's popular place serving delicious chicken, kebabs, vegetables and a few other small dishes inside or on the terrace. The freshly squeezed lime juice is excellent and you can request beer (E£12) and *sheesha*.

Getting There & Away

BUS

Upper Egypt Bus Co (Map p338; ☎ 782 4366; Midan al-Gamaa) runs buses at 7.30pm and 8.30pm to Cairo (E£55, eight to 10 hours) via Al-Kharga Oasis (E£16, one to two hours) and Asyut (E£25, four to five hours). Other services to Asyut leave at 6am, 6.30am and 10pm. You can also go to Cairo (E£55) via Farafra Oasis (E£18, three to four hours) and Bahariya Oasis (E£35, seven hours) at 6am and 5.30pm. There's a convenient **booking office** (Map p338; Midan al-Tahrir), where the bus also stops to pick up passengers.

Herz Bus Company (Map p338; ☎ 782 4914) recently started running a daily bus to Cairo (through Asyut) at 8pm (E£55) from the microbus and service taxi station.

SERVICE TAXI & MICROBUS

Microbuses leave when full from the old part of Mut, near the mosque, and cost E£11 to Al-Kharga, E£22 to either Farafra or Asyut and around E£60 to Cairo.

Getting Around

Abu Mohamed Restaurant (opposite) and Gardens Hotel (p337) rent out bicycles for E£10 per hour.

Most places in Dakhla are linked by crowded pick-ups, Peugeots or microbuses, but working out where they all go requires a degree in astrophysics. Those heading to Al-Qasr (E£1) depart from Sharia as-Sawra al-Khadra. You can take pick-ups to Balat and Bashendi from in front of the hospital for E£1. Most others depart from the service taxi station on Sharia Tamir.

It may prove easier on occasion to bargain for a 'special' pick-up.

AROUND MUT

The following sights are all marked on the Dakhla Oasis map (p336).

Hot Springs

There are several hot sulphur pools around the town of Mut, but the easiest to reach is **Mut Talata** (Mut Three). It's at the site of a small hotel, so unless you are staying there, you have to dip in the exposed 1.5m-deep pool outside the hotel's walls. The pool's funny-coloured water is both hot and actually relaxing, though it may stain clothes.

Bir al-Gedid (New Spring), located a short distance west of the Bedouin Camp (p337), is the latest artesian well to be dug and is also rust-coloured. A bit south of Bedouin Camp is the so-called **Magic Spring**, a cool, rock-lined pool where you can relax with soft drinks (E£5) served at a small cafeteria under a couple of palm trees.

Set among breathtaking desert scenery, **Bir al-Gebel** (Mountain Spring; admission E£10) has been turned into a day-trip destination where blaring music and hundreds of schoolchildren easily overwhelm any ambience it might have had. Sitting on the edge of a small palm-shrouded oasis, surrounded by rolling dunes and towering desert cliffs, this still has to be one of the most beautiful dipping-spots in the oases. It's best to come in the evening, when it's quieter and the stars blaze across the night sky. If you arrive during spring peak hour, there's a serene natural spring about 500m before Bir al-Gebel on the right, concealed behind a brick pump house. A sign marks the turn-off 20km north of Mut, from where it's about another 5km to the springs.

Sand Dunes & Camel Rides

A few kilometres out past the southern end of town you can have a roll around in sand dunes which, while not the most spectacular

WESTERN DESERT

THESE ARE A FEW OF OUR FAVOURITE SPRINGS...

There's nothing better after a hard day's rambling along the dusty roads of the desert than a soak or swim in one of the many springs that dot the Western Desert. The following are but a few of our best-loved waterholes:

Cleopatra's Bath (p358) No, the queen in question probably did not bathe here, but since this is one of the most famous, stunning and clear bubbling springs in the Western Desert, it's fine by us.

Bir Wahed (p359) This hot, jacuzzi-like spring sits among the dunes on the edge of the Great Sand Sea. Amazing sunsets guaranteed.

Ain Gomma (p354) A small, gushing, clear and cool isolated spring in a mini-oasis 45km south of Bawiti, surrounded on all sides by the vast desert expanse.

Bir al-Gebel (p339) Surrounded by breathtaking scenery, this spring can get packed with rowdy picnickers during the day. It's ideal in the evening, when the crowds die down.

Spring Etiquette

When bathing in the public springs of the oases, it's important to be mindful of generally accepted spring etiquette:

■ If locals are bathing, wait until they are finished before entering the water.

■ During the day, women should wear a long, baggy T-shirt over their bathing suit, although in some places even this may not be appropriate.

■ To locals, a woman bathing alone is about as provocative as running through a town's main drag in your underwear. Don't do it.

in the desert, are easy to reach for people without their own transport. Almost every hotel and restaurant in Mut offers day trips that include a sand-dune stop. Sunset camel rides out to the dunes can also be arranged (see Tours, p337).

Rock Carvings

Dakhla's cultivated land ends at the feet of some strange rock formations 45km towards Al-Kharga. This was the crossroads of two important caravan routes, the Darb al-Ghabari between Dakhla and Al-Kharga and another, now lost, track that linked the nearby village of Teneida with the Darb al-Arba'een to the south. Carved into the soft rock are prehistoric rock carvings, showing camels, giraffes and tribal markings. Long visited by desert travellers, some of whom left their names carved in the rock, it has recently suffered from the attentions of less-scrupulous travellers who have all but ruined most of these curious images with their own graffiti.

Balat

For a captivating glance into life during medieval times, pay a visit to the Islamic village of Balat, 35km east of Mut. Built during the era of the Mamluks and Turks on a site that dates back to the Old Kingdom, this is a living

monument to the possibilities of Sudanic-style mud architecture. Here in the old town, charismatic winding lanes weave through low-slung corridors past Gaudí-like moulded benches. Palm fronds are still used for shelter as smoothly rounded walls ease into each other. The tiny doors here were designed to keep houses cool and confuse potential invaders. A guide will happily take you onto the roof of one of the three-storey mudbrick houses for commanding views (a small tip is expected). To get to Balat, a pick-up from near the general hospital in Mut will cost E£1.

A dirt track that meets the main road 200m east of Balat heads north about 2km to **Ain al-Asil**, or Spring of the Origin, the site of a ruined fortress that's much less interesting than its name suggests. Continue another 1.5km to find **Qila al-Dabba** (adult/student E£25/15), Balat's ancient necropolis. The five mastabas (mudbrick structures above tombs that were the basis for later pyramids) here, the largest of which stands over 10m high, date back to the 6th dynasty. Four are ruined, but one has been restored and is now open to the public. Originally all five would have been clad in fine limestone, with three thought to have belonged to important Old Kingdom governors of the oasis. Opening hours are 8pm to 5pm October to April and 8am to 6pm May to September, but you may need to find a guardian in the nearby buildings. You'll need a private vehicle – or plenty of endurance – to get here.

Bashendi

This small village to the north of the main Dakhla–Al-Kharga road takes its name from Pasha Hindi, the medieval sheikh buried nearby. The **Tomb of Pasha Hindi** is covered by an Islamic-era dome, which sits over a Roman structure, clearly visible from the inside of the building. Locals make pilgrimages to pray for the saint's intercession. There's a **carpet-making cooperative** (admission E£3; ⊙ 9am-1pm Sun-Thu) in town, where you can see rugs being woven and browse through the showroom. Nearby is the sandstone **Tomb of Kitines** (adult/student incl Tomb of Pasha Hindi E£25/15; ⊙ 8am-5pm Oct-Apr, to 6pm May-Sep), which was occupied by Senussi soldiers during WWI and by a village family after that. Nevertheless, some funerary reliefs have survived and show the 2nd-century AD notable meeting the gods Min, Seth and Shu.

Al-Qasr

One of the must-see sights in Dakhla Oasis is the extraordinary medieval/Ottoman town of Al-Qasr, which lies on the edge of lush vegetation at the foot of the pink limestone cliffs that mark the northern edge of the oasis. Portions of the old village have been thoughtfully restored to provide a glimpse of how other oasis towns looked before the New Valley development projects had their way with them; the effect is pure magic. Several hundred people still live in the town that not so long ago was home to several thousand.

Al-Qasr is also a prime spot to romp around in the desert without a guide. Just north of town the plateau is textured with shallow, sandy wadis that weave around rocky benches and weirdly hewn hills. The ground is littered with fossils, including sharks' teeth. Meander with ease, or, for what may be the most sweeping vistas in any of the oases, hike to the top of the high bluffs that rise from the plateau like a limestone fortress – just choose the massive ramp of sand that looks most promising, and trudge on up! Running back down hundreds of feet of sand is an instant regression to childhood glee. From Al-Qasr, it takes about two hours to reach the top, and longer if you dawdle, so bring enough water and snacks for the round trip.

SIGHTS

The Supreme Council for Antiquities has taken responsibility for the town, but because people still live there, it is unable to enclose the site or charge an entrance fee. At some point while you meander around the mudbrick maze, it's helpful to hook up with one of the Antiquities guards (who will expect a 'donation' of up to E£10). They can lead you to the highlights listed below, which you'll have trouble finding on your own. A note to photographers: mid-day is actually a good time to take pictures here, since that's when the most light penetrates into the canyonlike corridors.

The old town is built on the ancient foundations of a Roman city and is thought to be one of the oldest inhabited areas of the oases. The gateway of a temple to Thoth is now the front of a private house, and inscribed blocks from the temple have been used in other local buildings. Most of what you can see today, however, dates to the Ottoman period (1516–1798). During its heyday, this was probably the capital of the oasis, easily protected by barring the fort's quartered streets. The size of the houses and the surviving fragments of decoration suggest a puzzling level of wealth and importance given to this town by the Ottomans.

The architecture of the narrow covered streets harks back to its ancient origins. The winding lanes manage to remain cool in the scalding summer and also serve to protect their inhabitants from desert sandstorms. Entrances to old houses can be clearly seen and some are marked by beautiful lintels – acacia beams situated above the door. Carved with the names of the carpenter and the owner of the house, the date and a verse from the Quran, these decorative touches are wonderfully preserved.

There are 37 lintels in the village, the earliest of which dates to the early 16th century. One of the finest is above the **Tomb of Sheikh Nasr ad-Din** inside the old mosque, which is marked by a restored 12th-century mudbrick minaret. Adjoining it is **Nasr ad-Din Mosque**, with a 21m-high minaret. Several buildings have been renovated, including one that appears to have been a **madrassa**, a school where Islamic law was taught and which doubled as a town hall and courthouse: prisoners were tied to a stake near the entrance.

Also of interest is the restored **House of Abu Nafir**. A dramatic pointed arch at the entrance frames a huge studded wooden door. Built of mudbrick, and on a grander scale than the surrounding houses, it incorporates huge blocks from an earlier structure, possibly a Ptolemaic temple, decorated with hieroglyphic reliefs.

Other features of the town include the **pottery factory**, a **blacksmith's forge**, a **waterwheel**, an **olive press** and a huge old **corn mill** that has been fully restored to function with Flintstone-like efficiency when its shaft is rotated. Near the entrance is the **Ethnographic Museum** (admission E£3; 9am-sunset). Occupying Sherif Ahmed's house, which itself dates back to 1785, the museum's everyday objects try to give life to the empty buildings around them.

Heading back to Mut from Al-Qasr, take the secondary road for a change of scenery. You can visit several **tombs** near the ruined village of Amhadah, dating from the 2nd century. About 10km further towards Mut is the village of **Al-Gedida**, where there's a **woodworking cooperative** (9am-1pm Sun-Thu), where you can watch palm and acacia trees being hewn and hammered into furniture and trinkets. Keep heading towards Mut and you'll soon reach the Mamluk village of **Qalamun**, with both Ottoman and modern houses built of mud. There are good views of the countryside from the cemetery.

SLEEPING

Al-Qasr Hotel (787 6013; r E£30) The sprightly and ever-helpful Mohamed captains this great little guest house, which sits above a cafe near the old town. The simple rooms with shared bathroom are fine for the price, and some even boast views onto Al-Qasr. There's a breezy upstairs communal sitting area where you can play games or relax, and for E£5 you can sleep on a mattress on the roof. The ground-floor coffeehouse and restaurant serves good basic fare (breakfast E£5). Mohamed rents bikes for E£5 a day and arranges camel tours into the surrounding desert.

Desert Lodge (772 7061/2, in Cairo 02-690 5240; www.desertlodge.net; s/d/tr half board €75/120/175;) This thoughtfully designed, eco-friendly mudbrick fortress of a lodge crowns a hilltop overlooking the old town of Al-Qasr. The restaurant is adequate, and there is also a bar, a private hot spring, a painting studio on the desert's edge, and many of the services you would expect for the price.

Bir Elgabal Camp (772 6600, 012 106 8227; elga balcamp@hotmail.com; s/d E£80/120;) This place has clean, plain, overpriced rooms next to Bir al-Gebel spring. It's in an idyllic position at the base of the soaring desert mountains, although fairly isolated from any amenities, 4km from the turn-off on the Mut road.

El Badawiya (Map p336; in Farafra 092-751 1163; www.badawiya.com; s/d €44/56;) This new luxury offering from the brothers in Farafra is perched above the fork in the road to Bir al-Gebel. It features comfortable domed rooms of stone, mud and tile, and the compound has some intriguing touches, like the palm-trunk stairways. The sweet spot is the swimming pool, with mesmerising desert views.

Al Tarfa Desert Sanctuary (Map p336; 910 5007/8/9; www.altarfa.com; s/d full board from €390/510;) Taking the high end to unheard-of heights in Dakhla, Al Tarfa is flat out desert-fabulous. The traditionally inspired decor is superbly tasteful and impeccably rendered, down to the smallest detail – from the embroidered bedspreads that look like museum-quality pieces to the mud-plastered walls that don't show a single crack. Even the golden dunes that flow behind the resort seem like they've been landscaped to undulating perfection. Each suite is unique, the pool is like a liquid sapphire, and the spa features massage therapists brought in from Thailand.

GETTING THERE & AWAY

Pick-ups to Al-Qasr leave from opposite Said Shihad restaurant in Mut and cost E£1, or take a minibus from Mut's minibus stand (E£1.25).

Deir al-Haggar

This restored Roman **sandstone temple** (adult/student E£25/15; 8am-sunset) is one of the most complete Roman monuments in Dakhla. Dedicated to the Theban triad of Amun, Mut and Khons, as well as Horus (who can be seen with a falcon's head), it was built between the reigns of Nero (AD 54–68) and Domitian (AD 81–96). The cartouches of Nero, Vespasian and Titus can be seen in the hypostyle hall, which has also been inscribed by almost every 19th-century explorer who passed through the oasis. If you look carefully in the adjacent Porch of Titus you can see the names of the entire expedition of Gerhard Rohlfs, the 19th-century desert explorer. Also visible are the names of famous desert travellers Edmonstone, Drovetti and Houghton.

The temple has been enclosed by a wall to help prevent wind and sand erosion. Deir al-Haggar is signposted about 7km west of Al-Qasr; from the turn-off it's another 5km to the temple.

FARAFRA OASIS

☎ 092 / pop 17,000

Blink and you might miss dusty Farafra, the least populated and most remote of the Western Desert's oases. Though little evidence has been found of Pharaonic occupation, Farafra does make a cameo appearance in the legend of King Cambyses' army (see boxed text, p345), which is purported to have disappeared in the 6th century BC on its way to Siwa.

Farafra's exposed location made it prone to frequent attacks by Libyans and Bedouin tribes, many of whom eventually settled in the oasis and now make up much of the population.

In recent years, the government has been increasing its efforts to revitalise this region, and the agriculture of olives, dates, apricots, guavas, figs, oranges, apples and sunflowers is slowly developing. Though light on tourist infrastructure or any real attractions, Farafra's proximity to the White Desert (only 20km away) and its torpid pace of life and extensive palm gardens manage to draw a small trickle of travellers each year.

QASR AL-FARAFRA

The only real town in Farafra Oasis, Qasr al-Farafra remains an undeveloped speck on the western Egypt circuit that is only now beginning to discover the cheap thrills of concrete. The town's tumbledown Roman fortress was originally built to guard this part of the desert caravan route, though these days all it has to show for it is a mound of rubble.

Some small, mudbrick houses still stand here against all the odds, their doorways secured with medieval peg locks and their walls painted with verses of the Quran.

Information

For tourist information, contact the tourist office in Mut (p336).

Hospital (Map p344; ☎ 751 0047; main Bahariya–Dakhla rd) For dire emergencies only.

Post office (Map p344; off main Bahariya–Dakhla rd; ☻ 8.30am-2.30pm Sat-Thu)

Telephone centrale (Map p344; off main Bahariya–Dakhla rd)

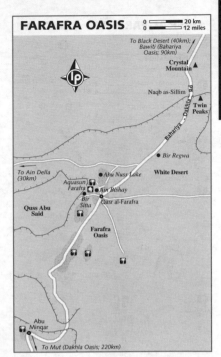

FARAFRA OASIS

0 — 20 km
0 — 12 miles

To Black Desert (40km); / Bawiti (Bahariya Oasis; 90km)

Crystal Mountain

Naqb as-Sillim

Twin Peaks

Bahariya–Dakhla Rd

Bir Regwa

To Ain Della (30km)

Abu Nuss Lake — White Desert

Aquasun Farafra
Ain Bishay
Bir Sitta
Qasr al-Farafra

Quss Abu Said

Farafra Oasis

Abu Minqar

To Mut (Dakhla Oasis; 220km)

Tourist police (Map p344; Sharia al-Mishtafa Nakhaz) No telephone.

Sights & Activities

BADR'S MUSEUM

Badr Abdel Moghny is a self-taught artist whose gift to his town has become its only real sight, bless 'im. **Badr's Museum** (Map p344; ☎ 751 0091, 012 170 4710; donation E£10; ☻ 8.30am-sunset), surrounded by a desert garden, is worth seeing for the enthusiasm that Badr puts into his interesting work, much of which records traditional oasis life. His distinctive style of painting and sculpture in mud, stone and sand has also won him foreign admirers; he exhibited successfully in Europe in the early 1990s and later in Cairo.

SPRINGS

A popular stop is **Bir Sitta** (Well No 6; Map p343), a sulphurous hot spring 6km northwest of Qasr al-Farafra. Water gushes into a jacuzzi-sized concrete pool and then spills out into a larger tank. This is a good place for a night-time soak under the stars.

WESTERN DESERT

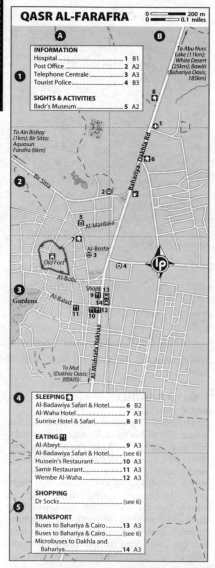

QASR AL-FARAFRA

0 —— 200 m
0 —— 0.1 miles

INFORMATION
Hospital 1 B1
Post Office 2 A2
Telephone Centrale 3 A3
Tourist Police 4 B3

SIGHTS & ACTIVITIES
Badr's Museum 5 A2

SLEEPING
Al-Badawiya Safari & Hotel 6 B2
Al-Waha Hotel 7 A3
Sunrise Hotel & Safari 8 B1

EATING
Al-Abeyt 9 A3
Al-Badawiya Safari & Hotel ..... (see 6)
Hussein's Restaurant 10 A3
Samir Restaurant 11 A3
Wembe Al-Waha 12 A3

SHOPPING
Dr Socks .... (see 6)

TRANSPORT
Buses to Bahariya & Cairo 13 A3
Buses to Bahariya & Cairo .... (see 6)
Microbuses to Dakhla and
Bahariya 14 A3

The Roman spring of **Ain Bishay** (Map p343) bubbles forth from a hillock on the northwest edge of town. It has been developed into an irrigated grove of date palms together with citrus, olive, apricot and carob trees, and is a cool haven. Several families tend the crops here; you should seek someone out and ask permission before wandering around.

If you're hanging around in the summer, a plunge in cool **Abu Nuss Lake** (Map p343) offers instant relief from oppressive afternoons. You might see some interesting bird life, too!

Tours

Farafra is nearer than Bahariya to the White Desert and yet there is a very limited choice of desert outfits. The sister hotels Al-Waha and Sunrise (see Sleeping, below) offer trips around Farafra and the White Desert, with prices starting at around E£500 per vehicle for an overnight stay, though some talented haggling will bring the price down a bit. Both Al-Badawiya and Aquasun are more expensive (see Sleeping, below), but are well prepared for long-range desert travel as well as trips closer to home; see also p328.

Sleeping

Al-Badawiya Safari & Hotel (Map p344; ☎ 751 0060, 012 214 8343; www.badawiya.com; s/d €25/35, villas with air-con €35/55; ▣ ▨) We hear mixed opinions about Al-Badawiya, but there is no escaping the dynamism of the Ali brothers, who dominate Farafra tourism with their hotel and safari outfit. Al-Badawiya has a range of stylishly designed and traditionally themed rooms and is dotted with cushioned sitting areas, has a refreshing pool, and boasts more than its fair share of arches and domes. Breakfast costs E£20, and reservations are recommended in winter. Saad Ali and Hamdy Ali lead camel and jeep trips into the Western Desert (see p328).

Al-Waha Hotel (Map p344; ☎ 016 209 3224, 012 720 0387; wahafarafra@yahoo.com; d with shared bathroom E£30, r E£50) A small, spartan hotel opposite Badr's Museum, Al-Waha is the only real budget choice in town. The location is convenient, and the rooms, with faux-oriental rugs, are acceptably clean. In summer, the cement walls pulse with heat.

Aquasun Farafra (Map p343; ☎ 012 7807 999; www .raid4x4egypt.com; Bir Sitta; s/d half board €35/50; ▨ ▨) Built beside Bir Sitta and nestled in its own idyllic oasis, Aquasun has 21 chalet-style rooms built around a peaceful garden. Each has its own porch, thatched with palm fronds, and piping-hot water from Bir Sitta fills the hotel pool. Owner Hisham Nessim has had years of hotel-owning experience in Sinai and is also a long-time desert-safari operator (see p329).

Sunrise Hotel & Safari (Map p344; ☎ 751 1530, 012 720 1387; wahafarafra@yahoo.com; s/d E£100/130) The

THE LOST ARMY OF CAMBYSES

Persian king Cambyses invaded Egypt in 525 BC, overthrowing Egyptian pharaoh Psamtek III and signalling the beginning of Persian rule over the country that was to last 193 years. This success, however, was not necessarily representative of this 'tyrannical despot's' skills as a military strategist. In the years immediately following his conquest of Egypt, Cambyses mounted several disastrous offensives. In one such campaign, he sent a mercenary army down the Nile into Ethiopia that was so ill-prepared and undersupplied it had to turn to cannibalism to survive. The soldiers returned disgraced, having never even encountered the enemy on the battlefield.

Cambyses' most famous failure, however, remains his attempt to capture the Oracle of Amun in Siwa (see also History, p355). As recounted by Greek writer Herodotus, Cambyses set out to destroy the famous oracle, which insolently predicted his tragic end, and legitimise his rule over Egypt. To this end, he dispatched an army of 50,000 men from Thebes, supported by a vast train of pack animals weighed down by supplies and weapons. The army is purported to have reached Al-Kharga and Farafra Oases before turning west to cover the 325km of open desert to Siwa – a 30-day march without any shade or sources of water. Legend has it that after struggling through the Great Sand Sea, the men were engulfed by a fierce sandstorm, which buried the entire army under the desert's shifting sands, never to be heard from again.

There have been dozens of unsuccessful expeditions over the centuries determined to find a trace of the lost men of Cambyses. Only time will tell if the shifting sands that buried this ancient army will ever reveal their archaeological riches.

---

newest hotel in Farafra is brought to you by the same family that owns Al-Waha Hotel (opposite). Here, they've gone for the Bedouin domed motif, and put refrigerators and televisions in brick bungalows that surround a rectangular courtyard. Some of the rooms have a strong septic stench, so check out a few if you need to.

Eating

As with most other facilities, eating choices are limited in Farafra.

Al-Badawiya Safari & Hotel (Map p344; ☎ 751 0060, 012 214 8343; meals E£25-50) Al-Badawiya serves freshly made, if rather expensive, dishes including pasta and simple three-course meals, using organic vegetables from its own farm. Serves beer and wine on occasion.

Aquasun Farafra (Map p343; ☎ 012 225 9660; meals E£30-60) Choice of the usual Western and Egyptian staples. It's been known to serve beer and wine.

A trio of restaurants in the centre of town, Wembe al-Waha, Hussein's Restaurant and Samir Restaurant (all Map p344) serve the typical Egyptian variety of grilled dishes for similar prices (about E£20 for a full meal, including rice, salad, beans, tahini and bread). Samir's is the most atmospheric of the three, but you'll pay a few pounds extra for the fancy tablecloths. For breakfast, hit **Al-Abeyt** (Map p344), a friendly felafel/*fuul* joint.

Shopping

It's a family affair. In the summer, Dr Socks takes wool from the neck and lower back of camels, spins it and knits. His sister makes sweaters, his uncle blankets, while he and his mother get on with the socks and scarves. Dr Socks and his wares can be found at Al-Badawiya Safari & Hotel (opposite) and beyond. Count on E£10 to E£30 for socks, and up to E£400 for a blanket.

Getting There & Away

There are Upper Egypt Bus Co buses from Farafra to Cairo (E£45, eight to 10 hours) via Bahariya (E£25, three hours) at 10am and 10pm. Buses from Farafra to Dakhla (E£25, four hours) originate in Cairo and leave around 2pm to 3pm and around 2am. Tickets are bought from the conductor. Two non-air-con Hashim company buses (they're green) head to Cairo (E£30) via Bahariya (E£15) between 5.30pm and 6.30pm and again at about 3.30am. Buses stop across from Al-Abeyt restaurant, at the petrol station, and sometimes at Al-Badawiya Hotel.

Microbuses to Dakhla (E£20, three to four hours) and Bahariya (E£20, three hours) leave from the town's main intersection when full (not often), so you're better off going early in the morning. Rare service taxis to Dakhla cost E£20, to Al-Kharga E£30.

FARAFRA OASIS TO BAHARIYA OASIS

The stupefying desert formations between the Farafra and Bahariya Oases are responsible for attracting more travellers to this far-flung corner of Egypt than any other sight. No surprises there: this unearthly terrain varies from the bizarre and impossibly shaped rock formations of the White Desert to the eerie black-coned mountains of the nearby Black Desert, with a healthy dose of sand dunes interspersed for good measure. These regions are relatively easy to get to from either Farafra or Bahariya Oases and are immensely popular with one-day and overnight safari tours.

AIN DELLA

Surrounded by cliffs on the north and east and dunes to the south and west, Ain Della (Spring of the Shade) lies about 120km from Qasr al-Farafra. The contrasting tawny hues of the surrounding landscape envelop this area in an alluring, almost soft glow. But Ain Della is more than a picturesque waterhole. Lying within 200km of the three major oases of Siwa, Bahariya and Farafra, it has been a strategic and extremely important source of water for desert travellers since ancient times. During WWII the British Army's Long Range Desert Group stored fuel and supplies here and used it as a jumping-off place for their raids behind German and Italian lines. Today, there's a base for Egyptian army patrols that search the desert for drugs and arms smugglers. Anyone coming here must have a guide and apply for a military permit a couple of weeks in advance (obtained through desert guides; see also boxed text, p353, or Tours, p359 and p344).

WHITE DESERT

Upon first glimpse of the White Desert (Sahra al-Beida; Map p343) dreamscape, you'll feel like a modern Alice fallen through the desert looking glass. Starting just 20km northeast of Farafra, the yellow desert sands east of the road start to become pierced by chalky rock formations. Blinding-white spires of rock sprout almost supernaturally from the ground, each frost-coloured lollipop licked into an ever odder shape by the dry desert winds. As you get further into the 300-sq-km

White Desert Protectorate, you'll notice that the surreal shapes start to take on familiar forms: chickens, ostriches, camels, hawks and other uncanny shapes abound. They are best viewed at sunrise or sunset, when the sun turns them hues of pink and orange, Salvador Dali–like, or under a full moon, which gives the landscape a ghostly, arctic, whipped-cream appearance. The sand around the outcroppings is littered with quartz and different varieties of deep-black iron pyrites, as well as small fossils.

On the west side of the road, away from the wind-eroded shapes, chalk towers called inselbergs burst from the desert floor like a smaller, more intimate (and, naturally, whiter) version of Arizona's Monument Valley. Between them run grand boulevards of sand, like geologic Champs-Élysées. The shade and privacy they provide makes them good camping spots.

About 50km north are two flat-topped mountains known as the **Twin Peaks**, a key navigation point for travellers. A favourite destination of local tour operators, the view from the top of the surrounding symmetrical hills, all shaped like giant anthills, is spectacular. Just beyond here, the road climbs a steep escarpment known as **Naqb as-Sillim** (Pass of the Stairs); this is the main pass that leads into and out of the Farafra depression and marks the end of the White Desert.

A few kilometres further along, the desert floor changes again and becomes littered with quartz crystals. If you look at the rock formations in this area you'll see that they are also largely made of crystal. The most famous of the formations is the **Crystal Mountain**, actually a large rock made entirely of quartz. It sits right beside the main road some 24km north of Naqb as-Sillim, and is easily recognisable by the large hole through its middle.

For information on getting to the White Desert, see opposite.

BLACK DESERT

The change in the desert floor from beige to black, 50km south of Bawiti, signals the beginning of the Black Desert (Sahra Suda). Formed by the erosion of the mountains, which have spread a layer of black powder and rubble over the peaks and plateaus, it's a mesmerising landscape straight out of Hades. The Black Desert is a popular stop-off for tours running out of Bahariya, though few

KNOW YOUR DUNE

Formal classification of types of sand dune was made in the 1970s, when scientists could examine photographs of dune fields taken on an early space mission. They identified five types of dune, four of which are found in Egypt.

Parallel Straight Dunes

Called *seif* (sword) in Arabic because they resemble the blades of curved Arab swords, these dunes are formed by wind and are primarily found in the Great Sand Sea and the northern Western Desert. Usually on the move, they will even fall down an escarpment, reforming at its base.

Parallel Wavy (or Barchan) Dunes

These are crescent-shaped dunes, with a slip face on one side. They are as wide as they are long and are usually found in straight lines with flat corridors between them. Usually on the move, they can travel as far as 19m in one year. They are predominant in Al-Kharga and Dakhla Oases and are also found in the Great Sand Sea.

Star Dunes

Created by wind blowing in different directions, these dunes are usually found alone. Instead of moving, they tend to build up within a circle. They are rare in Egypt.

Crescent (or Whaleback) Dunes

These are hill-like dunes formed when a series of smaller dunes collide and piggyback one another. Distinctive, with sides pointing in different directions, they can be seen in the area between Al-Kharga and Dakhla Oases.

stay there overnight. Other sights in the region include **Gebel Gala Siwa**, a pyramid-shaped mountain that was formerly a look-out post for caravans coming from Siwa. **Gebel az-Zuqaq** is a mountain known for the red, yellow and orange streaks in its limestone base. There is an easily climbed path leading to the top.

GETTING THERE & AWAY

Ordinary vehicles are able to drive the first kilometre or so off the road into the White or Black Deserts, but only 4WD vehicles can advance deeper into either area. Some travellers simply get off the bus and take themselves into the White Desert – but be very sure that you have adequate supplies, and remember that traffic between the neighbouring oases is rarely heavy. The megaliths west of the highway are relatively easy to access by foot, as are the so-called mushrooms to the east; the weirdest wonderland of white hoodoos is quite far to the east, and would be a real haul to reach on your own. Bir Regwa (Map p343), a small spring situated along the highway at one of the park entrances, usually has water; it's good to know where it is (just in case), though best not to rely on it.

There are plenty of safari outfits that can take you around these sights. See boxed text, p353, and p344 for listings. If you're considering a multiday camel safari to reduce the impact of motoring through the desert, think again. Virtually all camel trips are supported by gear vehicles that are driven ahead to set up camp. Since it's nearly impossible to convince tour operators to leave the car at home, the only reason to ride camels is because you want to – which is good enough!

BAHARIYA OASIS

☎ 02 / pop 34,500

Bahariya is one of the more fetching of the desert circuit oases, and at just 365km from Cairo is also the most accessible. Surrounded on all sides by towering ridges, much of the oasis floor is covered by verdant plantations of date palms and pockmarked with dozens of refreshing springs.

The conical hills that lie strewn around the valley floor may have once formed islands in the lake that covered the area during prehistoric times. During the Pharaonic

WESTERN DESERT

era, the oasis was a centre of agriculture, producing wine sold in the Nile Valley and as far away as Rome. Its strategic location on the Libya–Nile Valley caravan routes ensured it prospered throughout later ages. In recent years, stunning archaeological finds, such as that of the Golden Mummies (see boxed text, opposite), and easy access to the White and Black Deserts have earned Baharia a firm spot on the tourist map.

BAWITI

The sandy streets of the region's modern administrative capital may at first sight seem pretty underwhelming. But scratch beneath the surface and you might walk away with a different picture: stroll through its fertile palm groves, soak in one of the many hot springs or explore its quiet back roads, where donkeys still outnumber combustion engines.

Until recently, Bawiti was a quiet town dependent on agriculture, but it's gaining a new lease on life as more people head to the desert or come to see the Golden Mummies, and now has a good selection of hotels. Be warned, however, that upon arrival you're likely to be accosted by overzealous touts before you even step off the bus (see boxed text, p353).

Information

Hospital (Map p351; ☎ 3847 2390) Head to Cairo except in dire emergency.

Internet Centre (Map p351; per hr E£5; 🕙 11am-1am, closed some afternoons) Near Popular Restaurant.

National Bank for Development (Map p351; 🕙 9am-2pm Sun-Thu) Changes cash only. No ATM.

Net Cafe (Map p351; per hr E£5; 🕙 24hr) Has fast connection speeds.

Telephone centrale (Map p351; off Sharia Misr; 🕙 11am-7pm Sat-Thu)

Tourist office (Map p351; ☎ 3847 3035/9; 🕙 8am-2pm Sat-Thu, plus 7-9pm Sat-Thu Nov-Apr) Run by the eager and helpful Mohamed Abd el-Kader, who can also be contacted on ☎ 012 373 6567 or by email: mohamed _kader26@hotmail.com.

Tourist police (off Map p351; ☎ 3847 3900; Sharia Misr)

Sights & Activities

MUSEUM (AL-MATHAF)

Since the discovery of the Golden Mummies in the 1990s (see boxed text, opposite), growing interest in Baharia's ancient past has led

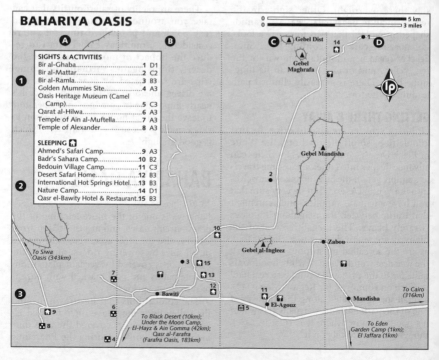

BAHARIYA OASIS

0 ————— 5 km
0 ————— 3 miles

SIGHTS & ACTIVITIES
Bir al-Ghaba	1 D1
Bir al-Mattar	2 C2
Bir al-Ramla	3 B3
Golden Mummies Site	4 A3
Oasis Heritage Museum (Camel Camp)	5 C3
Qarat al-Hilwa	6 A3
Temple of Ain al-Muftella	7 A3
Temple of Alexander	8 A3

SLEEPING
Ahmed's Safari Camp	9 A3
Badr's Sahara Camp	10 B2
Bedouin Village Camp	11 C3
Desert Safari Home	12 B3
International Hot Springs Hotel	13 B3
Nature Camp	14 D1
Qasr el-Bawity Hotel & Restaurant	15 B3

Gebel Dist
Gebel Maghrafa
Gebel Mandisha
Gebel al-Ingleez
Zabou
To Siwa Oasis (343km)
To Cairo (316km)
Bawiti
El-Agouz
Mandisha
El-Jaffara (1km)
To Eden Garden Camp (1km);
To Black Desert (10km); Under the Moon Camp, El-Hayz & Ain Gomma (42km); Qasr al-Farafra (Farafra Oasis, 183km)

BAHARIYA'S GOLDEN MUMMY CACHE

Put it down to the donkey: until 1996, no one had any idea of the extent of Bahariya's archaeological treasure trove. Then a donkey stumbled on a hole near the temple of Alexander the Great and its rider saw the face of a golden mummy peering through the sand. (Or so the story goes. Some locals wink knowingly at what they assert is a much-popularised myth.) Since then Dr Zahi Hawass, head of the Supreme Council of Antiquities, and his team have done extensive research in a cemetery that stretches over 3 sq km (see Map p348). Radar has revealed more than 10,000 mummies, and excavation has revealed more than 250 of them in what has come to be called the Valley of the Golden Mummies.

These silent witnesses of a bygone age could shed new light on life in this part of Egypt during the Graeco-Roman period, a 600-year interlude marking the transition between the Pharaonic and Christian eras. Bahariya was then a thriving oasis and, with its rich, fertile land watered by natural springs, was a famous producer of wheat and wine. Greek and, later, Roman families set up home here and became a kind of expatriate elite.

Research has shown that after a brief decline when Ptolemies and Romans fought for control of the oasis, Roman administrators embarked on a major public works program, expanding irrigation systems, digging wells, restoring aqueducts and building roads. Thousands of mudbrick buildings sprang up throughout the oasis. Bahariya became a major source of grain for the empire and was home to a large garrison of troops; its wealth grew proportionately. Researchers are hoping that continued excavation of the necropolis will provide more answers about the region's early history and its inhabitants.

to the opening of this new **museum** (Map p351; Sharia al-Mathaf; 🕒 8am-2pm). Yes, that building resembling a wartime bunker is the museum, but don't let that put you off (the ticket office is the hut situated 50m from the museum towards Sharia Misr; see boxed text, p350). This is where the mummies come to rest. Some of the 10 mummies on show are richly decorated and while the motifs are formulaic and the work is second-rate, the painted faces show a move away from stylised Pharaonic mummy decoration towards Fayoum portraiture (see boxed text, p208). Underneath the wrappings, the work of the embalmers appears to have been sloppy: in some cases the bodies decayed before the embalming process began, which suggests that these mummies mark the beginning of the end of mummification. Sadly, the exhibit embodies that spirit, and is entirely underwhelming.

QARAT QASR SALIM

This small mound (Map p351) amid the houses of Bawiti is likely to have been built upon centuries of debris. There are two well-preserved 26th-dynasty tombs here that were robbed in antiquity and reused as collective burial sites in Roman times. The rock-cut **Tomb of Zed-Amun-ef-ankh** (🕒 8.30am-4pm) is a fascinating glimpse of Bahariya in its heyday. It appears that Zed-Amun-ef-ankh was not a

government official but was given the richness of colourful tomb paintings anyway, hinting at his wealth and importance. Researchers assume he was a trader, perhaps a wine merchant or landowner making money out of Bahariya's thriving wine-export business. Unusually, his tomb contains only one chamber, with four circular (as opposed to the usual square) pillars and seven squat false doors.

Next to it lies the **Tomb of Bannentiu** (🕒 8.30am-4pm), Zed-Amun-ef-ankh's son. Consisting of a four-columned burial chamber with an inner sanctuary, it is covered in fine reliefs depicting Bannentiu in various positions with the gods. The most interesting pictures flank the entrance to the burial chamber. On one side, the journey of the moon is shown, with the moon, in the form of the god Khons, depicted as a source of life and flanked by the goddesses Isis and Nephthys. The other side of the entrance is decorated with the journey of the sun.

OASIS HERITAGE MUSEUM

You can't miss Mahmoud Eed's **Oasis Heritage Museum** (Map p348; ☎ 3847 3666; www.camelcamp.com; Bahariya–Cairo rd; admission E£5-10; 🕒 no set opening times), about 2km east of the town's edge on the road to Cairo: this hilltop bastion is announced by massive clay camels gazing longingly onto the street. Inspired by Badr's Museum (p343) in Farafra, its creator wishes to capture, in clay, scenes from traditional village life, among them men hunting or playing *siga* (a game played in the dirt with clay balls or seeds), women weaving and a painful-looking barber/doctor encounter. There is also a display of old oasis dresses and jewellery. Look for the sign saying 'Camel Camp', which is the plain and overpriced accommodation that's also offered here.

HOT & COLD SPRINGS

The closest springs to central Bawiti are the so-called Roman springs, known as **El-Beshmo** (Map p351), beside El-Beshmo Lodge. The view over the oasis gardens and the desert beyond is wonderful, but unfortunately the spring is not suitable for swimming.

The hot sulphurous spring of **Bir al-Ramla** (Map p348), 3km north of town, is very hot (45°C) and suitable for a soak, though you may feel a bit exposed to the donkey traffic passing to and fro. Women should stay well covered.

At **Bir al-Mattar** (Map p348), 7km northeast of Bawiti, cold springs pour into a viaduct, then down into a concrete pool, in which you can splash around during the hot summer months. As with all the springs, the mineral content is high and the water can stain clothing. One of the most satisfying springs to visit is **Bir al-Ghaba** (Map p348), located about 15km northeast of Bawiti. It's quite a trek to get out here but there is nothing quite like a moonlit hot bath on the edge of the desert.

A few kilometres south of the Bahariya–Cairo road, about 7km from Bawiti, is the mini-oasis of **El Jaffara** (off Map p348), where

---

YOUR TICKET TO ANTIQUITIES

In a move to make their lives a little easier, Bahariya's authorities have decided to issue a one-day ticket that gives entry to five of the oasis' ancient sites: the museum, the tomb of Zed-Amun-ef-ankh, the tomb of Bannentiu, the Ain al-Muftella and the Temple of Alexander. Tickets are available at the **ticket office** (adult/student E£45/25; ⏲ 8.30am-4pm) of the museum (Al-Mathaf; p348). This is annoying, as most visitors either don't have the time or the desire to see all the sights the oasis has to offer, yet have to pay for them.

---

two springs, one hot, one cold, make this a prime spot in winter or summer. Both are near Eden Garden Camp (p354).

Sleeping

Unlike most places in the New Valley, there is a very good selection of budget and mid-priced hotels in Bawiti, as well as elsewhere around Bahariya Oasis. The few options approaching the top-end range can be found outside the town; see p354.

BUDGET

It makes sense to sort out accommodation in Bawiti before you arrive, especially in high season, due to the fray of touts that swarm each bus arrival (see boxed text, p353). A tourist policeman now often escorts new arrivals to the Bawiti tourist office, where sleeping arrangements can be made in peace.

Desert Safari Home (Map p348; ☎ 3847 1321, 012 731 3908; www.desertsafarihome.com; dm E£25, s/d E£50/75, with shared bathroom E£35/50, with air-con E£80/120; 🖳 🖾) The friendly family that runs this place looks ready to sign your adoption papers the minute you walk in the door. The rooms are clean, if a tad musty, there's a pleasant vine-shaded sitting area in the garden, and an hourglass-shaped pool will probably be ready for soaking in by the time you read this. Wireless internet is free, bikes are available and patriarch Badry Khozam is happy to pick you up from the bus stand (it's about 2km from the centre of town).

New Oasis Hotel (Map p351; ☎ 3847 3030; max_rfs@hotmail.com; by El-Beshmo spring; s/d E£50/80, with air-con E£100/120) A study in curvaceous construction, this small but homely hotel has several teardrop-shaped rooms, some with balconies overlooking the expansive palm groves nearby. Inside, the rooms are aged but kept in good condition, though someone seems to have been a little overzealous with the powder-blue paint. It's one of the nicer budget options in town.

Alpenblick Hotel (Map p351; ☎ 3847 2184, 011 582 3356; alpenblick-bahariya.com; off Sharia Misr; s/d E£60/120, with air-con E£100/160) This granddaddy of the Bahariya hotel scene keeps getting dragged out of retirement by its consecutive owners; the current ones give a warm welcome. The small rooms are characterless and clean, but don't be surprised if you greet some cockroaches in the bathrooms.

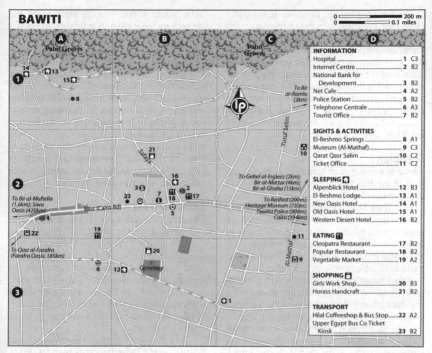

BAWITI

0 ————— 200 m
0 ————— 0.1 miles

INFORMATION	
Hospital	**1** C3
Internet Centre	**2** B2
National Bank for	
Development	**3** B2
Net Cafe	**4** A2
Police Station	**5** B2
Telephone Centrale	**6** A3
Tourist Office	**7** B2

SIGHTS & ACTIVITIES	
El-Beshmo Springs	**8** A1
Museum (Al-Mathaf)	**9** C3
Qarat Qasr Salim	**10** C2
Ticket Office	**11** C2

SLEEPING	
Alpenblick Hotel	**12** B3
El-Beshmo Lodge	**13** A1
New Oasis Hotel	**14** A1
Old Oasis Hotel	**15** A1
Western Desert Hotel	**16** B2

EATING	
Cleopatra Restaurant	**17** B2
Popular Restaurant	**18** B2
Vegetable Market	**19** A2

SHOPPING	
Girls Work Shop	**20** B3
Horass Handcraft	**21** B2

TRANSPORT	
Hilal Coffeeshop & Bus Stop	**22** A2
Upper Egypt Bus Co Ticket	
Kiosk	**23** B2

MIDRANGE & TOP END

El-Beshmo Lodge (Map p351; ☎ 3847 3500; www.elbeshmo
lodge.com; by El-Beshmo spring; s/d/tr E£80/150/180; ☒)
Another old-timer, El-Beshmo Lodge is
showing its age. While the 25 rooms are simply furnished and reasonably comfortable,
with fan and air-con rooms the same price,
the brick courtyard with crumbling plaster
walls is rundown and charmless. Safari sales
tactics are annoyingly aggressive here.

Old Oasis Hotel (Map p351; ☎ 012 232 4425; www
.oldoasissafari.com; by El-Beshmo spring; s/d/tr E£90/120/180,
with air-con E£120/180/220; ☒) Astute owner Saleh
Abdallah is at the helm of this hotel, which
is one of the most charming places to stay
in Bawiti town. The Old Oasis Hotel sits
above a pretty, shaded garden of palm and
olive trees and has 13 simple but impeccable
fan rooms, as well as a few fancier stone-
wall air-con rooms. A large pool receives
steaming hot water from the nearby spring;
the run-off waters the hotel garden and
its fountain.

Western Desert Hotel (Map p351; ☎ 012 433 6015,
012 301 2155; www.westerndeserthotel.com; off Sharia
Misr; s/d E£110/160; ☒ ☐) Right in the middle

of town, opposite Popular Restaurant, the
location is supremely convenient, if less
than serene. The clean, tiled rooms are good
value – the ones in back have views of the
gardens and desert in the distance – and
the comfortable beds even have two sheets!
The staff is a good bunch who aren't pushy
about their safaris.

Eating

The market area on Sharia Misr houses several
places that fire up the barbecue pits and roast
cheap chicken and kebab meals after dusk.
Fresh veggies can be bought from morning
until night along one of the streets running
south from Sharia Misr.

Cleopatra Restaurant (Map p351; meals E£5-35;
♥ 6am-10pm) It's worth popping in here just
for the smiling welcome and friendly evening
chats, though it's also popular for its yummy
chicken, *fuul, ta'amiyya* and eggs.

Rashed (off Map p351; meals E£15-25; ♥ 7am-late)
More a cafeteria than a restaurant, Rashed serves
hot and cold drinks and *sheeshas* (E£2) as well
as simple meals of rice, chicken or meat, and
vegetables. It's located near the petrol station

at the far eastern end of town. It's usually closed for a few hours in the afternoon.

Popular Restaurant (Map p351; meals E£20; 5.30am-10pm) Name it popular, and they will come. Off the main road in Bawiti, this small roadside restaurant is the chosen stopping-off point for many passing through Bawiti. The irrepressible Bayoumi serves the usual selection of chicken, soup, rice and vegetable dishes, though quality seems to be slipping while prices are creeping up. There's cold beer too.

Shopping

There is a living craft tradition in the oases, though puzzlingly many handicraft stores sell crafts made elsewhere.

Girls Work Shop (Map p351; south of Sharia Misr; 10am-1pm Sat-Thu) This great handicrafts store bucks the trend and sells only crafts made in Bahariya Oasis, providing local women with skills and much-needed work. Unique items include hand-embroidered greeting cards.

Horass Handcraft (Map p351; on the way to El-Beshmo spring; 8am-8pm) Sells some locally made crafts, including hand-decorated pouches cleverly marketed as 'mobile phone holders' or, our favourite, 'guidebook holders'. It also has standard adorned traditional Bedouin costumes and camel-hair socks. If the shop is closed, knock on the door directly across the street.

Getting There & Away
BUS

Upper Egypt Bus Co (Map p351; ☎ 3847 3610; Sharia Misr; roughly 9am-1pm & 7-11pm) runs buses from Bawiti to Cairo (E£30, four to five hours) at 6.30am, 10am and 3pm from the kiosk near the post office. These are often full, so it's strongly advised to buy tickets the day before travelling. There are two more Cairo-bound buses that originate in Dakhla and pass through Bawiti around noon and midnight, stopping at the Hilal Coffeehouse at the western end of town. For those, buy your ticket on the bus, and hope there are seats!

If you're heading to Farafra (E£20, two hours) and Dakhla (E£40, four to five hours), you can hop on one of the buses headed that way from Cairo. They leave Bahariya around noon and 11.30pm from the Upper Egypt kiosk and Hilal Coffeehouse.

SERVICE TAXI

Whenever they're full, microbus service taxis run from Bawiti to Cairo (E£30), ending in Giza, about a five-minute walk from the Moneib metro station. A microbus to Farafra (they're not very frequent) will cost E£20. All leave from Hilal Coffeehouse.

There are no service taxis to Siwa, so you will have to hire a private 4WD for the rough journey (permit required). Expect to pay around E£1300. If there is a 4WD that has arrived from Siwa and is returning empty, you might be able to get a ride with it for half that amount. Recent changes in legislation make it easy to arrange same-day permits to travel to Siwa (US$5 per person). Permits are purchased at the bank; drivers, or the tourist office, can help you arrange them.

AROUND BAWITI

The area's antiquities (eg Tomb of Alexander and Temple of Ain al-Muftella) have been recently spruced up and mostly reopened to the public. Surrounding the town are mud-brick villages and palm gardens, many fed by springs that are ideal for a night-time soak. Further afield lies some spectacular desert scenery; Black Desert, Gebel Dist and Gebel Maghrafa can be seen on a day trip or on an overnight safari.

The following sights and sleeping options feature on the Bahariya Oasis map (p348).

Sights
TEMPLE OF ALEXANDER

Southwest of Bawiti, just beyond Ahmed's Safari Camp, is the only place in Egypt where Alexander the Great's image and cartouche have been found – although since being uncovered by archaeologists in the late 1930s these have been mostly worn away by the wind. Alexander was known to have visited Siwa, but there is no evidence to suggest that he passed through Bahariya, so his likeness here is puzzling. The corrosive desert winds, combined with some insensitive restoration, have left this site pretty bare, with few clues to its original splendour.

TEMPLE OF AIN AL-MUFTELLA

Slightly south of the spring of the same name are four 26th-dynasty chapels that together form the Temple of Ain al-Muftella. The bulk of the building was ordered by 26th-dynasty high priest Zed-Khonsu-ef-ankh, whose tomb was recently discovered under houses in Bawiti (but is still closed to the public). Archaeologists suspect that

BAHARIYA TOURS

There is furious competition throughout the oases – and even in Cairo – for tour business, but it is particularly intense in Bahariya. Here, every hotel offers tours, as do a number of eager young men who have taken out bank loans to pay for their cars. The battle for customers is so fierce that most buses arriving in Bahariya are now greeted by a tourist-police officer, who will escort foreigners through the throng of aggressive touts to the safe haven of the tourist office. Here Mohamed Abd el-Kader can give you up-to-date information about local hotels and tour operators. He usually suggests only going with a driver approved by your hotel or the tourist office; others may be cheaper, but you will have no comeback if something goes wrong. And things do go wrong: there have been several serious injuries in the past few years and at least one death.

A typical itinerary will take you to the sights in and around Bahariya (Temple of Alexander, Ain el-Muftella, Gebel Dist and Gebel Maghrafa) then out through the Black Desert, with a stop at the Crystal Mountain and then into the White Desert.

A day trip to the local sights of Bawiti runs from E£150 to E£300, while a one-night camping trip into the White Desert will cost E£600 to E£1000 per day. If you're travelling into the remote corners of the desert on a multiday excursion, you'll be looking at E£800 to E£1250 per day. One of the variables is how much of the distance is covered off-road (which uses more fuel and is more wearing on the cars).

Before signing up, check vehicles to make sure they're roadworthy, confirm how much food and drink is supplied (and what this will be), ask how long the operators have been conducting safaris, confirm start and end times (some operators start late in the afternoon and return early in the morning but charge for full days) and try to talk with travellers who have just returned from a trip to get their feedback.

If you're planning on exploring remote parts of the desert such as Gilf Kebir, Gebel Uweinat or the Great Sand Sea, it is absolutely imperative that you go with an outfit that supplies new 4WDs (travelling in convoy), GPS, satellite phones and experienced Bedouin guides. You'll need an official permit for the Great Sand Sea (US$100; this takes 14 days to process, arranged through your outfitter).

If you are at all unsure of arrangements, check with Mohamed Abd el-Kader. And be sure to inspect the car, its spare tyres, water and communications before leaving.

the chapels could have been built during the New Kingdom and then significantly expanded during the Late Period and added to during Greek and Roman times. All have been extensively restored and have been given wooden roofs to protect them from the elements.

QARAT AL-HILWA

This sandstone ridge is about 3km southwest of Bawiti, northwest of the road to Farafra. In the New Kingdom this was a necropolis, a burial place of successive governors who, as representatives of the pharaoh, were the most powerful figures in the oasis. The 18th-dynasty **Tomb of Amenhotep Huy** is the only inscribed tomb left in the necropolis, but there is little to see there now. The faded, sunken reliefs here once showed scenes of Amenhotep's dreams for the afterlife: banquet tables groaning with fruit, cakes, flowers and casks of wine.

OTHER SIGHTS AROUND BAWATI

There are a number of other sights in Bahariya that are included as part of a tour by the many safari operators in Bawiti. Most can also be done on foot if the weather is cool.

Gebel Mandisha is a ridge capped with black dolomite and basalt that runs for 4km behind the village of the same name, just east of Bawiti.

Clearly visible from the road to Cairo, flat-topped **Gebel al-Ingleez**, also known as Black Mountain, takes its name from the remains of a WWI lookout post. From here Captain Williams, a British officer, monitored the movements of Libyan Senussi tribesmen.

Gebel Dist is an impressive pyramid-shaped mountain that can be seen from most of the oasis. A local landmark, it is famous for its fossils – dinosaur bones were found here in the early 20th century, disproving the previously held theory that dinosaurs only lived in North America. In 2001 researchers from the

University of Pennsylvania found the remains of another huge dinosaur, *Paralititan stromeri*. The discovery of this giant herbivore, which the team deduced was standing on the edge of a tidal channel when it died 94 million years ago, makes it likely that Bahariya was once a swamp similar to the Florida everglades. About 100m away is **Gebel Maghrafa** (Mountain of the Ladle).

One of the most magnificent springs we have yet seen is **Ain Gomma** (off Map p348), a fair distance away at 45km south of Bawiti. Cool and crystal-clear water gushes into this small spring as it sits surrounded by the vast desert expanse on all sides – the views are amazing. There's a shady, cushioned cafe here where you can buy tea and soft drinks. Situated near the town of El-Hayz, it's difficult to reach without your own transport, though many safari trips to the White Desert will stop here en route. You can also stay at nearby Under the Moon Camp (below).

Sleeping & Eating

BUDGET

Bedouin Village Camp (☎ /fax 3847 6811; www.sadiq1.20m.com; El-Agouz; s/d E£30/60) At this Bedouin-themed camp with slumlike quarters circling a central thatched area, the bathrooms are actually nicer than the bedrooms! The place is friendly and not entirely without charm, as owner Abdelsadiq Elbadrmani, an accomplished Bedouin musician, provides the evening entertainment. It's in the quiet village of El-Agouz, 3.5km east of Bawiti.

Badr's Sahara Camp (☎ 012 792 2728; www.badrysaharacamp.com; huts per person E£35; 🖳) A couple of kilometres from town, Badr's Sahara Camp has a handful of bucolic, African-influenced huts, each with two beds and small patio sitting areas out front. Hot water and electricity can't always be counted on but cool desert breezes and knockout views of the oasis valley can. Pick-ups are available and wi-fi is free.

Eden Garden Camp (off Map p348; ☎ 0100 710 707; www.edengardentours.com; huts with fan incl breakfast per person E£40, full board E£80) Located 7km east of Bawiti, in the small, serene oasis of El Jaffara, Eden Garden features simple huts, shaded lounge areas, fresh food and, best of all, two springs just outside its gates: one hot and one cold. Its desert safaris have a good reputation, and pick-ups from Bawiti are free.

Ahmed's Safari Camp (☎ /fax 3847 2090; www.ahmedsafaricamp.com; s/d E£60/80, with air-con E£120/150; 🖳 🖳) About 4km west of Bawiti, near the Siwa road, Ahmed's is an old favourite among travellers and trans-Africa groups. There are cool, pleasant, domed double rooms as well as more basic ones (some of which have air-con, the rest fans), or you can sleep under the stars on the roof (E£20). Simple meals (E£30) and beer are available, which is just as well, because it's a long walk to town if you have no transport. There's a hot spring a few steps from the hotel.

Under the Moon Camp (off Map p348; ☎ 012 423 6580; www.helaltravel.com; El-Hayz; huts s/d half board E£90/180, bungalows s/d half board E£140/240) Isolated in the small oasis hamlet of El-Hayz, 45km south of Bawiti, this beautiful camp features several round, stone huts (no electricity) and some new mudbrick bungalows (with lights) scattered around a garden compound. The accommodation is as simple as it gets but the hospitality and the setting can't be beat. The lovely Ain Gomma spring (left) is nearby and there's a cold spring pool right in the camp, with powerful desert views. Helal, the Bedouin owner who once trained Egyptian military units in desert navigation, runs highly recommended safari trips and arranges free pick-ups from Bawiti.

Nature Camp (☎ 847 2184, 012 337 5097; naturecamps@hotmail.com; Bir al-Ghaba; r half board per person E£100) At the foot of Gebel Dist, Nature Camp sets new standards for environmentally focused budget accommodation. The peaceful cluster of candlelit and intricately designed thatch huts looks out onto the expansive desert beside Bir al-Ghaba. The food is very good (meals E£25) and the owner, Ashraf Lotfe, is a skilled desert hand. Staff will drive you the 17km to and from Bawiti if you arrive without transport.

MIDRANGE & TOP END

International Hot Springs Hotel (☎ 3847 3014, 012 321 2179; www.whitedeserttours.com; s/d/tr half board US$45/70/90) About 3km outside Bawiti on the road to Cairo, this German-run three-star spa resort has forgettable architecture, but its 36 rooms and eight chalets are very comfortable, built around a hot spring and set in a delightful garden. As well as a deep pool of therapeutic spring water there's a gym, sauna, rooftop lounging area and a good restaurant. Owner Peter Wirth is an old Western Desert hand

and organises recommended trips throughout the area.

Qasr el-Bawity Hotel & Restaurant (☎ 3847 1880; www.qasrelbawity.com; s/d/ste half board from €50/80/120; ❌ ☲) The relatively new Qasr el-Bawity offers some of the swankiest accommodation in Bahariya. With a finely trained eye for environmentally friendly design, this place has sumptuous rooms finished in cool stonework and sporting ornate domed roofs, fine furniture and arty, frilly touches. There are two pools (one natural and one chlorinated) and the restaurant here is suitably good.

SIWA OASIS

☎ 046 / pop 22,000

If, like most visitors to Siwa, you are driving the 300km south from the coast through the monotonously featureless and desolate desert, you'll be rubbing your eyes thinking that your first sight of Siwa is an emerald mirage. Set against a backdrop of jagged sandstone hills, backed by the rolling silica ocean of the Great Sand Sea and carpeted thick with palm groves, this is the archetypal oasis. Here, an abundance of free-flowing freshwater springs support hundreds of thousands of olive and fruit trees and date palms, which also shade and cool the valley's mudbrick villages as they rest concealed in the greenery.

Siwa's very isolation helped protect a unique society that until today stands apart from mainstream Egyptian culture. Originally settled by Berbers (roaming North African tribes), Siwa was still practically independent only a few hundred years ago. For centuries the oasis had contact with only the few caravan traders that passed along this way via Qara, Qattara and Kerdassa (near Cairo), and the occasional determined pilgrim seeking the famous Oracle of Amun. Even today local traditions and Siwi, the local Berber language, dominate.

Siwa is less about rushing around any major sights than it is about sitting back with a cup of tea or a *sheesha* and letting the halcyon days wash over you. The hectares of palm groves invite casual strolling, numerous comfortable and cushioned cafes are perfect for chilling and meeting fellow travellers, and dozens of clear springs practically beg for you to dip your toes. As increasing numbers of independent travellers discover the tranquil joys of this remote paradise, local inhabitants are ever more mindful of retaining their traditions and limiting the sort of uncontrolled 'development' that has scarred more popular tourist destinations in Egypt.

HISTORY

Siwa has a long and ancient, ancient past: in late 2007 a human footprint was found that could date back three million years, making it the oldest known human print in the world. Flints discovered in the oasis further prove that it was inhabited in Palaeolithic and Neolithic times, but beyond that Siwa's early history remains shrouded in mystery.

The oldest monuments in the oasis, including the Temple of the Oracle, date from the 26th dynasty, when Egypt was invaded by the Assyrians. Siwa's Oracle of Amun (p358) was already famous then, and Egyptologists suspect it dates back to the earlier 21st dynasty, when the Amun priesthood and oracles became prominent throughout Egypt.

Such was the fame of Siwa's oracle that it threatened the Persians, who invaded Egypt in 525 BC and ended the 26th dynasty. One of the Western Desert's most persistent legends is of the lost army of Persian king Cambyses, which was sent to destroy the oracle and disappeared completely in the desert (see boxed text, p345). This only helped increase the prestige of the oracle and reinforce the political power of the Amun priesthood.

The oracle's power, and with it Siwa's fame, grew throughout the ancient world. The young conqueror Alexander the Great led a small party on a perilous eight-day journey across the desert in 331 BC. It is believed that the priests of Amun, who was the supreme god of the Egyptian pantheon and later associated with the Greek god Zeus, declared him to be a son of the god. On coins minted after this time, Alexander was often portrayed with the ram's horns associated with Amun. Ptolemaic leaders, anxious to prove their credentials, also made the trek. The tombs at Gebel al-Mawta (p358) are testament to the prosperity of the oasis during this period.

The end of Roman rule, the collapse of the trade route and the gradual decline in the influence of oracles in general all contributed to Siwa's gentle slide into obscurity. While Christianity spread through most of Egypt, there is no evidence that it ever reached Siwa,

WESTERN DESERT

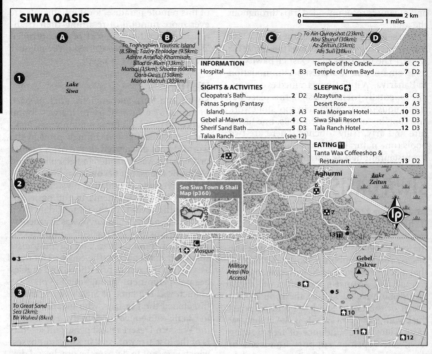

SIWA OASIS

0	2 km
0	1 miles

To Taghaghien Touristic Island (8.5km); Tazry Ecolodge (9.5km); Adrère Amellal; Kharmisah, Bilad ar-Rum (13km); Maraqi (15km); Shiatta (60km); Qara Oasis (150km); Marsa Matruh (303km)

To Ain Qurayshat (23km); Abu Shuruf (30km); Az-Zeitun (35km); Ain Sufi (38km)

Lake Siwa

INFORMATION
Hospital...1 B3

SIGHTS & ACTIVITIES
Cleopatra's Bath..............................2 D2
Fatnas Spring (Fantasy
  Island)..3 A3
Gebel al-Mawta................................4 C2
Sherif Sand Bath..............................5 D3
Talaa Ranch...............................(see 12)

Temple of the Oracle.......................6 C2
Temple of Umm Bayd.......................7 D2

SLEEPING
Alzaytuna...8 C3
Desert Rose......................................9 A3
Fata Morgana Hotel........................10 D3
Siwa Shali Resort............................11 D3
Tala Ranch Hotel............................12 D3

EATING
Tanta Waa Coffeeshop &
  Restaurant..................................13 D2

Aghurmi

Lake Zeitun

See Siwa Town & Shali Map (p360)

Mosque

Military Area (No Access)

Gebel Dakrur

To Great Sand Sea (2km); Bir Wahed (8km)

and priests continued to worship Amun here until the 6th century AD. The Muslim conquerors, who crossed the desert in 708, were defeated several times by the fierce Siwans. However, there was a cost to this isolation: it is said that by 1203 the population had declined to just 40 men, who moved from Aghurmi to found the new fortress-town of Shali. The oasis finally converted to Islam around the 12th century, and gradually built up wealth trading date and olive crops along the Nile Valley, and with Libyan Fezzan and the Bedouins.

European travellers arrived at the end of the 18th century – WG Browne in 1792 and Frederick Hornemann in 1798 – but most were met with a hostile reception and several narrowly escaped with their lives. The Siwans thus gained a reputation for being fiercely independent and hostile to non-Muslim outsiders. Throughout the 19th century, the Egyptian government also had problems trying to gain the loyalty of the oasis. Siwa was again visited in WWII, when the British and Italian/German forces chased each other in and out of Siwa and Jaghbub,

120km west in Libya, until Rommel turned his attention elsewhere. By then the Siwans were politically incorporated into Egypt, but the oasis remained physically isolated until an asphalt road connected it to Marsa Matruh in the 1980s. As a result, Siwans still speak their own distinct Berber dialect and have a strong local culture, quite distinct from the rest of Egypt. The oasis is now home to just over 20,000 Siwans and nearly 2000 Egyptians.

INFORMATION
Emergency
Tourist police (Map p360; ☎ 460 2047; Siwa Town)

Internet Access
There's a sprinkling of computers around the centre of town, most for E£10 per hour.
Desert Net Cafe (Map p360; Siwa Town; per hr E£3; ⏰ 11am-3pm & 7pm-3am) The cheapest internet access in town, usually with decent connection speeds.
Tiger Shali Net Cafe (Map p360; Abdu's Restaurant, central market sq, Siwa Town; per hr E£4; ⏰ 9am-1am) Above Abdu's Restaurant. Find it down an alley on the west side of the block. Its actual hours of operation are erratic.

Medical Services

Hospital (Map p356; ☎ 460 0459; Sharia Sadat, Siwa Town) Only for emergencies.

Pharmacy Al-Ansar (Map p360; ☎ 460 1310; Sharia Sadat, Siwa Town; 🕒 8am-2pm & 4pm-2am)

Money

Banque du Caire (Map p360; Siwa Town; 🕒 8.30am-2pm, plus 5-8pm Oct-Apr) Purported to be the only all-mud-brick bank in the world; there's an ATM here that works more often than not. Located next to the tourist-police station.

Permits

A permit is needed to venture off the beaten track from Siwa, but this is easily arranged by local guides. Mahdi Hweiti at the Siwa tourist office (below) will arrange permissions quite quickly (but not on Friday) at the fixed rate of US$5, plus an extra E£11 for the local Mukhabarat (Intelligence Police) office. The same rate applies for the permit needed to travel from Siwa to Bahariya. You'll need your passport.

Note that most permits will be valid for one day only, and although overnight trips can be easily arranged, they are often not permitted.

Post & Telephone

Main post office (Map p360; behind Arous al-Waha Hotel, Siwa Town; 🕒 8am-2pm Sat-Thu)

Telephone centrale (Map p360; Siwa Town; 🕒 24hr) Located at the beginning of the Marsa Matruh road.

Tourist Information

Tourist office (Map p360; ☎ 460 1338; mahdi_hweiti@yahoo.com; Siwa Town; 🕒 9am-2pm Sat-Thu, plus 5-8pm Oct-Apr) The local tourist officer, Mahdi Hweiti, is very knowledgeable and can help arrange trips to some of the surrounding villages or the desert. He can be reached on his mobile (☎ 010 546 1992). In the evening, you can watch an interesting documentary about Siwa in English, French or German.

SIGHTS & ACTIVITIES

Even though there are a number of fascinating sights hidden in the dense palm greenery of this oasis, the main attraction in Siwa remains its serene ambience. Strolling through the palm groves or relaxing over a cup of tea as the townspeople go about their languid paces seems to be the order of the day. Occasional visits to one of the wonderful springs in the area offer further distractions, and bicycles are a suitably geared form of transport that can be rented nearly everywhere.

> **RESPECTING LOCAL TRADITION**
>
> Siwans are very proud of their traditions, which are part of what makes the place so unique. They are particularly sensitive where female modesty is concerned. The least visitors can do to help preserve Siwa's culture is to respect local sensibilities and act accordingly. Modest dress is appreciated and women travellers in particular should make sure they cover their upper arms and their legs, and wear baggy T-shirts over bathing suits when taking a dip in any of the numerous springs. Do not, as the tourist office puts it, show 'displays of affection' in public.

Siwa Town

Siwa is a pleasant little town centred around a market square, where roads lead off into the palm groves in nearly every direction. Around the corner from the local council offices is the small **House of Siwa Museum** (Map p360; adult/student E£10/5; 🕒 9am-2.30pm Sun-Thu), which contains a modest display of traditional clothing, jewellery and crafts typical of the oasis. It was inspired by a Canadian diplomat who feared that Siwan culture and its mudbrick houses would disappear in a flood of poured cement and modernity. You can arrange to see the museum through the tourist office or find the custodian at the nearby Town Council Building (Map p360).

The centre of the town is dominated by the spectacular organic shapes of the remains of the 13th-century mudbrick **fortress of Shali** (Map p360). Built from a material known locally as *kershef* (large chunks of salt from the lake just outside town, mixed with rock and plastered in local clay), the labyrinth of huddled buildings was originally four or five storeys high and housed hundreds of people. For centuries, few outsiders were admitted inside – and even fewer came back out to tell the tale. But three days of rain in 1926 caused more damage than any invader had managed and, over the last decades, inhabitants moved to newer and more comfortable houses with running water and electricity. Now only a few buildings around the edges are occupied or used for storage, including the **King Fuad Mosque** (Map p360) with its old, chimney-shaped minaret. Those who wander around the outskirts of the fort are likely to be rewarded with glimpses of life as it used to be; there's an old donkey-powered oil press back here, and you should listen out for the clanging of a real-life metalsmith plying his trade.

Aghurmi

Before Shali was founded in the 13th century, Siwa's main settlement was at Aghurmi, 4km east of the present town of Siwa. It was here that in 331 BC Alexander the Great consulted the oracle (see p355) at the 26th-dynasty **Temple of the Oracle** (Map p356; adult/student E£25/15; ☾ 9am-5pm). Built in the 6th century BC, probably on top of an earlier temple, it was dedicated to Amun (occasionally referred to as Zeus or Jupiter Ammon) and was a powerful symbol of the town's wealth. One of the most revered oracles in the ancient Mediterranean, its power was such that some rulers sought its advice while others sent armies to destroy it (see boxed text, p345).

Today the Temple of the Oracle sits in the northwest corner of the ruins of Aghurmi village. Though treasure hunters have been at work here and the buttressed temple was poorly restored in the 1970s, it remains an evocative site, steeped in history. Surrounded by the ruins of Aghurmi, it has awesome views over the oasis palm-tops.

About 200m further along the track stands the remains of the almost totally ruined **Temple of Umm Ubayd** (Map p356), also dedicated to Amun. This was originally connected to the Temple of the Oracle by a causeway and was used during oracle rituals. Early drawings have revealed that the structure was built by Nectanebo II (360–343 BC) during the 30th dynasty. Nineteenth-century travellers saw more of it than we can: a Siwan governor in need of building material blew up the temple in 1896 in order to construct the town's modern mosque and police building. Only part of a wall covered with inscriptions survives.

Gebel al-Mawta

A small hill at the northern end of Siwa Town, **Gebel al-Mawta** (Map p356; adult/student E£25/15; ☾ 9am-5pm) – whose name means Mountain of the Dead – is honeycombed with rock tombs, most dating back to the 26th-dynasty, Ptolemaic and Roman times. Only 1km from the centre of town, the tombs were used by the Siwans as shelters when the Italians bombed the oasis during WWII. Many new tombs were discovered at this time but were not properly

excavated. In his book *Siwa Oasis,* Ahmed Fakhry recalls British soldiers paying Siwan families a few piastres to cut away large chunks of tomb paintings to keep as souvenirs.

Despite the damage, some paintings have survived. The best are in the **Tomb of Si Amun**, where beautifully coloured reliefs portray the dead man, thought to be a wealthy Greek landowner or merchant, making offerings and praying to Egyptian gods. Also interesting are the unfinished **Tomb of Mesu-Isis**, with a beautiful depiction of cobras in red and blue above the entrance; the **Tomb of Niperpathot**, with inscriptions and crude drawings in the same reddish ink you can see on modern Siwan pottery; and finally the **Tomb of the Crocodile**, whose badly deteriorating wall paintings include a yellow crocodile representing the god Sobek.

Hot & Cold Springs

Siwa has no shortage of active, bubbling springs hidden among its palm groves. Following the track that leads to the Temple of the Oracle and continuing past the Temple of Umm Ubayd will lead you to the most famous spring, **Cleopatra's Bath** (Spring of the Sun; Map p356). The crystal-clear natural spring water gurgles up into a large stone pool, which is a popular bathing spot for locals. Women should think twice about swimming here during the day, and if they decide to brave the stares then they should only bathe with their clothes on. There are changing rooms at the nearby Tanta Waa cafe.

The closest spring to town is **Ain al-Arais** (Map p360), a cool, inviting waterhole with a grotto-like bottom, just five minutes' walk from the central market. Beside the spring sits a casual cafe-restaurant.

There's a similar but slightly more secluded pool at **Fatnas Spring** (Map p356), the small island in the salty Birket Siwa (Lake Siwa) accessible across a narrow causeway. Nicknamed 'Fantasy Island' for its idyllic setting, the pool is about 6km from Siwa Town, and surrounded by palm trees and lush greenery. Although it is a safer place for a swim than Cleopatra's Bath, women should not swim alone and, again, should leave their bikinis for the Red Sea beaches. There's a small cafe among the palms, which is good for sitting and puffing on a *sheesha*, or drinking a cold beer if it's available. This is an idyllic place to watch the sunset. A Ministry of Agriculture project to try to improve the lake's drainage has left the 'island' high and dry, so that the cafe now looks out over salty mudflats rather than water.

A favourite excursion among local guides is the cold freshwater lake at **Bir Wahed** (off Map p356), 15km away on the edge of the Great Sand Sea. Once over the top of a high dune, you come to a hot spring, the size of a large jacuzzi, where sulphurous water bubbles in a pool and runs off to irrigate a garden. Cooling down in the lake, and then watching the sun setting over the dunes while soaking in a hot spring is a surreal experience. The thorns in this rose are the mosquitoes that bite at sunset. Because it's far from town, women can wear bathing suits here without offending locals. Bir Wahed can only be reached by 4WD, so if you don't have your own, you'll need to hire a guide and car. Permits are needed to visit Bir Wahed (see p357).

Palm Gardens

One of Siwa's greatest attractions is the oasis itself, which boasts more than 300,000 palm trees, 70,000 olive trees and a great many fruit orchards. The vegetation is sustained by more than 300 freshwater springs and streams, and the area attracts an amazing variety of bird life, including quail and falcons.

Outlying Villages

There are a few tumbledown villages about 15km northwest of Siwa Town (all shown off the Siwa Oasis map, p356). **Kharmisah** has five natural springs and is renowned for the quality of its olive gardens. **Bilad ar-Rum** (City of the Romans) has about 100 tombs cut into the rock of the nearby hills and the ruins of a stone temple, which is rumoured to be the final resting place of Alexander the Great. Both are Berber villages and can be reached by local bus.

About 2km west of here is **Maraqi**, where Liana Souvaltzi, a Greek archaeologist, claimed in 1995 to have found the tomb of Alexander the Great. Her findings proved

controversial and the Egyptian authorities revoked her permit and closed the site.

Sixty kilometres west of Siwa Town, the town of **Shiatta** sits lapping at the edge of the Great Sand Sea. There's a salt spring here, thought to be all that's left of a lake that once reached all the way to Siwa Town, where an ancient Egyptian boat, possibly used to sail to the Temple of the Oracle, was discovered lying 7m down. These days this area is mainly used by Bedouin tribes for grazing livestock and has some first-rate views of the desert mountains.

There are more springs to the east of Siwa Town (shown off the Siwa Oasis map, p356). **Ain Qurayshat** is 27km out from the town and has the largest free-flowing spring in the oasis. **Abu Shuruf**, a clean spring said by locals to have healing properties, is 7km further east from Ain Qurayshat in the next palm thicket. The clear water here is deliciously cold, but the ambience is somewhat spoilt by the sight and noise of the nearby Hayat water-bottling plant. Another 5km brings you to **Az-Zeitun**, an abandoned mudbrick village beaten by the sand and wind that sits alone on the sandy plain. Hundreds of Roman-era tombs have been discovered about 2km beyond Az-Zeitun and are currently under excavation, although little of interest has so far been found.

From Az-Zeitun, another 3km brings you to **Ain Safi**, the last human vestige before the overwhelming wall of desert dunes that stretches for hundreds of kilometres, all the way south to Al-Kharga Oasis. Some 30 Bedouin families live at Ain Safi.

To visit these sights you'll need your own sturdy vehicle. Mahdi Hweiti at the tourist office (p357), and almost every restaurant and hotel in town, organises trips. None of these sights, with the exception of Shiatta, require permits.

TOURS

Almost all restaurants and hotels in Siwa offer tours, ranging from half a day in the desert around Siwa Town to a full five- or six-day safari. Siwa Safari Paradise (p361) arranges tours using its own fleet of 4WDs, though this is an expensive option. The Palm Trees Hotel (p361) and Abdu's Restaurant (p363) have established a good reputation for their trips. The tourist office (p357) can also be a great help in organising tours around the oasis.

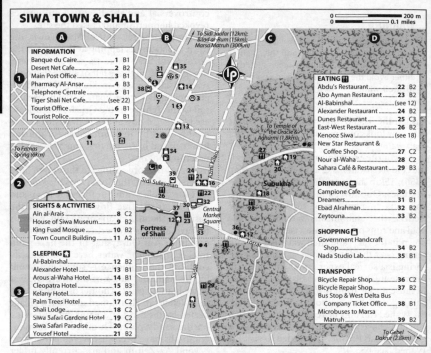

SIWA TOWN & SHALI

0 —————— 200 m
0 —————— 0.1 miles

INFORMATION
Banque du Caire................................1 B1
Desert Net Cafe................................2 B2
Main Post Office................................3 B1
Pharmacy Al-Ansar............................4 B3
Telephone Centrale............................5 B1
Tiger Shali Net Cafe........................(see 22)
Tourist Office....................................6 B1
Tourist Police....................................7 B1

SIGHTS & ACTIVITIES
Ain al-Arais......................................8 C2
House of Siwa Museum......................9 B2
King Fuad Mosque............................10 B2
Town Council Building......................11 A2

SLEEPING
Al-Babinshal....................................12 B2
Alexander Hotel................................13 B1
Arous al-Waha Hotel........................14 B1
Cleopatra Hotel................................15 B3
Kelany Hotel....................................16 B2
Palm Trees Hotel..............................17 C2
Shali Lodge......................................18 C2
Siwa Safari Gardens Hotel................19 C2
Siwa Safari Paradise........................20 C2
Yousef Hotel....................................21 B2

EATING
Abdu's Restaurant............................22 B2
Abo Ayman Restaurant......................23 B2
Al-Babinshal..................................(see 12)
Alexander Restaurant........................24 B2
Dunes Restaurant............................25 C3
East-West Restaurant........................26 B2
Kenooz Siwa..................................(see 18)
New Star Restaurant &
    Coffee Shop................................27 C2
Nour al-Waha....................................28 C2
Sahara Café & Restaurant..................29 B3

DRINKING
Campione Cafe................................30 B2
Dreamers..31 B1
Ebad Alrahman................................32 B2
Zeytouna..33 B2

SHOPPING
Government Handcraft
    Shop..34 B2
Nada Studio Lab................................35 B1

TRANSPORT
Bicycle Repair Shop..........................36 C2
Bicycle Repair Shop..........................37 B2
Bus Stop & West Delta Bus
    Company Ticket Office..................38 B1
Microbuses to Marsa
    Matruh..39 B2

To Sidi Jaafar (12km);
Bilad ar-Rum (15km);
Marsa Matruh (300km)

To Fatnas
Spring (6km)

To Temple of
the Oracle &
Aghurmi (1.8km)

Subukha

Sidi Suleyman

Central
Market
Square

Fortress
of Shali

Torrar

To Gebel
Dakrur (2.8km)

All desert trips require permits, which cost US$5 plus E£11 and are usually obtained by your guide from the tourist office. Prices and itineraries vary, but one of the most popular trips takes you to the desert hot spring at Bir Wahed, on the edge of the Great Sand Sea. Here you can have a simple meal or tea, then move on to the nearby spring-fed lake, where, in the summer, you can take a dip. Usually you will do a spot of dune driving, stop at fossil sites and see some fantastic desert vistas before returning to Siwa. This half-day trip costs about E£80 per person plus permission costs.

Other popular half-day itineraries include a tour of the springs Ain Qurayshat, Abu Shuruf, Az-Zeitun and Ain Safi (E£50 per person); and a tour of Siwa Town and its environs (Temple of the Oracle, Gebel al-Mawta, Cleopatra's Bath, Shali fortress and Fatnas; E£30). Overnight trips vary in length according to destination but a popular one-night trip is to Qara Oasis (E£300 to E£500 per vehicle, depending on whether asphalt or desert track is taken). Most trips are done by 4WD, so ensure that the vehicle is roadworthy before you set out and, as with any desert trip, that you have enough water.

Camels were recently introduced to the oasis to do desert trips. Sherif Fahmy of the **Tala Ranch** (Map p356; ☎ 010 588 6003; talaranchsiwa@ hotmail.com; Gebel Dakrur) can arrange camel tours to watch the sunset from the sand dunes or a longer desert safari, though prices are a bit steep at E£350 for a day and night or E£150 per half-day. Abdul at **Shali Camel Safaris Ranch** (☎ 010 194 1653) also organises camel tours, with all meals included, at a slightly lower cost. These are virtually impossible to arrange in summer, since daytime temperatures are too hot and guides won't travel by starlight.

FESTIVALS & EVENTS

Gebel Dakrur is the scene of the annual **Siyaha festival**. For three days around the October full moon, thousands of Siwans gather to celebrate the date harvest, renewing friendships and settling any quarrels that might have broken out over the previous year. All Siwans, no matter what their financial or social standing, eat together at a huge feast after the noon prayer each day during the festival. The festival is intertwined with Sufism, and each evening, hundreds of men form a circle and join together in a *zikr*, a long session of dancing, swaying and singing repetitive songs in praise of God. Siwan women do not attend the festivities, although girls up to about the age of 12 are present until sunset. Each year hundreds of non-Siwans – Egyptians and foreigners – attend the festival.

Once a year, just after the corn harvest in late summer, the small tomb shrine of Sidi Suleiman, behind the King Fuad Mosque in the centre of Siwa Town, is the scene of a *moulid* (saints' festival), known in Siwi as the **Moulid at-Tagmigra**. Banners announce the *moulid*, and *zikr*s are performed outside the tomb.

Occasionally on Thursday nights, after the evening prayer, local Sufis of the Arusiya order gather near the tomb shrine for a *zikr* and they don't mind the odd foreigner watching.

SLEEPING

Siwa has a great collection of places to bed down in, with everything from competitively priced budget pads to dazzling top-end options. The choices here are expanding yearly, and the competition helps keep standards high and prices down. Many midrange and top-end sleeping options can also be found further afield in Siwa Oasis, around Gebel Dakrur and Sidi Jaafar.

The police here are jittery about people camping close to town. If you really want to avoid other people, you're better off organising a trip to the desert with one of the many local operators (see p359).

Siwa Town
BUDGET
Yousef Hotel (Map p360; ☎ 460 0678; central market sq; dm/d without bathroom E£15/20, s/d E£20/25; ▣) With the cheapest beds in town, Yousef is perennially full with backpacking budgeters. The rooms are a bit tattered and kept barely above minimum hygiene levels, but the four-storey rooftop has great views of the oasis and a kitchen that guests are free to use. Noise can be an issue.

Cleopatra Hotel (Map p360; ☎ 460 0421; www.cleo patra-siwa.net; s/d/tr main bldg E£20/30/40, s/d/tr new bldg 35/45/65, ste with air-con E£130) A spartan budget option at the southern end of town. While the cheaper rooms in the main building are a little

scruffy, the quieter building out back is much neater and has balconied rooms.

Palm Trees Hotel (Map p360; ☎ 460 1703, 012 104 6652; m_s_siwa@yahoo.com; Sharia Torrar; s/d E£35/50, with shared bathroom E£20/35, bungalows s/d E£50/70) This deservedly popular budget hotel has sufficiently tidy rooms, all with screened windows, fans and balconies. The shady, tranquil garden with date-palm furniture is delightful (but mosquito-intensive), and the few ground-level bungalows have porches spilling onto the greenery. Breakfast costs E£5.

Alexander Hotel (Map p360; ☎ 460 0512; s/d E£25/50, with air-con E£30/60; ▣) The Alexander is badly in need of a maid, a plumber and an exterminator. However, it does boast the cheapest air-con abodes in town.

Arous al-Waha Hotel (Map p360; ☎ 460 0028; s/d E£38/50, with air-con E£50/100) If it wasn't for the sand-coloured paint job, we'd swear this old hotel had escaped from a communist housing block. The rooms at this former government rest house are austere, orderly and spacious, though the management seems a little bewildered by walk-in guests. It's opposite the tourist office, at the beginning of the Marsa Matruh road.

Kelany Hotel (Map p360; ☎ 460 1052, 012 403 9218; zaitsafari@yahoo.com; central market sq; r E£70, with air-con E£150) A modern hotel in a good location, the Kelany has comfortable rooms, spick-and-span bathrooms, hot and cold water and friendly management. The rooftop restaurant features views of Shali Fortress, Gebel Dakrur and everything in between.

Desert Rose (Map p356; ☎ 012 440 8164; ali_siwa@ hotmail.com; s/d/tr E£120/200/280, with shared bathroom E£80/150/180; ▣) Overlooking the magnificent dunes that stretch out to the southeast of Siwa, this friendly, cosy hotel has creatively decorated, spotless rooms in a funky octagonal building. Extremely good value, it has its own clear pool of natural spring water, a roof terrace for sunset adulation, indoor and outdoor fireplaces and a smattering of cushioned chill-out areas. Guests can prepare their own meals in the kitchen or eat food prepared by the staff. There are no electric lights, but there is a small generator to charge camera and phone batteries.

MIDRANGE & TOP END
Siwa Safari Paradise (Map p360; ☎ 460 1590; www .siwaparadise.com; s/d E£130/230, with air-con E£180/280; ▣) Laid out along a maze of garden paths,

this resort-style hotel mainly attracts northern Europeans looking to sunbake by the natural spring pool. The decoration is quite tacky and the place is showing its age, but the rooms are cool and comfortable, so it's not a bad option if other recommended hotels are full.

Shali Lodge (Map p360; ☎ 460 1299; info@eqi.com.eg; Sharia Subukha; s/d/tr E£260/340/420) This tiny, beautiful mudbrick hotel, owned by environmentalist Mounir Neamatallah, nestles in a lush palm grove about 100m from the main square. The large, extremely comfortable rooms have lots of curving mudbrick goodness, exposed palm beams, rock-walled bathrooms and cushioned sitting nooks. Tasteful and quiet, this is how small hotels should be.

Al-Babinshal (Map p360; ☎ 460 1499; www.siwa.com; s/d/tr E£260/340/420) Literally attached to the fortress of Shali, this place continues the ecolodge footprint left by Shali Lodge (above) and Adrére Amellal (right) owner Mounir Neamatallah. The cunning architects have seamlessly grafted this mudbrick hotel onto the front of Shali fort, and a maze of tunnels and stairways connects the spacious and cool cavelike rooms, making it impossible to tell where the hotel ends and the fort begins. Entirely made from the same materials as the original fort, each intimate abode has wood-floor panelling, traditional wooden-shuttered windows and exposed palm-log supports. Some locals, however, are not convinced that this augmentation of their town's landmark is necessarily for the better.

Siwa Safari Gardens Hotel (Map p360; ☎ 460 2801; www.siwagardens.com; s/d/tr half-board E£270/370/470; ✹ ✹ 🖳) This spanking-new hotel goes for a style that's simple but tasteful. Ground-floor rooms are surprisingly plain; those on the 2nd floor have domed ceilings and much more character, but might cost E£50 extra per person during high season. The serene palm-shaded courtyard is set around a gleaming, tourmaline, spring-fed pool. The kindly manager, Sami, speaks fluent English and German, and promises internet access in every room in the near future.

Sidi Jaafar

Taziry Ecolodge (off Map p356; ☎ 02-3337 0842, 012 340 8492; reservation@taziry.com; Gaary; s/d/s full board US$180/225/345; ✹) This lovely hotel was de-

signed and built by its friendly owners, an artist and an engineer, both from Alexandria. The large natural-material rooms are decorated with local crafts and Bedouin rugs, and have their own bathroom. Tranquil and laid back, with no electricity and a natural spring pool overlooking the lake, it is a great place to unwind and experience Siwa's magic.

our pick Adrére Amellal (off Map p356; ☎ in Cairo 02-736 7879, 02-738 1327; www.adrereamellal.net; Sidi Jaafar, White Mountain; s/d incl all meals, drinks & desert excursions US$415/550, ste from US$750; ✹) Backed by the dramatic White Mountain (called Adrére Amellal in Siwi), this impeccable desert retreat lies coddled in its own oasis, with stunning views over the salt lake of Birket Siwa and the dunes of the Great Sand Sea beyond. It is a truly unique place, built by environmentalist Mounir Neamatallah out of *kershef*, and using revived traditional building techniques. It's a real getaway from the regular pace of Egyptian life: mobile phones are banned outside the rooms and there is no electricity, with the gardens lit by torches and the rooms by candlelight. It offers the ultimate in spartan chic, as gourmet dinners are eaten under the stars or in salt-encrusted chambers. The swimming pool is an ancient stone natural spring and the rooms and suites are palatial, yet simple and beautiful. Together with inventive food that uses produce from its own organic garden and the feel-good factor of environmentally sound luxury, Adrére Amellal has featured in countless travel and style magazines and is one of the most innovative places to stay in the country.

Gebel Dakrur

Siwa Shali Resort (Map p356; ☎ 010 630 1017; www.siwashaliresort.com; s/d/ste half board €35/54/100; ✹ ✹) One of the few places in the desert that earns its 'resort' label, this self-contained village of traditionally styled bungalows snakes its way along a 500m spring-fed pool, and is quite beautiful. While the rooms are nothing special, suites have sitting rooms with two mattresses, which are perfect for young kids. You'll find all the mod cons, a restaurant, fitness facilities, a Bedouin-style cafe and gift shops.

Alzaytuna (Map p356; ☎ /fax 460 0037; www.alzaytuna.com; s/d E£90/180; ✹) Recently overhauled, Alzaytuna's newly finished bungalow rooms are pristine, with bathrooms seemingly trans-

---

SAND BATHING

If you thought a soak in a hot spring was invigorating, wait until you try a dip in one of the scalding-hot sand baths of **Gebel Dakrur**, several kilometres southeast of Siwa Town. From July to September, people flock here from all over the world to take turns being immersed up to their necks in a bath of very hot sand for up to 20 minutes at a time. Local doctors claim that a treatment regime of three to five days can cure rheumatism and arthritis – and judging by the number of repeat customers they get they might just be on to something. There are several places around the western slope of the mountain where you can get therapeutically sand-dunked; **Sherif sand bath** (Map p356) has a good reputation. Expect to pay around E£100 for each medicinal dip, which includes several necessary hours of recovery while sipping tea (though the tea is optional).

The mountain also supplies the oasis with the reddish-brown pigment used to decorate Siwan pottery. Siwans believe that the mountain is haunted and claim that *afrit* (spirits) can be heard singing in the gardens at night.

---

ported from Europe. A palm-shaded garden surrounds a swimming pool with views of Gebel Dakrur.

Fata Morgana Hotel (Map p356; ☎ 460 0237, 010 294 5850; s/d E£150/200; 🕮) The Fata Morgana has several cool and spacious rooms, jazzed up by tall, domed ceilings and curving arches. The two-storey, stonework building here stays amazingly chilled in the desert heat, and the small, clear pool will help you cool down if you're still breaking a sweat. Each chamber has a balcony with great views of either Gebel Dakrur or the desert expanse – top marks in the bang-for-buck department.

Tala Ranch Hotel (Map p356; ☎ 010 588 6003; www .talaranch-hotel.com; s/d E£300/400) This low-key ecoresort offers a very different experience of Siwa, with six stylish and comfortable rooms on the edge of the desert. It promises generous helpings of hush and is as relaxing as things get, with the camels, the desert and the wind as the only distractions. Sherif can organise camel trips or safaris for guests, while his wife, Siham, prepares commendable Egyptian food served in a Bedouin tent (four-course dinner E£120).

EATING

Many of the restaurants and cafes in Siwa cater to tourists. With the exception of the delicious restaurant at the Adrère Amellal, and the home-cooked food at places such as Taziry (opposite) and Tala Ranch (above), which is for guests only, most restaurants offer a similar menu of simple dishes, and the service and quality can vary from day to day. Most eateries are open from about 8am until late.

East-West Restaurant (Map p360; dishes E£2-15) Named after the historical divide between the two parts of Siwa Town, this restaurant serves a cheaper, more pedestrian version of Abdu's menu (see below) and has lethargic service.

Nour al-Waha (Map p360; ☎ 460 0293; Sharia Subukha; dishes E£5-20) A popular hang-out in a palm grove opposite Shali Lodge, Nour al-Waha has shady tables, and plenty of tea and games on hand for those who just want to while away the day in the shade. The food is a mixture of Egyptian and Western and, while it couldn't be called gourmet, it is generally fresh and good. At night *sheeshas* are available for E£5, and sometimes there is live music.

Alexander Restaurant (Map p360; off central market sq; dishes E£5-25) Alexander serves the usual budget-restaurant fare, with pizzas, veggie stews, very good chicken and, innovatively for Siwa, curries. Service can be slow here too, but the food usually arrives with a smile.

Abdu's Restaurant (Map p360; ☎ 460 1243; central market sq; dishes E£5-30; ⏰ 8.30am-midnight) Before internet and mobile phones, there were places like Abdu's – a village hub where people gathered nightly to meet, catch up and swap stories. This is the longest-running restaurant in town and remains the best eating option around, with a huge menu of breakfast, pasta, traditional dishes, vegetable stews, couscous, roasted chickens and fantastic pizza whipped to your table by the efficient service.

Dunes Restaurant (Map p360; ☎ 010 653 0372; Sharia Torrar; dishes E£8-30) With tables set under the palm trees and a large menu covering everything from herbal tea to couscous, Dunes is just another place to hang out and relax. The usual traveller stalwarts (from pancakes to smoothies) can be found here, as well as local specialities such as stuffed pigeon (by special order). *Sheeshas* are *de rigueur* and the owner can arrange special evenings with traditional Siwan music.

Tanta Waa Coffeeshop & Restaurant (Map p356; ☎ 010 472 9539; meals E£10-30; ☒ 8am-late) This super-chilled and creatively clad mudbrick cafe at Cleopatra's Bath is the perfect place for a cool drink or tasty meal in between splashes in the spring. The food here is surprisingly good, with a small selection of salads, pastas, meat dishes and fruit smoothies. The lasagne alone, which follows a genuine Italian recipe, is worth the trip out here. Slung with hammocks and with a background of funky tunes (it also occasionally holds evening parties), it's easy to while away an entire day at this haven.

Abo Ayman Restaurant (Map p360; meals E£13-23) Roasted on a hand-turned spit over coals in an old oil drum, the chickens at Abo Ayman are the juiciest in Siwa. They're well seasoned, and served with salad, tahini and bread. It sometimes takes an inconceivably long time for the birds to migrate from the grill to your table.

Kenooz Siwa (Map p360; ☎ 460 1299; Shali Lodge, Sharia Subukha; dishes E£20-50) On the roof terrace of Shali Lodge (p362), this cafe-restaurant is a great place to hang out while enjoying a mint tea or a cold drink, although the quality of the food, once the best in town, has definitely deteriorated.

Al-Babinshal Restaurant (Map p360; ☎ 460 1499; meals E£20-55) On the roof of the hotel of the same name (see p362), this might just be the most romantic dining spot found in the oases.

Moodily lit in the evenings, it's practically attached to the fortress of Shali and has sweeping views over all of Siwa. Though not bad, the food doesn't quite live up to the promise of the restaurant's chic ambience.

There are several other cosy palm-garden restaurants around Siwa serving the usual combination of Egyptian and Western fare. Following are a couple worth trying:

Sahara Café & Restaurant (Map p360; ☎ 010 856 9532; meals E£12-35) A nice place to chill, if you can find someone to serve you.

New Star Restaurant & Coffee Shop (Map p360; ☎ 460 0293; Sharia Subukha; dishes E£12-35) Also has a small shop selling traditional crafts.

DRINKING

Many of the cafes around town are no-name places where Siwan men gather to watch TV and chat, but no alcohol is served. The cafeteria at Fatnas Spring (p358) sometimes has beer.

Campione Cafe (Map p360; ☎ 460 1719; ☒ sunrise-late) We can't argue with Campione's slogan: 'life is too short for bad coffee'. Run by a groovy Alexandrian guy, it serves imported Italian coffee made with a bona-fide imported espresso machine and prepared any way you like it. Latte, anyone?

Dreamers (Map p360; opposite Arous al-Waha Hotel) Lively cafe open late where you can smoke a *sheesha* on an old-fashioned sofa while watching TV with locals, or drink a juice listening to reggae music.

Taghaghien Touristic Island (off Map p356; ☎ 921 0060; www.taghaghien-island.com; admission E£25) If you're desperate for a beer, this small island 12km northwest of Siwa Town and connected

---

GAY SIWA?

Much attention has been paid to Siwa's unique history of intimate male relations. Back when Siwa's citizens still lived in Shali fort, young men between the ages of 20 and 40 were expected to spend their nights outside the fortress to tend to the fields and protect the town from attack. These men of Siwa had a notorious reputation, not only for their bravery (they were known as *zaggalah*, or 'club bearers'), but for their love of palm wine, music and openly gay relations. Single-sex marriages were still practised in Siwa right up until WWII, although they had been outlawed in Egypt decades earlier.

Even though Siwa has been listed as a place to visit in several gay travel directories, the situation today is quite different. Residents of Siwa vehemently deny that local gay men exist in their town, and international travellers coming to Siwa in hope of 'hooking up' have been faced with increasingly homophobic sentiments. Siwan men are not amused at being propositioned by passing strangers – they are much more likely than foreigners to bear the brunt of antigay attitudes. Violent attacks on local men accused of homosexuality are not unheard of.

by a causeway is one of the few places selling the amber nectar (for a whopping E£35 a bottle). There is some humble accommodation and a restaurant here, but its many shaded tables and chairs, paddle-boat rentals and sweet sunset vistas make it better suited for a day trip or picnic. You'll need your own transport to get here.

Right in town, **Zeytouna** (Map p360; central market sq) and **Ebad Alrahman** (Map p360; central market sq) are two cafes facing each other at opposite ends of the square and taking turns nightly to fill up with locals smoking *sheesha*, downing tea and slapping backgammon pieces with triumphant vigour. Their tables often spill out onto the town square.

SHOPPING

Siwa's rich culture is well represented by the abundance of traditional crafts that are still made for local use as well as for tourists. Unfortunately, an estimated 98% of the older artefacts have become collectors' items and been sold to collectors worldwide. These pieces of Siwan heritage may be lost, but young Siwan craftworkers are slowly starting to make the pieces again.

Siwans love to adorn themselves and they are second only to the Nubians in their quest for the biggest and most ornate pieces of jewellery to be found in Egypt. Siwan women only wear the heavy silver jewellery on special occasions these days, but several interesting pieces are still made. Siwan wedding dresses are famous for their red, orange, green and black embroidery, which is often embellished with shells and beads. The black silk *asherah nazitaf* and the white cotton *asherah namilal* dresses can be found at the shops.

Baskets woven from date-palm fronds are still made here by women and girls. You can spot old baskets by their finer workmanship and the use of silk or leather instead of vinyl and polyester. The *tarkamt*, a woven plate that features a red leather centre, is traditionally used for serving sweets, the larger *tghara* is used for storing bread, and smaller baskets include the *aqarush* and the red-and-green silk-tasselled *nedibash*.

Local clays are mixed with straw and coloured with pigment from Gebel Dakrur to make pottery water jugs, drinking cups and incense burners. The *maklay,* a round-bottomed cup, and the *adjra,* used for washing hands,

are among the most popular buys, as are *timjamait* (incense burners).

There has been an explosion of craft shops around Siwa Town in recent years catering to the tourist demand for this traditional handiwork. Most sell very similar items, but a good place to get an idea of prices and what's available is at the **Government Handcraft Shop** (Map p360; opposite mosque; ☺ 9am-4pm Sun-Thu). If you blink, however, you might miss its erratic opening hours. From there you can wander through the many other handicrafts shops and stalls in town to compare the quality of the craftsmanship, the range of what's available and prices. Happy haggling.

Siwa is also known for its dates and olives, available in shops around the main market square. Usually someone will open a jar so you can try the olives to find the variety you like. Everyone has a favourite brand of dates; Jawhara are particularly good.

Camera film, SD memory cards, and batteries can be bought at **Nada Studio Lab** (Map p360), just past the Telephone centrale on the main road out of Siwa Town.

GETTING THERE & AWAY
Bus

Buses depart from the bus stop opposite the tourist police station, although when you arrive you'll be let off the bus in the central market square. You can purchase tickets to Marsa Matruh, Alexandria or Cairo at the West Delta Bus Company ticket office at the bus stop. It's sensible to buy your ticket ahead of time, as buses are often full.

There are three daily buses to Alexandria (E£33 to E£35, eight hours), stopping at Marsa Matruh (E£15, four hours); these leave at 7am, 10am and 10pm. There's an extra daily bus leaving at 3pm in the winter and 5pm in the summer. There's a daily service just to Marsa Matruh at 1pm. Buses to Cairo (E£60) leave only on Monday, Thursday and Saturday, at 8pm.

Service Taxi

Microbuses going to Marsa Matruh leave from the main square near the King Fuad Mosque (Map p360). They are more frequent but not as comfortable as the West Delta bus; tickets cost the same (see above).

A new road linking the oases of Siwa and Bahariya began construction in 2005, but funds dried up the following year and any finishing date is now a distant mirage. The old road, which passes through some jaw-dropping desert landscapes, is asphalted, though you can't tell by the awful shape it's in, and a permit (see p357) is needed to drive along it. In winter a police escort on this route is also usually required. There are no buses or service taxis here, but Siwan drivers are willing to make the 10-hour trip for about E£1300 per car. If you do go, ensure that the vehicle is a roadworthy 4WD and that you have food and water.

To/From Libya

Though Siwa is only about 50km from the Libyan border, it's currently illegal to leave or enter either country along this stretch of the frontier. Even if you're heading for the Libyan oasis of Jaghbub, which is closer to Siwa than any sizeable Egyptian town, you must travel north to the Mediterranean coast and cross at Sallum (see p405). Thanks to land mines scattered along the border west of Siwa, this rule is unlikely to change soon.

GETTING AROUND
Bicycle

Bicycles are one of the best ways to get around and can be rented from several sources, including most hotels and a number of shops dotted around the town centre. Getting a bike from one of the bicycle repair shops (see Map p360) gives you a better chance of finding a bike in good condition. The going rate is E£10 to E£15 per day.

Donkey Cart

Donkey carts, *careta*s, are a much-used mode of transport for Siwans and can be a more amusing, if slower, way to get around than bicycles or cars. Some of the boys who drive the carts speak English and can be fierce hagglers. Expect to pay about E£30 for two to three hours or E£10 for a short trip.

Motorcycle

Though not as enjoyable or tranquil as bicycles, motorbikes can also be rented from enterprising locals and can help you visit a lot more sights if you are short on time. You can pick one up from the bike shop next to Al-Babinshal Hotel, or at Palm Trees Hotel (p361). Expect to pay between E£100 and E£200 per day.

Service Taxi

Pick-up trucks serve as communal taxis linking Siwa Town with the surrounding villages. To get to Bilad ar-Rum costs E£1 each way; closer destinations are 50pt. If you want to hire your own to get to more remote sites, Mahdi Hweiti at the tourist office will be able to help, or head for the petrol station and talk directly to drivers. One reliable, English-speaking driver with a good-quality vehicle is Anwar Mohammed (☎ 012 687 3261). Prices are per truck, not per passenger, and depend on the duration of the trip, the distance to be covered and, of course, haggling skills.

BEYOND SIWA

QARA OASIS

About 120km northeast of Siwa, near the Qattara Depression, is another oasis, Qara. This remote oasis is home to 317 Berbers who, like the Siwans, built their fortresslike town on top of a mountain. According to legend, the harsh environment and scarce resources in the area meant that whenever a child was born in Qara an older person would have to leave in order to keep the population at a sustainable level. Whether or not this was ever true, it is no longer practised, although the Qarans remain small in number and their life is harsh. Unlike in Siwa, the old fortress is still inhabited, but an increasing number of new concrete houses are being built down below. To get there, take the narrow asphalt road that branches off the Siwa–Marsa Matruh road at the rest house, 150km from Siwa. You can either rent a pick-up to take you there for about E£400 or talk to the many people in town offering desert safaris. For more information, see p359.

GREAT SAND SEA

One of the world's largest dune fields, the Great Sand Sea straddles Egypt and Libya, stretching over 800km from its northern edge near the Mediterranean coast south to Gilf Kebir. Covering a colossal 72,000 sq km, it contains some of the largest recorded dunes in the world, including one that is 140km long. Crescent, *seif* (sword) and parallel wavy dunes are found here in abundance (see boxed text, p347) and have challenged desert travellers and explorers for hundreds of years. The Persian king Cambyses is thought to have lost an army here (see boxed text, p345), while the WWII British Long Range Desert Group spent months trying to find a way through the impenetrable sands to launch surprise attacks on the German army. Aerial surveys and expeditions have helped the charting of this vast expanse, but it remains one of the least-explored areas on the planet.

The Great Sand Sea is not a place to go wandering on a whim, and you will need military permits as well as good preparation. Guides will take you to the edges of the Great Sand Sea from Siwa and many safari outfits will take you on expeditions that skirt the area (see p328). Remember that you don't need to penetrate far into the desert to feel the isolation, beauty and enormous scale of this amazing landscape.

Alexandria & the Mediterranean Coast

The boundaries of Northern Egypt run smack bang into this dazzling 500km stretch of the Mediterranean seaboard. Here, the fabled city of Alexandria takes its rightful place as the cultural jewel in the coastal crown, while elsewhere the sea's turquoise waters lap up against pristine but mostly deserted shores. It has been dealt the short straw in life-giving fresh water, and Egyptian holidaymakers, and a few intrepid travellers, have only recently begun to discover the potential of its untouched beaches.

Alexandria wins the unfortunate accolade of being the 'greatest historical city with the least to show for it'. Although it was once the home of near-mythical historical figures and Wonders of the World, only fragmented memories of Alexandria's glorious ancient past remain. Today, however, the city is too busy gussying up its graceful 19th-century self to lament what's been and gone. The town shivers at the thought of its own potential: its streets and cafes buzz with the boundless energy of a new wave of creative youth.

Though the Nileside port of nearby Rosetta (Ar-Rashid) once rivalled Alexandria during that town's more woeful days, the town is most famous for the black-stone key that deciphered hieroglyphics and was unearthed here. Halfway across the coast to Libya, the memorials of El Alamein loom as solemn reminders of the lives lost during the North Africa campaigns of WWII. Meanwhile, not far off, a battalion of resorts offers a white-sand beach distraction from too much wartime reflection. Slumbering on a marvellous, aqua-lined bay for three-quarters of the year, Marsa Matruh screams into life in the summer months as half of the Nile Valley drops in for a visit.

HIGHLIGHTS

- Soak in the 19th-century grandeur through a puff of *sheesha* (water pipe) smoke or a kick-start-strong coffee at one of Alexandria's beautiful **period cafes** (see boxed text, p388)

- Try to grapple with the immense amount of ancient history made in Alexandria at the city's impressive **Alexandria National Museum** (p375)

- Wander down the dusty, donkey-filled streets of **Rosetta** (Ar-Rashid; p393) and admire the beautifully restored Ottoman architecture of this once-important seaport

- Be reminded of the ultimate toll paid by soldiers on all sides of the WWII North Africa campaign at **El Alamein** (p396)

- Soak in the stunning white sands and aqua waters of the *Dr Jekyll and Mr Hyde* town of **Marsa Matruh** (p401), a comatose hamlet in the low season or a heaving holiday metropolis in the summer months

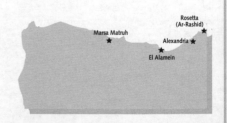

ALEXANDRIA

📞 03 / pop 4.1 million

The city of Alexandria (Al-Iskendariyya) is the stuff that legends are made of: the city was founded by none other than Alexander the Great; sassy queen Cleopatra made this the seat of her throne; the entrance to its harbour was marked by the towering Pharos lighthouse, one of the Seven Wonders of the World; and its Great Library of Alexandria was renowned as the ultimate archive of ancient knowledge. Alas, fate dealt the city a spate of cruel blows: today no sign remains of the great Alexander; the city of Cleopatra's day has been mostly swallowed up by the ocean; the Pharos lighthouse collapsed long ago; and the literary treasures of the Great Library were set to numerous torchings. To add insult to injury, Egypt's consequent Muslim rulers moved the capital to nearby Cairo, ignobly thrusting the once influential metropolis into near obscurity for centuries.

In the 19th century a cosmopolitan renaissance had Alexandria flirting with European-style decadence, but it was cut short in the 1950s by Nasser's wave of change. Today, even though the city plays second fiddle to Cairo, modern Alexandria feels like a teenager eager to forge its own identity. The daring new library of Alexandria signalled a brave new leap into modernity, the first tentative steps of a city ready to revamp itself for the future. This town is also swooping in on the role of Egypt's culture vulture – legions of young artists and writers are finding their voices and new cutting-edge venues are providing a stage for their prolific output. But whether the new Alexandria forges its own unique path forward, or follows the West's shopping-mall model of a brave new (air-conditioned) world, remains to be seen.

Alexandria, the famed ancient metropolis of the ages, is not easy to find in the city that bears its name today. Nevertheless, the city doffs its hat to an impressive past and successfully marries its 19th-century grandeur to the vibrancy of an energetic youth. This is an ideal place to spend a few days sipping coffee in grand, old-world cafes at breakfast; pondering the city's glorious past at its copious museums before or after lunch; and topping it all off with mouth-watering fish fare over sunset-lit dinners.

HISTORY

Alexandria's history is the bridging link between the time of the pharaohs and the days of Islam. The city gave rise to the last great Pharaonic dynasty (the Ptolemies), provided the entry into Egypt for the Romans and nurtured early Christianity before rapidly fading into near obscurity when Islam's invading armies passed it by to set up camp on a site along the Nile that later became Cairo.

The city was initiated with the conquests of Alexander the Great, who arrived from Sinai having had his right to rule Egypt confirmed by the priests of Memphis. Here, on the shores of his familiar sea, he chose a fishing village as the site for a new city that he hoped would become a bridge between the old Pharaonic world and the new world of the Greeks. Foundations were laid in 331 BC and almost immediately Alexander departed for Siwa in order to consult the famous oracle before then marching for Persia. His conquering army went as far as India, and after his death at Babylon in 323 BC, the rule of Egypt fell to the Macedonian general Ptolemy. Ptolemy won a struggle over Alexander's remains and had them buried in Alexandria.

Ptolemy masterminded the development of the new city, filling it with architecture to rival Rome or Athens in a deliberate attempt to establish it as the cultural and political centre of his empire. To create a sense of continuity between his rule and that of the Pharaonic dynasties, Ptolemy made Alexandria look at least superficially Egyptian by adorning the city with sphinxes, obelisks and statues scavenged from the old sites of Memphis and Heliopolis. The city developed into a major port and became an important halt on the trade routes between Europe and Asia. Its newfound economic wealth was equally matched by its intellectual standing. Its famed library (see boxed text, p382) stimulated some of the great advances of the age: this was where Herophilus discovered that the head, not the heart, is the seat of thought; Euclid developed geometry; Aristarchus discovered that the earth revolves around the sun; and Erastothenes calculated the earth's circumference. A grand tower, the Pharos (see boxed text, p380), one of the Seven Wonders of the World, was built on an island just offshore and acted as both a beacon to guide ships entering the booming harbour and, at a deeper level, as an ostentatious symbol of the city's greatness.

During the reign of its most famous regent, Cleopatra, Alexandria rivalled Rome in everything but military power – a situation that Rome found intolerable and was eventually forced to act upon. Under Roman control, Alexandria remained the capital of Egypt, but during the 4th century AD, civil war, famine and disease ravaged the city's populace and it never regained its former glory. Alexandria's decline was sealed when the conquering Muslim armies swept into Egypt in the 7th century and bypassed Alexandria in favour of a new capital further south on the Nile.

The city went into slow decline all through the Middle Ages and was even superseded in importance as a seaport by the nearby town of Rosetta. Over the centuries its monuments were destroyed by earthquakes and their ruins quarried for building materials, so much so that one of the greatest cities of the classical world was reduced to little more than a fishing village (now Anfushi) on the peninsula between two harbours, with a population of less than 10,000.

The turning point in Alexandria's fortunes came with Napoleon's invasion of 1798; recognising the city's strategic importance, he initiated its revival. During the subsequent reign of the Egyptian reformist Mohammed Ali, a new town was built on top of the old one. Alexandria once more became one of the Mediterranean's busiest ports and attracted a cosmopolitan mix of people, among them wealthy Turkish-Egyptian traders, Jews, Greeks, Italians and many others from around the Mediterranean. Multicultural, sitting on the foundations of antiquity, perfectly placed on the overland route between Europe and the East, and growing wealthy from trade, Alexandria took on an almost mythical quality and served as the muse for a new string of poets, writers and intellectuals. But the wave of anticolonial, pro-Arab sentiment that swept Colonel Gamal Abdel Nasser to power in 1952 also spelt the end for Alexandria's cosmopolitan communities. Those foreigners who didn't stream out of the country in the wake of King Farouk's yacht found themselves forced out a few years later in the wake of the Suez Crisis, when Colonel Nasser confiscated many foreign properties and nationalised many of the foreign-owned businesses.

Since that time the character of the city has changed completely. In the 1940s some 40% of the city's population was made up of foreigners, while today most of its residents are native Egyptians. And where there were 300,000 residents in the 1940s, Alexandria is now home to more than four million, a figure swelled by the steady drift of people from the country to the city.

ORIENTATION

Modern Alexandria lies protracted along a curving shoreline, stretching for 20km and rarely extending more than 3km inland. The centre of the city arcs around the Eastern Harbour, almost enclosed by two spindly promontories. The city's main tram station, Mahattat Ramla (Ramla Station) on Midan Ramla, where most lines terminate, is considered the epicentre of the city. Two of the city centre's main shopping streets, Sharia Saad Zaghloul and Sharia Safiyya Zaghloul, run off this square. Just west of the tram station is the larger and more formal square, Midan Saad Zaghloul, with a popular garden facing the seafront. Around these two *midan*s (city squares) are the central shopping areas, the tourist office, restaurants and the majority of the cheaper hotels.

To the west of this central area are the older quarters of the city, notably Anfushi, and further on the city's best beaches at the more upmarket resort town of Agami. Heading east, a succession of newer districts stretches along the coast to the upmarket residential area of Rushdy, the trendy suburbs of San Stefano and further on to Montazah, with its palace and gardens, which marks the eastern limits of the city. The Corniche (Al-Corniche) is the long coastal road that connects nearly all parts of the city, though crossing it involves playing chicken with swarms of hurtling buses and taxis.

If you're spending significant time in the city, the street map produced by Mohandes Mostafa el Fadaly (see Maps, opposite) is decidedly useful.

INFORMATION
Bookshops

All of the following stock only a smattering of fiction and nonfiction books in English.

ACML Bookshop (Map pp372–3; ☎ 545 3714; 181 Ahmed Shawky; ⏰ 10am-9pm Sat-Thu) Has one of the better selections in Alexandria.

ALEXANDRIA IN...

Two Days

Start day one sipping coffee at one of the city's many time-warp **period cafes** (see boxed text, p388), then get a taste of the past at the excellent **Alexandria National Museum** (p375). Follow that up with lunch at the unmissable **Mohammed Ahmed** (p386), deservedly regarded as the king of *fuul* (fava beans cooked with garlic and garnished with olive oil and spices) and *ta'amiyya*. Having gotten a view of the city's past, explore the future at the iconic **Bibliotecha Alexandrina** (p380), checking out several of its must-see museums and exhibits. Heading along the Corniche, stop at **El Qobesi** (p388) for the best mango juice ever. Wander **Fort Qaitbey** (p380), feeling the echoes of the legendary Pharos. Hungry, treat yourself to a fish dinner at one of Alexandria's marvellous local seafood restaurants, such as **Farag** (p387) or **Abu Ashraf** (p387), then work off supper by joining the crowds for a leisurely stroll down the **Corniche**. Finally, head to the wonderful seaside *ahwa* (coffeehouse) **Arous el Zilzila** (p389), to relax with a nightcap of *sheesha* (water pipe), tea and good conversation.

On day two, get an early start with an aromatic and strong Turkish coffee at the gorgeous **Sofianopoulos Coffee Store** (see boxed text, p388). Then, head to the **Roman Amphitheatre** and **Villa of the Birds** (p376) to see its exquisite ancient mosaics. After a quick pick-me-up meal at **Taverna** (p386), venture to the Roman **Catacombs of Kom ash-Shuqqafa** (p377). Get a sense of Alexandria's recent multicultural past by arranging a visit to the **Eliyahu Hanavi synagogue** (p378), then chow down on a spread of delectably grilled quail at **Malek es-Seman** (p386). Finish off your day with an evening drink at the atmospheric **Cap d'Or** (p389) or **Centro de Portugal** (p389), or, if you're in the mood for more quality *sheesha* time, head to the excellent **El Rehany** (p389).

Four Days

Follow the two-day itinerary, then add a day trip to **Rosetta** (p393) and the mouth of the Nile, and on the fourth day head to **El Alamein** (p396) and spend the afternoon on the beach in **Sidi Abdel Rahman** (p399).

Al Maaref Bookshop (Map p385; ☎ 487 3303; 32 Midan Saad Zaghloul; ☼ 10am-9.30pm Mon-Sat) Has a decent English-language section, including many titles on Egypt and Alexandria.

Cultural Centres

Many of the city's cultural centres operate libraries and organise occasional films, lectures, exhibitions and performances. Take along your passport as you may have to show it before entering.

Alexandria Centre of Arts (Map p385; ☎ 495 6633; Info@aca.org.eg; 1 Tariq al-Horreyya; ☼ 9am-9pm Sat-Thu) This active cultural centre, housed in a whitewashed villa, hosts contemporary arts exhibitions, poetry readings and occasional free concerts in its theatre. There is also an art studio, library and cinema on the 1st floor.

American Cultural Center (Map pp374-5; ☎ 486 1009; www.usembassy.egnet.net; 3 Sharia al-Pharaana, Azarita; ☼ 10am-4pm Sun-Thu)

British Council (Map pp372-3; ☎ 545 6512; www .britishcouncil.org.eg; 11 Sharia Mahmoud Abu al-Ela, Kafr Abdu, Rushdy; ☼ 11am-7pm Sat-Thu)

French Cultural Centre (Map p385; ☎ 391 8952; 30 Sharia al-Nabi Daniel; ☼ 9am-9pm Mon-Sat) Has a bookstore with extensive French and some English-language titles.

Goethe Institut (Map pp374-5; ☎ 487 9870; www .goethe.de/kairo; 10 Sharia al-Batalsa, Azarita; ☼ 9am-1pm Mon-Thu, to 2pm Sun)

Internet Access

Internet cafes in Alexandria seem to have the lifespan of a fruit fly, though as soon as one closes another opens not too far away. Here are but a few.

Farous Net Café (Map p385; ☎ 497 6905; Tariq al-Horreyya; per hr E£3; ☼ 10am-midnight)

Hightop Internet Café (Map p385; ☎ 484 0192; 71 Sharia al-Nabi Daniel; per hr E£4)

MG@Net (Map p385; ☎ 480 6981; www.mgnetalex .com;10 Sharia Shohada; per hr E£3; ☼ 10am-1am)

Maps

Mohandes Mostafa el Fadaly (Map p385; 2nd fl, 49 Sharia Safiyya Zaghloul; ☼ 9am-4pm Sat-Thu) An engineer *(mohandes)* who created and sells a street map (E£25) of

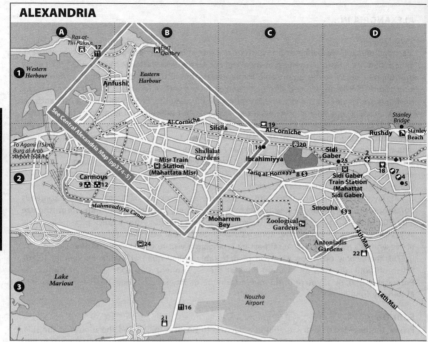

ALEXANDRIA

Alexandria, indispensable if you're spending any significant time in the city. Find Mostafa above the Mr Sanyo clothes store.

Medical Services

HOSPITALS

Al-Madina at-Tibiya (Map pp372-3; ☎ 543 2150/7402; Sharia Ahmed Shawky, Rushdy; ☯ 24hr) Well-equipped private hospital, also called Alexandria Medical City Hospital.

German Hospital (Map pp372-3; ☎ 584 0757; 56 Sharia Abdel Salaam Aarafa, Glymm; ☯ 8am-10pm) Near Saba Basha tram stop, line 2, and next to Al-Obeedi Hospital. Staffed by highly qualified doctors, with a day clinic for non-emergency patients.

PHARMACIES

There's no shortage of pharmacies around Midan Ramla, all with at least one English-speaking staff member.

Central Pharmacy (Map p385; ☎ 486 0744; 19 Sharia Ahmed Orabi; ☯ 9am-10pm Mon-Sat, 10am-1am Sun) This 100-year old establishment is worth visiting just for the soaring ceilings and beautiful display cabinets.

Khalil Pharmacy (Map p385; ☎ 480 6710; Sharia al-Ghorfa al-Tugareya; ☯ 9am-10pm Mon-Sat, 10am-10pm Sun) Next door to Drinkies.

Money

For changing cash or cashing travellers cheques it's simplest to use one of the many exchange bureaus on the side streets between Midan Ramla and the Corniche. Otherwise, try the following.

American Express (Amex; Map pp372-3; ☎ 420 2288; www.americanexpress.com.eg; Sharia 14th Mai, Elsaladya Bldg, Smouha; ☯ 9am-4pm Sun-Thu) This office is also a travel agency.

Thomas Cook (Map p385; ☎ 484 7830; www.thomas cookegypt.com; 15 Midan Saad Zaghloul; ☯ 8am-5pm)

ATMS

There are dozens of ATMs in central Alexandria, particularly on Sharia Salah Salem and Talaat Harb, the city's banking district. You can also find one at the following branch offices.

Banque du Caire Salah Salem (Map p385; 5 Sharia Salah Salem; ☎ 486 1245); Talaat Harb (Map p385; cnr Sharia Sisostris & Talaat Harb)

Barclays (Map p374-5; ☎ 16222; 11 Sharikat Misr, off Sharia Sultan Hussein, Azarita)

Credit Agricole (Map p385; ☎ 485 1790; 14 Sharia Salah Salem; ☯ 8.30am-2pm Sun-Thu)

ALEXANDRIA & THE MEDITERRANEAN COAST

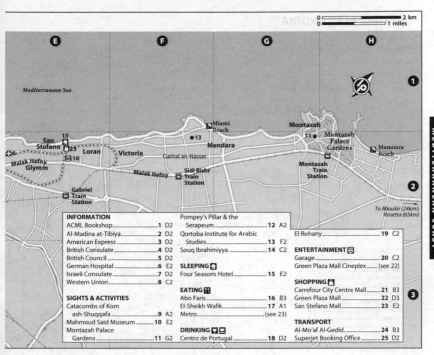

INFORMATION			Pompey's Pillar & the		
ACML Bookshop	1	D2	Serapeum	12	A2
Al-Madina at-Tibiya	2	D2	Qortoba Institute for Arabic		
American Express	3	D2	Studies	13	F2
British Consulate	4	D2	Souq Ibrahimiyya	14	C2
British Council	5	D2			
German Hospital	6	E2	SLEEPING		
Israeli Consulate	7	D2	Four Seasons Hotel	15	E2
Western Union	8	C2			
			EATING		
SIGHTS & ACTIVITIES			Abo Faris	16	B3
Catacombs of Kom			El-Sheikh Wafik	17	A1
ash-Shuqqafa	9	A2	Metro	(see 23)	
Mahmoud Said Museum	10	E2			
Montazah Palace			DRINKING		
Gardens	11	G2	Centro de Portugal	18	D2

El Rehany	19	C2
ENTERTAINMENT		
Garage	20	C2
Green Plaza Mall Cineplex	(see 22)	
SHOPPING		
Carrefour City Centre Mall	21	B3
Green Plaza Mall	22	D3
San Stefano Mall	23	E2
TRANSPORT		
Al-Mo'af Al-Gedid	24	B3
Superjet Booking Office	25	D2

HSBC (Map pp374-5; ☎ 487 2949; 47 Sharia Sultan Hussein; ◷ 8.30am-5pm Sun-Thu)
MIBank (Map p385; 45 Sharia Safiyya Zaghloul)

TRANSFERS
For receiving money from overseas or wiring money abroad, Western Union has two offices in town:
Western Union Tariq al-Horreyya (Map pp374-5; ☎ 420 1148; 281 Tariq al-Horreyya); Tariq al-Horreyya (Map pp372-3; ☎ 492 0900; 73 Tariq al-Horreyya)

Photography & Electronics
Kodak Express (Map p385; ☎ 486 4072; 63 Sharia Safiyya Zaghloul; ◷ 10am-11pm) Sells film and memory cards for digital cameras, and prints digital photos.
Radio Shack (Map p385; ☎ 480 0832; 68 Sharia Safiyya Zaghloul, ◷ 11am-midnight) Stocks standard electrical parts, and has a Vodafone desk for mobile services.

Post
The main post office is just east of Midan Orabi, and several other branches are dotted around the city.
DHL (Map p385; ☎ 485 1911; 9 Sharia Salah Salem; ◷ 9am-5pm Sat-Thu)

Express Mail Service (EMS; ◷ 8.30am-3pm Sat-Thu) At all post offices.
Main post office (Map p385; Sharia al-Bursa al-Qadima; ◷ 9am-9pm Sat-Thu)

Telephone
Menatel cardphones can be found all over the city, although the policy of placing them on street corners can make it hard to hear and be heard. Private call centres are everywhere, and are a much more convenient option. You can also buy an inexpensive cash line for your mobile; to work with a local SIM, your phone must be quad-band and unlocked.
Telephone centrale (Map p385; Sharia Saad Zaghloul; ◷ 8.30am-10pm)
Vodafone (Map p385; 68 Sharia Safiyya Zaghloul; ◷ 8.30am-10pm) Inside Radio Shack; sells cash (prepaid) SIM cards for E£20.

Tourist Offices
Mahattat Misr tourist office (Map pp374-5; ☎ 392 5985; Platform 1, Misr Train Station; ◷ 8.30am-6pm)
Main tourist office (Map p385; ☎ 485 1556; Midan Saad Zaghloul; ◷ 8.30am-6pm, reduced hours during Ramadan) Marginally useful.

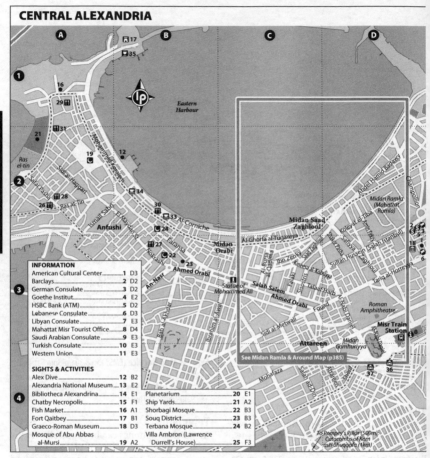

CENTRAL ALEXANDRIA

INFORMATION
American Cultural Center	**1** D3
Barclays	**2** D2
German Consulate	**3** D2
Goethe Institut	**4** E2
HSBC Bank (ATM)	**5** D2
Lebanese Consulate	**6** D3
Libyan Consulate	**7** E3
Mahattat Misr Tourist Office	**8** D4
Saudi Arabian Consulate	**9** E3
Turkish Consulate	**10** E3
Western Union	**11** E3

SIGHTS & ACTIVITIES
Alex Dive	**12** B2
Alexandria National Museum	**13** E2
Bibliotheca Alexandrina	**14** E1
Chatby Necropolis	**15** F1
Fish Market	**16** A1
Fort Qaitbey	**17** B1
Graeco-Roman Museum	**18** D3
Mosque of Abu Abbas al-Mursi	**19** A2
Planetarium	**20** E1
Ship Yards	**21** A2
Shorbagi Mosque	**22** B3
Souq District	**23** B3
Terbana Mosque	**24** B2
Villa Ambron (Lawrence Durrell's House)	**25** F3

See Midan Ramla & Around Map (p385)

Tourist police (Map p385; ☎ 485 0507) Upstairs from the main tourist office.

SIGHTS

The sights of Alexandria lie scattered along its extensive shore. As always, a good place to start is at the beginning: around Midan Ramla, the ancient heart of the city's many incarnations. From here you can explore the Alexandria National Museum, the Graeco-Roman Museum (if it's reopened), the Roman Amphitheatre, Pompey's Pillar and the Catacombs of Kom ash-Shuqqafa. Further afield, you can head west along the seafront to visit Fort Qaitbey, or go in the other direction to the Bibliotheca Alexandrina, the Mahmoud Said Museum and Montazah.

Ancient Alexandria

The history of ancient Alexandria borders on the mythical, a place of legends inspired by bedtime tales of Cleopatra, the Wonders of the World and that great library. Today a column, some catacombs and a few sculptures in the city's museums are the only tangible hints that it all might once have been real. All is not lost, however; thanks to ongoing archaeological research more and more evidence is being unearthed to give physical shape to the ancient city. While the Alexandria of Cleopatra's time lies buried 6m down, every now and then the city gives up more of its secrets as modern developers stumble across new antediluvian finds. In recent years underwater archaeology has been

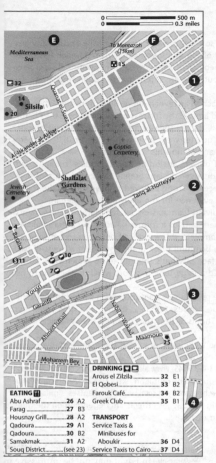

EATING ⊞
Abu Ashraf 26 A2
Farag 27 B3
Housnay Grill 28 A2
Qadoura 29 A1
Qadoura 30 B2
Samakmak 31 A2
Souq District ...... (see 23)

DRINKING ⊡⊡
Arous el Zilzila 32 E1
El Qobesi 33 B2
Farouk Café 34 B2
Greek Club 35 B1

TRANSPORT
Service Taxis &
Minibuses for
Aboukir 36 D4
Service Taxis to Cairo ... 37 D4

all the rage and has produced some dramatic discoveries (see boxed text, p376).

Nevertheless, Alexandria remains a city for nostalgics with a fertile imagination. The modern city, built directly on top of the ancient one, often follows the ancient street pattern. The street now known as Tariq al-Horreyya was the ancient Canopic Way, extending from the city's Gate of the Sun in the east to the Gate of the Moon in the west. Two thousand years ago Sharia al-Nabi Daniel was called the Street of the Soma. Standing at the intersection of Sharia al-Nabi Daniel and Tariq al-Horreyya (Map p385), you find yourself at the crossroads at the heart of the ancient city; according to the 1st-century-AD geographer Strabo, this was where Alexander's

tomb once stood. Heinrich Schliemann, who came to Alexandria in 1888 after rediscovering the ruins of Troy, believed that the tomb lay underneath the modern and fairly unnoteworthy Mosque of An-Nabi Daniel (Map p385). Recent trial excavations revealed that the mosque does indeed rest on the site of a 4th-century Roman temple, but religious authorities have placed a halt on any further digging. Since then some respected archaeologists have turned their attention elsewhere. The most likely location is now believed to be the intersection of Tariq al-Horreyya and a street known as R1, which runs through the middle of the Shatby necropolis. Here, where there are extensive Greek graveyards, archaeologists have discovered an impressive alabaster antechamber, which would originally have led to a massive tumulus tomb.

ALEXANDRIA NATIONAL MUSEUM
The excellent **Alexandria National Museum** (Map pp374-5; ☎ 483 5519; www.alexmuseum.org.eg; 110 Tariq al-Horreyya; adult/student E£35/20; ⊙ 9am-4.30pm) sets new benchmarks for summing up Alexandria's past. With a small, thoughtfully selected and well-labelled collection singled out from Alexandria's other museums, it does a sterling job of relating the city's history from antiquity until the modern period. Housed in a beautifully restored Italianate villa, it stocks several thousand years of Alexandrian history, arranged chronologically over three cryogenically air-conditioned floors.

The ground floor is dedicated to Graeco-Roman times, where highlights include a sphinx and other sculptures found during underwater excavations at Aboukir. Look for the small statue of the Greek god Harpocrates with a finger to his lips (representing silence), who was morphed from the original Egyptian god Horus. Also check out the beautiful statue of a Ptolemaic queen, with Egyptian looks and a Hellenistic body. The basement covers the Pharaonic period, with finds from all over Egypt, including an unusual New Kingdom pottery jar with the god Bes and the head of Queen Hatshepsut in painted limestone. The top floor displays artefacts from Islamic and modern periods, with coins, Ottoman weapons and jewels. Early coexistence of Alexandria's major religions is represented by a carved wooden cross encircled by a crescent. Well-written panels on the walls provide useful

NAUTICAL ARCHAEOLOGY

Alexandria has sunk 6m to 8m since antiquity, so most of what remains of the ancient city lies hidden beneath the modern city or the waters of the Mediterranean. On land, much has been destroyed as the city has grown. Rescue archaeologists are allowed to excavate before a new building, tunnel or road project goes ahead, but they are rarely given enough time – usually only a few weeks, or months at most.

But underwater the story is different and each year reveals more finds from the Ptolemaic period. So far, exploration has been concentrated around the fortress of Qaitbey where the Pharos (see boxed text, p380) is believed to have stood, the southeastern part of the Eastern Harbour, where parts of the submerged Ptolemaic royal quarter were found, and Aboukir (p393), where remains of the two sunken cities of Herakleion and Menouthis were found.

The Qaitbey dive has recorded hundreds of objects, including sphinx bodies, columns and capitals, and fragments of obelisks. Divers also discovered giant granite blocks broken as if by a fall from a great height, and, more recently, pieces of stone believed to have formed the frame of a massive gateway – all more circumstantial evidence for the likely end of the Pharos.

In the royal-quarter area, a French-Egyptian diving team has discovered platforms, pavements and red-granite columns that they speculate were part of a former palace ('Cleopatra's Palace', as it is being called), as well as a remarkably complete shipwreck carbon dated to between 90 BC and AD 130. In 1998 archaeologists raised a beautiful black-granite statue of a priest of Isis, followed by a diorite sphinx adorned with the face of what's thought to be Ptolemy XII, father of Cleopatra. And in December 2009 they raised a large temple pylon, which is believed to be part of the palace complex.

The most recent excavations in Aboukir have revealed *L'Orient* (Napoleon's flagship that sank in 1798); the city of Menouthis with a harbour, houses, temples, statues and gold jewellery; and another city believed to be Herakleion or Thonis, a port that guarded the Canopic branch of the Nile.

Some recovered treasures can be seen in the city's museums, and there are tentative plans for the world's first underwater museum. For now, it's possible to explore the submerged harbour sites through **Alex Dive** (Map pp374-5; ☎ 03-483 2045; www.alexandria-dive.com; Corniche, Anfushi), where a two-dive package costs US$100, with equipment rental an extra US$20. Another, newer company is **Blue Spot Divers** (☎ 961 1601; www.bluespotdivers.com), which organises similar trips. Several divers have reported that poor visibility in the bay (as little as 1m depending on the time of year) affected their enjoyment of the harbour dives.

---

insights into the life, art and beliefs of the Alexandrians through the centuries.

GRAECO-ROMAN MUSEUM

As part of Alexandria's effort to spruce itself up, many of its prime tourist attractions are undergoing renovation. Unfortunately, the wonderful **Graeco-Roman Museum** (Map pp374-5; ☎ 486 5820; 5 Al-Mathaf ar-Romani), normally home to one of the most extensive collections of Graeco-Roman art in the world, is one of them. There is no official completion date for the work, and the museum may be shuttered for the foreseeable future. Check with the tourist office for further information on opening dates.

ROMAN AMPHITHEATRE (KOM AL-DIKKA)

While the 13 white-marble terraces of the only **Roman Amphitheatre** (Map p385; ☎ 486 5106;

Sharia Yousef, off Midan Gomhuriyya; adult/student E£20/15; ⏰ 9am-5pm) in Egypt may not be impressive in scale, they remain a superbly preserved ode to the days of the centurion. This site was discovered when foundations were being laid for an apartment building on a site known unceremoniously as Kom al-Dikka (Mound of Rubble). Excavations continue to uncover more in the area; in early 2010 the ruins of a Ptolemaic-era temple were uncovered along with statues of gods and goddesses, including a number of the cat goddess Bastet.

In Ptolemaic times this area was known as the Park of Pan, a pleasure garden where citizens of Alexandria could indulge in various lazy pursuits. In the same complex is the **Villa of the Birds** (Map p385), a wealthy urban dwelling dating to the time of Hadrian (117–138 AD). Despite being redecorated at least four times in antiquity before being destroyed by fire in the 3rd century AD, its floor mosaic of pigeons, peacocks, quail, parrots and water hens remains astonishingly well preserved. Additional mosaics feature a panther, and a stylised flower design known as a rosette. To see the villa, buy a separate ticket (adult/student E£15/8) at the entrance to the amphitheatre.

POMPEY'S PILLAR & THE SERAPEUM

The massive 30m column that looms over the debris of the glorious ancient settlement of Rhakotis, the original township from which Alexandria grew, is known as **Pompey's Pillar** (Map pp372-3; ☎ 960 1315; Carmous; adult/student E£20/15; ◷ 9am-4.30pm). For centuries the column, hewn from red Aswan granite, has been one of the city's prime sights, a single, tapered shaft, 2.7m at its base and capped by a fine Corinthian capital. The column was named by travellers who remembered the murder of the Roman general Pompey by Cleopatra's brother, but an inscription on the base (presumably once covered with rubble) announces that it was erected in AD 291 to support a statue of the emperor Diocletian.

The column rises out of the disappointing ruins of the **Temple of Serapeum**, a magnificent structure that stood here in ancient times. It had 100 steps leading past the living quarters of the priests to the great temple of Serapis, the man-made god of Alexandria. Also here was the 'daughter library', the second great library of Alexandria, which was said to have contained copies and overflow of texts held in the Great Library of Alexandria, the Mouseion library (see boxed text, p382). These rolls could be consulted by anyone using the temple, making it one of the most important intellectual and religious centres in the Mediterranean. In AD 391, Christians launched a final assault on pagan intellectuals and destroyed the Serapeum and its library, leaving just the lonely pillar standing. The site is now little more than rubble pocked by trenches and holes with a few sphinxes (originally from Heliopolis), a surviving Nilometer and the pillar – the only ancient monument remaining whole and standing today in Alexandria.

It's possible to walk to the site from the square in front of Misr Train Station (about 1km) but taking a taxi is easier. Ask for it by the Arabic name, *amoud el sawari*. The fare should be E£5 to E£7 from Midan Saad Zaghloul.

CATACOMBS OF KOM ASH-SHUQQAFA

A short walk from Pompey's Pillar is **Kom ash-Shuqqafa** (Map pp372-3; ☎ 484 5800; Carmous; adult/student E£35/20; ◷ 9am-5pm). Discovered accidentally in 1900 when a donkey disappeared through the ground, these catacombs are the largest known Roman burial site in Egypt. This impressive feat of engineering was one of the last major works of construction dedicated to the religion of ancient Egypt. Demonstrating Alexandria's hallmark fusion of Pharaonic and Greek styles, the architects used a Graeco-Roman approach in their construction efforts. The catacombs consist of three tiers of tombs

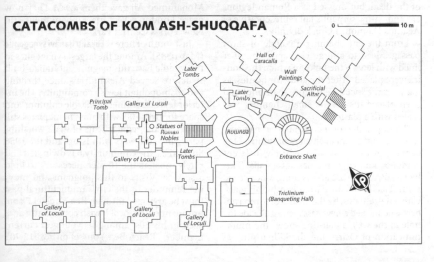

CATACOMBS OF KOM ASH-SHUQQAFA

0 — 10 m

Hall of Caracalla

Later Tombs

Wall Paintings

Later Tombs

Sacrificial Altar

Principal Tomb

Gallery of Loculi

Statues of Roman Nobles

Rotunda

Gallery of Loculi

Later Tombs

Entrance Shaft

Gallery of Loculi

Gallery of Loculi

Gallery of Loculi

Triclinium (Banqueting Hall)

and chambers cut into bedrock to a depth of 35m. The bottom level, some 20m below street level, is flooded and inaccessible but the areas above are impressive enough on their own.

Entering through a spiral staircase, the bodies of the dead would have been lowered on ropes down the centre of this circular shaft. The staircase leads off to a **rotunda** with a central well piercing down into the gloom of the flooded lower level. When the catacombs were originally constructed in the 2nd century AD, probably as a family crypt, the rotunda would have led to the **triclinium** (to your left) and principal tomb chamber (straight ahead) only. But over the 300 years that the tomb was in use, more chambers were hacked out until it had developed into a complex that could accommodate more than 300 corpses.

The triclinium was a banqueting hall where grieving relatives paid their last respects with a funeral feast. Mourners, who returned to feast after 40 days and again on each anniversary, reclined on the raised benches at the centre of the room around a low table. Tableware and wine jars were found when the chamber was excavated.

Back in the rotunda, head down the stairs to the **principal tomb**, the centrepiece of the catacombs. Here, an antechamber with columns and pediment leads through to an inner sanctum. The typical Alexandrian-style decoration shows a weird synthesis of ancient Egyptian, Greek and Roman funerary iconography. The doorway to the inner chamber is flanked by figures representing Anubis, the Egyptian god of the dead, but dressed as a Roman legionary and with a serpent's tail representative of Agathos Daimon, a Greek divinity.

From the antechamber a couple of short passages lead to a large U-shaped chamber lined with **loculi** – the holes in which the bodies were placed. After the body (or bodies, as many of the loculi held more than one) had been placed inside, the small chamber was sealed with a plaster slab.

Back up in the rotunda, four other passageways lead off to small clusters of tombs. One of these gives access to an entirely different complex, known as the **Hall of Caracalla**. This had its own staircase access (long-since caved in) and has been joined to Kom ash-Shuqqafa, which it pre-dates, by the efforts of tomb robbers who hacked a new passageway. Beside the hole in the wall, a painting shows the mummification of Osiris and the kidnapping of Persephone by Hades, illustrating ancient Egyptian and Greek funerary myths.

To walk to the catacombs from Pompey's Pillar, start from in front of the ticket office. With your back to the entrance, take the small street to the right, slightly uphill and away from the tram tracks. Follow this street for several hundred yards past a small mosque on the right, and the entrance to the catacombs is on the left.

Central Alexandria

'Like Cannes with acne' was Michael Palin's verdict on Alexandria's sweeping seafront **Corniche** (in his book *Around the World in 80 Days*). Right in the middle of the broad Corniche is the legendary **Cecil Hotel** (Map p385; see p386), overlooking Midan Saad Zaghloul. Built in 1930, it's an Alexandrian institution and a memorial to the city's belle époque, when guests included the likes of Somerset Maugham, Noel Coward and Winston Churchill, and the British Secret Service operated out of a suite on the 1st floor. The hotel was eternalised in Lawrence Durrell's *Alexandria Quartet*.

This area was roughly the site of the **Caesareum**, a large sanctuary and temple initiated by Cleopatra in honour of the deified Julius Caesar, and continued by Augustus, the first Roman ruler of Egypt. Two great obelisks brought up from Heliopolis marked the entrance to the sacred site. Long after the Caesareum disappeared the obelisks remained standing, until the 19th century when Mohammed Ali gave them away. They now grace London's Victoria Embankment and New York's Central Park.

Just south of here is **Eliyahu Hanavi synagogue** (Map p385). Among the largest synagogues in the Middle East, this magnificent Italian-built structure served Alexandria's once thriving and cosmopolitan Jewish community. The interior features immense marble columns and space for over 700, with brass nameplates still affixed to the regular seats of male worshippers. Since the wars with Israel and the 1956 Suez crisis, the community has dwindled and rarely musters the 10 men necessary to hold a service. Visits to this poignant and moving reminder of the city's multicultural past must be arranged through Ben Youssef Gaon, president of the local Jewish community and, aged in his 50s, among its youngest current members. Reach Ben Youssef on ☎ 012 703

1031; if you can't make contact this way, try asking at the front gate. A donation of E£10 to E£20 is appreciated but not required.

ANFUSHI

Charismatic Anfushi, the old Turkish part of town, was once where stuffy Alexandria came to let down its hair. While Midan Ramla and the Midan Tahrir area were developed along the lines of a European model in the 19th century, Anfushi remained untouched, an indigenous quarter standing in counterpoint to the new cosmopolitan city. This is where writer Lawrence Durrell's characters came in search of prostitutes and a bit of rough trade. Today it remains one of the poorest parts of the city, where a huge number of people live squeezed into atmospheric but old and decaying buildings, many of which seem to be teetering on the verge of collapse.

The beautiful little **Terbana Mosque** (Map pp374–5) stands at the junction of Sharia Faransa and Wekalet al Limon. This entire quarter, known as Gumruk, stands on land that was underwater in the Middle Ages. Late-17th-century builders managed to incorporate bits of ancient Alexandria in the mosque's structure, reusing two classical columns to support the minaret. The red-and-black-painted brickwork on the facade is typical of the Delta-style architecture. The **Shorbagi Mosque** (Map pp374–5; Sharia Nokrashi), nearby, is also built with salvaged remnants of antiquity.

Continuing on Sharia Faransa, the street narrows before opening suddenly onto a *midan* dominated by the stately **Mosque of Abu Abbas al-Mursi** (Map pp374–5), which was originally the tomb of a 13th-century Sufi saint from Murcia in Spain. Several successive mosques have been built and rebuilt on the site; though the current structure dates to the modern era, it's still an attractive octagonal building with a soaring central tower and interior decorated with eye-catching Islamic mosaics, tiling and woodwork. Under the main floor, devotees still flock to al-Mursi's shrine. As when visiting any mosque, leave your shoes at the entrance and slip the attendant a little baksheesh when you collect them.

Literary Alexandria

Many a traveller arrives at Misr Train Station with a copy of Lawrence Durrell's *Alexandria Quartet* in hand, for Alexandria is better known for its literature and writers than for any bricks-and-mortar monuments. Unlike the Alexandria of ancient days past, the Alexandria evoked by Durrell, EM Forster and the Alexandrian-Greek poet Constantine Cavafy can still be seen draped over the buildings of the city's central area.

Born of Greek parents, Cavafy (1863–1933) lived all but a few of his 70 years in Alexandria. In some poems he resurrects figures from the Ptolemaic era and classical Greece, in others he captures fragments of the city through its routines or chance encounters. He was born into one of the city's wealthiest families, but a reversal of fortune forced him to spend most of his life working as a clerk for the Ministry of Public Works, in an office above the Trianon cafe (see boxed text, p388).

Cavafy spent the last 25 years of his life in a 2nd-floor apartment, above a ground-floor brothel, on the former rue Lepsius (now Sharia Sharm el-Sheikh). With a Greek church (St Saba Church) around the corner and a hospital opposite, Cavafy thought this was the ideal place to live; somewhere that could cater for the flesh, provide forgiveness for sins and a place in which to die. The flat is now preserved as the **Cavafy Museum** (Map p385; ☎ 486 1598; 4 Sharia Sharm el-Sheikh; admission E£15, child free; ☯ 10am-4pm Tue-Sun), with two of the six rooms arranged as Cavafy kept them. Editions of the poet's publications and photocopies of his manuscripts, notebooks and correspondence lie spread out on tables throughout the rooms. Note that the museum is on a 2nd-floor walk-up and there are no elevators.

Cavafy was first introduced to the English-speaking world by EM Forster (1879–1970), the celebrated English novelist who'd already published *A Room with a View* and *Howards End* when he arrived in Alexandria in 1916. Working for the Red Cross, Forster spent three years in the city and, although it failed to find a place in his subsequent novels, he compiled what he referred to as an 'antiguide'. His *Alexandria: A History & Guide* was intended, he explained, as a guide to things not there, based on the premise that 'the sights of Alexandria are in themselves not interesting, but they fascinate when we approach them from the past'.

The guide provided an introduction to the city for Lawrence Durrell (1912–90), who arrived in Egypt 22 years after Forster's departure. Durrell had been evacuated from Greece and resented Alexandria, which he called a

---

THE PHAROS

The Egyptian coast was a nightmare for ancient sailors, the flat featureless shoreline making it hard to steer away from hidden rocks and sandbanks. To encourage trade, Ptolemy I ordered a great tower to be built, one that could be seen by sailors long before they reached the coast. After 12 years of construction, the tower, or Pharos, was inaugurated in 283 BC. The structure was added to until it acquired such massive and unique proportions that ancient scholars regarded it as one of the Seven Wonders of the World.

In its original form the Pharos was a simple marker, probably topped with a statue, as was common at the time. The tower became a lighthouse, so historians believe, in the 1st century AD, when the Romans added a beacon, probably an oil-fed flame reflected by sheets of polished bronze. According to descriptions from as late as the 12th century, the Pharos had a square base, an octagonal central section and a round top. Contemporary images of the Pharos still exist, most notably in a mosaic in St Mark's Basilica in Venice and another in a church in eastern Libya, and in two terracotta representations in Alexandria's Graeco-Roman Museum.

In all, the Pharos withstood winds, floods and the odd tidal wave for 17 centuries. However, in 1303 a violent earthquake rattled the entire eastern Mediterranean and the Pharos was finally toppled. A century later the sultan Qaitbey quarried the ruins for the fortress that still stands on the site.

'smashed up broken down shabby Neapolitan town'. But as visitors discover today, first impressions are misleading and between 1941 and 1945 Durrell found great distraction in the slightly unreal air of decadence and promiscuity engendered by the uncertainties of the ongoing desert war.

Committed fans of the *Alexandria Quartet* might like to search out **Villa Ambron** (Map pp374–5), where Durrell lived and wrote during the last two years of the war. Gilda Ambron, whose name appeared in the *Quartet*'s 'Balthazar', painted with her mother in a studio in the garden which they shared with their neighbour Clea Badaro, who provided inspiration for the character of Clea in the *Quartet*. Durrell's room was on top of an octagonal tower in the garden, though sadly the place has deteriorated badly over the past couple of decades. If you're in for a pilgrimage anyway, from Misr Train Station walk southeast down Sharia Moharrem Bey, then at the little square at the end turn left onto Sharia Nabil al-Wakad. Sharia Maamoun is about 200m along on the right. Villa Ambron is at No 19.

Fort Qaitbey

The Eastern Harbour is dominated by the fairy-tale-perfect **Fort Qaitbey** (Map pp374-5; ☎ 486 5106; Eastern Harbour; adult/student E£25/15; ⏰ 9am-4pm). Built on a narrow peninsula by the Mamluk sultan Qaitbey in AD 1480, it sits on the remains of the legendary Pharos lighthouse (see boxed text, above).

The lighthouse, which had been in use for some 17 centuries, was finally destroyed by an earthquake and was in ruins for more than 100 years when Qaitbey ordered the fortification of the city's harbour. Material from the fallen Pharos was reused, and if you get close to the outer walls you can pick out some great pillars of red granite, which in all likelihood came from the ancient lighthouse. Other parts of the ancient building are scattered around the nearby seabed.

The fort has been renovated and is now open to the public. It makes for a pleasant walk and the view back across the harbour is spectacular, with a foreground of colourful bobbing fishing boats and, in the distance, sunlike disk of the new library. There's also a lively fish market nearby (see p382).

From Midan Ramla, it's a 30- to 45-minute walk along the Corniche. Otherwise take yellow tram 15 from Midan Ramla or flag down any of the microbuses barrelling along the Corniche. A taxi should cost E£5.

Eastern Suburbs
BIBLIOTHECA ALEXANDRINA

Alexandria's ancient library was one of the greatest of all classical institutions (see boxed text, p382), and while replacing it might seem a Herculean task, the new **Bibliotheca Alexandrina** (Map pp374-5; ☎ 483 9999; www .bibalex.org; Corniche al-Bahr, Shatby; adult/student E£10/5; ⏰ 11am-7pm Sun-Thu, 3-7pm Fri & Sat) manages it with aplomb. Opened in 2002, this impressive piece of modern architecture is a deliberate attempt to rekindle the brilliance of the original centre of learning and culture. The complex has become one of Egypt's major cultural venues and a stage for numerous international performers.

The building takes the form of a gigantic angled discus embedded in the ground, evoking a second sun rising out of the Mediterranean. The granite exterior walls are carved with letters, pictograms, hieroglyphs and symbols from more than 120 different human scripts. Inside, the jaw-dropping main reading room can accommodate eight million books and 2500 readers under its sloping roof, with windows specially designed to let sunlight flood in but keep out rays that might harm the collection.

In addition to the main reading room, the library boasts a huge array of diversions: three permanent museums, four specialised libraries, a planetarium, a conference centre, temporary and permanent exhibitions, and a full schedule of events. To fully explore this very worthy attraction, you should allot half a day, though to gape at the astounding main reading room and do a tour, you'll need an hour or so.

The **Manuscript Museum** contains ancient texts, antiquarian books and maps, including a copy of the only surviving scroll from the ancient library. The **Antiquities Museum** holds some overspill from the Graeco-Roman Museum, including a fine Roman mosaic of a dog that was discovered when the foundations of the library were dug. The **History of Science Museum**, underneath the Planetarium, is targeted at children of school age.

The four specialised libraries are a children's library for ages six to 11; a youth library for ages 11 to 17; a multimedia library; and a library for the blind.

Regular exhibitions include **Impressions of Alexandria**, which does a sterling job of tracing the city's long history through drawings, maps and early photographs. There's also a video program on Egyptian history called the Culturama, displayed on nine screens, and, most recently added, an exhibition on Anwar Sadat.

The **Planetarium** (☎ 483 9999, ext 1451; admission E£25; ☽ shows at 11am, noon & 1pm Sat-Mon & Wed-Thu, plus 4pm & 5pm Thu-Fri) is a futuristic neon-lit sphere looming on the plaza in front of the library, like a mini Death Star from *Star Wars*.

It shows 3-D films on a rotating schedule (available on the library website), and has an Exploratorium as well as the aforementioned History of Science Museum.

Tickets to the library can be bought outside the main entrance, where all bags must be checked. The basic E£10 ticket includes free guided tours, entrance to the main reading room and any free exhibits or events. Hi-tech PDA (personal digital assistant) guides are also available in English, Arabic and French.

A combined ticket including the Antiquities and Manuscript Museums, but not the Planetarium, is E£45. You can also buy tickets to each of these individually at their respective ticket offices.

Note that while the library has a wide range of kid-friendly activities and diversions, little ones under the age of six are not admitted to the library complex. Helpfully, day care is available from 11am to 4pm daily except Friday and Saturday. The library is right on the Corniche, and you can easily get there by taxi or microbus.

MAHMOUD SAID MUSEUM

He might be little known outside his home country, but Mahmoud Said (1897–1964) was one of Egypt's finest 20th-century artists. A judge by profession, he moonlighted as a painter and became a key member of a group of sophisticates devoted to forging an Egyptian artistic identity in the 1920s and 1930s. Said's work has echoes of the past (some of his portraits bear resemblance to the Graeco-Roman Fayoum Portraits; see boxed text, p208), but he also blended European and American influences, at times experimenting with cubism and social realism. The **Mahmoud Said Museum** (Map pp372-3; ☎ 582 1688; 6 Sharia Mohammed Said Pasha, Gianaclis; adult/student E£10/5; ☽ 9am-1.30pm & 5-9pm Sat-Thu) presents about 40 of his works housed in the beautiful Italianate villa in which he once lived.

To get here take tram 2 from Midan Ramla to the San Stefano stop, then cross the tracks and go up the steps to the raised road. Go right and Sharia Mohammed Said Pasha is a short distance away on the left.

MONTAZAH PALACE GARDENS

Khedive Abbas Hilmy (1892–1914) built Montazah as his summer palace, a refuge

THE GREAT LIBRARY OF ALEXANDRIA

The original Library of Alexandria was the greatest repository of books and documents in all of antiquity. Ptolemy I established the library in 283 BC as part of a larger research complex known as the Mouseion ('Shrine of the Muses', the source of today's word 'museum'). This dedicated centre of learning housed more than 100 full-time scholars and boasted lecture areas, gardens, a zoo, shrines and the library itself. Uniquely, this was one of the first major 'public' libraries and was open to all persons with the proper scholarly qualifications.

Demetrius Phalereus, a disciple of Aristotle, was charged with governing the library and together with Ptolemy I and his successors established the lofty goal of collecting copies of all the books in the world. Manuscripts found on ships arriving at Alexandria's busy port were confiscated by law and copied, and merchants were sent to scour the markets of other Mediterranean cities looking for tomes of all descriptions. Most books back then consisted of papyrus scrolls, often translated into Greek, and rolled and stored in the library's many labelled pigeonholes. At its height the library was said to contain more than 700,000 works, which indicated some duplication as this was believed to be more than the number of published works in existence. The library soon exceeded its capacity and a 'daughter library' was established in the Temple of Serapeum (see p377) to stock the overflow. The vast collection established Alexandria's position as the pre-eminent centre of culture and civilisation in the world.

It is uncertain exactly who was responsible for the destruction of the ancient world's greatest archives of knowledge, though there are several suspects. Julius Caesar is the first. Caesar set fire to Alexandria's harbour, which also engulfed the part of the city the library stood in, in his scrap with Pompey in 48 BC. In AD 270 Zenobia, Queen of Palmyra (now Syria), had captured Egypt and clashed with Roman emperor Aurelian here, the resulting siege destroying more of the library. At this time Alexandria's main centre of learning moved to the 'daughter library'. Early Christians are next in line for the blame: the daughter library, located in the Temple of Serapeum, was finally destroyed as part of an antipagan purge led by Christian Roman Emperor Theodosius in AD 391.

when Cairo became too hot. Sited on a rocky bluff overlooking the sea, it's designed in a pseudo-Moorish style, which has been given a Florentine twist with the addition of a tower modelled on one at the Palazzo Vecchio. Now used by Egypt's president, the palace is off-limits to the public but the surrounding lush groves and **gardens** (Map pp372-3; admission E£5), planted with pines and palms, are accessible. They're popular with courting couples and picnicking locals. There's also an attractive sandy cove here with a semiprivate beach well suited to kids (E£13 to use it, although it's not particularly clean), and an eccentric Victorian-style bridge running out to a small island. If you ignore the fast-food restaurants, it makes a pleasant escape from the city centre's traffic and build-up. A second royal residence, known as the Salamlek and built in an Austrian style, has been converted into a luxury hotel.

The simplest way to get here is to stand on the Corniche or on Tariq al-Horreyya and flag down a microbus; when it slows, shout 'Montazah' and if it's going that way (and most of them are), it'll stop and you can jump on.

Souqs

Although you won't find the sort of antediluvian bazaars here that you do in Cairo, Alexandria has several busy souqs (markets) that are ideal spots for people-gazing. **Souq Ibrahimiyya** (Map pp372-3; Sharia Omar Lofty) is one of our favourite little markets in town for peeking into daily Egyptian life as it goes about its business. Down several tiny, covered side streets near the Sporting Club, it's packed to the brim with bright fruits and vegetables, piles of still-wet seafood, and stalls selling all kinds of clucking poultry and meats, both before and after they've seen the butcher's block. It's best in the morning, when the vendors are at their most vocal and enthusiastic.

For a city that devours more fish than a hungry seal, you'd expect to find a pretty impressive fish market – and Alexandria delivers. The **fish market** (Map pp374-5; Qasr Ras at-Tin) at the northern tip of Anfushi bustles daily with flapping seafood that's literally just been thrown off the boat. Here, vendors belt out the prices of their wares, while ever-sceptical buyers prod the merchandise and ponder the quality of the catch of the day. Be sure to get here early, when the market is at its bustling best, as things die down by midmorning.

At the southwestern corner of Midan Tahrir, the battered, grand architecture switches scale to something more intimate as you enter the city's main **souq district** (Map pp374–5). Sharia Nokrashi runs for about a kilometre and is one long, heaving bustle of produce, fish and meat stalls, bakeries, cafes and sundry shops selling every imaginable household item. Sharia Faransa begins with cloth, clothes and dressmaking accessories. The tight weave of covered alleys running off to the west are known as Zinqat as-Sittat, or 'the alley of the women'. Here you'll find buttons, braid, baubles, bangles, beads and much more, from junk jewellery to frighteningly large padded bras. Beyond the haberdashery you will find the gold and silver dealers, then herbalists and spice vendors.

Beaches

If you want to get in the water, there are plenty of public and private beaches along Alexandria's waterfront. But the shoreline between the Eastern Harbour and Montazah can be grubby and packed sardine-full in summer, and most locals head for beaches on the North Coast for the high season. If you're seeking an unspoilt beach experience, you're better off heading to El Alamein (p396), Sidi Abdel Rahman (p399), or Marsa Matruh (p401), too.

Women should note that at everywhere but the beaches owned by Western hotels, modesty prevails and covering up when swimming is recommend – wear a baggy T-shirt and shorts over your swimsuit.

Mamoura Beach (Map pp372–3), about 1km east of Montazah, is one of the better city beaches, with a few small waves rolling in. Local authorities are trying to keep this suburb exclusive by charging everyone who enters the area E£3.25, with a further fee of E£8 to get onto the sand, but it's still jammed during high season. There's a much less crowded private beach with nice frond-type umbrellas, at E£41 per person or E£80 for a family. To get there, flag down an Aboukir-bound microbus along the Corniche and let the driver know you want Mamoura. **Miami Beach** (pronounced

me-ami; Map pp372–3) has a sheltered cove with a waterslide and jungle gym set up in the sea for kids to frolic on, but note that these get almost comically crowded during peak season. The spectacular **Stanley Beach** (Map pp372–3), a tiny bay with Stanley Bridge soaring above it, has a modest patch of sand for bathing backed by three levels of beach cabins. The sight of the sea crashing against the bridge's concrete supports is dramatic, but note that this beach is less suitable for kids due to the wave action.

At these and any city beaches, expect to pay an entrance fee and more for umbrellas and chairs, if desired.

COURSES

Qortoba Institute for Arabic Studies (Map pp372–3; ☎ 556 2959; www.qortoba.net; cnr Muhammad Nabeel Hamdy & Khalid Bin Waleed, Miami; ⏰ 9am-4pm Sun-Thu) arranges private tuition starting at €4 per hour, with classes for everyone from absolute beginners to experienced speakers. The institute can arrange accommodation nearby in student apartments for €65 to €140 per month.

The French Cultural Center and the Goethe Institut (see Cultural Centres, p371) also offer language courses.

TOURS & SERVICES

Tamer Zakaria (☎ 012 370 8210; tamerzakaria@ yahoo.com) A highly recommended English-speaking guide and Egyptologist, friendly and knowledgeable, available for day guiding. He can also organise trips.

Ann and Medhat Hashem (☎ 012 035 4711; www .muzhela.com) This English expat and her Egyptian husband organise car and driver services starting at around E£200 per day. They also do short- and long-term flat rental.

Mena Tours (Map p385; ☎ 480 9676; menatoursalx@ yahoo.com; ⏰ 9am-5pm Sat-Thu)

SLEEPING

As Alexandria has had an overhaul, the accommodation scene is also slowly getting better. While several five-star hotel chains are setting up shop, hotels in the midrange category are still few and far between. Budget places run the whole gamut from downright seedy to pretty darn comfortable, but the selection from here mostly shoots straight into the US$100 a night top-end category.

The summer months of June to September are the high season in Alexandria, when half of Cairo seems to decamp here to escape the heat of the capital. At the peak of the season, in August, you may have difficulty finding a room at some of the more popular hotels.

Budget & Midrange

Quite a few of the budget hotels front at least partly onto the Corniche. One of the pleasures of staying in Alexandria is pushing open the shutters in the morning to get a face full of fresh air off the Mediterranean, but the unrelenting din of traffic on the Corniche can make it seem like you're trying to snooze next to an airport runway. Light sleepers may want to consider a room off the Corniche.

At any of these budget hotels, it's wise to bring along your own soap, towel and toilet paper, as supplies can be erratic.

Triomphe Hotel (Map p385; ☎ 487 1787; 3rd fl, Sharia Gamal ad-Din Yassin; s/d with shared bathroom E£60/80) This quiet and good value old-timer sits half a block off the Corniche, and features a reassuringly sturdy-looking lift opening onto a tiled, leafy lobby. The rooms cling to shreds of former elegance, with high ceilings, timber floors, handy washbasins, and wood furnishings. Shared bathroom, with fans only. Doubles have balconies with side sea view, singles have no view.

Nile Excelsior Hotel (Map p385; ☎ 480 0/99; nile_hotel@yahoo.com; 16 Sharia al-Bursa al-Qadima; s/d E£60/100, with air-con E£100/180; 🕸) A very central hotel on the same street as the Spitfire bar (handy for stumbling to bed). The stairs up to the hotel are rather dirty and uninviting, but the small rooms have high ceilings and fly the 'clean and comfortable' flag with pride.

Hotel Union (Map p385; ☎ 480 7312; 5th fl, 164 Sharia 26th of July; s E£70-140, d E£90-160; 🕸) While this used to be our budget place of choice in Alexandria, the Union let it go to its head a bit, with standards slipping and prices creeping up. The smallish rooms are still quite charming, relatively well maintained and come in a bewildering mix of bathroom/view/air-con options and rates. Our rates quoted include a Byzantine mix of taxes, but no breakfast.

Hotel Crillon (Map p385; ☎ 480 0330; 3rd fl, 5 Sharia Adib Ishaq; s/d incl breakfast E£72/99) Smack-dab on the Corniche, this place has oodles of character but is a little rough around the edges. It boasts high ceilings, cream and white painted walls, and balconies with cane furniture and a divine vista. That said, the furnishings are a bit worse for wear, the shared bathroom could be cleaner, and there's no fan or air-con. You can have breakfast served on your balcony – ask for the traditional Egyptian

spread of *fuul* (fava beans cooked with garlic and garnished with olive oil and spices), with cumin, paprika, salt and lime, and eat it while admiring the view of the graceful sweep of the harbour.

Swiss Canal Hotel (Map p385; ☎ 480 8373; 14 Sharia al-Bursa al-Qadima; s/d with fan E£78/90, with air-con E£90/113) The walls here are an iridescent shade of pink that really has to be seen to be believed, but if you look past that the rooms are generally clean, with towering ceilings, mammoth wooden doors, spongy, soft beds, en suite bathrooms, and windows overlooking a reasonably quiet souq area. In summer, the rooms with air-con *(takeef)* are better value.

Egypt Hotel (Map p385; ☎ 481 4483; 1 Sharia Degla; s incl breakfast US$40-63, d incl breakfast US$47-68) The Egypt single-handedly fills a desperate need for decent midrange digs. A noticeable step up from the budget choices, it's set in a renovated 100-year old Italian building right on the Corniche. The lobby is tiled floor to ceiling in a turgid cream and brown, but the rooms have lush beds, wood floors, clean en suite bathrooms, powerful air-con and small balconies with sea or street views. Wi-fi is available, but in the lobby only.

Top End

Metropole Hotel (Map p385; ☎ 486 1467; www.paradiseinnegypt.com; 52 Sharia Saad Zaghloul; s/d US$100/$150) Location, location, location! The Metropole sits right in the thick of things, with most rooms overlooking Midan Saad Zaghloul and the sea. It was entirely renovated in the 1990s, but don't be too put off by the magnificently tacky lobby with its fake Parthenon-style friezes – once past here, the lushly carpeted hallways lead to tastefully decorated rooms with gigantic gilded doors and walls panelled like a St Petersburg palace.

Windsor Palace Hotel (Map p385; ☎ 480 8123; www.paradiseinnegypt.com; 17 Sharia ash-Shohada; r with sea view US$150) This bejewelled Edwardian gem is an institution unto itself, towering over the Corniche and keeping a watchful eye on the Med since 1907. In the 1990s the Windsor was bought by Paradise Inn, after its success with the Metropole, and was given a much-needed nip and tuck. Thankfully the wonderful old elevators and grand lobby have been retained, and the rooms boast the sort of old-world, green- and gold-flavoured pizzazz that wouldn't be out of place on the *Orient Express*. The pricier rooms have splendid sea views.

MIDAN RAMLA & AROUND

0 ———— 200 m
0 ———— 0.1 miles

ALEXANDRIA & THE MEDITERRANEAN COAST

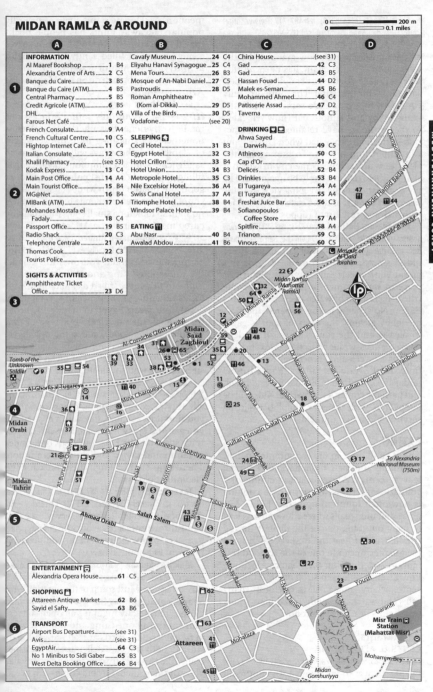

INFORMATION

Al Maaref Bookshop	1	B4
Alexandria Centre of Arts	2	C5
Banque du Caire	3	B5
Banque du Caire (ATM)	4	B5
Central Pharmacy	5	B5
Credit Agricole (ATM)	6	B5
DHL	7	A5
Farous Net Café	8	C5
French Consulate	9	A4
French Cultural Centre	10	C5
Hightop Internet Café	11	C4
Italian Consulate	12	C3
Khalil Pharmacy	(see 53)	
Kodak Express	13	C4
Main Post Office	14	A4
Main Tourist Office	15	B4
MG@Net	16	B4
MIBank (ATM)	17	D4
Mohandes Mostafa el Fadaly	18	C4
Passport Office	19	B5
Radio Shack	20	C3
Telephone Centrale	21	A4
Thomas Cook	22	C3
Tourist Police	(see 15)	

SIGHTS & ACTIVITIES

Amphitheatre Ticket Office	23	D6

Cavafy Museum	24	C4
Eliyahu Hanavi Synagogue	25	C4
Mena Tours	26	B3
Mosque of An-Nabi Daniel	27	C5
Pastroudis	28	D5
Roman Amphitheatre (Kom al-Dikka)	29	D5
Villa of the Birds	30	D5
Vodafone	(see 20)	

SLEEPING

Cecil Hotel	31	B3
Egypt Hotel	32	C3
Hotel Crillon	33	B4
Hotel Union	34	B3
Metropole Hotel	35	C3
Nile Excelsior Hotel	36	A4
Swiss Canal Hotel	37	A4
Triomphe Hotel	38	B4
Windsor Palace Hotel	39	B4

EATING

Abu Nasr	40	B4
Awalad Abdou	41	B6

China House	(see 31)	
Gad	42	C3
Gad	43	B5
Hassan Fouad	44	D2
Malek es-Seman	45	B6
Mohammed Ahmed	46	C4
Patisserie Assad	47	D2
Taverna	48	C3

DRINKING

Ahwa Sayed Darwish	49	C5
Athineos	50	C3
Cap d'Or	51	B4
Delices	52	B4
Drinkies	53	B4
El Tugareya	54	A4
El Tugareya	55	A4
Freshat Juice Bar	56	C3
Sofianopoulos Coffee Store	57	A4
Spitfire	58	A4
Trianon	59	C3
Vinous	60	C5

ENTERTAINMENT

Alexandria Opera House	61	C5

SHOPPING

Attareen Antique Market	62	B6
Sayid el Safty	63	B6

TRANSPORT

Airport Bus Departures	(see 31)	
Avis	(see 31)	
EgyptAir	64	C3
No 1 Minibus to Sidi Gaber	65	B3
West Delta Booking Office	66	B4

Cecil Hotel (Map p385; ☎ 487 7173; www.sofitel
.com; 16 Midan Saad Zaghloul; s/d US$205/245, with sea
view US$265/306) The historical Cecil Hotel,
an Alexandria legend, now managed by the
international Sofitel chain, has been refitted
several times over the last couple of decades,
sometimes for the better. The rooms are fully
equipped, though a little sombre, while the
grand lobby and famous bar (now relocated
to the 1st floor) have retained only a fraction of the lustre they had when Durrell and
Churchill came to visit. To that extent the
Cecil very much reflects the city in which it
stands, where the past has to be imagined. The
big consolation is the sweeping view over the
Eastern Harbour, and the excellent top-floor
China House restaurant (opposite).

Four Seasons Hotel (Map pp372-3; ☎ 581 8000; www
.fourseasons.com/alexandria; 399 Corniche, San Stefano; s/d
from US$320/350, ste US$800-9000) The much-loved
old Casino San Stefano made way for this
grand edifice, certainly the most luxurious
place to stay in town, if not the best value
(the little bottles of water in each room cost
E£25!). No expense has been spared: the marble lobby gleams, the army of staff is eager
to please, and the rooms sport all modern
conveniences while reflecting Alexandria's
Egyptian, Greek and French heritage. An in-
finity pool overlooks the sea, and a tunnel
under the Corniche leads to a private beach
and partially constructed marina. Kids will be
happy, too, with their own pool, babysitting
services and entertainment.

EATING

The old and once-grand restaurants, such as
Pastroudis and the Union, have long closed,
leaving central Alexandria something of a
culinary wilderness. Western-style cooking
is now often found in upmarket hotels and
noisy shopping malls where Alexandrians love
to hang out. Still, one of the delights in old
Alexandria is to eat the freshest catch from
the Mediterranean in one of the seafood restaurants overlooking the Eastern Harbour.
Equally enjoyable is to stroll around the city
centre, where you can sit in one of its many
cafes and watch Alexandrians at play. Many
restaurants don't serve alcohol.

Restaurants
CENTRAL ALEXANDRIA

Gad (Map p385; Sharia Saad Zaghloul; snacks E£1-9; ☼ 24hr)
Egypt's answer to (although a vast improve-

ment on) McDonald's, this chain of absurdly
popular takeaway joints has people flocking (think gadflies) day and night. It serves
a huge range of filled sandwiches, kebabs,
ta'amiyya and mouth-watering *shwarma*.
There's another branch on Sharia Mohammed
Azmy Tossoun.

Awalad Abdou (Map p385; Sharia Yousef; sandwiches
E£2-3; ☼ 24hr) With only minor concessions
made to hygiene, this uberbudget place is
nonetheless a smashing find. In two shakes
of a lamb's tail, these guys will whip up micro
sandwiches with a scrumptious, meat-centric
filling of your choice. Just point to what looks
good and quaff it down while standing at the
counter. It can be a challenge to find – there's
no sign, so look for a small shop with hanging
cured meats, near Sharia Attareen.

our pick **Mohammed Ahmed** (Map p385; ☎ 483
3576; 17 Sharia Shakor Pasha; dishes E£2-5) Under no
circumstances should you miss this classic,
the undisputed king and still champion of
fuul and *ta'amiyya*, filled day and night with
locals downing small plates of spectacularly
good and cheap Egyptian standards. From
the English menu, select your type of *fuul*
(*iskunduruni* is good), add some *ta'amiyya*,
and choose a few accompanying salads, such
as tahini, *banga* (beetroot) or pickles – then,
sit back and wait for the magic to happen.

Abu Nasr (Map p385; cnr Sharia Ibn el-Roumi & Sharia
al-Ghorfa al-Tugareya; large kushari E£4) This unusually tidy place serves good, filling *kushari*. If
you find it lacks mojo, throw in a dash of the
vinegar and spicy red sauce it's served with.
If it's still a bit plain for your taste, order sides
of tahini and *banga* and chuck them in too.
There's no sign in English, so look for the
gleaming gold bowls.

Taverna (Map p385; ☎ 487 8591; Mahattat Ramla;
shwarma sandwiches E£9, pizzas E£13-21) This deservedly popular establishment serves excellent
hand-thrown sweet or savoury *fiteer* (Egyptian
pancake), pizza, and some of the best *shwarma*
in town. Eat in or takeaway.

Malek es-Seman (Map p385; ☎ 390 0698; 48 Midan
el-Soriyin Masguid el-Attarine, off Sharia Attareen; two birds
E£25; ☼ 8pm-3am) Just south of the junction with
Sharia Yousef, by day this is a small courtyard
clothes market, by night it's an open-air restaurant doing one thing and doing it very,
very well: quail. Birds are served grilled or
stuffed; both ways are delicious, but we especially like the slightly charred and crispy flavour of the grilled. Orders come with bread

and six different salads. It's a bit hard to find, but look for a painted sign with a small bird. Serves beer.

China House (Map p385; ☎ 487 7173; Cecil Hotel, 16 Midan Saad Zaghloul; mains E£30-50; ⏰ 11am-11.30pm) Atop the Cecil Hotel (opposite), this highly recommended restaurant serves scrumptious Asian food beneath a tent with dangling lanterns and stunning views over the harbour. The ambience is breezy, the chicken dumplings and grilled beef with garlic first-rate, and the banana fritters unmissable. Beer and Egyptian wine are served.

ANFUSHI

For some authentic Alexandrian flavour and atmosphere, head for the simple good-value, streetside restaurants in Anfushi's *baladi* (working class, or 'of the land') district. Sharia Safar Pasha is lined with a dozen places where the fires are crackling and flaming under the grills barbecuing meat and fish. You could chance a table at any of them and probably come away satisfied, but those listed here deserve a special mention.

El-Sheikh Wafik (Map pp372-3; Qasr Ras at-Tin; desserts E£3-9; ⏰ 9am-4am) This unassuming and breezy corner cafe has a secret – the best dessert in town. You can get the usual ice cream in several flavours, but the real treats are Egyptian classics such as *couscousy* (E£8) – a yummy mix of couscous, shredded coconut, nuts, raisins and sugar, topped with hot milk.

Farag (Map pp374-5; ☎ 481 1047; 7 Souq al-Tabakheen, Manshey; fish per kg from E£45; ⏰ 12pm-3am) A highly recommended and very local seafood joint, a bit hard to spot – the sign is high above street level, so look up to be sure you don't miss it. If you do, just ask around; everyone knows it.

Hosny Grill (Map pp374-5; ☎ 481 2350; Sharia Safar Pasha, Bahari; meat per kg from E£80; ⏰ noon-4am) If you're a little fished out in Anfushi, Hosny Grill, opposite Abu Ashraf, is a semi-outdoor restaurant specialising in tasty grilled chicken, kebabs and other meats, served with the usual triumvirate of vegetables, salad and rice.

Abu Ashraf (Map pp374-5; ☎ 481 6597; 28 Sharia Safar Pasha, Bahari; dishes E£35-60; ⏰ 11am-3am) One of this street's fish specialists. Make your selection from the day's catch then take a seat under the green awning and watch it being cooked. Sea bass stuffed with garlic and herbs is a speciality, as is the creamy prawn *kishk* (casserole). Price is determined by weight and type of fish,

ranging from grey mullet at E£40 per kilo to jumbo prawns at E£150 per kilo.

Qadoura (Map pp374-5; ☎ 480 0405; 33 Sharia Bairam at-Tonsi; meals E£35-80; ⏰ 9am-3am) Pronounced 'Adora', this is one of Alexandria's most authentic fish restaurants. Pick your fish from a huge ice-packed selection, which usually includes sea bass, red and grey mullet, bluefish, sole, squid, crab and prawns, and often a lot more. Food is served at tables in the narrow street. A selection of mezze is served with all orders (don't hope for a menu). Most fish is around E£40 to E£80 per kilo, prawns E£180 per kilo. It has a second, air-conditioned (though less atmospheric) branch along the Corniche.

Samakmak (Map pp374-5; ☎ 481 1560; 42 Qasr Ras at-Tin; dishes E£40-90; ⏰ 1pm-2am) Owned by Zizi Salem, the retired queen of the Alexandrian belly-dancing scene, Samakmak is definitely one step up from the other fish eateries in the neighbourhood. The fish is as fresh as elsewhere, but customers flock to this place for its specials, including crayfish, marvellous crab *tagen* (stew cooked in a deep clay pot) and a great spaghetti with clams.

OUTSIDE THE CITY

Abo Faris (Map pp372-3; takeaway sandwiches E£10-20) An excellent eatery specialising in Syrian *shwarma*, a mouth-watering concoction of spicy grilled lamb or chicken slathered in garlicky mayonnaise and pickles, rolled up inside roasted flatbread. A full menu is available, and seating is indoors or in a garden patio (you can also do takeaway). It's about 500m before the Carrefour City Centre Mall, on the left as you're coming from the city. Most taxi drivers will know it.

Self-Catering

Hassan Fouad (Map p385; ☎ 485 9213; 7 Sharia Mahmoud Alam, cnr Sharia Sultan Abdel Aziz; ⏰ 9.30am-4am) This tiny and incredibly tidy market offers beautifully displayed produce, like grapes from Lebanon and tasty Egyptian mangoes, and a good selection of imported staples like digestive biscuits. There's no sign in English, so look for the place with artfully stacked fruits and a bright-red sign.

Patisserie Assad (Map p385; 14 Sharia Sultan Abdel Aziz; ⏰ 9.30am-4am) Just east of Midan Saad Zaghloul, this hole-in-the-wall bakery does good sweets, *fiteer* and croissants, sold by weight. It also offers a selection of hard-to-find local honey and olive oil. There's no sign, so look for the honey stacked in the window.

Metro (Map pp372-3; San Stefano Mall) A reliable supermarket chain with branches all around the city, including one at San Stefano Mall. It has a small organic section.

DRINKING

Juice

Freshat Juice Bar (Map p385; 18 Sharia Amin Fekry; juices E£1-5; ☯ 7am-1am summer, 9am-midnight winter) This sparkling little find has 26 different juices on offer, including all the standards plus some interesting and hard-to-find traditional drinks. If you're keen to try something new, ask the friendly owner, Ayman, to show you. All juices can be made without sugar on request.

El Qobesi (Map pp374-5; ☎ 486 7860; 51 Corniche; juices E£3-6; ☯ 24hr) El Qobesi has crowned itself the 'king of mango' but take one sip and you will bow down a loyal peon. Slivers of several ripe mangoes are cajoled nearly whole into a tall, chilled glass to make the single best mango juice we've ever tried. Ever. It's open around the clock and is always bustling, often with locals parked outside for a quick in-car slurp (we've even seen full microbuses stop by!). It's not signposted in English – but you can't miss the thousands of mangoes arranged out the front.

Cafes & Ahwas

During summer the 20km length of the Corniche from Ras at-Tin to Montazah seems to become one great strung-out *ahwa* (coffeehouse). With a few exceptions, these are not the greatest places – they're catering to a passing holiday trade and tend to overcharge. Nevertheless, Alexandria is a great place to get some quality *sheesha* (water pipe) time in. While many *ahwas* remain the exclusive domain of backgammon-playing men,

---

A MAGICAL (CAFFEINATED) HISTORY TOUR

In case you hadn't noticed, Alexandria is a cafe town – and we're not talking Starbucks double-decaf-soy-low-fat-vanilla grande lattes here. Ever since the first half of the 20th century, Alexandria's culture has centred around these venues, where the city's diverse population congregated to live out life's dramas over pastries and a cup of tea or coffee. Famous literary figures met here, chatted and pondered the city they could not quite grasp. Many of these old haunts remain and are definitely worth a visit for nostalgic purposes, historical associations and grand decor, but not always for the food or drink.

As good a place as any to start is by grabbing your first coffee of the day at **Athineos** (Map p385; ☎ 486 8131; 21 Midan Saad Zaghloul), opposite Midan Ramla. This place lives and breathes nostalgia. The cafe part on the Midan Ramla side still has its original '40s fittings, and pastries that taste like they've been sitting around since then. Come for the period character, skip the food.

Also facing Midan Ramla is **Trianon** (Map p385; 56 Midan Saad Zaghloul; ☯ from 7am; ✖), a favourite haunt of the Greek poet Cavafy, who worked in offices on the floor above. Stop here to admire the 1930s grandeur of its sensational ornate ceiling and grab one of its decent continental-style breakfasts, but give the adjoining restaurant a wide berth, as it's seen better days.

After you polish off breakfast, walk around the corner to check out **Delices** (Map p385; 46 Sharia Saad Zaghloul, Attareen; ☯ from 7am; ✖). This enormous old tearoom drips with atmosphere and it, too, can whip up a decent breakfast. It serves tea and cakes in the afternoon.

Now don't you think you've earned a dessert? **Vinous** (Map p385; ☎ 486 0956; cnr Sharias al-Nabi Daniel & Tariq al-Horreyya; ☯ 7am-1am) is an old-school patisserie with more grand art deco styling than you can poke a puff pastry at, but secretly we love it for the period scales labelled with the 'Just' brand. From here you can make a historical detour (to work off those extra calories you just imbibed) to the place where the famous **Pastroudis** (Map p385; Tariq al-Horreyya) once stood. Though now closed, this was a frequent meeting point for the characters of Lawrence Durrell's *Alexandria Quartet*.

Finally, exhausted, you might just need one last pick-me-up. Head over to the **Sofianopoulos Coffee Store** (Map p385; ☎ 484 5469; 21 Sharia Saad Zaghloul; ☯ 8am-midnight), a gorgeous coffee retailer that would be in a museum anywhere else in the world. Dominated by huge silver coffee grinders, stacks of glossy beans and the wonderful, faintly herbal aroma of roasted java, end your tour here with a flourish, sipping a thick Turkish coffee fit for a king.

families are welcome at these places, unless otherwise mentioned.

our pick **Arous el Zilzila** (Map pp374–5; Shatby Beach; 24hr) This fantastic *ahwa* across from the Bibliotheca Alexandrina is practically unique in Alexandria – you can sip tea and *sheesha* to the sound of waves rolling in, smelling sea air instead of petrol fumes. Directly on the water, it has rustic open-air tables and palm trees with cheerful coloured lights, set around a small curving beach where you can hardly hear the traffic. It's a great place to relax in the sultry breeze, enjoying the Mediterranean vibe. To find it, look for the modern sculpture with three white needles, directly across the Corniche from the library. Walk past the sculpture towards the sea; the entrance is down the steps to the right.

El Rehany (Map pp372–3; ☎ 590 5521; Corniche, Camp Chesar, cnr Sharia Ismail Fangary) This expansive and breezy Alexandrian classic is reputed to have the best *sheesha* in town, served with a flourish by attentive boys in smart two-toned waistcoats while waiters in black-and-white bring tea in silver urns. The decor is eclectically elegant, with lofty ceilings etched with elaborate floral patterns, tables and chairs in Islamic designs, and burgundy tablecloths. Check out the bizarre assortment of knick-knacks in the glass displays in back, too. There's no sign in English, so look for the place with green awnings, next to the Premiere Wellness and Fitness Centre.

El Tugareya (Map p385; Corniche; 9am–late) Although it may not look like much to the uninitiated (it doesn't even sport a sign), this 90-year-old institution is one of the most important *ahwas* in town. It's an informal centre of business and trade (the name roughly translates to 'commerce'), where deals are brokered in the time-honoured tradition – over a glass of tea. The cafe is separated into multiple rooms, covering a whole block. The southern side is a male-dominated area dedicated to games and informal socialising, while along the Corniche you're likely to be part of a rambunctious mix of writers, film-makers, students, expats, and courting couples filling the hall with a cacophony of animated conversation. Look for the cafe with the green window trim.

Farouk Cafe (Map pp374–5; ☎ 480 3103; Sharia Ismail Sabry, Anfushi; 24hr) This venerable *sheesha* joint doesn't look like it's changed an iota since it opened in 1928. It's a charmingly ramshackle

old place, with dusty bronze lanterns outside, and charmingly fusty old men arguing and playing board games at the tables. Women may not feel comfortable here.

Ahwa Sayed Darwish (Map p385; Sharia Abu Shusha) Named for the composer of Egypt's national anthem, this tiny and highly enjoyable local, near Sharia al-Nabi Daniel, is set on a quiet and leafy side street around the corner from the Cafavy Museum. The chairs are comfortably padded, and the *sheesha* is clean. The clientele is exclusively men.

Bars

Sixty years ago Alexandria was so famous for its Greek tavernas and divey little watering holes that the 1958 movie *Ice Cold in Alex* was entirely based around a stranded WWII ambulance crew struggling through the desert, dreaming of making it back to Alexandria to sip a beer. Times have changed and Alex isn't much of a drinking town any more; there are few places worth crossing the desert for.

our pick **Centro de Portugal** (Map pp372–3; ☎ 542 7599; 42 Sharia Abd al-Kader, off Sharia Kafr Abdou; admission E£10; 3pm–1am) This hard-to-find expat haven is fully equipped for fun: a garden bar in a leafy patio, an inside bar with darts, foosball and pool, plus a tiny disco complete with mirrored ball. Best of all, the beverages are very cold. Drinks are purchased via an unusual card system: E£70 gets you five credits; beers are one credit, while cocktails are two. The food menu (dishes E£40 to E£55) sports Western standards, from noodles to pasta to fish, along with the house speciality – pepper steak. It's a great place to unwind, hidden away from the hubbub of the city, and meet local expats while sucking down an icy gin and tonic. The entrance is unmarked; look for the gate on the south side of the street, about 90m from the intersection of Kafr Abdou.

Cap d'Or (Map p385; ☎ 487 5177; 4 Sharia Adbi Bek Ishak; 10am–3am) The Cap d'Or, just off Sharia Saad Zaghloul, is a top spot to relax, and one of the only surviving typical Alexandrian bars. With beer flowing generously, stained-glass windows, a long marble-topped bar, plenty of ancient memorabilia decorating the walls and crackling tapes of old French *chanson* (type of traditional folk music) or Egyptian hits, it feels very much like an Andalusian tapas bar. Crowds come to drink cold Stella beer, snack on great seafood, or just hang out at the bar and chew the proverbial fat with fellow drinkers. Thursday and Friday nights are more 'open-minded' than most nights in Alexandria.

Spitfire (Map p385; 7 Sharia L'Ancienne Bourse; 2pm-1.30am Mon-Sat) Just north of Sharia Saad Zaghloul, Spitfire feels almost like a Bangkok bar – sans go-go girls. It has a reputation as a sailors' hang-out and the walls are plastered with shipping-line stickers, rock-and-roll memorabilia and photos of drunk regulars. It's a great place for an evening out in one of the world's finest harbours, listening to American rock and roll from the 1970s.

Greek Club (Club Nautique Hellenique; Map pp374-5; 480 2690; Corniche, Anfushi; noon-11pm) The Greek Club is a great place for a sunset drink, inside its large newly restored rooms or, even better, on the wide terrace catching the afternoon breeze or watching the lights on this legendary bay. The menu has a selection of fresh fish cooked any way you like it (grilled with olive oil, oregano and lemon, baked or Egyptian style), as well as Greek classics such as moussaka (E£14) and souvlaki (E£32). An admission fee is sometimes charged.

Takeaway beer is available in the city centre at the aptly named **Drinkies** (Map p385; 19330, 480 6309 (delivery); Sharia al-Ghorfa al-Tugareya; noon-midnight), below the Hotel Acropole. It also delivers.

ENTERTAINMENT

Alexandria's cultural life has never really recovered from the exodus of Europeans and Jews in the 1940s and '50s, but in recent years things have started to change for the better. Since the opening of the Bibliotheca Alexandrina, the town is once again trying to compete with Cairo as the proprietor of Egyptian arts.

The **Alexandria International Film Festival** (http://alexandriafilm.org) takes place every September, offering Alexandrians a rare opportunity to see uncensored films from around the globe. Films are screened at several cinemas around town – ask at the tourist office for more information.

Music, Theatre & Dance

The free monthly booklet *Alex Agenda,* available at many hotels, is extremely useful for its extensive list of concerts, theatre events and live gigs throughout Alexandria. Also, check the French Cultural Centre (p371)

and Alexandria Centre of Arts (p371), as both organise occasional performances.

Bibliotheca Alexandrina (Map pp374-5; 483 9999; www.bibalex.org; Corniche al-Bahr, Shatby) The Bibliotheca Alexandrina is the most important cultural venue in town now, hosting major music festivals, international concerts and performances.

Alexandria Opera House (Map p385; 486 5106; www.cairoopera.org/sayed_darwish.aspx; 22 Tariq al-Horreyya) The former Sayed Darwish Theatre has been refurbished and now houses the city's modestly proportioned but splendid opera house. Most performances of opera and classical music are staged in this gorgeous auditorium.

Garage (Map pp372-3; tfetouh@yatfund.org; Jesuit Centre, Sharia Bur Said, Sidi Gaber) The renovated garage of the Jesuit Centre and maintained by the Young Arab Theatre Fund, Garage is a breath of fresh air on the city's cultural scene, presenting new performances by local and international youth theatre groups.

SHOPPING

There is a souq just west of Midan Tahrir (Map p385), and Sharia Safiyya Zaghloul and Sharia Saad Zaghloul are lined with an assortment of old-fashioned and more trendy clothes and shoe shops, but overall the city centre is not a shopper's paradise. Alexandrians have only recently discovered the joys of shopping malls, but there is no stopping them now. Today malls have replaced town squares as popular gathering spots, boasting entertainment, cafes, *ahwas* and restaurants. Younger Alexandrians find them great places to mingle with the opposite sex.

Carrefour City Center Mall (Map pp372-3; beginning of Cairo Desert Rd) A 20-minute drive south of the city, this is one of the largest malls, with the massive French superstore Carrefour. It sells everything from groceries to TVs.

San Stefano Mall (Map pp372-3; Sharia Abdel Salam Aref, San Stefano) The latest ode to international label shopping, this swanky mall sits behind the Four Seasons Hotel and has a big food court and cinemas. It is the current place to see and be seen for chic young Alexandrians.

Antique-collectors might have some fun diving through the confusion of backstreets and alleys of the Attareen district. When Alexandria's European high society was forced en masse to make a hasty departure from Egypt following the 1952 revolution, they largely went without their personal belongings – much of what they left has found its way over the years into the Attareen Antique Market (Map p385). Today there are fewer and fewer wonderful finds, and even fewer bargains. Dealers here recognise quality, and their bedtime reading may well include Christie's and Sotheby's catalogues.

One of the better ones, and certainly the most fun, is **Sayed el Safty** (Map p385; ☎ 392 2972; 63 Sharia Attareen; ⏲ 10am-10pm Mon-Sat), a 2nd-generation *antiquaire* who runs a small shop piled to the rafters with antique and reproduction Oriental furnishings in wood and metal – tables, chests, maps, bowls, beautifully inlaid backgammon sets, and more. The store itself is worth the trip alone, with graceful Arabic text carved into the stone walls. Sayed himself is enthusiastic, friendly and knowledgeable. The sign above the store says 'Ibrahim el Safty' (Sayed's father).

GETTING THERE & AWAY

Air

Internationally, Alexandria is served by multiple airlines: **EgyptAir** (Map385; ☎ 487 3357, 486 5937; 19 Midan Saad Zaghloul; ⏲ 8am-8pm), Emirates, Lufthansa, British Airways, British Midland, Air France, and more.

The airport infrastructure is undergoing significant change. There are two airports; the larger, **Burg al-Arab** (HBE; ☎ 459 1483), is 60km west of the city and at the time of writing was closed for a major overhaul and extension. While the work is ongoing, all air traffic is being routed to the smaller airport at **Nouzha** (ALY; Map pp372-3; ☎ 425 0527), much closer to the city.

However, once Burg al-Arab reopens, it will become the city's primary airport and most or all flights to Nouzha will cease. This is scheduled for late 2009/early 2010, but as always delays may occur, so check on the situation locally.

Transport to Burg el-Arab is via the air-con airport bus (one way E£6 plus E£1 per bag, one hour), leaving from in front of the Cecil Hotel (Map p385) three hours before all departures; confirm the exact bus departure time at the Cecil. A taxi to/from the airport should cost between E£100 and E£150. You can also catch bus 475 (one hour) from Misr Train Station.

If you do need to get to/from Nouzha, a taxi should cost between E£15 and E£25. There are also minibuses from Midan Orabi and Midan Ramla.

Bus

All long-distance buses leave from **Al-Mo'af al-Gedid** (New Garage; Map pp372-3). It's several kilometres south of Midan Saad Zaghloul; to get there either catch a microbus from Misr Train Station (50pt), or grab a taxi from the city centre (E£10 to E£15).

The main companies operating from here are **West Delta Bus Co** (☎ 362 9685) and **Superjet** (☎ 363 3552), which has more expensive but considerably nicer buses. West Delta has a convenient city-centre **booking office** (Map p385; ☎ 480 9685; Midan Saad Zaghloul; ⏲ 9am-9pm), while Superjet has a less convenient **booking office** (Map pp372-3; ☎ 543 5222; ⏲ 8am-10pm) opposite Sidi Gaber Train Station, next to the large fountain.

CAIRO

Superjet has hourly buses to Cairo (E£25, 2½ hours), also stopping at Cairo airport (E£35), from early morning. Services stop in the late evening, though there may be a single late service. West Delta also has hourly departures (E£25).

NORTH COAST & SIWA

West Delta has hourly departures to Marsa Matruh (E£20 to E£35, four hours); many of these buses continue on to Sallum (nine hours) on the border with Libya. Four services daily go to Siwa (E£27 to E£35, nine hours) between 8.30am and 10pm. Otherwise just take any Marsa Matruh bus and change there.

Superjet runs five buses to Marsa Matruh (E£30) daily during summer (June to September), the last one generally leaving in the late afternoon. Most Marsa Matruh buses stop in El Alamein (one hour), and will stop at Sidi Abdel Rahman if you want to get off, though you will have to pay the full Marsa Matruh fare.

SINAI

Superjet has one daily service to Sharm el-Sheikh (E£110, eight to 10 hours) at 9pm; West Delta has one at 9pm (E£80 to E£90).

SUEZ CANAL & RED SEA COAST

Superjet has a daily evening service to Hurghada (E£90 to E£100, nine hours). West Delta has several services a day to Port Said, two to Ismailia, and four to Suez. It also has two buses a day to Hurghada and Port Safaga (E£85 to E£100, six to eight hours). The

Upper Egypt Bus Co has three daily Hurghada buses (E£75 to E£90) that continue on down to Port Safaga.

INTERNATIONAL BUSES

For information on international services from Alexandria, see p525.

Service Taxi & Microbus

Service taxis and microbuses for Aboukir, and service taxis for Cairo, depart from outside Misr Train Station (Map pp374–5); all others go from the Al-Mo'af al-Gedid (New Garage; Map pp372–3) bus station out at Moharrem Bey. Fares cost around E£20 to Cairo or Marsa Matruh, depending on who you ask. To more local destinations, some sample fares are Zagazig E£10, Tanta E£8, Mansura E£10, Rosetta E£3 and Aboukir E£1.

Train

There are two train stations in Alexandria. The main terminal is **Mahattat Misr** (Misr Train Station; Map pp374–5; ☎ 426 3207), about 1km south of Midan Ramla. **Mahattat Sidi Gaber** (Sidi Gaber Train Station; Map pp372–3; ☎ 426 3953) serves the eastern suburbs. Trains from Cairo stop at Sidi Gaber first, and most locals get off here, but if you're going to the city centre around Midan Saad Zaghloul, make sure you stay on until Mahattat Misr.

There are more than 15 trains daily between Cairo and Alexandria, from 6am to 11pm. There are three train types: the special (*turbini*), Spanish (*espani*) and French (*faransawi*). Special and Spanish trains (1st/2nd class E£50/35, 2½ hours) are much better, as they make fewer stops. The French train (1st/2nd class E£35/22, 3½ to four hours) makes multiple stops. First class (*ula*) is well worth the additional cost, as you get a roomier seat and cleaner bathroom, though both classes have well-functioning *takeef* (air-conditioning). Seats are reserved, and your assigned car and seat should be printed on the ticket – ask a conductor for help finding it if needed.

At Mahattat Misr station, 1st- and 2nd-class tickets to Cairo are sold at the ticket office along the platform next to the tourist office; 3rd-class and 2nd-class ordinary tickets are purchased in the front hall. If you're getting a taxi from the station, it's advisable to bypass the drivers lurking outside the entrance – just walk out onto the street and flag one down there.

GETTING AROUND

As a visitor to Alexandria, you'll rarely use the buses, and while the tram is fun it's painfully slow. Taxis and microbuses are generally the best options for getting around.

Car

Driving yourself in Alexandria is not necessarily the suicide mission it might appear, as city traffic tends to move slowly. **Avis** (Map p385; ☎ 485 7400; Cecil Hotel, Midan Saad Zaghloul; per day incl 100kms from US$35; ☒ 8am-10pm) has cars, with drivers available for an additional US$20 per day. If you do rent, ensure that you're especially scrupulous with the initial and return inspections, to avoid any compensation claims for very minor vehicle damage.

The price of using a car and driver service (see Tours & Services, p383) can be comparable, and saves the headache of negotiating traffic yourself.

Microbus

Want to travel like the locals? Hop on a microbus. They go from pretty much anywhere to everywhere, but the most useful are the ones zooming along the Corniche – they can be nearly as fast as taxis and much cheaper. There are no set departure points or stops, so when one passes, wave and shout your destination; if it's heading that way it will stop to pick you up. You may have to clamber over others to get a seat, but that's all part of the fun. Once you sit down, pass the fare up to the driver. It's anywhere from 50pt for a short trip to E£1.50 to go all the way to Montazah. The easiest thing to do is just to pass up E£1 per person; if it's less, the change will be passed back to you.

Red Bus

The new air-conditioned red double-decker bus (E£3) plies the Corniche every 15 to 30 minutes between Ras el-Tin and the Sheraton in Montazah. You can flag it down anywhere along the route, but go to a major intersection like Midan Saad Zaghloul to be sure to catch it. Let the driver know when you want to get off. The fare is the same regardless of how far you travel.

Taxi

There are no working taxi meters in Alexandria. Locals simply pay the correct amount as they get out of the taxi, but since fares are both unpublished and subjective, this can be a challenge for a visitor to pull off (especially considering many drivers expect visitors to pay higher fares and won't hesitate to aggressively argue the point).

If you don't know the fare, or don't feel comfortable doing it the local way, negotiate a price before you get in. Don't worry about letting a cab or two go if you can't get the price you want; there'll usually be another one right behind. When you're dropped off, get out of the cab first, then hand the driver the exact amount. If you don't have exact change, you might have a bit of a tussle getting your correct change back.

Some sample fares are: Midan Ramla to Misr Train Station E£5 to E£7; Midan Saad Zaghloul to Fort Qaitbey E£5; Midan Saad Zaghloul to the Great Library E£5; Hotel Cecil to Montazah or Mamoura around E£22 to E£25.

Tram

Alexandria's rumbling, clackety old trams are fun to ride, but they can be almost unbearably slow and hence not the best option for getting around if you're short on time or patience. The system can be confusing, and the easiest way to get to grips with the various lines and stations is the English system map mounted on metal signposts at most larger stations (on the back of the Arabic system map).

The central tram station is Mahattat Ramla; from here lime-yellow-coloured trams go west. Tram 14 goes to Misr Train Station and Moharrem Bey, and tram 15 goes past the Mosque of Abu Abbas al-Mursi and Fort Qaitbey to Ras at-Tin.

The blue-coloured trams travel east: trams 2 and 36 to Sidi Gaber, Rushdy and San Stefano; tram 36 to Victoria via Rushdy and San Stefano; and tram 25 from Ras at-Tin to Sidi Gaber via Midan Ramla. The line numbers on each tramcar are in Arabic, but you can tell which line it is by the colour of the sign in front.

Some trams have two or three carriages, in which case one of them is reserved for women. Riding in the women's car is an interesting cultural experience, as long as you actually are female; it causes considerable amusement when an unsuspecting foreign man boards the wrong carriage. The standard fare is 25pt, and the conductors generally have plenty of change, so if you need to replenish your supply of small bills this is a good place to do it.

AROUND ALEXANDRIA

ABOUKIR

Aboukir (pronounced abu-eer), a small coastal town 24km east of Alexandria, was slingshot into fame by several major 18th-century battles that took place off its shores. The Battle of the Nile saw the British Admiral Horatio Nelson administer a crushing defeat over Napoleon's French fleet. Although Napoleon still controlled Egypt, his contact with France by sea was effectively severed. In 1799 the British landed 18,000 Turkish soldiers at Aboukir, but with a thirst for revenge the French force of 10,000 men, mostly cavalry led personally by Napoleon, forced the Turks back into the sea, drowning at least 5000 of them. In 1801, however, the French lost a further battle with the British troops at the same place and the French expeditionary corps was then forced out of Egypt.

Recent underwater excavation (see boxed text, p376) has revealed two sunken cities believed to be the legendary Herakleion and Menouthis, with several rescued treasures now on display at the Alexandria National Museum (p375). The beach here is rubbish-strewn, so the main reason to head in this direction is for lunch at one of the excellent fish restaurants, particularly at the **Zephyrion** (☎ 03-562 1319; seafront Aboukir; fish per kg E£40-160; ☽ 1pm-11pm). This old Greek fish taverna (the name is Greek for 'sea breeze') was founded in 1929 and serves first-class fish and seafood on the sweeping blue-and-white terrace that overlooks the bay. There is no wine list but you can bring your own bottle and it will be uncorked for you without complaint.

The easiest way to get to Aboukir is by flagging down an eastbound microbus along the Corniche (E£1.50). It will drop you at a roundabout; the sea is to your left as you face the large mosque beyond the roundabout.

Alternatively, a taxi from Alexandria city centre should cost around E£30, each way.

ROSETTA (AR-RASHID)

☎ 045 / pop 194, 700

It's hard to believe that this dusty town, squatting on the western branch of the Nile 65km from Alexandria, was once Egypt's most significant port. Also known as Ar-Rashid, Rosetta was founded in the 9th century and outgrew Alexandria in importance during that town's 18th- and 19th-century decline. Alas,

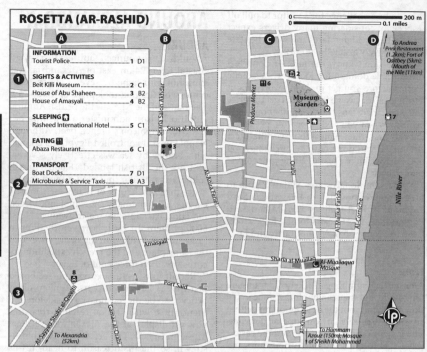

as Alexandria got back on its feet and regained its power in the late 19th century, Rosetta was thrust once again into near irrelevance.

Today Rosetta is most famous as the discovery place of the stone stele that provided the key to deciphering hieroglyphics (see boxed text, opposite). It strikes a contrast with the modern turmoil of nearby Alexandria – the streets are packed with donkeys pulling overloaded carts, basket-weavers artfully working fronds, and blacksmiths hammering away in medieval-looking shop fronts.

Rosetta's main draw is its striking Islamic architecture, in the form of beautifully crafted Ottoman-era merchants' houses. There are at least 22 of them tucked away along the streets but unfortunately most are undergoing renovation and are not open to visitors. While all the houses are scheduled to reopen in 2010, that could change, so if you're intent on seeing more than a few examples, check the situation with the **tourist police** (☎ 292 1733; Museum Garden) before making the trip.

The Beit Killi museum on the main square is also closed, and at present there's no official reopening date.

At the time of writing, the sights open to the public are the Hammam Azouz and House of Abu Shaheen (see opposite). Most houses have a similar layout, so whichever is open when you visit will likely be similar to the description of the House of Amasyali (opposite).

Information

There is no tourist office in Rosetta. Independent visitors must check in with the tourist police at the Museum Garden on arrival as the authorities are touchy about foreigners wandering around unescorted. You may be assigned a minder for the duration of your visit, whether you want one or not. Your minder can help arrange visits to sights, and a tip of E£10 to E£20 is appreciated. Note that the area around the fish market is best avoided within several days after any significant rain due to, ahem, reconstruction of the sewer system.

Sights

Built in the traditional Delta style using small, flat bricks painted alternately red and black,

Rosetta's Islamic houses are generally three-storey structures with the upper floor slightly overhanging the lower. Together with their jutting and ornate *mashrabiyyas* (the intricately assembled wooden screens that serve for windows), the buildings are reminiscent of an upside-down chocolate wedding cake.

One of the most impressive of all Rosetta's fine buildings is the **House of Amasyali**, one of two restored houses on Sharia al-Anira Feriel. The facade has beautiful small lantern lights and vast expanses of *mashrabiyyas*, which circulate cool breezes around the house. Although inside it's devoid of furniture – as are all the buildings – it's still possible to get a clear idea of how the house worked. A series of rough stone chambers, which would have been used for storage, make up the ground floor. The 1st floor was for the men. One of the rooms here is a reception room, where guests would have been entertained by groups of musicians, and is overlooked by a screened wooden gallery behind which the women would sit, obscured from view. The stairs to the gallery are hidden behind a false cupboard and there are some fine examples of mother-of-pearl inlay work in wooden panels along the same wall. Be sure to look up at the ceiling to see intricately carved decorations painted brilliant blue. Also notice the little revolving turn-table, designed so that women could serve tea and coffee without being seen. The nearby bedroom has several smaller rooms attached, one that was a walk-in wardrobe and another a hammam (bathhouse) with separate toilet.

Next door to the House of Amasyali is the **House of Abu Shaheen** (adult/student E£15/10), or Mill House, with a reconstructed mill on the ground floor, featuring enormous wooden beams and planks. You can actually see the gears and teeth rotate, which 200 years ago would have been pushed in an endless circle by a bored draught animal. In the courtyard, the roof of the stables is supported by granite columns with Graeco-Roman capitals. Tickets bought here are good for all of the open monuments in the town centre.

One of the most extraordinary buildings in Rosetta has to be the **Hammam Azouz**, a 400-year-old bathhouse still in operation as late as 1980, using water plumbed in from the Nile. It features a fine marble interior with elaborately carved wooden ceilings. Several bathing rooms encircle the main, fountain-

THE ROSETTA STONE

Now a crowd-pulling exhibit at the British Museum in London, the Rosetta Stone is the most significant find in the history of Egyptology. Unearthed in 1799 by a French soldier doing his duty improving the defences of Fort St Julien near Rosetta, the stone is the lower half of a large dark granitic stele. It records a decree issued by the priests of Memphis on 27 March 196 BC, the anniversary of the coronation of Ptolemy V (205–180 BC), and it announces their decision to honour the 13-year-old pharaoh with his own cult in return for tax exemptions and other perks. In order to be understood by Egyptians, Greeks and others then living in the country, the decree was written in the three scripts current at the time – hieroglyphic, demotic (a cursive form of hieroglyphs) and Greek, a language that European scholars would have read fluently. The trilingual inscription was set up in a temple beside a statue of the pharaoh. At the time of its discovery, much was known about ancient Egypt, but scholars had still not managed to decipher hieroglyphs. It was quickly realised that these three scripts would make it possible to compare identical texts and therefore to crack the code and recover the lost world of the ancient Egyptians.

When the British defeated Napoleon's army in 1801, they wrote a clause in the surrender document insisting that antiquities be handed to the victors, the Rosetta Stone being foremost among them. The French made a cast and the original was shipped to London, where Englishman Thomas Young established the direction in which the hieroglyphs should be read, and recognised that hieroglyphs enclosed within oval rings (cartouches) were the names of royalty.

But in 1822, before Young devised a system for reading the mysterious script, Frenchman Jean François Champollion recognised that signs could be alphabetic, syllabic or determinative, and established that the hieroglyphs inscribed on the Rosetta Stone were actually a translation from the Greek, and not the other way around. This allowed him to establish a complete list of signs with their Greek equivalents. His obsessive work not only solved the mystery of Pharaonic script but also contributed significantly to a modern understanding of ancient Egypt.

centred bathing room, and tall domed ceilings crown each chamber. Tiny round holes in the domes let in piercing shafts of light (and would have let out steam), with some still covered in colourful stained glass that further bathes the place in a faint rainbow of surreal colours. Tickets for the bathhouse are available at the House of Abu Shaheen.

About 5km north of Rosetta along the Nile is the **Fort of Qaitbey** (adult/student E£15/8; 8am-5pm), built in 1479 (just before the sultan's fort in Alexandria) to guard the mouth of the Nile 6km further on. It was here that the famous Rosetta Stone was found (see boxed text, p395), and there's a copy inside the fort. The mouth of the Nile is visible from atop the walls. Boats depart from the Corniche near the Museum Garden and make the trip to the fort for around E£50 to E£60 per person return (1½ hours), or you can hire a taxi to take you.

In the opposite direction, south along the Nile is the **Mosque of Sheikh Mohammed**. This small place of worship sits on the riverbank next to the ruins of Bolbitine, the ancient settlement and port dating back to Roman times which eventually grew into Rashid further north. It's locally famed for a well that supplies reliably cool, clean water, always offered to passers-by. Visits to the mosque must be arranged through the tourist police, who will organise the required boat transport (about E£60).

Sleeping & Eating

Rosetta sees few travellers and has limited tourist facilities, with only a handful of hotels and restaurants.

Rasheed International Hotel (045 293 4399; www.rosettahotel.jeeran.com, in Arabic; Museum Garden Sq; s/d/tr E£100/130/160;) This skinny 11-storey place has plainly decorated but spotless rooms, all with satellite TV, minibar and balconies with top views – on a clear day you can see the Mediterranean from the higher floors. Its restaurant serves some of the better food in town, with Egyptian favourites and some Western dishes thrown in to boot. Expect to pay around E£40 for dinner.

Abaza Restaurant (near museum) Just down the street from the museum, this hole-in-the-wall serves straight-ahead *kofta* (mincemeat and spices grilled on a skewer) and other grilled meats in a little upstairs room with a red carpet and single table. There's no sign

in English, so look out for the chickens spit-roasting in a metal grill at the front.

Andrea Park (010 260 6497) This breezy Nileside cafe, 1.2km north of town along the road to Fort Qaitbey, has outdoor seating in a pleasant garden. Meals are possible only with advance notice.

Getting There & Away

The easiest way to get to Rosetta from Alexandria is to organise a private car and driver (see Tours & Services, p383). Another option is to hire a taxi, which should cost you around E£100 to E£150, including waiting time.

Service taxis (E£35, one hour) and microbuses (E£3.50, one hour) to Rosetta leave from the Al-Mo'af al-Gedid bus station in Alexandria. Microbuses terminate at the Rashid Mo'af (station); the future of this station is uncertain, as there are rumblings it will be moved to a new location. At the time of writing there was no change in location nor announcement of official plans.

MEDITERRANEAN COAST

Almost the entire stretch of coastline between Alexandria and Sidi Abdel Rahman is jam-packed with resorts paying homage to the modern gods of concrete construction. This is where well-to-do Cairenes and the top brass of Egypt's military establishment now come to escape the oppressive city heat of the summer. It's so busy here that when driving past, the only glimpses you're likely to get of the ocean are through the skeletal structures of unfinished holiday villages. While some of these getaways border on the truly luxurious, there's little for the independent traveller. Halfway down the coast to Libya, El Alamein is home to several poignant memorials to the WWII battles that ensued here. Past here, and all the way to the Libyan border, the striking coast lies deserted until you reach Marsa Matruh, sitting on a brilliant, sandy bay. Marsa Matruh is either heaving with Egyptian holidaymakers in summer or completely deserted in the winter months.

EL ALAMEIN
046
This small coastal outpost (not a 'city' as the brochures would have you believe) is famed for the decisive victory doled out here by

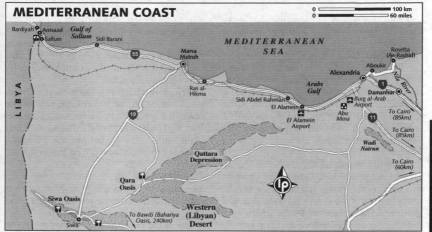

MEDITERRANEAN COAST

the Allies during WWII (see boxed text, p398). More than 80,000 soldiers were killed or wounded in the series of desert battles fought nearby which helped cement Allied control of North Africa. The thousands of graves in the Commonwealth, German and Italian war cemeteries in the vicinity of the town are a bleak reminder of the losses.

Much cheerier are the fine sands and heavenly water of the nearby beaches. Finding a place to access the sea is easier if you're staying at one of the local resorts, but there are also a few places where independent visitors can get in the water.

It's possible to stay overnight here and in nearby Sidi Abdel Rahman, but El Alamein is best visited as a day trip from Alexandria. Beaches aside, there really isn't that much that would detain any but the most enthusiastic of military historians for more than a few hours.

Sights

On the eastern side of town, along a side road that leaves the main highway at the Greek war memorial, is the **Commonwealth War cemetery** (admission free; 7am-2.30pm, key available outside of these hours). It's a haunting place where more than 7000 tombstones sit on a slope commanding a sweeping view of the desert. Soldiers from the UK, Australia, New Zealand, France, Greece, South Africa, East and West Africa, Malaysia and India who fought for the Allied cause lie here. As you enter, a separate memorial commemorating the Australian contingent is to your right; look here for a small plaque with

a relief map giving an insightful overview of the key battlefield locations. The memorial is supposedly visitable outside of regular hours via a key left outside the gate, but this may not be reliable.

The cemetery itself was a rear area during the fighting; the front line ran from nearby the Italian memorial and wound its way 65km south to the Qattara Depression. If you spend time in town, you may field offers of desert excursions to visit key battle sites, such as Ruweisat ridge or Alam el Halfa. Aside from the fact that millions of landmines were planted during the fighting and no one seems to know how many remain, officially you must obtain approval from the Egyptian military to access the battlefield. It's a controlled area and if you're caught without permission you risk serious trouble; what's more, if anything goes wrong in the desert you will not be able to rely on authorities for assistance.

A few kilometres west of the cemetery, the **War Museum** (410 0031/21; adult/student E£20/10; 9am-4pm) has a collection of memorabilia, uniforms and pictorial material of each country involved in the Battle of El Alamein and the North African campaigns, and maps and explanations of various phases of the campaign in Arabic, English, German and Italian complement the exhibits. There's also a 30-minute Italian-made documentary that you can watch. A range of tanks, artillery and hardware from the fields of battle is displayed outside the museum. The turn-off to the museum is along the main highway; just look for the large tank in the middle of the road.

About 7km west of El Alamein, what looks like a hermetically sealed sandstone fortress overlooking the sea is actually the **German War Memorial**. Inside this silent but unmistakable reminder of war lie the tombs of approximately 4000 German servicemen and, in the centre, a memorial obelisk. To reach the memorial, take the marked turn-off from the main highway; the entrance to the memorial is locked, but if you wait for a moment the very friendly Bedouin keeper will appear to let you in.

From the memorial, there's a panoramic view of the undeveloped stretch of shore in this area. Across roughly 1km of desert directly in front of the memorial is the tiny and glorious **German Memorial Beach**, which sees only the occasional busload and is relatively rubbish-free. The sea here is superb, in multiple shades of blue, and you'll feel miles away from Alexandria's teeming beaches. To get to the beach, you can ask the Bedouin keeper at the memorial to open the gate leading to the sand tracks across the desert. He may offer to accompany you, and even to set up a Bedouin tent on the beach and cook you lunch. The price for this service is negotiable.

There's also a road direct to the beach from the Alexandria–Matruh highway. It's an unmarked sand track, leading over some low hills to the beach. The turn-off is 150m east of the road to the German memorial.

About 4km further on, the **Italian Memorial** has a tall, slender tower as its focal point. This was roughly where the front line between the opposing armies ran.

Before reaching the German memorial, you'll notice on the left (south) side of the road what appears to be a large rock milestone. Inscribed on it is the plaintive Italian summary of the battle: '*Mancò la fortuna, non il valore*' – 'We were short on luck, not on bravery'.

Sleeping & Eating

The store opposite the War Museum has a small cafeteria where you can get a good spread of *fuul, ta'amiyya* and salads.

Max 24 (☎ 012 310 0006; s/d incl breakfast US$60/80) The only place to stay in town is this poorly marked new hotel and restaurant, just east of the War Museum. The en suite rooms are average and overpriced in high season, but the breezy bar and restaurant serves cold beer with a grand view towards the coastline. Camping may be possible in the garden but you'll need to negotiate this directly with the owner.

It also may be possible to camp on the beaches nearby but you'll have to hunt around for the police and attempt to get a *tasreeh* (camping permit).

TURNING POINT AT EL ALAMEIN

For a brief period in 1942, the tiny railway station at El Alamein commanded the attention of the entire world. Since 1940, the British had battled the Italians and Germans for control of North Africa; fighting raged back and forth from Tunisia to Egypt as first one side and then the other seized the advantage.

By 1942, Axis units under Field Marshal Erwin Rommel, the celebrated 'Desert Fox', had pushed the Allies back to the last defensible position before Cairo – a line running from El Alamein 65km south to the impassable Qattara Depression. The situation appeared hopeless. British staffers burnt their papers to prevent them from falling into enemy hands, the Germans were expected in Alexandria any day, and Mussolini flew to Egypt to prepare for his triumphal entry into Cairo.

However, in desperate fighting the Allies repulsed the next German thrust by late July. In early September, galvanised by the little-known General Bernard Law Montgomery, the Allies parried a second attack focused on the famous Alam al Halfa ridge.

Monty husbanded his strength for an all-out counteroffensive, which he launched on 23 October 1942. Intense fighting raged for 13 days, with each side suffering appalling losses, until the Axis line at last crumbled. Rommel's routed legions retreated westward, never to return to Egypt. The Desert Fox was recalled to Germany to spare him the disgrace of defeat, but 230,000 of his soldiers eventually surrendered in Tunisia.

Monty was knighted, and became the most famous British general of the war. In 1946 he was made the First Viscount Montgomery of Alamein, a title he used for the rest of his life. About the battle, Winston Churchill famously said 'Before Alamein we never had a victory. After Alamein we never had a defeat.'

CLEOPATRA'S TOMB?

Egypt's North Coast was heavily colonised during the Graeco-Roman period, and its potentially rich archaeological pickings are starting to be unearthed. The focus of much interest these days is the previously little-known temple of Taposiris Magna, about 45km west of Alexandria. The temple received newfound attention when Dr Zahi Hawass, the renowned and excitable secretary-general of Egypt's Supreme Council of Antiquities, theorised that it could be the final resting place of the legendary lovers Mark Antony and Cleopatra.

With imposing walls at least 10m high and 2m thick, Taposiris Magna was built by Ptolemy IV (221–205 BC) at the acropolis (the highest point) of a large city, whose remains lay south of the temple. The structure reflects the fusion of Greek and Egyptian influences typical of the era. Inside the walls, traces of the Romans, who converted the temple into a fort, are visible, as well as the remains of a 6th- to 7th-century-AD Christian church. Just east of the temple is an ancient 20m tower, built in the form of the Pharos, with a square base, hexagonal midsection and cylindrical upper section.

Excavations of the temple and city are ongoing, and finds include an alabaster bust of Cleopatra and coins with her visage, plus a mask that may bear some resemblance to Marc Antony. A recent radar survey has hinted at the presence of multiple large tombs, suggesting the tantalising possibility of a royal burial, but many archaeologists remain sceptical of the Cleopatra theory. One thing is clear, though – if Dr Hawass is correct, it could be the most significant find since King Tut.

Taposiris Magna is not open to visitors, but it is hoped that will change in the future. You can see the ruins from the Alexandria–Marsa Matruh highway; coming from Alexandria, just before the sign indicating km241 to Matruh, look on the left-hand side of the road. You'll see the smaller tower first, and the huge temple walls a few hundred metres further west. Coming from Marsa Matruh, the site is at km45–47.

If you want to stay on the beach – and who wouldn't with water like this? – the closest viable place is the Charm Life/Regency Ghazala Bay Hotel at Sidi Abdel Rahman (see p400), west of El Alamein town.

Getting There & Away

The easiest option is to organise your own car and driver (see Tours & Services, p383). A taxi will charge around E£250 to E£350 to take you to the War Museum, ferry you between the cemeteries and bring you back to Alexandria.

Alternatively, catch any of the Marsa Matruh buses from the Al-Mo'af al-Gedid long-distance bus station in Alexandria (see p391). You'll be dropped on the main road about 200m down the hill from the War Museum.

Charter flights have recently started operating from the UK and Germany to El Alamein airport in combination with a week's stay at Charm Life (p400).

SIDI ABDEL RAHMAN
☎ 046

The gorgeous beaches of Sidi Abdel Rahman are the raison d'être for this growing resort hamlet, and with charter flights starting between Europe and nearby El Alamein (23km east), development is likely to continue. Several resorts take prime position on the sparkling waters and white sands of the Mediterranean and are the major draw – though there is little else to see or do here.

Bedouins from the Awlad Ali tribe occasionally congregate in a small village about 3km in from the beach. Originally from the Libyan Cyrenaica, they came to the region several hundred years ago and settled, subduing the smaller local tribes of the Morabiteen. The Egyptian government has been attempting to settle these nomads, so today most Bedouins have forsaken their tents and herd their sheep and goats from the immobility of government-built houses, though you're still likely to see people ushering herds of livestock around.

Sights

A real find is **Shaat al-Hanna**, a free and blissfully uncrowded beach with splendid milky-blue water, great for swimming. Even out here, conservative dress for women applies. There are a few tents set up, and camping should be possible, but you'll need to ask around once there.

DIY NORTH COAST

While Egypt's North Coast generally offers slim pickings for the independent traveller, there are still some relatively unexplored areas ripe for anyone looking to get *seriously* off the beaten track. Along the Alexandria–Marsa Matruh road west of Sidi Abdel Rahman, the coastal development thins out considerably; there's really not much but the occasional half-completed resort, military installation, or Bedouin village. Every few hundred metres, tiny roads, usually sand tracks, lead off in the direction of the sea a few kilometres away. It's impossible to know where these lead without trying each one, but it's conceivable that some go to empty stretches of shore where you might have the water all to yourself.

To explore this area, you'll need transport capable of negotiating bumpy unpaved tracks. Language skills are also essential, because while passing through villages, you should greet anyone you happen to see and let them know what you're doing. Be especially mindful of local customs, remembering that this area sees few if any travellers. If the vibe doesn't feel right, turn around and try the next road.

Also, since there is so little accommodation between Sidi Abdel Rahman and Marsa Matruh, make sure to leave enough time to backtrack if you don't find anything.

Lastly, be prepared for nine out of 10 roads you try to be dead ends. But, one road may just go to that perfect, unspoilt beach – if you find it, let us know.

There's no sign in English; heading west along the Alexandria–Marsa Matruh road the turn-off for the beach is marked by three rusting yellow signs 1.9km after the 155km to Marsa Matruh milestone, or 4.9km after the checkpoint and turn-off for the Marassi Hotel. The road is part paved and part sand, but fine for regular cars.

Sleeping & Eating

Charm Life (☎ 419 0061/71; www.charmlifehotels.com; km140 on Alexandria–Marsa Matruh rd, Ghazala Bay; s/d incl breakfast E£1550, 1st child under 12yr stays free) Previously the Mövenpick and possibly to be renamed the Ghazala Regency, this resort caters to European families on package tours. The granite-floored rooms are large, but the decor uninspired, the housekeeping variable and the buffet meals bland. The beach, however, is out of this world, with azure water as clear as a pool, and empty stretches of sand perfect for walking. Youngsters are well catered for, with a kids' pool and artificial cove, plus jet-ski and kayak rental. There's little here in terms of culture or character, but if you're looking to lie about on a gorgeous beach checking out tanned Italians in skimpy swimwear (and we're not talking about the ladies), this fits the bill.

Getting There & Away

The same buses that can drop you at El Alamein en route to or from Marsa Matruh (see p391) can also drop you here. They generally stop for a break just after the Hanna Beach turn-off. There are service taxis operating between El Alamein and Sidi Abdel Rahman and to places further west, but nothing much happens after early afternoon.

MARSA MATRUH
☎ 046 / pop 159, 800

Your experience of the brilliant-white sand and turquoise-lined bays of Marsa Matruh will depend on what time of year you arrive. In the summer months of June to September, half of the lower Nile Valley descends on this sleepy Mediterranean town for their holiday spell. At this time the streets buzz with people late into the night, throngs of street stalls sell hot food and souvenirs, and impromptu street musicians bang out rhythmic tunes. But the beaches are sardine-packed full of picnicking families, hotels raise their rates to astronomical heights and buses to and from town overflow. The rest of the year, Marsa Matruh returns to its usual near-comatose state. Many hotels shut their doors at this time, the city's beautiful bay of white, sandy beaches lies empty, and the only visitors are Bedouins and Libyans stocking up on goods. Whatever the time of year, few foreign tourists make the trip out here, except to break the journey to Siwa.

Orientation

The two key streets in Marsa Matruh are the Corniche (Al-Corniche), which winds its way around the waterfront, and Sharia

Iskendariyya, which runs perpendicular to the Corniche, towards the hill behind the town. The pricier hotels are along the Corniche, while most others, as well as most of the restaurants and shops, are near Sharia Iskendariyya.

Information

There are several exchange bureaus on Sharia al-Galaa.

Banque Misr (Map p402; Sharia al-Galaa; ✆ 9am-2.30pm & 6.30-8pm Sun-Thu) Has an ATM.

CrazyNet (Map p402; Sharia ash-Shaati; ✆ 24hr) Internet cafe.

Main post office (Map p402; Sharia ash-Shaati; ✆ 9am-9pm Sat-Thu)

Military Hospital (Map p402; ☎ 493 5286; Sharia ash-Shaati)

National Bank of Egypt (Map p402; off Sharia al-Matar; ✆ 9am-2pm & 6-9pm Sun-Thu)

Passport office (Map p402; ☎ 493 5351; off Sharia Iskendariyya; ✆ 8am-3pm Sat-Thu) No sign, so look for the yellow/brown building with a line in front, or ask for the *gawezaat*.

Raafat Pharmacy (Map p402; ☎ 493 3939; 1 Sharia al-Galaa; ✆ 9am-3am)

Telephone centrale (Map p402; Sharia ash-Shaati; ✆ 8am-10pm)

Tourist office (Map p402; ☎ 493 1841; cnr Sharia Omar Mukhtar & Al-Corniche; ✆ 8.30am-7pm Jun-Sep, to 5pm Oct-May) Has updated transport details, and a free, handy street map.

Tourist police (Map p402; ☎ 493 5575; cnr Sharia Omar Mukhtar & Al-Corniche)

Sights & Activities

BEACHES

The luminescence of the water along this stretch of the coast is only marred by the town's overflowing hotel scene. Further away, the water is just as nice and you can still find a few places where the developers have yet to start pouring cement. During the hot summer months women cannot bathe in swimsuits, unless they can handle being the object of intense harassment and ogling. The exception is the private beaches at Hotel Beau Site and San Giovanni Cleopatra, although even here most Egyptian women remain fully dressed and in the shade.

If you do manage to get into the azure waters, offshore lies the wreck of a German submarine, and sunken Roman galleys reputedly rest in deeper waters off to the east.

The **Lido**, the main beach in town, has decent sand and clear water, but is jam-packed in summer. The unnamed beach on the east side of town, near the bridge over to Rommel's Beach, has a flat bottom and shallow water great for kids. At any of the town beaches, expect to pay from E£5 to E£10 for a chair and umbrella.

Possibly the most beautiful piece of coastline in the area is **Cleopatra's Beach**, about 14km west of town around the bay's thin tentacle of land. The sea here is an exquisite hue, and the rock formations are worth a look. You can wade to Cleopatra's Bath, a natural pool where legend has imagined the great queen and Mark Antony enjoying a dip, but there's no swimming these days due to the waves and rocks just offshore.

Three kilometres beyond Cleopatra's Beach, at the tip end of the tentacle of land, is **Shaati al-Gharam** (Lovers' Beach). Unsurprisingly, the water here is sublime but the sand is only marginally less busy than at the main city beaches. In summer, boats (E£3, until sundown) shuttle back and forth from near Hotel Beau Site across the bay. Taxis will charge about E£10 to E£20 each way, and more if you want the driver to wait while you enjoy the beach.

Agiba means 'miracle' in Arabic and **Agiba Beach**, about 24km west of Marsa Matruh, is just that. It is a small but spectacular cove, accessible only via a path leading down from the clifftop. The water here is a dazzlingly clear turquoise, though it isn't ideal for toddlers, as the waves roll in strongly. It's absolutely packed in summer and near empty the rest of the year. There is a cafe nearby (open in summer only) where you can get light refreshments. Microbuses (E£2) to Agiba leave from in front of the National Bank of Egypt (known locally as Ahly Bank).

About 1km to 2km east of the hilltop above Agiba is a long expanse of accessible beach, with fine sand and deep blue water, and far less crowded than the cove. Confusingly, this stretch of shore is also known as Agiba Beach. To get here, take the turn-off marked by a blue, white and yellow sign (in Arabic) 3km west of Carol's Beau Rivage (see p403). This paved road leads to the beachfront; entrance is gated, but at the time of writing there was no fee.

Along the highway to Agiba, there are multiple **roadside stands** selling excellent produce from Siwa, such as green and black olives, olive oil, spices, and lots of dates, which are considered the best in Egypt. The ones with

ALEXANDRIA & THE
MEDITERRANEAN COAST

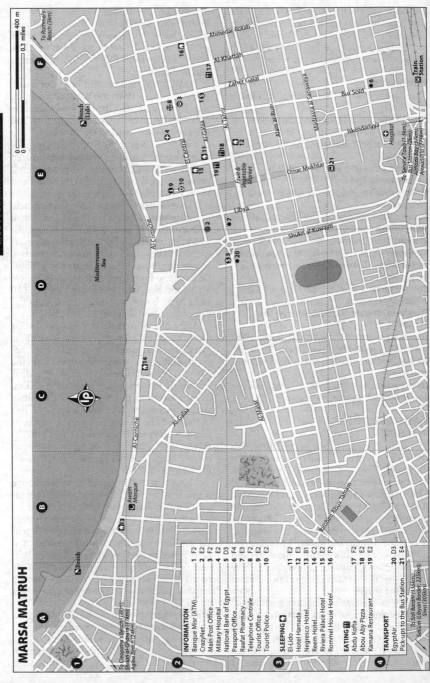

MARSA MATRUH

Mediterranean Sea

almonds stuffed inside make an excellent beach snack.

Sleeping

The accommodation situation in Marsa Matruh leaves a lot to be desired. With a few exceptions, hotels generally specialise in mediocrity at unreasonable rates, but demand for rooms over summer is such that hoteliers really don't need to try very hard. We list a few of the better, more central options.

Prices fluctuate wildly from winter to summer. In the June to September summer months you're advised to book well ahead, though note that many hotels will make you pay for a double room even if you are travelling solo.

BUDGET

Hotel Hamada (Map p402; ☎ 493 3300; Sharia al-Tahrir; s/d with shared bathroom E£30/60) Located right in the centre of town, the Hamada is a rudimentary budget option with reasonably clean rooms and friendly staff. Note that in summer the riotous party noise from Sharia Iskendariyya below can be deafening.

Rommel House Hotel (Map p402; ☎ 493 5466; fax 493 2485; Sharia al-Galaa; s/d E£60/90) Well away from the hubbub of the Corniche and Sharia Iskendariyya, rooms at this dependable, long-standing and cavernous hotel come with private bathroom, TV and refrigerator. Respect goes out to it for the relatively mild summer price hike.

MIDRANGE

El-Lido (Map p402; ☎ 493 2248; Sharia Iskendariyya; s/d incl breakfast Jun-Sep E£170/240; 🕸) Even though the rooms in this centrally located tower block see less daylight than Dracula, it's still a fair deal by Marsa Matruh's low standards – especially considering you get air-con thrown in.

Reem Hotel (Map p402; ☎ 493 3605; Al-Corniche; d without view/reg/VIP high season E£285/385/485) The Reem has institutionally white halls and rooms with balconies facing the ocean. While the abodes may suffer a serious charisma deficit, they do offer a spick-and-span place to sleep. View-deprived rooms are a little cheaper.

Riviera Palace Hotel (Map p402; ☎ 493 3045; Sharia Iskendariyya; s/d incl breakfast E£450/650) When not fully booked by holidaying Cairenes, you can get one of the big and tidy rooms here. Try as it might, the schizophrenic foyer design, oscillating from a chandelier-clad nautical theme

to a stuffed-tiger motif, does little to add any real character to the place.

Negresco Hotel (Map p402; ☎ 493 4491/2; Al-Corniche; s/d half board high season E£450/650, low season E£250/450) The Negresco adds a much-needed dollop of Mediterranean charm to Marsa Matruh's hotel scene, with whitewashed walls and pretty blue balconies. The rooms are overpriced but immaculate, and the facilities adequate.

TOP END

our pick **Almaza Bay** (off Map p402; ☎ 436 0000; www .jaz.travel; north coast 37km east of Matruh; s/d half board low season from €120/160) On a remote stretch of seafront 37km east of town, this resort includes three hotels: Almaza Bay, the Moroccan-themed Oriental, and Crystal, fitted out like a sophisticated New York cocktail bar. The lobby at Crystal is replete with chandeliers and accents of silver, white and purple velvet, but we like it for its large rooms with handsome wood doors, tasteful modern fittings, posh bathrooms with huge showers, and very comfortable beds. Crystal also offers larger family-sized rooms, which have an extra alcove with a crib and pull-out couch. The three hotels share a beachfront, and guests can use facilities at any of the three, including sampling the tasty buffets. The only drawbacks are the intrusive daytime 'entertainment', and the fact that the existing structures are just the beginning – the plan is to develop Almaza Bay into a megaresort with golf courses, villas and an artificial marina. This threatens to detract from the get-away-from-it-all feel, but as of now this place is unquestionably among the nicest on the North Coast.

Carol's Beau Rivage (off Map p404; 15km west of Marsa Matruh, on Sallum hwy; s/d rack rates US$350/400) Situated around a delightful bay with glowing aquamarine water, this recently opened resort has comfortable rooms in an incongruous safari theme, with elephant paintings, dark-wood furnishings and cane chairs on the balconies. In spite of this, or perhaps because of it, the overall feel is institutional, but the beach is certainly one of the nicest in the area.

Eating

The dining situation in Marsa Matruh is nothing to write home about. In winter you may have a hard time finding something to eat, although Abdu Kofta is open year-round.

Abdu Kofta (Map p402; ☎ 012 314 4989; Sharia al-Tahrir; dishes E£5-60; 🕸) Locals will swear black and blue that this is the best restaurant in

AROUND MARSA MATRUH

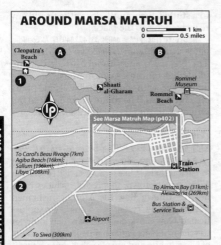

0 ——— 1 km
0 ——— 0.5 miles

Cleopatra's Beach Ⓐ

Ⓑ

❶

Shaati al-Gharam

Rommel Museum

Rommel Beach

See Marsa Matruh Map (p402)

To Carol's Beau Rivage (7km);
Agiba Beach (16km);
Sallum (196km);
Libya (208km)

Train Station

❷

To Almaza Bay (31km);
Alexandria (269km)

Bus Station & Service Taxis

Airport

To Siwa (300km)

town. In the clean and cool 1st-floor room, it serves *kofta* or grilled meat by the weight served with good mezze and salads.

Kamana Restaurant (Map p402; Sharia al-Galaa; meals E£8-20) This simple restaurant does a roaring daily trade in grilled meats (ie just chicken and kebabs). Follow your nose when you get to the Iskendariyya corner and you can't miss it.

Abou Aby Pizza (Map p402; Sharia Iskendariyya; pizzas E£12-18) For as-close-as-you'll-get-to-the-real-thing Western-style pizza, you can't go past Abou Aby. It has lots of seating upstairs, and as a bonus you can people-watch the action on Sharia Iskendariyya below while tucking in.

Getting There & Away

AIR
Twice-weekly flights between Cairo and Marsa Matruh are available with **EgyptAir** (Map p402; ☎ 493 6573; Sharia al-Matar) from June to September, leaving Cairo at 3.15pm and returning at 5pm. Tickets are about E£700 one way. A taxi to the airport should cost between E£5 and E£10. Microbuses leave from in front of the National Bank of Egypt.

BUS
Matruh's bus station (off Map p402) is 2km out of town on the main coastal highway. Expect to pay about E£5 to E£7 for a taxi to the town centre. There's also a microbus (50pt) leaving from Sharia Omar Mukhtar and 'Secondary School' road.

West Delta Bus Co (☎ 490 5079) has hourly services to Alexandria from 7am to 2am (E£17 to E£30, four hours). During summer, 17 departures daily serve Cairo (E£45 to E£55, five hours), leaving between 7.30am and 2am, with special 'VIP' buses at 8.30am and 3.30pm. In winter there are five daily buses to Cairo, again between 7.30am and 2am.

There are 16 buses daily to Barani and Sallum (E£13, four hours), departing around the clock. Six buses daily head to Siwa (E£13, four hours), between 7am and 2am.

Superjet (☎ 490 4787) has several services a day to Alexandria and Cairo from June to September only.

The tourist office in Marsa Matruh keeps updated details on bus schedules.

SERVICE TAXI
The service taxi lot is beside the bus station. Service taxis to Siwa, if there are enough passengers, cost E£13. Other fares include El Alamein E£10, Alexandria E£16, Cairo E£25 to E£30, Sallum E£12 and Sidi Barani E£12.

A MATRUH STREET PICNIC

The night-time street market running along and just off Sharia Iskendariyya sells a huge range of objects and consumables, and in particular offers plenty of produce from Siwa, the fertile desert oasis to the south – the olives and dates from there are especially delicious. Despite the crowds and blasting music, the market makes for good strolling, and by buying from different sellers, you can eat interestingly and inexpensively, too. Here's a sample street-food picnic:

2 pieces flatbread, hot from street oven – E£1
¼ kg mixed green and black Siwa olives – E£2
2 medium mangoes – E£1.50
¼ kg Siwa dates – E£2
1 bottle water or juice – E£2
total price – E£8.50

But don't take our word for it – wander the stalls, pick whatever suits your fancy, then take your feast down to the Corniche and dig in.

TRAIN

From 15 June to 15 September, there are three sleeper trains (www.sleepingtrains .com) weekly (single/double US$60/43, seven hours) between Cairo and Marsa Matruh. Trains depart Cairo Monday, Wednesday and Saturday, and leave Matruh on the return journey Sunday, Tuesday and Thursday. Going in both directions, trains depart at 11pm and arrive at 6am. Reservations can either be made in Cairo (☎ 02-2738 3682/4) or by purchasing your ticket on the train.

Air-conditioned 1st-/2nd-class express trains run daily between Cairo and Marsa Matruh (1st/2nd class E£58/34, seven hours) from June to September only.

Ordinary 2nd-/3rd-class trains without air-con run year-round between Marsa Matruh and Alexandria (6½ hours), but these are not recommended – even those working at the station have described the trains as 'horrible'.

Getting Around

Private taxis or pick-ups can be hired for the day, but you must bargain aggressively, especially in summer. Expect to pay E£80 to E£150, depending on the distance.

Bikes can be rented from makeshift rental places along Sharia Iskendariyya during the high season for around E£10 to E£20 per day. A taxi to the airport will cost around E£7 to E£10.

SIDI BARANI
☎ 046

About 135km west of Marsa Matruh on the way to Libya is this small but busy Bedouin town. It serves a bit of food and petrol to traffic coming from Libya, but that's about it. There are a few hotels, including the Arous al-Bahr and the Sidi Baruse (☎ 4400 142), and unsanitary places to eat.

SALLUM
☎ 46

Look up 'middle of nowhere' in the dictionary and you might just find the town of Sallum, a mere 12km from the Libyan border. Nestled at the foot of Gebel as-Sallum and lying on the Gulf of Sallum, the town was once the ancient port of Baranis. While

---

LIBYA BORDER CROSSING

The border crossing point of Amsaad, just north of Halfaya Pass, is open 24 hours (sometimes even in a row). It's 12km west of Sallum, which is about a E£5 ride in a service taxi. For information about visas for Libya, see p526.

---

a few Roman wells testify to its history, it is now mostly a Bedouin trading post that sees few international visitors.

The sea here, as along the rest of this stretch of coast, is crystal clear and aquamarine in colour, but don't think about frolicking in the water – dumped rubbish lines the sand, government property surrounds the town and permits are needed to be on the beach after 5pm.

On the eastern entrance to the town there is a modest WWII Commonwealth War Cemetery, commemorating the destruction of hundreds of British tanks by the Germans at nearby 'Hell Fire' pass.

Sallum has a National Bank of Egypt branch (☎ 480 0590), and some hotels may agree to exchange money.

Sleeping & Eating

If you can, you will want to avoid staying in Sallum, but if you have no choice the **Hotel al-Ahram** (☎ 480 0148; s/d E£14/21) is the best of an unattractive bunch. The rooms are spartan and when there is water, it's cold.

There are a couple of rough *lokanda*s (basic, cheap places to doss) with their names in Arabic only, of which the **Sirt Hotel** (☎ 480 1113) is the better one.

At the border, 12km further on, is Hotel at-Ta'un (signed in Arabic only). There are two modest *fuul* stands around, but check on the price first, as it may be higher for the lone foreigner passing by.

Getting There & Away

There are buses and the odd service taxi leaving from Alexandria (see p392) and Marsa Matruh (opposite).

From Sallum, buses for Marsa Matruh (E£15, four hours) depart hourly between 7am and 2am; some of these continue on to Alexandria (E£28, eight hours). A service taxi to Marsa Matruh will cost about E£12.

Suez Canal

The Suez Canal is truly one of the world's greatest engineering marvels. Slicing through the sands of the Isthmus of Suez, the canal separates mainland Egypt from the Sinai Peninsula as well as Africa from Asia. At 163km in length, the Suez Canal facilitates the transit of more than 20,000 ships a year between the Mediterranean and the Red Sea, and serves as the lifeline of the Egyptian economy.

Despite these impressive statistics, the Suez Canal is not well set up for tourism, unlike its Panamanian counterpart. Strict security measures prevent tourists from transiting the canal on private boats and independent travel in the region is tightly controlled. As a result, few foreigners set their sights on the Suez, aside from European yachties bound for the Red Sea.

The appeal of the region lies in the three cities that sit along the western banks of the canal, namely Port Said, Ismailia and Suez. Colonial creations that emerged when the canal grew in prominence, these cities were on the front line during the wars with Israel and suffered greatly from bombardments. However, their 19th-century beginnings still survive in the wide, leafy boulevards and graceful colonial architecture lining their picturesque town centres, setting them apart from the rest of Egypt.

If you have the time and the inclination to step off Egypt's more trodden trails, the canal's urban trio offers an altogether distinctive experience. In contrast with the temples, pyramids and ruins that characterise other parts of Egypt, the Suez Canal offers an intriguing combination of belle époque architecture, modern shipping infrastructure and portside energy.

HIGHLIGHTS

- Stroll along the waterfront while admiring the graceful 19th-century architecture of **Port Said** (opposite)

- Take the **ferry** (p408) from Port Said to Port Fuad to get a brief taste of life on the canal

- Step into Egypt's colonial past while wandering through the old European quarter of **Ismailia** (p411)

- Admire more than 4000 objects from Pharaonic and Graeco-Roman times at the rarely visited **Ismailia Museum** (p411)

- Watch supertankers appear to glide through the desert in the city of **Suez** (p413), the canal's southern terminus

Port Said ★★ Port Fuad

★ Ismailia

★ Suez

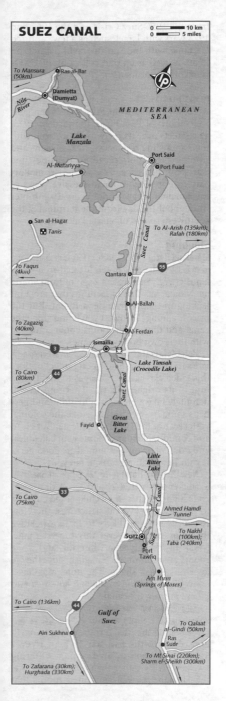

SUEZ CANAL

0 — 10 km
0 — 5 miles

To Mansura (50km)
Ras al-Bar
Damietta (Dumyat)
Nile River
MEDITERRANEAN SEA
Lake Manzala
Al-Matariyya
Port Said
Port Fuad
San al-Hagar
Tanis
To Al-Arish (135km); Rafah (180km)
To Faqus (4km)
Qantara
55
Al-Ballah
To Zagazig (40km)
Al-Ferdan
Ismailia
3
Lake Timsah (Crocodile Lake)
To Cairo (80km)
44
Great Bitter Lake
Fayid
Little Bitter Lake
To Cairo (75km)
33
Ahmed Hamdi Tunnel
Suez
Port Tawfiq
To Nakhl (100km); Taba (240km)
Ain Musa (Springs of Moses)
To Cairo (136km)
44
Gulf of Suez
Ain Sukhna
To Qalaat al-Gindi (50km)
Ras Sudr
To Mt Sinai (220km); Sharm el-Sheikh (300km)
To Zafarana (30km); Hurghada (330km)

SUEZ CANAL

PORT SAID

☎ 066 / pop 570,000

Port Said's main attraction, and the reason for its establishment on the Mediterranean, is the Suez Canal. The enormous ships and tankers lining up to pass through the canal's northern entrance are an impressive sight to behold. Although heavily damaged in the 1967 and 1973 wars with Israel, much of the city has been rebuilt along its historic lines. Today, Port Said exudes a prosperous and bustling air, particularly its historic waterfront of late 19th-century colonial buildings. The city is also home to the leafy suburb of Port Fuad, which can be reached by a free ferry that crosses the Suez Canal – perfect for anyone who doesn't own their own yacht.

Orientation

Port Said is connected to the mainland by a bridge to the south and a causeway to the west. There is also a ferry between Port Said and its sister town of Port Fuad on the opposite side of the canal.

Most banks and important services are on Sharia Palestine, which runs along the canal, or on Sharia al-Gomhuriyya, two blocks inland.

Information

CUSTOMS

Port Said was declared a duty-free port in 1976. In theory, everyone must pass through customs when entering and leaving the city, though in practice this is seldom enforced. Regardless, be sure to have your passport with you.

EMERGENCY

Tourist police (☎ 322 8570; post office bldg, off Sharia al-Gomhuriyya)

INTERNET ACCESS

Compunet (per hr E£3; ☼ 9am-midnight) Next to Ferial Gardens.

MEDICAL SERVICES

Delafrant Hospital (☎ 322 3663; Sharia Orabi)
Public Hospital (☎ 322 0694; Sharia Safiyya Zaghloul)

MONEY

Bank of Alexandria (Sharla al-Gomhuriyya; ☼ 8.30am-2pm & 6-8pm Sun-Thu)
National Bank of Egypt (Sharia al-Gomhuriyya; ☼ 9am-2pm & 6.30-8pm Sat-Thu)

POST
Main post office (Sharia al-Geish; ☉ 8.30am-2.30pm Sat-Thu)

TOURIST INFORMATION
Tourist office (☎ 323 5289; 8 Sharia Palestine; ☉ 9am-6pm Sat-Thu)

Sights

SUEZ CANAL HOUSE

If you've ever seen a picture of Port Said, it was probably of the striking green domes of the Suez Canal House, which was built in time for the inauguration of the canal in 1869. Unfortunately, the interior of the building is off limits to visitors.

TOWN CENTRE

The heart of Port Said is located along the edge of the canal, on and around Sharia Palestine. Here, the waterfront is lined with late 19th-century five-storey buildings complete with wooden balconies, louvered doors and high verandahs in grand belle époque style.

Take a stroll down Sharia Memphis, in particular, with its old Woolworth's building (now a souvenir emporium), and around the streets just north of the Commercial Basin. There are some wonderfully odd colonial remnants, such as the **old Postes Françaises**, a sign for the ship chandlers of the pre-Soviet 'volunteer Russian fleet' and another for the Bible Society.

Northeast of here, on Sharia 23rd of July, is the **Italian consulate building**, erected in the 1930s and adorned with an engraved piece of the propaganda of Fascist dictator Benito Mussolini: 'Rome – once again at the heart of an empire'.

Several blocks inland, on and around Sharia Salah Salem, is an impressive collection of churches, including the **Coptic Orthodox Church** of St Bishoi of the Virgin and the **Franciscan compound**.

At the very northern end of Sharia Palestine is a large **stone plinth** that once held a statue of Ferdinand de Lesseps, until it was torn down in 1956 with the nationalisation of the Suez Canal. Although the statue was restored at the expense of the French government in the early 1990s, it has yet to be re-erected.

MILITARY MUSEUM

This compact **museum** (☎ 322 4657; Sharia 23rd of July; admission E£5; ☉ 9am-4pm Sat-Thu) houses relics from the 1956 Suez Crisis and the 1967 and 1973 wars with Israel, such as a few captured US tanks with the Star of David painted on them, as well as an odd collection of UXOs (unexploded ordnance).

PORT FUAD

Across the canal from Port Said is the genteel suburb of Port Fuad, founded in 1925. The streets near its quay invite a stroll, with their sprawling residences, lush gardens and sloping tiled roofs recalling the one-time European presence. Free ferries from Port Said to Port Fuad offer impressive views of the canal and leave about every 10 minutes throughout the day from the terminal at the southwestern end of Sharia Palestine.

Sleeping

Mereland Hotel (☎ 322 7020; r E£50, with shared bathroom E£35) This tatty hotel, located in a small lane between Sharia Saad Zaghloul and Sharia an-Nahda, has shared facilities that are a bit lacking in the hygiene department. But the price is among the lowest you'll find along the canal and the largish rooms come complete with their own breezy balconies.

Hotel de la Poste (☎ 322 4048; 42 Sharia al-Gomhuriyya; s/d from E£75/100) Port Said's best budget option, this faded classic still manages to maintain a hint of its original charm. That said, it will definitely take a bit of imagination (and perhaps some hazy vision) to evoke the colonial yesteryear of the Hotel de la Poste. But clean and comfortable rooms (some with balconies) and a decent on-site restaurant are good perks if your imagination starts to fail you.

New Regent Hotel (☎ 323 5000; off Sharia al-Gomhuriyya; s/d from E£220/245; ☒ ☐) A drab concrete high-rise that stands in marked contrast to the nearby classical structures, the New Regent is not very likely to leave a positive first impression. However, this three-star hotel has a surprisingly smart interior, and while rooms are a bit on the smallish side, they're kept in spotless shape. The hotel also has a convenient location in a small lane just two blocks in from the canal.

our pick Helnan Port Said (☎ 332 0890; www.helnan .com; Sharia Atef as-Sadat; s/d from US$200/400; ☒ ☐ ☒) Overlooking the Mediterranean at the north end of town, the five-star Helnan is Port Said's most sophisticated option. Offering low-key luxury rather than opulent pleasure, the Helnan has well-appointed rooms that

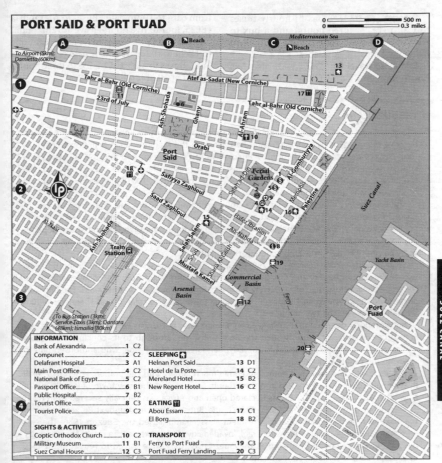

PORT SAID & PORT FUAD

INFORMATION		
Bank of Alexandria	1	C2
Compunet	2	C2
Delafrant Hospital	3	A1
Main Post Office	4	C2
National Bank of Egypt	5	C2
Passport Office	6	B1
Public Hospital	7	B2
Tourist Office	8	C3
Tourist Police	9	C2

SIGHTS & ACTIVITIES		
Coptic Orthodox Church	10	C2
Military Museum	11	B1
Suez Canal House	12	C3

SLEEPING		
Helnan Port Said	13	D1
Hotel de la Poste	14	C2
Mereland Hotel	15	B2
New Regent Hotel	16	C2

EATING		
Abou Essam	17	C1
El Borg	18	B2

TRANSPORT		
Ferry to Port Fuad	19	C3
Port Fuad Ferry Landing	20	C3

boast views over the end of the canal and the Mediterranean. The hotel is also home to a number of top-notch restaurants serving up some of the best eats in town. If you book over the internet, it's sometimes possible to snag discount rates and special packages.

Eating

For fruit and vegetables, try the lively market on Sharia Souq, three blocks north of Sharia al-Gomhuriyya.

El Borg (☎ 332 3442; off Sharia Saad Zaghloul; dishes E£10-25; 🕙 10am-3am) A local favourite, with an Arabic only menu and serve-yourself seafood grills.

Abou Essam (☎ 323 2776; Sharia Atef as-Sadat; meals E£25-35; 🍴) This favourite has a serve-yourself

salad bar featuring tahini, *baba ghanoug* (purée of grilled aubergines with tomato and onion) and other delicacies, as well as a selection of fish, pasta and grilled meat.

Getting There & Away

BOAT

Cruise ships ply the waters between Port Said and Limassol (Cyprus), with most sailing between April and October; see p527 for details.

BUS

The bus station is about 3km from the town centre at the beginning of the road to Cairo (about E£3 to E£5 in a taxi).

Superjet (☎ 372 1779) has bi-hourly buses to Cairo (E£25, three hours) and a bus to Alexandria (E£30, four hours) at 4.30pm daily. Bookings are advisable.

East Delta Travel Co (☎ 372 9883) also has hourly buses to Cairo (E£17, three hours) from 6am to 10pm daily. Buses to Alexandria (E£25, four to five hours) leave at 7am, 11am, 3.30pm and 7pm. Buses to Ismailia (E£7, one to 1½ hours) depart hourly between 6am and 7pm. Buses to Suez (E£14, 2½ to three hours) depart at 10am and 3.30pm.

THE SUEZ CANAL

The Suez Canal represents the culmination of centuries of effort to enhance trade and expand the empires of Egypt by connecting the Red Sea with the Mediterranean Sea. Construction of the first recorded canal was begun by Pharaoh Nekau II between 610 and 595 BC. The canal stretched from the Nile Delta town of Bubastis, near present-day Zagazig, to the Red Sea via the Bitter Lakes. After reputedly causing the death of more than 100,000 workers, construction of the canal was quickly abandoned.

The project was picked up again and completed about a century later under Darius, one of Egypt's Persian rulers. The canal was improved by the Romans under Trajan but over the next several centuries it was either neglected and left to silt up, or dredged for limited use depending on the available resources. The canal was again briefly restored in AD 649 for a period of 20 years by Amr ibn al-As, the Arab conqueror of Egypt.

Following the French invasion in 1798, the importance of some sort of sea route south to Asia was again recognised. For the first time, digging a canal directly from the Mediterranean Sea to the Red Sea, across the comparatively narrow Isthmus of Suez, was considered. The idea was abandoned, however, as Napoleon's engineers mistakenly calculated that there was a 10m difference between the two sea levels.

British reports detected that mistake several years later but it was Ferdinand de Lesseps, the French consul to Egypt, who pursued the Suez Canal idea through to its conclusion. In 1854, de Lesseps presented his proposal to the Egyptian khedive Said Pasha, who authorised him to excavate the canal; work began in 1859.

A decade later the canal was completed amid much fanfare and celebration. When two small fleets, one originating in Port Said and the other in Suez, met at the new town of Ismailia on 16 November 1869, the Suez Canal was declared open and Africa was officially severed from Asia.

Ownership of the canal remained in French and British hands for the next 86 years until, in the wake of Egyptian independence, President Nasser nationalised the Suez in 1956. The two European powers, in conjunction with Israel, invaded Egypt in an attempt to retake the waterway by force. In what came to be known as the 'Suez Crisis', they were forced to retreat in the face of widespread international condemnation.

Today, the Suez Canal remains one of the world's most heavily used shipping lanes and toll revenues represent one of the largest contributors to the Egyptian state coffers. Starting in 2010, the Suez will open up for the first time in its history to supertankers, which previously had been too wide to navigate the canal and instead were forced to either offload their wares at the canal's entrance, or take the long route around the Cape of Agulhas in South Africa. Unfortunately, security in the Suez is being threatened by the increase in piracy off the coast of Somalia and in the Gulf of Aden.

Despite that more than 50 ships pass through the Suez each day, canal enthusiasts who want to do the same will find that it's not so easy. Organised trips don't exist and the police do not allow private boats to cruise the canal, for security reasons. Still, if you want to try to hitch a ride, the yacht basin in Port Fuad (p408) is the best place to enquire about passage on a vessel plying the canal, as the captains are sometimes looking for crew members. If you do manage to get on some sort of vessel, remember that taking photographs is generally prohibited as there is a strong military presence all along the canal.

Of course, the easiest way to get a fleeting taste of life on the canal is to simply take the free ferry over to Port Fuad from in front of the tourist office on Sharia Palestine in Port Said. Note that ships only transit the canal during daylight hours, so it's best to visit early on in the day to maximise your chances of seeing a transit.

SERVICE TAXI

Service taxis have an area in the bus station (about E£3 to E£5 to get there in a taxi; ask for *al-mahattat servees*). Sample destinations and fares: Cairo (E£15 to E£20), Ismailia (E£7 to E£12) and Suez (E£10 to E£15).

TRAIN

The five daily trains to Cairo via Ismailia (2nd-class service E£13 to E£18) are slow (five hours) and run at 5.30am, 9.45am, 1pm, 5.30pm and 7.30pm. There are no 1st-class services. Delays on these routes are common; buses are more efficient and more comfortable than the non-air-con trains.

Getting Around
HANTOUR

The most enjoyable way to tour Port Said, especially around sunset, is by *hantour* (horse-drawn carriage). *Hantours* can be found along all the main streets, and cost about E£10 per hour after some bargaining.

MICROBUS

Microbuses run along main arteries such as Sharia Orabi and Sharia ash-Shohada, and cost 50pt for a short ride.

TAXI

There are plenty of blue-and-white taxis around Port Said. Fares for short trips within the town centre average E£1 to E£3.

ISMAILIA
☎ 064 / pop 750,000

Ismailia was founded by and named after Pasha Ismail, who was khedive of Egypt in the 1860s while the Suez Canal was being built. The city was also the temporary home of Ferdinand de Lesseps, the director of the Suez Canal Company, who lived here until the canal was completed. Not surprisingly, Ismailia grew in the image of the French masters who had ensconced themselves in Egypt during the colonial era. Today, Ismailia's historic town centre, with its elegant colonial streets, expansive lawns and late 19th-century villas, is one of the most peaceful and picturesque neighbourhoods in the country.

Orientation

The heart of Ismailia and the area most worth exploring is the old European quarter around Sharia Thawra and the central square, Midan

---

LIBERTY ON THE CANAL

New York's Statue of Liberty was originally designed to stand in Port Said at the entrance to the Suez Canal. Inspired by the colossal statues at Abu Simbel (see p323), French sculptor Frédéric-Auguste Bartholdi formulated the idea of a huge statue of a woman bearing a torch. She was to represent progress – 'Egypt carrying the light of Asia', to use Bartholdi's own words. The idea was ultimately abandoned due to the cost, and the 'Light of Asia', which had developed from one of Bartholdi's models, was sent to New York, where she became Lady Liberty.

---

al-Gomhuriyya. Sharia Thawra runs south from the train line to the placid Sweetwater Canal, with Midan al-Gomhuriyya several blocks to the west.

Information
INTERNET ACCESS
Rodu Internet Café (Sharia Thawra; per hr E£2; ⏰ 10am-8pm)

MEDICAL SERVICES
Hospital (☎ 337 3902/3; Sharia Mustashfa)

MONEY
Bank of Alexandria (Midan Orabi; ⏰ 9am-2pm & 6-8pm Sun-Thu)

POST
Main post office (Sharia al-Horreyya; ⏰ 8.30am-2.30pm Sat-Thu)

TOURIST INFORMATION
Tourist office (☎ 332 1078; 1st fl, New Governorate Bldg, Sharia Tugary, Sheikh Zayeed area; ⏰ 8.30am-3pm Sat-Thu) About 1.5km north of Midan Orabi.
Tourist police (☎ 333 2910; tourist village, beach area)

Sights & Activities
ISMAILIA MUSEUM

More than 4000 objects from Pharaonic and Graeco-Roman times are housed at the small but interesting **Ismailia Museum** (☎ 391 2749; Mohammed Ali Quay; adult/child E£6/3; ⏰ 8am-4pm, closed for Fri noon prayers), located on the eastern edge of town. The collection includes statues, scarabs, stelae and records of the first canal, built between the Bitter Lakes and Bubastis by the

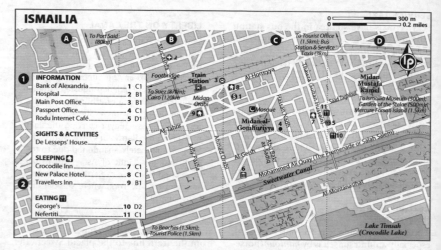

ISMAILIA

INFORMATION	
Bank of Alexandria	1 C1
Hospital	2 B1
Main Post Office	3 B1
Passport Office	4 C1
Rodu Internet Café	5 D1

SIGHTS & ACTIVITIES	
De Lesseps' House	6 C2

SLEEPING	
Crocodile Inn	7 C1
New Palace Hotel	8 C1
Travellers Inn	9 B1

EATING	
George's	10 D2
Nefertiti	11 C1

Persian ruler Darius. The highlight of the museum is a 4th-century-AD mosaic depicting characters from Greek and Roman mythology. At the top Phaedra is sending a love letter to her stepson Hippolytus, while below Dionysus is riding a chariot driven by Eros. The bottom section recounts the virtues of Hercules.

GARDEN OF THE STELAE
Just southwest of the Ismailia Museum is a garden containing a rather forlorn little sphinx from the time of Ramses II (1279–1213 BC). You need permission from the museum to visit the garden but you are able to see the unremarkable statue from the street. The attractive grounds of the majestic residence between the garden and the museum belong to the head of the Suez Canal Authority and are off limits to the public.

DE LESSEPS' HOUSE
The residence of the one-time French consul to Egypt used to be open to the public. These days you can see the interior only if you're a VIP of some sort, as the building currently serves as a private guest house for visitors of the Suez Canal Authority.

If you're not a privileged guest, you might be interested to know that de Lesseps' bedroom looks as if it has hardly been touched in over a century – old photos, books and various utensils are scattered around the desk and on the floor. Inside the grounds is also de Lesseps' private carriage, which has been encased in glass and remains in impeccable condition.

The house is located on Mohammed Ali Quay near the corner of Sharia Ahmed Orabi.

BEACHES
There are several beaches around Lake Timsah, on the southeastern edge of town. The better ones are owned by the various clubs dotting the shore and you'll need to pay to use them (on average about E£20). The public beaches charge between E£3 and E£5.

Sleeping
Travellers Inn (☎ 392 3304; Sharia Ahmed Orabi; r E£50, with shared bathroom E£35) This strictly shoestring place is one of the cheapest options in town but it's not for the faint of heart. Its musty rooms and grubby bathrooms are somewhat compensated for by a convenient location just west of Midan al-Gomhuriyya. This one's for the penny-pinchers.

New Palace Hotel (☎ 391 7761; Midan Orabi; r from E£85;) Occupying a grand old building near the train station in the city centre, the New Palace evokes a good measure of colonial flare. Recent renovations have kept the aged interior a bit closer to the times, though some rooms are much better than others. There is a sliding price scale here, so ask to look around and spring for some of the larger balcony-ringed rooms if they're available.

Crocodile Inn (☎ 391 2555; cnr Sharias Thawra & Saad Zaghloul; r from E£150;) While it's in a different class than the Mercure (opposite), the Crocodile Inn is without a doubt the best hotel in the town centre. Despite the spiffy exterior, the rooms themselves are a bit drab and decidedly lacking in character but overall it's a professional yet relaxed establishment. It's a good spot if you're looking for a base to explore the European quarter as historic Ismailia is right on your doorstep.

Mercure Forsan Island (☎ 391 6316; www.mercure.com; Gezirat Forsan; s/d from US$185/115; ❄ 🖥 ⚛) About 1.6km southeast of the old centre of town, the four-star Mercure is easily the most attractive hotel in town. It occupies a private island and overlooks a tranquil beach, making for a relaxing getaway that is surprisingly cheaper than you would imagine – check the web for special offers. Even if you're not staying here, stop by for a refreshing dip (day passes are available) or a gourmet dinner by the water.

Eating
Takeaway and budget places are concentrated on and around Sharia Thawra and around Midan Orabi.

Nefertiti (☎ 391 0494; Sharia Thawra; dishes E£20-55; ❄) This cosy little place serves fresh seafood and other meals, and has a bright interior, red-checked tablecloths and a bar.

George's (☎ 391 8327; 11 Sharia Thawra; dishes E£30-65; ❄) An Ismailia classic, George's has been around since 1950 and serves up seafood dishes amid a cosy British-pub-style ambience.

Getting There & Away
BUS
Ismailia's bus station is about 3km northwest of the old quarter; taxis to the town centre cost from E£3 to E£5. **East Delta Travel Co** (☎ 332 1513) has buses to Cairo (E£20, three hours) every half-hour between 6am and 8pm. Buses to Alexandria (E£30, five hours) leave at 7am, 10.30am and 2.30pm. Buses to Port Said (E£7, two hours) and Suez (E£6, 1½ hours) depart every hour from 7am to 6pm.

There are also hourly buses to Al-Arish (E£10 to E£12, three to four hours) between 8.30am and 5.30pm. Buses to Sharm el-Sheikh (E£45 to E£50, six hours) leave frequently throughout the morning, starting at 6.30am. Afternoon and evening departures include those at noon, 2.30pm, 5.30pm, 10pm and 11pm, with the 2.30pm and 11pm services going on to Dahab (E£55, eight hours).

SERVICE TAXI
These taxis depart from the bus station. Destinations include Suez (E£5 to E£10), Port

Said (E£5 to E£10), Zagazig (E£5 to E£10), Cairo (E£10 to E£15) and Al-Arish (E£10 to E£15).

TRAIN
Trains in the canal zone are slow and inefficient. Second-class trains to Cairo (four to five hours, eight daily) cost E£11 to E£14. To Port Said, there are six trains per day (E£2 to E£4) in 2nd class. There are also frequent trains to Suez (E£1 to E£3 in 3rd class only).

Getting Around
MICROBUS
Microbuses ply the main arteries of the city. Fares average 50pt.

TAXI
There are plenty of taxis around town. Short trips cost E£1 to E£3; between town and the beaches expect to pay E£5.

SUEZ
☎ 062 / pop 500,000
Balmy, bustling Suez sprawls around the shores of the gulf where the Red Sea meets the southern entrance of the Suez Canal. Although it was heavily damaged during the 1967 and 1973 wars with Israel, little evidence of the devastation remains. While the rebuilt main streets are mostly a facade hiding a maze of ramshackle back-street neighbourhoods, Suez remains one of the best places in the region to view colossal cargo ships gliding through the canal. Viewed from afar, they appear to be ploughing through the desert, a surreal and unforgettable sight.

Orientation
Suez is divided between Suez proper and Port Tawfiq – the latter is at the mouth of the canal and is an ideal place for watching the ships go by. Port Tawfiq also has several streets with gracious old colonial buildings that managed to escape the bombing.

Joining Port Tawfiq with Suez proper is Sharia al-Geish, a wide thoroughfare that cuts through an industrial area before leading through the heart of Suez. Here, you'll find a few staid old buildings and a surprising number of colonial-era churches crowded among a proliferation of sombre high-rises.

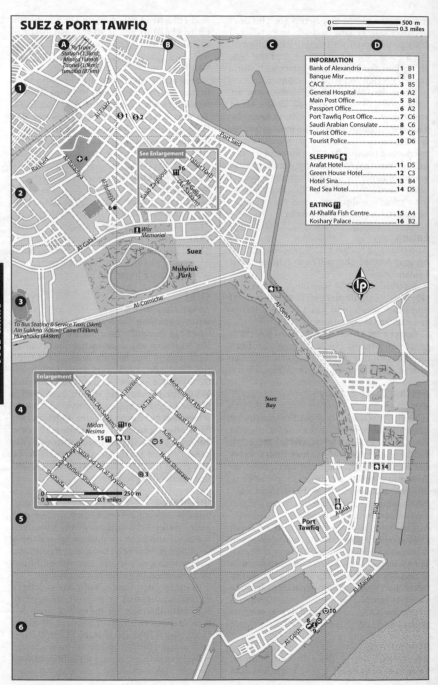

SUEZ & PORT TAWFIQ

INFORMATION	
Bank of Alexandria	**1** B1
Banque Misr	**2** B1
CACE	**3** B5
General Hospital	**4** A2
Main Post Office	**5** B4
Passport Office	**6** A2
Port Tawfiq Post Office	**7** C6
Saudi Arabian Consulate	**8** C6
Tourist Office	**9** C6
Tourist Police	**10** D6

SLEEPING	
Arafat Hotel	**11** D5
Green House Hotel	**12** C3
Hotel Sina	**13** B4
Red Sea Hotel	**14** D5

EATING	
Al-Khalifa Fish Centre	**15** A4
Koshary Palace	**16** B2

Information

INTERNET ACCESS

CACE (Sharia al-Geish, Suez; per hr E£2; ⊙ 9am-8pm)

MEDICAL SERVICES

General Hospital (☎ 333 1190; Sharia al-Baladiya, Suez)

MONEY

Bank of Alexandria (off Sharia al-Geish, Suez; ⊙ 9am-2pm Sun-Thu)

Banque Misr (Sharia al-Geish, Suez; ⊙ 9am-2pm Sun-Thu)

POST

Main post office (Sharia Hoda Shaarawi, Suez; ⊙ 8.30am-2.30pm Sat-Thu)

Port Tawfiq post office (Sharia al-Marwa; ⊙ 8.30am-2.30pm Sat-Thu)

TOURIST INFORMATION

Tourist office (☎ 333 1141; Sharia al-Marwa, Port Tawfiq; ⊙ 8am-8pm Sat-Thu, to 3pm Fri)

Tourist police (Sharia al-Marwa) Next to the tourist office.

Sleeping

Arafat Hotel (☎ 333 8355; Sharia Arafat, Port Tawfiq; r E£30, with shared bathroom E£25) This budget hotel is located near the port on a small side street off Sharia al-Geish. Like most portside hotels, the Arafat is a little rough around the edges but if you only want to crash for a night without being too picky about your surroundings, it'll do just fine.

Hotel Sina (☎ 333 4181; 21 Sharia Banque Misr, Suez; r with shared bathroom E£35; ⊗) This faded place is one of the better options if you want to be based in the town centre, though you're going to have to deal with shared bathrooms and lots of other guests. It has reasonably clean rooms with ceiling fans but it's not recommended for female travellers or people who need their privacy.

Green House Hotel (☎ 333 1553/4; Sharia al-Geish, Suez; s/d from E£240/265; ⊗ ▯ ▮) This large hotel is in a relatively quiet location at the southern edge of town and boasts attractive views of the canal. While it's showing its age much more than the Red Sea Hotel (right), it's a bit cheaper while still offering rooms of comparable grade. The property is centred on an attractive pool and garden, where you can do a few laps and then retire to a lounge chair.

Red Sea Hotel (☎ 333 4302; 13 Sharia Riad, Port Tawfiq; s/d from E£305/335; ⊗ ▯) One of the city's premier establishments is this affordable midrange hotel located near the yacht basin in Port Tawfiq – look for the large white-and-red sign poking out above the rooftops. No-nonsense rooms are a bit on the smallish side, though reasonably priced considering the quality of service here. If you're looking to sample the bounty of the Red Sea, note there is a good on-site restaurant.

Eating

For inexpensive favourites like *ta'amiyya* and *shwarma*, take a wander around the Sharia Talaat Harb area.

Koshary Palace (Sharia al-Geish, Suez; meals E£1.50-5) Clean and friendly, with lots of local flavour and good *kushari* in your choice of sizes. It's just around the corner from the Al-Khalifa Fish Centre.

Al-Khalifa Fish Centre (☎ 333 7303; Midan Nesima, Suez; dishes E£20-50) Tucked away on the edge of Midan Nesima in the congested town centre, this no-frills place sells the day's catch by weight; pick your fish, then wait for it to be grilled.

Getting There & Away

BOAT

In the past, it was possible to travel by boat from Suez to Jeddah (Saudi Arabia), though at the time of research all passenger services were being moved south to the port of Safaga (see p432).

BUS

The bus station is 5km out of town along the road to Cairo. **Upper Egypt Bus Co** (☎ 356 4258) has buses to Cairo (E£15 to E£20, two hours) every 15 to 30 minutes from 6am to 9pm daily. Buses to Hurghada (E£35 to E£40, four to five hours) leave almost hourly between 5am and 11pm. There are buses to Luxor (E£60 to E£70, nine to 10 hours) via Safaga (E£35 to E£45, four to five hours) and Qena (E£45 to E£50, five to six hours) at 8am, 2pm and 8pm. Buses to Aswan (E£55 to E£65, 11 to 12 hours) leave at 5am, 11am and 5pm.

East Delta Travel Co (☎ 356 4853) has buses to Sharm el-Sheikh (E£35 to E£40, five to six hours) departing at 8.30am, 11am, 1.30pm, 3pm, 4.30pm, 5.15pm and 6pm. There is a bus at 11am to Dahab (E£45 to E£50, five hours), and at 2pm to St Katherine Protectorate

(E£25, three to four hours). Buses to Taba and Nuweiba (both E£45 to E£50) leave at 3pm and 5pm. Buses to Ismailia (E£6, 1½ hours) depart every half-hour from 6am to 4pm. Departures to Port Said (E£14, 2½ to three hours) are daily at 7am, 9am, 11am, 12.15pm and 3.30pm.

SERVICE TAXI

Service taxis leave from beside the bus station to many of the destinations that are also serviced by buses and trains, including Cairo (E£10 to E£15), Ismailia (E£5 to E£10), Port Said (E£10 to E£15) and Hurghada (E£40 to E£55). The only place in Sinai that service taxis go to is Al-Tor (E£15 to E£20).

With a group of seven people you can hire a 'special' taxi to get you to various other destinations, including St Katherine's Monastery (around E£250 to E£300 per vehicle) and the Red Sea monasteries (around E£350 to E£400, return).

TRAIN

Six very slow and uncomfortable 2nd-class Cairo-bound trains depart Suez daily (E£15 to E£18, three hours) going only as far as Ain Shams, 10km northeast of central Cairo; the first Cairo-bound train leaves at 5.30am. There are eight very slow trains to Ismailia (E£1 to E£3 in 3rd class only, three hours).

Getting Around

MICROBUS

There are regular microbus services along Sharia al-Geish to Port Tawfiq. They will pick up or drop off anywhere along the route and cost 50pt.

TAXI

Taxis (painted blue) are easy to find almost everywhere. Expect to pay from about E£5 between the bus station and town, about E£10 between the bus station and Port Tawfiq, and about E£3 between Suez and Port Tawfiq.

Red Sea Coast

Arguably one of the world's most famous stretches of coast, it was here that Moses was said to have parted a great sea and set free the Hebrew slaves. Of course, Hollywood movie-magic and biblical allegory aside, most visitors to this coastline seem perfectly content in letting the Red Sea lie still. Famed for its brilliant turquoise waters and splendid coral reefs, the Red Sea coast attracts tens of thousands of tourists annually. In fact, it's Egypt's most rapidly developing area, with more hotels and resorts than anywhere else in the country.

Unfortunately, the overall picture is anything but pretty, especially since large tracts of the 800km coastline are nothing short of an environmental disaster. Fuelled by decades of European-driven package tourism, and compounded by the lack of any kind of sustainable development plan, illegal landfill operations and irresponsible mooring have destroyed off-shore reefs, and the construction of solid concrete jetties have simply eroded away parts of the coastline. Furthermore, declining tourism amid increasing fears of a wider Middle East war has spooked investors, and today much of the coastline remains a construction site of half-finished hotels.

For independent travellers weary of package tourism, the Red Sea coast can be a frustrating place to visit, though it shouldn't be overlooked altogether. Far removed from the coastal scene is the Eastern Desert, which harbours Christianity's two oldest monasteries, plus traces of Pharaonic, Roman and other settlements. The inland is also home to wadis, ancient rock art and nomad cultures, and offers countless opportunities for travellers seeking a healthy dose of desert adventure. And, if you do happen to find yourself in any of the Red Sea's coastal resort towns, you'll find the diving here truly is world-class.

HIGHLIGHTS

- Discover Christian monasticism's centuries-old roots at the **monasteries of St Anthony and St Paul** (p418)
- Trek though mountains and wadis, visit old mines and ruins and gaze at ancient rock art in the **Eastern Desert** (p437)
- Interact with the **Ababda** and **Besharin** (p438), two nomadic peoples of the Eastern Desert who maintain their traditions in a changing world
- Plunge into the underwater world of the **Red Sea** (p425 and p421) at Hurghada and El-Gouna
- Wander along the picturesque waterfront of the sleepy coastal town of **Al-Quseir** (p433)

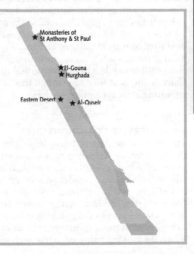

★ Monasteries of St Anthony & St Paul

★El-Gouna
★ Hurghada

Eastern Desert ★ ★ Al-Quseir

RED SEA COAST

RED SEA MONASTERIES

The Coptic monasteries of St Anthony and St Paul are Egypt's and Christianity's oldest monasteries, and are among the holiest sites in the Coptic faith. In fact, the establishment of the religious community of St Anthony's, hidden in the barren cliffs of the Eastern Desert, marks the beginning of the Christian monastic tradition.

If you're at all interested in Egypt's lengthy Christian history, both monasteries make for fascinating and inspiring visits, and the surrounding desert scenery is simply breathtaking. And, depending on where you're coming from, the Red Sea monasteries are a refreshing change of scene from the hassles and touts of Cairo and the Nile Valley, or the package tourism and rampant commercialism of the coastline.

Orientation & Information

The two monasteries are only about 25km apart but thanks to the cliffs and plateau of Gebel al-Galala al-Qibliya (which lies between 900m and 1300m above sea level), the distance between them by road is around 85km.

Both monasteries are open daily throughout the year (St Anthony's from 7am to 5pm, St Paul's from 8am to 3pm), except during Advent and Lent, when they can only be visited on Friday, Saturday and Sunday. During Holy Week they are closed completely to visitors. For enquiries or to confirm visiting times, contact the monasteries' headquarters: **St Paul's** (☎ 02-2590 0218; 26 Al-Keneesa al-Morcosia) or **St Anthony's** (☎ 02-2590 6025; 26 Al-Keneesa al-Morcosia), located off Clot Bey, south of Midan Ramses in Cairo.

If you don't have your own vehicle, the easiest way to visit the monasteries is to join an organised tour from Cairo or Hurghada (any hotel or travel agency can organise these). It's also possible to join a pilgrimage group from Cairo – the best way to arrange this is by enquiring at local Coptic churches.

Sights

MONASTERY OF ST ANTHONY

This historic monastery traces its origins to the 4th century AD when monks began to settle at the foot of Gebel al-Galala al-Qibliya, where their spiritual leader, Anthony (see boxed text, opposite), lived. Over the next few centuries, the community moved from being a loosely organised grouping of hermits to a somewhat more communal existence in which the monks continued to live anchoritic

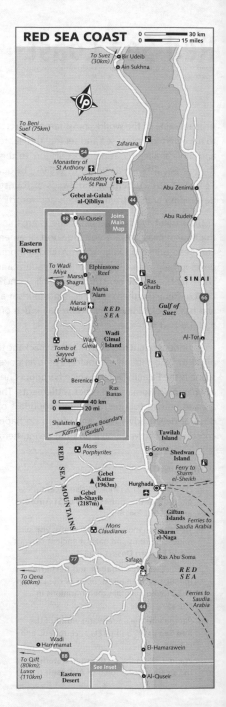

lives, but in cells grouped together inside a walled compound.

In the 8th and 9th centuries, the monastery suffered Bedouin raids, followed in the 11th century by attacks from irate Muslims and, in the 15th century, a revolt by bloodthirsty servants that resulted in the massacre of the monks. The small mudbrick **citadel** into which they would retreat during attacks can still be seen, although visitors are not usually admitted. It's also possible to see the large basket and wooden winch that were the only means of getting into the monastery in times of attack.

Today the monastery is a large complex surrounded by high walls (it's possible to walk along the top of some sections), with several churches and chapels, a bakery, a lush garden and a spring. The source of the latter, deep beneath the desert mountains, produces 100 cu metres of water daily, allowing the monks to cultivate olive and date trees as well as a few crops.

The oldest part of the monastery is the **Church of St Anthony**, built over the saint's tomb and containing one of Egypt's most significant collections of Coptic wall paintings. Painted in secco (whereby paint is applied to dry plaster), most date back to the early 13th century, with a few possibly much older. Stripped of the dirt and grime of centuries, the paintings are clear and bright, and demonstrate how medieval Coptic art was connected to the arts of the wider Byzantine and Islamic eastern Mediterranean (for more information on Coptic art, see p420). The monks who live here, following centuries-old traditions and the examples set by St Anthony, St Paul and their followers 16 centuries ago, have dedicated their lives to seeking God in the stillness and isolation of the desert, in a life built completely around prayer.

Perched about 300m – 1158 wooden steps – above the monastery on a nearby cliff is the **Cave of St Anthony**, where Anthony spent the final 40 years of his life. The climb up is hot and steep and takes about half an hour if you're reasonably fit. At the top is a small clearing (now littered with the graffiti of countless pilgrims) with wide vistas over the hills and valley below. In the cave itself, which is for the svelte and nonclaustrophobic only (you need to squeeze through a narrow tunnel to get inside), there is a small chapel with an altar as well as a tiny recessed area where Anthony lived – bring a torch (flashlight) along to illuminate the interior.

There is usually an English-speaking monk on hand to give tours of the monastery (free but a donation is expected). The monastery bookstore has a good selection of materials on Coptic Christianity.

MONASTERY OF ST PAUL

St Paul's monastery dates to the 4th century, when it began as a grouping of hermitages in the cliffs of Gebel al-Galala al-Qibliya around

---

THE FATHER OF MONASTICISM

Although St Paul is honoured as the earliest Christian hermit, it is St Anthony who is considered to be the Father of Monasticism. Anthony was born around AD 251, the son of a provincial landowner from a small Upper Egyptian town near Beni Suef. Orphaned with his sister at the age of 18, he was already more interested in the spiritual than the temporal, and soon gave away his share of the inheritance to the poor. After studying with a local holy man, Anthony went into the Eastern Desert, living in a cave and seeking solitude and spiritual salvation. Word of his holiness soon spread and flocks of disciples arrived, seeking to imitate his ascetic existence.

After a brief spell in Alexandria ministering to Christians imprisoned under Emperor Maximinus Daia in the early 4th century, Anthony returned to the desert. Once again, he was pursued by eager followers, though he managed to flee even further into the desert in search of solitude. After establishing himself in a cave on a remote mountain, his disciples formed a loose community at its base, and thus was born the first Christian monastery.

The number of Anthony's followers grew rapidly, and within decades of his death, nearly every town in Egypt was surrounded by hermitages. Soon after, the whole Byzantine Empire was alive with monastic fervour, which by the next century had spread throughout Italy and France.

It is ironic that, for all his influence, Anthony spent his life seeking to escape others. When he died at the advanced age of 105, his sole wish for solitude was finally respected and the location of his grave became a closely guarded secret.

COPTIC ART 101

Before you set foot into the Coptic monasteries of the Eastern Desert, here is a quick introduction to the history and tradition of Egyptian Coptic art.

Overview

Coptic art refers to the distinct Christian art of Egypt. Although it originated from the ancient Egyptian and Greek heritages, Coptic art has also been influenced by the Persians, Byzantines and Syrians. In fact, due to its myriad influences, the exact nature of Coptic art can be difficult to define, though it is fortunately easy to identify. Since early Christian artisans were extremely utilitarian in their aims, Coptic art typically manifests itself in daily items including textiles and religious illustrations. Furthermore, Coptic art has a strong tradition of painting, particularly portraits and wall paintings.

Textiles

The Coptic Church inherited a strong tradition of textile-making from the ancient Egyptians, particularly loom and tapestry weaving. For the most part, Coptic textiles are made from linen, though there is some evidence of sophisticated silk-weaving. In regards to design, Coptic textiles borrow heavily from Greek-Egyptian themes, and include traditional pattern motifs such as cupids, dancing maidens and animals. However, these are typically incorporated with unique Christian motifs such as fish, grapes and biblical scenes, especially the Immaculate Conception.

Religious Illustrations

Religious illustration originated in ancient Egypt when pharaohs started adorning papyrus texts with liturgies and prayers. Coptic Christians retained this tradition, and early papyrus texts maintained the original Egyptian design of protective illustrations surrounded by elaborate borders and text. Like the Egyptians, Coptic artisans used bright colours for vignettes, and striking black ink for all texts. Later on, however, Coptic illustrations began to take on greater complexity as they started to incorporate religious imagery, landscapes and intricate geometric designs.

Portraits

In comparison to other early Christian movements, the Coptic Church is unique in regard to their abundance of martyrs, saints and ascetics. Since the actions and deeds of these individuals helped to form the foundation of the church, their images were immortalised in portraits, and hung in every chapel and church throughout the land. In these paintings, the human figure is usually depicted in the front position, with placid, almond-shaped eyes and idealised expressions. Coptic portraits of Jesus Christ are unique in that they usually depict him enthroned by saints and angels as opposed to suffering on the cross.

Wall Paintings

Early Coptic wall paintings were unsophisticated in comparison to later endeavours, though this is primarily due to the fact that ancient Egyptian temples were being converted into churches. In order to complete the transformation, Pharaonic reliefs were covered with layers of plaster, and Christian themes were painted on top. However, as Coptic art developed and prospered, wall painting became increasingly complex, particularly following the mastery of dye mixing and gold stencilling. Some of the finest Coptic wall paintings depict spiritual scenes that are awash with vibrant colours and accented with gold.

Coptic Art Today

Long overshadowed by both ancient Egyptian and Islamic themes, Coptic art is not given much attention in Egypt despite its lengthy history and established tradition. Fortunately, this cultural heritage has been preserved in museums, churches and monasteries throughout Egypt and the world, and the artistic traditions continue to flourish among communities of modern-day Coptics.

the site where St Paul had his hermitage. Paul, who was born into a wealthy family in Alexandria in the mid-3rd century, originally fled to the Eastern Desert to escape Roman persecution. He lived alone in a cave here for over 90 years, finding bodily sustenance in a nearby spring and palm tree. According to tradition, in AD 343 the then 90-year-old St Anthony had a vision of Paul. After making a difficult trek through the mountains to visit him, Paul died, and was buried by Anthony's hands.

The heart of the monastery complex is the **Church of St Paul**, which was built in and around the cave where Paul lived. It's cluttered with altars, candles, ostrich eggs (the symbol of the Resurrection) and murals representing saints and biblical stories. The **fortress** above the church was where the monks retreated during Bedouin raids.

St Paul's monastery is quieter and much more low-key than St Anthony's, and is often bypassed in favour of its larger neighbour. But a visit is well worthwhile, and gives a glimpse into the life of silence, prayer and asceticism that has flowered here in the Eastern Desert for almost two millennia. Visitors are welcome and there is usually an English-speaking monk available to give a guided tour (free but a donation is appreciated).

Activities

HIKING

It is possible to hike between the two monasteries along a trail across the top of the plateau. However, hiking this rugged area, commonly known as 'Devil's Country', is only for the fit and experienced and should under no circumstances be attempted without a local guide. In 2001, a lone tourist attempting the walk died of thirst after losing his way – this is clearly not a trip to undertake lightly. Those who have made the hike recommend starting from St Paul's. The hike (about 30km) is possible in one long day but better broken up into two.

Sleeping & Eating

There is no official accommodation for the general public at either monastery, although male pilgrims are allowed to spend the night in dormitories with written consent from the monasteries' Cairo headquarters (see Orientation & Information, p418). Since both places are major destinations for Coptic Christians on religious pilgrimages, guests are expected to attend prayer sessions, respect

the atmosphere of the grounds and leave a donation at the time of departure.

If you haven't made reservations in advance, or your double X-chromosome prevents you from bedding down in the monasteries, consider spending the night in the nearby junction town of Zafarana. Here you'll find the **Sahara Inn Motel** (s/d from E£140/165; ⊠), which offers up some bare-bones concrete cubicles and a basic roadside restaurant. It's not the Hilton but, if a day trip to the monasteries from Cairo, El-Gouna or Hurghada just isn't enough time for you, this is a decent option.

Both monasteries have canteens that sell snacks, drinks and simple meals.

Getting There & Away

Zafarana is located 62km south of Ain Sukhna and 150km east of Beni Suef on the Nile. Buses running between Cairo or Suez and Hurghada will drop you at Zafarana but direct access to the monasteries is limited to private vehicles and tour buses from Cairo or Hurghada.

To get to St Anthony's, start from the main Zafarana junction and follow the road west to Beni Suef for 37km to the monastery turn-off. From here, it's 17km further south along an unsurfaced but good road through the desert to St Anthony's.

The turn-off for St Paul's is about 27km south of the Zafarana lighthouse along the road to Hurghada (watch for a small signpost). Once at the turn-off, it's then 10km further along a good tarmac road to the main gate of the monastery, and about 3km further to the monastery itself.

Buses running between Suez and Hurghada will drop you along the main road at the turn-off, from where the only options are walking or hitching. If you do decide to hike in from the main road (which isn't the best idea), don't go alone, and be sure you're properly equipped, especially with water, as it's a long, hot, dry and isolated stretch.

EL-GOUNA

☎ 065 / pop 10,000

The brainchild of Onsi Sawirie, the Egyptian multibillionaire who heads the Orascom conglomerate, El-Gouna was largely built from the ground up during the 1990s. Today, this self-contained resort town is largely frequented by Egypt's rich and famous, and increasingly by Westerners on package tours. Boasting more than a dozen hotels, several golf courses, countless shopping malls and the odd casino, El-Gouna serves up heaping amounts of family fun, albeit of the homogenised, vacation community variety. But, if you're looking for a place to laze on a beach surrounded by Western amenities and cushioned from the chaos of Egyptian life, you'll most definitely enjoy your time here.

Orientation & Information

Most of the action in El-Gouna takes place within the resorts and there is little reason to leave if you're on an all-inclusive package. Of course, if you do feel the need to motivate and venture into the 'real world', you can take one of the shuttle buses that connect the various hotels to the central 'downtown' area. This is where you'll find a cluster of banks and internet cafes as well as several dive centres, supermarkets, various shops and eateries. El-Gouna's 10km-long beachfront is also home to a growing number of private villas and luxury condo units.

Activities

El-Gouna is a veritable paradise for water sports. The various activity centres inside the resorts offer a laundry list of activities including sailing, ocean kayaking, boogieboarding, parasailing, jet-skiing, windsurfing, kitesurfing, waterskiing and many, many others. Offshore, you'll find a good number of excellent snorkelling and diving sites. For an overview of diving in the Red Sea, including recommended operators and dive sites in the El-Gouna area, see p450.

Sleeping

Unlike Hurghada, its brasher and less-refined neighbour to the south, El-Gouna is solely an upmarket destination. Although you will have to pay to play, splurging on a resort hotel will ensure a memorable vacation, especially if the kiddies are in tow.

Be advised that advanced reservations are necessary, though you can sometimes score cheaper rooms and discounted all-inclusive packages if you book through a travel agent or through the web. As such, rates given here should be taken as guides.

Also check out www.elgouna.com for more accommodation listings.

Dawar el-Omda (☎ 358 0063; www.dawarelomda -elgouna.com; Kafr El-Gouna; s/d half board from US$115/125; ☒ ☒ ☒) This tastefully decorated four-star

resort eschews European design in favour of classic Egyptian lines and arches. It's squeezed in among several other buildings in the heart of downtown El-Gouna, with cosy, well-appointed rooms and a convenient lagoonside location. Although there's no beach, shuttle boats can whisk you away to the sands, and you're within easy walking distance of El-Gouna's retail shopping hubs.

Mövenpick (☎ 354 4501; www.moevenpick-hotels.com; El-Gouna; s/d half board from US$145/165; ☒ ☒ ☒ ☒) A significant step up in quality to the five-star level, the Mövenpick offers all of the luxury amenities you'd expect in this price bracket. Drawing its inspiration from a desert oasis, the manicured grounds are lined with soaring palm trees, which shed ample shade on the swimming pools and lagoons. Rooms lack the sophistication of the Sheraton Miramar (below) but they're still first-class all the way.

our pick Sheraton Miramar (☎ 354 5606; www .starwoodhotels.com/sheraton; El-Gouna; s/d half board from US$175/215; ☒ ☒ ☒ ☒) A five-star, pastel-coloured, postmodern desert fantasy, the Sheraton was designed by well-known architect Michael Graves, and is one of the signature properties of El-Gouna. The entire complex is strung along a series of beach-fringed private islands, which seek to maximise intimacy despite being a large resort hotel. Accommodation of varying levels of opulence incorporates a dreamlike mix of Arabian, Nubian and Egyptian design motifs.

Getting There & Away
AIR

Several domestic charter companies serve El-Gouna, though most international flights touch down in Hurghada, about 20km south along the main coastal highway. For the vast majority of package travellers, flight arrangements are booked in conjunction with hotel packages.

BUS

El-Gouna Transport buses travel three times daily between the Hilton Ramses in Cairo, El-Gouna and Hurghada (E£85 to E£95, five hours), best booked a day in advance. The ticket office and bus stop in El-Gouna is on the main plaza downtown, opposite the tourist information centre.

TAXI

Taxis run frequently between El-Gouna and Hurghada, with fares ranging from E£60 to E£75, depending on your destination.

Getting Around

The El-Gouna sprawl is readily accessible by a fairly comprehensive network of local buses – a daily bus pass will only cost you E£5. *Tuk-tuks* also scan the streets for potential fares; prices for these are highly variable, around E£3 to E£10.

HURGHADA

☎ 065

Once an isolated and modest fishing village, Hurghada has metamorphosed into a sprawling collection of more than 100 hotels, and is today Egypt's most popular resort destination for foreign travellers. Despite its immense popularity, a good number of travellers in the know tend to shun Hurghada's frightful mix of rampant construction and largely unchecked environmental degradation.

Modern Hurghada is a dense band of concrete in the form of gated resorts, which stretch along the coastline for more than 20km. Scattered amid these ageing pleasure palaces are thousands of construction sites, all in varying degrees of abandonment and neglect. Not surprisingly, the reefs close to shore have been degraded by illegal landfill operations and irresponsible reef use.

To be fair, Hurghada was put on the map because of its superb diving, and there are some incredible offshore sites here. If you want to combine a diving holiday with a visit to Luxor and other Nile Valley sites, Hurghada is a convenient destination. However, independent travellers would be wise to press on to Dahab in Sinai (p476), while package-holiday seekers might prefer nearby El-Gouna (p421) or even Sharm el-Sheikh (p466).

Orientation

Hurghada is split into three main areas. To the north is Ad-Dahar, where most budget accommodation is located. This is also the most 'Egyptian' part of the city, with lively backstreet neighbourhoods and a bustling souq. The main inland artery through Ad-Dahar is Sharia an-Nasr.

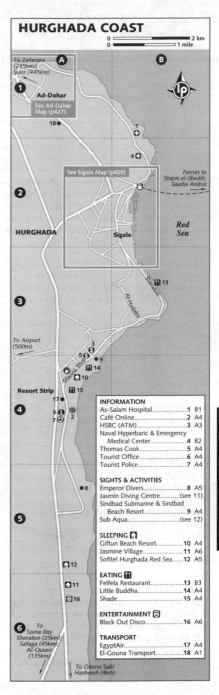

THE NEW RUSSIA

Although Western Europeans tend to prefer the airbrushed shine of El-Gouna and Sharm el-Sheikh, Russia's emerging middle class is flocking to Hurghada in droves. Attracted by the hot sun and warm sea, which are indeed rarities in the Motherland, Russians are cashing in on cheap flights and discount package deals. As a direct result, first-timer travellers in Hurghada are usually surprised to discover an abundance of Cyrillic signs and beet-red borscht.

For Egyptians, Russian travellers are viewed as something of a mixed blessing. On one hand, newly wealthy Russian travellers tend to have lots of disposable cash and are quick to inject a hefty amount of capital into the local economy. Tourism patterns also suggest that Russians seem to not be discouraged by semi-regular terrorist actions, which have sullied Egypt's image elsewhere.

On the other hand, Russians have been stereotyped among local Egyptians as heavy drinkers prone to promiscuity. While this is certainly a sweeping generalisation, it is to an extent based on local views of the behaviour of some Russian and other foreign tourists in Hurghada. By Egyptian standards, the town has a comparatively high number of prostitutes, and late-night drunken fights in the clubs are not uncommon.

But for the most part Russians in Hurghada are simply holidaymakers like anyone else, and their presence is evidence that the new Russia has finally arrived on the global tourism scene.

Separated from Ad-Dahar by a sandy mountain called Gebel al-Afish is the fast-growing and congested Sigala area, where resort hotels jostle for sea frontage, while smaller two- and three-star establishments and dozens of restaurants fill the spaces inland. This is also where you'll find the port for ferries to Sharm el-Sheikh. Sigala's main thoroughfare is Sharia Sheraton.

South of Sigala, lining the coastal road, and increasingly some inland arteries as well, is the resort strip. Here you'll find an increasingly lengthening row of mostly upmarket pleasure domes, Western-style shopping malls and half-finished shells of hotels.

Information

EMERGENCY
Air ambulance (☎ 010 154 1978)
Ambulance (☎ 354 6490, 123)
Police (Map p429; ☎ 354 6303/6; Sharia Shedwan, Sigala)
Tourist police Ad-Dahar (Map p427; ☎ 344 4774; Sharia Al-Tahrir); resort strip (Map p423; ☎ 344 4773/4) Next to the tourist office.

INTERNET ACCESS
There are internet cafes all over the city and in many hotels, most charging between E£5 and E£10 per hour.
Café Online (Map p423; resort strip; ☺ 10.15am-11.15pm; ⊠) Has a juice bar.
El Baroudy Internet (Map p427; Sharia Sheikh Sabak, Ad-Dahar; ☺ 24hr; ⊠)

Speed.Net (Map p429; Sharia Al-Hadaba, Sigala; ☺ 10am-midnight; ⊠)

MEDICAL SERVICES
Al-Saffa Hospital (Map p427; ☎ 354 6965; Sharia an-Nasr, Ad-Dahar)
As-Salam Hospital (Map p423; ☎ 354 8785/6/7; Corniche) Just north of Iberotel Arabella.
Decompression Chamber Naval Hyperbaric & Emergency Medical Center (Map p423; ☎ 344 9150, 354 8450; Corniche) Near Iberotel Arabella.
Public Hospital (Map p427; ☎ 354 6740; Sharia al-Mustashfa, Ad-Dahar)

MONEY
ATMs are all over the city, including at the following locations.
HSBC (Map p423; opposite Sindbad Beach Resort, resort strip)
National Bank of Egypt (Map p427; Sharia an-Nasr, Ad-Dahar; ☺ 8.30am-2pm & 6-9pm Sat-Thu)
Triton Empire Beach (Map p427; Sharia Sayed al-Qorayem, Ad-Dahar)

Other money outlets:
Thomas Cook Ad-Dahar (Map p427; ☎ 354 1870/1; Sharia an-Nasr; ☺ 9am-2pm & 6-10pm); Sigala (Map p429; ☎ 344 3338; Sharia Sheraton; ☺ 9am-3pm & 4-10pm); resort strip (Map p423; ☎ 344 6830; ☺ 9am-5pm)
Western Union (Map p429; ☎ 344 2771, 19190; Sharia Sheraton, Sigala; ☺ 8.30am-10pm Sat-Thu, 3-10pm Fri)

POST
Main post office (Map p427; Sharia an-Nasr, Ad-Dahar; ☺ 8.30am-2.30pm Sat-Thu)

RESCUING THE RED SEA

Conservationists estimate that more than 1000 pleasure boats and almost as many fishing boats ply the waters between Hurghada and the many reefs situated within an hour of the town. Fifteen years ago, there was nothing to stop captains from anchoring to the coral, or snorkellers and divers breaking off a colourful chunk to take home. However, due largely to the efforts of the Hurghada Environmental Protection & Conservation Association (HEPCA) and the Egyptian National Parks Office in Hurghada, the Red Sea's reefs are at last being protected.

Set up in 1992 by 15 of the town's larger, more reputable dive companies, HEPCA's program to conserve the Red Sea's reefs includes public-awareness campaigns, direct community action and lobbying of the Egyptian government to introduce appropriate laws. Thanks to these efforts, the whole coast south of Suez Governorate is now known as the Red Sea Protectorate. Over 570 mooring buoys have been set up at popular dive sites around Hurghada and further south, enabling boat captains to drop anchor on a buoy rather than on the coral itself, and marine rangers from the Egyptian National Parks Office police the waters.

The Egyptian National Parks Office is also trying to establish new dive sites to ease the pressure on existing sites, as well as trying to reduce the number of new boats licensed in the Red Sea. Finally, a symbolic 'reef conservation tax' of E£1 has been introduced, and is payable by anyone using the reefs for diving, snorkelling or any other boating activities. It is designed to make the public aware that the reefs and offshore islands are now protected areas, rather than simply a source of revenue.

For more information on safe diving practices or about how you can help **HEPCA** (Map p429; ☎ 344 6674; www.hepca.com; off Corniche, Sigala) in its efforts to protect the Red Sea's reefs, check the organisation's website or call in between 9am and 5pm Saturday to Thursday.

TELEPHONE
Telephone centrale Ad-Dahar (Map p427; Sharia an-Nasr; ☺ 24hr); Port area (Map p429; Midan Shedwan; ☺ 24hr); Sigala (Map p429; Sharia Sheraton; ☺ 24hr)

TOURIST INFORMATION
Tourist office (Map p423; ☎ 344 4420; resort strip; ☺ 9am-8pm Sat-Thu, 2-10pm Fri)

TRAVEL AGENCIES
Abanoub Travel (Map p429; ☎ 344 2843; abanoubt@menanet.net; 2nd fl, Cotton House Bldg, Sigala)
Thomas Cook (☎ 344 3338; www.thomascookegypt.com); Ad-Dahar (Map p427; Sharia an-Nasr; ☺ 9am-2pm & 6-10pm); Sigala (Map p429; Sharia Sheraton; ☺ 9am-3pm & 4-10pm); resort strip (Map p423; ☺ 9am-5pm)

Dangers & Annoyances
Although Hurghada is a resort town, many of the workers here come from the conservative towns that don't receive tourists, so their attitude towards women travellers is less than progressive (there have been rapes and assaults in the past). To avoid hassle, women should dress modestly when walking around town, especially in the souq area of Ad-Dahar.

Sights
BEACHES
Although many of Hurghada's beaches are bare and stark, developers have snapped up almost every available spot. Apart from the not-so-appealing **public beach** (Map p429; Sigala; admission E£2; ☺ 8am-sunset), the main option for enjoying sand and sea is to go to one of the resorts, most of which charge nonguests between E£25 and E£75 for beach access.

AQUARIUM
If you don't want to put your head under the water, you can still get an idea of some of the life in the Red Sea at the **aquarium** (Map p427; ☎ 354 8557; Corniche, Ad-Dahar; admission E£5; ☺ 9am-10pm). It's just north of the public hospital in Ad-Dahar and has a reasonable, if somewhat neglected, selection of fish and other marine creatures.

Activities
SNORKELLING & DIVING
Although there is some easily accessible coral at the southern end of the resort strip, the best reefs are offshore and the only way to see them is to take a boat and/or join a snorkelling or diving excursion. For all excursions, shop around a bit. Relying on your hotel may not

be the best way to do things as travellers often complain about not getting everything they expected. For any boat trip, take your passport as you'll need to show it at the port.

For an overview of diving in the Red Sea, including recommended operators and dive sites, see p441.

SUBMARINE RIDES

A ride in the yellow **Sindbad Submarine** (Map p423; ☎ 344 4688; www.sindbad-group.com; Sindbad Beach Resort; adult/child US$50/25), which takes up to 46 people to a depth of 22m, is one way to plumb the depths of the Red Sea while staying dry. Bookings can be made at any hotel or travel agency.

Tours

Tours to almost anywhere in Egypt can be organised from Hurghada, including whirlwind one-day jaunts to Cairo (from E£300), slightly more leisurely two-day tours (from E£600) and one-day excursions to Luxor (E£2300). The most popular option from Hurghada is a desert jeep safari (from E£200), which usually includes visits to either Mons Porphyrites or Mons Claudianus (p439). Other possibilities include a full-day excursion to the monasteries of St Paul and St Anthony (p418), camel treks and sunset desert excursions.

To arrange any of the tours mentioned above, enquire at either your hotel or a travel agency in town – there are dozens and dozens, so you shouldn't have a problem finding one. Note that a minimum number of people are needed for most trips, so it's best to enquire several days in advance.

Sleeping

Hurghada has the greatest selection of accommodation outside Cairo, though virtually everything in town is midrange to top-end resorts. Travel agencies in Europe and the UK can offer often-significant reductions if you book in advance, especially since prices fluctuate according to the season and state of the tourism industry. If you haven't booked a package deal in advance, you can still show up and request a room, though accommodation can get expensive. Fortunately, supply outstrips demand, so there is always room for negotiation – be patient and shop around.

Accommodation in Hurghada is split into three principal areas: Ad-Dahar, Sigala and the resort strip. Most budget accommodation is located within Ad-Dahar not far from the sea, though the water is rarely within sight. Sigala is a convenient base if you want to be near the nightlife but it is extremely congested and noisy. The resort strip, which extends south of Hurghada along the coast, is home to the majority of the city's four- and five-star resorts. If you stay down here, you will be able to enjoy a bit of privacy (a prized rarity in Egypt), though you will be dependent on your hotel for meals.

AD-DAHAR

Happy Land Hotel (Map p427; ☎ 354 7373; Sharia Sheikh Sebak; s/d from E£45/75) If you're heading out to Sinai by ferry, and just want a cheap place to crash for the night, the Happy Land will do just fine. The hotel's name is a bit optimistic given the dingy rooms and indifferent management but at this price level you get what you pay for. The location near the souq means it can be noisy at night; on the bright side you have plenty of cheap food options within easy walking distance.

4 Seasons Hotel (Map p427; ☎ 354 5456; fourseasons hurghada@hotmail.com; off Sharia Sayyed al-Qorayem; s/d from E£95/125;) A significant step up in quality, the 4 Seasons (not to be confused with the upmarket 'Four Seasons') is a small, friendly hotel that is popular with shoestringers and often fully booked. Simple rooms here have hot water, air-con and not much else. There is an attractive rooftop terrace for lounging about, and guests have free access to the pools and beach at the Geisum Village.

El-Arosa Hotel (Map p427; ☎ 354 8434; elarosa hotel@yahoo.com; off Corniche; s/d from E£115/165;) El-Arosa overlooks the sea in the distance from the inland side of the Corniche, though few of the rooms actually have ocean views. However, it is one of the best deals in town, especially considering that the rooms are equipped with modern amenities, and there's even a small pool for cooling off (albeit located in the dining room). If you're unimpressed, there's a much better option for cooling off at nearby Geisum Village.

Geisum Village (Map p427; ☎ 354 6692; Corniche; s/d from E£175/300;) Although it's seen way better decades, the Geisum Village is one of the cheapest resorts in Hurghada. The rooms themselves are fairly nondescript and in need of a fresh coat of paint, though the grounds

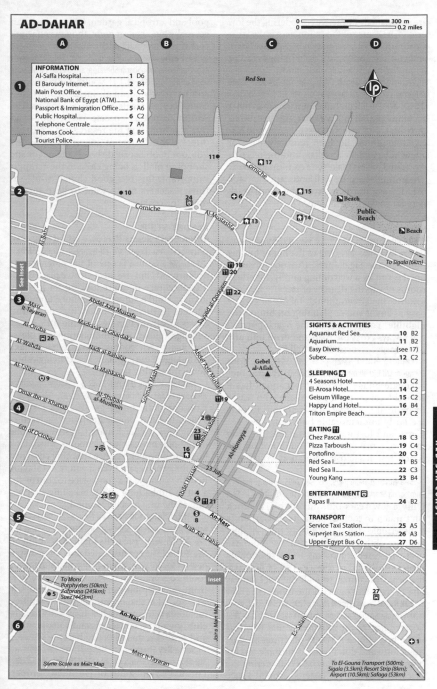

AD-DAHAR

0 — 300 m
0 — 0.2 miles

INFORMATION
Al-Saffa Hospital.....................**1** D6
El Baroudy Internet................**2** B4
Main Post Office.....................**3** C5
National Bank of Egypt (ATM)...**4** B5
Passport & Immigration Office...**5** A6
Public Hospital.......................**6** C2
Telephone Centrale.................**7** A4
Thomas Cook..........................**8** B5
Tourist Police.........................**9** A4

Red Sea

Public Beach
Beach
Beach

To Sigala (6km)

Corniche

Al-Mustashfa

Gebel al-Afish

SIGHTS & ACTIVITIES
Aquanaut Red Sea...................**10** B2
Aquarium................................**11** B2
Easy Divers.........................(see 17)
Subex.....................................**12** C2

SLEEPING
4 Seasons Hotel......................**13** C2
El-Arosa Hotel........................**14** C2
Geisum Village.......................**15** C2
Happy Land Hotel...................**16** B4
Triton Empire Beach................**17** C2

EATING
Chez Pascal............................**18** C3
Pizza Tarboush.......................**19** C4
Portofino................................**20** C3
Red Sea I................................**21** B5
Red Sea II...............................**22** C3
Young Kang............................**23** B4

ENTERTAINMENT
Papas II..................................**24** B2

TRANSPORT
Service Taxi Station.................**25** A5
Superjet Bus Station................**26** A3
Upper Egypt Bus Co................**27** D6

RED SEA COAST

Masr It-Tayaran
Al-Oruba
Al-Wahda
Al-Talitir
Omar Ibn al-Khattab
6th of October
Abdel Aziz Mustafa
Madrasat al-Ghardaka
Nadi al-Rahalat
Al-Mahkama
Al-Shuban al-Muslimin
Soliman Mazhar
Sayyed al-Qoraiyan
Abdel Aziz Mubarak
Al-Horreyya
Sheikh Saud
23 July
An-Nasr
Abdel Hassan
Arab Ad-Dahar
E-Salam
Al-Bahr
Corniche

Inset
To Mons Porphyrites (50km);
Zafarana (245km);
Suez (445km)
An-Nasr
Masr It-Tayaran
Same Scale as Main Map
Joins Main Map

To El-Gouna Transport (500m);
Sigala (3.5km); Resort Strip (8km);
Airport (10.5km); Safaga (53km)

are surprisingly attractive considering the low price. The centre of the action here is the large swimming pool surrounded by a grassy lawn, and you can always take a dip in the ocean or lie on the beach (er, spot of sand).

Triton Empire Beach (Map p427; ☎ 354 7816; www .threecorners.com; Sharia Sayyed al-Qorayem; s/d from US$60/80; ❌ 🖳 🛒) Decidedly more upmarket than other accommodation in Ad-Dahar, this enormous three-star hotel caters almost exclusively to foreign tour groups. But there is usually space for a few independent travellers and the recently renovated rooms make for a comfortable base. The grounds here are well landscaped and full of lush grass, and there's even a bit of real beach here for soaking up the sun.

SIGALA

White Albatross (Map p429; ☎ 344 2519; Sharia Sheraton; s/d from E£135/185; ❌) One of the better budget hotels in the Sigala area, this no-nonsense hotel is run by a welcoming family. Standard rooms of varying degrees of sterility face out towards the street, though this is as good a base as any if you're planning on hitting the nightlife. You're far from the beach but you can always cross the road and drop into any of the larger resorts for a small fee.

Lamera Hotel (Map p429; ☎ 344 2075; Sharia Sheraton; s/d incl all meals from E£155/90; ❌) Another adequate budget option, the Lamera has a central location good for anyone who wants to be in the middle of the action. Rooms are fairly unmemorable but some have sea views, and fortunately cleanliness isn't too much of a problem here. You're not on the beach but it's close enough if you don't mind walking.

Sea Garden (Map p429; ☎ 344 7493; www.seagarden .com.eg; off Sharia Sheraton; s/d from US$65/70; ❌ 🖳 🛒) Only a few years old, this high-rise block isn't much to look at but the Sea Garden is a discernible step up in quality from budget options. With a three-star rating you can expect well-cared-for rooms and a reasonably professional level of service. You're far from the beach of course, though the pool here is one of the nicer ones on the block.

Zak Royal Wings Hotel (Map p429; ☎ 344 6012; www .zakhotel.com; Sharia al-Hadaba; s/d from €40/60; ❌ 🖳 🛒) Located next to the infamous Papas Bar, this is the best choice if you're planning on getting blotto and don't want to stumble too far home. Rooms are slightly bare considering the price, though they're clustered around a nice

pool and a tropical garden. Obviously, it can get really loud here at night, though you won't care if you're a part of the mayhem.

Le Pacha Resort (Map p429; ☎ 344 4150; www .lepacharesort.com; Sharia Sheraton; s/d incl all meals from US$75/115; ❌ 🖳 🛒) If you're looking for a comparatively cheap all-inclusive, this centrally located Sigala hotel is a good choice. Although not as upscale as the four- and five-star hotels on the resort strip, Le Pacha offers a wide range of amenities including outdoor pools, a private beach and an on-site shopping mall. If being close to the action is important, this is a good choice, while intimacy seekers might want to head further down the coast.

RESORT STRIP

Giftun Beach Resort (Map p423; ☎ 346 3040; www .giftunbeachresort.com; s/d all-inclusive from US$65/85; ❌ 🖳 🛒) Giftun is one of the older resorts in Hurghada but this all-inclusive place is still a good choice if you're looking for low-key luxury. Unlike some of the more upmarket choices in this part of the city, the Giftun caters mostly to families looking for a cheap package holiday. Accommodation is in pleasant chalet-style rooms, and guests can take advantage of the popular on-site diving centre and windsurfing facilities.

Jasmine Village (Map p423; ☎ 346 0460; www.jasmine village.com; s/d all-inclusive from US$65/85; ❌ 🖳 🛒) Another oldie but a goodie, the Jasmine Village has also found a home among families trying to save a quick buck. Guests stay in one of 400-plus bungalow-style rooms, which look out onto a proper beach, a stunning coral reef and the open ocean. Even if you're not staying here the Jasmine is a good place to stop by for a bit of sunbathing and snorkelling as it has one of the best beaches around.

Sofitel Hurghada Red Sea (Map p423; ☎ 346 4641; www.sofitel.com; resort strip; s/d half board from US$150/175; ❌ ❌ 🖳 🛒) True to its high-class moniker, the Sofitel is a sophisticated and refined spot perfect for intimacy and seclusion. Immaculate rooms decorated in classical Arabesque style front the deep-blue expanse of the Red Sea. The Sofitel is also brimming with amenities, including a 700m-wide beach, as well as a kids' club, jogging track, tennis and squash courts and several restaurants and bars.

Soma Bay Sheraton (off Map p423; ☎ 354 5845; www .sheraton-somabay.com; s/d from €115/125; ❌ ❌ 🖳 🛒) Located 25km south of Hurghada proper,

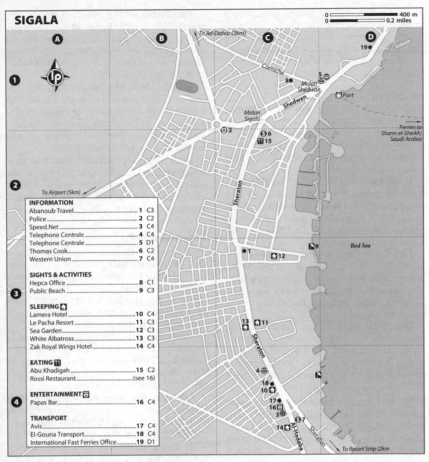

SIGALA

INFORMATION
Abanoub Travel.................................**1** C3
Police...**2** C2
Speed.Net...**3** C4
Telephone Centrale...........................**4** C4
Telephone Centrale...........................**5** D1
Thomas Cook....................................**6** C2
Western Union..................................**7** C4

SIGHTS & ACTIVITIES
Hepca Office.....................................**8** C1
Public Beach.....................................**9** C3

SLEEPING
Lamera Hotel...................................**10** C4
Le Pacha Resort...............................**11** C3
Sea Garden.....................................**12** C3
White Albatross...............................**13** C3
Zak Royal Wings Hotel.....................**14** C4

EATING
Abu Khadigah.................................**15** C2
Rossi Restaurant.........................(see 16)

ENTERTAINMENT
Papas Bar.......................................**16** C4

TRANSPORT
Avis..**17** C4
El-Gouna Transport.........................**18** C4
International Fast Ferries Office........**19** D1

this 298-room resort is part of the Ras Abu Soma 'resort cluster', one of a number of self-contained tourist centres being built along the coast south of Hurghada. Built in pseudo-Pharaonic style, the Sheraton boasts the typical five-star amenities including a golf course, tennis courts and a postcard-perfect beach of powdery sand. The Soma Bay is noteworthy for its continued efforts to foster a Red Sea sustainable-tourism initiative targeted at helping hotels become environmentally friendly.

ourpick **Oberoi Sahl Hasheesh** (off Map p423; ☎ 344 0777; www.oberoihotels.com; Sahl Hasheesh; ste from €200; ✕ ✕ 🖥 ☲) Peaceful, exclusive and opulent beyond your imagination, the Oberoi features palatial suites decorated in minimalist Moorish style. Each individually decorated accommodation comes complete with sunken marble baths, walled private courtyards – some with private pools – and panoramic sea views. Justifiably advertised as the most luxurious destination on the Red Sea, the Oberoi is world-class, and guests here are pampered to their hearts' content.

Eating

With its diverse expat population and large pool of tourists, Hurghada has a good variety of restaurants. If you're travelling on a budget, Ad-Dahar has dozens of inexpensive local-style eateries as well as several affordable Western-style ones. Sigala – and increasingly the northern end of the resort strip as well – has the

RED SEA COAST

greatest variety of restaurants in town, which primarily cater to upmarket tourists. Opening hours are generally irregular. The four- and five-star hotels along the resort strip are chock-full of eateries, and the vast majority are open to hotel guests and nonguests alike.

AD-DAHAR

Pizza Tarboush (Map p427; Sharia Abdel Aziz Mustafa; pizzas E£12-25) A popular takeaway pizzeria on the edge of the souq, Tarboush has a variety of topping choices, and a few chairs on the sidewalk for those who want to dine in and scope out the street scene.

Young Kang (Map p427; ☎ 012 422 9327; Sharia Sheikh Sabak; dishes E£25-35; 😊) This small and unassuming place might not look like much but it has a surprisingly good Far Eastern menu offering up traditional Korean and Cantonese favourites.

Portofino (Map p427; Sharia Sayyed al-Qorayem; dishes E£25-50; 😊) A Hurghada institution, Portofino serves authentic Italian wood-fired pizzas and homemade pastas as well as a few staple Egyptian dishes including homemade tahini and *baba ghanoug*.

Chez Pascal (Map p427; Sharla Sayyed al-Qorayem; meals E£30-65; 😊) This charming, European-style bistro is a good spot for eclectic cuisine served amid bright and clean surroundings – the perfect place to savour a Turkish coffee and indulge in a bit of people-watching.

Red Sea I (Map p427; ☎ 354 9630; off Sharia an-Nasr; dishes E£30-70; 😊) This and its sister restaurant, Red Sea II, on Sharia Sayyed al-Qorayem, offer a wide selection of seafood, plus Egyptian dishes and pizza, steaks, poultry and pleasant rooftop seating.

SIGALA & THE RESORT STRIP

Abu Khadigah (Map p429; Sharia Sheraton; meals E£2-20) Patronised by an intriguing mix of workers and local businessmen as well as the odd tourist, this no-frills place is known for its *koftas* (mincemeat and spices grilled on a skewer), stuffed cabbage leaves and other Egyptian staples.

Felfela Restaurant (Map p423; Sharia Sheraton; dishes E£15-55; 😊 8.30am-midnight) Sitting on a gentle bend in the coastline and overlooking the turquoise sea, this branch of the Felfela chain wins a prize for vistas, which you can enjoy while dining on Egyptian classics at reasonable prices.

Rossi Restaurant (Map p429; Sharia Sheraton; mains E£20-45) This popular hang-out for divers and expats serves a variety of pizza toppings on crispy crusts, and pasta dishes – the service is relaxed, and women can eat by themselves without being hassled.

our pick **Little Buddha** (Map p423; Marina Blvd; mains E£45-75) This is one of Hurghada's most well known Asian restaurants. The cuisine here is a fusion of sushi spreads, Chinese-style seafood dishes and plenty of rice and noodle concoctions to round things out.

Shade (Map p423; Marina Blvd; mains E£50-95) A uniquely Scandinavian spot directly on the waterfront, Shade is where you can sample fresh local seafood served up with a Northern European culinary sensibility.

Entertainment

Thanks to its large community of resident dive instructors, tour guides, hotel employees and other foreigners, Hurghada has some of Egypt's liveliest nightlife. Almost all the three- to five-star hotels and tourist villages have one or several bars, and there are many independent places as well.

Most of the large hotels offer some sort of spectacle – usually a Russian-themed show – as well as belly-dancing performances in their clubs. For dancing, most places don't get going until at least 11pm.

Papas Bar (Map p429; www.papasbar.com; Sharia Sheraton, Sigala) The centre of nightlife in Hurghada is this popular Dutch-run bar attached to Rossi Restaurant in Sigala. Filled with diving instructors and other foreign residents, it's very lively and has a great atmosphere most nights.

Papas II (Map p427; www.papasbar.com; Corniche, Ad-Dahar) Under the same management as Papas Bar (above), Papas II has a dark wooden interior, cold beers and regular live music. Both bars feature a constantly changing entertainment program – watch for their flyers around town or check the website.

Perhaps owing its inspiration to Paris' famed Buddha Bar, Little Buddha (above) doubles as a swanky nightspot where you can sip well-crafted cocktails in Zen-inducing surrounds.

For something a little less refined, the aptly named **Black Out Disco** (Map p423; Ali Baba Palace, resort strip) is where you should go to drink hard, dance harder and hopefully not black out before morning.

Shopping

Hurghada has a good selection of clothing boutiques in the small malls along the resort strip, as well as the obligatory abundance of overpriced T-shirts, hookahs, Pharaonic memorabilia, stuffed camels, etc. But avoid anyone selling marine curios. Stalls in the souq have been known to sell everything from stuffed sharks to lamps made from triggerfish – these are illegal and, frankly, would probably clash with your furniture anyway.

Getting There & Away

AIR

EgyptAir (Map p423; ☎ 344 3592/3; www.egyptair.com; resort strip) has daily flights to Cairo and Sharm el-Sheikh, though prices tend to fluctuate greatly depending on the season and availability. If you book in advance, it is sometimes possible to snag a ticket for as little as US$85, though prices can climb much higher during the busy summer and winter holiday seasons.

If you book a package holiday in either the UK or Europe, it is likely that your travel agent will arrange a charter flight directly to Hurghada for you. Even if you're an independent traveller, it's worth visiting a few travel agents before booking your ticket to Egypt – charter flights to Hurghada are often significantly cheaper than round-trip airfares to Cairo, and the city is a good jumping-off point for the Sinai Peninsula, Luxor and the Nile Valley.

BOAT

Ferry tickets to Sharm el-Sheikh are sold at the **International Fast Ferries office** (Map p429; Corniche, Sigala). Several travel agencies in town, including Thomas Cook (p425) also act as ticket agents. If you're staying at a four- or five-star hotel, the concierge can also help you book tickets in advance.

The ferry to Sharm el-Sheikh departs from Hurghada at 9.30am on Monday, Tuesday, Thursday and Saturday (one-way E£250/US$40, return E£450/US$70, 90 minutes). Note that departure times of the Sharm el-Sheikh ferry don't correspond with bus arrivals from Luxor, so you'll need to spend at least one night in Hurghada.

The rate of the dollar against the Egyptian pound and the whim of the ferry officials determine which currency you'll need to use for the Sharm ferry ticket – come prepared with dollars as they're not always available at banks in Hurghada. To avoid this extra hassle, it's wise to book your ticket in advance through either a travel agent or your hotel.

Note that the ferry is often cancelled during winter because of windy conditions, which unfortunately strands travellers in Hurghada for longer than they intended. For this reason, it's a good idea not to buy tickets in Luxor beforehand (trying to get refunds is difficult if not impossible). If the ferry is likely to be cancelled for a few days, you can then make alternative arrangements to get to Sharm by bus or service taxi.

Although the boarding process seems to make sense to the Egyptians, the entire system is somewhat lacking in clarity to foreign travellers. It's best to arrive at the ferry port at least one hour prior to departure. First, you will need to stop by the International Fast Ferries office to pick up your boarding pass, even if you've already purchased your ticket. Several touts will attempt to walk you through the process; it's worth declining their services and saving your baksheesh for a drink on board. After you pick up your boarding pass, cross the road and wait in line – about half an hour prior to departure, you will be ushered through security before boarding the ferry.

A few words of caution about the ferry – the Red Sea can get extremely rough, so much so that the staff on board hands out Dramamine prior to departure. If you've never had the pleasure of witnessing dozens of people simultaneously emptying out their stomach contents, you're in for a memorable trip. With that said, try to get a seat by the window, and keep your eyes fixed on the horizon – this is a great way to beat seasickness. Also note that if the seas are particularly rough, the advertised 90-minute journey can take as long as three hours.

For information on the ferries to Duba and Jeddah in Saudia Arabia, see p527.

BUS

Superjet (Map p427; ☎ 354 4722; Sharia al-Oruba, Ad-Dahar) has daily buses to Cairo (E£70, six hours) departing at noon, 2.30pm, 5pm and midnight. A 2.30pm service also goes to Alexandria (E£90, nine to 10 hours).

Upper Egypt Bus Co (Map p427; ☎ 354 7582; off Sharia an-Nasr, Ad-Dahar) has 10 daily buses to Cairo (E£60 to E£70, six to seven hours). There are also regular daily departures to Suez

RED SEA COAST

(E£35 to E£40, four to five hours) and Luxor (E£30 to E£35, five hours) via Safaga (E£10, one hour).

Finally, there are a few daily departures to Al-Quseir (E£20 to E£25, two to three hours), Marsa Alam (E£30 to E£35, four to five hours) and Shalatein (E£55, nine hours).

Schedules for the two companies listed above seem to change randomly. Confirm departure times at the bus station and try to book ahead for long-distance journeys such as to Luxor and Cairo.

SERVICE TAXI

The **service taxi station** (Map p427; off Sharia an-Nasr, Ad-Dahar) has taxis to Cairo (E£55 to E£60, six hours), Safaga (E£10, one hour), Al-Quseir (E£15 to E£20, two to three hours) and Marsa Alam (E£20 to £E25, three to four hours).

At the time of writing, forced convoys heading inland to the Nile Valley had been lifted, which means that it is now possible for foreigners to take service taxis to Luxor (E£20 to E£25, five hours).

Getting Around
TO/FROM THE AIRPORT

The airport is close to the resort strip. A taxi to downtown Ad-Dahar will cost between E£25 and E£30.

CAR

There are numerous car rental agencies along Sharia Sheraton in Sigala, including **Avis** (Map p429; ☎ 344 7400).

MICROBUS

Microbuses run throughout the day from central Ad-Dahar south along the resort strip (E£1), and along Sharia an-Nasr and other major routes. Short rides cost 25pt to 50pt.

El-Gouna Transport (Map p429; ☎ 354 1561) operates a more comfortable route (E£5 to E£10) between El-Gouna, Ad-Dahar and the end of Sharia Sheraton in Sigala about every half-hour, beginning at 9am. You can flag the bus down at any point along the way and pay on board.

TAXI

Taxis from Ad-Dahar to the start of the resort strip (around the Marriott hotel) charge about E£15. Travelling from the bus station to the centre of Ad-Dahar, expect to pay between E£5 and E£10.

SAFAGA
☎ 065

Safaga is a rough-and-ready port town that keeps itself in existence through the export of phosphates from local mines. It's also a major local terminal for the ferry to Saudi Arabia, and during the hajj thousands of pilgrims from the Nile Valley embark here on their voyages to Mecca. Despite the turquoise waters and the reefs that lie offshore, the town itself is unattractive, barely stretching beyond a few flyblown streets off a main thoroughfare. Unless you're into windsurfing (which is top notch here) or diving (which is decent here but better elsewhere), and are thus staying at one of the beach hotels along the resort strip at the northern end of the bay, it is hardly worth more than a brief stopover.

Orientation & Information

Safaga is a long town, stretched out over about 5km and based around Sharia al-Gomhuriyya, the main road running parallel to the waterfront. The bus station is near the southern end of town. Heading north there is a motley collection of small, cheap eateries, and beyond these the **post office** (⌚ 8.30am-2.30pm Sat-Thu). About 1.5km north of the bus station is the service taxi station, followed by the port entrance (for ferries to Saudi Arabia). At the far-northern end of town, near the roundabout with the large dolphin sculptures, a road branches northeast off Sharia al-Gomhuriyya leading to the northern resort strip.

Sights & Activities

The old Roman settlement of **Mons Claudianus** lies about 40km from Safaga along the Qena road; see p439.

Safaga is a famously windy place, with a fairly steady stream blowing in from the north, and most of the resort hotels have **windsurfing** centres, plus kitesurfing and other aquatic sports.

For an overview of diving in the Red Sea, including recommended operators and dive sites in the Safaga area, see p441.

Sleeping & Eating

Cleopatra (☎ 253 3926; opposite EgyptAir office; s/d E£65/85) This is about as cheap as it gets in these parts, so you shouldn't expect more than an old bed, an older TV and hopefully some clean sheets. On the plus side, the private bathrooms mean you don't have to share the sink with anyone else, and the central location is convenient for walking around and exploring the town. All in all a decent option if you're just in need of a bed for the night before hopping on the ferry to Saudi.

Holiday Inn Resort Safaga Palace (☎ 326 0100, 325 2821; www.ichotelsgroup.com; resort strip; s/d from US$55/65; ✿ 🖳 ☎) This large complex on the northern resort strip compensates for lack of ambience with good facilities and a great price. Generic rooms have little personality beyond the view from the window, though the grounds are home to a sweeping beach, an attractive pool and a well-equipped water-sports centre. If you're looking for a cheap but comfortable escape, the price is right here, particularly if you book in advance and snag lower rates online.

Menaville Village (☎ 326 0600; www.menadive.com /en/middle.html; resort strip; s/d from US$80/95; ✿ 🖳 ☎) Approximately 5km north of the town centre is this four-star resort, which has a reputable scuba centre and is very popular with European divers. Much more low-key than other resort hotels along the coast, the poolside scene is a modest affair where you can quietly unwind after your dive. Accommodation is in whitewashed two-storey villas that are a bit worn but remain spacious, bright and airy.

At the northern end of town, just south of the dolphin roundabout, are several inexpensive eateries, though nothing is particularly noteworthy. Most tourists prefer to eat in their hotels, and full-board and all-inclusive plans are generally available at upmarket properties.

Getting There & Away
BOAT
There are regular passenger boats from Safaga to Duba (Saudi Arabia), and services to Jeddah (Saudi Arabia) during the hajj – for more information, see p527.

BUS
Safaga is located along the main coastal highway, 53km south of Hurghada. There are seven daily buses to Cairo (E£65 to E£75, seven to eight hours). In addition, there are regular daily departures to Suez (E£40 to E£45, five to six hours), which also stop in Hurghada (E£10, one hour), and to Luxor (E£25 to E£35, four hours). Finally, there are a few daily departures to Al-Quseir (E£10, one hour), Marsa Alam (E£25 to E£30, three to hour fours) and Shalatein (E£50, eight hours).

SERVICE TAXI
Service taxis run to Cairo (E£55 to E£60 per person, seven hours), Hurghada (E£10, one hour), Al-Quseir (E£25 to E£30, one to two hours) and Marsa Alam (E£20 to £25, two to three hours).

AL-QUSEIR
☎ 065
The historic city of Al-Quseir was founded during Pharaonic times as the launching point for boats sailing to Punt, a fabled site in eastern Africa that was the alleged source of rare and exotic trade products. Although nothing remains of this ancient trading port, Al-Quseir's long history and sleepy present lend it a charm absent from other towns along the coast of the Red Sea. Dominated by an Ottoman fortress, lined with old coral-block buildings and home to domed tombs of various saints – mostly pious pilgrims who died en route to or from Mecca – Al-Quseir has a soothing vibe that can be difficult to find in the clamour of modern Egypt. Even if you're just passing through, it's worth spending an hour or two strolling along the waterfront and enjoying a quiet, reflective moment.

History
Prior to the 10th century, Al-Quseir was one of the most important ports on the Red Sea and a major exit point for pilgrims who were travelling to Mecca for the hajj. It also served as a thriving centre of trade and export between the Nile Valley and the Red Sea and beyond. Even during its period of decline, the city remained a major settlement and was sufficiently important for the Ottomans to fortify it during the 16th century. Later the British beat the French for control of Al-Quseir and for some time it was the main import channel for the spice trade from India to Britain. However, the opening of the Suez Canal in 1869 put an end to all this and the town's decline accelerated, with only a brief burst of prosperity as a phosphate-processing centre in the early decades of the 20th century.

Information
Hot Line Internet Café (Sharia Port Said; per hr E£10; ☽ 9am-3am)
Main post office (Sharia al-Sheikh Abdel Ghafaar; ☽ 8.30am-2pm Sat-Thu)

RED SEA COAST

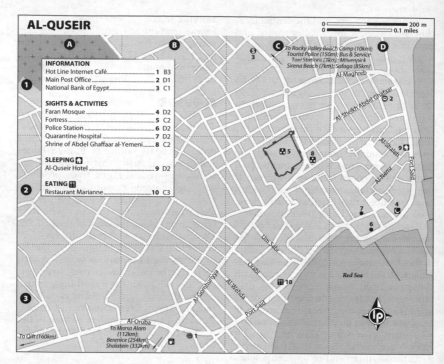

AL-QUSEIR

INFORMATION
Hot Line Internet Café...........................1 B3
Main Post Office.....................................2 D1
National Bank of Egypt........................3 C1

SIGHTS & ACTIVITIES
Faran Mosque...4 D2
Fortress..5 C2
Police Station...6 D2
Quarantine Hospital.............................7 D2
Shrine of Abdel Ghaffaar al-Yemeni.......8 C2

SLEEPING
Al-Quseir Hotel.....................................9 D2

EATING
Restaurant Marianne..........................10 C3

National Bank of Egypt (Safaga rd; 8.30am-2pm Sun-Thu) No ATM (yet).

Tourist police (335 0024; Safaga rd)

Sights

The 16th-century Ottoman **fortress** (admission E£10; 9am-5pm) is Al-Quseir's most important historical building. Much of the original structure remains intact, although it was modified several times by the French, as well as the British, who permanently altered the fortress by firing some 6000 cannonballs upon it during a heated battle in the 19th century.

Just across from the fortress is the 19th-century **shrine** of a Yemeni sheikh, Abdel Ghaffaar al-Yemeni, which is marked by an old gravestone in a niche in the wall.

A few blocks south along the waterfront is the picturesque **police station**, originally an Ottoman *diwan* (council chamber) and later the town hall. Photos aren't permitted and it's not open to the public.

Behind here is another fortresslike building, formerly a **quarantine hospital**, built during the reign of the Ottoman sultan Selim II –

just next to this is the **Faran Mosque**, dating to 1704.

Running between the waterside Sharia Port Said and the main street, Sharia Al-Gomhuriyya, are numerous small lanes good for wandering around to get a glimpse of local life. One of them, **Sharia Um Sabr**, has been restored – it's best reached from a turn-off on Sharia Al-Gomhuriyya.

For an overview of diving in the Red Sea, including recommended operators and dive sites in the Al-Quseir area, see p441.

Sleeping & Eating

Al-Quseir Hotel (333 2301; Sharia Port Said; s/d E£135/165;) This charismatic hotel has six simple but spacious rooms in a renovated 1920s merchant's house on the seafront. With its original narrow wooden staircase, high wooden ceilings and latticework on the windows, it's full of atmosphere, and staying here is a pleasure. There are also good views from the seafront rooms, and a tiny restaurant. Order ahead for meals.

Rocky Valley Beach Camp (333 5247; www .rockyvalleydiverscamp.com; 4-/8-day all-inclusive diving pack-

---

WARNING

Some coastal areas, especially in the southern Red Sea, are mined. While these remnants of earlier conflicts are being gradually removed, they remain a threat, particularly as sites are not always marked. Avoid entering any area demarcated with barbed wire, no matter how broken or old, and if you decide to check out that secluded beach, always look for tyre tracks or footprints. Better still, check with locals.

---

age €200/350; [icon]) Plopped down on a wilderness beachfront about 10km north of town, this remote camp is a veritable paradise for shoestringing scuba aficionados. Rocky Valley lures in divers by offering a variety of cheap all-inclusive packages, which include Bedouin-style tents, beachside barbecues and some incredible reefs right off shore. The management here fosters a wonderful communal atmosphere, and it's the kind of place where a late-night beach party under a blanket of stars might postpone any plans you have for an early-morning dive.

Mövenpick Sirena Beach ([icon] 333 2100; www.moevenpick-quseir.com; r from US$105; [icons]) This low-set, domed ensemble 7km north of the town centre is top of the line in Al-Quseir, and one of the best resorts along the coast, though it's surprisingly more affordable than you might imagine. Its amenities include excellent food and the usual five-star facilities, a Subex diving centre, quiet evenings and a refreshing absence of the glitz so common in other resort hotels. The management is known for its environmentally conscious approach.

Restaurant Marianne ([icon] 333 4386; Sharia Port Said; dishes E£15-50) One of the best places in town to sample the bounty of the Red Sea, this local favourite serves up some seriously delicious seafood. Opening hours are irregular.

Getting There & Away

The bus and service taxi stations are next to each other about 3km northwest of the Safaga road.

BUS

Buses run to Cairo (E£80 to E£85, 10 to 11 hours) and Hurghada (E£20 to E£25, three hours), departing at 6am, 7.30am, 9am, 7pm

and 8.30pm. Buses to Marsa Alam (E£10 to E£15, two hours) are at 5am, 9am, 7pm and 8pm.

SERVICE TAXI

Sample fares: Cairo (E£70 to E£75, 10 to 11 hours), Hurghada (E£15 to E£20, three hours) and Marsa Alam (E£5 to E£10, two hours).

Getting Around

Microbuses go along Sharia al-Gomhuriyya, with some also going to the bus and service taxi stations. Fares are between 50pt and E£1, depending on the distance travelled. Taxis also cover this route, with fares averaging a few pounds per ride.

MARSA ALAM
[icon] 065

The rather nondescript town of Marsa Alam is nothing more than a few scattered buildings surrounding a large army base, though this is all set to change in the years to come. Following the completion of its international airport in 2001, Marsa Alam has been heavily touted by the Egyptian government as the Red Sea Riviera's newest tourist drawcard. The primary reason for the heavy hype is simple – the seas just off the rugged coastline allow some of the best diving Egypt has to offer.

Until very recently, only serious divers accessed this far-flung destination, though tourist numbers in Marsa Alam are on the rise, perhaps due to growing dissatisfaction with traditional resort destinations such as Hurghada. And, while some local residents and diving aficionados are justifiably grumbling about the threat of overdevelopment, coastal construction has been comparatively slow and surprisingly sustainable. At present, the area around Marsa Alam is home to a collection of highly recommendable ecolodges and, for the time being, only a handful of upmarket luxury resorts.

History

Despite its current remote location, the area around Marsa Alam has an ancient history. Gold and emeralds were once mined in the barren, mineral-rich mountains just inland, and the road leading from Marsa Alam west to Edfu in the Nile Valley follows an ancient route that was originally built by Ptolemy II.

Today phosphate mining is the area's main industry, although it is fast being overtaken by tourism.

Orientation & Information

Marsa Alam itself is little more than a T-junction where the road from Edfu meets the coastal road. Just south of the junction is a modest collection of shops, a pharmacy, a telephone centre and a bustling market. The coast to the south and north is sprinkled with resorts.

EMERGENCY
Air ambulance (☎ 010 154 1978)
Decompression chamber (☎ 012 218 7550, 019 510 0262, emergency VHF code16; Marsa Shagra) Located 24km north of Marsa Alam.
Tourist police (☎ 375 0000; Quaraya Hotel, coastal rd)

Sights & Activities

Diving and desert excursions are the main activities around Marsa Alam. For more on diving, which is primarily for experienced divers only, see p441. For more on desert safaris, see opposite.

Sleeping

There are few places to stay in Marsa Alam village itself – at least for the time being. But north and south along the coast there's an ever-growing number of all-inclusive resorts, plus a handful of simple, diver-oriented 'ecolodges' or diving camps. These usually consist of no-frills reed or stone bungalows, sometimes with private bathrooms, generator-provided electricity, and a common area. They are run together with a dive centre and offer a rugged alternative to the resort scene for backpackers or backpackers-at-heart.

ECOLODGES
our pick **Shaqra Eco-Lodge** (☎ 02-337 1833; www.redsea -divingsafari.com; Marsa Shagra; tents/chalets per person €35/50) This simple place owned by Hossam Helmi – lawyer, committed environmentalist and diving enthusiast – was one of the first ecolodges along the southern Red Sea coast, and remains the best. It offers simple but spotless and comfortable accommodation in a choice of two-bed tents sharing bathroom facilities or stone chalets with en suite – all designed to be as kind to the environment as possible – plus first-rate diving (dives from €30). Nondivers in search of beautiful vistas

and tranquillity are welcome, too. It's along the main road, 24km north of Marsa Alam.

The same owner also runs a similar camp with the same prices at Marsa Nakari, 18km south of Marsa Alam, plus a camp with 25 tents and 16 stone chalets in Wadi Lahami, a remote mangrove bay just north of Ras Banas, near Berenice and 120km south of Marsa Alam. There are live-aboards based in each of the three camps used for offshore diving. With his legal qualifications, Helmi also has a sideline in underwater weddings.

ALL-INCLUSIVE RESORTS
Be advised that rooms at the following resorts listed are usually booked in advance as part of a package deal including return airfares from the UK and Europe and transfers from the airport to the resort. So, it's probably not a good idea to simply show up at the front door and request a room, though you can always stop by any of the ecolodges already listed.

Note that prices for the following all-inclusive resorts vary considerably depending on season and availability. It certainly pays to shop around and visit several travel agents in advance as it's sometimes possible to get a five-star holiday at a three-star price. Also note that the listings are by no means comprehensive as this stretch of the Red Sea is currently experiencing a construction boom.

Kahramana Beach Resort (☎ 02-748 0883; www.kahramanaresort.com/k_marsa/home.htm; s/d all-inclusive from US$120/135; 🅿 🖳 🖭) Located 26km north of Marsa Alam at Marsa Shagra, the Kahramana is built on two hills that surround an attractive beach. The entire complex is built of natural stone, and consists of attached chalets in shades of ochre. One of the larger complexes along this stretch of coastline, the Kahramana has a particularly festive atmosphere, which means you'll have plenty of fun above and below the water.

Lahami Bay Beach Resort (☎ 195 100 354; www .lahamibay.com; s/d all-inclusive from €105/135; 🅿 🖳 🖭) Located 123km south of Marsa Alam, Lahami Bay has the distinction of being the most southerly resort on the Egyptian Red Sea. Boasting a unique fusion of Eastern and Mediterranean architecture, the Lahami Bay welcomes visitors with plush lodgings overlooking the deep-blue sea. The real attraction of this lodge is its remote location, which means that nearby reefs are about as pristine as they come.

Sol y Mar Solaya (☎ 375 0015; www.solymar
-hotels.com; s/d all-inclusive from €110/140; ❄ ☐ ☎)
A plush pleasure-palace about 75km north
of Marsa Alam, this four-star resort is awash
in Romanesque arches and verdant gardens.
Boasting two swimming pools, a full spa complete with jacuzzis, steam baths and saunas,
and tennis courts overlooking the ocean, there
are enough amenities on offer to keep nondivers entertained. Of course, you're here to
dive, so don't spend too much time living
the resort life.

Palace Port Ghalib Resort (☎ 336 0000; www
.ichotelsgroup.com/intercontinental; s/d all-inclusive from
US$175/195; ❄ ☐ ☎) Run by the prestigious
InterContinental group of hotels and resorts,
the Palace is the new face of Marsa Alam and
the heart of the new Port Ghalib development
just 5km from the international airport. While
development has slowed considerably in light
of the global credit-crunch, the Palace opened
up to considerable fanfare, and can now easily compete with other luxury properties in
Hurghada and Sharm el-Sheikh. The Palace
is a slightly subdued yet wholly hedonistic
affair where you can lap up the beauty of
the coastline.

Eating

In Marsa Alam there are a couple of cafes
at the junction where you can find basic
fare as well as a small supermarket with a
modest selection. However, all of the resorts and lodges have restaurants as well as
full-board packages.

Getting There & Away

AIR

The Marsa Alam International Airport is
67km north of Marsa Alam along the Al-
Quseir road. There is no public transport, so
you'll need to arrange a transfer in advance
with your hotel.

EgyptAir (www.egyptair.com) has daily flights
to Cairo and Sharm el-Sheikh. Prices tend
to fluctuate wildly depending on the season
and availability. The airport is also served by
charter flights originating in either the UK
or Europe.

BUS

There is no bus station in Marsa Alam. For
transport to Shalatein, wait at the coffee shop
next to the police post at the entrance to Marsa
Alam. For transport to the Nile Valley, wait

at the petrol station in Marsa Alam, or at the
T-junction about 1km further along on the
Edfu road.

Buses from Shalatein pass Marsa Alam
en route to Edfu (E£35, three to four hours)
at around 7am and 9am daily. Buses to
Shalatein (E£20 to E£25, four hours) come
from Hurghada and depart Marsa Alam at
around 5am, 7am, noon and 8.30pm.

There are four daily buses to Al-Quseir
(E£10 to E£15, two hours) and Hurghada (E£30
to E£35, four to five hours), departing at 5am,
12.30pm, 2.30pm and 5pm. To Cairo direct, the
fare is E£85 to E£90 (10 to 11 hours).

EASTERN DESERT

The Eastern Desert – a vast, desolate area
rimmed by the Red Sea Mountains to the
east and the Nile Valley in the west – was
once criss-crossed by ancient trade routes
and dotted with settlements that played
vital roles in the development of many of
the region's greatest civilisations. Today
the desert's rugged expanses are filled with
fascinating footprints of this history, including rock inscriptions, ancient gold and
mineral mines, wells and watchtowers, and
religious shrines and buildings. Indeed, it
is one of the highlights of any visit to the
Red Sea coast, and a world apart from the
commercialised coastline.

Orientation & Information

None of the roads crossing the desert can be
freely travelled – some are completely closed
to foreigners, and others require a convoy –
and all the sites require a guide. As a result,
it is strongly advised (in fact necessary) that
you explore the Eastern Desert with the aid
of an experienced tour operator.

Although second-rate travel agencies
occupy every corner of the tourist hub of
Hurghada (p423), it is recommended that you
book a tour through **Red Sea Desert Adventures**
(☎ 012 399 3860; www.redseadesertadventures.com; Marsa
Shaqra). This extremely professional safari
outfit is run by Dutch geologist Karin van
Opstal and her Austrian partner, and offers
tailor-made walking, camel and jeep safaris
throughout the area. Van Opstal has lived
in Marsa Alam for over a decade and is an
authority on the local Ababda tribesmen, with
whom she works closely.

Tours start at approximately €40 per
person, though they vary depending on the

NOMADS OF THE EASTERN DESERT

Although the desert of the southern Red Sea may seem empty and inhospitable, the area has been home to nomadic Ababda and Besharin tribes for millennia. Members of the Beja, a nomadic tribe of African origin, they are thought to be descendents of the Blemmyes, the fierce tribesmen mentioned by classical geographers. Until well into the 20th century, the extent of the territory in which they roamed was almost exactly as described by the Romans, with whom they were constantly at war some 2000 years earlier.

Expert camel herders, the Ababda and Besharin lived a nomadic lifestyle that hardly changed until the waters of Lake Nasser rose and destroyed their traditional grazing lands. While most Besharin, many of whom do not speak Arabic, live in Sudan, most of the Arabic-speaking Ababda are settled in communities in the Nile Valley between Aswan and Luxor. A small number continue to live in their ancestral territory, concentrated in the area from Marsa Alam to Wadi Gimal, as well as on the eastern shores of Lake Nasser.

If you spend time in the region, you'll still likely see the traditional Ababda hut, lined inside with thick, hand-woven blankets, or hear Ababda music, with its rhythmic clapping and drumming and heavy use of the five-stringed lyre-like *tamboura*. At the centre of Ababda social life is *jibena* – heavily sweetened coffee prepared from fresh-roasted beans in a small earthenware flask heated directly in the coals.

With the rapid expansion of tourism along the southern Red Sea, long-standing Ababda lifestyles have become increasingly threatened. Tourism has begun to replace livestock and camels as the main source of livelihood, and many Ababda men now work as guards or labourers on the resorts springing up around Marsa Alam, while others have started working with travel companies, offering camel safaris to tourists.

There are differing views on the impact of tourism in this region. On one hand, revenue from tourism can play a vital role in the development of the region, particularly through the sale of locally produced crafts or payment for services of a local guide. However, indigenous tourism sometimes becomes exploitative and visits can take on an unfortunate 'human zoo' quality. If you are considering a visit, ask questions about the nature of your trip and consider the potential positive and negative impact that it may have on the community.

---

specifications of your uniquely catered tour, the size of your party and the time of year. In order for the necessary permits to be organised for multiday desert safaris, try to book at least one month in advance.

Alternatively, you can arrange your trip through Fustat Wadi El Gemal (see opposite).

Sights

One of the most impressive collections of **rock inscriptions**, many of which date to prehistoric times, is found in the barren tracts fringing the Marsa Alam–Edfu road, beginning close to Marsa Alam, where the smooth, grey rock was perfect for carving. They include hunting scenes with dogs chasing ostriches, depictions of giraffes and cattle, and hieroglyphic accounts of trade expeditions.

In the remote **Wadi Miya**, west of Marsa Alam, in what was likely an ancient mine works, are the remains of a temple said to be built by Seti I. **Wadi Sikait**, about 80km southwest of Marsa Alam, was an emerald-mining

centre at least as early as the Ptolemaic period. It provided emeralds that were used throughout the ancient world and was the exclusive source of emeralds for the Roman Empire.

The high, smooth walls of **Wadi Hammamat**, about halfway along the road connecting Al-Quseir to the town of Qift, display a remarkable collection of graffiti dating from Pharaonic times down to Egypt's 20th-century King Farouk. The road through the wadi runs along an ancient trade route, and remains of old wells as well as other evidence of the area's long history can be seen along the way. In Graeco-Roman times, watchtowers were built along the trail at short enough intervals for signals to be visible, and many of them are still intact on the barren hilltops on either side of the road.

Starkly beautiful **Wadi Gimal**, which extends inland for about 85km from its coastal opening south of Marsa Alam, is home to a rich variety of bird life, gazelles and stands of mangrove. In ancient times, the surrounding area was the source of emerald, gold and other minerals used in Pharaonic and Roman civilisations. Together with tiny Wadi Gimal Island, just offshore from the wadi's delta area, Wadi Gimal has been given protected status and targeted for development as an ecotourism destination. Because of its long history and abundance of historical monuments, the area has also been proposed as a Unesco World Heritage Site.

About 40km along the Safaga–Qena road, a signposted track breaks off northwest towards **Mons Claudianus**, an old Roman granite quarry/ fortress complex, and one of the largest of the Roman settlements dotting the Eastern Desert. This stark and remote place was the end of the line for Roman prisoners brought to hack the granite out of the barren mountains, and was a hardship post for the soldiers sent to guard them. It was more a concentration camp than a quarry – you can still see the remains of the tiny cells that these unfortunates inhabited. There is also an immense cracked pillar, left where it fell 2000 years ago, a small temple and some other ruins. Once the granite was mined, it was carved and transported more than 200km across the desert to the Nile, from where it then was taken to the Mediterranean and the heart of the empire. The site is about 25km north of the turn-off along deteriorated tarmac.

Mons Porphyrites – about 40km northwest of Hurghada – is the site of ancient porphyry quarries worked by the Romans. The precious white-and-purple crystalline stone was mined and then transported across the desert along the Via Porphyrites to the Nile for use in sarcophagi, columns and other decorative work elsewhere in the Roman world. The quarries were under the direct control of the imperial family in Rome, which had encampments, workshops and even temples built for the workers and engineers here. Evidence of this quarry town can still be seen, although not much of it is standing. A road leading to the site branches off the main road about 20km north of Hurghada.

In addition to the many traces of Pharaonic and other ancient civilisations, the Eastern Desert is also home to numerous Islamic tombs and shrines. One of the best known is the tomb of Sayyed al-Shazli, a 13th-century sheikh who is revered as one of the more important Sufi leaders. His followers believe that he wanted to die in a place where nobody

had ever sinned. Evidently such a place was difficult to find, as the site was a journey of several days from either the Nile Valley or the coast. Al-Shazli's tomb – which lies about 145km southwest of Marsa Alam at Wadi Humaysara – was restored under the orders of King Farouk in 1947, and there is now an asphalt road leading to it. His *moulid* (saints' festival), on the 15th of the Muslim month of Shawal, is attended by thousands of Sufis.

Sleeping

If you've booked a tour through Red Sea Desert Adventures (see p437), they'll organise a combination of desert camping and Bedouin village stays depending on the length and depth of your tour.

Another option is to bed down at **Fustat Wadi El Gemal** (☎ 240 5132; www.wadielgemal.com; prices vary), a permanent tented camp located in the impossibly scenic 'Valley of the Camels'. A locally run project aimed at generating a sustainable revenue for the Bedouin community, Fustat Wadi El Gemal serves as a base for all manner of excursions into the Eastern Desert, which shouldn't set you back more than US$50 to US$100 per person per day. The camp itself is a highly memorable affair modelled on a traditional nomadic camp, albeit with a healthy amount of artistic flourishes. Advance reservations are recommended.

Getting There & Away

With prior reservations, either Red Sea Desert Adventures (p437) or Fustat Wadi El Gemal (above) will organise your transport to and from the Eastern Desert as well as your travel between all of the sites. The only viable option for accessing the area is to make transport arrangements with local operators such as these.

BERENICE

The military centre and small port of Berenice, 150km south of Marsa Alam, was founded in 275 BC by Ptolemy II Philadelphus. From about the 3rd to the 5th century AD, it was one of the most important harbours and trading posts on the Red Sea coast, and is mentioned in the 1st-century AD mariner's chronicle *Periplus of the Erythraean Sea*.

The ruins of the ancient town, including ruins of the **Temple of Serapis**, are located just south of the present-day village, and have been the subject of ongoing archaeological investigations. About 100km to the northwest are ruins of the old Roman settlement of **Sikait**, which was once at the centre of major emerald-mining operations in the region.

Today the main activity is at Ras Banas peninsula – jutting into the sea just northeast of Berenice – which is an important military base. Because of this, and because of the region's proximity to the Sudanese border, independent visits are strongly discouraged – you can expect to be questioned by the tourist police, and to be accompanied by an escort even if you succeed in getting to Berenice.

There is no official accommodation, and camping needs to be cleared with the police.

Buses (E£50, nine hours) departing from Hurghada bound for Shalatein stop in Berenice. You will need to arrange your own transport in order to get out to the ruins.

SHALATEIN

This dusty outpost 90km south of Berenice marks the administrative boundary between Egypt and Sudan. With that said, Egypt considers the political boundary to be another 175km southeast, beyond the town of Halaib, a once-important Red Sea port that has long

since fallen into obscurity. Of course, Sudan strongly disagrees, resulting in a large swath of disputed territory that is probably worth avoiding in the interest of personal safety.

Shalatein's colourful camel market is a major stop on the camel-trading route from Sudan, which for many of the camels finishes in the Birqash camel market outside Cairo (p211). Amid the dust and the vendors, Rashaida tribesmen in their lavender *galabiyya*s (full-length robes) mix with Ababda, Besharin and other peoples from southern Egypt and northern Sudan.

As with Berenice, independent visitors are discouraged, and the area is sporadically closed to foreigners completely. You can expect to be questioned by the tourist police, and to be accompanied by an escort even if you succeed in getting to Shalatein. However, you can easily avoid hassles by simply organising an excursion to the camel market through Red Sea Desert Adventures (see p437).

There is no official accommodation and camping needs to be cleared with the police.

Buses (E£55, nine to 10 hours) departing from Hurghada via Berenice terminate in Shalatein.

Diving the Red Sea

Given Egypt's living history stretching back several millennia, it's no wonder that so many tourists never give a thought to exploring its underwater world. But while landlubbers are busy sweating and dodging touts in the desert, divers are plunging into the Red Sea's clear depths, and finding themselves surrounded by one of nature's most magnificent sights.

In 1989, a panel of scientists and conservationists chose the northern portion of this 1800km-long body of water as one of the Seven Underwater Wonders of the World. Here divers will find coral mountains, shallow reefs swarming with brightly coloured fish, sheer drop-offs disappearing into unplumbed depths and coral-encrusted shipwrecks, all bathed in an ethereal blue hue.

Indeed, the Red Sea boasts a legendary reputation among diving enthusiasts, and undoubtedly deserves its status as one of the world's premier underwater destinations. The two jewels in the Red Sea's crown are Ras Mohammed National Park, home to the 'Holy Trinity' of Shark Reef, Eel Garden and the Yolanda, and the WWII wreck of the *Thistlegorm*, a British warship first discovered in the 1950s by Jacques Cousteau.

The strongest appeal of the Red Sea is that you can tailor your diving holiday to your own travelling style. Independent travellers spend more time than they planned in the backpacker-friendly village of Dahab, and to a lesser extent Nuweiba, while package tourists enjoy the creature comforts in the resort towns of Sharm el-Sheikh, Hurghada and El-Gouna. If you truly want to maximise your underwater time, there's no better option than a week on a dive safari.

Regardless of your travelling style, the Red Sea never fails to impress and is one of the top highlights of any trip to Egypt.

HIGHLIGHTS

- Be overwhelmed at the magnificent underwater world of **Ras Mohammed National Park** (p449)

- Explore the remains of the **Thistlegorm** (p451), one of the top wreck dives in the world

- Push your limits by sinking into the deep blue abyss of Dahab's notorious **Blue Hole** (p447)

- Combine diving and Bedouin culture in a camel/dive safari from Dahab to **Gabr el-Bint** (p448)

- Spend your days sailing from one remote site to the next on a **live-aboard dive safari** (p456)

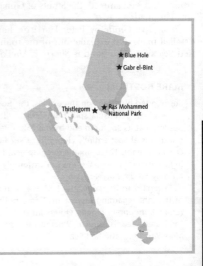

Orientation

Diving tends to be concentrated at the northern end of the Egyptian Red Sea, although increasing numbers of advanced divers are pushing further south. The most popular sites are around the southern tip of the Sinai Peninsula, most famously the thin strip of land that juts out into the sea and forms Ras Mohammed National Park.

Another major diving area is in the Straits of Tiran, which form the narrow entrance to the Gulf of Aqaba. The currents sweeping through the deep channel allow coral to grow prolifically, attracting abundant marine life. The reefs further north along the shores of the Gulf of Aqaba are also popular.

On the western side of the Sinai Peninsula lie the Straits of Gubal, a series of coral pinnacles just beneath the surface of the sea, famous for snagging ships trying to navigate north to the Suez Canal. This is where the majority of Egypt's shipwrecks, including the *Thistlegorm*, lie.

Heading south, the best reefs are found around the many offshore islands. Although most reefs near Hurghada have been damaged by uncontrolled tourist development, there is a plethora of pristine dive sites further south.

Information

BOOKS

Red Sea Diver's Guide from Sharm El Sheikh to Hurghada by Shlomo and Roni Cohen has excellent maps and descriptions of sites around Ras Mohammed, the Straits of Gubal and Hurghada.

Sinai Dive Guide by Peter Harrison has detailed maps and explanations of the main Red Sea sites. Also good is *Sharm el-Sheikh*

Diving Guide by Alberto Siliotti, with maps and ratings of numerous sites around Sharm el-Sheikh and Ras Mohammed National Park. *Red Sea Diving Guide* by Andrea Ghisotti and Alessandro Carletti covers Egyptian sites, as well as others in Sudan, Israel and Eritrea.

The Red Sea: Underwater Paradise by Angelo Mojetta is one of the better glossy coffee-table books, with beautiful photos of the flora and fauna of Egypt's reefs.

The Official HEPCA Dive Guide, produced by the Hurghada Environmental Protection & Conservation Association (HEPCA), details 46 sites with artists' drawings and a small fish index. Proceeds from the sale of this guide go towards maintaining mooring buoys on the Red Sea. For more on HEPCA, see Rescuing the Red Sea, p425.

INTERNET RESOURCES

GoRedSea.com (www.goredsea.com) A growing index of dive centres and live-aboards as well as links to jobs on offer for divers, and other information on the Red Sea.

H2O Magazine (www.h2o-mag.com) The website of the quarterly publication of the Red Sea Association for Diving and Watersports, with articles and updates on diving in the region.

Man & the Environment (MATE; ☎ 069-364 1091; www.mate-info.com) Environmental resource centre in Dahab where divers can learn more about the area's reefs and how to protect them. It also helps organise trash dives in an effort to keep rubbish off the reefs.

Red Sea Virtual Dive Center (www.redseavdc.com) Detailed descriptions of more than 73 dive sites.

Reef Check (www.reefcheck.org) A membership organisation working to save coral reefs in the Red Sea and elsewhere in the world.

South Sinai Association for Diving & Marine Activities (SSDM; ☎ 069-366 0418; www.southsinai

---

MARE ROSTRUM

Surrounded by desert on three sides, the Red Sea was formed some 40 million years ago when the Arabian Peninsula split from Africa, allowing the waters of the Indian Ocean to rush in. Bordered at its southern end by the 25km Bab al-Mandab Strait, the Red Sea is the only tropical sea that is almost entirely closed. No river flows into it and the influx of water from the Indian Ocean is slight. These unique geographical features, combined with the arid desert climate and high temperatures, make the sea extremely salty. It is also windy – on average the sea is flat for only 50 days a year.

In regard to its name (the Red Sea is in fact deep blue), there are two competing schools of thought regarding etymology. Some believe that the sea was named after the surrounding red-rock mountain ranges. Others insist it was named for the periodic algae blooms that tinge the water a reddish-brown. Whatever the spark, it inspired ancient mariners to dub these waters *Mare Rostrum* – the Red Sea.

.org) An NGO focused on raising the quality of dive sites and water sports, with an emphasis on the Sinai.

MEDICAL SERVICES

El Gouna Hospital & Hyperbaric Centre (☎ 065-358 0011, 012 218 7550, 012 219 0383; El-Gouna)

Marsa Shagra Decompression Chamber (☎ 012 218 7550, satellite 0195-100 262; Marsa Shagra) Located 24km north of Marsa Alam.

Naval Hyperbaric & Emergency Medical Center (Map p423; ☎ 065-344 9150, 065-354 8450; Corniche, Hurghada)

Sharm el-Sheikh Hyberbaric Medical Center (Map p467; ☎ 069-366 0922/3, 24hr emergency 012 212 4292; hyper_med_center@sinainet.com.eg; Sharm el-Sheikh; ⊙ 10.30am-6pm)

Sharm el-Sheikh International Hospital (Map p467; ☎ 069-366 0893/4/5; Sharm–Na'ama Bay rd, Sharm el-Sheikh)

Hyperbaric specialists:
Dr Adel Taher (☎ 012 212 4292; Sharm el-Sheikh)
Dr Hanaa Nessim (☎ 012 219 0383; Hurghada)
Dr Hossam Nasef (☎ 012 218 7550; Hurghada)

Dangers & Annoyances

There is no government regulatory body responsible for overseeing dive clubs in Egypt, although two nongovernmental organisations – the **Red Sea Association for Diving & Watersports** (RSADW; ☎ 065-344 4802; Hurghada), for the area from El-Gouna south to the Sudanese border, and the South Sinai Association for Diving & Marine Activities (opposite) for all of southern Sinai – are increasingly taking on this function.

All dive guides must have a valid ID card from one of these entities, and in the southern Sinai, all dive centres and live-aboards must be members of the SSDM. However, accidents still occasionally happen as a result of neglect and negligence. Before making any choices, carefully check out the club you're considering. Confirm with the relevant organisation that a club or guide is registered.

Before embarking on a scuba-diving, skin-diving or snorkelling trip, carefully consider the following points to ensure a safe and enjoyable experience.

■ Possess a current diving certification card from a recognised scuba diving instructional agency (if scuba diving).
■ Be sure you are in good health and feel comfortable diving.
■ Obtain reliable information about physical and environmental conditions at the dive site (eg from a reputable local dive operation).
■ Be aware of the local laws, regulations and etiquette about marine life and the environment.
■ Dive only at sites within your realm of experience; if available, engage the services of a competent, professionally trained dive instructor or dive master.
■ Be aware that underwater conditions vary significantly from one region, or even site, to another. Seasonal changes can significantly alter any site and dive conditions. These differences influence the way divers dress for a dive and what diving techniques they use.
■ Ask about the environmental characteristics that can affect your diving and how local trained divers deal with these considerations.

Watching Wildlife

The Red Sea is teeming with more than 1000 species of marine life, and is an amazing spectacle of colour and form. Fish, sharks, turtles, stingrays, dolphins, corals, sponges, sea cucumbers and molluscs all thrive in these waters.

Coral is what makes a reef a reef – though thought for centuries to be some form of flowering plant, it is in fact an animal. Both hard and soft corals exist, their common denominator being that they are made up of polyps, which are tiny cylinders ringed by waving tentacles that sting their prey and draw it into their stomach. During the day corals retract into their tube, only displaying their real colours at night.

Most of the bewildering variety of fish species in the Red Sea – including many that are found nowhere else – are closely associated with the coral reef, and live and breed in the reefs or nearby sea-grass beds. These include such commonly sighted species as the grouper, wrasse, parrotfish and snapper. Others, such as tuna and barracuda, live in open waters and usually only venture into the reefs to feed or breed.

When snorkelling or diving, the sharks you're most likely to encounter include white- or black-tipped reef sharks. Tiger sharks, as well as the enormous, plankton-eating whale sharks, are generally found only in deeper waters. If you're skittish about these apex predators, you can take comfort in the

DIVING THE RED SEA

DIVING THE RED SEA

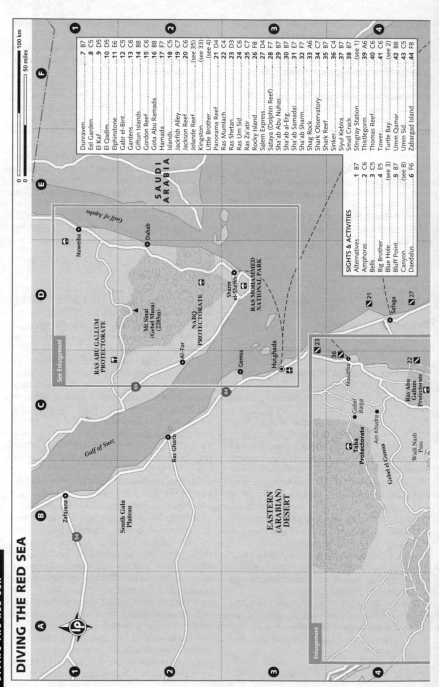

S A U D I
A R A B I A

Gulf of Aqaba

Nuweiba

Dahab

RAS ABÚ GALLUM
PROTECTORATE

Mt Sinai
(Gebel Musa)
(2285m)

NABQ
PROTECTORATE

Sharm
el-Sheikh

Al-Tor

RAS MOHAMMED
NATIONAL PARK

66

Gemsa

Hurghada

Gulf of Suez

Ras Gharib

44

SOUTH GALA
PLATEAU

Zafarana

54

EASTERN
(ARABIAN)
DESERT

21

Safaga
27

See Enlargement

Enlargement

23

36

Nuweiba

22

Taba
Protectorate

Gebel
Barqa

Ras Abu
Gallum
Protectorate

Ain Khudra

Gebel el Gunna

Wadi Nasb
Pass

0   100 km
0   50 miles

LP

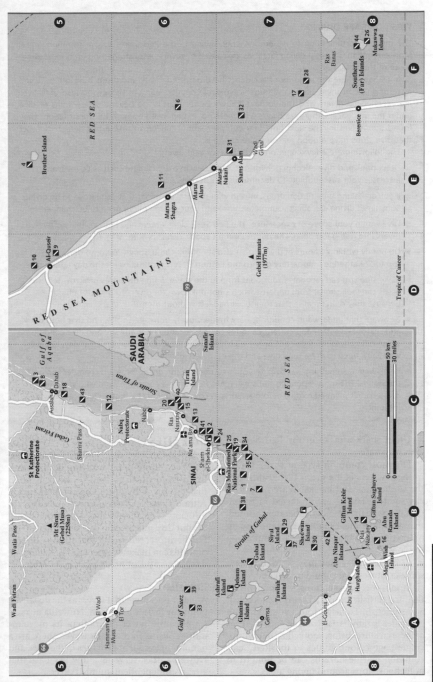

TIPS FOR SAFE DIVING

The most important thing to remember when diving in the Red Sea is to use common sense. More often than not, most diving fatalities are caused by divers simply forgetting (or disregarding) some of the basic rules.

In Dahab, where the majority of accidents have occurred, drink and drugs have often played a starring role in these tragic and largely avoidable deaths. Many of those who lose their lives are experienced divers who should have known better than to go beyond safety limits or dive under the influence. Others are divers who were not experienced enough for the situations they found themselves in. The next time you complain about having to take a test dive, remember that dive clubs have a good reason to be cautious.

The following are a few common-sense tips for safe diving:

■ Don't drink and dive. Alcohol dehydrates, especially in a dry climate such as Egypt's, and increases your susceptibility to decompression sickness.

■ If you are taking prescription drugs, inform your medical examiner that you intend to go diving. Sometimes diving can affect your metabolism and your dosage might need to be changed.

■ Dive within your scope of experience. The Red Sea's clear waters and high visibility often lull divers into going too deep. The depth limit for sports divers is 30m. Stick to it.

■ Do not fly within 24 hours of diving. You also shouldn't climb above 300m, so don't plan a trip to St Katherine's Monastery or into the Eastern Desert mountains for the day after a dive.

■ Make sure you can recognise your boat from in the water. Some dive sites get crowded and boats can look similar from underneath. It's not unknown for divers to get left behind because they didn't realise that their boat had left without them.

■ Be aware that underwater conditions vary tremendously from site to site, and that both daily and seasonal weather and current changes can significantly alter any site and dive conditions. These differences influence not only which sites you can dive on any particular day, but the way you'll need to dress for a dive and the necessary dive techniques.

■ Be insured. If something happens to you, treatment in the decompression chamber can cost thousands. The most reputable clubs will make insurance a condition for diving with them. If you hadn't planned to dive before arriving in Egypt, many of the better clubs can provide insurance.

fact that shark attacks in the Red Sea are extremely rare.

The most common type of turtle found in these waters is the green turtle, although the leatherback and hawksbill are occasionally sighted. Turtles are protected in Egypt, and although they're not deliberately hunted, they are sometimes caught in nets and end up on menus in restaurants in Cairo and along the coasts.

As intriguing as they may seem, there are some creatures that should be avoided, especially moray eels, sea urchins, fire coral, blowfish, triggerfish, feathery lionfish, turkeyfish and stonefish. To help protect yourself, it's a good idea to familiarise yourself with pictures of these creatures before snorkelling or diving – single-page colour guides to the Red Sea's common marine hazards can be bought in hotel bookshops around diving areas.

DIVE SITES

Following are brief descriptions of some of the Red Sea's more popular diving destinations, listed from north to south – keep in mind that this list is by no means comprehensive. Although we've given a general indication of difficulty, you should always seek the advice of your dive guide when deciding where to go. Furthermore, remember that strong currents or winds can make an otherwise fairly tame site dangerous and, at times, even undiveable.

Nuweiba

A major port town that serves as the departure point for ferries to Jordan, Nuweiba attracts significantly fewer divers than its more famous cousins in Sinai. However, there are a handful of excellent dive sites in the area, and Nuweiba does serve as a low-key base that attracts independent-minded divers.

RAS SHETAN
Location: 15km north of Nuweiba
Depth: 10m to 30m
Rating: Intermediate
Access: Shore

Although hard corals are not a strong point of the dive, there is a profusion of graceful soft corals between 10m and 20m, as well as the usual array of reef fish. The highlight of the dive is undoubtedly the contoured topography, including narrow valleys, sand-filled depressions and deep chasms.

SINKER
Location: Nuweiba
Depth: 6m to 35m
Rating: Intermediate
Access: Shore

A stone's throw away from the Hilton Coral Beach Resort, the Sinker is a massive submerged mooring buoy designed for cargo ships, which was sunk by mistake in the mid-1990s. Since then, it has developed into a fantastic artificial reef, attracting a host of small, colourful species.

RAS MUMLACH
Location: About 30km south of Nuweiba
Depth: 10m to 25m
Rating: Intermediate
Access: Shore

Although it takes a little longer to access Ras Mumlach, this site rewards divers with ample marine life and attractive topography. Entering from the shore, you'll cross a shallow sandy area carpeted with seagrass, followed by a sloping reef interspersed with enormous boulders and excellent table corals.

Dahab

Long dubbed the 'Ko Samui of the Middle East', the backpacker paradise of Dahab is a Thai-inspired collection of beachside hotels and restaurants. As well as the banana pancakes and apple *sheesha* (water pipes), the diving here is world-class, though independent travellers often use Dahab as a jumping-off point for dive sites around Sinai.

CANYON
Location: North side of Dahab
Depth: 5m to 33m
Rating: Intermediate
Access: Shore

One of the area's most popular dives, the Canyon is a long, narrow trench that runs perpendicular to the reef shelf, and is home to prolific hard and soft corals. If you're an experienced diver, you can descend to the bottom of the canyon (30m), and then swim towards shore through a chimney and past the 'fishbowl' (20m), a small chamber full of billowing curtains of glassfish and anthias.

EEL GARDEN
Location: North side of Dahab
Depth: 5m to 20m
Rating: Intermediate
Access: Shore

Eel Garden takes its name from the countless garden eels that carpet the seafloor not

---

BELLS & BLUE HOLE
Location: 8km north of Dahab
Depth: 7m to 27m
Rating: Intermediate
Access: Shore

The Blue Hole is Egypt's most infamous dive site. Carved into a reef just offshore, the Blue Hole is a gaping sinkhole that drops straight down – some say to as deep as 130m. Unfortunately, the site has claimed several lives, mainly thrill-seekers venturing well below the sport-diving limit.

An archway at approximately 65m connects the sinkhole to the open ocean – this is the trap. Solo divers have attempted to swim beneath this archway. Victims have succumbed to narcosis, missed the archway entirely, lost all sense of direction or simply run out of air. If you leave the depths to the experienced technical divers, you'll find the outer lip of the Blue Hole is full of marine life, and a reasonable plunge into the hole itself is somewhat akin to skydiving.

The entry point is at the Bells, a narrow breach in the reef table that forms a pool close to shore. From here, you descend through a chimney, exiting at 27m on a ledge that opens to the sea. If you swim south along the wall, a saddle in the reef at 7m allows you to enter the Blue Hole. As long as you monitor your depth carefully, you can finish up the dive by swimming across the sinkhole towards shore.

far from the entry point of the dive – as you approach, the eels vanish into their burrows like synchronised swimmers. Other highlights include huge coral boulders, dense congregations of barracudas and big groupers and snappers.

ISLANDS
Location: South side of Dahab
Depth: 5m to 18m
Rating: Novice
Access: Shore

Just south of Dahab before the lagoon, this underwater *Alice in Wonderland*–esque site offers an outstanding topography of coral alleyways, amphitheatres, valleys and gulleys. The quality and quantity of coral is phenomenal, with all varieties imaginable – from massive elkhorns to delicate table corals.

UMM SID
Location: 15km south of Dahab
Depth: 5m to 35m
Rating: Intermediate to advanced
Access: Shore

An impressive entrance through a wide corridor carved into a steeply sloping reef descends to a maximum depth of 25m, where you'll find a sandy slope inhabited by garden eels. The next major feature, a large sandy patch punctuated by table corals, quickly drops down further to 35m, where you'll find two enormous gorgonians.

GABR EL-BINT
Location: 25km south of Dahab
Depth: 10m to 30m
Rating: Intermediate
Access: 4WD/camel

What makes this dive so unique is the unorthodox means of transport you must take to get here – from Dahab, the journey combines a 4WD trip and a Bedouin-led camel convoy (yes, camels can actually carry full scuba tanks and a full complement of dive gear!). The dive itself features a dramatic seascape highlighted by a 60m wall cut by numerous chasms, faults and sandy ravines.

Sharm el-Sheikh & Na'ama Bay

Near the southern tip of Sinai and bordering Ras Mohammed National Park, Sharm el-Sheikh and adjacent Na'ama Bay together are one of the busiest dive destinations in the world. Unfortunately, in recent years package holiday and upscale resorts have become the norm, though the diving here still remains world-class.

JACKSON REEF
Location: Straits of Tiran
Depth: Surface to over 40m
Rating: Intermediate to advanced
Access: Boat or live-aboard

Midway between Tiran Island and the mainland, Jackson Reef is crowned with the remains of a Cypriot freighter, the *Lara*, which ran aground here in 1985. Home to sharks and large pelagic fish, Jackson Reef is stunning. Always enquire about sea conditions as the currents here can be dangerous.

THOMAS REEF
Location: Straits of Tiran
Depth: Surface to over 40m
Rating: Advanced
Access: Boat or live-aboard

The smallest, but easily the most spectacular of the Tiran reefs, Thomas is home to steeply plunging walls that are lined with soft coral, schooling fish and patrolling sharks. The strong currents here necessitate drift diving, so it's best to wait for ideal conditions before jumping in the water.

GORDON REEF
Location: Straits of Tiran
Depth: 15m to 30m
Rating: Intermediate
Access: Boat or live-aboard

This reef is famous for the battered remains of the *Louilla*, which eerily sits atop the northern end of Gordon Reef. Descending from the wide plateau on the south side of the reef, lucky divers can spot whitetip reef sharks in the morning hours in a large circular depression known as 'The Amphitheatre'.

GARDENS
Location: Between Shark and Na'ama Bays
Depth: Surface to over 40m
Rating: Intermediate
Access: Shore, boat or live-aboard

At the perennially popular Gardens there are actually three sites in one, each named for their respective proximity to Na'ama Bay. Near Garden is home to a lovely chain of pinnacles, Middle Garden features a sandy path leading to a scenic overlook, and Far Garden is home to 'The Cathedral', a colourful overhang in deep water.

TOWER

Location: Just south of Na'ama Bay
Depth: 12m to 30m
Rating: Intermediate
Access: Shore, boat or live-aboard

Named for the tower of fossilised coral that rises from the water on the south side of the bay, this site features a deep canyon with walls that drop below 120m. Between 15m and 30m, you'll find some beautiful coral pinnacles, while the shallower depths are home to several caves that can easily be penetrated.

AMPHORAS & TURTLE BAY

Location: Just north of Ras Um Sid
Depth: 10m to 35m
Rating: Intermediate
Access: Shore, boat or live-aboard

Named after the resident wreck of a 17th-century Turkish galleon that went down with a full cargo of mercury, Amphoras is renowned for its ancient history and its stunning topography. Leaving Amphoras, you can easily drift into Turtle Bay, which is home to a sloping reef that attracts schools of fish.

RAS UM SID

Location: Opposite Hotel Royal Paradise
Depth: 15m to 40m
Rating: Intermediate
Access: Shore, boat or live-aboard

One of the best dive sites in the area, Ras Um Sid features a spectacular gorgonian forest along a dramatic drop-off that hosts a great variety of reef fish. As you pass by the swaying fans, be sure to look out into the abyss as manta rays and whale sharks have been known to occasionally cruise by.

Ras Mohammed National Park

Without a doubt, Ras Mohammed is one of the best dive destinations in the world, with superb and extensive corals and an unparalleled diversity of fish and other marine life. The national park protects 200 hard coral species and about 120 soft coral species, and is home to approximately 1000-plus species of tropical fish.

RAS ZA'ATIR

Location: South lip of the mouth of Marsa Bareika
Depth: Surface to over 40m
Rating: Intermediate
Access: Boat or live-aboard

Marking the start of the Ras Mohammed wall, Ras Za'atir has a series of small caves and overhangs where black coral trees flourish. The highlight of the dive is the Point, where you'll encounter a solitary pinnacle topped by table coral, and surrounded by groupers waiting to be cleaned.

JACKFISH ALLEY

Location: Just south of Ras Za'atir
Depth: 6m to 20m
Rating: Intermediate
Access: Boat or live-aboard

A comparatively shallow site that is good for a second or third dive, Jackfish Alley has two enormous caves filled with shoaling glassfish. If you swim straight into the open cavern, you will see shafts of light filtering through the crevices and lighting up the sandy ocean floor.

SHARK OBSERVATORY

Location: Eastern tip of Ras Mohammed
Depth: Surface to over 40m
Rating: Advanced
Access: Boat or live-aboard

Shark Observatory is a high promontory that is used to spot sharks in the surrounding waters, though the wall beneath is extremely sheer and there are no ledges to mark your depth – this is for advanced divers only. With that said, the wall is truly stunning, covered with soft corals and gigantic gorgonians, and there is a good chance you'll see a shark or two cruising in the distance.

SHARK & JOLANDE REEFS

Location: Southern tip of Ras Mohammed
Depth: Surface to over 40m
Rating: Advanced
Access: Boat or live-aboard

This two-for-one special is among the most famous dives in the Red Sea, and rated one of the top five dives in the world – strong currents take divers on a thrilling ride along sheer coral walls, through vast schools of fish and eventually to the remains of the *Jolande,* a Cypriot freighter that sank in 1980. Although not much remains of the wreck, its cargo of bathtubs and toilets makes an interesting contrast to the deep blue water and surrounding reef shelves.

ALTERNATIVES & STINGRAY STATION

Location: Southeast tip of Sha'ab Mahmud
Depth: 10m to 30m
Rating: Intermediate
Access: Boat or live-aboard

The Alternatives are a 3km long stretch of seven coral pinnacles, which are sheltered from the weather conditions and home to varied wildlife including enormous leopard sharks and teeny-tiny nudibranchs. At the west end of the Alternatives is Stingray Station, marked by a large blocky coral outcrop at 15m, which is swamped with bluespotted, feathertail and honeycomb stingrays.

DUNRAVEN
Location: Southeast tip of Sha'ab Mahmud
Depth: 15m to 28m
Rating: Intermediate
Access: Boat or live-aboard

In 1876, the *Dunraven* was on her way from Bombay to Newcastle with a cargo of spices, timber and cotton when, in seemingly good weather, she hit the Sha'ab Mahmud reef and sank to the bottom. Today, this enigmatic wreck is encrusted in coral and home to various knick-knacks including china plates, metal steins and jars of gooseberries and rhubarb among the detritus.

SMALL CRACK
Location: Northwest side of Sha'ab Mahmud
Depth: 5m to 20m
Rating: Intermediate
Access: Live-aboard

A difficult to access but utterly unique dive site, the Small Crack is a shallow channel through the reef that can only be safely navigated by divers and dinghy shuttles. The walls of the crack are covered in soft corals, and guarded by titan triggerfish that fiercely protect their nests, especially from August to September.

SHAG ROCK & KINGSTON
Location: 1km southwest of Sha'ab Ali
Depth: 8m to 25m
Rating: Intermediate
Access: Live-aboard

On the northern side of a circular reef is the coral-encrusted wreck of the *Kingston*, a steam-driven cargo ship that sank after running aground in 1881. Her bow has been virtually destroyed, but the stern remains remarkably intact, and her twin boilers resting peacefully on the reef top are very photogenic.

El-Gouna & Hurghada

In recent years, the reefs close to El-Gouna and Hurghada have been heavily damaged by unfettered touristic development – experienced divers now generally prefer sites further afield. On a positive note, conservation measures are finally being implemented, spearheaded by local NGOs, and there is a chance that the situation around both towns will begin to improve.

BLUFF POINT
Location: Southern Straits of Gubal
Depth: 10m to 30m
Rating: Intermediate
Access: Live-aboard

A popular stop for live-aboards – you can overnight in a sheltered lagoon near the dive site – the reef here sports some graceful gorgonians and black coral bushes. The area is also home to two wrecks: a small sunken barge that is abuzz with morays, and the *Ulysses*, a 90m steamship that went down in 1887.

SHA'AB ABU NUHAS
Location: Southeastern Straits of Gubal
Depth: 5m to 26m
Rating: Intermediate
Access: Boat or live-aboard

This group of small, submerged islands at the southern entrance to the Straits of Gubal has snagged more ships than any other reef group since the opening of the Suez Canal in 1869. The most famous ships in this marine graveyard are the *Carnatic*, which went down in 1879, and the nearby wrecks of two Greek cargo ships, the *Giannis D* and the *Chrisoula K*, both of which sank in the early 1980s.

SIYUL KEBIRA
Location: Southern Straits of Gubal
Depth: 10m to 30m
Rating: Intermediate
Access: Boat or live-aboard

This site offers two dive plans: if the current is strong, you can drift along the wall while skirting along the edges of huge coral outcroppings. If there are calmer conditions, you can tour the upper section of the reef amid schools of bannerfish, angelfish, goatfish and snappers.

SHA'AB AL-ERG
Location: Off El-Gouna
Depth: 5m to 15m
Rating: Novice
Access: Boat or live-aboard

This huge horseshoe-shaped reef with a shallow lagoon is famous for attracting dolphins and manta rays as well as the occasional whitetip reef shark. The lack of strong currents and ease of access means that this is an excellent dive site for beginners, though veteran divers will still enjoy the towering brain corals and fan-encrusted rock formations.

THISTLEGORM

Location: Sha'ab Ali
Depth: 17m to 30m
Rating: Intermediate to advanced
Access: Boat or live-aboard

Built by the North East Marine Engineering Company, the 129m-long cargo ship christened the *Thistlegorm* was completed and launched in 1940 in Sunderland, England. Prior to setting out from Glasgow in 1941, she had previously made several successful trips to North America, the East Indies and Argentina. However, with a cargo full of vital supplies destined for North Africa, where British forces were preparing for Operation Crusader, the relief of Tobruk against the German 8th Army, the *Thistlegorm* met her end at 2am on 6 October, 1941.

While waiting in the Straits of Gubal for a call sign to proceed up the Gulf of Suez, four German Heinkel He 111s that were flying out of Crete mounted an attack on the ship. The planes were returning from an armed reconnaissance mission up the Sinai coast, and targeted the ship to off-load their unused bombs. One bomber scored a direct hit on the No 4 hold, which tore the ship into two and sent the two railway locomotives that the vessel was carrying hurtling through the air. Incredibly, they landed upright on the seabed, one on either side of the wreck. In less than 20 minutes, the ship sank to the ocean floor, taking along with it nine sailors out of a crew of 49.

The *Thistlegorm* lay undisturbed until 1956 when legendary French diver Jacques Cousteau located the wreck, lying at a depth of 17m to 35m to the northwest of Ras Mohammed. Cousteau found a cache of WWII cargo packed in the hold, including a full consignment of armaments and supplies, such as Bedford trucks, Morris cars, BSA 350 motorbikes and Bren gun carriers. Although Cousteau took the ship's bell, the captain's safe and a motorbike, he left the wreck as he found it, and proceeded to keep its location secret. However, it was rediscovered in 1993 when some divers stumbled upon its location and it has since become one of the world's premier wreck-dive sites.

The *Thistlegorm* is best dived on an overnight trip since it takes 3½ hours each way from Sharm el-Sheikh by boat; dive operators throughout Sinai can easily help you arrange this. On your first dive, you will do a perimeter sweep of the boat, which is highlighted by a swim along the soldier walkways on the side of the vessel. On your second dive, you will penetrate the ship's interior, swimming through a living museum of WWII memorabilia.

UMM QAMAR

Location: 9km north of the Giftun Islands
Depth: 10m to 27m
Rating: Intermediate
Access: Boat or live-aboard

A long, thin reef with a vertical wall plunging down on the east side, Umm Qamar is highlighted by three coral towers that are swathed in beautiful purple, soft coral and surrounded by glassfish. Experienced divers will enjoy diving along the drop-offs, particularly if there are large pelagics cruising by.

GIFTUN ISLANDS

Location: Off Hurghada
Depth: 5m to 30m
Rating: Intermediate
Access: Boat or live-aboard

The islands of Giftun Kebir and Giftun Sughayer (Big Giftun and Little Giftun) are a short boat ride from Hurghada, and rank as one of the most popular dive destinations in the Red Sea. They are surrounded by a number of spectacular reefs teeming with marine life, including Hamda, Banana Reef, Sha'ab Sabrina, Erg Somaya and Sha'ab Torfa.

GOTA ABU RAMADA

Location: 5km south of the Giftun Islands
Depth: 3m to 15m
Rating: Novice
Access: Boat or live-aboard

Also known as the Aquarium due to the mind-boggling abundance of marine life on display here, Gota abu Ramada is a popular spot for underwater photographers, snorkelers and night divers. The site comprises two impressive pinnacles on a flat and sandy seafloor in less than 15m of water.

Safaga

For the most part, Safaga defies the tourist hordes, which is a good thing as there are

DIVING THE RED SEA

some pristine reefs offshore from this unsightly port town. Unlike nearby Hurghada and El-Gouna, resorts here are extremely low-key, and cater almost exclusively to dedicated divers from overseas rather than families and package travellers.

PANORAMA REEF
Location: Outer Safaga Bay
Depth: 3m to 40m
Rating: Intermediate
Access: Boat or live-aboard

Down the outer edge of Safaga Bay runs a line of offshore reefs, which tumble steeply down to a sloping ledge that eventually plunges into the abyss. Panorama Reef in particular is famous for its schooling barracuda, as well as numerous dolphins, eagle rays, grey reef sharks and silvertips.

SALEM EXPRESS
Location: South Safaga Bay
Depth: 15m to 30m
Rating: Intermediate
Access: Boat or live-aboard

Sometimes described as one of the best wrecks in the Red Sea, the *Salem Express* is a stunning yet mournful sight. In 1991 this passenger ferry sank along with hundreds of pilgrims returning from the hajj – while diving, try to take a moment to pause and reflect on this watery graveyard.

Al-Quseir

A historic trade and export hub with a history stretching back centuries, the sleepy town of Al-Quseir holds a charm absent from other Red Sea towns. The comparative lack of tourist development means that the offshore dive sites here are generally empty, though you will have to contend with strong winds and rough seas.

EL QUADIM
Location: 7km north of Al-Quseir
Depth: 5m to 30m
Rating: Intermediate
Access: Shore

This dive site, located in a small bay abutted by the Mövenpick Resort, boasts a complex network of interconnecting caves and canyons. At the centre of the bay lies a large sandy patch that is occasionally interrupted by soaring coral spikes, which act as a playground for small species.

EL KAF
Location: 10km south of Al-Quseir
Depth: 18m to 25m
Rating: Novice
Access: Shore

An easy plunge that appeals to divers of all skill levels, El Kaf is a canyon pitted with small caves and passages, and accented by massive coral boulders and sandy ravines. This labyrinth topography is overwhelmingly spectacular in parts, especially when whitetip reef sharks pay the site a visit.

South Coast

As tourist development expands southwards, so too does the diving, though be advised that high winds and strong currents make the following sites best suited for experienced divers. Since this part of the coast remains remote, most diving is done from live-aboards, though the lack of crowds more than make up for the difficult access.

ELPHINSTONE
Location: 125km north of Marsa Alam
Depth: 20m to 40m
Rating: Advanced
Access: Boat or live-aboard

Elphinstone has steep reef walls covered with soft corals, and washed by strong currents that are ideal for sharks – seven species reportedly frequent its waters. Legend has it that a large arch in the reef, between 50m and 70m down, contains the sarcophagus of an unknown pharaoh.

SHA'AB SAMADAI
Location: 18km southeast of Marsa Alam
Depth: 10m to 15m
Rating: Novice to intermediate
Access: Boat or live-aboard

Nicknamed Dolphin Reef, Sha'ab Samadai is wrapped around a shallow lagoon that is home to a school of spinner dolphins. Even if the dolphins don't show up, the site offers beautiful coral ergs along the edges of the lagoon, as well as a series of caves and tunnels that can be explored if you are comfortable with overhead surfaces.

SHA'AB SHARM
Location: 30km northeast of Wadi Gimal
Depth: 15m to over 40m
Rating: Advanced
Access: Boat or live-aboard

This large, kidney-shaped offshore reef has steep walls hosting rich corals as well as shallow plateaus on both ends – it is an impressive underwater site in regards to topography. Currents are strong but marine life is excellent, with hammerheads, barracuda, groper, snapper and yellowmouth moray eels.

HAMADA
Location: 60km north of Berenice
Depth: 6m to 14m
Rating: Novice
Access: Boat or live-aboard

Atop an inshore reef lies the wreck of this 65m-long cargo ship, which was on its way to Jeddah from Suez with a cargo of polyethylene granules (better known as packing peanuts) when she sank on 29 June 1993. Lying on her side in just 14m of water, the *Hamada* is a fairly easy, extremely picturesque dive site.

SATAYA (DOLPHIN REEF)
Location: 50km north of Berenice
Depth: 4m to over 40m
Rating: Intermediate
Access: Boat or live-aboard

The horseshoe-shaped Dolphin is the main reef of Fury Shoal, and has steep walls leading down to a sandy slope scattered with coral heads. In addition to a great variety of corals, especially in the uppermost 10m, there are also abundant pelagics including frequent schools of dolphins and sharks.

The Far South

Egypt's southernmost waters are home to four islands, all of which are coveted and highly challenging destinations for experienced divers. Only accessible by live-aboard, the islands of the far south are home to spectacular and rarely visited reefs – as veterans of these parts will tell you, once you've dived here, nothing else will compare.

BIG BROTHER
Location: 67km east of Al-Quseir
Depth: Surface to over 40m
Rating: Advanced
Access: Live-aboard

The most northerly of the two 'brothers', Big Brother has a small lighthouse and two wrecks lying on its walls: one an English freighter (the *Numidia*) and the other an Italian ship (the *Aida II*). Currents are strong, though the soft corals are stunning, and the marine life is varied and plentiful.

LITTLE BROTHER
Location: 67km east of Al-Quseir
Depth: Surface to over 40m
Rating: Advanced
Access: Live-aboard

This magical island has a long reef protruding from its northern end, which is a popular spot for cruising thresher sharks, silvertips, hammerheads and grey reef sharks. Elsewhere, there are huge fan corals, caves and overhangs, though divers tend to simply slow down and be overwhelmed at the sheer number of apex predators about.

DAEDALUS
Location: 96km east of Marsa Alam
Depth: Surface to over 40m
Rating: Advanced
Access: Live-aboard

Lying right in the middle of the Red Sea nearly halfway to Saudi Arabia, this isolated dive spot is marked by a 19th-century British-built lighthouse lying in the centre of the circular reef. As you'd expect from a reef in the middle of nowhere, the coral here is pristine, and there's nary a dive boat in sight.

ZABARGAD ISLAND
Location: 20km south of Ras Banas
Depth: 10m to 40m
Rating: Advanced
Access: Live-aboard

This mountainous island emerges majestically from the sea, though this tranquil beauty has snared several ships over the years. Fortunately for divers, these wrecks, which include an ill-fated German dive boat known as the *Neptune*, lie at the bottom of a shimmering lagoon of turquoise water.

ROCKY ISLAND
Location: 5km southeast of Zabargad
Depth: Surface to over 40m
Rating: Advanced
Access: Live-aboard

Exposed Rocky Island, with its noisy seabirds and breaking waves, lies just north of the Sudanese border, and is one of Egypt's most far-flung dive sites. When the dive conditions are perfect, it's possible to see anything here – divers often jump in the water here and find themselves surrounded by everything from pods of dolphins to passing whale sharks.

DIVE OPERATORS

Whether you choose to plunge into the Red Sea with a small local shop, an established

REEF PROTECTION

The Red Sea's natural wonders are just as magnificent as the splendours of Egypt's Pharaonic heritage, and appear all the more stunning when contrasted with their barren desert backdrop. However, care is needed if the delicate world of coral reefs and fish is not to be permanently damaged. Almost the entire Egyptian coastline in the Gulf of Aqaba is now a protectorate, as is the Red Sea coast from Hurghada south to Sudan. Divers and snorkellers should heed the requests of instructors *not* to touch or tread on coral – if you kill the coral, you'll eventually kill or chase away the fish, too.

Overall, the paramount guideline for preserving the ecology and beauty of reefs is to take nothing with you, leave nothing behind. Other considerations:

- Never use anchors on the reef, and take care not to ground boats on coral.
- Avoid touching or standing on living marine organisms or dragging equipment across the reef. Polyps can be damaged by even the gentlest contact. If you must hold on to the reef, only touch exposed rock or dead coral.
- Be conscious of your fins. Even without contact, the surge from fin strokes near the reef can damage delicate organisms. Take care not to kick up clouds of sand, which can smother organisms.
- Practise and maintain proper buoyancy control. Major damage can be done by divers descending too fast and colliding with the reef.
- Take great care in underwater caves. Spend as little time within them as possible as your air bubbles may be caught within the roof and thereby leave organisms high and dry. Take turns to inspect the interior of a small cave.
- Resist the temptation to collect or buy corals or shells or to loot marine archaeological sites (mainly shipwrecks).
- Ensure that you take home all your rubbish and any litter you may find as well. Plastics in particular are a serious threat to marine life.
- Do not feed fish.
- Minimise your disturbance of marine animals. Never ride on the backs of turtles.

resort or a live-aboard, you will have no problem finding a dive operator. As the Red Sea and Sinai coasts continue to develop, the number of dive operators is mushrooming and there is something to suit everyone. Some clubs and live-aboards are laid-back and informal, while others are slick and structured. Regardless of which diving style you choose, you're going to get wet – and love every minute of it.

Dive Clubs

Almost all of the coastal hotels and resorts have a dive centre, though there are also smaller places – some long-standing, others fly-by-night outfits – cashing in on the area's popularity among divers. When deciding which dive club to use, among the considerations should be the club's attention to safety and its sensitivity to environmental issues.

Please be aware that there are literally hundreds of dive clubs along the Red Sea coast and in Sinai, so it's simply impossible to list any more than a fraction of these. We have chosen dive clubs that have a long-standing reputation for excellence, as well as a high PADI rating or equivalent, though there are certainly other dive clubs out there worth checking out.

Here are some tips to help you choose a respectable dive club:

- Take your time when choosing clubs and dive sites, and don't let yourself be pressured into accepting something, or someone, you're not comfortable with.
- Don't choose a club based solely on cost. Safety should be the paramount concern; if a dive outfit cuts corners to keep prices low, you could be in danger.
- If you haven't dived for more than three months, take a check-out dive. This is for

your own safety (and is required by many operators), and the cost is usually applied towards later dives.

■ If you're taking lessons, ensure that the instructor speaks your language well. If you can't understand them, you should request another.

■ Check that all equipment is clean and stored away from the sun, and check all hoses, mouthpieces and valves for cuts and leakage.

■ Confirm that wetsuits are in good condition. Some divers have reported getting hypothermia because of dry, cracked suits.

■ Check that there is oxygen on the dive boat in case of accidents.

■ If you're in Sinai, ask if the club donates US$1 per diver each day to the decompression chamber; this is often a reflection of the club's safety-consciousness.

NUWEIBA

Diving Camp Nuweiba (Map p485; ☎ 012 249 6002; www.scuba-college.com/en) Located at the Nuweiba Village Hotel in the centre of town, the Diving Camp has been in the business for more than two decades.

Emperor Divers (off Map p485; ☎ 069-352 0321; www.emperordivers.com) Situated at the Hilton Nuweiba Coral Resort, this place is part of the multibranch Emperor empire.

DAHAB

Desert Divers (Map p477; ☎ 069-364 0500; www.desert-divers.com; Masbat) A popular place offering a range of diving courses plus extras such as camel safaris, yoga classes and more.

Fantasea Dive Centre (Map p477; ☎ 069-364 0483; www.fantaseadiving.net; Masbat) This long-standing Australian-Egyptian-owned five-star PADI centre gets consistently good reviews.

Fish & Friends (Map p477; ☎ 069-364 0720; www.fishandfriendsdahab.com/eng/home.php; Masbat) A well-managed and highly personal British- and Egyptian-run diving centre.

Inmo Divers Home (Map p477; ☎ 069-364 0370; www.inmodivers.de; Inmo Hotel, Mashraba) Run by Mohammed and Ingrid al-Kabany, this family-friendly outfit was one of the first dive clubs to start operating in Dahab.

Nesima Dive Centre (Map p477; ☎ 069-364 0320; www.nesima-resort.com; Nesima Hotel, Mashraba) PADI. A reputable club owned by local environmental activist and veteran diver Sherif Ebeid.

Penguin Divers (Map p477; ☎ 069-364 1047; www.penguindivers.com; Penguin Village, Mashraba) A popular dive club aimed at budget travellers looking to have fun while saving a few pounds.

Sunsplash Divers (Map p477; ☎ 069-364 0932; www.sunsplash-divers.com; Mashraba) PADI. A long-standing German-run diving centre that has trained countless budding divers over the years.

SHARM EL-SHEIKH & NA'AMA BAY AREA

Camel Dive Club (Map p470; ☎ 069-360 0700; www.cameldive.com; Camel Hotel, King of Bahrain St, Na'ama Bay) A respected club owned by Sinai diver Hisham Gabr.

Divers International (Map p470; ☎ 069-360 0865; www.diversintl.com; Sharm–Na'ama Bay rd, Na'ama Bay) Large diving outfit offering a wide range of courses and dive excursions.

Emperor Divers (Map p470; ☎ 069-360 1734; www.emperordivers.com; Sharm–Na'ama Bay rd, Na'ama Bay) A branch of the five-star outfit offers courses aimed at families of all ages.

Oonas Dive Centre (Map p470; ☎ 069-360 0581; www.oonasdiveclub.com; Na'ama Bay) A popular centre at the northeastern end of Na'ama Bay.

Shark's Bay Diving Club (off Map p470; ☎ 069-360 0942; www.sharksbay.com; Shark's Bay) Also known as Umbarak, Shark's Bay is a Bedouin-run centre with years of experience and its own house reef.

Sinai Divers (Map p470; ☎ 069-360 0697; www.sinaidivers.com; Na'ama Bay) Based at the Ghazala Hotel, this is one of Sharm el-Sheikh's most established dive centres.

Subex (Map p470; ☎ 069-360 0122; www.subex.org; Na'ama Bay) CMAS, SSI. Swiss-based dive club at the Mövenpick Hotel with years of experience in the Red Sea.

HURGHADA & SAFAGA

Aquanaut Red Sea (Map p427; ☎ 065-354 9891; www.aquanaut.net; Corniche, Ad-Dahar, Hurghada) Founding member of the Hurghada Quality Dive Club, a group of clubs that tries to maintain basic standards of safety and service.

Easy Divers (Map p427; ☎ 065-354 7816; www.easy divers-redsea.com; Corniche, Ad-Dahar, Hurghada) This British-managed club has a long history of first-class service.

Emperor Divers (Map p423; ☎ 065-344 4854; www.emperordivers.com; resort strip, Hurghada) At the Hilton Hurghada Resort, this is a highly reputable dive school.

Jasmin Diving Centre (Map p423; ☎ 065-346 0475; www.jasmin-diving.com; resort strip, Hurghada) At Jasmine Village, this is a member of the Hurghada Quality Dive Club.

Menaville Divers (☎ 065-326 0060; www.menadive.com/en/middle.html; resort strip, Safaga) The centre of the scuba scene in Safaga is this diver-centric resort hotel.

Sub Aqua (Map p423; ☎ 065-346 4101; www.subaqua-divecenter.com; resort strip, Hurghada) Branch of

---

ACCESSING THE OFFSHORE MARINE PARK ISLANDS

Accessing the waters of Egypt's far south is strictly regulated. Divers must have completed a minimum of 50 dives before entering, night diving or landing on the islands is prohibited; and fishing, spear fishing and the use of gloves are banned.

Due to these restrictions, permission must be given for each trip, and a park ranger will often accompany boats to ensure that the rules are being enforced. In order to carry divers, boats must have special safety equipment, which national-park and Red Sea governorate officials inspect before each trip.

If you've been offered a trip to these remote areas, it's worth checking in with one of the organisations mentioned under Dangers & Annoyances, p443, to see that the boat is licensed. If you are caught on an unlicensed boat you could have your own equipment or belongings confiscated and find yourself in custody.

Diveteam Sub Aqua at the Sofitel Hotel, which specialises in diving around the world.

Subex (Map p427; ☎ 065-354 7593; www.subex .org; Ad-Dahar) Another branch of the well-known Swiss outfit.

AL-QUSEIR

Rocky Valley Divers (☎ 333 5247; www.rockyvalley diverscamp.com) This shoestringers' beach camp has a well-equipped dive centre offering a variety of cheap all-inclusive packages.

Mövenpick Sirena Beach Dive Centre (☎ 333 2100; www.moevenpick-quseir.com) Al-Quseir's signature property is also home to the town's most established dive centre.

SOUTH COAST

Red Sea Diving Safari (☎ in Cairo 02-337 1833, 02-337 9942; www.redsea-divingsafari.com; Marsa Shagra) PADI. Run by environmentalist and long-time diver Hossam Hassan, who pioneered diving in the Red Sea's deep south.

Diving Courses

Most dive clubs in Egypt offer **PADI** (www.padi .com) certification, though you'll occasionally find **NAUI** (www.naui.org), **SSI** (www.divessi.com), **CMAS** (www.cmas2000.org) and **BSAC** (www.bsac.com). Generally, PADI Open Water dive courses take five (intensive) days and cost between US$250 and US$400. When comparing prices, check to see whether the certification fee and books are included.

Beginner courses are designed to drum into you things that have to become second nature when you're underwater. They usually consist of classroom work, where you learn the principles and basic knowledge needed to dive, followed by training in a confined body of water, such as a pool, before heading out to the open sea. If you've never dived before and want to give it a try before you commit yourself, all dive clubs offer introductory dives for between US$30 and US$50, including equipment.

In addition to basic certification, most of the well-established clubs on the coast offer a variety of more advanced courses as well as professional-level courses or training in technical diving.

Live-Aboards

The vast majority of the clubs listed can organise dive safaris to remote sites ranging from one night to two weeks. The cost of these live-aboard dive safaris (also known as marine safaris) varies according to the boat and the destination, with the more remote sites in the far south generally the most expensive. While you won't see much of terrestrial Egypt, they allow you to access a greater range of dive sites, including many more distant areas that are too far to explore as day trips.

As a general rule, you should always ask to see the boat before agreeing to sail on it. Also, if a trip is very cheap, check whether or not the cost of diving and food are included. Furthermore, the Red Sea Association for Diving & Watersports (RSADW) has the following two rules in place for its jurisdictional area:

■ There should be a diver-guide ratio of one guide to every 12 divers (or every eight divers in marine park areas).

■ Divers on live-aboards entering marine park areas must be experienced, with a minimum of 50 logged dives, as well as insurance coverage.

WHERE TO GO?

With so many dive sites and operators to choose from, it can be difficult for first-time Red Sea divers to know where to base themselves. Here are our tips:

- **Nuweiba** (p484) Attracts independent travellers looking for low-key ambience and minimal crowds, though the diving here is not as rich and as varied as other spots in Sinai and the Red Sea.

- **Dahab** (p476) The preferred base for independent travellers, this Thai-style village is surrounded by spectacular dive sites, and abounds with cheap guest houses and chilled-out beach bars. It also serves as a quick and easy jumping-off point for diving Ras Mohammad National Park.

- **Sharm el-Sheikh & Na'ama Bay** (p466) Egypt's most famous resort strip is the most accessible base from which to reach Ras Mohammed. Sharm has gone high end in recent years and primarily caters to European package travellers looking for Western-style resorts brimming with four- and five-star amenities.

- **Hurghada** (p423) Egypt's original resort strip, ageing Hurghada has been plagued by overdevelopment and poor environmental management. As a result, serious divers now prefer to base themselves elsewhere, though there are cheap package deals to be had here.

- **Safaga** (p432) Despite being a rather unattractive port town just south of Hurghada, there is some decent and comparatively uncrowded diving off the coast here.

- **Al-Quseir** (p433) A historic port town with an authentically Egyptian character, Al-Quseir boasts a handful of good dive spots that are also overlooked by the crowds.

- **Marsa Alam** (p435) This up-and-coming resort town is staking its reputation on its proximity to the south coast dive sites. If you're looking for resort amenities with a remote outpost ambience and the chance for desert excursions, this is your choice.

- **Live-aboards** For on-the-edge diving away from the crowds, serious divers know that live-aboards are the only way to travel. If you're looking to explore the far south of the Red Sea (advanced divers only), live-aboards are your only option.

While it's quite possible to book yourself a basic package on a live-aboard after arriving in Egypt, there are numerous agencies that specialise in Red Sea diving holidays. Here is a small sampling:

Crusader Travel (☎ in UK 020-8744 0474; www.divers .co.uk) Diving packages in the Red Sea, including diving for people with disabilities.

Maadi Divers (☎ 02-2519-8644; www.maadi-divers .com) A friendly local outfit run by owner Magdy El-Araby and his wife, Barbara, Maadi Divers offers affordable trips in Egyptian waters.

Oonasdivers (☎ in UK 01323-648924; www.oonas divers.com) Diving tours based at Na'ama Bay, Red Sea diving safaris from the Marsa Alam region and live-aboard trips.

Thomson (☎ in UK 0845-644 7090; www.thomson .co.uk/explorers) Diving packages and live-aboards around Sharm el-Sheik, Dahab and elsewhere in the northern Red Sea.

Sinai

> Here, not for the first time, I fell deeply in love with the landscape…I longed to reach out and stroke the great gaunt flanks of the mountain falling away into bewildering foot-hills and plains of dazzling sand.
>
> *GW Murray,* Dare Me to the Desert

Sinai, a region of stark beauty, has been a place of refuge, conflict and curiosity for thousands of years. Wedged between Africa and Asia, it is an intercontinental crossroads *par excellence* – prophets, nomads, exiles and conquerors have all left their footprints here.

Sinai is bordered by the Mediterranean Sea to the north, and the Gulfs of Aqaba and Suez to the east and west respectively. From the palm-lined Red Sea coasts, rows upon rows of barren, red-brown mountains fill the southern interior. Heading north, the relentlessly dry desert plains metamorphose into many-hued panoramas under the rays of the morning and evening sun. Sinai abounds with contrasts but never ceases to captivate.

The majority of international tourists head to the glitzy European-style resorts of Sharm el-Sheikh, of which there are literally hundreds vying for beach space. Most are amenable enough places for sea-and-sand holidays, though independent travellers prefer the terminally laid-back town of Dahab. Sinai is also a convenient jumping-off point for southern Jordan, home to the 'Rose-Red City' of Petra, one of the New Seven Wonders of the World.

Of course, the real charm of Sinai is its stunning desert and marine environments – among the highlights are snorkelling or diving amid teeming coral reefs, close-up encounters with traditional Bedouin culture, and following pilgrims' roads to biblical sites. Whatever captures your fancy, a visit to Sinai will be one of the most memorable parts of your Egyptian travels.

HIGHLIGHTS

- Gorge yourself on banana pancakes by the oceanside in the backpacker paradise of **Dahab** (p476)
- Dive everything from coral mountains to ghostly shipwrecks in **Ras Mohammed National Park** (p464)
- Climb **Mt Sinai** (p497), the legendary mountain of biblical proportions
- Follow the footsteps of centuries of pilgrims on a visit to **St Katherine's Monastery** (p495)
- Leave Egypt behind (for a few days) on an excursion to the legendary city of **Petra** (see boxed text, p492)

History

Some 40 million years ago the African and Arabian continental plates began to move apart, creating the relatively shallow (95m-deep) Gulf of Suez and the much deeper (1800m) Gulf of Aqaba. The Gulf of Aqaba, which varies from 14km to 25km in width, is part of a rift (a crack in the top layer of the earth) that extends 6000km from the Dead Sea, on the border between Israel and Jordan, through the Red Sea, Ethiopia, Kenya, and all the way down to Mozambique in southern Africa.

In Pharaonic times the quarries of Sinai provided great quantities of turquoise, gold and copper. The importance of this 'Land of Turquoise' also made it the goal of empire builders, as well as the setting for countless wars. Acting as a link between Asia and Africa, it was of strategic value – many military forces marched along its northern coastline as they travelled to or from what is now known as Israel and the Palestinian Territories.

For many people, Sinai is first and foremost the 'great and terrible wilderness' of the Bible, across which the Israelites journeyed in search of the Promised Land, having been delivered from the Egyptian army by the celebrated parting of the Red Sea that allowed the 'Children of Israel' to safely gain access to the dry land of Sinai. It was here that God is said to have first spoken to Moses from a burning bush and it was at the summit of Mt Sinai that God delivered his Ten Commandments to Moses:

Tell the children of Israel; Ye have seen what I did unto the Egyptians… If ye will obey my voice and keep my covenant, then ye shall be a peculiar treasure unto me above all people: for all the earth is mine. And ye shall be unto me a kingdom of priests, and a holy nation.
And Mount Sinai was altogether in smoke, because the Lord descended upon it in fire; and the whole mount quaked greatly… And the Lord came down upon Mount Sinai…and called Moses up to the top of the mount… And God spoke all these words, saying, I am the Lord thy God, which have brought thee out of the land of Egypt, out of the house of bondage. Thou shalt have no other gods before me.
                        Exodus 19:4-6; 19:18-20:3

Early in the Christian era, Sinai was a place for Christian Egyptians to escape Roman persecution. Monasticism is thought to have begun here as early as the 3rd century AD, with most hermits settling in the caves of Wadi Feiran, on the assumption that Gebel Serbal, located nearby, was in fact the 'Mountain of God'. By the time the Emperor Justinian founded a monastery at the foot of Mt Sinai (Gebel Musa) in the 6th century, it had been decided that this was the mountain on which God had spoken. For centuries thereafter, the peninsula became a place of pilgrimage. It later became one of the routes taken to Mecca by Muslim pilgrims. Until recently the majority of its inhabitants were Bedouin, the only people who are capable of surviving in the harsh environment of the peninsula.

In recent years Sinai has become the focus of development and 'reconstruction' in much the same way that the New Valley in the Western Desert was during the 1970s and 1980s, when landless fellaheen (peasant farmers) from an overcrowded Nile Valley were encouraged to move to the oases. The government has built a new pipeline, called the Al-Salam Canal, to bring fresh water from the Suez Canal to various areas of North Sinai that have been targeted for resettlement. Agriculture is to be expanded dramatically, roads are being paved and desalination plants are being installed in coastal towns.

Tourism, too, has brought great changes, especially around the Gulf of Aqaba. Surveys estimate that the southern tourist town of Sharm el-Sheikh has seen a tenfold population increase in the past 15 years, and the small villages of Dahab and Nuweiba have grown into sprawling beachfront tourist towns. The Bedouin, the traditional inhabitants of Sinai, have become a minority in their native land, and have complained of marginalisation by Cairo-based tour operators and ill-treatment by the police (see also the boxed text, p486).

Climate

Sinai's climate is extreme: on one hand it can get very hot, so remember always to carry water, use copious amounts of sunblock and wear sensible clothes to avoid sunburn (wearing a T-shirt while snorkelling is advisable), as well as a hat or scarf. On the other hand, while summer temperatures can climb to 50°C, it gets very cold at night, and the mountains can be freezing during the day. Come prepared with warm clothing, especially if you'll be trekking or climbing Mt Sinai. Camping out in winter requires a warm sleeping bag and a good jacket – snow is frequent at this time of year.

Dangers & Annoyances

Because of the peninsula's unique position between cultures and continents, its occasionally tumultuous history, its mountainous terrain and – in more recent times – its tourist masses, Sinai has traditionally had a higher security profile than other parts of the country.

In recent years, the region of Sinai has been thrust into the international spotlight following a string of high-profile bombings. On 7 October 2004, three bomb attacks in the Taba area killed 34 people and injured over 150 people. The worst attack occurred when a truck drove into the lobby of the Taba Hilton and exploded – 10 floors of the hotel collapsed following the blast. According to the Egyptian government, the bombers were Palestinians who had tried to enter Israel to carry out attacks there but were unsuccessful.

On 23 July 2005 a series of coordinated bombings in the tourist market of Sharm el-Sheikh killed 88 people and injured close to 200 people. The bombing coincided with Egypt's Revolution Day, which commemorates Nasser's 1952 overthrow of King Farouk – it was the deadliest terrorist action in the country's history. A group calling itself the 'Abdullah Azzam Brigades' was the first to claim responsibility for the attacks. Additional claims were later made by two other groups calling themselves the 'Tawhid and Jihad Group in Egypt' and 'Holy Warriors of Egypt'.

On 24 April 2006, three bombs exploded in Dahab – two near the bridge in the centre of town and one near the Ghazala Supermarket – which killed 23 and injured over 75 people. The attacks occurred during a public holiday where crowds were celebrating Sham al-Nasseim (Spring Festival), and were carried out by Bedouin suicide bombers. The Egyptian government later stated that these attacks were the work of an organisation called Jama'at al-Tawhid wal-Jihad (Monotheism and Jihad).

It is impossible to offer anything other than blind speculation bordering on irrational fear regarding the possibility of a future terrorist attack in Sinai. With that said, it's worth checking your embassy's travel advisory to get an update on the situation before making any plans. However, it's important to remember that the overwhelming majority of travellers to Sinai enjoy their visits without incident.

On a different note, while G-strings and topless sunbathing seem to be *de rigueur* for some tourist groups in Sharm el-Sheikh, women should be aware that Egypt is a conservative country and tourists have been assaulted in Sinai. While rape is rare, it does occur, so do not sunbathe alone in an isolated location, and try to choose a somewhat modest bathing costume (best to leave the string bikini at home!). You should also keep in mind that as well as offending the local people, topless sunbathing is illegal in Sinai, as well as in the rest of Egypt.

Getting There & Away

Sinai's international air hub is at Sharm el-Sheikh, which receives regular charters from Europe in addition to local flights. There is also an international airport in Taba, though it currently receives only occasional charter flights. For overland travel, the peninsula is linked to the mainland by the Ahmed Hamdi Tunnel, and by the Mubarak Peace Suspension Bridge, both of which connect to main arteries to Cairo. The 1.6km-long tunnel, which goes under the Suez Canal near Suez, was completed in 1982 and named after a martyr of the 1973 war. It is open 24 hours. There are frequent buses connecting Cairo and other destinations with all major towns on the Sinai Peninsula. A railway has been built to part of North Sinai, but there are no passenger services.

Getting Around

Because of Sinai's rugged landscape, paved roads link only the permanent settlements, and public transport is not as regular as elsewhere in Egypt. You can get to all major destinations if you travel by bus, but in many cases there are only a couple of connections each day – and sometimes there is only one. Service taxis are a popular means of transport in northern Sinai (primarily along the route connecting Rafah and Al-Arish with Suez and Cairo). Elsewhere on the peninsula, with the exception of the coastal route to Al-Tor, it is only possible to arrange a service taxi by

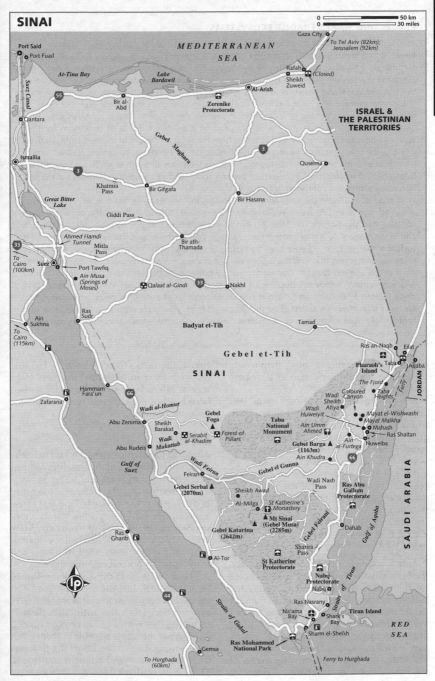

SINAI

0   50 km
0   30 miles

MEDITERRANEAN SEA

Gaza City

To Tel Aviv (82km);
Jerusalem (92km)

Port Said
Port Fuad

At-Tina Bay

Lake Bardawil

Rafah
Sheikh Zuweid

(Closed)

Al-Arish

Suez Canal

55

Bir al-Abd

Zerenike Protectorate

ISRAEL & THE PALESTINIAN TERRITORIES

Qantara

Gebel Maghara

3

Ismailia

3

Khatmia Pass

Bir Gifgafa

Quseima

Great Bitter Lake

Giddi Pass

Bir Hasana

33

To Cairo (100km)

Ahmed Hamdi Tunnel

Mitla Pass

Bir ath-Thamada

Suez

Port Tawfiq

Ain Musa (Springs of Moses)

Qalaat al-Gindi

33

Nakhl

Ain Sukhna

Ras Sudr

Badyat et-Tih

Tamad

To Cairo (115km)

Gebel et-Tih

Ras an-Naqb

Eilat

SINAI

Taba

Pharaoh's Island

JORDAN

Aqaba

Hammam Fara'un

The Fjord

Coloured Canyon

Taba Heights

Zafarana

66

Wadi al-Homur

Gebel Foga

Wadi Sheikh Atiya

Wadi Huweiyit

Mayat el-Wishwashi
Mayat Malkha

Abu Zenima

Sheikh Barakat

Serabit al-Khadim

Forest of Pillars

Taba National Monument

Ain Umm Ahmed

Mahash

Ras Shaitan

Wadi Mukattab

Gebel Barga (1163m)

Ain al-Furtega

Nuweiba

Abu Rudeis

Ain Khudra

66

Gulf of Suez

Wadi Feiran

Feiran

Gebel el Gunna

Ras Abu Gallum Protectorate

SAUDI ARABIA

Gebel Serbal (2070m)

Sheikh Awad

Wadi Nasb Pass

Al-Milga

St Katherine's Monastery

Mt Sinai (Gebel Musa) (2285m)

Gebel Féiráni

Ras Gharib

Gebel Katarina (2642m)

Dahab

Gulf of Aqaba

Al-Tor

Sharira Pass

St Katherine Protectorate

Nabq Protectorate

Nabq

Straits of Tiran

44

Ras Nasrany

Tiran Island

Na'ama Bay

Shark's Bay

RED SEA

Straits of Gubal

Sharm el-Sheikh

Ras Mohammed National Park

Gemsa

To Hurghada (60km)

Ferry to Hurghada

PROTECTING SINAI'S FRAGILE ECOSYSTEMS

Although much of Sinai is made up of hot, dry desert, it is full of life. Craggy mountains are sliced by dry gravel wadis in which sprout the odd acacia tree or clump of gnarled tamarisk, while a surprisingly rich variety of plants tenuously cling to the loose, sandy flanks of coastal dunes. Once every few years, when storm clouds gather over the mountains and dump buckets of water onto this parched landscape, the entire scene is transformed into a sea of greenery as seeds that have lain dormant for months burst into life. For Sinai's wildlife, such as the gazelle and rock hyrax (as well as for the goats herded by local Bedouin people), these rare occasions are times of plenty.

Yet these fragile ecosystems – which depend on a delicate balance of conditions for their survival – have come under increasing threat from the rapid onslaught of tourism. Until relatively recently, the only people to wander through this region were Bedouin on camels. Now adventure seekers in ever-multiplying numbers are ploughing their way through in 4WDs and quad bikes (four-wheeled motorcycles) in search of pristine spots, and in so doing, churning up the soil, uprooting plants and contributing to erosion.

In order to minimise the environmental damage, the government has banned vehicles from going off road in certain areas, including Ras Mohammed National Park and the protected areas of Nabq, Ras Abu Gallum and Taba. Yet enforcement in Sinai's vast wilderness areas is difficult, and while rangers do patrol protectorates, a large part of the responsibility is left with visitors to follow the rules. To do your part, try not to be persuaded by overeager guides wanting to show you something that's off the beaten track. If you really want to explore the region in depth, do it in the age-old fashion – go on foot or by camel, with the necessary provisions. Also be aware of rubbish, which has become an increasingly serious threat to Sinai's ecosystems. Dive clubs located in Dahab and Sharm el-Sheikh organise regular rubbish dives, and always find far more than they can collect. You should carry out all your litter with you, and dispose of it thoughtfully. And wherever you visit, treat Sinai's ecosystems – both those above and below the sea – with care.

bargaining and paying far more than would be the case over similar distances elsewhere in Egypt.

If you are driving yourself, you will need to exercise caution at all times. Stick to tracks when going off the road, as there are still mines left over from the wars with Israel. When at the wheel in winter, remember that it rains with some frequency in Sinai, and flash floods often wash out paved roads, particularly around Wadi Feiran. Bus drivers are a good source of information on trouble spots.

COAST

A barren coastline of extraordinary beauty, the Sinai coast is the meeting spot of choice for the world's political leaders, a booming package-tourism destination, and nirvana for the members of the international diving fraternity. Over the past several millennia some of human history's most significant events have played out against these isolated shores, and today the region remains sacred to all the world's major monotheistic religions. Of

course, this doesn't alter the simple fact that the majority of international travellers make regular pilgrimages to the coast for its isolated beaches, superb coral reefs and unique Bedouin culture.

AIN MUSA

Ain Musa (Springs of Moses) is said to be the place where Moses and the Israelites camped after crossing into Sinai, and where Moses – on discovering that the water was too bitter to drink – took the advice of God and threw a special tree into the springs, miraculously sweetening the water. Unfortunately, however, only one of the 12 original springs still exists, and is now sadly filled with litter and surrounded by a stand of date palms.

The site is about 25km south of the Ahmed Hamdi Tunnel, just off the main road and signposted only in Arabic. It is watched over by an officer from the antiquities department, together with a group of eager guides. Camping at the site is possible in theory, but unappealing due to the litter, the proximity of the roadway and a nearby settlement. There's also no drinkable water (as the spring water is too brackish, with no sign of Moses' special tree.

It's best to visit with your own vehicle, or on a tour organised through one of the hotels in Ras Sudr (see below). All buses heading south pass by here and will drop you off, though it can be difficult to find onward transport.

RAS SUDR
☎ 069

Ras Sudr (or simply Sudr) was originally developed as the base town for one of Egypt's largest oil refineries, though its coastline and proximity to Cairo have spurred its transition into a resort area. Due to the lack of offshore reefs, the international community has mostly bypassed Sudr, though wealthy Cairene families have been more than happy to snatch up coastal time-share villas. However, with uninterrupted winds blowing at mostly force five or six, Sudr does enjoy a fine reputation among windsurfers.

The town centre, which lies just off the main highway, boasts several small restaurants, a post office, a bank and various small shops. Well away from here, to the south and north, are a handful of ageing resorts interspersed with blocks of holiday villas.

One of the most famous places for wind- and kitesurfing, **Moon Beach** (☎ 581 0088; www .moonbeachretreat.com; 7-/14-night accommodation package per person £295/445, 7-/14-day kit hire £130/220, 4-day progression courses £85; 🔀 🖳) is where the British magazine *Boards* tests equipment each year. Located on the Gulf of Suez just off the main coastal road, Moon Beach has beachfront bungalows with all the trimmings. Additionally, there's a professionally staffed and stocked wind- and kitesurfing centre, as well as a fully licensed school for budding surfers of all kinds. Nightly rates and shorter-stay packages are available – check out the website for more detailed information.

East Delta has a bus station along the main road about 500m south of the main junction. Buses to Cairo (E£25 to E£30, two to three hours) depart at 7.30am, 2pm and 4pm. A taxi from the bus station in Ras Sudr to Moon Beach costs about E£25 to E£30.

HAMMAM FARA'UN

Hammam Fara'un (Pharaoh's Bath) is the site of a hot-springs complex that is commonly used by local Bedouin as a cure for various ailments ranging from arthritis to rheumatism. The springs are located in a cave beside the beach, but are too hot for all but the most dedicated hot-springs fans. Women who decide to brave the waters should avoid swimming in anything more daring than leggings and a baggy T-shirt.

Hammam Fara'un is about 50km south of Ras Sudr, and signposted only in Arabic. It's best to visit with your own transport or with a tour from Moon Beach (see left), especially since there is no place to stay near the springs.

AL-TOR
☎ 069

Al-Tor, also known as Tur Sinai, has been a significant port since ancient times, though today it primarily serves as the administrative capital of the South Sinai Governorate. With stiff and constant breezes similar to those buffeting the coastline further north around Ras Sudr, Al-Tor has been trying in recent years to establish itself as a wind- and kitesurfing destination.

National Bank of Egypt has a branch with an ATM; it's in the town centre near the post office. If you've overstayed your welcome in Egypt, you can extend your visa at the Mogamma, the large administrative building on the main road in the town centre.

About 5km from town are some hot springs known as **Hammam Musa** (admission E£20), which tradition holds to have been one of the possible stopping points used by Moses and the Israelites on their journey through Sinai. It's possible to bathe in the springs, and there are some paved walkways, a changing area and a small cafe.

The focal point of wind- and kitesurfing in Al-Tor is the **Moses Bay Hotel** (☎ 377 4343; www .oceansource.net/hotel; s/d 7-night half board with equipment rental £405/700, full board £720/1215; 🔀 🖳), which also happens to be the nicest place along this stretch of coast. Located approximately 3km from town smack-dab on the beach, Moses Bay has its own private stretch of sand, pleasant rooms, a restaurant, and a wind- and kitesurfing centre. Although it's not as upmarket as Moon Beach in Ras Sudr (see left), it offers great value if you're prepared to sacrifice a bit on the glitz.

The East Delta bus station is along the main road at the northern edge of town opposite the hospital, and about 700m from the Delmon Hotel. Buses depart from 7am onward

SINAI

HISTORY'S FOOTPRINTS

Sinai's rugged expanses are dotted with traces of early settlements and pilgrimage routes. One of the most impressive sites is **Serabit al-Khadim**, a ruined Pharaonic temple surrounded by ancient turquoise mines and starkly beautiful landscapes. Despite the remoteness of the location, turquoise was mined here as far back as the Old Kingdom. The temple itself dates back to the 12th dynasty and is dedicated to the goddess Hathor. Beside it is a New Kingdom shrine to Sopdu, god of the Eastern Desert. Throughout the temple's many courts, inscriptions list the temple's benefactors, including Hatshepsut (1473–1458 BC) and Tuthmosis III (1479–1425 BC). It is thought to have been abandoned during the reign of Ramses VII (1136–1129 BC).

Serabit al-Khadim can be reached via an unsignposted track just south of the coastal settlement of Abu Zenima or, more interestingly, from a track branching north off the road running east through Wadi Feiran via **Wadi Mukattab** (Valley of Inscriptions), which itself is well worth a visit. Here Sinai's largest collection of rock inscriptions and stelae, some dating back to the 3rd dynasty, give further evidence of ancient turquoise-mining activities. Unfortunately, many of the workings and stelae were damaged when the British unsuccessfully tried to revive the mines in 1901.

Heading inland from Serabit al-Khadim, another track takes you through the colourful wadis of **Gebel Foga** to the cliffs that edge Gebel et-Tih and the **Forest of Pillars**, a naturally occurring phenomenon accessible with 4WD and camel via a long track.

All of these destinations require guides and a 4WD. The most straightforward way to visit is to arrange a jeep trip with Moon Beach resort (see p463), or with an outfit in Na'ama Bay.

If you're travelling in your own vehicle, you can head into the village of **Sheikh Barakat** and get a guide: coming from Ras Sudr, follow the marked track that leads off into the desert, just south of Abu Zenima, for about 39km. When you see a white dome on your right, take the track to your left. After about 3km you'll come to Sheikh Barakat, where you can camp (the closest hotels are in Al-Tor and Ras Sudr), and organise a guide to take you the remaining 7km to the trail leading up to Serabit al-Khadim. At the end of this you'll need to park your vehicle and climb for about an hour. The track up the mountain is steep at times and involves a bit of scrambling but can be handled by anyone who is reasonably fit. Coming from Wadi Feiran, you can negotiate for a guide in the village of Feiran.

throughout the day to Sharm el-Sheikh (E£15 to E£20, two hours). From the bus station, you can hire a pick-up for E£10 to take you to the Moses Bay Hotel, or you can arrange transport directly with the hotel.

RAS MOHAMMED NATIONAL PARK

About 20km west of Sharm el-Sheikh on the road from Al-Tor lies the headland of **Ras Mohammed National Park** (admission per person €5, plus per vehicle €5; ☺ 8am-5pm), named by local fishermen for a cliff that resembles a man's profile. The waters surrounding the peninsula are considered the jewel in the crown of the Red Sea. The park is inundated with more than 50,000 visitors annually, enticed by the prospect of marvelling at some of the world's most spectacular coral-reef ecosystems, including a profusion of coral species and teeming marine life. Most, if not all, of the Red Sea's 1000 species of fish can be seen in the park's waters, including sought-after pelagics, such as hammerheads, manta rays and whale sharks.

History

The most ancient corals at Ras Mohammed are fossil reefs dating back some two million years. Because they are similar in composition and structure to present-day reefs, they are an invaluable source of scientific information about changing sea levels and past climatic conditions.

Ras Mohammed was declared a marine reserve in 1983 and became Egypt's first national park in 1989. At the time of its declaration, the park was the subject of controversy, but since then has proved its value in preventing the area's fragile environment from being destroyed by the sort of development that has transformed the Sharm el-Sheikh coast. Hotels are not permitted, only 12% of the park is accessible to visitors and limits are applied to the number of dive boats allowed.

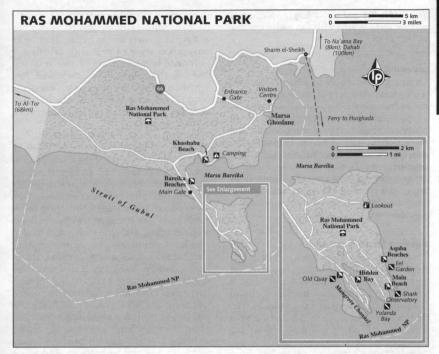

RAS MOHAMMED NATIONAL PARK

Orientation & Information

Ras Mohammed occupies a total of 480 sq km of land and sea, including the desert in and around the *ras* (headland), Tiran Island, and the shoreline between Sharm el-Sheikh harbour and Nabq Protectorate.

You'll need your passport to enter the park. Visitors on Sinai-only permits cannot go to Ras Mohammed overland as it is beyond the Sharm el-Sheikh boundary, but should not have any problem on dive-boat trips – check with the dive clubs if you have any doubts.

The entrance to the park is about 20km from the reefs. A **visitors centre** (10am-sunset Sat-Thu) with a restaurant is clearly marked to the left of the main access road in an area known as Marsa Ghoslane. Videos are shown here, and you may be able to pick up a booklet highlighting local fauna. The park is laid out with colour-coded trails and clearly marked pictograms of what each site offers.

Activities

If you're planning to dive in Ras Mohammed, you will need to arrive via a boat tour or a live-aboard, both of which typically depart from

Sharm el-Sheikh (p469) or Dahab (p478). For more information on dive operators, as well as an overview of the best dive sites in the national park, see p449.

If you arrive at the national park by private car, it's possible to hike to a variety of wilderness beaches and go snorkelling on a variety of offshore reefs – you will need to bring your own equipment.

At the park's laboratory, a pink trail leads to **Khashaba Beach** and a camping area. Yellow arrows lead to the sandy beaches and calm waters of **Marsa Bareika**, excellent for snorkelling and safe for children. Blue arrows take you to **Main Beach**, which gets crowded with day visitors, but remains one of the best places to see vertical coral walls. Brown arrows lead to **Aqaba Beaches**, which border the **Eel Garden**, named after a colony of garden eels 20m down. Just beyond here, orange arrows lead to the **Shark Observatory**, a cliff-top area where you can sometimes see sharks as they feed from Ras Mohammed's rich offerings. The red arrows lead to **Yolanda Bay**, another beach with good snorkelling, and green arrows lead to the **Mangrove Channel** and **Hidden Bay** and to **Old Quay**, a spectacular vertical reef teeming with fish and accessible to snorkellers.

Sleeping

Camping is permitted in designated areas, with permits (€5 per person) available from the entrance gate. You'll need to bring all supplies with you; the nearest shops are in Sharm el-Sheikh. If you camp, respect the environment and clean up. In particular, don't bury toilet paper or rubbish, as the relentless winds here mean that nothing stays under the sand for long. Camp rules are strictly enforced by rangers, and if you're caught violating them, you will be fined and possibly even prosecuted.

Getting There & Around

If you don't have a car, you can hire a taxi from Sharm el-Sheikh to bring you here, but expect to pay at least E£150 for the day. If you don't mind company, the easiest option is to join one of the many day tours by jeep or bus from Sharm el-Sheikh and Na'ama Bay, most of which will drop you at the beaches and snorkelling sites. Expect to pay from E£150. Alternatively, divers are often brought in by boat from tourist centres on the Red Sea.

To move around the park you'll need a vehicle. Access is restricted to certain parts of the park and, for conservation reasons, it's forbidden to leave the official tracks.

SHARM EL-SHEIKH & NA'AMA BAY
☎ 069

The southern coast of the Gulf of Aqaba, between Tiran Island and Ras Mohammed National Park, features some of the world's most amazing underwater scenery. The crystal-clear waters, rare and lovely reefs and an incredible variety of exotic fish darting in and out of the colourful coral have made this a snorkelling and scuba-diving paradise. Unfortunately, the proudly brash resort destination of Sharm el-Sheikh, which comprises the two adjacent bays of Na'ama Bay and Sharm al-Maya, does not always reflect this serene underwater beauty.

Known simply as Sharm by package travellers the world over, Sinai's largest and most famous beach town has undergone a miraculous transformation in recent years. What was once a small village that attracted mainly hard-core divers is now commonly described as Egypt's answer to Las Vegas, drawing in wave upon wave of primarily British and European holidaymakers in search of sun and sea. Here along the much-touted 'Red Sea Riviera', high-rise block hotels and dense condo developments stretch down the coastline, all the while jockeying for highly prized beachfront property.

Sharm has both adoring fans and harsh critics alike, and opinions tend to fall solely in either camp. Defenders of the town, particularly resident expats and package travellers, claim that Sharm simply is what it is, namely a pleasure-seeking European enclave on the edge of Sinai. If you want to indulge in resort living, party with foreigners into the wee hours of the morning, and dine on Western food to your heart's content – all at a surprisingly affordable price – welcome to paradise. Sharm is also touted as being a great destination for families who want to bring the little ones to Egypt for a beach holiday, though be advised that terror attacks have taken place here in the past (see Dangers & Annoyances, p469).

On the other hand, critics accuse Sharm of being a sterile and air-brushed facade that lacks any real authenticity, and worse yet covers up some serious environmental degradation and pressing issues of sustainability. Whether or not these claims are valid, independent travellers who are turned off by coastal sprawl and gated resorts would be wise to skip Sharm, passing through only en route to the more low-key and backpacker-friendly town of Dahab (p476).

Orientation

Most resorts are clustered along or just inland from the beach at Na'ama Bay. If you enjoy being in the centre of the action and don't mind the crush of pedestrians, central Na'ama Bay – consisting of a beachfront promenade and a pedestrians-only area lined with hotels, restaurants and shops – is the most convenient base. The further away from this central strip you go, the quieter things become: most of the resorts lining the coast north of Na'ama Bay are comparatively tranquil upmarket retreats with their own patch of sand and easy taxi access to the central area.

Sharm al-Maya, about 6km west of Na'ama Bay, centres on a large, walled market area known as Sharm Old Market, with a selection

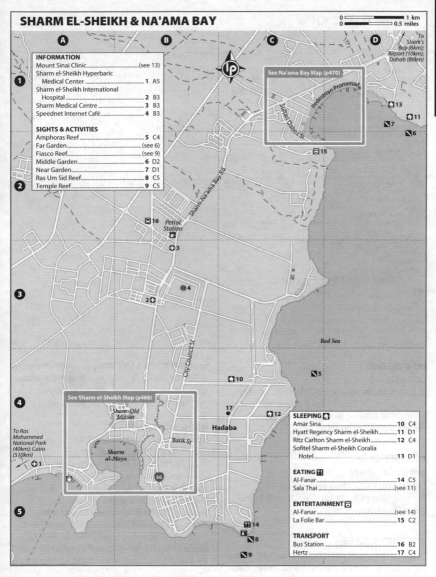

SHARM EL-SHEIKH & NA'AMA BAY

0 ——————— 1 km
0 ——————— 0.5 miles

INFORMATION
Mount Sinai Clinic...................................(see 13)
Sharm el-Sheikh Hyperbaric
  Medical Center..**1** A5
Sharm el-Sheikh International
  Hospital..**2** B3
Sharm Medical Centre.............................**3** B3
Speednet Internet Café...........................**4** B3

SIGHTS & ACTIVITIES
Amphoras Reef...**5** C4
Far Garden...(see 6)
Fiasco Reef..(see 9)
Middle Garden..**6** D2
Near Garden...**7** D1
Ras Um Sid Reef.......................................**8** C5
Temple Reef..**9** C5

See Na'ama Bay Map (p470)

To
Shark's
Bay (6km);
Airport (10km);
Dahab (80km)

Pedestrian Promenade

Sinai Dahab St

13
7
11
6

15

Sharm-Na'ama Bay Rd

Petrol
Station
16
3

4
2

Red Sea

City Council St

10
5

See Sharm el-Sheikh Map (p468)

*Sharm Old
Market*

17
12

Hadaba

Bank St

SLEEPING
Amar Sina...**10** C4
Hyatt Regency Sharm el-Sheikh............**11** D1
Ritz Carlton Sharm el-Sheikh..................**12** C4
Sofitel Sharm el-Sheikh Coralia
  Hotel...**13** D1

EATING
Al-Fanar...**14** C5
Sala Thai..(see 11)

To Ras
Mohammed
National Park
(40km); Cairo
(510km)
1

*Sharm
al-Maya*

66

ENTERTAINMENT
Al-Fanar...(see 14)
La Folie Bar...**15** C2

TRANSPORT
Bus Station..**16** B2
Hertz..**17** C4

14
8
9

of inexpensive eateries. A large section of the Old Market area was badly damaged in the tragic bombings of July 2005 and has been heavily rebuilt. On the southwestern edge of Sharm al-Maya is the port.

Spread out on a cliff top above Sharm al-Maya is the administrative area of Hadaba, which is rimmed by a barren network of long, treeless avenues lined with primarily midrange resorts. These are targeted at travellers flying in directly from Europe, and are connected to the beach via shuttle bus. To the southeast of the administrative area is Ras Um Sid, with an agreeable stretch of coastline, a lighthouse and a row of upmarket hotels.

SINAI

SINAI

SHARM EL-SHEIKH

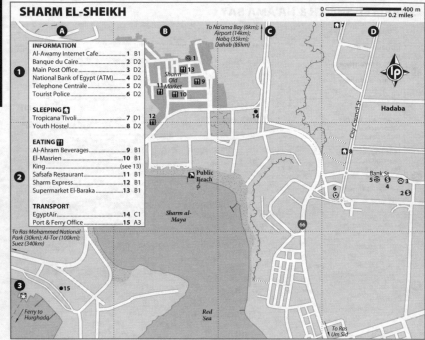

INFORMATION
Al-Awamy Internet Cafe	1 B1
Banque du Caire	2 D2
Main Post Office	3 D2
National Bank of Egypt (ATM)	4 D2
Telephone Centrale	5 D2
Tourist Police	6 D2

SLEEPING
Tropicana Tivoli	7 D1
Youth Hostel	8 D2

EATING
Al-Ahram Beverages	9 B1
El-Masrien	10 B1
King	(see 13)
Safsafa Restaurant	11 B1
Sharm Express	12 B1
Supermarket El-Baraka	13 B1

TRANSPORT
EgyptAir	14 C1
Port & Ferry Office	15 A3

To Na'ama Bay (6km); Airport (14km); Nabq (35km); Dahab (85km)

Sharm Old Market

Hadaba

City Council St

Bank St

Public Beach

Sharm al-Maya

To Ras Mohammed National Park (30km); Al-Tor (100km); Suez (340km)

Ferry to Hurghada

Red Sea

To Ras Um Sid

Information

BOOKSHOPS

Al-Ahram Bookshop (Map p470; Sharm–Na'ama Bay rd, Na'ama Bay; 10am-1.30pm & 6-8pm) Sharm el-Sheikh's best-stocked bookshop, with a reasonable selection of books and magazines.

EMERGENCY

Ambulance (☎ 123)

Tourist police Hadaba (Map p468; ☎ 366 0311); Na'ama Bay (Map p470; ☎ 360 0554, 366 0675; booth next to Marina Sharm Hotel)

INTERNET ACCESS

Many hotels have internet access and there are internet cafes dotted around town, each charging between £5 and £10 per hour depending on your length of use.

Al-Awamy Internet Cafe (Map p468; Sharm Old Market, Sharm el-Sheikh; 24hr)

Felicita.Net (Map p470; Na'ama Bay; 24hr) Above the Egyptian American Bank.

Naama Internet (Map p470; Na'ama Centre, Na'ama Bay; noon-3am)

Speednet Internet Café (Map p467; Sharm-Na'ama Bay rd, Sharm el-Sheikh; 24hr) In the Delta Sharm complex.

Yes Business Centre (Map p470; Na'ama Bay; 11am-1am) Between Mall 7 and Avis car rental.

MEDICAL SERVICES

Mount Sinai Clinic (☎ 012 218 9889; 24hr); Mövenpick Hotel (Map p470; Na'ama Bay); Sofitel Sharm el-Sheikh Coralia Hotel (Map p467; Na'ama Bay) Specialises in diving-related medical problems as well as ordinary ailments.

Omar & Omar Pharmacy (Map p470; ☎ 360 0960; King of Bahrain St, Na'ama Bay; 24hr)

Sharm el-Sheikh Hyberbaric Medical Center (Map p467; ☎ 366 0922/3, 012 212 4292; hyper_med _center@sinainet.com.eg; Sharm el-Sheikh; 24hr)

Sharm el-Sheikh International Hospital (Map p467; ☎ 366 0893/4/5; Sharm-Na'ama Bay rd, Sharm el-Sheikh; 24hr)

Sharm Medical Center (Map p467; ☎ 366 1744; Sharm-Na'ama Bay rd, Sharm el-Sheikh; 24hr) Next to the bus station.

MONEY

You will find ATMs every few metres in Na'ama Bay, including several in Na'ama Centre (Map p470), as well as ATMs in the lobbies of most larger hotels. Otherwise, all the major banks have branches in Hadaba.

Banque du Caire (Map p468; Hadaba; ☽ 8.30am-2pm Sun-Thu)

Commercial International Bank (Map p470; Na'ama Centre, Na'ama Bay; ☽ 9am-1pm & 6-10pm Sat-Thu, 10-11am Fri)

Egyptian American Bank (Map p470; ☎ 360 1423; Na'ama Bay; ☽ 8.30am-2pm Mon-Thu) American Express agent; diagonally opposite Cataract Resort.

National Bank of Egypt Hadaba (Map p468; Bank St; ☽ 8.30am-2pm & 6-9pm Sat-Thu, 9am-1pm & 6-9pm Fri); Na'ama Bay (Map p470; Na'ama Centre; ☽ 6pm-1am) ATM.

Thomas Cook (Map p470; ☎ 360 1808; Gafy Mall, Sharm-Na'ama Bay rd, Na'ama Bay; ☽ 9am-2pm & 6-10pm) Just west of Sinai Star Hotel.

Western Union (Map p470; ☎ 364 0466; Rosetta Hotel, Na'ama Bay; ☽ 8.30am-2pm & 6-10pm Sat-Thu, 3-10pm Fri)

POST

Main post office (Map p468; Bank St, Hadaba; ☽ 8.30am-2.30pm Sat-Thu)

TELEPHONE

There are several cardphones in Na'ama Bay and at least two on the beachfront promenade. Cards can be bought everywhere, but watch out for overcharging by shopkeepers. There are also several call centres where you can dial internationally for E£4 to E£7 per minute.

Telephone centrale (Map p468; Bank St, Hadaba; ☽ 24hr).

Dangers & Annoyances

In July 2005, three terrorist bombs exploded in Sharm el-Sheikh, killing 88 people and injuring over 200. The worst damage was in the Sharm Old Market area and near Ghazala Gardens hotel in Na'ama Bay. In the wake of the bombings, the Egyptian government increased security at all Sharm el-Sheikh hotels and began building a fence around the town. The government has also worked tirelessly to revive tourism to the city, with incentives ranging from discounted flight prices to free concerts.

At the time of writing, reconstruction of the affected establishments was complete, and tourist numbers had long since returned to normal. Although the scars of the attack clearly remain, Sharm is generally considered to be a safe destination, and – barring another major attack – it is a relaxed and hassle-free destination, even if you're travelling with young children.

For an overview of the history of terrorism in Sinai, see p460.

Activities
SNORKELLING & DIVING

It's something of a tragedy that Sharm's truly exquisite diving has been overshadowed by unfettered tourist development. However, offshore dive sites in both Sharm and the adjacent Ras Mohammed National Park are easily accessible by live-aboards, or even from boat trips departing from Dahab. For more information on diving in the Red Sea, see p441.

Snorkelling in the waters around Sharm is excellent. While there are some easily accessed reefs in central Na'ama Bay, it's better to make your way to the more impressive **Near and Middle Gardens** (Map p467), or the even more beautiful **Far Garden** (Map p467). The Near Garden is around the point at the northern end of the bay just below the Sofitel hotel, and the Middle and Far Gardens are below the Hyatt Regency hotel. All can be reached on foot, or you can take a boat organised by one of the diving centres; bring plenty of drinking water and sunblock along.

Another prime spot for snorkelling is **Ras Um Sid Reef** (Map p467), near the lighthouse at Sharm el-Sheikh, which is known for its fan corals and plethora of fish, although the small beach is parcelled up between several resorts and can get quite crowded. The popular **Temple** and **Fiasco Reefs** (Map p467) are within easy swimming distance, and while they're primarily dive destinations, snorkellers can still get a taste of their flora and fauna. Close by the Ritz Carlton hotel is **Amphoras Reef** (Map p467), another popular snorkelling spot. On the road to the airport, **Shark's Bay** (off Map p467) also has a good reef, which is frequented by large rays in springtime. Tickets for beach use cost E£15, and are issued at the camps on the left side of the beach.

It's possible to get to more distant sites by joining a dive boat, which can be arranged at most local dive clubs; expect to pay US$25 to US$50 for a day trip. Many of the clubs also do snorkelling trips to Ras Mohammed National Park, with prices starting at about US$50; see p465 for more information. While there is some excellent snorkelling in the park, be sure that you'll be taken to a suitable site, as some dive destinations are not always ideal for snorkellers, and some areas have strong currents that are not for the faint-hearted.

SINAI

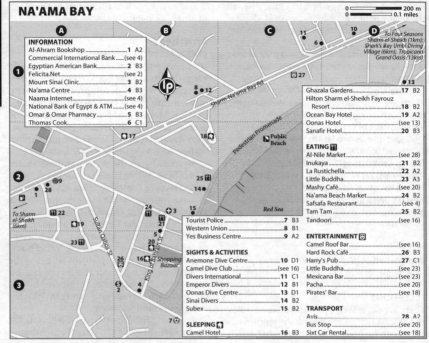

Most dive clubs rent out masks, snorkels and fins. Remember that the same reef-protection rules apply to snorkellers as to divers. As snorkellers tend to stick to shallower waters, their fins often do more damage to reefs than those of divers, so take care to keep your distance from the corals. For more on reef-protection measures, see boxed text (p454).

WATER SPORTS
Most major hotels offer a range of other water sports, including sailing lessons, windsurfing, parasailing, pedalos, banana boats and glass-bottom boats. Most hotels also have beach access – either their own stretch of waterfront, or by agreement with another resort. Check when booking, as the beaches of some hotels are fairly distant (up to 10km) from the hotel itself and can only be accessed via shuttle. There is a narrow stretch of public beach diagonally opposite Hilton Fayrouz Village on Na'ama Bay, but it is so crowded with rental chairs that it is difficult to see the sand. Keep in mind that it's illegal to swim off Na'ama Bay after 11pm, and that despite all the development, the beaches and waters of Na'ama Bay are part of Ras Mohammed National Park and its regulations apply here.

In Sharm al-Maya there is also a stretch of public beach. However, there's no reef, and women swimming here are likely to be ogled by young Egyptian men.

CAMEL RIDES
Camel rides to 'traditional Bedouin villages' can be easily arranged with most hotels, but it's usually a better and more authentic experience if you can negotiate treks directly with the Bedouin in Dahab (p479). If you decide to try one from Sharm, expect to pay US$40 to US$60, and to find yourself in the midst of a large group.

HORSE RIDING
Several top-end hotels, including **Sofitel Sharm el-Sheikh Coralia Hotel** (Map p467; ☎ 360 0081; www .sofitel.com; Na'ama Bay), offer horse riding from about US$20 to US$30 per hour.

Tours
Almost all travel agencies and large hotels organise jeep or bus trips to St Katherine's

Monastery (p495), and to desert attractions such as the Coloured Canyon (p479). However, most of the guides are Nile Valley dwellers, not Bedouin, and the groups are often large. Better, more sensitive trips can be arranged from Dahab (see p479) and Nuweiba (see p487).

Sleeping

Sharm el-Sheikh and the surrounding area has one of the greatest concentrations of hotels in Egypt, though you're going to have to pay to play here. Budget accommodation places are few and far between, with the all-inclusive resort being the standard rather than the exception. For anyone who is serious about pinching their pennies, it's probably wise to continue on to Dahab.

If you're looking for a decent hotel that won't break the bank, a cluster of midrange hotels has sprung up in the area rimming Hadaba. While lacking ambience – most hotels are spread along or near a wide concrete strip – prices are more reasonable than on the waterfront, and most places have shuttle buses to take guests to the beach at Ras Um Sid or to Na'ama Bay. Beachfront hotels in Na'ama Bay are generally pricey affairs, though for a better deal, choose one that's set back a bit.

The entire coast from Na'ama Bay northward towards the airport has been the target of a massive construction boom in recent years, and is now home to a large number of five-star resorts. Flaunting luxury names, all are geared to visitors on all-inclusive tours, and are usually booked from outside Egypt or as part of a package.

The Shark's Bay area, about 6km northeast of Na'ama Bay, was once home to a quiet Bedouin village, though over the past decade, it has been developed with amazing rapidity. Today this stretch of coast is now a row of ultra-exclusive luxury hotels – if you're staying at any of these top-end resorts, your every whim will be catered for.

Be advised that the hotel scene in Sharm is changing rapidly, which means that the following information is likely to become outdated quickly. Also keep in mind that prices in Sharm are more volatile than those in other parts of the country, and are subject to wild fluctuations depending on the number of tourists in town.

Although we've tried to give approximate prices for hotels, it's worth noting that cheaper rate are nearly always available if you book in advance, especially as part of an all-inclusive package.

BUDGET

Youth Hostel (Map p468; ☎ 366 0317; City Council St, Hadaba; dm from E£20; 🔀) The only attraction of this shabby affair is that it's the cheapest place to stay in the area. Rooms are utterly soulless, but at least a night here won't put you in the poorhouse. It's up on the hill in Hadaba, near the police station and mosque and away from the beach, though frequent microbuses pass by that can take you to Na'ama Bay or Ras Um Sid.

our pick **Shark's Bay Umbi Diving Village** (off Map p470; ☎ 360 0942; www.sharksbay.com; s/d/tr sea-view huts E£14/17/21, beach cabins E£22/33/43, village r E£32/43/52) This long-standing Bedouin-owned camp has a relaxed ambience, simple but clean huts with shared bathrooms up on the cliff, and pricier huts down below with air-con and bathroom, and a recently constructed village-style block of furnished rooms. There's also the Bedouin-tented Shark's Bay Umbi Restaurant (mains E£20 to E£35) overlooking the water, which is the perfect spot for a charcoal-roasted meal or a charcoal-roasted *sheesha* (water pipe). To reach the camp, just tell the taxi driver 'Shark's Bay Umbi'; expect to pay about E£25 from Na'ama Bay and E£50 from the port at Sharm. If you're driving, take the airport road from town to a right-hand turn-off for the Savoy and Conrad Concorde hotels, follow this road for 400m to the right-hand turn-off for Gardenia Plaza, then turn and continue 2km further to Shark's Bay.

Tropicana Tivoli (Map p468; ☎ 366 1384; www.tropicana hotels.com; Hadaba; r from €35; 🔀 🔊) A good option for families on a strict budget, the Tivoli is the Sharm-based Tropicana chain's lowest entry. But, despite the ridiculously cheap price tag, the Tivoli has simple but clean rooms with kitchenettes that are conducive to self-catering. There is a decent-sized pool for a quick dip, though you can always access the nearby beach at Ras Um Sid.

MIDRANGE

Ocean Bay Hotel (Map p470; ☎ 360 1012; r from US$50; 🔀 🖵 🔊) This relatively characterless concrete box is not exactly one of the most atmospheric hotels on the block. But, in the rapidly expanding sprawl that is Sharm, location is everything, and the Ocean Bay is within easy walking distance of Na'ama Bay's beachfront promenade. Although you might not want to linger on the stale hotel grounds for too long, the beach is right there whenever you want it.

Sanafir Hotel (Map p470; ☎ 360 0197; www.sanafirhotel .com; King of Bahrain St; r from US$80; ❄ ☐ ☒) Located smack-dab in the nerve centre of Na'ama Bay, the Sanafir was one of the first hotels to be built here. Over the years, however, the Sanafir has undergone extensive renovations to keep up with the rapidly increasing competition, though the Bedouin-style rooms that made this place so memorable are still intact. The Sanafir has also expanded its offerings of restaurants, lounges and bars, and with its nearly unbeatable location, Na'ama Bay is literally at your doorstep.

Oonas Hotel (Map p470; ☎ 360 0581; www.oonasdivers .com; s/d/tr from €45/60/85; ❄ ☐ ☒) One of the best bargains in Sharm is this combination hotel and scuba club, which has a 20-year history of certifying divers from around the world. Occupying a choice location on the beach in Na'ama Bay, Oonas allows you to comfortably relax on the beach or by the pool in between dives. Accommodation is in fairly standard rooms with decent furnishings, but they're a bargain if you book them in conjunction with a dive package.

Amar Sina (Map p467; ☎ 366 2222/9; www.minasegypt .com; Hadaba; r from US$85; ❄ ☐ ☒) With soaring domes, graceful arches and whitewashed walls adorned with brick ornaments, this *Arabian Nights*–styled hotel upholds Sharm's renowned kitsch factor. Of course, guests don't seem to be bothered by this one bit, especially when sunning themselves with drink in hand beside the palm-fringed free-form swimming pool. Although it's set a bit back from the shore, guests have access to beach space at Ras Um Sid.

Tropicana Grand Oasis (off Map p470; ☎ 360 1290/1; www.tropicanahotels.com; Sharm–Na'ama Bay rd; r from €90; ❄ ☐ ☒) One of the Tropicana chain's signature properties, this modest but affordable luxury resort is located right on the beach in Shark's Bay about 10km past Na'ama Bay. Catering mostly to families on package holidays, the Grand Oasis is an appealing place with attractive grounds, a series of pools, views out to sea and a children's play area. While it's certainly not the most lavish spot around, it's the kind of place where you won't feel too out of place if your kid is fussy during mealtimes.

Camel Hotel (Map p470; ☎ 360 0700; www.cameldive .com; King of Bahrain St; s/d from €60/100; ❄ ☐ ☒) This attractive, small and well-appointed four-star hotel is attached to a dive centre of the same name in the heart of Na'ama Bay. Needless to say, diving is the main attraction here – even the swimming pool is tiered, allowing for open-water skills to be practised in a confined environment. If you're looking to take a course or book a bunch of dives, you can save a bit of cash if you arrange a package in advance.

TOP END

Ghazala Gardens (Map p470; ☎ 360 0150; http://redseaho tels.com; r from US$100; ❄ ☐ ☒) The target of a massive truck bomb that claimed 45 innocent lives in 2005, the Ghazala Gardens has been completely rebuilt, and is now an enduring symbol of Egypt's commitment to endure in the face of terrorism. With Moorish stylings and expansive gardens, the Ghazala is an excellent upmarket retreat that boasts several hundred rooms as well as an impressive offering of international restaurants. Although it's not actually on the beach, guests can simply cross the road, and access the hotel's sister property, the Ghazala Beach, one of Na'ama Bay's classic spots.

Hilton Sharm el-Sheikh Fayrouz Resort (Map p470; ☎ 360 0137; www.hiltonworldresorts.com; r from US$130; ❄ ☐ ☒) This sweep of deluxe bungalows along the promenade somehow manages to capture a degree of intimacy absent from its giant neighbours. Although it pales in comparison to the shows of wealth and privilege found at competing hotels, you can easily bask in the lap of luxury here without being a millionaire. As you'd expect of any Hilton establishment the world over, the Fayrouz Village has the usual assortment of infinity pools, gourmet restaurants and top-notch resort facilities.

Hyatt Regency Sharm el-Sheikh (Map p467; ☎ 360 1234; www.sharm.hyatt.com; r from US$185; ❄ ☐ ☒) Luxuriously perched above the rich corals of the Near Garden reef, this five-star charmer is perfectly positioned to take in the rich turquoise and cobalt blue hues of the Red Sea. Even if you never leave the resort, the entire property is awash with panoramic views, giving the Hyatt an open feeling rarely found at resorts. And there's little reason to leave, as the Hyatt overwhelms guests with opulence, from the classically decorated rooms to the perfectly manicured gardens and lashings of marble at every turn.

Sofitel Sharm el-Sheikh Coralia Hotel (Map p467; ☎ 360 0081; www.sofitel.com; r from US$205; ✷ ☐ ☒) Dominating the bay's northern cliffs, this whitewashed hotel terraces majestically down towards the sea like a sultan's palace from a children's fairy tale. The distinctly Middle Eastern–style rooms are decked out in exotic wooden furniture, and boast stunning views over the bay. True to its name, the Sofitel offers an incredibly sophisticated resort experience to the guests privileged enough to be staying here.

Ritz Carlton Sharm el-Sheikh (Map p467; ☎ 366 1919; www.ritzcarlton.com; Ras Um Sid; r from US$260; ✷ ☐ ☒) Despite the smooth lines and spotless glass of its architecturally distinct but decidedly modern exterior, the Ritz brims with Old World elegance from the moment you step inside. Expansive rooms and suites are decorated in the finest European furnishings, transporting guests to some forgotten time. Although the entire affair is decidedly un-Egyptian, it's difficult to complain when you're suckling the bosom of luxury.

Four Seasons Sharm el-Sheikh (off Map p470; ☎ 360 3555; www.fourseasons.com/sharmelsheikh; r from US$325; ✷ ✷ ☐ ☒) Unmatched in elegance and sophistication, the Four Seasons is an arabesque-style pleasure palace built around palm-ringed courtyards and overlooking the Straits of Tiran. From the towering whitewashed walls and intricate geometric lattice workings to the ornate bronze fixtures and richly dyed Persian rugs, the Four Seasons is a model of perfection straight down to the last detail. Of course, you're going to need a small fortune to spend some time here, but it's difficult to put a price on over-the-top indulgence.

Eating

As the unashamed tourist capital of Sinai, Sharm has literally hundreds of restaurants spanning the culinary globe. Though most tourists on all-inclusive packages never seem to stray from their resort, it's certainly worth venturing outside the hotel walls. Although restaurants in Sharm are by no means cheap, the quality is extremely high, particularly as local seafood brought straight to your plate from the Red Sea. And, of course, if you've been in Egypt for any significant amount of time, the sight of international favourites, including Italian, Thai, Indian and Japanese, is likely to get the mouth watering.

Rebuilt after the 2005 bombings, the Old Market in Sharm el-Sheikh functions as the culinary hub of the town. Small, friendly, local-style restaurants predominate, the food is good and the service usually efficient. Na'ama Bay has a large selection of eateries, and it's easy to while away a few hours each evening walking along the beachfront promenade and sampling different places. Although it's easy to get suckered into the first restaurant you spot, shop around, compare prices and don't be afraid to let your stomach guide you.

If you're staying in the resort strip or in Shark's Bay, you'll either be wining and dining in luxury at your five-star all-inclusive resort, or self-catering at your Bedouin camp. Of course, frequent taxis and shuttles ply the coastal road, so you're never that far from the action in Sharm el-Sheikh and Na'ama Bay.

King (Map p468; dishes E£5-10; ⏱ from 7am) A clean and popular *fuul* (fava bean paste) and felafel takeaway in the centre of the Old Market, with a range of snacks and the additional advantage of being open early in the morning.

El-Masrien (Map p468; dishes E£5-25) Another popular neighbourhood-style restaurant, El-Masrien offers savoury kebabs and *kofta* (mincemeat and spices grilled on a skewer) to hungry locals and travellers alike – consider this spot the perfect antidote if you've been hitting the booze a bit too hard.

Tam Tam (Map p470; Ghazala Gardens hotel; dishes E£20-60) This popular restaurant along the waterside promenade is a laid-back place where you can delve into a range of Egyptian fare, including mezze, *kushari* and roast pigeon, while relaxing on cushions overlooking the beach and puffing on a *sheesha*.

Safsafa Restaurant (Map p468; dishes E£20-50; ✷) A small establishment offering some of the freshest and cheapest fish in Sharm (whole fish is priced from E£40 to E£50 per kilo) – don't skip on the homemade tahini and *baba ghanoug* (purée of grilled aubergines with tomato and onion).

Mashy Café (Map p470; Sanafir Hotel; dishes E£35-75) Lebanese is the undisputed king of the Middle Eastern gastronomic world, and this low-key open-air spot outside the Sanafir Hotel is as good a place as any to sample the full bounty of this refined cuisine.

La Rustichella (Map p470; pizzas E£25-40; mains E£40-75; ✷) This Sharm institution serves a variety of delectable meals, including Italian-style seafood dishes, brick-oven-roasted pizzas, and a good variety of chicken and beef dishes – stop by in the afternoon and cool off with an ice coffee and a creamy gelato.

Tandoori (Map p470; Camel Hotel, King of Bahrain St; dishes E£40-100; 6.30-11.30pm) This small place in the courtyard of the Camel Hotel has what many consider to be Sharm's best Indian food, including a selection of tandoori dishes and an excellent *dhal makhani* (dish of black lentils and red kidney beans).

Little Buddha (Map p470; Naama Bay Hotel; mains E£45-115;) One of the most popular Asian restaurants in Sharm, the Little Buddha serves excellent Asian fusion cuisine alongside a fresh and varied sushi bar – it's also a loungey bar (right).

Sala Thai (Map p467; Hyatt Regency Sharm el-Sheikh; dishes E£40-120;) Delicious Thai food (fiery curries and delicately spiced noodle dishes) and pleasing aesthetics (teak decor and an outdoor terrace) are yours to enjoy at this comfortable spot overlooking the sea.

Inukaya (Map p470; King of Bahrain St; dishes E£50-115;) Sushi is all the rage in Sharm these days, though this upmarket eatery serves up the highest-quality cuts amid mellow and subdued surrounds that stay true to its Nipponese roots.

our pick **Al-Fanar** (Map p467; Ras Um Sid; dishes E£40-150; 10am-10.30pm;) This upmarket restaurant boasts an excellent seafront location at the base of the lighthouse, cosy alcoves overlooking the water, Bedouin-influenced decor, indoor and outdoor dining, and a large Italian menu featuring thin-crust pizza and homemade pasta dishes.

There are several small but well-stocked supermarkets in Sharm Old Market, including Supermarket El-Baraka (Map p468) and the large Sharm Express (Map p468). Beer and wine can be bought at **Al-Ahram Beverages** (Map p468; 366 3133). There are also numerous supermarkets in central Na'ama Bay, including **Al-Nile Market** (Map p470; 24hr) and **Na'ama Beach Market** (Map p470; 9am-2am).

Entertainment

With a young resident population and a large number of relatively wealthy tourists, Sharm el-Sheikh has one of Egypt's liveliest bar and club scenes. Drinking starts during the day along the promenade, intensifies during the early-evening happy hours and starts to really take off once the sun goes down. Dancing gets going around midnight and ends at dawn, with a fair number of revellers passing out on the sand.

For the most part, nightlife in Sharm is casual – a clean shirt and a pair of decent sandals is perfectly acceptable – though the town's rising prosperity is drawing in greater numbers of the rich and beautiful. You won't be out of place if you dress to the nines, but female travellers should keep in mind that they will attract a lot of attention. Some Egyptian men in Sharm seem to have a penchant for Western women, though the attraction seems to go the other way as well.

Considering that Egypt is a fairly conservative country that typically shuns alcohol and excess pleasures of the flesh, Sharm can either be a shock to the senses or a welcome relief – depending on your own vices, of course. The entire charade may be wholly un-Egyptian, but after a few beers and a couple of uninhibited dancing sessions, fun is usually had by all.

Al-Fanar (Map p467; Ras Um Sid) Superb views, drinks nightly and an open-air party dance floor make this one of the most exciting bars around.

Camel Roof Bar (Map p470; Camel Hotel, Na'ama Bay) A favourite among dive instructors, this is the optimal place to start off the evening, especially if you've been diving all day and looking to swap stories from down under.

Hard Rock Café (Map p470; Sultan Qabos St, Na'ama Bay) A late-night disco-bar with dancing, and one of Sharm's most popular nightspots. Dancing starts at midnight and goes until the wee hours of the morn'.

Harry's Pub (Map p470; Marriott Beach Resort, Na'ama Bay) This English pub has a large selection of beers on tap and occasional special nights with unlimited draught beer at a very reasonable price.

La Folie Bar (Map p467; Iberotel Lido, Na'ama Bay; 2pm-2am) For a more sedate start to your evening, head to this quiet, pleasant bar on the water overlooking the bright lights of Na'ama Bay.

Little Buddha (Map p470; Na'ama Bay Hotel, Na'ama Bay; 11pm-3am) With dim lights, big, cushiony chairs and a mellow ambience, the bar at this Asian fusion restaurant gets going after the kitchen closes.

Mexicana Bar (Map p470; Na'ama Bay Hotel, Na'ama Bay) A small and sometimes happening bar close to the promenade, this is a great place to down a few bowls of nachos followed by some expertly mixed margaritas.

Pacha (Map p470; Sanafir Hotel, King of Bahrain St, Na'ama Bay) The hub of Sharm's nightlife, the Pacha goes wild pretty much every night of the week. Owner Adli Mestakawi also holds Echo Temple Concerts in the desert outside Sharm on Friday during the high season, bringing big-name singers to play to audiences of thousands under the stars – watch for Pacha's advertising around town to see what's playing.

Pirates' Bar (Map p470; Hilton Fayrouz Village, Na'ama Bay) A cosy, pub-style bar where divers congregate for an early evening drink or bar meal. Happy hour is from 5.30pm to 7.30pm.

Getting There & Away
AIR
Daily flights to Cairo, Luxor and Alexandria are available with **EgyptAir** (Map p468; ☎ 366 1056; www.egyptair.com; Sharm al-Maya; ☺ 9am-9pm), though prices tend to fluctuate wildly depending on the season and availability. If you book in advance, it is sometimes possible to snag a ticket for less than US$100, though prices can climb much higher during the busy summer and winter holiday seasons.

If you book a package holiday in either the UK or Europe, it's likely that your travel agent will arrange a charter flight directly to Sharm for you. Even if you're an independent traveller, it's worth visiting a few travel agents before booking your ticket to Egypt – charter flights to Sharm are often significantly cheaper than a round-trip airfare to Cairo, and the city is a quick and easy jumping-off point for the Sinai Peninsula, Luxor and the Nile Valley.

BOAT
Tickets for the high-speed ferry to Hurghada from Sharm el-Sheikh can be bought from various travel agencies in town, or at the port office (Map p468) on days that the ferry runs. Boats leave from the port west of Sharm al-Maya, and it's best to arrive at the ferry port at least one hour prior to departure

The ferry to Hurghada departs from Sharm el-Sheikh at 5pm on Monday, Thursday and Saturday and at 3am on Wednesday (one way E£250/US$40, round trip E£450/US$70, 1½ hours). The rate of the dollar against the Egyptian pound and the whim of the ferry officials determines which currency you'll need to use for the Sharm ferry ticket. Also note that the ferry is often cancelled during winter because of windy conditions – if the ferry is

likely to be cancelled for a few days, you can then make alternative arrangements to get to Hurghada by bus or service taxi.

A few words of caution about the ferry – the Red Sea can get very rough, so much so that the staff on board hands out Dramamine (an antihistamine that can help with seasickness) prior to departure; see p536 for more information. If you've never had the pleasure of witnessing dozens of people simultaneously emptying out their stomach contents, you're in for a memorable trip. With that said, try to get a seat by the window, and keep your eyes fixed on the horizon – this is a great way to beat seasickness. Also note that if the seas are particularly rough, the advertised 1½-hour journey can take as long as three hours.

BUS
The bus station (Map p467) is along the Sharm–Na'ama Bay road behind the Mobil petrol station. Seats on the buses to Cairo should be reserved in advance. Buy tickets from the following bus companies at the bus station.

Superjet (☎ 366 1622, in Cairo 02-2290 9017) runs buses to Cairo (E£65 to E£75, five to six hours) at noon, 1pm, 3pm, 5pm and 11pm.

East Delta Travel Co (☎ 366 0660) also has buses to Cairo (E£65 to E£75) at 7am, 10am, 11am, noon, 1pm, 2.30pm, 4.30pm and 5.30pm. There are daily buses to Suez (E£35 to E£40, five to six hours) at 7am, 9am and 10am; to Dahab (E£15 to E£20, one to two hours) and Nuweiba (E£25 to E£30, three to four hours) at 9am, 2.30pm and 5pm; and to Taba (E£30 to E£35, four to five hours) at 9am.

Getting Around
TO/FROM THE AIRPORT
Sharm el-Sheikh International Airport is about 10km north of Na'ama Bay at Ras Nasrany; taxis generally charge from E£20 to E£25 from the airport to Sharm or Na'ama Bay.

BICYCLE
Standard and cross country bicycles can be rented from stands along the promenade in Na'ama Bay from E£25 per day.

CAR
Car-rental agencies in Na'ama Bay include **Avis** (Map p470; ☎ 360 2400/0979; Sharm–Na'ama Bay rd, Na'ama Bay), just west of Mall 7; **Hertz** (Map p467; ☎ 366 2299; Bank St, Hadaba) and **Sixt Car Rental** (Map

SINAI

p470; ☎ 360 0137; Hilton Fayrouz Village). All charge about US$80 for a basic saloon, and US$120 and up for a roomier 4WD. Unlimited-kilometre arrangements generally require a minimum three- to four-day rental.

MICROBUS & TAXI

Toyota pick-ups and microbuses regularly ply the stretch between central Na'ama Bay and Sharm el-Sheikh. The going fare is E£2, though foreigners are often charged E£5. Taxis charge a minimum of E£10 between the two centres, and between Hadaba and Na'ama Bay, and from E£5 within Na'ama Bay. Many of the hotels above Ras Um Sid have their own shuttles to Na'ama Bay.

The usual warnings about hitching apply, and women should avoid it completely.

NABQ PROTECTORATE

Thirty-five kilometres north of Sharm el-Sheikh is **Nabq**, the largest coastal protectorate on the Gulf of Aqaba. Named after an oasis that lies within its boundaries, Nabq straddles 600 sq km of land and sea between the Straits of Tiran and Dahab. Because it is less frequently visited than Ras Mohammed, Nabq is a good place to see Sinai as it was before the arrival of mass tourism.

There is a **visitors centre** (admission €5; ⏰ 8am-5pm) located off the road leading from Sharm el-Sheikh past the airport and Ras Nasrany. Within the park itself, you'll find several hiking trails, clearly marked snorkelling spots and designated camping areas.

Nabq's main attraction is its **mangrove forest**, which runs along the shoreline at the mouth of Wadi Kid, and is the most northerly mangrove stand in the world. Mangrove root systems filter most of the salt from sea water and help to stabilise shorelines, while also providing an important habitat for birds and fish. Just inland from the mangrove forest are the dunes of Wadi Kid, which are home to one of the Middle East's largest stands of **arak bushes** (arak twigs were traditionally used by Bedouin to clean teeth). Gazelles, rock hyraxes and Nubian ibexes can be seen in the protectorate, as well as two villages of Bedouin from the Mizena tribe. Offshore there are rich reefs with easy access, although visibility can be poor because of sediment from the mangroves.

To visit Nabq, you'll need a vehicle or will have to join an organised tour. Most hotels and resorts in Sharm el-Sheikh and Dahab offer safaris, both on the land and in the water. If you drive, remember that vehicles are strictly forbidden to leave the tracks.

DAHAB
☎ 069

Long hailed as the 'Ko Samui of the Middle East', Dahab has a long history of luring travellers – and trapping them for days or weeks on end – with its cheap oceanside camps, golden beaches and rugged mountain backdrop. In recent years Dahab has expanded beyond its humble origins, and now boasts a smooth fusion of hippie mellowness and resort chic. The banana pancakes, moonlight spliffs and hard-core backpackers still remain, though they now coexist with upmarket restaurants, boutique hotels and holidaying European families. However, while the vast majority of Sinai is being packaged and sold for mainstream consumption, Dahab is a place where independent travellers are still the rule rather than the exception.

Meaning gold in Arabic, a reference to the area's sandy coastline, Dahab also boasts some of Egypt's most spectacular diving and trekking. A short walk, jeep ride or even camel trek will bring you to some of the Red Sea's most memorable dive sites, and a boat can bring you within easy striking distance of the world-class reefs in nearby Ras Mohammed National Park (p464). Predominantly a Bedouin enclave at its heart, Dahab is also the preferred base for organising guided excursions into the interior deserts, as well as to the lofty heights of nearby Mt Sinai (p497).

Unlike its airbrushed neighbour of Sharm el-Sheikh, Dahab is still trying to maintain its humble roots, determined to find a compromise between the lure of the tourist dollar and its fishing traditions. The balance isn't always easy, but Dahab remains one of the more authentic tourist towns in Egypt. True, a paved boardwalk now lines the beachfront area of Assalah, and the hard sell for pricey dinners by pushy restaurateurs can quickly test your nerves. However, Dahab remains what it has always been, namely a tranquil oceanside refuge from the unrelenting heat of the desert. If Dahab is in your sights, be forewarned – after a few days of crystal-clear diving, desert trekking, oceanside dinners and countless *sheesha* sessions, you're probably going to want to cancel the rest of your itinerary.

Orientation

There are two parts to Dahab: the small and newer area of Dahab City, with a smattering of resort hotels, the bus station, post and phone offices, and a bank; and Assalah, which runs along the beach and is the major tourist stretch. Assalah is further divided into Masbat, Mashraba and the Lagoon. Masbat starts at the northern end of Assalah and is made up of a stretch of 'camps', hotels and laid-back restaurants among the palm trees, as well as a busy little bazaar. To the south, starting roughly at the ruins (currently off limits as an excavation site) is the slightly more staid Mashraba, named after the freshwater springs that apparently exist around

DAHAB

0 — 400 m
0 — 0.2 miles

INFORMATION
Banque du Caire **1** A5
Call Centre .... (see 21)
Commercial International
  Bank ATM **2** C3
Dahab Hospital **3** A3
Download.Net .... (see 27)
Dr Sherif Salah .... (see 24)
Felopater Internet Café **4** D2
Felopater Internet Café **5** D2
Main Post Office **6** A4
National Bank of Egypt .... (see 33)
National Bank of Egypt (ATM) **7** A4
Police **8** D2
Telephone Centrale **9** A4
Tourist Police **10** A4
Western Union .... (see 21)

SIGHTS & ACTIVITIES
Accor Coralia Club Dahab .... (see 18)
Blue Beach Club **11** D1
Desert Divers **12** D2
Eel Garden **13** D1
Fantasea Dive Centre **14** D2
Fish & Friends **15** D2
Hilton Dahab Resort .... (see 24)
Inmo Divers Home .... (see 25)
Lighthouse Reef **16** D2
Nesima Dive Centre .... (see 27)
Penguin Divers .... (see 29)

Ruins **17** D2
Sunsplash .... (see 32)
Swiss Inn Golden Beach Resort .. (see 33)

SLEEPING
Accor Coralia Club Dahab **18** B4
Alaska Camp & Hotel **19** D2
Alf Leila **20** A5
Bamboo House Hotel **21** D2
Bishbishi Garden Village **22** A5
Christina Beach Palace **23** A5
Christina Pool .... (see 23)
Hilton Dahab Resort **24** A4
Inmo Hotel **25** A5
Jasmine Pension **26** A5
Nesima Resort **27** D3
New Sphinx Resort **28** A5
Penguin Village **29** A5
Red Sea Relax **30** D2
Seven Heaven Hotel **31** A5
Sunsplash Divers **32** D3
Swiss Inn Golden Beach Resort ... **33** A4

Telecommunications Tower

To Sharm el-Sheikh (85km);
Nuweiba (87km);
St Katherine's
Monastery (125km)

Mosque

EATING
Al Capone **34** D2
Blue Beach .... (see 31)
Carm Inn **35** D2
Funny Mummy **36** A5
Gado Restaurant **37** A5
Ghazala Supermarket **38** D2
Jay's Restaurant **39** D2
Lakhbatita **40** A5
Penguin Restaurant .... (see 29)
Tota Restaurant .... (see 41)

DRINKING
Shipwreck Bar .... (see 27)
Tota Dance Bar **41** D2

TRANSPORT
East Delta Travel Company
  Station **42** B3
Max Car Rental .... (see 24)

To Canyon & Blue Hole /
Dive Sites (6km)

Assalah

Masbat

Dahab Bay

Mashraba

See Enlargement

Gulf of Aqaba

Al-Mashraba

0 — 200 m
0 — 0.1 miles

Lagoon

Enlargement

the beach. In the centre of Masbat is a small pedestrian bridge, which makes a convenient landmark and is a good place to find taxis. Further south, and just below Dahab City, is a large lagoon shaped by a jutting peninsula that is home to several upmarket resort hotels.

Information

EMERGENCY
Police (☎ 364 0213/5; Masbat) Near Ghazala Supermarket.
Tourist police (☎ 364 0188; Dahab City)

INTERNET ACCESS
Download.Net (Nesima Resort, Mashraba; per hr E£5; 24hr)
Felopater Internet Cafe (per hr E£5); Masbat (100m south of police station on beachside promenade; 10am-midnight); Mashraba (Sharia al-Mashraba, just north of Nesima Resort; 24hr)

MEDICAL SERVICES
Dahab Hospital (☎ 364 0208; Dahab City)
Dr Sherif Salah (☎ 012 220 8484) Local doctor recommended by most hotels; office at the Hilton Dahab Resort (p482)

MONEY
Banque du Caire (Sharia Al-Mashraba, Mashraba; 9am-2pm & 6-9pm Sat-Thu, 9-11am & 6-9pm Fri) Near Inmo Hotel.
Commercial International Bank ATM (Blue Hole Plaza) About 1.5km northeast of the Hilton Dahab Resort, between the resort strip and Mashraba.
National Bank of Egypt Dahab City (9am-2.30pm & 6-8pm Sun-Thu); Swiss Inn Golden Beach Resort (resort strip; 9am-1pm) The Dahab City branch has an ATM.

POST
As well as the main post office, postboxes are also outside Ghazala Supermarket and next to Red Sea Relax Terrace Restaurant, both in Masbat.
Main post office (Dahab City; 8.30am-2.30pm)

TELEPHONE
In addition to the Telephone centrale and cardphones, you will find numerous call centres along the beachfront in Assalah where you can dial internationally for a few pounds a minute. Phonecards are sold at the Ghazala Supermarket in Masbat and at most small shops.
Call centre (Masbat; per min E£7; 10am-3pm & 6-9pm Sat-Thu, 3-9pm Fri)
Telephone centrale (Dahab City; 24hr)

Dangers & Annoyances
Although Dahab is one of the most relaxed destinations in Egypt, be advised that there is the potential for a future terrorist attack. In April 2006, suicide bombers killed 23 people and injured dozens. Although the government has cracked down on the seeds of Islamic fundamentalism since then, it remains to be seen whether or not its efforts have been effective. However, it is important to emphasise that the overwhelming majority of visitors to Dahab and the greater Sinai enjoy their time immensely, and never experience any sort of problem.

For an overview of the history of terrorism in Sinai, see p460.

Activities
SNORKELLING & DIVING
Other than just lounging around, snorkelling and diving are the most popular activities in

---

ONE TOKE OVER THE LINE

It's worth mentioning that Dahab's hippie roots and backpacker-friendly atmosphere often go hand in hand with drug use. At some point during your time here, you will most likely be offered marijuana or hashish (and possibly harder stuff), and you may see people around you openly using drugs. Although it should go without saying that the penalty for being caught with drugs in Egypt is stiff (to say the least), some misinformed travellers have the attitude that toking is legal – it's not.

While vets on the Dahab backpacking scene may fondly remember the days of smoking on the beach in broad daylight, these days police patrol their drug-sniffing dogs up and down the boardwalk, and are quick to bust travellers for smoking dope. Please heed our advice – if you're going to indulge, do it discreetly, either under cover of night or hidden away from prying eyes and sensitive nostrils. Of course, it's probably better to just stick to smoking *sheesha* (water pipe), and hold off on the herb until you get home. Trust us – you really don't want to see the inside of an Egyptian prison.

Dahab. The reefs off Assalah are often strewn with litter, but if you can ignore this, the reef at the northern end of Mashraba has table corals and impressive fish life. Also worthwhile are the reefs off the southern end of Mashraba, just before the lagoon; **Lighthouse Reef**, a sheltered snorkelling site at the northern tip of Assalah; and the popular **Eel Garden**, just north of Assalah, where a colony of eels lives on the sandy seabed.

About 6km further north are the **Canyon** and **Blue Hole** dive sites. Despite their intimidating reputation as danger zones for careless divers, the tops of the reefs are teeming with life, making them fine snorkelling destinations when the sea is calm. It's easy to find half-day tours to both sites, but watch for hidden 'extras', such as overpriced drinks and gear-minding fees at some of the cafes around the Blue Hole.

Many dive centres also organise snorkelling and dive safaris to the nearby **Ras Abu Gallum** (p483) and **Nabq** (p476) protectorates, as well as overnights to **Ras Mohammed National Park** (p464).

You can hire snorkelling gear from all the dive centres and many other places in Masbat for about E£25 to E£40 per day. Keep in mind that some of the reefs have unexpected currents – drownings have occurred in Dahab – so keep your wits about you. And, although this should go without saying, lay off the drinking and drugging if you're going to be in open seas.

For an overview of diving in the Red Sea, including recommended operators and dive sites, see p441.

CAMEL & JEEP SAFARIS

Dahab is one of the best places in Sinai to arrange camel safaris into the dramatic mountains lining the coast, especially the spectacular Ras Abu Gallum Protectorate. When choosing who to go with, try to find a Bedouin – or at least an operator that works with the Bedouin. Unfortunately, local communities have been excluded from the tourist industry, which tends to be dominated by migrants from the Nile Valley. A good place to look is the waterfront in the village, where camel drivers tend to congregate. Register with the police before beginning the safari, and don't pay the camel driver until you return to the village. Itineraries – and as a result prices – are generally custom designed, but expect to pay from E£75 to E£100 per person for an

evening trip into the mountains with dinner at a Bedouin camp, and from about E£300 to E£400 per person per day for a safari including all food and water.

Centre for Sinai (☎ 364 0702; www.centre4sinai.com .eg) is one organisation that tries to promote knowledge of the local culture. **Man & the Environment Dahab** (MATE; ☎ 364 1091; www.mate -info.com) is an environmental education group that helps arrange treks with Bedouin guides. Contact both organisations via telephone or email in order to arrange tours around Sinai.

One of the most popular jeep safaris is a trip to Coloured Canyon, between St Katherine and Nuweiba. The canyon derives its name from the layers of bright, multicoloured stones that resemble paintings on its steep, narrow walls, and is magnificently beautiful. As the canyon is sheltered from the wind, the silence – assuming you aren't there with a crowd – is one of its most impressive features. Unfortunately, the canyon has become overtouristed in recent years, and many operators have also begun offering trips to other sites, where the rock formations are equally impressive and the sense of wilderness more intact. All of the hotels, dive centres and travel agencies offer jeep safaris, though prices vary considerably depending on the time of year, your destination and the size of your party – don't be afraid to shop around and bargain hard.

WATER SPORTS

Pedalos, kayaks and jet skis can be rented at the northern end of Masbat and at the holiday villages on the lagoon. Although the golden hills of Saudi Arabia in the distance seem to make for an excellent destination, trust us – you don't want to try to cross. At least one Japanese backpacker we know of managed to touch Saudi soil, only to be rounded up and arrested by some rather unhappy border guards.

Windsurfing is another popular pastime, and the **Hilton Dahab Resort** (☎ 364 0310; www .hilton.com; resort strip) and **Swiss Inn Golden Beach Resort** (☎ 364 0054; www.swissinn.net/dahab; resort strip) have good windsurfing centres. The centre of the bay boasts the steadiest winds in Dahab, though strong gusts occasionally sweep across the northern end. Kitesurfing is also starting to take off in Dahab, although offshore winds limit the areas where it can be done.

There's no beach to speak of in Assalah itself – instead the rocky coastline leads straight out onto the reef. For the golden sands after which Dahab was named, you'll need to head down to the lagoon area where the resorts are clustered.

HORSE RIDING

If you want to go riding, just wait on the beach in Mashraba for one of the Bedouin who walk up and down with horses for hire. Rates start at about E£20 to E£40 per hour. You can also ask around the camps. **Blue Beach Club** (☎ 364 0411; www.bluebeachclub.com; Assalah) and the **Accor Coralia Club Dahab** (☎ 364 0301; www.accorhotel.com; resort strip) can also arrange organised horse-riding excursions.

Sleeping

For a small village perched on the tip of Sinai, Dahab has an incredibly diverse range of accommodation. Most budget travellers head straight for the camps of Assalah, which vary considerably, from spartan stone, cement or reed huts with a mattress tossed on the floor to attractive backpacker palaces with cushioned seating shaded by palm groves. Generally speaking, long gone are the days of grubby tented camps on the beach. Increased competition has raised the bar in Dahab, and there are some excellent rooms to be had for the price of a decent meal back home.

Dahab's upward push has also resulted in the construction of a good number of midrange hotels scattered among the budget accommodation in Assalah. And, if you want to enjoy the Dahab vibe in slightly more comfortable surroundings, there are a number of swish boutique hotels and resorts in town, particularly on the shores of the lagoon near Dahab City.

Be advised that the following list is a small sampling of what is available – new places are going up all the time, while older establishments are being knocked down. Also keep in mind that prices are not to be taken at face value – most places drop their prices considerably during the low season, and fixed prices only exist in name in Egypt.

Finally, if you're looking to arrange any activities, it's best to enquire through your hotel as discounts are readily available for guests.

BUDGET

Seven Heaven Hotel (☎ 364 0080; www.7heavenhotel .com; Masbat; huts/bungalows with shared facilities US$6/8,

r from US$14; 🖳) This pleasant family-run hotel is one of the cheapest places to crash in Dahab, though it offers surprising value for your money. Die-hard shoestringers can bed down in pairs in the rough but ready huts and bungalows lining the beaches, though a few extra dollars can net you a modern private room complete with tiled bathroom. As in most of the budget hotels in town, you'll find a good range of amenities including a dive shop, a tour booking centre and fairly reliable internet access.

Bishbishi Garden Village (☎ 364 0727; www.bish bishi.com; Mashraba; s €5-13, d €10-19, tr €21-23; 🗶 🖳) Set back from the sea on the street parallel to the waterfront is this classic backpacker spot. Guests congregate in several cushion-strewn and palm-shaded public spaces, as well as the adjacent Funny Mummy (see p482), one of Dahab's signature restaurants. Rooms are fairly basic, with air-conditioning and en-suite options available, though you'll spend most of your time here lounging about while chatting up travellers from near and far.

Penguin Village (☎ 364 1047; www.penguindivers .com; Mashraba; s €7-20, d €10-25, tr €22-30; 🖳) Another enduring backpacker favourite, the Penguin serves up its own brand of Bedouin chic, complete with pillow lounges overlooking the sand and sea that are best appreciated with several friends and a towering hookah. Once again, there is a mix of rooms to suit all budgets – from no-frills fan-cooled concrete boxes to air-con rooms with wooden balconies. Whether you desire a dive holiday or a pilgrimage up Sinai, the helpful and jovial staff are quick to sort you out.

Sunsplash Divers (☎ 364 0932; www.sunsplash -divers.com; Mashraba; r E£60-140; 🗶 🖳) A friendly German-run dive operation set on its own at the southern end of Mashraba, Sunsplash offers the standard Dahab formula of simple but comfortable bungalows and private rooms. Diving is the main attraction, and the highly professional centre has an excellent reputation built on years of experience. There's a good restaurant that offers a healthy mix of Deutschland favourites, as well as the obligatory beachside lounge.

Jasmine Pension (☎ 364 0852; www.jasmine pension.com; Mashraba; s €10-15, d €15-20, tr €25-30; 🗶 🖳) Located at the southern end of Mashraba, this low-key pension is a good choice for travellers looking for a tranquil yet affordable spot. Nine pleasantly decorated rooms with polished wood accents overlook the beach, and a few extra euros nets you a private balcony perfectly suited for quiet reflection. The on-site restaurant is a good choice for sipping a cold Stella while staring at the starry Sinai sky.

Inmo Hotel (☎ 364 0370; www.inmodivers.de; Mashraba; s €11-40, d €22-54; ✖ ▢ ✿) Boasting colourful rooms, domed ceilings and attractive furniture, this well-run, family-friendly hotel caters both to shoestringing backpackers in search of cheap but comfortable rooms, as well as more upmarket travellers on diving packages from Europe. With a presence in Dahab dating back over 20 years, Inmo is well regarded in town, especially when it comes to its highly recommended dive shop. Guests can also take advantage of the owners' knowledge of the Bedouin community, which makes for some memorable custom-tailored desert trips.

Alaska Camp & Hotel (☎ 364 1004; www.dahab escape.com; Masbat; r E£90-180; ▢) Another budget place that is friendly on the wallet, Alaska Camp & Hotel is looking shinier than ever thanks to some recent renovations. Offering an assortment of rooms with varying levels of comfort, this is more of a private-minded hotel than a boisterous camp, though it's still just steps away from the beach and the boardwalk. Simple fan-cooled rooms don't exactly evoke the feeling of Alaska, though slightly more expensive air-conditioned rooms cater to fussy sleepers who prefer the chill.

Bamboo House Hotel (☎ 364 0263; www.bam boohouse-dahab.com; Masbat; r US$20-35; ✖ ▢) Centrally located near the bridge in Masbat, this Asian-themed hotel is styled in cool, crisp lines and soft, pastel colours. The largish rooms positively lighten up when the sun is shining, and are expectedly heavy on the bamboo. Although it's lacking the community feeling found at other hotels, it's a good spot if you want to unwind in the comfort your own room.

Red Sea Relax (☎ 364 1309; www.red-sea-relax.com; Masbat; dm €12, s/d from €35/40; ✖ ▢ ✿) With a brand-new location a couple of hundred metres from the lighthouse in the north end of the bay, this surprisingly affordable hotel adds the 'Relax' to the Red Sea. The compound is centred on a glistening pool that adds a touch of resort class, as does the rooftop bar that beckons you with the promise of a fruit smoothie. Attractive dormitories are constructed of rich woods, while more expensive private rooms

have modern fixtures and provide quiet sanctuary from the bustling boardwalk.

MIDRANGE & TOP END
Some of the following hotels, particularly at the top end of the price scale, offer discounted rates if you book in advance via the internet.

New Sphinx Resort (☎ 548 8708; www.sphinxdahab .com; Mashraba; d from US$55; ✖ ▢ ✿) Somewhat akin to an upmarket backpacker spot, this perennially popular miniresort offers a slightly more refined take on the Bedouin camp theme that dominates Dahab's budget scene. There are still plenty of pillow lounges and *sheesha* spots to retire to, though the sprawling swimming pool and umbrella-shaded sun deck is a wonderfully swish complement. Accommodation at the New Sphinx is solely in privates, though its sibling property, the Sphinx Hotel, which offers dormitories and shoestringing singles and doubles, should open after extensive renovations during the shelf life of this book.

Alf Leila (☎ 364 0595; www.alfleila.com; Mashraba; r from US$60; ✖ ▢ ✿) At long last, Dahab has a boutique hotel that pays tribute to the distinct architectural design elements that have emerged over the centuries from the Arab world. With just eight rooms and four studios that are uniquely designed and decorated, Alf Leila offers individualised attention and service amid truly florid surroundings. While the property is 'A 1001 Arabian Nights' at every turn, the 1st-floor German bakery is an incongruous but wholly welcomed finishing touch.

Christina Beach Palace & Christina Pool (☎ 364 0390; www.christinahotels.com; Mashraba; s €28-40, d €36-52; ✖ ▢ ✿) These small Swiss-run hotels offer a degree of European sophistication that is matched by few other hotels in Dahab. Both hotels offer classically designed rooms – with just a touch of Arabic architectural accents – that boast modern amenities and luxurious bathrooms. Depending on your preference, the Christina Beach Palace is (appropriately enough) a palace-like compound on the beach, while the Christina Pool is more of a chateau fronted by an immaculate pool.

Nesima Resort (☎ 364 0320; www.nesima-resort.com; Mashraba; s/d/ste €55/65/90; ✖ ▢ ✿) Overlooking the beach in Mashraba, this modest resort is a compromise for those who want resort living without feeling as if they're isolated from the town. With pleasing stone and wood overtones

SINAI

and soaring domes, rooms at Nesima induce calm, relaxed feelings for all who stay here. The most attractive feature of the property is without a doubt the palm-tree-lined infinity-edge pool, which regally overlooks the beach and the boardwalk.

Accor Coralia Club Dahab (☎ 364 0301; www.accor hotel.com; resort strip; s/d from US$95/120; 🖾 💻 🖳) One of the most affordable top-end hotels in Dahab, this branch of the Accor Coralia chain offers 140 rooms of varying sizes, shapes and views. Set on 650m of sandy beach, the Club Dahab is one of the few hotels in town where you can lie out on a sandy beach to your heart's content. Much like other Accor hotels around the world, Club Dahab is brimming with amenities, including a dive centre, pool complex, gymnasium, health spa, and a whole slew of bars and restaurants.

Swiss Inn Golden Beach Resort (☎ 364 0054; www .swissinn.net/dahab; resort strip; s/d from €70/90; 🖾 💻 🖳) This family-friendly four-star resort has well-appointed rooms and a pleasantly unpretentious ambience. Entire days can be spent lounging around the flower-fringed pool and stunning stretch of golden sand, though there's always the on-site dive and windsurfing centre if you want to get active. The Swiss Inn is home to a number of recommendable restaurants, including a pleasant poolside cafe and a European-inspired bistro.

Hilton Dahab Resort (☎ 364 0310; www.hilton.com; resort strip; r from US$125; 🖾 💻 🖳) The five-star Hilton is the big boy on the block and easily the swankiest hotel in the Dahab area. Though it's more subdued than some of its flashier cousins around the world, the whitewashed, domed two-storey villas are still a class act. On offer are two pools, an immaculate beach, a play area for children and a full range of water sports, including a highly professional dive centre.

Eating

The waterfront is lined with restaurants, the majority of which are Bedouin-style beachfront seating areas where you can relax on cushions while gazing out over the sparkling waters of the Gulf of Aqaba. Seafood is on almost all menus, together with a good selection of pizza, pasta, meat and vegetarian dishes. All places also serve the requisite apple *sheesha* and mint tea, perfect for chilling out and letting Dahab work its magic on you.

Gado Restaurant (Sharia al-Mashraba; meals E£5-15) We don't know how it's possible to serve such generous portions of hearty cuisine at these prices, but we do know that the traditional Egyptian fare at Gado is damn good, and worth every pound.

Jay's Restaurant (Masbat; dishes E£25-55) A Dahab institution serving a mixture of Egyptian and Western fare at very reasonable prices – the menu changes weekly, and dishes such as coconut rice and curried vegetables make a welcome change from the usual offerings.

Tota Restaurant (Masbat; dishes E£25-60) This unmissable boat-shaped bar (see opposite) in the heart of Assalah also serves decent Italian cuisine, including large pizzas and pasta dishes, plus a range of other meals and desserts.

Carm Inn (Masbat; dishes E£30-70) This waterfront place is a favourite of local dive instructors, with a varied menu of Western, Indian and Indonesian dishes served in mellow surroundings with a hint of the South Pacific.

Blue Beach (Masbat; dishes E£35-85) The headlining restaurant at the Seven Heaven Hotel contributes to the Thai beach party flair that characterises much of Dahab by offering authentic South-East Asian–style curries.

our pick Funny Mummy (Mashraba; dishes E£35-85) One of the most popular restaurants on the boardwalk, this palm-fringed and pillow-decked spot offers all of your favourite Western and Asian dishes alongside traditional Egyptian delicacies.

Penguin Restaurant (Mashraba; dishes E£35-85) A traveller favourite, the oceanside restaurant at this backpacker hotel serves an eclectic menu ranging from pancakes and English fry-ups in the morning to Thai curries and Italian pasta dishes in the evening.

Al Capone (at the bridge; dishes E£40-95) Sure, it's packed to the brim with tourists, but the impressive seafood offering, bridgeside location, and the occasional live music and belly dancing make the strangely named Al Capone an obligatory stop.

Lakhbatita (Mashraba; dishes E£45-115) This eccentric beachfront establishment at the southern end of Mashraba is decorated with old Egyptian furniture, and serves gourmet food drawing on Egyptian, Middle Eastern, Asian and Continental influences.

For self-caterers, there are numerous supermarkets dotted around Assalah, including the **Ghazala Supermarket** (Masbat; 🕙 8am-2am), near the main junction at the southern end of Masbat.

Drinking

In comparison with Hurghada and Sharm el-Sheikh, Dahab is fairly quiet at night, but there is a good selection of lively bars, some of which turn into discos if the atmosphere is right. Of course, after a long day of diving and desert exploration, most travellers are content with sprawling out in any of Dahab's waterfront restaurants and nursing a few cold Stellas.

Shipwreck Bar (Nesima Resort, Mashraba) A popular rooftop bar with great views over the sea, which attracts a sophisticated crowd with its daily happy-hour specials.

Tota Dance Bar (Masbat) The centre of nightlife in Dahab, this nautically themed drinking spot has free movies from Sunday to Thursday, and turns into an impromptu disco on Friday and Saturday nights – the top deck is a good place to watch the sunset while sipping a cold beer, especially during the 5pm to 7pm happy hour.

Getting There & Away
BUS

From the bus station in Dahab City, well southwest of the centre of the action, **East Delta Travel Co** (☎ 364 1808) has buses to Sharm el-Sheikh (E£15 to E£20, one to two hours) departing at 8am, 8.30am, 10am, 11.30am, 12.30pm, 2.30pm, 4pm, 5.30pm, 8.30pm and 10pm. Buses to Nuweiba (E£15 to E£20, one hour) leave at 8.30am and 10.30am, with the 10.30am bus continuing on to Taba (E£35, two hours).

There is a 9.30am bus to St Katherine (E£20 to E£25, two to three hours), though it's much more convenient to organise a service taxi or private vehicle in the late afternoon. Buses heading to Cairo (E£60 to E£70, nine hours) depart at 8.30am, 12.30pm, 2.30pm and 7.30pm. There is also a bus to Luxor (E£130, 14 to 16 hours) departing at 4pm, which, while long, is a faster and less expensive option than going via Hurghada on a combination of bus and ferry.

Most hotels and camps can arrange your bus tickets for you, plus transport to the bus station, for about E£10 to E£15 extra. Be sure to check departure times with hotel staff as they're subject to change without notice, especially in the off season.

SERVICE TAXI

Service taxis in Dahab are generally more expensive than buses, and as travellers are a captive market, there's usually not much room for negotiation. Per-person rates (multiply these by seven to charter an entire taxi) average about E£45 for St Katherine, E£20 to Nuweiba and E£25 to Sharm el-Sheikh, though prices can fluctuate significantly depending on the price of fuel.

Getting Around

Pick-ups and minibuses go up and down the main street in Assalah and, less frequently, around the resort strip. The usual fare is E£1 for around town, and E£3 if you find one doing the entire stretch between Assalah and Dahab City. In addition to a handful of taxis, a minibus usually meets incoming buses at the East Delta Travel Co's Dahab City station and goes up to Assalah. Departing from Assalah, you'll need to rely on taxis to get to the bus station (E£5 to E£10).

Max Car Rental (☎ 364 0310; www.max-car-rental.com) has a branch at the Hilton Dahab Resort.

RAS ABU GALLUM PROTECTORATE

The starkly beautiful Ras Abu Gallum Protectorate covers 400 sq km of coastline between Dahab and Nuweiba, mixing coastal mountains, narrow valleys, sand dunes and fine-gravel beaches with several excellent diving and snorkelling sites. Scientists describe the area as a 'floristic frontier', in which Mediterranean conditions are influenced by a tropical climate. This, together with its 165 plant species (including 44 that are found nowhere else in Sinai) and wealth of mammals and reptiles, gives it great environmental importance and makes it a fascinating place to visit.

As in nearby Nabq, Bedouin of the Mizena tribe live within the protectorate confines, fishing here as they have done for centuries (although this is now regulated by the protectorate). There is a designated camping area and several walking trails, and you can hire Bedouin guides and camels through the ranger house at the edge of **Wadi Rasasah**. Otherwise, there are no facilities and no visitors centre. Popular destinations within the protectorate include **Bir el-Oghda**, a now-deserted Bedouin village, and **Bir Sugheir**, a water source at the edge of the protectorate.

SINAI

Dive centres and travel agencies in Nuweiba and Dahab offer camel and jeep excursions to Abu Gallum, often as part of a diving safari. If you are driving, remember that all vehicles should stick to the tracks. The entry track off the main highway is unsignposted. The protectorate can also be reached by hiking in from north of the Blue Hole near Dahab.

NUWEIBA

☎ 069

Turquoise waters edged by fine, sandy beaches and rimmed on both sides by barren, rugged mountain chains give Nuweiba one of the most attractive settings among Sinai's resort towns. Stretched randomly over about 15km, Nuweiba lacks a defined centre and a cohesive ambience, and functions primarily as a port town rather than a travellers' retreat. As a result, Nuweiba has never managed to attract the cult following of nearby Dahab, or the massive development of Sharm el-Sheikh. Most travellers pass through Nuweiba either on their way to the scenic camps and resorts near the Israeli border, or to catch the Aqaba-bound ferry en route to Petra in Jordan.

Yet the lack of crowds gives Nuweiba its own appeal, and the town makes a reasonable stop if you're working your way up or down the coast. Nuweiba is also a good place to organise jeep and camel safaris into the interior, and its modest diving scene means that its offshore reefs are comparatively uncrowded. Although it's perhaps not a tourist destination in itself, a number of low-key resorts and backpacker-friendly camps make Nuweiba a pleasant enough place to spend a few days.

History

Following the conquest of Sinai during the Six Day War in 1967, Nuweiba under Israeli occupation became the site of a large moshav (farming settlement), which drew in Israeli settlers and tourists alike. Following the Egypt-Israel peace treaty of 1979, Sinai was returned to Egypt, and Israeli settlements were disbanded, though a thriving Israeli tourist trade continued. For a brief period, Nuweiba could claim rivalry to Dahab and even to Sharm el-Sheikh. However, due to the vagaries of the regional political situation over the subsequent decades, coupled with the fallout from the two Persian Gulf wars, Israeli travellers have all for the most part shunned Nuweiba – and much of Sinai for that matter.

While Sharm has boomed under the waves of foreign and domestic investment, and Dahab has grown steadily into a low-key resort town, Nuweiba has been left to go to seed. Ambitious tourism projects aimed at transforming the region have ground to a halt, and today the outskirts of Nuweiba, and indeed much of the coastline north to Taba, is littered with the shells of half-built resorts. The skeletal remains of failed construction projects can certainly be a bit depressing, though the comparative lack of tourists means that Nuweiba is more authentically Egyptian than other coastal towns along the peninsula.

Orientation

Nuweiba is divided into three parts: to the south is the port, with a bus station, banks and a couple of scruffy hotels; about 8km further north is Nuweiba City, a small but spread-out settlement with a variety of accommodation options, a small bazaar and several cheap places to eat; and about a 10-minute walk north along the beach is Tarabin, Nuweiba's equivalent of Dahab's Assalah area.

Information

EMERGENCY

Tourist police Nuweiba City (☎ 350 0231; near Nuweiba Village hotel; ☯ 24hr); Nuweiba Port (☎ 350 0401)

INTERNET ACCESS

Al-Mostakbal Internet Café (☎ 350 0090; Nuweiba City; per hr E£4; ☯ 9am-3am)

MEDICAL SERVICES

Nuweiba Hospital (☎ 350 0302; Nuweiba City; ☯ 24hr) Just off the Main East Coast Hwy to Dahab.

MONEY

Neither of the banks at the port will handle Jordanian dinars.
Banque du Caire (Nuweiba Port; ☯ 9am-2pm Sun-Thu) Has an ATM.
Banque Misr (Nuweiba Port; ☯ 8.30am-2pm Sun-Thu) Has an ATM.
National Bank of Egypt (Nuweiba Village; ☯ 9am-1pm & 7-9pm Sat-Thu, 9-11am Fri) Has an ATM.

POST

Branch post office (Nuweiba Port; ☯ 8.30am-2.30pm Sun-Thu)

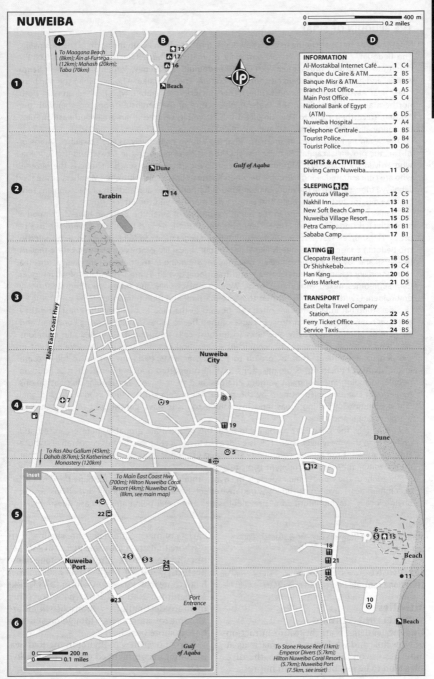

NUWEIBA

0 — 400 m
0 — 0.2 miles

To Maagana Beach
(8km); Ain al-Furtega
(12km); Mahash (20km);
Taba (70km)

Beach

Gulf of Aqaba

Dune

Tarabin

Main East Coast Hwy

Nuweiba
City

To Ras Abu Gallum (45km);
Dahab (87km); St Katherine's
Monastery (120km)

Dune

Inset

To Main East Coast Hwy
(700m); Hilton Nuweiba Coral
Resort (4km); Nuweiba City
(8km, see main map)

Nuweiba
Port

Beach

Port
Entrance

Gulf
of Aqaba

0 — 200 m
0 — 0.1 miles

Beach

To Stone House Reef (1km);
Emperor Divers (5.7km);
Hilton Nuweiba Coral Resort
(5.7km); Nuweiba Port
(7.5km, see inset)

INFORMATION		
Al-Mostakbal Internet Café	**1**	C4
Banque du Caire & ATM	**2**	B5
Banque Misr & ATM	**3**	B5
Branch Post Office	**4**	A5
Main Post Office	**5**	C4
National Bank of Egypt (ATM)	**6**	D5
Nuweiba Hospital	**7**	A4
Telephone Centrale	**8**	B5
Tourist Police	**9**	B4
Tourist Police	**10**	D6

SIGHTS & ACTIVITIES		
Diving Camp Nuweiba	**11**	D6

SLEEPING		
Fayrouza Village	**12**	C5
Nakhil Inn	**13**	B1
New Soft Beach Camp	**14**	B2
Nuweiba Village Resort	**15**	D5
Petra Camp	**16**	B1
Sababa Camp	**17**	B1

EATING		
Cleopatra Restaurant	**18**	D5
Dr Shishkebab	**19**	C4
Han Kang	**20**	D6
Swiss Market	**21**	D5

TRANSPORT		
East Delta Travel Company Station	**22**	A5
Ferry Ticket Office	**23**	B6
Service Taxis	**24**	B5

SINAI

THE BEDOUIN OF SINAI

Sinai's rugged tracts are home to desert dwellers, most of whom live in the north of the peninsula. The Bedouin – whose numbers are variously estimated to be between 80,000 and 300,000 – belong to 14 distinct tribes, most with ties to Bedouin in the Negev, Jordan and northern Saudi Arabia, and each with their own customs and culture. The Sukwarka, who live along the northern coast near Al-Arish, are the largest tribe. Others include the Tarabin, who have territory in both northern and southern Sinai; the Tyaha in the centre of the peninsula who, together with the Tarabin, trace their roots to Palestine; and the Haweitat, centred in an area southeast of Suez, and originally from the Hejaz in Saudi Arabia.

The seven Bedouin tribes in southern Sinai are known collectively as the Towara or 'Arabs of Al-Tor', the provincial capital. Of these, the first to settle in Sinai were the Aleiqat and the Suwalha, who arrived soon after the Muslim conquest of Egypt. The largest southern tribe is the Mizena, who are concentrated along the coast between Sharm el-Sheikh and Nuweiba. Members of the tiny Jabaliyya tribe, centred in the mountains around St Katherine, are descendants of Macedonians sent by the Emperor Justinian to build and protect the monastery in the 6th century.

Thanks to centuries of living in the harsh conditions of Sinai, the Bedouin have developed a sophisticated understanding of their environment. Strict laws and traditions govern the use of precious resources. Water use is closely regulated and vegetation carefully conserved, as revealed in the Bedouin adage 'killing a tree is like killing a soul'. Local life centres on clans and their *sheikhs* (leaders), and loyalty and hospitality – essential for surviving in the desert – are paramount. Tea is traditionally taken in rounds of three, and traditional dwellings are tents made of woven goat hair, sometimes mixed with sheep wool. Women's black veils and robes are often elaborately embroidered, with red signifying that they are married, and blue unmarried.

Sinai's original inhabitants are often left behind in the race to build up the coast, and they are sometimes viewed with distrust because of their ties to tribes in neighbouring countries, and allegations of criminal activity and links to terrorist cells throughout Sinai. Bedouin traditions also tend to come second to the significant economical benefits brought by development in the peninsula – benefits that, according to Bedouin activists, Bedouins are yet to fully experience. Egyptian human rights organisations have also reported ongoing persecution of Bedouin people, including imprisonment without charges, and there have been regular demonstrations by Bedouin claiming mistreatment by the police. These concerns, as well as loss of traditional lands, pollution of fishing areas, and insensitive tourism, have contributed to the sense of marginalisation and unrest.

Fortunately, the news isn't all bad – indeed, the Bedouin are arguably more organised and unified than they have ever been. This is evident in their recent formation of cooperatives whose aims are to grant the greater community sustained economic independence, and to ensure that their traditional desert environment is protected.

Throughout the world – and especially in Egypt – tourism has the power to shape the destinies of communities. Travellers can limit any negative effects by seeking out Bedouin-owned businesses, buying locally, staying informed of prevalent issues and never being afraid to ask questions.

Main post office (Nuweiba City; ✆ 8.30am-2.30pm Sun-Thu)

TELEPHONE
Telephone centrale (Nuweiba City; ✆ 24hr)

Activities
SNORKELLING & DIVING
Underwater delights are the feature attraction of Nuweiba, and while not as dramatic as at other resorts on the Gulf of Aqaba, the dive sites tend to be less busy, with an impressive variety of marine life. There are shallow reefs offshore that are reasonable places to snorkel, but the best snorkelling is the **Stone House Reef** just south of town. Divers sometimes head to nearby Ras Abu Gallum (p483), Ras Mohammed National Park (p464) or other offshore destinations – many of which are also fine for snorkellers – though most diving here is shore based.

For an overview of diving in the Red Sea, including recommended operators and dive sites, see p441.

CAMEL & JEEP SAFARIS

With the exception of Dahab, Nuweiba is the best place in Sinai to arrange camel safaris into the interior. When planning your trip, keep in mind that camels are a slower and – if budget is a worry – more expensive way of travelling. However, they allow you to reach places that are inaccessible to vehicles, and are the best way to see the area. Almost every camp and shop in Tarabin offers these trips, but take care that whoever you pick is a local Bedouin – not only are they marginalised by tour operators from the Nile Valley and therefore need the work, but there have been some instances of travellers lost in the desert without water because their so-called guides didn't know the routes.

Register with the police before beginning the safari, and don't pay the camel driver until you return to the village. Itineraries – and as a result prices – are generally custom designed, but expect to pay from E£75 to E£100 per person for an evening trip into the mountains with dinner at a Bedouin camp, and from about E£300 to E£400 per person per day for a safari including all food and water.

All of the camps and shops also offer jeep safaris, though prices vary considerably depending on the time of year, your destination and the size of your party – don't be afraid to shop around and bargain hard.

In addition to trips to the popular **Coloured Canyon** (see p479 for more information), other popular destinations are **Ain al-Furtega**, a palm-filled oasis 16km northwest of Nuweiba; and **Mayat el-Wishwashi**, a large cistern hidden between two boulders in a canyon – it used to be the largest cistern in Sinai but now has only a trickle of water, except after floods. Nearby is **Mayat Malkha**, a palm grove fed by the waters of Mayat el-Wishwashi and set amid colourful sandstone.

Wadi Huweiyit is an impressive sandstone canyon with lookouts giving panoramic views over to Saudi Arabia. **Ain Khudra** (Green Spring) is where Miriam was supposed to have been struck by leprosy for criticising Moses. The picturesque **Ain Umm Ahmed** is the largest oasis in eastern Sinai, with lots of palms, Bedouin houses and a famous stream that becomes an icy river in the winter months.

Further afield, **Wadi Sheikh Atiya** is named after the father of the Tarabin tribe – the largest tribe in the area – who lies buried here under a white dome. There is an oasis here

and Bedouin frequently come on pilgrimage. **Gebel Barga** is a mountain that is difficult to climb, yet affords stunning views over the mountains of eastern Sinai.

Sleeping

Nuweiba City is the area's principal population centre, and home to a collection of mostly midrange hotels plus a few low-key backpacker camps. Since Nuweiba primarily serves as a port city, this area is sprawling and decidedly lacking in character – getting around can be a pain, so it's best to grab a taxi and choose a camp instead of going door to door looking for the best price. However, there are a few decent accommodation options here, and it's a convenient place to spend the night if you're catching the ferry to Jordan the following day.

Most backpackers and independent travellers prefer Tarabin, which is essentially a pedestrian-only boardwalk that stretches along the waterfront for 1.5km. Since the resurgence of the intifada (the Palestinian uprising against Israeli authorities), Tarabin has been very quiet, although it continues to attract a trickle of visitors. While many of the original camps have either closed or gone upmarket, it's still possible to find a number of interesting spots.

Be advised that the following list is a small sampling of what is available – the listings below are well-established spots that have weathered the storm in light of decreasing tourism. Also keep in mind that prices are not to be taken at face value – most rooms are subject to bargaining, especially if there aren't too many tourists in town. If you also want to arrange activities, it's best to enquire through your hotel as discounts are readily available for guests.

For more sleeping options along the Nuweiba to Taba coastline, see p490.

Sababa Camp (☎ 350 0855; huts from E£20) One of the first beach camps to set up shop in Tarabin, Sababa has survived the dramatic upward and downward swings that have characterised tourism in Nuweiba. While there are many explanations for the camp's success, the fact is that Sababa has stuck to the simple but highly effective formula of offering dirt-cheap accommodation without sacrificing basic creature comforts. Spartan wooden shacks are hard-wired for electricity, shared bathrooms have reliable bursts of hot water,

SINAI

and the Bedouin staff members are keen to extend their hospitality.

Petra Camp (☎ 350 0086; huts from E£20) A much-loved camp that has also been rocking out the Tarabin scene since the very beginning, Petra Camp remains one of the nicest budget accommodation places in town. The centrepiece here is an atmospheric open-air restaurant that was constructed from recycled wood salvaged from a defunct Cairo theatre. As with Sababa Camp, you can rely on the basics while kicking back in your beach hut, though most travellers are here to maximise their pursuit of sun, sand and sea, which are thankfully served up in heaping portions.

New Soft Beach Camp (☎ 010 364 7586; www.soft beachcamp.com; huts per person from E£30; 🖳) Located at the quieter end of Tarabin near the dunes, the New Soft Beach has one of the best settings in Nuweiba. The camp consists of rustic but picturesque huts with communal outdoor showers and attractive gardens, and there is also a good restaurant on the premises where you can sample some local Bedouin favourites. Although Soft Beach has its fair share of adoring fans, we have unfortunately received a number of complaints regarding the camp's cleanliness, and it was starting to look a little rough around the edges during our most recent visit.

Fayrouza Village (☎ 350 1133; www.sinai-camp .com; huts per person from US$7) Yet another shoe-stringer's paradise, the Fayrouza Village has a convenient location at the edge of Nuweiba City and in front of a reef. Like the competition, the camp consists of simple but spotless huts overlooking the water, communal bathrooms, a small restaurant serving filling, tasty meals, and around-the-clock opportunities for snorkelling – quite literally at your doorstep. If you're arriving in Nuweiba by bus, ask to be dropped off at the hospital, from where it's a 10-minute walk down to Fayrouza.

Nakhil Inn (☎ 350 0879; www.nakhil-inn.com; r from US$40; 🖾) At the northern end of Tarabin is this charming inn, comprising attached wooden bungalows, which front a large patio area, and are strung along a private beachfront. Interiors are a soothing mix of stained woods and natural tiles (a pleasant alternative to much of the concrete that lines the beachfronts in Egypt), and the fireplace-warmed restaurant is wonderfully atmospheric on a cold winter's night. Guests

can also take advantage of the on-site yoga studio, which will put you in the right mood to enjoy the relaxing ambience of Tarabin.

Nuweiba Village Resort (☎ 350 0401; www.nuweiba villageresort.com; r from US$60; 🖾 🖳 🖳) The Village Resort is a good choice for affordable upmarket accommodation in Nuweiba – the main hotel area consists of a collection of attached bungalow-style rooms overlooking a central garden area. Most guests focus their time and energies on the sun-drenched beach, though you can always take a break from the sun and indulge in the three-star amenities including an attractive pool and a well-stocked water-sports centre. The Village has a private location at the southern end of Nuweiba City off the main coastal road.

Hilton Nuweiba Coral Resort (☎ 352 0320; www .hiltonworldresorts.com; Nuweiba Port; r from US$120; 🖾 🖳 🖳) Nuweiba's most sophisticated hotel is this immaculate resort, which boasts lush gardens, a free-form infinity pool, posh restaurants and bars, a private stretch of soft sand, and all the usual five-star amenities. Accommodation is in a variety of rooms ranging from contemporary designs with Western-style furnishings to whitewashed bungalows with Bedouin-style interiors. It's located about 2.5km south of the Tropicana, and about 4km via road from the port area.

Eating

At the port there is a cluster of *fuul* and *ta'amiyya* places in the area behind the National Bank of Egypt and before the ticket office for Aqaba ferries. If you'd prefer a bit more than a quick bite, however, the selection is much better in and around Nuweiba City, where you have a choice of several small eateries or the hotel restaurants. If you're out in Tarabin, you'll probably take meals at your camp or hotel – most of the camps also have self-catering facilities if you're cooking your own grub.

Swiss Market (Nuweiba City) Self-caterers can try this popular local market, which has a good selection of the basics, as well as a decent stock of local produce and fresh cuts of meat.

Dr Shishkebab (Bazaar Nuweiba City; dishes E£10-30) This place is just what the doctor ordered, with generous spreads of Egyptian favourites from hearty fried eggplant and hummus to delectable *daoud basha* (meatballs in a rich tomato sauce).

Han Kang (Nuweiba City; dishes E£20-40) Although you're a long way from the Far East, this surprisingly good Chinese restaurant hits the spot, especially if you've been on the road for a while and can't bear to look at another felafel sandwich.

Cleopatra Restaurant (Nuweiba City; dishes E£20-50) One of the more popular tourist restaurants in Nuweiba City, Cleopatra offers up the bounty of the sea, Lebanese-inspired mezze platters, wood-fired pizzas and a few Western fast-food favourites.

Getting There & Away
BOAT

There's a so-called 'fast-ferry' service between Nuweiba in Egypt and Aqaba in Jordan, leaving Nuweiba at 3.30pm and in theory taking between one and two hours assuming normal sea conditions. Heading back to Nuweiba, fast ferries depart from Aqaba at noon. One-way tickets cost US$70 for economy and US$90 for first class, while return tickets cost US$120 and US$155, respectively. You must be at the port two hours before departure to get through the shambolic departure formalities in the main ferry terminal building.

A word of caution: we have received numerous letters from readers detailing the aggravating specifics of interminable delays along this sea route. A small sampling of horror stories includes a monumental 20-hour delay due to heavy thunderstorms and rough seas, as well as a truly epic three-day delay due to severe power outages. While the majority of travellers either arrive on time, or experience a delay of no more than an hour or two, you might want to leave some flexibility in your travel schedule if you're planning on taking the ferry to Jordan. As an alternative, you can also travel overland to Jordan via Israel – for more information, see the boxed text, p492.

There's also a 'slow-ferry' service, leaving Nuweiba at 2pm and arriving in Aqaba on average between three and five hours later. Heading back to Nuweiba, slow ferries depart from Aqaba at midnight. One-way tickets cost US$60 for economy and US$65 for first class, while round-trip tickets cost US$100 and US$105, respectively. As previously mentioned, while the fast ferry isn't always fast – or even on time – we can't stress how much more comfortable it is than the slow ferry.

Tickets must be paid for in US dollars (note that these are not always available at the banks in Nuweiba) and can be purchased on the day of departure only at the **ferry ticket office** (☽ 9am), in a small building near the port. Note that the only exception to this rule is during the hajj (pilgrimage to Mecca), when boats are booked weeks prior to departure. During this period, it's necessary to buy your ticket as far in advance as possible.

To find the ticket office, turn right when you exit the bus station, walking towards the water, and turn right again after the National Bank of Egypt. Continue along one block, and you'll see the sand-coloured ticket office building ahead to your left. The office stops selling tickets approximately one hour before the ferry leaves.

Free Jordanian visas can be obtained on the ferry if you have an EU, US, Canadian, Australian or New Zealand passport. Fill out a green form on board, give it and your passport to the immigration officers and – hey presto – you can collect your passport and visa when you pass through Jordanian immigration at Aqaba. Other nationalities will need to organise a visa in advance.

BUS

East Delta Travel Co (☎ 352 0371; Nuweiba Port) has buses to Cairo (E£70 to E£80, seven to eight hours) at 9am, 11am and 3pm going via Taba (E£15 to E£20, one hour); and to Sharm el-Sheikh (E£25 to E£30, three to four hours) at 6.30am, 8.30am, 10am and 4pm going via Dahab (E£15 to E£20, one hour). If you're heading to St Katherine, it's best to arrange a service taxi in Dahab.

SERVICE TAXI

There is a service taxi station by the port, but unless you get there when the ferry has arrived from Aqaba, you'll have to wait a long time for the car to fill up. As with Dahab, this is one place in Egypt where service taxi fares can often be more expensive than riding the bus.

Per-person fares (multiply by seven for the entire car) average about E£30 to E£40 for Sharm el-Sheikh, E£20 to Dahab and E£75 to E£80 to Cairo (usually changing vehicles in Suez). It's also sometimes possible to find service taxis at the outskirts of Tarabin that will take you directly out on the road north towards Taba or south to Dahab and Sharm el-Sheikh.

SINAI

Getting Around

Since Nuweiba is so spread out, taxis are expensive. Expect to pay E£10 to E£20 for a taxi from the port/bus station to Nuweiba City, depending on your destination and negotiating powers, and from E£5 for the few kilometres between Tarabin and Nuweiba City. If you're arriving in Nuweiba by bus, you can usually ask to be dropped at the hospital, from where you can walk to Fayrouza Village and nearby camps/hotels.

NUWEIBA TO TABA

☎ 069

The stunning coastline between Nuweiba and Taba is fringed by aqua waters and rimmed by chains of low, barren mountains. While there are a few pristine spots left, much of it is lined by a string of 'tourist villages' in various stages of completion, interspersed with simple beach camps consisting of reed huts and an eating area. Many of these camps sprang up when the local Bedouin were forced off their land to make way for hotel and resort development.

Business, which traditionally came from visiting Israelis, has suffered greatly with the political turmoil of recent years, and you'll frequently have much of the coastline to yourself. As a result, at most places there's nothing much to do other than relaxing on the sands while gazing out at the turquoise panoramas stretching before you. If you're feeling energetic, you can take a break from all the vegging out, and organise camel and jeep safaris into the interior.

If you're debating whether or not to stop at any of the places listed here, it's worth asking yourself what kind of traveller you are. If you need constant stimulation, you're likely to go a bit stir-crazy. However, if you want to seriously slow things down, and spend some quality time with an interesting cast of characters, the Nuweiba–Taba coastline will appeal immensely.

Sights

About 7km south of Taba and 250m off the Egyptian coast is **Pharaoh's Island** (Gezirat Fara'un; adult/child E£20/10; ⊙ 9am-5pm), a tiny islet in turquoise waters, dominated by the much-restored Castle of Salah ad-Din. The castle is actually a fortress built by the Crusaders in 1115, but captured and expanded by Saladin in 1170 as a bulwark against feared Crusader penetration south from Palestine. At the height of Crusader successes, it was feared that they might attempt to head for the holy cities of Mecca and Medina. Some of the modern restoration is incongruous (concrete was not a prime building material in Saladin's time), but the island is a pleasant place for a half-day trip, with limpid and enticing waters and coral for snorkelling at the island's southern end. There is also a cafe serving soft drinks and snacks.

The only boat to the island runs from the Salah ad-Din Hotel, on the coast just opposite. Unfortunately, the service is unreliable, though if the boat is running, a return ticket costs only US$4. Tickets are available from the hotel reception, and tickets for the island are available on landing.

Sleeping

Note that accommodation options are listed from south to north – unless you have your own transport, the only way to reach them is by service taxi or bus. Meals are available at all of the properties we've listed, though a good number of visitors prefer to bring their own food and self-cater. All of the options listed can also arrange desert and diving safaris throughout Sinai.

Magana Beach Camp (☎ 012 795 2402; huts from E£45) Although it's close to the road and exposed to the wind, this stretch of sand is conveniently located just north of Nuweiba. Accommodation is in simple huts that lack much individual personality, but the helpful Bedouin staff really know how to bring this place together. If you want to explore the Nuweiba–Taba coastline, but don't want to venture too far from town, this is a good choice.

Ayyash Camp (☎ 012 760 4668; huts from E£45) Located on the rocky point of the frighteningly named Ras Shaitan (Satan's Head) about 3km north of Maagana Beach, this strip of coastline was also attacked in the 2004 Taba bombings (see p460). Since then the pace of life has returned to normal, and it's one of the most popular beach areas on the Nuweiba–Taba strip. Owned by a local Bedouin, Ayyash has a placid setting on a wide stretch of sand, canvas tents and simple huts with shared facilities, and no electricity.

Castle Beach (☎ 012 739 8495; http://castlebeach sinai.net/home.html; huts from E£50; 🖭) Just north of Ayyash Camp near the *ras*, Castle Beach is one of the few midrange camps along this stretch of coastline. Accommodation is in comfortable bungalows that boast dramatic views of Satan's Head. One of the perks of staying here is the beachside restaurant, which serves delicious meals that make the most of the local seafood.

our pick **Basata** (☎ 350 0480; www.basata.com; camping per person E£35, huts from E£60, 3-person chalets from US$60) Twenty kilometres north of Nuweiba in the Mahash area is Basata ('simplicity' in Arabic), an ecologically minded and hugely popular travellers' settlement that lives by its name – owner Sherif Ghamrawy's concern for the environment is reflected in the philosophy of the hotel, which uses organically grown produce and recycles its rubbish. There are simple huts sharing facilities, pleasant chalets with electricity and private bathroom, a large camping area, a kitchen (where you can self-cater or arrange to have prepared meals), a bakery and shower blocks. Any cooking ingredients you could want are available, the ambience is very laid-back and family friendly with a New Age twist, and TVs and loud music are thankfully prohibited.

Getting There & Away
Approximately 50km of well-paved coastal highway connects Nuweiba with its northerly neighbour of Taba. Buses and service taxis from either Taba or Nuweiba will drop you at any of the places mentioned previously. When you're ready to leave, staff will help you hail a bus from the road, or they can help you and some friends arrange a service taxi to pick you up from the premises.

TABA
☎ 069
Taba holds the dubious distinction of being the last portion of Sinai to be returned to Egypt under the terms of the 1979 Egypt-Israel peace treaty. It has been a minor point of contention between the two countries for nearly a decade. Egypt argued that Taba was on the Egyptian side of the armistice line agreed to in 1949, while Israel contended that it was on the Ottoman side of a border agreed between the Ottomans and British Egypt in 1906, and therefore the lines drawn in 1949 and 1979 were in error. After a dispute lasting nearly a decade, in 1988 the issue was submitted to an international commission, which ruled in Egypt's favour – Israel returned Taba to Egypt later that year.

As part of this agreement, Israeli travellers were permitted to visit Taba visa-free for up to 48 hours, which sparked tourism development throughout the town. However, following a series of deadly bomb attacks in 2004 that killed and injured a large number of Israeli travellers, tourism virtually ceased in Taba. Today the town primarily serves as a border crossing for overland travellers heading between Egypt and Israel and the Palestinian Territories. However, the recent unveiling of the Taba Heights project, aimed almost exclusively at high-rolling overseas travellers, is the latest attempt by the Egyptian government to reinvigorate the stagnant local economy.

Orientation & Information
The town centre is home to a couple of banks, a small hospital and various shops. Just inside the border are an ATM and several foreign-exchange booths. Cash and travellers cheques can also be exchanged at the Taba Hilton.

About 20km south of Taba is the massive new **Taba Heights** (www.tabaheights.com), one of the lynchpins in Egyptian efforts to create a 'Red Sea Riviera'. After years of construction, it now houses five luxury hotels, a casino, countless upmarket shops, bars and restaurants, a private medical clinic and extensive water-sports facilities.

Dangers & Annoyances
On 7 October 2004, three bomb attacks in the Taba area killed 34 people and injured over 150 people – the worst of these attacks occurred when a truck bomb brought down several floors of the Taba Hilton. Although subsequent attacks in Sinai have targeted tourists in Sharm el-Sheikh, another attack in Taba is still possible. However, it's worth mentioning that tourism in the town has since then slowed dramatically, which means that there are perhaps more likely targets in other parts of the country. Though the Israel–Egypt border remains perfectly safe and relatively hassle-free to cross, it's still worth paying attention to warnings.

For an overview of the history of terrorism in Sinai, see p460.

Sleeping & Eating
Sadly, the tourist potential of Taba was destroyed following the attacks of 2004. Although the Taba Heights project may yet

LONELY PLANET JORDAN (ABRIDGED)

Planning a brief excursion to Jordan? Wishing you had a bit of info on the ancient city of Petra? Here's a quick guide to one of the 'New Seven Wonders of the World'. For the full story on Jordan, pick up a copy of the guidebook, or buy and download individual chapters from the Lonely Planet website, lonelyplanet.com.

PETRA

Hewn from towering rock walls of multicoloured sandstone, the imposing facades of Petra's great temples and tombs are an enduring testament to the vision of the desert tribes who sculpted them. The Nabataeans – Arabs who dominated the region in pre-Roman times – chose as their capital a place concealed from the outside world, and fashioned it into one of the Middle East's most remarkable cities. Almost as spectacular as the monuments themselves are the countless shades and Neapolitan swirls formed in the rock. Petra is often called the 'Rose-Red City', but even this hardly does justice to the extraordinary range of colours that blend as the sun makes its daily passage over the site.

Orientation & Information

The base town for exploring Petra is Wadi Musa (Valley of Moses), a patchy mass of hotels, restaurants and shops located about 3km from the **visitors centre** (☎ 3-215 6020; ⊗ 6am-5.30pm May-Sep, to 5pm Oct-Apr). Entry fees are JD21/26/31 for one-/two-/three-day passes. Note that at the time of publication, one Jordanian dinar (JD) was approximately equal to US$1.40 and €0.97.

Sights & Activities

The ancient city is approached via the **Siq**, a canyon-like passage that is actually a single block that has been rent apart by tectonic forces – at various points you can see where the grain of the rock on one side matches the other. The Siq can seem to continue forever, and the sense of anticipation builds as you look around each corner for your first glimpse of the Treasury, Petra's most famous monument.

Tucked away in such a confined space, **Al-Khazneh**, or the Treasury, is where most visitors fall in love with Petra. The Hellenistic exterior is an astonishing piece of craftsmanship, with the sophistication, symmetry, scale and grandeur of the carving enough to take the breath away of first-time visitors. Standing before the Treasury is a magical introduction to the ancient city, especially since the building is the precise location of the Holy Grail – at least according to the Hollywood classic *Indiana Jones and the Last Crusade*.

Heading towards the ancient city centre are over 40 tombs and houses built by the Nabataeans and colloquially known as the **Street of Façades**. Continuing along you'll reach a Roman-style **theatre**, which was built over 2000 years ago and has a capacity of about 3000 in 45 rows of seats, with three horizontal sections separated by two corridors.

The Wadi Musa riverbed widens out after the theatre – to the right (or north), carved into the cliff face, are the impressive burial places known collectively as the **Royal Tombs**. There are more tombs dotted around Petra than any other type of structure, and for years archaeologists assumed that the city was just one vast necropolis. The simple reason why so few dwellings have been discovered is that the Nabataeans lived in tents, much as some Bedouin do today.

One of Petra's most magnificent sights is **Al-Deir**, or the Monastery, which is reached via a one-hour uphill slog from the **Colonnaded Street** (Cardo Maximus). Similar in design to the Treasury, the imposing Monastery – 50m wide and 45m high – is just as impressive. Built in the 3rd century BC as a Nabataean tomb, the Monastery gets its name from the crosses carved on its inside walls, suggesting that the building was used as a church in Byzantine times. The building has towering columns and a large urn flanked by two half-pediments, and like the Treasury has heavy Hellenistic influences. **Petra by Night** (admission JD12; ⊗ 8.30-10.30pm Mon & Thu) is a magical way to see the old city, taking you along the Siq (lined with hundreds of candles) in silence as far as the Treasury, where traditional Bedouin music is played and mint tea is served.

SINAI

Sleeping

Cleopatra Hotel (☎ 3-215 7090; s/d/tr JD12/16/21; 💻) Located in the centre of Wadi Musa, this popular backpacker spot offers the obligatory nightly screening of *Indiana Jones and the Last Crusade*. The rooms here, all with private bathroom and hot water, are on the small side, but there's a cosy communal sitting area that feels like your aunt's sitting room. You can sleep on the roof for JD4 or JD5 with breakfast.

Amra Palace Hotel (☎ 3-215 7070; www.amrapalace.com; s/d JD42/65; 💻 🏋) This lovely hotel lives up to its name with a magnificent lobby, marble pillars, giant brass coffeepots and Damascene-style furniture. The brothers who have run this establishment for more than a decade take a personal interest in the details, and they have a fine sense of interior design. Each room has spotless linen that's changed every day, in addition to wooden headboards, upholstered furniture and satellite TV.

Mövenpick Hotel (☎ 3-215 7111; www.moevenpick-petra.com; s/d JD155/170; 💻 🏋) This beautifully crafted Arabian-style hotel, 100m from the entrance to Petra, is worth a visit simply to admire the inlaid furniture, marble fountains, wooden screens and brass salvers. Petals are floated daily in the fountains, a roaring fire welcomes residents to the lounge, and pleasant views are afforded from the roof garden. As the hotel is in the bottom of the valley, there are not sweeping views, but the large and super-luxurious rooms all have huge picture windows regardless.

Eating & Drinking

Al-Wadi Restaurant (mains JD4-5; ☉ 7am-late) Right on Shaheed roundabout, this lively local spot offers pasta and pizza, as well as a range of vegetarian dishes and local Bedouin specialities.

Sandstone Restaurant (mains from JD6) Near the centre of town, this tourist restaurant special-ises in Jordanian dishes, including spit-roasted lamb and whole chickens, which are served up to hungry diners in an attractive outdoor beer garden.

Cave Bar (drinks from JD3) If you've never been to a bar in a 2000-year-old Nabataean rock tomb (and we're guessing you haven't!), then this memorable spot near the visitors centre is an absolute must.

Getting There & Away

Both fast and slow ferries depart from Nuweiba, Egypt, and arrive in Aqaba, Jordan. For more information on the crossing, see p489. From the ferry terminal in Aqaba, share taxis meet ar-riving ships in order to shuttle tourists to their desired hotel in Wadi Musa. When dealing with taxi drivers, it helps to be a good negotiator – and to have a lot of friends with you to bring down the price. Generally speaking, you can expect to pay approximately US$15 to US$20 per person to reach Wadi Musa. The ride takes approximately two hours, and winds through some attractive stretches of open desert.

Given that the ferry crossing to Jordan isn't always smooth sailing, a good alternative is to travel by bus via Israel. From Taba (see p491), you can cross the Egypt–Israel border, and then catch a quick taxi (US$15 to US$20) to the Wadi Araba border crossing between Israel and Jordan. Note that you can still cross into Jordan and return to Egypt with an Israeli stamp, though you will not be allowed to enter Lebanon, Syria and a whole slew of other Muslim countries. If this is an issue, kindly ask the border guards not to stamp your passport, though be advised that they will not always comply. Once you've crossed into Jordan, you can either hop a quick taxi to Aqaba for a few dollars, or try to arrange a taxi directly to Wadi Musa from the border.

Getting Around

In Wadi Musa, most hotels offer a free shuttle service to and from the visitors centre, though a taxi ride from anywhere in Wadi Musa to Petra shouldn't cost you more than JD1 or JD2. Although hikers have little difficulty exploring Petra's sights, donkeys accompanied with guides are available all around Petra for negotiable prices. Camel rides are more for the novelty value, though their photogenic appeal is undeniable, especially if you wrap yourself up like Lawrence of Arabia.

prove to be a major tourist draw, there is little in the town to warrant a visit, and today most of the hotels in Taba have simply closed their doors and shut down. Perhaps things will change in the years to come, though it's unlikely the damage will ever be entirely undone.

Hilton Taba Resort (☎ 353 0140; www.hilton.com; Taba Beach; r from US$125; ⬛ ▢ ⬛) The Hilton gained worldwide attention and sympathy in 2004 when much of it was destroyed in a terrorist attack. In the aftermath, it has been rapidly rebuilding, and now offers a good selection of rooms in its main tower and adjacent village-esque compound, set in lush grounds overlooking the turquoise waters of the Gulf of Aqaba. Although the scars of the attack are still evident, the Taba Hilton stands as a testament to Egypt's resolve to fight domestic terrorism.

Hyatt Regency Taba Heights (☎ 358 0234; www .taba.hyatt.com; r from US$175; ⬛ ⬛ ▢ ⬛) This tasteful desert-pastel hotel was designed by the famous American designer and architect Michael Graves, and seeks to replicate the opulence and elegance typical of the five-star resorts in Sharm el-Sheikh. Nestled beside the mountains close to the beach, it has excellent facilities, including several pools, a large health centre, extensive water sports and a rapidly expanding list of gourmet restaurants. The Hyatt Regency is one of the showpieces of the Taba Heights development project, and aims to recapture a slice of the tourist industry that was lost in the 2004 bombings.

Castle Zaman (☎ 350 1234, 012 214 0591; www.castle zaman.com; meals from E£100; ⏱ from 10am; ⬛) This atmospheric stone castle on a cliff with views over the gulf has the best cuisine along this stretch of coast, featuring huge portions of items such as a full rack of grilled lamb. There's also a bar, a pool, a small private beach and a couple of rooms (available per night from US$1000 only to those who want to rent the castle out in its entirety). It's a good idea to call in advance to confirm opening times, as the castle is sometimes booked for weddings or other events.

Getting There & Away

The Taba–Eilat border, which is open 24 hours daily, is the only safe and reliable crossing between Egypt and Israel. For more information, see p526.

AIR
Flights to Taba have been discontinued, though it's possible to fly either to Eilat, which is just across the border in Israel, or to Sharm el-Sheikh, further down the coast of Sinai.

BUS
East Delta Travel Co (☎ 353 0250) has its bus station along the main road about 800m south of the border. Buses to Nuweiba (E£15 to E£20, one hour) leave at 7am, 9am and 3pm. Departures to Cairo (E£70 to E£80, six to seven hours) are at 10.30am, 12.30pm and 4.30pm. Buses to Dahab (E£20, 2½ hours) and Sharm el-Sheikh (E£30 to E£35, four to five hours) leave at 7am (terminating in Dahab), 9am and 3pm (both continuing to Sharm el-Sheikh).

CAR
Car rental is available at **Max Car Rental** (☎ 353 0333; tabareservation@max.com.eg; ⏱ 6am-8pm), situated just before the border post, opposite the Taba Hilton.

SERVICE TAXI
Taxis and minibuses wait by the border for passengers. If business is slack, you may have a long wait for the vehicle to fill up – or you can pay the equivalent of all seven fares and leave immediately. Per-person fares are about E£15 to Nuweiba, E£30 to Dahab, E£45 to Sharm el-Sheikh and E£55 to Cairo. Your bargaining power increases if the bus is not too far off.

INTERIOR

Sinai's rugged interior is populated by barren mountains, wind-sculpted canyons and wadis that burst into life with even the shortest rains. The rocks and desert landscapes turn shades of pink, ochre and velvet black as the sun rises and falls, and what little vegetation there is appears to grow magically out of the rock. Bedouin still wander through the wilderness, and camels are the best way to travel, with much of the terrain too rocky even for a 4WD. Against this desolate backdrop some of the most sacred events in recorded human history took place, which has consequently immortalised the Sinai in the annals of Judaism, Christianity and Islam.

ST KATHERINE PROTECTORATE
☎ 069

The 4350-sq-km St Katherine Protectorate was created in 1996 to counteract the detrimental effects of rapidly increasing tourism on St Katherine's Monastery and the adjacent Mt Sinai. In addition to the area's unique high-altitude desert ecosystem, it protects a wealth of historical sites sacred to the world's three main monotheistic religions, and the core part around the monastery has been declared a Unesco World Heritage Site. Although at times it can be difficult to pry yourself away from Sinai's beaches, a visit to the St Katherine Protectorate is not to be missed.

Orientation

Rising up out of the desert and jutting above the other peaks surrounding the monastery is the towering 2285m Mt Sinai (Gebel Musa). Tucked into a barren valley at the foot of Mt Sinai is the ancient St Katherine's Monastery. Approximately 3.5km from here is the small town of Al-Milga, which is also called Katreen and is known as the 'Meeting Place' by local Jabaliyya Bedouin.

Information

The **St Katherine Protectorate Office** (☎ 347 0032), located at the tourist village near the entrance to Al-Milga, is where you'll find informative guides to four 'interpretive trails' established in the area, including one for Mt Sinai. These booklets take you through each trail, explaining flora and fauna as well as sites of historical and religious significance.

To allow the local population to benefit from tourism, visitors are also requested to hire a local Bedouin guide. If you haven't arrived on an organised tour from elsewhere in Sinai, this is the best place to enquire about local guides.

The following listings are located in the town of Al-Milga.

Banque Misr (beside petrol station; ☼ 10am-1pm & 5-8pm Sat-Thu) Cash advances on Visa and MasterCard.
Police (☎ 347 0046; beside the St Katherine Protectorate Office)
St Katherine Hospital (☎ 347 0263) Provides very basic care only.
Telephone centrale (beside the bakery; ☼ 24hr)

TREADING LIGHTLY IN THE PROTECTORATE

In order to limit the impact of tourists upon this special place, the following code is now in force:

■ Respect the area's religious and historical importance and the local Bedouin culture and traditions.

■ Carry your litter out with you, bury your bodily waste and burn your toilet paper.

■ Do not contaminate or overuse water sources.

The following acts are illegal:

■ Removing any object, including rocks, plants and animals.

■ Disturbing or harming animals or birds.

■ Cutting or uprooting plants.

■ Writing, painting or carving graffiti.

Sights
ST KATHERINE'S MONASTERY

The ancient **St Katherine's Monastery** (☎ in Cairo 02-482 8513; admission free; ☼ 9am-noon Mon-Wed, Fri & Sun, except religious holidays) traces its founding to about AD 330 when the Roman empress Helena had a small chapel and a fortified refuge for local hermits built beside what was believed to be the burning bush from which God spoke to Moses. In the 6th century Emperor Justinian ordered a fortress to be constructed around the original chapel, together with a basilica and a monastery, to provide a secure home for the monastic community that had grown here, and as a refuge for the Christians of southern Sinai. Since then the monastery has been visited by pilgrims from throughout the world, many of whom braved extraordinarily difficult and dangerous journeys to reach the remote and isolated site. Today St Katherine's is considered one of the oldest continually functioning monastic communities in the world, and its chapel is one of early Christianity's only surviving churches.

The monastery – which, together with the surrounding area, has been declared a Unesco World Heritage Site – is named after St Katherine, the legendary martyr of Alexandria, who was tortured on a spiked wheel and then beheaded for her faith. Tradition holds that her body was transported

SINAI

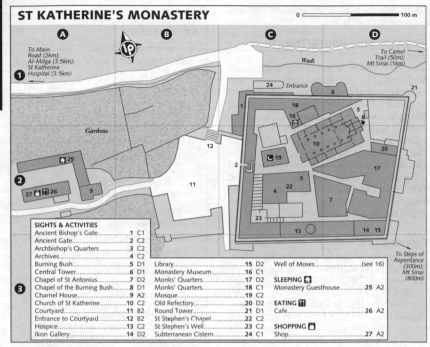

by angels away from the torture device (which spun out of control and killed the pagan onlookers) and onto the slopes of Egypt's highest mountain peak. The peak, which lies about 6km south of Mt Sinai, subsequently became known as Gebel Katarina. Katherine's body was subsequently 'found' about 300 years later by monks from the monastery in a state of perfect preservation.

Today a paved access road has removed the hazards that used to accompany a trip to the monastery, and both the monastery and the mountain are routinely packed with tour buses and people. It is especially full early in the morning, although somehow the monastery's interior tranquillity manages to make itself felt despite the crowds. When you visit, remember that this is still a functioning monastery, which necessitates conservative dress – no one with shorts is permitted to enter, and women must be sure to cover their shoulders.

Although much of the monastery is closed to the public, it is possible to enter the ornately decorated 6th-century **Church of the Transfiguration**, with its nave flanked by massive marble columns and walls covered in richly gilded icons and paintings. At the church's eastern end, a gilded 17th-century iconostasis separates the nave from the sanctuary and the apse, where St Katherine's remains are interred (off limits to most visitors). High in the apse above the altar is one of the monastery's most stunning artistic treasures, a 6th-century mosaic of the biblical account of the transfiguration of Christ, although it can be difficult to see past the chandeliers and the iconostasis.

To the left of and below the altar is the monastery's holiest area, the **Chapel of the Burning Bush**. Access is restricted, but it's possible to see what is thought to be a descendant of the original burning bush in the monastery compound. According to the monks, this bush was transplanted from the nearby chapel in the 10th century, and continues to thrive centuries later. Near the burning bush is the **Well of Moses**, a natural spring that is supposed to give marital happiness to those who drink from it.

Above the well is the superb **Monastery Museum** (adult/student E£25/10), also known as the Sacred Sacristy, which has been magnificently restored. It has displays (labelled in Arabic and English) of many of the monastery's artistic treasures, including some of the spectacular Byzantine-era icons from its world-famous collection, numerous precious chalices and gold and silver crosses.

Although it contains a priceless collection of ancient manuscripts and illuminated bibles, the monastery's **library** is unfortunately closed to the general public.

Outside the monastery walls is a gift shop selling replicas of icons and other religious items (with branches in the museum and inside the monastery compound just near the entrance), and a cafe with an array of cold drinks and snacks. The least crowded days for visiting the monastery are generally Tuesday and Wednesday, while Saturday and Monday tend to be the most crowded.

MT SINAI

Known locally as Gebel Musa, Mt Sinai is revered by Christians, Muslims and Jews, all of whom believe that God delivered his Ten Commandments to Moses at its summit. The mountain is easy and beautiful to climb, and although you'll invariably be overwhelmed with crowds of other visitors, it offers a taste of the magnificence of southern Sinai's high mountain region. For those visiting as part of a pilgrimage, it also offers a moving glimpse into biblical times.

There are two well-defined routes up to the summit – the **camel trail** and the **Steps of Repentance** – which meet about 300m below the summit at a plateau known as Elijah's Basin. Here, everyone must take a steep series of 750 rocky and uneven steps to the top, where there is a small chapel containing paintings and ornaments (although it is usually kept locked). Both the climb and the summit offer spectacular views of nearby plunging valleys and of jagged mountain chains rolling off into the distance, and it's usually possible to see the even higher summit of Gebel Katarina in the distance. Most people make the climb in the pre-dawn hours to see the magnificence of the sun rising over the surrounding peaks, and then arrive back at the base before 9am, when the monastery opens for visitors.

The camel trail is the easier route, and takes about two hours to ascend, moving at a steady pace. The trail is wide, clear and gently sloping as it moves up a series of switchbacks, with the only potential difficulty – apart from sometimes fierce winds – being gravelly patches that can be slippery on the descent. Most people walk up, but it's also possible to hire a camel at the base, just behind the monastery, to take you all or part of the way to where the camel trail meets the steps. If you decide to try a camel, it's easier on the anatomy (especially if you're male) to ride up the mountain, rather than down.

En route are several kiosks selling tea and soft drinks, and vendors renting out blankets (E£5) and mattresses (E£10) to help ward off the chill at the summit. Trust us – both are worthy investments as the mattresses will provide a layer of protection from the ice-cold rocks, and the blankets (even though they smell like camels) will protect you from the howling winds. The alternative path to the summit, the taxing 3750 Steps of Repentance, was laid by one monk as a form of penance. The steps – 3000 up to Elijah's Basin and then the final 750 to the summit – are made of roughly hewn rock, and are steep and uneven in many places, requiring strong knees and concentration in placing your feet. If you want to try both routes, it's best to take the path on the way up and the steps – which afford impressive views of the monastery – on the way back down.

During summer try to avoid the heat by beginning your hike by 3am. Although stone signs have been placed on the trail as guides, it can be a bit difficult in parts, and a torch (flashlight) is essential. The start of the camel trail is reached by walking along the northern wall of the monastery past the end of the compound. The Steps of Repentance begin outside the southeastern corner of the compound.

Due to the sanctity of the area, and the tremendous pressure that large groups place on the environment, the Egyptian National Parks Office has instituted various regulations. If you spend the night on the mountain, you are asked to sleep below the summit at the small Elijah's Basin plateau. Here you'll find several composting toilets and a 500-year-old cypress tree, marking the spot where the prophet Elijah heard the voice of God. Bring sufficient food and water, warm clothes and a sleeping bag, as there is no space to pitch a tent. It gets cold and windy, even in summer, and in winter light snows are common.

As late as mid-May, be prepared to share the summit with up to several hundred other visitors, some carrying stereos, others bibles and hymn books. With the music and singing, and people nudging each other for space, it can be difficult to actually sleep, especially in the small hours before sunrise. For more tranquillity, the dawn views are just as impressive from the upper reaches of the camel path, shortly before it joins the Steps of Repentance.

Activities

TREKKING

St Katherine's Monastery lies in the heart of South Sinai's high mountain region, and the surrounding area is an ideal trekking destination for anyone with a rugged and adventurous bent. Treks range from half a day to a week or more, and can be done either on camel or on foot. Even if you decide to walk, you'll need at least one camel for your food and luggage.

One of the most common circuits goes to the **Galt al-Azraq** (Blue Pools) and takes three to four days. The trail leaves Al-Milga via the man-made **Abu Giffa Pass** and goes through **Wadi Tubug**, taking a detour around **Wadi Shagg**, where there are springs, waterholes and lush, walled gardens *(bustans)*. The walk then goes through the picturesque **Wadi Zuweitin** (Valley of the Olives), with ancient olive trees said by local Bedouin to have been planted by the founder of the Jebaliyya tribe. The first night is often spent here, and there is a small stone hut in which hikers can sometimes sleep. The hike continues through **Wadi Gibal**, through high passes and along the valleys of **Farsh Asara** and **Farsh Arnab**. Many hikers then climb either **Ras Abu Alda** or **Gebel Abu Gasba** before heading to the spring of **Ain**

CLIMBING & DIVING: A WORD OF CAUTION

Altitude can kill, particularly if your body is full of residual nitrogen. If you've been diving recently, be advised that Mt Sinai is high enough to induce decompression sickness. As a general rule, avoid climbing the mountain for 12 hours after one dive, or 18 hours if you've been on multiple dives. Although this may complicate your travel plans, trust us – you'll be delayed a lot longer if you end up confined in a hyperbaric chamber. And, of course, decompression sickness is anything but fun.

Nagila and the ruins of a Byzantine monastery at **Bab ad-Dunya** (Gate of the World). On the third day the trail leads to the crystal-clear, icy waters of the **Galt al-Azraq**, a deep, dramatic pool in the rock, before continuing on the fourth day through more dramatic wadis to a camel pass on **Gebel Abbas Basha**. A one-hour hike up a fairly easy but steep path leads to a ruined palace built by the 19th-century viceroy Abbas Hilmi I, with stunning views from the summit (2304m). The trail then goes back to Wadi Zuweitin and retraces its way to Al-Milga.

Other destinations include **Sheikh Awad**, with a Sheikh's tomb and Bedouin settlement; the **Nugra Waterfall**, a difficult to reach, rain-fed cascade about 20m high, which is reached through a winding canyon called **Wadi Nugra**; and **Naqb al-Faria**, a camel path with rock inscriptions. A shorter trip is the hike to the top of **Gebel Katarina**, Egypt's highest peak at 2642m. It takes about five hours to reach the summit along a straightforward but taxing trail. The views from the top are breathtaking, and the panorama can even include the mountains of Saudi Arabia on a clear day. The **Blue Valley**, given its name after a Belgian artist painted the rocks here blue some years ago, is another popular day trip.

All treks must be done with a Bedouin guide and most are arranged through either the **Mountain Tours Office** (☎ 069 347 0457) in Al-Milga, or any of the camps and hotels we've listed (opposite). Guided treks typically start at around E£150 per day, with an additional E£30 to E£50 per day for food and equipment. You should also buy firewood here in order to discourage destruction of the few trees in the mountains. Whoever you go with, be sure to register with the police prior to leaving.

Make sure you bring water-purification tablets, unless you want to rely on the mountain springs. You'll also need comfortable walking boots, a hat and sunglasses, sunblock, a warm jacket, a good sleeping bag and toilet paper. Keep in mind that it can get very cold at night – frost, and even snow, are common in winter.

Tours

The majority of visitors arrive at the St Katherine Protectorate on an organised tour departing from either Sharm el-Sheikh (p470) or Dahab (p476). However, it's both cheap and easy to sleep within the confines of the protectorate, and to organise everything independently.

Sleeping

In addition to the aptly dubbed Monastery Guesthouse, which is in fact located at the monastery, there are also several hotels and guest houses in the village of Al-Milga (Katreen), approximately 3.5km from the monastery.

Desert Fox Camp (☎ 347 0344; www.desertfoxcamp .com; camping per person E£10, r per person E£25-50) Run by local Bedouin Soliman and Farag al-Gebaly (also known as the Fox), this is a relaxed budget camp with simple but clean facilities. The owners offer the obligatory treks up Mt Sinai, though the real treat is their custom-tailored desert safaris, which are priced according to your group size and your planned itinerary. The camp is in Al-Milga, on the road behind the Catherine Plaza Hotel about 200m from the main round.

El-Malga Bedouin Camp (☎ 010 641 3575; www .sheikhmousa.com; camping per person E£10, r per person E£30-60; ▣) Run by the affable Sheikh Musa, who can help you organise treks to Sinai and around the protectorate, this popular camp is a backpacker favourite. El-Malga is a rock-hewn single-storey structure offering a handful of rooms with sleeping mats and shared bathrooms with hot water – a blessing after a chilly night up in the mountains. The camp is located next to the mountain trekking office in Al-Milga, and is an easy 500m walk from the bus stand.

Al-Karm Ecolodge (Sheikh Awaad; camping/r per person E£25/75) A fine, albeit rugged, base for immersing yourself in the beauty of southern Sinai, the Bedouin-owned Al-Karm Ecolodge, well outside Al-Milga, is in a remote wadi near the small settlement of Sheikh Awaad. It offers simple rooms, solar-heated shared showers, a kitchen and endless tranquillity. To get here, follow the track from Tarfa village, about 20km from St Katherine on the Wadi Feiran road.

Monastery Guesthouse (☎ 347 0353; St Katherine's Monastery; dm per person half board US$25, s/d/tr US$40/60/75) If location is your thing, the Monastery Guesthouse can't be beat. It's right next to St Katherine's Monastery, so you can literally roll out of bed and walk to the monastery before having your breakfast. A favourite of pilgrims the world over, the Monastery Guesthouse offers well-kept

rooms with heaters and blankets to keep out the mountain chill, and a pleasant patio area with views towards the mountains. Meals at the on-site cafeteria are filling and tasty, and lunches can be arranged for a few extra dollars per person.

Daniela Village (☎ 748 2671; www.daniela-hotels .com/dstcvillage.htm; s/d half board from US$65/95; ▨) One of the nicest midrange hotels in Al-Milga, this reasonably priced three-star affair comprises stone-clad prefab huts that are scattered around attractive grounds. The on-site bar and restaurant is a popular tourist hang-out, and is especially good if you're in need of a Stella after an all-night trek. It's diagonally opposite the hospital and about 1.5km from the bus station.

St Catherine's Tourist Village (☎ 347 0333; www .misrsinaitours.com; s/d half board from US$85/100; ▨) This four-star establishment is Al-Milga's plushest accommodation option, with pleasant stone bungalow-style rooms that blend in with the surrounding landscape. If you want to sprawl out in comfort after punishing your body on any of the protectorate's rugged treks, you'll be glad you dished out the extra cash to stay here. It's located along the same road as Daniela Village hotel, about 500m past the hospital and about 2km from the bus station.

Eating

In Al-Milga, there's a bakery opposite the mosque and several well-stocked supermarkets in the shopping arcade – perfect for stocking up on supplies before hitting the trails. Just behind the bakery are a few simple restaurants, though most tourists either self-cater at the camps or take their meals at their hotel or in the monastery's cafeteria.

Getting There & Away

In addition to the transport options listed below, many hotels and camps in Sinai, as well as travel agencies in Cairo, also organise trips to the protectorate.

BUS

St Katherine's Monastery is about 3.5km from the village of Al-Milga (which is where buses from Dahab, Sharm el-Sheikh and Cairo will drop you), and 2km from the large roundabout on the road between the two.

SINAI

East Delta Travel Co (☎ 347 0250) has its bus station and ticket office on the main road near the post office. There is a daily bus to Cairo (E£60, six to seven hours) at 6am, via Wadi Feiran and Suez (E40, four hours), and another to Dahab at 1pm (E£20 to E£25, two to three hours), where you can get onward connections to Nuweiba and Taba. For Sharm el-Sheikh, Hurghada and Luxor, it's necessary to change buses in Dahab.

SERVICE TAXI

Service taxis usually wait at the monastery for people coming down from Mt Sinai in the morning, and then again around noon when visiting hours end. A lift to the village costs E£10 to E£15. Plan on paying about E£30/45 per person to Dahab/Sharm el-Sheikh. To Cairo, expect to pay about E£400 per vehicle.

WADI FEIRAN

This long valley serves as the main drainage route for the entire high mountain region into the Gulf of Suez. Sinai's largest oasis, it is lush and very beautiful, containing more than 12,000 date palms, as well as Bedouin communities representing all of Sinai's tribes. Stone walls surround the palms, and the rocky mountains on each side of the wadi have subtly different colours that stand out at sunrise and sunset, making the landscape even more dramatic.

Feiran also has biblical significance – it is believed to be the place where Moses struck a rock with his staff, bringing forth water, and later became the first Christian stronghold in Sinai. An extensively rebuilt early Christian convent remains from this time, although you need permission from St Katherine's Monastery if you want to visit.

The valley is also an ideal spot from which to trek into the surrounding mountains. To the south, the 2070m **Gebel Serbal** (believed by early Christians to have been the real Mt Sinai) is a challenging six-hour hike along a track also known as **Sikket ar-Reshshah**. Those who persevere are rewarded with fantastic panoramic views. You must be accompanied by a Bedouin guide for all hikes, though this is most easily arranged in Al-Milga, near St Katherine's Monastery.

QALAAT AL-GINDI & NAKHL

In the centre of Sinai, located about 80km southeast of the Ahmed Hamdi Tunnel, is Qalaat al-Gindi, which features the 800-year-old **Fortress of Saladin** (Salah ad-Din). In the 12th century Muslims from Africa and the Mediterranean streamed across Sinai on their way to Mecca. The three caravan routes they followed all converged at Qalaat al-Gindi, prompting Saladin to build a fortress here to protect the pilgrims making their hajj. He also planned to use the fort, which today is still largely intact, as a base from which to launch attacks on the Crusaders, who had advanced as far as Jerusalem. As it turned out, Saladin managed to evict the Crusaders from the Holy City even before the completion of his fortress.

Qalaat al-Gindi is well off the beaten track and seldom visited. From the coast, you must turn off at Ras Sudr and follow the unsignposted road from there. As there is no public transport, you'll need to either have your own vehicle or hire a taxi.

Continuing north from Qalaat al-Gindi for about 20km you'll reach the turn-off for Nakhl, another 60km east. This little community sits almost in the centre of the Sinai Peninsula, surrounded by a vast wilderness. It boasts a petrol station, a surprisingly well-stocked supermarket and a bakery. A road leads north from here to Al-Arish, but foreigners are forbidden to use it.

NORTHERN SINAI

Rarely visited by tourists, northern Sinai has a barren desert interior, much of which is off limits to foreigners, and a palm-fringed Mediterranean coast backed by soft white sands sculpted into low dunes. As a crossroad between Asia and Africa, the coastal highway follows what must be one of history's oldest march routes. Known in ancient times as the Way of Horus, it was used by the Egyptians, Persians, Greeks, Crusaders and Arab Muslims. In fact, the Copts believe that the infant Jesus also passed along this route with his parents during their flight into Egypt.

AL-ARISH

☎ 068 / pop 50,000

Much of the north coast of Sinai between Port Fuad and Al-Arish is dominated by the swampy lagoon of Lake Bardawil, separated from the Mediterranean by a limestone ridge. As a result of this inhospitable geography, Al-Arish is the only major city in the region, and by default the capital of North Sinai Governorate. Unsurprisingly, Al-Arish resembles a ghost town for much of the year, aside from the bustling central market that draws in thousands of Bedouin traders from around the peninsula. In summer, however, the long, palm-fringed coastline of Al-Arish comes alive when holidaying Cairenes arrive en masse.

Orientation

The main coastal road, Sharia Fuad Zikry, forms a T-junction with Sharia 23rd of July,

which runs a couple of kilometres south – changing name to Sharia Tahrir on the way – to the main market area.

Information

EMERGENCY

Ambulance (☎ 123)
Tourist police (☎ 336 1016; Sharia Fuad Zikry; ☻ 24hr)

INTERNET ACCESS

El Basha.Net (per hr E£2; ☻ 11am-3am)

MEDICAL SERVICES

Mubarak Military Hospital (☎ 332 4018; near Governorate Bldg, Rafah Rd; ☻ 24hr)

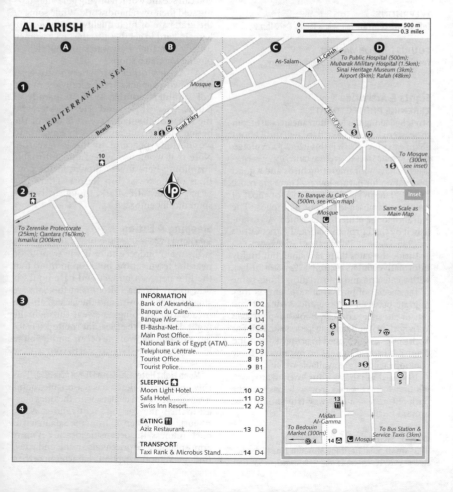

AL-ARISH

0 —— 500 m
0 —— 0.3 miles

To Public Hospital (500m); Mubarak Military Hospital (1.5km); Sinai Heritage Museum (3km); Airport (8km); Rafah (48km)

To Mosque (300m, see inset)

To Zerenike Protectorate (25km); Qantara (160km); Ismailia (200km)

Inset

To Banque du Caire (500m, see main map)

Same Scale as Main Map

To Bedouin Market (300m)

Midan Al-Gamma

To Bus Station & Service Taxis (3km)

INFORMATION
Bank of Alexandria.............................1 D2
Banque du Caire................................2 D1
Banque Misr......................................3 D4
El-Basha-Net.....................................4 C4
Main Post Office................................5 D4
National Bank of Egypt (ATM)..........6 D3
Telephone Centrale............................7 D3
Tourist Office....................................8 B1
Tourist Police...................................9 B1

SLEEPING
Moon Light Hotel............................10 A2
Safa Hotel.......................................11 D3
Swiss Inn Resort.............................12 A2

EATING
Aziz Restaurant..............................13 D4

TRANSPORT
Taxi Rank & Microbus Stand...........14 D4

Public Hospital (☎ 336 0010; Sharia Fuad Zikry; ⊙ 24hr) To be avoided except in the direst emergencies.

MONEY
Bank of Alexandria (Sharia 23rd of July; ⊙ 8.30am-2pm & 6-8pm Sun-Thu)
Banque du Caire (Sharia 23rd of July; ⊙ 8.30am-2.30pm Sun-Thu)
Banque Misr (off Sharia Tahrir; ⊙ 9am-2.30pm & 6-8pm Sun-Thu)
National Bank of Egypt (Sharia Tahrir; ⊙ 9am-2.30pm Sun-Thu)

POST
Main post office (off Sharia Tahrir; ⊙ 8.30am-2.30pm Sat-Thu)

TELEPHONE
Telephone centrale (off Sharia Tahrir; ⊙ 24hr)

TOURIST INFORMATION
Tourist office (☎ 336 3743; Sharia Fuad Zikry; ⊙ 9am-2pm Sat-Thu)

Sights & Activities
ZERENIKE PROTECTORATE
Stretched along the Mediterranean coast from the eastern edge of Lake Bardawil until about 25km east of Al-Arish is this 220-sq-km **protectorate** (☎ 010 544 2641; per person/car US$5/5; ⊙ sunrise-sunset), a haven for migrating birds and a good destination for nature lovers. There are more than 250 avian species here and for most of the year it's possible to spot flamingos. The entrance to the protectorate, which was established by the Egyptian National Parks Office in 1985, is about 35km east of Al-Arish.

Inside the gates there is a small but highly informative **visitors centre** (⊙ 9am-5pm Sun-Thu), with a cafeteria and information about some of the species of birds that stop here as they migrate between Europe and Africa. If you call in advance, you can book simple **rooms** (per person US$25) and **camping** (per person US$10). For both options, you'll need to bring all food and drink with you as there is no restaurant. Basic cooking facilities are available on site.

If you don't have your own transport, it's best to take a taxi from Al-Arish to the park entrance – a one-way trip should cost around E£30.

OTHER SIGHTS
The small **Sinai Heritage Museum** (Coast Rd; adult/student E£20/10, camera E£20; ⊙ 9.30am-2pm Sat-Thu),

on the outskirts of Al-Arish along the coastal road to Rafah, was established in order to inform visitors to the peninsula about traditional nomadic life in Sinai. Displays include Bedouin tools, handicrafts, clothing and traditional medicines, with the odd English explanation.

Much livelier is the **Bedouin market** (⊙ 9am-2pm Thu), held at the southern edge of town near the main market – note that it's signposted in Arabic and in English as the Souq al-Hamis. It's fascinating to watch as Bedouin come in from the desert in pick-up trucks or occasionally on camels, with the veiled women trading silver, beadwork and embroidered dresses, while the men sell camel saddles. Sometimes you can see the women buying gold after having sold their own handiwork. While some of the crafts are of high quality, you'll need to bargain hard to get these, as the savvy women usually save their best wares for middlemen buying for Cairo shops.

Al-Arish's other attraction is its long **beach**, which packs in the crowds in the hot summer months. With its parade of palms, fine white sand, clean water and the occasional small wave, it is one of the better Mediterranean spots in Egypt, and wonderfully peaceful in the low season. Note that women may feel uncomfortable swimming here unless they're in the confines of the Swiss Inn Resort. There is a beach curfew after dark, though it is only sporadically enforced.

Sleeping & Eating
Safa Hotel (☎ 335 3798; Sharia Tahrir; s/d E£30/40) Safa is the main budget choice if you want to be near the town centre, but keep in mind that the line between budget and bare-bones is thin to say the least. Rooms at the Safa are small and run-down, and the lack of air-con means you're going to sweat through the night. However, the pleasant rooftop terrace has a distant view of the ocean, and if you're looking for some serious local flavour, you've chosen correctly.

Moon Light Hotel (Sharia Fuad Zikry; r from E£50) This tiny hotel on the beach has reasonable rooms in small, detached chalets, with the ones closest to the water costing slightly more. While it's just barely a step up from the Safa in terms of cleanliness, the oceanside location is more atmospheric. The price is also right, and you'll find much more Egyptian character here than at other backpacker-oriented camps elsewhere in Sinai.

Swiss Inn Resort (☎ 335 1321; www.swissinn.net; Sharia Fuad Zikry; s/d from US$70/90; 🏊 🈯) Despite changing ownership several times, this faded but pleasant upmarket establishment is perfectly located on a long, breezy stretch of white-sand beach. It's incredibly understated compared with the resorts in Sharm el-Sheikh, but all of the rooms have sea views and balconies, enabling you to fall asleep to the sounds of the surf. There's also a restaurant and two large swimming pools on the grounds that are only filled during summer.

Aziz Restaurant (Sharia Tahrir; dishes E£5-25) With an inviting Bedouin-style inner room, this excellent and affordable restaurant offers filling meals of *fuul* and *ta'amiyya*, as well as grilled chicken, *kofta*, rice and spaghetti – with advance notice the owner can prepare multicourse meals for you featuring local specialities.

Getting There & Away

The main bus and service taxi stations are next to each other, about 3km southeast of the town centre (about E£2 in a taxi).

BUS

Superjet has buses to and from Cairo (E£25 to E£30, five hours) departing in each direction at 8am and 4pm. Similarly priced, **East Delta Travel Co** (☎ 332 5931) has buses to Cairo departing at 8am, 4pm and 5pm, and departures to Ismailia (E£10, three to four hours) at 7am,

10.30am, 11.30am, 1pm, 2pm, 3pm and 4pm. For Suez, change in Ismailia.

SERVICE TAXI

Service taxis from Al-Arish to Cairo cost around E£20 to E£25 per person. Service taxis to Ismailia coast E£5 to E£10, and to the border (or vice versa) for anywhere from E£10 to E£20.

Getting Around

The main taxi rank and microbus stand is at Midan al-Gamma, near the market at the southern end of town. Microbuses shuttle regularly between here and the beach (25pt).

RAFAH
☎ 068

This coastal town, 48km north of Al-Arish, marks the border with the Gaza Strip, an area that is a world away from the relative peace and calm of Sinai. Since Hamas took control of Gaza in 2007, the border has essentially been sealed off and at the time of research there was a heavy police presence on the Egyptian side. If you have a pressing reason to head to the border, you can take one of the service taxis that run daily between Al-Arish and the Rafah border crossing for about E£15. However, unless the political situation in Israel and the Palestinian Territories dramatically improves during the shelf life of this book, it is highly unlikely that you will be able to cross.

For border-crossing details and warnings, see p525.

Directory

CONTENTS

ACCOMMODATION

Egypt offers visitors the full spectrum of accommodation: hotels, flotels (Nile cruisers), all-inclusive resorts, pensions, B&Bs, youth hostels, camping grounds and even ecolodges.

Prices cited in this book are for rooms available in the high season and include taxes. Breakfast is included in the room price unless indicated otherwise in the review. We have roughly defined budget hotels as any that charge up to E£120 for a room, midrange as any that charge between E£120 and E£600 and top end as those that charge E£600 or more for a room. However, there is some variation in pricing brackets throughout the book as certain destinations are pricier than others.

Be advised that rates often go up by around 10% during peak times, including the two big feasts (Eid al-Fitr and Eid al-Adha; see p514), New Year (20 December to 5 January) and sometimes for the summer season (running approximately 1 July to 15 September).

Also note that just because a hotel has its rates displayed it doesn't mean they aren't negotiable. In off-peak seasons and during the middle of the week, haggling will often get you significant discounts, even in midrange places.

Resorts in Egypt typically offer half board (two meals), full board (three meals) or all-inclusive rates that usually include most drinks as well as some activities. Although prices are given throughout the book for all-inclusive resorts, it's worth booking these accommodation options in advance as considerable discounts are sometimes available.

Hotels rated three stars and up generally require payment in US dollars, which officially is illegal though no one seems to be paying much attention. Upmarket hotels are increasingly accepting credit-card payments, but you shouldn't take this as a given. A number of hotels, particularly along the coasts, list prices in euros, which is in response to the weakening dollar and the large European clientele. You can pay in other currencies but be advised that exchange fees sometimes apply.

Most top-end hotels and a few midrange hotels in Egypt offer nonsmoking rooms, though you can't always count on one being available. The smoking culture is extremely pronounced in Egypt, which is something that nonsmokers will be forced to get used to quickly.

Camping

Officially, camping is allowed at only a few places around Egypt, such as at Harraniyya near Giza in Cairo, Luxor, Aswan, Farafra and Ras Mohammed National Park. A few private hotels around the country also allow campers to set up in their backyards, such as at Abu Simbel, Al-Kharga, Nuweiba, Basata, Qena and Abydos. Facilities in most of these places, including official sites, are extremely basic. In Sinai the most popular budget choices are beach-side camps – all have electricity and 24-hour hot water unless noted in our reviews.

Hostels

Egypt has around a dozen hostels recognised by **Hostelling International** (HI; www.hihostels.com) in destinations including Cairo, Alexandria, Luxor and others. Having an HI card is not absolutely necessary as nonmembers are admitted, but a card will save you a bit of cash depending on the hostel.

Generally speaking, HI hostels tend to be noisy, crowded and often a bit grimy. In some there are rooms for mixed couples or families but on the whole the sexes are segregated. Most of the time you'll be much better off staying at a budget hotel instead. Reservations are not usually needed.

Hotels
BUDGET

The two-, one- and no-star hotels form the budget group. Of course, often the ratings mean nothing at all as a hotel without a star can be as good as a two-star hotel, only cheaper. Clearly, luck of the draw often applies – you can spend as little as E£25 a night for a clean single room with hot water, or E£80 or more for a dirty room without a shower. Generally, the prices quoted include breakfast, but don't harbour any great expectations –

more often than not, it's usually a couple of pieces of bread, a frozen patty of butter, a serving of jam, and tea or coffee.

Competition among the budget hotels in cities such as Cairo and Luxor is fierce, which is good news for travellers as it leads to an overall improvement in standards and services offered. Increasingly, hotels are offering rooms with private bathrooms and air-con (this costs an extra E£20 or so), improving the quality of their breakfasts and providing welcoming lounges with satellite TV, internet access and backgammon boards.

Some hotels will tell you they have hot water when they don't. They may not even have warm water. Turn the tap on and check, or look for an electric water heater when inspecting the bathroom. If there's no plug in your bathroom sink and you forgot to bring your own, then try using the lid of a Baraka mineral-water bottle – according to one cluey traveller, they fit 90% of the time.

Many budget establishments economise on sheets. If you aren't carrying your own sleeping sheet, just ask for clean sheets – most hotels will oblige. Toilet paper is usually supplied, but you'll often need to bring your own soap and shampoo.

MIDRANGE

Egypt has a great range of budget and top-end hotels, but midrange options are surprisingly limited. This is particularly so in Cairo and Alexandria, where foreign investment is channelled into top-end accommodation. In these cities local establishments often pitch themselves as midrange establishments but end up offering no-star facilities at three-star rates. Also, beware the extras: sometimes you'll be charged extra for the fridge, aircon and satellite TV in your room – before agreeing to take the room, always confirm what the quoted cost actually covers. This is particularly important when it comes to taxes, which are as high as 24% in many midrange and top-end establishments.

TOP END

Visitors are spoilt for choice when it comes to top-end hotels in Egypt. While prices and amenities are usually up to international standards, in some instances service and food can fall short. As always, it's a good idea to inspect your room before handing over any hard-earned cash.

ACTIVITIES

The incredibly varied desert and aquatic landscapes of Egypt are rife with opportunities for a wide range of activities. The following is a brief listing of some of the possibilities.

Ballooning

At the time of research, most hot-air balloons in Luxor were grounded after one crashed into a cellphone tower, injuring several tourists in the process. For more information, see p275.

Birdwatching

Egypt is an ornithologist's delight. The country boasts several excellent birdwatching areas holding a plethora of birds, both native and migrant species (see p89). The prime birdwatching spot among these areas is Lake Qarun, in the Al-Fayoum region, where species include the spoonbill and the marsh sandpiper. The saltwater lagoons in the northern

Delta and the Zerenike Protectorate on Lake Bardawil in northern Sinai are home to the greater flamingo, white pelican and spoonbill (all winter visitors). In Aswan twitchers can spot sunbirds, hoopoes, herons and kingfishers among other species. It is also possible to see huge flocks of pelicans around the small lakes near Abu Simbel in southern Egypt. In the desert you may see – or hear – eagle owls. In spring the cliffs at Ain Sukhna on the Red Sea coast offer opportunities for viewing eagles, vultures and other birds of prey.

A Photographic Guide to Birds of Egypt and the Middle East by Richard Porter and David Cottridge (E£40) and *Common Birds of Egypt* by Bertel Bruun and Sherif Baha el Din (E£35) are good illustrated references published by the American University in Cairo Press. Both are available in Egypt. Or visit the website of the Egyptian birding community, www.birdinginegypt.com, which lists top birding sites, rarities reports and travel tips.

Cycling

High temperatures, extreme distances and a limited road network don't exactly make for great cycle touring, though it's definitely doable – see p529 for ideas on making the best of what there is.

Desert Safaris

For desert safaris the options are the Western Desert, with its fantastic sand landscapes, weirdly eroded rocks and Roman ruins, or the more rugged, rocky surrounds of Sinai. Western Desert trips can be arranged cheaply in the oases (particularly Farafra) or, more expensively (involving 4WDs), in Cairo; for details, see p328.

Sinai safaris are perhaps easier to arrange. These typically involve a day or two (with overnight camping) travelling through desert canyons on foot, by camel or in a jeep. These expeditions can be organised on the ground at either Dahab or Nuweiba.

A growing number of travellers are choosing to combine an Eastern Desert safari (see p437) with a diving holiday on the Red Sea coast.

Diving & Snorkelling

Many visitors to Egypt rarely have their heads above water. No wonder, as some of the best diving in the world is to be found along the Red Sea coast (for more information, see p441).

It isn't necessary to dive to enjoy the marine life of the Red Sea. You can see plenty with just a snorkel, mask and flippers. Along the Sinai coast, the reefs are only 15m out, and in some places you don't need to go out of your depth to be among shoals of brightly coloured fish. The best places are Sharm el-Sheikh, Nuweiba and Dahab, all of which have equipment for hire for between E£25 and E£40 per day.

Fishing

Angling is seen more as a means of living than as a pastime in Egypt. Sport fishing does occur on Lake Nasser, where a couple of outfits organise 'big game' fishing safaris for Nile perch. There is also an annual International Fishing Tournament every February in Hurghada; for more details, check with the **Egyptian Angling Federation** (www.ega f.org).

Horse Riding

Horse riding is possible in Cairo around the Pyramids and in Luxor on the West Bank, where there are a couple of stables just up from the local ferry landing; see the relevant chapters for further details. There are also stables at the Sinai resorts of Sharm el-Sheikh, Dahab and Nuweiba that rent out steeds to tourists by the hour.

Sadly, most of the animals are not very well looked after. If a horse looks obviously unwell, request another.

Sandboarding

Avid sand-dune buffs can try out sandboarding at some of the oases in the Western Desert. Several hotels in Bahariya and Siwa rent out sandboards (mostly just planks of wood with foot straps) for around E£10 per day and will arrange transport to nearby dunes for some sand-surfing action. Note that sandboarding is considerably more difficult than snowboarding, and clambering back up the steep, sandy hills in the heat of the day can get exhausting pretty fast.

Windsurfing

If you're keen on windsurfing, Sinai is the place to go. Several resorts and hotels along the coastline have windsurfing centres on site, which offer full equipment rental and professional instruction. Safaga, on the Red Sea coast, is another good windsurfing spot.

BUSINESS HOURS

The following information is a guide only. The official weekend is Friday and Saturday. Note that during Ramadan offices, museums and tourist sites keep shorter hours.

Banks From 8.30am to 1.30pm Sunday to Thursday. Many banks in Cairo and other cities open again from 5pm or 6pm for two or three hours, largely for foreign exchange transactions. Some also open on Friday and Saturday for the same purpose. Exchange booths are open as late as 8pm. During Ramadan, banks are open between 10am and 1.30pm.

Bars and nightclubs Early evening until at least 3am, often later (particularly in Cairo).

Government offices From 8am to 2pm Sunday to Thursday. Tourist offices are generally open longer.

Post offices Generally open from 8.30am to 2pm Saturday to Thursday.

Private offices From 10am to 2pm and 4pm to 9pm, except Friday and holidays.

Restaurants and cafes Between noon and midnight daily. All restaurants except for those in top-end hotels remain closed throughout the day during the month of Ramadan, opening only at sundown. Cafes tend to open earlier and close a bit later. Their business hours are around 7am to midnight in the big cities, earlier in other parts of the country.

Shops From 9am to 1pm and 5pm to 10pm in summer, 10am to 6pm in winter. Hours during Ramadan are 9.30am to 3.30pm and 8pm to 10pm. Most large shops tend to close on Friday and holidays; many also close on Sunday.

CHILDREN

Egypt is a very child-friendly place, particularly in the big tourist destinations such as Luxor and Sharm el-Sheikh, and having kids with you can be a great ice-breaker with locals. There's a lot to keep the under-aged contingent happy – pyramids and temples can be explored by junior archaeologists, felucca rides please all aspiring pirates and beach outings are always popular. Also see p156 for things to see and do with children in Cairo.

Bookshops at most five-star hotels in Cairo and the major tourist centres stock a wide variety of Egyptology-related children's books that will help kids relate to what they're seeing. Locally produced history books, such as Salima Ikram's *The Pharaohs,* are excellent and reasonably priced. For books set in modern Egypt, look for *The Day of Ahmed's Secret* by Florence Parry Heide and Judith Heide Gilliland, a wonderful story of a day in the life of a small boy who delivers gas canisters in one of Cairo's poor neighbourhoods.

DIRECTORY

Apart from antiquities, there are the ever-popular camel or donkey rides. And horse riding can be great fun – the stables on Luxor's West Bank (p275) and around the Pyramids in Cairo (p145) have plenty of horses docile enough for young people and hard hats in all sizes.

Practicalities

There are a couple of things to keep in mind while you're out and about with kids in Egypt. One is that child-safety awareness is minimal. Seat belts and safety seats are nonexistent in the back seats of most cars and taxis; if you're renting a car remember to specify that you want them. Also, don't expect felucca or other boat operators to have children's life-jackets. If you can't do without them, bring your own.

Another potential worry is the high incidence of diarrhoea and stomach problems that hit travellers in Egypt. If children get sick, they tend to dehydrate more quickly than adults, and given the country's dry climate it is crucial to keep giving them liquids, even if they just throw them up again.

It's worth having some rehydration salts on hand. These are available at all pharmacies (ask for Rehydran) and usually cost less than a dollar for a box of six sachets. They can prevent a bad case of the runs from turning into something more serious. Just stir a packet into 200mL of bottled water and keep giving it until the diarrhoea has passed. See p535 for more details on preventing and dealing with potential health problems.

Formula is readily available in pharmacies, and supermarkets stock disposable nappies. High-chairs are often available in restaurants. Babysitting facilities are usually available in top-end hotels.

For great practical advice about taking the kids on your travels, pick up a copy of Lonely Planet's *Travel with Children*, written by a team of parent-authors.

CLIMATE CHARTS

Egypt's climate is easy to summarise: hot and dry, with the exception of the winter months of December, January and February, which can be quite cold in the north. Average temperatures range from 20°C (68°F) on the Mediterranean coast to 26°C (80°F) in Aswan. Maximum temperatures for the same places can get up to 31°C (88°F) and 50°C (122°F), respectively.

At night in winter the temperature sometimes plummets to as low as 8°C in Cairo and along the Mediterranean coast. In the desert it's even more extreme – often scorching during the day and bitterly cold at night.

Alexandria receives the most rain, approximately 19cm a year, while far to the south in Aswan the average is about 10mm over five years. Al-Kharga in the Western Desert once went 17 years without any rain at all.

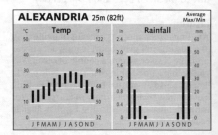

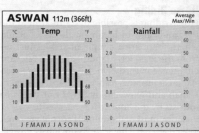

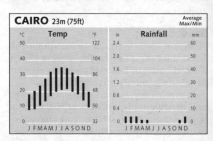

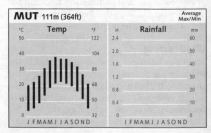

Between March and April the khamsin (a dry, hot wind) blows in from the parched Western Desert at up to 150km/h. The sky becomes dark orange and choked with dust and, even when everyone closes all doors and windows tightly, the inside of every house is covered with a patina of grit so that they resemble undisturbed tombs.

For more information on the best time to visit Egypt, see p18.

COURSES
Belly Dancing
For information about the belly-dancing courses available in Cairo, see p156.

Diving
For information on the various dive courses offered in Egypt, see p441.

Language
If you're serious about learning Arabic, the best option is to sign up at the **Arabic Language Institute** (Map pp120-1; www.aucegypt.edu; 113 Sharia Qasr al-Ainy, Cairo), a department of the American University in Cairo. It offers intensive instruction in both modern standard Arabic and Egyptian colloquial Arabic at elementary, intermediate and advanced levels in semester courses running over five months.

A cheaper option is to study at the **International Language Institute** (ILI; Map pp146-7; ☎ 02-3346 3087; www.arabicegypt.com; 4 Sharia Mahmoud Azmy, Sahafayeen, Mohandiseen, Cairo). This offers courses in modern standard Arabic and Egyptian colloquial Arabic over eight levels.

Another highly regarded school, **Kalimat** (Map pp146-7; ☎ 02-3761 8136; www.kalimategypt.com; 22 Sharia Mohamed Mahmoud Shaaban, Mohandiseen, Cairo) offers courses in modern standard Arabic and Egyptian colloquial Arabic over multiple levels.

Other Courses
The American University in Cairo is one of the premier universities in the Middle East. It offers degree, nondegree and summer-school programs. Any of the regular courses offered can be taken. Popular subjects include Arabic Language and Literature, Arab History and Culture, Egyptology, Islamic Art and Architecture, Middle East Studies and Social Science courses on the Arab world. Up to 15 unit hours can be taken per semester at the undergraduate level.

The summer programs offer similar courses. The term lasts from mid-June to the end of July. Two three-unit courses can be taken and several well-guided field trips throughout Egypt are usually included.

Applications for programs with the Arabic Language Institute (left) or undergraduate and graduate studies at the university are separate. Specify which you want when you request an application form. A catalogue and program information can be obtained from the American University in Cairo **Office of Admissions** (www.aucegypt.edu/admissions).

CUSTOMS REGULATIONS
The duty-free limit on arrival is 1L of alcohol, 1L of perfume, 200 cigarettes and 25 cigars. On top of that, once in the country, you can buy another 3L of alcohol plus a wide range of other duty-free articles, but this must be done within 24 hours of arrival at one of the special Egypt Free shops in the arrival and departure areas of the airport.

Sometimes the Customs Declaration Form D is given to arriving tourists to list all digital cameras, jewellery, cash, travellers cheques and electronics (laptop computers, MP3 players, video cameras etc). No one seems to be asked for this form on departure, and few tourists are given it on arrival. However, travellers are sometimes asked to declare their digital camera, and some have reported being hit with a hefty 'import tax'.

There are prohibited and restricted articles, including books, printed matter, motion pictures, photographs and materials that the government considers 'subversive or constituting a national risk or incompatible with the public interest'. Articles for espionage and explosives are banned.

DANGERS & ANNOYANCES
The incidence of crime, violent or otherwise, in Egypt is negligible compared with most Western countries. Most visitors and residents would agree that Egyptian towns and cities are safe to walk around in the day or night. Unfortunately, the hassle factor often means that this isn't quite the case for an unaccompanied foreign woman – for details, see p521.

Apart from the issues discussed here, you should be aware that the Egyptian authorities take a hard view of illegal drug use (see p515).

DIRECTORY

Terrorist acts against foreign tourists in 1997, 2004, 2005, 2006 and 2009 resulted in a great many deaths, and have led to the government giving security the highest possible priority – after all, the income derived from tourism constitutes an extraordinary 20% or so of the country's GDP.

While further incidents may occur at some point in the future, we'd say that Egypt is presently no more or less dangerous than any other country, your own included.

Theft

Theft never used to be a problem in Egypt but it seems to be becoming a bigger one. In the past couple of years we've received a stream of letters from readers concerning money disappearing from locked rooms, even hotel safes. Our advice is to keep your cash and valuables on your person at all times.

There are also a few areas where pickpockets are known to operate, notably on the Cairo metro and the packed local buses from Midan Tahrir to the Pyramids. Tourists aren't the specific targets, but be careful how you carry your money in crowded places.

Generally, though, unwary visitors are parted from their money through scams, and these are something that you really do have to watch out for.

DISCOUNT CARDS
Student Cards

Proof of student status is required before an International Student Identity Card (ISIC) will be issued. That proof must be a university ID card or a letter from your own college or university. You'll also need one photo, a photocopy of the front page of your passport and E£65. There are no age limits.

Most of Cairo's backpacker hotels and budget travel agencies can get the cards. Be aware that fake ISIC cards are sold by scam artists in Downtown Cairo.

SCAMS, HUSTLES & HASSLE

Egyptians take hospitality to strangers seriously. You'll receive a steady stream of *salaams* (greetings) and the odd *ahlan wa sahlan* (hello/welcome) inviting you to sit and have *shai* (tea). A lot of this is genuine, particularly in rural areas, where drink, food and transport are frequently offered with no expectation of remuneration.

But in more touristy places – notably around the Egyptian Museum and Pyramids in Cairo, and all around Luxor – a cheery 'Hello, my friend' is double-speak for 'This way, sucker'. One traveller wrote to us about feeling like a 'walking wallet' in Egypt.

Be warned that you'll become a magnet for instant friends who just happen to have a papyrus factory they'd like to show you. You'll be showered with helpful advice such as 'the museum is closed, take *shai* with me while you wait' – of course the museum isn't closed and refreshments will be taken at a convenient souvenir shop. As an English speaker you might be asked to spare a moment to check the spelling of a letter to a relative in the USA, and while you're at it how about some special perfume for the lady…

It's all pretty harmless stuff but it can become very wearing. Everyone works out a strategy to reduce the hassle to a minimum. Years ago, we heard a story about a traveller keeping touts away by jabbing his finger at his chest and saying, '*Ya Russki*' (I'm Russian). Not only were the hustlers defeated by the language, everyone expected that the Russians had no money. But now that Egypt is a popular holiday destination for newly rich Muscovites, the street entrepreneurs are just as fluent in Russian sales patter as they are in English, German, French, Dutch and Japanese.

About the only way to deal with unwanted attention is to be polite but firm, and when you're in for a pitch cut it short with 'Sorry, no thanks'.

Aside from the hustling, there are countless irritating scams. The most common involves touts who lie and misinform to get newly arrived travellers into hotels for which they get a commission – see p159 for examples of their ever-ingenious strategies.

If you do get stung, or feel one more 'Excuse me, where are you from?' will make you crack, it's best to take a deep breath and simmer down – by acting rudely or brusquely you may offend one of the vast majority of locals who would never dream of hassling a foreigner and is only trying to help a guest to the country.

TRAVEL ADVISORIES

Government websites that offer travel advisories and information on current hot spots:

Australian Department of Foreign Affairs (☎ 1300 139 281; www.smarttraveller .gov.au)

British Foreign Office (☎ 0845-850-2829; www.fco.gov.uk/travel)

Canadian Department of Foreign Affairs (☎ 800-267 6788; www.dfait-maeci.gc.ca)

US State Department (☎ 888-407 4747; http://travel.state.gov)

If you are looking for student cards in Luxor, make sure you get to the correct office; one office issues ISE (International Student & Youth Exchange) cards, which do not provide as many discounts as the ISIC. Several budget hotels issue ISIC cards but there are many fakes going around. The best places to get a genuine card are on **Sharia Ahmed Orabi** (Map pp244-5; ☎ 238 2163; ☼ 9am-6pm), next to the Egoth Institute, or at the Nefertiti Hotel (see p278).

It's worth having a student card as it entitles you to a 50% discount on admission to nearly all the antiquities and museums, as well as significant reductions on train travel. The ISIC card may sometimes get you a discount on your bus ticket but this is quite rare. Still, it's always worth asking.

Travellers have reported using a wide range of other cards to get student discounts for museum entry and transport, from HI cards to Eurail cards.

EMBASSIES & CONSULATES

Most embassies and consulates are open from around 8am to 2pm Sunday to Thursday. The addresses of some of the foreign embassies and consulates in Egypt are in the following list. If you need to ask directions to find an embassy ask, 'fayn sifarat' (where's the embassy), followed by the country name.

Australia (Map pp146-7; ☎ 02-2575 0444; 11th fl, World Trade Centre, 1191 Corniche el-Nil, Cairo)

Canada (Map pp112-13; ☎ 02-2791 8700; 26 Sharia Kamal el-Shenawy, Cairo)

Denmark (Map pp146-7; ☎ 02-2739 6500; www .ambkairo.um.dk/da; 12 Hassan Sabry, Zamalek, Cairo)

Ethiopia (Map p150; ☎ 02-3335 3696; 3 Sharia al-Misaha, Doqqi, Cairo)

France Cairo (Map pp120-1; ☎ 02-2394 7150; www .ambafrance-eg.org; 29 Sharia el-Fadl); Alexandria (Map p385; ☎ 03-487 5615; 2 Midan Orabi, Mansheyya)

Germany Cairo (Map pp146-7; ☎ 02-2728 2000; www .kairo.diplo.de; 8 Hassan Sabry, Zamalek); Alexandria (Map pp374-5; ☎ 03-4867 503; 9 Sharia el-Fawateem, Azarita)

Iran (Map p150; ☎ 02-3748 6400; 12 Sharia Refa'a, off Midan al-Misaha, Doqqi, Cairo)

Ireland (Map pp146-7; ☎ 02-2735 8264; www.embassy ofireland.org.eg; 22 Hassan Assem, Zamalek, Cairo)

Israel Cairo (off Map p152; ☎ 02-3332 1500; 8 Sharia Ibn Malek, Giza); Alexandria (Map pp372-3; ☎ 03-544 9501; 15 Rue Mina Kafr Abdou, Rushdy)

Italy Cairo (Map p150; ☎ 02-2794 3194; 15 Sharia Abdel Rahman Fahmy, Garden City); Alexandria (Map p385; ☎ 03-487 9470; 25 Sharia Saad Zaghloul)

Jordan (Map p150; ☎ 02-3748 5566; 6 Sharia Gohainy, Cairo)

Kenya (Map pp146-7; ☎ 02-3345 3628; 7 Sharia al-Quds al-Sharif, Mohandiseen, Cairo)

Lebanon Cairo (Map pp146-7; ☎ 02-2738 2823; 22 Sharia Mansour Mohammed, Zamalek); Alexandria (Map pp374-5; ☎ 03-484 6589; 64 Sharia Tariq al-Horreyya)

Libya Cairo (Map pp146-7; ☎ 02-735 1269; fax 735 0072; 7 Sharia el-Saleh Ayoub, Zamalek); Alexandria (Map pp374-5; ☎ 03-494 0877; fax 494 0297; 4 Sharia Batris Lumomba, Bab Shark)

Netherlands (Map pp146-7; ☎ 02-2739 5500; egypt .nlembassy.org; 18 Sharia Hassan Sabry, Zamalek, Cairo)

New Zealand (Map pp146-7; ☎ 02-2461 6000; www .nzembassy.com; lvl 8, North Tower, Nile City Towers, 2005C Corniche el-Nil, Cairo)

Saudi Arabia Cairo (Map p150; ☎ 02-3749 0775; 2 Sharia Ahmed Nessim, Giza); Alexandria (Map pp374-5; ☎ 03-482 9911; 9 Sharia Batalsa); Suez (Map p414; ☎ 497 7591-2; 12 Sharia el-Guabarty; Port Tawfiq) The consulate in Suez is around the corner from the tourist office.

Spain (Map pp146-7; ☎ 02-2735 6462; embespeg@mail .mae.es; 41 Sharia Ismail Mohammed, Cairo)

Sudan Cairo (Map pp112-13; ☎ 02-2794 9661; 3 Sharia al-Ibrahimy, Garden City); Aswan (Map p300; ☎ 097-230 7231; bldg 20, Atlas; ☼ 9am-3pm) Both consulates can issue same-day visas to Sudan. You need your passport, four passport photos, a letter from your embassy and US$100.

Syria (Map p150; ☎ 02-3749 5210; 18 Abdel Rahim Sabry, Doqqi, Cairo)

Turkey Cairo (Map pp112-13; ☎ 02-2794 8364; 25 Sharia al-Falaky); Alexandria (Map pp374-5; ☎ 03-393 9086; 11 Sharia Kamel el-Kilany)

UK Cairo (Map p150; ☎ 02-2791 6000; 7 Sharia Ahmed Ragheb, Garden City); Alexandria (Map pp372-3; ☎ 03-546 7001/2; Sharia Mena, Rushdy)

USA (Map pp120-1; ☎ 02-2797 3300; http://cairo.us embassy.gov; 8 Sharia Kamal el-Din Salah, Garden City, Cairo)

DIRECTORY

FESTIVALS & EVENTS

There aren't many events on the Egyptian cultural calendar, and those that are there don't always take place. The only events worth going out of your way to attend are possibly the *moulid*s (saints' festivals; see below).

JANUARY/FEBRUARY

Book Fair Held at the Cairo Exhibition Grounds over two weeks, this is one of the major cultural events in the city. It draws massive crowds, but far more burgers, soft drinks and balloons are sold than books.

FEBRUARY

Ascension of Ramses II 22 February – One of the two dates each year when the sun penetrates the inner sanctuary of the temple at Abu Simbel, illuminating the statues of the gods within.

International Fishing Tournament Held at Hurghada on the Red Sea and attended by anglers from all over the world.

Luxor Marathon (www.egyptianmarathon.com) Held on the West Bank. Competitors race around the main antiquities sites.

Nitaq Festival Excellent arts festival centred on Downtown Cairo with two weeks of exhibitions, theatre, poetry and music at galleries, cafes and a variety of other venues.

APRIL/MAY

South Sinai Camel Festival Camel races that prove these animals have fire in their bellies.

JUNE

Al-Ahram Squash Tournament International competitors play in glass courts set up for the occasion beside the Pyramids on the Giza Plateau.

International Festival of Oriental Dance (www .nilegroup.net) Held in Cairo, this is a festival of belly dancing in which famous Egyptian practitioners give showcase performances and lessons to international attendees.

AUGUST

Tourism & Shopping Festival A countrywide promotion of Egyptian products. Participating shops offer discounted prices.

SEPTEMBER

Experimental Theatre Festival Held over 10 days, this theatre festival brings to Egypt a vast selection (40

THE MOULID

A cross between a funfair and a religious festival, a *moulid* celebrates the birthday of a local saint or holy person. They are often a colourful riot of celebrations attended by hundreds of thousands of people. Those from out of town set up camp in the streets, close to the saint's tomb, where children's rides, sideshows and food stalls are erected. In the midst of the chaos, barbers perform mass circumcisions; snake charmers induce cobras out of baskets; and children are presented at the shrine to be blessed and the sick to be cured.

*Tartour*s (cone-shaped hats) and *fanous* (lanterns) are made and sold to passers-by and in the evenings local Sufis usually hold hypnotic *zikr*s in colourful tents. A *zikr* (literally 'remembrance') is a long session of dancing, chanting and swaying usually carried out to achieve oneness with God. The *mugzzabin* (Sufi followers who participate in *zikr*s) stand in straight lines and sway from side to side to rhythmic clapping that gradually increases in intensity. As the clapping gains momentum, the *zikr* reaches its peak and the *mugzzabin*, having attained oneness with Allah, awake sweating and blinking. Other *zikr*s are formidable endurance tests where troupes of musicians perform for hours in the company of ecstatic dancers.

Most *moulid*s last for about a week and climax with the *leila kebira* (big night). Much of the infrastructure is provided by 'professional' *mawladiyya*, or *moulid* people, who spend their lives going from one *moulid* to another.

For visitors, the hardest part about attending a *moulid* is ascertaining dates. Events are tied to either the Islamic or Gregorian calendars and dates can be different each year. You'll need to be prepared for immense crowds (hold on to your valuables) and females should be escorted by a male.

One of the country's biggest *moulid*s, the *moulid* of Sayyed al-Badawi, is held in Tanta in October, while Cairo hosts three major *moulid*s dedicated to Sayyida Zeinab, Sayyidna al-Hussein and Imam ash-Shafi (held during the Islamic months of Ragab, Rabei al-Tani and Sha'aban, respectively). You'll need to ask a local for the exact dates in any particular year.

There are a number of smaller *moulid*s in the area around Luxor – see p252 for more details on these celebrations.

at the last outing) of international theatre troupes and represents almost the only time each year when it's worth turning out for the theatre in Cairo.

OCTOBER
Alexandrias of the World Festival A four-day celebration attended by delegations from all the cities bearing the name Alexandria (there are over 40 in the world).
Birth of Ramses 22 October – the second date in the year when the sun's rays penetrate the temple at Abu Simbel.
Pharaohs' Rally An 11-day, 4800km motor-vehicle (4WDs and bikes) race through the desert, beginning and ending at the Pyramids, that attracts competitors from all over the world.

NOVEMBER
Arabic Music Festival A 10-day festival of classical, traditional and orchestral Arabic music held at the Cairo Opera House early in the month. Programs are usually in Arabic only but the tourist office should have details.

DECEMBER
Cairo International Film Festival (www.cairofilmfest .org) This 14-day festival, held in November/December, gives Cairenes the chance to watch a vast range of recent films from all over the world. The main attraction is that the films are all supposedly uncensored. Anything that sounds like it might contain scenes of exposed flesh sells out immediately.

FOOD
In this book, budget eateries are usually defined as those where you can get a meal (no drinks) for less than E£15. Midrange restaurants serve up main courses for under E£75 and often serve alcohol. Top-end joints are usually in five-star hotels, serve up main courses for over E£75, almost always serve alcohol and require diners to dress for dinner. Tipping is appreciated in budget places, advisable in midrange places and essential in all top-end restaurants.

For more information about eating out in Egypt, see p79.

GAY & LESBIAN TRAVELLERS
Homosexuality in Egypt is no more or less prevalent than elsewhere in the world, but it's a lot more ambiguous than in the West. Men routinely hold hands, link arms and give each other kisses on greeting – but don't misread the signals: this is not gay behaviour; it's just the local take on male bonding.

Beyond this a strange double standard goes on whereby an Egyptian man can indulge in same-sex intercourse but not consider himself gay because only the passive partner is

regarded as such. So it's not uncommon for foreign male visitors to receive blatant and crudely phrased propositions of sex from Egyptian men. But there's not necessarily any sort of gay scene – any that does exist is strictly underground. The concept of 'gay pride' is totally alien, and bar the occasional young crusader, no Egyptian man would openly attest to being homosexual for fear of being shunned by society and labelled as weak and effeminate.

While there is no mention of homosexuality in the Egyptian penal code, some statutes criminalising obscenity and public indecency have been used against gay men in the past. In May 2001, 55 Egyptian men were arrested when police raided a floating bar-restaurant moored on the Nile in Cairo. The state prosecutor's office labelled the men 'deviants', and following a retrial in 2003 (the sentences handed down at the first trial weren't tough enough on reconsideration), 21 of the men received prison time of three years.

The bottom line is that Egypt is a conservative society that condemns homosexuality but, at the same time, plenty of same-sex intercourse goes on.

There are no national support groups or gay- or lesbian-information lines at present. The premier gay and lesbian Egypt site is www.gayegypt.com.

HOLIDAYS
Egypt's holidays and festivals are primarily Islamic or Coptic religious celebrations, although all holidays are celebrated equally by the entire population regardless of creed.

The Hejira (Islamic calendar) is 11 days shorter than the Gregorian (Western) calendar, so Islamic holidays tend to fall 11 days earlier each Western year. The 11-day rule is not entirely strict, though, as the holidays can fall from 10 to 12 days earlier. The precise dates are known only shortly before they fall as they're dependent upon the sighting of the moon. See the Islamic Holidays table (p514) for the approximate dates of the major holidays for the next few years.

The following list details public holidays in Egypt.
New Year's Day 1 January – Official national holiday but many businesses stay open.
Coptic Christmas January – Coptic Christmas is a fairly low-key affair and only Coptic businesses are closed for the day.

ISLAMIC HOLIDAYS

Hejira year	Ras as-Sana	Moulid an-Nabi	Ramadan starts	Eid al-Fitr	Eid al-Adha
1431	18.12.10	26.02.10	11.08.10	10.09.10	16.11.10
1432	26.11.11	15.02.11	01.08.11	30.08.11	06.11.11
1433	15.11.12	15.02.12	20.07.12	19.08.12	26.10.12
Note that dates can vary slightly.					

Coptic Easter March/April – The most important date on the Coptic calendar, although it doesn't significantly affect daily life for the majority of the population.

Sham an-Nessim March/April – A Coptic holiday with Pharaonic origins, it literally means 'smell of the breeze'. It falls on the first Monday after Coptic Easter and is celebrated by all Egyptians, with family picnics and outings.

Sinai Liberation Day 25 April – Holiday celebrating Israel's return of Sinai in 1982 (Sinai only).

May Day 1 May – Official national holiday.

Liberation Day 18 June

Revolution Day 23 July – Official national holiday commemorating the date of the 1952 coup, when the Free Officers seized power from the puppet monarchy.

Wafa'a el-Nil 15 August – Literally 'the flooding of the Nile'.

Coptic New Year 11 September; 12 September in leap years

Armed Forces Day 6 October – Official national holiday celebrating Egyptian successes during the 1973 war with Israel. The day is marked by military parades and air displays and a long speech by the president.

Suez Victory Day 24 October

Victory Day 23 December

Islamic Holidays

Eid al-Adha Also known as Eid al-Kebir (Great Feast), this marks the time of the hajj (pilgrimage to Mecca). Those who can afford it buy a sheep to slaughter for the feast, which lasts for three days (many businesses reopen on the second day). Many families go out of town, so if you want to travel at this time, book your tickets well in advance.

Ras as-Sana Islamic New Year's Day. The entire country has the day off but celebrations are low-key.

Moulid an-Nabi This is the birthday of the Prophet Mohammed. One of the major holidays of the year, during which the streets are a feast of lights and food.

Ramadan Observant Muslims fast for a whole month during daylight hours. People are tired, listless and hungry during the day, but they come back to life again when the sun goes down and they can feast and get festive.

Eid al-Fitr A three-day feast that marks the end of Ramadan fasting.

INSURANCE

A travel insurance policy to cover theft, loss and medical problems is a good idea. There is a wide variety of policies available, so check the small print. Some policies specifically exclude 'dangerous activities', which can include scuba diving, motorcycling and trekking. A locally acquired motorcycle licence is not valid under some policies.

Check that the policy covers ambulances and an emergency flight home. For more information on health insurance, see p535.

Worldwide travel insurance is available at www.lonelyplanet.com/travel_services. You can buy, extend and claim online any time – even if you're already on the road.

INTERNET ACCESS

Travelling with a laptop is a great way to stay in touch with life back home, but unless you know what you're doing, it's fraught with potential problems. If you plan to carry your laptop computer with you, remember that the power-supply voltage may differ from that at home, which may damage your equipment. The best investment is a universal AC adaptor for your appliance, which will enable you to plug it in anywhere without frying the innards.

The good news is that Egypt has taken up the internet in a big way, and there are internet cafes throughout the country. We have listed the best of these throughout the book, and have also indicated which hotels offer internet access for guests (look for the icon 🖳). Most internet cafes will charge between E£5 and E£10 per hour for online access, will print for around E£1 per page and will burn CDs for between E£15 and E£25. Unfortunately, outside Cairo, Alexandria and tourist destinations in Sinai and along the Red Sea coast, internet connections can be infuriatingly slow at times – a result of too much demand on insufficient international bandwidth.

In recent years, a surprising number of wireless hotspots have started to appear in major tourist destinations. At the time of writing, wireless hotspots were a good bet to be found at hotels and resorts in major tourist destinations such as Luxor, Sinai and

MOHAMMED, MUHAMMAD...MU7AMMAD?

People have been wrestling Arabic into Roman letters for centuries, and now the rise of mobile phone and internet communication in the Middle East has spawned another method. Once you get over the confusion that it involves numbers, the so-called 'Arabic chat alphabet' might be the most sensible transliteration system to come along in a while. All the sounds peculiar to Arabic have been assigned a number, based very loosely on their shape in Arabic. A 3 for the back-of-the-throat letter *ayn* is the most common, so you could type 'Assalaam 3aleikum!' as a greeting. A 7 represents the aspirated 'h' ('Al-7amdulillah!'), and a 9 is the emphatic 's'. The system is popping up in ads, names of cool clubs and the like. Who knows – if it really catches on, we might be using it in the next edition of this book.

the Red Sea coast, Western-style cafes in both Cairo and Alexandria, and a select number of airports, cafes and fast food restaurants across the country. Considering that more and more travellers are lugging around their laptops, it's likely that this much-welcomed trend will continue to gain momentum.

See also p22 for a list of useful Egypt-related websites.

LEGAL MATTERS

Foreign travellers are subject to Egyptian laws and get no special consideration. If you are arrested you have the right to telephone your embassy immediately (see p511).

One of the first signs visitors see when entering the country via Cairo airport is a prominent billboard warning that the possible penalty for drug use in Egypt is hanging. Executions for such offences have been taking place since 1989 and you'll get no exemption from penalties just because you're a tourist – be very careful.

With that said, travellers tend to take a lax attitude towards smoking hashish in Sinai, particularly in the backpacker-friendly towns of Dahab and Nuweiba. Although you will no doubt be offered drugs during your travels, and will come across other travellers who are indulging, trust us – there are far better places to spend your golden years than rotting away in an Egyptian prison.

MAPS

The pick of the country maps available commercially is the Kümmerly & Frey map, which covers all of Egypt on a scale of 1:950,000. The same company also produces a map of Sinai and a pictorial (but fairly useless) map of the Nile. Similarly good is the Freytag & Berndt map, which includes a plan of the Pyramids of Giza and covers all of Egypt except the western

quarter, at a scale of 1:1,000,000. It includes insets of Cairo and central Alexandria.

Nelles Verlag has one of the most complete, though dated, general maps of Egypt (scale 1:2,500,000), including a map of the Nile Valley (scale 1:750,000) and a good enlargement of central Cairo.

Map of Egypt (scale 1:1,000,000), published by Macmillan, includes a map of the Nile Valley and a map of the country, plus good maps of Cairo and Alexandria and a variety of enlargements and temple plans.

Clyde Surveys of England has an excellent map of eastern Egypt titled *Clyde Leisure Map No 6: Egypt & Cairo*. It covers the Nile region from the coast to Aswan, and has detailed maps of Cairo, Alexandria, Luxor and Thebes, and the Pyramids, with notes in English, French and German.

MONEY

The official currency is the Egyptian pound (E£) – in Arabic, a *guinay*. One pound consists of 100 piastres (pt). There are notes in denominations of 5pt, 10pt and 25pt, but these are rarely spotted. The 50pt, E£1, E£5, E£10, E£20, E£50 and E£100 notes are widely used. There's also a rarely seen E£200 note. Coins in circulation are for denominations of 10pt, 20pt, 25pt, 50pt and E£1, but they seem to be almost nonexistent and are sometimes thought of as collector's items. Prices can be written in pounds or piastres; for example, E£3.35 can also be written as 335pt. In practice, however, vendors tend to round up, especially if you're a tourist.

There is a severe shortage of small change in Egypt, a reality that quickly becomes a nuisance for travellers frequenting ATMs. The 50pt, E£1, E£5 and E£10 notes, which are useful for tips, taxi fares and avoiding the painfully repetitious incidents of not being given

DIRECTORY

the correct change, are not always easy to come by. Even worse is that staff in businesses including upscale hotels and restaurants will sometimes scowl at you if you pay your bill in E£100 notes, thus forcing them to take to the streets to round up change.

As a good rule of thumb in Egypt, make sure you hoard small change wherever possible. Also, be sure to cash out large bills in upscale establishments, even if they initially appear unwilling. These two simple practices will save you a huge amount of frustration.

The black market for hard currency is negligible; few travellers can be bothered hunting it out for the fraction of difference it makes.

Because of the dire state of the national currency, many tour operators and hotels will only accept payment in American dollars or euros. This applies when it comes to purchasing tickets for the Abela Sleeping Car train running between Alexandria, Cairo, Luxor and Aswan; the Nuweiba to Aqaba (Jordan) ferry; and all international buses. Although technically illegal but never enforced, it is also becoming increasingly common for upscale hotels to demand payment in US dollars, though more times than not you can charge your room on a credit card. To be on the safe side, it's a good idea to travel around Egypt with a modest supply of dollars.

Exchange rates for a range of foreign currencies are given on the inside front cover of this book. For information on costs in Egypt, see p18.

ATMs

It's possible to travel in Egypt now relying solely on plastic as ATMs are becoming more and more widespread. Tourist-friendly cities such as Cairo, Alexandria, Luxor, Sharm el-Sheikh and Hurghada are saturated with cash dispensers, and you'll also find them in Alexandria, Dahab, Nuweiba and Aswan. Where it is difficult to find ATMs is anywhere between Cairo and Luxor (the towns of Minya and Asyut have just the occasional one) and out in the oases (there's just one each in Siwa and Kharga).

Of the numerous types of ATM in Egypt, the vast majority are compatible with Visa, MasterCard and any Cirrus or Plus cards. ATMs at Banque Misr, CIB, Egyptian American Bank (EAB), National Bank of Egypt and HSBC are particularly reliable.

Credit Cards

Amex, Visa, MasterCard and Diners Club are becoming more useful in Egypt. Generally speaking, they are accepted quite widely in foreign-friendly hotels, shops and restaurants, though away from tourist establishments, they are far less common, and in remote areas they remain useless. In many places you will be charged a percentage of the sale (anywhere between 3% and 10%) to use them.

Make sure you retain any receipts to check later against your statements as there have been cases of shop owners adding extra zeros. It's a dumb, easily detected crime, but the swindlers are playing on the fact that they will only be found out once the victim has returned home, and is thousands of kilometres from Egypt.

Visa and MasterCard can be used for cash advances at Banque Misr and the National Bank of Egypt, as well as at Thomas Cook offices.

International Transfers

Western Union, the international money-transfer specialist, operates jointly in Egypt with Misr America International Bank and IBA business centres. See also the Information sections for individual destinations.

Alexandria (Map pp374-5; ☎ 03-420 1148; 281 Tariq al-Horreyya)

Alexandria (Map pp372-3; ☎ 03-492 0900; 73 Tariq al-Horreyya)

Cairo (☎ 02-2755 5165) Downtown (Map pp120-1; 19 Qasr el-Nil); Garden City (8 Ibrahim Naguib)

Dahab (Map p477; ☎ 069-364 0466; just north of Bamboo House Hotel, Masbat)

Luxor (Map pp244-5; ☎ 095-372 292; Mina Palace Hotel, Corniche el-Nil)

Sharm el-Sheikh (Map p470; ☎ 062-602 222; Rosetta Hotel, Na'ama Bay)

The opening hours for these offices are the same as those of the banks. For further details and other branches, check the Egypt pages of the Western Union website (www.western union.com).

Moneychangers

Money can be officially changed at Amex and Thomas Cook offices, as well as commercial banks, foreign exchange (forex) bureaus and some hotels. Rates don't tend to vary much, especially for the US dollar but, if you're keen to squeeze out the last piastre, note that the forex bureaus generally offer slightly better rates than the banks, and usually don't charge commission.

Most hard currencies can be changed in Egypt, though US dollars, euros and British pounds are the easiest to switch out. As a rule of thumb, always look at the money you're given when exchanging, and don't accept any badly defaced, shabby or torn notes (there are plenty of them around) because you'll have great difficulty offloading them later. The same goes for transactions in shops, taxis etc.

Egyptian pounds can be changed back into hard currency at the end of your stay at some banks, forex bureaus, and Thomas Cook and Amex offices.

It is also possible to have money wired to you from home through Amex. This service operates through most Amex branches, and can be used by anyone, regardless of whether you have an Amex card. The charge is about US$80 to US$100, payable in the country from which the money is sent.

Taxes

Taxes of up to 25% will be added to your bill in most upmarket restaurants. There are also hefty taxes levied on four- and five-star accommodation – these have been factored into the prices we have cited.

Tipping

For information on tipping, see the boxed text, p65.

Travellers Cheques

While there is no problem cashing well-known brands of travellers cheques at the major banks such as Banque Misr or the National Bank of Egypt, many forex bureaus don't take them. Cheques issued on post office accounts (common in Europe) or cards linked to such accounts cannot be used in Egypt.

Banks can have a small handling charge on travellers cheques, usually a few Egyptian pounds per cheque. Always ask about commission as it can vary. Forex bureaus that take cheques tend not to charge any commission.

In addition, Amex and Thomas Cook travellers cheques can also be cashed at their offices, found in Cairo, Alexandria, Luxor, Aswan, Hurghada and Sharm el-Sheikh. A small handling charge usually applies.

POST

Postcards cost less than a dollar and take four or five days to get to Europe and a week to 10 days to the USA and Australia.

Sending a letter is also less than a dollar, and stamps are usually available at post offices, and some souvenir kiosks, shops, news-stands and the reception desks of major hotels. Sending mail from the post boxes at major hotels instead of from post offices seems to be quicker. If you use the post boxes, blue is for international airmail, red is for internal mail and green is for internal express mail.

Post offices are usually open from 8.30am to 2pm Saturday to Thursday. Poste restante in Egypt functions remarkably well and is generally free (though in Alexandria there's a small fee to collect letters). If you plan to pick up mail there, ensure that the clerk checks under Mr, Ms or Mrs in addition to your first and last names.

If you receive a package, you'll get a card (written in Arabic; you'll need a local to help you if you don't speak the language) directing you to some far-flung corner of the city to collect it. Take your passport, money and lots of patience, and allow plenty of time.

For more information on Egypt Post, contact ☎ 0800 800 2800 or check www.egypt post.org.

Parcels

Packages going by normal sea mail or airmail are sent from the main post office, although in Cairo they can only go from the huge post traffic centre located on Midan Ramses. As an indication of fees, a parcel that weighs 1kg costs between E£100 and E£200 to send via surface mail to the USA, Australia or Europe. Parcels of more than 20kg for western Europe and Africa, and 30kg for the USA, will not be accepted. Parcels should also not be bigger than 1m long and deep, and 50cm wide.

There is usually a long and complicated process of customs inspection and form filling – don't close the parcel until the process is over. You may have to get export licences or have goods inspected, depending on what they are. Printed matter and audio and visual material will be checked and foodstuffs (except dried food) and medicines also need clearance.

The easiest way to send a package is to pay someone else a small fee and have them do it

DIRECTORY

for you. Some shopkeepers will provide this service, especially if you've bought the article in their bazaar. It should include obtaining an export licence, packaging and mailing.

SHOPPING

Egypt is a shopper's dream – from traditional papyrus scrolls and original artwork to hand-made jewellery and the obligatory hookah, there is no shortage of trinkets and souvenirs on sale in souqs across the country. Of course, a good portion of tourist offerings tend to be low-quality junk, though anyone with a discerning eye can pick out the diamonds in the rough.

The undisputed shopping capital of Egypt is Khan al-Khalili in Cairo, which is just as much a tourist circus as it is one of the Middle East's most storied and historic markets. Although you're going to have to navigate a gauntlet of slimy touts and rip-off shops, there are some great finds to be had, assuming you have the time (and the patience) to shop around.

Other top-notch shopping areas include the tourist markets in Luxor, Aswan and Sharm el-Sheikh. Also, be on the lookout for traditional Siwan, Bedouin and Nubian handicrafts in the Western Desert, Sinai and Aswan, respectively.

SOLO TRAVELLERS

Other than where common sense dictates – for example, don't go wandering off into the desert on your own, don't go snorkelling or diving unaccompanied – there is nowhere in Egypt that can't be travelled solo, if you are a man, that is. Solo travel for women is slightly more difficult (see p521 and various warnings throughout the book) but is still viable as long as you use sensible caution and dress appropriately.

TELEPHONE

The country code for Egypt is ☎ 20, followed by the local area code (minus the zero), then the number. Local area codes are given at the start of each city or town section. The international access code (to call abroad from Egypt) is ☎ 00. For directory assistance call ☎ 140 or ☎ 141. The most common mobile-phone prefixes in Egypt are ☎ 010 and ☎ 012.

Two companies sell phonecards in Egypt. Menatel has yellow-and-green booths, while Nile Tel's are red and blue. Cards are sold at shops and kiosks and come in units of E£10, E£15, E£20 and E£30. Once you insert the card into the telephone, press the flag in the top left corner to get instructions in English.

THE ART OF BARGAINING

Bargaining is part of everyday life in Egypt, and almost everything is open to haggling, from hotel rooms to the price of imported cigarettes. Even in shops where prices are clearly marked, many Egyptians will still try to shave something off the bill. Of course, when buying in souqs, such as Cairo's Khan al-Khalili, bargaining is imperative unless you are willing to pay well over the odds. It can be a hassle for anyone not used to shopping this way, but keep your cool and remember it's a game, not a fight.

The first rule is never to show too much interest in the item you want to buy. Second, don't buy the first item that takes your fancy. Wander around and price things up, but don't make it obvious; otherwise, when you return to the first shop, the vendor knows that it's because he or she is the cheapest.

Decide how much you would be happy paying and then express a casual interest in buying. The vendor will state a price. So the bargaining begins. You state a figure somewhat less than the one you have fixed in your mind. The shopkeeper will inevitably huff about how absurd that is and then tell you the 'lowest' price. If it is not low enough, then be insistent and keep smiling. Tea or coffee might be served as part of the bargaining ritual but accepting it doesn't place you under any obligation to buy. If you still can't get your price, walk away. This often has the effect of closing the sale in your favour. If not, there are thousands more shops in the bazaar.

It is considered very bad form to offer an amount, have the shopkeeper agree and then to change your mind or try to get the price even lower – make sure you don't do this.

If you do get your price or lower, never feel guilty – no vendor, no matter what they may tell you, ever sells below cost.

Alternatively, there are the old telephone offices, known as Telephone centrales, where you can book a call at the desk, which must be paid for in advance (there is a three-minute minimum). The operator directs you to a booth when a connection is made.

You will find fax services are available at the main centrales in the big cities. A one-page fax costs E£7.65.

International Calling Cards

The following cards can be accessed through these Cairo numbers: **AT&T** (☎ 02-2510 0200) and **MCI** (☎ 02-2795 5770).

Mobile Phones

Egypt's mobile-phone network runs on the GSM system.

There are two main mobile-phone companies in Egypt: **MobiNil** (☎ 02-2574 7000; www .mobinil.com) and **Vodafone** (☎ 16888; www.vodafone .com.eg, www.mobileconnect.vodafone.com). Both sell convenient prepaid cards from their many retail outlets across the country. MobiNil sells its Alo Magic Scratch Card in denominations of E£10, E£25, E£50, E£100, E£200 and E£300; these have a validity period of 30 days and air-time credit is carried over if you recharge the card before the end of the validity period. Vodafone has a similar card available to Vodafone customers only, as well as a Mobile Connect card that enables wireless connection to the internet through your laptop.

TIME

Egypt is two hours ahead of GMT/UTC and daylight-saving time is observed (it begins on the last Thursday in April and ends on the last Thursday in September). So, without allowing for variations due to daylight saving, when it's noon in Cairo it is 2am in Los Angeles, 5am in New York and Montreal, 10am in London, 1pm in Moscow, and 7pm in Melbourne and Sydney.

TOILETS

Public toilets, when they can be found, are bad news. Some toilets are of the 'squat' variety. Only in midrange and top-end hotels will toilet paper be provided; most toilets simply come equipped with a water squirter for washing yourself when you're finished. It's a good idea to adopt this practice as toilets in Egypt are not capable of swallowing much

toilet paper and it's not uncommon to find toilets absolutely choked with the stuff in hotels frequented by Westerners. If you do use toilet paper, put it in the bucket that's usually provided.

In cities it's a good idea to make a mental note of all Western-style fast-food joints and five-star hotels, as these are where you'll find the most sanitary facilities.

When trekking in the desert, climbing Mt Sinai or camping on a beach, do not leave used toilet paper lying around. Don't bury it as strong winds can still blow it away. Place the paper in a plastic bag to throw away later or take matches to burn the paper.

TOURIST INFORMATION

The **Egyptian Tourist Authority** (www.egypt.travel) has tourist-information offices throughout the country, some of which are better than others. The usefulness of the offices depends largely on the staff. The Cairo, Aswan, Luxor, Dakhla, Siwa, Alexandria and Suez offices are staffed by people who have strong local knowledge and who will go out of their way to help you. Government-produced reference materials, such as maps and brochures, tend to be out of date and too general.

TRAVELLERS WITH DISABILITIES

Egypt is not well equipped for travellers with a mobility problem. Ramps are few and far between, public facilities don't necessarily have lifts, curbs are high (except in Alexandria, which has wheelchair-friendly sidewalks), traffic is lethal and gaining entrance to some of the ancient sites – such as the Pyramids of Giza or the tombs on the West Bank near Luxor – is all but impossible due to their narrow entrances and steep stairs.

Despite all this, there is no reason why intrepid travellers with disabilities shouldn't visit Egypt. In general you'll find locals quite willing to assist with any difficulties. Anyone with a wheelchair can take advantage of the large hatchback Peugeot 504s that are commonly used as taxis. One of these, together with a driver, can be hired for the day. Chances are the driver will be quite happy to help you in and out of the vehicle. Getting around the country should not be too much of a problem as most places can be reached via comfortable internal flights.

We have heard excellent reports of **Egypt for All** (www.egyptforall.com; 334 Sharia Sudan, Mohandiseen, Cairo), an Egyptian company specialising in travel arrangements for travellers who are mobility impaired.

Organisations

See the website **Access-Able Travel Source** (www .access-able.com) for general information for travellers with disabilities. Before leaving home, travellers can also get in touch with their national support organisation. Ask for the 'travel officer', who may have a list of travel agencies that specialise in tours for people with disabilities.

Access, The Foundation for Accessibility by the Disabled (☎ 516-887 5798; PO Box 356, Malverne, NY 11565, USA)

CNFLRH (☎ 01 53 80 66 66; 236 Rue de Tolbiac, Paris, France)

Radar (☎ 020-7250 3222; www.radar.org.uk; 12 City Forum, 250 City Rd, London EC1V 8AF, UK) Produces holiday fact-packs that cover planning, insurance, useful organisations, transport, equipment and specialised accommodation.

Society for the Advancement of Travel for the Handicapped (SATH; ☎ 212-447 7284; www.sath.org; 347 Fifth Ave, No 610, New York, NY 10016, USA)

VISAS & PERMITS

Most foreigners entering Egypt must obtain a visa. The only exceptions are citizens of Guinea, Hong Kong and Macau. There are three ways of doing this: in advance from the Egyptian embassy or consulate in your home country, at an Egyptian embassy abroad or, for certain nationalities, on arrival at the airport. This last option is the cheapest and easiest of the three.

Visas are available on arrival for nationals of all western European countries, the UK, the USA, Australia, all Arab countries, New Zealand, Japan and Korea. At the Cairo airport, the entire process takes only 20 minutes or so, and costs US$15. No photo is required.

Nationals from other countries must obtain visas in their countries of residence. Processing times and costs for visa applications vary according to your nationality and the country in which you apply.

If you are travelling overland, you can get a visa at the port in Aqaba, Jordan, before getting the ferry to Nuweiba. However, if you are coming from Israel, you *cannot* get a visa at the border unless you are guaranteed by an Egyptian Travel Agency. Instead, you have to get the visa beforehand at either the embassy in Tel Aviv or the consulate in Eilat.

A single-entry visa is valid for three months and entitles the holder to stay in Egypt for 40 days. Multiple-entry visas (for three visits) are also available, but although good for presentation for six months, they still only entitle the bearer to a total of one month in the country.

Sinai Entry Stamps

It is not necessary to get a full visa if your visit is confined to the area of Sinai between Sharm el-Sheikh and Taba (on the Israeli border), including St Katherine's Monastery. Instead you are issued with an entry stamp, free of charge, allowing you a 15-day stay. Note that this does not allow you to visit Ras Mohammed National Park. Points of entry where such visa-free stamps are issued are Taba, Nuweiba (port), St Katherine's airport and Sharm el-Sheikh (airport or port).

Visa Extensions & Re-Entry Visas

Six-month and one-year extensions of your visa for tourist purposes can easily be obtained at passport offices, and only cost a few dollars. You'll need one photograph and photocopies of the photo and visa pages of your passport. You have a short period of grace (usually 14 days) to apply for an extension after your visa has expired. If you neglect to do this there's a fine of approximately E£100, and you'll require a letter of apology from your embassy.

If you don't have a multiple-entry visa, it's also possible to get a re-entry visa that is valid to the combined expiry dates of your visa and any extensions. A re-entry visa for one to several entries costs less than US$5.

In Cairo all visa business is carried out at the **Mogamma** (Map pp120-1; Midan Tahrir, Downtown; ☺ 8am-1.30pm Sat-Wed), a 14-storey Egypto-Stalinist monolith that is rumoured to be closing at some point in the near future. In the meantime, foreigners should go to the 1st floor and confirm the following details at the information desk before proceeding.

On the 1st floor, go to window 12 for a form, fill it out and then buy stamps from window 43 before returning to window 12 and submitting your form with the stamps, one photograph, and photocopies of the photo and visa pages of your passport (photos and photocopies can be organised on the ground floor).

You can pick up your passport, hopefully with the visa extension granted, from window 38. Generally speaking, applications are processed overnight, though same-day service is sometimes possible if you drop your passport off very early in the morning.

Passport and visa offices elsewhere in the country:

Alexandria (Map p385; ☎ 482 7873; 25 Sharia Talaat Harb; ☒ 8.30am-2pm Mon-Thu, 10am-2pm Fri, 9-11am Sat & Sun) Does visa extensions, usually on the same day. You need one passport-size photo, a photocopy of the relevant pages of your passport, the passport itself and E£13. Go to counter eight on the 2nd floor; it's a good idea to get there in the morning.

Aswan (off Map p306; ☎ 231 2238; Corniche an-Nil; ☒ 8.30am-1pm Sat-Thu) For visa extensions. At the southern end of the Corniche.

Hurghada (Map p427; Sharia an-Nasr, Ad-Dahar; ☒ 8am-2pm Sat-Thu) For visa extensions and re-entry visas.

Ismalia (☎ 391 4559; Midan al-Gomhuriyya; ☒ 8am-2pm Sat-Thu)

Luxor (Map pp244-5; ☎ 238 0885; Sharia Khalid ibn al-Walid; ☒ 8am-8pm Sat-Thu, for information only 2-8pm)

Minya (☎ 236 4193; 2nd fl, above main post office; ☒ 8.30am-2pm Sat-Thu) Off Sharia Corniche an-Nil.

Port Said (window 7, left wing, 4th fl, Governorate Bldg, Sharia 23rd of July; ☒ 8am-2pm Sat-Thu)

Suez (Sharia al-Horreyya; ☒ 8.30am-3pm) Issues visa extensions.

Travel Permits

Military permits issued by either the Ministry of the Interior or Border Police are needed to travel in the Eastern Desert south of Shams Allam (50km south of Marsa Allam), on or around Lake Nasser, off-road in the Western Desert and on the road between the oases of Bahariyya and Siwa. These can be obtained through a safari company or travel agency at least a fortnight in advance of the trip.

WOMEN TRAVELLERS

Egyptians are conservative, especially on matters concerning sex and women – Egyptian women, that is, not foreign women.

An entire book could be written from the comments and stories of women travellers about their adventures and misadventures in Egypt. You're almost certain to hear chat-up lines such as 'I miss you like the desert misses the rain', which might be funny if they weren't

so constant and intimidating. Most of the incidents are nonthreatening nuisances, like a fly buzzing in your ear: you can swat it away and keep it at a distance, but it's always out there buzzing around.

The presence of foreign women presents, in the eyes of some Egyptian men, a chance to get around local cultural norms with ease and without consequences. This belief is reinforced by distorted impressions gained from Western TV and by the clothing worn by some female tourists. As a woman traveller you may receive some verbal harassment at the very least. Serious physical harassment and rape do occasionally occur, but more rarely than in most Western countries.

Attitudes Towards Women

Some of the biggest misunderstandings between Egyptians and Westerners occur over the issue of women. Half-truths and stereotypes exist on both sides: many Westerners assume all Egyptian women are veiled, repressed victims, while a large number of Egyptians just see Western women as sex-obsessed and immoral.

For many Egyptians of both genders, the role of a woman is specifically defined: she is mother and matron of the household. The man is the provider. However, as with any society, generalisations can be misleading and the reality is far more nuanced. There are thousands of middle- and upper-middle-class professional women living in Egypt who, like their counterparts in the West, juggle both work and family responsibilities. Among the working classes, where adherence to tradition is the strongest, the ideal may be for women to concentrate on the home and family, but economic reality means that millions of women are forced to work (but are still responsible for all the domestic chores).

The issue of sex is where the differences between Western and Egyptian women are most apparent. Premarital sex (or, indeed, any sex outside marriage) is taboo in Egypt. However, as with anything forbidden, it still happens. Nevertheless, it is the exception rather than the rule – and that goes for men as well as women.

For women, however, the issue is potentially far more serious. With the possible exception of the upper classes, women are expected to be virgins when they marry and a family's reputation can rest upon this point.

DIRECTORY

TIPS FOR WOMEN TRAVELLERS

- Wear a wedding ring. Generally, Egyptian men seem to have more respect for a married woman.

- If you are travelling with a man, it is better to say you're married rather than 'just friends'.

- Avoid direct eye contact with an Egyptian man unless you know him well; dark sunglasses help, mirrored ones are even better.

- Try not to respond to an obnoxious comment from a man – act as if you didn't hear it.

- Be careful in crowds and other situations where you are crammed between people as it is not unusual for crude things to happen behind you.

- On public transport, sit next to a woman if possible. This is not difficult on the Cairo metro where the first compartment is reserved for women only.

- If you're in the countryside (off the beaten track) be extra conservative in what you wear.

- Keep your distance. Remember that even innocent, friendly talk can be misconstrued as flirtation by men unused to close interaction with women. Ditto for any physical contact.

- If you need help for any reason (directions etc), ask a woman first.

- Be wary when horse or camel riding, especially at touristy places. It's not unknown for a guy to ride close to you and grab your horse, among other things. Riding with an unknown man on a horse or camel should be avoided.

- Egypt is not the place for acquiring a full suntan. Only on private beaches in the top-end resorts along the Red Sea and in southern Sinai are you likely to feel comfortable stripping down to a bikini. Along the Mediterranean coast and in oasis pools, you'll have to swim in shorts and a T-shirt at the very minimum, and even then you'll attract a flock of male onlookers. Egyptian women rarely go swimming at public beaches; when they do, they swim fully clothed, scarf and all.

- You may find it handy to learn the Arabic for 'don't touch me' (la' tilmasni). Also worth memorising are ihtirim nafsak (literally 'behave yourself') or haasib eedak (watch your hand). Swearing at would-be Romeos will only make matters worse.

- If you do get groped, don't expect people to be ashamed or apologise if you call them out. Most guys will just sort of stare at you blankly and wander away. So all the advice to ignore, ignore, ignore is really wiser – you won't be standing there with your adrenaline running, shouting and feeling like an idiot.

- Being befriended by an Egyptian woman is a great way to learn more about life in Egypt and, at the same time, have someone totally nonthreatening to guide you around. Getting to know an Egyptian woman is, however, easier said than done. All we can say is seize on whatever opportunities you get.

In such a context the restrictions placed on a girl – no matter how onerous they may seem to a Westerner – are to protect her and her reputation from the potentially disastrous attentions of men.

What to Wear

Away from the Sinai and Red Sea beaches, Egyptians are quite conservative about dress. As with anywhere, take your cues from those around you: if you're in a rural area and all the women are in long, concealing dresses, you should be conservatively dressed. If you're going out to a hip Cairo nightspot, you're likely to see middle- and upper-class Egyptian girls in the briefest designer gear and can dress accordingly – just don't walk there.

It is particularly important to cover up when visiting mosques and churches – you'll find that carrying a shawl to use as a head covering will come in very useful, particularly when visiting areas such as Islamic and Old Cairo.

Unfortunately, although dressing conservatively should reduce the incidence of harassment, it by no means guarantees you'll be left alone. Although it may or may not be comforting, Egyptian women get verbal and physical harassment as well – it's not just because you're foreign.

WORK

More than 40,000 foreigners live and work in Egypt. It is possible to find work with one of the many foreign companies, especially if you begin your research before you leave home. *Cairo: A Practical Guide,* edited by Claire E Francy and published by the American University in Cairo Press, has lots of information about working in Cairo. Once you have an employer, securing a work permit through an Egyptian consulate or from the Ministry of the Interior (if you are in Egypt) should not be difficult.

The most easily available work for native or fluent English speakers is teaching the language to the locals. The best places to do this are reputable schools such as the ILI in Cairo (see p509). However, all of these places require qualifications and the minimum requirement is a Certificate in English Language Teaching to Adults (CELTA). The ILI runs several one month intensive CELTA courses each year and sometimes employs course graduates.

If you are a dive master or diving instructor you can find work in Egypt's diving resorts fairly easily. As many divers fund their travels through such work the turnover is high and you're likely to find an opening if you can hang around for a couple of weeks. Owners say that apart from the basic diving qualifications, they look for languages and an ability to get along with people. If you're interested in a job, a dive centre will usually take you along on a few dive trips to assess your diving skills and to see how you interact with others before offering you work.

It is sometimes possible to find other types of work in resort towns. Sharm el-Sheikh and Dahab in particular have a relatively large number of travellers who find short-term work as bartenders or workers in the many hotels and dive centres dotted along the beach. There are also a few enterprising travellers who've financed their stay by setting up shop as masseurs, acupuncturists and herbalists.

Away from the beaches, some of the larger hotels in Luxor and Aswan occasionally take on foreigners as entertainment directors, but many of the large chains have their own staff sent in from abroad.

Transport

CONTENTS

GETTING THERE & AWAY

If you're heading to Egypt from Europe, the easiest way to get there is to fly direct. If you're coming from any other continent, it can sometimes be cheaper to fly first to Europe and then make your way to Egypt. And, of course, there are also the overland combinations of bus, taxi and ferry from other European, African and Middle Eastern countries to consider.

ENTERING THE COUNTRY

If you enter the country via Cairo International Airport, there are a few formalities. After walking past the dusty-looking duty-free shops, you'll come to a row of exchange booths. If you haven't organised a visa in advance, you'll need to pay US$15 to receive a visa stamp (see p520). You then fill in one of the pink immigration forms available on the benches in front of the immigration officials before queuing to be processed. The whole procedure usually takes about 20 minutes but, this being Egypt, it's probably best to expect delays.

Although formalities vary depending on which border you're crossing, generally speaking it's fairly straightforward to enter Egypt by land or sea.

Regardless of the means by which you enter Egypt, be sure that you have a passport that is valid for at least six months from the date of entry into the country.

If you're leaving Egypt by air, your departure tax will usually have been prepaid with your airfare. If you're departing by land, you'll need to pay E£2 (travellers who entered Egypt on a Sinai-only visa are exempt). Also note that Egyptian international ferries charge E£50 port tax per person on top of the ticket price.

AIR
Airports & Airlines

Egypt has quite a few airports, but only seven of these are official international ports of entry: Cairo, Alexandria, Luxor, Aswan, Hurghada, Sharm el-Sheikh and Marsa Alam. Most air travellers enter Egypt through Cairo, Alexandria or Sharm el-Sheikh, while the other airports tend to be used by charter and package-deal flights only.

Most tickets are sold for flights in and out of Cairo but sometimes it's possible to get cheaper deals to the airports serving resorts, such as Sharm el-Sheikh. While you could use Sharm as a starting point for travelling around the country, it is a good six-hour bus ride from Cairo, and the loss of time may outweigh any potential savings in money. However, Sharm serves as an excellent base for exploring Sinai or as a jumping-off point for Jordan and Israel and the Palestinian Territories.

THINGS CHANGE...

The information in this chapter is particularly vulnerable to change. Check directly with the airline or a travel agent to make sure you understand how a fare (and ticket you may buy) works and be aware of the security requirements for international travel. Shop carefully. The details given in this chapter should be regarded as pointers and are not a substitute for your own careful, up-to-date research.

CLIMATE CHANGE & TRAVEL

Climate change is a serious threat to the ecosystems that humans rely upon, and air travel is the fastest-growing contributor to the problem. Lonely Planet regards travel, overall, as a global benefit, but believes we all have a responsibility to limit our personal impact on global warming.

Flying & Climate Change

Pretty much every form of motor travel generates CO_2 (the main cause of human-induced climate change) but planes are far and away the worst offenders, not just because of the sheer distances they allow us to travel, but because they release greenhouse gases high into the atmosphere. The statistics are frightening: two people taking a return flight between Europe and the US will contribute as much to climate change as an average household's gas and electricity consumption over a whole year.

Carbon Offset Schemes

Climatecare.org and other websites use 'carbon calculators' that allow jetsetters to offset the greenhouse gases they are responsible for with contributions to energy-saving projects and other climate-friendly initiatives in the developing world – including projects in India, Honduras, Kazakhstan and Uganda.

Lonely Planet, together with Rough Guides and other concerned partners in the travel industry, supports the carbon offset scheme run by climatecare.org. Lonely Planet offsets all of its staff and author travel.

For more information check out our website: lonelyplanet.com.

Egypt's international and national carrier is **EgyptAir** (MS; ☎ national call centre 0900 70000; www .egyptair.com; ☘ 8am-8pm), which has its hub at Cairo International Airport. Humorously (or perhaps terrifyingly) dubbed 'Egypt Scare' or '*inshallah* Air' by some jaded travellers, EgyptAir doesn't have particularly good service and its fleet could certainly use an upgrade. If you're looking for an international flight to Egypt, you'd probably do better flying with a different airline.

For details of EgyptAir offices in Egypt, see the Getting There & Away sections of destination chapters throughout the book. For airport details, see To/From the Airport in the Getting Around section of destination chapters throughout the book.

AIRLINES FLYING TO/FROM EGYPT

Air France (AF; ☎ in Cairo 02-2770 6262; www .airfrance.com)

Alitalia (AZ; ☎ in Cairo 02-2578 5823; www.alitalia.com)

British Airways (BA; www.britishairways.com) Cairo (☎ 02-2480 0380); Cairo International Airport (☎ 02-2269 1690)

BMI (BMI; ☎ in UK 0870 6070 555; www.flybmi.com)

El Al Israel Airlines (LY; ☎ in Cairo 02-736 1620; www .elal.com)

Emirates Airlines (EK; ☎ in Cairo 02-19899; www .emirates.com)

KLM (KL; ☎ in Cairo 02-2770 6251; www.klm.com)

Lufthansa (LH; ☎ in Cairo 02-19380; www.lufthansa .com)

Royal Jordanian (RJ; ☎ in Cairo 02-2575 0875; www .rj.com)

Singapore Airlines (SQ; ☎ in Cairo 02-3749 2879; www.singaporeairlines.com)

Tickets

Recommended online booking agencies:

Expedia (www.expedia.com)

Flight Centre (www.flightcentre.com)

Lastminute (www.lastminute.com)

Lonely Planet (www.lonelyplanet.com/bookings)

STA Travel (www.statravel.com) Discounts for students.

Travel (www.travel.com)

Travelocity (www.travelocity.com)

LAND

Israel & the Palestinian Territories

The two official borders with Israel and the Palestinian Territories are Rafah and Taba.

RAFAH

At the time of research, the Rafah border crossing, which services a direct route from Cairo to Tel Aviv via the Gaza Strip, was closed. Responsibility for policing the border was relinquished by the Israelis after their withdrawal from Gaza in September 2005, and the Palestinian Authority and the Egyptian government subsequently policed the border.

In June 2007, the crossing was closed entirely after the Hamas takeover of the Gaza Strip and, in January 2008, Hamas-linked militants bombed the wall dividing the Egyptian and Palestinian portions of Rafah. In the aftermath, several hundred thousand Gazans entered Egypt to purchase food and supplies.

In December 2008, Egypt temporarily opened the crossing to care for the wounded after the Israeli airstrikes in Gaza, but it is unlikely that the border crossing will return to normalcy in the near future.

TABA

The border crossing at Taba is used for the majority of travel between Egypt and Israel and the Palestinian Territories. Travellers make their way to Taba from destinations across Egypt, and then walk across the border, which is open 24 hours. An Israeli visa is not required for most nationalities. Once the border is crossed, taxis or buses (city bus E£15) can be taken the 4km to Eilat, from where there are frequent buses onward to Jerusalem and Tel Aviv. Keep in mind that there are no buses operating in Israel and the Palestinian Territories on Friday evenings or before sundown Saturday, the Jewish holy day of Shabbat.

Heading back to Egypt, you must have a visa in advance unless your visit is limited to eastern Sinai or you have prearranged your entry with an Egyptian tour operator (see also p520). If you don't have a visa, you can go to the **Egyptian embassy** (☎ 03-546 4151; 54 Basel St; ☺ applications 9-11am Sun-Thu) in Tel Aviv or **consulate** (☎ 08-637 6882; 68 Afrouni St; ☺ 9-11am Sun-Thu) in Eilat. An Egyptian visa sourced through either of these offices will cost 65NIS for US and German citizens and 100NIS for everyone else. Deliver your passport, application and one passport-sized photo during opening hours in the morning and you'll be able to pick up the visa around 2pm on the same day.

At the **border crossing** (☎ 08-637 2104, 636 0999) you'll need to pay a 68NIS fee to leave. Once you've crossed the border, you'll need to pay an Egyptian entry tax of E£30 at a booth about 1km south of the border on the

main road. Alternatively, you can pick up a free Sinai-only entry permit (see p520). Vehicles can be brought into Egypt from Eilat, but no private vehicles are permitted to cross at Taba *from* Egypt to Israel and the Palestinian Territories.

For information on getting to/from Taba, see p494.

Jordan

From Cairo, there's a twice-weekly **Superjet** (☎ 02-2290 9017) service to Amman (US$85) leaving from Al-Mazah Garage on Sunday and Thursday at 5am. There is also a daily **East Delta Travel Co** (☎ 02-2574 2814) service from Cairo to Aqaba (US$45) at 8pm. Both of these bus services use the ferry between Nuweiba and Aqaba, so you will be liable for the port tax and the cost of a ferry ticket (see p489).

Libya

The border-crossing point of Amsaad, just north of Halfaya Pass, is 12km west of Sallum. Service taxis run up the mountain between the town and the Egyptian side of the crossing for E£5. Once you've walked through passport control and customs, you can get a Libyan service taxi on to Al-Burdi for about LD1. From there, buses run to Tobruk and Benghazi.

Be advised that at the time of writing it was still not possible to get a Libyan visa at the border. However, you should check with the Libyan embassy in Cairo (p511) as the regulations do seem to be becoming more user-friendly. It is also not possible to get an Egyptian visa at the border but this may change in the near future. Departure tax from Egypt is E£20; there is no Libyan departure tax.

Superjet has buses to Benghazi leaving on Tuesday, Thursday and Saturday at 11am (E£150, 17 hours), as well as buses to Tripoli leaving on Tuesday, Friday and Sunday at 10am (E£275, 24 hours). East Delta Travel Co also has buses to Benghazi, which leave at noon on Tuesday, Thursday and Saturday, and buses to Tripoli on Tuesday and Friday at 11am. Services leave from Al-Mazah Garage in Cairo (p178).

Sudan

Despite their sharing an enormous land border, the only way to travel between Egypt and

Sudan is to fly or take the Wadi Halfa ferry (see right).

SEA
Cyprus

From Port Said, boats to Limassol in Cyprus depart twice weekly from May to November (one-way US$120). For information and tickets, visit one of the many shipping agents in town. These include **Canal Tours** (☎ 066-332 1874, 012 798 6338; canaltours@bec.com.eg; 12 Sharia Palestine, Port Said; ☾ 8am-3pm & 7pm-midnight), a few blocks up from the tourist office. Note that some nationalities (mainly those from the subcontinent) must be in possession of a valid visa for Cyprus to be allowed on board the boats.

Europe

At the time of research no passenger boats were operating between Egyptian ports and any ports in Europe.

Israel & the Palestinian Territories

There's been talk about resuming the boat service from Port Said to Haifa. At the time of writing, this service was still nonexistent.

Jordan

There's ferry service between Nuweiba in Egypt and Aqaba in Jordan. For more information on this service, see p489.

Saudi Arabia

There are regular ferries from Hurghada and Safaga to Duba and Jeddah, though they are not recommended following the high-profile sinking of the *Al-Salam Boccaccio* in 2006, which resulted in almost 1000 deaths. Schedules change depending on weather conditions, the hajj and other factors, so it's best to enquire locally. Also note that tourist visas for Saudia Arabia are about as common as unicorns, and you will simply not be allowed to set foot on the ferry unless your passport is in order. If you're heading to Saudia Arabia either for business or to partake in the hajj, it's highly recommended that you fly.

PORT TAX

All Egyptian international ferries charge E£50 port tax per person on top of the ticket price.

Sudan

The **Nile River Valley Transport Corporation** Aswan (☎ 097-303 348; in the shopping arcade behind the tourist police office; ☾ 8am-2pm Sat-Thu); Cairo (☎ 02-2575 9058; next to the 3rd-class ticket window at Ramses station) runs one passenger ferry per week from Aswan to Wadi Halfa. One-way tickets cost E£385 for 1st class with bed in a cabin, E£240 for an airline seat and E£165 for deck class. At the time of research, the ferry was departing on Monday at around noon, though departure times regularly change. Tickets are also issued on Monday at the company's **office** (☎ 097-480 567) in Aswan port. No tickets will be issued, nor will you be able to board the ferry, unless you have a valid Sudanese visa in your passport.

The trip takes between 16 and 24 hours (usually closer to 24), and tea, soft drinks and snacks are available on board. Passengers should arrive at about 8.30am to allow time to clear customs and fight for a decent seat. Some of the Sudanese immigration formalities are carried out on the boat, and people are occasionally asked for a yellow-fever certificate. The return trip departs from Wadi Halfa on Wednesday.

The Nile Navigation Company attaches a pontoon to the ferry whenever it is needed. Prices are E£400 for a motorcycle and E£2500 for a car or 4WD. Drivers and passengers travel inside the ferry, for which they must also buy tickets. If you are taking a vehicle, you must have the usual *carnet de passage en douane* and allow plenty of time for customs procedures.

TOURS

There are countless possibilities for arranging organised tours in Egypt, with a plethora of agencies dealing with everything from guided trips and overland safaris to Nile cruises (see p93) and dive trips (see p441). The programs on such trips are usually fairly tight, leaving little room for roaming on your own. However, the advantages are that many of the time-consuming hassles, such as waiting for public transport and finding accommodation, are taken care of, maximising time for exploring and sightseeing. There's also the security that comes with being in a group, which allows you to do things such as camping in the desert or participating in off-the-beaten-track activities that might be unsafe for individuals or couples.

It pays to shop around. When considering a tour, ask what the price includes (ie flights, admission fees, food etc) – some companies include these in their prices, while others don't – you need to be aware of what you're paying for when you compare prices.

For listings of recommended tour operators, be sure to check out www.lonelyplanet .com/travel_services.

Adventure & Overland Safaris

In this kind of tour, you travel in a specially adapted 'overland truck' with anywhere from 16 to 24 other passengers and your group leader-cum-driver/navigator/ nurse/mechanic/guide/fixer/entertainer. Accommodation is usually a mix of camping and budget hotels. Food is bought along the way and the group cooks and eats together, and you are expected to pitch in with the chores.

Recommended tour companies:

African Trails (☎ 020-7706 7384; www.africantrails .co.uk) Offers a range of tours in the region that include Egypt. Offices in the UK, Australia, New Zealand and Europe.

Dragoman (☎ 870-499 4475; www.dragoman.co.uk) A UK-based overland specialist with numerous itineraries throughout North Africa and the Middle East.

Other Tours

Following is a list of specialist operators that organise Egypt packages tailored for travellers looking for more than just two weeks in the sun.

AUSTRALIA

Intrepid Travel (☎ 03-8602 0500; www.intrepidtravel .com) Highly regarded small-group tours with an emphasis on responsible tourism. Also has offices in the UK, North America, Europe and South Africa.

Peregrine Adventures (☎ 03-9663 8611; www .peregrineadventures.com) An agent for the UK's Dragoman, Exodus and the Imaginative Traveller.

EGYPT

Abercrombie & Kent (☎ in the US 800-554-7094, 630-954-2944; www.akegypt.com) Offers first-class packages using top-end hotels, domestic flights and its own custom-built Nile cruisers.

Experience Egypt (☎ 02-3302 8364; www.experience -egypt.com; 42 Sharia Abu el-Mahassen el-Shazly, Mohandiseen, Cairo) Part of Lady Egypt Tours. Organises small-group tours of Sinai, Alexandria and the Nile Valley that are marketed in the UK and Canada.

UK

Bales Tours (☎ 0870 752 0780; www.balesworldwide .com) Runs upmarket tours using five-star accommodation.

Egypt on the Go (☎ 020-7371 1113; www.egypt onthego.com) Tours of Egypt and PADI diving-course holidays. Also has an Australian office.

Exodus (☎ 0870 240 5550; www.exodus.co.uk) Includes Nile cruises and tours around Sinai and through the Western Desert.

Explore Worldwide (☎ 0800 227 8747; www.explore worldwide.com) A variety of short and long itineraries.

Hayes & Jarvis (☎ 0870 366 1636; www.hayes-jarvis .com) A respected Egypt specialist.

Imaginative Traveller (☎ 0800 316 2717; www .imaginative-traveller.com) Small-group tours. Also has offices elsewhere, including the US.

Wind, Sand & Stars (☎ 020-7359 7551; www .windsandstars.co.uk) A Sinai specialist that organises trips involving climbing and walking, desert camping, birdwatching and snorkelling.

USA & CANADA

Bestway Tours & Safaris (☎ 604-264 7378; www .bestway.com) A Canadian company offering small-group tours, including one from Siwa to Ghadames in Libya and one visiting Egypt, Israel and the Palestinian Territories, and Jordan.

GETTING AROUND

Egypt has a very extensive public and private transport system, and you can travel just about anywhere in Egypt relatively cheaply. However, it's worth mentioning that most Egypt streets lack names, which can make navigating on your own difficult. Fortunately, locals are usually more than willing to help you find your way.

In recent years there have been a number of highly publicised bus crashes and ferry disasters that have claimed local and foreign lives. Although there is no cause for alarm, it's worth keeping this in mind, particularly when debating the merits of questionable transport options, such as night buses or dodgy-looking taxis.

AIR

EgyptAir (www.egyptair.com) is the main domestic carrier, and flights are a surprisingly cheap and convenient means of bypassing countless hours on buses or trains. Fares vary considerably depending on season and availability, but sometimes it's possible to snag domestic

DOMESTIC AIRLINES

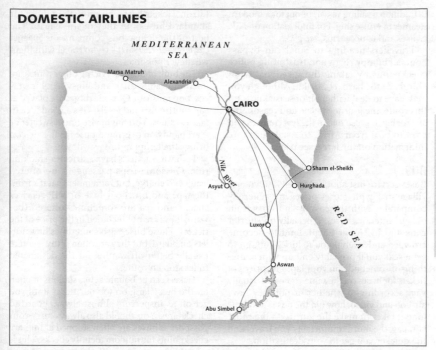

MEDITERRANEAN
SEA

Marsa Matruh
Alexandria
CAIRO
Nile River
Sharm el-Sheikh
Asyut
Hurghada
RED SEA
Luxor
Aswan
Abu Simbel

TRANSPORT

one-way fares for less than US$100. Prices can increase dramatically during the high season (October to April), and high demand means that it's wise to book as far in advance as possible. For EgyptAir contact details, see the Getting There & Away sections of individual cities and towns throughout this book.

BICYCLE

You meet very few cyclists touring Egypt – long distances combined with intense heat is the main deterrent. The blazing sun is at its worst from June to August, and even from May to mid-June and September to October it's necessary to make an early-morning start and finish by early afternoon.

Carrying a full kit with you is recommended, as spares are hard to come by, although in a pinch you'll find Egyptians are generally excellent 'bush mechanics'.

Members of **Cairo Cyclists** (www.cairocyclistsclub .com) reckon the best place in Cairo for repairs is Ghoukho Trading & Supplies near St Mark's Cathedral, 800m south of Midan

Ramses. It's quite hard to find, so be prepared to ask for directions.

If you are considering cycling Egypt but have a few pressing questions that first need answering, check the Thorn Tree travel forum on www.lonelyplanet.com – there's a dedicated forum section for cyclists. Post your query and there's a strong likelihood that somebody will respond with the information you're looking for.

Alternatively, you could contact the **Cyclists' Touring Club** (CTC; ☎ 01483-417 217; www.ctc.org .uk), a UK-based organisation that, among other things, produces information sheets on cycling in different parts of the world. The club also publishes a good, glossy bimonthly magazine that always carries one or two travel-type cycling pieces. Another handy resource is www.worldbiking.info.

BOAT

No trip to Egypt is complete without a trip down the Nile River. Egyptians have been plying these muddy waters for countless generations, and you can still take the trip on a felucca (a traditional sailing vessel) or opt for a modern steamer or cruise ship. For information on Nile cruises and felucca trips, see p93.

Travellers heading to Sinai can bypass hours of bumpy roads and frustrating police checkpoints by taking the speedboat from Hurghada to Sharm el-Sheikh. Although you may have to deal with a bit of seasickness on this route, the journey is safe and reasonably affordable. It's also one of the few chances you have to boat from Africa to Asia! For more information on the ferry, see p431.

BUS

Buses service just about every city, town and village in Egypt. Ticket prices are generally comparable with the cost of 2nd-class train tickets. Intercity buses, especially on shorter runs and in Upper Egypt, tend to become crowded and even if you're lucky enough to get a seat you'll probably end up with something or somebody on your lap. The prices of tickets for buses on the same route will usually vary according to whether or not they have air-con and video, how old the bus is and how long it takes to make the journey – the more you pay, the more comfortably you travel and the quicker you get to your destination.

Relatively comfortable, air-con 'deluxe' buses travel between Cairo, Alexandria, Ismailia, Port Said, Suez, St Katherine's Monastery, Sharm el-Sheikh, Hurghada and Luxor. Tickets cost a bit more than those for standard buses but they're still cheap. The best of the deluxe bus companies is **Superjet** (☎ in Cairo 02-2290 9017) – try to travel with them whenever possible.

The bulk of buses servicing other routes are uncomfortable, dirty and noisy. Arabic videos, pop music or Quranic dirges are played at ear-splittingly loud levels – it's a good idea to take earplugs. You might also find a sweater or scarf handy on overnight buses as the air-con brings the temperature way down.

Today most buses have a strict no-smoking rule. On some trips passengers are offered water (no charge, but remember that it's from the tap) and on the deluxe or VIP services snacks and tea are sometimes offered (beware: these are not included in the price of the ticket). These buses also sometimes have toilets on board, but they are often filthy – you're usually better off waiting for the designated toilet stop en route.

Tickets can be bought at bus stations or often on the bus. Hang on to your ticket until you get off as inspectors almost always board to check fares. You should also always carry your passport as buses are often stopped at military checkpoints for random identity checks. This is particularly common on the bus between Aswan and Abu Simbel, and on all Sinai buses.

It is advisable to book tickets in advance, at least on very popular routes (such as from

---

THE CURSE OF THE CONVOYS IS LIFTED...

Prior to 2009, tourists travelling by road in the Nile Valley, and along parts of the Red Sea coast, were forced to join a police-escorted convoy. A legacy of the Islamist insurgency of the 1990s, which reached its height with the 1997 massacre at the Temple of Hatshepsut in Luxor, the convoy system was introduced by the Egyptian government to give foreign tourists a sense of personal security. Later, this need for security had eased and the continuance of the convoy system seemed only to be a means of providing duties for the country's large and underemployed tourist-police force.

Now, after more than a decade of having your itinerary dictated by a frustratingly rigid schedule, and having to keep up with notoriously lead-footed police, it is possible to travel independently throughout an increasingly large swath of Egypt.

The implications are numerous: congestion is down at busy tourist sites (such as Luxor), far-flung destinations that were not previously serviced by the convoy route (such as Abydos) are now easily accessible, and foreigners are free to visit a larger number of towns and villages outside the standard tourist route without a police escort.

If you're travelling by local bus or minibus, the lifting of the convoys also means that forced early-morning departures between Luxor and the coast are no more. If you're travelling by rental car or private vehicle, which was until recently a very difficult proposition, you can now stop and go as you please throughout the country. If you're a self-drive adventurer, the easing of travel restrictions allows you to witness the real Egypt that lies well beyond the tourist- and tout-thronged temples and souvenir souqs.

Cairo to Sinai) and those with few buses running (from Cairo to the Western Desert). An International Student Identity Card (ISIC) now enables passengers to get discounts on some bus routes, so always remember to ask. Where you are allowed to buy tickets on the bus, you generally end up standing if you don't have an assigned seat with a booked ticket. On short runs there are no bookings and it's a case of first on, best seated.

CAR & MOTORCYCLE

Driving in Cairo is a crazy affair, so think seriously before you decide to hire a car there (see also p180). Driving in other parts of the country, at least in daylight, isn't so bad, though you should avoid intercity driving at night. And having a car – or better still a 4WD – opens up entire areas of the country where public transport is nonexistent.

At the time of research, it was no longer necessary to travel by police-escorted convoys (see boxed text, opposite), which opens large swaths of the Nile Valley and Red Sea coast that were previously difficult to access. While tourist infrastructure is limited out-side of major destinations, we have received numerous reports from intrepid readers that self-driving is a wonderful way to leave the tour buses behind in the dust.

A motorcycle would be an ideal way to travel around Egypt. The only snag is that you have to bring your own, and the red tape involved is extensive. Ask your country's automobile association and Egyptian embassy about regulations.

Petrol and diesel are readily available and very cheap, though unleaded petrol is only available at a handful of pumps in Cairo (mainly in Mohandiseen, Zamalek and Ma'adi) and Alexandria. When travelling out of Cairo, remember that petrol stations are not always that plentiful – as a rule, when you see one, fill up.

Bringing Your Own Vehicle

If you're bringing a car or motorcycle into the country, you'll need the vehicle's registration papers, liability insurance and an International Driving Permit in addition to your domestic driving licence. You'll also need multiple copies of a *carnet de passage en douane*, which

ROAD DISTANCES (km)

	Al-Arish	Al-Fayoum	Alexandria	Aswan	Asyut	Beni Suef	Cairo	Giza	Hurghada	Ismailia	Luxor	Marsa Matruh	Minya	Port Said	Sharm el-Sheikh
Al-Fayoum	431														
Alexandria	451	327													
Aswan	1238	822	1133												
Asyut	712	296	607	526											
Beni Suef	453	37	346	785	259										
Cairo	325	106	220	913	387	128									
Giza	333	98	228	903	377	118	8								
Hurghada	668	636	754	496	478	532	530	538							
Ismailia	185	246	266	1053	527	268	140	148	483						
Luxor	955	608	919	209	322	571	699	689	287	770					
Marsa Matruh	741	617	290	1473	897	638	510	518	1040	556	1209				
Minya	579	163	473	659	133	126	254	244	611	394	455	764			
Port Said	200	331	354	1138	612	353	225	233	563	85	850	644	479		
Sharm el-Sheikh	630	610	710	1279	909	632	504	512	783	444	1070	1000	758	529	
Suez	287	273	354	1047	521	262	134	142	395	88	682	644	388	168	388

TRANSPORT

is effectively a passport for the vehicle and acts as a temporary waiver of import duty. The *carnet* may also need to list any expensive spare parts you're planning to carry with you. If you're driving a car, you'll also need a fire extinguisher. Contact your local automobile association for details about documentation.

At the Egyptian border, you'll be issued with a licence valid for three months (less if your visa is valid for less time). You can renew the licence every three months for a maximum of two years, but you'll have to pay a varying fee each time. There is a customs charge of approximately US$200, and you must pay another US$50 for number-plate insurance.

If you plan to take your own vehicle, check in advance which spares are likely to be available. You may have trouble finding some parts for your car.

Driving Licence
Drivers with non-Egyptian licences need an International Driving Permit to drive in Egypt. Ensure that you keep this with you at all times while you are driving – if you cannot supply it when stopped, a hefty fine will be levied and you may have to leave your vehicle with the police until you can produce your permit. Likewise, ensure that you always have all car registration papers with you while driving.

Hire
Several international car-hire agencies have offices in Egypt, including Avis, Hertz, Europcar and Budget. See p181 for details of car-hire companies in Cairo. Their rates match international charges and finding a cheap deal with local agencies is virtually impossible – it's advisable to make arrangements via the web before you arrive. No matter which company you go with, make sure you read the fine print. If you choose to hire a car, rates are around US$50 to US$100 a day for a small Toyota to US$100 to US$200 a day for a 4WD.

An International Driving Permit is required and you can be hit with a heavy fine if you're caught hiring a car without one. Drivers should be over the age of 25.

Road Rules
Driving is on the right-hand side. The official speed limit outside towns is 90km/h (though it is often less in some areas) and 100km/h on four-lane highways, such as the Cairo–Alexandria Desert Hwy. If you're caught speeding, the police will confiscate your driving licence and you have to go to the traffic headquarters in the area to get it back – a lengthy and laborious process. A few roads, such as the Cairo–Alexandria Desert Hwy, the Cairo–Fayoum road and the road through the Ahmed Hamdi Tunnel (which goes under the Suez Canal near Suez), are subject to tolls.

Many roads have checkpoints where police often ask for identity papers, so make sure you've got your passport and International Driving Permit on hand or you may be liable for a US$100 on-the-spot fine.

Although city driving may seem chaotic, there is one cardinal rule: whoever is in front has the right of way – even if a car is only 1cm ahead of you and cuts across your path suddenly, you'll be liable if you hit it.

When driving through the countryside, keep in mind that children and adults are likely to wander into your path, even on main roads. If you do have an accident, get to the nearest police station as quickly as possible and report what happened.

HITCHING
Hitching is never entirely safe in any country in the world, and it is not recommended. Travellers who decide to hitch should understand that they are taking a small but potentially serious risk. People who do choose to hitch will be safer if they travel in pairs and let someone know where they are planning to go. Women must never hitch on their own in Egypt, as the general local assumption is that only prostitutes would do such a thing.

LOCAL TRANSPORT
As well as the local transport services described here, some cities and towns have their own options – most are variations on the pony-and-trap theme.

Bus & Minibus
Cairo and Alexandria are the only cities with their own bus systems. Taking a bus in either place is an experience far beyond simply getting from A to B. Firstly there's getting on board. Egyptians stampede buses, charging the entrance before the thing has even slowed. Hand-to-hand combat ensues as they run alongside trying to leap aboard. If you wait for the bus to stop, the pushing and shoving to get on is worse. Often several

passengers don't quite manage to get on and they make their journey hanging off the back doorway, clinging perilously to the frame or to someone with a firmer hold.

The scene inside the bus in this case usually resembles a *Guinness World Record* attempt on the greatest number of people in a fixed space. At some point during the trip, a man will somehow manage to squeeze his way through to sell you your ticket.

The buses rarely completely stop to let you off. You stand in the doorway, wait for the opportune moment and launch yourself onto the road.

Taking a minibus is an easier option. Passengers are not allowed to stand (although this rule is frequently overlooked), and each minibus leaves as soon as every seat is taken.

Metro

Cairo is the only city in Egypt with a metro system (for details, see p181).

Microbus

A slightly bigger version of the service taxi, the *meecrobus* is a Toyota van that would normally take about 12 people, but in Egypt takes as many as 22. Privately owned and usually unmarked, they shuttle around all the larger cities.

For the average traveller they can be difficult to use, as it is unclear where most of them go. Quite often there's a small boy hanging out of the doorway yelling the destination. In Cairo, you might have occasion to use a microbus to get out to the Pyramids, while in Alexandria they shuttle the length of Tariq al-Horreyya and the Corniche to Montazah, and in Sharm el-Sheikh they carry passengers between Old Sharm, Na'ama Bay and Shark's Bay. Most of the smaller cities and towns have similar microbuses doing set runs around town.

Intercity microbuses run on the same principle as service taxis and cost about the same, but operate on fewer routes.

Pick-Up

Toyota and Chevrolet pick-up trucks cover a lot of the routes between the smaller towns and villages off the main roads. The general rule is to get 12 people inside the covered rear of the truck, often with an assortment of goods squeezed in on the floor. After that,

it's a matter of how many can and want to scramble onto the roof or hang off the rear.

Covered pick-up trucks are also sometimes used within towns as local taxis. This is especially so in some of the oasis towns, on Luxor's West Bank and in smaller places along the Nile. Should you end up in one of these, there are a couple of ways you can indicate to the driver that you want to get out: if you are lucky enough to have a seat, pound on the floor with your foot; alternatively, ask one of the front passengers to hammer on the window behind the driver; or, last, use the buzzer that you'll occasionally find rigged up.

Service Taxi

Travelling by *servees* is one of the fastest ways to go from city to city. Service taxis are generally big Peugeot 504 cars that run intercity routes. Drivers congregate near bus and train stations and tout for passengers by shouting their destination. When the car's full, it's off. A driver won't leave before his car is full unless you and/ or the other passengers want to pay for all of the seats. Fares are usually cheaper than either the buses or trains and there are no set departure times – you just turn up and find a car.

Taxi

Almost every second car in Egypt (whether labelled or not) is a taxi, and they are by far the most convenient way of getting about. Stand at the side of the road, stick your hand out, shout your destination and get ready for some potential Indy race-car driving.

As a general rule, taxi etiquette is that you get in knowing what to pay, and when you arrive you get out and hand the money through the window. With that said, if a driver suspects you don't know what the correct fare is, you're fair game for fleecing. Since most travellers in Egypt don't speak fluent Arabic, it's probably best to agree on a price before getting into the taxi.

Often when it comes to bargaining, a driver will demand absurd amounts of money – don't be intimidated and don't be drawn into an argument. It's nothing but bluster; the driver is likely playing on the fact that you're a *khwaga* (foreigner) and don't know better. Eventually, the driver will probably accept your offer if it's appropriate, though you can always walk away if you feel like you're being taken advantage of and try again with another taxi.

TRANSPORT

TRANSPORT

'TAXI!'

Taxis are at once a blessing and a curse. They're a remarkably convenient and affordable way of getting around the city, but they can also be a frequent source of unpleasantness when it comes to paying the fare. The problem stems from the unmetered system of payment, which can lead to discontent. Passengers frequently feel that they've been taken advantage of (which they often have), while drivers are occasionally genuinely aggrieved by what they see as underpayment. So why don't the drivers use the meter? Because they were all calibrated at a time when petrol was ludicrously cheap. That time has long passed and any driver relying on his meter would now be out of pocket every time he came to fill up.

Taxi driving is far from being a lucrative profession. Of the more than 60,000 taxis on the road in Cairo, it would be a safe bet to assume that none of the drivers are yet millionaires. Average earnings after fuel has been paid are about E£8 per hour. Consider, too, that many drivers don't own their car and have to hand over part of their earnings as 'rent'.

Which isn't to say that the next time you flag a taxi for a short hop across town and the driver declares '10 pounds' that you should smile and say 'OK'. But it might make it easier to see that it was probably worth his while trying. After all, from the point of view of the local taxi driver, if you can afford to make it all the way to Egypt, you can probably afford to pay a bit more than the going rate.

Tram

Cairo and Alexandria are the only two cities in the country with tram systems. While Alexandria still has a fairly extensive and efficient network, Cairo now only has a handful of lines. See p393 and p182 for more details.

TRAIN

Although trains travel along more than 5000km of track to almost every major city and town in Egypt, the system is badly in need of modernisation (it's a relic of the British occupation). Most services are grimy and battered and are a poor second option to the deluxe bus. The exceptions are the *Turbini* and *Espani* services from Cairo to Alexandria and the tourist and sleeping trains from Cairo down to Luxor and Aswan – on these routes the train is the preferred option over the bus.

If you have an International Student Identity Card (ISIC), discounts are granted on all fares, except those for the sleeping-car services.

Classes & Services

Trains with sleeper cars are the most comfortable and among the fastest in Egypt. The cars, which are run by Abela Egypt, are the same as those used by trains in Europe. At least one sleeper train travels between Alexandria, Cairo, Luxor and Aswan daily. For details, see the Getting There & Away sections of those cities.

The Abela sleeper trains are 1st class only and reservations must be made in advance.

Compartments come with a seat that converts into a bed, a fold-down bunk (with clean linen, pillows and blankets) and a small basin with running water. Beds are quite short and tall people may spend an uncomfortable night as a result. It is worth requesting a middle compartment, as those at the ends of the carriages are located near the toilets and can sometimes be noisy. Shared toilets are generally clean and have toilet paper. Airline-style dinners and breakfasts are served in the compartments but you should not expect a gourmet eating experience. Drinks (including alcohol) are served by the steward.

Regular night trains with and without sleeper compartments and meals included leave for Luxor and Aswan daily and cost much less than the sleeper trains. Reservations must be made in advance at Ramses Station in Cairo. Unless you specify otherwise, you'll be issued with a ticket that includes meals on board. You may want to flout the rules and bring your own food. Both 1st- and 2nd-class compartments have air-con and they can get chilly at night; bring something warm to wear.

Trains without air-con are next down the scale. Classes are divided into 2nd-class ordinary, which generally has padded seats; and 3rd class, where seating is of the wooden-bench variety. These trains are generally filthy, tend to spend a lot of time at a lot of stations and can be subject to interminable delays.

Health Dr Caroline Evans

CONTENTS

> **TRAVEL HEALTH WEBSITES**
>
> It's usually a good idea to consult your government's travel health website before departure, if one is available.
> **Australia** (www.dfat.gov.au/travel)
> **Canada** (www.travelhealth.gc.ca)
> **UK** (www.dh.gov.uk)
> **USA** (www.cdc.gov/travel)

Prevention is the key to staying healthy while travelling in Egypt. Infectious diseases can and do occur here but these are usually associated with poor living conditions and poverty, and can be avoided with a few precautions. The most common reason for travellers needing medical help is as a result of accidents – cars are not always well maintained and poorly lit roads are littered with potholes. Medical facilities can be excellent in large cities but may be more basic in other areas.

BEFORE YOU GO

A little planning before departure, particularly for pre-existing illnesses, will save you a lot of trouble later. See your dentist before a long trip; carry a spare pair of contact lenses and glasses (take your optical prescription with you); and carry a first-aid kit.

It's tempting to leave planning to the last minute – don't! Many vaccines don't ensure immunity for the first two weeks so visit a doctor four to eight weeks before departure. Ask your doctor for an International Certificate of Vaccination (also known as the yellow booklet), which lists all the vaccinations you've received. This is mandatory for countries that require proof of yellow-fever vaccination, but it's a good idea to carry it wherever you travel.

Travellers can register with the **International Association for Medical Assistance to Travellers** (IAMAT; www.iamat.org). Its website can help travellers find a doctor with recognised training. Those heading off to very remote areas may like to do a first-aid course (Red Cross and St John's Ambulance can help) or attend a remote medicine first-aid course such as those offered by the **Royal Geographical Society** (www.rgs.org) and **Remote Medical International** (www.remotem edical.com).

Bring your medications in their original, clearly labelled containers. A signed and dated letter from your physician describing your medical conditions and medications, including generic names, is also a good idea. If you're carrying syringes or needles, be sure to have a physician's letter documenting their medical necessity.

INSURANCE

Find out in advance if your insurance plan will make payments directly to providers or reimburse you later for overseas health expenditures (in many places doctors expect payment in cash). It's also worth ensuring your travel insurance will cover repatriation home or to better medical facilities elsewhere. Not all insurance covers an emergency flight home or to a hospital in a major city, which may be the only way to get medical attention for a serious emergency. Your insurance company may be able to locate the nearest source of medical help, or you can ask at your hotel. In an emergency contact your embassy or consulate.

RECOMMENDED VACCINATIONS

The World Health Organization (WHO) recommends that all travellers, regardless of the region they are travelling in, should be vaccinated against diphtheria, tetanus, measles, mumps, rubella and polio, as well as hepatitis B. While making travel preparations, take the opportunity to ensure that your routine vaccination cover is complete. The consequences of these diseases can be very severe and outbreaks do occur in the Middle East.

MEDICAL CHECKLIST

Following is a list of other items you should consider packing in your medical kit.

- Acetaminophen/paracetamol (Tylenol) or aspirin
- Adhesive or paper tape
- Antibacterial ointment (eg Bactroban) for cuts and abrasions
- Antibiotics (if travelling off the beaten track)
- Antidiarrhoeal drugs (eg loperamide)
- Antihistamines (for hay fever and allergic reactions)
- Anti-inflammatory drugs (eg ibuprofen)
- Bandages, gauze, gauze rolls
- DEET-containing insect repellent for the skin
- Iodine tablets (for water purification)
- Oral rehydration salts
- Permethrin-containing insect spray for clothing, tents and bed nets
- Pocket knife
- Scissors, safety pins, tweezers
- Steroid cream or cortisone (for allergic rashes)
- Sunscreen
- Syringes and sterile needles (if travelling to remote areas)
- Thermometer

INTERNET RESOURCES

There is a wealth of travel health advice on the internet. For further information, the **Lonely Planet** (www.lonelyplanet.com) website is a good place to start. The **World Health Organization** (www.who.int/ith) publishes a superb book, *International Travel and Health,* which is revised annually and is available online at no cost. Another website of general interest is **MD Travel Health** (www.mdtravelhealth.com), which provides complete travel health recommendations for every country, updated daily, also at no cost. The **Centers for Disease Control & Prevention** (www.cdc.gov) website is also a useful source of travel health information.

FURTHER READING

Lonely Planet's *Africa: Healthy Travel* is packed with useful information including pretrip planning, emergency first aid, immunisation and disease information, as well as what to do if you get sick on the road. Other recommended references include *Travellers' Health* by Dr Richard Dawood (Oxford University Press); *International Travel Health Guide* by Stuart R Rose, MD (Mosby); and *The Travellers' Good Health Guide* by Ted Lankester (Sheldon Press), an especially useful health guide for volunteers and long-term expatriates working in the Middle East.

IN TRANSIT

DEEP VEIN THROMBOSIS (DVT)

Deep vein thrombosis (DVT) occurs when blood clots form in the legs during plane flights, chiefly because of prolonged immobility. The longer the flight, the greater the risk. Though most blood clots are reabsorbed uneventfully, some may break off and travel through the blood vessels to the lungs, where they may cause life-threatening complications.

The chief symptom of DVT is swelling or pain of the foot, ankle or calf, usually but not always on just one side. When a blood clot travels to the lungs, it may cause chest pain and difficulty breathing. Travellers with any of these symptoms should seek medical attention immediately.

To prevent the development of DVT on long flights, you should walk around the cabin, contract the leg muscles while sitting, drink plenty of fluids and avoid alcohol and tobacco.

JET LAG & MOTION SICKNESS

Jet lag is common when crossing more than five time zones; it results in insomnia, fatigue, malaise or nausea. To avoid jet lag try drinking plenty of fluids (nonalcoholic) and eating light meals. Upon arrival, seek exposure to natural sunlight and readjust your schedule (for meals, sleep etc) as soon as possible.

Antihistamines such as dimenhydrinate (Dramamine) and meclizine (Antivert, Bonine) are usually the first choice for treating motion sickness. Their main side effect is drowsiness. A herbal alternative is ginger, which works like a charm for some people.

IN EGYPT

AVAILABILITY & COST OF HEALTH CARE

The health care systems in Egypt are varied. Care can be excellent in private hospitals and those associated with universities but patchier elsewhere. Reciprocal payment arrangements with other countries rarely exist and you should be prepared to pay for all medical and dental treatment.

Medical care is not always readily available outside major cities. Medicine, and even sterile dressings or intravenous fluids, may need to be bought from a pharmacy. Nursing care may be limited or rudimentary, as this is something families and friends are expected to provide. The travel assistance provided by your insurance may be able to locate the nearest source of medical help, otherwise ask at your hotel. In an emergency contact your embassy or consulate.

Standards of dental care are variable and there is an increased risk of hepatitis B and HIV transmission via poorly sterilised equipment. Keep in mind that your travel insurance will not usually cover you for anything other than emergency dental treatment.

For minor illnesses such as diarrhoea, pharmacists, who are well qualified, can often provide valuable advice and sell over-the-counter medication. They can also advise whether more specialised help is needed.

INFECTIOUS DISEASES

The following diseases are all present within Egypt.

Diphtheria

Spread through close respiratory contact, diphtheria causes a high temperature and severe sore throat. Sometimes a membrane forms across the throat requiring a tracheostomy to prevent suffocation. Vaccination is recommended for those who are likely to be in close contact with the local population in infected areas. The vaccine is given as an injection alone or with the tetanus vaccine, and lasts 10 years.

Hepatitis A

This is spread through contaminated food (particularly shellfish) and water. It causes jaundice and, although it is rarely fatal, can cause prolonged lethargy and delayed recovery. Symptoms include dark urine, a yellow colour to the whites of the eyes, fever and abdominal pain. Hepatitis A vaccine (Avaxim, Vaqta, Havrix) is given as an injection: a single dose will give protection for up to a year, while a booster 12 months later will provide a subsequent 10 years of protection. Hepatitis A and typhoid vaccines can also be given as a single-dose vaccine (Hepatyrix or ViATIM).

Hepatitis B

Hepatitis B is transmitted by infected blood, contaminated needles and sexual intercourse. It can cause jaundice and affects the liver, occasionally causing liver failure. All travellers should make this a routine vaccination. (Many countries now give hepatitis B vaccination as part of routine childhood vaccination.) The vaccine is given alone, or at the same time as the hepatitis A vaccine (Hepatyrix). A course will give protection for at least five years. It can be given over four weeks or six months.

HIV

HIV is spread via infected blood and blood products, sexual intercourse with an infected partner and from an infected mother to her newborn child. It can be spread through 'blood to blood' contacts such as contaminated instruments during medical, dental, acupuncture and body-piercing procedures, and sharing used intravenous needles.

Malaria

Malaria is found in certain parts of some oases; risk varies seasonally. Risk of malaria in most cities is minimal but check with your doctor if you are considering travelling to any rural areas. It is important to take antimalarial tablets if the risk is significant. For up-to-date information about the risk of contracting malaria, contact your local travel health clinic.

Anyone who has travelled in a country where malaria is present should be aware of the symptoms of malaria. It is possible to contract malaria from a single bite from

HEALTH

an infected mosquito. Malaria almost always starts with marked shivering, fever and sweating. Muscle pains, headache and vomiting are common. Symptoms may occur anywhere from a few days to three weeks after the infected mosquito bite. The illness can start while you are taking preventive tablets if they are not fully effective, and may also occur after you have finished taking your tablets.

Poliomyelitis

This generally spreads through contaminated food and water. The vaccine is given in childhood and should be boosted every 10 years, either orally (a drop on the tongue) or as an injection. Polio may be carried asymptomatically but it can cause a transient fever and, in rare cases, potentially permanent muscle weakness or paralysis.

Rabies

Rabies spreads through bites or licks from an infected animal on broken skin. Rabies is fatal. Animal handlers should be vaccinated, as should those travelling to remote areas where a reliable source of postbite vaccine isn't available within 24 hours. Three injections are needed over a month. If you have not been vaccinated, you will need a course of five injections starting within 24 hours or as soon as possible after the injury. Vaccination does not provide you with immunity, it merely buys you more time to seek appropriate medical help.

Rift Valley Fever

This haemorrhagic fever is spread through blood and blood products, including those from infected animals. It causes a flulike illness with fever, joint pains and occasionally more serious complications. Complete recovery is possible.

Schistosomiasis

Also known as bilharzia, this is spread by the freshwater snail. It causes infection of the bowel and bladder, often with bleeding. It is caused by a fluke and is contracted through the skin from water contaminated with human urine or faeces. The Nile is known to be a source of bilharzia, but paddling or swimming in *any* suspect freshwater lakes or slow-running rivers should be avoided. Possible symptoms include a transient fever and rash. Advanced cases of bilharzia may cause blood in the stool or in the urine. However, there may be no symptoms. A blood test can detect antibodies if you have been exposed, and treatment is then possible in specialist travel or infectious-disease clinics.

Tuberculosis

Also known as TB, this is spread through close respiratory contact and occasionally through infected milk or milk products. BCG vaccine is recommended for those likely to be mixing closely with the local population. It is more important for people visiting family or planning on a long stay, and those employed as teachers and health-care workers. TB can be asymptomatic, or symptoms can include cough, weight loss or fever, months or even years after exposure. An X-ray is the best way to confirm if you have TB. BCG gives a moderate degree of protection against TB. It causes a small permanent scar at the site of injection and is usually only given in specialised chest clinics. As it's a live vaccine it should not be given to pregnant women or immunocompromised individuals. The BCG vaccine is not available in all countries.

Typhoid

This is spread through food or water that has been contaminated by infected human faeces. The first symptom is usually fever or a pink rash on the abdomen. Septicaemia (blood poisoning) may also occur. Typhoid vaccine (Typhim Vi, Typherix) will give protection for three years. In some countries the oral vaccine Vivotif is also available.

Yellow Fever

This vaccination isn't required for the Middle East. But the mosquito that spreads yellow fever has been known to be present in some parts of the region. It is important to consult your local travel health clinic for the latest details as part of your predeparture plans. Any travellers from a yellow-fever endemic area will need to show proof of vaccination against yellow fever before entry. This normally means if arriving directly from an infected country or if the traveller has been in an infected country during the previous 10 days. We would recommend, however, that travellers carry a certificate if they have been in an infected country during the previous month, to avoid any possible difficulties with immigration. There is always the possibility that a traveller without an up-to-date certificate will be vaccinated and detained in isolation at the port of arrival for up to 10 days, or even repatriated. The yellow-fever vaccination must be given at a designated clinic. It is valid for 10 years. It is a live vaccine and must not be given to immunocompromised or pregnant travellers.

In Cairo, you can obtain a yellow-fever vaccine at the medical clinic in Terminal 1 of Cairo airport (approximately E£60). Note that you must show proof of having a yellow-fever vaccination before being allowed entry to or from Sudan.

TRAVELLER'S DIARRHOEA

To prevent diarrhoea, avoid tap water unless it has been boiled, filtered or chemically disinfected (iodine tablets). Eat only fresh fruits or vegetables if cooked or if you have peeled them yourself, and avoid dairy products that might contain unpasteurised milk. Buffet meals are risky. Food should be piping hot; meals freshly cooked in front of you in a busy restaurant are more likely to be safe.

If you develop diarrhoea, be sure to drink plenty of fluids, preferably an oral rehydration solution containing lots of salt and sugar. A few loose stools don't require treatment but if you start having more than four or five stools a day, you should start taking an antibiotic (usually a quinolone drug) and an antidiarrhoeal agent (such as loperamide). If diarrhoea is bloody, persists for more than 72 hours, is accompanied by fever, shaking chills or severe abdominal pain, you should seek medical attention.

ENVIRONMENTAL HAZARDS
Heat Illness

Heat exhaustion occurs following heavy sweating and excessive fluid loss with inadequate replacement of fluids and salt. It is particularly common in hot climates, if you take unaccustomed exercise before full acclimatisation. Symptoms include headache, dizziness and tiredness. You're already dehydrated by the time you feel thirsty – aim to drink sufficient water so that you produce pale, diluted urine. Treatment consists of fluid replacement with water or fruit juice or both, and cooling by cold water and fans. The treatment of the salt-loss component consists of taking in salty fluids such as soup or broth, and adding a little more table salt to foods than usual.

Heatstroke is much more serious. This occurs when the body's heat-regulating mechanism breaks down. Excessive rise in body temperature leads to sweating ceasing, irrational and hyperactive behaviour and eventually loss of consciousness and even death. Rapid cooling by spraying the body with water and fanning is an ideal treatment. Emergency fluid and electrolyte replacement by intravenous drip is usually also required.

Insect Bites & Stings

Mosquitoes may not carry malaria but can cause irritation and infected bites. They also spread dengue fever. Using DEET-based insect repellents will prevent bites.

Bees and wasps only cause real problems to those with a severe allergy (anaphylaxis). If you have a severe allergy to bee or wasp stings, you should carry an adrenaline injection or similar.

Sandflies are located around the Mediterranean beaches. They usually only cause a nasty itchy bite but can also carry a rare skin disorder called cutaneous leishmaniasis. Bites may be prevented by using DEET-based repellents.

Scorpions are frequently found in arid or dry climates. They can cause a painful bite, which is rarely life-threatening.

Bed bugs are often found in hostels and cheap hotels. They lead to very itchy, lumpy bites. Spraying the mattress with an appropriate insect killer will do a good job of getting rid of them.

Scabies are also frequently found in cheap accommodation. These tiny mites live in the skin, particularly between the fingers. They cause an intensely itchy rash. Scabies is easily treated with lotion available from pharmacies; people who you come into contact with also need treating to avoid spreading scabies between asymptomatic carriers.

Snake Bites

Do not walk barefoot or stick your hand into holes or cracks. Half of those bitten by venomous snakes are not actually injected with poison (envenomed). If bitten by a snake, do not panic. Immobilise the bitten limb with a splint (eg a stick) and apply a bandage over the site and firm pressure, similar to a bandage over a sprain. Do not apply a tourniquet, or cut or suck the bite. Get the victim to medical help as soon as possible so that antivenin can be given if necessary.

HEALTH

Water

Tap water is not safe to drink throughout Egypt. Stick to bottled water or boil water for 10 minutes, use water-purification tablets or a filter. Do not drink water from rivers or lakes, as it may contain bacteria or viruses that can cause diarrhoea or vomiting.

TRAVELLING WITH CHILDREN

All travellers with children should know how to treat minor ailments and when to seek medical treatment. Make sure the children are up to date with routine vaccinations, and discuss possible travel vaccinations well before departure as some vaccines are not suitable for children aged under one year.

In hot, moist climates any wound or break in the skin may lead to infection. The area should be cleaned and then kept dry and clean. Remember to avoid contaminated food and water. If your child is vomiting or experiencing diarrhoea, lost fluid and salts must be replaced. It may be helpful to take rehydration powders with you, to be reconstituted with boiled water. Ask your doctor about this.

Children should be encouraged to avoid dogs or other mammals because of the risk of rabies and other diseases. Any bite, scratch or lick from a warm-blooded, furry animal should immediately be thoroughly cleaned. If there is any possibility that the animal is infected with rabies, immediate medical assistance should be sought.

WOMEN'S HEALTH

Emotional stress, exhaustion and travelling through different time zones can all contribute to an upset in the menstrual pattern. If using oral contraceptives, keep in mind that some antibiotics, diarrhoea and vomiting can stop the pill from working and lead to the risk of pregnancy – remember to take condoms with you just in case. Condoms should be kept in a cool, dry place or they may crack and perish.

Emergency contraception is most effective if taken within 24 hours after unprotected sex. The **International Planned Parent Federation** (www.ippf.org) can advise about the availability of contraception in different countries. Tampons and sanitary towels are not always available outside major cities in the Middle East.

Travelling during pregnancy is usually possible but there are important things to consider. Have a medical checkup before embarking on your trip. The most risky times for travel are during the first 12 weeks of pregnancy, when miscarriage is most likely, and after 30 weeks, when complications such as high blood pressure and premature delivery can occur. Most airlines will not accept a traveller after 28 to 32 weeks of pregnancy, and long-haul flights in the later stages can be very uncomfortable. Antenatal facilities vary greatly between countries in the Middle East and you should think carefully before travelling to a country with poor medical facilities or where there are major cultural and language differences from your home country. Taking written records of the pregnancy, including details of your blood group, is likely to be helpful if you need medical attention while in a foreign country. Try to find an insurance policy that covers pregnancy, delivery and postnatal care, but remember that insurance policies are only as good as the facilities available.

HEALTH

Language

CONTENTS

Arabic is the official language of Egypt. The Arabic spoken on the street differs greatly from the standard Arabic written in newspapers and spoken on the radio, which is known as Modern Standard Arabic (MSA). MSA is the written and spoken lingua franca common to all Arabic-speaking countries.

Egyptian Arabic is the local variety of the standard language and is different in many respects. It's the everyday language that differs the most from that of Egypt's other Arabic-speaking neighbours. More specialised or educated language tends to be pretty much the same across the Arab world, although pronunciation may vary considerably. An Arab from, say, Jordan or Iraq will have no problem having a chat about politics or literature with an Egyptian, but might have more trouble making themselves understood in a Cairo bakery.

There is no official written form of Egyptian Arabic, although Nobel Prize–winning author Naguib Mahfouz has no trouble writing out whole passages using predominantly Egyptian (or Cairene) slang. But people who specifically want to learn Egyptian Arabic instead of MSA are often told that it can't be written in script, and are then presented with one system or other of transliteration – none of them totally satisfactory.

But you certainly shouldn't let that stop you. If you take the time to learn even a handful of Arabic words and phrases, you'll discover and experience much more while travelling through the country.

If you'd like a more comprehensive guide to the language, pick up a copy of Lonely Planet's *Egyptian Arabic Phrasebook*, or *Middle East Phrasebook*, which includes both Egyptian Arabic and MSA. Both phrasebooks have script throughout.

Arabic uses masculine and feminine forms, which are indicated in this language guide by (m) and (f) respectively, or separated by a slash (m/f) if both forms are given.

TRANSLITERATION

Converting Arabic script into the Roman alphabet is a tricky business – in fact, no entirely 'correct' system of transliteration has been established. For this book, an attempt has been made to standardise some spellings of place names and common terms.

There is only one article in Arabic: *al* (the). It's also sometimes written as 'il' or 'el' and sometimes modifies to reflect the first consonant of the following noun. For example, in Saladin's name, Salah ad-Din, the 'al' has been modified to 'ad' before the 'd' of 'Din'. The article *el* is used only in a few instances in this book, such as for well-known places (El Alamein, Sharm el-Sheikh) or where locals have used it in restaurant and hotel names.

The business of transliteration is fraught with pitfalls, and even the locals often only guess at how to make the conversion – sometimes with amusing results. The fact that French and English have had a big influence (though the latter is now much more common in Egypt) has led to all sorts of interesting ideas on transliteration. Egypt's high rate of illiteracy doesn't help either. Don't be taken aback if you start noticing half a dozen different spellings for the same thing.

The letters **q** and **k** have caused many problems and are often interchanged in

THE STANDARD ARABIC ALPHABET

Final	Medial	Initial	Alone	Transliteration	Pronunciation
ـا			ا	ā/aa	as in 'father'/as the long 'a' in 'ma'am'
ـب	ـبـ	بـ	ب	b	as in 'bet'
ـت	ـتـ	تـ	ت	t	as in 'ten'
ـث	ـثـ	ثـ	ث	th	as in 'thin'
ـج	ـجـ	جـ	ج	g/zh	as in 'go'/(rarely) as the 's' in 'pleasure'
ـح	ـحـ	حـ	ح	H	a strongly whispered 'h', like a sigh of relief
ـخ	ـخـ	خـ	خ	kh	as the 'ch' in Scottish *loch*
ـد			د	d	as in 'dim'
ـذ			ذ	dh	as the 'th' in 'this'
ـر			ر	r	a rolled 'r', as in the Spanish word *caro*
ـز			ز	z	as in 'zip'
ـس	ـسـ	سـ	س	s	as in 'so', never as in 'wisdom'
ـش	ـشـ	شـ	ش	sh	as in 'ship'
ـص	ـصـ	صـ	ص	ş	emphatic 's'
ـض	ـضـ	ضـ	ض	ḍ	emphatic 'd'
ـط	ـطـ	طـ	ط	ţ	emphatic 't'
ـظ	ـظـ	ظـ	ظ	ẓ	emphatic 'z'
ـع	ـعـ	عـ	ع	ʾ	the Arabic letter *'ayn*; pronounce as a glottal stop – like the pause in the middle of 'uh-oh' (see Other Sounds, opposite)
ـغ	ـغـ	غـ	غ	gh	a guttural sound like Parisian 'r'
ـف	ـفـ	فـ	ف	f	as in 'far'
ـق	ـقـ	قـ	ق	q	a strongly guttural 'k' sound; in Egyptian Arabic often pronounced as a glottal stop
ـك	ـكـ	كـ	ك	k	as in 'king'
ـل	ـلـ	لـ	ل	l	as in 'lamb'
ـم	ـمـ	مـ	م	m	as in 'me'
ـن	ـنـ	نـ	ن	n	as in 'name'
ـه	ـهـ	هـ	ه	h	as in 'ham'
ـو			و	w	as in 'wet'; or
				oo	long, as in 'food'; or
				ow	as in 'how'
ـي	ـيـ	يـ	ي	y	as in 'yes'; or
				ee	as the 'e' in 'ear', only softer; or
				ai/ay	as in 'aisle'/as the 'ay' in 'day'

Vowels Not all Arabic vowel sounds are represented in the alphabet. For more information on the vowel sounds used in this language guide, see p543.

Emphatic Consonants To simplify the transliteration system used in this book, the emphatic consonants have not been included.

transliteration. You'll see, for example, *souq* (market) often written 'souk'; *qasr* (castle) sometimes written 'kasr'; and the Cairo suburb of Doqqi often written 'Dokki'. It's a bit like spelling language as it sounds – imagine the results if Australians, Americans, Scots and Londoners were all given free rein to write English as they pronounce it!

PRONUNCIATION

Pronunciation of Arabic can be somewhat tongue-tying for someone unfamiliar with the intonation and combination of sounds. But pronounce the transliterated words and phrases slowly and clearly and you will soon get the hang of it.

Following is a guide to get you started. Note that there are further rules governing pronunciation that we don't have the space to cover here – check out one of the Lonely Planet phrasebooks for more.

Vowels

a	as in 'had' (sometimes very short)
aa	like the long 'a' sound in 'ma'am'
ā	as the 'a' in 'father'
e	as in 'bet' (sometimes very short)
ee	as in 'beer', only softer
i	as in 'hit'
o	as in 'hot'
ō	as the 'o' in 'four'
oo	as in 'food'
u	as in 'put'

Diphthongs

ow	as in 'how'
ai	as in 'aisle'
ay	as in 'day'

Consonants

Pronunciation of all Arabic consonants is covered in the alphabet table, p542. Note that when double consonants occur in transliterations, each consonant is pronounced. For example, *hammam* (bathhouse) is pronounced ham-*mām*.

Other Sounds

Arabic has two sounds that can be tricky at first for Arabic learners: the *hamza* (glottal stop) and the *'ayn*. The glottal stop, which isn't represented in the alphabet, is like the short pause in the middle of 'uh-oh' in English. The letter *'ayn* represents a sound with no English equivalent – it is similar to the glottal stop but the muscles at the back of the throat are gagged more forcefully and air is allowed to escape, creating a sound that has been described as reminiscent of someone being strangled! In many transliteration systems *'ayn* is represented by an opening quotation mark, and the glottal stop by a closing quotation mark. To make the transliterations in this book easier to use, we have not distinguished between the glottal stop and the *'ayn*, using the closing quotation mark to represent both. You'll find that Arabic speakers will still understand you.

ACCOMMODATION

I'm looking for a ...	*a*·na ba·*dow*·war *'a*·la ...
hotel	*fun*·du'
pension	*ban*·syon
youth hostel	bait sha·*bāb*

Where can I find a cheap hotel?
a·*la*'·ee *fun*·du' ra·*khees* fayn
What is the address?
il *'un·waan* ay
Could you write the address, please?
mum·kin *tik·tib/tik·ti·*bee il' un·*waan* min *fad*·lak (m/f)
Do you have rooms available?
*'an·*dak/*'an·*dik *ghu·*raf *fad*·ya (m/f)

I'd like (a) ...	*a*·na 'aiz/'*ai·za* ... (m/f)
I'd like to book (a) ...	'aiz *aH*·gaz ... low sa·*maHt* (m)
	'*ai·za aH*·gaz ... low
	sa·*maH*·tee (f)
bed	si·*reer*
single room	*ghur*·fa li *waa*·Hid
double room	*ghur*·fa bi si·*reer* muz·*dow*·ag
room with two beds	*ghur*·fa bi si·reer·*ain*
room with a	*ghur*·fa bi Ham·*mām* khās
bathroom	
room with air-con/	*ghur*·fa bi tak·*yeef*/mar·*wa*·Ha
fan	
bed in a dorm	*ghur*·fa mush·*ta*·ri·ka

How much is it ...?	bi·*kam* ...
per night	li *lai*·la *waa*·Hid·a
per person	lil *fard*

May I see it?
mum·kin a·*shuf*·ha
Where is the bathroom?
fayn il Ham·*mām*
I'm/We're leaving today.
(*a*·na Ham·shi/*iH*·na Ha·*nim*·shi) inn·*har*·da

CONVERSATION & ESSENTIALS

Arabic is more formal than English, especially with greetings; thus even the simplest greetings, such as 'hello', vary according to when and how they're used. In addition, each greeting requires a certain response that varies according to whether it is being said to a male, female or group of people.

Hello.	sa-*lām* 'a-*lay*-kum
(response)	wa 'a-*lay*-kum es sa-*lām*
Hello./Welcome.	ah-*lan* wa *sah*-lan
(response)	ah-*lan* beek (to a man)
	ah-*lan* bee-*kee* (to a woman)
	ah-*lan* bee-*kum* (to a group)
Good morning.	sa-*bāH* al-*khayr*
(response)	sa-*bāH* an-*noor*
Good evening.	mi-*sa'* al-*khayr*
(response)	mi-*sa'* an-*noor*
Good night.	tis-baH '*a*-la khayr (to a man)
	tis-*baH*-ee '*a*-la khayr (to a woman)
	tis-*baH*-u '*a*-la khayr (to a group)
(response)	wen-ta bi-*khayr* (to a man)
	wen-tee bi-*khayr* (to a woman)
	wen-too bi-*khayr* (to a group)
Goodbye.	ma'-as sa-*laa*-ma
Yes.	ai-wa (or na-'am – more formal)
No.	la'
Please.	

min *fad*-lak/*fad*-lik/fad-*lu*-kum (to man/woman/group; used when asking for something in a shop)
low sa-*maH*t/sa-*maH*-tee/sa-*maH*-tu (to man/woman/group; similar, but more formal)
tfad-dal/*tfad*-da-lee/*tfad*-da-loo (to man/woman/group; used when offering something or inviting someone)
it-*fad*-dal/it-*fad*-da-lee/it-*fad*-da-loo (to man/woman/group; similar, or can mean 'Please, go ahead and do something')

Thank you (very much).	
shu-kran (ga-*zee*-lan)	
Excuse me.	
'an *iz*-nak, es-*maH*-lee (to man)	
'an *iz*-nik, es-ma-*Hee*-lee (to woman)	
'an iz-*nu*-kum, es-ma-*Hoo*-lee (to group)	
That's fine./You're welcome.	
'*af*-wan (or al-'*aff*-u)	
Sorry. (ie forgive me)	
'*as*-sif	

What's your name?	*is*-ma kay (to man)
	is-mi kay (to woman)
My name is ...	*is*-mee ...
Pleased to meet you.	ta-shar-*raf*-na (pol)
(when first meeting)	*fur*-sa sa-'*eed*-a (inf)

How are you?	iz-*zay*-yak (to a man)
	iz-*zay*-yik (to a woman)
	iz-*za*-yu-kum (to a group)
I'm fine.	kway-yis il-*Ham*-du lil-*lah* (to a man)
	kway-*yi*-sa il-*Ham*-du lil-*lah* (to a woman)
	kway-*seen* il-*Ham*-du lil-*lah* (to a group)

Where are you from?	en-ta/en-tee min-*ain* (m/f)
I'm from ...	*a*-na min ...
I like/don't like ...	*a*-na ba-*Hibb*/ma-ba-*Hib*-bish
Just a minute.	da-'*ee*-'a waa-*Hid*-a

A useful word to know is *imshee*, which means 'Go away'. This may be useful at the Pyramids or at other sites if you are being besieged by children. Don't say it to adults; instead just say, *la' shukran* (No thanks).

DIRECTIONS

Where is ...?	fayn ...
Go straight ahead.	'*a*-la tool
Turn left.	How-id shi-*māl*
Turn right.	How-id yi-*meen*
at the (next) corner	'*al*-al nas-ya (il-li gai-ya)
at the traffic lights	'and il i-*shā*-ra
behind	wa-ra
in front of	'ud-*daam*
far (from)	ba-'*eed* ('an)
near (to)	'u-ra-yib (min)
opposite	'u-*sād*
here	hi-na
there	hi-*naak*
this address	al-'*an*-waan da
north	shi-*maal*
south	ga-*noob*
east	shark
west	gharb

SIGNS	
Entrance	مدخل
Exit	خروج
Open	مفتوح
Closed	مغلق
Prohibited	ممنوع
Information	معلومات
Hospital	مستشفى
Police	شرطة
Men's Toilet	حمام للرجال
Women's Toilet	حمام للنساء

LANGUAGE

beach	al blaaj/ash·*shā*·ti
bridge	*ku*·bri
island	ga·*zee*·ra
main square	al·mai·*daan* ar·ra·*'ee*·si
mosque	al·*gaa*·me'
museum	al·*mat*·Haf
old city	al·me·*dee*·na al·'a·*dee*·ma
palace	al·*'asr*
pyramids	ah·ra·*māt*
The Pyramids (of Giza)	al·ah·*rām*
ruins	a·*sār*
sea	baHr
square	mi·*daan*
street	ash·*shaa*·ri'
tower	burg
university	al·*ga*·m'a
village	al·*qar*·ya

FOOD & DRINK
Basics

bakery	*makh*·baz
bread	'aish
coffeehouse	*ah*·wa
fork	*shō*·ka
glass	kub·*baa*·ya
knife	si·*kee*·na
menu	me·*nai*
plate	ta·ba'
restaurant	*ma*·t'am
rice	ruz
spoon	ma'·*la'*·a

Fruit & Vegetables

apple	tuf·*faaH*
banana	mooz
carrot	*ga*·zar
cauliflower	ar·na·*beet*
garlic	tom
grapes	*'i*·nab
guava	ga·*waa*·fa
mango	*man*·ga
okra	*bam*·ya
onion	*ba*·sal
orange	bur·tu'·*an*
parsley	ba'·*doo*·nis
peas	bı·*sıl*·la
pineapple	a·na·*naas*
potatoes	ba·*tā*·tis
strawberry	fa·*raw*·la
tomato	ta·*mā*·tim
watermelon	bat *teekh*

Meat

chicken	fir·*aakh*
lamb	*laH*·ma *dā*·ni

liver	*kib*·da
meat	*laH*·ma

Other Food & Condiments

butter	*zib*·da
cheese	*gib*·na
eggs	bayd
ice	talg
pepper	*fil*·fil
salad	sa·*lā*·ta
salt	*mal*·H
sugar	*suk*·kar
yoghurt	za·*baa*·di

Drinks

beer	*bee*·ra
coffee	*ah*·wa
lemonade	li·*moon*
milk	*la*·ban
mineral water	*may*·ya ma'·*dan*·*eey*·ya
water	*may*·ya
tea	shai

Eating Out

A table for (five), please.
ta·ra·*bay*·za li (*kham*·sa) low sa·*maHt*
May we see the menu?
mum·kin ni·*shoof* il mi·*nai*
Is service included in the bill?
il Hi·*saab* shaa·mil il *khid*·ma
I'm vegetarian.
a·na na·*baa*·tee/na·ba·*tee*·ya (m/f)
Do you have any vegetarian dishes?
'*an*·dak *ak*·la na·ba·*tee*·ya
I can't eat dairy products.
ma ba·*kulsh* il al·*baan*
Please bring us the bill.
low sa·*maHt* hat·*li*·na il Hi·*saab*

HEALTH

I'm ill.	a·na 'ai·*yaan*/'ai·*yaan*·a (m/f)
My friend is ill.	sa·*dee*·qi 'ai·*yaan*
It hurts here.	bi·yuw·*ga'*·ni *hi*·na

I'm ...	'*an*·dee ...
asthmatic	*az*·mit *ra*·boo
diabetic	is *suk*·kar
epileptic	sa·ra'

I'm allergic to ...	'*an*·dee Ha·sa·*siy*·ya min ...
antibiotics	mu·*dād* Hai·o·*wl*
aspirin	*as*·bi·reen
bees	naHl
nuts	mu·*kas*·sar·*āt*
penicillin	bi·ni·si·*leen*

LANGUAGE

EMERGENCIES

Help!	el·*Ha'*·nee
There's been an accident.	fee *Had*·sa
I'm lost.	*a*·na tā·yih/*tāy*·ha (m/f)
Go away!	*im*·shee
Call a doctor!	i·*tas*·sal bi·dok·*toor* (m)
	i·*tas*·sal·ee bi·dok·*toor* (f)
Call the police!	i·*tas*·sal bil·bo·*lees*
I've been robbed.	*a*·na it·*sa*·ra't
Where are the toilets?	fayn at·twa·*let*

LANGUAGE DIFFICULTIES

Do you speak English?
  en·ta bi·tit·*kal*·lim in·*glee*·zee (to a man)
  en·tee bi·tit·*kal*·li·mee in·*glee*·zee (to a woman)
Does anyone here speak English?
  fee Hadd bi·yit·*kal*·lim in·*glee*·zee
How do you say ... in Egyptian Arabic?
  iz·*zai* a·*'ool* ... bil *'a*·ra·bee
What does ... mean?
  ya'·ni ... ay
I understand.
  a·na faa·hem/*fah*·ma (m/f)
I don't understand.
  a·na mish faa·hem/*fah*·ma (m/f)
Please write it down.
  mum·kin tik·*ti*·buh/tik·*ti*·beeh (m/f)
Can you show me (on the map)?
  mum·kin ti·war·*ree*·ni (*'al*·al kha·*ree*·ta)

NUMBERS

Arabic numerals are simple to learn and, unlike the rest of the written language, run from left to right. Pay attention to the order of the words in numbers from 21 to 99. When followed by a noun, the pronunciation of 100 changes from *miyya* to *meet*, and the noun is always used in singular form. This rules also applies for numbers 300 to 900.

0	sifr	.
1	*waa*·Hid	١
2	it·*nayn*	٢
3	ta·*laa*·ta	٣
4	ar·*ba'a*	٤
5	*kham*·sa	٥
6	*sit*·ta	٦
7	*sa*·b'a	٧
8	ta·*man*·ya	٨
9	*ti*·s'a	٩

10	*'ash*·a·ra	١.
11	Hid·*'ash*·ar	١١
12	it·*n'āsh*·ar	١٢
13	ta·lat·*t'āsh*·ar	١٣
14	ar·ba·*'t'āsh*·ar	١٤
15	kha·mas·*t'āsh*·ar	١٥
16	sit·*t'āsh*·ar	١٦
17	sa·ba·*'t'āsh*·ar	١٧
18	ta·man·*t'āsh*·ar	١٨
19	ti·sa·*'t'āsh*·ar	١٩
20	*'ish*·reen	٢.
21	*waa*·Hid wi *'ish*·reen	٢١
22	it·*nayn* wi *'ish*·reen	٢٢
30	ta·la·*teen*	٣.
40	ar·ba·*'een*	٤.
50	kham·*seen*	٥.
60	sit·*teen*	٦.
70	sab·*'een*	٧.
80	ta·ma·*neen*	٨.
90	ti·sa·*'een*	٩.
100	miy·*ya* (*meet* before a noun)	١..
200	mi·*tayn*	٢..
1000	*'alf*	١...
2000	*'alf*·ayn	٢...

How many?	kam *waa*·Hid

QUESTION WORDS

Who?	meen
What?	ay
When?	*im*·ta
Where?	fayn
How?	iz·*zay*
Which?	ayy

SHOPPING & SERVICES

I'd like to buy ...	*'aiz*/*'ai*·za ash·*ti*·ri ... (m/f)
How much is it?	bi·*kam* da
I don't like it.	mish *'a*·gib·ni
May I look at it?	*mum*·kin a·*shoo*·fu
I'm just looking.	bat·*far*·rag bas
It's cheap.	da ra·*khees*
It's too expensive.	da *ghaa*·lee *'ow*·ee
No more than ...	mish *ak*·tār min ...
I'll take it.	*'a*·khud·ha
Can you give me ...?	*mum*·kin tid·*dee*·ni ...
a discount	takh·*feed*
a good price	sa'r *kway*·yis
Do you accept ...?	bi·*ta*·khud ... (m)
	bi·*ta*·khu·dee ... (f)
credit cards	*kre*·dit kard
traveller cheques	sheek si·*yaa*·Hi

more	*ak*·tar
less	a'·*all*
smaller	*as*·ghar
bigger	*ak*·bar

I'm looking for ...	a·na ba·*dow*·war '*a*·la
a bank	bank
the bazaar/market	as·*sooq*
the city centre	wust al·*ba*·lad
the (...) embassy	as·si·*fã*·ra (...)
the post office	al·*boos*·ta
the telephone centre	sen·*traal* it·te·li·fo·*naat*
the tourist office	*mak*·tab as·si·*yaa*·Ha

I want to change ...	a·na 'aiz/'*ai*·za u·*sar*·raf ... (m/f)
money	fu·*loos*
travellers cheques	shee·*kaat* si·ya·*Hiy*·ya

TIME & DATES

What time is it?	saa·'a kam
It's (8) o'clock.	saa'·a (ta·*man*·ya)
in the morning	sa·*ba*·Han
in the afternoon	ba'd id duhr
in the evening	bil layl
today	inn·*har*·da
tomorrow	*bo*·kra
yesterday	im·*be*·riH
day	yom
month	shahr
week	us·*bu*·'a
year	*sa*·na
early	*ba*·dree
late	mit·'*akh*·ar

Monday	(yom) al·it·*nayn*
Tuesday	(yom) at·ta·*laat*
Wednesday	(yom) al·*ar*·ba'a
Thursday	(yom) al·kha·*mees*
Friday	(yom) al·*gu*·m'a
Saturday	(yom) as·sabt
Sunday	(yom) al·Hadd

January	ya·*nay*·ir
February	fi·*bra*·yir
March	*maa*·ris
April	ab·*reel*
May	*ma*·yu
June	*yun*·yu
July	*yul*·yu
August	a·*ghus*·tus
September	sib·*tim*·bir
October	'uk·*too*·bir
November	nu·*fim*·bir
December	di·*sim*·bir

TRANSPORT
Public Transport

When does the ... leave/arrive?	*im*·ta qi·*yaam/*wu·*suul* ...
boat	al·*mar*·kib
bus	al·o·to·*bees*
ferry	ma'a·*diy*·ya
plane	al·tay·*yã*·ra
train	al·'*atr*

I'd like a ... ticket.	'aiz/'*ai*·za ... taz·*kar*·it (m/f)
one-way	zi·*haab*
return	'*ow*·da
1st-class	da·ra·ga *oo*·la
2nd-class	da·ra·ga *tan*·ya

I want to go to ...
a·na 'aiz/'*ai*·za a·*rooH* ... (m/f)
The train has been cancelled./delayed.
il·'*atr* it·'*akh*·khar/it·*la*·gha
Which bus goes to ...?
o·to·*bees* nim·ra kam ye·*rooH* ...
Does this bus go to ...?
al·o·to·*bees* da ye·*rooH* ...
Please tell me when we arrive in ...
min *fad*·lak, '*ul*·lee *em*·ta Ha·*noo*·sel ...
What is the fare to ...?
bi·*kam* at·taz·*ka*·ra li ...
Stop here, please.
wa·'if *hi*·na, min *fad*·lak
Wait!
is·*tan*·na

the first	il *aw*·wil/*oo*·la (m/f)
the last	il *aa*·khir
the next	*il*·li gayy
airport	ma·*tãr*
bus station	ma·*Hat*·tat a·lo·to·*bees*
bus stop	*maw*·'if a·lo·to·*bees*
platform number	ra·*seef* nim·ra
ticket office	*mak*·tab at·ta·*zaa*·ker
timetable	*qad*·wal
train station	ma·*Hat*·tat al·'*atr*

Private Transport

I'd like to hire a/an ...	'aiz/'*ai*·za a·'*ag*·gãr ... (m/f)
car	'*a*·ra·*biy*·ya
4WD	zheeb
motorbike	mu tu *sikl*
bicycle	'*a*·ga·la
camel	*ga*·mal
donkey	Hu·*mãr*
horse	Hu·*sãn*

Is this the road to …?
  i·ta·*ree'* da yi·*was*·sil li …
(How long) Can I park here?
  mum·kin *ar*·kin *hi*·na (*ad*·di ay)
I need a mechanic.
  miH·*taag*/miH·*taa*·ga me·ka·*nee*·ki (m/f)
The car/motorbike has broken down at …
  il 'a·ra·*biy*·ya/mu·tu·*sikl* '*i*·til 'and …
The car/motorbike won't start.
  il 'a·ra·*biy*·ya/mu·tu·*sikl* mish bit·*door*
I have a flat tyre.
  il ka·*witsh* nay·im
I've run out of petrol.
  il ben·*zeen* khi·lis
I've had an accident.
  kaan *'an*·dee *Had*·sa
Where's a service station?
  fayn ma·*Hat*·tet ben·*zeen*
Please fill it up.
  faw·*wil*·ha, low sa·*maHt*
I'd like (30) litres.
  'aiz/'*ai*·za (ta·la·*teen*) litr (m/f)

diesel	so·*lār*
petrol	ben·*zeen*

TRAVEL WITH CHILDREN

Is there a/an …?   fee …
I need a/an ….   'aiz/'*ai*·za … (m/f)
  car seat   *kur*·si 'a·ra·*biy*·ya li tifl
  child-minding   *khid*·mat ra'·*ai*·it tifl
    service
  children's menu   me·*nai* lil at·*fāl*
  (English-speaking)   ga·lis·at at·*fāl* (bi·tit·*kall*·im
    babysitter   in·*glee*·zee)
  formula (milk)   *la*·ban mu·*ga*·faf lil *bay*·bi
  highchair   *kur*·si lil at·*fāl*
  nappies/diapers   *bam*·bers (brand name)
  potty   as·*riy*·ya

Do you mind if I breastfeed here?
  mum·kin a·*rad*·da·'a *hi*·na
Are children allowed?
  mas·*mooH* bis·ti·*Haab* il at·*fāl*

Also available from Lonely Planet:
Egyptian Arabic Phrasebook and
Middle East Phrasebook

Glossary

For a glossary containing Pharaonic terms, see p61, and for food and drink terms, see p85 and p545.

abd – servant of
abeyya – woman's garment
abu – father, saint
ahwa – coffee, coffeehouse
ain – well, spring
al-jeel – a type of music characterised by a hand-clapping rhythm overlaid with a catchy vocal; literally 'the generation'

ba'al – grocer
bab – gate or door
baksheesh – alms, tip
baladi – local, rural
beit – house
bey – leader; term of respect
bir – spring, well
burg – tower
bustan – walled garden

calèche – horse-drawn carriage
caravanserai – merchants' inn; also called *khan*
centrale – telephone office

dahabiyya – houseboat
darb – track, street
deir – monastery, convent
domina – dominoes

eid – Islamic feast
emir – Islamic ruler, military commander or governor; literally 'prince'

fellaheen – (singular: fellah) peasant farmers or agricultural workers who make up the majority of Egypt's population; 'fellah' literally means ploughman or tiller of the soil

galabiyya – man's full-length robe
gebel – mountain
gezira – island
guinay – pound (currency)

hajj – pilgrimage to Mecca; all Muslims should make the journey at least once in their lifetime
hammam – bathhouse
hantour – horse-drawn carriage
Hejira – Islamic calendar; Mohammed's flight from Mecca to Medina in AD 622

ibn – son of
iconostasis – screen with doors and icons set in tiers, used in Eastern Christian churches
iftar – breaking the fast after sundown during the month of *Ramadan*

kershef – building material made of large chunks of salt mixed with rock and plastered in local clay
khamsin – a dry, hot wind from the Western Desert
khan – another name for a *caravanserai*
khanqah – *Sufi* monastery
khedive – Egyptian viceroy under Ottoman suzerainty
khwaga – foreigner
kuttab – Quranic school

madrassa – school, especially one associated with a mosque
mahattat – station
mammisi – birthhouse
maristan – hospital
mashrabiyya – ornate carved wooden panel or screen; a feature of Islamic architecture
mastaba – mudbrick structure in the shape of a bench above tombs, from which later pyramids developed; Arabic word for 'bench'
matar – airport
midan – town or city square
mihrab – niche in the wall of a mosque that indicates the direction of Mecca
minbar – pulpit in a mosque
Misr – Egypt (also means 'Cairo')
moulid – saints' festival
muezzin – mosque official who calls the faithful to prayer
mugzzabin – *Sufi* followers who participate in *zikr*s
muqarnas – stalactite-like decorative device forming tiers and made of stone or wood; used on arches and vaults

oud – a type of lute

piastre – Egyptian currency; one Egyptian pound consists of 100 piastres

qasr – castle or palace

Ramadan – the ninth month of the lunar Islamic calendar during which Muslims fast from sunrise to sunset
ras – headland

sabil – public drinking fountain
sandale – modified felucca
servees – service taxi
shaabi – popular music of the working class
sharia – road or street
sharm – bay
sheesha – water pipe
souq – market
speos – rock-cut tomb or chapel
Sufi – follower of any Islamic mystical order that emphasises dancing, chanting and trances to attain unity with God

tahtib – male dance performed with wooden staves
tarboosh – the hat known elsewhere as a fez
towla – backgammon

umm – mother of

wadi – desert watercourse, dry except in the rainy season
waha – oasis
wikala – another name for a *caravanserai*

zikr – long sessions of dancing, chanting and trances usually carried out by *Sufi mugzzabin* to achieve unity with God

The Authors

MATTHEW D FIRESTONE
Coordinating Author, Cairo, Egyptian Museum, Around Cairo, Suez Canal, Red Sea Coast, Diving the Red Sea, Sinai

Matthew trained as an anthropologist and epidemiologist, though he abandoned a promising academic career in favour of spending his youth living out of a backpack. With his best explorer's hat and hiking boots on hand, Matthew blazed a trail across the Middle East in the footsteps of Indiana Jones. Although a brief excursion to Petra failed to reveal the final location of the Holy Grail, Matthew's travels brought him from the depths of the Red Sea to the heights of Mt Sinai. He may not have found eternal life but at least he found a bit of adventure – and a whole lot of sand.

MICHAEL BENANAV
Western Desert

Michael cut his adventure-travelling teeth in Egypt back in 1998, and his experiences were so bizarre he figured he'd better start writing about them. Since then, he's authored the highly praised books *Men of Salt: Crossing the Sahara on the Caravan of White Gold,* for which he joined a working camel caravan on its mission schlepping salt to Timbuktu; and *Joshua & Isadora: A True Tale of Loss and Love in the Holocaust,* which took him through the vodka-soaked villages of rural Ukraine. He also writes and photographs for the *New York Times* and other publications. When he's not in some remote nook of Asia or Africa, he can often be found walking in the hills behind his home in northern New Mexico.

THOMAS HALL
Alexandria & the Mediterranean Coast

After a childhood in Mexico, Brazil, and the suburban Chicago of *Risky Business*, Tom attended the University of California, San Diego, and most likely graduated with Literature and Writing degrees. After ingloriously eking out a living as a trivia writer and musician, he moved to San Francisco and failed to strike it rich in the internet gold rush, though he made up for it with voracious consumption of vegetarian burritos. Spending 18 months in Egypt, Tom became a connoisseur of seriously good *sheesha* and learned to appreciate *fuul* and *ta'amiyya*. After working for Lonely Planet in Oakland and Melbourne, Tom now lives in London. This his first travel writing gig for Lonely Planet.

LONELY PLANET AUTHORS

Why is our travel information the best in the world? It's simple: our authors are passionate, dedicated travellers. They don't take freebies in exchange for positive coverage so you can be sure the advice you're given is impartial. They travel widely to all the popular spots, and off the beaten track. They don't research using just the internet or phone. They discover new places not included in any other guidebook. They personally visit thousands of hotels, restaurants, palaces, trails, galleries, temples and more. They speak with dozens of locals every day to make sure you get the kind of insider knowledge only a local could tell you. They take pride in getting all the details right, and in telling it how it is. Think you can do it? Find out how at **lonelyplanet.com**.

ANTHONY SATTIN
Cruising the Nile; Nile Valley: Beni Suef to Qena; Nile Valley: Luxor; Nile Valley: Esna to Abu Simbel

Anthony's highly acclaimed books include *The Pharaoh's Shadow,* a travel book about Egypt, and *The Gates of Africa,* an account of the search for Timbuktu. His latest book describes the winter that Florence Nightingale and Gustave Flaubert spent on the Nile. Anthony is a regular contributor to the *Sunday Times* and *Condé Nast Traveller* and his work has also appeared in *Vanity Fair, GQ* and a range of other publications. He has appeared in many television documentaries and presents features for BBC radio. He is the editor of Lonely Planet's *A House Somewhere: Tales of Life Abroad* and has contributed to Lonely Planet's *Morocco* and *Algeria* guidebooks.

CONTRIBUTING AUTHORS

Dr Joann Fletcher wrote the Pharaonic Egypt chapter and several boxed texts. Fascinated with Egypt since she was a small child, Joann Fletcher first visited the country in 1981 and this confirmed her decision to make it her career. A degree in Egyptology was followed by a PhD in the same subject and as a research and teaching fellow at the University of York, where she teaches Egyptian archaeology, she undertakes scientific research on everything from mummification to ancient perfumes. She is the Egyptologist for several UK museums and designed the UK's first nationally available Egyptology qualification. Having excavated at a number of sites in Egypt, including the Valley of the Kings, Joann regularly appears on TV, has contributed to the BBC History website and has written a number of books. When in Egypt she stays with her Egyptian family on Luxor's West Bank, or otherwise is at home on the Yorkshire coast or in Normandy.

Dr Caroline Evans wrote the Health chapter. Having studied medicine at the University of London, Caroline completed general practice training in Cambridge. She is the medical adviser to Nomad Travel Clinic, a private travel-health clinic in London, and is also a GP specialising in travel medicine. Caroline has acted as expedition doctor for Raleigh International and Coral Cay expeditions.

Behind the Scenes

THIS BOOK

This 10th edition of Lonely Planet's Egypt guidebook was researched by Matthew D Firestone (co-ordinating author), Michael Benanav, Thomas Hall and Anthony Sattin. The 9th edition was written by Matthew D Firestone, Zora O'Neill, Anthony Sattin and Rafael Wlodarski. Dr Joann Fletcher wrote the Pharaonic Egypt chapter as she has done for the past four editions. The 8th edition was researched and written by Virginia Maxwell, Mary Fitzpatrick, Siona Jenkins and Anthony Sattin. This guidebook was commissioned in Lonely Planet's Melbourne office and produced by the following:

Commissioning Editors Sasha Baskett, Emma Gilmour, Shawn Low
Coordinating Editor Laura Crawford
Coordinating Cartographers Xavier Di Toro, Marc Milinkovic
Coordinating Layout Designer Carol Jackson
Managing Editor Annelies Mertens
Managing Cartographers Adrian Persoglia, Amanda Sierp
Managing Layout Designer Sally Darmody
Assisting Editors Sarah Bailey, Helen Christinis, Melanie Dankel, Victoria Harrison, Kim Hutchins, Anne Mulvaney
Assisting Cartographers Owen Eszeki, Andy Rojas, Sam Sayer
Cover Research Naomi Parker, lonelyplanetimages.com

Internal Image Research Sabrina Dalbesio, lonelyplanetimages.com
Project Managers Chris Love, Glenn van der Knijff
Thanks to Brigitte Ellemor, Corey Hutchison, Lisa Knights, Yvonne Kirk, Peter Shields

THANKS
MATTHEW D FIRESTONE

Special thanks to the usual cast of characters, namely Mom, Dad, Kim and Akiko for always showering me with their unconditional support, regardless of how absurd my actions sometimes seem. On the Lonely Planet team, I would like to thank Anthony for yet another Egypt book under his belt, and to Michael and Thomas for joining the ranks and handing in veteran-worthy content. Also thanks to Emma Gilmour for giving me the chance to coordinate this veritable Pharaonic tome.

MICHAEL BENANAV

Big thanks go to Mohsen Abd al Moneam at the tourist office in Al-Kharga, and his colleagues Omar Ahmad in Mut and Mohamed Abd el-Kader in Bawiti. Thanks, too, to Fergany al-Komaty, my 'brother' in Giza, whose home is like my own. At Lonely Planet, I'd like to thank Matthew Firestone, Anthony Sattin and Emma Gilmour, who were valu-

---

THE LONELY PLANET STORY

Fresh from an epic journey across Europe, Asia and Australia in 1972, Tony and Maureen Wheeler sat at their kitchen table stapling together notes. The first Lonely Planet guidebook, *Across Asia on the Cheap,* was born.

Travellers snapped up the guides. Inspired by their success, the Wheelers began publishing books to Southeast Asia, India and beyond. Demand was prodigious, and the Wheelers expanded the business rapidly to keep up. Over the years, Lonely Planet extended its coverage to every country and into the virtual world via lonelyplanet.com and the Thorn Tree message board.

As Lonely Planet became a globally loved brand, Tony and Maureen received several offers for the company. But it wasn't until 2007 that they found a partner whom they trusted to remain true to the company's principles of travelling widely, treading lightly and giving sustainably. In October of that year, BBC Worldwide acquired a 75% share in the company, pledging to uphold Lonely Planet's commitment to independent travel, trustworthy advice and editorial independence.

Today, Lonely Planet has offices in Melbourne, London and Oakland, with over 500 staff members and 300 authors. Tony and Maureen are still actively involved with Lonely Planet. They're travelling more often than ever, and they're devoting their spare time to charitable projects. And the company is still driven by the philosophy of *Across Asia on the Cheap*: 'All you've got to do is decide to go and the hardest part is over. So go!'

BEHIND THE SCENES

able resources when I had technical (and sometimes, I'm sure, inane-seeming) questions. Special thanks to Kelly and Lucas, who make returning from a trip a good thing.

THOMAS HALL

Thanks to Carter Newman for connecting me to Ibrahim Abdallah, who connected me to everyone else. Islam Eweda and Mohammed Ossama el Akkad took me on a great late-night ramble and treated me to excellent *shwarma*. Tamer Zakaria shared his knowledge of everything Alexandria-related. Ehab el-Sayed and Rania Roushdy introduced me to the magnificent Arous el Zilzila. Cheers to Silke Martin, Petra Brown, Kyle Brown and Kevin Pruyn, who I accosted on the street after spotting them using this guidebook. Thanks also to Debbie Senters in Cairo and Adham Ibrahim. And to my family, who put the fun back in dysfunctional: Dad, Becky, Gill, Kira, the Gefiltefish, Padmapuzzo, and the Bean. And, Lucy.

ANTHONY SATTIN

Big thanks to Olivier Sednaoui, always an inspiration; Mamdouh, Enrique and Eleonore on the Nile; to Richard Launay, GM of the Winter Palace; Mourad at the Luxor tourist office; Hakim Hussein at the Aswan tourist office; Tarek and Sandra at Fikra; Muhammad Subhi on Elephantine; and Muhammad Arabi in Aswan. At Lonely Planet, thanks to Matt Firestone, Liz Abbott and Emma Gilmour.

OUR READERS

Many thanks to the travellers who used the last edition and wrote to us with helpful hints, useful advice and interesting anecdotes:

A Matt A, Tarek Abbady, Daniel Aeschlimann, Hasan Ahmed, Sylvia Andonopoulos, Scott Andrews, Andy Armitage, Robin Ashenden, Devang Asher, Vasco Asturiano, Joun Auvergne **B** Andrea Baer, Alan Bagot, Farah Baig, Mariam Banahi, Andrew Bannister, Adam Barnett, Emma Barnett, John Barry, David Bebarfald, Barbara Beck, Magnus Bengtsson, Lise Bentsen, Jonathan Bertman, Shirley Biggin, Lorella Binaghi, Susanne Binder, Reg Blakeley, Stephanie Bonnes, David Bowman, Dan Breslaw, James Broucek, Peter Brubacher, Mustafa Bulgu, Rollo Burgess **C** Jamie Caamano, Ariadne Calvo-Platero, Andreas Cameron, Dawn Campbell, Leslie Carolina, Katherine Chou, Gunnar Christiansson, Tracy Christmas, Garry Clark, Sally Coburn, Brian Connellan, Margie Cook, Ted Cookson, Monica Corrado, Joan Manuel Cortada, Suzanne Courteau, Bill Covington, Mary Jean Crouch, Rachel Curry **D** Elizabeth Dahab, Gavin Daly, Philip Davies, Clive Davies, Julie Davies, Cate Dawson, Conny De Waal, Marlon Dekker, Kaatje Delvaux, John Denard, Olivier Desvernois, Stephen Dipangrazio, Luke Dodd, Bizeul Dominique, Kelly Donaldson, Christine Down, Colin Doyle, Erica Dudas, Jane Dyer, Jane Dyer **E** Carina Ebnoether, Polly Edgar, Pedro Eichmann, Mohammed El-Razzaz, Anna Ely, Howard Evans **F** Sally Fairley, Eileen Farao, Rainer Feichter, Claas Feye, Raad Firas, Hans Fix, Aneka Flamm, Gibwa Fondaumiere, Leah Fox, Sverre Fredriksen, Michelle Freeman, Arthur Freeman, Jay Freyensee, Andreas Friedel **G** Mansi Gandhi Shah, Colleen Gerrity, Christy Gervers, Abigail Gibbs, Per Glad, Andrea Gonzalez Zuloeta, Ramin Goo, Bill Gosden, Carmela Grillone, Inge Groendahl, Farida Guindi, Leif Jr Gulddal **H** David Hackler, Maria Lykke Hansen, Nicholas Harding-Jackson, Leah Harmon, Allan Harris, Catherine Harrison, Teemu Havulinna, Michelle Hawes, Hansruedi Heeb, Daniel Hellendoorn, Neil Hewison, Richard Heyer, Richard Hoe, Nich Hogben, Emmanuelle Hulard, Debbie Hull, Selena Hurndell, Baher Ibrahim **J** Jussi Jääskeläinen, Emily Jamieson, Johan Jansen, Jendra Jarnagin, Peggy Jay, Paula Jephcott, Enrique Jimenez, Parker Johnson, Jenny Jones, Malcolm Joslyn, Diane Jumet **K** Michal Leah Kanovsky, Kathrin Kappmeier, Tim Karberg, Ronan Kenny, David Kerkhoff, Max Kim, Justus Klemperer, Kimberly Kohler, Mirjam Kruiniger, Hank Kryger, Stelios Kyparissis **L** Sanet Laing, Janet Langelaan, Mette Lansen, Lars Larsson, John Latham, Caroline Law, Gregorey Lee, Marja Lehtio, Brett Leighton, Stephen Lewin, Ian Lindley, Anne Llewellyn, Maria Lombardi **M** Tricia Mack, Ashraf Magdi, Alicja Malczewska, Zita Maliga, Bella Mandry, Bronwen Markham, Michael Martirena, Steven Mathers, Greg Mcelwain, Patrick Mcgrath, Andrew Medley, Sogoli Medo, Wim Meeussen, Andre Mershon, Omar

---

SEND US YOUR FEEDBACK

We love to hear from travellers – your comments keep us on our toes and help make our books better. Our well-travelled team reads every word on what you loved or loathed about this book. Although we cannot reply individually to postal submissions, we always guarantee that your feedback goes straight to the appropriate authors, in time for the next edition. Each person who sends us information is thanked in the next edition and the most useful submissions are rewarded with a free book.

To send us your updates – and find out about Lonely Planet events, newsletters and travel news – visit our award-winning website: **lonelyplanet.com/contact**.

Note: we may edit, reproduce and incorporate your comments in Lonely Planet products such as guidebooks, websites and digital products, so let us know if you don't want your comments reproduced or your name acknowledged. For a copy of our privacy policy visit lonelyplanet.com/privacy.

Molina, Anthony Moore, Przemyslaw Moranski, Alexandria (Alex) Morbey, Ibrahim Morgan, Shaun Morris, Jim Morris, Helmy Mourad, Samer Moussa, Jack Mui, Gordon Müller-Seitz, Robert Mundackal, Susan Muscovitch **N** Okechukwu Ndilemeni, Pamela Nelson, Jonathan Nelson, Benoit Nemery, Munjen Ng, Sarah Nicholas, Benedict Nicolson, Frank Norris, Paolo Notari **O** Greg O'Hern, Steve O'Sullivan, Saki Onda, Sylvia Osche, Alison Oswald **P** David Pavlita, Jossyl Peixoto, Matt Pepe, Bryce Petit, Slobodan Petrovich-English, Gabi Philips, Sandra & David Phillips, Wade Phillpott, Alberto Piccinni, David Pickering, Udai Pinnali, Kate Pounder, William Preston, Pam Prosser **R** Helen Rainger, Michael Raue, Timo Rautiainen, N Read, Christopher Reeve, Conrad Rein, Massot Rene, Giusi Renon, Torben Retboll, Zvika Rimalt, Vivian Robert, Barney Ross, Ahmed Rostom, Simone Rutkowitz, Clive Ryall **S** Valeska Schaudy, Fabian Schellhaas, Jasmin Scheuber, Almut Schindler, Leen Schmucker, Ulrike Schneider, Harvey Schwartz, Idunn Sem, Lesley Seymour, Akbar Sharfi, Tor Sheridan, Suhag Shirodkar, Flavio Alexandre Sisconeto, Alison Sloper, Ann Smith, Linda Smith, Mackenzie Evan Smith, Marika Snider, Dion Snyman, Vicki Somberg, Joseph Stanik, Karen Stash, Nancy Sternberg, Catherine Stevens, Michael Stevens, Jerome Stoll, Martin Straub, Rihana Sultan, Julia Szenthe **T** Rosealeen Tamaki, Elaine Tanabe, Emanuela Tasinato, Jack Tavares, Ilmar Tehnas, Elke Thape, John Thomson, Robyn Thorogood, Sustar Tina, Jane Tonkes, Jennifer Tonkovich, Bjorn Trompet, Nicole Troup, Matthew Tschoegl, Aino Tuominen, Denise Turcinov, Seema Turner **V** Martin Vallis, Peter Van Birgelen, Heidi Van Dael, Nathalie Van De Pol, Michel Van Eijk, Marleen Van Oosterhout, Ryan Van Wyk, Mike Vasey, Janita Venema **W** Katrin Wallner, James Waste, Elizabeth Webb, Philipp Wendtland, Sarah Wessel, Rob Wessels, Bella White, Simon Wickens, Rozie Wild, Kristina Wilson, Silke Wimme, Beau Winter, Ryanne Woltz, Jan Wouters, John Wren, Sheryl Wright **Y** Hsiao Ying Yang, Sullet Yoann, Gordon Young **Z** Michael Zappara

ACKNOWLEDGMENTS
Many thanks to the following for the use of their content:

Globe on title page ©Mountain High Maps 1993 Digital Wisdom, Inc.

BEHIND THE SCENES

Index

INDEX

INDEX

000 Map pages
000 Photograph pages

INDEX

GREENDEX

Going 'green' is a relatively new concept in Egypt but there are some trailblazers worth support-ing. The following have been selected by Lonely Planet authors because they demonstrate an active sustainable-tourism policy, are involved in conservation or environmental education, or are operated with a view to maintaining and preserving regional identity and culture.

We want to keep developing this content. If you think we've omitted someone or if you dis-agree with our choices, send us your feedback at www.lonelyplanet.com/feedback. And for more information, see www.lonelyplanet.com/responsibletravel.

572

MAP LEGEND

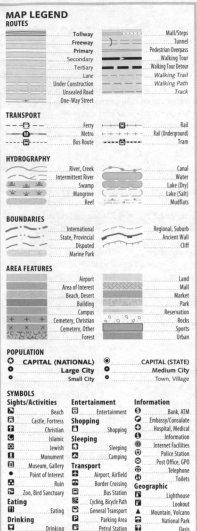

ROUTES
............Tollway
............Freeway
............Primary
............Secondary
............Tertiary
............Lane
Under Construction
Unsealed Road
One-Way Street

Mall/Steps
Tunnel
Pedestrian Overpass
Walking Tour
Walking Tour Detour
Walking Trail
Walking Path
Track

TRANSPORT
............Ferry
............Metro
............Bus Route

Rail
Rail (Underground)
Tram

HYDROGRAPHY
............River, Creek
Intermittent River
............Swamp
............Mangrove
............Reef

Canal
Water
Lake (Dry)
Lake (Salt)
Mudflats

BOUNDARIES
............International
............State, Provincial
............Disputed
Marine Park

Regional, Suburb
Ancient Wall
Cliff

AREA FEATURES
............Airport
Area of Interest
Beach, Desert
............Building
............Campus
Cemetery, Christian
Cemetery, Other
............Forest

Land
Mall
Market
Park
Reservation
Rocks
Sports
Urban

POPULATION
● **CAPITAL (NATIONAL)**
● **Large City**
○ **Small City**

◉ ....**CAPITAL (STATE)**
◎ ....**Medium City**
○ ....Town, Village

SYMBOLS

Sights/Activities
............Beach
Castle, Fortress
............Christian
............Islamic
............Jewish
............Monument
Museum, Gallery
Point of Interest
............Ruin
Zoo, Bird Sanctuary

Eating
............Eating

Drinking
............Drinking
............Cafe

Entertainment
............Entertainment
Shopping
............Shopping
Sleeping
............Sleeping
............Camping
Transport
Airport, Airfield
Border Crossing
Bus Station
Cycling, Bicycle Path
General Transport
Parking Area
Petrol Station
Taxi Rank

Information
............Bank, ATM
Embassy/Consulate
Hospital, Medical
............Information
Internet Facilities
Police Station
Post Office, GPO
............Telephone
............Toilets
Geographic
............Lighthouse
............Lookout
Mountain, Volcano
National Park
............Oasis
............River Flow

LONELY PLANET OFFICES

Australia (Head Office)
Locked Bag 1, Footscray, Victoria 3011
☎ 03 8379 8000, fax 03 8379 8111
talk2us@lonelyplanet.com.au

USA
150 Linden St, Oakland, CA 94607
☎ 510 250 6400, toll free 800 275 8555
fax 510 893 8572
info@lonelyplanet.com

UK
2nd fl, 186 City Rd,
London EC1V 2NT
☎ 020 7106 2100, fax 020 7106 2101
go@lonelyplanet.co.uk

Published by Lonely Planet
ABN 36 005 607 983

Mixed Sources
Product group from well-managed forests and other controlled sources
www.fsc.org Cert no. SGS-COC-005002
© 1996 Forest Stewardship Council
FSC